The Law of Public Communication, 2009 Update

The Law of Public Communication, 2009 Update

Seventh Edition

Kent R. Middleton
University of Georgia

William E. Lee
University of Georgia

PEARSON

A and B

Boston New York San Francisco
Mexico City Montreal Toronto London Madrid Munich Paris
Hong Kong Singapore Tokyo Cape Town Sydney

Senior Series Editor/Series Editor: Jeanne Zalesky
Series Editorial Assistant: Susan Brilling
Marketing Manager: Suzan Czajkowski
Production Editor: Patrick Cash-Peterson
Editorial Production Service: Elm Street Publishing Services
Manufacturing Buyer: Debbie Rossi
Electronic Composition: Integra Software Services Pvt. Ltd.
Cover Administrator: Kristina Mose-Libon

For related titles and support materials, visit our online catalog at www.ablongman.com.

ISBN-13: 978-0-205-57004-1 ISBN-10: 0-205-57004-6

Library of Congress Cataloging-in-Publication Data

Middleton, Kent.
The law of public communication / Kent R. Middleton, William E. Lee.—7th ed., 2009 update.
p. cm.
Includes bibliographical references and index.
ISBN 978-0-205-57004-1
1. Press law—United States. 2. Mass media—Law and legislation—United States.
3. Freedom of the press—United States. I. Lee, William E. (William Eyre) II. Title.
KF2750.M53 2009
343.7309'98—dc22

2008022257

Printed in the United States of America

10 9 8 7 6 5 4 3 2 1 12 11 10 09 08

New to This Edition

2009 Update

Media law changes rapidly, driven by technology, new Supreme Court justices, globalization, and the temporary fortunes of politicians. To ensure that the *Law of Public Communication* includes the most recent media law decisions, we update the text each year with new cases and laws. Every three years, we write a new edition reporting new judicial rulings, adding new sections and trimming others, reconsidering previous conclusions and identifying new trends. This text is the 2009 Update of Seventh edition of *The Law of Public Communication*. Pages x–xii of the Preface provide detailed chapter-by-chapter information on what is new to the seventh edition and the 2009 update. A brief overview follows:

- Supreme Court personnel changes (Ch. 1)
- New cases involving student speech (Ch. 2)
- Attorney General Gonzales' claim that the press can be punished for publishing classified information (Ch. 3)
- Cases involving libel judgments against Americans in foreign courts (Ch. 4)
- The latest developments in the Hewlett-Packard "pretexting" case (Ch. 5)
- New copyright developments relating to Internet technologies including filesharing and video postings on YouTube (Ch. 6)
- New section on music licensing for broadcasters, webcasters, and filmmakers (Ch. 6)
- New FEC rulings on the press exemption to federal election law and the FEC's actions against "527 groups" (Ch. 7)
- The Supreme Court's *Randall v. Sorrell* ruling on campaign contribution and expenditure limits (Ch. 7)
- New FCC rules regulating website addresses displayed during children's TV programs (Ch. 8)
- Fair information practices and rules protecting citizens' privacy in personal data collection (Ch. 8)
- Most recent FCC decisions regarding broadcast indecency and enactment of the Broadcast Decency Enforcement Act (Ch. 9)
- Fair trial–free press developments, including a ruling overturning a restriction on publication of juror identities in the trial of Wall Street figure Frank Quattrone (Ch. 10)
- New SEC rules limiting subpoenas to reporters (Ch. 11)
- New challenges to Patriot Act provisions (Ch. 11)
- Access to information about detainees in the "war on terror" (Ch. 12)

For Parker; for Theresa.

Contents

Chapter 4

◆ Libel 93

Chapter 5

◆ Privacy 176

Chapter 6

◆ Intellectual Property 233

Chapter 7

◆ Political Speech 281

Chapter 8

◆ Commercial Speech 326

Chapter 9

◆ Obscenity and Indecency 399

Chapter 10

◆ The Media and the Judiciary 454

Chapter 11

◆ Protection of News Sources, Notes, and Tape 510

Preface

The Law of Public Communication is designed primarily for an undergraduate liberal arts class in which professors wish to teach legal principles, demonstrate methods of analyzing cases, and provide practical knowledge for future communicators. The text explains the law as it applies to the daily work of writers, broadcasters, advertisers, cable operators, Internet service providers, public relations practitioners, photographers, and other public communicators. The many statutes and cases are presented in a cohesive narrative that is understandable even to students studying law for the first time. While presenting much of the rich complexity of communication law, we strive for readability. To help ensure understanding, we reinforce the narrative with frequent summaries of major points. Always, we hope to convey the fascination we maintain with the dynamic field of communication law.

In addition to acquiring practical knowledge, students learn legal principles and methods of analysis necessary to evaluate and keep abreast of a rapidly changing subject. We try to discuss cases in sufficient detail—often with quotations—for students to understand legal issues, identify court holdings, and appreciate the courts' rationale. We explain theories of media regulation and judicial tests in Chapter 2. Chapter 3 addresses prior restraints, post-publication penalties, and content-neutral regulations. We apply the theories and tools presented in Chapters 2 and 3 repeatedly throughout the text. As was true in earlier editions, this edition contains extensive but unobtrusive footnotes to document the scholarship on which assertions are based and to suggest further reading for the student and professor.

The authors recognize that publishers, broadcasters, and other media owners are not the only speakers with First Amendment rights. Thus, we cover the law of public relations and advertising as it affects political campaign coordinators, corporate spokespersons, and commercial advertisers. We offer separate chapters on commercial and political speech, while integrating issues of commercial communication into traditional chapters of libel, privacy, copyright, and access to courts.

The Law of Public Communication focuses on the law regulating the content of public communication, not on laws regulating the structure of corporate media, newsroom safety, or labor-management contracts. Thus, for example, taxes on the media are discussed only if they restrict what might be said or published. Important business and economic issues that do not directly affect the content of the media are left to courses in business law and communication management.

Chapter-By-Chapter Revisions

The 2009 Update of *The Law of Public Communication,* seventh edition, includes the most current information explaining the law as it applies to the daily work of writers, broadcasters, advertisers, cable operators, Internet service providers, public relations practitioners, photographers, and other public communicators. What follows are some of the most significant revisions to the seventh edition and 2009 Update.

Chapter 1

- What impact will the recent personnel changes to the Supreme Court have on the law of public communication law? Chapter 1 analyzes the changes in the Court's membership and the emergence of Justice Anthony Kennedy as the "swing" vote.
- Chapter 1 also shows that the Court under Chief Justice Roberts has not increased its caseload, continuing the limited caseload initiated by Chief Justice Rehnquist.

Chapter 2

- Do students have the same speech rights as adults? Chapter 2 reviews recent cases involving student speech, including *Morse v. Frederick* in which the Supreme Court decided a high school student in Alaska could be suspended for hoisting a "Bong Hits 4 Jesus" banner at a public event students were authorized to attend.
- Can college newspapers be regulated as extensively as the high school press? Chapter 2 considers the implications of an appellate court ruling that state university student newspapers enjoy no more freedom from administrative censorship than high school newspapers.
- Chapter 2 also examines the Supreme Court's ruling in *Garcetti v. Ceballos* limiting government work-place speech.

Chapter 3

- When do issues of national security supersede the rights of a free press? Chapter 3 reviews Attorney General Alberto Gonzales' claim that the press can be prosecuted for publishing classified information.
- Chapter 3 also examines the FCC's new rules for cable franchising and the movement within states to grant statewide cable franchises.

Chapter 4

- Are website operators responsible for defamation posted on their websites? Chapter 4 discusses cases interpreting Section 230 of the Telecommunications Act of 1996.
- Chapter 4 also discusses enforcement of libel judgments against Americans in foreign courts.

Chapter 5

- Is it illegal to acquire telephone records through "pretexting"? Chapter 5 discusses recent developments in the Hewlett-Packard case.
- Chapter 5 also discusses the Bush administration's warrantless wiretaps and developments in stalkerazzi and cyberstalking laws. The chapter analyzes the issues raised by *Boehner v. McDermott,* involving disclosure of an illegal telephone recording.

Chapter 6

- How is new technology affecting copyright law? Chapter 6 presents the Supreme Court ruling that Grokster's filesharing software contributed to infringement of copyrights owned by Metro-Goldwyn-Meyer Studios and other media producers.
- Chapter 6 also discusses the music license requirements for broadcasting, webcasting, and film and the "take down" issues posed by Viacom's suit against YouTube.
- Chapter 6 reviews efforts at sports venues to control media access and the use of recorded coverage.

Chapter 7

- What are the key provisions of the Honest Leadership and Government Act of 2007? Chapter 7 discusses the new law's impact on lobbying and campaign donations.
- Should corporations be permitted to refer to candidates in issue ads broadcast near an election? Chapter 7 examines *Wisconsin Right to Life v. FEC,* a challenge to the "electioneering communication" provision of the Bipartisan Campaign Reform Act (BCRA).
- Chapter 7 also explains recent FEC rules implementing the *Wisconsin Right to Life* decision.

Chapter 8

- Is it permissible to show commercial weblinks during children's television programs? Chapter 8 reviews the FCC's new rules regulating the display of website addresses during children's television programs.
- Is it legal for companies to share the personal data they collect about you? Chapter 8 discusses fair information practices and other rules protecting citizens' privacy in personal data collection and use.

Chapter 9

- How does the FCC determine when fines for indecency violations should be assessed? Chapter 9 covers the latest broadcast indecency cases and explains the Broadcast Decency Enforcement Act, which increased the indecency fines tenfold.
- Chapter 9 also discusses *United States v. Williams,* a 2008 Supreme Court decision upholding a restriction on the pandering of child pornography.

Chapter 10

- Is there a difference between restricting the media's access to information and preventing dissemination of information by the media once it's known? Chapter 10 analyzes the appellate ruling concerning press publication of juror identities in the Quattrone trial.
- Chapter 10 also discusses restrictions on access to information in the high-profile trial of media mogul Conrad Black.

Chapter 11

- In light of recent rulings limiting a First Amendment-based journalist's privilege, do journalists have a federal common law right to protect sources? Chapter 11 explores several recent journalist's privilege cases including Wen Ho Lee, Judith Miller, and Josh Wolf, and analyzes the prospects for a federal shield law.
- Chapter 11 also explains the *Doe v. Gonzales* ruling relating to National Security Letters.

Chapter 12

- What are the main points of the Open Government Act of 2007? Chapter 12 discusses the new law and the Bush administration's failure to fund an ombudsmen.
- When does the need to protect the public outweigh the public's right to know about government activities? Chapter 12 examines restrictions on access to information surrounding "the war on terror," including federal court rulings related to disclosure of names and photographs of detainees at Guantanamo Bay.

Acknowledgments

We thank the many people who have helped and encouraged us, particularly the scores of professors and students who have told us our book is comprehensive, accurate, and interesting. We appreciate our critics and reviewers who have pointed out errors and offered many suggestions we have incorporated into the text. The reviewers for this edition are Genelle Belmas, California State University, Fullerton; Lyombe Eko, University of Iowa; Marion Huttenstine, Mississippi State University; Barbara Morgenstern, Ithaca College; and Kirk Wolf, Delta College.

Kent R. Middleton
University of Georgia
kmiddlet@uga.edu

William E. Lee
University of Georgia
weyrelee@uga.edu

CHAPTER 1

Public Communication and the Law

The jailing of a journalist is an extraordinary event in the United States. On July 6, 2005, *New York Times* reporter Judith Miller was jailed, not for anything she wrote, but because she refused to testify before a grand jury investigating the leaking of a CIA agent's name. Miller claimed that the First Amendment protects reporters who, as part of their newsgathering activities, promise confidentiality to sources. Miller's claims were unsuccessful; a federal district court and appellate court ruled that reporters, like other citizens, must answer questions posed during legitimate law enforcement investigations. Miller's need to protect the confidentiality of her sources was outweighed by the government's need to investigate crimes.

The *Miller* case highlights many of the complex issues that will be discussed in this book. Should journalists have special status in our society, or should journalists be treated like other citizens? If journalists are entitled to special status, would the category of journalists be narrowly confined to reporters for newspapers and broadcast stations, or would it also include web bloggers? Is newsgathering by journalists entitled to the same level of constitutional protection as publishing? How should courts analyze the competing interests of journalists and other segments of society?

This book is concerned with law that affects journalists, as well as law affecting other public communicators such as advertising and public relations professionals. This book will discuss not only the law governing reporter-source relationships but also the law of libel, privacy, political communication, copyright, obscenity, coverage of court proceedings, and access to government-held information. The book focuses on the law affecting the content of public communication, including printed publications, electronic media, advertising, and public relations.

This chapter will examine legal concepts and procedures that are important to an understanding of the law of public communication. It will talk about the purpose and organization of law. It will also describe court procedures and discuss how communicators work with lawyers.

The Sources of Law

Law can be defined in many ways, but for our purposes, law is the system of rules that govern society. The system of rules serves many functions in our society, including regulating the behavior of citizens and corporations. Law prohibits murder and restricts what advertisers can say about their products. It provides a vehicle to settle disputes, such as when a reporter refuses to testify in court. Furthermore, law limits the government's power to interfere with individual rights, such as the right to speak and publish.

The law in the United States comes primarily from six sources: constitutions, statutes, administrative rules and regulations, executive actions, the **common law,**[1] and the law of **equity.**

Constitutional Law

Constitutions are the supreme source of law in the United States and are the most direct reflection of the kind of government desired by the people. Constitutions of both the federal and state governments supersede all other declarations of public policy. The Constitution of the federal government and the constitutions of the fifty states establish the framework for governing. They outline the structure of government and define governmental authority and responsibilities.

Frequently, a constitution limits the powers of government, as in the case of the Bill of Rights, the first ten amendments to the U.S. Constitution. The Bill of Rights, printed in Appendix B of this book, protects the rights and liberties of U.S. citizens against infringement

[1]Definitions for the terms printed in boldface can be found in the glossary at the end of the book.

by government. The First Amendment, particularly its prohibition against laws abridging freedom of speech and the press, provides the foundation for communication law.

The federal constitution is the country's ultimate legal authority. Any federal law, state law, or state constitution that contradicts the U.S. Constitution cannot be implemented; the U.S. Constitution prevails. Similarly, a state constitution prevails in conflicts with either the **statutory law** or the common law in the same state. However, federal and state laws that do not conflict with the federal constitution can provide more protection for communicators than is available under the First Amendment alone. For example, the majority of states shield journalists from revealing confidential news sources in more circumstances than the First Amendment as interpreted by the U.S. Supreme Court.

The Supreme Court, the nation's supreme judicial body, has the last word on the meaning of the federal constitution. Each state's supreme court is the interpreter of that state's constitution. Only the U.S. Supreme Court can resolve conflicts between the federal and state constitutions. The courts make constitutional law when they decide a case or controversy by interpreting a constitution. In 1980, the U.S. Supreme Court said the First Amendment requires that the public and press ordinarily be permitted to attend trials.[2] Constitutional law can be understood only by reading the opinions of the courts.

The U.S. Constitution is hard to amend and therefore is changed infrequently. Amendments to the U.S. Constitution can be proposed only by two-thirds of the members of both houses of Congress or by a convention called by two-thirds of the state legislatures. Amendments must be ratified by three-fourths of the state legislatures or by state constitutional conventions in three-fourths of the states.

Statutory Law

A major source of law in the United States is the collection of statutes and ordinances written by legislative bodies—the U.S. Congress, the fifty state legislatures, county commissions, city councils, and countless other lawmaking bodies. Statutes set forth enforceable rules to govern social behavior. Areas of communication law controlled by statutes include advertising, copyright, electronic media, obscenity, and access to government-held information.

Almost all of this country's criminal law, including a prohibition against the mailing of obscenity, is statutory. Statutes not only prohibit antisocial acts but also frequently provide for the oversight of acceptable behavior. For example, the federal Communications Act of 1934 was adopted so that the broadcast spectrum would be used for the public good.

The process of adopting statutes allows lawmakers to study carefully a complicated issue—such as how to regulate the use of the electromagnetic spectrum—and write an appropriate law. The process permits anyone or any group to make suggestions through letters, personal contacts, and hearings. In practice, well-organized special interests such as broadcasters, cable television system operators, and telephone companies substantially influence the legislative process. As shown in Chapter 7, highly regulated industries have the largest lobbying expenditures.

The adoption of a statute does not conclude the lawmaking process. Executive branch officials often have to interpret statutes through administrative rules. Judges add meaning

[2]Richmond Newspapers v. Virginia, 448 U.S. 555 (1980).

when either the statutes themselves or their application are challenged in court. Judges explain how statutes apply in specific cases, as when the U.S. Supreme Court ruled in 1984 that the Copyright Act allows homeowners to tape television programs on their VCRs.[3] In 1989, the Court said a provision in the federal Freedom of Information Act allows the FBI to withhold from the public a compilation of an individual's criminal records stored in a computer database. The Court said that giving the records to a reporter would constitute an "unwarranted" invasion of privacy.[4]

The courts can invalidate state and local laws that conflict with federal laws or the U.S. Constitution, including the First Amendment. In 1974, the U.S. Supreme Court declared unconstitutional a Florida statute that required newspapers to print replies to published attacks on political candidates.[5] In 2006, the Court struck down a Vermont law limiting both the amounts candidates for state office could spend on their campaigns and the amounts individuals and political parties could contribute to those campaigns.[6]

Sometimes federal laws **preempt** state regulation, thereby monopolizing governmental control over a specific subject. Article VI of the U.S. Constitution, known as the "supremacy clause," provides that state law cannot supersede federal law. In addition, under the Constitution, congressional regulation of the economy supersedes state law. In 1984, the U.S. Supreme Court nullified an Oklahoma statute banning the advertising of wine on cable television because it conflicted with federal law prohibiting the editing of national and regional television programming carried by cable systems.[7]

Administrative Law

Federal agencies such as the Federal Communications Commission (FCC) and the Federal Trade Commission (FTC) develop rules and decisions known as **administrative law.** These agencies dominate several areas of communication law. The FCC regulates the broadcast, cable, satellite, and telephone industries. The FTC regulates advertising and telemarketing. Other agencies overseeing communication include the Securities and Exchange Commission (SEC), which controls communication related to the securities industry, the Federal Election Commission (FEC), which regulates political campaign contributions and expenditures, and the Food and Drug Administration (FDA), which regulates prescription drug and medical product advertising. Table 1.1 lists these agencies, their areas of regulation, and key regulations.

Administrative agencies are often founded on the premise that they would be independent bodies of experts who set policy solely by analyzing facts. However, regulation by administrative agencies is an intensely political process involving complex interactions among the regulatory agency, the regulated industry, Congress, the President, and public interest groups. The President influences an agency by naming commissioners, subject to approval by the Senate, and designating an agency's chair. Through the Office of Management and Budget, the executive branch reviews proposed regulations to determine consistency with

[3]Sony Corp. v. Universal City Studios, 464 U.S. 417 (1984).
[4]Department of Justice v. Reporters Comm. for Freedom of the Press, 489 U.S. 749 (1989).
[5]Miami Herald Publishing Co. v. Tornillo, 418 U.S. 241 (1974).
[6]Randall v. Sorrell, 126 S. Ct. 2479 (2006).
[7]Capital Cities Cable, Inc. v. Crisp, 467 U.S. 691 (1984).

TABLE 1.1 Federal Regulatory Agencies

Agency	Areas of Regulation	Key Regulations
Federal Communications Commission (FCC)	Radio, television, cable, satellite, telephone	Political broadcasting rules, indecency regulations, children's television regulations
Federal Election Commission (FEC)	Federal elections	Contribution limits and prohibitions, disclosure of campaign finances, campaign expenditures
Federal Trade Commission (FTC)	Advertising (except prescription drugs and medical devices), telemarketing	Deceptive advertising, product labeling, unfair consumer practices, children's online privacy, tobacco health warnings
Food and Drug Administration (FDA)	Food, drugs, medical devices, cosmetics	Prescription drug advertising, medical device advertising, food, drug, cosmetic labels
Securities and Exchange Commission (SEC)	Securities brokers, investment advisors, stock exchanges	Insider trading, false/misleading information

the President's policies. Congress shapes regulation by telling agencies what industries or practices they can regulate. Moreover, Congress controls the budget of agencies, and Congressional committees closely monitor the actions of agencies. Regulated industries, such as telecommunications, are among the largest contributors to political campaigns. These industries use their ties to elected officials to influence regulatory agencies.

Successful nominees for agency positions have close ties to powerful political leaders. Michael Powell, chair of the FCC from 2001 to March 2005, is the son of former Secretary of State Colin Powell; Kevin Martin, the current FCC chair, was deputy counsel to President Bush's 2000 campaign committee and is married to a presidential assistant. The nominating process, like other aspects of agency regulation, involves the tug and pull of political factions. For example, because of a political stalemate, the position of FDA commissioner was vacant for nearly two years after President George W. Bush took office.[8] Senate Democrats insisted that the nominee not be tied to the pharmaceutical industry. The drug industry spent heavily on advertising in favor of Republican candidates in the 2000 and 2002 elections.[9] In return for its support of Republicans, the drug industry expected to influence President Bush's selection of a nominee. In July 2001, Senate Democrats rejected a nominee as being too closely tied to the industry; in February 2002, the drug industry complained to the Bush administration that a potential nominee would be too aggressive a regulator. Finally, the Bush

[8]Alan Murray, "Partisanship Leaves FDA Leaderless at Crucial Juncture," *Wall Street Journal,* June 18, 2002, at A4.
[9]Tom Hamburger, "Drug Industry Ads Aid GOP," *Wall Street Journal,* June 18, 2002, at A4.

administration found a nominee who was acceptable to both sides.[10] In October 2002, the Senate approved Mark McClellan as FDA Commissioner. McClellan, whose brother was President Bush's press secretary, comes from a prominent Texas political family.

McClellan left the FDA in 2004 to become the administrator of the Centers for Medicare and Medicaid Services. Because the FDA regulates one quarter of the nation's economy, and addresses controversial topics, such as the availability of the "morning-after" emergency contraception pill, the agency draws intense scrutiny from politicians. Politicians, upset over the agency's handling of the "morning-after" pill, fought over McClellan's successor for more than a year before confirming Lester Crawford as head of the FDA in July 2005.[11] Crawford suddenly resigned in September 2005 and joined a lobbying firm. Shortly after his resignation, it was disclosed that he was under investigation for conflict-of-interest due to his ownership of shares in companies regulated by the FDA. (Employees of regulatory agencies are barred from owning shares in companies regulated by the agency.) In October 2006, Crawford pleaded guilty to lying and conflict-of-interest charges in connection with stock ownership.[12]

Congress creates administrative agencies to supervise activities or industries that require more attention than legislators can provide. Administrative agencies serve a variety of functions, unique in the American system of government. First, agencies engage in **rule making,** a process that is similar to the legislative function. For example, the FCC developed a rule prohibiting a company from owning a television station and a newspaper in the same city. Second, agencies **adjudicate** disputes, resolving complaints initiated by business competitors, the public, or the agency itself. Administrative law judges conduct hearings resembling judicial proceedings at which evidence is submitted and witnesses are examined and cross-examined. After a hearing, an FTC administrative law judge found that advertisements for Extra Strength Doan's pills were deceptive because they contained an unsubstantiated claim that Doan's pills relieved pain more effectively than competing brands such as Tylenol. Third, agencies perform executive branch functions when they enforce rules against a firm or individual. In recent years, the FCC has fined broadcasters for violating indecency regulations by broadcasting sexual language. Before making its ruling, the agency reviewed the complaints of listeners and responses of broadcast licensees.

Regulatory agencies are bound by the requirements of the Administrative Procedure Act (APA).[13] This statute specifies the procedures that must be employed when an agency enacts rules or enforces regulations. For example, the APA requires that parties have the opportunity to comment on proposed rules. Parties may also petition an agency to issue, amend, or repeal a rule. And the APA establishes the procedures governing a hearing conducted by an administrative law judge, such as a party's right to cross-examine witnesses. Finally, under the APA, a party may seek judicial review of an agency action on a number of grounds, such as the agency has exceeded its statutory authority. Federal judges reviewing agency actions ensure that administrative agencies act within the boundaries set by the Constitution and statutory law.

---

[10]Sheryl Gay Stolberg, "After Impasse, F.D.A. May Fill Top Job," *Washington Post*, Sept. 25, 2002, at A18.
[11]Marc Kaufman, "Crawford Confirmed As Head of FDA," *Washington Post,* July 19, 2005, at A19.
[12]David Stout, "Ex-F.D.A. Chief Pleads Guilty in Stock Case," *N.Y. Times,* Oct. 18, 2006, at A21.
[13]5 U.S.C. §§ 551 et seq.

An administrative action may be challenged on the ground that the agency has exceeded its statutory authority. For example, the Supreme Court agreed with tobacco manufacturers that the FDA exceeded its authority when the agency banned outdoor tobacco advertisements near schools and playgrounds. Although the Supreme Court agreed that tobacco poses a serious health threat, the Court found Congress excluded tobacco products from the FDA's jurisdiction. The Court stated, "an administrative agency's power to regulate in the public interest must always be grounded in a valid grant of authority from Congress."[14]

An agency's action may be challenged on the ground that it is arbitrary and capricious. A federal appeals court recently ruled that the FCC was arbitrary and capricious when it decreed that one company could own two television stations in the same market but not a television station and a cable system.[15] The court said it was illogical for the FCC to conclude that television station and cable system ownership was harmful when the agency found that multiple television station ownership was in the public interest.

An agency's action may also be challenged as unconstitutional. The Supreme Court ruled that the FEC acted unconstitutionally when it sought to punish the Colorado Republican Party for purchasing radio advertising in a political campaign.[16] The Supreme Court ruled that a political party's advertising expenditures, like those of other individuals or groups, are constitutionally protected speech that cannot be limited as long as the expenditures are not coordinated with any candidate. "The independent expression of a political party's views is 'core' First Amendment activity no less than is the independent expression of individuals, candidates, or other political committees," the Court stated.

Executive Actions

The President and other governmental executive officers can also make law. The President exercises power by appointing regulators, issuing executive orders and proclamations, and forging executive agreements with foreign countries. Much of the President's authority derives from Article 2 of the U.S. Constitution, requiring the President to "take Care that the Laws be faithfully executed." The Supreme Court has allowed the chief executive broad regulatory powers under the clause. In addition, Congress often grants the President the authority to administer statutes.

Perhaps the President's greatest influence on communication law comes from the power to nominate judges to the federal courts, including the U.S. Supreme Court. The political and judicial philosophies of the judges, and particularly their interpretation of the First Amendment, determine the boundaries of freedom for communicators. The President also nominates the members of several administrative agencies, including the FCC, the FTC, and the SEC. The President seldom issues executive orders that directly affect the law of public communication. An exception is the order that determines the documents that should be "classified" and thereby withheld from public disclosure to protect national security.

[14]FDA v. Brown &Williamson Tobacco Co., 529 U.S. 120, 161 (2000).
[15]Fox Television Stations, Inc. v. FCC, 280 F.3d 1027 (D.C. Cir. 2002).
[16]Colorado Republican Campaign Committee v. FEC, 518 U.S. 604 (1996).

Common Law

The common law, often called judge-made law, was the most important source of law during the early development of this country. Unlike the general rules adopted as statutes by legislatures, the common law is the accumulation of rulings made by the courts in individual disputes. Judges, not legislatures, largely created the law of privacy, which allows individuals to collect damage awards for media disclosure of highly offensive personal information.

Common law in the United States grew out of the English common law. For centuries, judges in England, under the authority of the king, decided controversies on the basis of tradition and custom. These rulings established **precedents** that, together, became the law of the land. When the English colonized America, they brought the common law, including the precedents, with them.

The common law recognizes the importance of stability and predictability in the law. The common law is based on the judicial policy of **stare decisis,** which roughly means "let past decisions stand." In the common law, a judge decides a case by applying the law established by other judges in earlier, similar cases. The reliance on precedent not only provides continuity but also restricts judicial abuse of discretion. Thus, editors can use previous case law to help them determine whether a picture they want to publish is likely to be considered a violation of someone's privacy.

Although the common law promotes stability, it also allows for flexibility. The common law can adjust to fit changing circumstances because each judge can interpret and modify the law. Judges have five options when considering a case. They can (1) apply a precedent directly, (2) modify a precedent to fit new facts, (3) establish a new precedent by distinguishing the new case from previous cases, (4) overrule a previous precedent as no longer appropriate, or (5) ignore precedent. In most cases, precedent is either followed or adjusted to meet the facts at hand. Judges only rarely overrule previous precedents directly. Ignoring precedents greatly increases the risks of an opinion being overturned by a higher court.

Constitutional law and statutory law have a higher legal status than the common law, and therefore, the common law is relied on only when a statute or constitutional provision is not applicable. In a representative democracy, the people and their representatives in the legislatures, and not the courts, have the task of lawmaking. Sometimes legislatures incorporate portions of the common law into a statute, a process called *codification.* For example, in 1976, Congress rewrote the federal copyright statute to reflect a judicially created exception to a copyright owner's absolute control of a book, film, or musical score.

Sometimes, people confuse the common law with constitutional law. Both are created in part by judicial opinions based on precedent. However, constitutional law is based on judicial interpretation of a constitution, whereas common law is based on custom and practice.

The common law is not written down in one book. It can be understood only by reading recorded court decisions in hundreds of different volumes. Although the 1976 copyright statute is located in one volume of the *United States Code,* the common law of privacy can be discovered only by synthesizing numerous state and federal judicial opinions.

Common law is primarily state law. Each state has its own judicial traditions. However, as shown in Chapter 11, the Federal Rules of Evidence now allow federal judges to create common law testimonial privileges. In 1996, the U.S. Supreme Court ruled that a federal common law privilege covered confidential communications between therapists and patients.[17] Recently, journalists have argued that a federal common law privilege should also protect journalist-source relations. These claims have largely been rejected.

Law of Equity

The sixth source of law, equity, is historically related to the common law. Although *equity* is a legal term, it means what it sounds like. The law of equity allows courts to take action that is fair or just.

The law of equity developed because English common law allowed individuals to collect only monetary compensation after an injury had occurred. Under the law of equity, a **litigant** could petition the king to "do right for the love of God and by way of charity."[18] The law of equity allowed for preventive action and for remedial action other than monetary compensation. Although judges sitting in equity must consider precedent, they have substantial discretion to order a remedy they believe fair and appropriate.

Unlike England, the United States and most of the fifty states have never had separate courts of equity. Equity developed in the same courts that decided common law cases. However, juries are never used in equity suits.

Equity is significant in communication law primarily because of its preventive possibilities. Judges, for example, might use equity to halt the publication of a story considered a danger to national security. Punishment after publication would not protect national security.

◇ Summary ◇

Law in the United States comes from constitutions, statutes, administrative agencies, executive orders, common law, and equity. Constitutions outline the structure of government and define governmental authority and responsibilities. In the United States, the First Amendment to the federal Constitution protects the right to free speech and to a free press. Statutes are enforceable rules written by legislative bodies to govern social behavior. Administrative agencies make law as they adopt rules and adjudicate disputes, as authorized by statute. Executive orders are issued by the top officer in the executive branch of government. The common law is a collection of judicial decisions based on custom and tradition. Equity provides alternatives to the legal remedies available through the common law.

The Courts

Although agencies in all three branches of government in the United States make law, the judiciary is particularly important to a student of the law of public communication. There are fifty-two court systems in the country: the federal system, a system for each state, and another in the District of Columbia. The structures of the fifty-two systems are similar, but the state systems operate independently of the federal system under the authority of the state constitutions and laws.

[17] Jaffee v. Redmond, 518 U.S. 1 (1996).
[18] Henry Abraham, *The Judicial Process* 14 (1986).

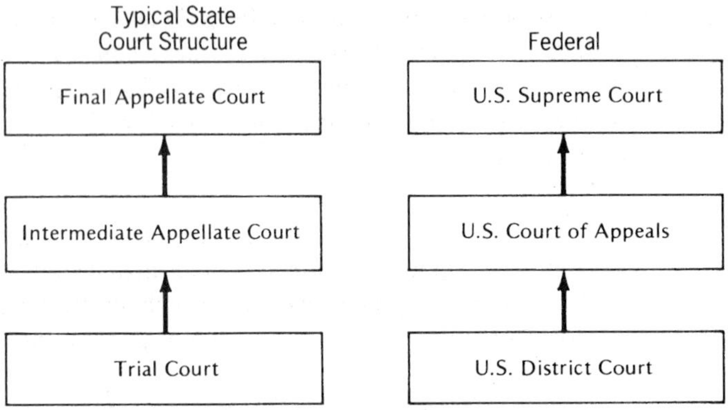

FIGURE 1.1 Comparative examples of state and federal court structures.

Most court systems consist of three layers (see Figure 1.1). At the lowest level are the trial courts, where the facts of each case are evaluated in light of the applicable law. The middle layer for both the federal system and many states is an intermediate **appellate court.** Finally, all court systems include a court of ultimate appeal, usually called a supreme court. The federal court system is the most important for the law of public communication.

The Federal System

The U.S. Constitution mandates only one federal court, the U.S. Supreme Court, but provides for "such inferior courts as the Congress may from time to time ordain and establish."[19] The Constitution also spells out the **jurisdiction,** or areas of responsibility, of the federal courts. The federal courts exercise ultimate authority over the meaning of the Constitution, including the constitutionality of statutes that impinge on the First Amendment. The federal courts also resolve conflicts in the interpretation of federal statutory law. The federal courts hear controversies involving the United States, such as when the U.S. Department of Justice seeks a court order to obtain the name of a confidential news source. The federal courts can hear controversies between citizens or corporations of different states. Frequently, for example, the two parties in a libel suit—the person suing and the publisher or broadcaster being sued—live in different states. Matters not specifically assigned to the federal courts by the Constitution are tried in state courts.

Congress created the federal judicial system in 1789 with the adoption of the Federal Judiciary Act. The federal system includes ninety-four trial courts, the U.S. district courts; thirteen intermediate appellate courts, the judicial circuits of the U.S. Courts of Appeals; and the highest appellate court, the U.S. Supreme Court. Courts with special jurisdiction, such as the U.S. Tax Court, are not generally important to the law of public communication.

TRIAL COURTS Almost all court cases begin in the trial courts, the U.S. district courts. These are also called courts of **original jurisdiction.** Trial courts examine the facts, or evidence, in a case and then apply the appropriate law. Only trial courts employ juries.

[19]U.S. Const. art. III, § 1.

There are ninety-four U.S. district courts. There is at least one federal district court in every state. Some states, such as Alaska, have only one district court. Other states, such as New York, have multiple districts. District courts also exist in the District of Columbia and in territories such as Guam. Many districts have more than one judge. By 2006, Congress had authorized 678 district court judgeships.

INTERMEDIATE APPELLATE COURTS Every person who loses in a trial court has the right to at least one **appeal.** In the federal system, that appeal is made to an intermediate appellate court. Appellate courts do not hold new trials and generally do not reevaluate the facts of cases. Rather, their responsibility is to ensure that trial courts use the proper procedures and apply the law correctly.

Appellate court judges decide cases primarily on the basis of lower court records and lawyers' written arguments, called *briefs.* The judges also hear a short oral argument by attorneys for both sides. If an appellate court discovers that a trial court has erred, the higher court may reverse, or overturn, the lower court and **remand** the case or send it back to a lower court for a new trial.

An appeal of a federal district court decision will ordinarily be considered in one of the thirteen circuits of the U.S. Courts of Appeals (see Figure 1.2). The jurisdictions of twelve of these courts are defined geographically. The thirteenth, the U.S. Court of Appeals for the Federal Circuit, handles only specialized appeals.

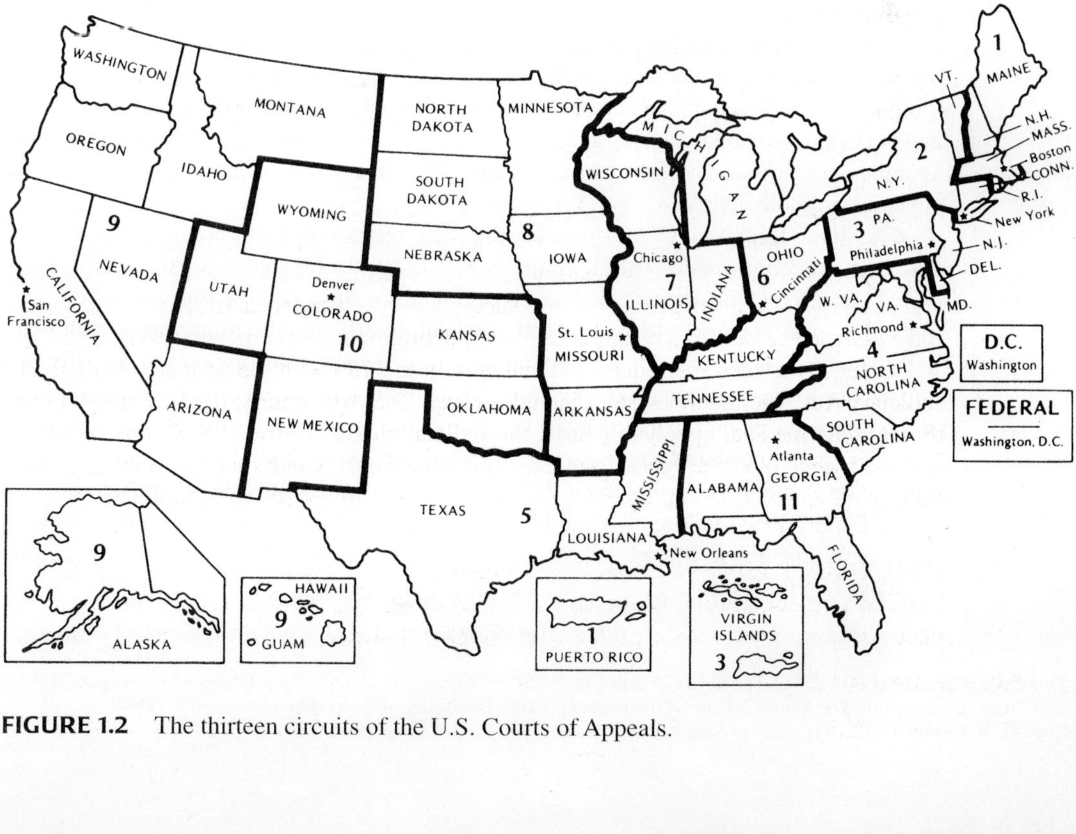

FIGURE 1.2 The thirteen circuits of the U.S. Courts of Appeals.

By 2006, Congress had authorized 179 appellate court judgeships. The Ninth Circuit, with twenty-eight judges, has the largest number of judges; the First Circuit, with six judges, has the smallest number. Most cases are heard by a panel of three judges. Particularly important cases will be heard **en banc,** that is, by all the judges of the court. For example, in 1993, the U.S. Court of Appeals for the Eighth Circuit affirmed en banc an FCC ruling that television stations are not required to provide balanced coverage of referenda, initiatives, or other ballot issues.[20]

The decisions of the U.S. Courts of Appeals must be followed by the federal district courts under their jurisdiction. Opinions of the Courts of Appeals may be persuasive authority but are not binding on state courts in the same jurisdiction deciding similar issues. Although federal appeals court decisions are not binding outside their jurisdiction, they are frequently influential.

Three circuits of the U.S. Courts of Appeals are particularly important to communication law. The Second Circuit, which hears appeals from federal courts in New York, decides a large number of media cases because New York City is the center of commercial telecommunications and the headquarters for many magazines, book publishers, advertising and public relations agencies, and newspapers. The Court of Appeals for the D.C. Circuit hears most of the appeals of decisions by the FCC and the FTC and many of the cases involving the federal Freedom of Information Act. The Ninth Circuit, with jurisdiction over the West Coast, frequently decides film, television, and copyright cases.

THE U.S. SUPREME COURT Although the U.S. Supreme Court can exercise both original and appellate jurisdiction, it is primarily an appellate court. The Constitution specifically limits the occasions when the Supreme Court can be the first court to consider a legal controversy, and the Court has decided cases in that capacity fewer than 250 times in the history of the country.[21] However, because the Court has the last word in the interpretation of federal law, the Court's appellate duties make it one of the most powerful institutions in the world. Appellate cases reach the Court from all other federal courts, federal regulatory agencies, and state supreme courts.

The nine Supreme Court justices, like all federal judges, are appointed by the President and confirmed by the Senate. Since 1789, the Senate has refused to confirm twelve Supreme Court nominees. Eleven nominations have been withdrawn when strong opposition was apparent. Most recently, Harriet Miers's nomination was withdrawn in 2005 when Senators questioned her qualifications. Justices are appointed for life, or as long as they choose to remain on the Court. They can be removed only by impeachment.[22] Of the nine justices on the Court in 2008, seven were appointed by Republican presidents. President Bush appointed two new conservatives in 2005, Chief Justice John Roberts Jr. and Justice Samuel Alito, replacing the conservative Chief Justice William Rehnquist and Justice Sandra Day O'Connor, a moderate (see Photo 1.1). Justice John Paul Stevens, 85, is arguably the most liberal justice on the Court. He was appointed by Republican President Gerald Ford.

[20]Arkansas AFL-CIO v. FCC, 11 F.3d 1430 (8th Cir. 1993).

[21]Lee Epstein et al., *The Supreme Court Compendium: Data, Decisions, and Developments* 63–65 (1994).

[22]U.S. Const. art. III, § 1; *see also* Samuel Mermin, *Law and the Legal System* 327 (2d ed. 1982).

PHOTO 1.1 Justices of the U.S. Supreme Court. *Standing:* Stephen G. Breyer, Clarence Thomas, Ruth Bader Ginsburg, Samuel A. Alito Jr. *Sitting:* Anthony Kennedy, John Paul Stevens, Chief Justice John G. Roberts Jr., Antonin Scalia, David H. Souter.

(Collection, The Supreme Court Historical Society. Photograph by Steve Petteway, Supreme Court.)

The Court is substantially more conservative than it was in the 1960s, when a majority of the justices had been appointed by Democrats. Conservative justices tend to interpret constitutional rights more narrowly than liberals. Conservatives also tend to favor states rights over central government regulations and to support individual property rights. Liberal justices are more concerned about protecting individual civil rights, including free speech and press. Liberal justices are also usually more willing to recognize new constitutional rights—such as a right of privacy—not explicitly stated in the Bill of Rights, and to increase access to government information. None of the justices on the Court in 2008 are considered as protective of civil liberties as former justices William Brennan Jr., Thurgood Marshall, and William Douglas.

During the period from 1994 to 2005, the Court had stable membership, and two distinct voting blocs emerged. The conservative bloc featured Rehnquist, Antonin Scalia, Clarence Thomas, and Anthony Kennedy. The liberal bloc featured Stevens, Ruth Bader Ginsburg, Stephen Breyer, and David Souter. Justice O'Connor, poised between the two blocs, was frequently the critical swing vote. With the replacement of Rehnquist and O'Connor by Roberts and Alito, the Court is in a period of transition. However, the first term of the Roberts Court shows the Court is becoming more conservative. Justice Alito, O'Connor's replacement, voted with the conservative bloc 15 percent more often than O'Connor had.[23] During the October 2005 Term, Justice Kennedy voted more often with the conservative bloc than with the liberal bloc, but abandoned the conservatives in several key cases; most notably Kennedy joined with Stevens, Breyer, Ginsburg, and Souter in striking down President Bush's plan to create military tribunals for suspected terrorists.[24] Thus, Kennedy is emerging as the new swing vote.[25] Although the Court may be more liberal or conservative at any given time, it seldom follows a prolonged extreme ideological course. As legal scholar Nelson Lund observes, "Our courts rarely make a lot of big lurches." If they do move in significant new directions, they are then apt to pull back toward the center.[26]

The justices who are considered "conservative" and those who are considered "liberal" do not always vote as blocs, nor do conservatives or liberals always have predictable votes in free expression cases. Many of the conservative justices have joined their more liberal colleagues to support freedom of expression. For example, Kennedy and Scalia joined Brennan, Marshall, Harry Blackmun, and Stevens in ruling unconstitutional damages assessed against a newspaper for publishing the name of a rape victim.[27] Kennedy and Scalia also voted with Brennan, Marshall, and Blackmun to hold that flag burning is protected by the First Amendment.[28] In a recent case in which the Court upheld a restriction on expressive activities occurring near health clinics, Scalia, Thomas, and Kennedy claimed in dissenting opinions that the Court's decision was harmful to freedom of expression.[29] Conversely, Justice Breyer dissented in two recent cases in which the Court struck down restrictions on sexual material on cable and the World Wide Web; Breyer believed the restrictions were necessary to protect children.[30]

As shown in Table 1.2, the number of cases filed with the Supreme Court has dramatically increased since 1954. While the number of cases accepted for oral argument and disposed of with a full opinion increased during the tenure of Chief Justices Warren (1953–69) and Burger (1969–86), Chief Justice Rehnquist (1986–2005) sought to reduce the number during his tenure. In the later part of Rehnquist's tenure, the Court usually received nearly 8,000 petitions annually and agreed to hear arguments in fewer that 100 cases a term. Although Chief Justice Roberts stated during his confirmation hearings he thought the Court could "contribute more to the clarity and uniformity of the law by taking more cases," the Court has yet to increase its caseload under Roberts. During the 2005 Term, the Court's first with Roberts as Chief Justice, the Court heard oral arguments in 87 cases; the Court heard oral arguments in only 78 cases during its 2006 Term. In 1988, Congress passed legislation giving the Supreme Court nearly total discretion in selecting the cases it will hear.[31] Until then, the Court was required to hear several kinds of appeals accounting for 20 percent of its caseload. Now, even more than before, most cases

[23]Linda Greenhouse, "Roberts Is at Court's Helm, But He Isn't Yet in Control," *N.Y. Times,* July 1, 2006, § 1, at 1.
[24]Hamdan v. Rumsfeld, 126 S. Ct. 2749 (2006).
[25]Jess Bravin, "Lawyers Swing for Kennedy Vote," *Wall Street Journal,* Oct. 3, 2006, at A2.
[26]Linda Greenhouse, "Court in Transition: The 2004–2005 Session," *N.Y. Times,* July 4, 2005, at 1.
[27]Florida Star v. B.J.F., 491 U.S. 524 (1989).
[28]Texas v. Johnson, 491 U.S. 397 (1989).
[29]Hill v. Colorado, 530 U.S. 703 (2000).
[30]Ashcroft v. ACLU 542 U.S. 656 (2004); United States v. Playboy Enter. Group, Inc., 529 U.S. 803 (2000).
[31]Supreme Court Case Selections, Pub. L. No. 100-352, 102 Stat. 662 (1988) (amending 28 U.S.C. §§ 1254, 1257 & 1258).

TABLE 1.2

United States Supreme Court Caseload 1954–2004 Terms

	1954 Term (Warren, C.J.)	1964 Term (Warren, C.J.)	1974 Term (Burger, C.J.)	1984 Term (Burger, C.J.)	1994 Term (Rehnquist, C.J.)	2004 Term (Rehnquist, C.J.)
Cases filed	1,397	2,288	3,661	4,046	6,996	7,496
Cases disposed of by full opinions	86	103	144	159	90	87
Disposed of by per curiam opinions	16	17	20	11	3	2

Sources: Administrative Office of the United States Courts, *Judicial Business of the United States Courts: 2005 Annual Report of the Director;* United States Supreme Court, *Chief Justice's Year-End Reports on the Federal Judiciary*, 2005; Lee Epstein et. al, *The Supreme Court Compendium: Data, Decisions & Developments* (2003).

reach the Court by a writ of **certiorari,** a Latin term indicating the Court is willing to review a case. As the Office of the Clerk of the Supreme Court explains, "review by this Court by means of a writ of certiorari is not a matter of right, but of judicial discretion. The primary concern of the Supreme Court is not to correct errors in lower court decisions, but to decide cases presenting issues of national importance beyond the particular facts and parties involved."[32]

The process of submitting a case to the Supreme Court for review begins when an attorney files a written argument, called a petition for certiorari, asking the Court to review a decision by a federal court or state supreme court. Four Supreme Court justices must vote yes if the Court is to grant a writ of certiorari and put the case onto its calendar. The Court rejects about 99 percent of the petitions for certiorari, usually with no explanation. When a petition for certiorari is denied, the lower court decision stands. The Supreme Court's refusal to accept a case does not affirm a lower court's opinion. Denial of certiorari "signifies only that the Court has chosen not to accept the case for review and does not express the Court's view of the merits of the case."[33] The Court denies certiorari for many reasons, perhaps because a case lacks legal significance or because there is no significant conflict in the lower courts to resolve.

If the Supreme Court accepts a case, the review process is much the same as for other appellate courts. The attorneys file briefs arguing their position. The briefs generally present the facts of the case, the issues involved, a review of the actions of the lower courts, and legal arguments. The Supreme Court justices review the written arguments and then listen to what is usually a half hour of oral argument from each attorney. The justices often interrupt attorneys to ask questions or challenge the arguments being presented. The time limit is precise. An attorney arguing before the Court is expected to stop in the middle of a sentence if the light in front of the lectern signals that time has expired.

Following oral arguments, the justices meet in chambers to discuss the case. No one except the justices is permitted in chambers. Once the justices have voted, a justice voting

[32]Office of Clerk, United States Supreme Court, *Guide for Prospective Indigent Petitioners for Writs of Certiorari* at 1, Oct. 2005.

[33]*Id.*

with the majority will be designated to write the Court's opinion. If the chief justice is part of the majority, he or she decides who will write the opinion of the Court. If the chief justice votes in the minority, the most senior justice in the majority decides who will write the Court's opinion. The choice of author for an opinion is significant because the author of the Court's opinion can weave in his or her political philosophy, view of the role of the Court, and interpretation of law.

After a justice drafts an opinion for the Court, the draft is circulated to the other justices for editing and comment. Drafts of dissenting opinions may be shared as well. The justices may bargain over the language in the drafts. Votes may shift. Ordinarily, at least a few justices will join the opinion of the Court without adding their own comments. However, justices often write their own **concurring** or **dissenting opinions** to explain their votes. They can also join, or sign onto, opinions written by other justices.

Sometimes none of the draft opinions presented to the Court attracts the five votes necessary for a majority. In such a situation, the draft with the most support becomes the **plurality** opinion of the Court, as occurred in *Richmond Newspapers v. Virginia.* Although the justices in *Richmond Newspapers* voted 7-1 that the First Amendment requires trials to be open to the public, no more than three justices agreed to any one opinion explaining why courtrooms should remain open during trials.[34] If many of the justices write their own opinions rather than joining an opinion of the Court, the high court offers little guidance to lower courts facing similar circumstances. A majority of the justices deciding a case, usually five, must agree to any point of law for the Court's opinion to become binding precedent.

In what is known as the Pentagon Papers case, discussed in Chapter 3, each of the nine justices wrote his own opinion. Although the Court voted 6-3 that the *New York Times* and the *Washington Post* could report a secret Defense Department study, the only opinion issued on behalf of the six-justice majority was an unsigned, three-paragraph **per curiam** opinion. A per curiam opinion is "by the court" rather than an opinion attributed to any one justice. The Court's opinion in the Pentagon Papers case said only that the government had not sufficiently justified barring news stories based on the Defense Department study.[35] The justices could not agree on the reasons a **prior restraint** was unjustified.

Technically, the Supreme Court's decisions apply only to the case being decided. The Supreme Court's opinions do not establish statutelike law. However, lower courts assume the Supreme Court will decide similar cases in similar ways, so they adjudicate conflicts before them accordingly. Otherwise lower court judges risk having their decisions overturned.

The Supreme Court, in its role as interpreter of the U.S. Constitution, can review the constitutionality of all legislation. This means that the Supreme Court can invalidate an act of Congress that violates the Constitution. The Court has declared all or part of a federal statute unconstitutional about 160 times in the history of the country. The Court has also declared provisions of about 1,250 state laws and constitutions to be unconstitutional.[36] The Supreme Court has frequently expanded freedom of expression by invalidating state and federal statutes found to conflict with the First Amendment.

[34] 448 U.S. 555 (1980).
[35] N.Y. Times Co. v. United States, 403 U.S. 713 (1971).
[36] Lee Epstein et al., *The Supreme Court Compendium: Data, Decisions, and Developments,* 163–93 (2003).

Neither the Supreme Court nor any other court can enforce its own decisions. The courts have no troops or police to force compliance. The executive branch enforces court decisions. Law enforcement officers ensure that fines are paid and sentences are served. When the Supreme Court rules against the executive branch, it relies on tradition and its own prestige to achieve compliance. In 1974, public respect for the Court forced President Nixon to obey an order to release secret White House tapes to a special prosecutor who was investigating the Watergate scandal.[37]

The State Systems

Most state court systems are organized much like the federal courts. Each state has trial courts, similar to the federal district courts, which handle nearly every kind of civil or criminal case. These courts, often called county courts, are ordinarily the first state courts to consider libel or privacy cases. These trial courts also handle appeals for a number of subordinate trial courts responsible for minor civil matters, traffic violations, and criminal misdemeanors. Most state court judges are elected, usually in nonpartisan elections.

State court systems provide either one or two levels of appellate courts. In some states, appeals go directly from the county courts to what is usually called the state supreme court. However, many states have intermediate appellate courts to moderate the workload of the supreme court. State courts of appeals, like the federal circuit courts, often use small panels of judges. State appellate court decisions interpreting state law are binding on both lower state courts and federal courts in the same jurisdiction.

The decisions of state supreme courts, usually made up of seven to nine justices, constitute the law of the state and are binding on all of the state's courts. Each state supreme court is the final arbiter of its own state constitution, provided there is no conflict with the federal constitution. A losing **party** in a state supreme court case may have recourse before the U.S. Supreme Court only if a substantial federal question is involved.

◇ Summary ◇

There are fifty-two court systems: one for the federal government, one for the District of Columbia, and one for each state. Most court cases originate in the trial courts, where the law is applied to the facts of each case. Appeals courts ensure that the trial courts use the proper procedures and apply the law correctly. The federal court system consists of federal district courts, the thirteen circuits of the U.S. Courts of Appeals, and the U.S. Supreme Court.

The Litigation Process: Civil and Criminal

In criminal law, the government punishes individuals who commit illegal acts such as murder, arson, and theft. Civil law ordinarily resolves disputes between two private parties. The dispute can be over a dog bite or a news story. Most communication cases are brought in civil court rather than criminal court.

[37]United States v. Nixon, 418 U.S. 683 (1974).

A crime is an antisocial act defined by law, usually a statute adopted by a state legislature. State criminal statutes forbid behavior such as murder and rape and specify punishment, usually a jail sentence, a fine, or both. Criminal law is enforced by government law enforcement officers. Once suspects are arrested, they are prosecuted by government attorneys. The state must prove its case beyond a reasonable doubt, a heavy **burden of proof** demanding that jurors be all but certain that the government's version of events is correct. One example of criminal law discussed in this book is obscenity. Both the federal and state governments prosecute individuals who distribute obscene publications.

Understanding criminal law is important to journalists who report news of the criminal courts. Several issues discussed in this book—access to courtrooms, pretrial publicity, and cameras in the courtroom—relate directly to criminal court proceedings.

In contrast to criminal cases intended to punish illegal behavior, civil cases often involve claims by individuals or organizations seeking legal redress for a violation of their interests. A person or organization filing a civil suit usually seeks compensation for harm suffered because of the actions of another. A woman may sue a neighbor for medical costs after being bitten by the neighbor's dog. Or a man may sue a newspaper for defamation if the paper inaccurately reports that he is an adulterer. A legal wrong committed by one person against another is often called a **tort.** Civil law provides the opportunity for a "peaceful" resolution when one person accuses another of committing a tort.

Litigants in civil cases can win by proving their cases by a preponderance of the evidence. Unlike criminal prosecutors, lawyers representing civil plaintiffs do not have to prove wrong beyond a reasonable doubt. Preponderance of the evidence means that litigants must convince jurors that their version of events is more probable—if by a narrow margin—than that of the opposing party. If the person suing wins a civil case, he or she often recovers monetary **damages.** If the person being sued wins, frequently no money changes hands except to pay the lawyers' fees. In civil law, there are no jail terms and usually no fines.

Civil law, including libel and privacy, is a significant part of the law of public communication. Civil suits are more likely to be based on common law than on statutory law. In media law, in particular, the government is not ordinarily involved except to provide neutral facilities—the judge, the jury, and the courthouse—to help settle the dispute. However, a civil suit can be based on a statute, and a person or group can sue, or be sued by, the government. Some states' open meetings and open records laws allow private citizens to sue officials to secure public access.

A Civil Suit

A civil case begins when the person suing, called the **plaintiff,** files a legal complaint against the person being sued, the **defendant.** In April 1976, Dr. Ronald Hutchinson, then the research director at a Michigan state mental hospital, filed a civil complaint against Senator William Proxmire of Wisconsin in the U.S. District Court for the Western District of Wisconsin. Hutchinson complained that Proxmire had libeled him by giving a "Golden Fleece" award to his research on monkeys. Proxmire had said that the American public was being "fleeced" by the nearly half-million dollars spent for Hutchinson's research by the National Science Foundation, the National Aeronautics and Space Administration, and the Office of Naval Research. The agencies were examining the problems faced by monkeys and humans confined in close quarters for long periods of time, as in space or underwater exploration.

Proxmire said, however, that the federal government ought to get out of the "monkey business." He said the "transparent worthlessness" of Hutchinson's research was taking a bite out of the American taxpayer. Hutchinson's civil complaint asked for $8 million in damages because, he said, Proxmire had humiliated him and held him up to public scorn, damaged his professional and academic standing, and damaged his ability to attract research grants.[38]

Once a complaint has been filed at the courthouse, a defendant, in this case Senator Proxmire, is served with a summons, a notice to appear in court. If defendants fail to appear, courts may hold them in contempt and require them to forfeit their cases. Defendants often respond to complaints by denying the accusations. Senator Proxmire "answered" the complaint, in part, by filing a motion for **summary judgment,** a common defense tactic in communication cases. A judge can grant a summary judgment to either a defendant or a plaintiff if the judge believes that the two sides in a case agree on the facts of the dispute and that one side should win as a matter of law. A summary judgment terminates a suit in its early stages, saving attorney fees and avoiding the often unpredictable outcome of a jury trial. Summary judgments are discussed more thoroughly in Chapter 4.

Hutchinson's complaint, Proxmire's answer, and a reply by Hutchinson are called the *pleadings,* documents stating the nature of a case. Sometimes the two sides in a dispute file a series of documents in an attempt to narrow the issues and thereby limit the length and expense of a trial. Frequently, the two sides will ask a judge for a pretrial conference in another attempt to narrow the issues or even to settle the case.

Meanwhile, the parties, sometimes called litigants, begin what is called **discovery.** Discovery is the information-gathering process. During discovery—which in major cases can take several years—each side finds out as much as possible about the evidence possessed by the other party. The lawyers often prepare interrogatories, written questions that must be answered under oath by people who might have relevant information. Then lawyers frequently take depositions, that is, ask questions in person that also must be answered under oath.

During discovery, lawyers may request that the judge issue a **subpoena** requiring a journalist or someone else to testify or bring documents or other evidence to court. A subpoena must be served to the person named in it. Failure to comply with a subpoena can result in a contempt of court ruling. Journalists frequently fight subpoenas on the grounds that revealing sources or evidence will limit their ability to gather news, a subject discussed in Chapter 11.

In the *Hutchinson* case, the judge granted time for discovery after receiving Senator Proxmire's motion for summary judgment. The two parties exchanged interrogatories and subsequently the answers. Hutchinson requested a jury trial. He also asked to amend his complaint, a motion that was granted over the objection of Senator Proxmire. In the amended complaint, Hutchinson said the Golden Fleece announcement not only libeled him but also infringed on his rights of privacy and peace and tranquillity. Both Hutchinson, the plaintiff, and Proxmire, the defendant, filed the results of depositions. Shortly thereafter, Hutchinson filed a brief, along with five volumes of exhibits, arguing against Proxmire's motion for summary judgment. Senator Proxmire filed a reply brief with exhibits.

[38]Hutchinson v. Proxmire, 443 U.S. 111 (1979).

About a year after Hutchinson filed his complaint, the district court judge granted Senator Proxmire's motion for summary judgment.[39] If the summary judgment had not been granted, the case would have gone to trial.

A jury trial is required if the two parties disagree on the facts of a case and one of the parties insists on a jury. After both sides present their cases, the judge explains the relevant law to the jurors. The jury is asked to apply the law to the facts, and it may set monetary damages as part of the verdict. If a judge believes the jury verdict is contrary to law or that the damage award is excessive, he or she can overturn the jury's decision. This occurred early in the 1980s when a judge decided that a jury verdict in favor of Mobil Oil president William Tavoulareas and against the *Washington Post* was contrary to libel law.[40]

Once a judgment has been recorded in a case, either party can appeal. The person who appeals is known as the **petitioner;** the person fighting the appeal is called the **respondent.** The petitioner in one appeal may be the respondent in another appeal. In Hutchinson's suit, Hutchinson became a petitioner when he appealed the grant of summary judgment to the U.S. Court of Appeals for the Seventh Circuit, where it was upheld. Hutchinson's petition for certiorari to the U.S. Supreme Court was granted. Proxmire was the respondent before both the Seventh Circuit and the Supreme Court. The Supreme Court reversed the decision of the Seventh Circuit and remanded the case to the lower courts for disposition consistent with the Supreme Court's opinion. Hutchinson and Proxmire eventually settled out of court. Hutchinson received $10,000 in damages and an apology from Senator Proxmire. The Supreme Court opinion, *Hutchinson v. Proxmire,* is discussed in Chapter 4.

A Criminal Case

The key steps in a criminal prosecution are substantially the same in most states. The procedures may be labeled differently or occur in a different sequence.

A criminal action begins with a law enforcement investigation. The government's case against an individual begins with the arrest, or apprehension, of the person suspected of committing a crime. The case of Dr. Sam Sheppard, important to communication law, began with his arrest in July 1954. Sheppard, a Cleveland, Ohio, osteopath, was arrested on a charge of murdering his wife, Marilyn. (Fictionalized accounts were presented in the 1960s television series *The Fugitive* and a 1990s movie of the same name.) The one-month investigation prior to the arrest established that Mrs. Sheppard had been killed with a blunt instrument, that Dr. Sheppard was in the house at the time, that no money was missing from the home, and that no readable fingerprints could be found.[41] The investigation included an inquest ordered by the coroner to determine whether a murder had been committed. Extensive, sensational publicity, discussed in Chapter 10, began immediately.

After an arrest, the person accused of a crime appears before a magistrate for a preliminary hearing. At the hearing, the person is advised of the nature of the crime and reminded of his or her right to counsel and the right to remain silent. The primary purpose of a preliminary hearing is to determine if there is sufficient evidence, or **probable cause,**

[39] 431 F. Supp. 1311 (W.D. Wis. 1977).
[40] Tavoulareas v. Washington Post Co., 567 F. Supp. 651 (D.D.C. 1983), *aff'd,* 817 F.2d 762 (D.C. 1987) (en banc).
[41] State v. Sheppard, 128 N.E.2d 471 (Ohio Ct. App. 1955).

to justify further detention or a trial. Sheppard appeared before a magistrate, was informed of the murder charge, and was bound over to the grand jury.

If the magistrate decides that there is probable cause, he or she will set the bail, that is, announce the amount of money that must be posted before the accused can be released from jail. The bail is intended to ensure that the accused appears in court. Sheppard was denied bail.

The next step, depending on the state, could be the filing by the prosecutor of a criminal information, a document formally accusing the person of a crime. Or the prosecutor may take the evidence to a grand jury to seek an **indictment,** a formal accusation by a grand jury. Not all states have grand juries, and their role in the criminal justice system varies. On August 17, 1954, a grand jury in Ohio indicted Sheppard for first-degree murder.[42]

An arraignment usually follows the formal accusation. The arraignment is the official, formal reading of the indictment or information to the accused. The accused is asked to plead guilty or not guilty.

If the defendant pleads not guilty, the focus turns to pretrial preparation and negotiation. Both the prosecution and defense engage in discovery, the pretrial fact-finding. Both sides may submit a variety of motions to the judge. The defense may move for an adjustment or dismissal of the charges. Or as in Sam Sheppard's case, a defense attorney may ask that a trial be relocated or delayed because of extensive pretrial publicity. The judge in the Sheppard trial denied both motions.

During the pretrial maneuvers, the prosecution and defense may agree to resolve the case through a plea bargain. In plea bargaining, a trial is avoided because the defendant is willing to plead guilty, often to reduced charges. Roughly 90 percent of criminal defendants plead guilty, thereby avoiding a trial.[43] Plea bargains not only save time and money but also avoid the uncertainty inherent in a trial.

A trial can take place before a judge or a jury. Criminal defendants can waive their right to a jury trial. After the jury announces the verdict of guilty or not guilty, a judge pronounces the sentence. A jury in the Common Pleas Court of Cuyahoga County, Ohio, decided that Sheppard "purposely and maliciously" killed his wife, the requirement for second-degree murder in Ohio. The judge sentenced Sheppard to life in prison, the mandatory penalty in Ohio for the crime of second-degree murder.

Sheppard appealed to the Court of Appeals of Ohio for Cuyahoga County, an intermediate appellate court. He argued that there were nearly forty errors in the conduct of the trial, including the denial of motions to move the trial and to postpone the trial. He also argued that the jury had been improperly selected and prejudicial evidence had been improperly allowed during the trial. The three-judge panel decided that Sheppard "has been afforded a fair trial by an impartial jury and . . . substantial justice has been done."[44] Sheppard also lost a 1956 appeal in the Ohio Supreme Court. The U.S. Supreme Court denied certiorari the same year.[45] Nine years later, the U.S. Supreme Court agreed to consider Sheppard's contention that he was denied a fair trial because of sensational media coverage. That story is told in Chapter 10.

[42]*Id;* Sheppard v. Maxwell, 384 U.S. 333 (1966).

[43]American Bar Association, *Law and the Courts: A Handbook of Courtroom Procedures* 44 (1995).

[44]State v. Sheppard, 128 N.E.2d at 504.

[45]State v. Sheppard, 128 N.E.2d 471 (Ohio Ct. App. 1955), *aff'd,* 135 N.E.2d 340 (Ohio 1956), *cert. denied,* 352 U.S. 910 (1956).

◇ Summary ◇

Criminal law prohibits antisocial behavior as defined by statute. Violations are punishable by jail sentences and fines. Criminal law is enforced by the government. A criminal action begins with an investigation and an arrest. A preliminary hearing is held to determine if there is sufficient evidence to justify a trial. Then either a prosecutor or a grand jury formally accuses a person of a crime. After the accused responds to the charge during an arraignment, the prosecution and the defense engage in pretrial fact-finding, known as discovery. Civil law ordinarily involves disputes between two private parties. A plaintiff sues a defendant for damages. After the plaintiff files a civil complaint and the defendant responds, the two parties engage in discovery. Civil and criminal cases can be dismissed or otherwise resolved before trial.

Working with the Law

Finding and Reading the Law

Many professional communicators value the ability to locate and understand the law by themselves. Communicators do not have to have legal training to find statutes and court opinions. Law libraries have knowledgeable personnel ready to help. Information in Appendix A in this book provides background to enable students to find court cases and other material. Although a nonlawyer can find the law with a little assistance, reading and understanding the law take time and practice. A few tips are offered in the appendix. Also in the appendix are explanations of the legal citations in this book. However, journalists should not try to be their own lawyers, even if they have law degrees.

Working with Lawyers

Because public communication often raises questions of law, professional communicators frequently need lawyers. Communicators should not fear or avoid lawyers; rather, communicators should use lawyers intelligently.

Most communicators will not have direct access to a lawyer in their first job. Newspapers, for example, generally prefer journalists to take legal questions to a supervisor. In newsrooms, city editors and managing editors ordinarily can answer routine legal questions and usually decide when a lawyer should be consulted. Some major daily newspapers and large advertising and public relations firms hire staff lawyers, known as in-house attorneys. Other media companies engage a law firm they can call as needed. Even the smallest communications organization should have experienced legal counsel to call when questions arise.

Lawyers, whose hourly fees are usually high, should be used when possible to prevent a legal conflict rather than to resolve one. A lawyer should be consulted in the following cases:

- When a communicator is served with a subpoena, a summons, or an arrest warrant. Communicators need the advice of a lawyer before responding to a legal document.
- When there is a concern that a story being considered for publication could lead to a libel or privacy suit. Attorneys can assess the risks of stories and suggest modifications.

- When a news medium is asked to print retractions or corrections. Some well-intentioned corrections can increase, rather than decrease, the risk of a suit if a lawyer is not consulted.
- When a communicator is approached by a lawyer hired by someone else. A layperson should not respond to the legal moves of a legal adversary.
- When a communicator is considering an action that may be illegal. Reporters pursuing a story sometimes consider trespassing, tape recording, or obtaining stolen documents. Sometimes it is obvious when an act is illegal; often it is not. Reporters need to understand the legal consequences of their actions. A lawyer may help.

Lawyers can do more than help limit the legal jeopardy of communication professionals. They can also help communicators do their jobs. For example, lawyers can help journalists obtain access to closed records or meetings by explaining to officials the rights of the public and press. Lawyers also help public relations specialists and broadcasters complete forms required by the Securities and Exchange Commission, the Federal Communications Commission, and other administrative agencies.

When communicators work with lawyers, they should remember that lawyers, like other professionals, are trained to do some tasks and not others. Lawyers can help resolve a legal conflict, but they cannot eliminate the sloppy writing or editing that may have caused a suit. Attorneys can explain the probable risks and consequences of a story or an ad. They can discuss the factors that ought to be considered in deciding how to avoid **liability.** An attorney should know the questions an opposing attorney will ask about a story and what arguments are likely to be made in a libel trial.

Lawyers are not usually qualified to tell a communicator what to write or how to edit. Some lawyers are insensitive to the problems, values, and commitments of journalists. Some attorneys regularly advise cutting stories to avoid trouble. They sometimes suggest eliminating the defamatory portions of stories without regard to the public importance of the information. The job of a lawyer, according to James Goodale, a prominent media attorney, should be "to figure out how to get the story published," not trimmed or killed.[46] The lawyer should explain legal risks; the communicator should make the editorial decisions after weighing those risks.

Public communicators may sometimes need a personal attorney. An employer might refuse to represent an employee in court, especially if the employee acts contrary to instructions or without consulting a supervisor. In the early 1970s, the *New York Times* refused to defend one of its reporters, Earl Caldwell, when he declined to testify before a grand jury. The *Times* wanted Caldwell to respond to a grand jury subpoena by entering the grand jury room, even if he refused to answer questions. However, Caldwell refused even to enter the grand jury room, which is closed to the public and the press. Caldwell believed that once he went behind closed doors, his sources would no longer trust his commitment to keep what he knew confidential. When Caldwell was found in contempt of court for refusing to testify, the *Times* did not provide him with a company attorney.

[46]Ann Rambo, "Litigious Age Gives Rise to Media Law," *presstime*, Nov. 1981, at 7.

Caldwell's case was considered by the Supreme Court in *Branzburg v. Hayes,* a case discussed in Chapter 11.

An attorney needs to know all of the facts that pertain to a legal issue. Communicators should hold nothing back. Although it is embarrassing for journalists to confess careless reporting or writing, the failure to tell a lawyer everything can be legally damaging, particularly if the errors are first revealed by an opposing lawyer in front of a jury. Attorneys need to know the worst in order to present the best case.

◇ Summary ◇

Legal advice can be an expensive but necessary part of modern communication. Lawyers should be called when a communicator must respond to an official document or someone else's attorney. Lawyers should be consulted when a communicator is considering an act that may be illegal. Lawyers should review stories that could lead to libel or privacy suits. Lawyers can explain the risks of publishing a story, but they should not be allowed to act as editors. Information about doing legal research is in Appendix A of this book.

Limitations of Law

This book focuses on the law. Professional communicators need to know the law in order to do their jobs effectively and without unnecessary risk. However, the law does not resolve all questions that may arise in public communication.

For one thing, the law does not necessarily protect every action that a professional communicator believes to be in the public interest. Libel law does not always protect a newspaper that wants to report an allegation of government corruption. In addition, reporters who refuse to reveal the names of sources for a story about government corruption could go to jail. At times, communicators have to decide whether the public benefit of a story is worth a jail sentence or a libel suit. The fact that journalists might not be protected by law is not the only factor to be considered when they are deciding whether to publish a story.

Conversely, the law may allow behavior that exceeds personal or professional ethics. Ethics is the consideration of moral rights and wrongs. Ethics involves honesty, fairness, and motivation. It also involves respect for the emotional well-being, dignity, and physical safety of others. The law, as reflected in statutes and court decisions, does not always parallel personal and professional codes of conduct. The First Amendment frequently permits expression, such as the publication of the names of rape victims, which many journalists consider unethical. Ethical questions are raised not only by the publication of highly personal information but also by pretrial publication of information about criminal defendants and by the refusal of journalists to reveal their news sources, all of which are sometimes permitted by law. Communicators base decisions to publish on whether behavior is morally "right" or "wrong" as well as on its legality. However, a discussion of ethics is left for another book. The purpose of this book is to help professional communicators understand the law that affects their performance.

CHAPTER 2

First Amendment

Americans enjoy greater freedom of expression than any other people. Other democracies protect freedom of expression, but not to the degree that the U.S. Constitution does. Unlike the citizens of many foreign lands, Americans are free to burn their country's flag, call the President a crook, carry swastikas in public demonstrations, and watch endless violence on television.

The legal foundation of the American freedom to speak and publish is the First Amendment. "Congress shall make no law," the First Amendment says, "respecting an establishment of religion, or prohibiting the free exercise thereof; or abridging the freedom of speech, or of the press; or the right of the people peaceably to assemble, and to petition the government for a redress of grievances." (The first fourteen amendments to the Constitution are reprinted in Appendix B.) The categorical language of the First Amendment, prohibiting government interference with freedom of expression, gives Americans a broad right to speak and publish on matters of conscience and consequence—and on trivial matters, too—without fear of government reprisal. Freedom of expression is in large measure a negative freedom: freedom from government interference.

Despite the categorical prohibition against government interference, the First Amendment does not establish an absolute freedom for citizens to speak and publish. Sometimes expression may be halted or punished. For example, the government may halt expression that threatens national security or incites a riot. Expression may also be punished after dissemination if it damages the reputation of others or invades their privacy. Communication law, the subject of this book, is the system by which society determines which expression is protected and which may be punished, when, and why. Exceptions to freedom of expression depend on what is said, who is speaking, and the harm that speech or writing causes. Whether speech may be prohibited or punished also depends on the standards of judgment employed by the courts and on the theory or purposes underpinning freedom of expression.

Theory of Freedom of Expression

A theory is a set of assumptions, principles, and procedures that categorize knowledge and explain behavior. Einstein's theory of relativity helps scientists to understand the relationship of time, space, and matter. Able scholars have attempted to formulate theories to explain when expression should be free and when it should be restricted. The researchers seek a set of assumptions, principles, and procedures that can consistently explain why freedom of expression should—or should not—protect such diverse expression as publishing stolen government documents, burning draft cards, proclaiming alcohol content on a beer label, and broadcasting four-letter words.

Forming a coherent theory of free expression might seem quite easy, considering the elegant economy of the First Amendment itself: "Congress shall make no law . . . abridging the freedom of speech or of the press." Yet few agree on the range of speakers, expression, and circumstances that such a theory should encompass.

Many thoughtful scholars have illuminated various values and purposes served by freedom of expression. Professor Vincent Blasi has emphasized the importance of protecting the powerful media that "check" government's power.[1] Professor Lee Bollinger stresses the importance of freedom of expression as a way to develop—and reflect—a tolerant society.[2] Yet, despite these and many other contributions to First Amendment theory, no all-encompassing theory of freedom of expression has emerged. This is because freedom of expression involves so many different media, social conflicts, and competing philosophies.

In the absence of a single theory of freedom of expression, perhaps one should adopt Professor Frederick Schauer's suggestion that there are several First Amendments, each with different theoretical justifications for different circumstances. One First Amendment, according to Schauer, serves the goals of democratic governance by forbidding government to suppress the political speech of its critics. Another First Amendment is justified by the search for truth in the "marketplace of ideas." This First Amendment protects open inquiry into the sciences at academic institutions. A third First Amendment, Schauer suggests, protects individual fulfillment by safeguarding expression in the arts.[3]

Like Schauer, the late law professor Harry Kalven saw so many conflicting values and complex facts in freedom of expression controversies that he thought it fruitless to try to construct an overarching theory. It is better, Kalven said, to "think small,"[4] deciding each court case as it arises without attempting to reconcile every decision with every other in a consistent structure. Thinking small offers the benefit of flexibility; if we treat each case separately, we do not necessarily have to protect the soap salesman's free speech to the same degree or for the same reasons we protect the speech of the soapbox orator. However, Kalven's particularized approach presents the drawback of complexity; if every free speech case is different, the First Amendment doctrine may become as complex as the Internal Revenue Code. Lawyers charging $400 per hour might welcome complexity, but newspaper publishers, broadcast station operators, and most journalism students prefer simpler guides to freedom of expression.

If decisions determining freedom of expression cannot be predicted or rationalized within an all-encompassing theory, neither must decisions about freedom of expression be abandoned to chaos. Communication law is guided by a number of procedures, traditions, and values that create unifying themes if not a consistent theory. Americans agree on the broad purposes and values of freedom of expression, even as they disagree on when the government may curb that freedom. Important values served by freedom of expression include the social goals of attaining the truth, making decisions in a democracy, checking government power, and managing change. Freedom of expression also serves the related personal value of individual fulfillment.

Attainment of Truth

The argument that freedom of expression aids the search for truth assumes that rational decisions emerge from consideration of all facts and arguments. An individual who seeks

[1]Vincent Blasi, "The Checking Value in First Amendment Theory," 1977 *Am. B. Found. Res. J.* 521, 538.

[2]Lee Bollinger, *The Tolerant Society* (1986).

[3]Frederick Schauer, "Must Speech Be Special," 78 *Nw. U. L. Rev.* 1284 (1983).

[4]*See* Kenneth L. Karst, "The First Amendment and Harry Kalven: An Appreciative Comment on the Advantages of Thinking Small," 13 *U.C.L.A. L. Rev.* 1 (1965).

knowledge and truth, said the late Professor Thomas Emerson, carries on a continuous Socratic dialogue. A citizen who seeks truth, Emerson said,

> must hear all sides of the question, especially as presented by those who feel strongly and argue militantly for a different view. He must consider all alternatives, test his judgment by exposing it to opposition, make full use of different minds to sift the true from the false. Conversely, suppression of information, discussion, or the clash of opinion prevents one from reaching the most rational judgment, blocks the generation of new ideas, and tends to perpetuate error.[5]

The belief that freedom of expression speeds the search for truth is frequently summarized in the metaphor of the marketplace of ideas. The best test of truth, according to the late Supreme Court Justice Oliver Wendell Holmes, is the power of a thought "to get itself accepted in the competition of the market."[6] Just as shoppers in the commercial marketplace are said to seek the best products, participants in the marketplace of ideas are said to seek the most original, truthful, or useful information. Like commercial shoppers, consumers of ideas must be wary that they do not accept inferior goods. In theory, good ideas—political, scientific, and social—will prevail in a free market.

The marketplace-of-ideas metaphor can be traced to the bad marital relations of John Milton, the English poet and essayist. In 1644, Milton published an essay titled *Areopagitica,* which was Milton's response to criticism he had received for publishing without a government license. Milton had published a tract urging that English divorce laws be liberalized so that he could dissolve an unpleasant union. In *Areopagitica,* Milton argued that Parliament should allow unlicensed printing.

Milton said that licensing is a bad idea because it deprives citizens of knowledge and ideas that could improve their lives. Furthermore, he argued, censorship is impractical because the censor's pencil does not prevent the circulation of influential ideas. In addition, Milton said that most people are not fit to be censors. Those with the intelligence to be discerning censors would not want such a boring and repulsive task. Besides, he concluded, citizens benefit from having to distinguish good ideas from bad. In his most famous passage, Milton said that the free competition of ideas furthered the search for truth:

> And though all the winds of doctrine were let loose to play upon the earth, so Truth be in the field, we do injuriously, by licensing and prohibiting, to misdoubt her strength. Let her and Falsehood grapple; who ever knew Truth put to the worse, in a free and open encounter?[7]

Despite his laissez-faire argument, Milton did not believe that all expression should be permitted. As a Puritan, he was not ready to allow free discussion of Catholicism or atheism.

Nineteenth-century philosopher John Stuart Mill thought it "idle sentimentality" to argue, as Milton did, that truth would not be "put to the worse" in combat with falsehood. "History teems," Mill wrote, "with instances of truth put down by persecution." Yet Mill valued free speech fully as much as Milton, not because truth would always prevail but because truth has no chance to prevail without freedom of expression. Silencing the opinion

---

[5]Thomas Emerson, *Toward a General Theory of the First Amendment* 7 (1966).
[6]Abrams v. United States, 250 U.S. 616 (1919).
[7]John Milton, *Areopagitica,* in 32 Great Books of the Western World 409 (1952).

of even one person robs the human race, Mill said. If a correct statement is suppressed, he said, people are "deprived of the opportunity of exchanging error for truth." If a false statement is suppressed, people "lose, what is almost as great a benefit, the clearer perception and livelier impression of truth, produced by its collision with error."[8]

Not all students of freedom of expression embrace the metaphor of the marketplace of ideas. One commentator, following Mill, questions whether citizens are sufficiently rational to choose truth over falsehood.[9] Another critic, feminist scholar Catharine MacKinnon, argues that the marketplace of ideas is an abstraction of little value to women because women are often too poor to buy speech. Indeed, MacKinnon argues that women are victimized in the marketplace by the avalanche of pornography depicting them as sexual objects. To MacKinnon, well-financed and often violent pornography constitutes the "free speech of men" that "silences the free speech of women."[10]

Critics of the marketplace metaphor also question whether consolidation of the media unduly restricts the circulation of ideas. Professor Jerome Barron has argued that the marketplace of ideas means little to minorities, dissidents, and fringe groups if they cannot gain access for their ideas in the monopoly daily newspapers found in most American cities.[11] Barron echoes the Commission on Freedom of the Press, a panel of scholars and intellectuals who warned in 1947 that concentration of media ownership threatened to create a private censorship as restrictive as government censorship.[12] More recently, Internet users fearful that too few companies will control access to the World Wide Web have advocated for "net neutrality" legislation that would require large Internet firms to allow equal access for all Internet traffic.

Although several large companies control vast holdings of newspapers, broadcast stations, cable outlets, and entertainment production facilities, there are more than a few voices in the marketplace of ideas. Weekly newspapers, niche magazines, radio stations, and the Internet challenge large dailies for advertisers, readers, and scoops. Cable television, offering scores of specialized channels, lures viewers from the once-dominant broadcast networks, even as telephone companies seek to become operators of local cable systems. In 2008, the Department of Justice approved the merger of the only competing satellite radio companies—Sirius and XM—on the grounds that satellite radio competes with terrestrial radio, iPods, and other mobile media. The rapidly expanding Internet offers interactive print, voice, and video.

Governance

Besides aiding the search for truth, freedom of expression contributes to democratic governance. "The root purpose of the First Amendment," Professor Thomas Emerson said, "is to assure an effective system of freedom of expression in a democratic society."[13] Alexander Meiklejohn, an influential philosopher and academic leader, was the best-known proponent of the theory that freedom of expression is to be valued primarily for its

[8]John Stuart Mill, *On Liberty* 24 (Gateway 1955).
[9]C. Edwin Baker, "Scope of the First Amendment Freedom of Speech," 25 *U.C.L.A. L. Rev.* 964 (1978).
[10]Catharine MacKinnon, *Feminism Unmodified: Discourses on Life and Law* (1987).
[11]Jerome Barron, *Freedom of the Press for Whom?* 6 (1973). *See also* Jerome Barron, "Access to the Press—A New First Amendment Right," 80 *Harv. L. Rev.* 1641 (1967).
[12]Commission on Freedom of the Press, *A Free and Responsible Press* (1947).
[13]Thomas Emerson, *System of Freedom of Expression* 17 (1970).

contribution to governance. For Meiklejohn, freedom of expression was more valued for its role in democratic governance than as a route toward truth. "No one can deny," Meiklejohn wrote, "that the winning of the truth is important for the purposes of self-government." However, Meiklejohn said, truth

> is not our deepest need. Far more essential, if men are to be their own rulers, is the demand that whatever truth may become available shall be placed at the disposal of all the citizens of the community. The First Amendment is not, primarily, a device for the winning of new truth, though that is very important. It is a device for the sharing of whatever truth has been won. Its purpose is to give to every voting member of the body politic the fullest possible participation in the understanding of those problems with which the citizens of a self-governing society must deal.[14]

Meiklejohn said the primary purpose of the First Amendment is to aid citizens' understanding of "the issues which bear upon our common life." Therefore, he said, "no idea, no opinion, no doubt, no belief, no counterbelief, no relevant information" may be kept from the people. "Under the compact upon which the Constitution rests, it is agreed that men shall not be governed by others, that they shall govern themselves."

Meiklejohn is often referred to as an "absolutist" because he said speech that contributes to "the business of government" should be absolutely protected from government intervention. Meiklejohn hoped that freedom of expression would protect discussion, beliefs, and associations necessary for responsible voting because, to him, voting was the key act of self-governance. Voting, he said, is "the official expression of a self-governing man's judgment on issues of public policy."

In response to criticism that his focus on political expression was too narrow, Meiklejohn expanded his definition of political speech. He said that governance in a democracy requires absolute First Amendment protection, not only for speech about elections and politics but also for communications about education, philosophy, science, literature, the arts, and public issues. From discussion of philosophy, science, and the arts, the voter derives the knowledge and sensitivity to human values necessary for "sane and objective judgment" in the voting booth, Meiklejohn said.[15] His expansive definition of political speech meriting "absolute" protection made it difficult to determine what expression would not deserve protection.

Check on Government Power

Professor Vincent Blasi offers a variation on the argument that freedom of expression serves primarily to further democratic governance. He argues that freedom of expression is to be valued as a check on abuses of governmental authority. He therefore sees the media as an institutional counterweight to government. To Blasi, freedom of expression, particularly as exercised by the larger media, is a countervailing power to federal, state, and local governments, in which corruption seems to increase with their budgets. Abuse of government, he says, "is an especially serious evil—more serious than the abuse of

[14]Alexander Meiklejohn, *Free Speech and Its Relation to Self-Government* 88–89 (1948). *See also* Robert Bork, "Neutral Principles and Some First Amendment Problems," 47 *Indiana L. J.* 1 (1971).

[15]Alexander Meiklejohn, "The First Amendment Is an Absolute," 1961 *Sup. Ct. Rev.* 245, 256–57. For criticism, *see* Zechariah Chafee, Book Review, 62 *Harv. L. Rev.* 891 (1949).

private power, even by institutions such as large corporations which can affect the lives of millions of people."[16]

The First Amendment, Blasi argues, is most valuable during such "pathological" periods as Watergate, when the pressure on democratic institutions is so intense that government may be tempted to suppress free expression.[17] He does not deny that freedom of expression serves other values besides checking government power, values such as promoting self-governance and enhancing individual dignity. But Blasi is more interested in power relationships. To him, the press can expose political corruption if it scrutinizes government operations in a system that recognizes the First Amendment checking function of the press.

Change with Stability

Another value related to governance is the contribution of free speech to orderly change. Free expression can act as a safety valve, allowing critics to participate in change rather than seek influence through antisocial acts. Those who believe this argue that racist militia groups must be allowed to express themselves at meetings and over the Internet. Suppression drives the opposition underground, Professor Emerson warned, "leaving those suppressed either apathetic or desperate. It thus saps the vitality of the society or makes resort to force more likely."[18]

If freedom of expression promotes change with stability, dissidents may work their ideas into the social fabric without resorting to a violent underground cell. Worthless ideas can be rejected with little threat to the equilibrium of society. Where freedom prevails, consensus may support orderly change. Free expression therefore promotes both stability and flexibility, tradition and change. As Emerson said, where there is freedom of expression, society is better able to maintain "the precarious balance between healthy cleavage and necessary consensus."

Fulfillment

Freedom of expression is valued not only because of the social values it promotes but also because speaking and publishing enrich one's life. Freedom of expression, Professor Emerson said, is justified as a right of the individual "purely in his capacity as an individual. It derives from the widely accepted premise of Western thought that the proper end of man is the realization of his character and potentialities as a human being."[19] Freedom of expression is a fundamental good, says Professor Laurence Tribe, "an end in itself, an expression of the sort of society we wish to become and the sort of persons we wish to be."[20]

The notion that freedom of expression is necessary to protect the integrity of the individual reflects the influence of natural law in American jurisprudence. Natural law, popular in the seventeenth and eighteenth centuries, posited that people are born, as English

---

[16]Vincent Blasi, "The Checking Value in First Amendment Theory," 1977 *Am. B. Found. Res. J.* 521, 538.

[17]Vincent Blasi, "The Pathological Perspective and the First Amendment," 85 *Colum. L. Rev.* 449 (1985). *See also* Floyd Abrams, "The Press Is Different: Reflections on Justice Stewart and the Autonomous Press," 7 *Hofstra L. Rev.* 563 (1979).

[18]Thomas Emerson, *Toward a General Theory of the First Amendment* 12 (1966).

[19]*Id.* at 4–5.

[20]Laurence Tribe, *American Constitutional Law* 785 (2d ed. 1988).

philosopher John Locke said, with fundamental rights of life, liberty, and property, rights that the government has a contract with its citizens to protect.[21] The influence of natural law can be seen in the American Declaration of Independence and in the guarantees of liberty and equality in the Bill of Rights. The Bill of Rights protects the integrity of the individual not only from government suppression of free speech but also from unreasonable searches and forced confessions.

Self-fulfillment is not an isolated value. When people fulfill themselves by speaking and writing, they also serve the social and political values of free speech. One might say that the individual's rights of liberty and equality find their highest fulfillment when a citizen participates in what Lincoln called "Government of the People."[22] Professor Steven Shiffrin captures a relationship between individual fulfillment and political speech when he suggests that the organizing symbol of the First Amendment should be neither fulfillment nor the marketplace, but the dissenter. Citing Ralph Waldo Emerson, Shiffrin argues that a major purpose of the First Amendment is "to protect romantics—those who would break out of classical forms: the dissenters, the unorthodox, the outcasts." The First Amendment, Shiffrin says, sponsors individualism, rebelliousness, and antiauthoritarianism.[23]

Some writers find the concept of natural rights too vague and sentimental for making principled decisions in free speech cases.[24] Does one's natural right to self-expression include the right to shout obscenities? Burn a draft card? Shoot an adversary? It is hard to answer these questions when freedom of expression is justified on the grounds of an unprovable natural right to fulfillment. Nevertheless, the American legal system, particularly the Bill of Rights, has been molded by the principles of natural law.[25] To most Americans, freedom of expression is an end in itself as well as a means to other ends.

◇ Summary ◇

Despite many attempts, scholars have failed to articulate a comprehensive theory of freedom of expression. Nevertheless, it is generally agreed that freedom of expression serves several important values, among them the search for truth, promotion of democratic governance, a check on government abuses, and orderly change. Freedom of expression is also valued because it contributes to human fulfillment.

Regulating Expression

Despite the categorical language of the First Amendment, freedom of expression is not protected absolutely. The language telling Congress it can pass "no law" abridging free expression has never meant absolutely no law. Justice Hugo Black argued that the federal

[21]John Locke, *Of Civil Government* (1955). *See also* Jean-Jacques Rousseau, *The Social Contract* (1960).
[22]*See* Wolfgang Friedman, *Legal Theory* 419–20 (5th ed. 1967).
[23]Steven Shiffrin, *The First Amendment, Democracy, and Romance* 5 (1990).
[24]*See, e.g.*, Frederick Schauer, "The Role of the People in First Amendment Theory," 74 *Calif. L. Rev.* 761 (1986).
[25]Wolfgang Friedmann, *Legal Theory* 136–37 (5th ed. 1967).

government was "without any power whatever under the Constitution to put any type of burden on speech and expression of ideas of any kind."[26] But Justice Black's **absolutism** never enjoyed the support of even a significant minority of the Supreme Court.

Other justices, with the exception of William Douglas, found Black's absolutism unrealistic. The Court's majority has concluded that there are times when freedom of expression must give way to other personal and social interests such as national security or public tranquillity. Even Justice Black conceded it was reasonable to limit when and where a constitutionally protected demonstration might be held.[27] Absolutists presumably would also concede that the government may abridge perjury and fraudulent speech.

Although absolutism has not prevailed as First Amendment doctrine, the First Amendment does protect two kinds of speech absolutely. One is speech critical of the government. Newspapers and broadcasters can say whatever they want about a city, state, or other government,[28] although the media may be sued if they defame individuals within the government. Another absolute protection is afforded to broadcasters fulfilling equal time requirements mandated by federal communications law. Because broadcast stations are required to provide opportunities of equal access for political candidates, the broadcasters are absolutely protected from libel suits resulting from those broadcasts.[29]

With absolutism failing to muster sufficient support, courts have developed tests to determine the point at which freedom of expression must give way to conflicting social interests, such as national security, individual reputation, orderly streets, and honest commercial markets. Whether regulations are constitutional depends on many factors, including the type of expression, who is speaking, and the medium of expression. These factors, in turn, determine the rigor with which the courts rule on the legality of regulations on expression. Generally speaking, the courts are less tolerant of regulations on political speech than on commercial speech or sexual expression. Generally, the courts are less tolerant of regulations on the print media than on broadcasting. Similarly, regulations on speech by adults are less likely to be constitutional than regulations on expression by students.

Judges determining the legality of media regulations employ a number of analytical and procedural tools designed to maximize freedom of expression. The assumptions and procedures that judges bring to their First Amendment decisions help ensure that their rulings will not be arbitrary, but will be consistent and unbiased. Among the most important judicial practices guaranteeing maximum freedom of expression are (1) judicial review, (2) First Amendment due process, and (3) a bias against regulating expressive content.

Judicial Review and the Fourteenth Amendment

Under the Constitution, judges have a duty to uphold the individual rights protected by the Bill of Rights. Because each federal court has the power of constitutional review, any federal judge has the authority to determine whether a law or regulation in the judge's jurisdiction unconstitutionally restricts freedom of speech or the press. Federal judges are the final arbiters of freedom of expression, deciding whether state and federal legislators,

[26] Ginzburg v. United States, 383 U.S. 463, 476 (1966) (dissenting opinion).
[27] Adderley v. Florida, 385 U.S. 39 (1966).
[28] For example, Philadelphia v. Washington Post, 482 F. Supp. 897 (E.D. Pa. 1979).
[29] Farmers Educ. and Coop. Union of Am. v. WDAY, Inc., 360 U.S. 525 (1959).

administrators, or lower courts have abridged freedom of expression in violation of the First Amendment.

It is proper that federal judges rather than legislators or executive branch administrators be the guardians of free expression. Federal judges, appointed for life, can be objective, free of political pressures. The late Professor Alexander Bickel pointed out that judges have "the leisure, the training, and the insulation to follow the ways of the scholar in pursuing the ends of government."[30] Only a judicial determination in First Amendment cases, the Supreme Court has said, "ensures the necessary sensitivity to freedom of expression."[31] Recognizing the importance of an independent judiciary as a guarantor of individual rights, emerging democracies often establish constitutional courts with the power to nullify legislation that infringes on freedom of speech, freedom of religion, and other civil rights.

The authority of American federal courts to review the constitutionality of state laws restricting speech derives from the **Fourteenth Amendment.** Without the Fourteenth Amendment, the First Amendment would only protect American citizens from abridgments of free expression by the federal government. The Fourteenth Amendment was intended to prohibit the states from violating citizens' rights protected by the Bill of Rights in the Constitution. The Fourteenth Amendment prohibits any state from enforcing a law that would (1) abridge the privileges or immunities of citizens of the United States, (2) deprive any person of life, liberty, or property, without due process of law, or (3) deny any person equal protection of the laws. (See Appendix B.)

The Fourteenth Amendment, adopted in 1868, was meant by its author, Representative John Bingham of Ohio, to end the "dual citizenship" under which Americans had lived from the time the Constitution was ratified through the Civil War.[32] Before the Civil War, Americans had two distinct citizenships: one state, one federal. A state legislature could limit speech, schooling, voting, or other rights in ways that the federal government could not.[33] This was because the Bill of Rights originally barred only Congress from passing legislation violating the First Amendment, the Fourth Amendment, and other amendments guaranteeing a citizen's rights. States could adopt poll taxes and create separate schools for blacks and whites without violating the Constitution.

The Fourteenth Amendment was supposed to give blacks full citizenship after the Civil War, guaranteeing to citizens of every state the same rights they enjoy as citizens of the United States. However, it was not until the late nineteenth century that the Supreme Court, employing the Fourteenth Amendment, began to challenge state laws that violated a citizen's property rights under federal law. By the twentieth century, the Supreme Court had begun to employ the Fourteenth Amendment to strike down state laws that denied citizens freedom of expression, freedom of religion, the right to a fair trial, and other rights guaranteed by the Bill of Rights. In several cases, the Supreme Court ruled that restrictive state laws violate a citizen's constitutional rights by denying the privileges and immunities, due process, or equal protection guaranteed by the Bill of Rights and the Fourteenth Amendment.

[30]Alexander Bickel, *The Least Dangerous Branch* 25–26 (1962).
[31]Freedman v. Maryland, 380 U.S. 51 (1965).
[32]Irving Brant, *The Bill of Rights* 325 (1965).
[33]See Barron v. Baltimore, 7 Peters 243 (1833).

In the 1925 case of *Gitlow v. New York,* the Court said it "assumed" that First Amendment rights protected from abridgment by Congress are "among the fundamental personal rights and 'liberties' protected by the due process clause of the Fourteenth Amendment from impairment by the states."[34] But the Court did not strike down a New York statute under which Benjamin Gitlow was convicted for publishing a little-noticed manifesto urging the overthrow of the government. The Supreme Court first struck down a state statute violating freedom of the press six years later in *Near v. Minnesota*.[35] The Minnesota statute declared unconstitutional in *Near* permitted prepublication restraints on "malicious, scandalous, and defamatory" publications. In declaring the restraints on publication unconstitutional, Chief Justice Charles Evans Hughes said,

> It is no longer open to doubt that the liberty of the press, and of speech, is within the liberty safeguarded by the due process clause of the Fourteenth Amendment from invasion by state action. It was found impossible to conclude that this essential personal liberty of the citizen was left unprotected by the general guaranty of fundamental rights of person and property.

Since *Near v. Minnesota,* almost all of the clauses of the Bill of Rights have been applied to the states in a process frequently called **incorporation.** Case by case, the Supreme Court incorporated the various clauses of the Bill of Rights into the Fourteenth Amendment, ruling that the state laws violate the Constitution by denying citizens either their privileges and immunities, equal protection of the law, or due process. Because the Fourteenth Amendment requires state and local governments to honor the federal Bill of Rights, an ordinance permitting a county sheriff to arbitrarily refuse a parade permit denies citizens their First Amendment rights as surely as if the U.S. attorney general denied the permit. Similarly, an unreasonable search by a county sheriff violates the Fourth Amendment just as if the illegal search were conducted by the FBI.

First Amendment Due Process

If the government wishes to ban an obscene movie, deny a parade permit, close a courtroom, or otherwise restrict expression, the First Amendment requires that careful procedures be followed. Procedures that are sometimes called **First Amendment due process** require that judges determine what restrictions are allowed after the government meets its burden of proving that a regulation is necessary.[36]

First Amendment due process requires the government to prove that speech is unprotected by the First Amendment rather than requiring the media to prove the expression is protected. The government bears the burden of proof so that the media will not become defensive and censor themselves. Citizens who know they must prove their conduct is lawful, the Supreme Court has said, will "steer far wider of the unlawful zone than if the State must bear these burdens."[37] Thus, the government must prove a film is obscene and therefore should not be shown; it is unconstitutional for the courts to assume that a film is

[34]268 U.S. 652, 666 (1925).
[35]283 U.S. 697 (1931).
[36]*See* Henry Monaghan, "First Amendment 'Due Process,'" 83 *Harv. L. Rev.* 518 (1970).
[37]Speiser v. Randall, 357 U.S. 513 (1958).

obscene and then require a theater owner to prove that it is not.[38] Similarly, the government bears the burden of proving why a publication might be so dangerous to the national security that publication should be halted,[39] or why a courtroom must be closed to the public to ensure a fair trial.[40]

When the government proposes halting freedom of expression, due process usually requires that the government post notice of a hearing at which media attorneys can challenge the proposed restriction.[41] At the hearing, attorneys for the media argue that the government cannot demonstrate a sufficient need for the restriction it proposes. In obscenity cases, due process requires that a censorship board hold a hearing at which attorneys for theater owners can argue against government charges that a work is obscene.[42]

Due process also requires that administrators regulating expression not act arbitrarily, but follow objective standards and explain how they arrived at their decision. Thus, it is unconstitutional for a government official to arbitrarily determine whether a fee will be charged for a parade permit and what that fee will be.[43] All demonstrators seeking a parade permit must pay the same reasonable fee, if any.

If an administrative board bans speech, due process also requires that the would-be speaker or theater owner be allowed a rapid appeal to a federal court. Only a judge can make the final determination whether expression can be banned. Statutes sometimes require a rapid—or expedited—judicial review.

Content Regulations

Central to First Amendment doctrine is the assumption that the government should not regulate the content of expression. Unless the government has a compelling interest, the Supreme Court has said, the constitutional guarantee of freedom of expression means that "government has no power to restrict expression because of its message, its ideas, its subject matter, or its content."[44] Where regulations restrict the content of political, social, and artistic expression, skeptical judges subject the regulations to an analysis called **strict scrutiny** to ensure that the regulations are (1) justified by a compelling government interest and (2) narrowly drawn so as to impose the minimum abridgment of free expression. The Constitution is more tolerant toward content-neutral regulations—such as restrictions on the times and routes of parades—that may impinge slightly on freedom of expression but are not aimed at regulating the content of the speaker's expression, only the time, place, and manner of expression. The Constitution is also more tolerant of regulations on advertising and other nonpolitical communications.

The application of strict scrutiny to **content regulations** reflects the skepticism with which judges view regulations that restrict a fundamental right such as freedom of expression. When courts review restrictions on a fundamental right, they abandon their usual deference to the legislature, a coequal branch of government. Instead, the courts adopt a

[38]Freedman v. Maryland, 380 U.S. 51 (1965).
[39]New York Times v. United States, 403 U.S. 713 (1971).
[40]Richmond Newspapers, Inc. v. Virginia, 448 U.S. 555 (1980).
[41]*See* Laurence Tribe, *American Constitutional Law* 1059–60 (2d ed. 1988).
[42]Freedman v. Maryland, 380 U.S. 51 (1965).
[43]Forsyth County v. Nationalist Movement, 505 U.S. 123 (1992).
[44]Police Dep't v. Mosley, 408 U.S. 92 (1972).

skeptical attitude of "prove to me this regulation is not unconstitutional." "Deference to a legislative finding cannot limit judicial inquiry when First Amendment rights are at stake," the Supreme Court has said.[45]

Content regulations are subjected to strict scrutiny to prevent government from unconstitutionally favoring or discriminating against a subject or viewpoint. In 1995, the Supreme Court employed strict scrutiny to strike down an Ohio law prohibiting anonymous campaign literature "designed to influence voters." In *McIntyre v. Ohio Elections Commission,* the Court invalidated the subject matter regulation, in part, because it unconstitutionally banned a category of political speech, the category designed to influence voters. Under the law, someone could distribute anonymous brochures about American literature but not about political issues—such as school taxes—that citizens might vote on.[46]

The Supreme Court found less than compelling Ohio's argument that the prohibition on anonymity was necessary to prevent fraud and libel. The Court said Ohio's ban on all unsigned fliers designed to influence voters was much broader than necessary to prevent what would be relatively few instances of fraud and libel in campaign literature. Furthermore, the Court said, fraud and libel in political literature would seldom pose a risk to democratic processes that would justify a ban on anonymity. The Court noted that the founders themselves signed fictitious names to the Federalist Papers when they argued for ratification of the Constitution.

The Supreme Court also struck down a law punishing desecration of the American flag because the law was aimed at the content of political messages. In *Texas v. Johnson,* the Court overturned the conviction of Gregory Lee Johnson, who burned a flag at the 1984 Republican National Convention in Dallas to protest policies of the Reagan administration. Johnson was convicted under a Texas law prohibiting intentional desecration of the flag where it caused "serious offense."[47] The Court ruled that the statute unconstitutionally punished political expression. "If there is a bedrock principle underlying the First Amendment," Justice William Brennan wrote for the Court majority, "it is that the Government may not prohibit the expression of an idea simply because society finds the idea itself offensive or disagreeable."

The Court found no compelling interest in the desire of Texas to preserve the peace or to preserve the flag as a symbol of national unity. Johnson's incendiary act posed no danger of a riot in Dallas, the Court noted. Brennan said the symbolic value of the flag would be better preserved not by punishing flag burners but by trying to persuade protesters they are wrong. A year later, the Supreme Court struck down a similar federal statute.[48] Since then, several members of the House and Senate have promoted a constitutional amendment prohibiting flag desecration.

A particularly egregious form of content regulation is **viewpoint discrimination.** When the government engages in viewpoint discrimination, it does not regulate a whole category of subject matter, such as political speech, but favors or disfavors a point of view within a category. For example, the Supreme Court ruled a school district in New York engaged in

[45]Landmark Communications, Inc. v. Virginia, 435 U.S. 829 (1978).
[46]514 U.S. 334 (1994).
[47]491 U.S. 397 (1989).
[48]United States v. Eichman, 496 U.S. 310 (1990).

unconstitutional viewpoint discrimination when it prohibited religious organizations from using classrooms after school to discuss child rearing and family values. The Court found unconstitutional viewpoint discrimination because the school permitted groups without religious affiliations to discuss child rearing in classrooms while prohibiting discussions of child rearing from religious viewpoints in the same classrooms. "[I]t discriminates on the basis of viewpoint," the Court said, "to permit school property to be used for the presentation of all views about family issues and child-rearing except those dealing with the subject matter from a religious standpoint."[49]

A federal district court found unconstitutional viewpoint discrimination when the Library of Congress—under pressure from Congress—ceased producing copies of *Playboy* magazine in braille because of the sexual orientation of the content. The court said the library might remove *Playboy* from the braille program for a content-neutral reason, such as the disproportionate expense of producing *Playboy* with its unusually large number of pages. But the court ruled that ceasing to produce *Playboy* in braille because of its sexual orientation constituted unconstitutional viewpoint discrimination.[50]

Sometimes justices disagree whether a regulation is aimed at content, and therefore must be subjected to strict scrutiny, or is content-neutral, and therefore will be acceptable if the law serves a substantial, but not compelling, government interest. The Supreme Court split 5-4 over whether a statute requiring cable operators to carry the programming of local over-the-air broadcasters is a content-neutral regulation or a content regulation.[51] The majority saw the "must-carry" law as a content-neutral business regulation requiring cable operators to carry all broadcasters, regardless of the content of their programming. The Court minority said the must-carry rules should be judged as content regulations because, the minority said, Congress demonstrated a preference for broadcast programming over cable programming when it required cable operators to carry the programming of broadcast stations.

In an abortion protest case, the justices again disagreed whether they were ruling on a content-neutral statute. The Colorado law in question barred speakers engaging in "oral protest, education, or counseling" from knowingly approaching within eight feet of another person without that person's consent.[52] The majority ruled the statute was a constitutional time, place, and manner regulation designed to protect the privacy of patients entering clinics. The majority said the law "applies equally to used car salesmen, animal rights activists, fundraisers, environmentalists, and missionaries." Two dissenting justices said the Colorado law restricted specific content, the message of those opposing abortion. They said the prohibition on "protest, education, and counseling" was aimed at antiabortion speakers, not used car salesmen.

Vagueness and Overbreadth

When scrutinizing a law or regulation for constitutionality, the Supreme Court is often making sure that the restriction is easily understandable and does not overreach into areas of protected expression. In legal terms, the courts examine content and content-neutral regulations

[49]Lamb's Chapel v. Center Moriches Union Free Sch. Dist., 508 U.S. 384 (1993).
[50]American Council of the Blind v. Boorstin, 644 F. Supp. 811 (D.D.C. 1982).
[51]Turner Broadcasting Sys., Inc. v. Federal Communications Comm'n, 520 U.S. 180 (1997).
[52]Hill v. Colorado, 530 U.S. 703 (2000).

for **vagueness** and **overbreadth.** Normally, citizens cannot challenge the constitutionality of a law unless the law has been invoked against them. However, a citizen can challenge a vague or overbroad law that restricts expression even if the plaintiff is not a victim of the law. That is to say, an overbroad or vague law that restricts freedom of expression can be challenged "on its face" because the very existence of the law may curtail freedom of expression.[53]

An unconstitutionally vague law is one that is written so unclearly that persons "of common intelligence must necessarily guess at its meaning and differ as to its application."[54] A vague law is unconstitutional because it inhibits speech by making speakers unnecessarily cautious.[55] A federal judge struck down a vague University of Michigan policy banning speech or action that "stigmatizes or victimizes."[56] The policy was designed to halt racial jokes, slurs, and other hate speech against women, minorities, and gays on campus. Striking the code down for being too vague, the court said that both "stigmatize" and "victimize" are general terms that elude precise definition. A university lawyer admitted to the judge that he could not distinguish between speech that is merely offensive, and therefore protected, and speech that stigmatizes or victimizes, and therefore would not be protected. A policy that does not define the line between protected and unprotected speech will inhibit speech and is therefore unconstitutionally vague.

The U.S. Supreme Court ruled that a federal law designed to protect children from indecency on the Internet was unconstitutionally vague. The Court struck down the Communications Decency Act in part because the statute failed to narrowly define the "indecency" that the statute prohibited for youth. Indecency, which can be thought of as raunchy four-letter words, is constitutionally protected for adults in print and on the Internet. But because the Communications Decency Act did not narrowly define indecency, an Internet user might avoid serious, constitutionally protected discussions of birth control or homosexuality, fearing a prosecution for "indecency," the Court said. The vagueness was of "special concern," the Court said, in a statute that regulated content, as the Communications Decency Act did.[57]

An overbroad law, unlike a vague one, may be quite clear about what it prohibits, but it prohibits too much. The Supreme Court ruled that the Communications Decency Act was overbroad, as well as vague. The statute was overbroad because it not only banned Internet sales to minors of indecent pictures and texts—a ban that would be constitutional—but also prohibited parents from searching the web for indecency with their children. The government cannot ban indecent expression for adults, whether or not the adults wish to show it to their children. The Court suggested the Communications Decency Act might have been constitutional if it could effectively limit indecency on the Internet only to minors, but the statute was unconstitutionally overbroad because it prohibited all Internet indecency.

The University of Michigan policy designed to halt racist and sexist speech was also overbroad. The federal court said the policy was too broad because it not only prohibited disruptive or obscene speech—speech that could be constitutionally prohibited—but also prohibited distasteful speech protected by the First Amendment.[58]

[53]New York v. Ferber, 458 U.S. 747 (1982); Brockett v. Spokane Arcades, Inc., 472 U.S. 491 (1985).
[54]Connally v. General Constr. Co., 269 U.S. 385, 391 (1926).
[55]*See* Anthony Amsterdam, "The Void for Vagueness Doctrine," 109 *U. Pa. L. Rev.* 67 (1960).
[56]Doe v. University of Michigan, 721 F. Supp. 852 (E.D. Mich. 1989).
[57]Reno v. American Civil Liberties Union, 521 U.S. 844 (1997).
[58]Doe v. University of Michigan, 721 F. Supp. 852 (E.D. Mich. 1989).

◇ Summary ◇

Federal courts, which have jurisdiction to determine what expression is protected by the Constitution, have the power under the Fourteenth Amendment to invalidate laws that violate the First Amendment. In reviewing the constitutionality of restrictions on free speech, the courts operate with a bias against regulations that limit the content of expression, a bias manifest through the application of strict scrutiny. Because of the important values at stake in freedom-of-expression cases, appellate courts do not assume the constitutionality of legislation or lower court decisions restricting speech. Furthermore, courts scrutinize restrictive rules for overbreadth and vagueness to ensure minimum curbs on freedom of expression. When considering banning or limiting expression, the courts also ensure First Amendment due process by placing the burden of justifying restrictions on the government and providing for adversary hearings at which the media may challenge restrictions.

Tests

A frequently employed test at the turn of the century was the now-discredited bad-tendency test, by which judges could easily punish expression that presented even a slight tendency to cause harm. More recently, courts have tested the constitutionality of some restrictions by whether the speech presents a clear and present danger to society. Another test, frequently employed, is a balancing test by which the Court weighs interests in free speech against conflicting social interests.

Bad-Tendency Test

The discredited **bad-tendency test,** accepted by a majority of the Supreme Court in the early twentieth century, provides virtually no First Amendment protection for speech. Under the bad-tendency test, expression may be halted or punished if it presents the slightest "tendency" to cause a substantial evil. The bad-tendency test is unconstitutionally vague because it fails to warn a speaker when speech may be punished.[59] The most innocuous threat might have a tendency—though extremely remote—to cause a disturbance.

The Supreme Court cited the bad-tendency test in *Gitlow v. New York* when it said the state could punish those who abuse freedom of expression by words that, among other things, are "inimical to the public welfare" or "tend . . . to corrupt public morals."[60]

Under the bad-tendency test, virtually any social or public interest justifies suppression of expression. The bad-tendency test therefore cuts off expression long before it poses a danger to society. Under the bad-tendency test, speech might be punished merely because the speaker intended harm, even if the speech was unlikely to cause harm.

Clear-and-Present-Danger Test

The repressive bad-tendency test was gradually replaced by the **clear-and-present-danger test,** which today protects much more speech than the bad-tendency test. The clear-and-

[59]Thomas Emerson, *Toward a General Theory of the First Amendment* 50–51 (1963); Zechariah Chafee, *Free Speech in the United States* 42–51 (1969).

[60]268 U.S. 652, 667 (1925).

present-danger test was first stated by Justice Oliver Wendell Holmes in *Schenck v. United States*.[61] Expression should be punished, Holmes said in the 1919 case, only when words "are used in such circumstances and are of such a nature as to create a clear and present danger that they will bring about the substantive evils that Congress has a right to prevent."

Despite the requirement that speech present a "clear" and "present" danger, Charles Schenck and another Socialist, Elizabeth Baer, were punished for distributing a pathetic circular that presented no immediate danger to anyone. Schenck's antidraft circular contained "impassioned language" urging that citizens were duty bound to oppose the draft because "conscription was despotism in its worst form and a monstrous wrong against humanity in the interest of Wall Street's chosen few." Evidence at Schenck's trial established that at least a few conscripts received a flier, but it apparently persuaded no one to avoid the draft. Schenck was convicted of conspiring to violate the Espionage Act of 1917, which, as strengthened in 1918, made it a crime to willfully cause or attempt to cause insubordination or disloyalty in military forces or to obstruct recruiting.[62] Convictions could result in fines of up to $10,000 and prison terms of up to twenty years.

Holmes could easily conclude that Schenck's ineffectual, one-page circulars presented a clear and present danger worthy of conviction because Holmes did not view the flyer as political speech. To Holmes, Schenck's fliers, which the justice noted were being distributed during wartime, were not speech on political matters so much as they were interjections, like falsely yelling "Fire!" in a theater, the punishment of which raised no First Amendment conflicts.[63]

Furthermore, freedom of expression enjoyed no special status in Holmes's mind at the time, despite his articulation of the clear-and-present-danger test. In fact, Holmes insisted at the time that free speech "stand no differently than freedom from vaccination," a "freedom" that a legislative majority could constitutionally curtail.[64] To Holmes and the Supreme Court in 1919, speech that presented a clear and present danger, like speech that presented a bad tendency, could be punished if it might cause harm at some time in the distant future.

That same year, Holmes began to see that freedom of expression enjoys little protection if speakers can be jailed because their speech has a tendency to cause some undefined harm at some undefined time. Giving voice to his new understanding, Holmes dissented when the Supreme Court upheld the conviction of five Russian aliens for distributing political fliers. In his famous dissent in *Abrams v. United States,*[65] Holmes said that even opinions we "loathe and believe to be fraught with death" should not be suppressed "unless they so imminently threaten immediate interference with the lawful and pressing purposes of the law that an immediate check is required to save the country." Holmes thought Abrams's fliers opposing the dispatch of American troops to Russia were opinions that presented no such imminent danger.

[61] 249 U.S. 47 (1919).

[62] Espionage Act of 15 June 1917, 40 Stat. 217.

[63] *See* Jeremy Cohen, *Congress Shall Make No Law: Oliver Wendell Holmes, the First Amendment, and Judicial Decision Making* (1989).

[64] Letter of Oliver Wendell Holmes Jr. to Judge Learned Hand, June 24, 1918, in Gerald Gunther, *Learned Hand: The Man and the Judge* 163 (1994).

[65] 250 U.S. 616 (1919) (dissenting opinion).

Several times after *Schenck* and *Abrams*, the Supreme Court purported to apply a clear-and-present-danger test but upheld convictions for expression that presented no imminent threat. During the McCarthy era in the 1950s, a Supreme Court plurality upheld the conviction of nearly a dozen members of the Communist party for "conspiring" to advocate the forcible overthrow of the government.[66] The defendants' crime in the case, *Dennis v. United States*, was belonging to the Communist party.

While applying a version of the clear-and-present-danger test in *Dennis*, the plurality admitted that the defendant and his comrades posed no immediate danger of violence. Nevertheless, the Court upheld the conviction, saying the government need not wait to stop speech "until the catalyst is added" if "the ingredients of the reaction are present." It was enough, the Court said, that Dennis and his friends established a "highly organized conspiracy, with rigidly disciplined members subject to call when the leaders . . . felt the time had come for action."

The Court's version of the clear-and-present-danger test in *Dennis* amounted to little more than a one-time balancing of free speech interests against general security considerations during a politically charged era. Whether or not one agrees with the Court's results, the justices in the plurality did not rigorously scrutinize the speech of Dennis and his cohorts to determine whether it presented a clear and present danger.

By 1957, the Court had begun to examine the facts of cases more carefully to determine if speech in fact presented an imminent danger. In *Yates v. United States*, the Court applied the clear-and-present-danger test more literally than before, ruling that a conspiracy to advocate the overthrow of the government was too far removed from immediate danger to be punished. The Court said that a clear and present danger could be found only if there were advocacy of direct illegal action.[67]

In 1969, in a decision that is still active precedent, the Court employed a variation of the clear-and-present-danger test requiring that speech be punished only if it incites lawless action. In the 1969 case *Brandenburg v. Ohio*,[68] the Court overturned the conviction of Ku Klux Klan members for racist provocations. The Court struck down an Ohio criminal syndicalism statute under which a Ku Klux Klan leader had been convicted for advocating unlawful methods of industrial or political reform. Brandenburg was fined $1,000 and sentenced from one to ten years in prison for telling Klansmen at a televised meeting:

> We're not a revengent organization, but if our President, our Congress, our Supreme Court, continues to suppress the white, Caucasian race, it's possible that there might have to be some revengence taken.

Brandenburg then told of plans to march on Congress "four hundred thousand strong" on the Fourth of July.

The Supreme Court overturned Brandenburg's conviction because the statute permitted convictions for "mere advocacy" of illegal action at some distant time. To be constitutional,

[66]Dennis v. United States, 341 U.S. 494 (1951).
[67]354 U.S. 298 (1957).
[68]395 U.S. 444 (1969) (*per curiam*). *See* Hans Linde, "'Clear and Present Danger' Re-examined: Dissonance in the Brandenburg Concerto," 22 *Stan. L. Rev.* 1163, 1166 (1970).

the Court said, an advocacy statute can punish only speech that "is directed to inciting or producing imminent lawless action and is likely to incite or produce such actions."

Four years later, the Court again employed its incitement variation of the clear-and-present-danger test to overturn the conviction of a street protester. In *Hess v. Indiana,* the Court reversed the conviction of a demonstrator who was arrested during an antiwar demonstration on a college campus for shouting, "We'll take the fucking street later."[69] The Court concluded that Hess's statement, at worst, "amounted to nothing more than advocacy of illegal action at some indefinite future time." To sustain a conviction, the Court said, it was necessary to show that the words "were intended to produce, and likely to produce, imminent disorder."

Balancing Test

The clear-and-present-danger test sets a standard for halting or punishing speech that presents an immediate danger of unlawful action. In many cases, however, such as those involving defamation or invasion of privacy, speech may be sufficiently harmful to justify compensation for an injured party, although the expression may not present immediate danger of unlawful action justifying a prior restraint or a criminal punishment. In such cases, which are much more common than cases in which speech incites unlawful action, the clear-and-present-danger test might not be appropriate. Instead, courts often employ a balancing test in such cases.

In effect, all judicial standards, including the clear-and-present-danger test, involve balancing of conflicting interests,[70] but judges employing the balancing test consciously weigh conflicting interests against each other. Chief Justice Vinson explained balancing when he said that it is the duty of the courts to determine which of two conflicting interests demands the greater protection in particular circumstances.[71]

Courts engage in what is called **ad hoc balancing** when judges treat each case separately, placing speech considerations on one side of the scales and conflicting values—such as individual reputation—on the other side. In ad hoc balancing, there are no definitions or single standards for guidance. Ad hoc balancing provides great flexibility because a judge can assign different weights to different facts of a case. One time, a judge could rule that freedom of expression was more important; another time, the judge could decide that a person's reputation outweighed freedom of expression.

But what is gained in flexibility is lost in predictability. In fact, ad hoc balancing risks making First Amendment protection indefinable; judges balancing speech interests against other personal and social interests may rule for either side in any case.[72] Ad hoc balancing creates opportunities for biased judgments because judges may impose their own values where there are no objective standards.

To put more uniformity and predictability into balancing, courts engage in what is sometimes called **definitional balancing.** In definitional balancing, courts define the outer limit of free speech before the balancing test is applied in individual cases. Thus, definitional

[69]414 U.S. 105 (1973). *See also* Healy v. James, 408 U.S. 169 (1972).
[70]Paul Freund, *The Supreme Court of the United States* 42–44 (1961).
[71]American Communications Ass'n. v. Douds, 339 U.S. 382 (1950).
[72]Rodney Smolla, *Smolla and Nimmer on Freedom of Speech* secs. 2:58–2:60 at 2-56 to 2-62 (1999).

balancing reduces the vagueness of ad hoc balancing by providing defined standards that can be applied in similar cases.

For example, in libel cases involving the media and a public official, the media's freedom of expression is balanced against the official's right to a good reputation. However, the media bring a defined advantage to the scales in each case. This is because the Supreme Court has ruled that the media's freedom of expression includes protection to publish false, defamatory statements about public officials, provided that the false statements are not published knowingly or recklessly, either of which constitutes what is called **actual malice.**

Because the Supreme Court has ruled that public officials must prove the media published defamatory statements with actual malice, officials know before they file a libel suit that the courts will not engage in ad hoc balancing of the officials' interest in reputation against the media's First Amendment rights. The media's constitutional freedom to make false but nonmalicious statements is defined beforehand.[73] Thus, the media have a preferred position—one mandated by the First Amendment because of the importance that political speech be robust and uninhibited—when an official's reputation is balanced against the media's freedom of expression. Public officials who sue the media for libel know at the outset they will have difficulty proving the defamatory statements were published with malice.

◇ Summary ◇

The First Amendment does not create absolute protection for freedom of expression, the courts say. Courts therefore apply tests in individual cases to determine whether freedom of expression or conflicting social and personal values will prevail. The discredited bad-tendency test permitted suppression of almost any expression that presented a vague danger to social or personal interests. A clear-and-present-danger test, if applied literally, provides more protection for freedom of expression by prohibiting speech only when there is clear evidence of an incitement to lawless action. Most often, the courts employ a balancing test. Ad hoc balancing gives judges great flexibility but makes First Amendment protections unpredictable. Definitional balancing brings more uniform standards to First Amendment adjudication.

Scope of the First Amendment: The Hierarchy of Protected Expression

The First Amendment says that Congress shall make no law abridging freedom of expression, and the Supreme Court has ruled that the constitutionality of content regulations on political speech will be subjected to strict scrutiny. Despite the staunch protections for content, however, not every type of content is protected by the First Amendment, and not every type of content that is protected is protected equally. Indeed, some content is so low in the hierarchy of freedom of expression that it is excluded from First Amendment protection and therefore can be banned.

[73]N.Y. Times v. Sullivan, 376 U.S. 254 (1964).

In the constitutional hierarchy of content, the most favored speech is political and social content, the regulation of which must be subjected to strict scrutiny. Less protected are advertising and nonobscene sexual expression, the regulation of which is subjected to more relaxed scrutiny or intermediate scrutiny. Excluded from constitutional protection are false advertising, fraud, obscenity, and fighting words.

Political and Social Expression

The most valued and most protected speech—the expression that arguably contributes most to individual fulfillment as well as to democratic governance—is expression dealing with political, social, religious, and cultural issues. Protected subject matter includes debate about elections, referenda, labor, race, health, agriculture, religion, education, and other political and social issues.

Protected political and social expression may take many forms. Protected content may be printed in newspapers, magazines, editorial advertisements, posters, and poetry. Protected content may be expressed orally through speeches, lectures, films, and broadcasts. It may be delivered symbolically through black armbands,[74] political campaign contributions,[75] marches, slogans, and political symbols.[76] One court ruled that a rugby match between the United States and South Africa was protected by the First Amendment and could not be canceled by the governor of New York because of the "singularly dramatic racial issue involved."[77] The Constitution, the Supreme Court has said, "looks beyond written or spoken words as mediums of expression."[78] Instead of protecting only "particularized" messages, the First Amendment also protects the "painting of Jackson Pollock, music of Arnold Schoenberg, or Jabberwocky verse of Lewis Carroll."

Commercial and Sexual Expression

Less protected in the First Amendment hierarchy than political and social expression are commercial advertising and nonobscene sexual expression. Despite the bias in First Amendment jurisprudence against content regulation, the Constitution tolerates more regulation on advertising and pornography because they are supposedly less valuable than political speech. Commercial advertising, the Supreme Court says, may be more heavily regulated than political and cultural expression because advertising, being motivated by economic gain, is hardier and can therefore withstand more regulation. Advertising is also more easily verified, the Court says.[79] Because of the hardiness and verifiability of commercial speech, the Supreme Court says there is less reason to tolerate inaccurate or misleading commercial speech than to tolerate false political speech. Political speech is said to be more vulnerable and less verifiable.

The Court applies a more relaxed scrutiny to regulations on commercial speech than to regulations on political content. Under this relaxed scrutiny, the government need not

[74]Tinker v. Des Moines Indep. Community Sch. Dist., 393 U.S. 503 (1969).
[75]Buckley v. Valeo, 424 U.S. 1 (1976).
[76]Spence v. Washington, 418 U.S. 405 (1974).
[77]Selfridge v. Carey, 522 F. Supp. 693 (N.D.N.Y. 1981).
[78]Hurley v. Irish-American Gay, Lesbian and Bisexual Group of Boston, 515 U.S. 557 (1995).
[79]Virginia State Bd. of Pharmacy v. Virginia Citizens Consumer Council, Inc., 425 U.S. 748 (1976).

demonstrate a compelling interest to justify a regulation; a substantial or significant government interest is sufficient to satisfy First Amendment standards. Thus, casino advertisements can be banned to serve the substantial government interest of discouraging gambling.[80] But discouraging gambling would not be a sufficiently compelling interest to justify a ban on political editorials promoting casinos.

Regulations on nonobscene sexual expression are also subject to less exacting scrutiny than regulations on political content. Nude dancing, the Supreme Court has said, enjoys less First Amendment protection than political speech because it is expressive conduct within the outer perimeters of the First Amendment.[81] Nonobscene sexual films, plays, and magazines may be examined for obscenity before distribution, whereas political and other more highly valued expression may not.[82] Furthermore, the display of nonobscene sexual plays, movies, and printed materials can be restricted to certain zones within a city without violating the First Amendment.[83]

Some expression is less protected if it is broadcast rather than printed. Indecency, which may be thought of as four-letter words, is fully protected content in magazines, books, and other printed media, but is less protected in broadcasting. The Supreme Court justifies less rigorous First Amendment protection for broadcast indecency because broadcasts supposedly intrude into the home, assailing vulnerable children.[84]

Sections on obscenity and indecency will discuss the Supreme Court's intermediate protection of cable content and the standard for protecting expression on the Internet. The section later in this chapter on noncontent regulations will explore the relaxed constitutional standards the Supreme Court applies to regulations on marches, demonstrations, and other forms of symbolic expression.

Fighting Words

A few narrow categories of content at the bottom of the First Amendment hierarchy have been excluded from constitutional protection. Under a two-tier theory of free speech,[85] some expression was protected by the First Amendment but other expression was not because it contributes nothing to self-fulfillment or to the robust debate that the First Amendment is supposed to foster.

Advertising was once among the categories of speech excluded by definition from constitutional protection, but truthful commercial speech now enjoys some constitutional protection from government regulation, although false advertising does not. Advertising will be discussed in Chapter 8. A second category, obscenity, which still is excluded from constitutional protection, will be discussed in Chapter 9. A third category, fighting words, a form of hate speech, will be discussed here, as will threats.

Hate speech, a problem worldwide, consists of written or spoken words that insult and degrade groups identified by race, gender, ethnic group, religion, or sexual orientation.

[80]Posadas de Puerto Rico Assocs. v. Tourism Co., 478 U.S. 328 (1986).
[81]City of Erie v. Pap's A.M., 529 U.S. 277 (2000).
[82]Freedman v. Maryland, 380 U.S. 51 (1965).
[83]City of Renton v. Playtime Theatres, Inc., 475 U.S. 41 (1986).
[84]*See* Glen Robinson, "The Electronic First Amendment," 47 *Duke L. J.* 899 (1998).
[85]*See* Cass Sunstein, *Democracy and the Problem of Free Speech* 121–65 (1993).

Hate speech includes the swastikas neo-Nazi marchers carry in a Jewish neighborhood, the ethnic "joke" on a campus radio station, and the burning cross in a black family's front yard.

Professor Richard Delgado argues that victims of racist speech should be able to sue for what Delgado considers the psychological, sociological, and political effects of racial insults. "The racial insult," Delgado says,

> remains one of the most pervasive channels through which discriminatory attitudes are imparted. Such language injures the dignity and self-regard of the person to whom it is addressed, communicating the message that distinctions of race are distinctions of merit, dignity, status, and personhood.[86]

Similarly, Professor Mari Matsuda argues that government's failure to punish racial and ethnic invective amounts to state support for hate speech. By failing to provide a legal remedy for the victims of hate speech, the government denies their personhood, Matsuda says.[87]

Most countries punish hate speech. Under a United Nations resolution, member nations are supposed to declare illegal "all dissemination of ideas based on racial superiority or hatred, [and] incitement to racial discrimination."[88] In Canada, it is a crime to wilfully promote hatred in public against an identifiable group, such as a religious or racial minority.[89] France criminalizes incitement to discrimination, hatred, or violence based on ethnicity, race, or religion.[90]

Although many would agree that hateful expressions "rape the soul" and undermine community tolerance,[91] support for legal sanctions against hate speech is not universal. Prohibitions on hate speech, it is argued, will have little beneficial effect because law cannot eradicate the prejudice and bias that motivate hate speech. Instead of benefiting society, it is argued, punishing hate speech may harm society by driving hate groups into dangerous underground cells. Furthermore, hate speech laws may be used to stifle the minorities the laws are supposed to protect.[92]

Whatever the real or imagined harms of hate speech, the U.S. Supreme Court has ruled that most expression of bigotry and prejudice is political speech protected by the First Amendment. Only words that amount to a slap in the face, expression that constitutes **fighting words,** are beyond constitutional protection, the Court has ruled.

The Supreme Court defines fighting words as those that "by their very utterance inflict injury or tend to incite an immediate breach of the peace."[93] Expression constitutes fighting words only if it is so offensive as to have "a direct tendency to cause acts of violence by

[86]Richard Delgado, "Words That Wound: A Tort Action for Racial Insults, Epithets, and Name-Calling," 17 *Harv. Civ. Rts.-Civ. Lib. L. Rev.* 133–36 (1982).

[87]Mari J. Matsuda, "Public Response to Racist Speech: Considering the Victim's Story," 87 *Mich. L. Rev.* 2320 (1989).

[88]*International Convention on the Elimination of All Forms of Racial Discrimination* art. 4(a), General Assembly Resolution 2106A of 21 Dec. 1965, entered into force 4 Jan. 1969.

[89]*See* John Manwaring, "Legal Regulation of Hate Propaganda in Canada," in *Striking a Balance: Hate Speech, Freedom of Expression and Non-discrimination* 107–108 (Sandra Coliver ed., 1992).

[90]*See* Roger Errera, "In Defense of Civility: Racial Incitement and Group Libel in French Law," in *Striking a Balance* 147 (Sandra Coliver ed., 1992).

[91]Rodney Smolla, *Free Speech in an Open Society* 153 (1992).

[92]*See, e.g.,* Sandra Coliver, "Hate Speech Laws: Do They Work?" in *Striking a Balance* 367 (Sandra Coliver ed., 1992).

[93]Chaplinsky v. New Hampshire, 315 U.S. 568 (1942).

the person to whom, individually, the remark is addressed."[94] Fighting words may be prohibited because they provoke a breach of the peace, not merely because their content offends.

The fighting words doctrine originated in the case of *Chaplinsky v. New Hampshire* in 1941.[95] Chaplinsky was convicted for calling a marshal in Rochester, New Hampshire, a "goddamned racketeer and a damned Fascist." Although the marshal did not strike Chaplinsky, the court said that "goddamned racketeer" and "damned Fascist" were epithets likely to provoke the average person to physical retaliation. Chaplinsky therefore had no First Amendment protection because he had uttered fighting words. Fighting words are outside of constitutional protection, the Court said, because they are "no essential part of any exposition of ideas, and are of such slight social value as a step to truth that any benefit that may be derived from them is clearly outweighed by the social interest in order and morality."

In 1971, the Court overturned the conviction of a war protester because the slogan on the back of his jacket—"Fuck the Draft"—did not constitute fighting words. In *Cohen v. California,* the Court said the slogan on Cohen's jacket, which he wore through a California courthouse, was a constitutionally protected comment on the unpopular war the country was then waging in Vietnam. Cohen's message did not constitute fighting words because it presented no immediate danger of a violent physical reaction in a face-to-face confrontation. No one, the Court said, could regard the words on Cohen's jacket as "a direct personal insult."[96]

The conviction of a St. Paul, Minnesota, racist was also overturned because of a faulty fighting words ordinance. The Supreme Court reversed the conviction of 17-year-old Robert A. Victoria, who was charged for burning a cross inside the fenced yard of the home of Russ and Laura Jones, a black couple, in violation of a city disorderly conduct ordinance. The ordinance made it a misdemeanor for anyone to place a symbol, object, or graffiti, including a swastika or burning cross, on public or private property if it was likely to arouse "anger, alarm, or resentment in others on the basis of race, color, creed, religion or gender."

In *R.A.V. v. City of St. Paul,*[97] the Court ruled that the ordinance was an unconstitutional content regulation. Writing for the majority, Justice Antonin Scalia said the St. Paul ordinance was unconstitutional because it prohibited only fighting words based on "race, color, creed, religion, or gender," while presumably permitting hate speech motivated by political party, union membership, homosexuality, or other protected interests. "The First Amendment," Justice Scalia said, "does not permit St. Paul to impose special prohibitions on those speakers who express views on disfavored subjects."

University codes designed to curb hate speech on campus have also been declared unconstitutional, in part because they are not narrowly drawn to prohibit only fighting words. In 1989 a federal district court struck down a University of Michigan regulation that prohibited verbal or physical behavior that "stigmatizes or victimizes an individual on the basis of race, ethnicity, religion, sex, sexual orientation, creed, national origin, ancestry, age, marital status, handicap or Vietnam-era veteran status."[98] The court said that the university enforced the policy "broadly and indiscriminately" in classrooms and other places.

[94]Gooding v. Wilson, 405 U.S. 518 (1972).
[95]315 U.S. 568.
[96]Cohen v. California, 403 U.S. 15, 20 (1971).
[97]505 U.S. 377 (1992).
[98]Doe v. University of Michigan, 721 F. Supp. 852 (E.D. Mich. 1989).

In effect, the court said, the university was proscribing speech "simply because it was found to be offensive," a rationale that would prohibit constitutionally protected speech as well as unprotected speech. The court said the university might prohibit obscenity, fighting words, criminal incitement, and sexual harassment in the workplace, but not speech that is merely offensive.

In the St. Paul case, Justice Scalia said that the cross burning might have been punished under laws that do not curb speech but prohibit illegal actions such as arson, terroristic threats, or criminal damage to property. After the *R.A.V.* decision, Arthur Morris Miller 3d, the only adult convicted under the St. Paul ordinance for the cross burning at the Jones home, pled guilty to the federal misdemeanor of interfering with the Joneses' right of access to housing by conspiring to burn crosses in the couple's yard.

Other courts have upheld convictions for burning crosses where the burning presented imminent physical danger. The U.S. Court of Appeals for the Seventh Circuit upheld the conviction of Kenneth Hayward, who burned crosses in a white couple's yard in Kenneyville, Illinois, after the couple entertained blacks at their home over a Labor Day weekend.[99] The Seventh Circuit viewed cross burnings that "portend violence" as fighting words devoid of First Amendment protection. Cross burning might also be a threat.

Although speech cannot be punished simply because it is motivated by racial, ethnic, religious, or gender bias, the Supreme Court has ruled that crimes that do not involve speech may be more severely punished if they are motivated by racial and ethnic bias. In *Wisconsin v. Mitchell,* the Supreme Court upheld a statute providing for higher penalties if a criminal selects victims because of their race, religion, or sexual orientation.[100] The Supreme Court upheld the punishment of a black Kenosha man whose sentence for aggravated battery had been increased because he selected his victim because he was white.

In 2006, a split federal appeals court dismissed on jurisdictional and other grounds a request by Yahoo! that a French order to remove anti-Semitic materials from its websites be declared unenforceable. French courts had ordered Yahoo! to remove from Yahoo's French and American servers web pages auctioning Nazi memorabilia, denying the Holocaust, and offering other anti-Semitic materials. French civil rights law prohibits disseminating and accessing Nazi hate speech.

Yahoo! "voluntarily" removed most offending materials from its French servers and some of the most hateful web pages from U.S. servers. In dismissing the case, the U.S. Court of Appeals for the Ninth Circuit did not rule whether the largely unenforced French court orders would violate the First Amendment rights of Yahoo! and of U.S. Internet users if enforced.[101]

Threats

Closely related to fighting words is another unprotected category of expression: threats. In *Watts v. United States,*[102] the Supreme Court upheld a federal criminal statute that prohibits knowing threats of violence against the President. But in *Watts,* as in other cases, the Court

[99] Hayward v. United States, 6 F.3d 1241 (7th Cir. 1993), *cert. denied,* 511 U.S. 1004 (1994).
[100] 508 U.S. 476 (1993).
[101] Yahoo! Inc. v. La Ligue Contre Le Racism et L'Antisemitisme, 433 F.3d 1199, *cert. denied,* 126 S.Ct. 2332 (2006).
[102] 394 U.S. 705 (1969) (*per curiam*).

ruled that vague threats, emotional hyperbole, and mere advocacy of violence are constitutionally protected speech. Only "true threats" can be punished. The Supreme Court has not formulated a test for determining when speech becomes a true threat, but the Court has said that context is important.

In *Watts,* the Court ruled that Robert Watts, an opponent of the war in Vietnam, had not threatened the life of the President when he told a discussion group at a Washington, D.C., rally that he might shoot Lyndon Baines Johnson. The 18-year-old war protester said that if he were inducted into the Army and made to carry a rifle, "the first man I want to get in my sights is L.B.J. They are not going to make me kill my black brothers." The teenager and his audience then laughed.

The Court considered Watts's warning to be "pure" political speech that could not be punished. The Court noted that the government had a compelling need to protect the President from true threats of physical harm, but the Court found no threat in Watts's statement, which was conditioned on his induction into the Army and was treated lightly by him and his audience. The Court said that Watts's only offense was to crudely state political opposition to the President.

The Court has also protected speech that intimidates and coerces if the speaker does not incite violence. In *NAACP v. Claiborne Hardware,* the Court ruled that the First Amendment protected warnings by civil rights leader Charles Evers. In a speech, Evers reportedly warned the 8,000-plus blacks of Claiborne County, Mississippi, that they would be answerable to him if they traded with white merchants.[103] He also warned that "Uncle Toms" who broke the boycott would "have their necks broken" by their own people. Blacks who traded with whites were indeed branded as traitors to the black cause, called demeaning names, and socially ostracized. The Court said the First Amendment does not protect violence or speech that incites unlawful action. But speech does not lose protection, the Court said, "simply because it may embarrass others or coerce them into action."

In 2003, the Supreme Court ruled that a state may constitutionally prohibit cross burning if the purpose of the burning is to intimidate. In *Virginia v. Black,* the Court said that burning a cross with the intent to intimidate constitutes a true threat "intended to create a pervasive fear in victims that they are a target of violence."[104] Writing for the Court, Justice Sandra Day O'Connor said cross burning is constitutionally protected if not intended to intimidate—such as burning a cross in a film—but is beyond constitutional protection if intended to intimidate—such as burning a cross in a black family's yard. O'Connor said punishing cross burning with intent to intimidate—"a particularly virulent form of intimidation"—is consistent with the *R.A.V.* case in which the Court invalidated an ordinance that punished hateful symbolic speech only if it offended people holding certain viewpoints.

While the majority of the Court held that cross burning intended to intimidate can be prohibited, the majority also ruled that the Virginia statute at issue in *Virginia v. Black* was unconstitutional because it allowed a jury to infer from the cross burning itself that the defendant intended to intimidate. The First Amendment requires a more detailed inquiry into intent in each case, O'Connor said.

◆

[103]458 U.S. 886 (1982).
[104]538 U.S. 343.

In dissent, Justice Souter agreed the Virginia statute was unconstitutional, but not because it allowed the intent to intimidate to be determined by the act of cross burning. Souter, joined by Justices Ginsburg and Kennedy, said the Virginia law was unconstitutional because it, like the law in the *R.A.V.* case, was content-based, punishing symbolic speech with ideological content. Cross burning is inherently symbolic, Souter said.

In an Internet case, a federal appeals court ruled 6-5 that posters and a website could be halted because they threatened doctors who perform abortions. The Court of Appeals for the Ninth Circuit enjoined posters and a website produced by the American Coalition of Life Activists; the posters contained the names and addresses of abortion doctors who were "GUILTY" of "CRIMES AGAINST HUMANITY." "Rewards" up to $5,000 were offered for the doctors' arrests and convictions. The posters did not advocate that the doctors be physically harmed, but several doctors testified they were terrified, and many quit providing abortions. Doctors sued under a federal statute punishing anyone who by "threat of force" intentionally intimidates a person who provides reproductive health services.[105]

The Ninth Circuit ruled that the posters and websites created a true threat that intentionally intimidated doctors, causing them to believe that the Coalition of Life Activists intended to harm them if they continued to perform abortions.[106] Important to the majority's decision was a context the court thought threatened murder. Although the posters did not advocate murder, they were similar to earlier posters identifying abortion doctors who had been killed or wounded. Furthermore, the website's "Nuremberg Files" named hundreds of abortion doctors with the avowed intent of "collecting dossiers on abortionists in anticipation that one day we may be able to hold them on trial for crimes against humanity." The website drew lines in black through the names of doctors who had been killed and highlighted in gray names of wounded doctors. The court said the more recent posters intimidated abortion doctors with the implied threat: "You're Wanted or You're Guilty; You'll be shot or killed."

In a dissent joined by four judges, Judge Alex Kozinski wrote that the "Wanted" posters and website contained protected expression by speakers who never threatened to harm a doctor. The posters and web page, Kozinski said, explicitly foreswore the use of violence and advocated lawful means of persuading doctors to stop performing abortions or punishing them if they continued. Kozinski argued the "Wanted" posters and website listings constituted emotional political rhetoric much like the constitutionally protected "threat" by Robert Watts, the young war protester, against Lyndon Johnson. Kozinski said the "Wanted" posters were less coercive to doctors than the constitutionally protected warnings issued by civil rights leader Charles Evers to coerce blacks to boycott white businesses in Claiborne County, Mississippi.

The Pennsylvania Supreme Court ruled that a teenager's website that disrupted a school and caused a teacher great emotional turmoil was not a "true threat." The website created by "J.S." said a teacher named Mrs. Fulmer should die. The site showed a picture of Mrs. Fulmer's head severed from her body and compared her to Hitler. The site sought twenty dollar donations to pay a hitman to kill Mrs. Fulmer.[107]

[105]Freedom of Access to Clinics Entrances Act (FACE), 18 U.S.C. § 248(a),(c).

[106]Planned Parenthood of Columbia/Willamette, Inc. v. American Coalition of Life Activists, 290 F.3d 1058 (9th Cir. 2002), *amended and rehearing en banc denied,* 2002 U.S. App. LEXIS 13829 (July 10, 2002).

[107]J.S. v. Bethlehem Area School Dist., 807 A.2d 847 (Pa. 2002).

Considering the totality of circumstances, the court concluded the site was not a true threat. The "reasons" for Mrs. Fulmer to die were ludicrous personal characteristics such as her "hideous smile, a zit, puke green eyes" and hair that may be a "rug, or God's Mistake." Threatening language was never transmitted to Mrs. Fulmer. Indeed, a disclaimer on the website urged readers not to convey the contents of the site to the school. There was no address to mail twenty dollar contributions. There was no reason to know whether J.S. had a propensity for violence. "We believe that the website, taken as a whole, was a sophomoric, crude, highly offensive and perhaps misguided attempt at humor," the court said. Although the website was ruled not to threaten Mrs. Fulmer, the site did disrupt the school, as will be discussed later in this chapter.

◇ Summary ◇

Despite the categorical language of the First Amendment prohibiting abridgments of free expression, the Supreme Court has structured a hierarchy of protected expression. Political and social commentary sit at the top of the hierarchy, enjoying the most protection under the First Amendment. Lower down and protected under a more relaxed constitutional scrutiny are commercial speech and nonobscene sexual expression. Excluded or enjoying almost no protection under the First Amendment are obscenity, false advertising, fighting words, and true threats.

Who Is Protected?

The First Amendment prohibits government from interfering with "the freedom of speech" but does not state whether all people and corporations enjoy the same degree of free expression. Do children have the same rights as adults? Do prison inmates have the same rights as the *New York Times?* Not surprisingly, perhaps, the courts have ruled that different speakers enjoy different levels of First Amendment protection, just as different categories of speech are protected differently. The average adult has greater First Amendment rights than students and government employees. Publishers enjoy fuller freedoms of expression than broadcasters and nonmedia corporations. But for most individuals, including publishers, the First Amendment guarantees a wide range of entitlements, including the right to speak, publish, associate, receive information, solicit contributions, and refuse to speak.

Adults

SPEAKING AND PUBLISHING The right to speak and publish is basic to freedom of expression. The First Amendment specifically protects the rights of speech and of the press. Any person enjoys the right to converse on a public sidewalk or expound on a political or religious theme at a public meeting or a speakers' corner. Any citizen with sufficient resources may publish and distribute a newspaper, pamphlet, or book. Some argue that the government has an affirmative obligation to encourage speech in "public forums" such as public parks and sidewalks.[108]

[108]Thomas Emerson, "The Affirmative Side of the First Amendment," 15 *Ga. L. Rev.* 795 (1981).

Freedom of expression includes the individual's right to participate in symbolic forms of expression such as marching, demonstrating, contributing money to a political campaign, and even burning the American flag. Symbolic expression, which is speech melded with conduct, is not permitted in all places and at all times but is nevertheless protected by the First Amendment along with more "pure" speech and publishing. As was noted earlier, anonymous speech is also protected, lessening the chances that outcasts will be persecuted for their unpopular viewpoints.

ASSOCIATING Besides the right to speak and publish, a citizen has a First Amendment right to associate with others. Alexis de Tocqueville noted that the "most natural privilege of man, next to the right of acting for himself, is that of combining his exertions with those of his fellow creatures and of acting in common with them."[109] The right of association is found in the First Amendment rights of assembly, speech, and petition. By joining a religious, political, or ideological group, individuals strengthen their individual right to speak. Thus, associations are protected from government interference not only because of the inalienable right of individuals to band together but also because associations advance political and social issues.

Citizens have a constitutional right to band together to advocate political change,[110] undertake litigation,[111] or worship their God.[112] Associations enjoying these rights include the conservative John Birch Society and the more liberal National Association for the Advancement of Colored People. The right of association guarantees these ideological groups the same rights enjoyed by individuals to speak, publish, pamphleteer, lobby, and march.

RECEIVING INFORMATION The First Amendment does not protect just the right to talk, write, and associate; it protects the interchange of ideas. Speaking and publishing mean little if one cannot also hear or acquire information. The right to speak and publish therefore implies an audience to hear, to read, and to respond.

The Supreme Court has recognized a limited constitutional right to receive information.[113] Workers, for example, have a right to hear what a labor organizer has to say.[114] Consumers have a right to receive some forms of commercial advertising[115] and corporate communication.[116] Regulations on broadcasting, too, are supposed to promote the rights of listeners and viewers to receive information.[117]

The constitutional right of a citizen to receive information is not as strong as the right to speak and publish. The right to receive derives from, and is subsidiary to, the right to speak and publish.[118] The right to receive, therefore, is difficult to assert. Indeed, in most circumstances,

---

109 *Democracy in America* 196 (Phillips Bradley ed., 1945). *See Freedom of Association* (Amy Gutman ed., 1998).
110 Cousins v. Wigoda, 419 U.S. 477 (1975).
111 NAACP v. Button, 371 U.S. 415 (1963).
112 Serbian Eastern Orthodox Diocese v. Milivojevich, 426 U.S. 696 (1976).
113 Martin v. Struthers, 319 U.S. 141 (1943).
114 Thomas v. Collins, 323 U.S. 516 (1945).
115 Virginia State Bd. of Pharmacy v. Virginia Citizens Consumer Council, Inc., 425 U.S. 748 (1976).
116 First Nat'l Bank of Boston v. Bellotti, 435 U.S. 765 (1978).
117 Red Lion Broadcasting Co. v. FCC, 395 U.S. 367 (1969). *See generally* William Lee, "The Supreme Court and the Right to Receive Expression," 1987 *Sup. Ct. Rev.* 303.
118 Ronald Dworkin, *Taking Rights Seriously* 93 (1977).

the government is not required to provide information, and citizens have no right of access to information. The Supreme Court has recognized a limited constitutional right of access to courtrooms,[119] but no constitutional right of access for the press and public to prisons,[120] to foreign countries that have been declared off-limits by the State Department,[121] or to the words of foreigners denied visas to speak in the United States.[122] Likewise, public access to government records and meetings depends on state and federal statutes,[123] not on a First Amendment right of access serving a public right to receive information.

SOLICITING FUNDS Individuals and ideological groups have a First Amendment right to contribute money and to solicit funds to further a cause. As part of their right of association, people may join political action committees associated with corporations and unions to raise and contribute money to support political candidates. The Supreme Court has also said that charitable appeals are protected by the First Amendment because they "involve a variety of speech interests—communication of information, the dissemination and propagation of views and ideas, and the advocacy of causes."[124] The solicitation of funds, the Court said, is "characteristically intertwined with informative and perhaps persuasive speech seeking support for particular causes or for particular views on economic, political, or social issues."

The First Amendment right to solicit funds, however, does not include begging in a subway.[125] The U.S. Court of Appeals for the Second Circuit ruled that the New York Metropolitan Transportation Authority did not violate the First Amendment when it prohibited panhandlers from the subways. Most individuals who beg are simply collecting money, the court said; they do not convey any social or political message meriting First Amendment protection. Furthermore, citizens in the closed environment of a subway are a "captive audience" that should not be assaulted by perhaps unwanted solicitations, the court said.

However, a federal district court ruled that the First Amendment does protect begging as a form of expression on the open street where pedestrians are not held captive.[126] A beggar has a legitimate interest, the judge said, in presenting the message that "social and economic conditions and opportunities and governmental services are such that many people are unable to support themselves and must rely on the freely given alms of others in order to eke out an existence while living on the streets of New York."

COMPELLING SPEECH The freedom of expression belonging to individuals and associations includes freedom from compelled speech. "The right to speak and the right to refrain from speaking are complementary components of the broader concept of 'individual freedom of mind,'" the Supreme Court has said.[127] Therefore, the government cannot compel schoolchildren to salute the flag if their families' religious beliefs forbid it.[128] Nor can the

[119]Richmond Newspapers, Inc. v. Virginia, 448 U.S. 555 (1980).
[120]Houchins v. KQED, 438 U.S. 1 (1978).
[121]Zemel v. Rusk, 381 U.S. 1 (1965).
[122]Kleindienst v. Mandel, 408 U.S. 753 (1972).
[123]*See, e.g.,* Freedom of Information Act, 5 U.S.C. § 552a.
[124]Village of Schaumburg v. Citizens for a Better Env't., 444 U.S. 620, 632 (1980).
[125]Young v. New York City Transit Auth., 903 F.2d 146 (2nd Cir. 1990), *cert. denied,* 498 U.S. 984 (1990).
[126]Loper v. New York City Police Dep't., 802 F. Supp. 1029 (S.D.N.Y. 1992).
[127]Wooley v. Maynard, 430 U.S. 705 (1977).
[128]West Virginia State Bd. of Educ. v. Barnette, 319 U.S. 624 (1943).

government, consistent with the First Amendment, compel citizens to affirm a belief in God,[129] associate with a political party in order to get a job,[130] adhere to an ideology,[131] or place their names on political campaign literature.[132]

In 1995, a unanimous Supreme Court ruled that private citizens who organize a parade may not be forced to include marchers conveying a message that the organizers do not wish to convey. In *Hurley v. Irish-American Gay, Lesbian and Bisexual Group of Boston,* the Court said that a veterans group that organized a St. Patrick's Day parade in Boston could exclude marchers expressing gay pride, a message the veterans said was inconsistent with their theme of traditional religious and social values.[133]

Writing for the Court, Justice David H. Souter said that the veterans' exclusion of gays did not constitute discrimination based on sexual orientation. Gays were permitted to march in the parade if they did not march under a gay banner. A private speaker—such as the Veterans Council—may permit "multifarious voices" in a parade without forfeiting the right to exclude others, including those who would openly celebrate being gay, Souter said.

The government is not supposed to withhold privileges or benefits from an association or compel disclosure of a group's membership.[134] Because of the right of association, minor political parties may be exempted from laws requiring disclosure of political contributions and expenditures if disclosure might subject the parties to threats, harassment, or reprisals.[135] An unpopular church might have difficulty collecting contributions, the Supreme Court has said, if the church were required to disclose the names of its members.[136]

A private newspaper may not be compelled to publish news stories, advertisements, letters, or replies. In *Miami Herald Publishing Co. v. Tornillo,*[137] the Supreme Court struck down a section of the Florida Election Code requiring a publisher to print a free reply by candidates attacked by a paper. The case arose when the *Miami Herald* refused to publish a reply to the paper's criticism of Pat Tornillo, a candidate for the state legislature. The paper charged that Tornillo, the executive director of the Classroom Teachers Association of Miami, had led an illegal teachers' strike a few years earlier.

Tornillo argued that the First Amendment rights of the public would be served if dominant newspapers like the *Herald* were required to print replies from political candidates. However, the Supreme Court ruled that compelling newspaper editors to publish replies violates the First Amendment. The Court said that requiring publication would unconstitutionally dampen the vigor and limit the variety of public debate because the replies would increase the cost of printing, require additional composing time, and take up space that could be devoted to other subjects. The Court also feared that editors forced to run political replies would avoid controversial election coverage, thus limiting public debate.

[129]Torcaso v. Watkins, 367 U.S. 488 (1961).
[130]Elrod v. Burns, 427 U.S. 347 (1976).
[131]Wooley v. Maynard, 430 U.S. 705 (1977).
[132]McIntyre v. Ohio Elections Comm'n., 514 U.S. 334 (1995).
[133]515 U.S. 557 (1995).
[134]Laurence Tribe, *American Constitutional Law* 1010–22 (2d ed. 1988).
[135]Buckley v. Valeo, 424 U.S. 1 (1976) (*per curiam*).
[136]Seattle Times v. Rhinehart, 467 U.S. 20 (1984).
[137]418 U.S. 241 (1974).

Furthermore, the unanimous Court said that compelling publication would interfere with the function of editors:

> The choice of material to go into a newspaper, and the decisions made as to limitations on the size of the paper, and content, and treatment of public issues and public officials—whether fair or unfair—constitute the exercise of editorial control and judgment. It has yet to be demonstrated how government regulation of this crucial process can be exercised consistent with First Amendment guarantees of a free press.[138]

Several years after *Tornillo*, the Supreme Court ruled that a public utility is protected from having to carry messages from a consumer group in the company's billing envelopes. A utility, like a newspaper and an individual, has a right to avoid associations it opposes.[139]

Nevertheless, the First Amendment does permit the government to require a number of disclosures by individuals and groups. Later chapters will discuss constitutionally acceptable compulsory disclosure by advertisers, corporations, lobbyists, contributors to political campaigns, and journalists ordered to testify before grand juries and courts.

The First Amendment also allows public access to electronic media. While citizens may not demand space in a newspaper or magazine, the Supreme Court has ruled that political candidates must be accorded "reasonable access" to broadcast channels. Cable operators, too, may be required to provide "access" channels for programs produced by local citizens. Access to the telecommunications media will be discussed in Chapter 7.

Public Forums

The government owns and manages numerous properties where communication occurs. People speak and distribute fliers on sidewalks built and maintained by government for public use; companies post mouthwash advertisements on government-owned buses; citizen groups discuss macrame and Islam in classrooms operated by local boards of education. Although the government owns and operates property, the government does not necessarily control the expression that takes place there. The degree of government control depends on the degree to which the property is a **public forum.**

The Supreme Court identifies three kinds of forums: traditional, dedicated, and nonpublic. Traditional public forums have historically been open for public discourse. They include streets, parks, and other public places that the Supreme Court says have "immemorially been held in trust for the use of the public" for assembly, communicating, and discussing public questions.[140] Speakers generally have as much right to discuss ideas and distribute information in traditional public forums as they would in their own front yards. The government can impose reasonable regulations on the loudness and hours of speech in a traditional forum, but the government can exclude speakers only by demonstrating a compelling interest—such as stopping a riot—and the exclusion is narrowly tailored. The government cannot favor one viewpoint over another in any forum.

A dedicated public forum is property that the government intentionally designates for public discourse. A state university dedicates a public forum in campus facilities when it

[138] *Id.* at 258.
[139] Pacific Gas & Elec. Co. v. Public Utilities Comm'n., 475 U.S. 1 (1986).
[140] Hague v. Committee for Indus. Org., 307 U.S. 496 (1939).

allows registered student groups to meet there.[141] A state legislature creates public forums when it declares citizens must be allowed to speak at school board meetings.[142] A municipal auditorium dedicated to expressive activities is a public forum.[143] A municipal bus system that accepts political as well as commercial advertisements may be a designated public forum.[144]

As with a traditional public forum, a speaker may be excluded from a dedicated forum only if the government has a compelling interest that is narrowly tailored. As with a traditional forum, the government cannot favor one viewpoint over another. But contrary to practice in a traditional forum, the government can limit the dedicated forum to certain speakers and topics in order to preserve the purpose for which the forum was created. Indeed, a dedicated public forum is often called a limited forum. Thus, a university that opens rooms after classes might limit access to student organizations discussing political and social issues, but the university cannot discriminate against viewpoints expressed by students on those issues.

The University of Virginia established an unconstitutional viewpoint regulation in a dedicated forum when it restricted funding of campus religious publications. The Supreme Court agreed that the university created a limited public forum by paying for various independent student organizations that often issued newsletters, newspapers, and other publications containing student news, information, opinion, entertainment, and academic communications. Trying to avoid using state money to support particular religions, the university operated under guidelines prohibiting funding for "religious activity," which was defined as activity that "primarily promotes or manifests a particular belief in or about a deity or an ultimate reality." Invoking the guidelines, the university barred funding of a student newspaper, "Wide Awake: A Christian Perspective at the University of Virginia."

The Supreme Court ruled in *Rosenberger v. Rector of the University of Virginia* that barring funding for "Wide Awake" was unconstitutional viewpoint discrimination.[145] The university was under no obligation to fund any student publications, but once it chose to do so, it could not discriminate on the basis of viewpoint. And the university did fund several publications representing a wide array of subjects and viewpoints; "Wide Awake" was one of fifteen newspapers and magazines containing news, humor, satire, and opinion. The university supported "The Yellow Journal," a humor magazine that satirized Christianity, and "Al-Salam," a publication that promoted a better understanding of Islam at the university. Given the wide array of religious and antireligious subject matter, the university could not discriminate against one religious viewpoint in "Wide Awake," a viewpoint based on faith in a deity.

The Supreme Court's third type of forum, the nonpublic forum, is property that is neither traditionally open for public debate nor dedicated by policy to public discourse. A military base is a nonpublic forum, dedicated to the training and discipline of soldiers not to the exploration of ideas. The government "has power to preserve the property under its control for the use to which it is lawfully dedicated," the Supreme Court has said.[146] In nonpublic forums, the government may permit speech, but the government need demonstrate no compelling reasons to justify barring speech. In nonpublic forums, the government needs only

[141]Widmar v. Vincent, 454 U.S. 263 (1981).
[142]Madison Joint School Dist. v. Wisconsin Employment Relations Comm'n., 429 U.S. 167 (1976).
[143]Southeastern Promotions, Ltd. v. Conrad, 420 U.S. 546 (1975).
[144]New York Magazine v. Metropolitan Transit Auth., 136 F.3d 123 (2nd Cir. 1998), *cert. denied,* 525 U.S. 824 (1998).
[145]515 U.S. 819 (1995).
[146]Greer v. Spock, 424 U.S. 828 (1976).

reasonable regulations that preserve the property for the purpose to which it is lawfully dedicated. As in all forums, the government may not favor one viewpoint over another.

A split Supreme Court ruled that large, publicly operated airports are not public forums, even though commerce, debate, and mass media are often found in airport concourses. In *International Society of Krishna Consciousness v. Lee,*[147] a six-justice majority held that the Krishna religious organization and other political and religious groups had no constitutional right to solicit funds in New York City airports operated by the Port Authority of New York and New Jersey. In an opinion written for five of the six justices in the majority, Chief Justice Rehnquist said that airports are not public forums because, unlike streets and sidewalks, airports do not have as their "principal purpose" the exchange of ideas, nor has the government intentionally opened airports as forums for public discourse. The purpose of air terminals, the Court said, is "the facilitation of passenger air travel, not the promotion of expression." Also, unlike other transportation centers, airports frequently restrict public access, often to preserve security. Groups soliciting funds may delay travelers, place them under duress, and expose them to fraud, Rehnquist said.

Although the majority ruled that airports are not public forums and solicitation of funds can be prohibited, a majority in a companion case that was decided at the same time ruled that religious and political groups can distribute leaflets and literature in airports.[148] Four justices consider airports to be public forums, much like a sidewalk or street, where the First Amendment permits political and religious discussion and leafleting. Justice Kennedy said a metropolitan airport, like a sidewalk, is "[o]ne of the places left in our mobile society that is suitable for discourse." Political and religious leafleters disrupt an airport concourse no more than they disrupt a sidewalk, a public forum that Kennedy noted is also dedicated to transporting people. Justice O'Connor also voted to permit leafleting in airports, but she did not consider airports to be public forums. She argued that the New York airport had not reasonably demonstrated that leafleting is incompatible with the purposes of an airport.

Privately owned shopping malls, like airports, are not public forums where protesters have a First Amendment right to express themselves.[149] However, the Supreme Court has ruled that state constitutions, which may be more protective of free expression than the Constitution, may require that private malls be open to free speech. In *Pruneyard Shopping Center v. Robins,* the Court ruled that a California shopping center could be required under the state constitution to permit high school students to oppose a United Nations resolution against Zionism.[150] The mall owner can disavow any association with the protest, the Court said.

Government Employees

The right to speak and publish does not belong only to private citizens. The government and its employees also share the right, but with limits. Government officials have a right, sometimes a legislated duty, to communicate with the public through press conferences, press releases, state of the union addresses, public reports, and paid public notices. Furthermore, government employees, like other citizens, may speak as private persons on public issues

[147]505 U.S. 672 (1992).
[148]Lee v. Int'l Soc. for Krishna Consciousness, Inc., 505 U.S. 830 (1992).
[149]Hudgens v. NLRB, 424 U.S. 507 (1976).
[150]Pruneyard Shopping Center v. Robins, 447 U.S. 74 (1980).

and vote for political candidates. The Supreme Court has ruled that midlevel government employees may accept payment for talks and articles they produce off the job.[151]

Government employees, as well as corporate employees, need freedom to reveal internal wrongs and cover-ups that might waste money and compromise the public interest. The law also recognizes special obligations on public employees that are not imposed on private citizens. Public employees must not distort the political process, disrupt the efficient operation of an agency, compromise the safety of fellow employees, or reveal confidential information, such as tax and health data, entrusted to an agency. The law therefore permits the government to restrict the speech of government employees and some private employees in ways that would not be permitted on speech by the general public.

Since the founding of the country, the government has attempted to preserve the neutrality of government officials by limiting their political participation. Thomas Jefferson ordered officers of his administration not "to influence the votes of others nor take any part in the business of electioneering, that being deemed inconsistent with the spirit of the Constitution and his duties to it."[152] The Hatch Act prohibits most federal executive branch employees from engaging in political activities on the job, running for political office, campaigning for or against a candidate, and collecting contributions for partisan candidates.[153]

To keep judicial races impartial, state ethics codes often prohibited judicial candidates, incumbents as well as challengers, from announcing positions on disputed legal or political issues. Such ethical canons, designed to maintain the impartiality of judges and campaigns, left judicial candidates to fill campaign talks with noncontroversial reviews of their resumes and general discussions of the role of the law and the courts.

But the Supreme Court ruled 5-4 that a code prohibiting a judicial candidate from "announcing his or her views on disputed legal or political issues" was unconstitutional. In *Republican Party of Minnesota v. White,* the Court ruled the Minnesota judicial cannon unconstitutionally restricted content at the core of First Amendment freedoms, speech about the qualifications of candidates for public office.[154] A law that prohibits speech about contested issues not only violates free speech rights but does not further impartiality, the Court said. "Proof that a Justice's mind at the time he joined the Court was a complete *tabula rasa* in the area of constitutional adjudication would be evidence of lack of qualification, not lack of bias," the Court said.

To ensure that government agencies are run efficiently, state and federal laws give government agencies considerable discretion to punish speech that supervisors think will disrupt an agency. Federal employees may be fired if supervisors "reasonably believe" that employees' remarks are even potentially disruptive. The Supreme Court upheld the firing of Cheryl Churchill for allegedly "knocking" the obstetrics department she worked in by discouraging another employee from switching departments. Churchill's remarks were disruptive, the Court said, because they "threatened to undermine management's authority."[155]

---

[151]United States v. National Treasury Employees Union, 513 U.S. 454 (1995).
[152]James Richardson, 10 *A Compilation of the Messages and Papers of the Presidents, 1789–1897,* at 98–99 (1898).
[153]5 U.S.C. §§ 7321–7326.
[154]536 U.S. 765 (2002).
[155]Waters v. Churchill, 511 U.S. 661 (1994).

Government employees are supposed to be protected if they "blow the whistle" on mismanagement and illegalities within their agencies. The Whistleblower Protection Act of 1989 is supposed to protect federal employees from retaliation if they reveal violations of law or regulations, gross mismanagement, waste of funds, abuse of authority, or substantial danger to public health or safety.[156] Federal law also protects whistle-blowing employees from retaliation in certain high-risk areas of private commerce, such as the nuclear and aviation industries, and employees in important policy areas, such as occupational safety, the environment, and civil rights. Following the Enron, Tyco Industries, and other business scandals, Congress passed legislation to protect employees against retaliation if they reveal securities law violations or fraud. Many states also have laws to protect whistle-blowers.

Nevertheless, the Supreme Court ruled in 2006 that government employees have no First Amendment protection if employers retaliate against them for statements made "pursuant to their official duties" as opposed to protected statements that contribute to "civic discourse." In *Garcetti v. Ceballos,* the Supreme Court ruled that Los Angeles County did not violate the First Amendment rights of Deputy District Attorney Richard Ceballos when the county demoted him after Ceballos wrote a memorandum to a supervisor questioning the truthfulness of a deputy sheriff's application for a search warrant.[157] "We hold," Justice Kennedy wrote for the 5-4 majority, "that when public employees make statements pursuant to their official duties, the employees are not speaking as citizens for First Amendment purposes, and the Constitution does not insulate their communications from employer discipline."

Although employees may be protected if they reveal mismanagement and illegalities in the workplace, government and private employees are not protected if they leak confidential information about the competitive practices of private businesses or the foreign policy and security practices of government. For better or worse, such leaked information is often central to news reporting about government, politics, foreign relations, and business.

The Supreme Court has never determined when, if ever, communicators may be punished for disseminating leaked national security information. However, the Court did refuse to review an appeals court decision upholding the conviction of a government employee who leaked classified photos to the press. In *Morison v. United States,* the Supreme Court refused to review the espionage conviction of a civilian Navy analyst who passed a secret satellite photo of a Soviet aircraft carrier to *Jane's Defense Weekly,* a prominent British defense magazine.[158] Samuel Loring Morison, who worked at the Naval Intelligence Support Center at Suitland, Maryland, received a two-year sentence for selling the picture and a typed summary of a secret report about an explosion at a Soviet naval base.

The government charged Morison with violating the Espionage Act of 1917 by intentionally giving national defense information to "a person not entitled to receive it." Morison was also charged with violating a federal theft statute and an employment agreement not to disclose classified information.

In 2006, Lawrence Franklin, a Department of Defense analyst, was sentenced to more than twelve years in prison and fined $10,000 for passing secret documents to lobbyists working for the American Israel Public Affairs Committee (AIPAC), one of Washington's

[156]5 U.S.C. § 2301(b)(9).
[157]126 S.Ct. 1951 (2006).
[158]844 F.2d 1057 (4th Cir.), *cert. denied,* 488 U.S. 908 (1988).

most influential lobbying organizations.[159] Franklin, an expert on the Middle East, held a top-secret security clearance and had signed a nondisclosure agreement in which he acknowledged he was not to disclose classified information to individuals lacking the appropriate security clearances. Frustrated with U.S. policy toward Iran, Franklin believed leaks of classified information would cause the National Security Council to take threats posed by Iran more seriously. Franklin disclosed classified information to Steven Rosen and Keith Weissman, lobbyists for AIPAC; because Rosen and Weissman lacked security clearances, Franklin's leaks of classified information to them violated the espionage laws.

Rosen and Weissman passed the information they received from Franklin to journalists and an Israeli government official. As part of a Bush administration crackdown on national security leaks, discussed in Chapter 3, the Department of Justice was prosecuting Rosen and Weissman for transmitting national defense information to persons not entitled to receive it. Rosen and Weissman claim they did what members of the press, lobbyists, and think-tank analysts do hundreds of times each day in Washington.

Judge T. S. Ellis III of the United States District Court for the Eastern District of Virginia in 2006 refused to dismiss the charges against Rosen and Weissman.[160] News organizations were watching the case closely with apprehension that journalists might someday also be charged with violating espionage laws for the common practice of receiving and transmitting sensitive government information, much of it leaked by government officials. In sentencing Franklin, Judge Ellis made clear his view that the espionage laws also apply to the press. All persons "who come into possession in an unauthorized way of classified information, must abide by the law," Ellis said. "That applies to academics, lawyers, journalists, professors, whatever."[161]

Students

First Amendment rights are not the exclusive property of adults. Speaking and publishing by young people are also constitutionally protected. As the Supreme Court said in 1969, students' First Amendment rights "do not stop at the schoolhouse gate."[162] However, the First Amendment rights of students at public high schools are weak.

For many years, courts followed the Supreme Court's ruling in *Tinker v. Des Moines Independent Community School District,* a case in which the Court said the First Amendment protected expression by high school students as long as it was not disruptive, obscene, or violative of the rights of other students. In *Tinker,* the Court upheld the right of high school students to wear black armbands as a silent political protest to the war in Vietnam. However, in 1986 the Court ruled that high school students have no First Amendment right to deliver "offensive" sexually oriented expression at a school-sponsored event. In *Bethel School District No. 403 v. Fraser,* the Court ruled that a school could constitutionally suspend a student for delivering a sexually suggestive nominating speech for a candidate for student office at a school assembly that "was part of a school-sponsored educational

[159]Jerry Markon, "Pentagon Analyst Given 12½ Years in Secrets Case," *Washington Post,* Jan. 21, 2006, at A1.
[160]United States v. Rosen, 445 F. Supp. 2d 602 (E.D. Va. 2006).
[161]Sentencing Hearing Transcript at 23-24, United States v. Franklin, Criminal No. 1:05CR225 (E.D. Va. Jan. 20, 2006).
[162]Tinker v. Des Moines Indep. Comm. Sch. Dist., 393 U.S. 503 (1969).

program in self-government."[163] Matthew Fraser was suspended for three days and removed from the list of student graduation speakers after he delivered a speech that resulted in disruptive hooting and yelling by students required to attend the assembly. Fraser told fellow students his nominee was "a man who will go to the very end—even the climax—for each and every one of you." The Court said a student has no First Amendment right to deliver speech containing pervasive, offensive sexual innuendo within the school context.

Two years later, the Supreme Court ruled a principal could censor nondisruptive stories containing no offensive innuendo in a school-sponsored newspaper if the censorship served the educational mission of the school. In *Hazelwood School District v. Kuhlmeier* the Court upheld deletions of two stories from *Spectrum,* the student newspaper at Hazelwood East High School near St. Louis.[164] Principal Robert Reynolds deleted an article about teen pregnancies and one about divorce.

Central to the decision was the Court's ruling that *Spectrum* was not a public forum where school officials would be prohibited from regulating expression. The Court said *Spectrum* was not a public forum because it had never been dedicated "by policy or by practice" to use by the public. Rather, the paper was produced in a journalism class under supervision of a teacher for academic credit. The Court said a school could impose virtually any reasonable regulation on school-sponsored expression, expression that includes student publications, plays, speeches at assemblies, and any other expression that the public might associate with a school. It was constitutional for the principal to remove the articles in *Spectrum,* the Court said, to protect younger students from "inappropriate" material, to allow the school to "disassociate itself" from expression it disliked, and to protect the privacy of students and parents.

In 2007, a divided Supreme Court ruled that high school students at an approved school event may be punished if they advocate—or appear to advocate—illegal drug use. The Court in *Morse v. Frederick* upheld the suspension of 18-year-old Joseph Frederick for hoisting a "Bong Hits 4 Jesus" banner on a sidewalk across from his high school as Frederick watched an Olympic Torch parade with fellow students.[165] Writing for five members of the Court, Chief Justice Roberts said a high school principal may constitutionally restrict student speech at approved school events when the speech is "reasonably viewed as promoting illegal drug use" in violation of high school rules.

As in earlier cases, the Court noted Frederick's limited speech rights because of the "special characteristics of the school environment." Frederick was subject to rules of his high school in Juneau, Alaska, the Court said, because he was attending a school-sanctioned event with fellow students during school hours. Teachers were also released from school to observe the parade and monitor students. Deterring drug use by school children is an important, perhaps compelling interest, Justice Roberts wrote.

Justice Stevens argued in a dissenting opinion, joined by Justices Souter and Ginsburg, that Frederick's banner was "nonsense" that should be protected by the First Amendment because it neither violated any rule nor expressly advocated illegal or harmful conduct.

After *Hazelwood,* the number of off-campus and "underground" newspapers and personal web pages increased as high school students sought to discuss drugs, sex, pregnancy,

[163] 478 U.S. 675 (1986).
[164] 484 U.S. 260 (1988).
[165] Morse v. Frederick, 2007 U.S. LEXIS 8514 (June 25, 2007).

and other issues that are frequently censored in school-sponsored publications.[166] The rights of off-campus publishers were strengthened when the U.S. Court of Appeals for the Ninth Circuit ruled that a school system may not review all non-school-sponsored student publications before they are distributed on campus.[167]

Some courts have ruled that student web pages created at home are beyond the administrative control of high schools. A federal court in the state of Washington ordered Kentlake High School to lift the suspension of 18-year-old Nick Emmett, an honor student, for his "Unofficial Kentlake High Home Page."[168] Emmett's private website, which claimed to be for entertainment only, included "mock obituaries" of students and asked readers to nominate the subject of the next obituary. The court found no intimidation, harassment, or disruption to the educational process. Indeed, the court said the private website was "entirely outside of the school's supervision or control."

Although most off-campus student expression may be beyond control of high school officials, courts have upheld punishment of off-campus expression that disrupts education at the school. The Pennsylvania Supreme Court ruled that J.S. could be expelled from high school for disrupting education from his home website, "Teacher Sux."[169] The court upheld the expulsion of J.S. for a website that recommended that a teacher, Mrs. Fulmer, die. On the site, her blood-dripping head was severed from her body. She was also compared to Hitler, and contributions were sought for a hitman. Although the court ruled that the tasteless website was not a true threat, the court said it was disruptive because it caused Mrs. Fulmer to lose several weeks of class as she treated the emotional and physical stresses she attributed to the site. Students were also distracted by fear, emotional distress, and low morale.

Although the Supreme Court's decision in *Hazelwood* allows high school principals to censor school-sponsored expression, the *Hazelwood* ruling does not require administrators to censor it. The decision says only that censorship of expression bearing the imprimatur of the school does not violate the First Amendment if reasonable regulations serve the school's educational purposes. In fact, several states, including California, Massachusetts, and Iowa, limit school officials' powers of censorship far more than *Hazelwood* permits. In 1988, Iowa adopted a law guaranteeing public school students freedom of expression similar to that guaranteed by the Supreme Court's 1969 ruling in *Tinker v. Des Moines School District.* The Iowa statute protects student expression except when speech is disruptive, obscene, or defamatory or would incite students to break the law.[170] To protect schools from liability for student speech, the Iowa law, like one in Massachusetts,[171] says student expression is not to be deemed an expression of school policy, nor is the school system liable if it fails to censor.

The *Hazelwood* decision, which allows officials to regulate high school expression, said nothing about the greater First Amendment freedoms usually enjoyed by students at state colleges and universities.[172] In 1972, the Supreme Court said that First Amendment

[166]James Hirsch, "Underground High School Papers Thrive as Teen-Agers Rebel Against Censorship," *Wall Street Journal,* June 8, 1992, at B1.
[167]Burch v. Barker, 861 F.2d 1149 (9th Cir. 1988).
[168]Emmett v. Kent School District, 92 F. Supp. 2d 1088 (W.D. Wash. 2000).
[169]J.S. v. Bethlehem Area School Dist., 807 A.2d 847 (Pa. 2002).
[170]Iowa Code § 280.22.
[171]Mass. Ann. Laws ch. 71, § 82.
[172]*See* Student Gov't. Ass'n. v. Board of Trustees, 868 F.2d 473 (1st Cir. 1989).

protections apply with the same force on college campuses as in the larger community.[173] A year later, the Court ruled that state university officials lack the authority to ban offensive student expression "in the name alone of the 'conventions of decency.'"[174]

In 2001, a federal appeals court reaffirmed that students at state universities and colleges enjoy more First Amendment freedoms than high school students do.[175] The U.S. Court of Appeals for the Sixth Circuit ruled that Kentucky State University violated the First Amendment when administrators confiscated 2,000 yearbooks because administrators objected to the "poor quality" and the theme, "destination unknown." Finding the yearbook to be a limited public forum, the appeals court rejected the university's claim that the Supreme Court's *Hazelwood* ruling allows university administrators to impose "reasonable" regulations as high school officials can. The Sixth Circuit ruled Kentucky State had failed to demonstrate the compelling interest needed to justify a prior restraint on content in a public forum at a state university.

However, in 2006, the U.S. Supreme Court refused to review a Seventh Circuit decision ruling that state university and college students enjoy no more freedom from administrative censorship than high school students.[176] An 11-member appellate court in Chicago ruled in 2005 that Governors State University might censor the campus paper, the *Innovator,* like a high school paper if it was not designated a public forum (See Fig. 2.1). The court also ruled that the administrator who censored the *Innovator* could not be held liable because she could not have known at the time whether the paper was a public or nonpublic forum. Four dissenters argued the majority ruling contradicted well-established precedent recognizing greater First Amendment rights for college students than for younger, less mature high school students.

Non-Media and Media Corporations

While First Amendment rights for adults, students, and government employees may differ, so, too, do rights of expression enjoyed by different media and non-media profit-making corporations.

Profit-making non-media corporations, such as General Motors, have First Amendment rights to spend from the corporate treasury for all manner of product advertising and issue advertising to bolster the corporate image and comment on public affairs. Corporate rights include the ability to buy advertising supporting or opposing ballot issues, such as whether a state should require a deposit on beverage containers to encourage conservation. However, profit-making non-media corporations are prohibited from spending corporate money to buy advertising on behalf of candidates in federal elections. Congress has concluded, and the Supreme Court has agreed, that profit-making non-media corporations should be barred from financial involvement in elections because they may corrupt the electoral process. However, as explained in Chapter 7, media corporations, such as newspaper publishers, have a First Amendment right to to criticize and comment on candidates.

The Supreme Court has ruled each medium of communication presents "peculiar problems"; consequently, different media enjoy different levels of protection under the First Amendment. For example, the government regulates newspaper publishers to a lesser degree than broadcasters.

[173]Healy v. James, 408 U.S. 169 (1972).
[174]Papish v. Board of Curators, 410 U.S. 667 (1973).
[175]Kincaid v. Gibson, 236 F.3d 342 (6th Cir. 2001).
[176]Hosty v. Carter, 412 F.3d 731 (7th Cir. 2005), *cert. denied* 126 S.Ct. 1330 (2006).

INNOVATOR

The Newspaper of Governors State University
Since 1971

October 31, 2000 Volume 29 Number 8

Leadership Conference Held at GSU

by Jeni Porche

By joining creative forces to develop a professional leadership conference, three Governors State University (GSU) campus organizations, *Students in Communication*, Kappa Kappa Chapter of *Lambda Pi Eta Communication Honor Society*, and the Student Life Division, hosted "Leadership on the Verge: A Conference on Professional and Personal Communication" on Saturday, October 21, 2000 in the Hall of Honors at GSU.

"We all wanted to find a way to raise awareness about the importance of good communication skills and get students, the community, and faculty members working and thinking together," said conference committee public relations representative and second-year communications graduate student, Amy Chmuras. Chmuras and the planning committee worked for nearly six months organizing presentation themes into a day-long program of events, and on contacting community leaders with substantive backgrounds and practical experience in communication theories, techniques, and applications. Keynote speaker, Phil Zepeda, from the American Red Cross' national headquarters in Washington D.C., kicked-off the event.

The conference breakout sessions tackled such communication concerns as listening, conflict management, cultural communication, and the role of media in conjunction with leadership. "This (conference) was an opportunity to brush up one's skills and network with experienced professionals," said Dr. Ana Kong, professor in the College of Arts and Sciences (CAS) at GSU, and academic advisor to the conference organizers.

GSU students, community members, area community college students, and a small group from the Netherlands were among the budding leaders in attendance. Students from various fields were asked to participate. The conference's central message was executed though modeling how inter generational, cultural/ethnic, sexual orientation, and even difference in one's field of study can impact perspective

(cont. on p.5)

Is Dr. Muhammad Failing Her Students?

A Trinity of Dubious Service

by M.L. Hosty

Dr. Rashidah Jaami' Muhammad, instructor and coordinator of the English department here at Governors State University (GSU) has certainly been receiving a lion's share of negative commentary from students enrolled in that discipline regarding her propriety and ability as a member of the university's academic community. Previous issues of the student newspaper have witnessed letters-to-the-editor about suspicious granting of scholarly awards, negligible course offerings, and negligent instructors in that department, and recently, even more disturbing information has made its way to the student press about program decisions made by Muhammad. (cont.on p.12)

Co-organizer Sheree Y. Sanderson (L) talks with conference presenter Debra Mubashshirthd, visiting from Beloit College

New Members Appointed to GSU Board of Trustees

Governors State University (GSU)President,Stuart Fagan, announced last week that Governor George H. Ryan has appointed two new trustees — Kathleen Field Orr and Lorine Skulark Samuels — to serve on the GSU Board of Trustees.

Orr, principal, *Kathleen Field Orr and Associates*, is a practicing attorney with a wealth of experience in municipal law and municipal finance. She has served as chairperson of the *Local Government Section Council of the Illinois Bar Association*, and is a member of the *Home Rule Attorneys Committee of the Illinois Municipal League*.

Orr's community involvement is extensive, and includes serving as one-time president of the *Abby Foundation*, a woman's organization with funding of more than $50,000 annually in grants and scholarships for young women. Orr's new appointment builds upon an established relationship with the GSU community as she currently serves as a member of the Board of Directors of the Center for Performing Arts at GSU, a position she has held since the Center opened in 1995.

Additionally, Orr was a member of the Board of Directors of the GSU Foundation from 1993 until 1998. She is a resident of Flossmoor, IL.

"I've been involved with GSU for many years. I am honored to serve as a trustee. Governors State University is a vital part of the far south suburban community. It provides educational opportunity for thousands of people who might not otherwise be able to advance their education," Orr said.

Samuels is the president/owner of *Strategic Business Services* in Homewood, Ill. She serves on the *Chicago Southland Chamber of Commerce* in Homewood, IL, and on the *New Lenox Chamber of Commerce* in that region. Samuels has served as a consultant with the *Women's Development Center* in Chicago, and the *Cosmopolitan*

(cont. on p. 6)

GSU to Host Open House

On Saturday, November 4, 2000, Governors State University (GSU) will hold its annual "Discovery Day" open house to give prospective students an opportunity to discover the possibilities that come with a quality college education. GSU will be opening its doors to prospective undergraduate and graduate students from 8:30 a.m. to noon.

All of the colleges within the university – Education, Arts and Sciences, Health Professions, and Business and Public Administration – will be on hand to answer any questions about the respective programs. Tours of the facilities will also be available. Additionally, individuals will have a chance to learn more about GSU's adult and continuing education programs, student life, and student development opportunities.

GSU is accredited by the *North Central Association of Colleges and Secondary Schools*. GSU is also a member of the *Illinois Council of Baccalaureate and Higher Degree Programs*, and nearly all eligible programs are accredited or in accreditation candidacy (for new programs) by their respective professional accrediting agencies. Individuals seeking more information about "Discovery Day" should call (708) 534-4490.

De Laforcade stands beside former Haitian President Aristide at a luncheon held in Aristide's honor at Chicago's Union League Club in 1999.

De Laforcade's Contract Dispute Reaches 3rd Phase Arbitration

by M. L. Hosty

On this, the tenth day past the allocated due date for personnel matters to enter into arbitration, Dr. Geoffroy de Laforcade, formerly employed by Governors State University (GSU) in its College of Arts and Sciences (CAS) as a Unit-B lecturer, is being forced to consider outside legal recourse in an attempt to resolve his grievance against the administration and the dean of the college for which he worked, Dr. Roger Oden. The decision to move towards external legislation is being mitigated by the university's failure to adhere to union contract guidelines for personnel matters.

De Laforcade, a Yale graduate specializing in Latin American, Caribbean, and African history, and who also taught courses on Europe and comparative world civilizations, came to GSU to help develop the Integrative Studies program, and contends that the university has violated its own contractual agreements per his employment, and that he has yet to receive either fair or satisfactory treatment in his dealings with the GSU administration as regards his official grievance for wrongful dismissal. De Laforcade states that neither he nor the union received official notice that his services would no longer be retained, despite having brought to the attention of the administration that the union-administrative contract stipulates that " the university administration shall provide the Union with a report on changes in status" of Unit-B employees. De Laforcade claims that he first had an indication that he was to be released from employment following the receipt of a copy of a missive indicating such from the division chair of CAS, Dr. Joyce Kennedy, which was addressed to Oden and which noted that de Laforcade's services were not recommended for retention due to shifts in (cont. on p. 6)

Rep. Scully Visits GSU Students Page 5

Students, Faculty, and Administrators work together to coordinate Leadership Conference Page 5

INSIDE

FIGURE 2.1 *Innovator* of Oct. 31, 2000. Reprinted with permission of Governors State University.

The degree of freedom a medium enjoys depends on several factors, including the availability of channels, the pervasiveness and intrusiveness of the medium, and the historic relationship between the government and the medium. As print, voice, and video merge into digital multimedia, the law struggles to categorize new media into old regulatory niches.

The print medium—the press mentioned in the Constitution—has historically enjoyed the most protection under the First Amendment. The First Amendment stoutly protects the right of newspaper, book, and pamphlet publishers to publish all manner of political and social commentary, whether tasteless or profound.

Broadcasters, who acquire a government license to operate over government-allocated frequencies, are—unlike newspapers—required to operate "in the **public interest.**" Unlike newspaper publishers, broadcasters must allow equal opportunities for political candidates to access their channels during the election cycle. The government also regulates the "decency" of broadcast programs during day and early evening hours because broadcasting is said to be an intrusive medium that might harm children if indecency were permitted.

Cable operators are licensed by local governments. However, the content of cable program channels is generally subject to minimal government control. For example, the courts see less need for control of indecency on cable than in broadcasting because cable is considered a less intrusive medium than broadcasating. Cable is a medium, like newspapers, that customers choose by purchasing it.

Congress has attempted to regulate indecency on the Internet, but the Supreme Court has ruled that contributors to the Internet enjoy much the same First Amendment freedom as newspaper publishers. Courts view the Internet as a dynamic, worldwide technology whose development should not be hampered. And the courts have found most attempts to protect children from offensive content on the Internet to be too broad, protecting children but also unconstitutionally banning access for adults to expression protected by the First Amendment.

Summary

First Amendment freedoms are enjoyed to a greater or lesser degree by average citizens, government employees, students, and corporations. The First Amendment freedoms of adults and ideological associations include the freedom to speak, publish, join with others, receive information, solicit funds, and refuse to speak. High school students may distribute nondisruptive personal communication on campus, but high school administrators may impose "reasonable"—highly restrictive—regulations on school-sponsored expression to advance the school's educational mission. Students may also be punished for off-campus websites that disrupt education. Government employees may speak and vote as private citizens, but high-level employees are barred from participating in political campaigns. Profit-making non-media corporations enjoy First Amendment freedoms to buy commercial and issue advertising, but not to buy advertising on behalf of federal political candidates. Among the media, print enjoys the most First Amendment protection; the Internet enjoys nearly the same. Broadcasters are subject to more control because of the limited public spectrum on which they operate and because of the intrusive nature of broadcasting. Cable operators enjoy less freedom than publishers, but more than broadcasters.

CHAPTER 3

Methods of Control

Because the First Amendment does not protect all expression, the question arises how best to curb unprotected expression that defames, invades privacy, incites riots, damages national security, or causes other harms. Should harmful expression be stopped by government censors before it is disseminated or punished after dissemination with financial penalties?

A consistent thread in the law of public communication favors the second choice, punishing the dissemination of harmful expression, not censoring speech before it is disseminated. In legal terms, First Amendment doctrine presumes that prior restraints on publication are unconstitutional. Nevertheless, a number of prior restraints on communication are permitted. The government can block false advertising, copyright violations, and dispatches from military combat sites.

This chapter explains the various forms of prior restraint. The chapter also explains why the Supreme Court generally disfavors licensing but allows licensing in special contexts such as broadcasting. Finally, this chapter discusses the Court's tests for determining the constitutionality of content-neutral regulations.

Prior Restraints and Postpublication Punishment

The legal bias against prior restraints precedes adoption of the First Amendment. William Blackstone, the English jurist, wrote long before the First Amendment was ratified that liberty of the press

> consists in laying no *previous* restraints upon publications, and not in freedom from censure for criminal matter when published. Every freeman has an undoubted right to lay what sentiments he pleases before the public: to forbid this is to destroy the freedom of the press: but if he publishes what is improper, mischievous, or illegal, he must take the consequences of his own temerity.[1]

Although prior restraints were imposed infrequently in the American colonies, the founders, who were familiar with Blackstone, adopted the First Amendment in part to end prior restraints.[2] The importance of having no restraints before publication has also been noted by the modern Supreme Court. "Prior restraints on speech and publication," the Supreme Court has said, "are the most serious and the least tolerable infringement on First Amendment rights."[3] Because of the presumption that prior restraints are unconstitutional, the courts will strictly scrutinize any proposal to restrict dissemination of news or information.

Although not all scholars would agree,[4] prior restraints are thought to be more inhibiting to free expression than subsequent punishment. For the publisher, prior restraints are a direct curb on publication, whereas the possibility of prosecution after publication is a more remote and perhaps less inhibiting threat.

Prior restraints may also bring a wider range of expression under government scrutiny than postpublication prosecution. Under a system of prior restraints, the government may require that all public expression be censored by a central authority. This creates a bottleneck that intimidates speakers and greatly diminishes the valuable facts and ideas the public receives. Where prior restraints are permitted, the public has no opportunity to judge the worth of suppressed ideas or to offer criticism that might strengthen weak proposals.

Although financial penalties or jail sentences imposed after publication may intimidate speakers, postpublication punishments offer the advantage of allowing ideas to circulate because expression is not throttled by a bureaucratic bottleneck. Furthermore, where a government engages in postpublication punishments instead of prior restraints, the government may lack the resources to prosecute every publisher it would have censored if given the opportunity.[5]

---

[1] 4 *Commentaries on the Laws of England* 151–52 (Gifford 1820) (emphasis in the original).
[2] Leonard Levy, *Emergence of a Free Press* (1985).
[3] Nebraska Press Ass'n v. Stuart, 427 U.S. 539 (1976).
[4] *See, e.g.* Martin Redish, *Freedom of Expression: A Critical Analysis* 127–71 (1984).
[5] Thomas Emerson, *The System of Freedom of Expression* 506 (1970).

The Supreme Court established the presumption that prior restraints are unconstitutional in the 1931 case of *Near v. Minnesota*.[6] In *Near*, the Court struck down a state nuisance statute that permitted an **injunction** to halt "malicious, scandalous, or defamatory" publications. Under the statute, publishers could avoid an injunction if they could prove that a publication was true and made with good motives for justifiable ends. Publishers who printed in defiance of an injunction could be held in contempt of court.

The constitutionality of the statute was tested by Jay Near, an anti-Semitic publisher from Duluth whose *Saturday Press* accused Minneapolis police chief Frank Brunskill of failure to pursue a "Jewish gangster" who allegedly controlled gambling, bootlegging, and racketeering in the city. Near's publication asserted that "[p]ractically every vendor of vile hooch, every owner of a moonshine still, every snake-faced gangster and embryonic yegg in the Twin Cities is a JEW." The trial court declared the paper a nuisance and issued an injunction to bar Near from publishing more defamatory and scandalous matter. The Minnesota Supreme Court upheld the trial court, but the U.S. Supreme Court, in a 5-4 decision, reversed.

Chief Justice Charles Evans Hughes, citing Blackstone and Madison, wrote that the main purpose of the guarantee of freedom of expression is to prevent previous restraints on publication. Hughes said the prohibition on prior restraints was even more important in the twentieth century than it was in the eighteenth because press exposures of official corruption—expression the government would most like to censor—multiply as the government becomes more complex.

Hughes said the Minnesota statute imposed unconstitutional prior restraints because it permitted courts to enjoin publication of expression critical of public officials. It is the essence of censorship, Hughes said, to suppress a newspaper, under threat of being held in contempt, for publishing charges of official dereliction. Defamed officials may sue a newspaper after publication for libel, the Court said, but it is unconstitutional to bar all publication because statements might be libelous.

The Court also rejected imposing prior restraints because a publication might be "scandalous." Charges of government misconduct may indeed cause public scandal, the Court said, but "a more serious public evil would be caused by authority to prevent publication."

The Court found unacceptable the statutory requirement that publishers trying to avoid injunctions prove their good motives, justifiable ends, and the truth of their publications. Under such vague standards, a legislature or court would have complete discretion to determine what are "justifiable ends" and to "restrain publication accordingly," Hughes said.

Chief Justice Hughes did not say that the constitutional prohibition on prior restraints is absolute. The Court suggested that prior restraints might be permissible in wartime to bar expression obstructing military recruiting or announcing the number and location of troops or the sailing dates of troop transports. Hughes also suggested prior restraints might be acceptable on obscene expression and on incitement to violence or to the forceful overthrow of the government. "The constitutional guaranty of free speech," Hughes said, does not "protect a man from an injunction against uttering words that may have all the effect of force."

Prior restraints may take many forms. They may appear as an injunction—the "classic" prior restraint—like that issued in the *Near* case, or they may appear as licensing, in contracts or other agreements, and in discriminatory taxes.

[6]283 U.S. 697 (1931).

Injunctions

Injunctions are quite easily permitted in some contexts. Courts willingly issue injunctions to halt obscenity, false advertising, and fraud, speech that is outside constitutional protection. As Professor Laurence Tribe suggests, prior restraints are justified in obscenity and commercial cases because the courts may determine as easily before publication as after whether a statement is obscene, false, or fraudulent.[7] Furthermore, delaying dissemination of such expression is less damaging to freedom of expression than delaying political speech, it is argued, because of the lesser value accorded to commercial and sexual expression.

The courts are less likely to issue a prior restraint on political speech and other expression in which the harm may be difficult to determine ahead of time and in which the harm caused by a restraint may be severe. *New York Times v. United States* is a dramatic case demonstrating the Supreme Court's unwillingness to grant prior restraints on political speech when the government cannot make a clear showing that publication will cause a severe harm.[8]

In *New York Times v. United States,* frequently referred to as the Pentagon Papers case, the Supreme Court refused to bar publication of a series of stories in the *New York Times* and other newspapers based on a secret Pentagon study of the Vietnam War. The Pentagon Papers, a forty-seven-volume classified history of American involvement in Vietnam, were commissioned by Defense Secretary Robert McNamara before he left office in 1968. The papers documented how Republican and Democratic administrations had misled the American people about the nation's objectives in Southeast Asia. One of the minor authors of the Pentagon Papers, Daniel Ellsberg, acting without authorization, provided the classified documents to the *Times* and later to the *Washington Post.*

After publication began in the *Times* on Sunday, June 13, 1971, President Nixon asked the Justice Department to seek an injunction on the grounds that continued publication would cause irreparable danger to the national interest. The government argued that publication would prolong the war in Vietnam and disrupt the administration's diplomacy. The country learned later that the Nixon administration also feared that publication of the Pentagon Papers might frighten the Chinese from then-secret negotiations to open diplomatic relations with the United States. The administration feared the Chinese would be wary of conducting confidential discussions with the United States if the details of the confidential Pentagon Papers were being exposed on the front page of the *New York Times.*

In New York, the U.S. Court of Appeals for the Second Circuit enjoined publication of the papers in the *Times,* but the Court of Appeals for the District of Columbia Circuit refused to stop publication in the *Post.* The Supreme Court temporarily stopped publication in the *Post* and, on June 25, granted expedited review of both cases. After oral arguments, the Court delivered its opinion in less than a week.

The Supreme Court ruled, 6-3, that the First Amendment did not permit an injunction. A brief, unsigned opinion for the court—a per curiam opinion—freed the papers to publish because the government, the Court said, had not met its "heavy burden" of proof to overcome the presumption that prior restraints are unconstitutional. While the newspapers

[7]Laurence Tribe, *American Constitutional Law* 1048 (2d ed. 1988).
[8]403 U.S. 713 (1971). *See generally* David Rudenstine, *The Day the Presses Stopped* (1996).

were pleased to resume publication, the Court's opinion provided little guidance about when injunctions violate the First Amendment. The terse majority opinion did not define the government's heavy burden or explain why the government had not met the burden in the Pentagon Papers case.

The Court's "real" opinion is found in nine separate opinions written by the six concurring and three dissenting justices. On the majority side, Justices Black and Douglas asserted their absolutism, arguing they could not imagine a situation in which the government could meet its "heavy burden" to justify a prior restraint. Justice Brennan, citing *Near v. Minnesota,* said prior restraints might be justified in wartime if the government presented clear evidence that publication presented an imminent danger. However, Congress had not declared war in Vietnam, and Brennan saw no evidence that publication of the Pentagon Papers presented an immediate danger to national security.

Three other justices in the majority, Potter Stewart, Byron White, and Thurgood Marshall, said a prior restraint might be justified if congressional legislation had authorized one in such a case. Justice Stewart, in an opinion joined by Justice White, suggested the Court might uphold an injunction against the *New York Times* even without congressional authorization if the government proved publication would "surely result in direct, immediate, and irreparable damage" to the nation. In any case, the government had not met that burden, Stewart said, although he was convinced that publication of the Pentagon Papers would cause some harm.

The three dissenters, Chief Justice Warren Burger and Justices John Harlan and Harry Blackmun, thought the Pentagon Papers case should not be decided so swiftly. The chief justice was also disappointed that the newspaper did not return the stolen papers as, in his view, any responsible citizen would return lost property to its owner.

Although the press considered the Pentagon Papers decision a great victory, the decision revealed for the first time that a majority of the Supreme Court might be willing to enjoin publication of political speech if a publication presented an immediate, irreparable danger to national security. The press was also put on notice that the government might prosecute the press under criminal statutes for publishing classified information. As shown later in this chapter, Attorney General Gonzales warned the press in 2006 that the government has the authority to punish those who publish classified information.

The government's power to halt national security publications was tested again in 1979, when a federal court in Wisconsin stopped publication of an article about the hydrogen bomb. The article, which described in general terms how easy it might be to build a bomb, was to appear in the small-circulation *Progressive* magazine. Using Justice Stewart's suggested test from the Pentagon Papers case, District Judge Robert Warren ruled that the article, "The H-Bomb Secret: How We Got It; Why We're Telling It," presented an "immediate, direct, irreparable harm to the interests of the United States."[9]

Even though the article was based in large measure on public information, the court found an imminent danger in publication of "concepts that are not found in the public realm, concepts that are vital to the operation of the bomb." The court said the article could allow a medium-size nation to move faster in developing a hydrogen weapon than it otherwise might

[9]United States v. Progressive, Inc., 467 F. Supp. 990 (W.D. Wis. 1979), *dismissed,* 610 F.2d 819 (7th Cir. 1979).

and thus irreparably harm the security of the United States. Publication also violated provisions of the Atomic Energy Act prohibiting disclosure of "restricted data," including information about the design and manufacture of atomic weapons. The media did not learn whether an appeals court would uphold the prior restraint on *Progressive* because the government dropped its suit after information similar to that in the *Progressive* article was published elsewhere.

Prepublication Agreements

Besides injunctions, prior restraints may take the form of a government contract or restrictive prepublication agreement. Although government employees have a right to speak as private citizens, their speech may be restricted in a number of ways. Just as private corporations may prohibit employees from revealing confidential business information, the government may prohibit its employees from divulging information that would jeopardize national security, reveal business secrets, or invade privacy.

Federal employees throughout the executive branch sign so-called standard nondisclosure forms prohibiting disclosure of "classified" and, on some forms, "classifiable" information. Employees who divulge information in violation of the agreements may lose their security clearances or their jobs.

CIA employees must sign an employment contract that subjects them to lifetime censorship. Former CIA intelligence officer Frank Snepp paid a heavy price for publishing a book in violation of his agreement with the CIA. Snepp, a former intelligence officer in Vietnam, published a book critical of the rapid American evacuation of Vietnam. Snepp violated his contract with the CIA by publishing before submitting the manuscript to the CIA, as his preemployment secrecy agreement required. Although the CIA conceded Snepp's book, *Decent Interval,* contained no classified material, the agency brought a suit for breach of contract. Upholding the CIA's contractual claims, the Supreme Court rejected Snepp's argument that the CIA imposed an unconstitutional prior restraint by subjecting all his expression to prepublication review.[10]

Even Snepp's publication of unclassified material relating to intelligence activities might damage national interests, the Court said. Snepp's publication, it said, might inadvertently reveal classified information and perhaps inhibit sources from confiding in the CIA if they thought the agency could not keep a secret.

In a footnote, the Court suggested that the CIA's censorship powers did not depend exclusively on the prepublication contract. Even in the absence of an agreement, the Court said, "the CIA could have acted to protect substantial government interests by imposing reasonable restrictions on employee activity that in other contexts might be protected by the First Amendment." To punish Snepp, the Supreme Court imposed a "constructive trust" on all of his earnings from the book, as well as earnings on movies and talks resulting from his work as an intelligence officer in Vietnam. Earnings in the trust revert to the government. In 1990, a federal appeals court denied Snepp's attempt to modify his prior censorship agreement with the government.[11]

[10]Snepp v. United States, 444 U.S. 507 (1980).
[11]United States v. Snepp, 897 F.2d 138 (4th Cir. 1990).

Military Security Review

Another and broader prior restraint is imposed by the military on press coverage of combat operations. American military officials carefully control press access to military bases and military operations. As a condition of access, the military imposes ground rules restricting what the press publishes. For example, during the opening stages of Operation Enduring Freedom, journalists aboard Navy ships in the Arabian Sea were not allowed to publish the full names of military personnel. Journalists accompanying Air Force flights over Afghanistan were not allowed to disclose sensitive information such as altitude and route. (The ground rules for coverage of Operation Iraqi Freedom are discussed in Chapter 12.) Journalists who violate the ground rules may be expelled from the combat zone.

Under Department of Defense policy, military commanders in the field have the option of subjecting news stories to review by military officials. Known as **security review,** this process is intended to ensure that journalists comply with the ground rules. Some commanders, fearful that the press will inadvertently disseminate information useful to the enemy, insist on security review of all news coverage. Other commanders carefully explain to journalists what can and cannot be reported and then trust journalists to follow the rules. In Operation Iraqi Freedom, security review was authorized when briefing of journalists did not sufficiently protect sensitive information.

Although Pentagon guidelines provide that security review be used only to excise information harmful to operational security, the system has also been used to control the military's image. During the 1991 Gulf War, military officers who supervised journalists understood that they "risked being called to task" by their commanders for negative stories.[12] This institutional imperative to burnish the organization's image is not unique to military officers; it is inherent in any system in which government officials engage in prepublication review. As Professor Thomas Emerson wrote, "The function of the censor is to censor. He has a professional interest in finding things to suppress. . . . The long history of prior restraint reveals over and over that the personal and institutional forces inherent in the system nearly always end in a stupid, unnecessary, and extreme suppression."[13]

Although members of the press have filed legal challenges to restrictions on access to battlefield settings, the system of security review has never been challenged. The press prefers that security review not occur but will accept it as a condition of gaining access to military operations or facilities.[14]

Licensing

Prior restraint by licensing was well known to the framers of the Constitution. In 1643, the English Parliament passed a law forbidding publication of any book, pamphlet, or paper without registration with the Stationers' Company, a group of ninety-seven London stationers who were given a monopoly by the Crown on all printing. Milton wrote *Areopagitica,* his famous pamphlet championing a free press, in opposition to this act.

[12]Jason DeParle, "After the War: Long Series of Military Decisions Led to Gulf War News Censorship," *N.Y. Times,* May 5, 1991, at A1.

[13]Thomas Emerson, "The Doctrine of Prior Restraint," 20 *Law & Contemp. Probs.* 648, 659 (1955).

[14]*See generally* William Lee, "'Security Review' and the First Amendment," 25 *Harv. J. L. & Pub. Pol'y* 743 (2002).

Under the Printing Act of 1662, London stationers controlled the printing, importing, and selling of all publications. Nothing could be printed, imported, or sold that was "heretical, seditious, schismatical, or offensive" to the Church of England. It was also forbidden to print anything offensive to any officer of government, to a corporation, or to any private person.[15] By the 1690s, economically powerful commercial printers forced an end to English licensing, but licensing continued in the colonies until the mid-1720s.

Contemporary First Amendment doctrine is hostile to licensing schemes in which government officials have unbridled discretion to control what may be communicated in public forums, motion pictures, and other media. In special contexts such as broadcasting, though, the Court allows licensing that would be unconstitutional in other media.

Anyone may start a newspaper without seeking a license from the government; newspaper publishers do not interfere with the voices of other publishers. The Court, however, believes that licensing of broadcasting is necessary to prevent interference among broadcasters and other users of the electromagnetic spectrum. Similarly, to minimize disruption of public streets and rights-of-way, cable system operators are required to obtain franchises from local governments. As with print media, communicators using the Internet do not need licenses; the Court believes the Internet lacks physical limitations similar to those of broadcasting.

PUBLIC FORUMS The modern Supreme Court has recognized that certain forms of public expression, such as the use of a street for a parade, require a license to protect public safety. However, the Supreme Court has consistently decried subjective licensing standards that allow government officials to discriminate among potential speakers on the basis of their messages. Licensing schemes for First Amendment activity on public property must contain "narrow, objective, and definite" standards to guide the licensing authority.

The Supreme Court believes that public facilities, such as streets, must be available to all, regardless of whether government officials agree with the views expressed. Subjective licensing laws are presumed unconstitutional, and plaintiffs challenging these laws need not prove that content discrimination has occurred. The Supreme Court believes that "the danger of censorship and of abridgment of our precious First Amendment freedoms is too great where officials have unbridled discretion over a forum's use. Our distaste for censorship—reflecting the natural distaste of a free people—is deep-written in our law."[16]

The line between permissible and impermissible licensing of public assemblies is illustrated in *Shuttlesworth v. City of Birmingham,* in which the Supreme Court found unconstitutional a Birmingham, Alabama, parade ordinance.[17] The law gave members of the city commission the authority to deny permits to parades that were harmful to the "public welfare," "morals," or "good order" of the community. The Court condemned the local officials' "virtually unbridled and absolute power" to prohibit parades. Writing for a unanimous Court, Justice Stewart said, "a municipality may not empower its licensing officials to roam essentially at will, dispensing or withholding permission to speak, assemble, picket, or parade, according to their own opinions regarding the potential effect of the activity in question on the 'welfare,' 'decency,' or 'morals of the community.'"

[15]Fredrick Siebert, *Freedom of the Press in England 1476–1776,* at 239–41 (1952).
[16]Southeastern Promotions, Ltd. v. Conrad, 420 U.S. 546, 553 (1975).
[17]394 U.S. 147 (1969).

Justice Stewart contrasted the Birmingham ordinance with a New Hampshire statute that had been found to be constitutional in *Cox v. New Hampshire.*[18] The New Hampshire law did not allow government officials to withhold a license if they disliked the message of a parade. Under the New Hampshire statute, marchers had a right to a license, subject only to content-neutral "time, place, and manner" regulations designed to accommodate competing demands for public use of the streets.

More recently, the Supreme Court struck down a Lakewood, Ohio, ordinance that required publishers to obtain a permit annually from the mayor before placing newsracks on public sidewalks. The ordinance contained no limits on the mayor's discretion, and the Court refused to presume that the mayor would act in good faith. A licensing statute "placing unbridled discretion in the hands of a government official," Justice Brennan wrote for the Court, "constitutes a prior restraint and may result in censorship."[19] The licensor's unfettered discretion intimidates parties into censoring their own speech, even if the discretion is never abused, Justice Brennan said. A newspaper that depends on the mayor's annual approval might feel compelled to support the mayor's policies, the Court said.

In 2002, the Supreme Court unanimously sustained a Chicago ordinance requiring individuals to obtain a permit before holding large-scale events in public parks.[20] The ordinance stipulated that permit applications could be denied on any of thirteen specified grounds. For example, a permit could be denied if the activity planned by the applicant conflicted with previously planned programs organized by the park district. Writing for the Court, Justice Scalia emphasized the content neutrality of the law:

> The Park District ordinance does not authorize a licensor to pass judgment on the content of speech: None of the grounds for denying a permit has anything to do with what a speaker might say. Indeed, the ordinance (unlike the classic censorship scheme) is not even directed to communicative activity as such, but rather to *all* activity conducted in a public park. The picnicker and soccer-player, no less than the political activist or parade marshal, must apply for a permit if the 50-person limit is to be exceeded.

Because the Chicago permit system did not raise the specter of censorship, the Court declined to impose the extraordinary procedural safeguards that had been developed in the context of film licensing.

MOTION PICTURES The Supreme Court believes that each medium of communication presents "peculiar problems." The Court has ruled that local governments may license motion pictures as a means of dealing with the "peculiar problems" posed by the film medium. The Court has also ruled, however, that film licensing must follow stringent procedural protections. In addition, a film licensing standard must not be unconstitutionally vague. Faced with these strict requirements, local governments no longer license films even though they have the legal authority to do so.

After the inception of motion pictures in the 1890s, government officials, fearful of the power of this new medium, began licensing films in various jurisdictions. Motion pictures

[18] 312 U.S. 569 (1941).
[19] City of Lakewood v. Plain Dealer Publishing Co., 486 U.S. 750, 757 (1988).
[20] Thomas v. Chicago Park District, 534 U.S. 316 (2002).

were not initially believed to be part of the press but were regarded as being similar to circuses and other "shows and spectacles" subject to government control without First Amendment limitations. In 1915, the United States Supreme Court unanimously upheld an Ohio statute requiring film licensing; only those films of a "moral, educational or amusing and harmless character" could be exhibited.[21] At that time, the Supreme Court did not interpret the Fourteenth Amendment as making the First Amendment applicable to the states. The Court ruled that motion pictures were not subject to the press protections of the Ohio constitution. The Court reasoned that motion pictures were not "organs of public opinion" but were "mere representations of events, of ideas and sentiments known." In addition, films were "capable of evil," especially because of "their attractiveness and manner of exhibition."

In 1925, the Court ruled that the First Amendment, through the Fourteenth Amendment, was applicable to the states.[22] It was not until 1952, though, that the Court invalidated on First Amendment grounds a state film-licensing statute. In *Joseph Burstyn, Inc. v. Wilson,* the Court concluded that motion pictures are important organs of public opinion, even though they are "designed to entertain as well as inform."[23] Furthermore, the "capacity for evil, particularly among the youth of a community," did not disqualify all motion pictures from First Amendment protection. The Court held that the New York licensing statute, which prohibited the exhibition of "sacrilegious" films, gave unbridled censorship powers to government officials. "It is not the business of government in our nation to suppress real or imagined attacks upon a particular religious doctrine, whether they appear in publications, speeches, or motion pictures," the Court wrote.

Although licensing is permitted to bar distribution of obscene films, the Supreme Court imposes strict procedural requirements to minimize unnecessary curbs on protected expression. In *Freedman v. Maryland* the Court unanimously ruled unconstitutional a Maryland film-licensing statute because it lacked the procedural protections necessary to protect free expression.[24] The Court ruled that a system of film licensing must contain three procedural safeguards. First, the burden of proving that the film is unprotected expression must rest upon the censor. Second, any restraint prior to judicial review can be imposed only briefly. Third, a prompt judicial determination of a film's protected or unprotected status must be assured. These safeguards, discussed more fully in Chapter 9, rest on the idea that communicators may assume their expression is entitled to constitutional protection until the government proves otherwise. Further, because the "censor's business is to censor," the Court feared that film licensors would be less responsive than the judiciary to free expression. Finally, if judicial review of an administrative decision is delayed, "the censor's determination may in practice be final."

A film-licensing scheme with careful procedures may nonetheless be unconstitutional if the licensing standard is vague. In *Interstate Circuit, Inc. v. Dallas,* the Court found unconstitutionally vague a municipal licensing scheme that classified films as "suitable for young persons" and "not suitable for young persons."[25] Unsuitable films included the portrayal

[21]Mutual Film Corp. v. Industrial Comm'n of Ohio, 236 U.S. 230 (1915).
[22]Gitlow v. New York, 268 U.S. 652 (1925).
[23]343 U.S. 495 (1952).
[24]380 U.S. 51 (1965).
[25]390 U.S. 676 (1968).

of "brutality, criminal violence or depravity" and "sexual promiscuity" in a manner that encouraged crime or sexual promiscuity by young people. The ordinance did not define terms such as "sexual promiscuity," leading the Court to conclude that the licensing board was "adrift upon a boundless sea." Although the Dallas law provided for prompt judicial review, the Court held that this did not cure the problem of vagueness. If local governments were to license films, they would have to create "definite standards" for licensing officials to follow.

During the social upheaval of the 1960s, American society became more tolerant of graphic film portrayals. Also, in 1968, the Motion Picture Association of America (MPAA) introduced its film rating system to offer parents advance information about films. This system of industry rating, discussed in detail in Chapter 9, reduced governmental interest in licensing films. These developments, along with the strict requirements of *Freedman* and *Interstate Circuit,* led to the cessation of film licensing in the late 1960s.

BROADCASTING The medium of mass communication receiving the least amount of First Amendment protection is broadcasting. The Court has approved licensing and content regulation for broadcasting that would be unconstitutional for the print media. The Court does not regard licensing of a broadcaster as a prior restraint, nor is FCC review of broadcast programming considered to be censorship. Nevertheless, the power to revoke or not renew a license for programming-related reasons has rarely been used. The threat of loss of license is sufficient deterrent to ensure that most broadcasters comply with programming regulations.

The Supreme Court has ruled that the physical limitations of the electromagnetic **spectrum** justify government licensing of broadcasters. Broadcast licensees, in return for receiving one of a limited number of spectrum assignments available, may be required to serve the **public interest** in ways not required of the print media. For example, the government cannot compel newspapers to provide space to political candidates. However, broadcasters are required to provide airtime to federal candidates, a requirement the Supreme Court regards as permissible under the First Amendment.[26]

To operate a radio or television station legally in the United States, a company or individual must have a license granted by the FCC. In *Red Lion Broadcasting Co. v. FCC,* the Supreme Court's most important discussion of the First Amendment and broadcasting, the Court described the electromagnetic spectrum as a scarce resource that requires a system of government allocation.[27] Justice White said as long as demand for spectrum space exceeds the frequencies available, no one can claim a First Amendment right to broadcast "comparable to the right of every individual to speak, write, or publish." Therefore, White said, the right to free speech is not violated when the FCC acts to ensure that the spectrum is used to benefit the public.

At the same time, White said, those who obtain broadcast licenses do not have an unfettered right to broadcast only their own views on public issues or the views of persons who agree with them. The First Amendment does not prevent the government "from requiring a licensee to share his frequency with others and . . . to present those views and voices which are representative of his community and which would otherwise . . . be

[26]CBS v. FCC, 453 U.S. 367 (1981).
[27]395 U.S. 367 (1969).

barred from the airwaves." Therefore, the Court sustained an FCC policy, known as the fairness doctrine, which required licensees to provide balanced coverage of public issues. As will be discussed in Chapter 7, the FCC rescinded the fairness doctrine in 1987, believing that the agency's supervision of public issue programming was unnecessary because of the explosive growth in the number and types of information outlets since the 1969 *Red Lion* decision.[28]

Red Lion introduced a new element to First Amendment analysis: the collective right of the people to receive expression justifies government regulation. "It is the right of the viewers and listeners, not the right of the broadcasters, which is paramount," the Court said. Thus, government supervision of broadcast speech is permissible because listeners benefit from the government's regulation.

To promote the public's interest in diverse views, Congress and the FCC have established limits on the number and types of media one licensee may own. For example, for many years a broadcaster could not own a newspaper in the same market. When the FCC adopted this rule in 1975, it ordered the divestiture of sixteen newspaper-broadcast combinations in small communities that had only one daily newspaper and one broadcast station. All other existing combinations were allowed to continue, but no new broadcast-newspaper combinations were permitted. The Supreme Court unanimously affirmed the FCC's authority to impose these conditions on broadcast licensees.[29] Citing *Red Lion,* the Court held that newspaper publishers had no First Amendment right to a broadcast license. Further, the FCC could use licensing criteria to promote more diverse media ownership. In 2007, the FCC revised this rule, allowing newspaper-broadcast combinations in the top twenty markets. All other proposed newspaper-broadcast transactions are presumed not in the public interest.[30]

Until recently, programming was also a significant factor considered by the FCC in awarding and renewing licenses. Despite the obvious dangers, courts permitted the agency to make licensing decisions based on subjective evaluations of the value of broadcast programming. As long as the FCC did not review the content of a specific program prior to its broadcast, there was no impermissible prior restraint.

The Radio Act of 1927, the first comprehensive regulation of broadcasting, established the Federal Radio Commission (FRC), forerunner of the FCC, and authorized the agency to grant and renew licenses and otherwise regulate broadcasters according to the "public interest, convenience, or necessity."[31] The Radio Act specifically stated that the FRC's licensing authority did not include "the power of censorship," but the Radio Act also banned obscene, indecent, or profane broadcasts. The statute also required that a licensee who allowed a political candidate to use broadcast facilities provide "equal opportunities" to opponents.

In spite of the no-censorship provision, key legislators believed a station's programming ought to be a factor in determining whether a licensee was acting in the public interest. A federal appeals court soon agreed, ruling that the FRC could refuse to renew a broadcast station's license if the station's programming did not serve the public interest.[32]

[28]Syracuse Peace Council, 2 F.C.C.R. 5043 (1987), *aff'd,* Syracuse Peace Council v. FCC, 867 F.2d 654 (D.C. Cir. 1989), *cert. denied,* 493 U.S. 1019 (1990).
[29]FCC v. National Citizens Comm. for Broadcasting, 436 U.S. 775 (1978).
[30]Cross-ownership of Broadcast Stations and Newspapers (FCC 07-216) (Dec. 18, 2007).
[31]Pub. L. No. 69-632, 44 Stat. 1162 (1927).
[32]KFKB Broadcasting Ass'n v. FRC, 47 F.2d 670 (D.C. Cir. 1931).

The government's authority to revoke or not renew a broadcast license for programming-related reasons stands in marked contrast to the limits on government power to control newspaper publishing.

Trinity Methodist Church, South v. FRC illustrates the distinction between the broadcasting and print media.[33] "Fighting Bob" Shuler, a Methodist minister, used his Los Angeles radio station to attack local government corruption; his broadcasts were laced with references to "pimps" and "prostitutes" as well as attacks on the Catholic Church. Shuler's broadcasts were strikingly similar to the newspaper attacks of Jay Near. In *Near v. Minnesota,* discussed earlier in this chapter, the Supreme Court ruled the government could not enjoin Near from publishing libelous and scandalous material. In the case of Shuler, though, a federal appellate court ruled that the FRC's refusal to renew Shuler's license because of defamatory and racist broadcasts did not violate the First Amendment. The appellate court said the FRC's action was neither "censorship nor previous restraint." Shuler remained free to continue his attacks on public officials in other forums, but he had no right to a broadcast license. To the appellate court, the power of the federal government to regulate interstate commerce meant that a broadcast licensee received a license "subject to the power of government, in the public interest, to withdraw it without compensation."

Despite the government's authority to revoke or not renew a broadcast license for programming-related reasons, such actions have been rare. As will be shown in Chapter 9, the FCC prefers to use sanctions such as fines to punish broadcasters for violations of programming rules. Also, Congress has recently substantially reduced the FCC's ability to evaluate programming in licensing decisions.

Before 1996, the FCC would hold a comparative hearing if more than one applicant wanted the same broadcast license. Among the criteria used were factors such as proposed program service and past broadcast record.[34] By comparing an existing licensee's program record with the proposed programming of a challenger, the FCC believed it could identify which programming would best serve the public. Congress significantly altered broadcast licensing in 1996, preventing the FCC from considering competing applications in license renewals.[35] Congress further altered broadcast licensing in 1997, giving the FCC the authority to award contested licenses for new nondigital commercial frequencies via an auction process; contested licenses for nondigital noncommercial licenses are awarded through a lottery process.[36] Comparative hearings will not be held for new digital television licenses; these frequencies are reserved for existing television broadcasters.

Currently, broadcasters have a renewal expectancy unless they have committed serious violations of statutory and regulatory requirements.[37] Broadcasters have an incentive to retain their valuable licenses and rarely offer programming that would justify a loss of license.

CABLE Cable television began in the late 1940s as a way to extend television service to small towns that were out of range of broadcast signals. Until the mid-1970s, cable systems merely functioned as a community antenna, facilitating the reception of broadcast signals.

[33] 62 F.2d 850 (D.C. Cir. 1932).
[34] Policy Statement on Comparative Broadcast Hearings, 1 F. C. C.2d 393 (1965).
[35] 47 U.S.C. § 309(k).
[36] 47 U.S.C. § 309(i) & (j).
[37] 47 U.S.C. § 309 (k).

In 1975, HBO became the first cable program service to distribute its programs to cable systems via communications satellite. Soon a variety of specialized services, such as ESPN, CNN, and MTV, also became available to cable systems via satellite. In addition, local cable systems began producing local programming, such as news and public affairs. As cable shed its community antenna function and began offering an expansive variety of programming, it was able to succeed in urban and suburban markets. Today, two-thirds of the country's households subscribe to cable. Modern digital cable systems offer hundreds of channels of video programming, high-speed Internet service, and telephony.

Cable signals are sent to homes through **coaxial cable** or **fiber-optic cable.** The cable is strung on utility poles or installed underground. Because local cable signals are not sent "over the air" through the broadcast spectrum, cable operators are not required to obtain broadcast licenses from the FCC. However, because cable installation involves disruption of city streets and the stringing of cable on utility poles, local governments grant licenses known as a **franchise** to cable operators. The franchise authorizes the construction and operation of a cable system.

Today, because most communities have at least one cable system, local government oversight of cable is directed at enforcing the franchise and its periodic renewal. During the 1970s and 1980s, the height of initial franchising, municipal governments generally followed a competitive bidding process to award a single cable franchise. The local government typically issued a request for proposals (RFP). This document described the cable system and the services the community desired. The RFP also outlined the information the franchising authority sought from applicants concerning their background, financial qualifications, proposed system design, construction plan, rates, and programming. After evaluating the bids, the local government selected a winning applicant and negotiated a franchise agreement.[38]

Because communities awarded only one franchise, they often exacted conditions, such as public access studios and channels, franchise fees, and free service to government offices and schools. And because communities awarded a single franchise, government officials believed that they must select the "best" applicant, which entailed a highly subjective evaluation of elements such as the bidder's character and the nature of the proposed service. Cable operators based critical features of bids, such as the monthly subscription fee, on predictions of construction costs and market penetration. When those predictions were incorrect, as they often were, and the cable company had to raise its fees or reduce its service package, subscribers could question whether the city had selected the "best" bid.

In *Los Angeles v. Preferred Communications, Inc.*, the Supreme Court unanimously held that the cable-franchising process would be subject to constitutional scrutiny.[39] The Court acknowledged for the first time that cable system operators are entitled to First Amendment protection. This meant that cities could not award exclusive franchises on the basis of assertions about the need to minimize the demands on public property.

Preferred involved a challenge to the franchise process in Los Angeles. The city was divided into different areas, and after a competitive bidding process, a single franchise was awarded for each area. Preferred Communications, Inc. (PCI), did not participate in the

[38] *See generally* William Lee, "Cable Franchising and the First Amendment," 36 *Vand. L. Rev.* 867 (1983).
[39] 476 U.S. 488 (1986).

bidding process. Nonetheless, PCI asked the city for an additional franchise to serve the South Central district. After this request was denied, PCI brought suit, claiming that its First Amendment right to construct and operate a cable system was violated by the city's exclusive franchising scheme.

The Supreme Court unanimously affirmed an appellate court ruling that Los Angeles violated the First Amendment when it prohibited competition among cable operators. Significantly, the Court held that cable television "partakes of some of the aspects of speech and the communication of ideas as do the traditional enterprises of newspaper and book publishers, public speakers, and pamphleteers." Specifically, cable operators exercise editorial discretion through original programming or by selecting which television stations or cable program services to offer to the public. However, the Court indicated that PCI's First Amendment rights would have to be balanced against the impact on the city caused by an additional cable operator stringing cable on poles and digging up city streets. The Court said it would not decide how to balance these competing interests because it needed more information about the impact of multiple cable systems on public property.

The Court remanded the *Preferred* case to the lower courts. In doing so, the Court rejected the claim that courts should defer to the city's judgment as to the need for exclusive franchising. Because the franchising scheme restricted speech protected by the First Amendment, the Court held that lower courts could not assume that the exclusive scheme actually served the city's interests. Los Angeles would have to prove that the installation of a second cable system was so disruptive that exclusive franchising was justified.

On remand, the district court found that the disruption the city feared was not sufficient to warrant an exclusive franchise scheme. The Court of Appeals for the Ninth Circuit affirmed; the appellate court held that although the interests advanced by the city were substantial, permitting only a single cable system "exacts too heavy a toll on the First Amendment interests at stake here. Competition in the marketplace of ideas—as in every other market—leads to a far greater diversity of viewpoints (and better service) than if a single vendor is granted a . . . monopoly."[40] Moreover, exclusive franchising created the risk that the cable operator would be a captive of city hall. The Supreme Court refused to hear the case for a second time.[41]

Congress has enacted several statutory provisions relating to cable franchising. Cable operators are required to have a franchise, but local governments may not grant an exclusive franchise.[42] Local governments may require cable operators to set aside channel capacity for public, educational, and governmental access channels and to pay franchise fees up to 5 percent of gross revenue.[43] Although franchising authorities may establish requirements for "broad categories of video programming," such as sports, news and public affairs, and children's programming, Congress said that franchising authorities could not require a particular program service, such as CNN or ESPN.[44] If both the cable operator and the local franchising authority agree, a franchise may be renewed through negotiations.

[40] 13 F.3d 1327, 1330 (9th Cir. 1994), *cert. denied,* 512 U.S. 1235 (1994).

[41] 512 U.S. 1235 (1994).

[42] 47 U.S.C. § 541.

[43] 47 U.S.C. §§ 531 & 542.

[44] 47 U.S.C. § 544. *See also* Time Warner Cable v. City of New York, 943 F. Supp. 1357 (S.D.N.Y. 1996), *aff'd sub nom.* Time Warner Cable v. Bloomberg L. P., 118 F.3d 917 (2nd Cir. 1997).

However, to protect cable operators from an arbitrary denial of a renewal, Congress has created procedures and standards that may be invoked for renewals.[45] For example, Congress said that local franchising authorities may consider the "quality of the operator's service," but this refers only to matters such as billing and response to consumer complaints, not to the quality or level of particular program services.

Recently, telephone companies such as Verizon have built fiber networks capable of carrying voice, video, and Internet communication. However, to offer video service on these networks, the telephone companies need cable franchises. Telephone companies claim that the process of gaining permission from thousands of individual communities will delay implementation of this service. Thus, the telephone companies have lobbied state legislatures for laws authorizing state-issued video franchises and a streamlining of the franchising process. Nine states have recently enacted laws allowing state-issued franchises.[46]

The phone companies have also sought federal streamlining of franchising. In 2006, Congress considered, but did not enact, legislation streamlining the franchising process. In late 2006, though, the FCC adopted rules designed to make it easier for phone companies to enter the cable television business.[47] The FCC found that local governments were acting unreasonably by delaying action on franchise applications and requiring franchise applicants to pay for the building of public swimming pools, recreation centers, and landscaping for parks. The FCC adopted rules requiring local franchise authorities to act on applications within ninety days, and the costs of in-kind contributions are counted toward the 5 percent cap on franchise fees.

Discriminatory Taxation

After licensing ended in England, the government controlled the press by taxing publications and advertisements. A discriminatory tax, or a "tax on knowledge" as it was called in colonial times, is not a prior restraint on a specific story. But a tax on the press may be considered a prior restraint because it curtails publishers' ability to disseminate information and, consequently, citizens' ability to receive it. Taxation by the English Crown made publications less profitable, thus making them vulnerable to control through government subsidies and bribery.[48] Taxes on the press did not end in England until 1855. The notorious Stamp Acts under which colonial publications were taxed helped precipitate the American Revolution.

The First Amendment does not exempt publishers and broadcasters from the laws regulating all businesses. The media must abide by tax, safety, antitrust, labor, and other laws that regulate businesses. However, the First Amendment may be used to strike down business regulations that are based on content or that place a disproportionate burden on the media.

The Supreme Court has consistently ruled that discriminatory taxes on the media are unconstitutional. In 1936, the Court struck down a tax on large newspapers in Louisiana because it was not a general business tax. The law imposed a license tax of 2 percent on the gross receipts of the thirteen newspapers in the state that had a circulation of more than 20,000

[45] 47 U.S.C. § 546.

[46] *See, e.g.,* S.C. Code Ann. 58-12-310; Tex. Utilities Code §§66.002-66.015.

[47] Implementation of Section 621(a)(1) of the Cable Communications Policy Act, Report and Order and Further Notice of Proposed Rulemaking (FCC 06-180) (Dec. 20, 2006).

[48] Fredrick Siebert, *Freedom of the Press in England 1476–1776,* at 305–22 (1952).

copies. Publishers subject to the tax were required to file sworn financial reports every three months under penalty of a fine of up to $500 and imprisonment of up to six months.

The tax was adopted to diminish criticism of Governor Huey Long by the large papers in the state. Notable among the more critical papers was the *New Orleans Times-Picayune*. Governor Long did not see the tax as a tax on knowledge, but rather as a tax on lying because, in his view, the big papers in the state lied about him. But to Justice George Sutherland, who delivered the opinion of the Supreme Court, the tax was an unconstitutional restraint on the press because it limited advertising revenue and restricted circulation.

The Court said that owners of newspapers are not immune from any of "the ordinary forms of taxation for support of the government," but they cannot be subjected to taxes "single in kind" that place a restraint on the press. Such a tax violates the First and Fourteenth Amendments, Justice Sutherland said, because it is "a deliberate and calculated device in the guise of a tax to limit the circulation of information to which the public is entitled."[49]

More recently, the Supreme Court struck down a Minnesota tax on newspapers that used large amounts of ink and paper. Although the Minnesota legislature was not trying to mute the state's large papers as the Louisiana legislature had, the tax was still ruled to be unconstitutional. Justice O'Connor, in her opinion for the Court, was willing to permit a special tax on newspapers if the state could meet its heavy constitutional burden to justify such a tax. But Minnesota had no interest of compelling importance to justify a special tax on large newspapers. The threat of a burdensome tax that discriminates against newspapers, O'Connor said, "can operate as effectively as a censor" to check critical comment on the government by the press.[50]

Similarly, the Supreme Court ruled in 1987 that an Arkansas sales tax imposed on general-circulation magazines, but not on religious, professional, trade, or sports journals, was unconstitutionally discriminatory. The law unconstitutionally discriminated against general-circulation magazines, the Court said.[51]

However, in 1991, the Supreme Court upheld for the first time the constitutionality of imposing a general business tax on one medium while exempting others. In *Leathers v. Medlock,* the Court ruled that Arkansas could apply a sales tax to cable television and satellite services while exempting the print media.[52] In a 7-2 opinion written by Justice Sandra Day O'Connor, the Court ruled that the state could constitutionally impose a 4 percent general business tax on programs delivered by cable and satellite because the tax was not based on content and was not intended to inhibit First Amendment activities.

The Court said the Arkansas tax was unlike the unconstitutional taxes in the *Grosjean* and *Minneapolis Star* cases, in which a small group of newspapers was singled out for a burdensome tax. In contrast, the Court noted that the Arkansas tax was applied to nearly 100 cable and satellite delivery systems. The Court envisioned no jeopardy to the dissemination of ideas by imposing "a tax on the services provided by a large number of cable operators offering a wide variety of programming throughout the State."

Nor did the Court view the Arkansas tax on cable and satellite services as being similar to the unconstitutional sales tax in *Arkansas Writers' Project v. Ragland* that applied to

[49]Grosjean v. American Press Co., 297 U.S. 233 (1936).

[50]Minneapolis Star & Tribune Co. v. Minnesota Comm'r of Revenue, 460 U.S. 575 (1983).

[51]Arkansas Writers' Project, Inc. v. Ragland, 481 U.S. 221 (1987). *See also* Texas Monthly, Inc. v. Bullock, 489 U.S. 1 (1989).

[52]499 U.S. 439 (1991).

general-interest magazines but not to religious and sports magazines. The tax on cable and satellite programming, the Court said, was not discriminatory but was a general tax applying equally to all tangible property and a number of services besides cable, including natural gas, electricity, water, telephone, repair services, and tickets to amusement parks.

In a sharp dissent, Justice Marshall, joined by Justice Blackmun, argued that the state of Arkansas discriminates unconstitutionally when it taxes electronic media but not print media.

The Supreme Court regards laws that impose a financial burden on speakers because of the content of their speech as being similar to discriminatory taxes. In *Simon & Schuster v. New York State Crime Victims Board,* the Court struck down a law requiring convicted criminals and those accused of crimes to deposit income from works describing their crimes in an account for the criminals' victims and creditors.[53] The "Son of Sam" law was enacted in 1977 to prevent serial killer David Berkowitz, known as Son of Sam, from profiting from the story of his crimes while families of Berkowitz's five dead victims and other injured people received nothing.

The Supreme Court found that the New York statute, like a discriminatory tax, would discourage creation of protected expression. Although the state had a compelling interest in ensuring that victims of crime are compensated by those who harm them, the law was not properly tailored to serve this interest. The law was too narrow because it singled out profits from crime stories but did not require profits from drug sales or other criminal activities to be paid to victims. The law was too broad because it applied to any work in which the author admitted to committing a crime, even if the crime was petty and the reference only incidental.

Punishment after Publication

The Blackstonian view of press freedom, discussed earlier in this chapter, regarded prior restraints as impermissible but left unchecked the government's power to impose sanctions after publication. Even in the early 1900s, the Supreme Court described the First Amendment as preventing prior restraints, but allowing subsequent punishment of communications "deemed contrary to the public welfare."[54] Beginning in the 1930s, the Court expanded its view of press freedom, announcing that the "mere exemption from previous censorship" was "too narrow a view of the liberty of the press."[55] Modern Supreme Court doctrine acknowledges the "chilling effect" or self-censorship that occurs when post-publication sanctions are severe. If a postpublication penalty chills the publication of constitutionally protected speech, the First Amendment is violated.[56]

The Court continues to regard prior restraints as the "most serious and least tolerable" form of regulating expression.[57] Thus, punishment after publication, rather than prior restraint, is the more common method of curbing harmful expression. Most of this book will discuss the circumstances under which communicators may be liable for disseminating dangerous, false, defamatory, private, obscene, or otherwise damaging communication.

[53] 502 U.S. 105 (1991).
[54] Patterson v. Colorado, 205 U.S. 454, 462 (1907).
[55] Grosjean v. American Press Co., 297 U.S. 233, 246 (1936).
[56] *See, e.g.,* New York Times Co. v. Sullivan, 376 U.S. 254, 278 (1964).
[57] Nebraska Press Ass'n v. Stuart, 427 U.S. 539, 559 (1976).

Of considerable legal and practical interest to communicators is whether they can be punished for publishing confidential information that they lawfully acquire from someone who deliberately leaks it or who inadvertently gives it to the media. In *Smith v. Daily Mail Publishing Co.,* the Court expressed the following principle: "If a newspaper lawfully obtains truthful information about a matter of public significance then state officials may not constitutionally punish publication of that information, absent a need to further a state interest of the highest order."[58] This principle indicates that although there is no categorical protection for truthful publications, it is extraordinarily difficult for the state to punish the publication of lawfully acquired truthful information of public significance.

While the contours of the phrase "lawful newsgathering" are imprecise, the Court's cases regard the mere receipt of information from a source to be legal, even when the source obtains the information illegally or is not supposed to disclose it. For example, in *Bartnicki v. Vopper,* the Court held that a radio talk show host acted lawfully when he received a copy of a recording of a telephone conversation that was illegally recorded by someone else.[59] Similarly, in *Florida Star v. B.J.F.,* police officials mistakenly gave the name of a rape victim to a reporter; the Court held that the receipt of this information by the press was lawful.[60]

In both *Bartnicki* and *Florida Star,* the Court ruled that privacy interests did not outweigh the right of the press to publish truthful information. Likewise, the Court ruled in *Daily Mail* that protecting the anonymity of juvenile offenders did not justify punishing the press for publishing a name that was lawfully acquired by monitoring the police band radio frequency and by questioning police and other officials. The Court has yet to find an interest of the "highest order" to warrant sanctions on the publication of truthful information.

An important theme appearing in cases applying the *Daily Mail* principle is the "chilling effect," which may occur if the press is punished for publishing truthful information. Especially when truthful information is lawfully obtained from government sources, the Court believes that the press should be free to publish without fear of a postpublication penalty. A press subject to "timidity and self-censorship" is unable to "inform citizens about the public business."[61]

As will be explained in Chapter 5, unlawful information gathering, such as trespass, can be punished. And as will be shown in Chapter 12, the government may withhold information from the press. Nonetheless, as Justice Potter Stewart wrote, though the government "may deny access to information and punish its theft, government may not prohibit or punish the publication of that information once it falls into the hands of the press, unless the need for secrecy is manifestly overwhelming."[62]

Stewart's reference to the need for secrecy left open the possibility that in rare cases, such as national security, punishment of publication would be constitutional. However, it is unclear that the existing espionage laws apply to press publication of classified information.

Although the press in America has never faced a criminal action for publishing information harmful to national security, in May 2006 Attorney General Alberto Gonzales

[58]443 U.S. 97, 103 (1979).
[59]532 U.S. 514 (2001).
[60]491 U.S. 524 (1989).
[61]Cox Broadcasting Corp. v. Cohn, 420 U.S. 469, 496 (1975).
[62]Landmark Communications, Inc. v. Virginia, 435 U.S. 829, 849 (1978) (Stewart, J., concurring in the judgment).

"fired a shot across journalism's bow, raising the possibility that news outlets might be criminally prosecuted if they publish classified government secrets."[63]

During 2005 and 2006, the press reported a series of secret government actions aimed at terrorists, such as the CIA's operation of secret prisons in Eastern Europe, the National Security Agency's warrantless wiretapping program, and a secret banking surveillance program. Each story was based on leaks of classified information. In response to these leaks, President Bush stated, "There can be no excuse for anyone entrusted with vital information to leak it—and no excuse for any newspaper to publish it."[64] After the press revealed these secret programs, the Bush administration began a series of leak investigations.

As part of the crackdown on leaks, the Department of Justice prosecuted Defense Department analyst Lawrence Franklin for unauthorized disclosures of classified information. As discussed in Chapter 2, Franklin pleaded guilty to disclosing classified information in January 2006. The Department of Justice is also prosecuting two lobbyists for receiving classified information from Franklin and passing it on to reporters.

Amidst the crackdown on leaks, Attorney General Gonzales told a television news audience the government has the legal authority under the espionage laws to prosecute the press for publishing classified information.[65] Gonzales's claim, along with the leak investigations, prompted two congressional committees to hold hearings in 2006 on the issues raised by national security leaks.[66] Some prominent members of Congress dispute Gonzales's claim, arguing that Congress has not authorized punishment of the press for publishing classified information.

Because the press has never been prosecuted for violating the espionage laws, judicial analysis of the application of these laws to the press is sparse. The federal district court considering the government's request for an injunction against the *New York Times* in the Pentagon Papers case ruled these laws to be inapplicable to "publishing."[67] The government in the Pentagon Papers case was not seeking to punish the press for publishing classified information; the government sought to rely on the espionage laws as support for an injunction. An authoritative 1973 study by two legal scholars concluded, "Neither the Congresses that wrote the laws nor the Executives who enforced them have behaved in a manner consistent with the belief that the general espionage statutes forbid acts of publication. . . ."[68]

◇ Summary ◇

Although prior restraints on content are presumed to be unconstitutional, they are permitted on a number of types of expression. Injunctions may be imposed on political speech in national security cases, but only if the government meets an undefined "heavy" evidentiary burden.

[63] "Chill Wind Blows in D.C.," *Boston Herald,* May 24, 2006, at 32.

[64] Scott Shane, "Behind Bush's Fury, a Vow Made in 2001," *N.Y. Times,* June 29, 2006, at A12.

[65] Adam Liptak, "Gonzales Says Prosecutions of Journalists Are Possible," *N.Y. Times,* May 22, 2006, at A14.

[66] *Examining DOJ's Investigation of Journalists Who Publish Classified Information: Hearing Before the S. Comm. on the Judiciary,* 109th Cong. (June 6, 2006); *Media's Role and Responsibilities in Leaks of Classified Information: Hearing Before the H. Permanent Select Comm. on Intelligence,* 109th Cong. (May 26, 2006).

[67] United States v. N.Y. Times, 328 F. Supp. 324, 328–29 (S.D.N.Y. 1971).

[68] Harold Edgar & Benno Schmidt, Jr., "The Espionage Statutes and Publication of Defense Information," 73 *Colum. L. Rev.* 929, 1077 (1973).

Injunctions may also be imposed on false advertising, publications that would violate a copyright, and obscenity. The courts have upheld preemployment contracts in which government employees agree to have all writings reviewed before publication. Courts also approve of general business taxes on the media, but discriminatory taxes based on the content of what is published are unconstitutional. Licensing that leaves unbridled discretion to government officials is an unconstitutional prior restraint, but the Supreme Court has approved licensing for broadcasting that would be unconstitutional for print media. Municipalities can issue nonexclusive cable franchises. Postpublication punishments are permitted for some libelous, false, fraudulent, and private communications. The Supreme Court has also said that the media may be liable for publication of confidential government information. However, the Court has never held the media liable for such a publication.

Content-Neutral Regulations

As was shown in Chapter 2, one of the most significant distinctions in the Supreme Court's contemporary First Amendment doctrine is between content-based and content-neutral regulations. Although content restrictions will generally be found unconstitutional under the strict scrutiny courts engage in, content-neutral regulations are subject to a less rigorous ad hoc balancing process.

Not all content-neutral regulations are treated alike. The burden on the government in content-neutral cases varies. Regulations that completely ban a form of expression, such as a law prohibiting billboards anywhere in a city, require greater justification than those with less impact on communication, such as a law banning billboards in historic neighborhoods. Similarly, regulations affecting a public forum are scrutinized more closely than those affecting nonforum public properties.

The Court has developed two tests that dominate content-neutral analysis: the *O'Brien* test and the **time, place, and manner** test.[69] The *O'Brien* test was developed for laws that incidentally regulate expression, such as a noise ordinance covering both amplified speech and the operation of construction equipment. The time, place, and manner test was designed for regulations targeting expressive activities, such as a restriction on where picketing may take place. The Court regards these tests as substantially similar.[70]

In each test, courts must assess whether the regulation is content-neutral, that is, whether the government has adopted the regulation to control something other than the message conveyed by expressive activities. A content-neutral regulation must not be based on government hostility to particular messages.[71] Second, courts assess whether the regulation is narrowly tailored to serve a significant governmental interest, such as preserving park property or keeping streets clean. The time, place, and manner test also asks whether the regulation leaves open "ample" alternative channels for communication.

[69]United States v. O'Brien, 391 U.S. 367, 377 (1968); Clark v. Community for Creative Non-Violence, 468 U.S. 288, 293 (1984).

[70]Clark, 468 U.S. 298 & n.8.

[71]Ward v. Rock Against Racism, 491 U.S. 781, 791 (1989).

Content Neutrality

One of the most important cases in the development of the Court's content-neutral methodology is *United States v. O'Brien.*[72] The Court upheld a military draft law prohibiting men from destroying or mutilating their draft cards, even when it was applied to a Vietnam war protestor who publicly burned his draft card. Writing for the Court, Chief Justice Warren noted that the law did not single out public protestors but applied to all men who destroyed their draft cards, even those privately destroying their cards without any communicative intent. The draft card law was content-neutral, the Court said, because it was adopted not to punish dissent but to allow the government to raise armies quickly and efficiently by requiring eligible men to carry classification certificates.

Another example of a content-neutral law restricting expressive behavior is a federal regulation prohibiting camping in Lafayette Park and other parks located near the White House. In *Clark v. Community for Creative Non-Violence,* the Court held that this law did not violate the First Amendment rights of protestors who sought to sleep in Lafayette Park to protest the Reagan administration's policies and to portray the plight of the homeless.[73] The Park Service issued a permit for the temporary erection of a symbolic tent city but would not allow the demonstrators to sleep in the tents. The Court held that the ban on camping, and on sleeping specifically, was not motivated by disagreement with the demonstrators' message. Damage to parks, the Court wrote, can as easily result from camping by demonstrators as by nondemonstrators. The government's substantial interest in preserving park property was served by uniformly applicable measures designed to limit wear and tear on parks.

It is not always easy to classify laws as content-based or content-neutral. Scholars recognize that many laws could be classified as both content-based and content-neutral, depending on the circumstances.[74] The Court has sought to clarify the content distinction, explaining that governmental claims of content neutrality will be unpersuasive when the harmful effect the government seeks to avert is tied to a particular message.[75] For example, in *United States v. Eichman,* the Court ruled unconstitutional a federal law protecting the American flag.[76] In *Eichman,* the Court rejected the government's claims that the law was content-neutral; the Court categorized the law as content-based because only messages of protest were punished.

Shortly after flags were burned to protest American involvement in Vietnam, Congress in 1968 enacted a statute to punish anyone who "casts contempt" on the flag "by publicly mutilating, defacing, defiling, burning, or trampling upon it." In response to the *Texas v. Johnson* decision, discussed in Chapter 2, Congress, in 1989, amended the flag desecration statute by deleting the words "casts contempt" and "publicly." Congress believed that these amendments made the flag law similar to the draft card law found to be content-neutral in *United States v. O'Brien.*

By removing the words "casts contempt," Congress claimed that the law was content-neutral because it did not refer to the communicator's message. Further, by removing "publicly"

[72]391 U.S. 367 (1968).
[73]468 U.S. 288 (1984).
[74]*See, e.g.,* Laurence Tribe, *American Constitutional Law* 803 (2d ed. 1988).
[75]*See, e.g.,* Boos v. Barry, 485 U.S. 312 (1988).
[76]496 U.S. 310 (1990).

Congress asserted that it was not concerned with how audience members would react to flag burning. Congress said it was merely protecting the physical integrity of the flag. However, the burning of worn flags was permitted as a form of disposal so that veterans' organizations that have ceremonial burnings on Memorial Day would not become criminals.

Justice Brennan's opinion for the Court rejected Congress's claim that the amended law was content-neutral. Congress's interest in protecting the flag as a symbol of the nation was not harmed by private destruction. Rather, this interest was implicated only when the flag was used to publicly protest against the government. Furthermore, the Court found that the terms used by Congress, such as "defile," which means "to dishonor," confirmed Congress's desire to punish acts communicating disrespect for the flag, while the exemption for disposal of worn flags protected acts traditionally associated with patriotic respect for the flag. As in *Texas v. Johnson,* the Court held that the government cannot promote orthodoxy by allowing flag burning only when such action promotes the flag's representation of nationhood.

Tailoring

After determining that a regulation is content-neutral, courts ask whether the regulation is narrowly drawn to advance a significant or substantial governmental interest. This prong of content-neutral analysis actually has three components: (1) assessing the substantiality of the government's interest, (2) determining whether the regulation advances that interest, and (3) examining the narrowness of the restriction.

SUBSTANTIAL GOVERNMENT INTEREST The Court requires a *compelling* governmental interest in cases involving a serious restriction on First Amendment rights, such as a content-based exclusion from a public forum. Because the Court regards content-neutral restrictions as less harmful to free expression than content-based restrictions, it applies the less demanding standard of a significant or *substantial* governmental interest. Such mundane interests as preserving the free flow of traffic or ensuring uncluttered sidewalks usually constitute a substantial interest.

In some cases, the Court balances the importance or substantiality of the government's interest against the regulation's impact on expression. For example, in *Ladue v. Gilleo,* the Court found the need to prevent clutter to be insufficient to justify a ban on political signs on residential property.[77] To the Court, residential signs were a "unique and important" form of expression. In other cases, the Court merely asks whether the government's interest, standing alone, has some value. For example, in *United States v. O'Brien,* the Court found that the preservation of draft cards was a substantial interest. Scholars have criticized *O'Brien* because the Court concluded only that the government's interest was nonimaginary or material; it did not weigh the interest against the law's impact on freedom of expression.[78]

ADVANCING THE INTEREST The Court employs two distinct approaches in determining whether a regulation advances the asserted governmental interest. First, in cases involving significant burdens on expression, the Court closely examines whether the regulation actually

[77]512 U.S. 43 (1994).

[78]Dean Alfange, "Free Speech and Symbolic Conduct: The Draft-Card Burning Case," 1968 *Sup.Ct. Rev.* 1, 23.

serves the interest. Second, in cases in which the Court perceives the burden on speech to be minimal, it defers to the judgment of legislators or other officials.

United States v. Grace shows the demanding scrutiny the Court employs in some content-neutral cases.[79] In *Grace,* the Court found unconstitutional a federal law in which the display of flags, banners, or other devices designed to draw attention to any party, organization, or movement was prohibited in the U.S. Supreme Court building or on its grounds, including the surrounding sidewalks. Because the appellees' sought to use only the sidewalks for communicative purposes, the Court considered only the statute's application to the sidewalks, which it characterized as a traditional public forum. As was shown in Chapter 2, traditional public forum property "occupies a special position in terms of First Amendment protection."

One purpose of the statute was to maintain proper order and decorum in the Supreme Court building and on its grounds. The Court questioned whether the presence of flags, banners, or devices on the sidewalks caused injury to others or interfered with the orderly administration of the building and grounds, especially since flags and banners could be displayed on other nearby sidewalks. A second purpose of the statute was to eliminate the appearance that the Supreme Court is subject to outside influence. The Court doubted that the "public would draw a different inference from a lone picketer carrying a sign on the sidewalks around the building than it would from a similar picket on the sidewalk across the street." Accordingly, the statute was unconstitutional because it advanced neither of the government's significant interests.

The careful scrutiny of *Grace* may be contrasted with the Court's assessment of the regulations in *Clark v. Community for Creative Non-Violence.* The Court found that the ban on camping advanced the government's interest in preserving park property. However, the demonstrators did not intend to cook, dig, or engage in any aspect of camping other than to sleep in tents. Because the Park Service permitted the erection of tents and feigned sleeping, the protestors claimed that the ban on sleeping barely advanced the governmental interest. The Court deferred to the expertise of Park Service officials, stating that the judiciary lacked "the competence to judge how much protection of park lands is wise and how that level of conservation is to be attained."

NARROWNESS In cases involving a serious restriction of expression, such as a total ban on leaflets, the Court asks whether the burden on expression is justified by the effectiveness of the state's chosen method. If the Court finds the burden to be too great, governments must use less restrictive methods, even if those methods are less effective. In cases involving a minimal burden on expression, the Court merely asks whether the regulation exceeds its purpose. Under this deferential standard, as long as the method of regulation serves the interest, it need not be the least restrictive means of doing so.

Ladue v. Gilleo, in which the Court invalidated an ordinance banning the display of political signs on residential property, illustrates the method employed in total ban cases.[80] Justice Stevens wrote that the city's interest in minimizing the visual clutter of signs was not sufficiently important to justify the ban on this "unique and important" form of expression.

[79] 461 U.S. 171 (1983).
[80] 512 U.S. 43 (1994).

"A special respect for individual liberty in the home has long been part of our culture and law," Justice Stevens wrote, and this principle "has special resonance when the government seeks to constrain a person's ability to *speak* there." The Court noted that "more temperate measures," such as limiting the size of signs, could minimize clutter without harming the First Amendment rights of homeowners.

The Court's less demanding approach to regulations only slightly burdening speech is shown in *Ward v. Rock Against Racism*.[81] The Court upheld a New York ordinance requiring that performers utilizing a stage area in Central Park use sound amplification equipment and a sound technician provided by the city. The city enacted the requirement so that performances would not be so loud as to disturb nearby residences. Rock bands, however, claimed the law interfered with their artistic freedom. The Court held that this type of regulation "need not be the least restrictive or least intrusive means" of serving the government interest. As long as the regulation did not include measures unrelated to the asserted interest, it was properly tailored. Had the law controlled amplified sound *and* banned pantomimes, it would not have been a narrowly tailored means of protecting nearby residences from loud noise.

Alternative Channels

In addition to narrowly advancing a content-neutral governmental interest, a constitutional time, place, and manner regulation must also leave open adequate alternative channels of communication. There is a pivotal relationship between the assessment of alternative means of communication and the level of scrutiny applied to whether the regulation narrowly advances a significant governmental interest. Where alternative methods of communication are presumed to be adequate, the Court also applies deferential scrutiny to whether the law narrowly advances the governmental interest. In cases in which the Court closely analyzes factors, such as cost, associated with alternative media, it also carefully examines the government's interests.

The ban on camping in parks in the District of Columbia was constitutional in part because demonstrators could convey the plight of the homeless without sleeping in the parks. Demonstrators were allowed to participate in day-and-night vigils, display signs, and erect a symbolic tent city. Similarly, the control of amplified sound in Central Park had "no effect on the quantity or content of that expression beyond regulating the extent of amplification." And a ban on picketing taking place solely in front of a particular residence still allowed protestors to march through a neighborhood and hand out literature.[82]

In contrast, the ban on residential signs in Ladue, Missouri, restricted "a venerable means of communication that is both unique and important." The alternative means of communication were either too expensive or time consuming to be constitutionally adequate, the Court said. "Even for the affluent," Justice Stevens wrote, "the added costs in money or time of taking out a newspaper advertisement, handing out leaflets on the street, or standing in front of one's house with a hand-held sign may make the difference between participating and not participating in some public debate."

[81] 491 U.S. 781 (1989).
[82] Frisby v. Schultz, 487 U.S. 474 (1988).

◇ Summary ◇

Regulations that are not directed at restricting expression but that incidentally impinge on free speech, are constitutional if they are content-neutral, serve a substantial government interest, are narrowly written, and leave alternative channels of communication. The Supreme Court has ruled that the government interest in efficient military mobilization justifies a prohibition on the burning of draft cards even though political expression is incidentally infringed. The Court has also ruled that officials may not ban citizens' use of public streets and parks but may limit expression to preserve public order, the integrity of parks, the privacy of residences, and the smooth flow of pedestrians and traffic.

Time, place, and manner regulations are not constitutional if they prohibit speech entirely in a forum. Time, place, and manner regulations must also leave alternative channels for communication, which may include the ability to communicate in a different way in the same forum or communicate from a nearby forum.

CHAPTER 4

Libel

Shakespeare in 1604 recognized the importance of reputation:

> Who steals my purse steals trash; tis something, nothing;
> Twas mine; tis his, and has been slave to thousands;
> But he that filches from me my good name
> Robs me of that which not enriches him,
> And makes me poor indeed.[1]

Four centuries later, the U.S. Supreme Court still recognizes **reputation** as one of a person's most important possessions. Society's willingness to protect individual reputation from "unjustified invasion and wrongful hurt," the late Justice Potter Stewart said, reflects the value that society attaches to the "dignity and worth of every human being."[2]

Stewart pointed to libel law, "as imperfect as it is," as the only legal means to vindicate or recover a falsely tarnished reputation. In the United States, people can sue for printed or spoken words that "diminish the esteem, respect, good will or confidence" others have in them or for language that incites "adverse, derogatory or unpleasant feelings or opinions" about them.[3] People who believe they have been libeled can sue to recover monetary compensation.

The law that allows individuals to sue for damaged reputations creates financial risks for the media and professional communicators. The Media Law Resource Center, an organization that monitors libel, privacy, and other suits against the media, reports that the average damage award in cases since 2000 where news media are defendants—most of them libel cases—is $2.6 million, the median $625,000.[4] In 2006 a judge finally dismissed a Philadelphia libel case in which a jury had awarded a state supreme court justice $23 million in litigation dating to 1983. Also in 2006, an Illinois jury awarded the chief justice of the state supreme court $7 million for a story in the 14,000-circulation *Kane County Chronicle* that said the judge's votes had been influenced by political favors.[5]

Actually, the number of successful libel and privacy cases brought against the news media is diminishing. The media have won nearly 54 percent of the suits brought against them since 2000. The media win rate in the 1980s was about 36 percent.[6] Even when the media lose before a jury, they often prevail on appeal, either winning a reversal or having the jury award reduced. About 90 percent of the cases are dropped, dismissed, or settled before trial.

Nevertheless, defamation is a costly threat to the media. Even when the media win libel cases, they pay heavy costs. If a libel case is tried before a jury, the defense can cost hundreds of thousands of dollars. The *Alton (Illinois) Telegraph,* a small paper, spent $600,000 to defend itself—unsuccessfully—in a libel suit. About a third of the cost was

[1] *Othello,* Act III, Scene 3.
[2] Rosenblatt v. Baer, 383 U.S. 75 (1966) (concurring opinion).
[3] W. Page Keeton et al., *Prosser and Keeton on the Law of Torts* § 111, at 773 (5th ed. 1984).
[4] Media Law Resource Center, "MLRC Annual Study of Media Trials," March 2, 2006.
[5] Reporters Committee for Freedom of the Press, "Jury Awards Judge $7 Million in Libel Suit," *News Media Update,* Nov. 16, 2006.
[6] Media Law Resource Center, "MLRC Annual Study of Media Trials," March 2, 2006.

paid by insurance.[7] The jury awarded the plaintiff $9.2 million. While appealing, the newspaper settled out of court for $1.4 million rather than risk bankruptcy.[8] For a feisty weekly in Queens, New York, winning reversal of a libel verdict on appeal came too late. The 10,000-circulation *Rockaway Press* died a year before an appellate court reversed a $2.1 million libel verdict.[9]

The costs of libel are intimidating. After the *Alton Telegraph*'s costly legal battle, the paper's editor refused to pursue a new lead about official misconduct. "Wouldn't you be gun-shy if you nearly lost your livelihood and your home?" the editor asked.[10] The publisher of four weekly newspapers in Pennsylvania said he stopped publishing investigative stories after being sued eleven times in seven years. "I decided to abandon my obligation to the First Amendment and run my newspapers as a business," he said.[11]

The fear of costly libel suits impeding robust public affairs journalism makes defamation one of the most important issues in the law of public communication. It also is one of the most complicated. Libel law is complex in part because it originated in fifty versions as state law. In addition, the U.S. Supreme Court added a transforming constitutional dimension by applying the First Amendment to libel in 1964. Finally, many aspects of libel law are illogical. In the words of a prominent legal scholar, "It must be confessed at the beginning that there is a great deal of the law of defamation which makes no sense."[12]

This chapter will explain the principles and application of libel law. The chapter begins with a discussion of libel terminology and the legal burden borne by the plaintiff suing for libel. Defenses to a libel suit are then discussed. Finally, the chapter reviews libel damage awards, media tactics to deter libel suits, and libel reform proposals.

Libel Terminology

Defamation is expression that tends to damage a person's standing in the community through words that attack an individual's character or professional abilities. Defamation also can cause people to avoid contact with the person attacked. Defamation can take the form of either libel or slander. Almost all defamation cases are taken to civil rather than criminal court.

Libel and Slander

Traditionally, written or printed defamation is **libel,** whereas spoken defamation is **slander.** Historically, plaintiffs could win larger damage awards in libel suits than in slander suits, in part because written defamation was believed to cause more harm to a person's reputation. The printed word was more enduring than speech and could be circulated more widely. In addition, the author of libelous words was considered to have deliberately damaged

[7]Gannett Center for Media Studies, "The Cost of Libel: Economic and Policy Implications" 5 (1986).

[8]John Curley, "How Libel Suit Sapped the Crusading Spirit of a Small Newspaper," *Wall Street Journal,* Sept. 29, 1983, at 1.

[9]George Garneau, "Appeal Succeeds but Weekly Paper Dies: In Pyrrhic Victory, Feisty Weekly Is Cleared on Appeal a Year after a Libel Suit Snuffed Its Life Out," *Editor & Publisher,* May 21, 1994, at 22.

[10]John Curley, "How Libel Suit Sapped the Crusading Spirit of a Small Newspaper," *Wall Street Journal,* Sept. 29, 1983, at 1.

[11]David Zucchino, "Publish and Perish," *Wash. Journalism Rev.,* July 1985, at 28.

[12]William Prosser, *Prosser on Torts* § 111, at 737 (4th ed. 1971).

someone's reputation, whereas slanderers were considered to have spoken spontaneously.[13] Because slander is considered less harmful, successful slander plaintiffs may have to show that the defamation caused them a financial loss. Only rarely do libel plaintiffs have to prove monetary loss.

However, broadcasting blurs the distinction between libel and slander because broadcasting carries the spoken defamation to a large audience. The **Restatement (Second) of Torts,** an influential summary of tort law, argues that defamation by broadcast should be treated the same as print defamation because defamation in radio and television can damage a reputation as badly as defamation in print. In fact, a network evening newscast reaches more homes than any single newspaper or magazine. In addition, the *Restatement* contends, broadcasting can damage a reputation as easily as print because, as a mass medium, it has the same credibility and prestige.[14] Courts also find defamation on the Internet to be libel rather than slander.[15]

Criminal Libel and Civil Libel

Most early libel law was criminal law. Governments adopted criminal libel statutes to prevent breaches of the peace and punish criticism of government. The government prosecuted defamation of public officials, disrespect for the dead, and aspersions on the chastity of women because such defamation—whether true or false—might cause disorder and violence. The defendant, if found guilty, could be fined or jailed. Government prosecution on behalf of the defamed, though not protective of free speech, was a civilizing improvement over earlier "self-help" remedies when the defamed sought to restore their honor by dueling or fighting.

In the twentieth and twenty-first centuries, virtually all libel cases in the United States have been civil suits. The defamed now sue for money damages. Seldom does the government seek a jail term or fine in criminal libel proceedings. The development of civil libel has given Americans an alternative to putting people in jail for something they say. The move away from criminal libel has come in spite of a 1952 Supreme Court opinion, *Beauharnais v. Illinois,* in which a divided Court upheld an Illinois statute that criminalized any publication that "portrays depravity, criminality, unchastity, or lack of virtue in any class of citizens of any race, color, creed or religion." The law had been used to prosecute a hatemonger who distributed racist literature. In a 5-4 decision, the U.S. Supreme Court ruled that libelous remarks directed at ethnic and racial groups are not protected by the First Amendment.[16]

Although *Beauharnais* never has been overturned, the decision has been eclipsed by more recent decisions abandoning breach of the peace as a justification for libel convictions. Under current libel law, ethnic and racial slurs directed at large groups are not considered defamatory because slurs on large groups do not identify a single individual. Under current law, a libel plaintiff must establish that he or she was identified individually.

In addition, the Supreme Court has ruled unconstitutional a state statute punishing speech that tends to breach the peace, thus knocking out an important rationale for criminal libel prosecutions. In *Ashton v. Kentucky,* the Court unanimously overturned the conviction

[13]Rice v. Simmons, 2 Del. (2 Harr.) 417, 422 (1838). *See Restatement (Second) of Torts* § 568(3).
[14]*Restatement (Second) of Torts* § 568A and 568A comment a.
[15]*E.g.,* Blumenthal v. Drudge, 992 F. Supp. 44 (D.D.C. 1998).
[16]343 U.S. 250 (1952).

of Steve Ashton under Kentucky criminal libel law allowing the state to punish conduct "calculated to create disturbances of the peace." Ashton had been fined $3,000 and sentenced to six months in prison for printing a pamphlet during a bitter labor dispute in Hazard, Kentucky. The pamphlet attacked the chief of police, the sheriff, and the co-owner of the *Hazard Herald* for their failure to support striking miners. The pamphlet said Sheriff Charles Combs had bribed a jury after "intentionally blinding a boy with tear-gas" and beating him while his hands were cuffed. The pamphlet also said Combs was indicted for murder in another incident: "Yet he is still the law in this county and has support of the rich man because he will fight the pickets and the strike." The U.S. Supreme Court said Kentucky's law was too vague and imprecise to withstand constitutional scrutiny. Vague laws give officials too much discretion to determine which speech is permissible, the Court said. Under the Kentucky breach-of-the-peace law, the Court asserted, speakers could not know when their speech was "calculated to create disturbances of the peace."[17]

Not only has the Supreme Court undermined criminal libel by finding breach-of-the-peace laws unconstitutionally vague, but the Court also has ruled that criminal prosecutions for criticism of the public conduct of public officials are unconstitutional unless the publication is false and made knowingly or recklessly. The Court reversed the conviction of New Orleans prosecutor Jim Garrison, who had accused eight judges of being lazy, inefficient, and sympathetic to "racketeer influences."[18] Some states still have criminal libel laws, but prosecutions are rare. There might not have been a successful prosecution in the last thirty-five years. The focus of libel law today is on civil libel, the topic of the rest of the chapter.

The Plaintiff

A person who files a libel complaint becomes the plaintiff in a libel suit. Any individual, business, nonprofit corporation, or unincorporated association can legally sue for lost reputation. A government or government agency may not sue for libel, although government officials may bring defamation suits.

Living Individuals

Every individual has a personal right to sue to protect his or her reputation. However, because reputation is personal to each individual, no person can sue for damage to the reputation of another. Relatives, partners, or subordinates of someone named in a defamatory story cannot ordinarily win suits by claiming that they were libeled. Because damage to reputation is an individual matter, defamation of one person does not "rub off" on another, even to close relatives or business associates.[19] One court said that Senate staff members close to Wisconsin Senator Joseph McCarthy could not claim they had been defamed by a film disparaging the late senator.[20] Friends, relatives, or associates of a person libeled can successfully sue for libel only if they have been defamed themselves.

[17]Ashton v. Kentucky, 384 U.S. 195 (1996).
[18]Garrison v. Louisiana, 379 U.S. 64 (1964).
[19]*Restatement (Second) of Torts* § 564 and comment e.
[20]Cohn v. NBC, 414 N.Y.S.2d 906 (N.Y. App. Div. 1979), *aff'd*, 430 N.Y.S.2d 265 (N.Y. 1980).

The right to sue for damage to reputation dies with each individual. No friend or relative can sue on behalf of a dead person whose reputation may be defiled.[21] Although people can bequeath houses, cars, copyright in books, and other property to heirs, they cannot bequeath personal rights such as reputation or privacy. Descendants of George Washington, Al Capone, Richard Nixon, and Dr. Martin Luther King, Jr., cannot sue publishers or broadcasters for defaming their famous ancestors or relatives. Rights of reputation die with an individual.

However, a relative may be able to continue a libel suit filed by an individual who dies before the suit is concluded. The U.S. Supreme Court ruled that the widow of Johnnie L. Cochran, Jr., could substitute for her husband in a libel suit the famous lawyer filed against a former client who picketed Cochran's offices, shouting insults and obscenities and claiming Cochran owed him money.[22]

After Cochran's death, the Supreme Court vacated and remanded a lower court decision enjoining the man, Ulysses Troy, from his libelous and slanderous statements about the public-figure lawyer. The majority said the injunction was an overly broad prior restraint, but left the door open to continuation of the injunction.

Some plaintiffs are "libel proof" because their reputations are "so hopelessly bad . . . that no words can affect [them] harmfully."[23] Libel-proof plaintiffs are relatively rare, but a court found that John Cerasani's reputation had been so "badly tarnished" by guilty pleas to racketeering, conspiracy to rob a bank, and possession of illegal drugs—as well as indictments for racketeering, extortion, and securities fraud—that his reputation could "suffer no further harm."[24] Therefore, Cerasani could not successfully sue the producers of a 1997 film that depicted him viciously beating a truck driver and participating in a gruesome murder.

Organizations

A business can sue for defamatory false stories about business practices, such as financial mismanagement or attempts to deceive the public through advertising. Nonprofit corporations, such as churches and charitable organizations, can sue for language that damages their ability to obtain donations.[25] Unincorporated associations, including labor unions, can sue for false stories that would damage their ability to attract members, conduct business, or obtain financial support.[26]

Government

Units of government cannot sue for criticism of governmental conduct. Governments cannot sue on their own behalf, on behalf of employees, or on behalf of the public they serve, no matter how false or unreasonable the criticism. Appellate courts consistently have held that

[21] *Restatement (Second) of Torts* § 560. *See also* Gugliuzza v. KCMC Inc., 593 So.2d 845 (La. 1992). *But see* Rodriguez v. El Vocero De Puerto Rico, Inc., 22 Media L. Rep. 1495 (P.R. 1994), *cert. denied,* 512 U.S. 1237 (1994).
[22] Tory v. Cochran, 544 U.S. 734 (2005).
[23] *Restatement (Second) of Torts* § 559 comment d.
[24] Cerasani v. Sony Corp., 991 F. Supp. 343, 346 (S.D.N.Y. 1998).
[25] *Restatement (Second) of Torts* § 561, 562, and 562 comment a.
[26] *Id.* at § 562 and 562 comment a.

governments cannot be defamed.[27] The U.S. Supreme Court has declared that libel suits by government institutions are unconstitutional.[28] The right to criticize government has been held to be too important to self-government for the law to permit governments to sue for libel.

The U.S. Supreme Court implicitly has endorsed the Illinois Supreme Court's rejection in 1923 of a libel suit by the City of Chicago. The Illinois court said, "no court of last resort in this country has ever held, or even suggested, that prosecutions for libel on government have any place in the American system of jurisprudence." The City of Chicago had sued the *Chicago Tribune* for printing that the city was "broke," its "credit was shot to pieces," and bankruptcy for the city was "just around the corner." The city claimed the articles damaged its credit in the bond market and accounted for a substantial financial loss. The Illinois Supreme Court said that even if the *Tribune*'s stories resulted in an increase in taxes, it was better that irresponsible individuals or newspapers go unpunished than for all citizens to be "in jeopardy of imprisonment or economic subjection" for criticizing "an inefficient or corrupt government."[29]

The fact that government cannot be libeled should not encourage careless statements about government. Besides, government employees can sue as individuals if they are defamed.

◇ Summary ◇

Defamation is expression that damages a person's reputation. Printed defamation and most broadcast defamation are considered to be libel. Slander is spoken defamation. Civil libel law—whereby one person or organization sues another for monetary damages—is most common, replacing criminal libel law, which is aimed at preventing breaches of the peace. Individuals and organizations, including businesses, may sue for libel, but governments may not.

The Plaintiff's Burden of Proof

To win damages in a libel suit, a plaintiff must establish certain claims to the satisfaction of a jury. This obligation is called the plaintiff's **burden of proof.** To sue successfully for libel, most plaintiffs must prove the following:

1. defamation, that there was defamatory language
2. identification, that the defamation was about the plaintiff
3. publication, that the defamation was disseminated
4. fault, that the defamation was published as a result of negligence or recklessness
5. falsity, that the statement was false, a burden only for persons suing for defamation related to matters of public concern
6. personal harm, such as a loss to reputation, emotional distress, or the loss of business revenues

[27]*See* College Savings Bank v. Florida Prepaid Postsecondary Educ. Expense Bd., 919 F. Supp. 756 *claim dismissed, in part, complaint dismissed,* 948 F. Supp. 400 (D.N.J. 1996), *aff'd,* 131 F.3d 353 (3d Cir. 1997), *aff'd in part,* 527 U.S. 666 (1999), *rev'd in part,* 527 U.S. 627 (1999).

[28]*See* Rosenblatt v. Baer, 383 U.S. 75 (1966); N.Y. Times Co. v. Sullivan, 376 U.S. 254 (1964).

[29]City of Chicago v. Tribune Co., 139 N.E. 86, 91 (1923).

Most plaintiffs have to satisfy all six elements of a libel suit. To prove only one—defamation, for example—is not enough to win a libel suit. However, even if libel plaintiffs meet their burden of proof, they might not win their suits. Defendants will present defenses based on the First Amendment and the common law, defenses that a plaintiff must refute. The defendant's case will be discussed later in the chapter.

Defamation

The *Restatement (Second) of Torts* defines defamation as statements that tend to expose a person "to hatred, ridicule or contempt." Defamation may reflect unfavorably on someone's morality or integrity or discredit a person in his or her occupation. Defamation may restrict a person's social contacts by asserting that the individual has a mental illness or a particularly undesirable and contagious disease.[30] Defamation can occur in news stories, press releases, advertising, broadcasts, in-house memos, Internet messages, and speeches.

In court, a judge usually determines whether a message is capable of a defamatory meaning. A jury determines whether that message, in its everyday meaning, defamed the person who is suing.[31]

DEFAMATORY CONTENT The words and phrases most often involved in libel suits are those stating or suggesting criminal activity, serious moral failings, or incompetence in business or professional life. More than 320 of 400 libel cases studied by a Stanford University law professor involved claims of either criminality, immorality, or incompetence.[32] Words also defame if they imply that a person is unpatriotic, mentally incompetent, alcoholic, or infected by a loathsome disease. Both businesses and business products can be libeled.

Crime Stories about crime make up a significant proportion of the news. Asserting that someone committed, or has been accused of committing, a crime is defamatory on its face. If a newspaper or broadcast station falsely reports that someone is suspected or convicted of rape, drug use, or drunken driving, that person may be able to win a libel suit. A court ruled the *Washington Post* printed libel when it erroneously reported that Michael Donaldson had plead guilty to a charge of murder. In fact, Donaldson was acquitted of the charge.[33] Similarly, a court said an Indiana couple defamed Marshall Agnew when they falsely told a real estate agent Agnew was a thief.[34] A court found that a magazine story calling a person an "eel" could be defamatory because everyone else called an eel in the story was "someone who has been convicted of or has plead guilty to violations of the Endangered Species Act."[35] The court said the story implied the plaintiff also had engaged in criminal activity.

Imprecision in crime reporting can result in a defamatory story. A New York court said Hazel Robart was defamed when the *Syracuse Post-Standard* falsely reported she had been charged with driving an uninsured motor vehicle. She instead had been ticketed and

[30] *Restatement (Second) of Torts* § 559.
[31] *Id.* at § 559 comment e, 563 comment c, and 614.
[32] Marc Franklin, "Winners and Losers and Why: A Study of Defamation Litigation," 1980 *Am. B. Found. Res. J.* 455, 481–82.
[33] Donaldson v. Washington Post Co., 3 Media L. Rep. 1436 (D.C. Super. Ct. 1977).
[34] Agnew v. Hiatt, 10 Media L. Rep. 2389 (Ind. Ct. App. 1984).
[35] Snider v. National Audubon Soc'y, Inc., 20 Media L. Rep. 1218 (E.D. Cal. 1992).

summoned to court—but was never charged—for failing to possess proof of state insurance. The ticket was dismissed when she provided proof of insurance coverage to the town justice. The New York court said that since the ticket was not an arrest and Robart was never charged with a crime, the newspaper's report was false and defamatory.[36]

Similarly, a reporter should not write that a defendant who fatally shoots his neighbor has committed murder. A prosecutor or jury may decide the man acted in self-defense or otherwise lacked the criminal intent required for a murder conviction.

Occupation Allegations of criminal activity, unethical practices, and incompetence related to work accounted for more than three-quarters of the libel cases in a study. Nearly 40 percent of the plaintiffs in the study worked in manufacturing or general business. Government employees, including law enforcement personnel and teachers, were the plaintiffs nearly 30 percent of the time. Professionals were the plaintiffs 14 percent of the time. Elected public officials or candidates for office were the plaintiffs 6 percent of the time.[37]

Libel law protects businesspeople, professionals, laborers, and government employees from false charges that they lack the intelligence, ability, or credentials to do their jobs. Defamation includes false statements that a doctor has only a mail-order medical degree or that a president of a savings and loan association is "incapable" of administration.[38]

Remarks that professionals do not perform the services promised or that they violate professional ethics could damage their reputations. A Kentucky appeals court said an article in the *Louisville Times* headlined "An Elderly Woman's Story of the Living Hell of Drugs" defamed Dr. Charles Pearce. The story recounted the tale of seventy-six-year-old Hattie Rose Ludwig, who said she became addicted to drugs while under Dr. Pearce's care. The court said the story left the impression that Pearce injected Ludwig with drugs for no valid medical purpose but only to take her money. The court said the "natural and probable effect of this story on the mind of the average lay reader" would be to hold Pearce up to hatred, contempt, or disgrace. The court ruled that Pearce should have the chance to prove in a trial that the story was false.[39]

Charges of corruption also may be defamatory. An Illinois jury awarded business executive Robert Crinkley $2.25 million for a *Wall Street Journal* article accusing him of making payoffs to foreign governments. The *Journal* falsely reported that Crinkley, president of a division of G. D. Searle and Company, resigned after disclosures that he made payments to foreign governments in order to obtain business. The court said the false allegations impugned Crinkley's integrity even though such payments were not illegal.[40]

Of course, not every story that generates a complaint is libelous. A federal appeals court said that criticism in *Newsweek* of a law class at Stanford University did not impugn the reputation of the professor. *Newsweek* said that Professor Stanley Kaplan's criminal law course was "recognized as the easiest five credits" at Stanford. The article reported that

[36]Robart v. Post-Standard, 425 N.Y.S.2d 891 (N.Y. App. Div. 1980), *aff'd*, 52 N.Y.2d 843 (N.Y. 1981).

[37]Marc Franklin, "Winners and Losers and Why: A Study of Defamation Litigation," 1980 *Am. B. Found. Res. J.* 455, 477–78, 482.

[38]Newton v. Family Fed. Sav. & Loan, 616 P.2d 1213 (Or. Ct. App. 1980).

[39]Pearce v. Courier-Journal & Louisville Times Co., 683 S.W.2d 633 (Ky. Ct. App. 1985).

[40]"Wall Street Journal Loses $2.25 Million Libel Judgment," *Editor & Publisher,* June 1, 1991, at 19; Crinkley v. Dow Jones & Co., 456 N.E.2d 138 (Ill. App. Ct. 1983).

some students listened to the lectures over the radio while they sunned themselves by the pool, the professor required only a midterm and a final, the grades "exactly mirror the curve" for grades at Stanford, and two students took the final exam in top hats and three-piece suits while drinking champagne. The U.S. Court of Appeals for the Ninth Circuit said that the story said nothing directly about the teacher's ability or integrity and maybe nothing derogatory about the course. The court said that any implication that the class was worthless because it was easy was "strained."[41]

Business Businesses may sue for stories claiming they provide poor service or have committed a crime. Businesses also may sue for language asserting they cheat their customers, are financially insolvent, or intentionally are selling harmful or ineffective products. Businesses can sue only for damage to the corporate reputation and not for damage to any individual's reputation.

Writers need to be particularly wary of such loaded words as *fraud, deception, cheated, ripped off,* and *gypped.* Charges that a business is deceptive could cause the loss of customers. A federal court said a broadcast report that a retail meat company deceptively advertised the price and quality of its beef could be defamatory. Donna Deaner, a reporter for WTAE-TV in Pittsburgh, broadcast that a Steaks Unlimited sales agent said the beef at a sale was "lovely, fully dressed and trimmed" and a "fantastic bargain." But Deaner said the beef came from "old tough animals" and was tenderized "with a variety of chemicals to make it palatable." She also said the meat was not much cheaper than what could be purchased in supermarkets. Although the U.S. Court of Appeals for the Third Circuit said the report could be defamatory, it ruled Steaks Unlimited could not meet the other elements of its burden of proof to win a suit.[42]

The reputation of a business also can be damaged by allegations that it is financially unstable or insolvent, reports that could damage bank credit and result in the loss of customers. In a case that will be discussed more thoroughly later in the chapter, a construction company named Greenmoss Builders won $350,000 when a credit-reporting agency falsely said the company had filed for bankruptcy. A seventeen-year-old employee of the credit agency had inadvertently attributed the bankruptcy petition of a former Greenmoss employee to the company itself.[43]

A business also may be able to win a libel suit if a publication or broadcast contends that it manufactures or promotes products that could damage the public health or safety. The Brown & Williamson Tobacco Corporation won $3.5 million in damages after a Chicago television commentator accused the company of trying to sell Viceroy cigarettes to children. Walter Jacobson of WBBM-TV said Viceroy's strategy was to convince young people that smoking cigarettes was an "illicit pleasure" like drinking alcoholic beverages, smoking pot, and engaging in sexual activities. Jacobson said Viceroy wanted to "present the cigarette as an initiation into the adult world" and a "declaration of independence." Jacobson's commentary said Viceroy lied when it contended it was not trying to sell cigarettes to children. However, Brown & Williamson proved the accusation false—the company

[41]Kaplan v. Newsweek Magazine, Inc., 776 F.2d 1053 (9th Cir. 1985).
[42]Steaks Unlimited, Inc. v. Deaner, 623 F.2d 264 (3d Cir. 1980).
[43]Dun & Bradstreet, Inc. v. Greenmoss Builders, Inc., 472 U.S. 749 (1985).

had rejected the "illicit pleasure" strategy aimed at children and fired the ad agency that proposed it.[44]

At least a few states limit libel suits related to business and occupation through what is called the *single instance rule.* Courts in New York and Florida have held that "language charging a professional person with ignorance or error on a single occasion" is not defamatory without proof of specific monetary loss. The courts have suggested that readers and viewers know that everyone makes mistakes at some time, and therefore a report of a single error will not damage a professional's reputation.

Thus, a New York court said former district attorney Nat Hentel could not claim his reputation was damaged by criticism of his handling of one murder case. A book, *The Alice Crimmins Case,* suggested that Hentel's political aspirations dictated his interest in the prosecution of a mother accused of murdering her children. Author Ken Gross said Hentel was out for "a quick kill," worried that he would be "dismissed at the polls as an impotent prosecutor" if he allowed the Crimmins case to "dribble away." The court said the criticism fell under the single instance rule.[45]

Product Disparagement or Trade Libel Libel of products—called **product disparagement** or **trade libel**—defames the quality or usefulness of a commercial product rather than the company that produced it. Stories suggesting that a brand of scissors cannot cut, a manufacturer's basketball does not bounce, or a prescription drug causes cancer are examples of product disparagement. The assertions criticize the products without contending that the companies are trying to cheat their customers. Product disparagement awards compensate for the loss of sales rather than for damage to reputation.

Plaintiffs have difficulty winning product disparagement suits. They not only must meet the burden of proof required of all libel plaintiffs but also must prove financial loss and malice. Bob Diefenderfer, businessman in Sheridan, Wyoming, lost a libel suit because he was unable to prove financial loss after a radio station suggested merchandise he wanted to sell after a fire was not

> worth the paper cartons it was packed in. . . . Radios had picked up moisture, dishes and glassware, subjected to terrific heat, were brittle. . . . The Navajo rugs were scorched and the colors ran together. The record stock was wet and useless.[46]

A trial judge ruled the merchandise on sale at Bob's War Surplus Store was worth more than the paper cartons. However, the judge said Diefenderfer had not proven his store had lost money because of the broadcast. Diefenderfer's claims of trade damage were "uncertain, conjectural and speculative," said the court.

In addition to proving a loss of business, a plaintiff in a product disparagement case must establish that defamation was published with either **common-law malice**—intent to

[44]Brown & Williamson Tobacco Corp. v. Jacobson, 644 F. Supp. 1240 (N.D. Ill. 1986), *aff'd in part,* 827 F.2d 1119 (7th Cir. 1987), *cert. denied,* 485 U.S. 993 (1988).

[45]Hentel v. Alfred A. Knopf, Inc., 8 Media L. Rep. 1908 (N.Y. Sup. Ct. 1982). *See Restatement (Second) of Torts* § 573 comment d.

[46]Diefenderfer v. Totman, 280 P.2d 284 (Wyo. 1955).

do harm—or **actual malice**—knowledge of falsity or reckless disregard for the truth.[47] The malice requirement prevented the Bose Corporation from winning damages for a false statement printed in *Consumer Reports* about the Bose 901 speaker system. The magazine said that sound from the speakers wandered "about the room." A violin appeared to be "10 feet wide and a piano stretched from wall to wall." A district court judge was persuaded that the publication caused an eight-month decline in the sales growth of the speaker system, a loss for which Bose should be compensated. However, a federal appeals court overturned the ruling, deciding that Bose had not adequately established that *Consumer Reports* knew the publication was false, a requirement imposed by the First Amendment. That ruling was upheld by the U.S. Supreme Court.[48]

A single story can constitute both business defamation and product disparagement. Disparaging a product can imply that the manufacturer is dishonest, fraudulent, or incompetent. Such was the ruling of the highest New York state court when the manufacturers of Snooze, a sleep aid, sued NBC and Jack Paar for a televised comment that the product was full of habit-forming drugs, led to weight loss, and would make a person feel like "a run-down hound dog." The court said the broadcast not only defamed the product but also implied fraud and deceit on the part of the company that would put such an "unwholesome and dangerous" product on the market.[49]

In a highly publicized case, a federal appeals court ruled that the *Oprah Winfrey Show* did not defame Texas beef in violation of a state food disparagement statute.[50] Texas, like more than a dozen states, has a "veggie libel statute" that makes the media liable if they knowingly disseminate false information about the safety of a perishable food. The U.S. Court of Appeals for the Fifth Circuit ruled that guests on the *Winfrey Show* presented protected opinion when one warned that the deadly mad cow disease could migrate rapidly from Great Britain, and another guest compared mad cow disease to AIDS. Sales of Texas beef plummeted after the show.

The appeals court said the opinion about the spread of mad cow disease was protected because it was based on known fact about how cattle were fed at the time. The comparison of mad cow disease to AIDS was protected exaggeration. The court did not determine whether a lower court had correctly ruled that cattle producers could not sue under the Texas statute because cattle were not "perishable."

Although the media won the Texas case, the media were not able to challenge the constitutionality of the Texas statute. The Texas law and so-called veggie libel statutes in other states are vulnerable to constitutional attack because they inhibit food critics, environmental writers, and agricultural experts who criticize how American foods are grown and processed. The First Amendment protects wide-open debate on public issues—a debate in which experts often disagree—but the veggie libel statutes make critics responsible for large payments unless their statements are based on scientific fact. However, environmentalists, biologists, agronomists, geneticists, and other scientists often disagree even about facts.

[47]*E.g., Restatement (Second) of Torts* § 623A comment d, 626, 633, 634; Rodney Smolla, *The Law of Defamation* § 11.02[2][e], at 11-33 (1998).

[48]Bose Corp. v. Consumers Union of United States, Inc., 508 F. Supp. 1249, *enforced,* 529 F. Supp. 357 (D. Mass. 1981), *rev'd,* 692 F.2d 189 (1st Cir. 1982), *aff'd,* 466 U.S. 485 (1984).

[49]Harwood Pharmacal Co. v. NBC, 174 N.E.2d 602 (N.Y. 1961).

[50]Engler v. Winfrey, 201 7.3d 680 (5th Cir. 2000).

Character, Habits, and Obligations Although a majority of recent libel suits have involved criticism of people for their work, a libel study demonstrated that many suits are filed for attacks on personal character traits or lifestyle. For example, personal reputations can be damaged by stories that suggest people are dishonest, cruel, or do not live up to their social obligations. A federal district court said that a broadcast news segment that could be interpreted to portray Amrit Lal as a slum landlord could be defamatory. The court said WCAU-TV in Philadelphia may have defamed Lal when it reported an allegation by students that he would not make necessary repairs on his property. The tenants complained of leaky roofs, faulty wiring, and "other eyesores." The court said the broadcast could be interpreted as accusing Lal of being an "unscrupulous" person who "preys upon the economically disadvantaged."[51] The court said the report could deter people from associating or dealing with Lal, an issue that needed to be determined at trial. Other courts have said that people were libeled when they were accused of being hypocrites, liars, cowards, or cheats, or unwilling to pay their bills.[52]

Assertions that either a husband or wife has not fulfilled marital or familial obligations also may be libelous. A court said a woman defamed her ex-husband when she said "he abandoned me, made no provisions for my support, treated me with complete indifference and did not display any affection or regard for me."[53]

Assertions that a person's sexual conduct deviates from generally accepted norms usually are defamatory. A jury awarded a Virginia woman $25,000 after the *Charlottesville Daily Progress* falsely said she was pregnant and unmarried.[54] Juries are also likely to decide that stories falsely reporting that a woman has been raped are defamatory. Many people, unfortunately, consider rape victims to be social outcasts. A story asserting that a man has made improper advances toward a woman also may be considered to have damaged his reputation.[55]

Although alcoholism is legally an illness, false accusations that someone is an alcoholic, a drunkard, a drunk driver, or a member of Alcoholics Anonymous may be libelous.[56] To say that someone had a drink is not defamatory under most circumstances, but a report of raucous activity because of drinking can be. Actress Carol Burnett settled out of court with the *National Enquirer* for an undisclosed amount of money after the publication inaccurately reported that she drank too much and became obnoxious at the Rive Gauche, a restaurant in Washington, D.C.[57]

A story can be libelous if it has a tendency to inhibit personal contact. Persons reported to have a particularly undesirable and contagious disease may be shunned.[58] Therefore, people can successfully sue for inaccurate reports that they have a sexually transmitted

[51]Lal v. CBS, 551 F. Supp. 356 (E.D. Pa. 1982), *aff'd*, 726 F.2d 97 (1984).

[52]*Restatement (Second) of Torts* § 569(g); W. Page Keeton et al., *Prosser and Keeton on the Law of Torts* § 111, at 775 (5th ed. 1984).

[53]Brown v. Du Frey, 134 N.E.2d 469 (N.Y. 1956).

[54]*E.g.*, Gazette Inc., v. Harris, 325 S.E.2d 713 (Va. 1985).

[55]W. Page Keeton et al., *Prosser and Keeton on the Law of Torts* § 111, at 775 (5th ed. 1984); *Restatement (Second) of Torts* § 569(f).

[56]W. Page Keeton et al., *Prosser and Keeton on the Law of Torts* § 111, at 775 (5th ed. 1984).

[57]Burnett v. National Enquirer, Inc., 144 Cal. App. 3d 991 (Cal. Ct. App. 1983), *appeal dismissed*, 465 U.S. 1014 (1984); "Settlement in Burnett-Enquirer Suit," United Press International, Dec. 19, 1984, BC cycle.

[58]*Restatement (Second) of Torts* § 559(c).

disease such as AIDS, genital herpes, or syphilis. Cancer is not believed to be contagious and is not considered to be damaging to esteem or reputation.[59]

In fact, many statements that embarrass, annoy, or hurt someone's feelings do not necessarily damage reputation. Ordinarily, a story that falsely asserts a woman is fifty-two years old rather than thirty-two does not defame her even though it might embarrass her and make her angry. Neither is it libelous to claim that someone has no sense of humor or is angry. Age and a lack of humor usually have little to do with bad character. Similarly, people described as poor can probably not sue successfully unless a story implies the poverty is the result of character flaws such as laziness or incompetence. Ordinarily, the assertion that someone is poor does not suggest the individual is immoral, insane, or a criminal.[60]

Politics, Religion, and Race People can lose face if a story questions their patriotism or accuses them of being aligned with a political group that is considered a threat to the nation's well-being. It can be defamatory to assert falsely that someone is a traitor or a spy, believes in anarchy, or wants to overthrow the government by force. A former Arizona state attorney general was awarded $485,000 after an editorial in the *Arizona Republic* said he had Communist sympathies.[61] A story falsely reporting that an individual is a member of a discredited organization—such as the Nazi party—is defamatory.[62]

However, courts have held that the use of derogatory nationalistic and racial terms might not damage reputation. To call someone a *spic, chink, polack, nigger,* or *cracker* is degrading and offensive but probably not libelous. An individual might be able to win a libel suit only if there is proof of harm to reputation. Ordinarily, the courts say that highly offensive terms do not reflect on the individual character or beliefs of the persons subjected to the verbal abuse.

Humor and Ridicule A publication that generates laughs at someone's expense or makes a person the butt of a joke is not necessarily libelous. But humor can become libelous if it subjects people to ridicule by suggesting they do not deserve respect. A major difficulty for writers is that even the courts disagree on where to draw the line between nondefamatory humor and defamatory ridicule.

"The reports of my death are greatly exaggerated," Mark Twain is reported to have said after his obituary appeared prematurely in a New York newspaper. Most courts have ruled that false obituaries, even those planted in newspapers, may be bad jokes but are not libelous.[63] A New York court ruled that it was not defamatory to assert that the corpse of someone who was very much alive was lying in state at the address of a saloon. Even if readers had known the address was that of a bar, the judge said, the obituary did not expose the plaintiff to public hatred, shame, odium, ridicule, aversion, or disgrace. The judge said that, at worst, the publication "might cause some amusement to plaintiff's friends."[64]

[59]Chuy v. Philadelphia Eagles Football Club, 595 F.2d 1265 (3d Cir. 1979).

[60]*See generally* Robert Sack & Sandra Baron, *Libel, Slander, and Related Problems* 69–76 (2d ed. 1994).

[61]Phoenix Newspapers, Inc. v. Church, 537 P.2d 1345 (Ariz. 1975), *appeal dismissed,* 425 U.S. 908 (1976), *reh'g denied,* 425 U.S. 985 (1976).

[62]Holy Spirit Ass'n v. Sequoia Elsevier Publishing Co., 4 Media L. Rep. 1744 (N.Y. Sup. Ct. 1978).

[63]*E.g.,* Cohen v. New York Times Co., 138 N.Y.S. 206 (1912).

[64]Cardiff v. Brooklyn Eagle, Inc., 75 N.Y.S.2d 222 (Kings Co. 1947).

FORMS OF LIBEL Libel suits most often result from words printed or broadcast in news stories, editorials, letters to editors, and press releases. But defamation can also appear in headlines and advertisements. Sometimes words are defamatory only in combination or because of circumstances not known to a reasonably prudent writer or editor. Libel also can occur in the use of photographs, cartoons, caricatures, and video in all media, including the Internet.

Words Some words are defamatory on their face; they are "libelous per se." Courts have held that these words can, by themselves, damage a person's reputation. Words that are libelous per se have clear, unambiguous, and commonly agreed-upon meanings. Among the many "red flag" words that are defamatory on their face are "unethical," "adulterer," "thief," "drunkard," and "cheat."

Quotation marks indicate to readers that a speaker's words are being reproduced verbatim. Therefore, fabricated quotes can defame speakers by attributing untrue assertions to them. Fabricated quotes may also tar people with unattractive personal traits they do not possess.[65]

Many words and phrases have more than one meaning. At least one state has adopted what is called the **innocent construction rule,** which provides that language should be considered nondefamatory if it can be read that way. The Illinois Supreme Court said courts should find no libel if words, "given their natural and obvious meaning," can reasonably be interpreted "innocently."[66] Applying the innocent construction rule, an Illinois appellate court said it was not defamatory for a school board member, Charles Garrison, to say that "legal ramifications" from a state investigation might result in school superintendent Gene Cartwright's losing certification and being fined or jailed. Cartwright said Garrison's statements libeled him by suggesting he was a criminal. But the Illinois court said Cartwright was not defamed because Garrison did not imply Cartwright was unfit to be a school administrator. Relying on the innocent construction rule, the court said Garrison's comment could reasonably be interpreted to mean he was leaving to the state's attorney whether Cartwright had done anything "legally wrong" that might result in "legal ramifications."[67]

In a libel case, the meaning of words must usually be considered in the context of a complete article, book, or broadcast.[68] A plaintiff cannot successfully contend that an isolated word or sentence is defamatory when the thrust of the article or book in which it appears creates a neutral or favorable impression of the person. A New York court said the survivor of a terrorist attack was not defamed by a book that falsely portrayed him fleeing the scene of the attack alone, without warning companions. The court said the book, *The Blood of Israel,* did not defame the survivor, Shaul Ladany, as a coward even though it inaccurately described his fleeing alone from an attack on Israeli athletes during the 1972 Olympic Games. In fact, Ladany had left his apartment with several Olympic teammates.

A federal district court ruled Ladany was not defamed by isolated passages that made him look less than heroic. The book as a whole, the court said, provided the more accurate and nonlibelous impression that Ladany thought he was alone in the apartment before he fled.

[65]Masson v. New Yorker Magazine, 501 U.S. 496 (1991).

[66]*E.g.,* Chapski v. Copley Press, 442 N.E.2d 195 (Ill. 1982). *See also* Kyu Ho Youm, "The Innocent Construction Rule: Ten Years after Modification," 14 *Comm. & L.* 49 (Dec. 1992).

[67]Cartwright v. Garrison, 447 N.E.2d 446 (Ill. App. Ct. 1983).

[68]*Restatement (Second) of Torts* § 563 comment d.

In addition, the court said, the book implied that escape "was the only prudent course." Although individual passages in the book might have been defamatory, the court said, the thrust of the book was not.[69]

Words also have to be considered in their social context. Whether language is considered defamatory may change with circumstances. In most areas of the country, it would be defamatory to falsely accuse a person of being a member of the Ku Klux Klan because the racist, violent Klan is held in contempt. However, in some communities where the Klan's commitment to white superiority is widely shared, a jury might conclude that falsely labeling a person a Klan member is not defamatory.[70]

In 1976, a federal judge ruled that falsely asserting that a citizen worked for the CIA could be defamatory, a ruling that would have been unlikely twenty years earlier. For many years following World War II, being wrongly associated with the CIA would not make most people an object of hatred, contempt, or ridicule. But the judge said falsely calling someone an employee of the CIA during the 1960s and 1970s might be defamatory because many citizens during that period believed the CIA engaged in illegal activities.[71]

Implication, Innuendo, and Circumstance Whereas some defamatory words are libelous on their face, others defame more subtly by implication or **innuendo.** The Tennessee Supreme Court, in remanding a case for trial, said omissions in a newspaper "so distorted the truth" that the story libeled Ruth Ann Nichols and her husband by falsely accusing her of adultery. The story in the *Memphis Press-Scimitar* truthfully reported that Mrs. Nichols was shot by a Mrs. Newton who "arrived at the Nichols home and found her husband there with Mrs. Nichols." Although the story, gathered from a police arrest report, was true, it omitted information from a second police report noting that Mr. Nichols and two neighbors were talking in the living room when Mrs. Newton arrived in the middle of the afternoon. The court said that readers could not have "conceivably" concluded that Mrs. Nichols was committing adultery if a complete account of the incident had been reported.[72] Nevertheless, a jury later ruled in favor of the newspaper at a trial in which Mrs. Nichols failed to meet her burden of proving defamation, falsity, fault, and damages.[73]

In some states, libel by implication or innuendo is called *libel per quod.*[74] More frequently, *libel per quod* means libel that is apparent only to readers who know facts not included in the story. For example, birth notices mistakenly naming the parents of a baby are usually not libelous. However, a birth notice wrongly identifying a new father might be libelous if readers know that the named father is single or happily married to someone other than the correctly identified mother.[75]

The distinction between *libel per se* and *libel per quod* is no longer as significant as it once was because the U.S. Supreme Court has said that plaintiffs must prove defamatory stories

[69]Ladany v. William Morrow & Co., 465 F. Supp. 870 (S.D.N.Y. 1978).
[70]*See Restatement (Second) of Torts* § 559(e).
[71]*See* Oliver v. Village Voice, Inc., 417 F. Supp. 235 (S.D.N.Y. 1976).
[72]Memphis Publishing Co. v. Nichols, 569 S.W.2d 412 (Tenn. 1978).
[73]Barbara Dill, *The Journalists Handbook on Libel and Privacy* 64–67 (1986).
[74]*See, e.g.*, Bruck v. Cincotta, 371 N.E.2d 874 (Ill. App. Ct. 1978).
[75]*See* W. Page Keeton et al., *Prosser and Keeton on the Law of Torts* § 111, at 776 (5th ed. 1984); Karrigan v. Valentine, 339 P.2d 52 (Kan. 1959).

are published negligently or recklessly. Editors cannot be held liable for stories that are defamatory only because of facts they had no reason to know. Some states require a plaintiff claiming *libel per quod* to prove a monetary loss and ill will on the part of the publisher.[76]

Headlines Courts are split over whether a headline alone can result in a successful libel suit. In many jurisdictions, a suit will not be successful if a defamatory headline is clarified in the accompanying story. In those states, the headline and article must be read as a whole. The Hawaii Supreme Court rejected Councilman William Fernandes's contention that a headline in the *Honolulu Advertiser* was libelous because the headline implied he exercised improper influence on behalf of his brother. The court said that although the headline said "Brother Helps in Kauai Zoning Request," the article explained that Fernandes's efforts had been approved by the Kauai County Board of Ethics. The headline and the story together were not defamatory.[77]

However, some courts hold that a headline by itself may be considered libelous even if the article provides clarification. As the *Restatement (Second) of Torts* notes, readers often miss important parts of a story because they see only the headlines or read an article "hastily or imperfectly."[78] The *New Orleans Times-Picayune* paid $10,000 in damages for the headline "Bid Specs Reported 'Rigged.'" The article below the headline correctly reported that a consultant concluded that bid specifications for a school for the deaf appeared to favor specific manufacturers. A Louisiana appellate court said that favoring some manufacturers over others may or may not be illegal or improper but that the word *rigged* in the headline was defamatory because it denoted "fraudulent, illegal and improper" activity.[79]

Advertisements Advertisements can also be defamatory. Although ads that claim one business is better than another are usually not libelous, an ad that claims the competitor provides poor service may be. For example, an advertisement is not defamatory if it asserts that a camera shop develops film faster and produces color prints that fade more slowly than prints made at another camera shop. However, the Pennsylvania Supreme Court said that Cal Pane may have defamed a competitor, the Cosgrove Studio and Camera Shop, when Pane's advertisement implied that Cosgrove misled consumers, ruined film, and produced poor prints. In response to a Cosgrove advertisement promising customers a free roll of film for every roll brought in for processing, Pane warned readers in an advertisement to "Use Common Sense—You Get Nothing for Nothing." Without naming Cosgrove, Pane's ad told consumers that he would not inflate the price of film processing to give customers free film, implying that Cosgrove had. In the court's view, Pane's ad suggested Cosgrove lacked integrity and provided poor service when Pane's ad said that his shop would not print blurred negatives, would not ruin film by speeding up the developing process, and would not use inferior chemicals and paper.[80]

[76]*See* Robert Sack & Sandra Baron, *Libel, Slander, and Related Problems* 131–33 (1998); Rodney Smolla, *Law of Defamation* § 7.06, at 7-12.2 to 7-15 (1998).
[77]Fernandes v. Tenbruggencate, 649 P.2d 1144 (Haw. 1982).
[78]*Restatement (Second) of Torts* § 563 comment d.
[79]Forrest v. Lynch, 347 So.2d 1255 (La. Ct. App. 1977).
[80]Cosgrove Studio & Camera Shop, Inc. v. Pane, 182 A.2d 751 (Pa. 1962).

Photographs, Cartoons, and Layout Photographs can also be the basis of a successful libel suit if the lens creates an illusion or the picture is altered.[81] More often, however, defamation occurs because of the combination of a picture and a nearby headline, story, or cutline. The Supreme Judicial Court of Massachusetts said a Boston lawyer was entitled to a jury trial to determine whether he had been libeled when his name and picture appeared just below a headline reporting a kickback in a land scandal. Mitchell Mabardi's picture and name, without further explanation, appeared in the *Boston Herald-Traveler* immediately below the headline "Settlement Upped $2,000: $400 Kickback Told." The headline applied to a story about an official—pictured and named in the story—who had been convicted for taking a kickback in a government land purchase. Mabardi had nothing to do with the kickback story. Mabardi's picture was supposed to appear next to another story on the page about a different land deal.[82]

Using photos out of context can be libelous. A jury decided that Drotzmann's, Inc., a South Dakota trucking firm, was defamed when a magazine erroneously implied the company was going out of business by using the picture of a Drotzmann sales poster out of context. A jury awarded Drotzmann $245,000 after *Fleet Owner,* a trucking industry magazine, illustrated a story about trucking companies going out of business with a picture of a Drotzmann poster announcing an equipment auction, not a going-out-of-business sale. The article and picture announcing Drotzmann's auction combined to create the false impression that Drotzmann's was going out of business. An appellate court ordered a new trial.[83]

◇ Summary ◇

Libel plaintiffs must establish that a publication or broadcast holds them up to hatred, ridicule, or contempt. Most defamation involves assertions that individuals committed a crime or are incompetent or unethical in their occupation. Both businesses and products can be defamed. Also defamatory are suggestions of deviant sexual habits, irresponsible or unethical behavior, mental deficiencies, loathsome diseases, and a lack of patriotism. Defamation can occur because of photographs, layouts, and headlines as well as stories. Judges determine whether words are capable of defamatory meaning, and jurors determine whether the person suing was actually defamed. Isolated words taken out of context cannot be defamatory. However, a person can be libeled by the implication of words or by words that take on a defamatory meaning because of facts known to some readers but not to writers and editors.

Identification

Libel plaintiffs, in addition to establishing that an expression is defamatory, must also prove that the defamatory language is about them individually. Persons who are part of a large group that is libeled are usually unable to sue because they cannot show the defamation is about them individually.

[81] *See* Robert Sack & Sandra Baron, *Libel, Slander, and Related Problems* 101–04 (1994); Rodney Smolla, *Law of Defamation* § 4.07[2] [a], at 4-28.6 to 4.-28.8 (1998).

[82] Mabardi v. Boston Herald-Traveler Corp., 198 N.E.2d 304 (Mass. 1964).

[83] Drotzmanns, Inc. v. McGraw-Hill, Inc., 500 F.2d 830 (8th Cir. 1974).

IDENTIFYING INDIVIDUALS The identification requirement means that plaintiffs must prove the defamatory language is "of and concerning" them. They must show that at least one reader or viewer could identify them as the object of the defamatory remarks. A person can be identified by name, picture, description, nickname, signature, caricature, or set of circumstances.[84] For example, a newspaper printed an article with the headline "Whitewater counsel kicks off first prosecution." Two photographs accompanied the article, one appearing over the name "Fitzhugh." The article discussed a defendant named "Eugene Fitzhugh" and then used the name "Fitzhugh," without a first name, seven times. The photograph was of a J. Michael Fitzhugh, who was not connected with the Whitewater case and who sued the newspaper for libel. Several people testified that at first they thought the article was about J. Michael Fitzhugh. A state supreme court said there was sufficient evidence allowing the impression J. Michael Fitzhugh had been charged with a crime.[85]

Many libel suits involve the inadvertent naming of the wrong person. A careless police reporter can erroneously copy the name "Adams" instead of "Adamson" from police records. Or a reporter might use the wrong middle initial or address. In a case of a wrong address, the *Springfield (Massachusetts) Union* lost a $60,000 suit for reporting that Anthony Liquori of Agawam had pleaded guilty to conspiring to break into two businesses. A reporter for the paper obtained Anthony Liquori's name from the court record. Because the court record did not include Liquori's address, the reporter wrote the address of the only Anthony Liquori listed in the Agawam telephone book. Unfortunately for the paper, the Anthony Liquori who had pleaded guilty was then living in Springfield, not Agawam, and the Anthony Liquori listed in the Agawam phone book successfully sued for libel.[86]

The Liquori case demonstrates that checking identification in one place is not always enough. The case also demonstrates the importance of a thorough identification. Media lawyers recommend identifying story subjects three ways: full name, including a middle initial; address; and occupation. Listing ages can also help to identify people with certainty. In 1980, the now-defunct *Washington Star* won a libel suit because it printed a complete identification, including name, age, and address. The paper, relying on a police officer at the scene, said the person who shot Dr. Michael Halberstam was Jerry Summerlin, twenty-two, of the 5500 block of Dana Place, N.W., Washington, D.C. Jerry Gene Summerlin of 8809 Plymouth Street in Silver Spring, Maryland, sued, claiming he had been wrongfully identified as the man who killed Halberstam. But a federal district court judge said the *Star*'s story had provided enough information to ensure that someone with the same name as the murder suspect would not be erroneously identified and unfairly stigmatized. Jerry Gene Summerlin was not twenty-two and did not live on Dana Place. Furthermore, Jerry Gene Summerlin had not been hospitalized with internal injuries, as the man arrested for Halberstam's murder had been. Halberstam had hit his assailant with his car as he was driving himself to the hospital.[87]

Courts have ruled that libel plaintiffs can establish a libelous story "of or concerning" them even if their name does not appear in the story. The Supreme Court of Massachusetts

[84]*See Restatement (Second) of Torts* § 564; W. Page Keeton et al., *Prosser and Keeton on the Law of Torts* § 111, at 783 (5th ed. 1984).
[85]Little Rock Newspaper, Inc. v. Fitzhugh, 954 S.W.2d 914 (Ark. 1997), *cert. denied,* 523 U.S. 1095 (1998).
[86]Liquori v. Republican Co., 396 N.E.2d 726 (Mass. App. Ct. 1979).
[87]Summerlin v. Washington Star Co., 7 Media L. Rep. 2460 (D.D.C. 1981).

ruled that Haim Eyal, the owner of Haim's Delicatessen in Brookline, Massachusetts, might be able to prove that he was identified by a broadcast that said, "The owner of a Brookline delicatessen and seven other people are arrested in connection with an international cocaine ring."[88] Although the broadcast did not name Haim or his delicatessen, the court noted that a significant number of residents thought the report referred to Haim.

A Kentucky court ruled that twelve-year-old Donnie Cholmondelay was identified in a newspaper story that falsely portrayed him—without naming him—as having savagely killed an acquaintance in a fight. The story reported that Jeff Gridler, eleven, with whom Cholmondelay had a fight, died after being "beaten into insensibility." In fact, Gridler died from one blow to the head from Cholmondelay. The court said that the story was of or concerning Cholmondelay because friends and acquaintances "familiar with the incident were certain to recognize Donnie as the unnamed perpetrator of the offense."[89]

People who provide the basis for unflattering characters in fiction may sue for libel if the author fails to adequately disguise the fictionalized characters.[90] In a case in which a real person and a fictionalized character had the same name, a federal appeals court ruled Melanie Geisler should have the chance to prove in court that she was identified as the central character in a fictionalized book titled *Match Set* about a transsexual who helped fix tennis tournaments and participated in graphic sexual conduct. Geisler said she was defamed because she was an "upstanding individual" and the mother of two children.[91]

GROUP LIBEL Because defamation is a matter of personal reputation, large groups—such as union members, doctors, Republicans, or Mexican Americans—cannot usually sue successfully for libel over comments made about their group. Individual members of large groups cannot successfully sue for such allegations as "all doctors are quacks" or "most politicians are corrupt." The courts consistently rule that people belonging to groups of more than one hundred members cannot claim that defamatory comments about the group as a whole are "of and concerning" them individually.[92]

The Kentucky Supreme Court ruled that a Kentucky Fried Chicken outlet in Bowling Green, Kentucky, belonged to too large a group to be identified when Colonel Harland Sanders, the chain's original owner, criticized the food produced and served by the chain. The Bowling Green outlet sued Sanders for telling the *Louisville Courier-Journal* that the gravy the chain served was a combination of "wallpaper paste" and "sludge" and the crispy recipe was "nothing in the world but a damn fried doughball stuck on some chicken." The court said that nothing in the article identified the Bowling Green restaurant from the more than 5,000 Kentucky Fried Chicken outlets around the world. A reference to all did not identify one.[93]

Courts and legal commentators suggest that individuals in a group that is smaller than one hundred may be able to establish they were identified and therefore can sue over a

[88]Eyal v. Helen Broadcasting Corp., 583 N.E.2d 228 (Mass. 1991).
[89]E.W. Scripps Co. v. Cholmondelay, 569 S.W.2d 700 (Ky. Ct. App. 1978).
[90]*E.g.*, Rodney Smolla, *The Law of Defamation* § 4.09[7][a], at 4-40 (1998).
[91]Geisler v. Petrocelli, 616 F.2d 636 (2d Cir. 1980).
[92]*Restatement (Second) of Torts* § 564A; W. Page Keeton et al., *Prosser and Keeton on the Law of Torts* § 111, at 784 (5th ed. 1984).
[93]Kentucky Fried Chicken, Inc. v. Sanders, 563 S.W.2d 8 (1978).

story that slurs the whole group. For example, the Oklahoma Supreme Court said an assertion that University of Oklahoma football players used illegal drugs libeled all sixty members of the football team. An article in *True* magazine said that team "members" used an amphetamine nasal spray, thereby increasing their aggressiveness and competitive spirit. The article did not name any team members or say how many players received the "spray jobs." However, a jury awarded fullback Dennit Morris $75,000 for defamation, an award affirmed by the Oklahoma Supreme Court, which said that the magazine's drug accusations exposed every player to hatred and contempt.[94]

The smaller the group, the more likely it is that every individual in it might be able to sue. Courts have suggested that defamatory language aimed at groups of fewer than fifteen people may be "of or concerning" each of the individuals in the group. A Michigan appellate court said that two officers of a union local could sue the *Detroit News* for accusing the local union leadership of being "thieves," "thugs," and "union hoods." The court allowed the president and secretary-treasurer of the local to sue for libel because the reference was to a group of seven leaders, "whose identities are readily ascertainable from the content of the article."[95]

However, members of even relatively small groups may fail to establish they were identified if defamation does not slur the whole group. A federal appeals court said that a story charging immorality by one unidentified policeman did not libel any of the twenty-one officers in the Bellingham, Massachusetts, police department. A column in the *Woonsocket Call and Evening Reporter* closed with the question: "Is it true that a Bellingham cop locked himself and a female companion in the back of a cruiser in a town sandpit and had to radio for help?" The U.S. Court of Appeals for the First Circuit said that "by no stretch of the imagination" could the question in the newspaper be considered a blanket slur, applying to each of the twenty-one officers. The court added that to allow every member of a small group to sue when only one unidentified member is defamed "would chill communication to the marrow." The court said that it might not have dismissed the libel suit if a number of members of the group were defamed.[96]

Other courts have said that statements encompassing *most* of a small group could be seen as a blanket slur, defaming everyone. In one case, all twenty-five salesmen in the menswear section of the Neiman-Marcus department store in Dallas were allowed to sue when a book, *U.S.A. Confidential,* asserted that "most of the sales staff" were "fairies."[97]

◇ Summary ◇

Libel plaintiffs must demonstrate that defamatory language refers to them individually. Many suits result from inaccurate identification. People who can show they can be recognized as characters in defamatory works of fiction may be able to successfully sue for libel. Communicators should be careful that libelous language about a group will not be considered to identify any single individual. Defamation of groups larger than one hundred people

[94]Fawcett Publications, Inc. v. Morris, 377 P.2d 42 (Okla.), *appeal dismissed, cert. denied,* 376 U.S. 513 (1962), *reh'g denied,* 377 U.S. 925 (1964). *See also* Brady v. Ottaway Newspapers, Inc., 445 N.Y.S.2d 786 (App. Div. 1981).

[95]Lins v. Evening News Ass'n., 342 N.W.2d 573 (Mich. Ct. App. 1983).

[96]Arcand v. Evening Call Publishing Co., 567 F.2d 1163 (Mass. 1977). *See also Restatement (Second) of Torts* § 564A comment c; W. Page Keeton et al., *Prosser and Keeton on the Law of Torts* § 111, at 784 (5th ed. 1984).

[97]Neiman-Marcus Co. v. Lait, 13 F.R.D. 311 (S.D.N.Y. 1952).

is reasonably safe. However, individuals may be able to sue successfully for defamatory language pertaining to all members of groups of fewer than one hundred. For groups of fewer than one hundred, restrictive phrases such as "a few of" or "a couple of" can sometimes thwart individuals' claims that they were identified. However, any member of a group of fifteen or fewer might claim identification in stories defaming members of the group.

Publication

Libel plaintiffs, in addition to proving that defamatory language identifies them, must prove that the libel is communicated to someone beyond the defamed. The *publication* of defamation, in the legal sense, requires at least three persons—the person uttering or publishing the defamation, the person being defamed, and a person hearing or seeing the defamation. A third person must be exposed to the defamation before the person defamed can suffer damage to reputation.

Newspapers and magazines *publish* when they circulate one copy of one issue. Radio and television stations *publish* when they air a broadcast. A libel plaintiff is not required to prove that subscribers or viewers heard or read a defamatory publication; courts assume publications and broadcast signals reach an audience.[98]

Libel can be *published* not only in newspapers and broadcasts but also in press releases, interoffice memos, conversations, interviews, business letters, and the Internet. Joseph Melosi and William Lhotka, reporters for the *Alton (Illinois) Telegraph,* published defamation in a memo to a U.S. Justice Department investigator. In the memo, Melosi and Lhotka said they suspected a local builder, James Green, was connected to organized crime. The memo was passed to federal bank regulators, who forced a savings and loan association to cut off credit to Green. Even though nothing was published in the paper, Green sued, claiming that he lost his business as a result of the memo. Green won a jury verdict and settled with the paper for $1.4 million.[99]

Reporters can also *publish* defamation during an interview. Theodor Schuchat, a freelance writer, was ordered to pay $1,500 after he falsely stated in interviews that insurance executive Leonard Davis was a convicted felon. Davis had been tried for perjury but not convicted. Schuchat said he made the remark as part of his interview technique of "throwing a lot of things out" in an attempt "to get a response." A federal appeals court refused to protect Schuchat's comments even though they were made in private conversations.[100]

Communicators are usually liable for repeating, or *republishing,* defamation if the defamation does not have an official government source. Plaintiffs are not restricted to suing the first person to utter or write a libelous comment; they can also sue anyone—including the media—who disseminates the libel. A citizen who accuses a doctor of malpractice can be sued for libel, but so can the reporter who quotes the accusation in a news story, the editors who review the copy, and the newspaper's publisher. Similarly, a reader who is libeled in a letter to the editor can sue the editor and publisher of the newspaper as

[98]*See Restatement (Second) of Torts* § 559 comment e; Hornby v. Hunter, 385 S.W.2d 473 (Tex. Civ. App. 1964).
[99]*See* John Curley, "How Libel Suit Sapped the Crusading Spirit of a Small Newspaper," *Wall Street Journal,* Sep. 29, 1983, at 1; Green v. Alton Telegraph, 438 N.E.2d 203 (Ill. App. Ct. 1982).
[100]Davis v. Schuchat, 510 F.2d 731 (D.C. Cir. 1975).

well as the author of the letter.[101] A newspaper or broadcast station also can be sued for defamation in an advertisement, regardless of who wrote the copy. Therefore, newspapers and broadcast stations take risks if they copy defamatory ads or stories from other media. Persons responsible for the republication of defamation are liable even if they properly attribute stories or indicate they are "only publishing a rumor."[102] The negligence section of this chapter will explain how print and broadcast journalists are protected when they republish defamation contained in wire reports.

Publishing companies and broadcasters are responsible for libel because their employees select, write, edit, and distribute information to the public. With the publishers' control of content comes liability for defamation. Thus, **common carriers,** such as telephone companies and some microwave system operators, are not responsible for libelous messages because they typically exercise no control over the information they transmit. Common carriers simply carry the messages of others, unedited, for a fee. Owners of bookstores, too, have been absolved of liability for defamatory and obscene materials that the store owners have no reason to know are contained in the books they sell.[103] Bookstore owners are not publishers who control the content of their offerings, and asking owners to review each book for libel would unconstitutionally hinder the flow of information.

ONLINE PUBLISHERS Under American law, operators of online bulletin boards and discussion groups, like common carriers and bookstore operators, are not considered to be publishers responsible for libel posted to their electronic information services. Even if an electronic service provider attempts to screen libelous and obscene messages from the service, the system operator is not liable for defamatory and offensive postings on the system. In Section 230 of the Telecommunications Act of 1996, Congress said providers and users of interactive computer services will not be considered publishers, even if they restrict "objectionable" messages on their services.[104] Section 230 was intended to overturn a New York court ruling that made electronic service operators liable for defamation if they, like a publisher, attempted to control the content of their system.[105]

A federal appeals panel upheld a ruling that Section 230 bars a libel suit against an Internet service provider over third-party postings, even if the service provider is notified that libelous material has been posted. In the case, Kenneth Zeran sued America Online over anonymous Internet advertisements for T-shirts, advertisements linking Zeran to offensive messages about the bombing of the Alfred Murrah Federal Building in Oklahoma City.[106] One advertisement said, "Visit Oklahoma . . . It's a BLAST!!!" Another proclaimed, "McVeigh for President 1996." Readers were invited to call "Ken" at Kenneth Zeran's phone number in Seattle. Zeran, a commercial publisher with no connection to the Oklahoma City bombings, tried to sue America Online for negligently allowing libelous

[101]*See, e.g.,* W. Page Keeton et al., *Prosser and Keeton on the Law of Torts* § 113, at 799 (5th ed. 1984); Weaver v. Pryor Jeffersonian, 569 P.2d 967 (Okla. 1977).

[102]*Restatement (Second) of Torts* § 578 comment a and comment b; W. Page Keeton et al., *Prosser and Keeton on the Law of Torts* § 113, at 799 (5th ed. 1984).

[103]*E.g.,* Smith v. California, 361 U.S. 147 (1959).

[104]47 U.S.C. § 230.

[105]Peter Lewis, "Judge Allows Libel Lawsuit Against Prodigy to Proceed," *New York Times,* May 26, 1995, at D4.

[106]Zeran v. America Online, Inc., 129 F.3d 327 (4th Cir. 1997), *cert. denied,* 524 U.S. 937 (1998).

material to appear on its bulletin board, even after Zeran asked that it be removed. Zeran received many abusive phone calls after AOL disseminated the bogus advertisements.

Ruling for America Online, the federal court said the Telecommunications Act of 1996 exempts Internet providers from liability when third parties post libelous electronic messages. Freedom of expression would be chilled, the court said, if online service providers were saddled with the "staggering" task of reviewing the millions of interactive messages disseminated daily on their electronic networks. An equally impossible burden would be placed on electronic service providers if they were held responsible for removing libelous messages after being "notified" of their presence, the court concluded. "In light of the vast amount of speech communicated through interactive computer services," the court said, "these notices could produce an impossible burden for service providers, who would be faced with ceaseless choices of suppressing controversial speech or sustaining prohibitive liability."

Similarly, a federal district court ruled Section 230 protected America Online from a libel suit brought after AOL distributed accusations of marital violence contained in the "Drudge Report," written by Matt Drudge. The Drudge Report said a White House aide beat his wife, a statement Drudge later withdrew as false. Although the aide could continue his libel suit against Drudge, Section 230 of the 1996 Telecommunications Act blocked action against America Online.[107] In a 2006 ruling consistent with earlier cases, the California Supreme Court ruled that federal law not only protects Internet service providers from defamation suits, but it also protects individual users who republish defamatory information in Internet postings.[108] The California court held that Ilena Rosenthal was immune from liability for distributing statements that two doctors operating websites exposing medical fraud were dishonest, disturbed, incompetent, unethical, and worse. Citing *Zeran,* the court said that Rosenthal was an Internet user under the terms of Section 230 with immunity to distribute defamatory content, even though she had no supervisory role over a website.

FOREIGN JURISDICTIONS Foreign courts sometimes rule that American journalists may be liable for "publishing" defamation in foreign countries, even if only a small number of issues circulate in the country or the defamatory article is downloaded abroad from an American Internet server. American journalists must be aware they may be sued for libel in virtually any country, including countries with little press freedom and substantial penalties for defamation. It is unlikely that American courts will enforce foreign libel judgments against American journalists because the same publication in the United States is usually protected by the First Amendment. However, American journalists may face harsh penalties if they visit countries where a libel judgment is outstanding against them.[109]

◇ Summary ◇

Publication, one element of the burden of proof for libel plaintiffs, means that defamation is communicated to a third party. Anyone participating in the process of publishing defamation

[107]Blumenthal v. Drudge, 992 F. Supp. 44 (D.D.C. 1998).

[108]Barrett v. Rosenthal, 40 Cal.4th 33 (2006).

[109]See Sarah Lyall, "High Court in Britain Loosens Strict Libel, Law," *New York Times,* Oct. 12, 2006; Michael Overing, "Defining Jurisdiction on the Internet," *Online J. Rev.* (USC Annenberg), Sep. 26, 2002.

may be liable. A republication of a libel is a new libel. Although print companies and broadcasters, who control the content of their media, are publishers responsible for libel, common carriers and bookstore owners are not. Operators of interactive computer services, like common carriers, do not assume the responsibility of publishers for obscene, defamatory, and otherwise objectionable postings on their electronic services.

Fault

A libel plaintiff proving defamation, identification, and publication also must prove that a medium erred in the preparation of a story. The U.S. Supreme Court has said that the First Amendment bars plaintiffs from collecting damages for loss of reputation unless they can show that defendants published or broadcast with **fault,** usually **negligence** for private plaintiffs, recklessness for public officials and figures. The Court revolutionized libel law by providing constitutional protection for false, defamatory statements when the journalist's error does not rise—or sink—to the level of negligence or recklessness. The degree of the journalist's fault is the central issue in many libel suits, the court never determining whether a plaintiff has been defamed.[110]

The degree of fault that a plaintiff must prove depends on who is suing. Public officials and public figures have the heavy burden of establishing that the media published defamation knowing that their story was false or that they recklessly disregarded the truth. The burden of proof for private persons suing for libel depends on state law. Most states require that private persons prove the media acted negligently, which is much easier to prove than proving knowing falsehood or reckless disregard for the truth.

Before the 1964 Supreme Court case *New York Times v. Sullivan,* libel plaintiffs in most states could win suits simply by proving that someone had defamed them. Journalists were said to be held to *strict liability.* That is, journalists were liable for defamation simply because they libeled someone. It did not matter if the journalist was careful or sloppy, whether the libel was deliberate or unintentional, whether the journalist thought his story was true or false. There was no standard of fault.

In *New York Times v. Sullivan,* the U.S. Supreme Court declared unconstitutional the common law of strict liability when the media defame a public official. In a decision that "constitutionalized" libel law, the Court ruled that the robust political debate necessary in a democracy is inadequately protected by a common law that failed to require public officials to prove that defamation was false and published with fault. Indeed, the Court said some false statements must be protected by the First Amendment in political debate if freedom of expression is to have the "breathing space" needed to flourish. The large jury awards often accompanying libel judgments in the common law regime of strict liability inhibited press freedom, the Court said, just as physical punishments inhibited freedom under the English and colonial criminal law of seditious libel.

SEDITIOUS LIBEL IN THE UNITED STATES During the formative years of the United States, the country relied substantially on English common law. In England during the seventeenth

[110] *See* John Soloski, "The Study and the Libel Plaintiff: Who Sues for Libel," 71 *Iowa L. Rev.* 217, 218 (1985); Randall Bezanson, "Libel Law and Realities of Litigation: Setting the Record Straight," 71 *Iowa L. Rev.* 226, 229–31 (1985).

and eighteenth centuries, criticism of government officials—always proclaimed by the officials to be false, scandalous, and malicious—was called **seditious libel.** A person convicted of seditious libel could be fined, imprisoned, pilloried, and whipped. The government said seditious libel should be punished to prevent public unrest—a breach of the peace—that criticism of government would often provoke. Truth was no defense to seditious libel charges because true criticism, officials said, was more likely to provoke violence than false statements. The legal adage "the greater the truth, the greater the libel" was accurate at a time when the criminal law of seditious libel was designed to prevent breaches of the peace. Moreover, judges decided the legal question of whether expression was seditious. The members of the public sitting on the jury could determine only the fact of whether the accused printed or said the words as charged.[111]

In a famous case, a colonial jury in New York rebelled against the common law of seditious libel. In 1735, the jury found the now-legendary printer John Peter Zenger, publisher of the *New York Weekly Journal,* not guilty of seditious libel even though he had printed stories of New York Governor William Cosby's high-handed land deals and manipulation of the courts. Zenger's lawyer, Andrew Hamilton, conceded that Zenger had published the remarks critical of Cosby, thereby conceding the only fact the jury could legally determine. However, the jury, affirming a citizen's right to truthfully criticize public officials, returned a verdict of not guilty. The judge could have overturned the jury verdict but chose not to.

The Zenger verdict, as welcome as it was to advocates of unfettered political expression, did not change the law. Zenger was acquitted in spite of the law. When the Bill of Rights was adopted in 1791, decades after the Zenger trial, critics of government could still be jailed and fined for truthful statements ruled to constitute seditious libel. Even when the First Amendment was adopted, truth was not a defense in libel cases, and juries were still limited to determining whether the defamation had been published as charged.

In fact, seven years after the Bill of Rights was ratified, Congress passed a seditious libel statute. Despite the First Amendment, Federalists in Congress adopted the Alien and Sedition Acts in 1798 to punish their Republican critics, led by Thomas Jefferson. The Federalists were afraid that the Republicans would destroy the young American republic by fostering the radical ideas that had led to the French Revolution. The Alien Act allowed the president to deport anyone not born in the United States who was "dangerous to the peace" or suspected of "secret machinations against the government." The Sedition Act prohibited any conspiracy to oppose the government and "any false, scandalous and malicious writing" against the government or government officials. Violators could be punished by fines of up to $2,000 and jail terms for as long as two years.[112]

Ironically, the Sedition Act did bring reform. The Sedition Act permitted the defense of truth and accorded juries the power to determine, as a matter of law, whether publications were seditious. But these reforms meant little because juries were dominated by Federalists. In addition, literal Federalist judges required the accused to prove the truth "to the marrow"—documenting every word of every statement. Critical opinions that could not be proven true were judged false.

[111]Leonard Levy, *Emergence of a Free Press* 9 (1985).
[112]James Morton Smith, *Freedoms Fetters* 321, 438–42 (1956).

The Federalists prosecuted more than a dozen people under the Sedition Act, including newspaper editors and writers in Boston, Philadelphia, and Richmond. Congressman Matthew Lyon was fined $1,000 and sentenced to four months in jail after he wrote for the *Vermont Journal* that President Adams was continually grasping for power and possessed "an unbounded thirst for ridiculous pomp, foolish adulation, and selfish avarice."[113] Individual Supreme Court justices sat on circuit courts that prosecuted government critics under the act.

The Federalists shrewdly wrote the Alien and Sedition Acts so that the laws could not be used against them. In today's terminology, the Alien and Sedition Acts were written with a sunset clause. The acts expired at the end of Federalist President John Adam's term. This was a thought precaution in case the Federalists lost the election of 1800, which they did, to Thomas Jefferson and the Republicans. Jefferson did not renew the acts when the Republicans took office in 1801.

The Republicans argued that the Alien and Sedition Acts violated the First Amendment because they punished criticism of government. However, historian Leonard Levy contends that the statutes reflected the conventional understanding of the term *freedom of the press* at the time. Levy argues that most politicians in the late eighteenth century believed in freedom of expression as it was defined by famed English legal commentator William Blackstone. Blackstone said liberty of the press meant only freedom from prior restraint on publication and not freedom from punishment for publishing words that were "improper, mischievous, or illegal."[114]

Levy contends that prosecutions under the Alien and Sedition Acts helped to sensitize Americans to the dangers of punishing criticism of government and government officials. Republican theorists argued fiercely that freedom of expression was hollow unless criticism of government—including false statements—was tolerated, and their message seems to have been heard.[115] In 1812, the Supreme Court terminated the federal common law of seditious libel.[116] In 1840, Congress repaid fines levied under the Sedition Act on the grounds that the law was unconstitutional.[117] Prosecutions for seditious libel under state statutes became less frequent, and the courts declared that the government itself could not be libeled; only individuals within a government might pursue a defamation suit. The constitutionality of the Sedition Act of 1798 was never tested before the Supreme Court, but in 1964 the Supreme Court stated in *New York Times v. Sullivan* that the Sedition Act of 1798 had been unconstitutional.

CONSTITUTIONAL PROTECTION FOR LIBEL ABOUT PUBLIC OFFICIALS In *New York Times v. Sullivan,* the Supreme Court said for the first time that the First Amendment protects criticism of government officials even if the remarks are false and defamatory. The Court said that public officials cannot successfully sue for libel unless they establish that defamation has been published with actual malice: knowing falsity or reckless disregard for the truth. This burden of proof for public officials has come to be known as *New York Times* actual malice.

[113] *Id.* at 226, 235, 421–22.

[114] William Blackstone, *Commentaries on the Laws of England,* London, 1765–69, book 4, 151–52. *See generally* Leonard Levy, *Emergence of a Free Press* (1985).

[115] Leonard Levy, "Liberty and the First Amendment: 1790–1800," 68 *Am. Hist. Rev.* 29 (1962).

[116] United States v. Hudson & Goodwin, 7 Cranch 32 (1812).

[117] See N.Y. Times Co. v. Sullivan, 376 U.S. 276.

The new constitutional protection for criticism of public officials announced in *New York Times v. Sullivan* effectively ended the law of seditious libel in the fifty states.

Breathing Space for Falsity The case that provided the media with constitutional protection for the criticism of public officials was a product of the civil rights struggle in the South in the early 1960s. L. B. Sullivan, a Montgomery, Alabama, police official sued the *New York Times* for publishing a March 29, 1960, advertisement purchased by a committee of civil rights activists, including the well-known labor leader A. Philip Randolph. The full-page ad, titled "Heed Their Rising Voices," said that "thousands of Southern Negro students are engaged in widespread nonviolent demonstrations" affirming "the right to live in human dignity." The efforts were being met, the ad said, "by an unprecedented wave of terror." The ad purported to document the "wave of terror" and sought support for the civil rights movement in the South and for its leader, Dr. Martin Luther King Jr. (See ad, Figure 4.1.)

The ad contained several false statements, some of them minor inaccuracies. Nine student leaders were not expelled for singing at the state capitol, as the ad stated. The students were expelled for demanding service at a Montgomery courthouse lunch counter. Contrary to statements in the ad, the dining hall at the Alabama State College campus had not been padlocked, and there was no attempt "to starve" students into "submission." The only students barred were those without tickets. The police, although deployed in large numbers, had not "ringed" the campus, as the advertisement claimed. Nor had Martin Luther King been arrested seven times, as the ad declared. King had been arrested four times. There was conflicting evidence about the ad's claim that King had been assaulted. The *New York Times* ad staff could have checked the accuracy of the ad against the *Times*'s news stories of the same events, but the newspaper staff did not.

The Montgomery commissioner in charge of police, L. B. Sullivan, demanded that the *Times* publish a retraction. The paper refused, asking Sullivan why he believed the ad referred to him. Sullivan did not respond but sued the *Times* for $3 million along with three other Montgomery officials and the Alabama governor, John Patterson. At the trial, Sullivan argued the charges of police abuse in the advertisement defamed him—even though he was not named in the advertisiment—because he supervised the police department. The Alabama judge trying the case instructed the jury that the ad was libelous on its face and that damage to reputation need not be proved.

The judge told the jury that it had to decide only that the statements were published in the *Times* and were "of and concerning" Sullivan. Under rules of strict liability in effect at that time, a newspaper was liable for defamation regardless of the intent of the publisher or the care the paper exercised publishing a libelous story. The jury awarded Sullivan $500,000, the largest libel judgment in Alabama to that time.[118] The judgment was upheld by the Supreme Court of Alabama. The U.S. Supreme Court voted unanimously to reverse the Alabama court.

Justice William Brennan, Jr., writing for the Supreme Court, said that Alabama's libel law, which presumed defamation to be both false and harmful to reputation, did not adequately safeguard freedom of speech and press as required by the First and the Fourteenth Amendments. Brennan said that at issue was "a profound national commitment to the principle

[118]Anthony Lewis, "Annals of Law: The Sullivan Case," *New Yorker,* Nov. 5, 1984, at 52, 55.

"*The growing movement of peaceful mass demonstrations by Negroes is something new in the South, something understandable. . . . Let Congress heed their rising voices, for they will be heard.*"

—New York Times editorial Saturday, March 19, 1960

Heed Their Rising Voices

As the whole world knows by now, thousands of Southern Negro students are engaged in wide-spread non-violent demonstrations in positive affirmation of the right to live in human dignity as guaranteed by the U. S. Constitution and the Bill of Rights. In their efforts to uphold these guarantees, they are being met by an unprecedented wave of terror by those who would deny and negate that document which the whole world looks upon as setting the pattern for modern freedom. . . .

In Orangeburg, South Carolina, when 400 students peacefully sought to buy doughnuts and coffee at lunch counters in the business district, they were forcibly ejected, tear-gassed, soaked to the skin in freezing weather with fire hoses, arrested en masse and herded into an open barbed-wire stockade to stand for hours in the bitter cold.

In Montgomery, Alabama, after students sang "My Country, 'Tis of Thee" on the State Capitol steps, their leaders were expelled from school, and truck-loads of police armed with shotguns and tear-gas ringed the Alabama State College Campus. When the entire student body protested to state authorities by refusing to re-register, their dining hall was pad-locked in an attempt to starve them into submission.

In Tallahassee, Atlanta, Nashville, Savannah, Greensboro, Memphis, Richmond, Charlotte, and a host of other cities in the South, young American teen-agers, in face of the entire weight of official state apparatus and police power, have boldly stepped forth as protagonists of democracy. Their courage and amazing restraint have inspired millions and given a new dignity to the cause of freedom.

Small wonder that the Southern violators of the Constitution fear this new, non-violent brand of freedom fighter . . . even as they fear the upswelling right-to-vote movement. Small wonder that they are determined to destroy the one man who, more than any other, symbolizes the new spirit now sweeping the South—the Rev. Dr. Martin Luther King, Jr., world-famous leader of the Montgomery Bus Protest. For it is his doctrine of non-violence which has inspired and guided the students in their widening wave of sit-ins; and it this same Dr. King who founded and is president of the Southern Christian Leadership Conference—the organization which is spearheading the surging right-to-vote movement. Under Dr. King's direction the Leadership Conference conducts Student Workshops and Seminars in the philosophy and technique of non-violent resistance.

Again and again the Southern violators have answered Dr. King's peaceful protests with intimidation and violence. They have bombed his home almost killing his wife and child. They have assaulted his person. They have arrested him seven times—for "speeding," "loitering" and similar "offenses." And now they have charged him with "perjury"—a *felony* under which they could imprison him for *ten years*. Obviously, their real purpose is to remove him physically as the leader to whom the students and millions of others—look for guidance and support, and thereby to intimidate *all* leaders who may rise in the South. Their strategy is to behead this affirmative movement, and thus to demoralize Negro Americans and weaken their will to struggle. The defense of Martin Luther King, spiritual leader of the student sit-in movement, clearly, therefore, is an integral part of the total struggle for freedom in the South.

Decent-minded Americans cannot help but applaud the creative daring of the students and the quiet heroism of Dr. King. But this is one of those moments in the stormy history of Freedom when men and women of good will must do more than applaud the rising-to-glory of others. The America whose good name hangs in the balance before a watchful world, the America whose heritage of Liberty these Southern Upholders of the Constitution are defending, is *our* America as well as theirs . . .

We must heed their rising voices—yes but we must add our own.

We must extend ourselves above and beyond moral support and render the material help so urgently needed by those who are taking the risks, facing jail, and even death in a glorious re-affirmation of our Constitution and its Bill of Rights.

We urge you to join hands with our fellow Americans in the South by supporting, with your dollars, this Combined Appeal for all three needs—the defense of Martin Luther King—the support of the embattled students—and the struggle for the right-to-vote.

Your Help Is Urgently Needed . . . NOW !!

Stella Adler
Raymond Pace Alexander
Harry Van Arsdale
Harry Belafonte
Julie Belafonte
Dr. Algernon Black
Marc Blitztein
William Branch
Marlon Brando
Mrs. Ralph Bunche
Diahann Carroll
Dr. Alan Knight Chalmers
Richard Coe
Nat King Cole
Cheryl Crawford
Dorothy Dandridge
Ossie Davis
Sammy Davis, Jr.
Ruby Dee
Dr. Philip Elliott
Dr. Harry Emerson Fosdick
Anthony Franciosa
Lorraine Hansbury
Rev. Donald Harrington
Nat Hentoff
James Hicks
Mary Hinkson
Van Heflin
Langston Hughes
Morris Iushewitz
Mahalia Jackson
Mordecai Johnson
John Killens
Eartha Kitt
Rabbi Edward Klein
Hope Lange
John Lewis
Viveca Lindfors
Carl Murphy
Don Murray
John Murray
A. J. Muste
Frederick O'Neal
L. Joseph Overton
Clarence Pickett
Shad Polier
Sidney Poitier
A. Philip Randolph
John Raitt
Elmer Rice
Jackie Robinson
Mrs. Eleanor Roosevelt
Bayard Rustin
Robert Ryan
Maureen Stapleton
Frank Silvera
Hope Stevens
George Tabori
Rev. Gardner C. Taylor
Norman Thomas
Kenneth Tynan
Charles White
Shelley Winters
Max Youngstein

We in the south who are struggling daily for dignity and freedom warmly endorse this appeal

Rev. Ralph D. Abernathy (*Montgomery, Ala.*)
Rev. Fred L. Shuttlesworth (*Birmingham, Ala.*)
Rev. Kelley Miller Smith (*Nashville, Tenn.*)
Rev. W. A. Dennis (*Chattanooga, Tenn.*)
Rev. C. K. Steele (*Tallahassee, Fla.*)
Rev. Matthew D. McCollom (*Orangeburg, S. C.*)
Rev. William Holmes Borders (*Atlanta, Ga.*)
Rev. Douglas Moore (*Durham, N. C.*)
Rev. Wyatt Tee Walker (*Petersburg, Va.*)
Rev. Walter L. Hamilton (*Norfolk, Va.*)
I. S. Levy (*Columbia, S. C.*)
Rev. Martin Luther King, Sr. (*Atlanta, Ga.*)
Rev. Henry C. Bunton (*Memphis, Tenn.*)
Rev. S. S. Seay, Sr. (*Montgomery, Ala.*)
Rev. Samuel W. Williams (*Atlanta, Ga.*)
Rev. A. L. Davis (*New Orleans, La.*)
Mrs. Katie E. Whickham (*New Orleans, La.*)
Rev. W. H. Hall (*Hattiesburg, Miss.*)
Rev. J. E. Lowery (*Mobile, Ala.*)
Rev. T. J. Jemison (*Baton Rouge, La.*)

COMMITTEE TO DEFEND MARTIN LUTHER KING AND THE STRUGGLE FOR FREEDOM IN THE SOUTH

312 West 125th Street, New York 27, N. Y. UNiversity 6-1700

Chairmen: A. Philip Randolph, Dr. Gardner C. Taylor; *Chairmen of Cultural Division:* Harry Belafonte, Sidney Poitier; *Treasurer:* Nat King Cole; *Executive Director:* Bayard Rustin; *Chairmen of Church Division:* Father George B. Ford, Rev. Harry Emerson Fosdick, Rev. Thomas Kilgore, Jr., Rabbi Edward E. Klein; *Chairman of Labor Division:* Morris Iushewitz

Please mail this coupon TODAY!

Committee To Defend Martin Luther King
and
The Struggle For Freedom In The South
312 West 125th Street, New York 27, N. Y.
UNiversity 6-1700

I am enclosing my contribution of $______ for the work of the Committee.

Name ______ (PLEASE PRINT)
Address ______
City ______ Zone ____ State ______

☐ I want to help ☐ Please send further information

Please make checks payable to:
Committee To Defend Martin Luther King

FIGURE 4.1 Advertisement published March 29, 1960 that led to U.S. Supreme Court decision in *New York Times v. Sullivan*.

that debate on public issues should be uninhibited, robust, and wide-open, and that it may well include vehement, caustic and sometimes unpleasantly sharp attacks on government and public officials."

Brennan said that a civil libel suit brought by a public official such as Sullivan created the same kind of dangers to First Amendment freedoms as a seditious libel prosecution initiated by the government. He said "the court of history" had found that the Sedition Act of 1798, which had authorized punishment for criticism of government and public officials, was inconsistent with the First Amendment. He argued that the media's fear of large damage awards under civil libel laws such as the one in Alabama created greater "hazards to protected freedoms" than the criminal penalties of seditious libel laws. Brennan said First Amendment freedoms could not survive if a "pall of fear and timidity" was imposed on those who otherwise offer public criticism.

Brennan said a privilege to criticize official conduct was "appropriately analogous" to protection accorded a public official sued for libel by a private citizen. Private citizens cannot sue public officials for libelous statements uttered in their official capacity in a legislative chamber, in an executive statement, or from the bench. Officials speaking in an official capacity are immune from libel suits so that they are not inhibited from engaging in "fearless, vigorous, and effective administration." The "citizen-critic" who libels an official should have a similar immunity, Brennan said. "It is as much his duty to criticize as it is the official's duty to administer," the justice said.

Brennan rejected Sullivan's argument that constitutional guarantees did not protect the *Times* because the defamation had occurred in an advertisement. Sullivan had cited the Supreme Court's 1942 decision in *Valentine v. Chrestensen,* in which the Court denied constitutional protection to a handbill it had called "purely commercial advertising."[119] In *Sullivan,* however, Brennan argued that the civil rights ad in the *Times* was not purely commercial speech. Although the ad had been purchased, it was political speech that "communicated information, expressed opinion, recited grievances and sought financial support" on behalf of a cause "of the highest public concern." Brennan said the fact that the *Times* was paid for the ad was as immaterial as the fact that books and newspapers are sold. He added:

> Any other conclusion would discourage newspapers from carrying "editorial advertisements" of this type, and so might shut off an important outlet for the promulgation of information and ideas by persons who do not themselves have access to publishing facilities.

Brennan also rejected the argument that falsehoods cannot be protected by the First Amendment. He said constitutional protection did not depend on the "truth, popularity, or social utility" of the ideas and beliefs expressed. The national commitment to the free expression of political beliefs presumed exaggeration and error. Indeed, truth for one person could be error for another, Brennan said. If critics of public officials could be penalized for false statements, Brennan said, they would tend to avoid controversy:

> A rule compelling the critic of official conduct to guarantee the truth of all of his factual assertions—and to do so on pain of libel judgments virtually unlimited in amount—leads to a comparable "self-censorship."

[119] *See* 316 U.S. 52 (1942).

Brennan said potential critics of government could be "chilled" from even speaking the truth for fear of the expense and uncertainty of a libel trial.

Because a requirement that defendants prove the truth of their remarks "dampens the vigor and limits the variety of public debate," the Supreme Court established a new constitutional rule to provide better protection for the criticism of public officials. No longer would courts, such as those in Alabama, be able to presume the falsity of defamation and require the defendant to prove the truth, often a very difficult task. Instead, the Court said that plaintiffs—public officials—must shoulder the heavy responsibility of proving published statements about them are false and defamatory. Not only that, but public officials must also prove that libelous statements about their official conduct were published with "actual malice." To prove *New York Times* actual malice, an official has to establish that a defendant published the statement either (1) knowing it was false or (2) exercising reckless disregard for the truth.

The Court ruled the ad in the *Times* had not been published with actual malice. The Court said the fact that stories contradicting the ad existed in the *Times*'s own files did not mean that employees responsible for the ad knew it was false. Brennan said a statement by a *Times* employee that he thought the advertisement was "substantially correct" was reasonable and suggested the employee did not know the ad was false. The *Times*'s failure to check the ad against the news stories might be evidence of negligence, the Court said, but it did not demonstrate recklessness. The Court was also satisfied with the *Times*'s reliance for the accuracy of the advertisement on the good reputation of those listed as sponsors of the ad, particularly the chair of the "committee" submitting the ad, well-respected civil rights advocate A. Philip Randolph. Furthermore, the Court said the *Times*'s failure to retract the errors in the ad was not evidence of actual malice. The *Times* reasonably responded to Sullivan's request for a retraction by asking him why he believed the ad referred to him, the Court said. The *Times*'s unacknowledged letter to Sullivan did not constitute a final refusal to retract.

Although the Supreme Court ruled the *New York Times* was not liable for the civil rights ad, the *Sullivan* opinion left many unanswered questions about the new constitutional protection for libel. For example, who would be considered a public official? What kind of conduct constituted *New York Times* actual malice? Would anyone besides public officials have to prove *New York Times* actual malice to win a libel suit?

Defining Public Officials The Sullivan Court said that public officials would have to prove actual malice to collect damages for defamation relating to their official conduct, but the Court did not define *public official* or *official conduct.* The Court said only that Sullivan was a public official because he was an elected commissioner, and the allegations in the ad related to his conduct as the commissioner in charge of the police department.

In the four decades since *Sullivan,* courts have ruled that public officials include persons elected to public office and nonelected government employees who play major roles in the development of public policy. Public officials include federal and state legislators, mayors, town council members, school board members, and elected judges.[120] In addition, courts have said that nonelected government employees responsible for public policy are

[120]Bruce Sanford, *Libel and Privacy* § 7.2.3.1, at 264–67 (2d ed. 1999).

public officials. Shortly after *New York Times v. Sullivan,* the Supreme Court declared that a former supervisor of a county-owned ski resort might be a public official. In that case, *Rosenblatt v. Baer,* the Court said the decision in *New York Times v. Sullivan* was motivated by "a strong interest in debate" about public issues and the people in positions to significantly influence the resolution of those issues. Therefore, the Court said, public officials are government employees "who have, or appear to the public to have, substantial responsibility for or control over the conduct of governmental affairs."[121] It is not necessary that officials exercise great power or possess a lofty title. Rosenblatt was only the supervisor of a ski resort, but the Court said he might be a public official if his position "would invite public scrutiny and discussion of the person holding it."

Lower courts have ruled that persons supervising public funds and maintaining the public health and welfare are public officials. The likelihood of being designated a public official increases as an employee's contact with the public and authority to make governmental decisions increase. Among public employees designated public officials are a school superintendent, a town tax assessor, an administrator of a county motor pool, a county medical examiner, a director of financial aid at a state college, a director of an antipoverty agency, and various military officers. Paid consultants, police informants, and the director of a university print shop were ruled not to be public officials because they lacked influence over public policy.[122]

The courts' criteria indicate that the head of a city public works department would be considered a public official because of the position's inherent responsibility for public policy, public safety, and public funds. An auditor might be a public official. An auditor is usually not responsible for public policy but does play a key role in the government's use of public funds. Receptionists and janitors are generally not public officials. They exercise little if any control over public policy and do not, in their government jobs, play an important role in the debate of public issues.

Law enforcement personnel, regardless of rank, are ordinarily considered public officials. The courts have said that a police chief, a deputy sheriff, and a federal drug enforcement agent are public officials. Frequently, police officers without rank, "the cops on the beat," are also categorized as public officials. The courts are conscious of the frequent contact the police have with the public, their authority, and their ability to exercise force. That force "can result in significant deprivation of constitutional rights and personal freedoms, not to mention bodily injury and financial loss."[123]

Public officials are required to prove *New York Times* actual malice only for defamatory statements about their official conduct, not for statements about their private lives. However, the Supreme Court has interpreted official conduct broadly. In *Garrison v. Louisiana,* the Court said that an assertion that judges were lazy, "vacation-minded," and sympathetic to criminals was a comment about their official conduct. The Court unanimously reversed the Louisiana Supreme Court's determination in a criminal libel case that Jim Garrison, the district attorney for New Orleans Parish, had attacked the judges' private reputations rather than their official or public reputations. Writing for the Supreme Court, Justice Brennan conceded that accusing the judges of dishonesty, malfeasance, and

[121]Rosenblatt v. Baer, 383 U.S. 85.
[122]*See* Bruce Sanford, *Libel and Privacy* § 7.2.2.2, at 260–64 (2d ed. 1999).
[123]Gray v. Udevitz, 656 F.2d 588 (10th Cir. 1981).

improper motivation affected their private as well as public reputations. But, Justice Brennan said, the *New York Times* rule protects the free flow of criticism about the public conduct of an official even if the criticism hurts an official's private as well as public reputation. Indeed, Brennan said, the *New York Times* rule is so broad that it protects any statements "which might touch on an official's fitness for office." Brennan said few personal attributes were more germane to an official's fitness for office "than dishonesty, malfeasance, or improper motivation."[124]

A few years later, the Court said that any accusation that a public official had committed a crime was related to the person's fitness for office. The Court ruled that Leonard Damron, the mayor of Crystal River, Florida, had to prove *New York Times* actual malice to win a suit he had filed against the Ocala Star-Banner Company over a false report in the *Star-Banner* that Damron had been charged with perjury.[125] The courts have routinely held that discussions of the official conduct of former public officials is protected under the *New York Times v. Sullivan* rule.

◇ Summary ◇

In *New York Times v. Sullivan,* the U.S. Supreme Court ruled for the first time that the First Amendment protects the publication of false statements that may damage an official's reputation. The Court said that public officials suing the media for statements about their official conduct must prove that defamation was published with knowing falsehood or reckless disregard for the truth. The Court said that such a heavy burden of proof on public officials was necessary to protect a robust debate on public issues. *New York Times v. Sullivan* eliminated state common law holding that officials could win libel suits by showing only that the media had disseminated defamatory information about them. After *New York Times v. Sullivan,* courts have defined public officials to include anyone elected to public office as well as government employees responsible for policy making or for public funds, health, or safety.

EXTENDING *NEW YORK TIMES* TO PUBLIC FIGURES As we have seen, the courts extended the *New York Times* actual malice requirement to a wide range of public officials, all the way down to fairly low-level former government employees. In 1967, three years after *Sullivan,* the Court in effect extended the *New York Times* malice requirement to **public figures.** In *Curtis Publishing Co. v. Butts,* the Court required two well-known libel plaintiffs, a football coach and a segregationist, to prove that defamatory statements about them were published with what amounted to *New York Times* actual malice.[126] Public figures, the Court said, include those who are "intimately involved in the resolution of important public questions or, by reason of their fame, shape events in areas of concern to society at large."

In 1971, a badly split Court extended the actual malice requirement even further, requiring private libel plaintiffs involved in an issue of public importance to prove *New York*

[124]Garrison v. Louisiana, 379 U.S. 64 (1964).
[125]Ocala Star-Banner Co. v. Damron, 401 U.S. 295 (1971).
[126]388 U.S. 130 (1967).

Times actual malice, even if the private person was little known and had little influence. In the 1971 case, *Rosenbloom v. Metromedia, Inc.,* the Court plurality said that George Rosenbloom, a little-known businessman, had to prove that stories falsely saying he sold obscenity were disseminated with knowing falsehood or reckless disregard for the truth.[127] If *Rosenbloom* had remained a strong precedent, virtually any libel plaintiff misidentified in a news story about drunk driving, rape, arson, or other issues of public concern would have had to prove actual malice to win a libel suit. But a more conservative court in the 1970s backed away from *Rosenbloom,* largely limiting the malice requirement to public official and public figure libel plaintiffs.

In 1974, the Supreme Court ruled in *Gertz v. Welch* that private libel plaintiffs—those who are neither public officials nor public figures—are not required to prove *New York Times* actual malice. But, the Court said private libel plaintiffs, like public officials and public figures, would have to prove more than the fact that they were defamed. Private libel plaintiffs, too, would have to prove that a libelous publication was published with fault, but a lesser degree of fault than the malice that public figures and officials were required to prove. *Gertz* ended strict liability for the press in private-person libel suits just as *Sullivan* ended strict liability in cases of public officials.

Elmer Gertz was a prominent Chicago civil rights attorney who was libeled by *American Opinion,* a magazine representing the right-wing John Birch Society. The libelous article said Gertz engineered a frame-up of Richard Nuccio, a Chicago police officer convicted of second-degree murder for killing a boy. Gertz represented the parents of the boy in a civil suit filed against Officer Nuccio; Gertz had nothing to do with Nuccio's criminal trial.

Besides accusing Gertz of a frame-up, *American Opinion* pictured Gertz as part of a nationwide conspiracy to discredit local law enforcement agencies and replace them with a national police force that would support a Communist dictatorship. Gertz was inaccurately called a "Leninist," a "Communist-fronter," and an official of the Marxist League for Industrial Democracy. *American Opinion* also said that Gertz had been an officer of the National Lawyers Guild, which the magazine described as a Communist organization. The magazine falsely reported that the police had a file on Gertz that took "a big Irish cop to lift."[128]

Relying on *Rosenbloom v. Metromedia, Inc.,* the trial court and appeals court ruled that Gertz was involved in an issue of public interest and therefore had to prove that *American Opinion* published the defamatory article with *New York Times* actual malice. The trial court and an appellate court said Gertz was involved in an issue of public importance because Gertz represented the family in a well-publicized suit against Richard Nuccio over the death of their son. The lower courts said the public had a legitimate interest in trials of a police officer and the broader controversy of a nationwide conspiracy to discredit local police officers. The Supreme Court reversed the lower court decisions, 5-4, ruling that Gertz was a private person who did not have to prove actual malice to win his libel suit.

Writing for the Court, Justice Lewis Powell identified two kinds of public figures, since labeled (1) "all-purpose" and (2) "limited," or "vortex," public figures. All-purpose public figures "occupy positions of such pervasive power and influence that they are deemed public figures for all purposes." More commonly, Powell said, those classed as

[127] 403 U.S. 29 (1971).
[128] Gertz v. Robert Welch, Inc., 418 U.S. 323 (1974).

public figures have "thrust themselves to the forefront of particular public controversies in order to influence the resolution of the issues involved." Powell implied that individuals who voluntarily inject themselves into a public controversy would have to prove *New York Times* actual malice only for defamatory falsehoods related to that controversy, thus the labels of "limited" and "vortex" public figures. Private persons, like George Rosenbloom or Elmer Gertz, who are involuntarily drawn into public issues would seldom have to prove actual malice, Powell said.

The Court said public figures, like public officials, should meet heavier burdens of proof when suing the media for libel than private plaintiffs meet. Powell said libel law should be more generous to private plaintiffs than to public figures because public figures expect to be commented on and have better means of self-defense. Public figures, unlike private citizens, invite attention and comment; they seek their status by playing an influential role in the affairs of society and thereby voluntarily expose themselves to an increased risk of public scrutiny and defamatory falsehoods. Private persons, on the other hand, have not embraced the risk of public exposure. The private person has relinquished "no part of his interest in the protection of his own good name, and consequently he has a more compelling call on the courts for redress of injury inflicted by defamatory falsehood."

Public figures, unlike private citizens, also have access to "channels of effective communication" so that they can counteract false statements about them, Powell said. Because of their access to media, public figures can minimize damage to their reputations; they can "contradict the lie or correct the error." In contrast, private persons, Powell said, are more "vulnerable to injury"; they lack effective opportunities for rebuttal.

Powell said that Elmer Gertz was neither an all-purpose public figure nor a vortex public figure. Although Gertz had published several books and articles on legal subjects and had served as an official in several civic and professional associations, he was not an all-purpose public figure. None of the jurors at the libel trial had heard of him. In any case, Powell said that a citizen who participates in community and professional affairs does not become a public personality "for all aspects of his life" unless there is "clear evidence of general fame or notoriety in the community, and pervasive involvement in the affairs of society."

If Gertz did not have widespread fame and notoriety, neither had he "thrust himself into the vortex" of the public issue involving the trials of the police officer Richard Nuccio. Gertz had not "engage[d] the public's attention in an attempt to influence" the outcome of an issue, the Court said. Gertz never discussed the criminal or civil litigation in the press. A lawyer did not become a public figure simply by representing a client in a controversial case.

After determining that Gertz was a private person who did not have to show actual malice, the Court sent the case back to the trial court. In 1983, more than fourteen years after Gertz sued, he was awarded $482,000 in damages, interest, and court fees.[129]

The *Gertz* case, like *New York Times v. Sullivan,* raised several questions. Justice Powell used several terms—*fame, notoriety, pervasive power, influence, voluntarily thrust,* and *public controversies*—that he did not define. Shortly after *Gertz,* one federal judge said trying to define a public figure is "much like trying to nail a jellyfish to the wall."[130] Lower courts still struggle to distinguish between public figures and private persons.

[129]Anthony Lewis, "Annals of Law: The Sullivan Case," *New Yorker,* Nov. 5, 1984, at 52, 79.
[130]Rosanova v. Playboy Enterprises, Inc., 411 F. Supp. 440 (S.D. Ga. 1976), *aff'd,* 580 F.2d 859 (5th Cir. 1978).

All-Purpose Public Figures One of Powell's two categories of public figures in *Gertz* included people with special prominence in society—those who exercise general power or influence and those who occupy a position of continuing news value. Such *all-purpose* public figures have achieved widespread fame or notoriety. The public figures must prove *New York Times* actual malice for libelous stories about their private lives as well as their public activities.

One federal appeals court said that the all-purpose public figure

> is a well-known "celebrity," his name a "household word." The public recognizes him and follows his words and deeds, either because it regards his ideas, conduct, or judgment as worthy of its attention or because he actively pursues that consideration.[131]

Courts have had limited opportunities to categorize nationally known persons as all-purpose public figures. A federal appeals court said the long-time host of a popular television program was an all-purpose public figure.[132] Other federal courts put a prominent political writer, William Buckley, Jr.,[133] and a publicly owned insurance company with assets of a billion dollars into the all-purpose public figure category.[134] Actress Carol Burnett was presumed without explanation to be a public figure in her suit against the *National Enquirer.*[135] Presumably, former President Jimmy Carter and General Colin Powell would be all-purpose public figures for defamation related to their activities after they left office. Film star and activist Jane Fonda and cable television innovator and philanthropist Ted Turner also probably have sufficient fame and notoriety to be considered all-purpose public figures.

In a series of cases, the U.S. Supreme Court ruled that plaintiffs who may be quite well known in their own professional or social circles nevertheless may remain private persons as libel plaintiffs. Elmer Gertz, the reader will recall, was a private person even though he published articles, represented controversial clients, and participated in civic affairs. The Supreme Court also ruled that a prominent member of Palm Beach society and former wife of Firestone tire heir Russell Firestone was not a public figure.[136]

Mary Alice Firestone sued *Time* magazine after a "Milestones" item incorrectly reported that Russell Firestone had won a divorce on the grounds "of extreme cruelty and adultery." Although cruelty and adultery were issues in the divorce trial, the trial court did not say they were the reasons the divorce was granted.

The Supreme Court categorized Firestone as a private person for the purpose of her suit even though she was "prominent among the '400' of Palm Beach Society" and an "active" member of the "sporting set." She subscribed to a clipping service to keep track of the times she was mentioned in the newspapers. Her marital difficulties were "well known," and her suit for divorce became a "veritable cause *celèbre* in social circles across the country." However, the Supreme Court said that Firestone remained a private person because she "did not assume any role of especial prominence in the affairs of society, other than perhaps Palm Beach society."

131 Waldbaum v. Fairchild Publications, Inc., 627 F.2d 1287 (D.C. Cir.), *cert. denied,* 449 U.S. 898 (1980).
132 Carson v. Allied News Co., 529 F.2d 206 (7th Cir. 1976).
133 Buckley v. Littell, 539 F.2d 882 (2d Cir. 1976), *cert. denied,* 429 U.S. 1062.
134 Reliance Ins. Co. v. Barrons, 442 F. Supp. 1341 (S.D.N.Y. 1977).
135 Burnett v. National Enquirer, Inc., 144 Cal. App. 3d 991 (Cal. Ct. App. 1983).
136 Time, Inc. v. Firestone, 424 U.S. 448 (1976).

Limited, or Vortex, Public Figures Justice Powell's second category of public figures in *Gertz* included people who inject themselves into a public controversy to affect its outcome. Such people are *limited* public figures, who have to prove *New York Times* actual malice only for defamation directly connected to their voluntary acts. These limited public figures remain private persons for libelous statements about their private lives. The Supreme Court said Elmer Gertz was a private person because he had not actively thrust himself into any issue related to the trials of policeman Richard Nuccio. Gertz had not tried to influence public opinion.

In cases after *Gertz,* the Supreme Court has made it clear that persons will be classified as limited, or vortex, public figures only if (1) the alleged defamation involves a public controversy, (2) the person suing for libel has voluntarily participated in the discussion of that controversy, and (3) the person suing for libel has tried to affect the outcome of the controversy.

All three criteria must be met before a person will be considered a limited public figure, although court discussions of the last two criteria are frequently merged. In addition, lower courts sometimes consider other factors discussed by the Supreme Court in *Gertz,* including access to the media for the purpose of rebutting a defamatory remark.

The Court has not carefully defined the term *public controversy,* in which vortex figures become involved. However, the Court has indicated that public controversy should be understood narrowly. In *Time v. Firestone,* the Court said the term did not refer to all controversies that attracted the public's interest. When the Court declared that Firestone was not a public figure, it asserted that a divorce proceeding was not the sort of "public controversy" referred to in *Gertz,* even though the marital difficulties of extremely wealthy individuals may be of interest to some members of the public.

The U.S. Court of Appeals for the D.C. Circuit said that a public controversy has to be a "real dispute" over a specific issue affecting a segment of the general public. In *Waldbaum v. Fairchild Publications,* the D.C. Circuit said the outcome of a public controversy has "foreseeable and substantial ramifications" for those not directly participating in the debate. News coverage is an indication of a public controversy, the court said, but newsworthiness itself is not a sufficient criterion.[137]

The D.C. Circuit said Eric Waldbaum was a public figure in his suit against a trade publication called *Supermarket News* because he injected himself into controversy as the president of an innovative consumer cooperative, Greenbelt Consumer Services. Greenbelt, the second of its kind in the country, owned retail supermarkets, furniture and gift outlets, and service stations. Waldbaum sued *Supermarket News* over a five-sentence item that announced his ouster as Greenbelt president. The article said that the co-op had been "losing money" and "retrenching" with Waldbaum in charge.

The D.C. Circuit said Waldbaum was a limited public figure because he set policies and standards in the supermarket industry. The court said Waldbaum thrust himself into public controversies over unit pricing and open dating in supermarkets by fighting traditional industry practices. He also invited the public and press to meetings about topics ranging from "supermarket practices to energy legislation and fuel allocation." The court said that Waldbaum's activities generated considerable comment from trade journals and

[137]627 F.2d at 1292.

newspapers, including the *Washington Post.* His policies were debated within the supermarket industry and by retailers and consumers in the Washington, D.C., area.

Public controversies identified by the courts, in addition to supermarket business practices, include the value of protein supplements in the human diet[138] and alleged recruiting violations in a college basketball program.[139] A court said the infamous rape trial of black youths known nationally as the "Scottsboro Boys" focused on the controversy of fair justice for blacks in the court system.[140] The courts have also considered controversial a campaign to recall city council members,[141] the firing of an administrator of a large public hospital,[142] and the impact on a community when a company closes a manufacturing plant.[143]

Issues that the courts have not considered to be public controversies include a fight among company stockholders that would have no impact on the general public[144] and the demonstration of an air-powered automobile. A court said the car may be of some interest to the public but had not been part of a dispute.[145]

Once the courts determine that a story is about a public controversy, they must determine the nature and purpose of a person's participation in that controversy. Five years after *Gertz,* the Supreme Court said that limited public figures must thrust themselves into controversies with the intent of affecting the outcomes. Public figures must initiate their own participation in the debate over a public controversy. It is not enough for someone to become involuntarily involved in a controversy or to do something controversial, such as using government funds for questionable research or committing a crime. Public figures must also make an effort to affect the resolution of the controversy.

In *Hutchinson v. Proxmire,* the Supreme Court said that receiving substantial federal funds did not make a research scientist a public figure. Neither did the scientist's publication of research findings in professional journals. The scientist, Dr. Ronald Hutchinson, sued Senator William Proxmire for criticizing the half-million dollars spent by three government agencies on Hutchinson's study of monkeys. Senator Proxmire gave one of his Golden Fleece awards for wasteful government spending to the National Science Foundation, the Office of Naval Research, and the National Aeronautics and Space Administration for sponsoring Hutchinson's research. Hutchinson was trying to help federal agencies resolve problems faced by humans confined in close quarters in space and under the ocean. He was looking for visible ways to determine aggressive tendencies in animals, such as the clenching of jaws. Senator Proxmire ridiculed the research on the U.S. Senate floor, in a newsletter to constituents, and in comments made on a nationally televised talk show. Proxmire said that Hutchinson "has made a fortune from his monkeys and in the process made a monkey out of the American taxpayer." Hutchinson contended that the comments had damaged both his reputation among his professional colleagues and his ability to obtain research grants.

[138] Hoffman v. Washington Post Co., 433 F. Supp. 600 (D.D.C. 1977).
[139] Barry v. Time, Inc., 584 F. Supp. 1110 (N.D. Cal. 1984).
[140] Street v. NBC, 645 F.2d 1227 (6th Cir.), *cert. granted,* 454 U.S. 815, *cert. dismissed,* 454 U.S. 1095 (1981).
[141] Weingarten v. Block, 102 Cal. App. 2d 129, *cert. denied,* 449 U.S. 899 (1980).
[142] Gadd v. News-Press Publishing Co., 10 Media L. Rep. 2362 (Fla. Cir. Ct. 1984).
[143] Thompson v. National Catholic Reporter Pub. Co., 4 F.Supp. 2d 833 (E.D. Wis. 1998).
[144] Denny v. Mertz, 318 N.W.2d 141 (Wis. 1982).
[145] Re v. Gannett Co., 480 A.2d 662 (Del. Super. Ct. 1984).

The Supreme Court, in an opinion written by Chief Justice Warren Burger, said that simply being the recipient of public money does not make a person a public figure. If such were the case, Burger said, "everyone who received or benefited from the myriad public grants for research could be classified as a public figure." Burger said that Hutchinson had not thrust himself or his views into a public controversy for the purpose of influencing others. Hutchinson had become involved in a controversy created by Senator Proxmire, but Hutchinson had never assumed a role of prominence in the broad question of how public money should be spent, Burger said. "Neither his applications for federal grants nor his publications in professional journals can be said to have invited that degree of public attention and comment . . . essential to meet the public figure level."[146] In addition, Burger noted that Hutchinson had not enjoyed the regular access to the media necessary for a public figure. He was offered access only after Proxmire directed attention to him.

If receiving public funding does not make a person a public figure, neither does involvement in a criminal proceeding. In *Wolston v. Reader's Digest Ass'n.,* the Court said that a man who refused to testify in 1958 before a federal grand jury investigating Soviet spy activities was not a public figure, even though he received substantial media attention. The Court said that people did not automatically become public figures because they were the focus of public attention, even if they had been convicted of a crime. The Court said Ilya Wolston did not thrust himself into the forefront of the controversy over Soviet espionage in the United States but was "dragged unwillingly" into the spotlight. Nor had he tried to create public support for himself or public antagonism against the investigation.

If Ronald Hutchinson and Ilya Wolston are private persons, despite their prominence, it is unlikely that many private libel plaintiffs will have to prove malice if they are involuntarily drawn into issues of public importance. Indeed, the Court in *Gertz* said that only in "exceedingly rare" circumstances would private persons become public figures through no purposeful action on their part. Lower courts rarely determine that a plaintiff is an involuntary public figure.[147]

Instead, the courts almost always find that people who do not seek public attention or controversy are not public figures, even though they may be controversial themselves. A California court said that Virginia Franklin, a high school teacher who became the focus of a book-banning controversy, did not become a public figure because there was no evidence that she intentionally triggered a controversy when she told students to read a book of underground writings of the 1960s. A parent complained about the book to a chapter of the Elks Lodge, and protests of the lodge led to a public hearing before the school board and an administrative evaluation. The court said Franklin did not initiate media contact. She participated in the controversy only to the extent required by her job.[148]

Businesspeople do not ordinarily become public figures simply because their business practices or products are criticized, even if they respond to the charges.[149] Nor will they usually be considered to have injected themselves into controversial public issues solely

---

[146] 443 U.S. 111 (1979).

[147] *E.g.,* Rodney Smolla, *Law of Defamation* § 2-14[1], at 2-43 (1998). *But see, e.g.,* Dameron v. Washington Magazine, Inc., 779 F.2d 736 (D.C. Cir. 1985).

[148] Franklin v. Lodge No. 1108, 97 Cal. App. 3d 915 (Cal. Ct. App. 1979).

[149] *E.g.,* General Prod. Co. v. Meredith Corp., 526 F. Supp. 546 (E.D. Va. 1981).

because they advertised or practiced public relations.[150] However, businesses or businesspeople may become public figures if they initiate aggressive advertising or public relations campaigns related to controversial issues. A federal appeals court categorized Greenbelt co-op executive Eric Waldbaum as a public figure because he promoted precedent-breaking business policies vigorously. Waldbaum, who knew how to use the news media, held press conferences to discuss Greenbelt's policies and operations. He conducted an aggressive consumer education campaign in a monthly newspaper, *Co-op Consumer.* In the words of the trial judge, Waldbaum was "an activist, projecting his own image and that of the cooperative."[151]

Courts regularly conclude that political candidates are public figures if defamatory comments are made about their candidacies. The Supreme Court has said that criticism about political candidates must be accorded as much constitutional protection as criticism about officeholders. In *Monitor Patriot v. Roy,* a losing candidate for a New Hampshire seat in the U.S. Senate sued after a syndicated political columnist called him a former small-time bootlegger. The Court said that the candidate, Alphonse Roy, was a public figure who, like most political candidates, puts before the voters "every conceivable aspect of his public and private life that he thinks may lead the electorate to gain a good impression of him."[152] The Court said that a candidate's integrity or qualities as a father or husband may become matters of public concern.

Courts usually decide that people who voluntarily try to change the minds of others about public issues are limited public figures. Among persons the courts have determined to be public figures for trying to affect the outcome of public controversies were an outspoken foe of fluoridating water[153] and a person who circulated a petition and purchased advertising to oppose county land acquisition.[154] Also designated a limited public figure was Liberty Lobby, a self-avowed citizens' lobby. Liberty Lobby claims to promote "patriotism, nationalism, lawfulness, protection of the national interests of the United States and the economic interests of its citizens."[155]

Other Limited Public Figures Besides recognizing the all-purpose public figure and the vortex figure, some courts confer limited public figure status on entertainers, athletes, and others who attract attention because of visible careers. Public figures in this category do not have the widespread fame or notoriety of an all-purpose public figure, nor have they injected themselves into a controversial public issue with the intent of affecting the outcome. Nevertheless, many lower courts believe those who seek public attention during their careers ought to have to prove *New York Times* actual malice for the limited purpose of defamation about their public performances.[156]

[150]*See, e.g.,* Vegod Corp. v. ABC, 603 P.2d 14 (Cal. 1980). *But see* Steaks Unlimited, Inc. v. Deaner, 468 F. Supp. 779 (W.D. Pa. 1979), *aff'd,* 623 F.2d 264 (3d Cir. 1980).
[151]Waldbaum v. Fairchild Publications, Inc., 627 F.2d 1300.
[152]*See* Monitor Patriot Co. v. Roy, 401 U.S. 265 (1971).
[153]Yiamouyiannis v. Consumers Union of the United States, 619 F.2d 932 (2d Cir. 1980).
[154]Cloyd v. Press, Inc., 629 S.W.2d 24 (Tenn. App. 1981).
[155]Liberty Lobby, Inc. v. Anderson, 562 F. Supp. 201 (D.D.C. 1983), *aff'd,* 746 F.2d 1563 (D.C. Cir. 1984), *vacated on other grounds,* 477 U.S. 242 (1986).
[156]*See, e.g.,* Bruce Sanford, *Libel and Privacy* § 7.4.2, at 317–22 (2d ed. 1999).

Indeed, while the U.S. Supreme Court has not directly recognized this category of public figure in *Gertz* or since, one of the first public figures to be recognized by the Court would probably fit. In a case to be discussed later, University of Georgia athletic director Wally Butts was considered a public figure in his suit against the *Saturday Evening Post* after the *Post* said that Butts plotted to fix a football game. Although Butts was what the Supreme Court called a "well-known and respected figure in coaching ranks," his fame did not extend beyond the sports world. Nor had Butts voluntarily injected himself into a controversy. Yet the Supreme Court recognized Butts as a public figure.[157]

Similarly, the U.S. Court of Appeals for the Fifth Circuit said entertainer Anita Brewer was a public figure for a story that focused on her romance with Elvis Presley, a relationship that advanced her career. The Fifth Circuit said Brewer had entered a profession that required public appearances and invited press attention.[158] Other plaintiffs treated similarly include a football player,[159] a prominent writer for *Sports Illustrated,*[160] a person promoting newly acquired radio stations,[161] and a seminude dancer.[162]

Time Lapse The Supreme Court has not said whether a public figure becomes a private person over time. In the absence of Supreme Court direction, several lower courts have said that public figures do not lose their public figure status with a lapse of time, at least when the libel concerns the same issues that led to the public attention in the first place.

For example, a federal appeals court said that Victoria Price Street, who accused the nine black "Scottsboro Boys" of raping her in 1931, was a public figure fifty years later. Street sued NBC for a network docudrama that portrayed her as a woman trying to send innocent young men to the electric chair. The U.S. Court of Appeals for the Sixth Circuit said that Street had been a public figure in the 1930s because of her prominent role in the controversy over justice for blacks, her access to the media, and her effort to aggressively promote her version of the case outside of the courtroom. She was still a public figure nearly fifty years later because "once a person becomes a public figure in connection with a particular controversy, that person remains a public figure for purposes of later commentary or treatment of *that controversy*" (emphasis in original).

Public figures of the past do not lose access to the media where they can discuss their role in a continuing controversy, the court said. In addition, the Sixth Circuit said, vigorous public debate must be protected even though fading memories and disappearing sources make it more difficult for the media to verify the accuracy of their reports. At the same time, the court said the passage of time "does not automatically diminish the significance of events or the public's need for information." The Sixth Circuit said the case of the Scottsboro Boys, "the most famous rape case of the twentieth century," focused the nation's attention on the courts' treatment of blacks. The court said the Scottsboro case would remain "a living controversy" as long as fair justice for blacks is an issue.[163]

---

[157]Curtis Publishing Co. v. Butts, 418 U.S. at 334.
[158]Brewer v. Memphis Publishing Co., 626 F.2d 1238 (1980).
[159]*E.g.,* Chuy v. Philadelphia Eagles Football Club, 595 F.2d 1265 (3d Cir. 1979) (en banc).
[160]Maule v. NYM Corp., 429 N.E.2d 416 (N.Y. 1981).
[161]Howard v. Buffalo Evening News, Inc., 453 N.Y.S.2d 516 (App. Div. 1982).
[162]Griffin v. Kentucky Post, 10 Media L. Rep. 1159 (Ky. Cir. Ct. 1983).
[163]Street v. NBC, 645 F.2d at 1235, *cert. granted,* 454 U.S. 815, *cert. dismissed,* 454 U.S. 1095 (1981).

◇ Summary ◇

The Supreme Court said in *Gertz v. Welch* that public figures are either persons of widespread fame or notoriety or people who inject themselves into the debate about controversial public issues for the purpose of affecting the outcome. Public figures, unlike private libel plaintiffs, voluntarily subject themselves to public exposure and have ready access to the media, in which they can rebut defamatory remarks. The Supreme Court said that persons of widespread fame and notoriety are public figures for all purposes either because of their prominence or because of the influence they exercise in society. Limited public figures are persons who voluntarily thrust themselves into a public controversy with the intent of having an impact on the way that controversy is resolved. Limited public figures must prove *New York Times* actual malice only for media discussion of that issue.

***NEW YORK TIMES* ACTUAL MALICE** Once a court decides that a person is a public official, a public figure, or a private person, the focus of the libel case turns to the question of *fault,* that is, whether communicators published the alleged libel carelessly or maliciously. To win a libel suit, each plaintiff must prove not only that the publication was false and defamatory but also that it was published with fault. Private persons must prove that a publisher acted negligently or carelessly. Public officials and public figures must prove *New York Times* actual malice: that the publisher knew the publication was false or published it with reckless disregard for the truth. Actual malice, which must be proven with "clear and convincing evidence,"[164] is a subjective decision, not susceptible to a precise definition. But a communicator who acts with actual malice demonstrates much more than ill will or carelessness. *New York Times* actual malice is also more flagrant than an "extreme departure" from the professional journalistic practices that most communicators would follow.[165]

Reckless Disregard for the Truth Public officials and public figures most often try to prove *New York Times* actual malice by establishing that communicators demonstrated a reckless disregard for the truth. The Supreme Court has said that plaintiffs can establish reckless disregard only if they can prove that defamatory statements were made with a "high degree of awareness of their probable falsity."[166] In *St. Amant v. Thompson,* the Court said a candidate for sheriff in Baton Rouge did not exercise reckless disregard because he believed the truth of false statements he made in a televised speech. Phil St. Amant implied during his speech that his opponent, a deputy sheriff named Herman Thompson, had been bribed by a local union officer. St. Amant based his charges on an affidavit of a union member, but St. Amant did not consider that his accusations might be defamatory and made no effort to verify his information. The U.S. Supreme Court, finding no reckless disregard for the truth, overturned lower court rulings for Thompson.

Justice Byron White, writing for the Court's eight-person majority, said reckless conduct is not measured by whether a reasonably prudent person would have published or investigated before publishing. Rather, White said, "There must be sufficient evidence to

[164] *See, e.g.,* Philadelphia Newspapers Inc. v. Hepps, 475 U.S. 767 (1986).
[165] Harte-Hanks Communications, Inc. v. Connaughton, 491 U.S. 657 (1989).
[166] Garrison v. Louisiana, 379 U.S. at 74.

permit the conclusion that the defendant in fact entertained serious doubts as to the truth of his publication."[167]

However, White emphasized that the Court's decision did not automatically protect journalists who argue they believe their stories are true. A journalist cannot successfully contend a story is written in good faith if there are "obvious reasons" to doubt the credibility of a source or the accuracy of the source's information, White said. Nor can remarks be "based wholly on an unverified anonymous telephone call." White said courts may find *New York Times* actual malice if defamatory remarks are fabricated or "so inherently improbable that only a reckless man would have put them into circulation."

The inquiry into whether a journalist entertained "serious doubts" about the truth or falsity of a story requires the courts to try to reconstruct the publishing process. The courts ask whether a journalist adequately investigated a story given the time available. The courts consider whether the reporter chose reliable sources, ignored warnings that the story was wrong, or disregarded inconsistencies. Other factors that could contribute to a finding of actual malice include a mistake in interpretation, the use of the wrong terms, and a biased selection of facts. Proof of motives such as ill will or hatred could be one of the factors in actual malice. So could a publisher's intent to print sensational stories to attract readers and the failure to print a retraction. Ordinarily, one of these items alone is not sufficient evidence of reckless disregard for the truth; actual malice is usually a combination of reckless practices.

The Supreme Court found actual malice in an Ohio case in which journalists, according to the Court, purposely avoided the truth. The *Hamilton (Ohio) Journal News* deliberately evaded the truth, the Court said, when the paper relied on a highly questionable source and failed to investigate contradictions before publishing a front-page story charging a judicial candidate with planning blackmail and promising favors for help in smearing his opponent. The story said that the unsuccessful judicial challenger, Daniel Connaughton, promised Alice Thompson and her sister jobs, a trip to Florida, and fancy dinners "in appreciation" for their help in the investigation of corruption in the incumbent judge's office. Connaughton supposedly made these unethical promises during a taped conversation with Thompson and her sister, a conversation at which several other people were present. The paper also reported that Thompson said Connaughton planned to quietly blackmail the incumbent judge with a tape of the sisters' damning information.

Connaughton denied threatening blackmail and offering the sisters favors, a denial supported by five others who witnessed the taped conversation between Connaughton and the sisters. The Supreme Court upheld the jury's award of $200,000, finding that the newspaper published with actual malice.[168]

The Court cited several reportorial practices that added up to actual malice:

- Relying on a questionable source—Thompson, who had a criminal record, had been treated for mental instability and had told the paper that she opposed Connaughton's candidacy
- Failing to interview Thompson's sister and several other people who later refuted Thompson

[167] 390 U.S. 727 (1968).
[168] Harte-Hanks Communications, Inc. v. Connaughton, 491 U.S. 657 (1989).

- Failing to listen to the tape, which Connaughton made available to the newspaper, a tape that would have corroborated or disproved Thompson's claims of Connaughton's offers and threats
- Ignoring Connaughton's denials
- Ignoring the improbability that Connaughton would quietly blackmail the incumbent judge with the taped interview when the newspaper knew Connaughton had already given the tape to the police
- Revealing the newspaper's prejudice by publishing an editorial accurately predicting the conclusions of the investigative story it later published about Connaughton
- Claiming that staff members were assigned to conduct key interviews that staffers testified they had not been assigned

In sum, the Supreme Court concluded that the *Journal News* had published with actual malice by its "deliberate decision not to acquire knowledge of facts that might confirm the probable falsity of Thompson's charges. Although failure to investigate will not alone support a finding of actual malice," the Court said, "the purposeful avoidance of the truth is in a different category."

The Court saw similarities between the Connaughton case and an earlier case in which the *Saturday Evening Post* lost a libel suit because of slipshod investigatory techniques that three justices thought constituted actual malice. In the earlier case, *Curtis Publishing Co. v. Butts,* reporters failed before publication to check the story of an unreliable source who said that Georgia football coach Wally Butts had fixed a football game with Alabama. Although the staff of the *Saturday Evening Post* was under no deadline pressure, it failed to interview witnesses or view game films. The *Post* instead relied on the unsupported testimony of a check forger who claimed he acquired information about the fix when he was mysteriously connected to a telephone conversation between Butts and Alabama coach Bear Bryant.

In a case decided at the same time as *Butts,* a unanimous Court determined that the Associated Press had acted responsibly when it reported that retired Army Major General Edwin Walker had encouraged violence and led a charge against federal marshals during the integration of the University of Mississippi in 1962. In *Associated Press v. Walker,* the Court reversed a $500,000 award for Walker, who denied that he encouraged violence.

The AP reporter, the Court said, gave "every indication of being trustworthy and competent." He checked his story with apparently reliable sources, leaving no reason for AP editors to doubt the reporter's story about a former general known for his vehement opposition to integration. Furthermore, the Court recognized that some errors might creep into a news story written under deadline pressure.[169]

Knowing Falsehood Although public officials and public figures who have to prove *New York Times* actual malice usually try to establish reckless disregard for the truth, a few cases provide evidence that journalists published with knowledge that a defamatory story was false. Potent evidence of knowing falsehood is fabrication; a journalist who makes up a story knows it is false.

[169]Curtis Publishing Co. v. Butts, 388 U.S. 130 (1967).

In *Cantrell v. Forest City Publishing Co.,* a case that will be discussed in Chapter 5, the U.S. Supreme Court said that a reporter acted with *New York Times* actual malice when he fabricated an interview with a West Virginia widow named Margaret Cantrell. Although Cantrell was not home when the *Cleveland Plain Dealer* reporter visited the Cantrell home, he nevertheless quoted her in his story. The story also exaggerated the family poverty following the death of Cantrell's husband in a bridge accident.[170]

In *Goldwater v. Ginzburg,* the U.S. Court of Appeals for the Second Circuit said that *Fact* magazine knowingly published defamatory falsehoods about 1964 presidential candidate Barry Goldwater. In *Goldwater,* the court said *Fact* editor Ralph Ginzburg and managing editor Warren Boroson decided shortly after the Republican nominating convention to attack Goldwater's character "on preconceived psychiatric or psychological grounds of their own fabrication."[171] Before Boroson had begun his research, the court said, he wrote that the Goldwater profile would say that the candidate had "deep-seated doubts about his masculinity." Ginzburg wrote in one of the magazine's articles that Goldwater had experienced two nervous breakdowns, although Ginzburg knew that Goldwater and his physician denied the charge. Ginzburg also asserted, without consulting experts in psychiatry, that Goldwater suffered from a serious mental disease. For a second article in *Fact,* Ginzburg edited psychiatrists' responses to a mail survey to distort the doctors' comments about Goldwater. The Second Circuit, noting that Ginzburg had created numerous false statements to support his predetermined views about Goldwater's mental condition, affirmed a jury verdict that the *Fact* articles were published with actual malice.

Performer Carol Burnett proved that the *National Enquirer* knowingly printed a false story when it said she made a fool of herself in an expensive Washington, D.C., restaurant. The four-sentence item in the *Enquirer* said that "a boisterous" Carol Burnett argued with former Secretary of State Henry Kissinger. Burnett supposedly "traipsed around the place offering everyone a bite of her dessert" and "really raised eyebrows when she accidentally knocked a glass of wine over one diner and started giggling instead of apologizing."

The trial court established that the story was based on tips from a freelancer who emphasized that Burnett was not drunk. One *Enquirer* writer expressed doubts that the tip about Burnett's behavior could be trusted. Another could verify only that Burnett shared her dessert and "carried on a good-natured conversation" with Kissinger. No one told *Enquirer* columnist Brian Walker, the author of the story, that Burnett and Kissinger had an argument. The reports of Burnett's "boisterous" behavior and the wine spilling were only unverified hearsay. The trial judge suggested that Walker added "embellishment . . . 'to spice up' the item." The judge said the *Enquirer* published with actual malice because Walker had serious doubts about the truth of the publication and there was "a high degree of probability" that he fabricated part of the story.[172]

Although fabrication by itself can constitute *New York Times* actual malice, the Supreme Court has ruled that a writer who deliberately modifies a speaker's words within quotation marks does not necessarily knowingly falsify the speaker's statement. Unless the

[170]419 U.S. 245 (1974).

[171]414 F.2d 324 (2d Cir. 1969).

[172]Burnett v. National Enquirer, Inc., 7 Media L. Rep. 1321 (Cal. Super. Ct. 1981), *aff'd on other grounds,* 144 Cal. App. 3d 991 (Cal. Ct. App. 1983).

change substantially increases damage to a person's reputation, altering the words in quotation marks is not "knowing falsehood," the Court said. In *Masson v. New Yorker Magazine Inc.*, the Court rejected, 7-2, Freudian scholar Jeffrey Masson's argument that writers act with actual malice when they deliberately change a speaker's remarks inside quotation.

Masson sued *New Yorker* author Janet Malcolm for falsely quoting him as calling himself an "intellectual gigolo" and "the greatest analyst who ever lived." Masson claimed these phrases were exaggerations that made him appear unscholarly, irresponsible, vain, and lacking honesty and moral integrity. Malcolm said her quotes were accurate.[173]

Without deciding whether the quotes libeled Masson, the Supreme Court said that writers must be left some leeway to re-create quotes that reflect the substance if not the exact words spoken in an interview. Writers, the Court said, often alter words inside of quotation marks to correct grammar and syntax, including making intelligible the remarks of "rambling speakers." In addition, the Court said, writers working from notes often put into quotation marks statements that are incomplete or inexact. Even writers using tape recorders must add punctuation and edit for publication, the Court said. Only if the alterations add significantly to defamatory meaning would the alterations constitute knowing falsehood.

In dissent, Justice White, joined by Justice Scalia, argued that any deliberate change in a direct quotation ought to be, by definition, knowledge of falsity. Quotation marks, White said, suggest that a person spoke the exact words quoted. Changing those quotes is evidence of malice, White said. After two trials, a federal court jury ruled against Jeffrey Masson, a decision affirmed on appeal.[174]

Inquiry into a Journalist's Mind The proof necessary for *New York Times* actual malice, evidence of knowing falsehood or reckless disregard of the truth, seemingly requires courts to know what journalists think as they prepare a story. The need to prove knowing falsehood or a "high degree of awareness" of the probable falsity encourages plaintiffs' lawyers to examine the thought processes, or "the state of mind," of journalists. Plaintiffs' lawyers ask writers whether they believed what their sources told them. Editors are asked whether they doubted the truth of the story and, if so, whether they told reporters to provide more documentation. Both writers and editors are asked how they decided what to publish.

Many journalists argue that detailed examinations of news decisions violate the First Amendment by interfering with editorial processes. They contend that writers and editors are reluctant to express doubts about a story in the newsroom if those doubts might be used against them in court. Journalists claim that juries cannot understand why journalists under deadline pressure might decline to pursue tips that could make a story more complete. Nevertheless, in *Herbert v. Lando,* the Court said the First Amendment does not bar inquiry into the editorial process.

In *Lando,* the Court said a producer for *60 Minutes* could be asked how he evaluated information for a segment on Colonel Anthony Herbert, a controversial retired Army officer. A 1973 *60 Minutes* broadcast questioned allegations by Herbert of an official cover-up of atrocities committed by U.S. troops in Vietnam. Herbert sued CBS, claiming that *60 Minutes* falsely suggested he made up the war-crimes charges to explain why he was

[173]501 U.S. 496 (1991).
[174]Masson v. New Yorker, 85 F.3d 1394 (9th Cir. 1996).

relieved of his command. Herbert conceded he was a public figure and therefore had to prove *New York Times* actual malice.

The Supreme Court said that it had not intended, when constitutionalizing libel law, to prevent plaintiffs from obtaining evidence needed to prove actual malice. Indeed, Justice Byron White, who wrote the Court's opinion, said the *New York Times* actual malice rule "made it essential" that public officials and public figures understand both the conduct and state of mind of media defendants. If public officials and public figures were prevented from asking about the thoughts, opinions, and conclusions of journalists, White said, the balance between the protection of reputation and the protection for the First Amendment guarantees of freedom of speech and press would be unacceptably skewed in favor of the press.

White rejected the argument that investigations into the journalist's state of mind would have "an intolerable chilling effect" on editorial decision making. He contended that the media have a self-interest in taking any necessary precautions, including a "frank interchange of fact and opinion," to avoid publishing a knowing falsehood or reckless error. White said he did not believe that discussions between reporters and editors were "so subject to distortion and . . . misunderstanding" that they should be immune from courtroom examination. However, he said, investigations into the editorial process should be permitted only when someone suing for libel has to prove *New York Times* actual malice. Inquiry into the state of mind should not be permitted "merely to satisfy curiosity."[175]

The Supreme Court returned the *Herbert v. Lando* case to the federal district court judge for trial. The trial judge eventually ruled for CBS on most of Herbert's complaint on grounds he could not prove *New York Times* actual malice. In 1986, a federal appeals court dismissed the case.[176]

◇ Summary ◇

Public officials and public figures are required to prove *New York Times* actual malice, knowing falsehood or reckless disregard of the truth, to win libel suits. The Supreme Court has said plaintiffs must demonstrate that journalists had serious doubts about the truth of a defamatory story before publication. To determine whether writers and editors are reckless, courts examine whether journalists employ standard news-gathering techniques in the time available to prepare a story. Courts also consider the believability of the story, the depth and breadth of the investigation, the credibility of sources, and motives for publication. Plaintiffs can also establish actual malice if they can prove a journalist fabricated a story or otherwise knowingly printed false defamation. The Supreme Court has ruled that public communicators can be required to testify about what they knew and were thinking when they wrote and edited defamatory stories.

FAULT FOR PRIVATE PERSONS The 1974 Supreme Court case *Gertz v. Welch* not only defined public figures but also eliminated the doctrine of strict liability in libel law for **private figures.** When the law holds the media to strict liability, publishers are automatically

[175] 441 U.S. 153 (1979).
[176] 781 F.2d 298 (2d Cir.), *cert. denied,* 476 U.S. 1182 (1986).

liable if they defame a private person, even if the media observe normal journalistic practices. Just as *New York Times v. Sullivan* established that the media could not be held liable by public officials who simply proved they had been defamed, *Gertz* established that the media could not be held liable by private persons who proved only that they had been defamed. Justice Powell, writing for the majority, said that private libel plaintiffs, who are more vulnerable and have less access to the media than public figures, should perhaps not have to prove *New York Times* actual malice as public officials and public figures must to collect general damages. On the other hand, Powell said, publishers and editors should not be automatically liable—subject to strict liability—if they defame a private person while observing the normal standards of journalism. Powell said holding the media strictly liable for libel of private persons would threaten the vigorous public debate the Court wanted to protect in *New York Times v. Sullivan.*[177] Since *Gertz v. Welch,* every person suing the media for libel must prove some level of fault.

All plaintiffs, public or private, must prove actual malice to collect punitive damages, but the Court in *Gertz* said the states may decide what level of fault private libel plaintiffs must meet to collect general damages. Four states require private persons involved in matters of public interest to prove actual malice, the same high standard that public officials and public figures must meet.[178] New York State sets a slightly lower standard, requiring private persons to prove "gross irresponsibility,"[179] a standard more rigorous than negligence but less demanding than actual malice. About thirty states,[180] the District of Columbia, and Puerto Rico impose the lesser standard of negligence, requiring private persons to prove that defamation was published with a lack of due care.

Negligence Negligence, the fault requirement most states have adopted for private persons suing for libel, is a standard of liability that is used widely in tort law. Negligence means a failure to act as a reasonable person would in similar circumstances. In libel law, the issue is whether a writer exercised reasonable care in determining whether a story was true or false.[181]

States apply the term *negligence* in one of two ways. Many states define negligence by an *average person standard:* the failure to do what "a reasonably prudent person" would do.[182] Other states define negligence by a *professional standard:* a failure to be as careful as an ordinarily prudent person in the same occupation.[183] The difference between the two standards is whether journalists' efforts to be accurate are to be judged by the standards of an average person who is perhaps unfamiliar with communications or by

[177] 418 U.S. 34548.

[178] Alaska, Colorado, Indiana, and New Jersey. *See* John McCrory & Robert Bernius, "Constitutional Privilege in Libel Law," 1 *Communications Law 1997* 53, 427–29.

[179] *See* Chapadeau v. Utica Observer-Dispatch, Inc., 341 N.E.2d 569 (N.Y. 1975).

[180] The states are Alabama, Arizona, Arkansas, California, Delaware, Florida, Georgia, Hawaii, Illinois, Iowa, Kansas, Kentucky, Maine, Maryland, Massachusetts, Michigan, Minnesota, Mississippi, New Jersey, New Mexico, North Carolina, Ohio, Oklahoma, Oregon, Pennsylvania, Tennessee, Texas, Utah, Vermont, Virginia, Washington, and Wisconsin. *See* John McCrory & Robert Bernius, "Constitutional Privilege in Libel Law," 1 *Communications Law 1997* 53, 419–26.

[181] *See Restatement (Second) of Torts* § 580B comment g.

[182] Memphis Publishing Co. v. Nichols, 569 S.W.2d 412 (Tenn. 1978). For lists of states adopting each standard, *see, e.g.*, John McCrory & Robert Bernius, "Constitutional Privilege in Libel Law," 1 *Communications Law 1997* 53, 433–39.

[183] Martin v. Griffin Television, Inc., 549 P.2d 85 (Okla. 1976).

what professional writers and editors would ordinarily do in similar circumstances. The average person standard does not take into consideration the daily difficulties of journalism, such as deadline pressures or uncooperative sources. When the professional standard is used, witnesses can testify to the kinds of behavior considered acceptable within the profession.

No court has provided a definitive list of journalism practices considered to be negligent. The Supreme Court suggested in *New York Times v. Sullivan* that a failure to check facts may be negligent. In *Sullivan,* the *Times*'s advertising staff may have acted negligently, the Court said, when it failed to check the paper's news columns to verify the accuracy of an advertisement calling for support for civil rights activities in the South.[184]

A single lapse in generally accepted reporting practices may constitute negligence, while it probably would not constitute actual malice. Negligence can arise through errors in note taking and mistakes in typing. Negligence often occurs because journalists rely on the wrong sources or fail to check facts. One academic study reported that juries are likely to decide a journalist was negligent if they find the following:

1. a failure to contact the person who is being defamed (unless there was a thorough investigation otherwise)
2. a failure to verify information through the best sources available
3. an unresolved disagreement between the sources and the reporter over what the source told the journalist[185]

A South Carolina reporter made several mistakes that constituted negligence when he erroneously reported that James Jones pleaded guilty to pirating stereo tapes in violation of copyright laws. Jones had been arrested and arraigned with his father, an uncle named Jack Jones, and two others. Two months later, the father and uncle pleaded guilty, but the charges against James Jones were dismissed. The reporter who wrote the defamatory story said a U.S. attorney had told him that James Jones pleaded guilty. But the official said he had read the reporter the names of the guilty directly from the record, a record that did not include the name of James Jones.

The South Carolina Supreme Court said a jury understandably decided that the reporter violated acceptable reporting standards because he did not check court records himself or contact the Joneses, whom he knew. The court said the six days between the guilty pleas and publication of the story gave the reporter ample time to check his information. The state supreme court reinstated a jury verdict of $35,000, which had been set aside by the trial judge.[186]

In a case mentioned earlier, a court found a Springfield, Massachusetts, reporter to be negligent when he relied only on a phone book for the address of Anthony Liquori, a man who pleaded guilty to conspiring to break into a business. The reporter obtained Liquori's name from the court record, which did not list an address. Instead of tracking down the address through official records, the reporter looked up Anthony Liquori in the phone book, assuming the person listed in the book was the man in the court record. However,

[184]New York Times Co. v. Sullivan, 376 U.S. 287–88.
[185]W. Wat Hopkins, "Negligence Ten Years after Gertz v. Welch," *Journalism Monographs,* Aug. 1985, at 93.
[186]Jones v. Sun Publishing Co., 191 S.E.2d 12 *cert. denied,* 459 U.S. 944 (1982).

the reporter attributed the guilty plea to the wrong Liquori; the Liquori who pleaded guilty did not live in the community.[187]

A reporter is not apt to be found negligent, however, if a story is based on several sources who told the same story or if a single source verifies the reporter's version of events. A Florida appeals court said a reporter was not negligent in falsely reporting that Hersh and Ogenia Karp faced deportation after being charged with illegally entering the country. In fact, no such charges were filed. But the reporter's source was an officer of the Immigration and Naturalization Service who had provided accurate information before. Fortunately for the journalist, the official testified that the published article accurately reflected what he had told the reporter. The court also noted that the reporter had tried to reach the Karps for their version of the events.[188]

Most courts expect that public communicators will make a good-faith effort to determine the accuracy of a news story. Courts do not usually demand that communicators investigate exhaustively before a story is published or broadcast. A journalist who contacts the persons directly affected by a story and checks information carefully with sources known to be reliable will not ordinarily be found negligent, even if a story is false.

Wire Services and Live Transmissions Courts have held the media are ordinarily not negligent if they publish defamatory wire service stories without checking facts in the stories. In one case, Massachusetts courts affirmed a summary judgment for newspapers sued for publishing wire service stories about a criminal investigation of Kenneth Appleby. Appleby, of West Springfield, said the media published false defamatory stories about an investigation culminating in his conviction for rape, kidnapping, and assault and battery. Appleby said he was damaged by false statements about his homosexuality, the torture and murder of young homosexual men, and his interest in the Nazi party. In all, Appleby sued ninety-four newspapers and broadcast stations in the region as well as the Associated Press and United Press International.

The Massachusetts Supreme Judicial Court, affirming the judgment of the trial court, said that the media's "reasonable reliance" on stories obtained from a "reputable wire service" was not negligence, even in the case of the *Holyoke Transcript-Telegram,* located about ten miles from West Springfield, near the sources for the story. The court noted that both the AP and UPI had excellent reputations for accuracy. The court said requiring individual newspapers and broadcast stations to corroborate wire service stories would be impractical, imposing a heavy burden on the media's ability to report national and world news.[189]

The Massachusetts court did not, however, indicate that newspapers and broadcast stations could always rely on wire service copy without checking it. If a newspaper or broadcast station has reason to doubt a wire service story, the Massachusetts court said, publication without verification could become the basis of a negligence suit. However, the court noted that none of the Appleby stories was "so inherently improbable or inconsistent" that the newspapers should have doubted their accuracy. Nor, said the court, was there evidence

[187]Liquori v. Republican Co., 396 N.E.2d 726 (Mass. App. Ct. 1979).
[188]Karp v. Miami Herald Publishing Co., 359 So. 2d 580 (Fla. Dist. Ct. App. 1978).
[189]Appleby v. Daily Hampshire Gazette, 478 N.E.2d 721 (Mass. 1985).

that the newspapers knew, or should have known, information about Appleby that raised doubts about the truth of the wire service stories.

The Michigan Supreme Court ruled the wire service defense protected the *Detroit Free Press* against a libel suit. The paper published an article quoting a former professional baseball player saying his cocaine addiction was due to the player's father having a drinking problem. The *Free Press* received the article from the Knight Ridder Tribune News Wire and republished it.[190] The state supreme court said the news service was reputable, the *Free Press* did not know the article contained any false information, and nothing in the story could have alerted the *Free Press* to any potential inaccuracies.[191]

The requirement that libel plaintiffs prove fault also provides broadcast stations with protection for defamatory statements on call-in shows and other live broadcasts. Some states have adopted statutes that protect broadcast stations exercising "reasonable care." A few states have passed laws that either provide broadcasters with immunity for defamation by callers or require private persons who sue to prove *New York Times* actual malice when libelous statements are made during controversial programs. Some states also limit damages for defamatory broadcasts.[192]

In the states that do not protect defamatory statements made during call-in shows, the courts have provided inconsistent guidelines for precautions broadcasters should take. In cases in which recklessness was at issue, courts have disagreed whether the failure to use a delay system during live broadcasts was reckless. The Montana Supreme Court said that a broadcaster is not reckless in failing to install a delay device that allows a talk-show host a few seconds to censor calls before they are broadcast. In *Adams v. Frontier Broadcasting Co.,* Bob Adams sued radio station KFBC after an anonymous caller said on a talk show that Adams had been discharged as state insurance commissioner because he was dishonest. The Montana Supreme Court said that use of a delay system could restrict a robust public debate because the device might be used to screen out only those ideas unacceptable to the broadcaster.[193] However, in Louisiana, a state appeals court said the direct broadcast of anonymous defamatory remarks without any attempt to monitor or delay them constituted reckless disregard for the truth.[194] Conduct that is not reckless may be negligent.

◇ Summary ◇

In *Gertz v. Welch,* the U.S. Supreme Court said that even persons who are not public officials or public figures must show fault to win their libel suits. Most states have said that private persons must prove negligence or a lack of reasonable care on the part of journalists. Negligence often involves the failure to check information adequately or to use the most appropriate sources.

[190]Jack Weiss & Amy Neuhardt, "Recent Developments in the Law of Defamation," 2 *Communications Law 1998* 21.
[191]Howe v. Detroit Free Press, 586 N.W.2d 85 (Mich. 1998).
[192]*See* Robert Hughes, "Radio Libel Laws: Relics That May Have Answer for Reform Needed Today," 63 *Journalism Q.* 288 (1986); Bruce Sanford, *Libel and Privacy* § 9.4.3, at 447–48 (2d ed. 1999).
[193]555 P.2d 556 (Mont. 1976).
[194]Snowden v. Pearl River Broadcasting Corp., 251 So. 2d 405 (La. Ct. App. 1971).

Falsity

Public officials, public figures, and private persons involved in matters of public concern must prove not only recklessness or negligence to win libel suits but also falsity.

PROOF OF FALSITY The Supreme Court made clear in *New York Times v. Sullivan* and its progeny that public officials and public figures must prove falsity in order to document *New York Times* actual malice.[195] But the Court did not establish in *Gertz v. Welch* that private persons must also demonstrate falsity to win libel suits. In *Gertz,* the Court said only that a private plaintiff must show fault, often negligence.

At least a few state courts had continued to hold that private-person plaintiffs could win libel suits without proving a defamatory statement was false. In those states, the media might have to prove the truth of their publications, and plaintiffs did not have to prove negligence. In 1986, the Supreme Court declared that private persons involved in matters of public interest must prove falsity as well as fault.

In *Philadelphia Newspapers, Inc. v. Hepps,* the Supreme Court ruled that the private persons suing, rather than the media defending, bear the responsibility for proving their version of a case.[196] In *Hepps,* a corporation that franchised a chain of Thrifty stores sued the *Philadelphia Inquirer* for linking the chain to organized crime. The *Inquirer* had said the Thrifty chain, which sold beer, soft drinks, and snacks, used its criminal connections to obtain favorable rulings from the state liquor control board. Pennsylvania law, consistent with *Gertz,* required the corporate plaintiff, General Programming, to prove negligence to win its suit. However, Pennsylvania common law did not require General Programming or other plaintiffs to prove the defamatory language to be false. Rather, Philadelphia Newspapers, Inc., and other defendants had the burden of proving truth to avoid losing the suit.

The Supreme Court ruled, in a 5-4 decision, that the Constitution required General Programming to prove the falsity of defamatory remarks as well as negligence. Justice Sandra Day O'Connor, who wrote the majority opinion, noted that public officials and public figures already had to prove falsity as part of *New York Times* actual malice. This First Amendment requirement protects speech about public figures and matters of public concern. To ensure that truthful speech was not deterred, O'Connor said the Constitution requires that private libel plaintiffs involved in matters of public interest must also establish falsehood. O'Connor said the question of who has the burden of proof in private-person cases becomes important only when the evidence is ambiguous—when truth or falsity cannot be proven in court. She said when it is impossible to "resolve conclusively" whether speech about matters of public concern is true or false, the Constitution requires the scales to be tipped in favor of protecting speech that might be true.

O'Connor said that as a practical matter, requiring private persons to prove falsity will not significantly add to their burden of proof. She said that if plaintiffs can prove that defamation was false, they will ordinarily have an easier time proving the media acted negligently. Justice O'Connor said the Court was not deciding whether a plaintiff, even one involved in matters of public interest, would have to prove falsity when suing a nonmedia

[195]N.Y. Times Co. v. Sullivan, 376 U.S. 279; Garrison v. Louisiana, 379 U.S. 64 (1964); Herbert v. Lando, 441 U.S. 153 (1979).
[196]475 U.S. 767 (1986).

defendant. Although private persons claiming to be defamed in a speech or an unpublished memo must prove negligence, they may not have to prove falsity.

MATTERS OF PUBLIC CONCERN The ruling in *Hepps* does not apply to all defamation involving private persons, only to defamation about matters of public interest. Private persons who are not involved in matters of public concern still must prove negligence but not necessarily falsity. The Supreme Court in *Hepps* said that it provided extra protection to speech about issues of public interest to encourage debate.

The U.S. Supreme Court has never defined "matters of public concern." In *Hepps,* the state licensing of a chain of stores that sold beer was a matter of public concern. In *Rosenbloom v. Metromedia,* discussed earlier, the Court said that a police campaign against obscenity was an event of "public or general interest." Other matters of public concern include investment reports sent to a readership of 200,000,[197] comments about product reliability on *60 Minutes,*[198] and criticism of the refereeing of a boxing match reported in the *National Sports Daily.*[199]

Private plaintiffs not involved in matters of public concern do not have to prove actual malice to collect punitive damages. In *Dun & Bradstreet v. Greenmoss Builders,* the Court ruled that Greenmoss Builders did not have to prove actual malice to collect punitive damages after the firm was libeled in a confidential credit report that was not a matter of public concern.[200] Dun & Bradstreet, a credit-reporting agency, had mistakenly told five subscribers confidentially that Greenmoss Builders had filed for bankruptcy. Dun & Bradstreet inadvertently attributed the bankruptcy petition of a former Greenmoss employee to Greenmoss itself.

The Court said the private credit report was not a matter of public concern and did not affect the debate on public issues, including "the free flow" of information about business. The Court did not indicate what other kinds of speech might be considered private. The term *matter of public concern* could refer to any issue discussed in the mass media but not to private conversations or materials released only to those with a direct personal interest in the information.

Summary

In 1986, the Supreme Court ruled that private persons involved in matters of public concern must also prove that defamation is false.

Damage, Injury, or Harm

Under American libel law, persons who have been defamed are prohibited by the First Amendment from halting a publication or forcing publication of a retraction, but they can sue for monetary rewards for the harm they have suffered. Proof of harm is the sixth element of a plaintiff's libel case. A plaintiff cannot sue successfully over a harmless libel,

[197]Straw v. Chase Revel, Inc., 813 F.2d 356 (11th Cir. 1987).
[198]Unelko Corp. v. Andy Rooney, 912 F.2d 1049 (9th Cir. 1990).
[199]Don King Productions, Inc. v. James Buster Douglas, 742 F. Supp. 778 (S.D.N.Y. 1990).
[200]472 U.S. 749 (1985).

although some harm to reputation may be "presumed." Libel plaintiffs may sue for *presumed damages,* the loss of reputation that a defamation is assumed to cause. They may also sue for two kinds of *compensatory damages:* **actual damages,** which are awards for proven loss of good name, shame, humiliation, and stress, and **special damages,** which compensate for lost revenues and other out-of-pocket losses resulting from defamation. A libel plaintiff may also sue for **punitive damages,** awards imposed not to compensate for lost reputation but to punish the libeler.

PRESUMED DAMAGES Since *New York Times v. Sullivan,* the Supreme Court has made it more difficult for libel plaintiffs involved in public affairs to receive awards for presumed damages. Before *Sullivan,* successful libel plaintiffs won damages on the presumption that their reputations were damaged because a publication had defamed them. When libel damages were presumed and fault did not have to be proven, juries had wide latitude to make large damage awards to plaintiffs who were not necessarily harmed. If juries wished, they could punish unpopular ideas, thus inhibiting the press.

In *New York Times v. Sullivan,* the Supreme Court held that public officials could be awarded damages, including presumed damages, only if they proved *New York Times* actual malice. In *Gertz,* the Court said that public figures and private plaintiffs too must prove actual malice if they are to collect presumed damages from the media. Writing for the Court, Justice Powell said that the First Amendment required curbing the "uncontrolled discretion of juries to award damages" when the plaintiff has not been harmed.[201] However, private plaintiffs who are not involved in a matter of public concern may collect presumed damages without proving fault. In *Dun & Bradstreet,* a divided Supreme Court upheld a jury award of $50,000 for presumed damages to a building company libeled in a private credit report.

COMPENSATORY DAMAGES Compensatory damages compensate a plaintiff for the harm a libel causes a reputation. When determining compensatory damage awards, juries consider the degree of fault, the number of people who may have read or heard the defamation, the seriousness of the defamatory charge, the degree of injury suffered, and the character and reputation of the litigants. Two forms of compensatory damages are actual damages and special damages.

Actual Damages In *Gertz,* the Supreme Court said plaintiffs who cannot prove *New York Times* actual malice can collect only for "actual injury." Actual injury may include financial loss, such as a restaurant might suffer after a defamatory review. But the Court in *Gertz* used the term *actual injury* more broadly. "Actual injury," the Court said, includes "impairment of reputation and standing in the community, personal humiliation, and mental anguish and suffering." The Court said that such actual injuries must be supported by "competent evidence," although the Court said plaintiffs do not have to assign a dollar value to their actual injuries.

Elmer Gertz, the Chicago lawyer called a Communist by a John Birch Society publication, won $100,000 in actual damages. A federal appeals court said that Gertz had

[201] 418 U.S. 349–50.

demonstrated actual injury in part by testifying to his own mental distress, anxiety, and embarrassment. Several attorneys testified that lawyers' professional reputations would be damaged by false claims that they were Communists.[202]

In another case, a court awarded $50,000 in actual damages to a Virginia couple, E. Grey and Carolyn Lewis, who were falsely accused of physically abusing their son. Two articles and an editorial in the *Alexandria Port Packet* "horrified," "mortified," and "humiliated" Mrs. Lewis. She was "scared to death" she was going to be put into prison. She isolated herself for six months, lost sleep, and suffered stomach pains because of her "public humiliation." The Lewises also became afraid to discipline their five-year-old daughter for fear that someone would hear about it.[203]

The Supreme Court's requirement that injury to reputation be proven rather than presumed has had little practical effect on the size of damage awards. The Court has provided no guidelines for acceptable proof of injury. Proof of damage to reputation is necessarily speculative when monetary loss is not demonstrated. Personal humiliation and mental anguish, in particular, do not carry price tags. If a jury is convinced that a plaintiff has not been seriously damaged by a defamatory remark, the jury may award only *nominal damages*—an award as little as $1. Nominal damages also may be awarded when libel trials are held before judges, without juries. Comedian Rodney Dangerfield won his libel suit against *Star Magazine,* which had falsely said Dangerfield "swills vodka by the tumblerful, smokes pot all day and uses cocaine." The judge said Dangerfield had not proven serious damage to his reputation and awarded $1 in nominal damages. However, the judge also gave Dangerfield $45,000 in presumed damages because *Star Magazine* had acted with actual malice.[204]

Special Damages Special damages, unlike actual damages, require proof of out-of-pocket loss, such as financial harm to a business. Monetary loss is the only kind of injury sufficient to justify special damages. Evidence of special damages is required before plaintiffs can win trade libel suits. Some states also require plaintiffs to prove special damages when suing for slander or *libel per quod,* libel based on circumstances not apparent to the reasonably prudent editor.[205] Plaintiffs often have difficulty proving that their loss of business was due to a defamatory article.

PUNITIVE DAMAGES The large money awards in libel cases are usually assessed for punitive damages. Punitive damages are intended to punish a publication for defamation rather than to compensate the plaintiff for injury to reputation. Justice Powell said in *Gertz* that punitive damages are "private fines" levied by juries "to punish reprehensible conduct and to deter its future occurrence." Justice Powell and many commentators have said that punitive damages fail to serve the social interest of libel law: that of vindicating reputation.

Richard DiSalle, a former judge, was awarded $2.2 million, of which $2 million was for punitive damages, for an article in the *Pittsburgh Post-Gazette* saying DiSalle helped

[202]Gertz v. Robert Welch Inc., 680 F.2d 527 (7th Cir. 1982).
[203]Gazette, Inc. v. Harris, 325 S.E.2d 713 (Va. 1985).
[204]Dangerfield v. Star Editorial, Inc., 25 Media L. Rep. 1379 (9th Cir. 1996).
[205]*E.g.,* Rodney Smolla, *Law of Defamation* § 9.07, at 9-16.1 (1998).

to draft a fraudulent will.[206] Vic Feazel, a former district attorney, won $58 million in 1991 when he sued Dallas television station WFAA for accusing him of taking bribes to fix drunk driving cases. Forty-one million dollars of the verdict, the largest ever in a libel trial, was for punitive damages. The suit was eventually settled for $20 million.[207] If large jury verdicts are not cut back through out-of-court settlements, they are often reduced by judges.

Many commentators and the Supreme Court itself have been concerned that large punitive damage awards lead journalists to censor themselves.[208] To reduce the chances of self-censorship, the Supreme Court requires that all libel plaintiffs, except for private plaintiffs involved in private issues, prove *New York Times* actual malice to collect punitive damages. Some states, including Washington, Oregon, and Massachusetts, do not permit punitive damages.[209] Other states require plaintiffs seeking punitive damages to prove not only actual malice but also that the media intended to harm their reputations.[210]

The Supreme Court has upheld the right of plaintiffs to sue for "reasonable" punitive damages. Reasonable punitive damages can be very high. In a case that did not involve the media, a divided Supreme Court affirmed a $10 million award of punitive damages, an award more than 500 times greater than the compensatory awards in the case.[211] In 1989, the Supreme Court denied review of a newspaper's argument that punitive damage awards violate not only the First and Fourteenth Amendments but also the Eighth Amendment's prohibition against excessive fines. The Court rejected a petition for certiorari by the *Pittsburgh Post-Gazette,* appealing a $2.2 million libel judgment, all but $200,000 for punitive damages.[212]

In 1996, the Supreme Court for the first time overturned an award of punitive damages as "grossly excessive" in violation of the Fourteenth Amendment. In a 5-4 decision, the Court overturned a $2 million punitive damage award to an Alabama doctor, an amount that had been awarded because the manufacturer of his new BMW failed to tell him that his car had been repainted before it was sold. The Court did not define what is "grossly excessive" but said courts should consider the reprehensibility of the defendant's conduct, the disparity between the award and the harm suffered, and the difference between the award and the civil penalties authorized in comparable cases.[213]

The Court said the $2 million BMW award was not reasonable because the car manufacturer's failure to inform the doctor of the paint job was not particularly "reprehensible." Furthermore, there was a great disparity between the $2 million award and the minor

---

[206] "Aftermath of Libel Case Bodes Ill for Media," *Broadcasting,* July 10, 1989, at 37.

[207] "$58 Million Libel Award against TV Station," *Editor & Publisher,* Apr. 27, 1991, at 16; Kim Cobb, "Attorney Considered by Turner Gains Prestige in Libel Lawsuits," *Houston Chronicle,* Feb. 10, 1992, at A11.

[208] *See* Gertz v. Robert Welch, Inc., 418 U.S. 349.

[209] *E.g.,* Stone v. Essex County Newspaper, 330 N.E.2d 161 (Mass. 1975); Taskett v. King Broadcasting Co., 546 P.2d 81 (Wash. 1976).

[210] *E.g.,* Rodney Smolla, *Law of Defamation* § 9.08(3)(b)(ii), at 9-20.2 (1998).

[211] TXO Prod. Corp. v. Alliance Resources Corp., 509 U.S. 443 (1993).

[212] *See* DiSalle v. P. G. Publishing Co., 544 A.2d 1345 (Pa. Super. 1988), *appeal denied,* 557 A.2d 724 (Pa. 1989), *cert. denied,* 492 U.S. 906 (1989).

[213] BMW of North America, Inc. v. Gore, 517 U.S. 559 (1996).

economic harm—about $400—the doctor suffered, and there was a great difference between the $2 million award and the maximum civil penalty of $2,000 the doctor might have collected under Alabama's Deceptive Trade Practices Act.

Summary

The U.S. Supreme Court has said that public officials, public figures, and private persons involved in matters of public concern can collect presumed and punitive damages only if they prove *New York Times* actual malice. Presumed damages do not require proof of harm. Punitive damages are intended to punish a publication for false defamatory remarks. Public officials, public figures, and private persons involved in matters of public concern who do not prove *New York Times* actual malice must show actual injury in order to be eligible for damage awards. Actual injury is proof of damage to reputation or mental anguish as well as actual monetary loss. Special damages are awarded only after proof of monetary loss.

The Defendant's Case

Although the media are protected by the high evidentiary burdens placed on libel plaintiffs, media are not required to passively observe whether libel plaintiffs can meet their constitutionally imposed burdens of proving defamation, falsity, and fault. Libel defendants also have a number of defenses they can actively assert.

A complete defense in a libel suit is the truth, although truth may be difficult to prove. Besides, the truth is often unknown or unprovable, particularly in statements made during official proceedings. Thus, a common law privilege allows the media to accurately report to the public about the courts, legislature, and executive branch, even when reporters are repeating defamatory statements from trial testimony, courthouse filings, senate speeches, and executive press conferences. Communicators also have common-law and constitutional protection to express opinions about the quality of public presentations, including films, books, lectures, restaurant meals, video games, and recitals.

This section will discuss libel defenses that predate and often overlap the constitutional protections established in *New York Times v. Sullivan* and related cases. This section covers the defenses of truth, the media privilege to report official records and proceedings, and the protection for opinion. Other defenses that are discussed in this section are statutes of limitations, the absolute privilege enjoyed by government officials, a privilege for broadcasters fulfilling political programming requirements, consent, neutral reportage, self-defense, and a qualified privilege for internal communications. Any one of the defenses may defeat the plaintiff seeking damages.

Before the media defend themselves in court, however, they try to prevent a trial from starting. Often they seek *summary judgment,* asking a judge to terminate a case before it starts because the plaintiff has no chance of winning.

Summary Judgment

For plaintiffs to win libel suits, they must prove defamation, identification, publication, fault, harm to reputation, and usually falsity. If judges are satisfied before trial that plaintiffs cannot prove their cases, the judges may terminate the case before trial by awarding defendants **summary judgment.** During 1995 and 1996, defendants prevailed on summary judgment motions 82 percent of the time.[214]

The media understandably favor summary judgments because libel cases that end before trial do not go to juries; when they do, the media are apt to lose three times out of four. Summary judgments, which avoid lengthy trials, not only save time, avoid stress, and preclude big damage awards but also save lawyers' fees.

A judge should issue a summary judgment if the plaintiff's case is too weak to prevail and there is no "genuine" dispute over a "material" fact that the jury must decide. Judges cannot resolve factual disputes, such as whether the defendant published defamatory language or the plaintiff is a public figure. But if both parties agree on the facts, then judges can determine as a matter of law whether the plaintiff lacks any realistic chance of winning. If so, the judge may issue summary judgment for the media.

Summary judgments have been particularly useful in cases involving public officials and public figures, who must prove *New York Times* actual malice. The Supreme Court has ruled that trial courts must issue summary judgment for the media unless public officials and public figures can make their case with "clear and convincing evidence." Thus, the Court requires that libel plaintiffs meet the same demanding standards of proof before trial as during trial. In *Anderson v. Liberty Lobby, Inc.,* the Supreme Court approved a district court's decision to require the founder of a self-described citizens lobby to prove with clear and convincing evidence before trial that investigative journalist Jack Anderson libeled him with actual malice.[215] Anderson called the lobbyist an "American Hitler." The district court had issued summary judgment for Anderson, ruling that Anderson's thorough investigation precluded a jury from finding *New York Times* actual malice.

◇ Summary ◇

Judges issue summary judgments, in effect dismissing libel cases, when there are no factual issues in dispute and plaintiffs lack sufficient evidence to succeed at trial.

Statutes of Limitations

A state's **statute of limitations** is a sure and often easy way to defeat a libel suit. For almost all criminal and civil actions, prosecutors and plaintiffs must file a suit within a specified period which in a libel suit is usually from one to two years from the date of publication. A plaintiff may not initiate an action after the deadline for filing a suit has passed. Statutes of limitations serve freedom of expression by narrowing the period during which publishers must be concerned that a libel suit will result from the mass of information disseminated through many different media.[216]

In most jurisdictions, the statute of limitations is governed by the *single-publication rule.* This means the clock starts running when the libel is first published. Would-be plaintiffs may not claim a new publication—and bring a new libel suit—each time a defamatory

[214] "Group Reports Media Won More Libel Suits," *New York L.J.*, Aug. 13, 1997, at 6.
[215] 477 U.S. 242 (1986).
[216] For a list of state statutes of limitations, *see* Bruce Sanford, *Libel and Privacy,* App. C, at 819-822.1 (2d ed. 1999).

publication is sold or displayed.[217] However, a new edition of a publication or a new newscast may allow a person to sue a second time for what could be the same libel.[218]

A few states cling to the common-law rule that a libel is published every time the article is displayed, sold, or circulated to a third party.[219] In these jurisdictions, the media are in constant jeopardy because a plaintiff can sue any time after the first publication date, even long after the statute of limitations has run out on the original publication. How is the date of original publication decided? Most states use the date that the libelous publication is released for sale. For magazines and books, the release date—the date the magazine is generally available for readers—is usually before the date on the cover. Paperback books, too, are often distributed to the public before the dates their publishers declare as publication dates. Attorney Michael J. Morrissey unwittingly waited too long to sue the publishers of the book *Spooks: The Haunting of America—The Private Use of Secret Agents*. Morrissey sued on December 1, 1980, within a year of December 19, 1979, the official publication date of the paperback edition of the book in which he claimed to be libeled. However, a federal appeals court said the one-year clock for the statute of limitations began running on November 20, 1979, the date the paperback version "was generally available for sale in bookstores throughout the United States."[220]

Most courts have ruled that the statute of limitations clock begins ticking when defamation is published online, rejecting the position that online publication is "continuous."

◇ Summary ◇

Under most statutes of limitations, persons who wish to sue for libel must file suits within a year or two of the publication of the alleged defamation.

Truth

In most states, libel defendants will win if they can prove the defamation they published is true. Although proving the truth will still defeat a libel suit, the defense of truth is less important than it was before 1964 when defamation was presumed and defendants bore the burden of proving the truth. Truth became less important to media defendants when *New York Times v. Sullivan* and the constitutional cases that followed required libel plaintiffs to prove falsity and fault. Now if a plaintiff fails to establish that a remark is false, the defendant wins without having to prove the publication is true.

The truth of a publication or broadcast may be hard to prove because evidence is unavailable. A reporter's confidential sources may refuse to testify or may lack credibility if they do testify. Furthermore, reporters who testify about events they witnessed have no

---

[217]*E.g.*, W. Page Keeton et al., *Prosser and Keeton on the Law of Torts* § 113, at 800 (5th ed. 1984); *Restatement (Second) of Torts* § 577A (3) and comment on subsection (3).

[218]*Restatement (Second) of Torts* § 577 comment d; *e.g.*, Cox Enterprises, Inc. v. Gilreath, 235 S.E.2d 633 (Ga. Ct. App. 1977).

[219]*See* W. Page Keeton et al., *Prosser and Keeton on the Law of Torts* § 113, at 800 (5th ed. 1984); Bruce Sanford, *Libel and Privacy* § 13.2.4, at 630-31 (2d ed. 1999).

[220]Morrissey v. William Morrow & Co., 739 F.2d 962 (4th Cir. 1984), *cert. denied*, 469 U.S. 1216 (1985).

certainty that a jury will believe them. Convincing witnesses for the opposing party and skilled attorneys on the other side can cloud the truth.

The determination of truth rests on the overall impression, or "gist," of a statement. A story must be substantially true but need not be true in every detail. Minor errors will not destroy the defense of truth. The Connecticut Supreme Court upheld a summary judgment in favor of a Stamford newspaper, *The Advocate,* for a substantially true story linking state senator William E. Strada, Jr., to reputed crime figures. The story accurately reported that the FBI investigated a Strada trip to the West that involved talks with a crime figure, but the paper misreported the actual trip the FBI investigated. The newspaper inaccurately said that the FBI investigated a Strada trip to Las Vegas and New Orleans, when the paper should have reported that the FBI investigated Strada's trip to Reno, where he met a crime figure. The court said the story linking Strada to a crime figure was substantially true; the impact of the story would have been no different if the details of the trip had been accurate.[221]

The media will not be able to prove the truth of a story if important omissions create a false, defamatory impression even though the story contains true statements. In *Memphis Publishing Co. v. Nichols,* a case discussed earlier, the *Memphis Press-Scimitar* was held liable because it omitted critical facts from an article about a shooting.[222] The *Press-Scimitar* truthfully reported that a Mrs. Newton shot Ruth Nichols when she found Nichols and Mr. Newton in the Nichols home. However, the paper mistakenly implied that Nichols and Mr. Newton were having an affair because the paper failed to report that Nichols, Mr. Newton, and two neighbors were sitting and talking in the living room when Mrs. Newton arrived at the Nichols's house. The court said the paper's failure to report the innocent conversation between Mr. Newton and Nichols created the false impression that Mr. Newton and Nichols were committing adultery. The Tennessee Supreme Court said that literal truth of statements in a story does not protect an article that conveys a defamatory meaning.

◇ Summary ◇

Libel suits can be successfully defended with proof that defamatory statements are substantially true. Minor errors will not defeat the truth defense. Although defendants were once required to prove truth to win libel suits, the Supreme Court has shifted the burden so that libel plaintiffs must now prove falsity.

Protection for Opinion

Libel plaintiffs, as we have seen, must prove that a defamatory statement is false and published with fault. If plaintiffs can't prove falsity, they can't win their libel suit. Often plaintiffs can't prove falsity because the story they claim libeled them consists of **opinion** that can't be proven to be false. Thus, a Southern chef had no libel suit, even though he felt "defamed," when a newspaper reviewer wrote that his dinner was covered with "hideous sauces" and that he had been served "trout a la green plague."[223]

[221] Strada v. Connecticut Newspapers, Inc., 477 A.2d 1005 (Conn. 1984). *See also Restatement (Second) of Torts* § 581A comment f.

[222] 569 S.W.2d 412 (Tenn. 1978).

[223] Mashburn v. Collin, 355 So. 2d 879 (La. 1977).

The chef had no libel suit because the reviewer had stated an opinion that could not be considered a false, defamatory fact. The reviewer did not say the chef was transmitting communicable diseases, a statement that could be proven true or false in a laboratory. The reviewer simply said his taste buds rebelled at the sauces and entrees. Diners at the next table might have loved the food. How the food tasted is a matter of nondefamatory opinion.

The Supreme Court has established constitutional protection for statements of opinion. Indeed, the Supreme Court once said, "there is no such thing as a false idea. However pernicious an opinion may seem, we depend for its correction not on the conscience of judges and juries but on the competition of other ideas."[224] While constitutional protection for opinion is generous—extending to biting, caustic criticism inevitable in a democratic society—the First Amendment, the Supreme Court has said, has not created a "wholesale defamation exemption for anything that might be labeled 'opinion.'" Statements of purported opinion, such as "In my opinion John Jones is a child molester," are not protected opinion, the Supreme Court says, if they connote provably false statements of fact.[225] When a speaker says, "In my opinion, John Jones is a child molester," the speaker implies he or she knows unstated facts about Jones's activities.

Distinguishing opinion from false facts is no easy undertaking. Traditionally, courts have distinguished fact from opinion by considering such factors as the ordinary meaning of words, their verifiability, the social context in which they were uttered, and the media in which they were disseminated. Although the Supreme Court is mindful of these factors—and indeed employs some of them in its analysis of opinion—the Court has refused to adopt these criteria as a formal test for determining constitutionally protected opinion. Instead, the Court has proclaimed that an assertion is protected as opinion unless it contains "a provably false factual connotation." Libel plaintiffs who establish that statements contain or imply false facts still have the constitutional requirement to prove the statements defame them and are published with negligence or malice, but the media cannot claim constitutional protection for false facts couched as opinion. There are no connotations of false facts, the Supreme Court has said, when a writer employs exaggerated or figurative terms that are incapable of a factual meaning. Other expressions protected as opinion include vague terms, evaluations based on stated facts, and statements that are opinion because of the circumstances in which they are uttered.

EXAGGERATION AND FIGURATIVE TERMS Some words are so exaggerated or are used in such a figurative sense that the Supreme Court has said they are incapable of a factual interpretation. One case of exaggeration is that of Charles Bresler, a land developer in Maryland, who lost a libel suit against the *Greenbelt News Review* because the newspaper published "rhetorical hyperbole," not fact, when it said Bresler might have engaged in "blackmail." The paper repeated the epithet hurled by citizens who charged that Bresler blackmailed the city when he offered to sell land to the city only after the city rezoned a different parcel he owned.

In *Greenbelt Cooperative Publishing Ass'n v. Bresler,*[226] the Supreme Court said the term *blackmail* clearly did not imply the false, defamatory fact that Bresler was guilty of

[224]Gertz v. Welch, 418 U.S. 339–40.
[225]Milkovich v. Lorain Journal Co., 497 U.S. 1 (1990).
[226]398 U.S. 6 (1970).

a crime. "Even the most careless reader," the Court said, "must have perceived that the word was no more than rhetorical hyperbole, a vigorous epithet used by those who considered Bresler's negotiating position extremely unreasonable." As a matter of constitutional law, the Court said, the word *blackmail* was not libelous, at least in the context of a heated city council debate over a political and economic issue of intense public interest. However, the term *blackmail* could be defamatory if it was intended to mean that a person employed criminal means to gain advantage.

In another case of exaggerated language, the Supreme Court ruled that a newspaper did not defame a laborer in the charged context of a labor dispute when the paper referred to him as a "scab" and a "traitor to his God, his country, his family and his class." Noting that exaggerated rhetoric is "commonplace in labor disputes," as it is at city council meetings, the Supreme Court said the word *traitor* in a union newsletter did not convey a defamatory meaning when applied to an employee who crosses a picket line. Rather, the Court said in *National Ass'n of Letter Carriers v. Austin,* the word was used in a "loose, figurative sense."[227] It is impossible to believe, the Court said, that any reader "would have understood the newsletter to be charging" the workers "with committing the criminal offense of treason." The case might have come out differently if the word *scab* had been taken out of context to create a false impression.

The Virginia Supreme Court held the phrase *Director of Butt Licking* did not have a literal meaning and therefore was not defamatory. A student newspaper used the words to fill space until it could determine the plaintiff's actual job title. However, the newspaper inadvertently published the phrase without changing it.[228] The state supreme court rejected the plaintiff's argument the words implied "that she curries favor with others by disingenuous behavior" or "performs the duties of her job in an artificial, shallow, or other manner that generally lacks integrity," or that the words accuse her of committing "a crime of moral turpitude." The court said the "phrase is disgusting, offensive, and in extremely bad taste" but "cannot reasonably be understood as stating an actual fact."[229]

Courts also have ruled that words may be too vague to connote facts. The statement "That's the worst play I've ever seen" is protected opinion because it is so subjective that it is not "susceptible of being proven true or false."[230] Likewise, critics cannot be sued for libel if they conclude that a book is "uninteresting" or, as the cartoon character Butthead might say, "It sucks." Although vague terms may be offensive, they do not give rise to successful libel claims because they connote no facts that might be proven false.

OPINION BASED ON FACT If writers understandably prefer to avoid exaggerated, hyperbolic, and vague language, they can ensure that their expression is understood as opinion by stating the facts on which the opinion is based. Readers of opinions based on stated facts, like readers of hyperbole, have no reason to think that statements are factual. Opinion based on stated facts is sometimes called "pure opinion."[231]

---

[227] 418 U.S. 264 (1974).
[228] Jack Weiss & Amy Neuhardt, "Recent Developments in the Law of Defamation," 2 *Communications Law 1998* 11.
[229] Yeagle v. Collegiate Times, 497 S.E.2d 136 (Va. 1998).
[230] Phantom Touring, Inc. v. Affiliated Publications, 953 F.2d 724 (1992).
[231] *See id.; see also* KCNC-TV, Inc. v. Living Will Ctr., 879 P.2d 6 (Colo. 1994).

The U.S. Court of Appeals for the First Circuit ruled that two columns by *Boston Globe* writer Kevin Kelly were protected opinion in part because Kelly fully disclosed the facts supporting his conclusion that producers of a touring version of the musical *The Phantom of the Opera* were deliberately confusing the public.[232] Kelly said producers of the touring version were trying to make the public think they were seeing a more popular nontouring version produced by Andrew Lloyd Webber. Kelly wrote that Phantom Touring, Inc., was trying to boost the popularity of its modestly successful road version of *Phantom* by causing patrons to mistakenly think the show was related to Webber's smash London hit of the same name.

Kelly spelled out in his columns why he thought the touring company was "trying to score off the success" of Webber's play by deliberately employing "confusing marketing." In his columns, Kelly recounted how the touring company proclaimed in large type that its production was "The Original London Stage Musical," a headline that was technically true but, Kelly said, deceptively overlooked the fact that Webber's *Phantom* was the only version popular in London. Kelly also made clear he doubted the touring company sincerely wished to distinguish its *Phantom* from Webber's *Phantom* because the touring company's advertisements employed small type to state that the plays were different. Kelly also admitted in his column that he was being subjective when he concluded the success of Phantom Touring's show must be tied to the reputation of Andrew Lloyd Webber because the road show "lacked artistic merit" and any recognizable stars.

Because Kelly presented the facts on which he based his opinion, the court said Kelly's allegations against the touring company "could only be understood" as personal opinions, not facts that might be proven true or false. Just as exaggeration and rhetorical hyperbole are incapable of being considered factual, the court said, statements are recognizable as "pure opinion because their factual premises are revealed." Perhaps most important, neither of Kelly's columns indicated that he had more information about Phantom Touring's marketing practices than he reported in the articles. In other words, Kelly's columns contained no connotations of unprinted facts that might be proven false and defamatory.

Opinions may be supported not only by stated facts but also by widely known or easily accessible facts.[233] It is unlikely that O. J. Simpson could successfully sue for libel if critics continue to call him a murderer. Even though a jury cleared the former football star of criminality, widely known facts about blood evidence, Simpson's alibi, and earlier episodes of domestic violence would allow a reasonable person to express an opinion that Simpson killed his ex-wife.

Although opinions based on facts are protected, the facts must be stated accurately and interpreted plausibly. "Even if the speaker states the facts upon which he bases his opinion," the Supreme Court has said, "if those facts are either incorrect or incomplete, or if his assessment of them is erroneous, the statement may still imply a false assertion of fact."[234] The Supreme Court said a jury should determine whether an Ohio journalist made a false factual statement when he said that a high school wrestling coach lied to a panel investigating a brawl following a wrestling match. In *Milkovich v. Lorain Journal Co.*, the

[232]Phantom Touring, Inc. v. Affiliated Publications, 953 F.2d 724 (1st Cir.), *cert. denied,* 504 U.S. 974 (1992).
[233]Bruce Sanford, *Libel and Privacy* § 5.4.2.1, at 161 (2d ed. 1999).
[234]Milkovich v. Lorain Journal Co., 497 U.S. 1 (1990).

Court said a jury might conclude that the term *liar* in a column by journalist Theodore Diadiun was a false fact because it could be read to mean that the coach committed perjury.

The Court ruled 7-2 that wrestling coach Michael Milkovich may have been libeled when Diadiun wrote in the Willoughby, Ohio, *News-Herald* that anyone attending the wrestling match "knows in his heart" that Milkovich "lied at the hearing after . . . having given his solemn oath to tell the truth." Diadiun said in his column that Milkovich inspired fans to attack opponents from Mentor High School, although Milkovich testified that he was not responsible for the brawl in which seven were injured following a wrestling match between Maple Heights and Mentor. After the hearing, Diadiun wrote that Milkovich taught Maple Heights students a lesson: "If you get in a jam, lie your way out."

Writing for the Supreme Court, Chief Justice Rehnquist saw in Diadiun's column a factual statement—Milkovich committed perjury—that could be proven true or false. Diadiun's use of the term *liar,* the Court said, "is not the sort of loose, figurative or hyperbolic language which would negate the impression" that Diadiun "was seriously maintaining" that Milkovich "committed the crime of perjury." The Court remanded the case so that a lower court could examine testimony in an earlier hearing and trial to determine the truth of Diadiun's charge that Milkovich lied. Milkovich later settled out of court with the *News-Herald* for an estimated $100,000.[235]

TOTALITY OF THE CIRCUMSTANCES By the time the Supreme Court established constitutional protection for rhetorical hyperbole and opinion that does not connote verifiable fact, many courts had developed a more comprehensive protection for opinion that they were reluctant to abandon. Indeed, the Supreme Court does not escape contextual analysis when it distinguishes fact from opinion. Following a tradition reaching back into common law, courts examining the totality of circumstances distinguish fact from opinion by evaluating various factors, usually including an examination of the ordinary meaning of the statement, whether the statement is verifiable, and the linguistic and social context in which a statement occurs. These factors in various mutations are often called the "totality of the circumstances" test.

There is much overlapping of analysis whether courts distinguish opinion from fact by searching for factual connotations or by examining the totality of circumstances. When courts do distinguish fact from opinion by reviewing the circumstances, one factor they often analyze is the common usage or meaning of words, that is, whether a statement has a "precise core of meaning for which a consensus of understanding exists, or, conversely, whether the statement is indefinite and ambiguous."[236] Average readers are more likely to consider vague, subjective terms such as *undistinguished* and *embarrassing* to be opinion than they are more precise, definable terms such as *robber* or *child molester.* Journalists need to be wary of terms that have a legal—and therefore factual—meaning, terms such as *obscene* publication, *substandard* housing, and *thief.*

A second criterion often examined in the multifactor distinction between fact and opinion is whether a statement is verifiable, that is, whether it is objectively capable of proof or disproof. Value-laden, subjective statements such as *scumbag, dandy,* or *shrill* are

[235]"Wrestling Coach Settles Suit over Column," *News Media & L.*, Spring 1991, at 23.
[236]Ollman v. Evans, 750 F.2d 970 (D.C. Cir. 1984).

unverifiable opinion, whereas more objective, verifiable statements are factual. The Supreme Court in *Milkovich v. Lorain Journal Co.* said the term *liar* connoted facts the truth of which could be determined by a jury. The professional reviewer and critic wants to avoid statements that imply the existence of derogatory facts the writer cannot verify.

A third factor is the social context in which a statement occurs. Abusive words that in some contexts might be understood literally as fact in other contexts are understood to be exaggeration, rhetorical hyperbole, or opinion. The Supreme Court recognized the importance of social context when it ruled the word *traitor,* as applied to an employee who crossed a picket line, was protected hyperbole because "such exaggerated rhetoric was commonplace in labor disputes."[237] Readers expect opinion in heated political debates and public controversies.

Another criterion for distinguishing fact from opinion is the linguistic context. Adding verbal cues such as "in my opinion" or "it seems to me" may indicate opinion but not, of course, if the statement implies false facts. Courts are more likely to find opinion where statements are phrased as hypotheses rather than assertions. The First Circuit said that Kevin Kelly's *Boston Globe* columns about the Phantom Touring company established a tone of opinion by raising rhetorical questions—instead of making bald statements—about the integrity of the touring company's marketing. The Supreme Court considered linguistic context in *Milkovich* when it noted that Diadiun's article did not contain the "hyperbolic language" that might "negate the impression" that Diadiun was asserting as fact that Milkovich committed perjury.

Courts also consider the format of a statement when distinguishing fact from opinion. Readers are more apt to expect opinion in bylined columns and reviews than in objective news stories. The First Circuit noted that Kevin Kelly's *Boston Globe* columns appeared in a regularly published theater column, "a type of article generally known to contain more opinionated writing than the typical news report." The Supreme Court considered the whole of Diadiun's column in *Milkovich* when Chief Justice Rehnquist noted that the "general tenor" of the article did not negate the impression that Diadiun was asserting a fact about Coach Milkovich.

The U.S. Court of Appeals for the Fourth Circuit held the "context and 'general tenor'" of a *Forbes* magazine piece showed it was protected opinion. *Forbes* published three paragraphs about Biospherics Inc., a company that sells its shares through the stock market. In a column called "Streetwalker" and with a headline "Sweet-Talkin' Guys," the *Forbes* story said, "Hype and hope for a natural, noncaloric sugar substitute—called Surgaree—that the company's been 'developing' for 15 years." The story also said Biospherics's stock was overvalued. Biospherics sued *Forbes,* saying its stock went down in value because *Forbes* injured the company's reputation. But the court said the article was protected opinion, not fact, because it was irreverent in tone—the words "hype and hope," for example—and used "imprecise, casual language." Also, the court said "the article clearly disclosed the factual bases for its views."[238]

Book reviews are "a genre in which readers expect to find spirited critiques of literary works that they understand to be the reviewer's description and assessment."[239] In contrast,

---

[237]National Ass'n of Letter Carriers v. Austin, 418 U.S. 264 (1974).
[238]Biospherics, Inc. v. Forbes, Inc., 151 F.3d 180 (4th Cir. 1998).
[239]Moldea v. N.Y. Times Co., 22 F.3d 310 (D.C. Cir. 1994), *cert. denied,* 513 U.S. 875 (1994).

facts are more apt to be found in a "lengthy, copiously documented newspaper series" written after thorough investigation.[240]

Some courts distinguishing fact from opinion by examining surrounding circumstances say they are simply distinguishing opinion from statements connoting false facts as the Supreme Court did in *Milkovich*.[241] Other courts employ the multifactor fact-opinion distinction to protect a broader range of opinion than statements not connoting false facts. Courts in New York and Ohio, for example, employ a contextual fact-opinion test to protect a broader range of opinion under their state constitutions than the Supreme Court protects under the First Amendment.[242]

Although largely obsolete, the common-law protection of opinion, known as the privilege of fair comment and criticism, also relies on an evaluation of several contextual factors to distinguish fact from opinion.[243] Long before the First Amendment protected statements of opinion, the defense of fair comment and criticism protected critics, reviewers, reporters, and essayists who criticized public officials, persons involved in public issues, cultural presentations, consumer goods, and other matters of public interest. The common-law defense of fair comment and criticism, like state constitutions and statutes, may supplement the constitutional protection for opinion. But the media rely on fair comment and criticism infrequently because the common law often imposes the difficult and perhaps unconstitutional burden on the media to prove that facts are reasonable, that an opinion reflects the writer's actual beliefs, and that opinion is offered without ill will.[244]

◇ Summary ◇

Opinion is protected by the First Amendment, by state constitutions and statutes, and by common law. Statements may be protected as opinion, the Supreme Court said in *Milkovich v. Lorain Journal Co.*, provided they do not connote false facts. Protected expression includes exaggerated and vague expression that cannot be understood as factual. Also protected are statements reasonably based on known or stated facts. To distinguish fact from opinion, courts sometimes examine the circumstances surrounding a statement, including the common meaning of a statement, its verifiability, its social and linguistic context, and the format in which it appears. Opinion is apt to be found when terms are used hyperbolically or figuratively in columns and reviews.

Absolute Privileges

Some false and defamatory statements are completely protected by law. **Absolute privileges** protect the speaker of a defamatory message regardless of the speaker's accuracy or motives. Three absolute privileges are important to professional communicators. First, the

[240]Gross v. N.Y. Times Co., 82 N.Y.2d 146 (1993).

[241]*E.g.*, Phantom Touring, Inc. v. Affiliated Publications, 953 F.2d 724 (1st Cir. 1992); KCNC-TV, Inc. v. Living Will Ctr., 879 P.2d 6 (Colo. 1994).

[242]Immuno AG v. Moor-Jankowski, 567 N.E.2d 1270 (N.Y.), *cert. denied*, 500 U.S. 954 (1991). *See also* Vail v. Plain Dealer Publishing Co., 649 N.E.2d 182 (Ohio 1995), *cert. denied*, 516 U.S. 1043 (1996).

[243]Robert Sack & Sandra Baron, *Libel, Slander, and Related Problems*, 234–42 (2d ed. 1994).

[244]Bruce Sanford, *Libel and Privacy* § 5.2, at 142–43 (2d ed. 1999).

spoken and written words of public officials acting in their official capacity are privileged. Second, the media have an absolute privilege to defame a person who consents to be defamed. Third, broadcasters have been granted an absolute privilege to air the false defamatory speech of political candidates.

PRIVILEGE FOR GOVERNMENT OFFICIALS Government officials acting in their official capacity have absolute privilege from libel litigation. The courts have decided that open and uninhibited communication in government must be protected at the risk of damaging individual reputations. Public officials, it has been said, must be able to do their jobs without "the constant dread of retaliation."[245] Therefore, the official statements of executive branch officers and the remarks of legislators during official proceedings are privileged. Also privileged are all of the comments made during judicial proceedings—including those by judges, lawyers, and witnesses.[246]

U.S. senators and representatives are protected from libel suits by the Constitution, which declares that they "shall not be questioned in any other place" for "speech or debate in either house" of Congress.[247] This privilege, however, is not confined to statements made within the legislative chambers. Federal legislators enjoy the privilege when they communicate in committee hearings, legislative reports, and other activities integral to the consideration and adoption of legislation. However, the Supreme Court has said the federal legislative privilege does not extend to written and spoken statements beyond the legislative process. In *Hutchinson v. Proxmire,* the Court said that Senator William Proxmire's libelous criticism of Dr. Ronald Hutchinson's research on monkeys was privileged on the floor of the Senate but not outside the Senate.[248] Proxmire could be sued for defamatory remarks repeated in press releases, in his constituent newsletter, and during a nationally televised talk show. The Constitution shields senators and members of Congress from libel suits only for matters that are an "integral part of the deliberative and communicative processes," the Court said. Communication with constituents and promotional activities are not privileged.

States have enacted privileges for state legislators similar to those granted to members of Congress by the U.S. Constitution. Many states also provide either an absolute or a **qualified privilege** for lower-level legislators such as city council members. A qualified privilege protects speech only on certain conditions that vary from state to state. A qualified privilege can be defeated by such "abuses" as inaccuracies or common-law malice, to be discussed later.[249]

Federal executive branch officials with policymaking authority have a broader absolute privilege than members of Congress. In *Barr v. Matteo,* the Supreme Court said public officials are absolutely privileged for libelous comments made in the line of duty. Defamation by an official is protected, the Court said, even if the speech or document is not mandated by the job and is disseminated beyond the office. In *Matteo,* the Court ruled

[245]Gregoire v. Biddle, 177 F.2d 579 (2d Cir. 1949).
[246]*See* Bruce Sanford, *Libel and Privacy* § 10.4, at 491–98 (1999).
[247]U.S. Const. art. I, § 6.
[248]443 U.S. 123–30.
[249]*E.g.,* Rodney Smolla, *Law of Defamation* § 8.09[3], at 8-33, and 8.10[3], at 8-43 to 8-45 (1998).

that William Barr, acting director of the U.S. Office of Rent Stabilization, was protected from a libel suit arising from a press release in which Barr condemned two agency officials.[250] The press release said that the two officials, John Madigan and Linda Matteo, would be suspended for violating the spirit, if not the letter, of a federal law when they permitted employees to receive cash for accumulated leave time. Members of Congress called the cash payments "a conspiracy to defraud the Government of funds."

When Madigan and Matteo sued, the Supreme Court ruled that Barr's press release was absolutely privileged. It has long been thought important, the Court said, that "officials of government should be free to exercise their duties unembarrassed by the fear of damage suits" for libel they disseminate in the course of their duties. In issuing the press release, Barr was operating within the sphere of his responsibilities, the Court said. "It would be an unduly restrictive view of the scope of the duties of a policy-making executive official to hold that a public statement of agency policy in respect to matters of wide public interest and concern is not action in the line of duty," the Court said.

The *Barr* ruling has also been extended to protect officials when they send libelous letters or make libelous statements to grievance boards. States have also adopted an absolute privilege for governors and cabinet-level officers. In addition, most states provide a qualified privilege to lower-echelon officers of state and local government.[251]

CONSENT A settled area of law prohibits people from collecting compensation if they are harmed by activities they agree to. In libel, this means that people cannot successfully sue for libel if they initiate or authorize publications that damage their own reputations.[252] Explicit consent to defamatory publication is rare. Few people authorize the publication of remarks that may damage their reputations. However, in addition to explicit consent, the courts have, on rare occasions, recognized an implied consent. Consent can be inferred when the person suing for libel encouraged or participated in the defamatory publication, knowing what was about to be printed.

The Tennessee Supreme Court said that the Reverend Robert Langford consented to a defamatory publication when he agreed to talk to the Vanderbilt student newspaper, *Hustler,* about his suit for libel and privacy against the campus humor magazine. Langford, a Methodist minister, was suing *Chase,* the humor magazine, for falsely implying that his wife was sexually promiscuous and his one-year-old daughter wanted to be. Langford told the newspaper reporters that he wanted publicity about his suit against *Chase.* Langford encouraged the students to see his lawyers for details of the suit. Subsequently, *Hustler* published that Langford was suing *Chase,* reproduced the page in *Chase* that triggered the suit, describing the charges in Langford's words. Langford sued the paper and the magazine, but the Tennessee court said that *Hustler*'s presentation of the dispute was privileged because Langford had either invited it or consented to it.[253]

[250] 360 U.S. 564 (1959).

[251] *E.g., Restatement (Second) of Torts* § 598A; Rodney Smolla, *Law of Defamation* § 8.05[2] [a], at 8-19 to 8-20, 8.07[2], at 8-20.2 to 8.20.3 (1998).

[252] *See* W. Page Keeton et al., *Prosser and Keeton on the Law of Torts* § 114, at 822 (5th ed. 1984); Bruce Sanford, *Libel and Privacy* § 10.4.6, at 513–16 (2d ed. 1999).

[253] Langford v. Vanderbilt University, 318 S.W.2d 568 (Tenn. 1958).

PRIVILEGE FOR BROADCASTS BY POLITICAL CANDIDATES Broadcast stations have been granted an absolute privilege to air libel during political broadcasts. In 1959, the Supreme Court said that broadcasters would not be held accountable for defamatory remarks made by political candidates during time provided under the equal opportunities provision, Section 315, of the 1934 Communications Act. Section 315 requires stations to provide time to all candidates for an office once it has provided time to one. Yet the communications act also prohibits stations from censoring the remarks of political candidates.

In the 1959 case of *Farmers Educational and Cooperative Union of America v. WDAY*, the Supreme Court ruled that broadcasters are immune from liability if political candidates defame someone while the broadcaster is providing airtime under Section 315. The Court ruled that WDAY-TV of Fargo, North Dakota, was not liable when W. C. Townley, a colorful independent candidate for the U.S. Senate, accused the North Dakota Farmers Union of being controlled by Communists. Townley was granted time on WDAY under Section 315.[254]

In a 5-4 vote, the Supreme Court ruled that stations could not be held responsible for libelous comments they were required to air and could not censor. The Court said it would be "unconscionable" to hold broadcasters liable for defamation by candidates after compelling the stations to grant the candidates airtime.

◇ Summary ◇

Defamatory statements made by public officials in their official capacity are absolutely privileged and cannot be the basis of a successful libel suit. In addition, persons who have consented to the publication of defamation about themselves cannot successfully sue for libel. Broadcasters are also protected from liability when providing time to political candidates under the equal opportunities rule of the 1934 Communications Act.

Qualified Privileges

Whereas participants in official government activities may be absolutely protected from libel suits, reporters have a **qualified privilege** to report on official activities. Journalists do not enjoy an absolute privilege, but they too are protected from libel suits if their reports on legislative, judicial, and executive proceedings are fair and accurate. Professional communicators are also protected if they employ defamation in self-defense, while discussing matters of "mutual interest," and sometimes in news reports of public, but unofficial, events of public concern.

REPORTER'S PRIVILEGE A qualified privilege protects journalists who report defamatory comments made in official proceedings as long as the stories are fair and accurate. In many states, the stories also have to be attributed and printed without ill will. The reporter's privilege to repeat libel is justified by the public's need to be informed about government actions. Because most citizens cannot observe government directly, they depend on journalists who might not report on city council meetings, court sessions, and legislative hearings if the

[254] 360 U.S. 525.

journalists were liable for repeating defamatory statements at these official government proceedings.

The reporter's qualified privilege, the most important common-law defense in the post–*Times v. Sullivan* era, is one of the few protections for the publication of false defamatory statements by news sources. The defense not only defeats libel claims but also frustrates the filing of many suits.

The privilege usually protects only the reports of *official* proceedings, including legislative, executive, and judicial activities at all levels of government. The privilege covers reports of government actions and records as well as reports of meetings and hearings. For the privilege to apply, proceedings must have a legal basis and must deal with a matter of public concern. Usually, meetings must be open to the public, and documents must be available to the public.[255] Some states limit the privilege to the press.[256]

Official Proceedings: Legislative Branch The reporter's qualified privilege protects news reports of official proceedings of governmental bodies authorized to enact or repeal statutes. The privilege applies to reports of the activities of the U.S. Congress, state legislatures, county commissions, city councils, community school boards, and university boards of trustees.[257] There is usually no privilege from libel suits for reports of organizations, such as a local parent-teacher association, that do not enact enforceable legislation.

The privilege applies to fair and accurate stories about official meetings, hearings, and reports of legislative bodies and their committees. The privilege protects reports of the comments of anyone recognized to speak during official meetings. Reporters need not worry about the truth of the remarks in official proceedings or reports. Hence, the Barton County, Missouri, *Democrat* was privileged when it reported that a man speaking at a city council meeting accused Gregg Shafer, a local police officer, of "knocking up" the man's sixteen-year-old daughter. The comments came during a discussion of who should run the police department. A Missouri appeals court said the *Democrat* was not responsible for investigating the truth or falsity of the accusation. If a newspaper were responsible, the court said, it would be fearful of fully reporting derogatory statements made at public meetings of official bodies.[258]

Journalists will probably be protected by the privilege as long as a quorum is present, minutes are being taken, and the legislative body appears to be conducting official business. The *Passaic (New Jersey) Daily News* was privileged when it reported a defamatory comment made during an official meeting even though the meeting was not held in its usual place and the defamatory comment was beyond the subject for which the meeting was called.

The New Jersey Supreme Court recognized a privilege for the *Daily News* to report defamatory statements made by the Clifton city manager during a special meeting of the city council convened in a conference room rather than the usual chamber to consider fiscal issues. In response to a question during the meeting, City Manager John Fitzgerald said he did not promote Chester Swede and Raymond DeLucca to the rank of police sergeant because Swede and DeLucca had been "insubordinate" and "should have been fired."

[255]*Restatement (Second) of Torts* § 611 and § 611 comment d.
[256]*See* Medico v. Time, Inc., 643 F.2d 134 (3d Cir. 1981), *cert. denied,* 454 U.S. 836 (1981).
[257]*Restatement (Second) of Torts* § 611 comment d.
[258]Shafer v. Lamar Publishing Co., 621 S.W.2d 709 (Mo. Ct. App. 1981).

Fitzgerald admitted to having a few drinks before the meeting. After Fitzgerald retired a few months later, the council exonerated Swede and DeLucca of all charges. When the officers sued the *Daily News* for printing Fitzgerald's charges, the New Jersey court said the report of the council meeting was privileged. The court said that although the meeting took place in a conference room rather than the regular meeting room, the council conducted official business and minutes were taken. The meeting was not only official but also public, since the press was allowed to attend.[259]

The reporter's privilege applies to reports of defamatory statements in petitions or complaints officially received by a legislative body. Defamatory petitions to recall a public official may not be protected until the documents are accepted by the appropriate government office. In addition, reports of meetings and discussions by citizens' groups planning to submit petitions may not be protected before the petitions are submitted. Also unprotected are reports of defamatory comments in the halls outside a council meeting or legislative session. The remarks may not be considered part of a legislative proceeding, even if they are made by a council member or legislator and relate to the official proceedings.

Official Proceedings: Executive Branch The reach of the privilege to report executive branch activities is not always clear. But stories based on official reports are usually privileged. For example, the *New York Times* was protected when it reported the damaging conclusions of an investigation by New York City's Department of Consumer Affairs into the sales practices of air conditioner repair shops.[260] Likewise, the *Tampa Tribune* was privileged when it reported that the Stable Lounge was identified as a "trouble spot" in information provided by the county sheriff.[261] Also privileged, by a Massachusetts court, was an accurate report of defamatory statements contained in a commissioned government report prepared by private contractors.[262]

Generally speaking, accurate stories about officials acting and speaking in their official capacity will be protected. Most legal authorities argue that the reporter's qualified privilege is triggered when official conduct is clothed by an official's absolute privilege.[263] The higher the position of the officials, the more likely the reporter will enjoy a qualified privilege to report them. Articles based on official press conferences often will be privileged.[264] The California Supreme Court recognized a privilege for media to report libelous statements contained in a document released at a press conference convened by the state attorney general. The court said the press was privileged to report the names of ninety-two people named in a report by the state's Organized Crime Control Commission as being suspected of connections to organized crime. The court ruled against Gerald Hay Kilgore, who sued several media for reporting that he was identified in the report as a bookie. The court said that the media reports were privileged because they were accurate stories about a public meeting legally convened by a public official for a lawful purpose.[265]

[259]Swede v. Passaic Daily News, 153 A.2d 36 (N.J. 1959).

[260]Freeze Right Refrigeration & Air Conditioning Servs., Inc. v. City of New York, 475 N.Y.S.2d 383 (N.Y. App. Div. 1984).

[261]Hatjioannou v. Tribune Co., 8 Media L. Rep. 2637 (Fla. Cir. Ct. 1982). *See also Restatement (Second) of Torts* § 611 comment d.

[262]*E.g.*, Bruenell v. Harte-Hanks Communications, Inc., 23 Media L. Rep. 1378 (Mass. Super. Ct. 1994).

[263]*See* W. Page Keeton et al., *Prosser and Keeton on the Law of Torts* § 114, at 793 (5th ed. 1984); *Restatement (Second) of Torts* § 612 comment c.

[264]*See, e.g.*, Rodney Smolla, *Law of Defamation* § 8.10[2] [d], at 8-41 to 8-42 (1998).

[265]Kilgore v. Younger, 640 P.2d 793 (Cal. 1982).

In many jurisdictions, journalists are not privileged to report defamation contained in informal remarks by public officials made independently of an official proceeding or report. Journalists had no privilege to repeat libelous accusations contained in an argument between Anthony Mitchell, a prosecuting attorney in Camden County, New Jersey, and a local police chief. The argument took place in a judge's chambers after court had been adjourned. The New Jersey Supreme Court said the media had no privilege to report Mitchell's assertions that Les Rogers, a prominent Camden politician, had ordered the police to "fix" criminal cases. The court said Mitchell's comments were not made during official court proceedings and did not constitute an official statement of the county prosecutor's office.[266]

Stories about quasi-judicial proceedings in the executive branch are usually protected. In 1985, the *Louisville Times* was protected for most of a story reporting that Dr. Charles Pearce was being investigated for prescribing excessive or unneeded drugs. The article was primarily based on proceedings before the Kentucky Board of Medical Licensure.[267] Stories about public hearings may be privileged if the hearings are supervised by an official with the power to investigate complaints.[268] However, stories based on pending government investigations and on nonpublic investigatory documents have generally not been privileged.[269]

Arrest reports are privileged but usually only after a suspect has been officially booked.[270] The suspect usually must be officially charged with a crime, and the name of the suspect must be entered on a police blotter. The blotter itself—the suspect's name, address, age, and charge—is privileged in those states where it is a public record.

Journalists need to be particularly careful not to report arrests prematurely. It may be libelous to say that police "arrested" someone if police only question a suspect or "invite" someone to the police station. Furthermore, journalists may not have a privilege against a libel suit if no charges are filed against a suspect after the media report that police plan to file charges.

Reports of informal disclosures by law enforcement officers may not be privileged. Reporters may not be privileged when they rely on an officer's word at a crime scene, obtain information from an officer over the phone, or take information from a police hot line. For example, a court ruled that there was no privilege attached to information provided by a hot line in the District of Columbia that provided recorded crime reports. The *Washington Evening Star* relied on the hot line to write that John Phillips was charged with homicide after shooting his wife during an argument. The police later classified the shooting as an accident. The Court of Appeals for the District of Columbia said the hot line consisted of unofficial police statements rather than a privileged official police report. The appeals court allowed a jury award of $1 in nominal damages to Phillips to stand.[271]

[266]Rogers v. Courier Post Co., 66 A.2d 869 (N.J. 1949).

[267]Pearce v. Courier-Journal & Louisville Times Co., 683 S.W.2d 622 (Ky. Ct. App. 1985).

[268]Restatement (Second) of Torts § 611 comment d.

[269]But *see* Medico v. Time, Inc., 643 F.2d 134 (3d Cir. 1981).

[270]*See* W. Page Keeton et al., *Prosser and Keeton on the Law of Torts* § 115, at 836–37 (5th ed. 1984); *Restatement (Second) of Torts* § 611 comment h.

[271]Phillips v. Evening Star Newspaper Co., 424 A.2d 78 (D.C. 1980), *cert. denied,* 451 U.S. 989 (1981), *aff'g* 2 Media L. Rep. 2201 (D.C. Super. Ct. 1977).

Informal police reports may not only lack privilege but may also be unverifiable. The media often have no protection for defamatory statements if the police officer on the scene or the desk officer on the telephone denies a reporter's version of a conversation.

Journalists must also be careful not to lose a privilege to report from official proceedings by adding defamation from unofficial sources. Although the *Louisville Times* was privileged when it reported from official proceedings that the drug prescriptions written by Dr. Charles Pearce were being investigated, other information in the same story was not privileged. The *Times* was not protected for a paragraph reporting that seventy-nine-year-old Hattie Rose Ludwig contended she became a drug addict while a patient of Dr. Pearce. Although Ludwig's allegation had been used only to illustrate the charges under investigation in an official proceeding, it arose during an interview that was not privileged. When Dr. Pearce sued the paper for libel, a Kentucky appeals court affirmed a summary judgment for the newspaper in the case of the information taken from official proceedings. However, the court allowed Pearce to sue for the information obtained from Ludwig.[272]

Journalists should have little faith that the word *alleged* will protect them from a libel suit if the journalists are not quoting official sources. Journalists cannot claim a privilege to report that a crime is "alleged" if they lack an official source that the press is privileged to report, even if the source is wrong. The use of *alleged* may tell readers that the reporter is not the source of a charge, but reporters can still be sued for libel if they have no privilege to repeat false, defamatory charges originated by others. If journalists choose to employ the verb *allege* in a crime story, the subject of the sentence should be "police," "the grand jury," "an indictment," or some other official source, which is then accurately reported. Many good police reporters avoid the legalistic term *alleged,* preferring instead to report that "police charge" or "the indictment says."

Official Proceedings: Judicial Branch The privilege to cover judicial proceedings is particularly important because almost every issue taken to court is potentially defamatory. The reporter's privilege pertains to any statements during the official judicial process by all legitimate participants, including judges, witnesses, jurors, litigants, and attorneys. The *Flint Journal* successfully relied on the privilege after it reported from defamatory court testimony that a former local law enforcement officer had offered to protect drug activities.[273]

Also protected are opinions and conclusions that fairly represent court testimony. Federal courts in Massachusetts ruled that television station WCVB-TV fairly and accurately linked Willis Brown, Jr., to the disappearance and death of his wife in a report based on a divorce trial. The court said the station accurately reflected testimony at the trial when the station reported that Brown was a prime suspect even though Brown was never charged with a crime. Linking Brown to his wife's disappearance accurately reflected the "gist" of trial testimony that Brown was an abusive husband whose wife feared for her life, the courts said.[274]

[272]Pearce v. Courier-Journal & Louisville Times Co., 683 S.W.2d 633 (Ky. Ct. App. 1985). *See Restatement (Second) of Torts* § 611 comment f.

[273]Dicks v. Fiedler, 16 Media L. Rep. 2391 (Mich. Ct. App. 1989).

[274]Brown v. Hearst Corp., 862 F. Supp. 622 (D. Mass. 1994), *aff'd,* 54 F.3d 21 (1st Cir. 1995).

The privilege applies to fair and accurate reports of all judicial proceedings, no matter how minor the court. The privilege covers the report of indictments, trials, judicial orders, verdicts, and judgments entered at the court clerk's office. The privilege also covers reports of documents filed to support requests for search warrants. California courts ruled that the *Los Angeles Herald-Examiner* was protected from a libel suit by nightclub owners named as arson suspects in a police request for a search warrant. Arson investigator Gary Cooper's request suggested that club owners had set fire to their own clubs.[275]

In many recent rulings, courts have held that the privilege pertains to any aspect of a legal proceeding, from the beginning to the end. In California, for example, a news story about the filing of a complaint in a civil proceeding is privileged,[276] but the same would not be true in every jurisdiction. The reporters' privilege may also protect reports of depositions, which are sworn statements by witnesses under oath.

The press might not have a privilege to report about documents that are irrelevant to the case they are filed with. The New Jersey Supreme Court said that a newspaper was not privileged to report an unsigned document charging a male policeman with fondling a female suspect in violation of federal law. The document containing the allegations was attached to one filed in an unrelated state court proceeding involving disorderly conduct. The New Jersey court recognized no privilege for a misleading and unfair newspaper report and headline falsely implying that federal charges were pending against the officer for improper treatment of the female suspect.[277]

In some states, the press has a privilege to report only after a judge takes action in a case by setting a court date or meeting with the parties in chambers. In these states, if a judge has not taken action, news stories about the instigation of a civil lawsuit may not be privileged even though a complaint is filed with the court clerk.[278] Courts historically were reluctant to provide a privilege for news stories about the filing of civil complaints because the courts wanted to discourage frivolous suits filed only to obtain news coverage protected by libel law. For example, the courts did not want to allow vindictive divorced spouses to file complaints falsely charging their ex-spouses with various wrongs and then withdraw the suits after the press reported the charges. More recently, judges and legal scholars have expressed doubts that withholding the privilege to report judicial filings can frustrate a frivolous suit.[279]

Reports based on copies of court documents may not be privileged even though the copies are identical to filed documents for which coverage is privileged. A California appeals court ruled that a faxed copy of a civil complaint filed against a computer company was not privileged because the copy faxed to the press was not part of the judicial process.[280]

Ordinarily, the privilege to cover the judicial process extends only to proceedings that are public. Closed court sessions for juvenile cases and for the testimony of victims in sexual

[275]Cox v. Los Angeles Herald-Examiner, 286 Cal. Rptr. 419 (Cal. Ct. App. 1991).
[276]*See, e.g.*, Dorsey v. National Enquirer, Inc., 17 Media L. Rep. 1527 (C.D. Cal. 1990).
[277]Costello v. Ocean County Observer, 643 A.2d 1012 (N.J. 1994).
[278]*See* W. Page Keeton et al., *Prosser and Keeton on the Law of Torts* § 115, at 837 (5th ed. 1984); *Restatement (Second) of Torts* § 611 comment e.
[279]*E.g.*, Hoelficker v. Higginsville Advance Inc., 818 S.W.2d 650 (Mo. Ct. App. 1991); Bruce Sanford, *Libel and Privacy* § 10.2.3.1, at 469 (2d ed. 1999).
[280]Shahvar v. Superior Court, 30 Cal. Rptr. 2d 597.

assault cases are often not privileged. Similarly, in most states, stories relying on documents or records officially withheld from the public are not privileged.[281] Nonpublic documents often include papers filed in juvenile and divorce cases.

Although journalists should know the breadth of privilege in their state, they are not expected to make technical determinations of what constitutes an official legal proceeding. If a proceeding appears to be legal and if the officials participating act as if it is legal, an accurate report of the proceeding should be protected even if false, defamatory statements are made at a proceeding during which the tribunal exceeds its authority.[282]

Unofficial Proceedings In some states, reporters are privileged to report unofficial but open meetings held to discuss matters of public concern.[283] The privilege may apply to public meetings of union members, churches, political parties, civic groups, and medical and bar associations. The privilege could be used to report a chamber of commerce "forum" or a meeting to discuss the removal of public officials. The U.S. Court of Appeals for the Ninth Circuit ruled that the *Moscow Idahonian* was privileged when it reported defamatory comments made at an unofficial public meeting of citizens at Moscow High School. Some at the meeting had argued that a grand jury ought to investigate the legal maneuvers that followed a fight between a University of Idaho student and a lawyer named Murray Estes. One speaker had implied that Judge John Borg acted unethically when he dismissed a charge brought against Estes for assault with a deadly weapon. Borg sued the paper for libel, using Estes as his attorney. After a trial court ruled that the story in the *Idahonian* was accurate, the Ninth Circuit said the press was privileged. The court said the newspaper performed "its most valuable function" when it truthfully reported proceedings related to the administration of law. The court said the public in a representative government must be informed.[284]

Reports of private gatherings, such as the annual meetings of corporations, are not generally privileged. Such meetings usually are not concerned with public problems but with private interests, such as those of stockholders. However, in some states, a report of a meeting of a private organization may be privileged if the meeting pertains to matters of public interest and is open to the public.[285]

Conditions of Privilege: Accuracy and Fairness Any story and headline based on an official proceeding must accurately reflect what was said. Relatively minor errors will not defeat the privilege, but a substantial error or distortion can. *Time* magazine could not claim a privilege when it erroneously reported the reason Russell Firestone was granted a divorce from his wife Mary Alice, a case discussed in the section on public figures.[286] *Time* mistakenly reported that the divorce was granted because of Mrs. Firestone's adultery. Unfortunately, the *Time* reporter apparently did not know that, under Florida law, Mrs. Firestone

[281] *See* W. Page Keeton et al., *Prosser and Keeton on the Law of Torts* § 115, at 837 (5th ed. 1984).

[282] *See* Lee v. Brooklyn Union Publishing Co., 103 N.E. 155 (N.Y. 1913); *Restatement (Second) of Torts* § 611 comment g.

[283] *See Restatement (Second) of Torts* § 611 comment i.

[284] Borg v. Boas, 231 F.2d 781 (1956).

[285] *See* W. Page Keeton et al., *Prosser and Keeton on the Law of Torts* § 115, at 836 (5th ed. 1984); *Restatement (Second) of Torts* § 611 comment i.

[286] Time, Inc. v. Firestone, 424 U.S. 457–58.

could not have been granted the alimony the court awarded her had adultery been the justification for the divorce.

To be privileged, a story must not only be accurate but also provide a balanced presentation of the proceeding. A federal appeals court refused NBC a privilege when the network presented only one side of the famous trial of the "Scottsboro Boys." The court said that NBC's portrayal of the trial was not balanced enough to justify a privilege against a libel suit by Victoria Price Street, the white woman who had accused the nine black "Scottsboro Boys" of raping her in 1931. The court said NBC's docudrama inaccurately emphasized the boys' defense. NBC failed to include witnesses who corroborated the story of the former Victoria Price, the court said, while emphasizing portions of the trial that portrayed Price as promiscuous and a perjurer. The flashbacks the network used to dramatize events before the trial reflected only the story of the defense, the court said.[287] Of course, journalists can report the events in court for a day even if only the prosecution is presenting its case. However, reporters will be expected to report the case when the defense is presenting its side.[288]

Conditions of Privilege: Attribution and Common Law Malice In most cases, the media can claim a privilege only if they inform readers, viewers, and listeners that a story reports an official proceeding. This means that both the story and the headline must include an attribution. The former *Washington Daily News* lost a libel suit because it failed to attribute a counterfeiting charge to the Secretary of the Treasury. The *Daily News* printed a story without attribution asserting that William and Josephine Hughes were charged with making bogus money and passing the bills during an air tour of the country. The newspaper told the court it had obtained the information from an announcement by the U.S. Secretary of the Treasury. The U.S. Court of Appeals for the District of Columbia said, however, that the newspaper had no privilege to publish an unattributed defamation even though the newspaper report was similar to the official announcement.[289]

A few courts have ruled that journalists can rely on the reporter's privilege only if they base their stories on official documents rather than media reports about the documents. In Louisiana, a court ruled that the Baton Rouge *State Times* had no privilege to report false defamatory information from another newspaper, the *Morning Advocate.* The *Morning Advocate* was privileged when it made a "reasonable interpretation" of an ambiguous press release reporting that Ronald Melon had been arrested on three drug charges. However, the court said it could not grant a privilege to the reporter for the *State Times* who did not see the press release and relied on the report of the other paper.[290]

NEUTRAL REPORTAGE Historically, the media have not been privileged to report newsworthy but defamatory charges made outside an official proceeding. However, a few courts have adopted a legal defense that protects reporters who accurately repeat defamatory charges made about public figures. A doctrine called **neutral reportage** allows the media to report newsworthy statements by reliable sources even if the reporter doubts the accuracy

[287]Street v. NBC, 645 F.2d 1223
[288]*Restatement (Second) of Torts* § 611 comment f.
[289]Hughes v. Washington Daily News Co., 193 F.2d 922 (1952).
[290]Melon v. Capital City Press, 407 So.2d 85 (La. Ct. App. 1981).

of the remarks. Indeed, in the give-and-take of public controversy, reporters often know that one side or the other is lying, although they often don't know who.

The few courts that have adopted neutral reportage say the protection is important to permit the public debate of controversial issues encouraged by the First Amendment. Critics of neutral reportage oppose a legal defense for publishing statements a reporter knows might be false. Knowingly publishing falsity, after all, is actual malice, the critics of neutral reportage observe.

Legal recognition of neutral reportage arose from the controversy over the pesticide DDT. Three scientists sued the *New York Times* for reporting that the National Audubon Society called them "paid liars" when the society said "scientist-spokesmen" of the pesticide industry were being paid to say that DDT did not kill birds. The *Times* obtained the names of the scientists from officials of the Audubon Society, which earlier had accused unnamed industry scientists of misusing bird-count data to conclude that bird life in North America was thriving in spite of pesticides. The scientists' claims, the society said, were "false and misleading, a distortion of the facts for the most self-serving reasons."

A federal jury awarded $20,000 to each of the scientists, but the U.S. Court of Appeals for the Second Circuit reversed the judgment. The appeals court said the First Amendment protected the "accurate and disinterested reporting" of charges made by a "responsible, prominent organization" such as the National Audubon Society, even if a reporter believes the accusations are untrue, which was not the case in the Audubon story. The court said the public interest in being informed about "sensitive issues" requires that the press be able to accurately report, without fear of liability, newsworthy accusations made by responsible, well-noted organizations.[291]

Other courts have adopted the privilege of neutral reportage in narrowly defined circumstances. Usually, the charges must be

1. newsworthy and related to a public controversy
2. made by a responsible person or organization
3. about a public official or public figure
4. accurately reported alongside opposing views
5. reported impartially

In addition to the Second Circuit, neutral reportage has been adopted in only a few jurisdictions, including the Eighth Circuit, several federal district courts, and state appellate jurisdictions in Florida, Ohio, Vermont, and Wyoming. The privilege has been rejected by the state supreme courts in Kentucky and South Dakota and an appeals court in Michigan.[292] Courts rejecting neutral reportage object to protecting the media when they print statements known to be, or suspected to be, false. Indeed, some courts say they cannot shield knowingly false statements from liability because the Supreme Court has ruled that constitutional protection for defamation crumbles when statements are published with knowing falsehood.

[291]Edwards v. National Audubon Soc'y, Inc., 556 F.2d 113 (2d Cir.), *cert. denied*, 434 U.S. 1002 (1977).
[292]*See* John McCrory & Robert Bernius, "Constitutional Privilege in Libel Law," 1 *Communications Law 1997* 53, 500–12.

SELF-INTEREST OR SELF-DEFENSE People can use reasonable means to defend themselves against an assault, an unfair business practice, or libel. Thus, individuals and businesses are protected from defamation suits when they publish libelous statements to combat attacks on their own reputations.[293] For example, a manufacturer has a qualified privilege to defame a critic in response to charges the company puts the safety of its employees at risk.

Courts have held that the news media can use the self-defense privilege not only to reply on their own behalf but also on behalf of others whose character or professional competency have been maligned in their newspapers and broadcast programming. For example, the Virginia Supreme Court of Appeals ordered a trial court to consider whether libelous attacks by the *Virginia Beach Sun-News* on a competing paper's editor were privileged publications in self-defense and in defense of public officials criticized by the editor. Virginia's supreme court said a trial court had not adequately considered self-defense when it awarded $30,000 in damages to the competing editor, J. Willcox Dunn, after the *Sun-News* called him a "deliberate liar" and a "fugitive from truth." The *Sun-News* defamed Dunn, editor of the *Princess Anne Free Press,* after Dunn charged that the *Sun-News* and a majority of local officeholders were part of a political machine associated with criminals.[294]

PRIVILEGES FOR MESSAGES OF MUTUAL INTEREST Two related privileges protect communications among persons with common interests. In the first, members of an organization are privileged in their discussions of mutual affairs. The privilege protects communications between business partners and corporate employees that defame third parties. Therefore, the mutual interest privilege protects conversations in newsrooms about potentially defamatory stories. The privilege also applies to defamation involving mutual interests among members of religious or professional societies, fraternities, sororities, labor unions, and educational organizations.

A second privilege protects defamatory messages that affect the welfare of the receiver, particularly if the receiver has requested the information. This privilege usually protects credit agencies, authors of letters of reference, and employees who comment to employers about fellow employees and customers. The Illinois Supreme Court said that a freight company would be privileged if it, in good faith, warned a mortgage company that a former freight company employee might be a risky mortgage applicant. The court ruled a jury should determine whether the freight company in fact acted in good faith when it reported to the mortgage company that the freight company was owed a "substantial sum of money" when the employee left.[295]

People or companies cannot claim a privilege for defamatory messages of common interest if they communicate the messages to people not sharing the same interests. Thus, a company cannot claim the common-interest privilege if it tries to damage a former employee by leaking defamatory comments to the press. The privileges can also be defeated with ill will or *New York Times* actual malice.[296]

[293]*Restatement (Second) of Torts* § 594 comment k; W. Page Keeton et al., *Prosser and Keeton on the Law of Torts* § 115, at 825 (5th ed. 1984).
[294]Haycox v. Dunn, 104 S.E.2d 800 (Va. 1958).
[295]Zeinfield v. Hayes Freight Lines, Inc., 243 N.E.2d 217 (Ill. 1968).
[296]W. Page Keeton et al., *Prosser and Keeton on the Law of Torts* § 115, at 828–30 (5th ed. 1984).

COUNTERING SLAPP SUITS The media are not the only libel defendants. Non-media businesses and nonprofit corporations are also sued for comments they make about employee performance or for comments to reporters when trying to protect their own business interests. Recently, citizen activists have been the subject of libel suits by the businesses and government officials they criticize.

The libel suits against citizen activists are called **SLAPP suits—Strategic Lawsuits Against Public Participation.** University of Denver professors coined the term to refer to lawsuits filed to muffle political expression. SLAPPs are filed to stifle opposition to a developer's plans to cut trees or to silence protests of police brutality.[297] Even though SLAPP suits are seldom successful, they often discourage citizen activism because defending libel suits is so time consuming and expensive.

A California court dismissed a $40 million SLAPP suit it said had been filed to silence critics of a housing development in the foothills of the Santa Cruz mountains. Parnas Corporation sued Victor Monia for libel after he circulated a flier that linked Parnas to alleged conflicts of interests by the mayor of Fremont. Monia, the president of the West Valley Taxpayers and Environment Association, had been leading a fight to prevent the building of million-dollar homes by Parnas, a San Francisco development company. The Parnas suit was dismissed after Monia argued in court that the claims in the flier were substantially true. A California appellate court affirmed a trial court's decision that the Parnas suit was filed to chill the environmentalists' speech, a strategy the appeals court said was "repugnant to the ideal of American democracy."[298]

One way citizens fight SLAPP suits is to countersue, as Monia did Parnas, contending the original suit was filed from spite and maliciousness rather than on legitimate legal grounds. In the countersuit, Monia won a jury award of $260,000 for Parnas's malicious prosecution of the libel suit. Citizens confronted with a SLAPP suit may also contend their constitutional rights have been violated. Citizens can argue that their First Amendment right "to petition the government for a redress of grievances" is violated when they are "SLAPPed" for complaining to the government about a business or governmental activity.[299] A third protection for SLAPP suit defendants, in at least California and New York, is an anti-SLAPP statute. In New York, plaintiffs in SLAPP suits must prove *New York Times* actual malice. In addition, defendants can recover court costs and attorneys' fees if suits do not have a "substantial basis" in law. Defendants can also recover compensatory damages of their own if the suit can be shown to have been filed to harass, intimidate, punish, or inhibit free speech.[300] Defendants in SLAPP suits can also claim their statements are protected opinion.

◇ Summary ◇

The reporter's qualified privilege to report official proceedings is the most important of the common-law defenses. Reporters will be protected from libel suits as long as they report

[297]Penelope Canan & George Pring, "Strategic Lawsuits against Public Participation," 35 *Soc. Prob.* 506 (1988).

[298]Monia v. Parnas Corp., 227 Cal. App. 3d 1349 (1991).

[299]*E.g.*, NAACP v. Claiborne Hardware, 458 U.S. 886 (1982); Westfield Partners, Ltd. v. Hogan, 740 F. Supp. 523 (N.D. Ill. 1990).

[300]N.Y. Civ. Rights Law § 70-a, 76-a); N.Y. Civ. Prac. L. & R. § 3211 (g). *See also* Cal. Civ. Proc. Code § 425.16.

official proceedings and records fairly and accurately, with proper attribution, and, in some jurisdictions, without ill will. The privilege does not protect the reporting of an official's informal comments outside of an official meeting. A few courts have declared that the defense of neutral reportage protects journalists who accurately report false defamatory statements by responsible parties about public officials and public figures. The charges usually must be newsworthy, related to a public controversy, and reported impartially, including a reaction from the person defamed. The courts also protect libelous remarks that are communicated only among members of a group with a strong common interest. The courts also protect defamatory information provided to individuals or organizations for their well-being. Businesses can publish defamation to protect their interests. An individual or mass medium cannot be successfully sued for libel if the defamatory remarks were made in reply to libelous remarks first uttered by the plaintiff. Communicators critical of government and business have been harassed by libel suits designed to intimidate, but some communicators have successfully sued back.

Preventing Libel Suits

Legal defenses may protect a publication once a libel suit is filed, but litigation is expensive and exhausting. Often communicators can avoid libel suits if they respond promptly and respectfully to disgruntled readers and viewers. People who think the media have defamed them might decide not to sue if they believe the media take their complaints seriously, respond to their questions, and, if warranted, publish a retraction. In some states, communicators lessen damage awards for libel if they publish a retraction.

Handling Complaints

A study published by three scholars at the University of Iowa suggests that old-fashioned courtesy may be one of the best deterrents to a libel suit. Professors Randall Bezanson, Gilbert Cranberg, and John Soloski found that libel plaintiffs usually sue only after they decide that they have been treated rudely by the press. Plaintiffs typically do not sue immediately after seeing what they believe to be an inaccurate story about them in the media. The Iowa researchers found that about half of the 160 libel plaintiffs studied said they asked the media for an explanation before contacting a lawyer or filing a complaint. The readers became plaintiffs, the researchers said, after media personnel assured them the media make no mistakes, gave them the bureaucratic runaround, or cursed them for complaining.

The Iowa professors noted that journalists are conditioned to resist businesses, politicians, and average citizens who attempt to use the media for publicity of dubious news value. Arnold Garson, then of the *Des Moines Register,* said that limited space forces journalists "to say no every day"—to the couple seeking publication of their daughter's beauty contest photo, to the business with a commercial promotion, and to the politician cutting a ribbon. Garson said that the same tough mind-set unfortunately carries over to communicators' dealings with readers and viewers who may have been wronged by a story. "We ought to have a good deal more compassion and understanding and take a good deal more time in hearing people out," Garson said.[301]

[301]Gilbert Cranberg, "Fanning the Fire: The Media's Role in Libel Litigation," 71 *Iowa L. Rev.* 221, 222 (1985).

The Iowa project stressed communicators' need to become less defensive about complaints. People agitated by news coverage want to believe they have been listened to. The researchers said that editors should teach reporters how the press can damage reputations, and journalists should respond promptly and courteously to complaints. The professors also suggested the media develop systematic procedures for handling complaints, a recommendation that many media organizations have followed.

Retractions

Publishers may also avoid a libel suit by printing a retraction. Some people who believe they have been defamed refrain from suing if a newspaper or broadcast station corrects the error.

A retraction can be a part of a written settlement, signed by both parties, in which the person complaining agrees not to sue. In addition, more than thirty states have retraction statutes providing protection to media willing to retract false defamatory publications. The retraction statutes vary widely. Some prohibit the recovery of punitive damages if a newspaper or broadcast station retracts a defamatory falsehood. Other statutes restrict the plaintiff to recovering special damages through proof of out-of-pocket loss if a retraction is published.[302]

In many states, a reader or viewer must request a retraction within a certain time after the publication. Often, a statute requires that the media be given an opportunity to retract before a suit is filed. Even if a retraction does not reduce damages by law, a jury may award lower damages if the media publish a retraction.

Wisconsin prohibits plaintiffs from suing a "newspaper, magazine or periodical" before first allowing the publication a chance to correct the error. Plaintiffs are denied punitive damages if a proper, timely correction is published. However, a Wisconsin appeals court recently ruled that a libel plaintiff could sue the SportsNet electronic bulletin board without first asking for a retraction that would preclude punitive damages. The court said a plaintiff need not ask a bulletin board for a retraction before filing suit because a bulletin board is not a newspaper, magazine, or periodical. An electronic bulletin board is a "random communication," the court said, not a publication that appears at regular intervals.[303]

To reduce damages, retractions must ordinarily be complete, fair, and free of damaging innuendoes. Retractions need to be an honest effort to repair damage. They often need to be published within a limited amount of time and given the same emphasis and prominence as the defamatory statement. A California court said the *San Francisco Examiner* did not meet the statutory requirement that a retraction be given the same prominence as the defamation when the paper retracted on a Wednesday a libel that was published on a Sunday. A Sunday edition of the paper with a circulation of 450,000 erroneously identified the suspect in a shooting as Willie Lee Beasley instead of Willie Ray Beasley. The court was not satisfied when the paper published a retraction in a Wednesday edition with a circulation of 150,000. The court said the retraction was not published "in as conspicuous a manner" as the libel.[304]

It is usually best for communicators to consult an attorney before printing a retraction. A lawyer can ensure that a retraction does not exacerbate a complaint. A retraction that

[302] *E.g.*, Bruce Sanford, *Libel and Privacy* § 12.3, at 589–94; App. B, at 773–812 (2d ed. 1999).
[303] Its In the Cards, Inc. v. Fuschetto, 535 N.W.2d 11 (Wis. App. 1995).
[304] Beasley v. Hearst Corp., 11 Media L. Rep. 2067 (Cal. Super. Ct. 1985).

repeats a libel may provoke a suit instead of keeping a publication or broadcast station out of court. In addition, a retraction written without legal assistance might not meet state statutory requirements.

◇ Summary ◇

The media may avoid libel suits if they respond to informal complaints promptly and courteously. Sometimes the media can avoid damages by printing retractions, particularly if the retractions meet the requirements of state retraction statutes.

Ideas for Reform

Despite media efforts to handle complaints professionally and publish retractions, libel suits and threats of suits are a continuing burden. Media companies lose two-thirds of the libel suits tried before a jury, and plaintiffs are frequently awarded more than a million dollars in damages. Even the costs of successful defenses are high. Premiums for libel insurance policies are also high.

Like the media, libel plaintiffs are usually unsatisfied with libel law. Expensive trials seldom vindicate reputations because the litigation focuses on constitutional questions of malice rather than on the truth or falsity of a defamatory story. Although libel plaintiffs frequently win awards from juries, they usually lose on appeal. Even if libel plaintiffs prevail in court, they win money, not a restored reputation.

Because libel law is so unsatisfying to communicators and consumers, several reforms have been proposed by scholars, lawyers, and reform groups.[305] Many of the proposals recommend streamlining the process of settling libel disputes and focusing on issues of truth and falsity rather than on issues of negligence and *New York Times* actual malice. The University of Iowa project suggested that both sides to a libel dispute voluntarily submit to arbitration, after which the press would publish whether the offending story was found to be true or false. Under the Iowa proposal, no money would change hands. However, the Iowa project floundered because people were unwilling to experiment with resolving disputes outside the judicial system.[306]

Several libel reform proposals recommend judicial declarations, called *declaratory judgments,* on the truth or falsity of disputed stories. One proposal would allow defamed parties to vindicate their reputations by determining truth rather than seeking a large payment. Under this plan, aggrieved persons could not sue for damages if the media retracted the libel or allowed the potential plaintiff to reply. If the parties were to refuse retractions and replies, a plaintiff could sue for compensatory but not punitive damages.[307]

Critics of the proposed declaratory judgments, argue that defendants would be required, in effect, to waive their constitutional protections—the constitutional requirement

[305]*See generally, Reforming Libel Law* (John Soloski & Randall P. Bezanson eds., 1992), and Donald Gillmor, *Power, Publicity, and the Abuse of Libel Law* (1992).

[306]*See generally* Roselle Wissler et al., "Resolving Libel Disputes Out of Court: The Libel Dispute Resolution Program," in *Reforming Libel Law* (John Soloski & Randall Bezanson eds., 1992).

[307]Rodney Smolla, "The Annenberg Libel Reform Proposal," in *Reforming Libel Law* (John Soloski & Randall P. Bezanson eds., 1992).

that libel plaintiffs prove fault—if a plaintiff sued for a declaratory judgment of the truth. On the other side, plaintiffs' lawyers argue that plaintiffs should not have to abandon large damage awards as would be required if the media sought a determination of the truth instead of large damage awards.[308] Both sides object that attorneys' fees might be the biggest awards in lengthy litigation whose only goal was to determine the truth.

One reform proposal would deny libel plaintiffs all damages, except for "economic loss," if the media publish a "timely" and "sufficient" correction or clarification. North Dakota adopted the proposal, the Uniform Correction or Clarification of Defamation Act in 1995,[309] but other states failed to follow, despite an endorsement for the model statute by the American Bar Association.[310] The uniform defamation law would halt huge jury awards of general and punitive damages when there is no economic loss. Under the North Dakota correction or clarification law, an individual or corporation can sue only for out-of-pocket loss caused by "a false and defamatory publication" if the publisher or broadcaster corrects or clarifies the false statements in a manner "reasonably likely to reach" the same audience as the libel. The correction might be made at the initiative of the publisher or, more likely, in response to a request by a plaintiff. Under the law, requesters can sue only for monetary damages if the correction appears within forty-five days after the plaintiff requests it. Plaintiffs have ninety days to make the request after they learn of the defamation.

Summary

Dissatisfaction with libel law by both the media and persons who contend that they have been defamed has led to several reform proposals. Fearing loss of constitutional protections, the media have opposed many reform efforts. There was limited support for the Uniform Correction or Clarification of Defamation Act, which would allow damages only for economic loss if the media adequately corrected or clarified defamation.

[308] Tony Mauro, "The Annenberg Libel Plan," *Wash. Journalism Rev.*, Apr. 1989, at 7.
[309] "News Notes: North Dakota Adopts Uniform Correction Act," 23 *Media L. Rep.*, May 2, 1995.
[310] "ABA Approves Defamation Act," *Editor & Publisher*, Apr. 2, 1994, at 13.

CHAPTER 5

Privacy

The right of privacy is a relatively new area of the law. Unlike libel law, the roots of which go back centuries, privacy law is largely a development of the twentieth century. The origin of privacy law is often traced to an 1890 article in the *Harvard Law Review* written by two Boston attorneys, Samuel Warren and Louis Brandeis. Warren and Brandeis argued that advances in technology and the voyeurism of urban newspapers necessitated new legal protections for privacy. "Instantaneous photographs and newspaper enterprise have invaded the sacred precincts of private and domestic life," Warren and Brandeis declared. "Numerous mechanical devices threaten to make good the prediction that 'what is whispered in the closet shall be proclaimed from the house-tops.'"

Gossip had become a business, in the opinion of Brandeis and Warren, and details of sexual relations were "broadcast in the columns of the daily papers."[1] Warren, who belonged to a socially prominent family, and Brandeis, who would later sit on the U.S. Supreme Court, argued that the individual had a "right to be let alone," a right to be free from publication of intimate information by a callous and increasingly powerful press.

It has been suggested that the two law partners were motivated to write their article by lurid press coverage of the Warren family, particularly by the *Saturday Evening Gazette*.[2] However, the *Gazette* seldom mentioned the Warrens' social life and then not in intimate detail. The *Gazette* did call Warren's father-in-law, Senator Thomas Francis Bayard, a "pompous turkey-cock," but such political hyperbole hardly invaded anyone's privacy.[3]

Whatever their motivation, Brandeis and Warren argued that a right of privacy is rooted in the dignity of the individual, a dignity then recognized in the law of trespass and copyright. The lawyers said a person's right to prevent trespassers on private property protects the integrity of the personality in a way that should also be protected from journalists who would disclose intimate information. The two authors saw the same personal dignity inherent in the copyright law, which protects writing and other creative expression from unauthorized copying. If the creative expression of one's personality can be protected by law, the Boston lawyers argued, so, too, should the privacy essential to the integrity of the personality.

The seeds that Warren and Brandeis planted were slow to take root in the law, but today nearly all fifty states and the District of Columbia recognize a legal right of privacy. The core of privacy still is, as Warren and Brandeis described it, the right to be let alone. The right to be let alone by the government is recognized in the Fourth Amendment to the Constitution which—though never mentioning "privacy" by name—prohibits unreasonable government searches of citizens' homes and papers. Broadly speaking, the Constitution protects from government intrusion places and personal effects in which a citizen has a "reasonable expectation of privacy."[4] Common law and statutes, too, protect a citizen's spatial or physical privacy from snooping, peeping, and secret electronic and photographic surveillance.

In many states, privacy law also includes the right to be portrayed accurately in the media and the right to prohibit the unauthorized commercial exploitation of one's name or picture in advertising and public relations. The Supreme Court has also extended the constitutional right of privacy to protect one's ability to make important decisions about marriage and the family, including decisions about employing birth control,[5] having an abortion,[6] and choosing one's sexual practices.[7]

---

[1]"The Right of Privacy," 4 *Harv. L. Rev.* 193 (1890).

[2]Alpheus Mason, *Brandeis, A Free Man's Life* 70 (1946); William Prosser, "Privacy," 48 *Calif. L. Rev.* 383 (1960).

[3]Lewis Paper, *Brandeis* 33–35 (1980).

[4]*See* Will Thomas DeVries, "Annual Review of Law and Technology: III. Cyber Law: A. Privacy: Protecting Privacy in the Digital Age," 18 *Berkeley Tech. L. J.* 283 (2003).

[5]Griswold v. Connecticut, 381 U.S. 479 (1965).

[6]Roe v. Wade, 410 U.S. 113 (1973).

[7]Lawrence v. Texas, 539 U.S. 558 (2003).

Beyond spatial and decisional privacy, the law protects informational privacy, an increasingly important arena as electronic databases store vast amounts of personal data gathered by banks, schools, credit card companies, brokerage houses, retailers, and the government. Privacy concerns become more urgent as computers—whose security is sometimes breached—amass private information in central databases that can be disseminated instantaneously over the Internet.

The Fourth Amendment recognizes citizens' reasonable expectation of privacy in their "papers," an interest in controlling information about oneself. Federal and state statutes, too, recognize a privacy interest in information by permitting citizens to inspect, correct, and control the release of medical, tax, and other personal information held by businesses and government. Statutes protecting information privacy include the Fair Credit Reporting Act, the Right to Financial Privacy Act, the Children's Online Privacy Protection Act, and the Health Insurance Portability and Accountability Act. These laws and others will be discussed in later chapters on commercial speech and access to information.

This chapter is concerned with four areas of common law and statutory privacy that affect the media. One is the publication of intimate private facts, a concern of Warren and Brandeis. A second is intrusion, a physical or technological invasion of a person's privacy. A third is "false light," which is the public portrayal of someone in a distorted or fictionalized way. The fourth is appropriation, the unauthorized commercial exploitation of someone's identity.[8] Related issues, which will also be discussed in this chapter, include the media's rare infliction of emotional distress and violation of civil rights.

Private Facts

Brandeis and Warren were concerned over dissemination of what they considered to be intimate information. One outgrowth of their concern is the private-facts or embarrassing-facts tort. The private-facts tort is defined in the *Restatement (Second) of Torts,* a summary of the common law, as a publication of private information that "(a) would be highly offensive to a reasonable person and (b) is not of legitimate concern to the public."[9] In other words, the private-facts tort involves the disclosure of very personal information, a disclosure that is not justified by the newsworthiness of the information. The U.S. Court of Appeals for the Second Circuit said the private-facts tort is publication of information that is "so intimate" and the publication of which is "so unwarranted" as to shock or "outrage the community's notions of decency."[10] In California, the line between legitimate public interest and invasion of privacy is drawn where publicity "becomes a morbid and sensational prying into private lives for its own sake, with which a reasonable member of the public, with decent standards, would say that he had no concern."[11]

Relatively few courts have found publication of private information sufficiently offensive and sufficiently lacking in newsworthiness to justify punishing the media. The Supreme Court has further diminished successful suits against the media by establishing a nearly impermeable right for the media to publish truthful information if the information

[8] William Prosser, "Privacy," 48 *Calif. L. Rev.* 383 (1960).
[9] *Restatement (Second) of Torts* § 652D (1977).
[10] Sidis v. F-R Publishing Corp., 113 F.2d 806, 809, (2d Cir. 1940).
[11] Virgil v. Time, Inc., 527 F.2d 1122, 1129 (9th Cir. 1975).

is lawfully acquired—usually from public records and public officials—and the information involves an issue of public importance.[12] Yet, there are instances when the media may be liable for the highly offensive publication of private information.

Unlike a libel plaintiff, the private-facts plaintiff does not sue for lost reputation resulting from false statements. Successful private-facts plaintiffs sue over publication of truthful information that is so intimate that revelation robs them of a part of their personality. Truth, therefore, is not a defense in private-facts cases. The successful private-facts plaintiff sues for shame, humiliation, and mental anguish. Also unlike libel, the publication of private facts is usually a tort only if dissemination is widespread. A defamation plaintiff can sue if a defamatory statement is communicated to one other person, but a private-facts plaintiff must usually show that a wide audience was exposed to the publication. The publication of private facts is a tort of publicity.

Highly Offensive Disclosure of Private Information

For a private-facts plaintiff to be successful, he or she must establish that the information publicized is in fact private and that dissemination of that information is highly offensive to the average person. It is generally true, as the *Restatement (Second) of Torts* concludes, that "There is no liability when the defendant merely gives further publicity to information about the plaintiff that is already public"[13] or if publication is not offensive.

The media are most likely to be held liable for the private-facts tort if they reveal intimate information about illnesses, mental disorders, intimate medical procedures, and hospitalizations without the consent of the subject. Because offensiveness is a jury question, what constitutes a highly offensive revelation of private facts varies from community to community.

In one well-known case, the Missouri Supreme Court ruled that *Time* magazine invaded the privacy of Dorothy Barber when the magazine published Barber's picture and a story about her unusual eating disorder. *Time* published a photo of Barber taken against her wishes as she lay in a Missouri hospital room. Barber's disease caused her to lose weight even though she consumed large amounts of food. *Time* referred to her as the "starving glutton."[14]

The Missouri Supreme Court considered *Time*'s acquisition and publication of the picture and story to be an invasion of Barber's privacy, a privacy supported by the legally recognized confidential relationship between a doctor and a patient. The Missouri court said the public could be told of Barber's newsworthy disease without the embarrassing revelation of her identity. Because Barber's unusual malady was not contagious, there was no need to reveal Barber's identity to the public to alert people who had been in contact with her.

Public revelations of children, particularly about their medical treatment, may also invade privacy. In 1992, Lifetime Cable Network and the BBC agreed to pay $175,000 to settle a privacy claim brought on behalf of nine-year-old Hilary Foretich.[15] The suit was brought by Hilary's father, Eric Foretich, after Hilary was featured in a television documentary on child abuse. In the documentary, Hilary was shown talking to her mother during

[12]Florida Star v. B.J.F., 491 U.S. 524 (1989)

[13]*Restatement (Second) of Torts* § 652 D comment b (1977).

[14]Barber v. Time, Inc., 159 S.W.2d 291 (Mo. 1942).

[15]"BBC, Lifetime Settles Foretich Privacy Suit," *News Media & L.* 10 (Spring 1992).

a therapy session. She was demonstrating with anatomically correct dolls how her father allegedly abused her sexually. After a federal court agreed that Foretich could sue for invasion of privacy,[16] Lifetime and the BCC settled without admitting liability.

Ruling that Foretich should be allowed to pursue a private-facts claim, the court said a jury could find the broadcast to be highly offensive. The court noted that seven-year-old Hilary Foretich would have to live for many years with "whatever consequences, good or ill," of the global broadcast of "what appear to be very intimate details about her personal life."

A plastic surgeon invaded the privacy of one of his female patients by revealing highly offensive photos in a public relations promotion without the patient's written consent. Dr. Csaba Magassy showed slides at Garfinckel's Department Store in Washington and in a television promotion of his patient, Mary Vassiliades, both before and after her plastic surgery. The public relations department of Garfinckel's arranged the presentations as part of a promotion on creams versus plastic surgery.[17]

A Washington, D.C., court upheld the jury finding that Magassy's presentation without Vassiliades's written consent was highly offensive. The court said the doctor and Garfinkels disseminated to a large audience medical information that was embarrassing and emotionally distressing. The Washington court agreed with the Missouri court in the *Barber* case when it said: "[C]ertainly if there is any right of privacy at all, it should include the right to obtain medical treatment at home or in a hospital for an individual personal condition (at least if it is not contagious or dangerous to others) without personal publicity." While agreeing with Dr. Magassy that the subject of plastic surgery was newsworthy, the court ruled that it was not necessary to identify Mary Vassiliades.

While Dr. Magassy was liable for disclosure of private facts, Garfinckel's was not because the store had reason to believe that Ms. Vassiliades had consented to the use of her picture. Garfinckel's public relations director had justifiably relied on Dr. Magassy, an authority in his field, when the doctor assured the department store that Vassiliades had given oral permission for the use of her pictures. The public relations director had asked Magassy specifically whether he had permission to use some of the more graphic pictures.

The South Carolina Supreme Court ruled that talking to a reporter does not constitute consent to have one's name published if the source does not understand the subject of a personalized story. The South Carolina Supreme Court ruled that Craig Hawkins, the teenage father of an illegitimate child, did not consent to having his name published in a story about teen pregnancies when he spoke by phone with a reporter. Although the reporter identified herself to Hawkins and to his mother during brief telephone conversations, the reporter did not ask Hawkins's permission to use his name in the story. Hawkins said he understood the newspaper was conducting a "survey" on teenage pregnancy, not writing a story in which individual minors would be identified as parents of illegitimate children, as Hawkins was. The court ruled Hawkins gave no implied consent because he never understood enough about how his name might be used to make an informed choice. Whether publication of Hawkins's name was newsworthy should be left to a jury, the court said. Hawkins obtained a verdict against Multimedia for $1,500 actual and $25,000 punitive damages.[18]

[16]Foretich v. Lifetime Cable, 777 F. Supp. 47 (D.D.C. 1991).
[17]Vassiliades v. Garfinckel's, 492 A.2d 580 2057 (D.C. 1985).
[18]Hawkins v. Multimedia, Inc., 344 S.E.2d 145 (S.C. 1986), *cert. denied*, 479 U.S. 1012 (1986).

The Public Domain

Private-facts plaintiffs can successfully sue only if the highly embarrassing information revealed about them is, in fact, private. In common law, courts refused the claims of private-fact plaintiffs whose "private" information appeared on public records, thus placing the information in the public domain. Robin Howard provides an example of the plaintiff denied relief because her deeply personal information—a sterilization—appeared on a public record and therefore was not private. The Iowa Supreme Court ruled that Howard could not sue for invasion of privacy when a newspaper published that she had been sterilized involuntarily while a patient at a government home. The fact of her sterilization, the court said, was a public fact because it was part of a record forwarded to the governor's office in a file of complaints against the home. "Because the documents were public," the court said, "the information which they contained was in the public domain," and Howard could not sue for invasion of privacy.[19]

In 1975, the U.S. Supreme Court created a constitutional right for the media to report information contained in records available in an open courtroom. In *Cox Broadcasting Corp. v. Cohn,*[20] the Court established nearly complete First Amendment protection for the media to report information from official records available in open court. The Court ruled 8-1 that a Georgia father could not bring a privacy suit against a television station for reporting the name of his daughter in violation of a Georgia statute. The statute made publication or broadcast of the name of a rape victim a misdemeanor.

The case arose from the 1971 rape and murder of a seventeen-year-old girl. Six youths were indicted for murder and rape, but the murder charges were later dropped. The victim's name was never publicized during the initial media coverage of the crime. Eight months after the murder, the six youths appeared in court to enter pleas to indictments for rape. During a recess in the proceedings, a reporter for Atlanta station WSB-TV learned the name of the rape victim by reading the indictments provided by the court clerk. Later that day, the station named the victim in a report about the court proceedings. The victim's father brought a civil suit claiming that his privacy was invaded by WSB's broadcast of his daughter's name.

The Georgia Supreme Court ruled that the father's privacy suit should go to trial, but the U.S. Supreme Court reversed. The U.S. Supreme Court said the First Amendment does not permit a privacy suit against the media for disseminating private information contained in public records that are part of an open court proceeding. "The commission of crime, prosecutions resulting from it, and judicial proceedings arising from the prosecutions," Justice Byron White wrote for the majority, "are without question events of legitimate concern to the public and consequently fall within the responsibility of the press to report the operations of Government." By their very nature, the Court said, public records "are of interest to those concerned with the operation of government, and a public benefit is performed by the reporting of the true contents of the records by the media."

The Court was reluctant to forbid publication of public records that might be "offensive to the sensibilities of the supposed reasonable man." Punishing the press for disseminating "offensive" public records "would invite timidity and self-censorship and very likely

[19]Howard v. Des Moines Register, 283 N.W.2d 289 (Iowa 1979), *cert. denied,* 445 U.S. 904 (1980).
[20]420 U.S. 469 (1975).

lead to the suppression of many items" that should be available to the public, White said. If there are matters at a trial that should remain private, the government should not put them in the public domain, White said.

Matters of Public Importance

Justice White noted in *Cox v. Cohn* that court records, which belong in the public domain, contain information about crime, prosecutions, and judicial proceedings that are "events of legitimate concern to the public." The *Restatement of Torts* defines private facts as information *not* of legitimate concern to the public. In 1989, the Supreme Court extended First Amendment protection to publication of nearly all information dealing with matters of public importance if the information is truthful and lawfully acquired. In *Florida Star v. B.J.F.*, the Court said the First Amendment protects publication of lawfully acquired truthful information about a matter of public importance unless prohibiting publication will further a state interest "of the highest order." The First Amendment requires that each privacy case be weighed individually, the Court said.

In *B.J.F.*, the Court reversed a judgment against a weekly Jacksonville newspaper for publishing the full name of B.J.F., a rape victim, in violation of a 1911 state statute.[21] The statute barred an "instrument of mass communication" from printing, publishing, or broadcasting the name of the victim of a sexual offense. A reporter-trainee for the weekly *Florida Star* acquired the name of B.J.F. from a government news release prepared by the Duval County sheriff's department. Although the sheriff's department distributed B.J.F.'s name, a sign at the department warned that names of rape victims were not matters of public record. The *Star* published B.J.F.'s name in violation of the paper's own policy not to publish names of rape victims.

In her privacy suit, B.J.F. claimed that publication of her name caused her emotional distress. She testified that her mother received phone calls in which a man threatened to rape B.J.F. again. She testified she had been compelled to move to a new residence, change her phone number, and begin mental health counseling. A jury awarded B.J.F. $75,000 in compensatory damages and $25,000 in punitive damages for the paper's violation of the statute. A Florida appeals court affirmed the jury award, and the Florida Supreme Court refused review. The U.S. Supreme Court reversed.

Relying on an earlier decision in *Smith v. Daily Mail Publishing Co.*, a case discussed in Chapter 10, the Supreme Court said the government may constitutionally punish a newspaper for publishing lawfully obtained, truthful information about a matter of public significance only if the government can show that punishment is "narrowly tailored to a state interest of the highest order." The Court agreed that the newspaper published lawfully obtained, truthful information about a matter of public importance. The *Florida Star* acquired B.J.F.'s name lawfully from the sheriff's department. Indeed, the department disseminated the information about B.J.F.'s rape, information about a violent crime that the Supreme Court said was of "paramount public import." The press would censor itself, the Court said, if it feared liability for publishing news stories based

[21] 491 U.S. 524 (1989).

on government press releases. If the government wishes to keep information confidential, the Court said, it should establish stronger safeguards on disclosure, not punish the press.

The Court also seemed to agree that the Florida statute served a state interest of a very high—if not the highest—order. The goals of the Florida statute—to protect rape victims' privacy and safety and encourage victims to report rapes without fear of exposure or reprisal—were "highly significant," the Court said. Nevertheless, the Court ruled for the newspaper because the Florida statute was not narrowly tailored.

First, the Court objected to the categorical nature of the statute's prohibition. The Florida law made the press liable whether or not the rape victim's name was already public, regardless of whether publication was offensive or inoffensive to anyone, and without consideration of the publisher's motives. Such automatic liability, without case-by-case weighing of competing values, motives, and damages, is unconstitutional when important First Amendment interests are at stake, the Court said.

Second, the statute would be ineffective, the Court said, because it punished only one means of publication: "instruments of mass communication." The statute permitted dissemination of rape victims' names by other methods, including word of mouth, thus failing to serve the purpose of protecting a rape victim's privacy. "When a State attempts the extraordinary measure of punishing truthful publication in the name of privacy, it must demonstrate its commitment to advancing this interest by applying its prohibition evenhandedly, to the smalltime disseminator as well as the media giant," the Court said.

Justice White, in a dissenting opinion joined by Chief Justice William Rehnquist and Justice Sandra Day O'Connor, argued that the majority opinion would "obliterate" liability for publication of private facts. "If the First Amendment prohibits wholly private persons . . . from recovering for the publication of the fact that she was raped, I doubt that there remain any 'private facts' which persons may assume will not be" disseminated by the media, Justice White wrote.

Although the *B.J.F.* court ruled that media cannot be held liable automatically for publishing the names of sexual assault victims, the Court said the media might be punished under a narrowly drawn statute or under common law. In either case, the courts must balance privacy interests against the public interest, the Court said.

In *B.J.F.,* the Supreme Court appeared to nullify the 1911 Florida statute. However, even after the *B.J.F.* decision, prosecutors in Florida charged the supermarket tabloid *The Globe* with violating the statute when the paper published the name of a Palm Beach woman whom William Kennedy Smith allegedly raped. Relying on the U.S. Supreme Court's decision in *B.J.F.,* the Florida Supreme Court declared unconstitutional the Florida statute prohibiting the publication of sexual assault victims' names in the mass media.[22]

Newsworthiness

Long before the Supreme Court ruled that the First Amendment protects publication of court records and matters of public importance, the common law had protected publication of an ever-widening range of newsworthy information. Many newsworthy events involved crime, official actions, and events of significant public importance. Some newsworthy

[22]Florida v. Globe Communications Corp., 648 So.2d 110 (Fla. 1994).

events are more ephemeral, in which case the disclosure of private information is usually less embarrassing.

A man who saved President Gerald Ford's life lost a private-facts case because the fact of his homosexuality was ruled to be in the public domain and was related to significant newsworthy issues. Oliver Sipple, a decorated Vietnam veteran and a well-known leader in the San Francisco gay community, deflected the hand of Sarah Jane Moore as she aimed a gun at President Ford during his visit to San Francisco in 1975. Sipple unsuccessfully sued several newspapers for revealing his homosexuality to friends and family far from San Francisco.[23] Sipple agreed that saving the president's life was newsworthy but contended that his sexual life was not.

A California appellate court ruled that Sipple's sexual orientation was not a private matter. Sipple's homosexuality was part of the public domain in San Francisco because of his activism in the gay community. His homosexuality was also of legitimate public interest, the court said, because his courageous act cast often-stereotyped homosexuals in a positive light. There was also a newsworthy question whether President Ford delayed public expression of gratitude because of Sipple's homosexuality.

Publishing Sipple's sexual identity was ethically complicated. Although Sipple said he was embarrassed, other members of the gay community, seeking positive publicity about gays, had urged the media to tell the public of Sipple's homosexuality. In ruling against Sipple in his privacy suit, the court said the publication was not intended to embarrass him. The court said publication was an attempt to "dispel the false public opinion that gays were timid, weak and unheroic figures."

Private-facts plaintiffs often lose their cases because they have the misfortune of being involved in significant newsworthy events that reveal personal or embarrassing information. Hilda Bridges lost a privacy suit against a Florida newspaper over publication of a photograph of her fleeing the apartment where her husband had just committed suicide. The photo in *Cocoa Today* showed Bridges running nude across a parking lot on the arm of a police officer. Bridges was rushed from her former apartment after her estranged husband fatally shot himself. He had earlier forced Bridges to disrobe and threatened to kill her. Police surrounded the apartment when they learned that Bridges was a hostage. The media arrived shortly thereafter. Police stormed the apartment at the sound of gunfire from within.

Although Bridges was holding a towel over her front as she fled the apartment, her hips were exposed in the published picture. The jury awarded Bridges $10,000 in her privacy suit against *Cocoa Today,* but an appellate judge ruled for the newspaper because the picture recorded a newsworthy event in a public place. Bridges's public exposure in an event involving a suicide, threatened murder, and police was of legitimate public interest, the court said, just as other crimes, arrests, police raids, accidents, and fires are of public interest.[24]

Courts have also cited newsworthiness to justify rulings against private-facts plaintiffs in cases in which the public was merely curious. Newsworthiness has proven to be an elastic term, encompassing the sad, the macabre, the hair-raising, and the tasteless. "News" has been said to include "all events and items of information that are out of the ordinary humdrum

[23]Sipple v. Chronicle Publishing Co., 201 Cal. Rptr. 665 (Cal. Ct. App. 1984).

[24]Cape Publishing, Inc. v. Bridges, 423 So.2d 426 (Fla. Dist. Ct. App. 1982), *cert. denied,* 464 U.S. 893 (1983). *See also* Taylor v. KTVB, 525 P.2d 984 (Idaho 1976).

routine, and which have 'that indefinable quality of interest which attracts public attention.'"[25] Courts have found newsworthiness in the family of a man kicked to death by a youth gang,[26] in pictures of auto accident victims,[27] and in the picture of the juvenile victim of a street accident.[28] News can include not only information in official records and events of significant public interest, but also revelation of people's oddities, foibles, skills, and talents.

Sometimes the privacy forfeited in a press story of ephemeral newsworthiness is itself insignificant. Michael S. Virgil is an example of an unsuccessful private-facts plaintiff whose story was deemed newsworthy but the personal embarrassment of his "private" revelation also seemed minimal. Virgil, once one of the greatest surfers on the California coast, lost a private-facts suit against *Sports Illustrated* because the magazine's revelations about his unusual ocean-side exploits were more newsworthy than personally embarrassing. *SI* told readers true stories of Virgil eating insects, diving off stairs to impress women, extinguishing cigarettes in his mouth, and deliberately hurting himself to collect unemployment insurance so he could surf more. The court said the magazine's revelations were not sufficiently embarrassing to outweigh their newsworthiness. The publication was not morbid or sensational and was related to a "legitimate journalistic attempt" to explain Virgil's daring surfing style.[29]

NEWSWORTHINESS OVER TIME Once people are newsworthy, they may remain newsworthy. Unusual intellectual talents made William James Sidis a newsworthy public figure as a boy, newsworthiness that he retained into adulthood. When Sidis was only eleven years old, his intellectual ability was so developed that he gave lectures to the math department at Harvard. Several years later, the *New Yorker* published a "Where Are They Now?" piece on Sidis. The article described the life of a man who had become a reclusive clerk who collected streetcar transfers and lived in a simple room in a shabby Boston neighborhood.[30] As a child prodigy, the court said, Sidis inspired both admiration and curiosity. Nearly three decades after he lectured at Harvard, the question of whether Sidis had fulfilled his early promise remained a matter of public concern, the court said.

The court continued:

> Regrettably or not, the misfortunes and frailties of neighbors and "public figures" are subjects of considerable interest and discussion to the rest of the population. And when such are the mores of the community, it would be unwise for a court to bar their expression in the newspapers, books, and magazines of the day.

Sidis died shortly after the article was published.

Information from old public records may retain its newsworthiness even if the information is published in stories of little newsworthiness. The Louisiana Supreme Court ruled a weekly newspaper, the *Iberville South,* did not invade Carlysle Roshto's privacy when it

[25]William Prosser, "Privacy," 48 *Calif. L. Rev.* 383, 412 (1960) (*quoting* Sweenek v. Pathe News, 16 F. Supp. 746, 747 (E.D.N.Y. 1936)).
[26]Jenkins v. Dell Publishing Co., 251 F.2d 447 (3d Cir. 1958).
[27]Kelley v. Post Publishing Co., 98 N.E.2d 286 (Mass. 1951).
[28]Leverton v. Curtis Publishing Co., 192 F.2d 974 (3d Cir. 1951).
[29]Virgil v. Sports Illustrated, Inc., 424 F. Supp. 1286 (S.D. Cal. 1976).
[30]Sidis v. F-R Publishing Corp., 113 F.2d 806 (2d Cir. 1940). *See also* Cohen v. Marx, 211 P.2d 320 (Cal. Ct. App. 1949).

republished a twenty-five-year-old story about Roshto's conviction for cattle theft. Publication of Roshto's criminal record had no relation to any current public issue; the item appeared in the paper's "Page from Our Past" feature, which was made up of randomly chosen stories from earlier issues. Roshto sued for invasion of privacy because he had worked hard after his release from prison, had been pardoned, and had hidden his conviction from the people in the community. The court suggested that the paper was insensitive to publish Roshto's story but ruled that the paper would not be punished for publishing truthful, accurate, and nonmalicious information.[31]

Consent

Besides asserting a First Amendment or newsworthiness defense, defendants in private-facts cases may also argue that the plaintiff consented to publication. Consent may be explicit or implied. One who is involved in a newsworthy public event, whether voluntarily or involuntarily, will usually be held to have given an implied consent to be photographed and written about. Similarly, people who talk to a reporter give implied consent for use of their names because they should anticipate publication. However, consent might not be implied if people interviewed fail to understand who they are talking to or that their interview might be published or broadcast.[32]

The more private the facts, the stronger the need for a journalist or public relations practitioner to obtain explicit written consent to publish a name or picture. Journalists and public relations practitioners should be particularly careful to obtain consent when intending to publish information about medical and psychological conditions and private facts about children. Legally, minors cannot give consent.

It can be difficult to know who has authority to give consent to disseminate private information at institutions housing the sick, the retarded, and the young. Releases obtained by television journalist Bill Moyers permitting CBS to film mental patients at Creedmoor State Hospital in New York were invalid because they were not signed by the proper authority. The hospital's Consent for Patient Interview form required that a patient's consent be witnessed by a physician who had determined that a patient was capable of giving consent. The court said that permission forms secured by Moyers were invalid because they were signed by a psychologist, not by a medical doctor.[33]

The media may invade an individual's privacy if they exceed the bounds of the consent granted. For example, a book publisher that has permission to publish the picture of a woman bathing should not pass the picture to a newspaper for publication to a much broader audience.[34] Consent to have one's picture published in news columns does not include consent to have the picture used in a commercial context.

When proper consent is lacking, a court may enjoin dissemination of intimate private information. The Massachusetts Supreme Court barred filmmaker Frederick Wiseman from showing to the general public his documentary about the Massachusetts Correctional Institution at Bridgewater because Wiseman lacked permission to disseminate private

[31]Roshto v. Hebert, 439 So.2d 428 (La. 1983). *See also* Shifflet v. Thomson Newspapers, 431 N.E.2d 1014 (Ohio 1982).
[32]Prahl v. Brosamle, 295 N.W.2d 768 (Wis. Ct. App. 1980).
[33]Delan v. CBS, 445 N.Y.S.2d 898 (N.Y. Sup. Ct. 1981), *modified,* 458 N.Y.S.2d 608 (N.Y. App. Div. 1983).
[34]McCabe v. Village Voice, 550 F. Supp. 525 (E.D. Pa. 1982).

information. Wiseman was blocked in part because the filmmaker had failed to get written releases from all inmates. The documentary, *Titicut Follies,* showed deplorable conditions in the institution. Because consent was lacking, the court said Wiseman could show his documentary only to doctors, lawyers, social workers, and others with a professional interest in the institution.[35]

Nearly twenty-five years after Frederick Wiseman filmed *Titicut Follies,* a Boston judge lifted the injunction on the film, allowing Wiseman to show it to the public. "As each year passes," the judge wrote, "the privacy issue of this case is less of a concern to the court than the prior restraint issue."[36] However, the judge did require Wiseman to maintain the confidentiality of the names and addresses of the individuals shown in the motion picture.

Summary

The private-facts tort is the highly offensive revelation of true, private information that is not newsworthy. Defendants in private-facts cases may claim the information in question in fact is in the public domain. The Supreme Court has ruled that publication of private information contained in court records is constitutionally protected. So is lawfully acquired truthful information of significant public interest, unless a plaintiff can demonstrate that punishment would advance a state interest of the highest order. Newsworthiness is also a broad defense, including information gathered in public places and information about public figures and interesting events. However, information about the ill or the retarded and private information about children might not be newsworthy and publication may be highly offensive. Consent may be explicit or implied. The media should be most careful to get written consent when acquiring information about mental and physical illness and minors.

Intrusion and Trespass

In recent years, citizens have brought an increasing number of suits against the media for their newsgathering techniques. In these cases, subjects of news coverage sue the media for reporters' use of secret recording and video equipment and for accompanying officials into private property. In these suits, the media are charged with intrusion, trespass, and related torts.

The common law protects citizens not only from disclosure of their intimate information but also from intrusion into private places. In the common law of privacy, the tort of intrusion is said to be a highly intrusive physical, electronic, or mechanical invasion of another's solitude or seclusion.[37] Intrusion includes the secretly recorded conversation, the overly aggressive surveillance, and the long-distance photograph made with a telephoto lens. Intrusion is part of privacy law because an intrusion violates citizens' rights to be left alone and to control information about themselves.

Intrusion is a tort of information gathering, not a tort of disseminating information by publishing or broadcasting. Journalists gathering information with a secret camera or

[35]Commonwealth v. Wiseman, 249 N.E.2d 610 (Mass. 1969).
[36]"Judge Lifts Ban on 'Titicut Follies' Film," 15 *News Media & L.* 36–37 (Fall 1991).
[37]*Restatement (Second) of Torts* § 652B (1977).

recorder may be liable for intrusion regardless of what they learn or whether they publish their information. "Where there is intrusion," a federal circuit judge said, the intruder should

> generally be liable whatever the content of what he learns. An eavesdropper to the marital bedroom may hear marital intimacies, or he may hear statements of fact or opinion of legitimate interest to the public; for purposes of liability that should make no difference.[38]

Whether an act intrudes on the privacy of another depends on whether that person has a reasonable expectation of privacy. Is the person in a place where he or she can reasonably assume that secret photographs will not be taken or secret recordings made? One may have an expectation of privacy in some public places, such as an enclosed phone booth, but generally, the more public the surroundings, the less the expectation of privacy.

Intrusion in Public and Quasi-Public Places

Common-law decisions generally hold that people in public and quasi-public places must assume they might be photographed or recorded, particularly if they are officials carrying out their public duties. Media personnel therefore can photograph, film, and record what they easily see or hear in public places, provided they do not harass, trespass, or otherwise intrude. A California statute reflects the law generally when it says tape-recording at public meetings is not an intrusion when "the parties to the communication may reasonably expect that the communication may be overheard or recorded."[39]

PERMITTED NEWSGATHERNG It is not an intrusion for a TV crew to record police publicly frisking a suspect[40] or to take a picture of private property from a public sidewalk. Thus, John W. Bisbee lost an intrusion suit over a picture of his Ocean Township estate taken from a sidewalk. Bisbee had no suit for intrusion, a New Jersey court said, because the picture "merely represented a view which is available to any bystander."[41]

A person dining in a public restaurant has little expectation that he or she will not be photographed. A federal court in Maine ruled that a *National Enquirer* reporter did not intrude when she persistently sought to interview and photograph Henry Dempsey at a restaurant as well as outside his home.[42] The court said it is not intrusive to attempt to take a photograph in a restaurant open to the public or to attempt interviews without passing the threshold of the home. The reporter's attempts to interview may have been "annoying," the court said, but they were not "highly offensive" and therefore did not constitute intrusion. Although one court suggested that filming a person in a private dining room "might conceivably be a highly offensive intrusion upon that person's seclusion,"[43] filming someone in a public dining room probably is not.

[38]Pearson v. Dodd, 410 F.2d 701 (D.C. Cir. 1969).
[39]Cal. Penal Code § 632(c).
[40]Prahl v. Brosamle, 295 N.W.2d 774.
[41]Bisbee v. Conover, 9 Media L. Rep. 1298, 1299 (N.J. Super. Ct. App. Div. 1982). *See also* Mark v. King Broadcasting Co., 618 P.2d 512 (Wash. App. 1980); Neff v. Time, Inc., 406 F. Supp. 858 (W.D. Pa. 1976).
[42]Dempsey v. National Enquirer, Inc., 702 F. Supp. 927 (D. Maine 1988).
[43]Stessman v. American Black Hawk Broadcasting Co., 416 N.W.2d 685 (1987).

Aggressive interviewing that stops short of harassment is not an intrusion. One federal court ruled an "aggressive and possibly abrasive" interview is not an intrusion in a public or semipublic place as long as it does not amount to "unabated hounding." In *Machleder v. Diaz,* a reporter entered the property of a hazardous waste company without permission and asked questions of the company's president. There was no intrusion because the executive's willingness to talk constituted consent to the interview.[44]

A lower court in Washington ruled that aggressive phoning—ten unwanted calls over several months—to obtain comments on newsworthy events was not intrusive, but constituted "routine newsgathering activities."[45]

Journalists may record and photograph what they easily see or overhear in the public sections of jails. Radio reporter Carl Connerton did not intrude on attorney Marvin Holman when he recorded Holman hollering and banging in an Arkansas jail cell after he was charged with drunk driving. "The boisterous complaints which were recorded were not made with the expectation of privacy or confidentiality," the federal court said.[46]

Whether it is an intrusion to photograph an inmate in his cell without permission is not clear. On the one hand, an inmate is housed in a quasi-public institution and has almost no right of privacy. Because prisoners have little privacy to protect, at least one court ruled a prisoner could not sue over a surreptitious picture taken while he was asleep.[47] On the other hand, jail inmates are not completely without civil rights. Inmates are protected, for example, by the Fourth Amendment from having to undress in front of guards of the opposite sex.[48] One court ruled that a prisoner could pursue a civil rights suit against a warden who permitted a camera crew to film the prisoner.[49] Even though no intrusion suit was brought against the film crew, a warden may be reluctant to permit press photographers and camera crews into a prison if inmates can then bring suits charging a violation of their civil rights.

HARASSMENT AND STALKING Journalists whose aggressive tactics result in harassment or overzealous surveillance may be liable, even if they pursue their stories in public places. Society has been particularly repulsed by very aggressive newsgathering since Diana, Princess of Wales, died in a car crash as she was being chased by photographers in Paris.

A famous case involving Jacqueline Onassis, the widow of President John F. Kennedy, illustrates how aggressive journalism can cross over to illegal harassment. Although the case of *Galella v. Onassis* is not an intrusion case, it illustrates where overzealous reporting becomes intrusive.[50] Photographer Ron Galella, in his pursuit of photos and information about Onassis, bumped the parents of the Kennedy children's schoolmates, blocked passages, temporarily blinded people with his flashbulbs, impersonated family employees, spied with telephoto lenses, and trailed Onassis hour after hour. When Onassis sued over this list of intrusive activities, Galella complained that Onassis was camera-shy and uncooperative. However, the court ruled that Galella was liable for assault, battery, harassment,

[44]538 F. Supp. 1364 (S.D.N.Y. 1982).
[45]Lee v. The Columbian, Inc., 16 Media L. Rep. 1264 (Wash. Super. Ct. 1989).
[46]Holman v. Central Arkansas Broadcasting Co., 610 F.2d 542 (8th Cir. 1979).
[47]Jenkins v. Winchester Star (W.D. Va. 1981). *See also* Rifkin v. Esquire, (C.D. Cal. 1982).
[48]Lee v. Downs, 641 F.2d 1117 (4th Cir. 1981).
[49]Smith v. Fairman, 98 F.R.D. 445 (C.D. Ill. 1982).
[50]353 F. Supp. 196 (S.D.N.Y. 1972), *aff'd,* 487 F.2d 986 (2d Cir. 1973).

and infliction of emotional distress. "The essence of the privacy interest," the federal district court said, includes a general "right to be left alone" and to define one's circle of intimacy, to shield intimate and personal characteristics and activities from public gaze, to have moments of freedom from the unremitted assault of the world and unfettered will of others in order to achieve some measure of tranquillity for contemplation or other purposes, without which life loses its sweetness.

A federal district court enjoined Galella from taking pictures of Onassis from closer than 150 feet. A federal appeals court affirmed most of the lower court ruling but reduced to twenty-five feet the distance that Galella was to remain from Onassis. After several violations, Galella was held in contempt of court and ordered to pay Onassis $10,000.[51]

A federal court in Pennsylvania enjoined *Inside Edition* from persistent, technologically sophisticated monitoring of a prominent family from public property. The federal judge enjoined the *Inside Edition* reporters from "harassing, hounding, following, intruding, frightening, terrorizing or ambushing" Richard and Nancy Wolfson, officers at U.S. Healthcare. Two *Inside Edition* reporters had been monitoring the Wolfsons for a story about the high salaries U.S. Healthcare paid its executives.[52]

In Pennsylvania, *Inside Edition* monitored the Wolfson family's comings and goings from a van parked near the Wolfson home. *Inside Edition* denied the Wolfsons' charges that reporters also followed the couple's young children, causing the Wolfsons great concern for the youngsters' safety. In Florida, the reporters observed the Wolfson family home from a boat, employing videocameras, binoculars, and a "shotgun mike" capable of picking up conversations sixty yards away. *Inside Edition* was also accused of attempting to create ambush interviews.

The federal judge concluded that Lewis's and Wilson's "unreasonable surveilling, hounding and following" drove the Wolfson family from their Pennsylvania home. In another family home in Florida, the Wolfsons and their children were made captives by the media's "relentless surveillance, conducted with the aid of sophisticated sound and video equipment aimed directly at the home," the judge said.

To curb aggressive surveillance from public property, California passed a "stalkerazzi" law. The California statute makes journalists liable for "constructive" trespass if they use a "visual or auditory enhancing device" to obtain images or recordings they could not otherwise collect without physically trespassing.[53]

◇ Summary ◇

Intrusion is the physical or technological violation of another's privacy. Generally, the media can record or take pictures of what is easily seen or heard in public and quasi-public places. However, the media are not permitted to engage in harassment, assault, or overzealous surveillance, even in a public place.

[51]Galella v. Onassis, 533 F. Supp. 1076 (S.D.N.Y. 1982).
[52]Wolfson v. Lewis, 924 F. Supp. 1413 (E.D. Pa. 1996).
[53]Cal. Civ. Code § 1708.8.

Intrusion in Private Places

Of more concern to citizens and the media than intrusion into public places is intrusion into private places. Even the most well-known public figures have a right to private retreats where they are free to talk, joke, and lower their guard without being accountable to the outside world. A person has a justifiable expectation in a private place to be free from the telephoto lens,[54] the hidden microphone, and the trespasser crouching below the window. The law has long held that it is illegal to peep, snoop, or eavesdrop on people in private places. Peering in someone's window or pressing one's ear to the door may be trespass, intrusion, or both.[55] It is also an invasion of privacy to open someone's mail[56] or to tap someone's telephone or illegally access their computer files.

ELECTRONIC HARASSMENT Stalkers and harassers may follow, annoy, and physically threaten their victims, but increasingly stalkers and harassers employ electronic communications—the Internet, e-mail, blogs, and the telephone—to harass and threaten their prey. Stalkers of any stripe usually wish to exercise control over their targets. Victims, who often know their tormentor, are more apt to be women than men. With the growth of the Internet, it is increasingly easy for "cyberstalkers" to acquire personal information about their subjects—often from MySpace, Facebook, and other social networking sites—and to harass their victims anonymously with repeated threatening messages. A woman in New York was repeatedly contacted after someone posted her name, address, and phone number in an online "adult personals" advertisement concluding, "I can make you very happy and satisfied. In my den of love pad."[57] Federal, state, and local law enforcement authorities have set up special units to investigate and prosecute online harassment.

Federal law makes it a crime punishable by up to five years in prison to threaten someone through interstate communication.[58] Federal communications law, which for decades has prohibited the use of telephones to "annoy, abuse, harass, or threaten," was extended in 2006 by the Violence Against Women and Department of Justice Reauthorization Act to punish the same offenses perpetrated through computer communications if the sender does not reveal his true identity.[59] The federal statute prohibits annoying, threatening, and harassing computer communications directly to a victim; the statute does not apply to harassing or terrorizing messages posted on a bulletin board or chat room. California and more than forty other states also prohibit cyberstalking.[60]

The federal cyberstalking law was immediately challenged by an Arizona company claiming a statute that prohibits annoying communications is unconstitutionally overbroad and vague. The government said the law would be invoked only if the cyber sender has the

[54]Souder v. Pendleton Detectives, Inc., 88 So.2d 716 (La. Ct. App. 1956).

[55]Alan Westin, *Privacy and Freedom* 333–34 (1967); Souder v. Pendleton Detectives, Inc., 88 So.2d 716 (La. Ct. App. 1956).

[56]Vernars v. Young, 539 F.2d 966 (3d Cir. 1976).

[57]Tom Zeller Jr., "Despite Laws, Stalkers Roam on the Internet," *New York Times,* April 17, 2006.

[58]18 U.S.C. § 875(c).

[59]47 U.S.C. § 223.

[60]Cal. Penal Code § 422; Cal. Civil Code §§ 1708, 653m. *See,* Tom Zeller Jr., "Despite Laws, Stalkers Roam on the Internet," *New York Times,* April 17, 2006.

intent to "instill fear in the victim."[61] A federal court ruled in 1999 that the federal statute prohibiting annoying, abusive, and harassing telephone calls could not be applied constitutionally to protected political speech. The court refused to hold liable a caller who repeatedly criticized a public official in caustic telephone messages that the court determined constituted political speech.[62]

THIRD-PARTY MONITORING Only law enforcement officers operating under a valid search warrant may legally bug a room, secretly monitor telephone conversations, or intercept computer communications. The Fourth Amendment to the Constitution, which protects citizens from unreasonable government searches of their homes and property, requires that government officials acquire a court-approved warrant before conducting searches and seizures, including "searches and seizures" of citizens' telephone conversations and e-mail messages. The search warrant, a fundamental element of a criminal suspect's rights of due process, is issued after law enforcement officers have convinced a judge there is probable cause to believe that the search of a specific place or monitoring of specific conversation will reveal evidence related to a specific crime. Warrants are required to authorize bugging, wiretapping, and eavesdropping because these intrusions are a form of third-party monitoring conducted without the knowledge of parties to a conversation. Third-party monitoring is a particularly intrusive monitoring because, as Justice Douglas observed, it may intrude "upon the privacy of those not even suspected of crime and intercepts the most intimate of conversations."[63] State and federal courts authorized some 1800 interceptions of wire, oral and electronic communications in 2005, an increase of 4 percent from 2004.[64] Only one application for a wiretap was denied.

However, after the attacks of September 11, 2001, President Bush secretly authorized the National Security Agency to conduct warrantless wiretapping on Americans to acquire evidence of terrorist activity. The president claimed power as commander-in-chief to authorize secret monitoring of e-mails and telephone calls between U.S. citizens and persons abroad with alleged links to terrorist activities. The secret monitoring, which stimulated sharp criticism when disclosed by the *New York Times,* was conducted without judicial warrants or warrants issued by a Foreign Intelligence Surveillance Court, a secret court authorized to issue warrants in national security cases more quickly and with less evidence of suspected criminal activity than civilian American courts require. President Bush said the secret courts were too slow. In winter 2008, the House and Senate fought over limitations on continued warrantless eavesdropping and over immunity from lawsuits—including retroactive immunity—for telephone companies that help the administration conduct warrantless surveillance.[65]

Although the Fourth Amendment in normal times constrains surveillance by government officials, private citizens, too, are prohibited by federal and state statutes and the

---

[61] "The Anonymous Email.com Successfully Obtains Clarification of Federal 'Annoyance Law' in Its Suit Against Attorney General Gonzalez and the Federal Government," *Market Wire,* Aug. 3, 2006.

[62] United States v. Popa, 187 F.3d 672 (D.C. Cir. 1999).

[63] Berger v. New York, 388 U.S. 41, 64–65 (1967) (concurring opinion).

[64] News Release, Administrative Office of the U.S. Courts, "Authorized Wiretap Intercepts Increase 4 Percent in 2005," May 1, 2006.

[65] *See,* Penelope Sheets, "Wiretap Updates: Administration's Domestic Spying Program Raises Constitutional Questions," *Bulletin,* Silha Center, University of Minnesota, Winter 2006, at 9; Eric Lichtblau, "House Votes to Reject Immunity for Phone Companies Involved in Wiretaps," *N.Y. Times,* Mar. 15, 2008, at 14.

common law from bugging, wiretapping, and eavesdropping.[66] Federal and state law prohibit third parties—parties not involved in a conversation—from intercepting and recording conversations transmitted over wired, wireless, microwave, or cellular phones; electronic mail; and satellite transmissions of video teleconferences and data.[67] Furthermore, federal law and many states prohibit receiving and disclosing illegally intercepted wire, electronic, and oral communications.[68]

However, the U.S. Supreme Court ruled in 2001 that the First Amendment allows journalists to disseminate illegally taped conversations if the conversations are of great public interest and if the journalist breaks no law to acquire them. In *Bartnicki v. Vopper,* the Court ruled that radio talk show host Frederick Vopper could not be punished under federal and Pennsylvania statutes for broadcasting an illegally recorded cell phone conversation between two participants in negotiations over teacher pay raises.[69] In the surreptitiously recorded tape, the head of a local teachers' union suggested blowing off the porches of school board members if they failed to offer higher raises. The tape was left anonymously in a mailbox and then passed to the radio station.

Relying on *Smith v. Daily Mail* and *Florida Star v. B.J.F.,*[70] the Supreme Court ruled 6-3 that the media's dissemination of lawfully acquired information about an issue of public importance outweighs the legislatures' interest in discouraging unlawful interceptions and protecting the privacy of wire and electronic conversations. To deter unlawful recordings, it is better to punish the interceptors than the journalists who innocently acquire and disseminate the recordings, Justice Stevens wrote for the majority. Stevens suggested the First Amendment might not protect dissemination of some private conversations and trade secrets, but the majority ruled the public interest outweighed privacy when a station broadcast a secret recording of a conversation by participants in an issue of public importance. The subject of the conversation recorded in the *Bartnicki* case was an issue of public importance—negotiations over teacher pay. "One of the costs associated with participation in public affairs is an attendant loss of privacy," the Court said.

In *Bartnicki*, no one was charged under the federal statute with knowingly receiving a stolen recording, as journalists sometimes do. The radio station acquired the tape from a source who received it from an anonymous provider. But in 2007 a federal appeals court majority reaffirmed the First Amendment privilege established in *Bartnicki* while ruling that a congressman who disseminated an illegally recorded conversation violated confidentiality rules he had pledged to uphold as a member of the House Ethics Committee.[71]

In a 5-4 ruling, the U.S. Court of Appeals for the District of Columbia Circuit ruled that Democratic Congressman Jim McDermott violated House ethics rules when he passed to journalists a recording he knew had been illegally created by a Florida couple. The couple, John and Alice Martin, each paid a $500 fine for illegally recording a cell-phone conference call among leading Republicans about ethics issues in the House of Representatives.

66Omnibus Crime Control and Safe Streets Act of 1968, 18 U.S.C. § 2511; Katz v. United States, 389 U.S. 347 (1967); Hamberger v. Eastman, 206 A.2d 239 (N.H. 1964).
67Electronic Communications Privacy Act of 1986, 18 U.S.C. § 2510.
6818 U.S.C. §2511(1)(c).
69532 U.S. 514 (2001).
70See text, pp. 196–198.
71"Privacy: Courts Revisits Spying Case Against Rep. McDermott," *Technology Daily,* Oct. 31, 2006.

The Martins chanced upon the conversation while driving in Florida and listening to their police radio scanner. The Martins passed the recording to McDermott, then the ranking Democrat on the House Ethics Committee. McDermott gave the recording to reporters for the *New York Times* and the *Atlanta Journal-Constitution.* McDermott's release of the recording resulted in stories embarrassing to Republican Congressman John Boehner, one of the participants in the conversation. A three-member panel of the court of appeals ruled that McDermott violated the wiretapping statute.[72]

In 2007, a majority of the full court of appeals, including concurring Judge Thomas B. Griffith, held that Rep. McDermott, as a member of the House Ethics Committee, "voluntarily accepted a duty to confidentiality that covered his receipt and handling of the Martins' illegal recording." But in his concurring opinion, Judge Griffith said that if McDermott had not been required to withhold the tape under House ethics rules, Griffith would have voted that McDermott had a First Amendment right under the Supreme Court's *Bartnicki* ruling to disclose the illegally recorded tape containing subject matter of public importance. Judge Griffith joined four dissenters—creating a majority of five—reaffirming the *Bartnicki* principle that the First Amendment protects disclosure of lawfully acquired conversations of public importance even if they are unlawfully recorded.

Besides prohibiting tapping phones and intercepting wireless calls, the law also prohibits hacking into telephone systems to acquire previously recorded conversations. Michael Gallagher, a former reporter for the *Cincinnati Enquirer,* pleaded guilty to violations of Ohio wiretap and computer access laws for stealing voice mail messages from Chiquita Brands International, Inc. Gallagher used the recordings to write unflatteringly about Chiquita's operation of banana plantations in Latin America. *The Enquirer* apologized to Chiquita for the reporter's intrusion and theft and reportedly paid Chiquita $10 million.[73] Similarly, it is illegal to implant "keylogging" software on computers so that users unknowingly transmit private and confidential information—such as passwords and account numbers—to outside monitors.[74]

It is also illegal to acquire a person's phone records from a phone company by posing as someone authorized to see the records. Gaining phone records through a false identity is called "pretexting." Congress passed legislation in 2006 outlawing pretexting after a scandal in which private investigators working for Hewlett-Packard executives used pretexting to acquire phone records of Hewlett-Packard board members and journalists covering boardroom fights at the company.[75] Telephone pretexting is illegal in about a dozen states.

Hewlett-Packard agreed to a $14.5 million settlement approved by a California Court after private investigators hired by HP executives engaged in pretexting and other invasive practices to find the source of leaks from the company.[76] The corporate leaks revealed information about Hewlett-Packard's acquisition strategies and product plans. Reporters whose records were accessed included Dawn Kawamoto and Tom Krazit of CNET News.com,

[72]Boehner v. McDermott, 441 F.3d 1010 (D.C. Cir. 2006).

[73]See 3 *Communications Law 1998* at 466–68 (Practising Law Institute).

[74]Tom Zeller Jr., "Cyberthieves Silent Copy Your Passwords as You Type," *N.Y. Times,* Feb. 27, 2006, at 1.

[75]David Rogers and Robert Guy Matthews, "Congress Approves Bill to Criminalize 'Pretexting,'" *Wall St. J.,* Dec. 11, 2006, at A6.

[76]Reporters Committee for Freedom of the Press, "HP to Pay $14.5 Million Settlement in 'Pretexting' Scandal," Dec. 8, 2006, http://www.rcfp.org/

who wrote a story based on an anonymous source reporting HP's strategies and plans. Investigators also accessed the phone records of reporters for the *Wall Street Journal,* the *New York Times, BusinessWeek,* and the *Associated Press.* At one point, Kawamoto was sent an e-mail containing spyware allowing Hewlett-Packard executives to learn with whom Kawamoto was corresponding.[77]

The settlement will fund future prosecutions for privacy crimes and requires Hewlett-Packard to restructure the company's ethical and legal standards. Criminal charges against former Hewlett-Packard chairwoman Patricia Dunn were dismissed.

PARTICIPANT MONITORING The law is generally more tolerant of participants who record their own conversations than of third parties who record conversations to which they are not a party. **Participant monitoring** occurs when at least one party to a conversation is aware of a secret recorder or transmitter. Some people contend that secret participant tape-recording is unethical and unnecessary, but lawyers, businesspeople, public relations practitioners, and journalists sometimes secretly record conversations to establish an accurate record without inhibiting candor. Unannounced recording protects journalists against false charges that a source was misquoted. Investigative reporters, like police informants, will sometimes carry a secret tape recorder or transmitter to document drug deals and other wrongdoing. Federal law and most states permit participant monitoring if not conducted for criminal purposes, but participant monitoring in particularly private places may still be a tort in common law.

Federal Law Federal law permits one party to a conversation to record or transmit a conversation without telling the other party. Participant tape-recording is considered no more intrusive than orally retelling a conversation to a third party. Citizens are generally free to recount conversations, even private conversations, to friends, neighbors, colleagues, or journalists. Doctors, lawyers, and ministers are prohibited by law from divulging confidential conversations with their clients, but other citizens are not.[78]

Although federal law permits participant recording, Section 2511 of the federal wiretap statute forbids a participant to secretly record a conversation for the purpose of committing a crime or a tort.[79] Civil penalties for violation of the act can result in a fine of $10,000.[80] It is a crime or a tort for a participant in a conversation to make a recording with the intent to blackmail or threaten someone with the recording.[81] However, Congress intended that the federal statute not be invoked against journalists simply because their surreptitious recordings may result in news stories that "embarrass" someone.[82] Similarly, it is probably not tortious to gather news through secret participant recordings even though the resulting news story may contain defamation.[83]

[77]Ellen Nakashima and Yuki Noguchi, "Extensive Spying Found at HP," *Washington Post,* Sep. 20, 2006.

[78]See generally Kent Middleton, "Journalists and Tape Recorders: Does Participant Monitoring Invade Privacy," 2 *Comm/Ent L.J.* 287 (1979–80).

[79]18 U.S.C.S. § 2511 (2)(d) (1999); Katz v. United States, 389 U.S. 347 (1967).

[80]18 U.S.C.S. § 2520 (c)(2)(B). *See* United States v. Turk, 526 F.2d 654 (5th Cir. 1976).

[81]United States v. Phillips, 540 F.2d 319, 325 (8th Cir.), *cert. denied,* 429 U.S. 1000 (1976).

[82]*See* Boddie v. American Broadcasting Cos., 694 F. Supp. 1304 (N.D. Ohio 1989).

[83]Russell v. ABC, Inc., 23 Media L. Rep. 2428 (N.D. Ill. 1995).

Contrary to the federal wiretap statute, the Federal Communications Commission requires telephone companies to prohibit telephone subscribers from recording conversations unless all parties to the conversation are told of the recording in advance, with either an announcement or a beep tone.[84] However, telephone company regulations prohibiting participant recording are seldom enforced. Highly competitive phone companies have little incentive to seek out violators, and the penalty—removal of a subscriber's phone—is only a slight deterrent because one can easily obtain another number. In any case, federal law permitting participant monitoring may preempt telephone company regulations prohibiting it.

A rule the FCC does enforce requires broadcasters to notify callers immediately if a telephone conversation is being recorded for broadcast.[85] The FCC assessed a $5,000 penalty against radio station WXLO in Fitchburg, Massachusetts, for recording a telephone conversation for broadcast without telling the party called.[86] But broadcasters, like anyone else, need provide no notice of a secret participant telephone recording not intended for broadcast, provided that participant recording is legal under state law. Furthermore, the FCC rule requiring notice of telephone conversations taped for broadcast does not require notice of face-to-face taped conversations intended for broadcast.

State Prohibitions The law in thirty-eight states, like the federal law, permits participant monitoring. However, statutes in twelve states prohibit participant tape-recording.[87] At least one state court has upheld the constitutionality of the prohibition on participant monitoring. In a case involving a reporter's unannounced telephone recordings, the Florida Supreme Court rejected reporters' arguments that secret tape-recording was needed to corroborate a journalist's story. The court said that secret recording is not an "indispensable" tool of newsgathering and that the First Amendment does not include a right to corroborate news stories with secret recordings.[88]

The California Supreme Court ruled that an accident victim, Ruth Shulman, could bring an intrusion suit against Group W Productions for videotapes of Shulman as she conversed with a nurse at the scene of an auto accident and in a medical helicopter.[89] But affirming a lower court, the California high court agreed with Group W that Shulman had no claim for the disclosure of embarrassing private facts. The court concluded that broadcast of Shulman's identity, injuries, and conversations were not embarrassing invasions of privacy but were truthful, relevant additions to a newsworthy video documentary, *On Scene: Emergency Response,* about medical evacuations.

Although the broadcast did not reveal embarrassing facts, the court said a jury should decide whether Group W intruded on a zone of privacy that Shulman might reasonably expect in the medical helicopter, much as patients in a hospital room or ambulance have an expectation that they will not be photographed or their conversations with doctors and

---

[84]47 C.F.R. § 64.501; § 73.1206.

[85]*In re* Amendment of Section 1206: Broadcast of Telephone Conversations, 65 P & F2d 444(1988).

[86]*In re* Montachusett Broadcasting, Inc., 7 F.C.C.R. 3594 (1992).

[87]California, Delaware, Florida, Hawaii, Illinois, Maryland, Massachusetts, Minnesota, Montana, New Hampshire, Pennsylvania, and Washington. *See* 3 *Communications Law 1998* at 518 (Practising Law Institute).

[88]Shevin v. Sunbeam Television Corp., 351 So.2d 723 (Fla. 1977), *appeal dismissed,* 435 U.S. 920, *reh'g denied,* 435 U.S. 1018 (1978).

[89]Shulman v. Group W Productions, Inc., 18 Cal.4th 200 (1998).

nurses recorded. Even though the journalist was invited into the helicopter by an employee of Mercy Air, operator of the rescue service, the court said, "It is neither the custom nor the habit of our society that any member of the public at large or its media representatives may hitch a ride in an ambulance and ogle as paramedics care for an injured stranger."

The court also said that a jury should decide whether Group W intruded into Shulman's privacy by recording her conversations with a nurse at the accident scene. The nurse attending to Shulman transmitted the conversations from a wireless microphone. Any bystander might videotape the accident in plain view near a highway without intruding, the court noted, but Group W was able to record conversations between Shulman and the nurse only because the nurse wore a transmitter. "A patient's conversation with a provider of medical care in the course of treatment, including emergency treatment, carries a traditional and legally well-established expectation of privacy," the court said.

In another newsgathering case, ABC paid more than $900,000 to settle an intrusion claim brought by an employee of a telephone psychic service whose office conversations were secretly recorded and broadcast. ABC settled the case with Mark Sanders, an employee of Psychic Marketing Group, after the California Supreme Court ruled that Sanders had an expectation of privacy during the secretly recorded workplace conversations, even though Sanders's coworkers could overhear his conversations. An appellate court also ruled that ABC could be asked to pay damages not only for its intrusive secret recording but also for broadcasting the recordings. Damages from the intrusion were increased by the broadcast, the court said. Sanders was secretly recorded during conversations at his work cubicle by ABC's Stacy Lescht, who took a job temporarily as a tele-psychic.[90]

Secret Recording as a Tort Regardless of federal and state statutes, secret recording by a participant to a conversation may be an intrusion, particularly if subterfuge is used to bring electronic eavesdropping equipment into a private place, such as a home. In one well-known case from California, a federal court ruled secret transmitting and photographing by two journalists in a private home were an intrusion. In *Dietemann v. Time, Inc.*, the U.S. Court of Appeals for the Ninth Circuit ruled that A. A. Dietemann, a quack doctor, could collect damages from Time, Inc., for invasion of his privacy by two *Life* magazine employees who secretly used a voice transmitter and camera in the doctor's den. The journalists gained entrance to Dietemann's house by giving false names. One *Life* staffer secretly photographed the doctor as he waved a wand over bottles of body tissue and rubbed what he said was the cancerous breast of the other journalist. Meanwhile, a transmitter in the journalist's purse transmitted the conversation to a tape recorder in a nearby police car.[91]

The federal appeals court affirmed a lower court ruling awarding $1,000 to Dietemann for the journalists' electronic intrusion into a private place. Dietemann's den, the Ninth Circuit said, "was a sphere from which he could reasonably expect to exclude eavesdropping newsmen." When a person invites another into a private place, the court said,

[90]Sanders v. American Broadcast Cos., 978 P.2d 67 (Cal. 1999); Sanders v. American Broadcast Cos., 28 Media L. Rep. 1183 (BNA) (Cal. App. 999) (unpub.), Reporters Committee for Freedom of the Press, "Network Pays Out $900,000 in Hidden Camera Claim," http://www.rcfp.org/news/2000/0223sander.html.

[91]Dietemann v. Time, Inc., 449 F.2d 245 (1971).

> he does not and should not be required to take the risk that what is heard and seen will be transmitted by photograph or recording, or in our modern world, in full living color and hi-fi to the public. . . . A different rule could have a most pernicious effect upon the dignity of man and it would surely lead to guarded conversations and conduct where candor is most valued, *e.g.*, in the case of doctors and lawyers.[92]

The court rejected *Life*'s claim that concealed electronic instruments are essential to investigative reporting and that their use is protected by the First Amendment. "We agree," the court said, "that newsgathering is an integral part of news dissemination. We strongly disagree, however, that the hidden mechanical contrivances are 'indispensable tools' of newsgathering."

In a passage that has been cited frequently, the court wrote,

> The First Amendment has never been construed to accord newsmen immunity from torts or crimes committed during the course of newsgathering. The First Amendment is not a license to trespass, to steal, or to intrude by electronic means into the precincts of another's home or office.[93]

◇ Summary ◇

Bugging and wiretapping are prohibited. But secret recording by one party to a conversation is permitted by federal statute and statutes in thirty-eight states. However, participant monitoring may violate federal law if done to commit a crime or a tort. Unannounced telephone recordings also violate seldom-enforced telephone regulations. Unannounced participant telephone recordings also violate FCC regulations if the recordings are intended for broadcast. Participant monitoring violates statutes in twelve states and may be a tort, particularly if conducted in very private settings under false pretenses. Surreptitious recording may not be an intrusion in business settings where expectations of privacy are lower, particularly if no deceit is used to gain entry.

Trespass

Closely related to intrusion and often claimed simultaneously with intrusion is trespass. But whereas an intrusion usually involves newsgathering with a secret electronic or photographic technique, a trespass usually requires a physical invasion of someone's property. The trespasser enters private property without consent of the owner or "possessor" of the property.[94] Merely going onto private property or posted public property without permission may be a trespass, whether or not the trespasser uses intrusive tape recorders, secret cameras, or other technological devices. As with intrusion, the violation lies in the act of trespass, not in what is learned or published as a result of the trespass. Property owners need not prove their property was damaged, but punitive damages usually will be awarded only if the trespass is willful or malicious.[95]

[92]*Id.* at 249; 1 Media L. Rep. at 2420.
[93]*Id.*
[94]*Restatement (Second) of Torts* § 158 at 277 (1965).
[95]Le Mistral, Inc. v. Columbia Broadcasting Sys., 402 N.Y.S.2d 815 (App. Div. 1978); Belluomo v. KAKE TV & Radio, Inc., 596 P.2d 832 (Kan. Ct. App. 1979).

A federal court in the Midwest extended trespass law to the Internet. The Federal District Court for the Southern District of Ohio enjoined an advertiser from trespassing on Compuserve's proprietary computers by sending unsolicited "junk mail" to Compuserve customers. The federal court said mass electronic mailings by Cyber Promotions, Inc., hurt Compuserve by burdening its computers and causing irritated subscribers to abandon the Internet provider. When Compuserve consented to transmit e-mail messages, it retained authority to deny access to unauthorized parties, the court said.[96] In other filings, America Online has asserted that unauthorized companies transmitting unsolicited e-mail over AOL's network with false header information trespass and violate the federal Computer Fraud and Abuse Act.[97]

It is not a trespass to enter private property with the consent of the owner or possessor of the property. Usually, the possessor of private property is the owner, but a person who rents also "possesses" property. A tenant may grant or deny access to an apartment or rental house, regardless of the wishes of the property owner.[98] For brief periods during emergencies, fire and police officials may also control access to private property, but even during an emergency, the owner of property can deny access to the media.[99] Once journalists enter private property to ask questions, they gain an implied consent to remain if the property owner agrees to talk.[100] However, journalists may become trespassers if they refuse to leave when asked. They may also be trespassers if they misrepresent the purpose of the interview with a private person,[101] fail to identify themselves as reporters,[102] or unnecessarily disrupt a business.[103]

Courts are divided on whether journalists trespass when they misrepresent themselves to acquire information from public businesses. In a decision the Supreme Court let stand, a federal appeals court dismissed trespass and fraud claims against ABC for allowing reporters to pose as patients to investigate Midwest eye clinics after allegedly promising not to work surreptitiously. The U.S. Court of Appeals for the Seventh Circuit dismissed trespass and other claims by the Desnick Eye Center against ABC and *Prime Time Live* reporter Sam Donaldson for using reporters with hidden cameras at Desnick facilities in Wisconsin and Indiana to gather information about allegedly unnecessary cataract operations. This deception occurred after ABC gained the cooperation of the Desnick Center in Chicago by promising no "ambush" interviews or "undercover" surveillance.[104]

The appellate court said ABC reporters did not trespass when they posed as patients any more than food critics trespass when they conceal their identity from restaurant owners. Owners of restaurants and eye clinics consent to entry by customers, knowing that some might not be who they say, the court said. Desnick should have remained skeptical, the court said, when ABC promised not to employ investigative journalists as patients.

However, a federal court ruled that a supermarket should receive more than $300,000 because ABC employees, misrepresenting themselves, surreptitiously gathered information

[96]CompuServe, Inc. v. Cyber Promotions, Inc., 962 F. Supp. 1015 (1997).
[97]"AOL Asserts 'Spammers' Violate Computer Fraud Act," News Notes: 25 Media L. Rep., Nov. 11, 1997.
[98]Lal v. CBS, 551 F. Supp. 356 (E.D. Pa. 1982), *aff'd*, 726 F.2d 97 (3d Cir. 1984).
[99]Prahl v. Brosamle, 295 N.W.2d 768 (Wis. Ct. App. 1980); Anderson v. WROC-TV, 441 N.Y.S.2d 220 (Sup. Ct. 1981).
[100]Machleder v. Diaz, 538 F. Supp. 1364 (S.D.N.Y. 1982).
[101]Belluomo v. KAKE TV & Radio, Inc., 596 P.2d 832 (Kan. Ct. App. 1979).
[102]Prahl v. Brosamle, 295 N.W.2d 768 (Wis. Ct. App. 1980).
[103]Le Mistral, Inc. v. Columbia Broadcasting Sys., 402 N.Y.S.2d 815 (App. Div. 1978).
[104]Desnick v. ABC, 44 F.3d 1345 (7th Cir. 1995).

for a report about low-quality meat. The court awarded Food Lion $1,400 in actual damages and $315,000 in punitive damages,[105] a significant reduction from the $5.5 million awarded by a North Carolina jury.

In a widely watched case, the court ruled that ABC employees were liable for trespassing into nonpublic areas of a Food Lion facilities under false pretenses and fraudulently concealing their identities on their job applications. The two ABC producers also violated a legal duty of loyalty to their supermarket employer, the court said.

The court awarded Food Lion only $1,400 actual damages to reimburse the supermarket chain for the costs of training and paying two ABC producers who were briefly employed by the company.[106] By limiting actual damages to $1,400, the court refused to allow Food Lion to collect for lost sales, lost profits, and a diminished stock price following the broadcast.[107] The court said Food Lion's losses were not the result of ABC's trespass, fraud, and breach of duty. The broadcast may have damaged Food Lion, but the broadcast itself was not on trial in the suit over newsgathering practices.

ACCOMPANYING OFFICIALS Much of the news that journalists report results from the day-to-day activities of police, firefighters, rescue crews, and others who protect and serve—and are often paid by the community. What better way to get close to the news than for journalists to ride along with police on a drug raid or with the medic on an emergency mission? Journalists have a long history of watching public servants at close range as they search for evidence, arrest suspects, rescue the injured, and revive the stricken. Public servants often perform their duties on public streets and in public buildings, but they are often called into private homes and businesses, where journalists accompanying them are increasingly considered to be trespassers. The trend to view journalists accompanying officials as trespassers runs counter to a famous Florida case.

In *Florida Publishing Company v. Fletcher*, the state supreme court ruled that a *Florida Times Union* photographer did not trespass when he accompanied firefighters into a private home after a major fire that killed a seventeen-year-old girl, Cindy Fletcher. Cindy's mother, Kleena Ann, who was not at home when the fire destroyed the house, sued the *Florida Times Union* for trespass after reading a story about the fire that was accompanied by a photograph of Cindy Fletcher's silhouette outlining where she lay after she was overcome.[108]

The Florida Supreme Court ruled that the *Times Union* photographer did not trespass because he had been invited into the Fletcher home by fire officials. The court reasoned that the practice of journalists accompanying officials into private places following a calamity was so common that the law created an implied consent for the journalists' entry. The court said that journalists accompanying officials onto private property following a catastrophe is similar to a magazine salesperson knocking on a householder's front door. Both acts are so customary, the court reasoned, that the law recognizes a privilege for the entries, a privilege in "custom and usage."

---

[105]Food Lion, Inc. v. Capital Cities/ABC, Inc., 984 F. Supp. 923 (M.D.N.C., 1997).

[106]Barry Meier, "Jury Says ABC Owes Damages of $5.5 Million," *N.Y. Times*, Jan. 23, 1997, at 1; Scott Andron, "Food Lion versus ABC," *Quill*, Mar. 1997, at 15.

[107]Food Lion, Inc. v. Capital Cities/ABC Inc., 887 F. Supp. 811 (M.D.N.C. 1995).

[108]Florida Publishing Co. v. Fletcher, 340 So.2d 914 (Fla. 1976), *cert. denied*, 431 U.S. 930 (1977).

Although the *Fletcher* case has never been overturned, its legal influence is limited primarily to Florida cases involving catastrophes such as fires and hurricanes when the property owner is absent. In most other cases, courts have rejected the conclusion that journalists are not liable for trespass or intrusion if they accompany officials into private domains. A New York court ruled that WROC-TV employees trespassed when they accompanied Ronald Storm of the Humane Society of Rochester and Monroe County on an investigation of a private home. Storm, who had a search warrant, was investigating a complaint that animals were being mistreated at the home of Joy E. Brenon.[109] Brenon, unlike Kleena Ann Fletcher, was home when the official arrived. Brenon objected when the TV crew accompanied Storm into the house and shot footage.

The New York court said the authority of officials to enter private property to perform their duty "does not extend by invitation, absent an emergency, to every and any other member of the public, including members of the news media." The court said the Florida Supreme Court's ruling in the *Fletcher* case expanding the custom-and-usage doctrine to journalists accompanying officials is a "self-created custom and practice" that gives the media greater right to go onto private property than an official who needs a warrant. The authority of state officials to enter private property with a search warrant, the court said, does not extend to people the officials might invite to accompany them.[110]

Not only might journalists trespass and intrude if they accompany officials into private places, but they might also be considered to be officials themselves–acting under **color of law**–who violate citizens' rights of privacy under the Fourth Amendment.

OFFICIALS' LIABILITY In 1999, the U.S. Supreme Court ruled unanimously that officials violate citizens' Fourth Amendment rights when they invite journalists to accompany them into private places while executing a warrant. In *Wilson v. Layne,* the Court ruled that U.S. marshals violated the rights of Charles and Geraldine Wilson in 1992 when the officers allowed two *Washington Post* reporters to observe and photograph an early morning attempt to arrest the Wilsons' son at their home in Rockville, Maryland. The marshals were participating in "Operation Gunsmoke," a national program to apprehend dangerous criminals. A *Post* photographer took pictures of Charles Wilson, dressed only in undershorts, held face down on the floor, and of his wife in a sheer nightgown. The Wilsons' son was not at his parents' home. No photographs were published.[111]

The Supreme Court agreed with officials that the presence of journalists might beneficially publicize law enforcement efforts to combat crime. But the Court said, "the possibility of good public relations for the police is simply not enough . . . to justify the ride-along intrusion into a private home." Furthermore, the need for accurate reporting on police issues "bears no direct relation" to the constitutionally permissible police intrusion into a home to execute an arrest warrant, the Court said.

[109] Anderson v. WROC-TV, 441 N.Y.S.2d 220 (N.Y. Sup. Ct. 1981).

[110] *See also* Miller v. National Broadcasting Co., 232 Cal. Rptr. 668 (Cal. Ct. App. 1987); Green Valley Sch., Inc. v. Cowles Florida Broadcasting, Inc., 327 So.2d 810 (Fla. Dist. Ct. App. 1976); Prahl v. Brosamle, 295 N.W.2d 768 (Wis. Ct. App. 1980); and Kent Middleton, "Journalists, Trespass, and Officials: Closing the Door on Florida Publishing Co. v. Fletcher," 16 *Pepp. L. Rev.* 259 (1989).

[111] 526 U.S. 603 (1999).

The Court also rejected arguments that the presence of reporters during a search might minimize police abuses and protect suspects and officers. Although the presence of third parties might be constitutionally permissible in some cases, the Court said that the *Washington Post* reporters were not in the Wilsons' home to protect the Wilsons or the officers; the reporters were working on a story for their own purposes.

Although the Court held that officials violate the Fourth Amendment when they invite the media into private places, a nearly unanimous Court also ruled that the federal marshals in the Wilson case would not be held liable because they did not know in 1992 that they would violate the Fourth Amendment if they invited journalists to accompany them.

The Court came to a similar conclusion for federal officials in Montana who arranged for the media to accompany them on a search for illegal pesticides. In *Hanlon v. Berger,* the Court ruled that U.S. Fish and Wildlife agents may have violated the Fourth Amendment privacy rights of a Montana couple when the agents coordinated a search with journalists from CNN. However, as in the *Wilson* case, the Court ruled the officers were immune from liability because the law was not clear in 1993 when the search was conducted on the 75,000-acre ranch of Paul and Emma Berger.[112]

While ruling that officials executing a search warrant may not invite journalists onto private property, the Supreme Court did not review a Ninth Circuit ruling that journalists accompanying officials act under **color of law** and therefore may also be liable for violating a citizen's Fourth Amendment right of privacy.[113] The Ninth Circuit ruled that CNN personnel were not acting as independent journalists but were acting under color of law when they signed an agreement with officials and closely coordinated the search of the Bergers' property for evidence the couple were illegally killing eagles. Conversations inside the home were transmitted to CNN recorders from a microphone worn by agent Joel Scrafford. The agreement signed earlier with officials left editorial control of CNN broadcasts with the cable network, while CNN agreed to withhold broadcasts until a potential defendant's rights to a fair trial had been secured. In no other cases, the Ninth Circuit said, "did law enforcement officials engage in conduct approaching the planning, cooperation and assistance to the media that occurred in this case." The court remanded the case to see whether CNN could be liable for trespass and infliction of emotional distress. Paul Berger was acquitted of all charges except for failing to follow the label when using a toxic chemical.

Journalists, like other private citizens, do not become arms of the police simply because they voluntarily help officials[114] or, at their own initiative, accompany officials onto private property to gather news but play no official role.[115] To act under color of law, a journalist must act in "collusion" with[116] or willingly participate in joint activities with state officials.[117] The Ninth Circuit found sufficient coordination between CNN and Wildlife officials for journalists to act "under color of law."

[112]Hanlon v. Berger, 526 U.S. 808 (1999), *vacating and remanding* Berger v. Hanlon, 129 F.3d 505 (9th Cir. 1997).

[113]Berger v. Hanlon, 129 F.3d 505, on remand from the Supreme Court, *aff'd* in part, *rev'd* in part and *remanded,* 188 F.3d 1155 (9th Cir. 1999).

[114]*E.g.,* Marshall v. United States, 352 F.2d 1013 (9th Cir. 1965). *See* Kent Middleton, "Journalists, Trespass, and Officials: Closing the Door on Florida Publishing Co. v. Fletcher," 16 *Pepp. L. Rev.* 259, 290–94 (1989).

[115]Prahl v. Brosamle, 295 N.W.2d 768 (Wis. Ct. App. 1980).

[116]United States v. Gibbons, 607 F.2d 1320 (10th Cir. 1979).

[117]Adickes v. S.H. Kress & Co., 398 U.S. 144 (1970).

Even in those cases in which journalists might act as agents of the government, they are not liable for a civil rights violation unless they violate the Constitution or a federal law. A journalist's defamation or invasion of privacy will generally not give rise to a civil rights claim because neither reputation nor most privacy interests are protected by the Constitution or by federal law.[118]

RECEIVING STOLEN INFORMATION Although journalists may be liable for trespass, at least one court has ruled that they are not liable if they receive the fruits of someone else's trespass. In the major case on this question, national columnist Drew Pearson was not held liable for obtaining private information about Senator Thomas Dodd, information Pearson knew was stolen by the senator's staff. Pearson was not liable for intrusion or trespass because Pearson himself had not trespassed and had not encouraged what might have been a trespass by Dodd's staff.[119]

In addition, the federal appeals court rejected Senator Dodd's assertion that Pearson should be held liable for "conversion" of the senator's property. Conversion is the unauthorized exercise of ownership rights over someone else's property, usually denying the owner use of his or her own property.[120] The court of appeals ruled that there was no conversion because Dodd was not deprived of the use of his files. Pearson received photocopies of originals that had been immediately returned to their proper place in the senator's office.

Furthermore, the court did not consider the letters from constituents, office records, and other routine business of a senator to be "property" because it had no economic value. The court said information in a senator's files was not like a literary creation, scientific invention, or secret business plan whose economic value depends on its being confidential.

Although *Pearson v. Dodd* is the major case on receiving stolen property, people in the media should not feel secure that stolen documents can be published with impunity as long as media personnel themselves do not trespass, steal, or encourage theft. Chief Justice Warren Burger, in his dissent in the *Pentagon Papers* case, said the *New York Times* should have been held liable under a theory of stolen property for publishing the stolen government history of the Vietnam War.[121] Since the 1971 *Pentagon Papers* case, some of the liberals who prevailed against the chief justice in 1971 have been replaced with justices more in tune with the views of Burger and other conservative justices. Furthermore, receiving stolen property could violate a state statute prohibiting the receipt of such goods.[122]

◇ Summary ◇

Trespass, the physical entry onto private property, is closely related to the tort of intrusion. A journalist, like any citizen, can be held liable for trespass. Courts disagree over the circumstances in which journalists employing false identities are trespassers. The Florida

[118] *See* Paul v. Davis, 424 U.S. 693 (1976).

[119] Pearson v. Dodd, 410 F.2d 701 (D.C. Cir.), *cert. denied,* 395 U.S. 947 (1969). *See also* Bilney v. Evening Star, 406 A.2d 652 (Md. Ct. App. 1979).

[120] 89 *Corpus Juris Secundum* (Trover and Conversion) § 1 at 531 (1955). *See* Everette Dennis, "Purloined Information as Property: A New First Amendment Challenge," 50 *Journalism Q* 456 (1973).

[121] New York Times v. United States, 403 U.S. 713 (1971).

[122] People v. Kunkin, 100 Cal. Rptr. 845, *rev'd,* 107 Cal. Rptr. 184 (1973).

Supreme Court said that journalists may accompany authorities onto private property at a disaster scene, but several jurisdictions have rejected the Florida court's reasoning in cases in which the owner is present to object. Officials themselves may violate a citizen's Fourth Amendment right of privacy by inviting journalists to accompany them onto private property, and journalists coordinating raids or searches with officials may themselves be considered to be government agents. A journalist may avoid liability for trespass or intrusion for receiving stolen documents, but the Supreme Court has not ruled on this point.

False Light

A third privacy tort, after embarrassing facts and intrusion, is called *false light.* It is illustrated by the case of John W. Gill, whose picture was snapped as he sat with his arm around his wife Sheila at the counter of their ice cream concession at the Farmers' Market in Los Angeles. As Gill leaned forward, touching his cheek to his wife's, the famous photographer Henri Cartier-Bresson took a photograph without the Gills' knowledge or consent.

The photograph was published a short time later in the *Ladies Home Journal* to illustrate a story about love. But the story didn't portray love as affectionate gestures, like the one Cartier-Bresson caught between the Gills. Under the Gills' picture in the *Journal* appeared the caption, "Publicized as glamorous, desirable, 'love at first sight' is a bad risk." The accompanying story said that love at first sight, the kind the Gills were portrayed as representing, is the "wrong" kind because it is founded on "100% sex attraction."[123]

The Gills sued the publisher of the *Journal* for invasion of privacy. Their complaint was not that their affectionate moment was captured and publicized, but that their picture, with the caption and article, portrayed them falsely. The California Supreme Court ruled the Gills had a cause of action for invasion of privacy. "It is not unreasonable," said the court, to believe that the portrayal of the couple's relationship as based solely on sex "would be seriously humiliating and disturbing."

The *Restatement (Second) of Torts* defines the false-light tort as the dissemination of highly offensive false publicity about someone with knowledge of, or reckless disregard for, the falsity.[124] The interest protected by the law, the *Restatement* says, "is the interest of the individual in not being made to appear before the public in an objectionable false light or false position, or in other words, otherwise than he is."

The false-light tort provokes disagreement over its relationship to libel and other privacy torts, over what constitutes a "highly offensive" publication, and over how much the First Amendment should protect the media from plaintiffs, like the Gills, who assert difficult-to-prove injuries of mental anguish and emotional distress. "False light invasion of privacy has caused enough theoretical and practical problems," one commentator concludes, "to make a compelling case for a stricter standard of birth control in the evolution of the common law."[125]

As the Gill case illustrates, the false-light tort has much in common with libel. Dean William Prosser contended the interest protected by the false-light tort, like the interest protected by libel law, "is clearly that of reputation with the same overtones of mental

[123]Gill v. Curtis Publishing Co., 239 P.2d 630 (Cal. 1952).
[124]*See Restatement (Second) of Torts* § 632E (1977).
[125]Diane Zimmerman, "False Light Invasion of Privacy: The Light That Failed," 64 *N.Y.U. L. Rev.* 364, 366 (1989).

distress as in defamation."[126] Not surprisingly, false-light claims are often filed at the same time as defamation suits. In their suit against the *Ladies Home Journal,* the Gills claimed that the picture, caption, and story not only cast them in a false light but also hurt their reputation for industry, decency, and morality.

In libel and false-light litigation, a plaintiff claims to be the victim of falsehood. Defenses are also similar. False-light defendants, like libel defendants, may claim that the plaintiff is not identified by the publication and that the publication is true. Furthermore, because false-light privacy, like libel, has been "constitutionalized," false-light defendants, like libel defendants, may claim that the plaintiff must prove fault, usually actual malice as required in *New York Times v. Sullivan.*

Although false light shares similarities with libel, the false-light plaintiff does not sue for lost reputation but, like someone suing over publication of embarrassing facts, is seeking recompense, as the Gills were, for the psychic harms of mental distress and humiliation. The late law professor Melville Nimmer thought the false-light tort was a natural derivative of the private-facts tort. Comparing false light and embarrassing facts, Nimmer said an individual has the same privacy interest in "maintaining a haven from society's searching eye" whether true or false information is being revealed.[127] "The injury to the plaintiff's peace of mind which results from the public disclosure of private facts may be just as real where that which is disclosed is not true."

The false-light tort also shares similarities with the embarrassing-facts tort. One similarity is the requirement that a plaintiff in both cases prove the offending material is widely disseminated. Libel plaintiffs must prove that a defamatory remark is "published" to at least one other person besides the plaintiff; a business letter sent to only one person may constitute publication in a libel case. But a false-light plaintiff, like an embarrassing-facts plaintiff, must prove that the false information is widely disseminated. False-light privacy is a tort of publicity.

Several states have refused to recognize the false-light tort. Some states find little relationship between false light and privacy, while others see the law of libel adequately covering what might be considered false light.[128]

Highly Offensive Publications

Although there is substantial inconsistency in judicial rulings in false-light cases, the highly offensive publications that result in false-light suits may be seen to belong to two broad categories: distortion and fictionalization. Cases of only minor falsification do not support a false-light claim.

DISTORTION The most common false-light claim against the media is for the distortion resulting when a broadcaster or publisher omits information or uses it out of context. In a Pennsylvania case, a federal district court refused to set aside a nominal jury award to

[126]Privacy, 48 *Calif. L. Rev.* 383, 400 (1960).

[127]"The Right to Speak from *Times* to *Time:* First Amendment Theory Applied to Libel and Misapplied to Privacy," 56 *Calif. L. Rev.* 935, 958 (1968).

[128]States that do not recognize the false-light tort include Minnesota, Missouri, North Carolina, and Ohio.

Clare Randall Uhl, who sued CBS over editing of a documentary that Uhl claimed falsely suggested he was an unsportsmanlike hunter.

In the documentary titled *The Guns of Autumn,* CBS opened a sequence with wild geese walking in a clearing next to a field. Next, the viewer saw Uhl and other hunters, their guns aimed nearly parallel to the ground, firing from behind nearby cornstalks. Finally, Uhl was shown picking up a goose from the ground. Uhl said the editing erroneously portrayed him shooting birds on the ground instead of in flight. A federal district court agreed with the jury finding that falsely suggesting that a hunter shoots birds on the ground is highly offensive to the average person, at least in areas of the country, such as western Pennsylvania, where wild geese "darken the noonday sky."[129]

The context in which information is used can also distort, particularly when one is portrayed in an offensive sexual milieu. The U.S. Court of Appeals for the Fifth Circuit ruled that Mrs. Ed Braun was portrayed falsely when her picture was published in Larry Flynt's *Chic* magazine, a publication devoted to sex. The picture Flynt published showed Braun in a conservative bathing suit feeding a diving pig named Ralph at a family amusement park in Texas where Braun worked. *Chic* acquired the picture of Braun from the park management by misrepresenting the nature of the magazine. Although *Chic* did not alter Braun's picture, Braun objected to its publication next to stories and pictures about enlarging men's breasts, preparing a Chinese concoction from animals' sexual organs, and demonstrating navel jewelry on nude models.[130] Braun said she was terrified, embarrassed, and humiliated when she learned of the publication.

The court ruled that a jury could have reasonably found that *Chic* cast Braun in a false light by the unauthorized publication of her picture in a magazine "devoted exclusively to sexual exploitation and to disparagement of women." The court said that it could consider the "overall impression" of the magazine in determining that the publication cast Braun in a false light. The court agreed that publication of the photo might erroneously imply that Braun consented to publication of her picture or that she approved of the opinions expressed in *Chic.* A jury might reasonably conclude, the court said, that either misrepresentation was highly offensive.

File photos and television footage of street scenes used to illustrate stories may cast a person in a false light if offensive characteristics are wrongly ascribed to individuals shown. A federal court allowed Linda K. Duncan to pursue a suit against a Washington, D.C., television station for broadcasting scenes falsely suggesting she had herpes. The suit arose from footage WJLA shot of pedestrians, including Duncan, in the capital. Duncan had no false-light claim for the 6 o'clock news broadcast that showed her walking down K Street with other pedestrians. It was not an invasion of privacy for the station to show a close-up of Duncan while the reporter made general statements about herpes. These statements did not suggest Duncan had the disease.

The false-light claim arose from an edited version of the report shown on the 11 o'clock news. As the camera focused on Duncan in the late-night newscast, the reporter said, "For the 20 million Americans who have herpes, it's not a cure." In refusing summary judgment

[129]Uhl v. CBS, 476 F. Supp. 1134 (W.D. Pa. 1979).

[130]Braun v. Flynt, 726 F.2d 245 (5th Cir. 1984). *But see* Faucheux v. Magazine Management, 5 Media L. Rep. 1697 (E.D. La. 1979).

for WJLA, the court said the juxtaposition of the close-up of Duncan and the commentary about twenty million Americans with herpes supported an inference that Duncan had the disease. A jury could decide whether the false inference was sufficiently offensive for Duncan to prevail in a false-light suit.[131]

In contrast, the New York Court of Appeals ruled that Clarence Arrington had no false-light suit against the *New York Times* because characteristics of blacks that Arrington found offensive in an article were not attributed to him. Arrington's picture ran on the cover of the *New York Times Magazine* to illustrate a story about middle-class blacks. Arrington's picture was snapped without his knowledge as he walked down a Manhattan street in a dark business suit. The article portrayed middle-class blacks as "materialistic, status-conscious and frivolous individuals without any sense of moral obligation to those of their race who are economically less fortunate."

Arrington said the cover photo falsely cast him as one of the insensitive, callous blacks discussed in the article.[132] However, the New York Court of Appeals, while not ruling whether New York recognizes the false-light tort, said the article did not portray Arrington himself as holding the ideas or opinions of insensitive blacks. Furthermore, unlike the *Braun* case, in which the sexual context was offensive, Arrington's photo was not published in a news context. The picture and article about the upward mobility of minorities, a newsworthy social issue, were not sufficiently offensive to allow Arrington to sue, the court said.

The Michigan Court of Appeals upheld a trial court ruling that the rap artist Eminem did not place a high school classmate in a false light when Eminem, also known as Marshall Bruce Mathers III, referred to the classmate as a bully. In the song "Brain Damage," Eminem said high school classmate Deangelo Bailey "banged my head against the urinal til he broke my nose, / Soaked my clothes in blood, grabbed me and choked my throat."

The court said the rap song and similar charges of Bailey's bullying in a *Rolling Stone* article were essentially true, although sometimes stated in hyperbolic language that the court said was not believable or highly offensive.[133]

The appeals court affirmed the trial court's granting of Eminem's motion for summary disposition. Trial judge Deborah A. Servitto noted in a footnote:

> Those false light charges that so disturbed
> Prompted from Bailey not a single word
> So highly objectionable, it could not be
> —Bailey was happy to hear his name on a CD
> Bailey also admitted he was a bully in youth
> Which makes what Marshall said substantial truth
> This doctrine is a defense well known
> And renders Bailey's case substantially blown.[134]

FICTIONALIZATION A second category of false light is fictionalization, the addition of fictional dialogue or characters to what are otherwise essentially factual works. Fictionalization

[131]Duncan v. WJLA-TV, Inc., 106 F.R.D. 4 (D.D.C. 1984).

[132]Arrington v. New York Times, 5 Media L. Rep. 2581 (N.Y. Sup. Ct. 1980), *aff'd,* 433 N.Y.S.2d 164 (App. Div. 1980), *aff'd in part,* 449 N.Y.S.2d 941 (N.Y. 1982), *cert. denied,* 459 U.S. 1146 (1983).

[133]Bailey v. Mathers, 2005 Mich. App. LEXIS 930 (per curiam, unpublished, April 14, 2005).

[134]Bailey v. Mathers, Case No. 2001-3606-NO, Macomb County Circuit Court, Oct. 17, 2003.

ranges from the relatively limited embellishment of news stories to the much more elaborate addition of dialogue, characters, scenes, mannerisms, beliefs, and thoughts in fictionalized books, short stories, and "docudramas." An example of embellishment of the news is a story in the *Cleveland Plain Dealer* about Margaret Cantrell and her family five months after the Silver Bridge crashed into the Ohio River, killing Cantrell's husband, Melvin. *Plain Dealer* reporter Joseph Eszterhas wrote the story after a visit to the Cantrell home in Point Pleasant, West Virginia. The article implied that Eszterhas had interviewed Cantrell when he hadn't. Without seeing or interviewing Cantrell, who was not at home when Eszterhas visited, the reporter wrote, "Margaret Cantrell will talk neither about what happened nor about how they are doing. She wears the same mask of non-expression she wore at the funeral."[135]

Margaret Cantrell sued for invasion of privacy, arguing that she was cast in a false light through Eszterhas's deliberate falsifications that implied she was interviewed. She also charged that the article exaggerated the family's poverty. Cantrell said the article made the family objects of pity and ridicule and caused her and her son mental distress, shame, and humiliation. Agreeing with Cantrell, a majority of the Supreme Court ruled that Eszterhas placed Margaret Cantrell in a false light with *New York Times* actual malice through his "significant misrepresentations," primarily the false implication that the reporter interviewed Cantrell during his visit and that he observed her wearing "the same mask of non-expression" that he had seen at Melvin Cantrell's funeral.

Fictionalization that portrays a plaintiff falsely need not be negative or disparaging to be highly offensive. The Hill family was portrayed positively but falsely in a 1955 *Life* magazine article that led to a false-light suit. In the article "True Crime Inspires Tense Play," *Life* reported on a Broadway play that depicted the "ordeal" of the Hill family when three convicts held the Hills hostage in their home for nineteen hours during a weekend in 1952. *Life* said that the play was a "heart-stopping account of how a family rose to heroism in a crisis." *Life* photographed scenes from the play that were said to be reenacted at the house where the Hills were "besieged." One picture, over the caption "brutish convict," showed the son being "roughed up." Another picture, captioned "daring daughter," showed the daughter biting the hand of a convict.[136]

Although the weekend in 1952 was most unpleasant for the Hill family, the convicts, contrary to the *Life* article, did not mistreat the family. In fact, the three convicts treated the Hills courteously and released them unharmed. The Hills neither displayed the heroics nor endured the intimidation portrayed in the article. After their captivity, the family moved from Pennsylvania to Connecticut, but the fictionalized article in *Life* renewed memories that the Hill family was trying to forget. The lower courts upheld the false-light claim, but the Supreme Court reversed on other grounds.

The Supreme Court in *Time, Inc. v. Hill* recognized the false-light tort but ruled that plaintiffs, even private plaintiffs like the Hills, must, like public-figure libel plaintiffs, prove *New York Times* actual malice if they are involved in a newsworthy issue. The fault requirement in false-light cases will be discussed shortly.

[135]Cantrell v. Forest City Publishing Co., 419 U.S. 245 (1974).
[136]Time, Inc. v. Hill, 385 U.S. 374 (1967).

MINOR FALSIFICATION Minor falsehoods that offend only hypersensitive individuals are not sufficiently offensive to support a false-light suit. A federal court ruled that a false statement that parents "instituted a suit" against a psychiatrist for the death of their daughter "but later abandoned" it was too insignificant an error to support a false-light suit. The story should have said that the parents consulted an attorney about bringing a suit but had not begun legal action.[137]

A federal district court ruled that a photo and story that falsely suggested a couple resold American consumer goods in Latin America was also insufficiently offensive to permit a false-light suit. The photo appeared in *Forbes* magazine, illustrating a story about Latin American tourists who boost the Miami economy by buying consumer goods in Florida and reselling them at high profits in Latin America. In the photo, Maxwell Fogel, a Philadelphia dentist, and his wife Anna were shown standing at an airport counter in Miami next to several boxes. The photo accompanied an article about the benefit to the Miami economy of sales to Latin Americans who ship their purchases home, sometimes reselling them at four times the purchase price. The caption under the Fogels' picture said, "The Load: Some Latins buy so much in Miami they've been known to rent an extra hotel room just to store their purchases."[138]

The Fogels, who said they were photographed while waiting to acquire ticket information, charged in their false-light and libel suit that the photograph created the false impression that they were buying merchandise for resale in Latin America and were masquerading as citizens of another country. A federal judge granted summary judgment for the magazine on both libel and false-light claims. The judge said the Fogels' appearance in the photo at the ticket counter did not imply that the couple participated in the Latin American trade. Furthermore, the judge said neither the Fogels' reputation nor privacy would be violated if the photo and story did imply they bought goods in the United States for legal resale elsewhere.

Clearly unbelievable falsification will usually not support a false-light suit. The U.S. Court of Appeals for the Tenth Circuit ruled that a beauty queen had no libel or false-light suit against *Penthouse* magazine because the story that offended her was so obviously unbelievable. The story told of a fictional Miss Wyoming's memories of making men levitate during sex.[139] The court said the story was neither libelous nor an invasion of the privacy of a real Miss Wyoming who sued. The court said the story "described something physically impossible in an impossible setting." The reader would realize, the court said, that the offensive sections of the story were "pure fantasy and nothing else."

However, an Arkansas jury awarded $1.5 million to a ninety-six-year-old woman for published statements about her pregnancy that the average reader would have trouble believing. The jury said that Globe International, publisher of the tabloid *Sun,* should pay Nellie Mitchell $650,000 compensatory damages and $850,000 punitive damages for maliciously publishing her photo to accompany an article entitled "World's oldest newspaper carrier, 101, quits because she's pregnant."

Refusing to overturn the judgment, a federal district court ruled that a jury could reasonably conclude that the publication was highly offensive to Mitchell. The publication

[137]Rinsley v. Brandt, 700 F.2d 1304 (10th Cir. 1983).
[138]Fogel v. Forbes, Inc., 500 F. Supp. 1081 (E.D. Pa. 1981).
[139]Pring v. Penthouse Int'l, Ltd., 695 F.2d 438 (10th Cir. 1982), *cert. denied,* 462 U.S. 1132 (1983).

was, the court said, like being "dragged slowly through a pile of untreated sewage." The court said that even if readers could not believe that a woman in her nineties was pregnant, they could reasonably believe from the picture and story that she was sexually promiscuous. Affirming the district court, a federal appeals court said readers might reasonably believe the stories because the paper continuously "mingles factual, fictional, and hybrid stories" about "the weird, the strange, and the outlandish."[140]

Summary

The false-light tort is the knowing dissemination of highly offensive false publicity. A person may be placed in a false light through highly offensive distortion resulting from omissions and from the use of pictures and broadcast footage out of context. Plaintiffs may also be cast in a false light through embellishment of news and fictionalization in books, short stories, docudramas, and other media. One is not necessarily cast in a false light by minor or fanciful fictionalization or by creative embellishment.

Fault

The media are protected in false-light suits by the First Amendment fault requirement imported by the Supreme Court from the law of libel. In *Time, Inc. v. Hill,* decided three years after *New York Times v. Sullivan,* the Court ruled that false-light plaintiffs involved in issues of public interest may not successfully sue for false light without proving that publication was made with *New York Times* actual malice.

As in *Sullivan,* the *Hill* Court said that the press would be saddled with too great a burden if it had to verify "to a certainty" the accuracy of the facts in news articles. The Court said that sanctions against either innocent or negligent misstatement in stories of public interest could discourage the press from exercising its First Amendment freedoms. Thus, the Hills had to prove malice even though they were private persons involuntarily drawn into an issue of public interest.

Malice in false-light cases, like malice in libel, comprises a combination of reckless or knowing practices, such as fabrication of quotes, reliance on unreliable sources, and failure to heed warnings. Eszterhas published with actual malice in the *Cantrell* case because he misrepresented that he had interviewed Cantrell. Similarly, the author of an unauthorized biography of baseball player Warren Spahn published with malice when he invented dialogue, created imaginary incidents, and attributed imagined thoughts and feelings to Spahn. The author of the Spahn book, like Eszterhas, failed to interview the subject of the work. The author of the Spahn biography also failed to interview any members of Spahn's family or any baseball player who knew him.[141]

A federal court also found actual malice in the case of Larry Flynt's *Chic* magazine and its publication of Braun's photo. The magazine "acted with entire disregard for the falsity of their portrayal of Mrs. Braun," the court said. Not only was her picture published

[140]Peoples Bank & Trust Co. v. Globe Int'l, Inc., 786 F. Supp. 791 (W.D. Ark. 1992), *aff'd,* 978 F.2d 1065 (8th Cir. 1992), *cert. denied,* 510 U.S. 931 (1993).

[141]Spahn v. Julian Messner, Inc., 221 N.E.2d 543 (N.Y. 1966), *appeal dismissed,* 393 U.S. 1046 (1969).

in an offensive sexual context, but the editor misrepresented the nature of the magazine to acquire permission to publish the picture.[142]

Since *Cantrell,* some courts, citing *Gertz v. Welch,* have argued that private false-light plaintiffs, like private libel plaintiffs, should have a lesser burden of proof than actual malice. These courts, which see the false-light tort as paralleling libel, focus on the status of the plaintiffs—whether they are private persons or public figures—rather than on public interest in the subject. These courts see a natural symmetry in requiring private plaintiffs in libel and false-light cases to shoulder a similar burden of proof.

Other courts require private and public false-light plaintiffs to prove reckless disregard as public figures must in libel suits. Courts requiring all false-light plaintiffs to prove malice focus on protecting publication of newsworthy issues. These courts argue that the First Amendment imposes a heavier burden on private false-light plaintiffs than on private libel plaintiffs because the false-light plaintiffs' claims of mental suffering and shame are less demonstrable than the reputational harm asserted by private libel plaintiffs. The press would be exposed to excessive liability to private false-light plaintiffs, it is argued, if the plaintiff were not required to prove malice.

The fault requirement poses a particularly troublesome problem when real people recognize themselves as "fictional" characters in novels and docudramas. Fiction writers usually write from their own experience, but they disguise the real people on whom their work is based by transforming them, making composite characters, and using other literary devices. However, real people may be identified in works that purport to be pure fiction or fictionalizations of real events. Plaintiffs identified in either type of work might sue for libel or false-light privacy.

The identification problem is illustrated in a libel case in which author Gwen Davis Mitchell, in her popular novel *Touching,* did not adequately disguise a psychologist who conducted nude encounter groups. *Touching* was a fictionalized account of the author's experiences in a California nude therapy group called the "Nude Marathon." The encounter group was conducted by Dr. Paul Bindrim.

Mitchell thought she had transformed her experiences in the Nude Marathon sufficiently that she created a work of fiction in which Bindrim could not be identified. The leader of the therapy group in the novel was a Dr. Simon Herford, a crude, vulgar psychiatrist who used four-letter words frequently with his patients. Herford was "a fat Santa Claus type" with "long white hair, white sideburns, a cherubic rosy face and rosy forearms." Bindrim was a clean-shaven, trim psychologist—not a psychiatrist—who did not use profanity with his patients.[143]

Despite the differences between Herford and Bindrim in speech, physical appearance, and professional credentials, a few witnesses said that they recognized Bindrim in the character of Herford by the pattern of Herford's conduct in situations similar to actual occurrences in the Nude Marathon. Thus, fabricated dialogue that Mitchell thought would increase the distance between her fictional doctor and the real one was ruled to have libeled Bindrim by making him out to be crude and unprofessional. Bindrim won $75,000 in damages from Doubleday and Mitchell.

[142]Braun v. Flynt, 726 F.2d 245 (5th Cir. 1984). *But see* Faucheux v. Magazine Management, 5 Media L. Rep. 1697 (E.D. La. 1979).

[143]Bindrim v. Mitchell, 155 Cal. Rptr. 29 (Cal. Ct. App. 1979), *cert. denied,* 444 U.S. 984 (1979).

The *Bindrim* case is a warning that once real people convince a jury they are identified in a fictional work, the author's attempts at disguise become evidence of falsification and, in the *Bindrim* case, defamation. Attempts to disguise real people may also be evidence of malice because malice is knowing falsehood. As the court said in *Bindrim,* "Mitchell's reckless disregard for the truth was apparent from her knowledge of the truth of what transpired at the encounter, and the literary portrayals of that encounter."

Summary

All false-light plaintiffs must meet a fault requirement. Public figures must prove actual malice, but courts divide over whether private plaintiffs must prove actual malice or some lesser degree of fault.

Commercialization

The fourth branch of privacy law is appropriation. The *Restatement (Second) of Torts* says that a person is liable for invasion of privacy if he or she "appropriates to his own use or benefit the name or likeness of another."[144] An appropriation is usually the unauthorized commercial use of another's name or picture in an advertisement, poster, public relations promotion, or other commercial context.

The injury suffered by an appropriation plaintiff may take two forms. A plaintiff whose identity is used for commercial purposes may suffer shame and humiliation similar to that suffered by a private-facts plaintiff, or the plaintiff may suffer loss of a commercial property. Celebrities, in particular, lose the "publicity" value in endorsements and other commercial opportunities when their identities are appropriated without their consent.

Appropriation and Unauthorized Publicity

Appropriation was the first branch of privacy law to develop following publication of Brandeis and Warren's 1890 article in the *Harvard Law Review.* Although Brandeis and Warren did not discuss commercial appropriation, the appropriation tort, as it developed at the turn of the century, is consistent with Brandeis and Warren's concern that people be able to control what is said about them. To publish peoples' names or pictures in commercial contexts without their permission is, in a sense, to deny them the right to be left alone. Pirating one's identity for commercial gain may cause the same mental distress as the revelation of personal information, the disclosure that concerned Brandeis and Warren.

The law of appropriation originated in New York, where a disproportionate number of appropriation cases are still filed because of the concentration there of publishing, broadcasting, public relations, and advertising companies. Under the New York civil rights statute, adopted in 1903, it is a tort and a misdemeanor to use a person's name, portrait, or picture without consent for "advertising purposes or for the purposes of trade."[145]

[144] *Restatement (Second) of Torts* § 652C (1977).
[145] N.Y. Civ. Rights Law § 50–51.

The appropriation sections of the New York civil rights statute were adopted in response to a case in 1902 in which the New York Court of Appeals, the state's highest court, refused to recognize a right of privacy. In *Roberson v. Rochester Folding Box Co.,* the Court of Appeals ruled that Abigail Roberson of Albany had no legal claim to assert when the Franklin Mills Company used the young girl's picture, without her permission, in advertisements for the company's flour.[146] The Franklin Mills advertisements, which referred to Roberson as "The Flour of the Family," were circulated in stores, warehouses, saloons, and other public places. Roberson said she had been "greatly humiliated by the scoffs and jeers of persons who recognized her face and picture."

When the Roberson family sued for invasion of privacy, the New York court ruled in a 4-3 decision that there was no law of privacy. While sympathetic to the Roberson claim, the court was unwilling to recognize a legal remedy for such a purely mental injury as invasion of privacy. The court feared it could not contain the privacy tort if the new category of legal wrong were recognized. If the commercial publication of unauthorized photos may be barred, the court said, what is to prevent the courts from halting the publication of unauthorized photos in news columns? If the unauthorized publication of a person's likeness can be barred, then why not a description or commentary about a person's looks?

Furthermore, the court wondered how it could adequately distinguish between public figures, who abandon much of their right of privacy, and private persons like Abigail Roberson, who do not. Not the least of the court's fears was a deluge of litigation by plaintiffs with ill-defined claims of mental suffering. This imagined barrage of lawsuits would place too great a burden on the press to defend itself, the court said.

After a storm of public disapproval over the court's refusal to recognize a right of privacy, the New York legislature passed a privacy statute prohibiting the unauthorized commercial use of a person's name, portrait, or picture. About the same time, the Georgia Supreme Court became the first state supreme court to recognize commercial appropriation as a violation of a right of privacy.[147] On learning of the Georgia decision, Louis Brandeis wrote he was glad that the right to privacy was finding judicial recognition.[148]

Since the turn of the century, many courts have compensated private citizens like Abigail Roberson for the shame, humiliation, and mental distress suffered when their privacy is invaded through the unauthorized commercial exploitation of their identities. Celebrities and public figures, too, have sued successfully for invasion of privacy when their names, pictures, acts, and talents have been commercially appropriated without their permission. However, some courts have balked at compensating baseball stars, movie actors, singers, and other celebrities for loss of privacy when their identities are commercially appropriated. These courts argue that celebrities, who make their living from public performances, do not suffer a loss of privacy as a private person does when their identities are appropriated for commercial purposes. Celebrities, these courts say, suffer a commercial loss, not the shame and humiliation of an invasion of privacy. In a word, celebrities lose their right of publicity.

The right of publicity, recognized in more than twenty states, is the right of celebrities and public figures to exploit the significant commercial value in their names, pictures,

[146]63 N.E. 442 (N.Y. 1902).
[147]Pavesich v. New England Life Ins. Co., 50 S.E. 68 (Ga. 1905).
[148]1 *Letters of Louis D. Brandeis* 306 (Melvin Urofsky & David Levy eds., 1971).

styles, voices, and other distinctive features and talents. Unlike a right of privacy, the right of publicity is a property right that can be marketed and, in some jurisdictions, willed to one's heirs. "[I]nfringement of the right of publicity looks to an injury to the pocketbook," one commentator notes, while "an invasion of appropriation privacy looks to an injury to the psyche."[149] Unauthorized appropriation of celebrities' identities does not necessarily cause mental distress but may diminish their publicity value, particularly if the appropriation is extensive or tasteless.

A privacy right, tied as it is to a person's personality, dies when the person dies. However, the right of publicity, which is a property right, does not necessarily die with the owner.[150] The right of publicity may be willed to one's heirs. In legal jargon, the right of publicity may be "descendible." Several states have adopted statutes allowing people to will the publicity value in their name or identity to their estate or heirs.[151]

States recognizing the inheritability of publicity rights tend to emphasize one's right to enjoy and pass to one's heirs the fruits of one's industry. In California, a publicity statute prohibits for fifty years after death the commercial use of the name, voice, signature, photograph, or likeness of any "deceased personality" without prior consent of the person or his agent. A deceased personality is anyone who has commercial value in his or her identity at the time of death. However, it is not a violation of the California law or other state statutes recognizing the descendibility of publicity rights to use the identity of a dead person in news, public affairs, sports stories, or political campaigns or in a book, magazine, musical work, film, or television program.[152]

Some states do not recognize a right for people to will publicity rights to their heirs, whether or not the celebrities exploit the rights commercially during their lifetime.[153] In these states, rights of publicity die with the person. Instead of emphasizing the right of individuals to pass the product of their work to their descendants, these states tend to emphasize the personal nature of the right of publicity and the difficulties in treating such rights as independent of the people who made them valuable.

Whether an unauthorized commercial appropriation violates privacy or publicity, the appropriation most often involves the unauthorized use of a person's name or identity in a commercial advertisement, including look-alike and sound-alike advertisements. Appropriation may also occur in other commercial trade contexts.

ADVERTISEMENTS In a typical case, businessperson Donald Manville was allowed to collect damages for invasion of privacy when his picture ran without his permission in newspaper advertisements for Norge self-service laundries. Manville had posed for a picture in front of a laundry with the understanding that the photo would be used in a news story, not as it was published, as an advertisement in which he endorsed Norge laundries as good investments.[154]

---

[149] J. Thomas McCarthy, "Public Personas and Private Property: The Commercialization of Human Identity," 79 *Trademark Rep.* 681, 687 (1989).

[150] W. Page Keeton et al., *Prosser and Keeton on the Law of Torts* 778 (5th ed., 1984).

[151] *See* American Law Institute, *Restatement (Third) of Unfair Competition* § 46–47 (1995).

[152] Cal. Civ. Code § 990.

[153] *E.g.,* N.Y. Civ. Rights Law § 50; R.I. Gen. Laws § 9-1-28; *see generally,* Peter Felcher & Edward Rubin, "The Descendibility of the Right of Publicity: Is There Commercial Life after Death?" 89 *Yale L. J.* 1125 (1980).

[154] Manville v. Borg-Warner Corp., 418 F.2d 434 (10th Cir. 1969).

Identification resulting in commercial appropriation can also be made through nicknames and slogans. The S. C. Johnson & Son Company violated football player Elroy Hirsch's right of publicity by using his nickname, Crazylegs, as the name of a women's shaving gel.[155] Johnny Carson's right of publicity was violated by the manufacturer of portable toilets. The manufacturing company never used Carson's full name or picture but appropriated his identity by using the phrase "Here's Johnny," the same phrase used to introduce Carson on his nightly television program. The company also appropriated Carson's personality by calling its portable toilet "The World's Foremost Commodian."[156]

The Shaklee Corporation appropriated the identity of the author Heloise Bowles in a motivational campaign for the company's distributors. Heloise was the author of books and a syndicated newspaper column of household hints. Shaklee, which makes and sells household cleansers, food supplements, and cosmetics, appropriated Heloise's identity by making it appear that Heloise endorsed Shaklee's products.[157]

Shaklee bought 100,000 copies of *All Around the House,* one of several of Heloise Bowles's writings containing hints on how to make household chores easier. Distributing the books to the company's distributors was not an appropriation of Heloise's name. However, a federal district court said Shaklee advertisements sent to the distributors did appropriate Heloise's name. The ads said, "Welcome to a new Shaklee Woman, Heloise," a woman who "will soon be helping you to open doors and make more sales with Shaklee." Shaklee also altered the back cover of the book to say, "Heloise and Shaklee all around the house just naturally make your day easier." The court said Shaklee's unauthorized association of Heloise's name with the company's products amounted to an unauthorized endorsement for which the court awarded $75,000 in damages.

The court rejected Shaklee's argument that there was no appropriation because the promotional advertisements and book were sent only to company distributors, not to the general consumer. The court noted that the ads went to 240,000 distributors who, besides being employees, were themselves consumers of Shaklee products. More than half a million consumers saw the Heloise advertisements if one counts, as the court did, the spouses and friends who read the company materials sent to distributors.

LOOK-ALIKES AND SOUND-ALIKES A celebrity might successfully sue if he or she is identified through a "look-alike." Jacqueline Onassis obtained an injunction to stop magazine fashion advertisements in which Barbara Reynolds, an Onassis look-alike, was shown at a "legendary" private wedding—"no tears, no rice, no in-laws, no smarmy toasts, for once no Mendelssohn." Reynolds appeared in the Christian Dior ad with actress Ruth Gordon and television personality Gene Shalit. A *Newsweek* magazine story characterized the actors in the much-discussed ads as "idle, rich, suggestively decadent, and aggressively chic."[158]

In ruling for Onassis in her appropriation suit, the court said that imitators can simulate the voice or hairstyle of the famous in noncommercial settings but that "no one is free to trade on another's name or appearance and claim immunity because what he is using is

[155]Hirsch v. S.C. Johnson & Son, Inc., 280 N.W.2d 129 (Wis. 1979).
[156]Carson v. Here's Johnny Portable Toilets, Inc., 698 F.2d 831 (6th Cir. 1983).
[157]National Bank of Commerce v. Shaklee Corp., 503 F. Supp. 533 (W.D. Tex. 1980).
[158]Onassis v. Christian Dior-New York, Inc., 472 N.Y.S.2d 254 (Sup. Ct. Spec. Term 1984).

similar to but not identical with the original." Reynolds "may capitalize on the striking resemblance of facial features at parties, TV appearances, and dramatic works," the court said, but she may not use her face in commercial advertisements that are deceptive or would promote confusion.

In a "sound-alike" case, a California jury awarded Bette Midler $400,000 for an automobile advertisement in which a singer imitated Midler's voice.[159] The U.S. Court of Appeals for the Ninth Circuit had earlier held that a jury should determine whether the Ford Motor Company and the advertising agency Young & Rubicam, Inc., appropriated Midler's identity by broadcasting an ad with a singer who was hired because she sounded like Midler when she sang "Do You Want to Dance."[160] Several people testified that they thought Midler was singing in the commercials.

The Ninth Circuit said it is a tort in California for advertisers to deliberately imitate the distinctive voice of a widely known professional singer to sell a product. Young & Rubicam had acquired permission to use the song but not to imitate Midler's voice. The Ford Motor Company was dropped from the suit. In a similar case, the Ninth Circuit upheld an award of more than $2 million to singer Tom Waits for imitation of his distinctive singing voice in radio ads for SalsaRio Doritos.[161] In 2006, Waits was awarded damages in a case against the Audi division of Volkswagen for a Spanish commercial in which a voice like Waits's sang music similar to Waits's "Innocent When You Dream."[162]

TRADE PURPOSES Appropriations do not always occur in advertisements for commercial products. It is also possible to appropriate peoples' identities or violate their right of publicity through the unauthorized use of their names or likenesses in public relations promotions, posters, and other commercial purposes that do not advertise a product. The New York privacy statute bars the unauthorized commercial use of someone's name not only in advertising but also for other "purposes of trade."

The model Christie Brinkley sued successfully under the trade section of the New York law to stop unauthorized use of her picture on posters sold in stores. The posters did not advertise any products but traded on Brinkley's good looks and popularity without her consent.[163] In another trade case, a man was allowed to bring an appropriation suit when his picture was used without permission in a Minox camera manual. The manual served an educational purpose but also was ruled to be an appropriation of the man's identity for commercial purposes.[164]

It is not an appropriation to make an *incidental* reference to a real person in a book, film, play, musical, or other work, whether fact or fiction. Even identifying persons in a corporate documentary that builds goodwill but does not advertise a product has been ruled not to be a misappropriation. The U.S. Court of Appeals for the Fifth Circuit ruled that Anheuser-Busch Companies did not appropriate Roy Benavidez's identity by depicting him as a hero in a documentary about valiant Hispanic soldiers. Benavidez appeared in an

---

[159]Midler v. Young & Rubicam, 944 F.2d 909 (9th Cir. 1991), *cert. denied,* 503 U.S. 951 (1992).
[160]Midler v. Ford Motor Co., 849 F.2d 460 (9th Cir. 1988).
[161]Waits v. Frito-Lay, Inc., 978 F.2d 1093 (9th Cir. 1992), *cert. denied,* 506 U.S. 1080 (1993).
[162]Ben Sisario, "Still Fighting for the Right to His Voice," *N.Y. Times,* Jan. 20, 2006.
[163]Brinkley v. Casablancas, 438 N.Y.S.2d 1004 (App. Div. 1981).
[164]Selsman v. Universal Photo Books, Inc., 238 N.Y.S.2d 686 (App. Div. 1963).

eighty-second segment of the thirteen-minute film titled *Heroes*. The documentary recounted the exploits of Hispanic Congressional Medal of Honor recipients.

The Corporate Relations Department of Anheuser-Busch Companies supervised and paid for the film, which was developed at the request of the National Association of Latino Elected and Appointed Officials from information supplied by the Department of Defense. The film was made available to schools, government agencies, veterans' organizations, and Hispanic organizations. It may also have been shown at Anheuser-Busch hospitality centers where the company distributes free beer.[165]

The appeals court said there was insufficient commercial benefit to Anheuser-Busch to support a misappropriation claim. No beer was sold at the hospitality centers, no orders were taken or solicited, and no one was forced to watch the film. Undoubtedly, Anheuser-Busch "may enjoy increased good will in the Hispanic community" as a result of the film, the court said, but the "incidental" commercial benefit did not support a claim for misappropriation.

◇ Summary ◇

Appropriation is the unauthorized commercialization of another. Appropriation may or may not be accompanied by the mental stresses associated with invasions of privacy. A violation of one's right of publicity, however, is the taking of the marketable, sometimes inheritable, property interest celebrities own in their looks, voices, and talents. Appropriation and violation of publicity rights may occur in unauthorized advertisements and promotions.

Defenses

Traditional defenses in appropriation and publicity suits have been newsworthiness and consent. However, the First Amendment is appearing more frequently as a defense for disseminating someone's name, picture, or identity without their consent.

THE FIRST AMENDMENT An emerging defense in publicity cases is a constitutional privilege to disseminate information of public interest. The Utah Supreme Court ruled that the First Amendment protected a U.S. senator from a publicity suit when he published constituents' pictures in campaign literature. Postal workers who posed with Senator Orrin Hatch said the picture reproduced in reelection literature constituted an implicit endorsement of the senator, which they did not intend and which they said violated their publicity rights. But the Utah court ruled that the campaign literature was newsworthy information protected by the First Amendment. The court said persons who pose with, or inadvertently appear with, public officials or candidates may not claim their identity has been appropriated if the picture is taken in a public or semipublic place.[166]

Even without constitutional protection, Senator Hatch would have defeated the postal workers' publicity claim because the court ruled the senator appropriated nothing of value from them. A political endorsement by an unknown member of the general public has no

[165]Benavidez v. Anheuser-Busch, Inc., 873 F.2d 102 (5th Cir. 1989).
[166]Cox v. Hatch, 761 P.2d 556 (Utah 1988).

"intrinsic value," the court said. In addition, the court said the workers had no appropriation claim because use of their names and likenesses was "incidental to the purpose of showing Senator Hatch in the company of workers. Other workers' pictures would have sufficed as well."

A political poster has also been ruled to be constitutionally protected newsworthy expression. In *Paulsen v. Personality Posters, Inc.,*[167] the New York Supreme Court said that a poster of presidential candidate and comedian Pat Paulsen was protected by the First Amendment even though it was being sold for profit. Unlike the poster of Christie Brinkley, which merely capitalized on the model's good looks, the Paulsen poster provided political comment on a mock presidential campaign in which Paulsen was participating. The poster showed Paulsen holding an unlit candle in one hand and cradling a rubber tire in his other arm. A "For President" sash was draped across his chest as if he were a contestant in a beauty pageant.

The court said the poster was constitutionally protected political commentary even though Paulsen was "only kidding" about his candidacy for president. "When a well-known entertainer enters the presidential ring, tongue in cheek or otherwise, it is clearly newsworthy and of public interest," the court said. "A poster which portrays plaintiff in that role, and reflects the spirit in which he approaches said role, is a form of public interest presentation to which protection must be extended." The protected status of the poster was not altered, the court said, because the poster might be merely entertaining to some.

Entertainment news may also be constitutionally protected. A federal court in New York ruled that the First Amendment protected a magazine that published a photo of actress Ann-Margret partially nude. Ann-Margret brought a publicity and appropriation suit against *High Society* magazine for publishing the photograph taken from a film. Ruling against the actress, the court said that newsworthy matters protected by the First Amendment include items "of entertainment and amusement." Ann-Margret's movie appearance would be of great interest to many people, the court said.[168]

In the only publicity case on which the Supreme Court has ruled, the high court held that the First Amendment does not protect the media from appropriation suits brought under state law if the media appropriate an entertainer's whole act. In *Zacchini v. Scripps-Howard,* the Supreme Court ruled that the First Amendment did not bar a human cannonball from pursuing a publicity suit under Ohio law against a television station that broadcast his entire act during a news program.[169]

WEWS-TV in Cleveland broadcast Zacchini's act on the news even though Zacchini asked the news team not to. WEWS's coverage consisted of a fifteen-second news clip of Zacchini from the time he blasted from the cannon until he landed safely in a net. The segment did not show Zacchini inspecting the cannon and net as drumrolls built tension. In the newscast, the station's freelance reporter said the film did not do justice to Zacchini's exciting act and that viewers should see it at the fair.

Zacchini sued for $25,000, saying that WEWS-TV had appropriated his professional property without consent. He did not seek to stop publicity about his act but wanted to be paid for it. The Supreme Court of Ohio ruled that the news broadcast was protected by the First

[167]299 N.Y.S.2d 501 (Sup. Ct. 1968).
[168]Ann-Margret v. High Society Magazine, Inc., 498 F. Supp. 401 (S.D.N.Y. 1980).
[169]Zacchini v. Scripps-Howard Broadcasting Co., 433 U.S. 562 (1977).

Amendment because it was of legitimate public interest. But the U.S. Supreme Court held that the First Amendment did not provide a privilege to broadcast someone's whole act. The Court did not consider the drumrolls and Zacchini's inspections before blastoff to be part of the act. Writing for a five-person majority, Justice White said WEWS appropriated Zacchini's entire "professional property." White said Zacchini might have had no case if WEWS had simply reported that Zacchini was performing at the fair. But broadcasting his entire act, the Court said, posed "a substantial threat to the economic value of that performance" because viewers of the broadcast might not pay to see Zacchini in person. In dissent, Justice Powell, joined by Justices William Brennan and Thurgood Marshall, argued that the broadcast segment about Zacchini's act was a constitutionally protected report of a newsworthy event.

Although the media lost the *Zacchini* case, the Court's decision does not greatly inhibit reporting. The case is limited by its unusual facts, facts that would seldom be duplicated. Rarely would reporters risk violating a right of publicity by reporting "all" of an act or performance. Football games, ice pageants, and plays are too long for the evening news, and admission of the media is usually controlled by the promoter.

◇ Summary ◇

Courts have recognized a First Amendment privilege for newsworthy information used in campaign literature, commercial political posters, and entertainment news but not in broadcasts of a performer's whole act.

NEWSWORTHINESS The traditional defense at common law in commercialization cases is newsworthiness. Newsworthiness is a broad defense in appropriation cases as it is in private-facts cases. Publication or broadcast of names and pictures in news reports of political, social, and entertainment events are not commercial appropriations. The fact that the media are commercial enterprises motivated by profit and supported by advertising does not diminish the newsworthiness of the items they publish and broadcast. "It is the content of an article or picture, not the media's motive to increase circulation, which determines whether an item is newsworthy," the New York Court of Appeals has said.[170]

Events may be newsworthy even if they are commercially sponsored. The newsworthiness of an Elvis Presley press conference allowed producers of a "talking magazine" to reproduce and distribute large segments of the conference even though the event was staged as a commercial promotion by Presley's record company.[171] The recorded segments of the conference appeared in *Current Audio,* a magazine that included written and photographic material supplemented with a stereo record that included interviews and commentary. RCA Corporation, which sponsored the press conference, said the extensive coverage of the conference, including the voice recording, violated the company's exclusive contract with Presley.

But the court said a press conference of a popular singing star is newsworthy. "To hold, as [RCA] urges, that one who has freely and willingly participated in a press conference has some property right which supersedes the right of its free dissemination . . . would

[170]Stephano v. News Group Publications, Inc., 474 N.E.2d 580 (1984).
[171]Current Audio, Inc. v. RCA Corp., 337 N.Y.S.2d 949 (Sup. Ct. 1972).

constitute an impermissible restraint upon the free dissemination of thoughts, ideas, newsworthy events, and matters of public interest," the court said.

The picture on the cover of a book or magazine is newsworthy if the subject is a newsworthy event or is reasonably related to a newsworthy subject inside the publication. *New York* magazine won an appropriation suit brought by Duncan Murray after the magazine published a cover photo of Murray at the city's St. Patrick's Day parade. In a picture taken by a freelance photographer, Murray was dressed in the "striking attire" of an Irish hat, a green bow tie, and a green pin. The New York Court of Appeals said the picture was newsworthy because Murray participated in "an event of public interest to many New Yorkers." Furthermore, the picture was related to a newsworthy article on Irish immigrants in the magazine.[172]

If a cover picture is not related to newsworthy content inside a publication, the use may be considered an appropriation. A black teen received $1,500 under the New York appropriation statute for the unauthorized use of her picture on the cover of a book about getting into college. The picture was used not because the teen was a subject of the book but to promote sales to minorities. The publisher was unaware that the freelancer who took the picture lacked written consent to use the picture for a commercial purpose.[173]

Media Promotion Courts have consistently ruled that it is not an appropriation for publishers and broadcasters to promote the media's own publications and programs with advertisements containing previously published or broadcast news and photos. In one well-known case, *Holiday* magazine successfully defended itself against an appropriation suit brought when the magazine advertised itself with previously published pictures of actress Shirley Booth.

Holiday had photographed Booth wearing a fashionable hat and immersed in water up to her neck at a resort in the West Indies.[174] After the picture was published in a newsworthy travel story, *Holiday* published the photo again in an advertisement for the magazine. Booth sued for appropriation under the New York Civil Rights Statute. In ruling for *Holiday,* New York Appellate Judge Charles Breitel said:

> so long as the reproduction was used to illustrate the quality and content of the periodical in which it originally appeared, the statute was not violated, albeit the reproduction appeared . . . for purposes of advertising the periodical.[175]

Such commercial uses are not an appropriation because they do not imply that the person pictured endorses the publication. The use of the person is said to be only "incidental" to the media advertisement for its news and entertainment.

The media may also advertise books, broadcasts, and other presentations with photos and footage not previously disseminated. The U.S. Court of Appeals for the Second Circuit said that the First Amendment may require that a book publisher be allowed to publish in

[172]Murray v. New York Magazine, 267 N.E.2d 256 (N.Y. 1971).
[173]Spellman v. Simon & Schuster, 3 Media L. Rep. 2406 (N.Y. County 1978).
[174]Booth v. Curtis Publishing Co., 223 N.Y.S.2d 737 (App. Div.), *aff'd,* 182 N.E.2d 812 (N.Y. 1962). *See also* Namath v. Sports Illustrated, 363 N.Y.S.2d 276 (Sup. Ct. 1975), *aff'd,* 371 N.Y.S.2d 10 (App. Div. 1975), *aff'd,* 352 N.E.2d 584 (N.Y. 1976).
[175]223 N.Y.S.2d 744.

an advertisement the picture of the author of a competing book. The Second Circuit said Random House could publish the picture of Robert Groden, the author of a book arguing that several conspirators killed President Kennedy, in an advertisement for Random House's *Case Closed* by Gerald Posner. Posner's book about the Kennedy assassination rejected conspiracy theories.

The Second Circuit concluded that the ad fell within the incidental use exception to the appropriation law, an exception that "implements, and might even be required by, First Amendment considerations." What drives the incidental use exception, the court said, "is the First Amendment interest in protecting the ability of news disseminators to publicize, to make public, their own communications."[176] Similarly, the Oregon Supreme Court ruled that a station did not appropriate the identity of an accident victim receiving emergency medical care when the station broadcast tape of the woman in an advertisement for the station's special report on emergency medical services.[177]

Summary

Newsworthiness is a broad defense allowing the use of information of public interest in commercial contexts. Newsworthiness has been recognized in reports of commercially staged press conferences and in the photos on book covers. Newsworthy names and photos may also be used in incidental advertising for a publication or broadcast.

CONSENT Besides the First Amendment and newsworthiness, consent is a defense in commercialization cases. A broadcaster or publisher generally need not acquire consent to present people in newsworthy reports because newsworthy uses of a person's identity are not considered commercial appropriations. However, advertisers and public relations practitioners normally should acquire written consent from participants in commercial advertisements and public relations promotions. As with any contract, consent agreements should be written, should state the parties to the agreement, state the scope and duration of the terms, and should provide for consideration. Consideration is the payment for the use of the name or picture.

A name or picture should not be used commercially after consent has expired. Actor Charles Welch was awarded $1,000 compensatory damages and $15,000 punitive damages because the Mr. Christmas company broadcast Welch's commercials after his contract expired. Under terms of the contract, Mr. Christmas could run the ads for two years, but the company ran them for three.[178]

Altering or falsifying materials may also violate a consent agreement. Maryland Manger, the author of a prize-winning letter on "Why I Am Glad I Chose Electrolysis as a Career," won an appropriation suit against the Kree Institute of Electrolysis because the institute changed her letter into an endorsement for the institute's electrolysis machine.[179]

---

[176] Groden v. Random House, 61 F.3d 1045 (2d Cir. 1995).
[177] Anderson v. Fisher Broadcasting Co., 712 P.2d 803 (Or. 1986).
[178] Welch v. Mr. Christmas, Inc., 447 N.Y.S.2d 252 (App. Div. 1982), *aff'd*, 57 N.Y.2d 971 (1982).
[179] Manger v. Kree Institute of Electrolysis, Inc., 233 F.2d 5 (2d Cir. 1956).

Manger was the winner of a contest conducted by Kree, an institute that taught electrolysis and sold the Radiomatic electrolysis machine that permanently removed superfluous hair. Manger, who used a different machine, signed a consent form permitting Kree to publish her winning letter and picture in Kree's magazine. A jury ruled that Kree appropriated Manger's identity in violation of the consent agreement when the institute's publication referred to her as a "Kree operator" and changed her letter into an endorsement of the Radiomatic, an electrolysis machine she did not use.

Releases must be signed by mentally competent adults. Parents must sign for minors. Actress Brooke Shields learned that agreements signed by parents on behalf of minors are usually binding. When Shields turned seventeen, she tried to enjoin publication of nude photos taken of her in a bathtub when she was ten. Shields's mother had signed a contract granting photographer Gary Gross unlimited rights to take and use the innocent photos of Brooke in return for $450.

Shields, who as a teen made provocative advertisements for Calvin Klein clothes, said the nonpornographic bathtub photos embarrassed her simply because "they are not me now." But the court ruled that a parent's consent is binding for a minor. "A parent who wishes to limit the publicity and exposure of her child," the court said, "need only limit the use authorized in the consent."[180]

An oral or implied agreement is not satisfactory under the New York Civil Rights Law and may not be binding in other jurisdictions. Betty Frank Lomax, a radio announcer and interviewer, was allowed to sue in New York for appropriation because her employer had not acquired written consent to use her identity commercially. To keep her job, Lomax had reluctantly agreed orally to appear at sales meetings and to hand out autographed pictures promoting the station. Lomax was allowed to sue because her employer had not acquired written consent to use her identity.[181]

Consent may often take the form of a broad model release. The broadest releases give the advertiser unrestricted rights to take, copyright, alter, sell, and publish a model's or actor's photograph. Unrestricted-use contracts allow great flexibility to advertisers and the media, but a model who signs such an open-ended contract may later regret the broad terms.

A New York court ruled that a model who signed an unrestricted consent form was blocked from suing for appropriation when her photo was sold for uses she disliked. The highly paid model, Mary Jane Russell, was barred from an appropriation suit when Springs Mills retouched one of her photos the company bought from Marboro Books. Russell signed a release granting unrestricted use of her picture to photographer Richard Avedon, who took several pictures of Russell for advertisements of Marboro Books. Russell had no objection to Marboro's use of her picture showing her in bed, next to her "husband's" bed, reading an educational book. The caption said, "For People Who Take Their Reading Seriously."

Russell objected, however, when the picture was sold to Springs Mills, Inc., a manufacturer of bedsheets, and retouched so that Russell appeared to be reading a pornographic book. Springs Mills also added captions suggesting a "lost weekend" and other risque activities.

[180]Shields v. Gross, 451 N.Y.S.2d 419 (App. Div. 1982), *aff'd as modified,* 58 N.Y.2d 338 (1983). A federal court also refused an injunction in Shields v. Gross, 563 F. Supp. 1253 (S.D.N.Y. 1983).

[181]Lomax v. New Broadcasting Co., 238 N.Y.S.2d 781 (App. Div. 1963).

Russell said the bedsheet ad contradicted her modeling image as an intelligent, well-bred young wife in socially approved situations.

A New York court said the unrestricted consent form Russell signed barred an appropriation suit for Marboro's sale or Springs Mills's purchase of the original photograph. However, the court said unrestricted consent did not block a suit for libel. The court said Springs Mills might have so altered the emphasis, background, and context of Russell's picture as to make it an essentially different—and perhaps libelous—picture.[182]

◇ Summary ◇

Communicators should have written consent to use a person's name or picture for commercial purposes. Oral consent may be unsatisfactory. Consent agreements, signed by competent adults, should state the parties to the agreement and the scope and duration of the terms and should provide for consideration. A name or picture should not be used commercially after consent has expired.

Emotional Distress and Personal Injury

As the libel and privacy chapters illustrate, plaintiffs suing the media for libel and invasion of privacy often claim anxiety, humiliation, and other emotional distress. Sometimes, however, plaintiffs claim emotional distress as a separate tort, independent of defamation, invasion of privacy, or other wrong. Courts have been reluctant to recognize liability for the intangible harms of emotional distress just as they have been reluctant to recognize liability for the mental suffering of the privacy plaintiff. Damages are not easily awarded when, as in emotional distress and privacy cases, it may be difficult to prove what, if anything, a plaintiff suffers. Besides, minor insults and threats are an unfortunate fact of life. "It would be absurd," a legal text notes, "for the law to seek to secure universal peace of mind."[183] Law may be an especially inappropriate remedy when the source of mental discomfort is a publisher or broadcaster with a First Amendment mandate to promote robust debate that may be disquieting.

Nevertheless, courts do occasionally recognize the tort of intentional infliction of emotional distress where "outrageous" conduct by the media is thought to cause severe anxiety in private persons. Of related concern are cases in which plaintiffs argue, usually unsuccessfully, that the media cause physical harm either by "inciting" readers and viewers to illegal action, or through negligence, where the media fail to foresee that members of an audience will emulate violent acts they see or read about. A few courts have held the media liable for failing to foresee physical harm that would result from publication.

Intentional Infliction of Emotional Distress

A plaintiff can sue for intentional infliction of emotional distress when another's conduct is "so outrageous in character, and so extreme in degree, as to go beyond all possible bounds of decency, and to be regarded as atrocious, and utterly intolerable in a civilized

[182]Russell v. Marboro Books, Inc., 183 N.Y.S.2d 8 (Sup. Ct. 1955).
[183]W. Page Keeton et al., *Prosser and Keeton on the Law of Torts* 56 (5th ed. 1984).

community."[184] The intentional infliction tort is also called "outrage." Conduct is sufficiently shocking to support an emotional distress suit when, for example, a person delivers a rat to a customer who ordered bread[185] or harasses a debtor with repeated abusive threats of lawsuits and ruined credit.[186] The victim suffers rather ill-defined, subjective mental anguish and emotional upset. The victim may also suffer tangible damages such as ulcers and lost wages.

The media have been sued several times for intentional infliction of emotional distress, but usually unsuccessfully. Whether a publication or broadcast constitutes outrageousness is a particularly subjective judgment based on the facts of a case. Statements insufficiently outrageous to sustain a lawsuit include disclosing the identity of undercover narcotics agents,[187] publishing the details of a loved one's death in an emergency room,[188] calling a leading opponent of pornography the "Asshole of the Month,"[189] and saying that a murdered daughter had "no family support."[190] Whatever the lack of taste or sensitivity displayed by the media in these cases, the courts found insufficient grounds to hold them legally liable for intentional infliction of emotional distress.

However, in recent years, several courts have refused to dismiss intentional infliction claims in cases of aggressive news coverage of vulnerable private people. In 1993, CBS settled a suit wth Yolanda Baugh, who claimed the network intentionally inflicted emotional distress by broadcasting a videotape of her made shortly after she was allegedly attacked by her husband.[191] A federal district judge in California had earlier ruled that Baugh might have an emotional distress claim against a CBS news crew that broadcast the taped conversation between Baugh and a crisis intervention worker at Baugh's home after the alleged attack.[192]

The judge denied CBS's motion for summary judgment in a suit in which Baugh charged that a CBS crew acted "outrageously" when it taped her for segments of *Street Stories*. The court said CBS might have acted outrageously when the news crew taped Baugh, knowing that she was psychologically vulnerable shortly after an alleged incident of domestic violence. In addition, the court said the CBS team may have contributed to the emotional distress by acting fraudulently if the CBS employees misrepresented themselves—as Baugh claimed they did—as a camera crew from the district attorney's office.

An Orlando television station also settled an outrage case rather than go to trial after a Florida court refused to dismiss a suit over the grisly broadcast of a girl's skull.[193] WESH-TV, Channel 2, agreed to pay Robert and Donna Armstrong $175,000 for

[184] *Restatement (Second) of Torts* § 46 comment d (1965). *See* Robert Drechsel, "Negligent Infliction of Emotional Distress: New Tort Problem for the Mass Media," 12 *Pepp. L. Rev.* 889 (1985).

[185] Great Atl. & Pac. Tea Co. v. Roch, 153 A. 22 (Md. 1931).

[186] W. Page Keeton et al., *Prosser and Keeton on the Law of Torts* 61 (5th ed. 1984).

[187] Ross v. Burns, 612 F.2d 271 (6th Cir. 1980).

[188] Reichenbach v. Call-Chronicle, 9 Media L. Rep. 143 (Penn. Ct. C. P. Lehigh County 1982).

[189] Ault v. Hustler, 13 Media L. Rep. 2232 (D. Or. 1987), *aff'd,* 860 F.2d 877 (9th Cir. 1988), *cert. denied,* 489 U.S. 1080 (1989).

[190] Holtzscheiter v. Thomson Newspapers, Inc., 411 S.E.2d 664 (S.C. 1991).

[191] Baugh v. CBS, No. C93-0601 FMS (ARB), 1993 WL 280319 (N.D. Cal. July 20, 1993).

[192] Baugh v. CBS, 828 F. Supp. 745 (N.D. Cal. 1993).

[193] "Orlando TV Station Settles Outrage Case," *Brechner Report* (University of Florida), November 1991, at 1.

broadcasting a dramatic close-up of a police officer lifting the skull of their daughter, Regina Mae, from a box.[194] The broadcast began with an emotional story about the memorial services held that day for six-year-old Regina Mae, who had been abducted three years earlier. The Armstrongs, who had not been warned of the broadcast, watched the news program in shock, the court reported.

A California court refused to dismiss a case in which television journalists, knowing no adult was present, told three young children in their home that their neighbor had killed herself and her three children. Even though the station never broadcast the children's reactions to the murders and suicide, the court said the broadcasters' conduct might be sufficiently outrageous for a jury to award damages.[195] Citing the *Restatement of Torts,* the court concluded a jury could find that a television reporter who "attempts deliberately to manipulate the emotions of young children for some perceived journalistic advantage has engaged in conduct 'so outrageous in character, and so extreme in degree, as to go beyond all possible bounds of decency.'"

Although private persons may occasionally be allowed to pursue outrage suits against the media, the Supreme Court has all but eliminated such suits by public figures and officials. For a time, public figures viewed intentional infliction of emotional distress suits as an alternative to libel and false-light privacy claims because the person claiming emotional distress, unlike the plaintiff suing for libel or false-light privacy, did not have to prove the media published with malice.

However, in a case pitting *Hustler* magazine against the Reverend Jerry Falwell, the U.S. Supreme Court ruled that public figures may not successfully sue the media for intentional infliction without proving—as in a libel suit—that they are the subject of a false statement of fact published with *New York Times* actual malice. The Court's decision, in the case of a crude parody portraying Falwell as an incestuous drunkard, means that public officials and public figures will be unable to sue successfully for even the most biting satire or criticism unless it contains a provably false fact and is published with actual malice.[196]

Falwell charged that *Hustler* magazine engaged in outrageous conduct by publishing an advertisement satirizing an advertisement for Campari Liqueur. In the real Campari advertisement, celebrities talk about their "first time," that is, their first encounter with Campari Liqueur, often in glamorous settings. But in the *Hustler* parody (see Figure 5.1), Falwell's "first time" is a sexual encounter with his mother in a Lynchburg, Virginia, outhouse. Falwell's mother is portrayed as a drunken and immoral woman, and Falwell appears as a hypocrite and habitual drunkard. At the bottom of the page is a disclaimer stating, "ad parody—not to be taken seriously."

Falwell sued for libel, invasion of privacy, and intentional infliction of emotional distress. The U.S. Court of Appeals for the Fourth Circuit ruled that the parody did not invade privacy under Virginia law because it was not used for commercial purposes. There was no libel, the court said, because no reasonable person would believe that the statements about Falwell in

[194]Armstrong v. H&C Communications, Inc., 575 So.2d 280 (Fla. Dist. Ct. App. 1991).
[195]KOVR-TV, Inc. v. Superior Court of Sacramento County, 37 Cal. Rptr. 2d 431 (Cal. App. 1995).
[196]Hustler Magazine, Inc. v. Falwell, 485 U.S. 46 (1988).

FIGURE 5.1 Reproduced with permission of L.F.P, Inc. and Larry Flynt.

the parody were factual. However, the Fourth Circuit did rule the outrageous language of the parody caused Falwell emotional distress. In *Hustler Magazine, Inc. v. Falwell,* the Supreme Court reversed in a unanimous decision written by Chief Justice William Rehnquist.

Chief Justice Rehnquist agreed with Falwell that the *Hustler* advertisement was "doubtless gross and repugnant in the eyes of most." But the Court said the caricature of Falwell contained constitutionally protected ideas and opinions about a public figure. The ad did not contain "actual facts" about Falwell "or actual events in which [he] participated." Rather, the ad contained statements about Falwell that were so outrageous that they could not be true, the Court said. The very outrageousness of the parody placed it in the realm of ideas and opinion, not false and possibly defamatory facts. The Court said that the *Hustler* cartoon was a tasteless version of political cartoons that have flayed public figures through American history. Justice Rehnquist compared the advertising parody to political cartoons of Thomas Nast castigating the Tweed Ring in New York and cartoons of George Washington portrayed as an ass. Cartoons may be offensive, but they contain constitutionally protected ideas and opinion.

The Court said an "outrageousness" standard of liability is unconstitutional because it is too subjective and would punish the publisher's motives. Rehnquist said public debate might suffer no harm if courts could punish outrageous cartoons, but the chief justice said he doubted there is any principled way to make a distinction between outrageous and reasonable cartoons. "'Outrageousness' in the area of political and social discourse," he said,

> has an inherent subjectiveness about it which would allow a jury to impose liability on the basis of the jurors' tastes or views, or perhaps on the basis of their dislike of a particular expression. An "outrageousness" standard thus runs afoul of our longstanding refusal to allow damages to be awarded because the speech in question may have an adverse emotional impact on the audience.[197]

The Court also said that holding *Hustler's* publisher, Larry Flynt, liable for outrageous political opinions would unconstitutionally punish him for bad motives. In debate about public affairs, the First Amendment protects many things "done with motives that are less than admirable," the Court said. Indeed, the Court noted, a political cartoon is often "intentionally injurious"; the purpose of a political cartoon is to be "a weapon of attack, of scorn and ridicule and satire." In a word, the cartoonist's motive is to be outrageous.

◇ Summary ◇

The media seldom are sued successfully for intentional infliction of emotional distress, conduct so outrageous as to be beyond human decency. However, several courts have recently permitted private persons to pursue intentional infliction suits over aggressive reportorial practices. Attempts by public figures to employ intentional infliction suits as

[197]*Id.* at 55. *See generally* Rodney Smolla, "Emotional Distress and the First Amendment: An Analysis of *Hustler v. Falwell,*" 20 *Ariz. St. L. J.* 369 (1988).

substitutes for libel and privacy suits were stalled when the Supreme Court ruled that the First Amendment bars outrage suits by public figures who cannot prove the statements are false and published with actual malice.

Physical Harm

Besides being charged with inflicting emotional distress, the media are also accused of causing physical harm, the most frequent instances being when someone emulates or copies what they have seen or read. Some plaintiffs argue the media "incite" harm when mimics of the media harm themselves or others. Courts have tended to reject the incitement arguments as they have also rejected claims that the media should be held liable for negligence, that is, failing to foresee that audience members might hurt themselves or others by copying what they read and hear.

INCITEMENT When stories or programs appear to cause physical harm, some courts have ruled that the First Amendment prohibits holding the media responsible unless it can be shown that the media "incited" the harmful action. The U.S. Court of Appeals for the Fifth Circuit ruled that *Hustler* magazine was not liable for the death of a fourteen-year-old because the magazine story that led to the death did not incite the dangerous act. In *Herceg v. Hustler,* the appeals court reversed a $169,000 jury award to Diane Herceg for the death of her son, Troy D., from experimenting with "autoerotic asphyxia," a masturbatory practice he had read about in *Hustler.*

Hustler published a detailed article about autoerotic asphyxia, the practice of masturbating while "hanging" oneself. Practicing autoerotic asphyxia, one is supposed to increase sexual pleasure by cutting off the blood supply to the brain at the moment of orgasm. *Hustler* warned its readers not to attempt autoerotic asphyxia because it is dangerous. The article began with accounts of people who died trying it.[198] Nevertheless, Troy D. attempted it. Troy's nude body was found hanging by the neck in his closet. A jury decided that the article had incited Troy's fatal act. The Fifth Circuit reversed.

The appeals court first determined that the article on autoerotic asphyxia was constitutionally protected speech because it was not obscene or otherwise outside of First Amendment consideration. The court then ruled that *Hustler* should not be held liable because it did not incite the death. The incitement test the court employed is drawn from *Brandenburg v. Ohio,* a case discussed in Chapter 2. In *Brandenburg,* the Supreme Court ruled that speech might be punished if it is "directed to inciting or producing imminent lawless action."

The Fifth Circuit said no fair reading of the *Hustler* article "can make its content advocacy, let alone incitement to engage in the practice." Noting that the incitement test is usually invoked in cases of speech agitating a crowd, the court questioned whether a magazine purchased for solitary reading could ever incite a reader to imminent lawless action.

With similar reasoning, a California appeals court ruled that CBS Records and singer Ozzy Osbourne did not incite the suicide of a young listener. The court ruled that the First Amendment barred the parents of nineteen-year-old John McCollum from suing Osbourne

[198]Herceg v. Hustler Magazine, Inc., 814 F.2d 1017 (5th Cir. 1987).

and the record company for the suicide of their son after he listened to an Osbourne song with the lyrics:

> Ah know people
> You really know where it's at
> You got it
> Why try, why try
> Get the gun and try it
> Shoot, shoot, shoot[199]

There is no incitement, the court said, in art that evokes "a mood of depression as it figuratively depicts the darker side of human nature."

The incitement requirement has protected the media not only when members of the audience hurt themselves, as in *Hustler* and Osbourne cases, but also when they hurt others by imitating or copying media violence. An NBC program in which a girl is raped with a "plumber's helper" was ruled not to have incited four youths, who had seen the program, to rape a girl with a bottle on a California beach shortly after the program was aired.[200] Similarly, CBS was not liable for the death of a woman killed by a youth who argued the network had inspired the deed by saturating him with years of violent episodes.[201] The California court also ruled that CBS was not negligent.

Although media offerings are seldom held to incite physical harm, a federal appeals court ruled that a publisher might be liable for disseminating a book that, in effect, incites crime by aiding and abetting murder. The U.S. Court of Appeals for the Fourth Circuit reversed summary judgment for Paladin Enterprises, publisher of *Hit Man: A Technical Manual for Independent Contractors,* a book James Perry relied on as a guide when he murdered three members of a family.[202] Relatives of the family sued Paladin for aiding and abetting murders by contract. *Hit Man* openly taught would-be killers how a professional "gets assignments, creates a false identity, makes a disposable silencer, leaves the scene without a trace, watches his mark unobserved and more." Perry followed *Hit Man* closely, even shooting his victims through the eyes, as the book advised.

The court rejected Paladin's claim that *Hit Man* was constitutionally protected speech because it did not incite anyone to murder. The Fourth Circuit overturned a district court ruling that the Supreme Court's decision in *Brandenburg v. Ohio* barred liability for Paladin because the book only "advocated" or "taught" lawlessness but was not "directed to inciting or producing imminent lawless action." The Fourth Circuit determined that although *Brandenburg* protects "abstract" teaching, it does not protect the intentional, detailed direction of murderers the court found in *Hit Man.* Paladin's book was not constitutionally protected, the Fourth Circuit said, because the publisher "intended that *Hit Man* would immediately be used by criminals and would-be criminals in the solicitation, planning, and commission of murder and murder for hire." The court said few other publications describing potentially illegal activities would be unprotected by the First Amendment because few other publishers

[199]McCollum v. CBS, 249 Cal. Rptr. 187 (Cal. Ct. App. 1988).
[200]Olivia N. v. NBC, 178 Cal. Rptr. 888 (Cal. Ct. App. 1981).
[201]Zamora v. CBS, 480 F. Supp. 199 (S.D. Fla. 1979).
[202]Rice v. Paladin Enters, Inc., 128 F.3d 233 (4th Cir. 1997), *cert denied,* 523 U.S. 1074 (1998).

would demonstrate the specific intent to aid criminality that Paladin demonstrated. As part of a settlement, Paladin agreed to take *Hit Man* off the market.[203]

NEGLIGENCE People act negligently if they breach a duty of care owed to the plaintiff and that breach causes injury.[204] Surgeons, for example, are negligent if they leave scissors in a patient. Surgeons have a duty to their patients to foresee that forgetting scissors will cause serious injury.[205] Plaintiffs have argued that the media are negligent when they fail to foresee that publications and programs containing violence and antisocial behavior may inspire readers and viewers to cause harm to themselves or others. Courts, however, generally hold the media owe no duty of care under the common law of negligence to a general audience, either for physical harms or for financial losses.

In the *Osbourne* case, the California court said that CBS owed no duty to the McCollums or to anyone else to foresee all the harms that listeners and viewers might inflict on themselves and others. CBS and Osbourne owed no duty of care to the McCollums because the company and the artist could not reasonably have foreseen that suicide would result from listening to the song, the court said. The music and lyrics had been recorded and distributed years before McCollum killed himself.

Furthermore, the court said, Osbourne and CBS had no relationship with the public creating a duty to prevent harm. Unlike the relationship between doctors and their patients, there was no "dynamic interaction" between the singer and his audience justifying media liability, the court said. In addition, the court said, the social costs of imposing a duty on the media to withhold a song that might inspire suicide would be too burdensome. "[I]t is simply not acceptable to a free and democratic society," the court said, to impose a duty upon performing artists to avoid the dissemination of artistic speech, "which may adversely affect emotionally troubled individuals."

Courts have also ruled the media are not liable when false information causes financial harm. In *Gutter v. Dow Jones, Inc.*, the Supreme Court of Ohio ruled that the owner of the *Wall Street Journal* was not liable to a reader for an error in listings of corporate bond interest. Phil Gutter, an investor, lost nearly $1,700 when the interest rate turned out to be different than the paper reported. However, the Ohio Supreme Court dismissed a suit for negligent misrepresentation.[206]

The court said that the newspaper owed no duty to Gutter, a member of the broad newspaper readership. Like other courts, the Ohio court said holding a newspaper liable to the public imposes too great a burden on freedom of expression. Furthermore, the court said it was not justifiable for Gutter to rely on the mistaken news account to buy his bonds without first checking the status of the bonds with a broker. Similar legal rulings have been reached when unintentional errors have appeared on a ticker tape,[207] in commercial loose-leaf summaries of corporate finances,[208] and in advertisements for investment opportunities.[209]

[203] "'Hit Man' Case Settles," News Notes: 27 Media L. Rep., June 15, 1999.
[204] W. Page Keeton et al., *Prosser and Keeton on the Law of Torts* 164–65 (5th ed. 1984).
[205] *Id.*
[206] Gutter v. Dow Jones, Inc., 490 N.E.2d 898 (1986).
[207] Jaillet v. Cashman, 194 N.Y.S. 947 (App. Div. 1922), *aff'd,* 139 N.E. 714 (N.Y. 1923).
[208] First Equity Corp. v. Standard & Poor's Corp., 869 F.2d 175 (2d Cir. 1989).
[209] Pittman v. Dow Jones, Inc., 662 F. Supp. 921 (E.D. La. 1987), *aff'd,* 834 F.2d 1171 (5th Cir. 1987).

FORESEEABLE HARMS A few courts have ruled that the media may be liable for causing serious physical harm to an individual. In two commercial cases, courts have held the media liable when particularly serious risks—in one case murder—were thought to be too obvious for the media to ignore. In another case, a newspaper placed a crime victim at risk of further violence by publishing her name.

In the most significant media negligence case, the U.S. Court of Appeals for the Eleventh Circuit upheld a jury verdict finding *Soldier of Fortune* magazine liable for negligently publishing an advertisement that resulted in a contract killing. Saying that a magazine has a legal duty to refrain from publishing advertisements that subject the public to a "clearly identifiable unreasonable risk of harm," the court upheld an award of more than $4 million to Michael and Ian Braun, the sons of a man murdered by an assassin hired through a classified ad.[210]

A jury determined that *Soldier of Fortune* negligently published an advertisement that resulted in the killing of Richard Braun and the wounding of his sixteen-year-old son in front of the family's Atlanta home. The killer, Michael Savage, was hired after he placed a "Gun for Hire" ad in the personal services section of *Soldier of Fortune.* In the ad, Savage said a "Thirty seven-year-old professional mercenary desires jobs. Vietnam Veteran. Discrete [sic] and very private. Body guard, courier, and other special skills. All jobs considered."

The court ruled that *Soldier of Fortune* violated a public duty not to publish a clearly identifiable unreasonable risk of harm that in fact led to Richard Braun's death. Onc determines whether a risk is unreasonable, the court said, by balancing the risk of a serious harm against the costs of guarding against it. *Soldier of Fortune* was held liable because the advertisement presented a grave risk—murder—that outweighed the burden of requiring the publisher to foresee the likely consequences of the ad.

The court said its holding did not violate the First Amendment because publishers were not being subjected to burdensome responsibilities to check the danger and legality of each advertisement. The court said a publisher could be held liable only if an advertisement on its face, without further investigation, would alert a reasonably prudent publisher to the unreasonable risk.

The Savage ad presented a clearly identifiable unreasonable risk, the court said, because it

> (1) emphasized the term "Gun for Hire," (2) described Savage as a "professional mercenary," (3) stressed Savage's willingness to keep his assignments confidential and "very private," (4) listed legitimate jobs involving the use of a gun—bodyguard and courier—followed by a reference to Savage's "other special skills," and (5) concluded by stating that Savage would consider "[a]ll jobs."[211]

In another commercial case, the California Supreme Court ruled that the First Amendment did not bar a negligence action against a radio station whose on-air promotion stimulated reckless conduct among teenage drivers, conduct that resulted in the death of a motorist. The case resulted from a station's public relations promotion in which a popular disc jockey

---

[210]Braun v. Soldier of Fortune Magazine, Inc., 968 F.2d 1110 (11th Cir. 1992), *cert. denied,* 506 U.S. 1071 (1993).
[211]968 F.2d 1121.

drove from place to place in southern California. Meanwhile, the station encouraged its teenage audience to hurry to the disc jockey's next stop to claim a prize. One youthful listener, following the disc jockey at high speeds on the California freeways, forced another car to overturn, killing the driver.

In *Weirum v. RKO General, Inc.*, the California Supreme Court ruled the station was liable because it was "foreseeable that defendant's youthful listeners, finding the prize had eluded them at one location, would race to arrive first at the next site and in their haste would disregard the demands of highway safety." Although the court did not say that the station "incited" the reckless driving, the station's broadcast promotion stimulated the teenage audience to irresponsible, dangerous conduct that resulted in a death.[212] Giving short attention to the station's First Amendment claims, the court said, "The First Amendment does not sanction the infliction of physical injury merely because achieved by word, rather than act."

The *Soldier of Fortune* and *Weirum* cases involve advertising and commercial promotion that have less constitutional protection than political speech. But a Missouri court ruled that a newspaper might be liable for subjecting a person to violent threats by publishing a crime story. The Missouri Supreme Court ruled that Sandra Hyde could bring an emotional distress suit against the City of Columbia and a Columbia newspaper over a story about her successful escape from an abductor who was still at large. After the story appeared, Hyde was followed and threatened by telephone. In one call, a man said, "I'm glad you're not dead yet; I have plans for you before you die."[213]

The Missouri court imposed an obligation on the press to investigate the risk of publishing information from a law enforcement document the paper argued was a public record. The court said the newspaper could reasonably foresee from the assailant's past conduct, reported character, and tendency toward violence that the publication of Hyde's name and address would create a temptation for the abductor to harm her. Hyde settled the case for $6,000 from the city.[214]

◇ Summary ◇

The media are seldom liable for the physical harms that media users inflict on themselves or others. Some courts have ruled that violent acts on television do not incite members of the audience to harm themselves or others, but one federal appellate court ruled that a book publisher might be liable for distributing a manual for murder.

Some courts find the media have no duty under the common law of negligence to foresee harms to a general audience and that the burden of preventing violence or financial hardship would be too inhibiting. However, the Fifth Circuit has found the media liable for publishing an advertisement containing a "clearly identifiable unreasonable risk" of murder. The media have also been exposed to liability for encouraging reckless behavior in a commercial promotion and for subjecting a woman to threats from an abductor known to be at large.

[212] 539 P.2d 36 (Cal. 1975).

[213] Hyde v. City of Columbia, 637 S.W.2d 251 (Mo. App. 1982), *cert. denied*, 459 U.S. 1226 (1983).

[214] *News Media & L.* 41 (Sept.–Oct. 1983).

CHAPTER 6

Intellectual Property

Whereas privacy law allows people to limit public dissemination of private information about themselves, copyright allows authors to control how their creative expression is copied, distributed, and performed. Copyright protects books, musical compositions, newspaper articles, recordings, software, TV programs, advertisements, podcasts, e-mail, and other original expression from unauthorized copying and performance. Copyright law punishes those who infringe the rights of authors to control the reproduction, adaptation, distribution, display, and performance of their original works.

Copyright is an increasingly important mass communication issue in post-industrial countries whose information economies depend in large measure on the creation and sale—including exports—of intellectual property.

Copyright law is implicated when students download iTunes in the dorm or upload videos to YouTube, when Google links to other websites, and when a magazine scoops a competitive publication with a purloined manuscript. A 2005 federal statute prohibits members of the audience from recording motion pictures with portable cameras from a theater screen.[1] The Motion Picture Association of America estimates that 43 percent of all movies illegally recorded with camcorders in the United States are copied in New York City.[2] Anger over Chinese piracy of American intellectual property has fueled threats of higher duties on U.S. imports from China.[3] The United States was considering blocking Russia's entrance into the World Trade Organization because of Russian tolerance of unauthorized file-sharing sites.[4] Google set up a reserve fund of more than $200 million for possible lawsuits over copyrighted material shown on its video website YouTube.[5]

Intellectual property was protected in the Constitution before adoption of the First Amendment. Article I, Section 8, of the U.S. Constitution gives Congress the power "to promote the Progress of Science and useful Arts, by securing for limited Times to Authors and Inventors the exclusive Right to their respective Writings and Discoveries." Section 8 encourages intellectual creativity of benefit to the society by granting creative people exclusive control over their intellectual expression for a fixed period, after which the work passes into the public domain. Thus, copyright not only benefits society by spurring creative expression; it also benefits "authors" by allowing them to control and profit from their creative expression for a limited time. There is great tension between copyright owners who tend to emphasize their property rights to control the distribution and copying of their works and creative entities that want to create new works by borrowing from works still under copyright protection and from works that have passed into the public domain. Critics say powerful content producers, such as The Walt Disney Company and SONY, are creating a "tyranny" of copyright by supporting ever-longer terms before copyrighted works pass into the public domain and by suing creators who borrow even small phrases and samples from copyrighted works.[6] Opposition to long, rigid copyright terms has spawned a counter "Creative Commons" by which copyright owners grant more generous terms of use, particularly to nonprofit organizations promising also to share their expressive content.[7]

Yet, it is increasingly difficult in a digital age for copyright owners to protect the valuable property in their copyrights. Digitization allows pirates worldwide to instantly copy music, video, and text, each copy as perfect as the previous one, unlike the often diminishing quality of successive copies of works on paper, tape, and film. Producers of copyrighted music and film have lost millions of dollars to companies that manufacture illicit CDs and DVDs and transmit copyrighted works for royalty-free digital downloads. Thus, media companies are both plaintiffs and defendants in copyright cases—plaintiffs when they are

[1]Artists' Rights and Theft Prevention Act of 2005 in the Family Entertainment and Copyright Act of 2005, § 102, S.167
[2]Sewell Chan, "With Economics in Mind, City Takes Aim at Movie Piracy," *N.Y. Times*, Dec. 2, 2006, at 16.
[3]Edward Cody, "U.S. Warns China on Piracy, Market Access," *Wash. Post*, Nov. 15, 2006, at D8.
[4]Frank Ahrens, "U.S. Joins Industry in Piracy War; Nations Pressed on Copyrights," *Wash. Post*, June 15, 2006, at A1.
[5]"Technology Briefing," *Wash. Post*, Nov. 16, 2006, at D5.
[6]*E.g.*, Robert Boynton, "The Tyranny of Copyright?" *N.Y. Times*, Jan. 25, 2004.
[7]Visit, http://creativecommons.org.

trying to halt the unauthorized copying of protected works; defendants when media companies are charged with copying, performing, or displaying copyrighted works without a license.

Article I, Section 8, recognizes two kinds of intellectual property: inventions and writings. Inventions are protected under patent law, which provides inventors up to 20 years in which to enjoy exclusive commercial exploitation of the machines, processes, manufactured products, and designs they create.[8] "Writings," which include books, poems, screen plays, songs, and DVDs, are protected by the federal copyright statute, the primary subject of this chapter.[9] This chapter will also discuss trademark law, which prohibits companies from confusing the public about the origin of a product.

Copyright

The British originated copyright as a method of censorship after Gutenberg invented the printing press in the 1440s. In 1556, the British Crown granted the Stationers' Company a monopoly on printing, primarily to check the spread of the Protestant Reformation. By requiring that all published works be registered with the Stationers' Company, the government made it easier to block dissemination of heretical writings that threatened the Crown.

In time, the government's interest in controlling heresy was outweighed by authors' and publishers' desire to curb unauthorized copying of their publications. Under pressure from authors and publishers, the British government relinquished its copyright control. The first statute to recognize the rights of authors was the Statute of Anne of 1710, which granted authors the exclusive right to publish their new works for a renewable fourteen-year term. Works had to be registered at Stationers' Hall, not so that the government could easily identify the dangerous, but so that copyright holders could prove their claims of originality when they believed others had copied their work.

In the United States, the first federal copyright law was adopted in 1790.[10] The first copyright act protected an author of any "book, map or chart" from unauthorized copying for a renewable fourteen-year term. Protection for prints was added in 1802,[11] musical compositions in 1831,[12] photographs in 1865,[13] and paintings in 1870.[14]

The federal copyright statute was revised twice in the twentieth century, once in 1909[15] and again in 1976,[16] with numerous amendments before and after 1976. The 1909 Act was continually strained by the development of new technologies used to create copyrighted works or exploit them—the motion picture, phonograph, radio, television, the computer, tape recorder, photocopy machine, and satellite, cable, and other communication technologies.

[8] 35 U.S.C. §§ 154 and 173.
[9] Federal copyright law is found in Title 17 of the United States Code, chapters 1–13, § 101–1332.
[10] 1 Stat. 124 (1790).
[11] 2 Stat. 171 (1802).
[12] 4 Stat. 436 (1831).
[13] 13 Stat. 540 (1865).
[14] 16 Stat. 212 (1870).
[15] 35 Stat. 1075 (1909).
[16] 90 Stat. 2541 (1976).

Congress adopted the 1976 Copyright Act after twenty years of study. The Copyright Act of 1976 included several changes that made it easier for authors to control when and how their works are used by others. The 1976 revision also made copyright law more uniform by preempting state copyright law. Since 1976, technological advances have forced Congress and the courts to make changes in copyright law in response to the development of cable television, satellite transmissions, home recording of television programs, rental movies, software, cell phones, video games, and the Internet.

Copyrightable Works

Copyright, which the Constitution says protects "writings," protects much more expression than words on a page. Copyright subsists in "original works of authorship fixed in any tangible medium of expression . . . from which they can be perceived, reproduced, or otherwise communicated."[17] Copyrightable works of authorship include literary, musical, dramatic, audiovisual, pictorial, graphic, and sculptural works. Literary works include books, newspapers, magazines, corporate house organs, newsletters, annual reports, and computer programs.

To be original, a work need not be unique, novel, or good. Rather, the work must be created independently—not copied from another work—with a modicum of intellectual effort.[18] Students own copyright in their exam essays, the videos they shoot, and their e-mail postings. The U.S. Copyright Office in Washington will register a work whether or not it is of high quality. The office will not deny copyright because a work may be obscene[19] or fraudulent.[20]

A work is fixed in a tangible medium of expression as soon as it is created or recorded so that it can be perceived. A short story is fixed when it is saved on a computer disk or printed on paper. A photo is fixed—whether on film or a memory card—when the shutter clicks. The tape of a televised football game becomes a fixed work of authorship as a camera crew and director select shots and simultaneously broadcast and record the game. An unedited video of a plane crash is also an original work of authorship.[21] Loading expression into the random access memory of a computer also "fixes" a copy if the expression resides in RAM long enough to be "perceived."[22]

Copyright protects expression, not the ideas or the facts contained in the expression. An author owns the copyright in a review of a Pink concert but not in the idea of writing the review or in the facts within it. Others are free to write a review of the concert employing the same facts, provided these authors employ their own language, style, and sequencing. To be ethical, writers should acknowledge the sources of facts and ideas they borrow from others. But borrowing facts and ideas—with or without attribution—does not violate the first author's copyright. Copyright infringement occurs when an author copies the expression of another without permission or a privilege to do so. Copying an author's copyrighted

[17] 17 U.S.C. § 102.
[18] Bleistein v. Donaldson Lithographing Co., 188 U.S. 239 (1903).
[19] *See, e.g.*, Clancy v. Jartech, 666 F.2d 403 (9th Cir. 1982), *cert. denied*, 459 U.S. 826 (1982).
[20] *E.g.*, Belcher v. Tarbox, 486 F.2d 1087 (9th Cir. 1973).
[21] Los Angeles News Serv. v. Tullo, 973 F.2d 791 (9th Cir. 1992).
[22] MAI Systems Corp. v. Peak Computer, Inc., 991 F.2d 511 (9th Cir. 1993).

FIGURE 6.1 Napoleon Sarony's photo of Oscar Wilde.

words, music, or other expression without permission infringes copyright in the original work even if the copier acknowledges the source of the expression.

The Supreme Court ruled in 1884 that photographs are "writings" that can be protected by copyright. In *Burrow-Giles Lithographic Co. v. Sarony,* the Court ruled that a photograph of the playwright Oscar Wilde sitting in a Victorian interior with a book in his hand (see Figure 6.1) was an original work authorship.[23] Napoleon Sarony, therefore, could bar unauthorized copying of his photograph by a lithographer. The Court rejected the argument that a photograph is a mere mechanical reproduction requiring no originality and therefore no authorship. On the contrary, the Court said, Sarony gave visible form to his original mental conception by posing Wilde, selecting and arranging the costume and draperies, arranging and disposing the light and shade, and thereby evoking the desired expression. Photographers may not protect the idea of taking a picture or the individual elements of the picture under copyright law. Rather, the copyright owner owns the copyright in the composition, the placement of the elements within the whole.[24] An advertiser

[23]111 U.S. 53 (1884)

[24]Bleistein v. Donaldson Lithographing Co., 188 U.S. 239 (1903).

is given copyright protection, not for the choice of a particular actor or a special editing technique, but for the expression resulting from a combination of artistic choices, including the selection of actors, the composition of each frame, the pace of editing, camera angles, hairstyle, jewelry, decor, and makeup.[25]

Copyright is recognized not only for individual stories, photos, and programs but also for compilations and derivative works. A **compilation** is a work formed by collecting and assembling preexisting materials or data that are "selected, coordinated, or arranged in such a way" as to create a new original work. A compilation may be the assembly of discrete facts that, individually, would not be copyrightable. Trivia dictionaries, some databases, and Dow Jones's stock lists are copyrightable compilations even though the individual items in them may not be copyrightable.[26]

An alphabetized list of names in a telephone directory is not sufficiently original to constitute a copyrightable compilation. In *Feist Publications, Inc. v. Telephone Services Company,* the Supreme Court ruled that the publisher of a regional telephone directory did not violate the copyright of a smaller local directory when the publisher of the regional directory borrowed names and addresses from the local book.[27] The publisher of the larger directory merely took facts whose compilation and arrangement were "devoid of even the slightest trace of creativity," the Court said. However, in a different case, the U.S. Court of Appeals for the Eleventh Circuit ruled that the compilation of the Yellow Pages embodied enough originality to merit a copyright.[28] The court found sufficient originality for a copyright based on the compilers' judgments about which commercial categories to establish and which businesses to place in those categories.

In *Feist,* not only did the Supreme Court fail to find originality in an alphabetized list, but the Court also refused to recognize a copyright based on the time, money, and effort—the "sweat of the brow"— the telephone company expended to create the book. The Constitution requires originality, not effort alone, as a condition for successful copyright claims, the Court said.

One kind of compilation that can be copyrighted is a collective work. A **collective work** is a gathering of preexisting works that may already be copyrighted. Collective works include magazines, anthologies, and corporate reports, each of which may contain several copyrighted works. The publisher of a magazine or anthology must have permission from the individual copyright holders to compile the collective work. The collective work can be separately copyrighted as original expression while contributions to the collective retain their separate copyrights.

A **derivative work** may also be copyrighted. A derivative work is a transformation or adaptation of an existing work. The copyright owner has the exclusive right to create derivative works. Derivative works include translations from foreign languages, movie versions of plays and novels, and dolls based on cartoon characters. Derivative works are created when a work is recast, transformed, or adapted.[29] A federal appeals court ruled that encircling or

[25]C. Blore & Don Richman, Inc. v. 20/20 Advertising Inc., 674 F. Supp. 671 (D. Minn. 1987).

[26]Eckes v. Card Prices Update, 736 F.2d 859 (2d Cir. 1984); Dow Jones & Co. v. Board of Trade of Chicago, 546 F. Supp. 113 (S.D.N.Y. 1982).

[27]Feist Publications, Inc. v. Tel. Serv. Co., 499 U.S. 340 (1991).

[28]Bellsouth Advertising and Publishing Corp. v. Donnelley Information Publishing, Inc., 933 F.2d 952 (11th Cir. 1991).

[29]17 U.S.C. § 101.

"framing" another's web page in advertising may constitute a derivative work for which the framer should get permission.[30]

Facts, procedures, and processes are too unoriginal to be copyrighted. Also uncopyrightable are systems, methods of operation, concepts, principles, and discoveries.[31] A federal appellate court ruled that the user interface—the system of menus and commands—in popular spreadsheet software was an uncopyrightable method of operation, much like the familiar QWERTY arrangement of keys on a typewriter keyboard.[32] Copyright also does not protect useful items such as tables, chairs, and typefaces.

Formats and layouts are also not copyrightable. A format is the general plan or organization of a work, the shape and size of a publication, the length of a broadcast, or the number of minutes of music to be included at a certain time each week in a television show. The layout is the plan or arrangement of elements on the page. Fomats and layouts cannot be copyrighted because the number of ways in which stories, pictures, and type can be placed on a page is too limited to allow one person or company to claim exclusive ownership. Opposing copyright in formats, the U.S. Copyright Office feared that copyright disputes over relatively unimportant layout and format issues might halt publication of constitutionally protected literary works. A federal appeals court ruled that the arrangement of citations and the pagination in a commercial publication of legal opinions were too unoriginal for the publisher to claim a copyright.[33]

NOTICE, REGISTRATION, AND DEPOSIT The term of copyright protection continually lengthens, extending the time at which copyrighted works pass into the public domain and are then available for use by other creative authors without permission or royalty payments. Copyright protection for works created after 1977 lasts for the life of the author plus seventy years. The benefit of copyright, therefore, can be willed to one's survivors for seventy years after the death of the copyright holder. If a company is the copyright holder, copyright runs for 120 years from the date of creation or ninety-five years from the date of publication, whichever is shorter.[34]

In 2003, the Supreme Court ruled 7–2 that Congress did not exceed its authority when it lengthened the term of copyright by twenty years to seventy years after the life of the author. Writing for the majority in *Eldred v. Ashcroft,* Justice Ruth Bader Ginsburg said the Constitution did not set a specific duration for copyright terms when it provided for "limited" terms.[35] Ginsburg rejected the argument that Congress—in effect—unconstitutionally establishes a perpetual copyright when the legislature continually lengthens the term from its original renewable fourteen-year duration.

Ginsburg also rejected arguments that an extended copyright term violates the First Amendment by excessively delaying the time at which copyrighted works pass into the public domain and can be incorporated into new expressive creations. Ginsburg noted that copyright does not prohibit creators from disseminating ideas and facts contained in copyrighted works.

[30]Futuredontics, Inc. v. Applied Anagramics, Inc., 45 U.S.P.Q.2d 2005 (C.D. Cal. 1998).
[31]17 U.S.C.A. § 102(b).
[32]Lotus Dev. Corp. v. Borland Int'l Inc., 49 F.3d 807 (1st Cir. 1995), *aff'd by evenly divided vote,* 516 U.S. 233 (1996).
[33]Matthew Bender & Co., v. West Publishing Co., 158 F.3d 693 (2d Cir. 1998).
[34]17 U.S.C. §302.
[35]537 U.S. 186 (2003).

She also noted that the fair use defense—to be discussed later—permits commentators and scholars to publish limited portions of copyrighted works without permission for purposes of commenting on and criticizing the original work. Backers of the copyright term extension, which include the Disney Corporation, argue longer protections will encourage original and often-expensive creative expression by allowing long-term financial incentives.

Notice Although authors are not required to protect copyright, they should place copyright notices on their works and register them. If a work is published, two copies must be deposited with the Copyright Office in Washington, D.C. Copyright notice is the voluntary sign attached to a work warning would-be copiers that they need permission to reproduce that work. Copyright notice signifies that authors have not abandoned their work to the public domain. Notice has three elements: (1) the letter C in a circle ©, the word copyright, or the abbreviation copr.; (2) the year of first publication; and (3) the name of the copyright owner. A copyright notice looks like this: © 2006 John Dude.

A copyright notice should be placed where it will be easily seen. A copyright notice will normally be placed on, or just after, the title page of a book, on the title page or the masthead of a magazine, or near the title of a film. If notice on the front of a photograph or painting would damage the work, notice can be placed on the back. Notice should be placed on a computer program so that it appears on a user's terminal at sign-on. Although copyright notice is not required on American works distributed after March 1, 1989, placing notice on copyrighted works is advisable.[36] Besides warning would-be infringers that copyright is claimed, a copyright notice also bars infringers from claiming they infringed "innocently." A court may reduce the money paid to a copyright owner by an infringer who "was not aware and had no reason to believe that his or her acts constituted an infringement of copyright."[37] Copyright notice is also necessary for freelancers' bulk registration of works.

Copyright notice on a newspaper, periodical, anthology, or other collective work covers all contributions to the work except for advertisements inserted on behalf of outside businesses or organizations.[38] For example, one copyright notice on the *New York Times* covers all staff and freelance stories and pictures, even though freelance writers and photographers may retain separate copyright ownership in their works. But the overall *Times* copyright notice does not cover advertisements, except ads for the *Times* itself. Advertisers who want to protect themselves from innocent infringement of advertisements published in newspapers and magazines should put a separate copyright notice on each ad.

Individual contributors to collective works may attach separate copyright notice to their contributions if they and the publisher agree. A separate copyright notice on a story or picture can serve as the credit line. Freelance writers and other contributors to collective works will want a separate notice on their contributions if they wish to take advantage of the efficiency and low cost of bulk registration of their work.

Registration and Deposit In the days of the English Star Chamber, the British Crown required registration of all works in London so that the government could more easily

[36]*But see* Thomas Arden, "The Questionable Utility of Copyright Notice: Statutory and Nonlegal Incentives in the Post-Berne Era," 24 *Loyola Univ. Chicago L.J.* 259 (1993).
[37]17 U.S.C. § 504(c)(2).
[38]17 U.S.C. § 404(a).

check for heresy and sedition. Now, however, registration is not a tool of suppression but a way of establishing who first wrote a disputed work. The person who first registers a work has strong legal evidence of copyright ownership.

An author may register a work—published or unpublished—with the Register of Copyrights in Washington by submitting the proper form and a registration fee of $45. To obtain all the benefits of registration, it should be done within three months of publication. An author must "deposit" two copies of a published work and may deposit one copy of an unpublished work. The deposit requirement is separate from the voluntary registration system but is usually fulfilled at the time of registration.

To save time and money, freelance writers and photographers can register twelve months of work in a group for one fee.[39] Publishers of magazines, newspapers, and newsletters can register from one to three months of publications with a single application and fee.

Although unregistered works are protected under the copyright law, the law includes incentives for authors to register their work. Authors of works originating in the United States may not sue for infringement until a work is registered, although foreign authors can.[40] Copyright owners of registered works may sue an infringer for "actual damages"—lost sales and for profits the infringer illegally gained. Copyright owners may also ask a court to issue injunctions to stop further infringement.

If a copyright owner registered the work before the infringement took place, he or she can seek "statutory" damages instead of actual damages. Statutory damages are awarded to owners of registered copyrights simply because the copyright is infringed, without proof of financial damage. The court may award the copyright owner statutory damages of between $750 and $30,000 for each work infringed and up to $150,000 if the work was infringed "willfully."[41]

COPYRIGHT OWNERSHIP Copyright belongs to the "author" of a work. The author may be an individual or joint author. Joint authors are two or more authors who collaborate with the intent that their contributions be combined into a unified, copyrightable whole.[42] A composer and a lyricist, for example, may be joint authors of a collaborative song. Each joint author may authorize use of a work without permission of the other, provided both authors receive royalties. An editor usually is not considered to be a joint author of a work. However, publishers sometimes claim joint copyright ownership with freelancers if editors employed by the publishers make creative contributions to works. As computers have become the standard workstation, determining the "author" of digital works becomes more difficult. Working at computers, often in different locations, several writers, editors, photographers, and illustrators can make simultaneous contributions to a digital work, contributions that might never be separately identified.

Works Made for Hire The legal author of a work is not necessarily the same as the creator. When a work is "made for hire," the "author"—who owns the copyright—is the party who hires an employee or commissions a freelancer to create a work. A **work made for hire**

[39] 17 U.S.C. § 408(c)(2).
[40] 17 U.S.C. § 411(a).
[41] 17 U.S.C. § 504(c).
[42] *See, e.g.,* Childress v. Taylor, 945 F.2d 500 (2d. Cir. 1991).

is either (1) "a work prepared by an employee within the scope of his or her employment" or (2) "a work specially ordered or commissioned" that falls within one of nine specified categories. Works for hire include freelance contributions to a collective work—such as a magazine—if a work-for-hire agreement is signed.[43] Works created by employees within the scope of their employment include stories, photos, and videos created by staff reporters, artists, publicists, photographers, and copywriters while on the job. Copyright in those works belongs to the publisher, broadcaster, public relations firm, or advertising agency that employs the creators.[44] All rights in works for hire belong to the employer on the theory that the company that assigns the task, risks the resources to carry it out, and directs the work of the creator should own the copyright. Employers, as copyright owners, may grant permission to employees to publish or display their works elsewhere.

Even an article written in off-hours may be a work for hire if the article is the direct result of one's employment. A federal court in Indiana ruled that Miles Laboratories owned the copyright in a scientific article written outside the office by an employee because the article resulted directly from the employee's work at Miles. The court said the article was within the scope of the employee's work because the company initiated and supported the research that led to the article. Company policy also required employees to submit articles to the firm for review before publication.[45]

Independent writers and artists are not considered "employees" who create works for hire unless several elements of the employer-employee relationship are present. In *Community for Creative Non-Violence v. Reid,* the Supreme Court said that independent contractors are not considered employees unless they meet several criteria of employment such as being supervised, being provided a place to work, receiving fringe benefits, and having a long-term, salaried relationship with an employer.[46] The Court ruled that James Earl Reid, a sculptor working on commission, was not an employee because he was a skilled professional who supplied his own tools, worked in his own studio, received no regular salary or benefits, and had only a short-term business relationship with the homeless shelter that commissioned the sculpture. After *Reid,* freelance photographers and writers are seldom considered to be employees.

Even if freelance writers and artists working on commission seldom meet the criteria of "employees," they may create a "work for hire" in which they own no rights if a work is "specially ordered or commissioned" for a collective work—such as a magazine or newspaper—and both parties sign a work-for-hire agreement. Freelancers who are not employees create a work for hire only if both parties "expressly agree" in a written contract that "the work shall be considered a work made for hire."[47] Absent a written contract containing the term *work for hire,* freelance photographers and writers who sell a work to a publisher, advertising agency, or other producer grant permission only for one-time publication. All other rights remain with the freelancer unless a contract states otherwise.

While publishers often demand that freelance writers and artists sign work-for-hire contracts, publishers sometimes demand freelancers transfer copyright to the publisher

[43]17 U.S.C. § 101.

[44]*See, e.g.,* United States Ozone Co. v. United States Ozone Co. of Am., 62 F.2d 881 (7th Cir. 1933) (company owns copyright in pamphlet written by employee during working hours).

[45]Marshall v. Miles Laboratories, Inc., 647 F. Supp. 1326 (N.D. Ind. 1986).

[46]476 U.S. 693 (1989).

[47]17 U.S.C. § 101.

without signing a work-for-hire contract. In such cases, the law allows freelancers to negotiate the return of the copyright after thirty-five years.[48] Freelancers prefer if publishers are even less demanding, negotiating only "First North American serial rights," "First English-language serial rights," or "one-time rights," leaving other rights to the author. More established writers, photographers, and artists, who themselves have strong bargaining positions, are better able to negotiate transferring fewer rights to a publisher.

Government and Copyright The copyright statute prohibits the federal government or its employees from owning a copyright in works created by government employees as part of their official duties.[49] However, government employees own the copyright in speeches and writings composed on their own time. The U.S. Court of Appeals for the District of Columbia Circuit ruled that Admiral Hyman Rickover owned the copyright to speeches he wrote during his off-duty hours because the speeches were not "statements called for by his official duties."[50]

Private firms that contract with the government may own the copyright in works commissioned by the government if the government agrees. Public television station WQED in Pittsburgh was permitted to own the copyright of a bicentennial series called *Equal Justice Under Law,* a series that had been commissioned by the Judicial Conference to increase public understanding of the courts.[51]

State executive, legislative, and judicial branches may not copyright their statutes, judicial opinions, or regulations—laws binding on all citizens,[52] but states may copyright the annotations and comments added to a set of laws and regulations. Some states do assert copyright in government tax maps and other documents lacking the force of law, thus allowing state and local agencies to control copying of the records after public inspection.[53] However, copyright claims by state and local governments may conflict with citizens' rights to copy records under state open records laws.[54]

Summary

Copyright encourages creativity by granting authors exclusive rights in original works of authorship for a limited period. Copyrightable works include literary, pictorial, and graphic creations as well as compilations and derivative works. Copyright does not depend on notice or registration, although both are recommended for protection from claims of "innocent" infringement and for eligibility to file suit and receive statutory damages in infringement cases. Works created by employees are works made for hire, and the employer is deemed to be the author and copyright owner. Freelance writers, photographers, and video operators create a work for hire—and do not own the copyright—only if a contract specifies

[48]17 U.S.C. § 203.
[49]17 U.S.C. §§ 101, 105.
[50]Public Affairs Assoc. v. Rickover, 284 F.2d 262 (D.C. Cir. 1960), *vacated for insufficient record,* 369 U.S. 111 (1962).
[51]Schnapper v. Foley, 667 F.2d 102 (D.C. Cir. 1981).
[52]Banks v. Manchester, 128 U.S, 244 (1888).
[53]*E.g.,* County of Suffolk v. First American, 261 F.3d 179 (2d Cir. 2001).
[54]*See,* Becky Dale, "Can the Government Copyright Public Records?" *Virginia Lawyers Weekly,* July 26, 2004.

that the work is a work for hire. Neither the federal government nor its employees may own the copyright in works created by federal employees on the job, but some states claim copyright in works other than laws and judicial opinions. Private companies sometimes may copyright works created under government contract.

Rights

The Copyright Act grants a "bundle" of rights to copyright owners. These rights include the exclusive right to copy or reproduce a work, to create adaptations or derivative works, to distribute copies of a work, and to perform and display the work publicly.[55] These exclusive rights give authors the legal ability to control the use of their work.

COPYING One of the most important rights of the copyright owner is the exclusive right to control the copying, or reproduction, of a work. Photocopying a book is a form of reproduction or copying, as is downloading a copyrighted film, recording from the Internet or sampling musical phrases from a recording for inclusion in another musical work. The copyright owner of the expression in a book, magazine article, compact disk, recorded song, motion picture, or computer program has the right to control when and if that expression is reproduced. By prohibiting unauthorized copying, copyright law protects the commercial incentive for authors to produce creative expression that benefits society.

It is particularly hard to prohibit illicit copying of digital information on the Internet because thousands of copies can be produced quickly and flawlessly. American music and film producers say 85 million songs and 400,000 movies are downloaded illegally each day.[56] Pirating is augmented by some copiers' cavalier notion that digital information "ought to be free." American producers of copyrighted works are estimated to lose $250 billion per year to Internet pirates who trade illicit copies of *The DaVinci Code*, Chamillionaire's new album, and the latest *Grand Theft Auto* videogame.[57] The major American movie studios estimate they alone lost $6.1 billion to pirates worldwide in 2005.[58] This is a large loss in an industry in which U.S. companies producing copyrighted films, music, software, and video games account for more than 5 percent of the nation's gross domestic product. Exports of copyrighted materials are worth $626 billion annually.[59]

Courts and governments are beginning to curb some of the gravest excesses of illegal copying. A 2005 federal statute prohibits members of the audience from recording motion pictures with portable cameras from a theater screen.[60] The statute permits theater operators to detain suspects until law enforcement authorities can be summoned. American courts have recently ruled that companies cannot lawfully provide software or servers that allow pirates to download and trade copyrighted works without paying royalties. Under American pressure, the Swedish government closed Pirate Bay, a major center for illegal trading of copyrighted music, film, and games. Russia and China have been pressured to comply with

[55]17 U.S.C. §106.
[56]"The day Grokster music died," *Toronto Star*, Nov. 8, 2005, at D1.
[57]Frank Ahrens, "U.S. Joins Industry in Piracy War," *Wash. Post,* June 15, 2006, at A1.
[58]Michelle Keller, "Sweden Pulls the Plug on Pirate Bay," *L.A. Times,* June 1, 2006, at C1.
[59]Frank Ahrens, "U.S. Joins Industry in Piracy War," *Wash. Post,* June 15, 2006, at A1.
[60]Artists' Rights and Theft Prevention Act of 2005 in the Family Entertainment and Copyright Act of 2005, 119 stat. 218, § 102.

rules of the World Trade Organization prohibiting illegal copying.[61] The right of copyright owners to control the reproduction of their work is not absolute. The legal doctrine of "fair use," to be discussed shortly, allows critics, commentators, reviewers, scholars, and others to copy limited portions of copyrighted expression for comment and criticism. The copyright statute also allows limited copying by public libraries. Public libraries have a statutory privilege to photocopy an article to fill individual requests by noncommercial users. In a decision upheld by an evenly divided U.S. Supreme Court, the federal Court of Claims ruled that government libraries run by the National Institutes of Health and the National Library of Medicine could make numerous copies of articles from a single scientific journal to fill requests for single copies from library patrons.[62] In *Williams & Wilkins Co. v. United States,* the Court of Claims said that finding copyright infringement in such noncommercial copying would hamper medical research. The court also thought there was insufficient evidence that the multiple copies hurt the journal publishers financially. On review, the Supreme Court split 4-4, thus upholding the lower court decision. Commercial entities do not have a privilege to make such multiple copies of copyrighted works.[63]

Furthermore, the Library of Congress may record copyrighted newscasts and spot coverage of news events off the air for the American Television and Radio Archives.[64] The Library of Congress may make these tapes available to researchers and scholars and also deposit them in nonprofit libraries that may make them available for research.[65]

DERIVATIVE WORKS The owner of a copyright controls the creation of derivative works. Derivative works are transformations or adaptations of existing works.[66] The author of a novel, for example, may create—or authorize others to create—any number of derivative works, including sequels, films, plays, and cartoons, all based on the original novel. A separate copyright can be owned in each derivative work, which is important in cases of infringement of the derivative work. Film producers need their own copyrights in motion pictures based on novels so that they can sue if the film is illegally copied. Similarly, book publishers want their own copyrights so that they can protect their commercial interest in their publications.

Because copyright is divisible, authors can authorize separate copyrights on any number of derivative works while retaining copyright in the underlying work. Divisibility of copyright is much like the power of a landowner to grant water rights to one person, oil rights to another, and a road right of way to a third, while retaining ownership in the land.[67] Likewise, the author of a novel can authorize creation of a film script and production of a movie. The producer of the film can own a separate copyright. Meanwhile, the author of the novel can retain the right to license the creation of comic strip characters, T-shirts, and other works derived from the novel.

Giles Martin and his father, a former producer of the Beatles, derived a new album, *LOVE,* from 80 minutes of "reimagined" Beatles' music. The Martins' album began as a

[61]Frank Ahrens, "U.S. Joins Industry in Piracy War," *Wash. Post,* June 15, 2006, at A1.

[62]Williams & Wilkins Co. v. United States, 487 F.2d 1345 (Ct. Cl. 1973), *aff'd,* 420 U.S. 376 (1975).

[63]Princeton University Press v. Michigan Document Services, Inc., 99 F.3d 1381 (6th Cir.1996) (en banc), *cert. denied,* 520 U.S. 1156 (1997).

[64]2 U.S.C. § 170.

[65]17 U.S.C. §108(f)(3).

[66]17 U.S.C. § 101.

[67]*See* William Strong, *The Copyright Book* 36 (2d ed. 1984).

FIGURE 6.2 Reproduced with permission of MPAA.

soundtrack for an evening of acrobatics and dance for Cirque du Soleil. Giles Martin took apart some of the Beatles' recordings and put them back together again in different ways with the support and approval of Paul McCartney, Ringo Starr, Yoko Ono Lennon, and Olivia Harrison.[68] A reviewer in the *Wall Street Journal* called the reconfigured works "fresh, seamless and musically cohesive."

A federal court in Colorado ruled that an editing firm did not create derivative works when the company removed "sex, nudity, profanity and gory violence" from motion pictures for home viewing on DVDs the company sold.[69] The court said the editing changes by Clean Flicks, which consisted of simple deletions, were too unoriginal to result in a derivative work. The court ruled the sanitized DVDs were merely unauthorized copies of the original films, copies that interfered with the market of such producers as SONY Pictures and Time Warner Entertainment—companies that sold their own edited versions of their films. The court ordered Clean Flicks to stop copying and distributing the Hollywood motion pictures.

DISTRIBUTION The copyright owner's exclusive right to distribute includes the author's authority to publish, sell, loan, or rent copies of a copyrighted work. A book publisher, who usually owns the copyright in a book, distributes the work in physical form to bookstores or digitally over the Internet. Musical recordings, or "sound recordings," may be distributed in the physical form of compact disks (phonorecords) or in digital form through electronic dissemination. A webcast, whether by an independent Internet "station" or, more frequently, by websites operated by existing radio and TV stations, distributes and publicly performs copyrighted material. Playboy's distribution right in the magazine's copyrighted photographs was infringed when 170 Playboy photographs were made available without authorization on an electronic bulletin board.[70]

Although distribution rights include the right to sell a copy of a work, distribution rights do not include control over resale of a copy. The author's control and receipt of royalties stop with the "first sale" of each lawfully produced copy of a book, film, or other work. The author receives a royalty on the first sale but not on subsequent sales. Thus, a library may sell or loan copies of books it purchased without consulting or paying the copyright owner. Similarly a video store, which pays when it purchases cassettes, may resell or rent videos to private individuals without additional payments. Individuals can give a CD they purchase to a friend but may not distribute copies of the CD. An exception to the "first sale doctrine" prohibits the commercial rental of copies of computer programs and sound recordings without the copyright owner's permission. This is because computer programs and sound recordings are so easily copied, and are likely to be.[71]

The distribution right includes the right to pick the time when, or if, a work will be distributed. The right of copyright owners to pick the time of publication or distribution was reiterated by the Supreme Court in a case in which the *Nation* magazine pirated excerpts from President Ford's memoirs. In *Harper & Row, Publishers, Inc. v. Nation Enterprises,* the Supreme Court ruled that the *Nation* violated the copyright held by Harper & Row by

[68]Jim Fusilli, Beatles Music, "Reimagined With 'LOVE,'" *Wall. St. J.,* Nov. 29, 2006, at p 10.
[69]Clean Flicks of Colorado, LLC v. Soderbergh, 433 F. Supp. 2d 1236 (D. Colo. 2006).
[70]Playboy Enters., Inc. v. Frena, 839 F. Supp. 1552 (M.D. Fla. 1993).
[71]17 U.S.C. § 109.

publishing several stolen excerpts of Ford's memoirs that were to be published in *Time* magazine. *Time* had an exclusive contract with Harper & Row to publish excerpts from the memoirs before the hardbound book was distributed. "Publication of an author's expression before he has authorized its dissemination," the Supreme Court said, "seriously infringes the author's right to decide when and whether it will be made public."[72]

In a case involving distribution from electronic databases, the Supreme Court ruled that freelancers should control whether their newspaper and magazine work is republished in electronic databases. In *New York Times Company v. Tasini,*[73] the Court ruled that the *Times, Newsday, Time, Atlantic Monthly,* and other publishers infringe freelancers' copyright if they make available freelancers' printed stories and photos in electronic databases without getting the freelancers' permission or paying them for the electronic distribution.

The Court rejected the publishers' argument that distributing articles electronically is similar to preserving a publication on microfiche or creating a "revision" of the original magazine or newspaper, both of which publishers are allowed to do. Preserving a publication in microfiche or creating a revision maintains the freelancers' work in its original context, formatted with other articles, photographs, and advertisements. The Court ruled the publishers' electronic distribution of individual articles from a database created new works infringing freelancers' copyrights because the electronic database, unlike a revision or archive, presents articles and photos individually, without the context and format of the original compilation.

Following *Tasini,* a federal appellate court ruled that a magazine publisher does not violate a freelancer's distribution rights if the publisher includes freelance photographs and articles in CD-ROM collections. Relying on *Tasini,* the U.S. Court of Appeals for the Second Circuit ruled that *National Geographic Magazine* did not violate the copyright of freelance photographers and authors when the magazine archived 108 years of the magazine on CD-ROMs. The court said the digital archive is not a new work, but is similar to bound volumes or microfilms, which present the copyrighted work in the same visual context as the original published magazine.[74] There are no modifications to the original.

As a result of the *Tasini* decision, the *Times* and other publications began removing freelancers' work from databases unless freelancers granted permission for uncompensated online publication.[75] Even before *Tasini*, publishers were requiring freelancers to sign contracts—often work-for-hire contracts—granting electronic distribution rights to publishers.

DISPLAY Copyright owners have a right not only to copy, to authorize derivative works, and to distribute copies of their works but also to perform and display their work publicly. To "display" a work publicly means to show a copy "either directly or by means of a film, slide, television image" or other device to a substantial number of people beyond the normal circle of friends and acquaintances.[76] Thus, the copyright owner has a right to control when and if photographs are placed on exhibit, projected on a screen in a public place, or made available to the public browsing the Internet. When 170 Playboy photographs were

[72] 471 U.S. 539 (1985).
[73] 533 U.S. 483, 29.
[74] Faulkner v. National Geographic Enterprises, Inc., 409 F.3d 26 (2d Cir. 2005), *cert. denied,* 126 S. Ct. 833 (2005)
[75] *See* http://www.survey.nytimes.com/survey/restore. A challenge to the *New York Times* was dismissed. Tasini v. New York Times Co., 30 Media L. Rep. 1407 (S.D.N.Y. 2002).
[76] 17 U.S.C. §101.

posted without authorization on a bulletin board, not only was Playboy's right to distribute infringed but also the company's right to display the original expression.[77]

Courts have ruled it does not infringe a copyright owner's display rights if one computer links to a website in order for the viewer to see text and images stored there. Even "deep links" that bypass a website's important home page and advertising in favor of pages within a website are not considered to be an infringement.[78] A federal appeals court ruled that Google did not violate the display rights of *Perfect 10,* a magazine and website, when Google linked to *Perfect 10*'s website and "framed" full-size nude pictures stored at *Perfect 10*'s server. The court ruled that pictures are "displayed" by the websites that store and serve them, not by a search engine such as Google that links to a server and "frames" pictures stored at a distant website.[79] Google, the court said, neither displayed nor distributed *Perfect 10*'s full-size pictures. Nor, the court said, did Google infringe *Perfect 10*'s display rights in reduced or thumbnail photos. Even though Google created and stored the thumbnail photos of *Perfect 10*'s images on Google computers, Google's search engine transformed the use—thus creating a fair use—of the thumbnails from entertainment to an Internet pointer, "directing a user to a source of information."

PERFORMANCE The performance right allows owners of literary, musical, and dramatic works, dance, and audiovisual works "to perform the copyrighted work publicly."[80] Composers, playwrights, record companies, and film producers can authorize—or not authorize—public performances and demand royalties. A public performance can be live, projected from film or tape, broadcast to an audience, webcast, or otherwise performed. One may perform a work "publicly" by performing it at clubs, factories, theaters, summer camps, and large business establishments. A podcast—a digital file sent over the Internet to many receivers through a "syndication feed" for later playback on an MP3 player—is a public performance. To be a copyright infringement, the work must be performed at public places or transmitted to the public without authorization.[81] Broadcasting a Hollywood film is a public performance; playing a DVD at home for family and friends is not.

Performance rights in music have always been complicated because the user must get separate permissions to use copyrighted musical compositions and musical recordings. Music publishers usually own the copyright in the musical composition and lyrics—often referred to as the "song"—while a record label is apt to own the copyright in the "sound recording"—the track fixed on a CD. Broadcasters, webcasters, filmmakers, advertising agencies, theater producers, and others wishing to perform music publicly may need assistance of a lawyer, a trade association, or a performance rights organization—or perhaps all three.

Performance Licenses for Musical Compositions Say, for example, an oldies radio station wishes to broadcast a recording of the John Lennon-Paul McCartney song, "Yesterday," from the Beatles' album, *Help*. The station needs permission to perform the

[77]Playboy Enters. Inc. v. Frena, 839 F. Supp. 1552 (M.D. Fla. 1993). *See* Working Group on Intellectual Property Rights, Bruce Lehman, chair, Intellectual Property and the National Information Infrastructure 70–72 (1995).
[78]Michelle Finley, "Attention Editors: Deep Link Away," *Wired News,* March 30, 2000.
[79]Google, Inc. v. Amazon.com, Inc., 2007 U.S. App. LEXIS 11420 (9th Cir. May 16, 2007).
[80]17 U.S.C. § 106(4).
[81]17 U.S.C. § 101.

music and lyrics, that is, the song, written by Lennon and McCartney. Rather than negotiate separately with the publisher or owner of copyrighted Lennon-McCartney music, radio stations, film producers, and others acquire musical performance rights from one of the performing rights organizations.

The three main performing rights organizations are the American Society of Composers, Authors and Publishers (ASCAP), Broadcast Music, Inc. (BMI), and SESAC, companies that license the majority of the copyrighted music played on the air. BMI represents more than 300,000 songwriters, composers, and music publishers, encompassing music styles from classical to hip-hop and song writers from John Lennon to Faith Hill and Snoop Dogg. The clearinghouses collect the performance fees and distribute them to member composers and copyright holders according to a formula.[82]

Theater producers, including producers of campus productions, must get copyright clearance to perform copyrighted music in musical reviews and other nondramatic public performances. A filmmaker, television producer, commercial advertising agency, or other creators of audiovisual works must acquire a "synchronization" license controlled by the music publisher. A "synch" license allows use of music in a motion picture, television program, commercial advertisement, or music video. Often, the music is timed with—synchronized with—the moving or still visual images in the film or other audiovisual work.[83] General Motors would need a synchronization license to use the underlying music in Bob Seger's "Like a Rock" in Chevrolet truck advertisements. Artists sampling recorded music or remixing recordings in digital "mashups" need authorization to perform copyrighted music. Similarly, a podcaster needs a musical performance right if the podcast contains a copyrighted song disseminated for later playback on an MP3 player. If the podcast contains an audiovisual work, the podcaster should acquire a synchronizaztion license to time the music to the video.[84]

Performance Licensing for Sound Recordings Radio broadcasters with a license to play the McCartney-Lennon song, "Yesterday," do not need a separate performance right to broadcast a particular recording of "Yesterday," whether the recording is the Beatles' track on the *Help* album or the "Yesterday" recording by the Cincinnati Pops Orchestra directed by Erich Kunzel. For better or worse, broadcasters have never had to pay royalties to record companies—which usually own the performance rights in a recording—or to musicians—who sing and play instruments in a recording.[85] Radio stations pay royalties only for performing the musical composition. Furthermore, radio stations pay no performance royalties for the sound recording if they simultaneously webcast a recording on the Internet while they are broadcasting the same recording over the air.[86] However, other performances of sound recordings in films, dance halls, and other public places do require licenses, not only for the performance of the underlying music but also for the performance of a particular recording. A television station, for example, would need permission from the record label—a master

[82]United States v. American Soc. of Composers, Authors, & Publishers, 782 F. Supp. 778 (S.D.N.Y. 1991), *aff'd,* 956 F.2d 21 (2d Cir. 1992) (per curiam), *cert. denied,* 504 U.S. 914 (1992); National Cable Television Ass'n v. Broadcast Music Inc., 772 F. Supp. 614 (D.C.D.C. 1991).

[83]David Powell, "'All Clear?' A Music Clearance Primer," www.themusicbridge.com.

[84]Colette Vogel & Mia Garlick, *Podcasting Legal Guide: Rules for the Revolution* at 18.

[85]17 U.S.C. § 114(a)

[86]17 U.S.C. § 114(d)(1).

use license—to perform the Cincinnati Pops' recording of "Yesterday" in a broadcast program, an audiovisual work. Likewise a film producer would need a license.[87]

Stand-alone Internet "stations"—whether operated by broadcasters or independently—need licenses to perform digital sound recordings on the Internet if the Internet webcaster is operating like a radio station, with playlists and featured recordings, or is webcasting to subscribers or an interactive audience that chooses the tracks it hears.[88] Napster.com, an Internet webcaster, must acquire performance rights to play sound recordings for the company's digital jukebox, a service for subscribers who pay a fee to listen to selected recordings.

Webcasters can obtain performance rights for a musical composition from BMI or one of the other performance rights organizations, but the independent webcasters negotiate their own deals to perform copyrighted sound recordings over the Internet. Podcasters downloading audio files should also obtain performance licenses. Webcasters that intentionally transmit music over the Internet without paying royalties may be subject to payments up to $150,000 per infringement.[89]

Compulsory Licenses If webcasters are not serving subscribers and are not streaming with the regular schedule of a radio station, webcasters can play music under a compulsory license. A compulsory license is an exception to copyright allowing the media to perform a copyrighted work without explicit permission as long as the user pays royalties. Compulsory licenses save the media the cumbersome and expensive process of negotiating licenses. The time-consuming, costly licensing process reduces public performances of copyrighted works, thereby diminishing the number of public performances of a work the public might otherwise enjoy and cutting royalties for copyright owners. Therefore, Congress concluded that the public and copyright owners would benefit if the media were guaranteed the ability under a compulsory license to carry some copyrighted works without having to ask permission. In return, the media pay royalties.

Cable operators enjoy compulsory licenses that allow cable systems to carry non-network signals from superstations such as WGN in Chicago and various independent stations.[90] Under the compulsory license, cable operators cannot be refused permission by the copyright owners to retransmit the programs from "distant" signals. The distant stations, in effect, are compelled to license their broadcasts and programs to the cable operators at fixed rates. The purpose of the license is to increase the diversity of programming delivered by cable subscribers.

Similarly, operators of direct broadcast satellites have a compulsory license to transmit network signals to homes that are not served by over-the-air television.[91] Satellite operators are guaranteed content for which they pay, and broadcasters earn revenues for delivery of their programs to households the broadcasters would not otherwise reach. In 2006, the U.S. Copyright Office ruled that cell-phone companies have a statutory license to use

[87]*See,* David Powell, "All Clear?—A Music Clearance Primer," The Music Bridge LLC (http://www.themusicbridge.com/id38.htm).

[88]David Oxenford, "Internet Radio—The Basics of Music Royalty Obligations," First Amendment Law Letter (Davis, Wright Tremaine LLP) (Fall 2006) at 2.

[89]Andrea Bates, "Webcasters Face Retroactive Royalties in October," *National L. J.*, Sep. 23, 2002, at B8.

[90]17 U.S.C. § 119 XXX CHK.

[91]17 U.S.C.A. §119(a); Satellite Broadcasting & Communications Ass'n of Am. v. Oman, 17 F.3d 344 (11th Cir. 1994).

copyrighted music in the ring tones announcing cellular phone calls, once the copyright owners have made the music available to the public.[92]

Webcasters, too, have a compulsory license to play copyrighted digital sound recordings if the web system is not interactive and listeners do not subscribe.[93] Musicians and performers benefit from the compulsory license because they receive royalties on the digital web transmissions, royalties they are denied when their performances are broadcast over the air or simulcast by a radio station over the Internet. To qualify for the compulsory license, the webcaster must not operate like a radio station from which it might be easy for listeners to record scheduled music. The webcaster cannot publish a schedule of broadcast plays and must limit the number of songs played by a particular artist or from a single album. The webcaster must also employ technology to discourage illicit copying.

Several webcasters, including non-profit college webcasters, stopped streaming music over the Internet when royalty payments required under statutory licenses were pegged at thousands of dollars. Congress provided relief with the passage of the Small Webcaster Settlement Act, setting low yearly fees. However in 2007, the Copyright Royalty Board declared that statutory royalty rates would more than double by 2010, again causing dire prophesies and much lobbying not only from small non-profit webcasters but also from larger commercial webcasters.[94]

Under the Digital Millennium Copyright Act of 1998, half the statutory fee goes to the performers and half to the copyright owner in the performance—usually the record company. Rates for compulsory licenses are set, distributions determined and disputes settled by the three-member Copyright Royalty Board convened by the Librarian of Congress. Cable and wireless systems pay royalties into a general copyright fund that is then distributed to copyright owners. The royalty board determines the shares of the fund to be distributed to each type of work—motion pictures, sports, religious programming—and, if necessary, the appropriate share for individual copyright owners.[95] A new clearing agency, SoundExchange, collects royalties under the statutory license for digital Internet music performances.[96]

MORAL RIGHTS Countries that belong, as the United States does, to the Berne Convention for the Protection of Literary and Artistic Works are required to protect artists' and writers' "moral rights" in their work. Moral rights include the right to be known as the author of one's work and to withdraw a work from distribution. Moral rights also allow an author to protect the integrity of a work by preventing others from deforming it or using it in a way that reflects poorly on the author.[97] A related right permits artists to profit from resales of their work. The United States generally considers its moral rights obligations under the Berne Convention to be met when creators seek remedies under the law of libel, privacy, misappropriation, and rights of publicity.

[92] In the Matter of Mechanical and Digital Phonorecord (Docket No. RF 2006-1 Delivery Rate Adjustment Proceeding), Copyright Office, Library of Congress, Memorandum Opinion, Oct. 16, 2006.

[93] David Wittenstein & M. Lorrane Ford, "The Webcasting Wars," *J. of Internet L.* (1999).

[94] See David Oxenford, "Copyright Royalty Board Releases Music Royalties for Internet Radio Streaming for 2006–2010—Clarifying the Confusion," Davis Wright Tremaine *Broadcast Advisory Bulletin* (April 2007).

[95] 70 Fed. Reg. 30901-30916 (May 31, 2005).

[96] David Oxenford, "Internet Radio—The Basics of Music Royalty Obligations," First Amendment Law Letter (Davis, Wright Tremaine LLP) (Fall 2006) at 3.

[97] Harry Henn, *Copyright Law: A Practitioner's Guide* 176 (1988).

The Copyright Act grants additional moral rights for works of visual art under the Visual Artists Rights Act of 1990.[98] The act protects artists' rights of attribution and integrity in some paintings, drawings, prints, sculpture, and photographs produced for exhibition. An artist whose work is violated can sue to stop the violation and to claim monetary damages.

The right of attribution gives artists the right to have their names associated with works they create and to prevent use of their names with works they do not create. The law also allows artists to disassociate themselves from their works if the works have been distorted or mutilated. To protect the integrity of a work, the law prohibits intentional distortion, mutilation, or other modification of an artist's work if the changes "would be prejudicial to his or her honor or reputation." Several states, including New York[99] and California,[100] have also adopted moral rights statutes for artists.

The Visual Artists Rights Act does not protect the moral rights of journalists or news photographers. Moral rights for journalists must be found in other laws, such as the law of publicity, privacy, libel, or misappropriation. It is not a violation of a moral right protected under federal law to reproduce a picture of a painting, sculpture, or other artistic work in a book, newspaper, magazine, or audiovisual work, although the reproduction may infringe the copyright in the work.[101]

Congress has not prohibited the "colorization" of black-and-white films, a practice that some directors say violates the integrity of their work. Although colorization is permitted if no copyright infringement occurs, some films must be labeled if color has been added. Congress created a National Film Registry of distinguished motion pictures that must be labeled if copies are altered. Congress created a National Film Preservation Board that each year selects up to twenty-five "culturally, historically, or aesthetically significant" films for inclusion on the registry.[102] Under the terms of the act, registered black-and-white films must be labeled if copies are colorized or otherwise altered. Among the first twenty-five significant films named to the registry were *Citizen Kane, Casablanca, Gone With the Wind,* and *Snow White and the Seven Dwarfs.*

◇ Summary ◇

Copyright owners are granted a bundle of rights. These include the rights to reproduce and distribute their works, create derivative works, and publicly perform and display their works. The right to copy, perform, or exercise the other rights of the copyright owner include the power to deny copying, creation of a derivative work or a performance. Copyright law recognizes separate copyrights in musical compositions and sound recordings, resulting in a complicated mix of requirements for broadcasters, digital webcasters, and producers of audiovisual works. The federal government and a few states have enacted moral rights legislation granting certain artists protection of the integrity of their works of fine art after they are sold and the right to be accurately identified with their work.

[98] 17 U.S.C. § 106A.
[99] N.Y. Arts & Cult. Aff. Law § 14.03 (McKinney 1996).
[100] Cal. Civ. Code § 986–987.
[101] H.R. Rep. No. 514, 101st Cong., 2d Sess., *reprinted in* 1990 U.S.C.C.A.N. 6915, 6927.
[102] 2 U.S.C. § 179. Sec. 179 repealed.

Infringement

Plaintiffs in copyright cases must prove they own copyright in an original work and that the defendants violated one or more of the copyright owners' exclusive rights. Infringers may be criminally liable for unauthorized copying whether or not they profit from the copying.[103] Once likely infringement is established, a court may enjoin dissemination of the infringing copies. It does not violate the First Amendment to halt distribution of copies that infringe a copyright.[104] Halting a copyright infringement is viewed by the courts as a protection of a property interest rather than an interference with free speech.

Unless works are so strikingly similar that unauthorized copying is a certainty, it cannot be assumed that a work that resembles another was copied. Copyright protects any original literary or artistic expression even if, by coincidence, it resembles someone else's work. Thus, even if plaintiffs can prove that their work is original, that they own the copyright and that someone else's work is similar, they may have difficulty proving that the defendant's work was copied. Typically, a plaintiff has no witnesses to testify to the copying. Lacking direct evidence, copyright owners can nevertheless prove copying by showing that the defendant had reasonable access to the copyrighted work and that the alleged copy is substantially similar to the original.

ACCESS It is easy to prove access to a widely disseminated work that anyone might see and copy. Thus, Miller Brewing Company had no difficulty establishing that Carling O'Keefe Breweries had access to Miller Lite advertisements that were broadcast on television and on cable.[105] Similarly, Universal City Studios, producer of the movie *Jaws,* easily established that Film Ventures International, producer of the movie *Great White,* had easy access to *Jaws*. Both the movie *Jaws* and the book on which it was based had been seen or read by millions.[106] Copiers have easy access to works distributed online.

SUBSTANTIAL SIMILARITY Besides proving access, a copyright plaintiff must prove that the works are substantially similar. It is easy to prove substantial similarity in cases in which the pirate copies the original work verbatim. There was no question of substantial similarity in *Quinto v. Legal Times of Washington, Inc*. because it was easily demonstrated that a Washington legal publication reprinted without change 92 percent of a copyrighted work.[107] More often, however, copying will not be as obvious. Indeed, determining substantial similarity between two works is one of the more difficult questions in copyright law.[108] "[T]he test for infringement of copyright is of necessity vague," Judge Learned Hand observed.[109]

In determining substantial similarity, courts often examine whether the underlying ideas and the manner of expression are similar in the two works.[110] The film *Great White* was so similar to the movie *Jaws* that a court issued a preliminary injunction against

[103]17 U.S.C. § 506(a).
[104]*In re* Capital Cities/ABC, Inc., 918 F.2d 140 (1990).
[105]Miller Brewing Co. v. Carling O'Keefe Breweries, 452 F. Supp. 429 (W.D.N.Y. 1978).
[106]Universal City Studios, Inc. v. Film Ventures Int'l, Inc., 543 F. Supp. 1134 (C.D. Cal. 1982).
[107]506 F. Supp. 554 (D.D.C. 1981).
[108]Melville Nimmer & David Nimmer, *Nimmer on Copyright* § 12.10[3].
[109]Peter Pan Fabrics, Inc. v. Martin Weiner Corp., 274 F.2d 487 (2d Cir. 1960).
[110]Sid & Marty Kroft Television Prods. v. McDonald's Corp., 562 F.2d 1157 (9th Cir. 1977).

infringement of *Jaws*. Both films starred sharks that threatened coastal towns on the Atlantic seaboard. The manner of expression was also the same in the two films. The films shared similar major characters, sequences of events, and development and interplay of characters, including teenage victims of the shark, a crusty sea captain, and a shark expert. Each had an explosive ending. "In light of the great similarity of expression," the court said, "it would seem fair to conclude that the creators of *Great White* wished to be as closely connected with the plaintiff's motion picture *Jaws* as possible."[111]

In contrast, a federal appeals court ruled that ABC's *The Greatest American Hero* was not substantially similar to Warner Brothers' *Superman* movies. The idea of each was similar—a character with superhuman powers battles evil—but the characters were very different. Unlike Superman, ABC's hero, Ralph Hinckley, was slight, informally dressed, and weak-chinned, "the antithesis of the Superman character image." Unlike Superman, the flying Hinckley crashed into buildings and penetrated walls only with great difficulty. Although he was impervious to bullets, Hinckley, unlike Superman, feared being shot. Warner Brothers, the court said, could not "claim a protected interest in the theme of a man dressed in a cape and tights who has the power to fly, resist bullets, crash through walls and break handcuffs with his bare hands."[112]

TYPES OF INRINGEMENT Infringement takes three forms: direct, contributory, and vicarious.

Direct Infringement A person directly infringes a copyright by copying, performing, or otherwise violating a copyright owner's exclusive rights without permission. It's a direct infringement to photocopy a book or duplicate a DVD without permission. Those who share files of copyrighted music and film without permission are direct infringers. In an online case, Dennis Erlich directly infringed the copyright in the published and unpublished works of L. Ron Hubbard, the late founder of the Church of Scientology, by uploading copies of Hubbard's writings onto an electronic bulletin board without authorization. Expression posted on the bulletin board, which had 500 paying subscribers, was distributed worldwide on the Internet through Netcom On-Line Communications Services, Inc., a large commercial provider of Internet access.[113] Even though Erlich made no money from the Hubbard expression he placed on the bulletin board, a federal court in California said that he was a direct infringer because he copied copyrighted material into a forum where it would be read by others and more widely distributed and copied.

Anyone distributing a computer program, musical work, motion picture, or sound recording in advance of its commercial distribution is also a direct infringer. Under terms of the Artists' Rights and Theft Prevention Act of 2005, a person distributing even one copy of a work in advance of its commercial release could be imprisoned for up to three years. The music industry won $220,000 from a Minnesota woman who allegedly uploaded 24 songs illegally.[114]

Contributory Infringement Contributory infringers contribute to the infringement of others or knowingly cause others to infringe, but they do not necessarily infringe directly themselves.

[111]Universal City Studios, Inc. v. Film Ventures Int'l, Inc., 543 F. Supp. 1134 (C.D. Cal. 1982).
[112]Warner Bros. Inc. v. American Broadcasting Co., 523 F. Supp. 611 (S.D.N.Y. 1981).
[113]Religious Technology Ctr. v. Netcom On-Line Communication Servs., Inc., 907 F. Supp. 1361 (N.D. Calif. 1995).
[114]Artists' Rights and Theft Prevention Act of 2005, in the Family Entertainment and Copyright Act, Pub. L. No. 109-9, 119 Stat. 218; Sarah McBride, "Music Industry Wins Digital Piracy Case," *Wall St. J.*, Oct. 5, 2007.

A federal appeals court ruled that Napster, the online file-sharing company in a former incarnation, contributed to infringement by computer users who traded music recordings through the Napster online system.[115] Napster, which now sells music legitimately, provided the server from which music files were shared. Without Napster's support services, the court said, "Napster users could not find and download music they want with the ease of which defendant boasts." Driven from hosting a server that contributed to illegal file sharing, Napster reappeared as a service allowing patrons to lawfully download music files for a fee.[116]

In 2005, a unanimous Supreme Court ruled that providers of free "peer-to-peer" file-sharing software may also be contributory infringers. The Supreme Court ruled that Grokster, Ltd., and StreamCast Networks, Inc., may have been contributory infringers by inducing users through advertising to illegally download copyrighted music and film on what the Court called "a gigantic scale." The Court said Grokster and StreamCast profited from the illegal file trading by directing advertising to an estimated 10 million users of company software, many of them former users of Napster fileservers.[117]

The Supreme Court overturned a lower court, which had held Grokster was not a contributory infringer because the Grokster software was capable of many lawful, non-infringing uses, including trading articles among libraries or trading uncopyrighted music. The lower court relied on a 1982 Supreme Court ruling that the SONY Corporation was not a contributory infringer when it produced and sold videocassette recorders on which home viewers could record programs from their television sets. In *Sony Corporation of America v. Universal City Studios* the Supreme Court noted that the SONY recorder, the Betamax, had many lawful uses and that the SONY Corporation had no intent to encourage illegal copying.[118] The Court concluded the videocassette recorder's principle use was for "time-shifting," allowing viewers to record programs for viewing at times of their choosing.

In contrast, the Supreme Court ruled that Grokster and Streamcast may have been contributory infringers because the companies' intent was to induce users—as a substitute for Napster—to illegally download copyrighted works, a practice from which Grokster would profit by directing advertising to users' screens. The Supreme Court remanded the *Grokster* case for determination whether the two companies should be held liable for "purposeful culpable expression and conduct" constituting contributory infringement.

Four months later, Grokster settled with record producers, agreeing to halt distribution of its file-swapping software and agreeing to pay $50 million in damages.[119] In 2006, a federal court in California ruled against Streamcast Networks.[120] After the litigation, Grokster planned to sell music lawfully, joining such companies as Apple iTunes, Rhapsody, Apple iPod, and the new Napster.

[115] A&M Records v. Napster, 239 F.3d 1004 (9th Cir. 2001).
[116] *See,* Napster.com.
[117] Metro-Goldwyn-Meyer Studios, Inc. v. Grokster, Ltd., 125 S. Ct. 2764 (2005).
[118] 464 U.S. 417 (1984).
[119] Jeff Leeds, "Grokster Calls It Quits on Sharing Music Files," *N.Y. Times,* Nov. 8, 2005, at C1.
[120] Charles Duhigg, Chris Gaither, & Dawn Chinielewski, "Creator of Morpheus Is Found Liable," *L.A. Times,* Sep. 28, 2006, at C1.

Vicarious Infringement Vicarious liability is found when someone has the right and ability to supervise the infringer's activity—and therefore can stop it—and benefits from the infringement.[121] Vicarious infringement is found when someone with supervisory powers profits from an infringement.[122] Unlike the contributory infringer, the vicarious infringer does not necessarily encourage or provide the means for infringing.

The federal appeals court determined Napster to be a vicarious infringer as well as a contributory infringer because the company had a direct financial interest in building the user base on which future profits depended. Furthermore, Napster had the ability to police the system by blocking illegal downloads of copyrighted music. Podcasters might also be vicarious or contributory infringers if they profit from or encourage distribution of unlicensed copies of copyrighted recordings or films.

Safe Harbors In 1998, Congress adopted legislation that protects online service providers from liability for money damages for infringement when the service providers merely transmit or temporarily store digital information for their subscribers.[123] Under the statute, online service providers are not liable for monetary damages for copyright infringements on their systems or networks if they act as mere conduits of information sent or received by others. If, like a common carrier, a service provider merely transmits information but does not select or alter the content or choose the recipients, the provider will not have to pay the copyright owner monetary damages for the infringements of others.[124] The provider is also exempt from monetary liability for the temporary storage or "caching" of information—a form of temporary copying—that is, an automatic process designed to reduce congestion on the Internet. Online service providers may also avoid monetary liability for innocently storing infringing copies provided by subscribers and innocently providing hyperlinks to sites that contain infringing material. ISPs include web hosting companies, search engines such as Google, and e-tailers such as Amazon.com.[125]

To maintain their safe harbors, Internet service providers must "take down" Internet postings if notified they are hosting or linking to infringing material.[126] To have an allegedly infringing website removed from an ISP, the copyright owner must provide notice containing the name and address of the complaining party and identify the infringing materials.[127] The ISP must return the questionable material to the website if a subscriber who posted it swears the material was wrongly removed. The party claiming copyright violation can then sue the party posting the materials, but not the Internet service provider. Bloggers, too, can enjoy a safe harbor as a "provider of online services" if the bloggers designate an agent for notification of infringing materials with the Copyright Office and have a policy against repeat copyright infringement by their subscribers and account holders.[128]

---

[121]Fonovisa, Inc. v. Cherry Auction, Inc., 76 F.3d 259 (9th Cir. 1996); Shapiro, Bernstein & Co. v. H. L. Green Co., 316 F.2d 305 (1963).

[122]*Id.*

[123]Digital Millennium Copyright Act, Pub. L. 105–304, codified at 17 U.S.C. § 512.

[124]17 U.S.C. § 512(a).

[125]Corbis Corp. v. Amazon, Inc., 351 F. Supp.2d 1090 (W.D. Wash. 2004).

[126]17 USC § 512.

[127]512(c)(3)(A)(i)–(vi).

[128]*See* Electronic Frontier Foundation, "Bloggers FAQ," at 6 (www.eff.org/bloggers/lg/faq-ip.php).

Shortly after the announcement that Google, the dominant Web search engine, would pay $1.65 billion to purchase YouTube, the video posting site, YouTube deleted some 30,000 files in response to a "take down" notice from a Japanese organization representing the rights of composers and publishers rights group.[129] In 2007, Viacom sued Google for $1 billion, alleging YouTube was willfully infringing Viacom's copyrights. Meanwhile, YouTube was developing methods to remove unlawfully posted copyrighted materials quickly and was arranging licensing agreements with the Warner Music Group, Sony, and other major copyright holders to share YouTube's advertising revenues when copyrighted materials are posted. In 2007, Disney, Microsoft, and other media companies agreed not to sue for illegally uploaded content if website operators remove the materials expeditiously.[130]

Circumventing Technology Audio and video producers have long hoped they could protect their copyrighted works from illicit copying through technological means, such as scrambling the content, inserting software that blocks or limits copying, adding digital watermarks that allow copyright owners to trace the origin of illegal copies, and installing technology in receivers and recorders to limit or prohibit recording. These efforts to protect copyrights are often called digital rights management, or DRM.

In 1998, Congress adopted the Digital Millennium Copyright Act, a law criminalizing acts that disable or circumvent technology designed to prevent illegal copying.[131] A 1992 law permits householders to copy digital recordings for noncommercial personal use, but also requires that digital recorders be programmed to prevent digital dubbing beyond one generation, and the statute requires royalty payments on digital recorders and blank digital media.[132] The FCC issued a ruling requiring manufacturers of digital television receivers as of 2005 to include technologies that would prohibit copying and retransmission of copyrighted programs, a ruling that was overturned by a federal appeals court.[133]

Technological protections for copyrighted expression have often failed. Consumers with only modest computer programming skills may be able to discover the "key" to unlock the technological barriers to copying. Furthermore, a federal appeals court ruled the FCC lacked jurisdiction to require that digital television signals not be copied or retransmitted *after* the signals were received in a home television set. The recording industry would like to require similar technology on digital radio recorders.[134] Viewers, listeners, and hardware manufacturers adamantly oppose content producers' attempts to limit citizens' ability to back up copyrighted content for personal use or transfer it to a second television or media player. After causing customers' great irritation, SONY BMG recalled music disks and paid compensation for hiding "digital rights management" software on disks to prevent copying. The software had the unintended effect of allowing hackers to easily install viruses and worms on users' PCs.[135]

129 "YouTube Deletes 30,000 Files After a Copyright Complaint," *N.Y. Times*, Oct. 21, 2006, at B4.

130 Kevin J. Delaney and Merissa Marr, "Disney, Microsoft Lead Copyright Pact," *Wall St. J.*, Oct. 19, 2007, at B4; Dan Frost, "Tech Bubble 2.0," *Toronto Star*, Dec. 10, 2006, at A19.

131 17 U.S.C. §1201.

132 Audio Home Recording Act, 17 U.S.C. §§1002–1004.

133 American Library Association v. Federal Communications Commission, 406 F.3d 689 (D.C. Cir. 2005).

134 "Digital Radio Restrictions: RIAA's Attempt to Control Recording From the Radio," Electronic Frontier Foundation (http://www.eff.org/IP/digitalradio, Nov. 15, 2006).

135 Stephen Manes, "You Can't Do That to Me!" *Forbes*, Oct. 30, 2006, at 82.

With spotty success at preventing unauthorized copying through technological means, the recording and film industries have reluctantly sued their own customers for illegal "file sharing." But content producers are encouraged by the growth of legal markets for downloading copyrighted music, film, and software. iTunes and other distributors of copyrighted digital music control illegal copying by requiring their subscribers to sign contracts pledging to limit copying. Subscribers to iTunes agree to download products only for personal, noncommercial use on up to five Apple devices. Under the contract, an audio playlist can be burned up to seven times. No video products can be burned. The subscribers also agree not to circumvent security technology.[136]

◇ Summary ◇

Authors who think their copyrights have been infringed must prove that their works are original, that they own valid copyrights, that the alleged infringer had access to the copyrighted work, and that the alleged copy is substantially similar to the original. In determining substantial similarity, courts examine whether the works have the same idea and manner of expression. Infringers of copyright may violate the law by directly copying, knowingly contributing to infringement by others or by vicariously profiting from unlawful copying in circumstances they supervise. Federal law protects online service providers from monetary liability if they merely carry and temporarily store infringing material of cyberspace users and if they take down copyrighted materials when notified that posted materials violate copyright. It is illegal to circumvent technologies designed to prevent unauthorized copying.

Fair Use

The fair-use doctrine creates an exception to the law prohibiting unauthorized copying of copyrighted expression. The fair-use doctrine is the law's attempt to reconcile the "exclusive rights" granted to authors to encourage creativity with a sometimes conflicting interest in ensuring that knowledge of creative achievement is widely disseminated and discussed. For a journalist or critic to discuss and evaluate a copyrighted work, it is usually necessary to copy at least small portions of the original work. Therefore, the copyright law permits limited copying for comment and criticism under the doctrine of fair use.

Fair use, one expert declared, is "a privilege in others than the owner of a copyright to use the copyrighted material in a reasonable manner without his consent, notwithstanding the monopoly granted to the owner" by the copyright.[137] To make fair use of a copyrighted work, it is not necessary to ask permission or pay a royalty. The fair-use doctrine, which developed in the common law, was embodied in Section 107 of the Copyright Revision Act.[138] Section 107 permits limited copying of copyrighted work, usually only for "productive" purposes such as news reports, criticism, and comment. For copying to be a fair use, the copier should usually be "engaged in creating a work of authorship whereby he adds

[136]"Terms of Service," iTunes Store, http://www.apple.com/legal/itunes/us/service.html.

[137]Rosemont Enters., Inc. v. Random House, Inc., 366 F.2d 303, 306 (2d Cir. 1966), *cert. denied,* 385 U.S. 1009 (1967), (quoting Ball, *The Law of Copyright and Literary Property* 260 (1944)).

[138]H.R. Rep. No. 1476, 94th Cong., 2d Sess. 66 (1976), *reprinted in* 1976 U.S.C.C.A.N. 5659, 5680.

his own original contribution to that which is copied."[139] Copying is a fair use, the Supreme Court has said, when the new work is "transformative," that is, the author "adds something new" by altering the original with "new expression, meaning, or message."[140] It is also important that copying not be so extensive as to damage the copyright owner's commercial market. The factors to be considered when a court is determining if copying constitutes a fair use are as follows:

1. The purpose and character of the use, including whether such use is of a commercial nature or is for nonprofit educational purposes
2. The nature of the copyrighted work
3. The amount and substantiality of the portion used in relation to the copyrighted work as a whole
4. The effect of the use on the potential market for, or value of, the copyrighted work

Purpose and Character of the Use Section 107 of the Copyright Revision Act does not define the uses of copyrighted material that are "fair," but the preamble to Section 107 says that fair use is likely to be found when the purpose is "criticism, comment, news reporting, teaching, . . . scholarship or research." A purpose least favored by courts is "mere reproduction," creating a work in which the new author has contributed little effort or original expression.[141] At the time the copyright law was adopted, the Senate suggested fair use would include

> quotation of excerpts in a review or criticism for purposes of illustration or comment; quotation of short passages in a scholarly or technical work, for illustration or clarification of the author's observations; use in a parody of some of the content of the work parodied; summary of an address or article, with brief quotations, in a news report . . . reproduction by a teacher or student of a small part of a work to illustrate a lesson; reproduction of a work in legislative or judicial proceedings or reports; incidental and fortuitous reproduction, in a newsreel or broadcast, of a work located in the scene of an event being reported.[142]

News and Comment One purpose of the copyright law is to encourage the dissemination of knowledge. The law therefore permits reporters and scholars to quote brief excerpts from copyrighted works without paying royalties. Scholars may quote short passages of a written work or reproduce small sections of a painting for the purpose of discussion and criticism. Journalists may quote briefly from copyrighted works for the purpose of disseminating news. When the Senate said that incidental and fortuitous reproduction of a copyrighted work is fair use, it meant that copyrighted material may appear by chance as background to events being reported. A federal district court in New York City found such incidental copying when WABC, Channel 7, broadcast footage of a high school band playing a copyrighted song, "Dove sta Zaza," in a parade. The court said the station's brief segment of the

[139]Melville Nimmer & David Nimmer, 3 *Nimmer on Copyright* § 13.05[A], at 13–163.
[140]Campbell v. Acuff-Rose Music, Inc., 510 U.S. 569 (1994).
[141]Working Group on Intellectual Property Rights, Bruce Lehman, chair, *Intellectual Property and the National Information Infrastructure* 77 (1995).
[142]S. Jud. Comm. Rep. No. 983, A Report to Accompany S. 1361, Copyright Law Revision, 93d Cong., 2d Sess. 115 (1974).

copyrighted song was fair because the use was incidental to a news event.[143] Similarly, broadcast or publication of a copyrighted painting as background in news footage or a news photograph would be fortuitous and therefore a fair use.

Parody Another purpose permitted by the fair-use doctrine is parody. A parody distorts or closely imitates another work to make fun of the original work. The Supreme Court acknowledged that parody "needs to mimic an original to make its point."[144] It is unlikely to be a fair use when a communicator uses a copyrighted work merely to "get attention" or "avoid the drudgery in working up something fresh," rather than commenting on the "substance or style" of the original.

The U.S. Supreme Court ruled that a parody may be a fair use even though it has a commercial purpose and copies the "heart" of the original work. Reversing a lower court, the Supreme Court ruled in *Campbell v. Acuff-Rose Music, Inc.,* that 2 Live Crew's parody of Roy Orbison's "Oh, Pretty Woman" could be sufficiently transformative not to violate the copyright held by Acuff-Rose. The lyrics to the original song state: "Pretty woman, walking down the street, Pretty woman, the kind I like to meet." 2 Live Crew's parody, though, restates the original as: "Bald headed woman, girl your hair won't grow, Bald headed woman, you got a teeny weeny afro."

In a unanimous opinion written by Justice David Souter, the Court said the 2 Live Crew parody of "Oh, Pretty Woman" may be a transformative use of the original because it "depart[s] markedly" from the Orbison lyrics, creating its own comment and criticism of the Orbison song. Although the Court did not find the parody to be of "high rank," the Court said the 2 Live Crew version

> juxtaposes the romantic musings of a man whose fantasy comes true, with degrading taunts, a bawdy demand for sex, and a sigh of relief from paternal responsibility. The later words can be taken as a comment on the naivete of the original of an earlier day, as a rejection of its sentiment that ignores the ugliness of street life and the debasement that it signifies.

The Supreme Court said the lower court placed too much emphasis on the commercial purpose of a parody. Although a commercial use weighs against a finding of fair use, Justice Souter wrote, commercialism is not the only factor. Indeed, the Court said, if a commercial use were presumptively unfair, most copying of copyrighted works for news reporting, comment, criticism, research, and parodies would be unfair because these activities are usually conducted for profit. Justice Souter noted Samuel Johnson's adage that "no man but a blockhead ever wrote, except for money."

Although the Court ruled that a parody might be a fair use, it remanded the case for a determination whether 2 Live Crew's repetition of the opening musical phrase from Orbison's song amounted to excessive copying. The Court noted that some quotation of this musical phrase, the "heart" of the Orbison song, would be a fair use. Indeed, a parody, the Court said, must quote "the original's most distinctive or memorable features" if the audience is to recognize the original. "It is the heart at which parody takes aim," the Court said.

The Supreme Court also remanded the case for a determination whether 2 Live Crew's rap version of "Oh, Pretty Woman" would interfere with the potential market for other rap

[143]Italian Book Corp. v. ABC, 458 F. Supp. 65 (S.D.N.Y. 1978).
[144]Campbell v. Acuff-Rose Music, Inc., 510 U.S. 569 (1994).

versions of "Oh, Pretty Woman" should Acuff-Rose ever wish to produce and distribute its own rap versions. However, the Court concluded that the 2 Live Crew parody would not interfere with a potential market for parodies of "Oh, Pretty Woman" that Acuff-Rose might wish to produce. The Court doubted that Acuff-Rose would ever want to market a parody of its own copyrighted song. It is unlikely, the Court said, for creators of imaginative works to license parodies, critical reviews, or lampoons of their productions.

The Court also noted that Acuff-Rose cannot complain if the success of the 2 Live Crew parody diminishes the value of the Orbison song. Copyright violation is found when the copy becomes a substitute for the original, not when the copy successfully lampoons the original. "Parody may quite legitimately aim at garroting the original, destroying it commercially as well as artistically," the Court said.

Following the decision in *Acuff-Rose,* courts have emphasized that parodies must make fun of the original work, not some other target or people's foibles. Thus, drawing on copyrighted work to create satire is less likely to be a fair use than drawing on copyrighted work to create a parody. "Parody copies from the object it mocks, while satire uses recognizable elements from the original work to mock something else or society in general."[145]

In *Dr. Seuss Enterprises v. Penguin Books USA, Inc.,* the Court of Appeals for the Ninth Circuit upheld an injunction preventing distribution of *The Cat NOT in the Hat! A Parody by Dr. Juice,* rejecting the publisher's claim that the book was a parody of the famous book *The Cat in the Hat* by Dr. Seuss.[146] *The Cat NOT in the Hat!* retold the O. J. Simpson story in Dr. Seuss's characteristic style. For example, the book described the hiring of Simpson's defense lawyers, headed by attorney Johnnie Cochran, for Simpson's trial for murder:

> When you're accused of a killing scheme
> You need to build a real Dream Team.
> Cochran! Cochran!
> Doodle-doo
> Johnnie, won't you join the crew?
> Cochran! Cochran!
> Deedle-dee
> The Dream Team needs a victory.

The Ninth Circuit held the book was not a fair use because it failed to ridicule the original work by Dr. Seuss. The authors of *The Cat NOT in the Hat!* merely used the Seuss title and style to call attention to their own work.

In another parody case, the U.S. Court of Appeals for the Ninth Circuit ruled that artist Tom Forsythe did not violate the copyright or trademark of Matell, the toy company, with his series of photographs titled "Food Chain Barbie."[147] Forsythe, a self-described "Absurdist," produced a series of photographs depicting nude Barbie dolls juxtaposed with various vintage kitchen appliances, often in sexualized positions. Forsythe chose to parody Barbie because she "is the most enduring of those products that feed on the insecurities of our beauty and perfection-obsessed consumer culture." Forsythe displayed his photographs at art festivals and promoted his works through postcards, business cards, and a website. (See "Missionary Barbie," Figure 6.3.)

[145]Electronic Frontier Foundation, "Bloggers FAQ," at 4 (www.eff.org/bloggers/lg/faq-ip.php).
[146]109 F.3d 1394 (9th Cir. 1997).
[147]Mattel Inc. v. Forsythe, 353 F.3d 792 (9th Cir. 2003).

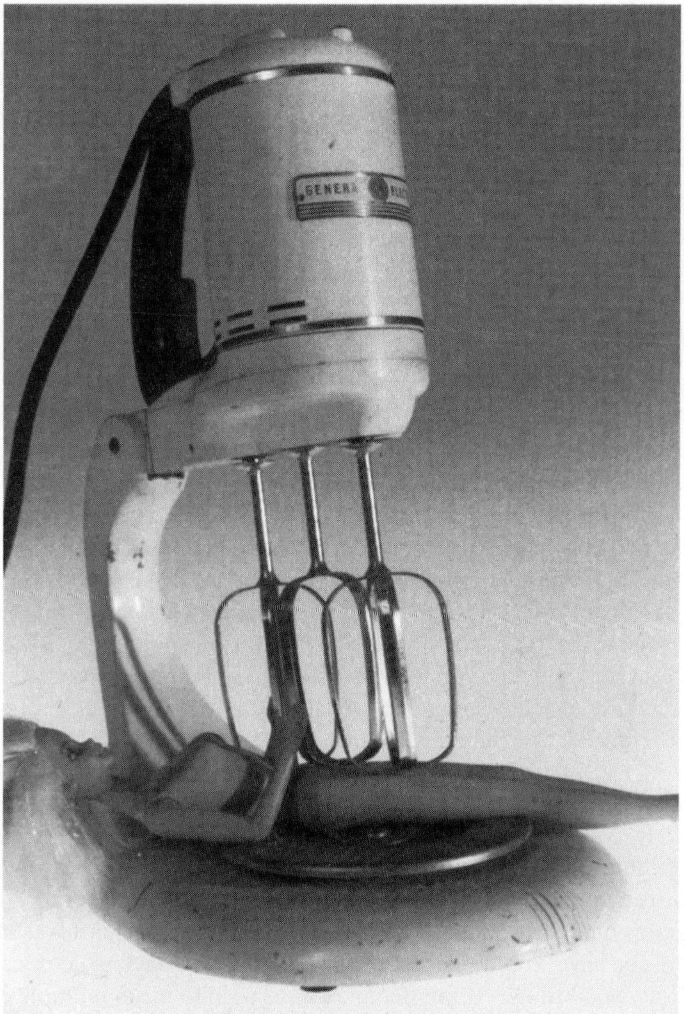

FIGURE 6.3 "Missionary Barbie" by Tom Forsythe. Copyright, Tom Forsythe. Reproduced with permission.

The Ninth Circuit affirmed a district court ruling that artist Tom Forsythe's use of Mattel's copyrighted work was fair use. The court of appeals agreed with the lower court that Forsythe's photographs were a parody of Barbie and everything the doll has come to signify. Mattel markets Barbie by portraying her in glamorous situations; Forsythe criticizes Barbie's meaning by portraying her in ridiculous and apparently dangerous situations.

Due to the nudity, Forsythe's photographs could only substitute for a work in the market for adult-oriented artistic photographs of Barbie, a market Mattel would not enter. Thus, Forsythe's work did not diminish the market for Barbie licensing. The appellate court found the public benefited from Forsythe's social criticism. "It is not in the public's interest to allow Mattel complete control over the kinds of artistic works that use Barbie as a reference for criticism and comment," the Ninth Circuit wrote.

Because the court said Mattel's action was frivolous and designed to force Forsythe to abandon use of Barbie in this artwork, the court ordered Mattel to pay more than $1.8 million for Forsythe's legal fees.

Teaching and Noncommercial Research Teaching and noncommercial research are also purposes for which limited copying is permitted under the fair-use doctrine. Guidelines often cited by courts allow a teacher or researcher to make a single copy of a chapter in a book or to copy a single article from a periodical or newspaper. The guidelines also permit a teacher to make multiple copies for a class, provided that the copies are short and maximum teaching effectiveness does not allow time to obtain permission from the copyright owner.[148]

Personal Entertainment Copying a work, particularly a whole work, for one's own pleasure or entertainment is normally not a fair use. Such copying is not a fair use because it has no transformative purpose. Photocopying a book or sharing a digital music file simply to avoid the cost of purchasing it violates copyright, even if the copier intends only to read the book or listen to the music, not lend it, sell it, or make more copies.

Thus, one may ask, is it lawful to record a song or television program for one's personal use? Yes, if one is making a single recording of a song or program that is broadcast free of charge to the listener or viewer. The Audio Home Recording Act of 1992 authorized listeners to make single recordings of music on recording machines programmed to block serial recording, machines on which royalties are paid for the benefit of copyright owners.

In 1982, the Supreme Court ruled in *Sony Corp. of America v. Universal City Studios, Inc.,* that homeowners can record complete copyrighted television shows off the air for their personal, noncommercial use. The case is known as the Betamax decision after Sony's home recorder, the Betamax. The Court ruled that home recording for the purpose of "time-shifting"—watching the program at a more convenient time—is a fair use.[149] Instead of requiring that living room copiers justify their recording of entire broadcast programs with a transformative purpose, the Supreme Court was satisfied that home copiers do not have a commercial purpose and that copying does not damage the market for Hollywood films. "If the Betamax were used to make multiple copies for a commercial or profit-making purpose, such use would presumptively be unfair," the Court said. But most people record television shows so that they can watch them at a later time. This time-shifting is "a noncommercial, nonprofit activity," which constitutes fair use, the Court said.

The limited legal protection for single copies made for individual use does not extend to multiple copies. The Betamax case was decided at a time when analog videocassette recorders were relatively new. The Supreme Court thought it "speculative" whether millions of householders creating home libraries of recorded programs would damage Hollywood's commercial market. There was little fear in 1982 of serial copying of copyrighted television programs because successive copies produced on analog copiers rapidly diminished in quality. The Audio Home Recording Act permitted digital recordings for individual use,

[148]H.R. Rep. No. 1476, 94th Cong., 2d Sess., 68–70 (1976), reprinted in 1976 U.S.C.C.A.N. 5659, 5681–83.
[149]464 U.S. 417 (1984).

but the 1992 Act prohibited serial recording and did not contemplate widespread distribution of perfect digital copies via computer networks and DVDs.

Record companies attempt to require consumers to purchase even single musical tracks from an authorized subscription service such as iTunes or Rhapsody, often at 99 cents per track. Company contracts may authorize subscribers to make digital copies for use on other platforms or at other locations but prohibit file sharing, a practice that demonstrates no transformative use.

Advertising Copying copyrighted materials for commercial purposes is unlikely to be a fair use. Courts are apt to find copyright infringement if copyrighted material is used in commercial advertising. For example, a federal court ruled that the Vogue School of Fashion Modeling infringed the copyright of *Vogue* magazine when the school copied the magazine's covers for a promotional campaign. The Vogue School had no relation to the magazine.[150]

In a case involving *Consumer Reports*, a federal court ruled that an advertiser may infringe the consumer magazine's copyright by accurately quoting a favorable product evaluation. The court said a trial should be held to determine whether the New Regina Corporation and its advertising agency violated *Consumer Reports'* copyright by quoting the magazine's positive rating of the vacuum cleaner. New Regina quoted *Consumer Reports'* high rating for its vacuum cleaner in a television advertisement.[151]

The federal district court, in its four-part analysis of fair use, said that the vacuum cleaner advertisements appropriated the most significant portion of *Consumer Reports'* product research and used it for a commercial purpose. Harm to a copyright is presumed, the court noted, where copyrighted expression is used for commercial purposes.

Most important to the court, however, was the effect the advertisement might have on *Consumer Reports'* potential market. Consumers Union claimed that the public would lose confidence in the organization's neutrality if manufacturers could associate Consumers Union with advertised products by routinely publishing its evaluations. Circulation of *Consumer Reports* would decline as public confidence waned, Consumers Union argued.

Although reprinting copyrighted material in commercial advertisements may constitute an infringement, it may be a fair use for competitors to reprint copyrighted materials in comparative advertisements. The U.S. Court of Appeals for the Fifth Circuit ruled that it was a fair use for the *Miami Herald* to copy the copyrighted covers of *TV Guide* in ads for the newspaper's competing television listings booklet. The court recognized that the *Miami Herald* copied the *TV Guide* covers for commercial purposes. But the court said that reproducing copyrighted material in a comparative advertisement is a productive fair use because the ad comments on, criticizes, and presents information about competing products. The Fifth Circuit also noted that comparing competing products in advertisements furthers the public interest by helping consumers make more rational decisions.[152] The *Miami Herald* case would have been different, the court noted, had the *Herald* copied *TV Guide*'s listings—the essence of a television booklet—instead of merely its descriptive cover. The court also said that the case would have been different if the *Herald* had misrepresented *TV Guide*.

[150]Conde Nast Publications, Inc. v. Vogue Schl. of Fashion Modeling, Inc., 105 F. Supp. 325 (S.D.N.Y. 1952).
[151]Consumers Union of United States, Inc. v. New Regina Corp., 664 F. Supp. 753 (S.D.N.Y. 1987).
[152]Triangle Publications, Inc. v. Knight-Ridder Newspapers, Inc., 626 F.2d 1171, 6 Media L. Rep. 1734 (1980).

Scooping a News Competitor The Supreme Court has ruled that a news organization that steals and publishes a competitor's news may infringe copyright. In *Harper & Row, Publishers, Inc. v. Nation Enterprises, Inc.,* the Supreme Court held that the political magazine *Nation* violated Harper & Row's copyright when the *Nation* printed 300 to 400 words from President Ford's then-unpublished memoirs, *A Time to Heal.*[153] After the *Nation* published its article, *Time* canceled an agreement with Harper & Row to publish excerpts from the book just before the hardbound edition went on sale. The *Nation*'s purpose, to "scoop" *Time,* weighed heavily in the Court's decision that the use was not fair. The Court did not question that the passages the *Nation* published were newsworthy; the quoted passages explained Ford's pardon of President Nixon. Nevertheless, the Court said that the passages infringed copyright because the *Nation*'s purpose and effect of the use were not to report news but to beat Harper & Row and *Time* to the marketplace. "The *Nation*'s use," wrote Justice Sandra Day O'Connor for the majority, "had not merely the incidental effect but the intended purpose of supplanting the copyright holder's commercially valuable right of first publication." The *Nation,* in the Court's opinion, was less interested in reporting news than in creating a news event of its own. Furthermore, the character of the use was hardly fair, the Court said, when the *Nation* acted in bad faith by knowingly exploiting a stolen manuscript.

Corporate Copying Corporate copying for commercial purposes is generally not a fair use. Thus, corporations that copy journal articles for different internal departments violate a publisher's copyright. A federal appeals court ruled that Texaco violated the copyright in scientific journals when company scientists photocopied articles from several scientific and technical journals for their research files.[154] Copying entire articles for one's files is not a transformative use, the court said. On the contrary, the court said that copying by a profit-making corporation was for a commercial purpose and that it damaged the publishers' market. The court suggested that if the company did not wish to purchase a subscription for each of its scientists, it could negotiate licenses with individual publishers, buy copies of articles from a document delivery service that would pay royalties to the publishers, or acquire a license to copy through the Copyright Clearance Center.

Commercial copying of broadcast programs, even segments of news programs—like commercial copying of printed articles—is generally not a fair use. The U.S. Court of Appeals for the Eleventh Circuit ruled that a commercial broadcast "clipping service" infringed the copyright in newscasts that the service copied off the air. WXIA-TV in Atlanta obtained an injunction against Carol Duncan's TV News Clips, a company that taped the evening news and sold segments to individuals and institutions that wanted a record of televised coverage of their activities.

The Eleventh Circuit said Duncan's "unabashedly commercial" purpose heavily influenced the court's decision to rule that the recording and sale of broadcast news segments was not a fair use.[155] The court distinguished TV News Clips from a newspaper clipping service that buys the newspapers it clips and sends the clippings to customers. TV News Clips was buying nothing. In fact, the court said that TV News Clips could impair WXIA's market for news clips if the station chose to sell them.

[153] 471 U.S. 539 (1985).
[154] American Geophysical Union, Inc. v. Texaco, Inc., 60 F.3d 913 (2d Cir. 1994).
[155] Pac. & S. Co. v. Duncan, 744 F.2d 1490 (11th Cir. 1984).

NATURE OF THE COPYRIGHTED WORK Besides considering the purpose and character of copying, courts ruling on fair use also consider the nature of the copyrighted work: its length, its factual or fictional nature, the effort involved in creating it, and its availability. Some works, because of their nature, are subject to more fair use than others. Works such as databases, lists, and stock tables, which require much effort but not much originality, in effect receive less copyright protection than works such as novels and plays that embody more originality.[156] News reports are less protected than movies and novels because the news contains facts, which cannot be copyrighted and which are used in comment and criticism of public events.

Some works are of such a nature that copying even a small amount might not be a fair use. A few words from a brief poem or song, for example, might be an infringement. Copying a small excerpt from a commercial newsletter might also be an infringement, particularly if the copying is for a commercial purpose. Commercial newsletters typically have only a few pages, a modest circulation, and a hefty subscription price. Publishers of newsletters of this nature cannot afford much free copying by others. Copying even a few lines might significantly damage the market value of the newsletter.[157] Courts are quite protective of unpublished manuscripts and letters. In the case in which the *Nation* published excerpts from Gerald Ford's memoirs, the Supreme Court said that the unpublished nature of the memoirs was a "key, though not necessarily determinative, factor" tending to negate a defense of fair use. In the *Nation* case, the Court was concerned that the copyright owner had lost the right of first publication.[158]

The U.S. Court of Appeals for the Second Circuit twice ruled that publishers of biographies violated the copyright in unpublished letters by copying or paraphrasing significant portions.[159] Copyright in letters belongs to the person who writes them. However, after complaints from historians and journalists, Congress passed legislation clarifying that courts were placing too much emphasis on the unpublished nature of works. The Court reminded that copying portions of an unpublished work might be a fair use. All four of the fair-use factors must be weighed to determine whether copyright in an unpublished work has been infringed, Congress said.[160]

AMOUNT AND SUBSTANTIALITY OF THE PORTION USED The greater the amount of work copied, the weaker is the fair-use defense. But determining substantiality is more than a question of the quantity copied; it is also a question of the quality of the portion used.

Quantity It is generally not a fair use to copy all or most of a copyrighted work, regardless of the purpose. For example, the *Legal Times* of Washington violated the copyright of Dave Quinto when it published 92 percent of an article Quinto wrote for the *Harvard Law Record*.[161]

The Betamax case is unusual because the Supreme Court ruled it was a fair use for householders to record entire copyrighted television programs off the air for shifting the

[156]N.Y. Times Co. v. Roxbury Data Interface, Inc., 434 F. Supp. 217 (1977).
[157]Wainwright Sec., Inc. v. Wall Street Transcript Corp., 558 F.2d 91 (2d Cir. 1977), *cert. denied,* 434 U.S. 1014 (1978).
[158]Harper & Row, Publishers, Inc. v. Nation Enters., 471 U.S. 539 (1985).
[159]Salinger v. Random House, Inc., 811 F.2d 90 (2d Cir. 1987), *cert. denied,* 484 U.S. 890 (1987); New Era Publications Int'l, ApS v. Henry Holt & Co., 695 F. Supp. 1493 (S.D.N.Y. 1988), *aff'd,* 873 F.2d 576 (2d Cir. 1989), *cert. denied,* 493 U.S. 1094 (1990). *But see* Wright v. Warner Books, Inc., 953 F.2d 731 (2d Cir. 1991).
[160]17 U.S.C. § 107.
[161]Quinto v. Legal Times, Inc., 506 F. Supp. 554 (D.C.D.C. 1981).

time of viewing. In this atypical case, the court reasoned that home copying by individuals for noncommercial purposes is a fair use that would not damage the commercial market for the copyright holder. As a general rule, one is prohibited from copying whole works. A critic or reporter should not quote more than a few paragraphs of a book or a few lines from an article at one time in a criticism or review. A reviewer might copy a few lines from a stanza of a poem or a single chart or graph from a technical treatise, even if the copying is for the purpose of criticism or comment.

Quality Even if the amount of material copied is small, copying may be an infringement if the "quality" of material taken is high. In *Harper & Row v. Nation,* the Supreme Court said that the 300 to 400 words quoted by the *Nation* from President Ford's memoirs constituted a small portion of Ford's book but were substantial because they were "the heart of the book." The *Nation* took "the most interesting and moving parts" of the manuscript, the Court said. The quoted passages qualitatively embodied Ford's distinctive expression.

The Supreme Court said the *Nation*'s copying was similar to CBS's infringement of Charlie Chaplin films when the network copied brief but important segments. CBS used no clips longer than four minutes from Chaplin films in a broadcast running more than an hour. But a federal court found an infringement because the network took the highest quality scenes.[162]

The U.S. Court of Appeals for the Second Circuit ruled that biographer Ian Hamilton violated the copyright in novelist J. D. Salinger's unpublished letters, in part, because the passages Hamilton quoted and paraphrased "make the book worth reading." The biography copies "virtually all of the most interesting passages of the letters, including several highly expressive insights about writing and literary criticism."[163]

A continually perplexing question is whether it is a fair use for composers and artists to "sample" from copyrighted songs. Digital music sampling is the exact reproduction in a new work of an existing musical phrase. Sometimes whole musical compositions are created with bits and snippets sampled from other works. Several courts have ruled that sampling is not a fair use.

A federal district judge ruled that musician Biz Markie violated the copyright in the song "Alone Again (Naturally)" when he digitally copied and repeated a ten-second phrase without authorization.[164] Courts in the federal sixth circuit have been particularly protective of copyright owners, ruling that even the briefest sampling may constitute a copyright infringement. In 2006, a federal judge in Nashville halted distribution of the million-selling classic hip-hop album "Ready to Die" after a jury determined that the producer, Sean "Diddy" Combs, had failed to get permission to include a three-note horn riff lasting only a few seconds from the 1992 recording, "Singing in the Morning," by the Ohio Players.[165] The jury awarded the copyright owners $4.2 million.

[162]Roy Export Co. v. Columbia Broadcasting Sys., Inc., 672 F.2d 1095, 8 Media L. Rep. 1637 (2d Cir. 1982), *cert. denied,* 459 U.S. 826 (1982).

[163]Salinger v. Random House, Inc., 811 F.2d at 99, 13 Media L. Rep. at 1960.

[164]Grand Upright Music Ltd. v. Warner Bros. Records, Inc., 780 F. Supp. 182 (S.D.N.Y. 1991).

[165]K. Matthew Dames, "Uncleared Sample Halts Sales of Seminal Hip Hop Album," *Copycense,* Mar. 20, 2006 (http://www.copycense.com/2006/03/uncleared_sampl.html).

On the one hand, sampling would appear to be a fair use because the sampler usually "borrows" only a few bars of music and transforms them into a new work. However, sampling suggests infringement because the sampler copies a musical phrase exactly, often a distinctive musical phrase, possibly the "heart" of the work. Because of the risk that musical sampling might not be deemed a fair use, many record companies go through the time-consuming, expensive process of negotiating an agreement for each musical phrase borrowed from another composition.[166]

Visual artists, like musicians, can also engage in digital sampling to create new images on magazine covers, in newspaper montages, and in works of art. *Newsday* reportedly paid FPG International, a stock photo agency, $20,000 to settle a copyright infringement claim and agreed to give proper credit for two digital photos *Newsday* edited for a front-page montage.[167]

EFFECT ON THE PLAINTIFF'S POTENTIAL MARKET The effect of copying on the plaintiff's commercial market is the most important factor for determining fair use.[168] This last criterion is a question of the effect of copying not only on the present market but also on the potential market for the copyrighted work. Critical to a determination of the commercial effect of copying is whether the copy has the same function as the original and therefore competes with, or supplants, the original work in the marketplace.

In *Wainwright Securities, Inc. v. Wall Street Transcript Corp.*, the U.S. Court of Appeals for the Second Circuit ruled that summaries of commercial reports infringed a copyright because they made it unnecessary to purchase the original.[169] *The Wall Street Transcript,* a financial newspaper, printed 250- to 300-word abstracts of research reports published by Wainwright Securities. Each year, Wainwright wrote 275 in-depth analyses of corporations, evaluating their financial characteristics, ability to take advantage of changes in their industry, growth prospects, and profit expectations. *The Wall Street Transcript* summarized Wainwright Securities' reports very effectively—so effectively that the *Transcript* advertised that it was not necessary to buy the reports.

In ruling that the *Wall Street Transcript*'s summaries violated Wainwright's copyright, the Second Circuit said that the *Transcript* was not making its own analysis and was not commenting on or criticizing Wainwright's work. Nor was the *Transcript* taking only brief quotes or seeking the opinions of others on the work. Instead, the *Transcript* "appropriated almost verbatim the most creative and original aspects of the reports, the financial analyses and predictions, which represent a substantial investment of time, money and labor." By summarizing the reports, the *Transcript* lowered the commercial value of Wainwright's reports. The *Transcript*'s summaries were, in effect, serving the same function as Wainwright's reports, the court said.

A detrimental commercial affect also figured in the infringement found in *Harper & Row v. Nation.* The Supreme Court ruled that the 300 to 400 words quoted in the *Nation* from President Ford's memoirs had a potential and actual effect on the market for the

[166]Carl Falstrom, "Note: Thou Shalt Not Steal: Grand Upright Music Ltd. v. Warner Bros. Records, Inc. and the Future of Digital Sound Sampling in Popular Music," 45 *Hastings L. J.* 359, 361 (1994).

[167]"Photo Suit Settled," *National Law Journal,* Jan. 16, 1995, at A10.

[168]Harper & Row, Publishers, Inc. v. Nation Enters., 471 U.S. 539 (1985); Triangle Publications, Inc. v. Knight-Ridder Newspapers, Inc., 626 F.2d 1171 (5th Cir. 1980).

[169]558 F.2d 91 (2d Cir. 1977), *cert. denied,* 434 U.S. 1014 (1978).

Ford book.[170] Almost immediately, Harper & Row lost $12,500 as a result of the *Nation*'s publication because *Time* magazine canceled a contract to serialize parts of the memoirs. The *Nation,* by quoting from sections of the book licensed to *Time,* took the part of the market *Time* would have had. More important, the Court said, the *Nation*'s publication of portions of the unreleased manuscript "poses substantial potential for damage to the marketability of first serialization rights."

In the Sony Betamax case of home taping, the majority and the dissenters on the Court disagreed sharply about how much home recording of copyrighted television shows might damage the commercial market for TV production studios. The majority said the potential harm to the market for studio productions was merely speculative. The Court was not satisfied that copying programs off the air for noncommercial use presented a "meaningful likelihood of future harm" to the Hollywood producers. On the contrary, the Court said, producers, broadcasters, and advertisers might benefit from home recording because time-shifting allows more people to view a broadcast.[171]

Four dissenters in the Betamax case argued home recording of complete over-the-air broadcasts did present a potential risk to the producers' market. The dissenters saw a potential danger to the producers' market for televised reruns, rentals, and re-releases in theaters if millions of homeowners build tape libraries with recordings. Potential damage to the copyright holders' market was sufficient, the dissenters argued, to negate a finding of fair use. Perhaps these arguments hold greater force today with the emergence of an extensive DVD market for television programs.

A federal appeals court ruled that downloading copyrighted music to consider whether to buy it is an infringement that damages the copyright owner's market.[172] The court rejected Cecilia Gonzalez's argument that downloading songs on a "try-before-you-buy" basis is good advertising for the copyright owners. On the contrary, the court said, most consumers testing downloaded songs fail to purchase them, thus undermining an already declining market for recorded music.

A federal appeals court rejected a claim by *Perfect 10,* an adult magazine and website, that Google's use of *Perfect 10*'s thumbnail nude photos damaged *Perfect 10*'s market for full-size nude photos or for cell phone downloads.[173] The court ruled that Google's transformative use of thumbnails as a search engine pointer was a fair use, a use that would not substitute for *Perfect 10*'s full-sized entertainment photos. The court also rejected *Perfect 10*'s unproven claim that Google's use of thumbnail nude photos in a search engine might harm *Perfect 10*'s market for downloading small photos to cell phones.

Copying book and magazine excerpts for professors' course packs is also an infringing commercial use, damaging to a publisher's market. A federal district court in New York awarded ten publishers more than $500,000 and enjoined Kinko's Graphics Corporation from unauthorized reprinting of copyrighted articles and book excerpts in students' course packets.[174] The district court rejected Kinko's claim that "anthologizing"

[170]471 U.S. 539 (1985).
[171]Sony Corp. of Am. v. Universal City Studios, Inc., 464 U.S. 417 (1984).
[172]BMG Muisic v. Gonzalez, 430 F.3d 888 (7th Cir. 2005).
[173]Perfect 10, Inc. v. Amazon.com, Inc., 2007 U.S. App. LEXIS 11420 (9th Cir. May 16, 2007).
[174]Basic Books, Inc. v. Kinko's Graphics Corp., 758 F. Supp. 1522 (S.D.N.Y. 1991).

substantial sections of copyrighted works for student source books is an educational purpose permitted by the fair-use doctrine. The court determined that Kinko's purpose in copying the professors' packets was commercial and that the copying—often more than a chapter from each source—would damage the publishers' market. "The use of the Kinko's packets, in the hands of the students, was no doubt educational," the court said. "However, the use in the hands of Kinko's employees is commercial."

◇ Summary ◇

The fair-use doctrine attempts to balance the competing social interests of encouraging creativity by granting authors exclusive rights in copyright while allowing limited copying for comment and criticism. In determining fair use, courts consider the purpose of the copying, the nature of the copyrighted work, the substantiality of the copying, and the effect of the copying on the market for the copyrighted work. Courts are least likely to find a fair use when works are copied for a commercial purpose and the copyright owner's commercial market is damaged. Nevertheless, copying may be a fair use, even in commercial advertising, if the new work is transformative or is an original work in its own right, commenting on or criticizing the original.

Unfair Competition

Copyright protects the property value in the expression of information and ideas. However, copyright does not protect the property value in signs, titles, names, and slogans that businesses use to differentiate themselves. These commercial symbols are considered too "trivial" for protection under copyright law. Nevertheless, the considerable originality and commercial value of these symbols can be protected from theft and misleading uses by the law of unfair competition.[175]

In early common law, unfair competition was often equated with "passing off." A company passes off or "palms off" when it offers a product as someone else's by using similar labeling, packaging, or advertising. Unfair competition now has a broader consumer orientation, encompassing several commercial practices that confuse or mislead the consumer. Prohibited forms of unfair competition include misappropriating the work of others, using similar titles in a misleading way, stealing trade secrets, and advertising falsely. False advertising is discussed in the chapter on advertising. Theft of trade secrets is treated in the chapter about access to government records. Misappropriation and trademark infringement are discussed here.

Misappropriation

Misappropriation is the unauthorized taking of the benefit of someone else's investment of time, effort, and money. Misappropriation is often referred to as "piracy." The Supreme Court established misappropriation as a separate tort in 1918 in a case in which the Court

[175]J. Thomas McCarthy, 1 *McCarthy on Trademarks and Unfair Competition* § 1.2 (1995).

ruled that the International News Service (INS) misappropriated news from the Associated Press (AP). INS employees misappropriated AP news by taking fresh dispatches from the AP office bulletin boards and putting the dispatches on the INS wire, sometimes after rewriting them, sometimes not.[176]

The misappropriation that the Supreme Court recognized in the INS case was the taking by INS of AP's expenditure of time and effort in gathering and assembling facts. The Supreme Court noted that facts in a news report cannot be copyrighted. Nor can the effort and money expended to gather news be copyrighted. Furthermore, AP placed no copyright notice on its news reports. However, INS was liable for misappropriation, which, the Court said, "is taking material that has been acquired . . . as the result of organization and the expenditure of labor, skill, and money, and which is salable."

A news organization, the Court said, may use a story by another news agency as a tip from which a new story can be developed through independent effort and expense. But the "bodily appropriation of a statement of fact or a news article, with or without rewriting, but without independent investigation or other expense" is misappropriation. Radio stations that broadcast verbatim newspaper reports without permission of the publisher misappropriate the time and effort invested by the newspaper staff in researching, writing, and publishing its reports.[177] Under European law, it is a misappropriation to take data from computerized scientific, business, or financial databases. The facts in a database cannot be copyrighted, and the organization may be too unoriginal to merit copyright protection. However, the time and effort invested to assemble the facts can be protected against misappropriation.[178]

Collecting and further disseminating already-broadcast sports scores is not a misappropriation, a federal appeals court ruled. The court said companies that transmitted broadcast sports scores to hand-held pagers did not misappropriate time-sensitive information belonging to the National Basketball Association.[179] The retransmitted facts were in the public domain.

However, a number of sports organizations are controlling media access to sports news and the subsequent dissemination. The sports organizations prefer to profit from their own Web sites and from exclusive news contracts with broadcasters and webcasters.

In 2007, the National Football League told news organizations they could post no more than 45 seconds per day of video shot at the facilities of the league's 32 teams. News organizations previously had been able to post unlimited online video clips of players and coaches.[180] Major League Baseball has limited the number of photos journalists can post online from each game and restricted audio and video coverage. MLB contemplated barring news organizations from hosting online photo galleries.

A professional golfers' organization, the PGA Tour, prohibits journalists from electronically disseminating real-time golf scores gathered by the PGA and posted on leader

[176] International News Serv. v. Associated Press, 248 U.S. 215 (1918).

[177] *See* Veatch v. Wagner, 116 F. Supp. 904 (D. Alaska 1953); Pottstown Daily News Publishing Co. v. Pottstown Broadcasting, 192 A.2d 657 (Pa. 1963).

[178] *See* John Flock & James Rosini, "Little Protection for Published Data Bases," *Nat'l L. J.,* March 22, 1993, at 19.

[179] National Basketball Ass'n v. Motorola, Inc., 105 F.3d 814 (2d Cir. 1997).

[180] Paul Farhi, "Under NFL Rule, Media Web Sites Are Given Just 45 Seconds to Score," washingtonpost.com, June 30, 2007.

boards and in media centers during tournaments. Journalists cannot disseminate the scores until 30 minutes after a shot or until after the scores are posted online by PGA Tour. Journalist organizations are also prohibited from selling the scores compiled in the tournament media centers. A federal appeals court ruled PGA Tour did not violate the antitrust laws by operating a monopoly system at tournaments for gathering scores and licensing their dissemination.[181]

Trademarks

Another form of unfair competition is misuse of another's trademark so as to confuse the public. A trademark is the word, name, or symbol a company uses to identify itself as the source of goods. The amended Lanham Trademark Act of 1946 defines a trademark as "any word, name, symbol, or device" used by a manufacturer in commerce "to identify and distinguish his or her goods . . . from those manufactured or sold by others and to indicate the source of the goods."[182] Familiar trademarks include Apple, M&M's, McDonald's, Scrabble, and Kleenex. Slogans such as "Where There's Life There's Bud" can also be trademarks as can titles of newspapers and columns. Trademarks associate a product with a specific source, whether or not the consumer can name the company that distributes M&M chocolate candies or Budweiser beer. iTunes is a trademark belonging to Apple Computer Incorporated.

Closely related to trademarks are service marks. A service mark is a symbol that is used in sales or advertising to identify services instead of products. "Elvis" and "Elvis in Concert" are service marks identifying entertainment services that Elvis Presley provided while alive and that Presley's estate owns rights to.[183] A broadcaster's call sign, such as "WXBQ," may also be registered as a service mark identifying the source of news, entertainment, and advertising services. Titles, character names, and other distinctive features of radio and television programs may also be service marks.

Trademarks and service marks have value as intellectual property because they represent a portion of the goodwill of a company. Trademarks and service marks are signals to consumers of the quality of goods and services. Trademarks and service marks reduce the time and effort customers expend to buy products. Because of the commercial value of trademarks and service marks, a company can acquire exclusive use of a distinctive mark.[184]

REGISTRATION Trademark and service mark rights are created through adoption and use on goods in trade. Unlike copyright and patent, trademark does not depend on originality, invention, or discovery, although a company's trademark may indeed embody imagination. Owners of trademarks and service marks are given exclusive use of their marks because of their marks' distinctiveness. The distinctiveness depends on the ability of the mark to cause the public to associate a product or service with the company that provides it.

[181] Morris Communications Corp. v. PGA Tour, Inc., 364 F.3d 1288 (11th Cir. 2004).
[182] 15 U.S.C. § 1127.
[183] Estate of Presley v. Russen, 513 F. Supp. 1339 (D.N.J. 1981).
[184] J. Thomas McCarthy, 1 *McCarthy on Trademarks and Unfair Competition* § 2.10, at 2-55 to 2-57.

Trademarks and service marks are protected under common law, but registration with the federal government under the Lanham Trademark Act provides recorded notice worldwide of a company's claim to ownership in a trademark or service mark. Trademark registration applications include a drawing of the mark and payment of a fee. A registered mark is denoted with a circled R, ®, and the phrase Registered in the U.S. Patent and Trademark Office or the abbreviated version Reg. U.S. Pat. & Tm. Off. If a trademark registration is pending, companies sometimes print "Trademark Pending" or "TM." Once the mark is used, the Patent and Trademark Office can issue a registration certificate.[185] Registration must be renewed every ten years and can be renewed for as long as the mark is used.[186] Trademarks can also be registered in each state, usually with the secretary of state's office.

Inherently Distinctive Marks To be registered, either a mark must be inherently distinctive or it must be a descriptive mark that has acquired a "secondary meaning." Words such as *reader, best,* or *nationwide* cannot normally be registered as trademarks because they merely describe the function, use, size, or quality of goods. Names such as "Tasty" candy, "Oyster House" restaurant, and "Ivy League" clothes cannot be registered as trademarks because, as merely descriptive terms, they are in the public domain.

A mark is inherently distinctive—or a strong mark—if it is fanciful, arbitrary, or suggestive.[187] A mark is fanciful if it is coined specifically to be a trademark. "Kodak" photographic equipment and "Clorox" bleach are coined terms that have no meaning other than to identify the source of certain products.

A mark is also inherently distinctive if it is arbitrary. An arbitrary mark consists of common words or symbols whose usual meaning has no relation to the product or service to which the words are attached. The "Stork Club" restaurant is an arbitrary trademark because storks have nothing to do with a restaurant. "Old Crow" whiskey, the "Flash" music group, and "Apple" computers are all arbitrary marks. These are strong marks, immediately identifying the source of specific products or services.

Suggestive marks, a third type of inherently distinctive or strong marks, are distinctive because they suggest what a product does without describing it. "Brilliant" furniture polish suggests the quality of the product. The polish in the bottle is not brilliant, but the mark suggests one's furniture will be. The same word, *brilliant,* could not ordinarily be a trademark for a diamond because brilliant would merely describe a gem. "Vanish" toilet bowl cleaner and "Coppertone" suntan lotion are other suggestive trademarks that do not merely describe a product.

Federal appeals courts disagree whether the "LA" on the label of low-alcohol beers is descriptive or suggestive. The U.S. Court of Appeals for the Eighth Circuit ruled that "LA" is a distinctive mark that suggests, but is not the descriptive initials for, light-alcohol, low-alcohol, or less-alcohol beer. Ruling that the Anheuser-Busch Company owns the LA trademark, the Eighth Circuit enjoined the Stroh Brewery Company from using the term "Schaefer LA." The court said initials are not descriptive unless they have become synonymous with specific descriptive words. "LA," however, was not associated in the public

[185] 15 U.S.C. § 1051.
[186] *Id.* at § 1058.
[187] J. Thomas McCarthy, 1 *McCarthy on Trademarks and Unfair Competition* §§ 11:1–11:4, at 11-5 to 11-18.

mind with a specific descriptive term such as light alcohol, the court said. The court based its ruling in part on a consumer survey in which only 24.4 percent of the people polled thought "LA" was a descriptive term, and three-quarters of those surveyed supported Anheuser-Busch's contention that "LA" suggested Anheuser-Busch's LA beer.[188]

Nevertheless, the U.S. Court of Appeals for the Seventh Circuit ruled that "LA" is descriptive and therefore is not protected under the Lanham Trademark Act.[189] In a ruling against Anheuser-Busch, the court agreed that G. Heileman Brewing Company and other brewers could use the "LA" designation on their light beers. The Seventh Circuit said that the L and the A are merely initials that describe the low-alcohol content of the beer. Furthermore, the court saw no danger of confusion among consumers if several companies used the "LA" designation. Confusion would not occur, the court said, because beer companies also put their names on their labels.

Secondary Meaning Although marks cannot be registered if they merely describe goods or services, descriptive marks can be registered if they acquire a secondary meaning. A secondary meaning is the drawing power or the commercial magnetism that develops over time in a title or in a corporate, business, or professional name. A secondary meaning is the mental association in a buyer's mind between a mark or symbol and the source of a product, even though the mark is not inherently distinctive.[190] A mark acquires a secondary meaning when the name and the business become one in the public mind.

Vogue is a word of common usage, but it has acquired a secondary meaning, at least when the term appears on a magazine. Over time, Vogue acquired an association between the magazine and the clothing and accessories "worn by the American woman of discriminating and fashionable tastes."[191] Other marks that began as descriptive names but developed secondary meanings include American Airlines, Kentucky Fried Chicken, and Payless drugstores. The Supreme Court has ruled that a distinctive color may be a trademark.[192]

INFRINGEMENT The purpose of a trademark is to protect consumers from being misled about the source of goods or services. When one company infringes the trademark of another, it confuses the consumer. In deciding whether a trademark has been infringed, courts consider such things as the strength of the marks, the similarity in appearance of the products, the meaning of the marks, the kinds of goods in question, and the intention of the defendant in using the mark. A plaintiff in a trademark case may sue to have the infringing use stopped and to collect illegal profits, damages, attorneys' fees, and court costs.

A federal court in New Jersey found sufficient likelihood of confusion to constitute infringement when Bob Russen used trademarks belonging to Elvis Presley's estate in promotions for Russen's "The Big El Show," an entertainment program imitating the dead singer's performances. Promotion for "The Big El Show" included use of "Elvis Presley," "TCB," and the "Elvis Pose," all words and symbols that are registered to Presley's estate. TCB with a lightning bolt is a trademark Presley placed on letterheads, jackets, and the

[188] Anheuser-Busch, Inc. v. Stroh Brewery Co., 750 F.2d 631 (8th Cir. 1984).
[189] G. Heileman Brewing Co. v. Anheuser-Busch, Inc., 873 F.2d 985 (7th Cir. 1989).
[190] J. Thomas McCarthy, 2 McCarthy on Trademarks and Unfair Competition § 15.01, at 15-4 to 15-7.
[191] Conde Nast Publications, Inc. v. Vogue Sch. of Fashion Modeling, Inc., 105 F. Supp. 325, 331 (S.D.N.Y. 1952).
[192] Qualitex Co. v. Jacobson Products Co., 1514 U.S. 159 (1995).

tails of airplanes to identify his entertainment services. The Elvis Pose is an image of Elvis in a jumpsuit hunched over a microphone and singing.[193]

The federal court said that "Elvis Presley," the "Elvis Pose," and "TCB" are strong marks distinguishing entertainment services provided first by Presley and then by his estate. Russen was using marks essentially identical to Presley's. Furthermore, the services Russen offered were very similar to Presley's. "The Big El Show" was a careful imitation of Presley's performances, and Russen's intent was to capitalize on Elvis's popularity. In finding a likelihood of confusion, the court did not suggest that people who bought tickets for "The Big El Show" would think that Elvis was alive—even though some of them might. But, the court said, the ordinary ticket buyer would likely believe incorrectly that "The Big El Show" was "related to, associated with, or sponsored by" Elvis Presley's estate.

The Washington Post, CNN, and other media stopped a company from "framing" their web pages in a manner that the media companies said infringed their trademarks. In a negotiated settlement, Total News, Inc., which operates an Internet news site, agreed to discontinue making it appear that the *Washington Post* and other prominent news sources were associated with *Total News* on the World Wide Web.[194] *Total News* agreed to stop framing web pages belonging to the *Post, CNN,* and other news sources with the *Total News* name and advertising. In a trademark and copyright infringement suit,[195] the *Post, Cable News Network, Wall Street Journal,* and other news organizations claimed that *Total News* pirated their products and reduced the value of their business by presenting their web pages diminished and partially obscured by the *Total News* frame. The news organizations that argued the public would be confused when they saw the companies' news and advertising under the *Total News* name next to *Total News* advertising. In the settlement, *Total News* agreed to avoid any practices that are "likely to imply" that *Total News* is affiliated with the *Post, CNN,* or the other news organizations. Visitors to the *Total News* site are able to jump to the web pages of the news organizations by clicking on plain text hyperlinks. But the news organizations' pages appear with no names or advertising associated with *Total News*.

FIRST AMENDMENT If a trademark is used in an unauthorized comedy, parody, or criticism, the use may be protected by the First Amendment. The U.S. Court of Appeals for the Second Circuit has ruled that the rights of the trademark owner must be balanced against the interests of free speech when the unauthorized use is for expressive purposes.

The Second Circuit ruled that the public interest in free expression and parody outweighed the slight risk of consumer confusion when *Spy* magazine published a parody of *Cliff's Notes*, the trademarked college study guides to the great books.[196] The parody, *Spy Notes,* purported tongue-in-cheek to summarize *Slaves of New York* and other hip urban novels.

Noting that "the expressive element of parodies requires more protection than the labeling of ordinary commercial products," the Second Circuit determined that consumers would not be confused because *Spy Notes* used red, blue, and white on the cover, colors very different from the distinctive yellow cover of *Cliff's Notes*. In addition, *Spy Notes,*

[193]Estate of Presley v. Russen, 513 F. Supp. 1339 (D.N.J. 1981).

[194]"Settlement Halts Internet Framing and Permits Text-Only Hyperlinking," 54 *Pat., Trademark & Copyright J.* (BNA) 165 (June 19, 1997).

[195]Wash. Post Co. v. Total News, Inc., 97 Civ. 1190 (S.D.N.Y., filed Feb. 20, 1997).

[196]Cliff's Notes, Inc. v. Bantam Doubleday Dell Publishing Group, Inc., 886 F.2d 490, 16 Media L. Rep. 2289 (1989).

which condensed trendy novels instead of great books, contained the word *satire* five times on the front cover and sold for twice the price of *Cliff's Notes*. Whatever minimal likelihood of confusion *Spy Notes* presented, it was insufficient to justify an injunction against a constitutionally protected parody, the court said.

Another federal court ruled that the First Amendment protects those who borrow trademarks to gather news. The district court for the Central District of California ruled that *Star* magazine and *USA Today* did not infringe the trademark of the singing group New Kids on the Block when the publications used the New Kids trademark while conducting a "900" telephone survey to determine the group's most popular member.[197] The court held that the First Amendment protects the use of the trademark for newsgathering even though participants in the survey had to pay for calls to vote for their favorite musician. The court rejected New Kids' claim that use of their trademark in the survey falsely implied that New Kids sponsored or endorsed use of the 900 number. "The risk that some people might think that the New Kids implicitly endorsed or sponsored the *Star* magazine's and *USA Today*'s 900-number services is outweighed by the danger of restricting news-gathering and dissemination," the court said. The court also rejected New Kids' claim that polling over a pay-per-call 900 network was a commercial misappropriation. First Amendment protection does not hinge on whether a constitutionally protected activity such as newsgathering is profitable or unprofitable, the court said.

A contrary result was reached when Miller Brewing Company and its advertising agency, Backer & Spielvogel, hired three performers who looked and sounded like the Fat Boys' rap group. In this case, the court decided that the advertisement was not a parody but a commercial appropriation of the Fat Boys' look and style that would confuse the public, thus infringing the Fat Boys' trademark.[198]

DILUTION Even if use of a trademark would not deceive or confuse the public, a use might be prohibited if it would tarnish or dilute the value of a mark. The dilution theory has frequently been successful in preserving the value of a trademark that has been used in an unwholesome or degrading context. At the request of the Coca-Cola Company, a federal district court in New York enjoined a company from selling posters reading "enjoy cocaine." The posters were printed in a script and color identical to those used by Coca-Cola. The poster company said that the posters were only a satirical spoof, but the court said that the unwholesome association of Coca-Cola with an illegal drug could dilute the value of the Coca-Cola trademark. The court did not suggest that consumers would confuse Coca-Cola with cocaine. Rather the court said consumers might be offended in their mistaken belief that the Coca-Cola Company treated a dangerous drug humorously.[199]

About half the states have antidilution statutes. Federal trademark laws also protect the aura and uniqueness of famous trademarks from dilution. The Federal Trademark Dilution Act protects famous trademarks such as Kodak from uses that would lessen the distinctiveness of the mark.[200] While state antidilution statutes require that a trademark owner only prove a "likelihood" of harm, the federal statute requires proof of actual dilution.

[197]New Kids on the Block v. News America Publishing, Inc., 745 F. Supp. 1540 (C.D. Cal. 1990).
[198]Tin Pan Apple, Inc. v. Miller Brewing Co., 737 F. Supp. 826 (S.D.N.Y. 1990).
[199]Coca-Cola Co. v. Gemini Rising, Inc., 346 F. Supp. 1183 (E.D.N.Y. 1972).
[200]15 U.S.C. § 1125 (c).

The United States Supreme Court held that the owners of the Victoria's Secret trademark had not proven that Victor's Little Secret, an adult video and "novelty" store, diluted the value of the Victoria's Secret trademark.[201] A federal district court had enjoined Victor's Little Secret from using that name, assuming that its continued use would likely tarnish the Victoria's Secret mark, the mark of a national chain of stores selling high-end, sexy clothing and beauty products. The Supreme Court, however, held that the dilution act requires proof of harm, such as a loss of a mark's distinctive identity, rather than speculation about future harm. The Supreme Court remanded the case to the lower courts for further proceedings on proof of dilution. The Court indicated that Victoria's Secret must prove that Victor's Little Secret had lessened the capacity of the Victoria's Secret mark to identify and distinguish lingerie and other goods sold through the Victoria's Secret catalog or stores.

A growing number of dilution and infringement claims are resulting from the unauthorized use of trademarks as Internet domain names. Domain names tell Internet users where an individual or company is located in cyberspace. Sometimes the names are used in an unsavory context. A federal judge in Washington enjoined a company from using the domain name "candyland.com" to identify a sexually explicit website. The Hasbro company, manufacturer of children's toys and games and owner of the "Candy Land" trademark, argued successfully that the value of its mark was diminished by the unsavory "candyland.com."[202] Similarly, Toys "R" Us, the toy store chain, convinced a federal judge to enjoin use of the name "Adults R Us" to identify a website for adult entertainment.[203]

Cybersquatting, another practice relating to Internet domain names, became common in the 1990s. Cybersquatters profit by registering domain names of well-known trademarks and then selling the domain names back to the trademark owners. Cybersquatting became profitable because registration was inexpensive and domain name registrars did not require that requesters of famous domain names own the trademarks. Once a cybersquatter registered a domain name, the trademark owner was prohibited from using its brand name for electronic commerce and was often forced to pay "ransom" to get its name back.

To halt cybersquatting, Congress passed the Anticybersquatting Consumer Protection Act of 1999.[204] The act makes a person liable for profiting from the domain name registration of another's trademark. Under the act, a court may order the cybersquatter to forfeit the domain name and transfer it to the owner of the mark. The United States Court of Appeals for the Fourth Circuit ruled that Virtual Works violated the act when it registered vw.net as a domain name. The firm was ordered to relinquish vw.net to Volkswagen, owner of the VW trademark.[205]

ABANDONMENT Unlike copyrights and patents, which are protected for limited times, a trademark lasts as long as it is used in commerce. Trademarks are lost when they are abandoned. A company can deliberately abandon its trademark by ceasing to use it or by willingly giving it up. More likely, a mark will be lost because companies do not guard against use of the mark as a generic term. Words such as aspirin, cellophane, and linoleum were

[201] Moseley v. V Secret Catalogue, Inc., 537 U.S. 418 (2003).
[202] Hasbro, Inc. v. Internet Entertainment Group, Ltd., 40 U.S.P.Q.2d (BNA) 1479 (W.D. Wash. 1996).
[203] Toys "R" Us, Inc. v. Akkaoui, 40 U.S.P.Q.2d (BNA) 1836 (N.D. Calif. 1996).
[204] 15 U.S.C. § 1125 (d).
[205] Virtual Works, Inc. v. Volkswagen of America, Inc., 238 F.3d 264 (4th Cir. 2001).

once trademarks but gradually passed into the public domain because people used the terms to signify generic pain relievers, food wrappings, and synthetic floor coverings. Escalator, shredded wheat, and thermos were also once trademarks but lost their association with a particular manufacturer and passed into the public domain.

Companies place great value in their trademarks and go to great lengths to keep them from passing into the public domain. A company lawyer might call a journalist reminding him to avoid using a trademark as a generic term. Trademark owners frequently buy advertisements reminding the media to use trademarks as proper adjectives, not as nouns or verbs. (See the Kimberly-Clark advertisement, Figure 6.4.) A writer may refer to a photocopying machine or a Xerox photocopying machine, but one should not

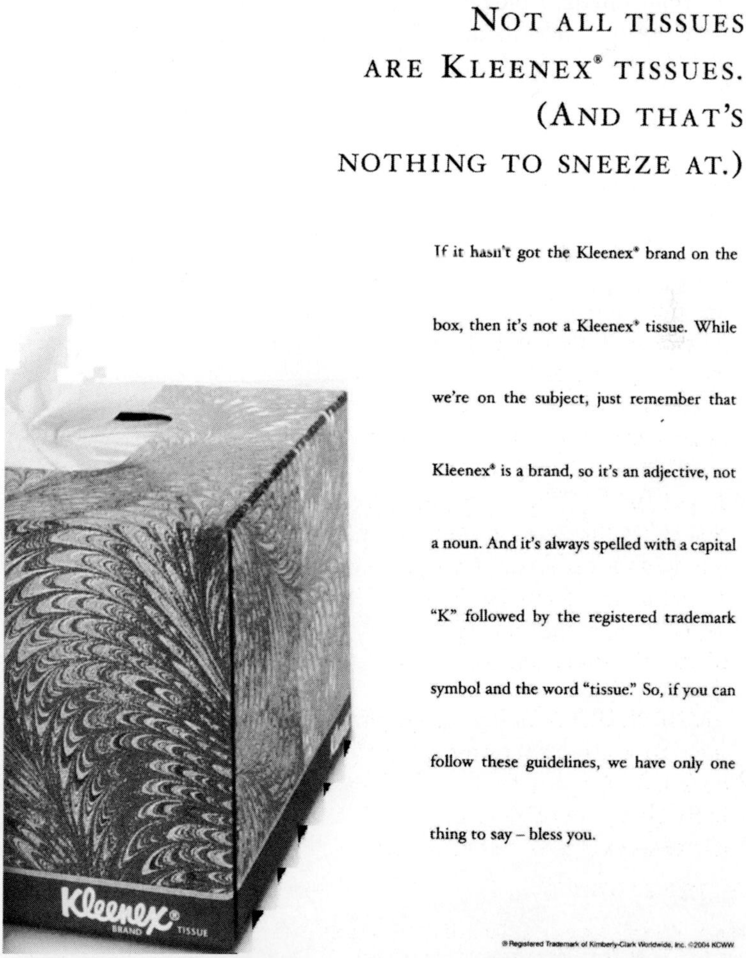

FIGURE 6.4 © 2004 Kimberly-Clark Worldwide, Inc. Reprinted with permission.

refer to the xerox or write that a person xeroxed a copy. "Xerox" and other trademarks are proper adjectives that should appear capitalized or in distinctive type with a lowercase generic noun such as photocopying machine. One wears a Stetson hat or perhaps a Stetson but not a stetson. One plays Scrabble crossword game or Scrabble but not scrabble. Journalists can avoid infringing trademarks and providing free advertising by describing students wearing western hats who photocopy their class assignments before playing a crossword game.

Summary

The law of unfair competition protects intellectual property not protected by copyright. Under the common law of misappropriation, a person can sue for damages if someone steals uncopyrightable facts or appropriates the time and expense invested in gathering and disseminating information. Trademark law protects trademarks and service marks—including slogans and titles that identify the source of a product—from misleading use by others. Both strong marks and descriptive marks that have acquired a secondary meaning can be protected from infringement. When trademarks are used in parodies, newsgathering, and other expressive purposes, the public's First Amendment interest in free expression may outweigh the trademark owner's property interests. Trademarks may be diluted through unsavory, though not necessarily confusing, associations. Owners of trademarks insist that their marks be capitalized and used as proper adjectives so that the marks do not lose their property value by acquiring a generic meaning.

CHAPTER 7

Political Speech

For many years, **corporations** have been held to be "persons" entitled to equal protection and due process of the laws.[1] Like individuals, corporations are protected by the Fifth Amendment against being charged twice for the same crime.[2] Yet corporations, unlike individuals, have no personality and no way to achieve personal fulfillment. A corporation is, as Chief Justice John Marshall observed in 1819, a "mere creature of law" and therefore possesses "only those properties which the charter of creation confers upon it."[3] Because corporations are artificial creations of the state, they have never enjoyed all the rights of personhood. For example, corporations, unlike individuals, can be required to testify against themselves[4] and have no right of privacy.[5]

For many years, profit-making non-media corporations also had no First Amendment rights. Thus, government regulations of corporate expression in elections, **referenda,** and lobbying raised few First Amendment issues. The law reflected Justice Byron R. White's view that speech by impersonal, state-chartered corporations deserves little or no First Amendment status because it does not further the First Amendment values of "self-expression, self-realization and self-fulfillment."[6]

Yet, although non-media corporations are impersonal entities, they contribute political and social commentary as well as commercial information to public debate. The ExxonMobil Corporation, for example, frequently prints editorial advertisements in *The New York Times.* The Pacific Gas & Electric Company's monthly newsletter of consumer advice and information circulates to three million customers. Other corporations contribute to public communication through advertisements, corporate reports, and video productions.

The Supreme Court now has recognized that profit-making non-media corporations have First Amendment interests in speaking and that consumers have First Amendment interests in hearing corporate messages. In 1978, the Court ruled that a company could buy advertisements to oppose an income tax on the ballot in Massachusetts. A short time later, the Court held that a New York utility could not be stopped from telling customers about the advantages of nuclear power. In addition to expressing their views on public issues, corporations are protected from having to disseminate messages they oppose. However, corporations operating broadcast stations have a unique obligation to provide broadcast time to political candidates.

The first section of this chapter examines expanding corporate rights to speak on referenda and social issues. The second section examines the continuing legal restraints on corporate speech in political elections. The third section explains the regulation of political broadcasting. Finally, the chapter discusses lobbying.

[1]Santa Clara County v. Southern Pac. R.R., 118 U.S. 394, 396 (1886) (equal protection); Smyth v. Ames, 169 U.S. 466, 522 (1898) (due process).

[2]United States v. Martin Linen Supply Co., 430 U.S. 564 (1977).

[3]Dartmouth College v. Woodward, 4 Wheat. 518, 636 (1819).

[4]Andresen v. Maryland, 427 U.S. 463 (1976); Wilson v. United States, 221 U.S. 361 (1911).

[5]California Bankers Ass'n v. Shultz, 416 U.S. 21 (1974); United States v. Morton Salt Co., 338 U.S. 632 (1950).

[6]First Nat'l Bank of Boston v. Bellotti, 435 U.S. 765, 804–05, (1978) (White, J., dissenting).

Referenda and Other Public Issues

The First Amendment rights of non-media corporations are most developed in cases involving referenda and public issues. In a referendum, citizens vote on propositions such as whether to establish an income tax, require deposits on beverage containers, institute rent control, or build a nuclear power plant. Referenda were initiated early in the century to neutralize the power of well-financed lobbyists over the legislatures. The reform was supposed to provide citizens a direct voice in governmental policy and discourage legislators from acting only in response to powerful, narrow interests.[7]

Some firms hire people to circulate petitions, paying the circulators for each signature they solicit. The firms are paid by the interest groups hoping to have the referenda or initiatives placed on the ballots. To ensure fraud or deceit does not corrupt the referendum process, whether or not petition circulators are paid, some states have adopted laws circumscribing how petitions may be circulated and signatures gathered. In 1999, the U.S. Supreme Court ruled that certain limits Colorado placed on the ballot initiative process violated the First Amendment's protection of political speech.[8] The Court said requiring petition circulators to be registered voters limited the number of possible people who could gather signatures. The Court also said it would inhibit political discussion to force petition circulators to wear badges stating their names and requiring referendum initiators to submit to the state, monthly and when turning in all the petitions, the names of the circulators and the amount paid, if any, to those who gathered signatures. The Court said anonymity is an important protection for political discussion. Anonymity should be protected when asking someone to sign an initiative petition and when the petitions are submitted, the Court said. The Court noted Colorado had a number of other protections in place to ensure a fair initiative process.

States also have expressed concern that commercial corporations may dominate political debate through the referendum and initiative process. To prevent this, several states, including Massachusetts, passed statutes prohibiting corporate financial participation in referenda. The Massachusetts law said corporations could not buy ads supporting or opposing a referendum issue unless the ballot measure related directly to the business of the corporation. The First National Bank of Boston challenged the law because the bank wanted to buy newspaper advertisements opposing a personal income tax. The attorney general of Massachusetts, Francis Bellotti, said First National's ads would violate the statute because the personal income tax proposal did not relate directly to the bank's business. First National then sued Bellotti, arguing that the state law infringed the company's First Amendment rights.

In ruling for the bank in *First National Bank of Boston v. Bellotti*,[9] and for other corporations in later cases, the Supreme Court has created an almost unlimited First Amendment freedom for non-media corporations to spend money to support referenda questions and other social issues. *Bellotti* is founded on the right of citizens to receive political speech by corporations.

---

[7] *See* Jeffrey Even, "A Discourse on the People's Powers of Initiative and Referendum," 32 *Gonzaga L. Rev.* 247 (1996/97).
[8] Buckley v. American Constitutional Law Foundation, 525 U.S. 182 (1999).
[9] 435 U.S. 765 (1978).

The Right to Receive Political Content

Central to the Court's ruling in *Bellotti* was the political nature of First National's proposed advertisement. Speech about a tax referendum, the Court said, is constitutionally protected political speech "at the heart of the First Amendment's protection." In making its ruling, the Court did not say that non-media corporations have the same broad First Amendment rights as an individual or a newspaper has. Instead, the Court focused on the political nature of the speech and the rights of citizens to receive it. The constitutional question, the Court said, was "whether the corporate identity of the speaker deprives this proposed speech of what otherwise would be its clear entitlement to protection." Because the Court concluded that political speech retains its constitutional status regardless of its corporate source, the Court declared the Massachusetts statute unconstitutional.

Although the Court recognized the constitutional value of the bank's political advertisements, the Court also recognized citizens' rights to receive corporate information. Corporate speech on a referendum is constitutionally protected, the Court said, "not so much because it pertains to the seller's business as because it furthers the societal interest in the 'free flow of commercial information'" to the public. Explaining the First Amendment right to receive information, the Court drew on *Virginia State Board of Pharmacy v. Virginia Citizens Consumer Council,*[10] an advertising case decided two years before *Bellotti.* In *Virginia Pharmacy,* the Court said a state statute prohibiting price advertising of prescription drugs violated citizens' First Amendment right to receive information. Citizens need price information, the Court said, to make thoughtful consumer choices that in the aggregate affect political issues, including the allocation of resources. Similarly in *Bellotti,* the Court said citizens have a right to receive political information about a tax referendum, information that is "indispensable to decision-making in a democracy."

To the Supreme Court, a referendum is just one of many social and political issues about which corporations might speak. "The freedom of speech and of the press guaranteed by the Constitution," the Court said in *Bellotti,* "embraces at the least the liberty to discuss publicly and truthfully all matters of public concern without previous restraint or fear of subsequent punishment."[11] The Court's broad vision of constitutionally protected corporate speech was confirmed two years later when the justices ruled that the Public Service Commission of New York could not bar a regulated utility from telling its customers about the benefits of nuclear power. Citing *Bellotti,* the Court in *Consolidated Edison Co. of New York, Inc. v. Public Service Commission of New York, Inc.*[12] struck down a state regulation barring the utility from including political brochures in its monthly bills. As a general matter, the Court said, "the First Amendment means that the government has no power to restrict expression because of its message, its ideas, its subject matter or its content."[13]

The Court did not rule in *Bellotti* that all corporate political speech is constitutionally protected. The government might regulate corporate expression, the Court said, if the government demonstrates a compelling interest, such as the need to preserve the integrity

[10] 425 U.S. 748 (1976).

[11] 435 U.S. at 776 (quoting Thornhill v. Alabama, 310 U.S. 88, 101–02 (1940)).

[12] 447 U.S. 530 (1980).

[13] *Id.* at 537 (quoting Police Dept. v. Mosley, 408 U.S. 92, 95 (1972)).

of the electoral process from corporate domination. However, the Court saw no evidence that "the relative voice of corporations has been overwhelming or even significant in influencing referenda in Massachusetts, or that there has been any threat to the confidence of the citizenry in government." To be sure, the Court said, corporate advertising may influence the outcome of a referendum, but "the fact that advocacy may persuade the electorate is hardly a reason to suppress it." People in a democracy, the Court said, bear the responsibility to judge which speech they choose to believe, whether that of the powerful or the weak.

The Court also rejected the Massachusetts government's contention that the statute barring corporate speech in referenda was necessary to protect shareholders from association with ideas they might oppose. The Court said the Massachusetts legislature did not intend to protect shareholders when it adopted the statute. If the legislature were concerned about shareholders' rights of association, it might have given shareholders a choice, the Court said. However, the Massachusetts statute barred corporate referendum advertisements even if all shareholders voted to buy them. The Court said a legislative intent to protect shareholders was also belied by other Massachusetts laws allowing corporations to lobby and buy political advertising without consulting shareholders. If shareholders are disgruntled, the Court said, they can vote against corporate directors who spend corporate funds on inappropriate or unpopular speech.

Justice White, who dissented in *Bellotti,* argued that non-media corporations enjoy no First Amendment right to speak or publish about matters unrelated to their businesses. White thought the Massachusetts statute prohibiting corporate spending in referenda should prevail because speech by an impersonal corporation, chartered by the government, does not serve the First Amendment value of self-fulfillment. The ideas expressed by a company "are not a product of individual choice," White said.

Justice William Rehnquist, who also dissented in *Bellotti,* argued that the government's power to create a for-profit corporation encompasses the power to regulate it, including regulation of the corporation's speech. The corporation, as a creature of the state, possesses no right to speak or publish, in Rehnquist's view.

Freedom from Compelled Speech

Corporations not only may express themselves on public issues but also are protected from having to disseminate messages they oppose. In *Pacific Gas & Electric Co. v. Public Utilities Commission of California,* the Supreme Court ruled a California utility could not be forced to include a newsletter from a consumer group in the company's billing envelopes.[14] In *Pacific Gas & Electric,* the Court overturned a Public Utilities Commission regulation requiring the utility to include materials from a consumer group that often challenged PG&E in rate-making proceedings. The commission had ruled that a monopoly utility must carry the messages of its critic.

The consumer group, Toward Utility Rate Normalization (TURN), tried to raise money through PG&E's billing envelopes. Four times a year, the Public Utilities Commission required PG&E to include TURN's consumer messages in the "extra space" of the utility's billing envelopes. The "extra space" was space that could be filled without additional postage

[14] 475 U.S. 1 (1986).

after the company's bills and legal notices were inserted. During the four months when TURN's messages were carried, Pacific Gas & Electric could not include its own newsletter, *Progress,* unless the utility paid extra postage.

In a 5-3 decision, the Supreme Court ruled it was unconstitutional for the Public Utilities Commission to force Pacific Gas & Electric to carry political views with which the utility disagreed. In an opinion written by Justice Louis Powell, Jr., and joined by three other justices, the Court equated the rights of a corporate utility with the rights of a newspaper publisher. The Court said forcing a utility to carry unwanted consumer messages was unconstitutional, just as the Court had earlier ruled it was unconstitutional to force a newspaper to publish a reply by a political candidate the paper attacked editorially. As will be discussed later in this chapter, broadcasters are required to carry speech by political candidates.

Requiring either utilities or newspapers to carry unwanted messages inhibits their right to speak, the Court said. Speakers may be reluctant to speak if they know their expression may entail an obligation to carry a response. A government-imposed right of access to a newspaper or a corporate billing envelope therefore inescapably dampens freedom of expression and limits the variety of public debate.

In addition, the Court said the California Public Utilities Commission order was unconstitutional because it forced PG&E to associate with expression with which the corporation disagreed. Forcing PG&E to carry TURN's messages might either make the utility appear to agree with TURN or force PG&E to respond. Compelling either an uncomfortable silence or a forced response violates the First Amendment, the Court said.

In dissent, Justice Rehnquist argued PG&E was not forced to associate with views it opposed because the utilities commission required TURN to publish a disclaimer saying PG&E did not necessarily agree with the consumer group's messages. Justice John Paul Stevens, in his dissent, argued that consumer messages are little different from other messages that corporations have traditionally been required to carry without First Amendment confrontations. Corporations often have been required to disseminate legal notices, print messages on loan forms, publish proposals by dissident stockholders, and disclose management plans and information about the accuracy and sponsorship of their advertisements.

Just as corporations need not disseminate messages they oppose, a federal district court held that advertising agencies cannot require online service providers to carry commercial material on the Internet. A federal court in Pennsylvania said America Online (AOL) had the right to prevent Cyber Promotions, an Internet advertising agency, from sending 1.9 million of its clients' ads per day to AOL subscribers without paying AOL or obtaining AOL's permission.[15]

The court held that because AOL is a private company, not a government agency, the First Amendment does not require AOL to open its system to all comers. Merely because the Internet is widely used does not mean an online service provider is a "public system" that must provide access to everyone, according to the court. The court said by refusing to allow Cyber Promotions to send its advertisements, AOL was protecting its computers, which are AOL's own property. But, the court said, AOL's refusal did not limit Cyber

[15]Cyber Promotions Inc. v. America Online Inc., 948 F. Supp. 436 (E.D. Pa. 1996); *see also* Cyber Promotions Inc. v. America Online Inc., 948 F. Supp. 456 (E.D. Pa. 1996) (court said AOL did not intend to limit expression but to protect its own communication system).

Promotions' access to the Internet. For example, Cyber Promotions could reach AOL subscribers through mail, television, and newspapers, the court said. Also, the court said, AOL has a system allowing AOL's subscribers to receive only the advertisements they want. Cyber Promotions could send its messages by that method under a contract with AOL.

In another case involving Cyber Promotions, a federal court in Ohio said the online advertising agency trespassed when it used CompuServe's online system without permission.[16]

Corporations can be required to subsidize generic advertising programs if the advertising is classified as government speech. If the speech is private, the permissibility of subsidies depends on the extent to which the industry is regulated.

In a 2005 case, *Johanns v. Livestock Marketing Association,*[17] the Supreme Court ruled the First Amendment rights of beef producers were not violated by compelled funding of a generic beef marketing program. Justice Scalia, writing for the majority, categorized the advertising as government speech because the message of the program was controlled by the federal government; the Secretary of Agriculture "exercises final approval authority over every word used in every promotional campaign. All proposed promotional messages are reviewed by Department [of Agriculture] officials both for substance and wording, and some proposals are rejected or rewritten by the Department." Just as taxpayers are unable to constitutionally challenge government expenditures for roads or wars they do not support, the beef producers have no First Amendment grounds to challenge the assessments for the advertising program. "Citizens may challenge compelled support of private speech, but have no First Amendment right not to fund government speech," Justice Scalia said.

In a dissenting opinion, Justice Souter claimed that the advertisements, which frequently include the tag line, "Funded by America's Beef Producers," masked the government's role in producing the ads. "No one hearing a commercial for Pepsi or Levi's thinks Uncle Sam is the man talking behind the curtain," Souter said. "Why would a person reading a beef ad think Uncle Sam was trying to make him eat more steak?" Unless the speech appears to be coming from the government, its governmental origin "cannot possibly justify the burden on the First Amendment interests of the dissenters targeted to pay for it," Souter wrote.

In two private speech cases, the Court reached contrasting results. In a 1997 case involving a requirement that fruit growers contribute to a program urging consumers to buy fruit, the Court ruled that the program was an economic regulation—not a speech regulation—within Congress' power.[18] The Court emphasized that the collective advertising was part of a regulatory scheme that extensively controlled the production and marketing of fruit. Moreover, the growers were not forced to support any political or ideological views. The ads created no "crisis of conscience" because the growers presumably agreed with the advertising, which urges people to purchase fruit. However, in a 2001 case involving the less regulated mushroom industry, the Court held that a statute requiring mushroom growers to pay for advertising—but otherwise leaving growers unregulated—unconstitutionally infringed the growers' free speech.[19] The Court treated the forced contributions as a speech regulation rather than an economic regulation because the mushroom program's sole objective was advertising.

[16]CompuServe Inc. v. Cyber Promotions, Inc., 962 F. Supp. 1015 (S.D. Ohio 1997).
[17]544 U.S. 550 (2005).
[18]Glickman v. Wileman Bros. & Elliott, Inc., 521 U.S. 457 (1997).
[19]United States v. United Foods, Inc., 533 U.S. 405 (2001).

◇ Summary ◇

The Supreme Court has created a First Amendment right for non-media corporations to speak on matters of public importance. Included among corporate rights are freedom from compelled dissemination of someone else's political messages.

Corporate First Amendment protections are based primarily on the right of citizens to receive messages on referenda and other political and social issues. A corporation can use its own channels of communication, such as billing envelopes and newsletters, or it can buy advertising in another medium, as the First National Bank of Boston did.

Corporate speech may be halted if the government demonstrates a compelling interest, such as an imminent threat to democratic processes. So far, according to the Supreme Court, corporate expenditures have not presented such a threat.

Elections

If the First Amendment permits corporations to buy advertising to support referenda and other political and social issues, it might seem likely that corporations also could buy advertising to support political candidates. After all, the Supreme Court has said, freedom of expression "has its fullest and most urgent application precisely to the conduct of campaigns for political office."[20]

However, the majority of the Supreme Court in *First National Bank of Boston v. Bellotti* said a profit-making corporation's right to speak on issues of general public interest "implies no comparable right in the quite different context of participation in a political campaign for election to public office."[21] Indeed, federal election law prohibits corporate contributions and expenditures for political candidates. The election law is supposed to restrict "the influence of political war chests funneled through the corporate form"[22] and to "eliminate the effect of aggregated wealth on federal elections."[23] Law in some states also prohibits corporations and unions from using treasury money to support candidates for state office.

Federal Election Campaign Act

The Federal Election Campaign Act of 1971 prohibits a corporation or union from using money from its treasury to make a contribution or expenditure in connection with candidates for federal office.[24] Corporations may not draw funds from their treasuries either to make contributions to a candidate or to make expenditures on a candidate's behalf. *Contributions* are gifts of money or services given directly to a candidate or a candidate's campaign committee. *Expenditures* are monies spent independently of candidates to advocate their election. A number of states also have restrictions on corporate contributions and expenditures.

Early campaign reform laws prohibited only corporate contributions to candidates. But the Taft-Hartley Act of 1947, which is still in effect, also barred corporate and union

[20]Monitor Patriot Co. v. Roy, 401 U.S. 265, 272 (1971).
[21]435 U.S. 765.
[22]FEC v. National Conservative Political Action Comm., 470 U.S. 480, 501 (1985).
[23]Pipefitters Local Union No. 562 v. United States, 407 U.S. 385, 416 (1972).
[24]2 U.S.C. § 441b(a).

expenditures "expressly advocating the election or defeat of a clearly identified candidate."[25] If corporate expenditures are not prohibited along with contributions, Senator Taft argued, "a candidate for office could have his corporation friends publish an advertisement for him in the newspapers every day for a month before election."[26]

The purpose of the Federal Election Campaign Act and earlier election reform laws is to prevent the corruption that might result if massive corporate capital enters the electoral process. Corporate contributions to candidates, it is feared, might lead to favored treatment for a contributing corporation if a candidate is elected to office. It is also feared that corporate expenditures may lead to corporate dominance of the electoral marketplace of ideas. The Supreme Court has upheld the constitutionality of a state statute, similar to the federal law, that bars profit-making corporations from spending corporate funds on behalf of a political candidate. Nonprofit corporations, however, are not similarly barred.

In late 2003, in *McConnell v. FEC,*[27] the Supreme Court upheld the key provisions of the Bipartisan Campaign Reform Act (BCRA), a 2002 law amending the FECA. The FECA allowed corporations and unions to give unlimited amounts of "soft money" to political parties for get-out-the-vote drives and other purposes not directly related to electing federal candidates. In 2000, the national political parties received over $500 million in "soft money." Political parties often improperly used this money to influence federal elections. Corporations and unions also circumvented FECA's ban on the use of corporate or union funds to influence federal elections by sponsoring sham issue ads that did not expressly say "Vote for John Doe," but supported or attacked a candidate's position on an issue.

In enacting BCRA, Congress sought to reduce the role of "soft money" in the political process and to prohibit sham issue ads near elections. The law prevents individuals, corporations, and unions from making "soft money" donations to the national political parties, but permits donations to state parties. The law also prohibits unions and corporations from sponsoring broadcast ads that refer to federal candidates within sixty days of a general election.

Profit-Making Corporations

In *Austin v. Michigan Chamber of Commerce,* the Supreme Court upheld a section of the Michigan Campaign Finance Act prohibiting business corporations from spending corporate treasury funds to support or oppose a candidate running for state office. In a 6-3 decision written by Justice Thurgood Marshall, the Court ruled that restrictions on corporate political speech are constitutional if narrowly tailored to serve a compelling government interest. The Court said Michigan's desire to "avoid corruption or the appearance of corruption" was a compelling interest justifying a prohibition on election expenditures by the Michigan Chamber of Commerce. The Chamber had wished to purchase a newspaper advertisement supporting a candidate in a special election for the Michigan House of Representatives.

The Court viewed the "corporate form" as the primary danger to the integrity of the elections that Michigan wished to preserve. By state charters, corporations are granted limited legal and financial liability, perpetual life, and favorable tax treatment. Operating with

[25]Labor-Management Relations Act, ch. 120, § 304, 61 Stat. 159 (1947) (current version at 2 U.S.C. § 441b(a)).
[26]93 Cong. Rec. 6439, *quoted in* United States v. United Auto Workers, 352 U.S. 567, 583 (1957).
[27]540 U.S. 93 (2003).

special privileges granted by the state, corporations develop power that should not be permitted to dominate the political marketplace, the Court said. Thus, the Michigan election law was properly aimed at

> the corrosive and distorting effects of immense aggregations of wealth that are accumulated with the help of the corporate form and that have little or no correlation to the public's support for the corporation's political ideas.[28]

Justice Marshall said the Michigan statute was sufficiently narrow because it prohibited corporations only from spending money from their treasuries; the statute did not bar corporations from operating political committees that collect and spend money contributed from corporate employees. Unlike money from corporate treasuries, money contributed by employees may be spent on behalf of candidates because the money reflects the employees' political views, not a corporation's economic interests, the Court said.

The Court distinguished the Chamber of Commerce from nonprofit ideological corporations that the Court had earlier ruled could spend money on behalf of candidates in an election. In *Federal Election Commission v. Massachusetts Citizens for Life, Inc.,*[29] the Court ruled that federal election law did not bar an antiabortion group from spending $10,000 to distribute a newsletter urging the public to vote for named pro-life candidates. In an opinion written by Justice Brennan, the Court said ideological groups such as Massachusetts Citizens for Life pose little threat to the integrity of an election because they are formed to disseminate political ideas rather than to amass capital. Thus, the government has no compelling interest to bar election expenditures by nonprofit ideological corporations.

Any organization, whether incorporated or not, might qualify as an ideological corporation, the Court said, if it were established to promote political ideas, if it had no shareholders, and if it were not influenced by business corporations. The Michigan Chamber of Commerce, although technically a nonprofit corporation, was much more like a profit-making business than a nonprofit ideological organization, the Supreme Court said. The Chamber was created by profit-making businesses for several nonideological purposes, including training workers and promoting the business goals of members. Although the Michigan Chamber had no shareholders, the Court said the Chamber's corporate members were like shareholders because they joined for nonideological purposes such as promoting profitability, not to further their political ideology. Finally, the Chamber of Commerce was heavily influenced by business corporations, the Court said.

In a strong dissent in *Michigan Chamber of Commerce,* Justice Anthony Kennedy, joined by Justices Sandra Day O'Connor and Antonin Scalia, said the Court's ruling was "the most severe restriction on political speech ever sanctioned by this Court." Kennedy said the Court's hostility to the "corporate form" and corporate wealth is too imprecise a reason to justify a ban on independent corporate campaign expenditures. In another dissent, Justice Scalia said the fact that corporations amass large treasuries is "not sufficient justification for the suppression of political speech." If corporations may be barred because they have large amounts of money, then wealthy individuals should also be barred, he said.

[28] 494 U.S. 652, 659 (1990).
[29] 479 U.S. 238 (1986).

Prohibited Contributions and Expenditures

Despite the dissents of Kennedy and Scalia in *Michigan Chamber of Commerce,* profit-making corporations can be barred from making expenditures or contributions in an election. Corporate—and union—contributions prohibited by the federal election law include gifts of money, advertising, securities, discounts, membership lists, use of facilities, broadcast time, and services to candidates and their campaigns.[30] Thus, an advertising firm that gives free or reduced-price services to a candidate or takes a loss to benefit a candidate makes an illegal contribution. Advertisers and public relations firms may provide services to candidates at regular prices.

However, a broadcaster who gives free time or news tapes to one candidate but not to his or her opponent makes an illegal campaign contribution.[31] Similarly, a corporate public affairs department makes an illegal contribution if it gives taped interviews of candidates to broadcasters. The Federal Election Commission ruled that the Atlantic Richfield Company made an illegal contribution when its public affairs department gave taped interviews with the major presidential candidates to 145 commercial and cable broadcast stations. Although the tapes did not favor the Republicans or Democrats, the Federal Election Commission said Atlantic Richfield's tapes were "something of value" given on behalf of the candidates by a non-media company. The distribution might not have been considered a contribution if the tapes had been obtained from a civic or other nonprofit, nonpartisan group, the FEC said.[32]

It is also an illegal contribution for a corporation or union to allow its stockholders, employees, or members the free use of its facilities for more than an "occasional, isolated, or incidental" amount of time to voluntarily produce election materials.[33] In 2006, the FEC amended its rules, allowing employees to use corporate computers and Internet facilities for voluntary Internet political activities, such as e-mail and blogging. These voluntary Internet activities are permissible provided the activity does not prevent the employee from completing the normal amount of work and does not increase overhead or operating costs.[34]

THE PRESS EXEMPTION Congress recognized that press entities have a First Amendment right to distribute news and commentary about federal candidates. Consequently, Congress crafted an exemption in federal election law, known as the press exemption, which allows recognized press entities, such as newspapers and broadcast stations, to disseminate news stories, commentary, or editorials discussing federal candidates as long as the press outlet is not owned by a candidate, political party, or political committee.[35] This exemption is narrow. It does not allow corporations and unions with in-house publications to distribute campaign material to the general public.[36] Nor does it allow media corporations to fund

[30] 11 C.F.R. § 100.52(d)(1).

[31] A.O. 1978-60, Fed. Election Camp. Fin. Guide (CCH) ¶ 5350 (Sept. 1, 1978).

[32] A.O. 1980-90, Fed. Election Camp. Fin. Guide (CCH) ¶ 5538 (Sept. 9, 1980). *See also* A.O. 1979-70, Fed. Election Camp. Fin. Guide (CCH) ¶ 5448 (Jan. 11, 1980).

[33] 11 C.F.R. § 114.9.

[34] Internet Communications, 71 Fed. Reg. 18589 (Apr. 12, 2006) (modifying 11 C.F.R parts 100, 110 & 114).

[35] 2 U.S.C. § 431 (9)(B)(i).

[36] *See* Massachsetts Citizens for Life v. FEC, 479 U.S. 238, 251 (1986) (pro-life group's newsletter is not entitled to the press exemption).

campaign activities, such as purchasing billboard advertisements, which are not news, commentary, or editorials. For example, the Walt Disney Company is able to disseminate news and commentary about candidates via its ABC television network. However, the Disney Company is prohibited from endorsing a candidate in brochures distributed at campaign rallies. As the Supreme Court stated in *McConnell v. FEC,* the press exemption applies to news, commentary, and editorials only; "it does not afford *carte blanche* to media companies generally to ignore" federal election restrictions.[37]

The FEC applies a multipart analysis in determining whether the press exception applies. First, the agency asks whether the entity engaging in the activity is a press entity as described by federal election law and FEC regulations. Congress recognized broadcast stations, newspapers, magazines, or other periodical publications as press entities.[38] Subsequently, the FEC ruled that entities producing cable news programming are entitled to the press exemption. In 2006, the FEC ruled that online news and commentary also be included within the press exemption.[39] Second, the agency considers whether the entity is owned by a political party, political committee, or candidate. Third, the FEC asks whether the entity is engaging in a "legitimate press function."[40] Under this prong, the FEC distinguishes the dissemination of news or commentary from other activities that are not typically performed by press entities. Thus, MTV was acting in a legitimate press function when it posted election-related content on its website during the 2004 elections; posting news on a press entity's website was a common media practice, the FEC said. However, the FEC concluded that MTV's plan to provide educational materials at community events did not qualify as a press function "because this activity is not one typically performed by a press entity."[41]

The FEC's interpretation of the press exemption favors entities that either operate news media outlets or have a record of regularly producing "news, commentary, or editorials" for media outlets.[42] For example, the FEC concluded that a series of websites operated by Fired Up, a for-profit company, were entitled to the press exemption. The websites included Fired Up's commentary on, quotes from, summaries of, and hyperlinks to news articles appearing on other entities' websites, along with Fired Up's original reporting and editorials. Although readers could submit comments to the sites, Fired Up maintained editorial control over the content displayed on its sites. The FEC found Fired Up to be a legitimate press entity because the websites were the online equivalent of a newspaper, magazine, or other periodical publication described in federal election law and FEC regulations. Fired Up was not owned or controlled by a political party, political committee, or candidate, and its websites were available to the general public. The provision of news stories, commentary, and editorials was within Fired Up's "legitimate press function."[43] In contrast, the FEC determined that Citizens United, a corporation seeking to produce and market a

[37]540 U.S. 93, 208 (2003).

[38]2 U.S.C. § 431 (9)(B)(i).

[39]Internet Communications, 71 Fed. Reg. 18589 (Apr. 12, 2006) (modifying 11 C.F.R parts 100, 110 & 114).

[40]*See* Federal Election Comm'n v. Phillips Publishing, Inc., 517 F. Supp. 1308 (D.D.C. 1981); Readers Digest Ass'n v. FEC, 509 F. Supp. 1210 (S.D.N.Y. 1981).

[41]A.O. 2004-07 (Apr. 1, 2004).

[42]*See, e.g.*, A.O. 2005-19 (Dec. 9, 2005) (concluding that producer of regularly scheduled political radio programs is qualified for the media exemption).

[43]A.O. 2005-16 (Nov. 18, 2005).

documentary film about John Kerry and John Edwards in 2004, was not a "bona fide" press entity. Citizens United promoted the "free enterprise system, belief in God, and the family as the basic unit in society" through a variety of educational activities, but it had not regularly produced documentaries for television.[44]

In interpreting the press exemption, the FEC does not measure whether the content is biased or balanced. Nor does express advocacy of the election or defeat of a candidate disqualify a press organization's news or commentary from the press exemption. Press organizations may even solicit contributions for candidates in their news and commentary.

Permitted Election Communications

The prohibition on corporate and union campaign expenditures and contributions does not completely bar corporations and unions from participating in election campaigns. Corporations and unions may form and support **political action committees (PACs)** that can spend unlimited amounts on behalf of a candidate. Corporations and unions may also promote candidates within their corporate or union "family."

ISSUES, ORGANIZATIONS, AND VOTER REGISTRATION Consistent with the Supreme Court's First Amendment ruling in *First National Bank of Boston v. Bellotti,* corporations may buy advertising to discuss issues, provided that corporate and union treasury funds are not used to urge the election or defeat of a named candidate. Prior to the enactment of BCRA in 2002, corporations and unions were allowed to refer to federal candidates in issue ads as long as so-called "magic words" such as "Elect John Smith" or "Vote Against Jane Doe" were not used. During the 2000 election cycle, an estimated $500 million was spent on issue ads. In 2002, Congress found that many broadcast issue ads lacking the "magic words" were nonetheless intended to influence candidate elections by condemning or supporting a candidate's record on a particular issue. For example, one 1996 ad referred to a candidate's failure to pay child support and urged viewers to call the candidate and "tell him to support family values."

In 2002, Congress prohibited corporations and unions from using their general treasury funds to pay for "electioneering communications." BCRA defined "electioneering communications" as any broadcast, cable, or satellite communication that refers to a federal candidate during the sixty days before a general election or the thirty days before a primary and is broadcast in the area in which that candidate is running for office. (Figure 7.1 summarizes federal restrictions on candidate-related public communication.) The Supreme Court found this law facially constitutional in *McConnell v. FEC.*[45] The Supreme Court agreed with Congress that the prior "magic words" requirement of express advocacy had become "functionally meaningless" and did not prevent "real or apparent" corruption of the political process. Both Justices Scalia and Kennedy wrote dissenting opinions adhering to the views they expressed in *Michigan Chamber of Commerce:* corporations should be free to speak on political issues and candidates.

[44]A.O. 2004-30 (Sept. 10, 2004).
[45]540 U.S. 93 (2003).

	Type of Speech	
Sponsor	**Electioneering Communication** (Reference to a federal candidate in a broadcast, cable or satellite communication reaching the "relevant electorate" within 30 days of a primary or 60 days of a general election)	**Express Advocacy** (Advocating the election or defeat of a federal candidate)
For-Profit corporation or union	Prohibited, but exception is permissible under *WRTL* ruling	Prohibited, except when directed only to respective corporate or union "family"
Qualified nonprofit corporation	Unlimited amounts may be spent if uncoordinated with candidate	Unlimited amounts may be spent if uncoordinated with candidate
PAC	Unlimited amounts may be spent if uncoordinated with candidate	Unlimited amounts may be spent if uncoordinated with candidate
Individual	Unlimited amounts may be spent if uncoordinated with candidate	Unlimited amounts may be spent if uncoordinated with candidate

FIGURE 7.1 Federal Restrictions on Candidate-Related Public Communication.

In 2006, in a case brought by a nonprofit ideological advocacy corporation, the Supreme Court ruled that *McConnell* did not mean that the BCRA restriction was constitutional in all cases.[46] Wisconsin Right to Life (WRTL) sought to broadcast advertisements in 2004 in Wisconsin concerning Senate inaction on judicial nominations. One radio advertisement airing before BCRA's blackout period included the following:

> Sometimes it's just not fair to delay an important decision. But in Washington it's happening. A group of Senators is using the filibuster delay tactic to block federal judicial nominees from a simple "yes" or "no" vote. So qualified candidates aren't getting a chance to serve. It's politics at work, causing gridlock and backing up some of our courts to a state of emergency. Contact Senators Feingold and Kohl and tell them to oppose the filibuster.

The advocacy group sought an injunction allowing it to continue airing the ads during the periods immediately before the September 14 primary and the November 2 general election. The group's request for an injunction was denied and the District of Columbia Court of Appeals ruled that the challenge to the BCRA restriction was foreclosed by the Supreme Court's *McConnell* ruling. The Supreme Court remanded the case so WRTL's challenge could be considered.

On remand, the District Court for the District of Columbia ruled that BCRA's "electioneering communications" restriction was unconstitutional as applied to WRTL's ads because those ads were not the equivalent of express advocacy. The Supreme Court affirmed the district court by a 5-4 vote in June 2007.[47] Chief Justice Roberts announced the judgment of the Court, stating "the First Amendment requires us to err on the side of

[46]Wisconsin Right to Life, Inc. v. FEC, 126 S. Ct. 1016 (2006).
[47]2007 U.S. LEXIS 8515 (June 25, 2007).

protecting political speech rather than suppressing it." In the portion of his opinion joined by Justice Alito, Roberts found the WRTL ads were permissible because the ads focused on a legislative issue and did not mention an election, nor did the ads take a position on a candidate's character, qualifications, or fitness for office.

Justice Scalia, in a separate opinion joined by Justices Kennedy and Thomas, concurred in the judgment, but would have declared the law unconstitutional. He believed the Court was overruling *McConnell* without saying so, commenting that "[t]his faux judicial restraint is judicial obfuscation." He predicted lower courts would have difficulty in the future separating issue advocacy from express advocacy.

Justice Souter, in a dissenting opinion joined by Justices Stevens, Ginsburg, and Breyer, also believed the Court was "effectively overruling" *McConnell* and claimed the country loses "when an important precedent is overruled without good reason . . . ." Furthermore, he found the law to have a minimal impact on political speech. "WRTL could have run a newspaper ad, could have paid for the broadcast ads through its PAC, . . . or could have said 'call your Senators' instead of naming Senator Feingold in the ads," Souter wrote.

Certain nonprofit corporations, technically known as "qualified nonprofit corporations" or QNCs, already are exempt from BCRA.[48] QNCs have no shareholders, are not established by nor accept donations from business corporations or labor organizations, and have the sole purpose of promoting political ideas. WRTL, however, is not a QNC. Because the Supreme Court did not distinguish WRTL from business corporations, the ruling allows business corporations to refer to candidates in issue ads broadcast near elections, so long as those ads are not the equivalent of express advocacy.

In response to the *WRTL* ruling, the FEC in November 2007 announced corporate- or union-sponsored broadcast advertisements near elections are legal if: (1) the advertisement does not mention any election, candidacy, or political party; (2) does not take a position on any candidate's character, qualifications, or fitness for office; and (3) focuses on a legislative, executive, or judicial matter or issue. Advertisers may urge a candidate to support or oppose a position or may urge the public to tell a candidate to support or oppose a position. In interpreting the statute, the FEC stated any doubt about the legality of an ad will be resolved in favor of the advertiser.

Corporations and unions may contribute $10,000 a year to state and local political parties for activities such as voter registration drives. In 2002, Congress outlawed such "soft money" contributions to national political parties; this ban was upheld in *McConnell v. FEC*. Congress may enact laws to prevent corruption or the appearance of corruption, the Court said.

As will be shown below, political parties may receive "hard money"—money lawfully intended to influence federal elections—from the political action committees (PACs) of corporations and unions. The parties may use this "hard money" to purchase unlimited advertising to support candidates if the parties do not coordinate that spending with the

[48] 11 C.F.R. § 114.10; 11 C.F.R. § 114.2(b)(2).

candidates. In 1996, the Supreme Court ruled the Colorado Republican Party did not violate FECA's spending limits by purchasing radio ads attacking a Democrat running for the U.S. Senate.[49] If the party had coordinated spending with a candidate, the ads would constitute "contributions," which the Supreme Court earlier ruled may be limited.

POLITICAL ACTION COMMITTEES Federal election law permits corporations and unions to form and support political action committees (PACs) that can raise and spend large amounts of campaign money. A PAC is the political arm organized by a corporation, labor union, or trade association to support candidates for elective office. PACs raise funds for their activities by seeking voluntary contributions from members and pooling them into larger, more meaningful amounts that are contributed to favored candidates or political party committees or spent on behalf of candidates. Several media corporations, including 20th Century-Fox Film Company, the Magazine Publishers Association, and the American Advertising Federation, have their own political action committees.

PACs are perhaps the most visible and controversial outgrowth of the campaign finance reform of the 1970s. The number of PACs now is in the thousands, and they contribute hundreds of millions of dollars to federal campaigns. Some PACs favor Republicans. During the 2005–2006 election cycle, the National Association of Homebuilders PAC gave 74 percent of its campaign contributions to Republican candidates; similarly, the American Bankers Association PAC gave 69 percent of its contributions to Republicans. Other PACs, especially those associated with organized labor, favor Democrats. For example, the American Federation of Teachers PAC and the United Auto Workers PAC respectively gave 99 and 98 percent of their 2005–2006 contributions to Democrats. Many PACs, however, support both parties. In the 2005–2006 election cycle, Democrats and Republicans respectively received 47 and 53 percent of the campaign contributions from the National Association of Realtors PAC.[50]

PACs generally favor incumbents over challengers. Thus, even Democrats, especially those with powerful leadership positions or assignments on committees overseeing regulated industries, are able to tap business interests for campaign contributions. For example, 54 percent of the PAC contributions received by House Minority Leader Nancy Pelosi in the 2005–2006 election cycle were from business groups.[51] Pelosi became Speaker of the House when the Democrats won control of the House in the 2006 elections.

Sponsorship of PACs Corporations and unions can provide sponsorship critical to the success of PACs. A sponsoring company or union can pay for all costs of establishing and operating the *separate segregated funds,* as corporate- or union-sponsored PACs are known legally. The sponsoring corporation, union, or trade association may pay the salaries, overhead, and costs of soliciting contributions. Corporate and union officers also may control company PACs and direct their contributions to candidates.[52]

---

[49]Colorado Republican Fed. Campaign Comm. v. FEC, 518 U.S. 604 (1996).

[50]The Center for Responsive Politics operates a website, opensecrets.org, detailing campaign finances and expenditures. *See* http://opensecrets.org/pacs/topacs.asp.

[51]*See* http://opensecrets.org/politicians/index.asp.

[52]2 U.S.C. § 441b; 11 C.F.R. § 114.5(b) and (d); Pipefitters Local Union No. 562 v. United States, 407 U.S. 385 (1972).

PACs also may be unsponsored or independent of corporations and unions. Independent PACs are established by independent organizations, partnerships, or unincorporated associations such as the California Medical Association. Unlike sponsored PACs, which can receive unlimited funds for overhead and administrative expenses, unsponsored PACs must pay for overhead and administrative expenses out of money solicited. However, independent PACs can solicit money from a wider range of contributors than sponsored PACs can.

Solicitation of Funds Corporate PACs can solicit voluntary contributions from management, stockholders, and their families; union PACs can solicit funds from members and their families. PACs are not supposed to solicit funds beyond their management or union class. Neither management nor union PACs may solicit funds from the general public. Corporations that have no stock, such as a cooperative or nonprofit organization, are restricted to soliciting contributions from members of the organization.[53] The Supreme Court ruled that the National Right to Work Committee, an organization opposing unions, violated the campaign financing laws when it solicited PAC funds from members of the general public who had contributed money to the committee but were not otherwise members.[54]

Contributions PACs can contribute only $5,000 to each candidate per election, but they can contribute to as many candidates as they want. They can also contribute $15,000 per year to national political parties and up to $5,000 per year to other committees. Furthermore, and most important, PACs and committees can make unlimited "independent expenditures" on advertising and other expenses that benefit a campaign.

Individuals may contribute up to $5,000 to a PAC per year. Contributions to candidates are indexed for inflation. During the 2007–2008 election cycle, individuals may contribute up to $2,300 to a candidate's primary campaign and up to an additional $2,300 for the general election. Overall contributions by an individual to all PACs, parties, and candidates are capped at $108,200 during the 2007–2008 election cycle. However, wealthy individuals, like PACs, may make unlimited expenditures independent of a candidate.[55] The unlimited expenditures for PACs and individuals are the result of a Supreme Court decision loosening expenditure restrictions imposed by the 1971 federal election law. In *Buckley v. Valeo,* the Supreme Court struck down the expenditure limits on PACs and individuals while upholding the constitutionality of limits on contributions.[56]

The Court in *Buckley* accepted the legislative purpose of contribution limits, which is to discourage political favoritism for large contributors. The Court then said contributions could be limited because they constitute a form of indirect expression but that expenditures could not be curtailed because they constitute direct speech. The Court said limits on contributions by PACs and individuals impose only a "marginal restriction upon the contributor's ability to engage in free communication" because the contributions are indirect or symbolic speech, often amounting to simply writing a check. Limiting contributions involves little "direct restraint" on a person's political communication, the Court said.

[53]*See* Bread Political Action Comm. v. Federal Election Comm'n, 635 F.2d 621 (7th Cir. 1980), *rev'd on other grounds,* 455 U.S. 577 (1982).

[54]Federal Election Comm'n v. Nat'l Right to Work Comm., 459 U.S. 197 (1982).

[55]2 U.S.C. § 441a(a).

[56]424 U.S. 1 (1976).

Furthermore, the Court in *Buckley* rejected the argument that limitations on contributions violate the right of association of contributing groups. Individuals are still free, the Court said, to make unlimited independent purchases of campaign advertising.

In 2000, the Supreme Court again said campaign contributions limits are constitutional.[57] The Court upheld a Missouri law restricting campaign contributions to candidates for statewide office to $1,075. The Court said the amounts, similar to the $1,000 limit approved in *Buckley,* were not so low that candidates' voices would not be heard and contributions would be ineffective. The Court rejected arguments that nearly twenty-five years of inflation made *Buckley*'s $1,000 limit outdated. The Court said the question is not "about the power of the dollar" but whether a candidate has "the power to mount a campaign" with a contribution limit.

Missouri said its campaign contribution limits were intended to prevent political corruption or the appearance of corruption that could result from large donations to candidates. As in *Buckley*, the Court found this concern justified campaign contribution limits. Justice Souter, writing for the 6-3 majority, said, " Leave the perception of impropriety unanswered, and the cynical assumption that large donors call the tune could jeopardize the willingness of voters to take part in democratic governance."

In 2006, a sharply divided Court found Vermont's low contribution limits to be unconstitutional. Under Vermont law, individuals, parties, and committees could contribute only $400 to a candidate for governor during a two-year general election cycle. Six members of the Court in *Randall v. Sorrell* found the contribution limits to be a violation of the First Amendment, but their reasons for reaching this conclusion varied.[58]

Justice Breyer's plurality opinion, joined by Chief Justice Roberts and Justice Alito, argued that contribution limits that were "too low" would prevent candidates from amassing the resources necessary for effective campaigns, especially against incumbents. The plurality suspected that incumbents in the legislature set low contribution limits to make challenges difficult. The plurality was troubled by the fact that Vermont's limits were substantially lower than those approved by the *Buckley* Court in 1976. (Adjusted to reflect its value in 1976, the year *Buckley* was decided, the Vermont limit for contributions to candidates for governor was $113.91 per two-year election cycle, as compared to the $1,000 per election limit on individual contributions at issue in *Buckley*.) Vermont's limits were the lowest in the nation and, unlike the Missouri limits approved by the Court in 2000, Vermont's limits were not indexed for inflation. There was no proof that corruption was greater in Vermont than in other states; consequently, the plurality concluded the limits were too restrictive.

The plurality also questioned the Vermont requirement that political parties comply with the same limits that apply to individuals. "That means, for example, that the Vermont Democratic Party, taken together with all its local affiliates, can make one contribution of at most $400 to the Democratic gubernatorial candidate," the plurality noted. This severely inhibited collective political activity and reduced the voice of political parties in Vermont to a "whisper," all in violation of the First Amendment.

Justice Thomas, joined by Justice Scalia, concurred in the result, but found the plurality's analysis did not offer a principled basis for assessing contribution limits. "The atmospherics—

[57]Nixon v. Shrink Missouri Government PAC, 528 U.S. 377 (2000).
[58]126 S. Ct. 2479 (2006).

whether they vary with inflation, whether they are as high as those in others States . . . no doubt contribute to the plurality's sentiment" that the limits are too low, Justice Thomas wrote. "But a feeling does not amount to a workable rule of law." Thomas claimed that contribution limits should be subjected to strict scrutiny; under this demanding standard contribution limits would almost always be unconstitutional. In a separate concurring opinion, Justice Kennedy agreed that the Vermont contribution limits were unconstitutional. Kennedy had earlier dissented in the Missouri contribution limits case, claiming the Court's lenient approach was harmful to the First Amendment. He found the Vermont limits to be "even more stifling" to First Amendment rights than the limits approved in the Missouri case.

Justice Souter's dissenting opinion, joined by Justices Stevens and Ginsburg, argued that the contribution limits were constitutional. Souter questioned the plurality's suspicion that low limits were designed by incumbents to favor incumbents. There was no proof that the contribution limits favored incumbents, thus there was no reason to "dispense with respect" for the judgment and expertise of the Vermont legislature, Souter said.

Expenditures In contrast to limits on contributions, limits on expenditures, the *Buckley* Court said, were unconstitutional. In *Buckley,* the Court invalidated federal limits on independent expenditures, expenditures by candidates made from personal or family funds, and limitations on overall campaign expenditures by candidates. (Independent expenditures are made by noncandidates and must not be controlled by or coordinated with the candidate. An example of an independent expenditure would be a PAC-sponsored television ad supporting a particular candidate; the ad would be considered to be an independent expenditure as long as the PAC produced and placed the ad without consulting with the candidate's campaign.) Because expenditures are more like pure speech than are monetary contributions, limits on expenditures, the Court said, "impose direct and substantial restraints" on political speech. A limit on campaign expenditures "necessarily reduces the quantity of expression by restricting the number of issues discussed, the depth of their exploration, and the size of the audience reached." The *Buckley* Court also argued that limits on expenditures would not necessarily curb corruption.

The Court rejected the argument that expenditure ceilings are needed to equalize the relative power of rich and poor in an election. In a far-reaching endorsement of the role of money in the marketplace of ideas, the Court said,

> the concept that government may restrict the speech of some elements of our society in order to enhance the relative voice of others is wholly foreign to the First Amendment. . . . The First Amendment's protection against governmental abridgment of free expression cannot properly be made to depend on a person's financial ability to engage in public discussion.

The Court added that the First Amendment "denies government the power to determine that spending to promote one's political views is wasteful, excessive, or unwise." The people, not the government, must retain "control over the quantity and range of debate on public issues in a political campaign," the *Buckley* Court wrote.

Recently, in *Randall v. Sorrell,* the Court found unconstitutional a Vermont law limiting the amounts a candidate for state office could spend during a two-year election cycle. The members of the *Randall* plurality offered different reasons for finding the expenditure limits unconstitutional. *Randall* shows the current members of the Court to be seriously divided over whether *Buckley* should be followed in cases involving expenditure limits.

Vermont asked the Court to overrule *Buckley,* claiming that the post-*Buckley* experience has shown that contribution limits alone cannot effectively deter corruption. Justice Breyer and Chief Justice Roberts stated that **stare decisis,** the legal principle that adherence to precedent is the norm, meant that special justification was required to overturn *Buckley*. Breyer and Roberts concluded that there had been no dramatic increase in corruption, nor had the respondents shown that expenditure limits are a necessary means of attacking corruption.

Justice Alito, in a concurring opinion, claimed it was inconsistent for Vermont's defense of its contribution limits to rely on *Buckley* while its defense of the expenditure limits sought to overturn *Buckley*. Justice Thomas, joined by Justice Scalia, argued that *Buckley* should be overruled, but only so that both contribution and expenditure limits would be subjected to strict scrutiny, a type of scrutiny almost always fatal to the law under review.

In a dissenting opinion, Justice Stevens argued the Court should overrule *Buckley*'s treatment of expenditure limitations. Stevens, a nonparticipating member of the *Buckley* Court, drew upon the earlier views of Justice White, who argued that expenditure limits were akin to content-neutral time, place, and manner regulations.[59] Stevens saw expenditure limits as a complement to corruption-reducing contribution limits. Stevens, along with Justice Ginsburg also joined Justice Souter's dissenting opinion in *Randall*. Souter claimed *Buckley* did not categorically foreclose the possibility that some spending limits might be constitutional; Souter believed *Randall* should be remanded so the district court could consider whether the expenditure limits were narrowly tailored.

527 Groups In 2006 and 2007, the FEC settled with eleven groups that illegally funneled millions of dollars into advertisements opposing 2004 presidential candidates John Kerry and George W. Bush. The groups agreed to pay fines of $3 million—a small fraction of the millions they spent in the campaign—for acting as PACs in 2004 without registering with the FEC and for failing to comply with contribution limits. The groups also failed to file FEC reports listing donors, contributions, and expenditures as PACs are required to do.[60]

The most prominent group, Swiftboat Veterans and POWS for Truth spent $22.6 million on television advertisements to defeat Democratic candidate John Kerry, a Vietnam War Veterans, by claiming Kerry misrepresented his combat record and charging he betrayed his fellow servicemen by opposing the war after his honorable discharge. Swiftboat Veterans and other groups, technically known as 527s, named for a section of the Internal Revenue Service code,[61] unsuccessfully claimed to be exempt from federal campaign restrictions because they were not engaged in express advocacy. Swiftboat Veterans, for example, asserted it was merely setting the record straight with regard to John Kerry's conduct in the Vietnam War.

The groups had registered under IRS regulations as section 527 organizations, a status that allowed them to pay no taxes for moneys received for get-out-the-vote activities or issue advocacy. The IRS allows 527 organizations to receive unlimited "soft money" contributions from any type of donor, such as a corporation or individual, to support issue

[59] *See, e.g.*, FEC v. National Conservative Political Action Comm., 470 U.S. 480, 508–09 (1985) (White, J., dissenting).
[60] *See, e.g.*, MUR 5511 & 5525; MUR 5573; MUR 5754 (Dec. 13, 2006); MUR 5487 (Feb. 28, 2007).
[61] 26 IRC § 527.

advocacy. The 527s file reports about their activities with the IRS, not the FEC. However, if a 527 seeks to engage in activities related to the election or defeat of a federal candidate, it must establish a separate segregated fund, register the fund with the FEC, must not accept contributions for these activities from corporations and unions, and individual contributions are limited to $5,000 per year. Moreover, these candidate-related activities become taxable.

The FEC applies a case-by-case approach to determining whether 527s must also register as PACs.[62] If the group receives contributions or makes expenditures in excess of $1,000 and its major purpose is the election or defeat of a federal candidate, it must register as a PAC. For example, the FEC found that Swiftboat Veterans solicited and received $25 million during the 2004 election cycle. The group's solicitations clearly stated the money would be spent on candidate-related speech. One letter thanking a donor for a $100,000 contribution stated, "We will do our utmost to assure that this timely donation will be expended directly and prudently in our quest to derail Senator Kerry's well organized and funded campaign to become the Commander in Chief of the United States Armed Forces. We are adamantly opposed to the political self serving ambitions of this man who betrayed us in 1971." The FEC also found the group's ads expressly advocated the defeat of Kerry. The group spent $22.6 million on advertisements explicitly challenging Kerry's "capacity to lead," asserting that he could not be "trusted" and asking why citizens should be willing to "follow" him as a leader. In addition, the group violated federal law regarding the amount and source of contributions. Approximately $12.5 million in individual contributions were in excess of the $5,000 per year limit. It also illegally accepted $715,050 in prohibited corporate contributions.

In announcing the fines, FEC Chairman Michael Toner stated 527 groups were on clear notice for the 2008 presidential election: Organizations seeking to influence the presidential election "will have to register with the F.E.C. and follow hard-dollar limits."[63] However, Fred Wertheimer, head of Democracy 21, a group that has filed complaints with the FEC over spending by 527 groups, called the FEC's action "too little, too late." The amounts of the fines were small in comparison with the groups' fundraising efforts, raising the possibility that fines may become simply the "cost of doing business," Wertheimer said.[64]

Despite the FEC's efforts, 527 groups were highly visible in the 2008 presidential primaries, prompting candidate John Edwards to publicly ask 527s to "stay out of the political process." In February 2008, supporters of Barack Obama complained to the FEC that the American Leadership Project, registered as a 527, was acting as a PAC. The ALP purchased television ads praising Senator Hillary Clinton's work on economic issues and asked voters to "tell Hillary to keep working on those solutions for the middle class." A spokesperson for the ALP said, "We're an issues campaign, and we're talking about issues."

[62]*See* Shays v. FEC, 511 F. Supp. 2d 19 (D.D.C. 2007).

[63]Kate Phillips, "Settlements Including Fines Are Reached in Election Finance Cases of Three Groups," *N.Y. Times*, Dec. 14, 2006, at A38.

[64]R. Jeffrey Smith, "FEC Fines 3 '527' Groups for Use of Large Donations in '04," *Wash. Post*, Dec. 14, 2006, at A5.

PARTISAN COMMUNICATIONS Profit-making corporations and unions may support PACs and engage in partisan communication—including advocating the election of specific candidates—provided the communications are directed only to the corporate or union "family." A corporation may use corporate funds to urge management, shareholders, and their families to vote for a specific candidate, and unions may use union funds to urge their executive and administrative personnel, members, and their families to support specific candidates.[65] Partisan messages by corporations and unions may include extremely opinionated, even vitriolic, messages urging election or defeat of specific candidates, provided the messages are delivered only to the respective "families" of the corporation or union. Corporations and unions may expressly advocate the election or defeat of a candidate on the corporate or union websites that are solely available to their restricted class. These restricted websites, however, may not accept advertising from political parties or candidates.[66]

Partisan communications, paid for from corporate or union treasuries, become illegal contributions if they are offered beyond the restricted class of eligible recipients.[67] However, the law permits a corporation or union to invite press coverage of endorsements, candidates' speeches, or other partisan communications to the corporate or union family.

Disclosure

When Congress adopted the campaign finance laws, the legislative goal was to curtail corruption, not political speech. Congress decided that corruption could be reduced and political speech preserved—even increased—if the donors and amounts of contributions and expenditures were disclosed. Thus, the Federal Election Campaign Act requires each political committee and federal candidate to register with the Federal Election Commission and to keep detailed records of both contributions and expenditures made "for the purpose of . . . influencing" the nomination or election of a person to federal office.[68] The records must include the name and address of everyone making a contribution of more than $50, along with the date and amount of the contribution.

Federal law also requires disclosure of the source of funding for advertising that "expressly advocates the election or defeat of a clearly identified candidate, or that solicits any contribution, through any broadcasting station, newspaper, magazine, outdoor advertising facility, poster, yard sign, direct mailing or any other form of general public political advertising."[69] The identity of the sponsor must be presented clearly and conspicuously, telling who paid for the ad and whether the ad was authorized by the candidate.

Candidates and their committees also must file periodic reports containing the name of each person who has contributed to a campaign and the names of candidates and committees that have received more than $200 in a calendar year. Reports filed with the Federal

[65]2 U.S.C. § 441b (b)(2)(A); 11 C.F.R. § 114.3(a).
[66]Internet Communications, 71 Fed. Reg. 18589 (Apr. 12, 2006) (modifying 11 C.F.R. parts 100, 110, and 114).
[67]11 C.F.R. § 114.3(a).
[68]2 U.S.C. §§ 431(9)(A)(i), 432(e)(1) and (f)(1).
[69]11 C.F.R. § 110.11(a)(1).

Election Commission and similar reports filed under state disclosure laws must be made available for public inspection and copying. A person who fails to comply with the requirements on making, receiving, or reporting contributions or expenditures aggregating $2,000 or more in one year may be imprisoned for up to a year and fined up to $25,000.[70]

The Supreme Court upheld the constitutionality of the election disclosure requirements in *Buckley v. Valeo.* The Court noted that disclosure requirements, unlike limitations on contributions and expenditures, impose no ceiling on campaign-related activities. The disclosure requirements are justified, the Court said, because they tell a voter to whom a candidate may be responsive when in office. Furthermore, the disclosure requirements deter corruption by exposing large contributions and expenditures and providing the records essential for monitoring contributions. The Court concluded that disclosure regulations "appear to be the least restrictive means of curbing the evils of campaign ignorance and corruption."

The Court admitted disclosure requirements may limit the right of association by deterring some contributions. But the Court said the minor infringement on the right of association was justified by the importance of disclosure to the political process. Nevertheless, the Supreme Court said that minor political parties would not have to disclose contributions and expenditures if there was "a reasonable probability" that disclosure of contributors would subject the party to threats or harassment from government or private individuals.

In a case involving potential harassment of a political organization, the Supreme Court allowed the Socialist Workers party to withhold the names of contributors. In *Brown v. Socialist Workers '74 Campaign Committee,* the Court forbade the state of Ohio to require disclosure of contributors to the Socialist Workers party because there was a history of government and private harassment of the party.[71] Similarly, the U.S. Court of Appeals for the Second Circuit ruled that the Communist party was exempt from record-keeping and disclosure requirements because there was undisputed evidence of a reasonable probability that disclosure would subject contributors to threats, harassment, or reprisals.[72]

Even without threats or harassment, some disclosure requirements may violate the First Amendment, particularly as applied to individuals. The U.S. Supreme Court struck down an Ohio law banning the distribution of anonymous campaign literature in *McIntyre v. Ohio Elections Commission.*[73] The 7-2 decision by the Court upheld the right of an Ohio woman to hand out anonymous leaflets opposing a proposed school tax levy. The Supreme Court pointed out the importance of anonymous political tracts throughout American political history, including the *Federalist Papers,* written by James Madison, Alexander Hamilton, and John Jay, but attributed to "Publius." Authors might seek anonymity to avoid economic retribution or social ostracism or for other reasons, the majority opinion pointed out. Regardless of motive, anonymous authorship alone should not prevent expression from entering into the marketplace of ideas. "Anonymity is a shield from the tyranny of the majority," the Court wrote.

---

[70]2 U.S.C. § 437g(d)(1)(A).
[71]459 U.S. 87 (1982).
[72]Federal Election Comm'n v. Hall-Tyner Election Campaign Comm., 678 F.2d 416 (2nd Cir. 1982), *cert. denied,* 459 U.S. 1145 (1983).
[73]514 U.S. 334 (1995).

The implications of the Court's opinion are limited, however. The Court noted that its ruling did not pertain to disclosure requirements that apply to political communications over the broadcast media. In its recent *McConnell v. FEC* ruling, the Supreme Court upheld a statute requiring disclosure of individuals or organizations spending $10,000 or more a year for broadcast advertisements referring to candidates in preelection periods. All individuals who contribute $1,000 or more for such purposes must also be identified.[74]

Summary

Campaign finance laws prohibit corporate and union contributions to candidates and independent expenditures on behalf of candidates in federal elections. Gifts of "anything of value" are prohibited, including free advertising, air time, and tapes. The Supreme Court has ruled that a ban on expenditures by business corporations is constitutional to prevent corruption or potential corruption of the election process. Corporations and unions can also participate in elections by forming and soliciting funds for political action committees. Contributions to PACs and the amount that PACs may contribute to candidates are limited by the election law, which was upheld by the Supreme Court in *Buckley v. Valeo.* However, PACs and individuals may spend unlimited amounts independent of a candidate. The Court has also upheld the constitutionality of laws requiring disclosure of campaign contributions and expenditures, although requiring individual advocates to identify themselves may be unconstitutional.

Regulation of Political Candidate Broadcast Programming

Broadcasting is one of the most important means by which candidates and interest groups communicate with voters. In 2006, $2 billion was spent on political television advertising, up from $771 million in 2000. From the inception of broadcast regulation in 1927, broadcasters have been subject to regulations concerning candidate use of their stations. Today, the FCC settles disputes involving two requirements of the 1934 Communications Act that provide access to the airwaves for political candidates. One, the equal opportunities rule, requires a broadcast station to provide time for a political candidate if it has provided time for an opponent. The other, the reasonable access law, requires broadcasters to provide reasonable amounts of time for candidates running for federal office.

Both laws also apply to cable system operators and direct broadcast satellite (DBS) system operators. FCC rules, however, sharply limit the equal opportunity and reasonable access laws to "origination programming," which is under the exclusive control of the cable operator or satellite provider.[75] Programming services that cable or satellite systems merely retransmit, such as CNN or Fox News, are not subject to the political broadcasting laws. Because cable and DBS system operators originate little of their own programming, FCC interpretations of the cable and DBS "origination programming" rules have been rare; consequently, this discussion focuses on broadcasting.

[74] 2 U.S.C. § 434(f).
[75] 47 C.F.R. § 76.5(p) (cable); 47 C.F.R. §25.701 (b)(2) (DBS).

If any licensee shall permit any person who is a legally qualified candidate for any public office to use a broadcasting station, he shall afford equal opportunities to all other such candidates for that office in the use of such broadcasting station: Provided, That such licensee shall have no power of censorship over the material broadcast under the provisions of this section. No obligation is imposed upon any licensee to allow the use of its station by any such candidate. Appearance by a legally qualified candidate on any—

(1) bona fide newscast,
(2) bona fide news interview,
(3) bona fide news documentary (if the appearance of the candidate is incidental to the presentation of the subjects covered by the news documentary), or
(4) on-the-spot coverage of bona fide news events (including but not limited to political conventions and activities incidental thereto),

shall not be deemed to be use of a broadcasting station within the meaning of this subsection. Nothing in the foregoing sentence shall be construed as relieving broadcasters, in connection with the presentation of newscasts, news interviews, news documentaries, and on-the-spot coverage of news events, from the obligation imposed upon them under this chapter to operate in the public interest and to afford reasonable opportunity for the discussion of conflicting views on issues of public importance.

FIGURE 7.2 The Equal Opportunities Statute.

Equal Opportunities for Political Candidates

The **equal opportunities** requirement (see Figure 7.2), initially a part of the 1927 Radio Act, states that broadcasters who provide airtime for "legally qualified" political candidates must "afford equal opportunities to all other such candidates for that office."[76]

The equal opportunities rules, sometimes inaccurately called the equal time rule, requires that candidates for the same office have the same opportunity to purchase broadcast time during a period of the day when they are likely to attract the same size and type of audience. However, broadcast stations do not have to limit the time provided for one candidate because an opponent cannot afford to buy the same amount of time. The FCC has recognized that Section 315 does not "equalize disparities in the financial resources of candidates."[77] If a station provides free time to one candidate, it must offer free time to any qualified opponents for the same office.

Critics of the equal opportunities rule, Section 315 of the 1934 Communications Act, complain the law does not stop a rich candidate from buying far more time than an opponent can afford. Nor does Section 315 require equal treatment for independent and minority party candidates, often excluded from televised debates between candidates of the major parties, for reasons explained in this section of the chapter.

[76]47 U.S.C. § 315(a).

[77]*See* Hon. Thomas Eagleton, 81 F.C.C.2d 423, 426 (1980) (quoting Carter/Mondale Reelection Committee, 81 F.C.C.2d 409, 419–20 (1980)).

Critics even say the equal opportunities requirements discourage broadcasters from providing time for political candidates. Stations may be reluctant to sell or otherwise provide airtime to the major political candidates, knowing they also will have to provide time to candidates they do not think merit attention.

In enforcing the political broadcasting requirements, the FCC only responds to complaints about programs or advertisements that have been broadcast. The agency will not intervene prior to a broadcast. During the 2004 presidential election, Sinclair Broadcasting announced plans to air "Stolen Honor," an anti-Kerry documentary on sixty-two of its television stations two weeks before the election. Eighteen senators, all Democrats, requested that the FCC determine the legality of the proposed broadcast. FCC Chair Michael Powell responded, "Don't look to us to block the airing of a program. I think it would be an absolute disservice to the First Amendment and I think it would be unconstitutional if we attempted to do so," Powell said.[78] Faced with intense public and advertiser pressure, Sinclair backed down from airing "Stolen Honor" in its entirety. Instead, Sinclair aired portions of the documentary, along with pro-Kerry material.

The FCC and federal courts have exclusive jurisdiction of Section 315 cases. In 2008, the Nevada Supreme Court overturned a lower state court's injunction ordering MSNBC to either include Representative Dennis Kucinich in a scheduled debate among Democratic Party presidential candidates or not televise the debate.[79] MSNBC's lawyers successfully argued Kucinich was trying to make an "end run" around the FCC and federal courts by seeking an injunction from a state court; the Nevada Supreme Court held the lower court had no jurisdiction over the matter. Kucinich's proper remedy was to complain to the FCC after the televised debate, the court said. The state supreme court also said the lower court's order was also an unconstitutional prior restraint because it prohibited MSNBC from televising the debate unless Kucinich participated.

QUALIFIED CANDIDATES Section 315 requires broadcasters to provide equal opportunities only to "legally qualified" political candidates once other "legally qualified" candidates have been given or sold airtime. The FCC has said a person must meet three requirements to qualify as an official political candidate.

First, a candidate must have publicly announced an intention to run for office. The commission considers filing for office or fulfilling state requirements to appear on the ballot the equivalent of a public announcement. A person is not a "legally qualified" candidate simply because supporters are raising funds or because political observers expect an individual to run for office. Extensive news coverage of incumbents does not mean that they have announced their intention to run again for office. The FCC said then President Lyndon Johnson was not a candidate for the 1968 Democratic presidential nomination when the television networks broadcast an interview with him in December 1967 because he had not publicly announced his bid for reelection.[80] Senator Eugene McCarthy, who had announced his candidacy, complained he should receive airtime because he and Johnson were the opposing candidates for their party's nomination. In fact, Johnson did not run for reelection.

[78] "FCC Won't Block Anti-Kerry Film," Associated Press, Oct. 15, 2004.
[79] NBC Universal v. Eighth Judicial District, Case No. 50889 (Nev. Sup. Ct., Jan.15, 2008).
[80] Sen. Eugene J. McCarthy, 11 F.C.C.2d 511, *aff'd sub nom.* McCarthy v. FCC, 390 F.2d 471 (D.C. Cir. 1968).

The FCC's decision in the Johnson-McCarthy dispute encourages incumbents with substantial public exposure to delay official announcements that would trigger the equal opportunities rule for their opponents. However, the commission said it would be "unworkable" for the FCC to decide which potential but undeclared candidates in fact were candidates.

The second requirement to be met before triggering Section 315 requirements is that a candidate meets the qualifications prescribed by law for the office. For example, any candidate for president of the United States must have been born in the United States and be at least 35 years old. Arnold Schwarzenneger, a naturalized citizen, is not eligible to be president and therefore could not be a "legally qualified" presidential candidate. Schwarzenneger, however, is qualified to hold the office of governor of California and was a "legally qualified" candidate in that state's 2003 and 2006 gubernatorial elections.

The third requirement for a legally qualified political candidate under Section 315 is the most complicated. A candidate seeking an elective office must qualify for a place on the ballot or publicly commit to seeking election as a write-in candidate. For example, a state may require candidates for any statewide office to represent parties receiving 5 percent of the vote in the preceding election or submit a nominating petition signed by a required number of registered voters.

Under Section 315, a person seeking election as a write-in candidate must meet any legal requirements for write-in candidates. A write-in candidate also must make a "substantial showing" as a candidate—that is, engage in such campaign activities as making speeches, distributing literature, maintaining a campaign committee, and establishing a headquarters. A candidate seeking nomination to public office by a convention or caucus must also make a "substantial showing" to be considered an official candidate.[81] A broadcast station cannot deny equal opportunities to any candidate simply because the person appears to have little chance of winning.

Broadcasters must provide equal opportunities only to legally qualified candidates who are competing for the same votes in a specific election. In a November general election, anyone running for the same office, regardless of party affiliation, is an "opposing candidate." In primary elections, candidates can claim equal opportunities for appearances by opponents within their party, but not for appearances by candidates running for the same office in another party.

TIME REQUIREMENTS The FCC has said emphatically that Section 315 requires stations to provide candidates with equal broadcast opportunities rather than only equal time. When a station sells time to one candidate, it must be willing to sell opponents the same amount of time at a time of day when a comparable audience can be reached. An hour of television time at 9 A.M. on Sunday is not equivalent to one hour during prime time on Sunday evening because substantially fewer people are likely to watch the morning program.

The FCC relies on a broadcaster's reasonable judgment when mechanical difficulties or other problems make it impossible to provide equal opportunities for opposing candidates. The FCC upheld a broadcast station's use of a still picture of former Indiana

[81] 47 C.F.R. § 73.1940 (3)(f).

Senator Birch Bayh when the video failed during the senator's closing remarks in a thirty-minute debate. The sound was not affected during the three-minute video interruption.[82]

Under Section 315, political candidates cannot demand that broadcast stations allow them to go on the air at any time the candidates choose. A candidate for mayor in Chicago could not demand hour-long blocks of time instead of the five-minute segments and spot announcements the station offered.[83] Nor are stations required to provide any individual candidate free time unless free time first was given to an opponent.

In fact, under Section 315, a broadcaster need not offer any time at all to political candidates. However, broadcasters cannot avoid election coverage completely. The FCC has said broadcast licensees must provide "substantial" amounts of time for political candidates as part of the stations' requirement to serve the public interest. In addition, the candidate access law, discussed later in the chapter, requires broadcasters to provide "reasonable" amounts of time to each candidate running for federal office.

A broadcast station is not required to notify a legally qualified political candidate when an opponent has been granted airtime. It is up to the candidate to request the time within a week of the broadcast triggering the statute.[84]

"USE" OF BROADCAST TIME Section 315 provides that any "use" of a broadcast station by a political candidate entitles opponents to an equal opportunity. Any positive presence of candidates in a sixty-second ad or a thirty-minute program, including their pictures or voices, triggers Section 315. Candidates "use" broadcast time under Section 315 even if they only announce the sponsorship of an ad in a voice that can be recognized.

Campaign advertising that does not "use" a candidate's image or voice, however, does not trigger the equal opportunities doctrine. For example, it is not a "use" when an ad describes a candidate's voting record but the candidate does not appear.

Only a "positive" appearance of a candidate's voice or picture constitutes a "use" under Section 315.[85] An unfavorable depiction of a candidate by an opponent or other critic is not a "use" of a broadcast station that triggers the equal opportunities requirements, the FCC has said. The commission wanted to ensure that candidates could not claim equal opportunities after airing ads critical of their opponents but containing their opponents' pictures and voices.

A broadcast station must offer a candidate's opponents equal opportunities to buy time whenever any favorable ad containing the candidate's voice or image is aired, whether the ad is purchased by the candidate or independently by a political supporter, political party, or special interest group. The FCC has repealed a 1991 ruling that political candidates "used" a broadcast station under Section 315 only if they or their campaign committee approved, controlled, or sponsored the ad containing the candidate's picture or voice.[86]

[82]Sen. Birch Bayh, 15 F.C.C.2d 47 (1968).

[83]Martin-Trigona, 64 F.C.C.2d 1087 (1977). However, federal candidates may have some control over the kind of time they can demand, as discussed in the next section of this chapter.

[84]47 C.F.R. § 73.1920(b).

[85]Codification of the Commission's Political Programming Policies, 9 F.C.C.R. 651 (1994).

[86]Codification of the Commission's Political Programming Policies, 7 F.C.C.R. 678 (1991).

A candidate's appearance need not be political to be a "use" for the purpose of Section 315. The FCC has said that distinguishing between political and nonpolitical broadcasts would require highly subjective judgments about content and could lead to increased governmental oversight of programming content. Therefore, public officials "use" the airwaves when they appear on-air on behalf of charities such as the United Fund and Community Chest campaigns. Television evangelists also "use" the airwaves when they participate in televised worship services, crusades, and their own talk shows if the evangelists are candidates for office.

Candidates who appear in televised entertainment programming, including movies, "use" the airwaves whether or not they approve of the timing of a broadcast. The airing of Ronald Reagan's movies when Reagan was an official candidate for president allowed opponents to claim equal opportunity for airtime even though Reagan was probably not consulted before the broadcasts.[87] Indeed, the FCC has ruled that an opponent may be granted time equal to the duration of a broadcast movie or radio or television program if the candidate's appearance is "substantial" and "integral" to the plot. If the candidate's appearance is not "substantial," opponents receive under Section 315 time roughly equal to the candidate's airtime. However, for candidates' appearances to constitute a use, the FCC has traditionally said, candidates must have sufficient control over the production of a movie or program that they can control the presentation of themselves to the voters.[88]

A candidate's control over a broadcast is a key criterion in determining whether an appearance requires a broadcaster to offer opponents equal opportunity for the time of an entire program or only for the amount of time a candidate appears. A candidate's presence in a political spot, however brief, obligates a broadcaster to provide the opponent time equivalent to the entire ad. If a candidate is present in only ten seconds of a sixty-second ad, the opponent has the right to sixty seconds. Political campaign ads are presumed to be controlled by the candidate or the candidate's political campaign staff. However, if a candidate appears as part of a talk show or variety show controlled by an emcee, an opponent is entitled only to the amount of time the candidate is "on camera or on mike." When Representative Sidney Yates appeared on a talk program called *Kup's Show* in Chicago, his opponent for the Democratic nomination wanted time equal to the duration of the entire program. The FCC said the station was obligated for only the ten minutes and nine seconds of Yates's appearance rather than the forty minutes of the complete show.[89]

EXEMPT PROGRAMMING Some programming is exempt from the equal opportunities requirement. In a 1959 amendment to the 1934 Communications Act, Congress said broadcasters do not have to provide equal opportunities for candidate appearances during newscasts, news interviews, news documentaries, and "on-the-spot coverage" of news events, including political conventions and many political debates.[90]

---

[87]Adrian Weiss, 58 F.C.C.2d 342, *review denied,* 58 F.C.C.2d 1389 (1976); Walt Disney Productions, Inc., 33 F.C.C.2d 297, *aff'd sub nom.* Review of the Pat Paulsen Ruling, 33 F.C.C.2d 835 (1972), *aff'd,* Paulsen v. FCC, 491 F.2d 887 (9th Cir. 1974).

[88]Gray Communications Systems, Inc., 19 F.C.C.2d 532 (1969).

[89]*See, e.g.,* Robert R. Benjamin, 51 P & F Rad. Reg. 2d 91 (1982).

[90]47 U.S.C. § 315(a).

Newscasts In 1959, Congress adopted the equal opportunities exemption for political candidates on newscasts to override a decision by the FCC. The commission had decided that a third-party mayoral candidate in Chicago should be granted airtime comparable to the news coverage accorded incumbent Mayor Richard Daley and his Republican opponent. Third-party candidate Lar Daly, no relation to the incumbent, said he was entitled to time when the mayor appeared in news film accepting his nomination and meeting the president of Argentina at the Chicago airport. The FCC agreed.[91]

The Daly decision created such a furor that Congress amended the Communications Act the same year. Congress feared the FCC's interpretation of Section 315 would "dry up" broadcast coverage of political campaigns. A Senate report said broadcasters would be reluctant to show a political candidate on a news program if broadcasters would have to offer free time to opponents. Broadcasters would fear the "parade of aspirants" who would seek free airtime, the report said.[92]

For a news program to qualify as a newscast under the 1959 amendment, it must be regularly scheduled and emphasize news. The content must be determined by network or station personnel rather than by a candidate. The FCC has ruled that the *Today* show on NBC qualifies as a news show because it is regularly scheduled and emphasizes news coverage. The FCC also has ruled that *Entertainment Tonight* and *Entertainment This Week,* syndicated programs that provide spot news coverage and news interviews about entertainment, are bona fide news programs that do not trigger the equal opportunities requirement. The commission said the news exemption from Section 315 is not based "on the subject matter reported" in a show but on "whether the program reports news of some area of current events." The commission said that any effort on its part to determine "whether particular kinds of news are more or less bona fide would involve an unwarranted intrusion into program content and would be, thus, at least suspect under the First Amendment."[93]

In 1994, a federal appellate court affirmed an FCC determination that *The McLaughlin Group* was a bona fide newscast exempt from equal opportunities requirements of the 1934 Communications Act.[94] The U.S. Court of Appeals for the D.C. Circuit said that since Section 315 of the act does not precisely define the newscasts that are exempt, the court would defer to the commission's interpretation. A unanimous three-judge panel said the commission could reasonably decide that *The McLaughlin Group* format—several segments that each included a news report, accompanied by video news clips, and a panel discussion—qualified as *news* under the statute. The commission had concluded that the *McLaughlin* reports on national and world news used "methods of traditional newscasts." The commission, said the court, also reasonably found the *McLaughlin* news segments were selected for their news value and not to advance or harm the cause of any particular political candidate.

When a journalist seeking elective office appears on a news show in the role of reporter or anchor, the newscast exemption does not apply. A federal appeals court affirmed an FCC decision that on-the-air appearances by reporter William Branch would have required a

[91]CBS, 26 F.C.C. 715, 18 P & F Rad. Reg. 238, *reconsideration denied,* 18 P & F Rad. Reg. 701 (1959).
[92]S. Rep. No. 562, 86th Cong., 1st Sess. 9, 10 (1959).
[93]Paramount Pictures Corp., 3 F.C.C.R. 245 (1988).
[94]Telecommunications Research and Action Center v. FCC, 26 F.3d 185 (D.C. Cir. 1994).

Sacramento television station to provide equal opportunities to Branch's opponents.[95] Branch wanted to keep his job while he ran for a town council position in Loomis, California, but KOVR said he would have to take an unpaid leave of absence during his political campaign. The station said it would not provide the airtime necessary to meet the equal opportunities requirements of Branch's opponents during the election campaign.

News Interviews and Documentaries News interviews are exempt from the equal opportunities requirement if they take place on a bona fide news interview program. Shows such as *Meet the Press* and *Face the Nation* and similar local programs are considered bona fide news interview programs. The FCC also considers news interview segments appearing on programs such as *The Tonight Show with Jay Leno* to be exempt from equal opportunities requirements.

The FCC, when deciding whether a news interview program should be exempt, considers how long the program has been on the air, and whether

1. the program is regularly scheduled,
2. broadcasters or broadcast journalists control the program content and format,
3. the decisions about content and format are based on reasonable journalistic judgments rather than an intention to advance a candidate's political career, and
4. the selection of persons to appear is based on their newsworthiness.

For twenty-five years following the enactment of the news interview exemption, the FCC narrowly applied the exemption only to programs with a "traditional" question-and-answer format such as *Meet the Press*. In 1984, the FCC adopted a broader view of the news exemption, ruling that interviews of political candidates on the *Donahue* show were exempt from equal opportunities obligations. The fact that other *Donahue* segments did not include discussions pertaining to politics was immaterial, the FCC stated.

In an earlier decision, the FCC had said the audience participation in the *Donahue* show did not leave Donahue with enough control over the contents of the program to qualify it as an exempt news interview program. In 1984, however, the commission said it did not want to stifle what it called innovative approaches to the coverage of political news.[96] Following the *Donahue* decision, other interview programs or segments with "unique and innovative format elements," such as the *Sally Jessey Raphael Show, Jerry Springer, Politically Incorrect,* and *The Howard Stern Show,* have qualified for the news interview exemption.[97]

Recently, the FCC ruled the news interview segments of *The Tonight Show with Jay Leno* qualified for the news interview exemption.[98] An interview with California governor Arnold Schwarzenegger airing during the 2006 campaign period was exempt because *The Tonight Show* was regularly scheduled the producers controlled all aspects of the program; and decisions about format, content, and participants are based on the producers' independent news judgment and not motivated by partisan purposes. The FCC's decision did

[95]Branch v. FCC, 824 F.2d 37 (1987), *cert. denied,* 485 U.S. 959 (1988).

[96]Multimedia Entertainment, Inc., 56 P & F Rad. Reg. 2d 143 (1984).

[97]*See, e.g.,* Infinity Broadcasting Operations, Inc., Declaratory Ruling (DA-03-2865) (Sept. 9, 2003).

[98]Equal Opportunities Complaint Filed by Angelides for Governor Campaign Against 11 California Television Stations, Order (DA 06-2098) (Oct. 26, 2006).

not apply to all aspects of *The Tonight Show*; skits, comedy monologues, musical entertainment, and similar segments did not serve the congressional intention in adopting the news interview exemption.

The fact that *Donahue, The Tonight Show,* and other programs had been regularly scheduled for years is a key factor in the commission's news interview rulings. One-time news interviews or special candidates' programs begun only weeks before an election do not qualify for the news interview exemption.

In 1994, the U.S. Court of Appeals for the D.C. Circuit upheld an FCC decision that allows news interviews produced by independent producers, as well as those provided by stations and networks, to qualify for the news interview exemption under Section 315.[99] The court affirmed the FCC's judgment that Congress, when it adopted the news interview exemption in 1959, intended that professional journalists rather than candidates produce and control news interview programs. The court also accepted the FCC's contention that limiting the exemption to programming produced by stations and networks prevents political programming by independent producers from reaching the air. The court recognized Congress had clearly intended to encourage rather than discourage news coverage of political campaigns.

The court said the FCC still could effectively enforce the news interview exemption because the broadcasters who aired independently produced programs remained subject to FCC jurisdiction. In addition, an independently produced show would lose its exempt status if the producers permitted political candidates to control the program for their own political advantage.

Although an interview on a bona fide news interview program is exempt from equal opportunities requirements, an appearance by a candidate in a news documentary is exempt only if the appearance is incidental to the discussion of an issue of genuine news value. The FCC rejected a request for equal time by Richard Kay, who was competing against Robert A. Taft, Jr., and Howard M. Metzenbaum in 1970 for a seat in the U.S. Senate. Taft and Metzenbaum appeared for ninety-three seconds in a CBS news documentary, *Television and Politics*. The commission ruled that the program focused on the use of television by candidates rather than on either of Kay's opponents.[100]

On-the-Spot Coverage of News Events The 1959 exemption for on-the-spot coverage of news events includes live broadcasts of presidential speeches such as the State of the Union and reports to the nation during international crises. Spot news events include candidates' announcements that they are running for office and candidate appearances at parades, court proceedings, and baseball games. The spot news exemption also applies to political conventions, press conferences held by political candidates, and many debates among political candidates.

The FCC first said in 1975 that broadcasts of press conferences were exempt news events if (1) a broadcaster made a good-faith judgment that the press conference was a bona fide news event and (2) the licensee did not intend by the broadcast to provide one candidate with an advantage over another.[101]

[99] Telecommunications Research & Action Center v. FCC, 26 F.3d 185 (D.C. Cir. 1994).
[100] Richard B. Kay, 26 F.C.C.2d 235 (1970).
[101] Petitions of Aspen Institute and CBS, 55 F.C.C.2d 697 (1975), *aff'd sub nom.* Chisholm v. FCC, 538 F.2d 349 (D.C. Cir.), *cert. denied,* 429 U.S. 890 (1976).

Applying those guidelines a few years later, the FCC said that the broadcast of a press conference held by President Jimmy Carter was a bona fide news event. Senator Edward Kennedy, who was challenging Carter's renomination, complained that the president had used more than five minutes of a press conference to attack him. The networks refused to give Kennedy time under the equal opportunities rule, and the FCC affirmed the broadcasters' decision. The commission said the press conference was carried live and the networks had covered Kennedy press conferences as news before he was a candidate. In addition, the commission said it would not overrule the news judgments of broadcasters absent evidence they intended to promote one candidate over another. The FCC acknowledged that its decision could favor incumbents because they might attract more media coverage than their opponents.[102]

In addition to exempting live press conferences under Section 315, the FCC has decided in a series of rulings to exempt the broadcast of many debates between political candidates. Before 1975, presidential debates had not been televised since the 1960 broadcasts featuring Richard M. Nixon and John F. Kennedy. Congress had temporarily suspended the equal opportunities rule to allow broadcasters to carry the Nixon-Kennedy debates.

However, beginning in 1975, the commission gradually has exempted debates sponsored by civic organizations, broadcasters, political parties, and the candidates themselves. The commission has said the factor determining whether a debate is exempt under Section 315 is its bona fide news value and not its sponsor. In 1988, the commission ruled that debates between presidential candidates George H. W. Bush and Michael Dukakis were exempt from the equal opportunities requirement even though the two major political parties sponsored them. The commission rejected a complaint by minor party presidential candidate Lenora Fulani that the Bush-Dukakis debates did not qualify for the spot news exemption under Section 315. The FCC said debates can be exempt as long as broadcasters make good-faith journalistic decisions that the debates are newsworthy. Televised debates, the commission said, do not give the candidates "unbridled power" to advance their candidacies. "Indeed, the adversarial nature of the debate format reduces greatly the chance of any broadcast favoritism."[103]

A few years earlier, a federal appeals court agreed with a commission decision that minor party candidates for president and vice president do not have a constitutional right to participate in televised debates. In 1987, the U.S. Court of Appeals for the D.C. Circuit rejected the appeal of the 1984 nominee for the Citizens party, Sonia Johnson, who was not included in the 1984 presidential debates and finished with less than 1 percent of the vote. The D.C. Circuit said the FCC had operated within its statutory authority when it had decided that debates between political candidates are news events exempt from Section 315. The court said no individual has a First Amendment right of access to the broadcast media.[104]

The U.S. Supreme Court has ruled that government-owned public broadcast stations may exclude candidates from debates as long as the exclusions are not made on the basis

[102]Kennedy for President Comm., 77 F.C.C.2d 64 (Broadcast Bureau), *review denied*, 77 F.C.C.2d 971, *aff'd*, Kennedy for President Comm. v. FCC, 636 F.2d 432 (D.C. Cir. 1980).

[103]*In re* Fulani, 65 P & F Rad. Reg. 2d 644, 645 (1988).

[104]Johnson v. FCC, 829 F.2d 157 (D.C. Cir. 1987).

of a candidate's views.[105] A public station may limit debate participants to candidates who are viable and "serious" without infringing the First Amendment rights of candidates not invited to participate, the Court said.

The Court upheld the decision of the Arkansas Educational Television Commission (AETC) to invite only major party candidates and others "who had strong popular support" to participate in a 1992 debate. Independent candidate Ralph Forbes, who was not included, sued AETC, claiming his First Amendment rights were abridged. The U.S. Court of Appeals for the Eighth Circuit ruled for Forbes, saying he could be excluded only if AETC had a compelling reason.[106]

Holding that political debates on public television are not a public forum, the Court said journalists need not demonstrate a compelling interest to justify excluding candidates the journalists consider unnewsworthy. As long as the publicly funded stations do not try to stifle a particular point of view, they may exercise editorial discretion when broadcasting debates among political candidates, the Court said.

Operating a nonpublic forum, broadcasters can limit participants in political debates to "serious" candidates from "major" parties. The Court said AETC did not violate Forbes's First Amendment rights when it denied him a place in the candidates' debate because he had no chance to win. The Court said the station's decision to exclude Forbes as based on viewpoint neutral journalistic discretion, not on an unconstitutional judgment to exclude Forbes because of his political views.

Any other result could lead the approximately 230 government-supported public television stations not to carry any candidate debates, the Court said. For example, the Court said, after the U.S. Court of Appeals for the Eighth Circuit ruled AETC was wrong in not including Forbes, the Nebraska Educational Television Network canceled a debate among U.S. Senate candidates because of concerns even minor candidates had to be included.

Three dissenting justices said AETC used "standardless" criteria in deciding to exclude Forbes. Stevens said AETC is a government agency and those who decided not to invite Forbes were government employees. Stevens said "pre-established, objective criteria" must be applied when the government is so intimately involved in choosing who may use a government forum to speak.

LIMITS ON BROADCASTER CENSORSHIP OF POLITICAL CONTENT A broadcast station has no control over the content of programming aired by political candidates. Section 315 prohibits broadcasters from censoring the candidates even if their statements are racist, vulgar, or defamatory. Hence, the FCC refused to tell stations they could reject the spot announcements of Georgia Senate candidate J. B. Stoner, who proclaimed himself to be a "white racist" candidate. Stoner's ad campaigned against a law he said "takes jobs from us whites and gives those jobs to the niggers." Stoner, chairman of the neo-Nazi National States Rights party, said he was for "law and order with the knowledge you cannot have law and order and niggers too." The commission said it could not, under the First Amendment, override the provision of Section 315 prohibiting stations from censoring candidates without evidence of a "clear and present danger of imminent violence."[107] The prohibition against

---

[105] Arkansas Educational Television Commission v. Forbes, 523 U.S. 666 (1998).

[106] Forbes v. Arkansas Educational Television Communication Network Foundation, 93 F.3d 497 (8th Cir. 1996).

[107] Letter to Lonnie King, 36 F.C.C.2d 635 (1972).

censoring candidate programming applies only when the candidate's voice or picture is a part of the broadcast.

Since the remarks of candidates cannot be edited for libel under Section 315, the U.S. Supreme Court decided candidates in broadcasts subject to the equal opportunities rule could not hold licensees responsible for libelous remarks. If the licensees were liable for the defamatory remarks of a candidate they could not censor, the Court said, they would be penalized for doing what the law intended them to do—provide broadcast time for political candidates.[108] Of course, the candidates themselves are legally responsible for defamatory remarks they make over the air.

RATES AND SPONSOR IDENTIFICATION The equal opportunities provision requires broadcasters to charge political candidates the station's lowest advertising rates forty-five days before a primary election and sixty days before a general election. Before the forty-five- and sixty-day time periods, broadcasters can charge candidates what they normally charge advertisers buying the same amounts of time.[109]

When fulfilling equal opportunities obligations, broadcasters can charge candidates only what they charge their largest-volume advertisers for the same amount of time at the same time of the broadcast day. If a radio station charges $200 for a single one-minute commercial but $125 for each of fifteen one-minute commercials sold as a package, the station must sell a single one-minute commercial to a candidate for $125. Federal candidate advertisements referring to an opponent qualify for the reduced rates only if the candidate's voice or image appears, accompanied by a statement that the candidate approved of the ad. The Supreme Court dismissed a challenge to this provision in *McConnell v. FEC.* Federal law also requires that an announcement specify who paid for the ad.[110]

Broadcasters must allow politicians the same flexibility to negotiate rate packages as commercial customers and must fully disclose policies for rescheduling ads that have been bumped. Stations cannot favor one candidate over another in the price charged for an ad, just as stations cannot offer one candidate substantially more airtime than another.

Broadcasters must maintain, and make available for public inspection, extensive records documenting purchase requests for ads relating to elections or national legislative issues.[111] These requirements were ruled constitutional in *McConnell v. FEC.*

In 2005, the FCC reminded broadcasters and cable operators that airing "video news releases," or VNRs, requires disclosure of sponsorship. VNRs are prepackaged news stories using actors to portray reporters, a practice opposed by journalists; VNRs are often prepared by government agencies or corporations.[112] The FCC ruled that if a VNR deals with a political matter or controversial issue, the station must disclose the source of the material, even if the station airs the material free of charge. Sponsorship announcements must be made at both the beginning and end of VNRs lasting longer than five minutes. Shorter VNRs require sponsorship identification only at the beginning or end of the material.

[108]Farmers Educ. & Co-op. Union of America v. WDAY, Inc., 360 U.S. 525 (1959).
[109]47 U.S.C. § 315(b).
[110]47 U.S.C. § 317. *See also* Codification of the Commission's Political Broadcast Rules, 9 F.C.C.R. 5288 (1994) (visual but not audio identification required for television).
[111]47 U.S.C. § 315 (e).
[112]*See, e.g.,* Joe Mandese, "The Art of Manufactured News," *Broadcasting & Cable,* Mar. 28, 2005, at 24.

If a corporation or association furnishes the VNR, the station must include in its public inspection file a listing of the officers of the group.[113] In August 2006, the FCC sent letters of inquiry to seventy-seven television stations, asking whether the stations had properly labeled VNRs.[114]

Access for Political Candidates

Although Section 315 of the Communications Act requires broadcasters to provide equal opportunities to political candidates, it does not require broadcast licensees to provide time to political candidates in the first place. If only Section 315 regulated political campaign advertising, stations could avoid equal opportunity requirements by refusing to run any political ads. To ensure that broadcasters accept ads from each legally qualified candidate running for *federal* office, Congress adopted Section 312(a)(7). Under the law, a broadcast station could lose its license for willfully or repeatedly refusing to provide "reasonable access" or to permit the "purchase of reasonable amounts of time" by federal candidates. Section 312(a)(7) does not require broadcast stations to provide airtime to candidates for state or local offices.

Congress adopted Section 312(a)(7) in 1971 to ensure that broadcasters would provide time to candidates for the presidency, the U.S. Senate, and the U.S. House of Representatives. Section 312(a)(7) was adopted in part to offset the fact that Congress was amending Section 315 to require broadcasters to charge political candidates the station's lowest advertising rates. Congress feared that imposing the low advertising rates would discourage broadcasters from selling time to political candidates when the time could be sold to others at higher prices. Even before the amendment, broadcasters were often reluctant to offer time to one candidate because of the requirement that they provide time to opponents.

The FCC has said the best way to balance the desires of the candidates for airtime and the interests of the broadcasters under Section 312(a)(7) is "to rely on the reasonable, good faith discretion" of broadcast licensees. Therefore, the commission has not established a set of rules interpreting "reasonable access" in Section 312(a)(7). However, the commission has said reasonable access means that broadcasters should try to accommodate the requests for airtime of individual candidates and avoid "blanket bans" of candidate advertising except during newscasts.

The commission has said "reasonable access" to broadcast facilities for candidates to federal office means that broadcasters ordinarily must provide some time for advertising during prime listening and viewing hours. Stations cannot, as a matter of policy, reject all candidate advertising during the most popular hours to accommodate commercial advertisers, the FCC said.[115]

Also, broadcasters may not put political advertising showing pictures of aborted fetuses only in the 10 P.M. to 6 A.M. time period, even if the broadcaster determines the graphic images would be "harmful to children."[116] The U.S. Court of Appeals for the District of Columbia Circuit said Congress intended to provide candidates for federal office with a

[113]Commission Reminds Broadcast Licensees, Cable Operators and Others of Requirements Applicable to Video News Releases (FCC 05-84) (Apr. 13, 2005).

[114]Frank Aherns, "FCC Queries TV Stations on Video News Releases," *Wash. Post,* Aug. 25, 2006, at D1.

[115]1984 Political Primer, 100 F.C.C.2d at 1524–25.

[116]Becker v. FCC, 95 F.3d 75 (D.C. Cir. 1996).

reasonable opportunity to reach potential voters with their messages. Federal candidates might not reach potential voters if their ads could be seen only late at night.

In addition, the court said, if station personnel were to apply the "harmful to children" criterion, they would have "standardless discretion." It might be difficult in some instances to separate a broadcaster's objection to a commercial's graphic images from objections to a candidate's message, the court said. A candidate might engage in self-censorship by changing the content of a commercial to ensure it would escape being channeled into the late-night hours. The court held stations are to broadcast political commercials containing graphic material just as they would advertisements without such images.

The D.C. Circuit's decision concerning political advertisements showing pictures of aborted fetuses involved a candidate for federal office. However, broadcast stations may not channel into late-night hours advertisements run by candidates for any office.

The FCC also has said broadcasters are not obligated to disrupt contracts with commercial sponsors to give candidates their choice of time.[117] Additionally, in 1994, the FCC said broadcasters need not sell political candidates odd blocks of time—such as five minutes or twenty minutes—that might disrupt station program schedules and station contracts with networks and program syndicators. However, in 1999, the FCC said stations' decisions not to sell odd blocks of time should not be based "solely" on whether a program schedule will be disrupted. Rather, stations and candidates should engage in "good-faith negotiations" about commericial lengths. The commission said it would accept a stations' decision about lengths of political commericals unless a station acts unreasonably.[118]

The FCC says stations deny "reasonable access" if they refuse to run any federal candidate advertising once a political campaign begins. The commission requires that broadcasters decide "reasonably," election by election, when campaigning has begun. In a decision upheld by the U.S. Supreme Court, the commission ruled that three national television networks violated Section 312(a)(7) when they turned down requests by the Carter-Mondale Presidential Committee to buy time eleven months before an election.

The case, *CBS v. FCC,* reached the Court after the networks refused to broadcast a thirty-minute Carter-Mondale campaign film in December 1979.[119] Campaign officials wanted the broadcast to coincide with President Carter's announcement that he would seek reelection. CBS offered the committee only five minutes of prime time. NBC and ABC said that they were not yet prepared to sell any time for the 1980 campaign. The networks said that demands for equal opportunity to the Carter-Mondale presentation by other presidential candidates so long before the election would disrupt their programming schedule.

The Court, following its reasoning in *Red Lion,* said the First Amendment rights of the candidates and the public outweigh those of the broadcasters. Chief Justice Burger, for the Court majority, said the access requirement "makes a significant contribution to freedom of expression by enhancing the ability of candidates to present, and the public to receive, information necessary for the effective operation of the democratic process." Burger said the Supreme Court was approving only a limited right of access for legally qualified federal candidates during a political campaign rather than a general right of access to the broadcast media.

[117]1984 Political Primer, 100 F.C.C.2d at 1524–25.
[118]Section 312(a)(7), 17 P & F Rad. Reg. 186 (1999).
[119]453 U.S. 367 (1981).

Burger said the FCC reasonably decided that once a campaign has begun, broadcasters must weigh the merits of each request for time from a federal candidate. Burger said the FCC requires each broadcaster to tailor the response to a request "as much as reasonably possible" to meet a candidate's purpose in seeking the airtime. Each broadcaster can consider such factors as the amount of time previously sold to the candidate, the disruption of regular programming, and the likelihood of requests for time by rival candidates under the equal opportunities provision of Section 315. However, to justify a refusal of a candidate's request, a broadcaster must make a counteroffer or be able to explain to the commission why access would pose "a realistic danger of substantial program disruption."

Burger said the commission determines when a campaign has begun only by examining the facts in individual cases after receiving a complaint. In the Carter-Mondale case, Burger said, the FCC's decision that the 1980 presidential campaign had begun by late 1979 was reasonable. He noted that twelve candidates had formally announced their intentions to run. They were collecting endorsements and otherwise campaigning. National campaign organizations were functioning, states had started to select delegates, and the national print media had been covering the candidates for months.

After the Carter-Mondale decision, one federal appeals court said the ruling that broadcasters cannot refuse all candidate advertising does not mean that broadcasters must provide free time to federal candidates. The U.S. Court of Appeals for the D.C. Circuit rejected a plea by Senator Edward Kennedy that he be granted free time to offset network coverage of President Carter, whom Kennedy was opposing in the 1980 Democratic primaries. The networks had broadcast a half-hour Carter speech and a half-hour presidential news conference four days before the Illinois primary. The networks said they would be willing to sell Kennedy time but would not grant him free time. Kennedy contended that the FCC's decision in the Carter-Mondale case meant that there could be no across-the-board rejection of his request. However, the FCC and the D.C. Circuit said Section 312(a)(7) did not mandate that candidates be given free time. Broadcasters can either provide reasonable access free or sell reasonable amounts of time.[120]

In his January 1998 State of the Union speech, President Clinton suggested campaign spending could be curbed if broadcasters were required to give candidates free time. FCC Chair William Kennard said the FCC would consider adopting rules governing broadcast political advertisements, including free time for presidential candidates. Members of Congress balked. Some congressional leaders argued the FCC did not have authority to require free time and said Congress, if necessary, would prevent the FCC from forcing networks to give away time. Several representatives threatened to cut the FCC's budget if the agency considered requiring free time. Broadcasters and Congress remain opposed to a free time requirement.

◇ Summary ◇

Section 315 of the 1934 Communications Act requires broadcast licensees to provide equal opportunities to legally qualified political candidates. To be considered legally qualified, candidates must satisfy the requirements for office, must publicly announce an intention to

[120]Kennedy for President Comm. v. FCC, 636 F.2d 432, 436 (D.C. Cir. 1980).

run for office, and must qualify for a ballot position or publicly seek election as a write-in candidate. Candidates running for the same office must have access to the same amount of airtime and the chance to appear before about the same size audience. The equal opportunities rule does not apply to spokespersons for political candidates. Nor does it apply to newscasts, news interview programs such as *Face the Nation,* news documentaries, or live coverage of news events, including political debates. Entertainment programs are not exempt from Section 315.

Broadcast licensees must charge political candidates the lowest advertising rates within forty-five days of primary elections and sixty days of general elections. Broadcasters cannot censor the remarks of legally qualified candidates during political broadcasts and are not liable for defamatory candidate comments.

Section 312(a)(7) of the Communications Act requires broadcast licensees to provide "reasonable access" or permit the "purchase of reasonable amounts of time" by legally qualified candidates for federal office. Stations are not required to provide free time to federal candidates, nor must they give candidates the time of the broadcast day that is requested. However, in the Carter-Mondale case, the Supreme Court affirmed an FCC determination that broadcasters cannot categorically refuse all candidate ads once a political campaign begins. Broadcasters must consider the individual circumstances of each request for broadcast time by federal political candidates, including whether a political campaign has begun. Neither Section 312(a)(7) nor Section 315 requires broadcasters to provide time for state or local candidates.

Regulation of Public Issue Programming: The Fairness Doctrine

In 1987, the FCC repealed the fairness doctrine, the most widely debated broadcast programming regulation of the 1960s and 1970s. Although the commission said broadcasters would not be required to air a diversity of views on important public controversies, two fairness doctrine-related policies, the personal attack and political editorializing rules, remained in effect until 2000. A third fairness doctrine-related policy, the Zapple Rule, is still in effect.

Fairness: 1949–1987

Broadcasters' obligation to air diverse views on public issues was first declared a policy of the Federal Radio Commission in 1929.[121] In 1949, the Federal Communications Commission announced the twofold duty of broadcasters that became known as the fairness doctrine.[122] The FCC required broadcasters (1) to devote a reasonable percentage of airtime to the discussion of public issues and (2) to present contrasting views in the case of controversial issues of public importance.

The fairness doctrine, unlike the equal opportunities rule, governed discussions of controversial issues and not broadcasts by political candidates. In addition, the fairness doctrine did not require the equal treatment imposed by Section 315. Rather, the fairness

[121]Great Lakes Broadcasting, 3 F.R.C. Ann. Rep. 34 (1929).

[122]*In re* Editorializing by Broadcast Licensees, 13 F.C.C. 1246 (1949).

doctrine imposed a more general obligation on broadcasters to ensure that diverse ideas were presented. If broadcasters aired a program stressing the problems of nuclear power, they were also expected to discuss the advantages of nuclear power sometime during their overall programming. Broadcasters determined which views were to be presented and by whom. No one person or group could claim airtime under the fairness doctrine.

In 1969, the U.S. Supreme Court in *Red Lion Broadcasting Co. v. FCC* declared at least one form of the fairness doctrine, the personal attack rules, to be constitutional. However, in 1987, an FCC with a deregulatory philosophy said the two-prong fairness doctrine itself would no longer be enforced because it conflicted with the public interest and the First Amendment. The FCC said the fairness doctrine requirement that broadcasters provide a diversity of views on controversial issues actually thwarted the discussion of public issues. The commission said broadcasters censored themselves because they feared complaints to the FCC would damage their reputations and be expensive to defend. The commission also found that the fairness doctrine required a government scrutiny of programming that "perilously treads upon the editorial prerogatives of broadcast journalists."[123] In addition, the FCC suggested, the fairness doctrine "may have penalized or impeded the expression of unorthodox or unpopular opinions." The commission said that several of the broadcasters who had been the focus of fairness inquiries aired particularly provocative opinions.

The commission argued that its intrusion into the editorial judgments of broadcasters was no longer necessary to ensure the airing of diverse views on important public issues. The commission said there had been "an explosive growth" in the number and variety of information outlets since the U.S. Supreme Court upheld the fairness doctrine in *Red Lion* in 1969. In 1989, the U.S. Court of Appeals for the D.C. Circuit upheld the FCC's decision to eliminate the fairness doctrine.[124]

Fairness Policies: Post-1987

After the FCC abandoned the general fairness doctrine, the commission later announced it had eliminated fairness requirements for broadcast discussions of referenda, initiatives, recall efforts, and bond proposals. The commission said that it had concluded in 1987 that the fairness doctrine thwarted the discussion of controversial issues of public importance, based in part on evidence that fairness requirements led broadcasters to refuse airtime for any discussion of ballot measures. However, the commission has not eliminated the Zapple Rule. In 2000, a federal court ordered the FCC to eliminate the personal attack and political editorializing rules.

ZAPPLE RULE The Zapple Rule holds that supporters of opposing candidates must be given about the same amount of airtime during election campaigns. The Zapple Rule complements Section 315 of the Communications Act, which requires only that broadcasters provide equal opportunities to legally qualified political candidates. Under the Zapple Rule, if the supporters of one candidate pay for airtime, the supporters of opposing

[123]Syracuse Peace Council, 2 F.C.C.R. 5043, 5051 (1987) (quoting General Fairness Doctrine Obligations of Broadcast Licensees (1985 Fairness Report), 102 F.C.C.2d 142, 191 (1985)).

[124]Syracuse Peace Council v. FCC, 867 F.2d 654 (D.C. Cir. 1989), *cert. denied,* 493 U.S. 1019 (1990).

candidates must be allowed to buy about the same amount of time. If the first group is given free time, the other groups must receive free time as well.[125]

The Zapple Rule governs political advertising that does not include the voice or picture of a political candidate, such as a review of a candidate's voting record or a discussion of the candidate's position on abortion. The Zapple Rule was created by the commission in response to a letter by a former congressional staff member, Nicholas Zapple.

PERSONAL ATTACKS AND POLITICAL EDITORIALS For two decades, broadcasters urged the FCC to eliminate two vestiges of the fairness doctrine: the personal attack and political editorial rules. The FCC adopted the two rules in 1967 as corollaries to the fairness doctrine.

The FCC's personal attack rule said that broadcasters had to offer reply time if the honesty, character, or integrity of an identified person or group was attacked during the discussion of a controversial issue of public importance. The broadcaster had to provide a script, tape, or accurate summary to the person attacked, who could use the station free of charge to reply. The FCC said personal attacks included allegations of criminal activity, moral turpitude, Communist activity, or the promotion of violence. However, disagreements over political issues and charges of bad judgment or incompetence usually were not considered personal attacks. The rule exempted newscasts, spot news interviews, and news coverage, including any commentary or analysis, but did not exempt news documentaries. The personal attack rule did not govern attacks on foreign groups or public figures. Nor did the rule apply to attacks made by legally qualified candidates or their campaign staffs during political campaigns.

The political editorial rule required broadcasters to provide a candidate notification, script or tape, and time to reply to station editorials that opposed a candidate or endorsed a competing legally qualified candidate. The rule applied only to editorials representing the station owner's or manager's views. Because editorials ordinarily do not feature pictures or voices of political candidates that would trigger the equal opportunities requirement, the rule said representatives of candidates, rather than candidates themselves, could respond.

In 2000, the Court of Appeals for the District of Columbia Circuit ordered the FCC to abolish the personal attack and political editorializing rules.[126] In light of the FCC's earlier decision to eliminate the fairness doctrine, the court held that the agency had not justified the retention of these fairness doctrine-related rules.

A federal statute prohibiting noncommercial educational broadcast stations from supporting or opposing any candidate for public office remains in effect.[127] A broader ban on all editorializing by noncommercial educational broadcasting stations receiving government funding was ruled unconstitutional by the Supreme Court in 1984.[128] Justice Brennan, writing for the Court, said the ban on editorializing restricted the very kind of political and social commentary the First Amendment was designed to encourage.

[125]Letter to Nicholas Zapple, 23 F.C.C.2d 707 (1970); 1984 Political Primer, 100 F.C.C.2d at 1534–35.
[126]Radio-Television News Directors Ass'n v. FCC, 229 F.3d 269 (D.C. Cir. 2000).
[127]47 U.S.C. § 399.
[128]FCC v. League of Women Voters, 468 U.S. 364 (1984).

◆ Summary ◆

Before 1987, the fairness doctrine required that broadcasters provide airtime for the discussion of important and controversial public issues and, in doing so, that they offer a reasonable opportunity for the presentation of contrasting viewpoints. The FCC eliminated the fairness doctrine in 1987, a decision upheld by the courts.

Although the commission abandoned the fairness doctrine, it retained a few related policies. However, an appellate court required the FCC to eliminate the rule requiring stations to provide reply time for personal attacks aired during discussions of controversial public issues. The court also ordered the commission to eliminate the rule allowing political candidates opportunities to respond to editorials attacking them or supporting their opponents. The FCC continues to require licensees to provide time to supporters of political candidates whose opponents' supporters use time on broadcast stations. Public broadcasters cannot support or oppose political candidates, but they can editorialize on public issues.

Lobbying: The Right to Petition

Lobbying is part of everyone's First Amendment right to speak and to petition the government for redress of grievances. This right is not denied because the petitioner is a corporation or union whose motives might be no more lofty than to seek legislation to damage a competitor.[129] In 2006, $2.6 billion was spent on lobbying the federal government; the largest spender was the pharmaceutical and health products industry.

Lobbying the government may be carried out through direct contacts with legislators or through indirect public relations campaigns, sometimes called *grassroots lobbying.* Either form is protected by the First Amendment. However, lobbyists are required to comply with extensive disclosure requirements. For many years, lobbying was regulated by the Federal Regulation of Lobbying Act of 1946. However, in 1995, Congress passed a new law—the Lobbying Disclosure Act of 1995—designed to oversee lobbying more effectively and increase public confidence in government.[130] The old law, Congress found, had been "ineffective because of unclear statutory language, weak administrative and enforcement provisions, and an absence of clear guidance as to who is required to register and what they are required to disclose."[131] Congress amended the LDA in 2007.

Lobbying Disclosure Act of 1995

The lobbying disclosure act requires registration by any person whose total income for lobbying "contacts" with government is expected to exceed $2,500 over a quarterly reporting period. The act also requires organizations with in-house lobbyists to register if the organization's lobbying expenses will be more than $10,000 over a quarter. Lobbying "contacts" are defined as any oral or written communication, including electronic communication,

[129] Eastern R.R. Presidents Conference v. Noerr Motor Freight, Inc., 365 U.S. 127 (1961).
[130] 2 U.S.C. § §1601-12.
[131] *Id.* at § 1601(2).

with legislative or executive branch officials, designed to influence federal policy. As a result of this definition, grassroots lobbying is not covered by the act. About 10,000 Washington lobbyists were registered prior to the passage of the lobbying disclosure act; approximately 35,000 lobbyists were registered in 2005.[132]

Nonprofit organizations, such as labor unions and trade associations, often must register because their principal purpose may be to influence legislation. Registered lobbyists are required to file quarterly statements identifying their clients and detailing the general areas and specific issues on which they have lobbied, including specific references to legislative bill numbers and executive branch actions. Registered lobbyists need not, however, report the names of legislators or executive branch officials they lobbied. Under the act, lobbyists must give estimates of income and expenses, although for amounts larger than $5,000, these estimates need only be rounded to the nearest $10,000. The reports are filed with the secretary of the Senate and the clerk of the House of Representatives. Violation of the lobbying disclosure act can result in a fine of up to $200,000.

Excluded from registration requirements are public officials acting in an official capacity, newspapers and other mass media, and persons who testify on legislation before a Congressional committee. Congress excluded those who testify from registering as lobbyists because Congress did not want to discourage testimony and thereby impair its ability to gather information necessary to legislate. Nor did Congress want to infringe on a citizen's right to petition by requiring citizens who testify to register as lobbyists. In any case, people who testify publicly usually disclose their affiliations and political interests during their testimony. Also excluded from registration are persons for whom lobbying makes up less than 20 percent of their work for a particular client per quarter. For example, a lawyer whose main responsibilities involved legal work for a client but who also did some lobbying for the client would not have to register if the lobbying involved less than 20 percent of the lawyer's total time spent working for that client.

Foreign Agents

Lobbyists who work for foreign "principals" are also supposed to disclose their activities. Just before World War II, Congress was disturbed to learn of well-organized, pro-German and Communist groups distributing large quantities of "anti-democratic material" in the United States. To mitigate the efforts of these new "subverters of democracy, and foreign-policy propagandists," Congress passed the Foreign Agents Registration Act of 1938.[133]

The Foreign Agents Registration Act (FARA), like the domestic lobbying act, relies on disclosure of agents' activities, not on suppression of their speech. Under the act, agents must report their affiliations, the way they carry out their activities, how they receive and spend money, and how they disseminate information to influence public opinion. However, foreign agents are prohibited from spending money to influence an American political election. In *Communist Party v. Subversive Activities Control Board,* the Supreme Court said Congress could require registration or disclosure when "secrecy or the concealment

[132]Jeffrey Birnbaum,"The Road to Riches is Called K Street," *Wash. Post,* June 22, 2005, at A1.
[133]22 U.S.C. § 611–22.

of associations has been regarded as a threat to public safety and to the effective, free functioning of our national institutions."[134]

Foreign "agents" who are supposed to register include any person or organization that acts as an agent or representative of a foreign principal or "at the order, request, or under the direction or control" of a foreign principal. Foreign principals include governments, political parties, businesses, and organizations. The foreign principal may be a friend or enemy of the United States.[135] A foreign agent also includes anyone in the United States who acts "as a public relations counsel, publicity agent, information-service employee or political consultant" for a foreign principal. For example, if a foreign government hires an American public relations firm, the firm becomes an agent subject to registration under the act because the firm is "indirectly supervised, directed, controlled, financed, or subsidized" by a foreign principal.

However, lobbyists for foreign businesses and trade organizations who register under the Lobbying Disclosure Act are exempt from registration under FARA. As a result, registration under FARA will be limited primarily to agents of foreign governments and political parties.

In addition to registration requirements, foreign agents are also required to label the "informational materials" they distribute and file copies of the material with the U.S. Justice Department.[136] "Informational material" is any communication designed to influence the American public about the political interests or policies of a foreign government or to influence the foreign policy of the United States. These materials must be labeled with information about the agent's identity and the identity of the principal for whom he or she acts. The Supreme Court upheld the labeling requirement in *Meese v. Keene,*[137] stating that the labeling requirement did not involve censorship or a restraint on distribution. "To the contrary," the Court stated, "Congress simply required the disseminators of such material to make additional disclosures that would better enable the public to evaluate" the materials.

Lobbying Reform

Jack Abramoff, once regarded as among the most powerful lobbyists in Washington, pleaded guilty on January 3, 2006, to charges of fraud, tax evasion, and conspiracy to bribe public officials.[138] Abramoff used his close ties to Republican leaders to collect $82 million in lobbying fees from casino-rich Indian tribes. As part of his lobbying practice, Abramoff offered "things of value" to public officials in exchange for official acts. "Things of value" included lavish trips, meals and entertainment, and employment for relatives of officials. Abramoff stated, "I can't imagine there's anything I did that other lobbyists didn't do and aren't doing today." In October 2006, Representative Bob Ney pleaded guilty to charges that he sponsored legislation to benefit Abramoff's clients in exchange for lavish golf and gambling trips.

[134] 367 U.S. 1, 97 (1961).
[135] 22 U.S.C. § 611(c)(1).
[136] 22 U.S.C. § 614.
[137] 481 U.S. 465 (1987).
[138] Susan Schmidt & James Grimaldi, "Abramoff Pleads Guilty to Three Counts," *Wash. Post,* Jan. 4, 2006, at A1.

Congress responded to the Abramoff scandal by enacting the Honest Leadership and Open Government Act of 2007.[139] Under the law, lobbyist-sponsored travel and gifts are severely restricted. House candidates are prohibited from flying on private aircraft; Senate and presidential candidates must pay the fair market value for flights on private aircraft. Lobbyists are prohibited from giving gifts or meals that violate House or Senate rules. Meals must be of nominal value, such as light appetizers; within the lobbyist community this is known as the "toothpick test." Members of Congress who are convicted of accepting bribes lose their retirement benefits.

The 2007 act seeks to restrict the "revolving door" between former legislators and the lobbying industry. For example, in 2003 former Representative Billy Tauzin began negotiating for a job as head of the lobby for drug companies shortly after President Bush signed a Medicare drug law authored by Tauzin. The 2007 act requires departing members of Congress to disclose negotiations with potential employers and to recuse themselves during their final months in the case of a conflict of interest. Former Senators must wait two years before they lobby Congress; former House members are banned for one year. The one- and two-year bans also apply to top Congressional staff members. The 2007 act also revokes the floor privileges of former lawmakers who become lobbyists.

The 2007 act also requires disclosure of "bundling," the practice whereby lobbyists combine campaign contributions from multiple donors. Candidate committees, political parties, and PACs controlled by candidates (known as leadership PACs) must disclose to the FEC the identities of registered lobbyists who provide two or more bundled contributions exceeding $15,000 per six-month period. The FEC is required to make this information available on its Web site.

The new law requires the Secretary of the Senate and the Clerk of the House to maintain searchable electronic databases of the reports filed by registered lobbyists. Senate and House members must also file travel reports and this information is also publicly available on the Internet.

Summary

Although petitioning the government is a right guaranteed by the First Amendment, Congress requires disclosure of lobbying to prevent corruption of democratic processes. Lobbyists are supposed to register and disclose income and expenditures as well as the laws or regulations they have attempted to influence. Foreign agents, too, are supposed to register and disclose their income and expenditures. Congress enacted lobbying reforms in 2007.

[139] Pub. L. No. 110-81, 121 Stat. 735 (2007).

CHAPTER 8

Commercial Speech

Until the late nineteenth century, advertisements were usually simple announcements much like today's classifieds. In the 1700s and 1800s, artisans and merchants used small notices to tell their patrons that fabrics and other manufactured goods had arrived from abroad. The truth of advertisements was seldom an issue because consumers could usually examine the products and shun merchants who sold inferior merchandise.[1]

With the growth of mass production, advertising became more sophisticated. By the beginning of the twentieth century, manufacturers were using national advertising to convince consumers in distant markets to buy mass-produced, undifferentiated products. As markets grew and became impersonal, opportunities for profitable misrepresentations increased. Patent medicine manufacturers, in particular, were notorious for their exaggerated advertising promises. Some patent medicine makers bragged that with the right advertising, they could sell dishwater.

As mass marketing developed, truth in advertising took on new importance to reputable companies. Procter & Gamble, Burpee Seeds, Quaker Oats, and other producers of brand-name products wanted consumers to have faith in the truth of national advertisements.[2] Believing the "rotten apple theory," reputable national advertisers feared that false advertising by one company damaged the credibility of the others.

Manufacturers' concerns for truth in advertising led to the formation of regulatory organizations within the business community. Truth in advertising was a major theme at the 1911 convention of the Associated Advertising Clubs of America. In 1912, the National Vigilance Committee—later the Better Business Bureau—was created. By the 1930s, a movement within the industry to clean up advertising had resulted in several codes discouraging false and misleading advertising.[3]

New legal regulations were an important tool in the effort to keep advertising honest. Most states adopted a law similar to one proposed in 1911 by the trade magazine *Printers' Ink.* The *Printers' Ink* statutes, which still form the basis for much state regulation, made it a misdemeanor to disseminate misleading advertising. On the national level, the Federal Trade Commission Act of 1914 established federal authority to outlaw deceptive acts and practices, including false advertising. Later, the Food and Drug Administration was established to oversee labeling of food, drugs, cosmetics, and medical devices and to regulate the advertising of prescription drugs. The Bureau of Alcohol, Tobacco and Firearms, a division of the Treasury Department, oversees advertising and promotion of alcoholic beverages.

For many years, state and federal regulation of advertising evolved without raising questions of freedom of expression. Until recently, advertising was outside First Amendment consideration. In 1942, the Supreme Court ruled in a short, almost casual opinion that the government could regulate advertising without infringing freedom of expression because commercial speech, like fighting words and obscenity, was not protected by the Constitution. However, by the 1990s, the Supreme Court had long since abandoned its 1942 ruling and had established limited First Amendment protections for commercial advertising.

[1]Daniel Pope, *The Making of Modern Advertising* 4–5 (1983).
[2]*Id.* at 184–226.
[3]*See* S. Watson Dunn et al., *Advertising: Its Role in Modern Marketing* 24–28 (1990).

First Amendment and Advertising

The Supreme Court first ruled that "purely" commercial advertising enjoys constitutional protection in a 1976 case involving advertising for prescription drugs. In *Virginia State Board of Pharmacy v. Virginia Citizens Consumer Council,*[4] the Court struck down a state statute prohibiting pharmacists from advertising the prices of prescription drugs. Since 1976, the Court has developed a complicated "commercial speech" jurisprudence that has limited government regulation of billboards, "For Sale" signs, lawyers' advertisements, and other commercial messages, including advertisements for abortion referral services. However, until shortly before the *Virginia Pharmacy* decision, commercial advertising had always been outside constitutional consideration.

Commercial Speech Doctrine

The Supreme Court placed advertising outside First Amendment protection in 1942, in a case called *Valentine v. Chrestensen.*[5] In that case, the Court ruled that F. J. Chrestensen had no First Amendment right to distribute handbills advertising tours of a former Navy submarine. Chrestensen distributed handbills to pedestrians in lower Manhattan, advertising 25-cent tours of his $2 million submarine moored at a state-owned pier in the East River in New York City. The handbills promised visitors a glimpse of the kitchen, torpedo compartment, and crew's sleeping quarters on the S-49 submarine, also known as the "fighting monster." Children could take the tour for 15 cents.

City officials, however, told Chrestensen to stop distributing his handbills because he was violating the New York City Sanitary Code, which prohibited the distribution of "commercial and business advertising." Chrestensen then added a message to the back of his fliers protesting the restrictions imposed on him under the sanitation code. With a "political" message on one side of his submarine handbills, Chrestensen sought an injunction barring police from interfering with distribution of his constitutionally protected expression.

The U.S. Supreme Court, in a four-page decision, ruled that New York officials could stop distribution of Chrestensen's fliers without violating the First Amendment. The Court said the fliers were "purely commercial" advertising that fell outside constitutional protection. The Court dismissed the political message appended to the fliers as a ruse not to be taken seriously. With its curt decision in *Valentine v. Chrestensen,* the Court originated the "commercial speech doctrine," which was to deny constitutional protection to commercial advertising until the mid-1970s.

In 1964, the Supreme Court took a small step toward constitutional protection for commercial advertising when it ruled in *New York Times Co. v. Sullivan* that political criticism of public officials is protected by the First Amendment even if it is paid for. The Supreme Court rejected Police Commissioner Sullivan's argument that the criticism of Alabama law enforcement officers should have no constitutional status because the criticism was part of a paid advertisement. Another commercial element of the advertisement, according to Sullivan, was its solicitation of funds to support the civil rights movement. The Supreme Court,

[4]425 U.S. 748 (1976).
[5]316 U.S. 52 (1942).

however, said that it was "immaterial" whether the editorial advertisement was purchased; the ad was protected political speech because it "communicated information, expressed opinion, recited grievances, protested claimed abuses, and sought financial support on behalf of a movement whose existence and objectives are matters of the highest public interest and concern."[6]

Although *Times v. Sullivan* established that paid political speech enjoys constitutional protection, the case did not create constitutional protection for "purely commercial advertising" such as a dog food ad or Chrestensen's original handbills. The Supreme Court came a bit closer to protecting commercial speech in 1973 when it suggested in *Pittsburgh Press Co. v. Pittsburgh Commission on Human Relations* that it might be willing to grant constitutional status to "an ordinary commercial proposal."[7] But the Court in *Pittsburgh Press* upheld an advertising regulation that prohibited unnecessary discrimination by gender in newspaper classified advertisements.

A short time later, in *Bigelow v. Virginia,*[8] the Court struck down a state statute that prohibited advertising of abortion referral services. But ads for abortion referral services too were not "purely commercial" speech. Unlike product ads, the abortion referral ads contained factual material similar to the political content of editorials and news columns. For example, the ad at issue in *Bigelow* declared, "Abortions are now legal in New York." The *Bigelow* ad was also different from purely commercial advertisements because the service advertised was itself constitutionally protected. The Supreme Court had ruled in 1973 that a woman's constitutional right of privacy includes the right to an abortion.[9] It is more difficult to square advertising restrictions with the First Amendment if the service advertised is itself constitutionally protected.

The Supreme Court established First Amendment protection for "purely commercial" advertisements in *Virginia State Board of Pharmacy v. Virginia Citizens Consumer Council,*[10] a case in which the Supreme Court struck down a Virginia statute prohibiting licensed pharmacists from advertising the prices of prescription drugs. The pharmacists' ads were purely commercial because they did "no more than propose a commercial transaction," the Court said.

The Virginia State Board of Pharmacy argued that the prohibition on price advertisements for prescription drugs did not violate the First Amendment because purely commercial speech had not been protected by the First Amendment since *Valentine v. Chrestensen.* The board also argued that aggressive price competition among pharmacists would harm consumers because pharmacists would have less time to compound and dispense drugs. The pressures of advertising, the board said, would force conscientious pharmacists either to diminish their painstaking professional services or to go out of business. Furthermore, the Board of Pharmacy argued that competitive advertising would not necessarily result in the lower drug prices anticipated by the Virginia Citizens Consumer Council.

[6]376 U.S. 254 (1964).
[7]413 U.S. 376 (1973).
[8]421 U.S. 809 (1975).
[9]Roe v. Wade, 410 U.S. 113 (1973).
[10]425 U.S. 748 (1976).

The Consumer Council, representing a number of prescription drug users, particularly the elderly and infirm, argued that the Virginia statute was a violation of consumers' First Amendment right to receive information necessary to their good health. The Consumer Council also argued that prohibitions on advertising forced consumers to spend more time and money finding the best drugs at the cheapest prices.

In *Virginia Pharmacy,* the Supreme Court recognized a constitutional protection for purely commercial speech motivated by a desire for profit. Justice Harry Blackmun, writing for the Court, said that the price advertising of prescription drugs is protected by the First Amendment even though a pharmacist does

> not wish to editorialize on any subject, cultural, philosophical, or political. He does not wish to report any particularly newsworthy fact, or to make generalized observations even about commercial matters. The "idea" he wishes to communicate is simply this: "I will sell you the X prescription drug at the Y price."

Although price advertising for drugs is "purely commercial," the Court said commercial advertising, like editorial comment, contributes to democratic decision making served by the First Amendment. In a statement merging the commercial marketplace and the marketplace of ideas, the Court said,

> Advertising, however tasteless and excessive it sometimes may seem, is nonetheless dissemination of information as to who is producing and selling what product, for what reason, and at what price. So long as we preserve a predominantly free enterprise economy, the allocation of our resources in large measure will be made through numerous private economic decisions. It is a matter of public interest that those decisions in the aggregate be intelligent and well informed. To this end, the free flow of commercial information is indispensable.

The Court's First Amendment protection for commercial advertising depended very little on the right of pharmacists to speak or publish. After all, the professional association representing pharmacists opposed lifting the ban on advertising. Of more importance to the Court than a right to speak was the consumer's constitutional interest in receiving information about drug prices. The right to receive would be honored, Justice Blackmun said, because the individual consumer's interest "in the free flow of commercial information may be as keen, if not keener by far, than his interest in the day's most urgent political debate." The Court rejected as "paternalistic" the State Board of Pharmacy's claim that allowing pharmacists to advertise prices of prescription drugs would undermine their professionalism and thereby hurt consumers.

In a very sharp dissent, Justice William Rehnquist feared that the "logical consequences" of the *Virginia Pharmacy* decision would be to elevate "commercial intercourse between a seller hawking his wares and a buyer seeking to strike a bargain to the same plane as has been previously reserved for the free marketplace of ideas." Rehnquist did not agree with the majority's assertion that commercial advertising should be protected by the First Amendment because purchasing decisions based on advertising contribute to public decision making in a democracy. To Justice Rehnquist, the First Amendment protects public decision making on political, social, and other public issues. It does not protect "the decision of a particular individual as to whether to purchase one or another kind of shampoo." Justice Rehnquist thought the Court's decision in *Virginia Pharmacy* devalued the First Amendment.

Advertising's Lower Status

According constitutional status to advertising has not necessarily devalued the First Amendment, but advertising itself still does not enjoy the full First Amendment protection of political speech. Although the majority of justices in *Virginia Pharmacy* appeared to equate commercial advertising with political speech, in fact commercial speech came under the constitutional umbrella in *Virginia Pharmacy* as a second-class form of expression. Starting in *Virginia Pharmacy* and continuing through other commercial speech decisions, the Court has permitted many regulations on commercial speech that would not be tolerated on political speech. For example, although the government must demonstrate a compelling interest to justify restraints on political speech, the government needs to demonstrate a lesser "substantial" or "important" need to justify restraints on commercial advertising.

A major difference in the protection of political and commercial speech can be seen in the Court's tolerance for falsehood in each. Although considerable falsehood is permitted in the political arena because government censorship is considered worse than false political speech, the Court said in *Virginia Pharmacy* that the government may constitutionally ban commercial promotions that are "false or misleading in any way" or that promote products or services that are illegal. The Court also said that prior restraints, which are presumed to be unconstitutional in the political arena, may be invoked to halt misleading commercial speech. Furthermore, although political expression may not be compelled, the Court said that commercial advertisers might be required to disseminate warnings, disclaimers, and other messages to ensure that commercial speech is not misleading. Since *Virginia Pharmacy* was decided, the Supreme Court has ruled that even truthful advertising may be prohibited.[11]

The constitutional protections for commercial speech are weaker than those for political speech, the Supreme Court said, because of "common sense" differences between commercial and political speech. First, the Court said that commercial speech is hardier than other kinds of expression because of the need of businesses to advertise in a market economy. Advertisers will not be as intimidated by government regulations as political speakers might be, the Court said, because of the unrelenting economic pressure on businesses to advertise. In other words, commercial advertising may be regulated more than political speech because advertising can more easily withstand regulation.

The other "commonsense" difference between commercial and political speech is that commercial speech is more easily verified. Advertisers, the Court said, know their products well and often make factual statements that can be proven objectively, perhaps by scientific test. Political statements, in contrast, are often assertions of fact or opinion that cannot be proved and should not have to be. But because advertisers easily may verify their statements,

[11]Posadas de Puerto Rico Assocs. v. Tourism Co., 478 U.S. 328 (1986).

the Court said there is less reason to tolerate false and misleading statements in commercial ads than in political debate.

Although commercial speech has occupied a second-class status constitutionally since *Virginia Pharmacy* was decided in 1976, the Supreme Court has issued a number of decisions broadening the range of commercial content protected—at least partially—by the First Amendment. In 1977, the Court ruled that attorneys have a constitutional right to advertise the prices of routine services, such as a simple will or uncontested divorce.[12] The Court has also extended constitutional protection to illustrations and pictures in attorneys' ads,[13] "For Sale" and "Sold" signs on private houses,[14] advertisements for contraceptives,[15] and promotions for electrical power by a utility.[16] However, the Supreme Court has also ruled that the First Amendment does not protect ads for casinos[17] or sales promotions in college dormitories.[18]

The Court's commercial speech decisions have been criticized for being inconsistent and therefore providing little guidance for advertisers who want to know whether government restrictions are constitutional. The Court employs a four-part analysis when determining the constitutionality of advertising regulations.

The Four-Part Test

The four-part test for determining the constitutionality of regulations on commercial speech was set forth by the Supreme Court in *Central Hudson Gas & Electric Corp. v. Public Service Commission,*[19] a case in which the Court upheld a utility's right to promote the use of electricity. In *Central Hudson,* the Court struck down a state regulation that prohibited electric utilities from running all advertisements promoting the use of electricity. The prohibition, which was instituted to conserve energy, barred ads promoting efficient uses of electricity as well as those advocating inefficient or wasteful uses. The Supreme Court ruled that a blanket ban on all electricity ads violated the First Amendment.

Under the four-part test promulgated in *Central Hudson* and later cases, a court must determine first whether speech is commercial expression eligible for First Amendment protection. Second, a court examines whether the government asserts a substantial interest in regulating the expression. If the speech is eligible and the government asserts a substantial interest, a court next considers whether the regulation directly advances the governmental interest asserted. If so, the court in the fourth step decides whether the regulation is sufficiently narrow.

COMMERCIAL SPEECH ELIGIBLE FOR CONSTITUTIONAL CONSIDERATION Speech passes the first part of the *Central Hudson* test and is eligible for constitutional protection if it is accurate and advertises a lawful product or service. False and misleading advertising and

[12]Bates v. State Bar of Arizona, 433 U.S. 350 (1977).
[13]Zauderer v. Office of Disciplinary Counsel, 471 U.S. 626 (1985).
[14]Linmark Assocs., Inc. v. Township of Willingboro, 431 U.S. 85 (1977).
[15]Bolger v. Youngs Drug Prod. Corp., 463 U.S. 60 (1983); Carey v. Population Servs. Int'l, 431 U.S. 678 (1977).
[16]Central Hudson Gas & Elec. Corp. v. Public Serv. Comm'n, 447 U.S. 557 (1980).
[17]Posadas de Puerto Rico Assocs. v. Tourism Co., 478 U.S. 328 (1986).
[18]Board of Trustees v. Fox, 492 U.S. 469 (1989).
[19]447 U.S. 557 (1980).

advertising for illegal products and services are not eligible for constitutional consideration. The first task of a court, therefore, is to determine whether the expression at issue is commercial speech for a lawful product or service.

Defining Commercial Speech An advertisement is commercial speech, the Court said in *Virginia Pharmacy,* if it does "no more than propose a commercial transaction."[20] The Court also has said that commercial speech is expression "related solely to the economic interests of the speaker and its audience." Similarly, Justice Brennan once referred to "pure advertising" as "an offer to buy or sell goods and services or encouraging such buying and selling."[21] Although these definitions do not encompass all commercial speech, they adequately describe ads that expressly offer a product or service for sale, particularly at a specific price.

Price advertising for prescription drugs, the Supreme Court said in *Virginia Pharmacy,* was a purely commercial proposal. Similarly, a lawyer's offer to write a will at a predetermined price, a homeowner's offer to sell a house, and a salesperson's attempt to sell Tupperware in a university dormitory are purely commercial speech because they do no more than "propose a commercial transaction."

Associating an advertisement with a political issue does not necessarily transform commercial speech into political speech, the Supreme Court has said. F. J. Chrestensen's commercial fliers for submarine tours remained commercial advertisements, the Supreme Court said, even though he appended a political protest to the back. In *Central Hudson,* the Court said that an electric utility's bill inserts promoting the efficient use of electricity were commercial speech even though the inserts served a political plan, the state-approved energy conservation program.

Likewise, in *Bolger v. Youngs Drug Products Corp.,*[22] the Court ruled that leaflets distributed by a condom manufacturer were commercial speech even though they contained political and social information about preventing venereal disease. Leaflets distributed by a condom manufacturer were not transformed into fully protected political speech simply because they "link a product to a current public debate," the Court said. The Court said in *Bolger* that a condom manufacturer's "direct comments" on public issues such as venereal disease would merit full constitutional protection, but not statements "made in the context of commercial transactions." The Court said it feared advertisers would try to immunize false or misleading product information from government regulation if commercial messages were considered to be political when the two were blended.

The informational pamphlets at issue in *Bolger* did not propose that readers buy Youngs's condoms. One pamphlet discussed the use of condoms generally as a method of preventing the spread of venereal disease. At the end, the pamphlet identified Youngs as the distributor of the flier. Another VD pamphlet described various Trojan-brand condoms manufactured by Youngs without offering them for sale. Nevertheless, the Court ruled the pamphlets were commercial speech because they (1) were conceded to be paid advertisements,

[20] 425 U.S. 762.
[21] Dun & Bradstreet v. Greenmoss Builders, 472 U.S. 749 (1985) (Brennan, J., dissenting).
[22] 463 U.S. 60 (1983).

(2) made reference to a specific product, and (3) were economically motivated. Not all of these three criteria must be met for an advertisement proposing no commercial transaction to be considered commercial speech. Corporate image ads, for example, might be considered commercial speech even though they mention no products, the Court said.

The definition of commercial speech was clouded in 2004 when the Supreme Court let stand a California ruling that corporate reports, press releases, and letters to the editor are less protected commercial speech—subject to penalties if found to be false—rather than the more protected political speech.[23] The California Supreme Court had ruled that Marc Kasky, a consumer activist, should be allowed to prove in court that Nike Inc. violated a state consumer protection law by issuing false statements about workers' conditions in the footwear company's Southeast Asian manufacturing plants. When the U.S. Supreme Court dismissed review, Nike settled with Kasky for $1.5 million to be used to educate workers, increase training, and monitor manufacturing in Southeast Asia.[24]

Nike issued several press releases and comments in response to charges that its manufacturing operations in Southeast Asia were "sweatshops" that paid low wages and exploited women and children. The California court said Nike's public comments were not fully protected political speech, but were commercial speech—like product advertising—because they were directed "to an audience of persons who may be influenced by that speech to engage in a commercial transaction with the speaker." Nike claimed its press releases and letters were political speech because they did not attempt to sell athletic footwear, but responded to politically motivated criticism about its manufacturing processes. (See excerpts from a Nike release in Figure 8.1.) More than 40 entities, including Microsoft, the *New York Times,* and public relations organizations, supported Nike's claim.

When the U.S. Supreme Court dismissed the Nike appeal, Justice Breyer dissented, arguing the high court should rule Nike's communications are protected speech about controversial public issues. Breyer, joined by Justice O'Connor, noted that Nike's letter to college presidents and athletic directors was not in an advertising format, proposed no product purchases and contained facts, and responded to criticism about Nike's labor practices. Breyer warned that fear of law suits would chill corporations' willingness to engage in public debate.[25] Afterward, Nike said it would withhold a report on corporate responsibility.

Lawful Products and Services Once a court has determined that commercial speech is at issue, it asks whether the expression promotes a lawful product or service. Under the first part of the *Central Hudson* analysis, commercial expression entitled to constitutional protection must promote products and services that are themselves legal. Ads for prescription drugs, houses, and lawyers' services are eligible for constitutional consideration because they promote lawful products and activities. Similarly, ads promoting electricity and condoms also meet the first part of the test. However, ads for explosives, obscene materials, criminal activities, and discriminatory job opportunities are outside constitutional consideration because they promote illegal products or services.

[23]Kasky v. Nike, 27 Cal. 4th 939 (2002), *cert. dismissed,* 539 U.S. 654 (2003).
[24]Stephanie Kang, "Nike Settles Case with an Activist for $1.5 Million," *Wall Street Journal,* Sept. 15, 2003, at A10.
[25]539 U.S. 654.

BEAVERTON, Ore.—June 6, 1996—NIKE, Inc. today responded to claims made by Joel Joseph, chairman of the Made in the USA Foundation, of under-age Indonesian workers making NIKE's line of Air Jordan shoes for 14 cents an hour by stating that his allegations are completely false and irresponsible.

"Perhaps Mr. Joseph should have looked at an Air Jordan shoe on store shelves to learn that the product is made in Taiwan," said Donna Gibbs, NIKE's director of corporate communications. "One has to question the credibility of an individual whose organization is largely financed by labor unions opposed to free trade with developing nations," she said. "It's also too bad that Kathie Lee Gifford has found it necessary to avoid the media spotlight by pushing Michael Jordan onto it."

Wherever NIKE operates around the globe, it is guided by principles set forth in a code of conduct that binds its production subcontractors to a signed Memorandum of Understanding. This Memorandum strictly prohibits child labor and certifies compliance with applicable government regulations regarding minimum wage, overtime, as well as occupational health and safety, environmental regulations, worker insurance and equal opportunity provisions.

NIKE enforces its standards through daily observation by NIKE staff members. Every factory in the world that manufactures NIKE components and finished goods has NIKE staff assigned to it who are responsible for monitoring adherence to the Memorandum of Understanding. The next level of enforcement is a system of third-party audit, conducted by Ernst & Young. These thorough reviews conducted over several days include interviews with workers, examination of safety equipment and procedures, review of free health-care facilities at the work site, investigation of worker grievances and audits of payroll records.

The average line-worker's wage in Asian subcontracted facilities is double the governmentmandated minimum. In addition, compensation extends beyond wages to include subsidies for transportation, housing, free meals and health care, bonuses for attendance and improved skills; and legally mandated paid holidays, pregnancy and menstrual leave. These benefits significantly increase the value of the daily wage.

The income level of an Indonesian entry-level worker at a NIKE subcontracted facility is five times that of a farmer, and in China, an assistant line-supervisor earns more than a surgeon with 20 years of experience.

FIGURE 8.1 Excerpts from a Nike Press Release Responding to Sweatshop Allegations.

Federal appellate courts have disagreed whether housing ads omitting pictures and references to minorities discriminate in violation of federal law. The federal Fair Housing Act prohibits advertising "indicat[ing] any preference . . . based on race." In one case, the U.S. Court of Appeals for the Second Circuit refused to dismiss a discrimination suit against the *New York Times* by minorities who claimed housing ads in the newspaper violated the federal law. Plaintiffs in the case, several African Americans joined by the Open Housing Center of New York, charged that *Times* real estate ads published over a twenty-year period violated the Fair Housing Act because they rarely depicted blacks as potential home buyers or renters. In refusing to dismiss the case, the Second Circuit said a jury "plausibly may conclude" that ads with models of a particular race and not others violate the Fair Housing Act by indicating a racial preference. Ads demonstrating a racial preference would not be protected by the First Amendment, the court noted, because they would "further an illegal commercial activity." The Supreme Court refused to review the Second Circuit's ruling to let the *Times* be sued.[26]

In contrast, the Sixth Circuit dismissed a similar discrimination suit against the *Cincinnati Enquirer,* ruling that the Fair Housing Act is not violated merely because minority models are absent from housing advertisements.[27] Unlike the Second Circuit in the *New York Times* case, the Sixth Circuit ruled that housing ads would violate the Fair Housing Act only if they constituted a discriminatory "campaign" by a specific realtor or if the ads illegally promoted discrimination at specific housing projects. But ads that are independent of a campaign are not discriminatory merely because they contain white models only, the court said. Indeed, the Sixth Circuit concluded that independent housing ads depicting whites only are lawful statements protected by the First Amendment.

In another twist to the question of what constitutes commercial speech for lawful products, the Supreme Court has ruled that ads and logos promoting unlawful uses of lawful products may be unprotected by the First Amendment. In *Village of Hoffman Estates v. Flipside, Hoffman Estates,* the Court ruled that logos and slogans on cigarette papers, water pipes, "roach clips," and other drug paraphernalia were outside First Amendment protection because the paraphernalia were marketed for illegal purposes.[28] In *Hoffman Estates,* drug paraphernalia were displayed next to books and magazines entitled *High Times, Marijuana Grower's Guide, A Child's Garden of Grass,* and *The Pleasures of Cocaine.* A sign in the store referred to the "head" supplies used by frequent drug users. A design on cigarette papers showed a person smoking drugs.

The *Hoffman Estates* decision did not say that commercial speech may be prohibited for all products that might be used for an illegal purpose. Such reasoning could lead to prohibitions on almost all commercial expression. "Peanut butter advertising cannot be banned," a federal judge once observed, "just because someone might throw a jar at the presidential motorcade."[29] However, the commercial expression in *Hoffman Estates* was not protected commercial speech because it promoted the illegal use of drugs.

False, Misleading, and Deceptive Advertising To merit constitutional consideration, commercial speech not only must promote a lawful product or service but also must be true and not misleading. The state has a legitimate interest, the Court said in *Virginia Pharmacy,* in ensuring that the "stream of commercial information flows cleanly as well as freely." The Supreme Court ruled that ads offering prescription drugs, simple legal services, and houses for sale were eligible for constitutional protection because the ads were not false, misleading, or deceptive. The promotion of electricity by Central Hudson Gas & Electric was also eligible for constitutional protection because it did not mislead consumers. A later section will discuss deception in detail.

Generally, ads mislead if they make important false statements or leave the wrong impression. A federal appeals court ruled that the term *invoice* in a car dealer's advertisement is inherently misleading because many customers mistakenly believe that a car dealer's profit

[26]Ragin v. New York Times Co., 923 F.2d 995 (2d Cir.), *cert. denied,* 502 U.S. 821 (1991).
[27]Housing Opportunities Made Equal v. Cincinnati Enquirer, Inc., 943 F.2d 644 (6th Cir. 1990).
[28]455 U.S. 489 (1982). *See also* Camille Corp. v. Phares, 705 F.2d 223 (7th Cir. 1983).
[29]Dunagin v. City of Oxford, 718 F.2d 738 (5th Cir. 1983), *cert. denied,* 467 U.S. 1259 (1984).

is the difference between the sale price to the customer and the invoice price to the dealer. In fact, a dealer's invoice may have little relationship to the cost of a car to a dealer.[30]

The Supreme Court has said advertising the price of a drug or simple legal procedure is not misleading but that price advertising of complex services is. In *Bates v. State,*[31] the Court said that price advertisements for complex legal services, such as complicated divorces and estate settlements, could be prohibited because they would be misleading. Ads for complex services are misleading, the Court said, because attorneys cannot accurately fix a price before work begins on open-ended, time-consuming tasks. Only routine legal services that take a fixed amount of time can be accurately priced in advertising that does not mislead, the Court said. Routine services for which the price might be advertised include uncontested divorces and simple adoptions.

The Court also has ruled that attorneys' use of in-person sales talks can be prohibited because of the potential for deception. In-person solicitations can be prohibited because they, unlike lawyers' advertisements in the media, present dangers of coercing, intimidating, misleading, and invading the privacy of potential clients. The Court said an attorney's in-person appeal for business—often to a vulnerable potential client who is distraught by a divorce, an accident, or a death—is deceptive because it "may exert pressure and often demands an immediate response, without providing an opportunity for comparison or reflection."[32]

In 2003, Congress enacted the Can-Spam Act to reduce unsolicited commercial e-mail messages.[33] The law makes it illegal to send commercial e-mail messages, known as spam, with intent to deceive recipients about who is sending the message or the subject of the message. The Can-Spam Act also requires commercial e-mailers to provide a functioning address and an opportunity for recipients to stop the commercial messages. The law does permit companies to send warranty and safety information to customers who have purchased products.

LEGITIMATE GOVERNMENT REGULATORY INTEREST Once it has been determined that an advertisement is eligible for constitutional consideration because it accurately promotes a legal product or service, a court's analysis focuses on the constitutionality of the proposed government regulation. The second criterion of the *Central Hudson* test is whether a regulation serves a legitimate or substantial government interest. If the speech in question were political rather than commercial, government suppression would require proof of a *compelling* state interest under the standards of strict scrutiny. The lesser value of commercial speech is reflected in the more relaxed standard that the government demonstrate only a *legitimate* or *substantial* interest to justify regulation.

The government frequently has met the second part of the *Central Hudson* test quite easily by demonstrating an interest in preserving the health, safety, morals, or aesthetic quality of the community. In *Central Hudson,* the Supreme Court recognized the legitimacy of the New York Public Service Commission's desire to conserve energy. The Public Service Commission tried to curb Central Hudson's promotional advertising for electricity

[30]Joe Conte Toyota, Inc. v. Louisiana Motor Vehicle Comm'n, 24 F.3d 754 (5th Cir. 1994).
[31]433 U.S. 350 (1977).
[32]Ohralik v. Ohio State Bar Ass'n, 436 U.S. 447, 457 (1978).
[33]Pub. L. No. 108-197, 117 Stat. 2699 (2003) (codified at 15 U.S.C. §§ 7701–7713).

as part of a national policy of energy conservation. The Supreme Court declared the commission's complete ban on the utility's electricity promotions to be unconstitutionally broad but not before recognizing the legitimacy of the Public Service Commission's goal of saving energy. The Supreme Court also has said that traffic safety and the physical appearance of a city are sufficient state interests to justify banning commercial billboards if the other criteria of the *Central Hudson* test are met.[34]

In *Posadas de Puerto Rico Associates v. Tourism Co.,* a case in which the Supreme Court upheld a ban on truthful casino advertising, the Court recognized as a legitimate state interest a desire by the government of Puerto Rico to preserve the morality and welfare of the Puerto Rican people by discouraging gambling.[35] The gambling promoted by the casino ads on the island, Justice Rehnquist said for the Court majority, could result in "disruption of moral and cultural patterns, the increase in local crime, the fostering of prostitution, the development of corruption, and the infiltration of organized crime." Although the Supreme Court has struck down laws prohibiting the advertising of alcoholic beverages, the Court has recognized that governments have a legitimate interest in curbing the consumption of alcohol.[36]

DIRECT ADVANCEMENT OF THE GOVERNMENT'S REGULATORY INTEREST The third part of the *Central Hudson* test is whether a regulation on commercial speech "directly and materially" advances the government's legitimate interest. It is one thing to conclude that the government has a legitimate interest in establishing a regulation; it is a more demanding requirement for the government to then establish that the proposed advertising regulation would directly advance the state's interest. In *Central Hudson,* the Court said there is an "immediate connection between advertising and demand for electricity." Therefore, a ban on the electricity promotions would advance the state's interest in conserving electricity. Thus, when the Supreme Court struck down the blanket prohibition on energy advertising in *Central Hudson,* it was not because the Court was convinced the ban would ill serve the goal of conserving energy. The ban was struck down because it barred all advertising for electricity, even ads that promoted efficient uses of electricity.

Sometimes the Supreme Court has assumed, without hard evidence, that a regulation on advertising would advance a governmental interest. In the *Posadas* case, the Court assumed, without concrete data or anecdotes, that barring casino advertising in Puerto Rico would serve the government goal of keeping Puerto Ricans out of the casinos. Writing for the majority, Justice Rehnquist said it was "reasonable" for the Puerto Rican legislature to believe that advertising gambling on the island would increase the number of gamblers. Therefore, Rehnquist concluded that banning casino advertising would directly advance the state interest in curbing prostitution, crime, and other demoralizing activities the legislature said gambling spawned.

Since *Posadas,* the Supreme Court has been less willing to assume, without evidence, that a government regulation will serve a government interest. Instead of deferring to state regulators, the Court now says states must present evidence that a regulation will advance

[34]Metromedia, Inc. v. City of San Diego, 453 U.S. 490 (1981).
[35]478 U.S. 328 (1986).
[36]44 Liquormart, Inc. v. Rhode Island, 517 U.S. 484 (1996); Rubin v. Coors Brewing Co., 514 U.S. 476 (1995).

a legitimate interest. The government's burden, the Supreme Court has said, "is not satisfied by mere speculation and conjecture; rather, a governmental body seeking to sustain a restriction on commercial speech must demonstrate that the harms it recites are real and that its restriction will in fact alleviate them to a material degree."[37]

The Supreme Court has not been convinced that prohibitions on alcohol advertising would further the government's legitimate interest in curbing drinking. In *Rubin v. Coors Brewing Co.,* the Court struck down a federal regulation prohibiting statements of alcohol content on beer labels because the ban would not sufficiently advance a government interest in preventing "strength wars,"[38] contests in which brewers attempt to increase market share by advertising the high alcohol content of their beverages. In an opinion written by Justice Clarence Thomas and joined by seven other justices, the Court said that the government ban on labels containing the alcohol content of beer would not prevent strength wars because the regulations were so contradictory as to be "irrational."

The Court recognized that the labels were accurate and that the government had a substantial interest in protecting the health, safety, and welfare of its citizens by preventing brewers from competing on the basis of alcohol strength, a competition that might increase alcoholism. However, the Court said it could not uphold the constitutionality of irrational regulations that prohibited statements of alcohol content on beverage labels but permitted them in beverage advertising. Justice Thomas also found it irrational that federal law would prohibit alcohol statements in beer labels but permit them on labels of wines and spirits. There is little chance, Thomas said, that a statute combating strength wars will advance its aim "while other provisions of the same act directly undermine and counteract its effects."

Similarly, the Court struck down a Rhode Island ban on advertising alcohol prices in part because the government did not demonstrate that the ban would discourage drinking. In *44 Liquormart, Inc. v. Rhode Island,* the government of Rhode Island argued, but did not document, that competing advertisements would lower the prices of alcohol, thus encouraging consumption.[39] In the principal opinion for the Court, joined by three other justices, Justice John Paul Stevens said that "without any findings of fact, or indeed any evidentiary support whatsoever, we cannot agree with the assertion that the price advertising ban will significantly advance the State's interest in promoting temperance." Furthermore, there was no evidence that eliminating the ban on advertising would raise alcohol consumption. With no evidence that the ban would curb alcohol consumption, the Court was unwilling to uphold what Stevens considered a paternalistic ban on truthful speech about a lawful product.

In contrast, a federal appeals court ruled that the federal do-not-call registry does directly advance the federal government's interests in reducing intrusions upon consumer privacy and the risk of fraud and abuse.[40] Commercial telemarketers are prohibited from calling consumers who voluntarily sign on to the national do-not-call registry, which was created by the FCC and the FTC. The appeals court also ruled the law was sufficiently narrow to be constitutional.

[37]Edenfield v. Fane, 507 U.S. 761 (1993).
[38]514 U.S. 476 (1995).
[39]517 U.S. 484 (1996).
[40]Mainstream Marketing Services, Inc. v. F.T.C., 358 F.3d 1228 (10th Cir. 2004).

NARROWLY DRAWN BAN Besides directly advancing a legitimate state interest, a constitutional regulation on truthful commercial speech for a lawful product must be narrowly drawn. Courts have sometimes interpreted the fourth *Central Hudson* requirement to mean that a regulation on commercial speech has to be the "least restrictive" possible. However, the Supreme Court ruled in *Board of Trustees v. Fox* that restrictions on commercial speech may be constitutional even if they are not the least restrictive.[41] The *Fox* Court said there should be a reasonable "fit" between legislative interests and the regulations employed to achieve them.

The Court remanded the *Fox* case for a determination whether university regulations barring all private commercial activities in dorm rooms represented the proper fit of legislative goal and regulatory means. The regulations were challenged by companies prohibited from selling housewares in university dorms. The State University of New York at Buffalo defended the regulations, designed to prevent commercial exploitation of students and to create an educational atmosphere at the university. The Supreme Court recognized the legitimacy of the state's goals but returned the case to the lower courts for determination of the reasonableness of the ban.

In *Central Hudson,* the Court found the ban on electricity promotions to be unconstitutionally broad because it was more extensive than necessary to further the government interest in energy conservation. The Court recognized that the New York Public Service Commission had a legitimate interest in regulating advertising to conserve energy. But the ban was unconstitutional, the Court said, because it barred promotional information about efficient as well as inefficient uses of electricity.

The Court said the Public Service Commission had failed to demonstrate that its interest in energy conservation could not be advanced adequately by more limited regulation. Rather than ban all promotions, the Court said the Public Service Commission might further its conservation policy by ensuring that the utility's advertisements include information about the relative efficiency and expense of different uses of electricity.

The city of Cincinnati also failed to constitutionally match a regulation to a legitimate government goal. In *Cincinnati v. Discovery Network, Inc.,* the Supreme Court ruled unconstitutional a city ordinance that prohibited sixty-two newsracks distributing commercial handbills but allowed more than 1,500 other newsracks containing newspapers.[42] The ordinance was challenged by companies that distribute real estate and adult education booklets.

The Court agreed that the city had a legitimate goal of preserving the safety and aesthetics of the community by limiting the number of newsracks. However, the Court saw no relationship between the total ban on sixty-two commercial newsracks and the city's interests in preserving safety and aesthetics. Removal of the sixty-two racks would be a minuscule improvement, the Court said, if more than 1,500 equally ugly newspaper racks were allowed to remain. After struggling unsuccessfully to find a clear distinction between noncommercial newspapers and "commercial" real estate and education promotions, the Court was "unwilling to recognize Cincinnati's bare assertion that the 'low value' of commercial speech is a sufficient justification for its selective and categorical ban on newsracks dispensing 'commercial handbills.'"

[41] 492 U.S. 469 (1989).
[42] 507 U.S. 410 (1993).

In a case of alcohol advertisements, eight justices of the Supreme Court agreed that Rhode Island's total ban on truthful price advertising for alcohol did not fit properly with the state's goal of reducing drinking. Rhode Island had several alternatives to a ban on price advertising, alternatives that would reduce drinking without curbing speech, the Court said. The state could discourage drinking by raising prices of alcoholic beverages, raising taxes on alcohol, putting limits on purchases of alcohol as the government limits the purchase of prescription drugs, and conducting education campaigns to discourage drinking.

While striking down the Rhode Island law, the Supreme Court rejected a contention from the *Posadas* case that the government's power to regulate the sale of a product includes the right to ban commercial expression about the product. "The First Amendment directs that government may not suppress speech as easily as it may suppress conduct, and that speech restrictions cannot be treated as simply another means that the government may use to achieve its ends," Justice Stevens wrote in *Liquormart.* Under the Twenty-First Amendment, states may regulate—even prohibit—the sale of alcohol. But the Twenty-First Amendment does not permit states to restrict truthful speech about a lawful product, the Court said.

The Supreme Court also emphasized the importance of truthful speech about lawful products when it struck down tobacco advertising regulations. In *Lorillard Tobacco Company v. Reilly,* the Court found that Massachusetts had a compelling interest in protecting the health of children, but a prohibition of outdoor advertising of cigars and smokeless tobacco products within 1,000 feet of schools or playgrounds failed the fourth prong of the *Central Hudson* test.[43]

Writing for the Court, Justice O'Connor held that the breadth and scope of the outdoor restrictions did not represent a "careful calculation" of the burden on speech. Massachusetts had not appropriately considered the varying impact of the 1,000 foot boundary in rural, suburban, and urban locations. In a large city such as Boston, tobacco manufacturers and retailers would be unable to advertise in 87 percent to 91 percent of the city. To Justice O'Connor, the geographic reach of the restrictions would "constitute nearly a complete ban on the communication of truthful information about smokeless tobacco and cigars to adult consumers."

The Court also struck down a Massachusetts prohibition on indoor smokeless tobacco and cigar advertisements lower than five feet from the ground. This regulation failed both the third and fourth prongs of the *Central Hudson* test. "Not all children are less than 5 feet tall, and those who are certainly have the ability to look up and take in their surroundings," O'Connor said.

Although states have the authority to enact narrowly tailored advertising restrictions on smokeless tobacco and cigars, a federal statute governing the advertising of cigarettes preempts states from restricting cigarette advertisements to promote health. The Federal Cigarette Labeling and Advertising Act, however, does not preempt state power to control the sale of cigarettes. Thus, a Massachusetts ban on self-service displays of tobacco products was found to be constitutional.

A federal appeals court did find a "reasonable fit" between a ban on all "junk faxes" and a legislative attempt to prevent advertisers from shifting the costs of advertising to consumers.[44] Upholding a section of the Telephone Consumer Protection Act of 1991, which

---

[43]533 U.S. 525 (2001).
[44]Destination Ventures, Ltd. v. FCC, 46 F.3d 54 (9th Cir. 1995).

bans unsolicited faxed advertising, the Ninth Circuit ruled the ban advances the government's substantial interest in protecting consumers from having to pay to receive unsolicited messages that tie up their fax machines. The law can constitutionally prohibit companies from burdening consumers with paper costs and loss of time, the court said, even though technology may eventually allow all consumers to receive faxes instantaneously at no cost.

Furthermore, the court said the law is not too broad, even though it prohibits all unsolicited commercial faxes even if the sender is not motivated by profit. "The ban is even-handed," the court said, "in that it applies to commercial solicitation by any organization, be it a multinational corporation or the Girl Scouts."

◇ Summary ◇

The First Amendment protects commercial speech but to a lesser degree than it protects political expression. The Supreme Court has said that the hardiness and verifiability of commercial speech justify lesser constitutional protections on advertising than on political and social commentary. Commercial speech has been defined as expression promoting a commercial transaction.

Under a four-part test developed by the Supreme Court, restrictions on commercial speech are permitted even if the expression is accurate and promotes a lawful product or service. Under the four-part test, truthful commercial speech may be restricted if the government asserts a substantial interest that will be advanced by a regulation. The regulation must also be narrowly tailored to serve government objectives.

Unfair and Deceptive Advertising

Because false and deceptive commercial advertisements are outside constitutional protection, they may be banned. Advertisers also may be ordered to alter ads so that they cease to be deceptive. The required alterations may include warnings, disclosures, and corrections of earlier deceptive ads. Advertisers are also required to substantiate advertising claims.

Advertisements are regulated under a number of federal and state laws. The leading regulatory body is the Federal Trade Commission (FTC), which operates under the Federal Trade Commission Act of 1914 and is a five-person commission whose members are appointed by the president to staggered seven-year terms. The commission has a large staff of attorneys, economists, and accountants who originate inquiries, issue reports, and conduct investigations.

The FTC's rulings and reports not only define the scope of federal regulation but also determine standards for state and industry regulatory bodies. In some states, an advertiser who complies with the Federal Trade Commission Act may not be penalized under state antideception laws.

The FTC's primary mission is to protect consumers from unfair or deceptive market practices and to promote vigorous competition. The primary statutory authority for the FTC's activities is the Federal Trade Commission Act, which prohibits unfair methods of competition and unfair or deceptive acts or practices in or affecting commerce. The Federal Trade Commission Act gives the FTC authority not only over advertising but also over monopolistic and other anticompetitive activities. In recent years, the FTC has been especially concerned with preventing deception in advertisements claiming environmental, nutritional, and other health benefits.

The FTC shares jurisdiction or coordinates with the Department of Justice, the Food and Drug Administration, the Environmental Protection Agency, the Consumer Product Safety Commission, and numerous other federal agencies. The FTC also works with state agencies, notably the National Association of Attorneys General.

The Federal Trade Commission originally had jurisdiction only over unfair and deceptive acts or practices that hurt competing companies. In 1938, however, the scope of the Federal Trade Commission Act was broadened to provide protection for consumers as well as competitors.[45] At the heart of FTC advertising regulation is its power to require that advertisers substantiate the accuracy of advertising claims.[46] Since the 1980s, the FTC has narrowed the definition of deception and demanded more empirical evidence than before to establish that an advertisement is deceptive or misleading.

Unfairness

The FTC may stop both unfair and deceptive advertising. Section 5 of the Federal Trade Commission Act declares unfair competition and unfair or deceptive acts or practices in commerce to be unlawful.[47] The Federal Trade Commission has referred to its authority to stop unfairness as its "general law of consumer protection for which deception is the one specific but particularly important application."[48]

In the early 1970s, unfairness was described very broadly as whether a practice offended public policy, was immoral or unethical, or caused substantial injury to consumers or businesses.[49] In 1980, the FTC narrowed the focus of its unfairness inquiries to whether an advertisement or commercial practice causes substantial consumer injury.[50] In 1994, Congress defined an unfair act or practice as one that "causes or is likely to cause substantial injury to consumers which is not reasonably avoidable by consumers themselves and not outweighed by countervailing benefits to consumers or to competition."[51] The Federal Trade Commission Act permits the FTC to issue broad rules curbing unfairness in a whole industry if the harmful acts or practices are "prevalent." These "Trade Regulation Rules" and the advertising industry's resentment of them will be discussed in a later section.

Unfairness is more likely to arise in a company's treatment of customers than in advertising. Because the commission looks for substantial harm, the FTC is not concerned with trivial or merely speculative harms. In most cases of unfairness, substantial injury involves monetary harm, as when sellers coerce consumers into purchasing unwanted goods or services. In one case, a company acted unfairly by requiring consumers to buy expensive parts before company service personnel would reassemble furnaces they had dismantled.[52]

[45] 15 U.S.C. § 53.
[46] Kenneth Plevan & Miriam L. Siroky, *Advertising Compliance Handbook* 109 (2d ed. 1991).
[47] 15 U.S.C. § 45(a)(1).
[48] International Harvester, Inc., 104 F.T.C. 949 (1984).
[49] FTC v. Sperry & Hutchinson, 405 U.S. 223 (1972).
[50] "Statement of Policy on the Scope of Consumer Unfairness Jurisdiction," 4 Trade Reg. Rep. (CCH) 13,203 (Dec. 17, 1980).
[51] 15 U.S.C. § 45(n).
[52] Holland Furnace Co. v. FTC, 295 F.2d 302 (1961).

The FTC ruled that the Orkin Exterminating Company acted unfairly when it raised the yearly fee for more than 200,000 homeowners who had signed a contract to pay a certain yearly fee for a termite-free house. Finding Orkin's unilateral fee increase to be an unfair breach of contract, the FTC ordered the increase rescinded. The FTC said the fee hike caused substantial damage that consumers could not avoid and offered no compensating benefits, such as better service.[53]

Unwarranted health and safety risks also may support a finding of unfairness. A razor blade manufacturer was found to have acted unfairly when it distributed free samples of blades in newspapers, thus creating the possibility that small children might hurt themselves.[54] A tractor manufacturer also was found to have acted unfairly when it failed to tell customers that opening the gas cap after the engine was hot might result in dangerous "geysering" of gasoline.[55]

The FTC also may find it unfair to not protect customers' privacy. In 1998, the FTC and the popular website host GeoCities agreed to a consent order requiring GeoCities to post a clear privacy notice informing its customers what personal information the website collected and what it did with that information. Also, GeoCities agreed to obtain parents' permission before collecting any personal information from children under 12 years old. The GeoCities action was the agency's first involving privacy on the Internet.[56] GeoCities, purchased in 1999 by Yahoo! Inc., helps Internet users create their own websites.[57]

Congress took action of its own to protect privacy on the Internet. In 1998, Congress authorized the FTC to establish rules regulating collection of personal information by commercial websites directed at children. The Children's Online Privacy Protection Act[58] requires parents' permission before these sites collect information such as names, addresses, phone numbers, or social security numbers from children less than thirteen years old. The FTC's rules implementing the Child Online Privacy Protection Act took effect in April 2000.[59]

Deception

The FTC is more concerned with deception than with unfairness. Although deception is not defined in the Federal Trade Commission Act, the FTC has defined a deceptive ad as one that is likely to mislead a reasonable consumer with a material statement or omission.[60]

LIKELY TO MISLEAD Deceptive advertisements are those that either contain express falsehoods or create false impressions that tend to mislead. Courts and the FTC have long held that ads do not have to deceive someone to be deceptive; rather, ads must possess a "tendency," or "capacity," or be "likely" to mislead a reasonable consumer.[61] It does not matter whether the advertiser intends to mislead; an advertisement may have a tendency to

[53]Orkin Exterminating Co., 108 F.T.C. 263 (1986), *aff'd,* 849 F.2d 1354 (11th Cir. 1988).
[54]Philip Morris Inc., 82 F.T.C. 16 (1973).
[55]International Harvester Co., 104 F.T.C. 949 (1984).
[56]"FTC Files First Internet Privacy Case," *Communications Daily,* Aug. 14, 1998.
[57]"Yahoo! Will Purchase GeoCities," *Baltimore Sun,* Jan. 29, 1999, at 1C.
[58]15 U.S.C. §§ 6501-6506.
[59]64 Fed. Reg. 59888 (Nov. 3, 1999).
[60]FTC, "Policy Statement on Deception," appended to Cliffdale Assocs., Inc., 103 F.T.C. 110, 165 (1984).
[61]*Id.* at 184.

deceive regardless of the advertiser's intent. Deceptiveness is determined by the overall impression of an advertisement, not by isolated statements within it. Statements that might be susceptible to both a misleading and a nonmisleading interpretation will be considered deceptive.

REASONABLE CONSUMER Whether an advertisement is deceptive depends on the likelihood the ad will deceive a consumer "acting reasonably in the circumstances."[62] An advertisement is not deceptive if it would mislead only a few particularly gullible consumers. After all, the FTC has said, a company "cannot be liable for every possible reading of its claims no matter how far-fetched."[63] Thus, for example, the law does not help the consumer who thinks Danish pastry is always made in Denmark.[64]

Sometimes the FTC determines an advertisement is deceptive simply by reading or viewing it. However, often the FTC relies on the testimony of experts and the results of consumer surveys to determine the likelihood of deception. An ad is deceptive if it is likely to deceive a "substantial number" of consumers in the group to which it is directed.[65] An ad that tends to deceive 20 percent to 25 percent of the consumers in a survey is said to deceive a "substantial number."

Although many ads are aimed at the reasonable consumer in the general public, others are targeted at subgroups, such as children, the aged, or the ill. An ad that exaggerates the medicinal powers of a product might not deceive average, healthy adults but could be deceptive if directed to terminally ill consumers desperately seeking a cure.[66] Misleading promises of easy weight loss might not deceive the consumer of average weight but could deceive the obese consumer to whom it is directed.[67]

For many years, the FTC has been especially attentive to ads aimed at children, who are "unqualified by age or experience to anticipate or appreciate the possibility that representations may be exaggerated or untrue."[68] In an important children's case, the FTC ruled that advertisements for Galoob Toys were deceptive because they falsely represented the company's Micro Machines as a set when, in fact, they were sold separately.[69] The commission said the toy company and its advertising agency also deceived children by misrepresenting the ability of a doll to twirl on one foot and of a missile to travel a long way.

The FTC also has taken action against alcohol and tobacco advertising that appears to threaten youth.[70] In one case, the FTC halted the use of logos and messages for Redman smokeless tobacco in televised tractor- and truck-pulling contests watched by young people. The commission said televising Redman logos, flags, and other commercial symbols at

[62]*Id.*
[63]International Harvester Co., 104 F.T.C. 949, 1057 (1984).
[64]*See* Heinz W. Kirchner, 63 F.T.C. 1282, 1290 (1963).
[65]Patricia Bailey & Michael Pertschuk, "Deception Policy Statement Prepared by Commissioners Bailey and Pertschuk and Transmitted on Feb. 29 to the House Energy and Commerce Committee," 46 *Antitrust & Trade Reg. Rep.* 372, 393 (1984).
[66]Travel King, Inc., 86 F.T.C. 715, 719 (1975).
[67]Porter & Dietsch, Inc., 90 F.T.C. 770, 864-65 (1977), *aff'd,* Porter & Dietsch, Inc. v. FTC, 605 F.2d 294 (7th Cir. 1979), *cert. denied,* 445 U.S. 950 (1980).
[68]Ideal Toy Corp., 64 F.T.C. 297, 310 (1964).
[69]Lewis Galoob Toys, Inc., 56 Fed. Reg. 11,516 (consent order, March 19, 1991).
[70]*E.g.,* Canandaigua Wine Co., 56 Fed. Reg. 32,575 (consent order, July 17, 1991).

the contests violated the federal law prohibiting televised advertising of smokeless tobacco products.[71] Similarly, the Philip Morris Company agreed to stop placing signs behind scoring tables and other locations at baseball, basketball, hockey, and football games where television cameras would fix on them.[72]

The FTC reached an agreement with Audio Communications, Inc., to make it less likely that children will run up large phone bills by calling 900 telephone numbers. Audio Communications and at least one other company agreed to explain in television ads aimed at children that calls to 900 numbers cost money and that the children should get permission from their parents before placing a call to hear a message, buy a toy, or receive a gift.[73]

Advertisers are not liable if accurate ads aimed at doctors, lawyers, and other specialists are misunderstood by the average consumer. Laypersons read at their own risk the technical language in ads directed to experts.[74]

MATERIALITY To be deceptive, advertising that has a tendency to deceive the average consumer must be material. A material statement in advertising, like a material statement in corporate securities transactions, is one that is likely to affect a purchasing decision. A material advertising claim need not actually influence a consumer's decision to buy a product; nor must the consumer lose money for the ad to be considered deceptive. An ad is deceptive if it is likely to, or has the capacity to, affect consumer choices.

Material statements include express claims and deliberately implied claims about a product or service. An omission in an advertisement may also be material if the seller knows or should know that consumers need the omitted information to form an accurate impression. The FTC has found advertising claims or omissions about health, safety, durability, performance, warranties, quality, and cost to be material. Indeed, the FTC considers most factual advertising claims about a product to be material. After all, the commission has observed, advertisers would not make factual claims if the advertisers did not intend to influence consumers' choices.[75]

Consumer decisions would be affected, for example, by a material claim that only one brand of air conditioner ensures cooling on extra hot, humid days.[76] Likewise, a claim that aspirin relieves pain better than other pain relievers is material,[77] as is a claim that a skin cream contains aspirin. However, it would not be material to say in a tire advertisement that the tire manufacturer's main office is red when it is white. The color of the building would not be germane to a consumer's decision to buy tires.

Material statements that are likely to deceive may consist of express falsehoods. More often, deceptive ads contain statements that are literally true but create a false implication.

[71]Pinkerton Tobacco Co., 57 Fed. Reg. 4634 (consent order, Feb. 6, 1992).

[72]"Phillip Morris Agrees to Settle DOJ Charge of Violating Ban on Cigarette Advertising," *BNA Management Briefing,* June 7, 1995.

[73]*In re* Audio Communications, Inc., FTC File No. 892-3231 (consent order to cease and desist) (April 3, 1991). *See* Edmund L. Andres, "F.T.C. Obtains Accord Regulating '900' Numbers Aimed at Children," *N.Y. Times,* May 9, 1993, at A1, B5.

[74]Koch v. FTC, 206 F.2d 311 (6th Cir. 1953).

[75]*See* "Policy Statement on Deception," appended to Cliffdale Assocs., Inc., 103 F.T.C. at 182 (1984).

[76]Fedders Corp. v. FTC, 529 F.2d 1398 (2d Cir.), *cert. denied,* 429 U.S. 818 (1976).

[77]American Home Prods., 98 F.T.C. 136 (1981), *aff'd,* American Home Prods. Corp. v. FTC, 695 F.2d 681 (3rd Cir. 1982).

EXPRESS FALSEHOODS Expressly false statements about product attributes are almost always deceptive. The FTC has defined express claims as ones that make a direct representation. The meaning of express falsehoods, like the meaning of *libel per se,* can be determined from the plain meaning of the words.[78] The message is stated unequivocally. Express falsehoods include claims that merchandise is "antique" when it is not old enough to qualify as antique,[79] that coffee is "caffeine free" when the brew contains caffeine, or that goods are "fireproof" when they are only fire resistant.[80] Explicit falsity has also been found when merchandise was called "genuine" when it was a simulation or imitation.[81]

An ad also is deceptive if it contains an expressly false demonstration of a product. In the famous sandpaper shave case, Rapid Shave was made to appear in a television commercial to have the moistening power to soak sandpaper for an effortless shave. The voice in the television commercial told viewers they were seeing proof that Rapid Shave could shave "tough dry sandpaper." However, viewers were not shown sandpaper being shaved. Instead, they saw a piece of Plexiglas on which sand had been spread. After Rapid Shave was applied, a razor whisked the sand away.[82]

The ability of Rapid Shave to soften sandpaper was not disputed, at least if considerable time was allowed. But the viewer was not seeing sandpaper shaved. The FTC and the Supreme Court ruled the Plexiglas mock-up was materially deceptive because it was used as "actual proof of an advertising claim." Even though Rapid Shave could shave sandpaper if enough soaking time were allowed, the Supreme Court said the demonstration was deceptive because it falsely told viewers they were seeing objective proof of a product's performance. The Court said the false demonstration was similar to false testimony by a celebrity or expert.

Colgate-Palmolive, the makers of Rapid Shave, said it substituted Plexiglas for sandpaper only to compensate for the technical distortions of television. Colgate-Palmolive said sandpaper on television looked like unattractive, plain, brown paper. But the Court said simulations should not be employed if they cannot represent a product truthfully. The Rapid Shave case indicates, the Court said, "that television is not a medium that lends itself to this type of commercial, not that the commercial must survive at all costs."

The Court's ruling did not foreclose the use of mock-ups to overcome the technical distortions of television. Mock-ups may be used if they are not employed falsely to prove a product claim. For example, an advertiser could use mashed potatoes to represent ice cream in an ad for table linen if ice cream would melt too quickly under hot television lights. However, mashed potatoes should not be used in an ice cream advertisement to demonstrate the velvety texture and enticing colors of ice cream. Props are deceptive if they are used falsely as proof of a product claim.

IMPLIED FALSEHOODS More common and more difficult to identify than express falsehoods are statements or omissions in advertisements that create a false impression by

[78]Thompson Medical Co., 104 F.T.C. 648, 788 (1984).
[79]State v. Cohn, 188 A.2d 878 (Conn. Cir. Ct. 1962).
[80]Perfect Mfg. Co., 43 F.T.C. 238 (1946).
[81]Masland Duraleather Co. v. FTC, 34 F.2d 733 (3rd Cir. 1929).
[82]FTC v. Colgate-Palmolive Co., 380 U.S. 374 (1965).

implication. The FTC defines implied claims circularly as claims that are not express.[83] An implication can be thought of as a false meaning added to a truthful advertisement by the reader or viewer because of an impression the advertisement creates. For example, a consumer might infer that a tire manufacturer's claims are backed by scientific tests if "technicians" in white jackets attest to the tires' superior stopping power. If no scientific tests support the tire manufacturer's claims, the advertiser's use of white-jacketed technicians creates a false implication of scientific validity. Advertising claims that are technically true but deceptive because they create a false implication can be divided into at least fifteen categories.[84] Several categories are discussed below.

Reasonable Basis Implication The Federal Trade Commission requires that advertisers have a *reasonable basis* for the objective claims in their advertisements. Advertisers should be able to support all material claims with results from scientific tests or other appropriate evidence. Thus, an advertiser who says its tires stop faster than others should have scientific evidence to substantiate the claim.

An advertiser's ability to support substantive claims is a material element, the absence of which is deceptive. Consumers, the FTC says, are less likely to rely on claims for products and services if they know that the advertisers have no reasonable basis for making them.[85] Thus, the FTC may find an advertisement deceptive, even if the claim is true, if the advertiser has no reasonable basis for making the claim.

The FTC originated the substantiation requirement in 1972 when it ruled that an advertising claim by Pfizer Pharmaceutical lacked a reasonable basis.[86] Although *Pfizer* was technically an unfairness case, the FTC has frequently cited *Pfizer* for the proposition that advertising claims must be substantiated if an advertiser is to avoid deception.[87] In *Pfizer,* the FTC was not satisfied that the pharmaceutical company had adequate substantiation for its claims that Unburn suntan lotion "actually anesthetizes nerves" to relieve pain. In fact, the company could offer no scientific data to support the claim.

The FTC said that "failure to possess substantiation amounts to a lack of reasonable basis, which in turn is an unfair act or practice under Section 5" of the Federal Trade Commission Act. The FTC said in *Pfizer* that substantiation might be provided through scientific studies, existing medical literature, tests conducted by makers of similar competing products, or in some cases, the successful wide use of a product. Pfizer, however, had virtually no evidence for its claims for Unburn tanning lotion.

Advertisers should possess substantiation before they make claims about safety, performance, efficiency, quality, and price. If an advertisement asserts a certain level of scientific support by saying "tests prove" or "studies show," the advertiser must be able to provide supportive results for the claim from two scientifically valid tests. If an ad does not claim a certain level of supporting data, the FTC determines a reasonable basis for claims by considering the type of claim, the product, and the consequences for consumers

[83] Thompson Medical Co., 104 F.T.C. 648, 788 (1984).
[84] *See* Ivan Preston, "The Federal Trade Commission's Identification of Implications as Constituting Deceptive Advertising," 57 *U. Cin. L. Rev.* 1243 (1989).
[85] "FTC Policy Statement Regarding Advertising Substantiation," *in* Thompson Medical Co., 104 F.T.C. at 839–40 (1984).
[86] Pfizer, Inc., 81 F.T.C. 23 (1972).
[87] Gary Ford & John Calfee, "Recent Developments in FTC Policy on Deception," 50 *J. of Marketing* 98 (1986).

of a false claim. The FTC also considers the benefits to consumers of a truthful claim, the cost to the company of developing substantiation, and the amount of substantiation experts in the field believe is reasonable.[88]

The Firestone Tire & Rubber Company was found to have issued deceptive and unfair advertisements by failing to substantiate a claim that the company's Super Sport Wide Oval tires "stop 25 percent quicker." The tires did stop a car more quickly than other tires on wet concrete, but the company lacked "substantial scientific test data" to prove that the tires performed significantly better in the many different road conditions American motorists encounter.[89] Similarly, a company marketing Acne-Satin, a skin medication promoted by singer Pat Boone, lacked substantiation for its claims that the product "cures acne, eliminates or reduces the bacteria and fatty acids responsible for acne blemishes."[90]

The FTC may reconsider a substantiation ruling if scientific opinion changes. In 1974, the commission prohibited the Sterling Drug Company from claiming that Lysol Disinfectant Spray prevents colds. The FTC's ruling was based on the best scientific evidence of the time, which concluded that colds were transmitted by airborne viruses that would not be affected by Lysol. Lysol was thought to have no effect on airborne viruses because it was used to clean counters, tables, and other surfaces. However, the commission lifted its ban when new scientific evidence indicated that colds may be transmitted through contact with surfaces that can be cleaned with Lysol. As new research began to appear, the FTC said Sterling could advertise that Lysol can prevent colds as long as successive claims were supported by "competent and reliable scientific evidence."[91]

Proof Implication Another deceptive advertisement is one that falsely creates the impression that evidence presented proves a claim. A false implication of proof is created if an advertiser misrepresents the evidence presented to substantiate an advertising claim. Ads are deceptive if they misuse test data, create a phony aura of scientific support, or otherwise imply proof that does not exist. In the Firestone advertisement just mentioned, the company created a false implication of proof by saying that the company's "racing research" established that Firestone tires "stop 25 percent quicker." The implication was deceptive because, although the company had conducted tests, it had no tests comparing the ability of Firestone and other tires to stop a car under normal driving conditions.[92]

Bayer Corporation agreed to undertake a $1 million campaign telling viewers the company had made unsubstantiated claims for Bayer Aspirin. The Federal Trade Commission said Bayer had no substantiation for its advertised claims that taking an aspirin daily can prevent heart attacks and strokes. The FTC said a regular aspirin regime will not benefit some adults and others will be adversely affected by taking an aspirin each day. Bayer's aspirin-a-day advertisements ran for three years. Bayer consented to distributing

---

[88]"FTC Policy Statement Regarding Advertising Substantiation Program," *in* Thompson Medical Co., 104 F.T.C. at 839–40 (1984).

[89]Firestone Tire & Rubber Co. v. FTC, 481 F.2d 246 (6th Cir. 1973), *cert. denied,* 414 U.S. 1112 (1973).

[90]*In re* National Media Group, Inc., 94 F.T.C. 1096 (1979).

[91]*In re* Sterling Drug Co., Order Reopening and Modifying 1974 Cease and Desist Order, 48 Fed. Reg. 14,891, 14,892 (1983).

[92]Firestone Tire & Rubber Co. v. FTC, 481 F.2d 246 (6th Cir.), *cert. denied,* 414 U.S. 1112 (1973).

brochures and running advertisements providing substantiated information about aspirin's effectiveness in preventing heart attacks and strokes.[93]

Demonstration Implication Product demonstrations in advertisements may also create deceptive implications. In the Rapid Shave case discussed earlier, a mock-up was misleading because it falsely demonstrated the moistening power of a shaving cream. More often, however, a demonstration is true but nevertheless creates a false impression about how the product will perform in normal circumstances. The FTC found misleading an advertisement in which a sandwich was kept dry under water in a Baggies lunch bag while the sandwich in a competitor's bag was soaked. The demonstration was accurate, but it falsely implied that Baggies were superior to other sandwich bags for keeping food fresh in a refrigerator or lunchbox. "Dunking the sealed bags in a sink of water and swishing them vigorously . . . is not proof of the comparative abilities of the two bags to prevent food spoilage," the FTC said.[94]

The Standard Oil Company of California falsely implied through a demonstration of clean air and a pollution meter that Chevron gasoline with F-310 removed all or most pollutants from engine exhaust. In one ad, a car burning Chevron with F-310 emitted clear exhaust into a large see-through balloon tied to the exhaust pipe of the car. In another ad, the exhaust was contained in a transparent bag encircling the car. In a third, a meter dial labeled "exhaust emissions" pointed to "100" at the "dirty" end of the scale before Chevron with F-310 was used. After "just six tankfuls," the meter pointed to "20," four-fifths of the way toward "0" at the "clean" end of the scale. Meanwhile, another car in the ads, a car whose gasoline did not contain F-310, continued to emit dirty exhaust that clouded the balloon and bag.

The balloon ads were deceptive, the FTC said, because the clear Chevron exhaust appeared to contain no pollutants, when in fact it contained invisible but significant amounts of carbon monoxide and hydrocarbons. Independent scientific tests revealed that the F-310 additive did reduce pollutants but not as much as the balloon and bag demonstrations indicated. The ads were deceptive, the FTC said, "because of the substantial disparity between the visual impact of the demonstrations and the evidence which showed the actual average reductions."[95] The meter, too, was misleading because the drop of eighty units from the dirty end to the clean end did not correspond to the much smaller percentage reduction in pollutants a typical motorist would experience from using Chevron with F-310.

The U.S. Court of Appeals for the Ninth Circuit ruled that BBD&O, the advertising agency in the Chevron case, bore responsibility for the deceptive demonstrations. It is not enough that an advertising agency know that products will perform as the manufacturer claims, the court said. The agency also has a responsibility to represent that performance accurately. BBD&O argued that it should not be liable because it based the ads on information that had been validated by independent tests and approved by several departments at Chevron, including engineering, research, and law.

[93]Caroline Mayer, "Bayer Settles Ad-Claim Dispute," *Wash. Post,* Jan. 12, 2000, at E2.
[94]*In re* Colgate-Palmolive Co., 77 F.T.C. 150 (1970).
[95]*In re* Standard Oil Co., 84 F.T.C. 1401, 1470 (1974).

However, the Ninth Circuit said it was not sufficient for BBD&O to satisfy itself only that F-310 did in fact reduce pollution. The agency also had a responsibility to ensure the accuracy of the implicit representations the ads conveyed. Said the court:

> No specialized engineer was needed to put BBD&O on notice that a gauge which drops from a reading of 100 ("dirty") to 20 ("clean") implies a sweeping representation with reference to the change in level of pollution discharge. In light of the advertising agency's active participation in developing this advertising, it was BBD&O's responsibility to assure itself not only that the gauge was not rigged, but also that use of the gauge did not convey a distorted impression.[96]

No Qualification Implication Advertisements are also misleading if they omit a necessary qualification. The FTC ruled, for instance, that a Firestone tire advertisement was misleading because it claimed without qualification that Firestone was "The Safe Tire." The company's claim was supported by the statement that Firestone tires pass all of the company's inspections.[97]

However, although it was true that Firestone marketed no tires that failed company inspections, the FTC ruled that the unqualified claim that Firestone tires were "safe" was deceptive because it falsely implied that the tires were free of all defects. Indeed, 15 percent of the respondents in a consumer survey thought the company was claiming that its tires were free of defects. But tests available at the time of the advertisement were insufficiently accurate to detect all defects in a tire.

Ineffective Qualification Implication Consumers are always warned to read the small type in an advertisement for qualifications, but the FTC says ads may be deceptive even if they contain accurate but ineffective qualifications. "A qualification presented weakly has the same impact as a qualification completely absent," Professor Ivan Preston observes.[98]

The FTC ruled that the advertisements for Chevron gasoline with F-310 were deceptive not only because the clear bags belied scientific tests for pollution, but also because the visual impact of the clear bags overwhelmed the verbal and written qualifications in the broadcast and print versions of the ads. The verbal and written parts of both balloon ads did not claim that the Chevron exhaust was completely "clean," only that it was "cleaner" than the other exhaust. Nor did the ads claim that Chevron eliminated pollution, only that it reduced it. Despite this qualifying language, the Federal Trade Commission ruled that the ads were misleading because the "strong, predominant visual message" of the clear balloons and bags implied a complete reduction in pollutants. "The net impression," the FTC said, "is overwhelmingly influenced by the striking visual portions of the advertisements."[99]

Significance Implication Insignificant facts stated so that they appear to be significant also create a false implication in advertising. In one case, advertisements for Old Gold

---

[96]*In re* Standard Oil Co. v. FTC, 577 F.2d 653, 660 (1978).
[97]*In re* Firestone Tire & Rubber Co., 81 F.T.C. at 457 (1972).
[98]"The Federal Trade Commission's Identification of Implications as Constituting Deceptive Advertising," 57 *U. Cin. L. Rev.* 1243 (1989).
[99]*In re* Standard Oil Co., 84 F.T.C. at 1471 (1974).

cigarettes were deceptive even though they truthfully claimed that Old Golds were found "lowest in throat-irritating tars and resins." Though true, the ads created the false implication that smokers would benefit from choosing Old Golds over other brands.[100]

The study on which the cigarette ad claims were based was reported in *Reader's Digest.* In its report of the study, *Reader's Digest* concluded that the difference in tar and nicotine among cigarette brands was too insignificant to be important to smokers. One cigarette is "just about as good as another" to "nail down" a smoker's coffin, the *Digest* said.

The FTC ruled, in a decision upheld by a federal appeals court, that the Old Gold ads were deceptive because they falsely implied a significant difference among cigarettes. The advertisements, the court said, used the truth in a perverted way "to cause the reader to believe the exact opposite of what was intended" in the *Reader's Digest* article.

Similarly, advertisements for Carnation Instant Breakfast were ruled to be misleading when they claimed the product provided "as much mineral nourishment as two strips of bacon." Bacon, it turns out, is not a good source of the most commonly recommended minerals.[101] Likewise, claims that Gainesburgers dog food provides all the milk protein a dog needs were of misleading significance because dogs do not need milk protein.[102]

Puffery Implication Although advertising claims are supposed to be factual and represent the experience of the people making them, the law of advertising, like the law of libel, leaves room for subjective statements of opinion. Advertisers may exaggerate or "puff" their products on such subjective matters as taste, feel, appearance, and smell. The commission assumes that ordinary consumers do not take **puffery** seriously.

It is acceptable puffery for an advertiser to say that a foreign sports car is "the sexiest European,"[103] that "Bayer works wonders,"[104] or that a motor oil is the "perfect" lubrication, allowing a car to travel an "amazing distance" without an oil change.[105] "So far as we know," a federal appeals court said, "there is nothing 'perfect' in this world, which undoubtedly means nothing more than that the product is good or of high quality." Such exaggeration is recognized as puffery and creates no false implication.

Puffery becomes deception when exaggerated claims falsely imply material assertions of superiority. However, determining when puffery becomes a materially misleading statement is very difficult. The FTC ruled that Jay Norris Company went beyond acceptable puffery when it advertised that a television antenna was an "electronic miracle." The FTC said the statement was one of several exaggerated claims that could lead consumers to believe falsely that the antenna was generally superior.[106]

Expertise and Endorsement Implications The FTC defines an expert as someone who has acquired superior knowledge of a subject as a result of experience, study, or training.

[100]P. Lorillard Co. v. FTC, 186 F.2d 52 (4th Cir. 1950).
[101]*In re* Carnation Co., 77 F.T.C. 1547, 1549 (1970).
[102]*In re* General Foods Corp., 84 F.T.C. 1572, 1573 (1974).
[103]*In re* Bristol-Myers Co., 102 F.T.C. 21 (1983), *aff'd,* 738 F.2d 554 (2d Cir. 1984).
[104]*In re* Sterling Drug, Inc., 102 F.T.C. 395, *aff'd,* 741 F.2d 1146 (9th Cir. 1984).
[105]Kidder Oil Co. v. FTC, 117 F.2d 892 (7th Cir. 1941).
[106]*In re* Jay Norris, Inc., 91 F.T.C. 751 (1978), *aff'd,* Jay Norris, Inc. v. FTC, 598 F.2d 1244 (2d Cir.), *cert. denied,* 444 U.S. 980 (1979).

Endorsements by experts and celebrities, unlike statements by company spokespersons, are regulated because testimonials by experts and celebrities are thought to carry special weight with consumers.[107] If experts claim in an advertisement that a product is superior, FTC guidelines require that the experts have expertise relevant to their product endorsements. Experts are also supposed to have compared a product they endorse with others. Astronaut Gordon Cooper's endorsement of a fuel-saving automobile engine attachment was ruled to be deceptive because the astronaut's expertise was not in the field of automobile engines.[108]

If an organization endorses a product, the product should meet professional standards set by the organization.[109] Thus, mattresses endorsed by a chiropractic association should perform to standards set by the profession. A police department or sports team should base its selection of a product for official use on comparative tests with other products.

Neither celebrities nor ordinary citizens need possess special expertise to endorse a product. However, endorsements by celebrities and average citizens imply that consumers generally will experience the same personal satisfaction as the endorser. If the typical consumer's experience might be different, a disclaimer should say so.

According to FTC guidelines, celebrities and common citizens who claim to use a product they endorse should actually use it; if they discontinue use, they should also stop their testimonials. Singer Pat Boone's endorsement of Acne-Satin, a skin medication, was ruled to be deceptive in part because, contrary to his testimonials, not all his daughters used the product. Boone was ordered to contribute his share of profits from Acne-Satin sales as restitution for people who bought the product. The advertising agency also had to pay because it too was responsible for the deception.[110]

At one time, it was necessary to tell consumers whether celebrities were paid for their endorsements. Such disclosure is no longer necessary because the FTC reasons that consumers will assume that celebrities are paid for their testimonials. But an advertisement is supposed to reveal if a noncelebrity actor is paid to endorse a product. Twin Star Productions, Inc., agreed to pay $1.5 million to consumers deceived by program-length "infomercials" in which seemingly independent consumers made false and unsubstantiated endorsements for the EuroTrym Diet Patch, Foliplexx hair-loss product, and Y-Bron impotence treatment.[111] At the conclusion of an FTC proceeding, Twin Star agreed to stop airing infomercials as independent consumer programs when, in fact, they were paid advertisements.

Besides halting false statements about the ability of the products to reduce weight, restore hair, and revive potency, Twin Star agreed to discontinue the deceptive format in which actors are paid to appear as ordinary, independent consumers expressing honest opinions about the products. All future Twin Star infomercials are required to begin with this disclosure: "The program you are watching is a paid advertisement for [the product or service]." The company and its officers also were ordered to pay the FTC $1.5 million for distribution to purchasers of EuroTrym, Foliplexx, and Y-Bron.

---

[107]*See* Whitney Washburn, "FTC Regulation of Endorsements in Advertising: In the Consumer's Behalf?" 8 *Pepp. L. Rev.* 697 (1981).

[108]*In re* Cooper, 94 F.T.C. 674 (1979).

[109]Guides Concerning Use of Endorsements and Testimonials in Advertising, 16 C.F.R. § 255.4.

[110]*In re* Cooga Mooga, 92 F.T.C. 310 (1978).

[111]*In re* Twin Star Productions, Inc., 55 Fed. Reg. 45,656 (1990).

State Regulations

All fifty states have enacted legislation that, like the Federal Trade Commission Act, prohibits unfair competition and unfair acts and practices or otherwise allows citizens and companies to sue over deceptive advertising.[112] Under many state laws, consumers as well as competitors can sue not only to stop deceptive advertising but also to recover damages and attorneys' fees.

Although states can regulate advertising only within their borders, regulations in important commercial states, such as Texas or Florida, have a national impact. During the administrations of Presidents Ronald Reagan and George H. W. Bush, state legislatures introduced and occasionally passed bills to regulate the sale of cigarettes, ban tobacco and alcohol advertisements, and require warnings on tobacco packages, including the Surgeon General's finding that nicotine is addictive.

During the Reagan and Bush years of less government regulation, federal monitoring of deceptive advertising diminished, spurring greater regulatory efforts in the states. State attorneys general, in particular, became more aggressive, suing airlines, car rental companies, and other corporations over advertising that violated state laws, laws that sometimes reflected guidelines issued by the National Association of Attorneys General. National advertisers objected that they could not meet fifty different state standards for deception.

In a blow to state efforts to regulate national advertising, the Supreme Court ruled that states could not regulate airline advertising because federal airline rules preempt state law.[113] Because Congress claimed federal jurisdiction for regulation of airline advertising, the Court said that states could not sue airlines for failing to disclose ticket restrictions and charges in their advertisements.

Congress has not claimed exclusive federal jurisdiction over all national advertisements. Plaintiffs have been allowed to sue under state law for a variety of claims, including one that national ads falsely claimed a diet plan was safe when, in fact, it caused gallbladder disease.[114] The Supreme Court has opened a way for consumers to sue cigarette manufacturers who conceal or misrepresent information about smoking and health. In *Cipollone v. Liggett Group,* the Court ruled 7-2 that federal law did not bar smokers from suing cigarette companies for misleading advertising.[115]

◇ Summary ◇

A number of federal and state agencies prohibit harmful trade practices. However, the Federal Trade Commission is the main enforcer of truth in advertising. Deceptive advertisements contain material statements or omissions that are likely to mislead reasonable consumers. Ads are deceptive if they contain expressly false statements or demonstrations. Ads are also deceptive if they contain true statements that convey a misleading implication. Deceptive implications may be found in advertisements that lack substantiation, lack

[112] Kenneth Plevan & Miriam Siroky, *Advertising Compliance Handbook* 289 (2d ed. 1991).
[113] Morales v. Trans World Airlines, Inc., 504 U.S. 374 (1992).
[114] Maria Maldonaldo v. Nutri-System, Inc., 776 F. Supp. 278 (E.D. Va. 1991).
[115] 505 U.S. 504 (1992).

sufficient qualification, contain misleading proofs or demonstrations, imply false significance, puff excessively, and rely misleadingly on expertise and endorsements. Plaintiffs may also bring suits for deceptive advertising under state law.

Federal Remedies

The FTC has a number of powers to prevent or remedy deceptive advertising. Some are future-looking, providing guidance to advertisers so that they can avoid deceptive advertising. These powers include staff opinion letters, industry guidelines, and rules. Some FTC powers focus on the present, permitting the agency to halt or correct a misleading or deceptive ad. These include **consent decrees,** cease-and-desist orders, affirmative disclosure, and corrective advertising. In addition, the FTC, advertisers, and consumers can seek court injunctions to halt deceptive ads. One of the FTC's most important powers is the authority to require advertisers to substantiate advertising claims before they are disseminated.

The FTC has issued no special regulations to prevent fraud and deception on the rapidly expanding Internet. However, the FTC has sued several Internet advertisers for violating current law on deceptive or fraudulent advertising. The FTC has not determined whether cyberspace, with its convergence of telephones, broadcast media, and computers, is more like a magazine in which, for example, cigarettes may be advertised or more like television broadcasting, in which cigarette advertising is prohibited.

Most large national and international corporations, as well as many smaller businesses, have established sites on the web. There were more than 1.5 billion business and personal World Wide Web pages in 2000,[116] and the number of websites grows by seventy per minute.[117] The FTC has had a website since 1995 that includes advice about credit, fitness, working at home, and many other topics. In 2001, more than 400 million people worldwide used the Internet.[118] Approximately 100 million American adults used the Internet in early 2001,[119] a marked increase from the twelve million American users in 1995 and fifty-six million in 1998.[120]

Prospective Remedies

The FTC's opinion letters, advisory opinions, industry guides, and trade regulation rules are broad statements that tell advertisers before they disseminate advertisements the kinds of statements and practices that may be deceptive. These are *prospective,* or future-looking, guidelines that help advertisers to avoid deceptive practices.

STAFF OPINION LETTERS Staff opinion letters are not specifically mentioned in the FTC's rules. They are a form of quick, free advice that does not bind the commission. If an advertiser wants an informal opinion on whether an ad might violate the law, the advertiser can ask for an opinion letter from the commission.

---

[116]Michael Downey, "Life Is More Like 'Star Trek' Than '2001,'" *Boston Globe,* Jan. 5, 2001, at A15.
[117]Michael Kanell, "What Happened to WorldCom?," *Atlanta Journal and Constitution,* Jan. 31, 2001, at 1D.
[118]*Id.*
[119]Jefferson Graham, "Suspended Animation," *USA Today,* Feb. 12, 2001, at 3D.
[120]Charles Stein, "The Wild '90s: The Pleasures and Perils of Prosperity," *Boston Globe Magazine,* Jan. 17, 1999, at 10.

ADVISORY OPINIONS If advertisers want to know more than they can learn in a staff opinion letter about whether a contemplated activity would be legal, they can write to the FTC for an advisory opinion. An advisory opinion, which is more formal than a staff opinion letter, is placed in the public record and protects the requesting party who follows the advice from litigation until such time as the commission might shift its position.[121] However, although the advertiser who follows an advisory opinion is protected from a suit, an advertiser might find the commission's advice burdensome because the commission tends to be stricter in its advisory opinions than in its litigation.

INDUSTRY GUIDES Under Section 18 of the Federal Trade Commission Act, the FTC may prescribe "interpretive rules and general statements of policy with respect to unfair or deceptive acts or practices." One form of general statement is an industry guide. Unlike an advisory opinion, an industry guide is written for a whole industry. An industry guide is the FTC's interpretation of federal law but does not itself have the force of law. An advertiser who violates an industry guide may or may not be charged with deception or some other violation of federal law.[122]

FTC industry guides prescribe, often in minute detail, acceptable advertising and labeling of products as diverse as adhesives,[123] dog food,[124] and toupees.[125] FTC regulations on product endorsements and testimonials are issued in the form of industry guidelines, as are regulations on deceptive pricing, fuel economy advertising for new automobiles, the women's handbag industry, and cigarette labeling.[126] Sometimes industry guides are required by Congress. For example, a section of the Fur Products Labeling Act required the FTC to establish a fur products name guide so that animals used for furs would be uniformly identified. One FTC industry guide specifies that the word *free* may be used in an advertisement even if a consumer is charged a small fee for postage and handling.[127]

The FTC has issued guidelines to limit deception when advertisers claim environmental benefits from their products.[128] The guidelines prohibit general environmental claims such as "Eco-Safe" if the environmental benefits are not specifically listed. Use of the term *biodegradable,* the FTC said, should be reserved for advertising claims that can be substantiated with competent scientific evidence that the product will decompose in nature within a reasonably short period.

The FTC also has issued guidelines explaining when the agency will consider health and nutrition claims such as "low fat" or "high fiber" to be deceptive or misleading.[129] The FTC's policy derives from regulations issued by the Food and Drug Administration (FDA) for the labeling of foods.[130] Under FDA regulations, food labels must tell consumers what

[121]Advisory Opinions, 16 C.F.R. § 1.1-1.4 (1995).
[122]*See generally*, George Rosden & Peter Rosden, 3 *Law of Advertising* § 32.04[2] (1995).
[123]Guides Against Deceptive Labeling and Advertising of Adhesive Compositions, 16 C.F.R. § 235.
[124]Guides for the Dog and Cat Food Industry, 16 C.F.R. § 241.
[125]Guides for Labeling, Advertising, and Sale of Wigs and Other Hairpieces, 16 C.F.R. § 252.
[126]*See* George Rosden & Peter Rosden, 3 *Law of Advertising* § 32.04[2] (1993).
[127]Guide Concerning Use of the Word "Free" and Similar Representations, 16 C.F.R. § 251.
[128]Guides for the Use of Environmental Marketing Claims, 16 C.F.R. § 260.
[129]Enforcement Policy Statement on Food Advertising, 59 Fed. Reg. 28,388 (1994).
[130]"Food Labeling Regulations Implementing the Nutrition Labeling and Education Act of 1990: Opportunity for Comments," 58 Fed. Reg. 2066 (1993) (codified in part at 21 C.F.R. parts 5, 20, 104, 105, and 130).

nutrients, fat, calories, cholesterol, salt, and fiber are contained in labeled food, and the FDA sets criteria allowing food manufacturers to describe a food as "low fat" or "high fiber."

After the FDA issued its labeling regulations, the FTC announced the agency would look to the FDA's regulations for guidance when determining whether health and nutrition claims in food advertising are deceptive. The FTC said, for example, it would adopt the FDA's definition of serving size for judging whether advertised claims of nutritional benefits in food are truthful. The FTC also said it would rely on the FDA's standards of scientific evidence to substantiate health claims in advertising. The FDA requires that there be "significant scientific agreement" to support claims that a food may prevent disease. A year after the nutrition labels began appearing on food, an Illinois research organization found consumers are more knowledgeable about nutrition, but they eat more beef, chocolate chip cookies, and butter than before.[131]

RULES A more sweeping and legally potent FTC power is the agency's rule-making authority. Rules may be required by statute or may be issued under the FTC's broad authority to prevent unfair and deceptive practices. The commission favors rules, like industry guides, because they allow for a more uniform and efficient policy than individual commission decisions. Rules, like industry guides, affect whole industries, not just an individual company or advertiser.

Rules are more potent than industry guides because they have the force of law. Advertisers who violate a rule may be sued for engaging in deceptive acts or practices in violation of Section 5 of the Federal Trade Commission Act. Violators may be required to refund money, return property, pay damages, and pay civil penalties of up to $10,000 a day.[132]

When the FTC wishes to issue a rule, it must publish the text of the rule and reasons for proposing the rule. Advertisers, manufacturers, and the public can then present written comments and testify at hearings. A final rule can be challenged in a federal appeals court within sixty days of its promulgation.

Several rules are mandated by statute. For example, the Comprehensive Smokeless Tobacco Health Education Act of 1986 requires health warnings on smokeless tobacco products and advertising.[133] The Hobby Protection Act of 1973 requires that imitation political posters, literature, and buttons be marked with the year of publication.[134]

The FTC has issued a rule required by statute to curb misleading telemarketing. Under the Telemarketing Sales Rule, telemarketers must disclose "promptly and clearly" their identities and that they are attempting to make a sale.[135] The caller must also disclose the nature of the goods or services offered. Costs of purchasing, receiving, or using any good or service must also be conspicuously disclosed. The rule also prohibits calls before 8 A.M. and after 9 P.M. and prohibits threats and intimidation, profane or obscene language, and repeated calling that abuses or harasses. However, the rule does permit telemarketers, including publishers and cable operators, to call more than once within any three-month period.

[131]Jennifer Steinhauer, "Food Labels Don't Change Eating Habits," *N.Y. Times,* May 10, 1995, at B1.
[132]15 U.S.C. § 45(m)(1).
[133]Regulations Under the Comprehensive Smokeless Tobacco Health Education Act of 1986, 16 C.F.R. § 307.
[134]Rules and Regulations Under the Hobby Protection Act of 1973, 16 C.F.R. § 304.
[135]16 C.F.R. pt. 310.

Besides issuing rules mandated by statute, the FTC also issues trade regulation rules, often called *TRRs,* under its own authority. The commission first asserted the power to issue trade rules in the early 1960s, when it issued the rule requiring a health warning on cigarette packages.[136] In the years following, the commission issued a number of rules, often specifying detailed requirements such as what information must be included in advertising about the power output of home amplifiers[137] and how the size of television screens is to be measured (diagonally).[138]

Backed by a Supreme Court decision[139] and legislation,[140] the FTC in the 1970s issued several broad rules to prevent unfairness in advertising for eyeglasses, vocational schools, funeral homes, used cars, and other products and services. Businesses objected, arguing that rules based on "unfairness" were too vague to follow without undue uncertainty and expense. Opposition to the FTC prevailed when the agency proposed to ban all televised children's advertising as unfair. The ban was justified, the FTC argued, because the relationship between powerful, sophisticated corporate advertisers and susceptible children was inherently unfair.[141] The networks, advertisers, and toy manufacturers, with $661 million in advertising revenues at stake, disagreed. If corporate advertising to children is inherently unfair, they asked, why isn't all advertising unfair? Is even the average adult a match for the refined marketing and psychological skills of Madison Avenue professionals with millions to spend on an ad campaign?

Responding to the criticism of the FTC's aggressive campaign against unfairness, Congress passed legislation requiring the FTC to halt issuing broad unfairness rules, including its proposed ban on televised children's advertising.[142] By 1994, after years of acrimony, Congress again authorized the FTC to issue trade regulation rules but not vague rules attempting to prohibit a generalized "unfairness." The FTC is now authorized to issue trade regulation rules to halt unfair acts and practices that cause or are likely to cause "substantial injury" to consumers, when consumers cannot reasonably avoid the injury, and when the injury is not outweighed by countervailing benefits to consumers or to competition.[143]

To reduce the likelihood of vague rules, Congress limited FTC discretion in two ways. First, the Federal Trade Commission Act bars the FTC from relying on "policy" considerations alone in determining what is unfair. The new law permits the FTC to consider "established public policies"—such as the desirability of reducing smoking, protecting children, and curbing consumers' fat intake—when determining unfairness. But the agency may not base a trade regulation rule primarily on such public policies. The FTC must base a trade regulation rule on a likelihood of substantial injury that the consumer cannot avoid.

Second, the Federal Trade Commission Act permits the FTC to issue a trade regulation rule only to halt harmful acts and practices that are "prevalent." Congress did not want

[136]FTC Trade Regulation Rule for the Prevention of Unfair or Deceptive Acts or Practices in the Sale of Cigarettes, 29 Fed. Reg. 8325 (1964).

[137]Trade Regulation Rule: Relating to Power Output Claims for Amplifiers Utilized in Home Entertainment Products, 16 C.F.R. § 432.

[138]Deceptive Advertising as to Sizes of Viewable Pictures Shown by Television Receiving Sets, 16 C.F.R. § 410.

[139]FTC v. Sperry & Hutchinson Co., 405 U.S. 233 (1972).

[140]Magnuson-Moss Warranty Federal Trade Commission Improvement Act of 1975, 15 U.S.C. § 45.

[141]FTC Staff Report on Television Advertising to Children (1978).

[142]Federal Trade Commission Improvements Act of 1980, Pub. L. No. 96-252 (1980).

[143]15 U.S.C. § 45(n).

to regulate practices that cause only isolated, insignificant harms. Harmful acts or practices are prevalent, the statute says, if they are the type the FTC has already ordered to be halted or if they present a "widespread pattern of unfair or deceptive acts or practices."[144] A review every ten years is supposed to weed out rules no longer necessary.

Halting Advertisements

If the FTC's warnings in advisory opinions, industry guides, and rules fail to prevent deceptive advertising, the FTC can halt illegal ads through the use of consent decrees and cease-and-desist orders. In addition, competing advertisers who might be hurt by a deceptive advertisement can seek a court injunction.

CONSENT DECREES More than 90 percent of FTC cases are settled by consent decrees in which a party agrees to discontinue an advertising practice.[145] Advertisers have a strong incentive to sign consent decrees. If they do not, the FTC may file a formal complaint against them. The formal complaint is often accompanied by considerable bad publicity, much more than accompanies a consent decree. In addition, an advertiser who signs a consent decree is not required to admit to false or deceptive advertising. Furthermore, a consent decree saves the costs and time of litigation. A signed consent order is published for public comment and becomes final after sixty days. Failure to abide by a consent order subjects a company to fines of up to $10,000 a day for as long as the advertising campaign continues.

The FTC has been actively seeking consent agreements to halt misleading infomercials and require advertisers to reimburse consumers who are misled. In a consent agreement with the Synchronal Corporation, the FTC ordered the New York company not to broadcast infomercials containing unsubstantiated claims for a baldness cure and ordered the company to pay $3.5 million into a consumer reimbursement fund.[146] In another consent order, the National Media Corporation agreed not to advertise Cosmetique Francais in infomercials making false claims about the efficacy or safety of skin treatments.[147] The company agreed to place $275,000 into a fund to be paid to consumers.

In response to the first complaint filed by the FTC against an Internet advertiser, Brian Corzine, who operated as Chase Consulting on America Online, agreed to refund the $99 customers paid him for advice to repair bad credit ratings. Corzine allegedly advised customers to use new federal taxpayer identification numbers on credit applications in place of their social security numbers.[148] The FTC said customers who followed Corzine's advice would be providing false information.

Most consent decrees originate when a citizen or—more frequently—a competitor sends a letter to the FTC complaining about an advertising practice. Commission staff members, either in Washington, D.C., or at one of the several regional FTC bureaus, may also originate an inquiry. If it appears that ads are deceptive, the staff conducts an investigation. If the investigation reveals that corrective action may be necessary, a proposed

---

[144]15 U.S.C. § 57a(b)(3).
[145]George Rosden & Peter Rosden, 3 *Law of Advertising* § 33.01 (1999).
[146]Synchronal Corp., 59 Fed. Reg. 33,293 (1993).
[147]National Media Corp., 58 Fed. Reg. 41,095 (1993).
[148]Stuart Elliott, "Court Halts Ad for Credit Repair," *N.Y. Times*, Sept. 15, 1994, at D17.

complaint may be submitted to the commission. The commission notifies the party of the proposed complaint and asks whether the party would sign a consent order agreeing to discontinue the deceptive practice.[149] If so, the complaint can be abandoned.

CEASE-AND-DESIST ORDERS If consent cannot be reached, the FTC may issue a formal complaint leading to a cease-and-desist order. Once the formal complaint is issued, the advertiser loses the opportunity to sign a consent order. The commission begins the cease-and-desist proceedings if it determines that the action would be "to the interest of the public" as required by Section 5 of the Federal Trade Commission Act. As Justice Brandeis said, that interest must be "specific and substantial."[150] If deception is trivial, the commission may decide that seeking a cease-and-desist order is not in the public interest.

The FTC has wide discretion to decide whether the public interest would be served by legal action against an advertisement. In deciding whether to take action, the FTC will answer such questions as how many consumers were deceived, how much money they lost, whether market forces would fix the problem without government intervention, and whether government intervention would be an effective deterrent.[151]

When the FTC issues a complaint against an advertiser, an investigation proceeds to adjudication. The FTC announces the complaint in a widely distributed press release sometimes accompanied by a press conference, either of which may damage a company's sales.[152] When the complaint is issued, the case is assigned to an FTC administrative law judge, who conducts a hearing much like a trial. The agency has the burden to establish substantial evidence that an advertiser has violated the law. The administrative law judge either dismisses the case or issues a cease-and-desist order that can be appealed to the full commission and then to a federal appeals court.

A cease-and-desist order becomes final after all appeals or after time runs out to make an appeal. Failure to abide by a cease-and-desist order, as with failure to abide by a consent decree, can lead to fines of up to $10,000 a day, but the fines are usually much less. In fact, a company might decide it makes better business sense to continue the ads and sustain the fines than to stop a successful ad campaign.

In one of the most famous and long-running cases, the FTC won a judgment against the makers of Geritol fourteen years after a complaint was filed to halt misleading advertisements. The FTC filed a complaint in 1962 charging that the J. B. Williams Company's television advertisements for Geritol were misleading. The FTC said the ads for the vitamin-and-iron tonic misleadingly said the product was an effective remedy for tiredness, loss of strength, and that "run-down" feeling. The FTC found the ad deceptive because Geritol is effective only in a minority of cases, in which tiredness is caused by a lack of the iron and vitamins in Geritol. In most cases, fatigue is caused by factors not affected by Geritol.

In 1964, the FTC issued a cease-and-desist order telling J. B. Williams to include statements in its ads that the vast majority of people who are run down do not suffer from iron or vitamin deficiencies that Geritol might correct. Two years later, the case was given

[149]George Rosden & Peter Rosden, 3 *Law of Advertising* § 33.02[2] (1999).
[150]FTC v. Klesner, 280 U.S. 19, 28 (1929).
[151]Deceptive and Unsubstantiated Claims Policy Protocol, 4 Trade Reg. Rep. (CCH) 39,059 (1975).
[152]George Rosden & Peter Rosden, 3 *Law of Advertising* § 34.03 (1999).

to the Justice Department when J. B. Williams did not comply with the cease-and-desist order. The company was fined $800,000 in 1973 for violating the FTC's order, but a court of appeals ordered a new trial.[153] In 1976, fourteen years after the complaint was filed, the FTC won a $280,000 judgment against the makers of Geritol.

INJUNCTIONS In some cases of deceptive advertising, particularly when public health might be at risk, the most important FTC goal is to stop the offending advertisement quickly. This can be accomplished with an injunction. Under Section 13 of the Federal Trade Commission Act, the commission can ask a federal district judge for an injunction to stop deceptive advertising for food, drugs, or cosmetics.[154] For example, in *FTC v. National Commission on Egg Nutrition,* the FTC obtained a temporary injunction stopping statements asserting there is no scientific evidence linking egg consumption and heart disease.[155]

Although the commission obtained a temporary injunction in the *Egg Nutrition* case, the agency usually does not seek a permanent injunction, preferring to act through the slower and more thorough administrative process of seeking consent decrees or cease-and-desist orders. However, these processes are much too slow for consumers whose health is being harmed by a product or for companies being hurt commercially by a competitor's deceptive advertisements. Advertisers damaged by competitors' ads often seek injunctions in federal court under the Lanham Act, a subject addressed shortly.

Required Statements

Not only can the FTC halt deceptive advertising and punish the advertiser, but the agency can also order alterations in advertisements to make them accurate. Besides requiring substantiation, the FTC can tell advertisers that they must include certain words or phrases in their ads and correct false impressions created by deceptive ad campaigns.

The FTC's power to alter the content of advertisements is a power not usually enjoyed by the government. Critics charge that such a power violates the First Amendment as well as the purpose of the Federal Trade Commission Act. The FTC, critics say, is supposed to prevent deception, not require the dissemination of information. But defenders of affirmative disclosure requirements say that the FTC cannot meaningfully prohibit deception unless it can sometimes require that statements be added to advertisements.

AFFIRMATIVE DISCLOSURE The Federal Trade Commission Act does not explicitly grant the FTC power to order disclosure. But Congress did recognize that advertisers must reveal facts necessary to keep ads from being deceptive.[156] Silence by an advertiser is not always deceptive, but silence is deceptive if it means a consumer might be hurt.[157]

Often a consent decree contains an affirmative disclosure requirement. In one case, the Morton Salt Company agreed to stop advertising Lite Salt in such a way that consumers would think it was more healthful than ordinary salt. In signing the consent order,

[153]United States v. J. B. Williams Co., 498 F.2d 414 (2d Cir. 1974).
[154]*See* FTC v. Sterling Drug, Inc., 317 F.2d 669, 671 (2d Cir. 1963).
[155]517 F.2d 485 (7th Cir. 1975).
[156]Committee on Interstate and Foreign Commerce, H.R. Rep. No. 1613, 75th Cong., 1st Sess. 5 (1937).
[157]Alberty v. FTC, 182 F.2d 36 (D.C. Cir. 1949), *cert. denied,* 340 U.S. 818 (1950).

the company agreed that future advertising of Lite Salt would contain the statement: "Not to be used by persons on sodium- or potassium-restricted diets unless approved by a physician."[158] In another case of affirmative disclosure, the FTC ordered the J. B. Williams Company to tell customers in Geritol ads that a vitamin-and-iron supplement will probably not correct a run-down feeling. Health warnings on cigarette packages are also a form of affirmative disclosure.

CORRECTIVE ADVERTISING In rare cases, the FTC requires that advertisements contain statements to correct misrepresentations created by a long-term, misleading advertising campaign. In a case involving Doan's pills, the FTC may impose corrective advertising if consumers develop false beliefs due to an advertising campaign and if consumers are likely to hold those false beliefs into the future.[159] To determine whether corrective ads are necessary, the FTC considers consumer surveys, the duration of the ads, the persuasiveness of the ad claims, and how sophisticated the audience for the ads is.

In the Doan's case the FTC imposed a corrective advertising requirement on the maker of for eight years advertisements said that Doan's was an effective remedy for back pain and that the pills contained special ingredients not found in other nonprescription pain relievers. The FTC said that the ads made an unsubstantiated claim that Doan's pills were better for relieving back pain because of special ingredients. The FTC said the pills do contain ingredients not found in other nonprescription pain relievers, but there was no evidence Doan's pills were more effective because of the ingredients. The FTC told Novartis Corporation, Doan's pills' manufacturer, to stop making the "special ingredients" claims. The FTC also ordered Novartis to include a disclaimer in their ads: "Although Doan's is an effective pain reliever, there is no evidence that Doan's is more effective than other pain relievers for back pain."

In the Doan's decision, the FTC said that it did not consider corrective advertising to be a "drastic remedy." It said that requiring a truthful message to counteract beliefs created by deceptive advertising is an "appropriate method" to tell the public the original ad was incorrect and to stop a company profiting from its deception. The FTC said corrective advertising may be required when "a preponderance of the evidence"shows a false belief will remain after the advertising campaign. The agency said it did not have to show with "certainty" that misbeliefs will linger. The FTC also said it could require corrective advertising even if the deceptive advertising campaign was not effective in boosting sales.

The U.S. Court of Appeals for the District of Columbia Circuit upheld the FTC's Novartis decision.[160] The court said the FTC may impose a corrective advertising requirement if (1) deceptive advertising substantially has helped to create false beliefs in the public's mind, (2) the false beliefs likely will remain after the advertising campaign stops, and (3) consumers continue making purchase decisions based on the false beliefs. The court said the FTC supported its finding that the Doan's pills advertisements met this test. The court said the FTC's use of survey research results and expert testimony was sufficient.

---

[158]Morton-Norwich Products, Inc., [1973-1976 Transfer Binder] Trade Reg. Rep. (CCH) ¶ 20,891 (1975).
[159]Novartis Corp., 1999 FTC LEXIS 90 (May 13, 1999).
[160]Novartis Corp. v. FTC, 223 F.3d 783 (D.C. Cir. 2000).

In the well-known Listerine case, the FTC required the Warner-Lambert Company to make statements in its advertising to correct a long-running campaign claiming that use of Listerine mouthwash would help to prevent colds.[161] The FTC ordered Warner-Lambert to include in $10 million of its advertising the statement that Listerine "will not help prevent colds or sore throats." The FTC also ordered the company to use the phrase, "Contrary to prior advertising." However, the U.S. Court of Appeals for the District of Columbia Circuit said requiring that phrase violated Warner-Lambert's First Amendment rights. The court said the FTC had required more speech than needed to correct the false impression. The FTC's order, the court said, was broader than necessary to set the record straight. The court did uphold the FTC's requirement that Warner-Lambert say Listerine would "not help prevent colds or sore throats."

In a 2006 fraud and racketeering case, Federal District Judge Gladys Kessler ordered the major cigarette companies to make corrective statements about the harm to health caused by smoking.[162] Judge Kessler also ordered Philip Morris, Lorillard, R.J. Reynolds and other cigarette manufacturers to point out to consumers the addictiveness of smoking and nicotine and the lack of any significant health benefit from smoking a "low tar," "light," "mild," or "natural" cigarette. The judge ordered the major tobacco companies to place full-page corrective statements in major newspapers on successive Sundays and to air 15-second corrective advertisements once a week on network television during prime-time for a year. In addition, the companies were told to run corrective statements on their websites and on cigarette packs themselves.

The FTC first required corrective advertising in 1971. In a consent order, the FTC told the ITT Continental Baking Company to correct a false impression created by a long-term series of ads for the company's Profile bread.[163] The ads suggested Profile bread contained fewer calories than other breads. Rather, Profile bread contained the same number of calories but was sliced thinner than other breads. In televised corrective ads, ITT Continental fulfilled the FTC requirement to correct a long-running, misleading ad campaign without unnecessarily damaging the company's credibility.

Competitor Remedies

Consumers, of course, are not the only people hurt by deceptive advertisements. Advertisers, too, may be hurt by the false and deceptive claims of competing companies. However, the FTC offers little immediate relief for a competitor whose major concern is to quickly stop a deceptive ad that may hurt business. Even if the FTC agrees to seek an injunction, the process may be too slow to be of much help to the damaged competitor. Therefore, companies often seek court injunctions themselves to stop the deceptive ads of competing companies.

Companies seek injunctions under Section 43(a) of the Lanham Trademark Act of 1946, the same act discussed earlier in the intellectual property chapter. Besides protecting trademarks, the Lanham Act, as amended in 1988, prohibits any person's "false or misleading representation of fact" in "commercial advertising or promotion" that "misrepresents the

[161]Warner-Lambert Co. v. FTC, 562 F.2d 749 (D.C. Cir. 1977), *cert. denied*, 435 U.S. 950 (1978).
[162]United States v. Philip Morris USA, Inc., 499 F. Supp. 2d 1 (D.C.D.C. 2006).
[163]ITT Continental Baking Co., 79 F.T.C. 248 (1971).

nature, characteristics, qualities, or geographic origin of his or her or another person's goods, services, or commercial activities."[164] Anyone, whether a competitor or not, who believes that he or she "is or is likely to be damaged" by deceptive advertising may seek an injunction. Courts, however, have often restricted recovery under the Lanham Act to those who have suffered "competitive injury." The U.S. Court of Appeals for the Third Circuit has ruled that consumers may not sue sellers for false advertising under the Lanham Act.[165] Plaintiffs usually seek to halt an offending ad, but they may also be entitled to significant monetary damages.

Before the 1988 amendments to the Lanham Act, competitors could sue under Section 43(a) only if the defendant's advertisement contained false statements about his or her own products. After the 1988 amendments, anyone may sue to stop advertisements in which defendants make false claims either about their own products or about the plaintiff's.

Employing the law before 1988, the makers of Minute Maid orange juice halted Tropicana orange juice ads that contained falsehoods about Tropicana. In the ads, Olympic champion Bruce Jenner squeezed fresh oranges and poured the juice into a Tropicana carton as a voice proclaimed, "It's pure, pasteurized juice as it comes from the orange."[166]

The Coca-Cola Company, which sells Minute Maid, claimed the Tropicana ads were misleading because Tropicana orange juice, like most ready-to-serve orange juices, is not packaged as it "comes from the orange." It is pasteurized and sometimes frozen before packaging. Even though the Tropicana ad said the juice was pasteurized, the U.S. Court of Appeals for the Second Circuit granted a preliminary injunction to stop the ads because they were likely to harm Minute Maid. A "not insubstantial" number of consumers surveyed mistakenly believed Tropicana juice came unprocessed from the orange.

Often competitors attempt to stop deceptive comparative advertisements under Section 43(a). All ads invite comparison, but so-called comparative ads point out the similarities and differences between an advertiser's product and its competitors'. The FTC has defined comparative advertising as ads that compare named or identified competing brands for objectively measurable attributes or price.[167] Although advertisers, the networks, and the FTC once frowned on comparative advertisements, the FTC now encourages companies to name and compare competitors' products in advertisements.[168] Comparative ads, which are popular today, are thought to help consumers make better choices.

In a well-known comparative ad case, Johnson & Johnson, the manufacturer of Tylenol, obtained an injunction against Anacin ads that falsely claimed Anacin was a superior pain reliever.[169] The televised ads claimed Anacin could reduce inflammation from muscle strain, backache, and tendonitis faster than other pain relievers. "Your body knows the difference between these pain relievers . . . and Adult Strength Anacin," the ad said. Unlike the Tropicana ad, which did not mention Minute Maid by name, the Anacin ad showed the competing products—Datril, Tylenol, and Extra Strength Tylenol—on the screen. A federal court enjoined the Anacin ads because they left the impression with consumers

[164] 15 U.S.C. § 1125(a).
[165] Serbin v. Ziebart Int'l Corp., 11 F.3d 1163 (3d Cir. 1993).
[166] Coca-Cola Co. v. Tropicana Prods., Inc., 690 F.2d 312 (2d Cir. 1982).
[167] 16 C.F.R. § 14.15(b) n.1.
[168] 16 C.F.R. § 14.15(b).
[169] American Home Prods. Corp. v. Johnson & Johnson, 577 F.2d 160 (2d Cir. 1978).

surveyed that Anacin was a better pain reliever overall. The real superiority of Anacin, if any, was its ability to reduce inflammation.

Although companies usually seek an injunction under Section 43(a) to stop a competitor's deceptive advertisement, plaintiffs may also seek monetary damages—large monetary damages. In 1986, the U.S. Court of Appeals for the Ninth Circuit upheld a $40 million damage award against Jartran rental truck company for its deceptive ads during a marketing battle with U-Haul.[170] Jartran's ads deceptively portrayed the company's rates as lower and its trucks as newer than U-Haul's. The court awarded U-Haul $6 million in benefits that Jartran received from its deceptive advertising campaign and $13.6 million that U-Haul had to spend to counter Jartran's deceptive ads. Then the court doubled the award to U-Haul as the Lanham Act allows when ads hurt a competitor.

A federal appellate court found Papa John's slogan and comparative advertising campaign were not false or misleading under the Lanham Act.[171] Using the slogan "Better Ingredients. Better Pizza," Papa John's ads said its superior ingredients made its pizza better than Pizza Hut's. Pizza Hut sued, claiming false advertising. The Fifth Circuit said the slogan was puffery, a vague "expression of opinion." The court also found Papa John's slogan and advertising campaign were truthful: Papa John's used different ingredients than Pizza Hut. The ads also were not misleading, the court said, since Pizza Hut did not present sufficient evidence to show that consumers purchased Papa John's pizza because they believed the company used better ingredients.

The authors of a treatise on advertising have offered several suggestions for avoiding litigation over comparative advertisements, including the following:[172]

- Make comparative ads truthful.
- Avoid subjective claims. Use objective claims that can be substantiated.
- Use reliable independent testing services or public surveying firms to substantiate claims.
- Keep the results of the substantiation.
- Present the comparison fairly.
- Avoid knocking the competitor's business practices.

Racketeering

Because individual consumers cannot sue over deceptive advertising under the Federal Trade Commission Act and often cannot sue under the Lanham Act, consumers sometimes can sue under racketeering statutes. Recently, consumers have joined class action suits under state or federal racketeering laws against advertisers whose deceptive advertising caused them harm. The federal law is the Racketeer Influenced and Corrupt Organizations Act, or RICO.[173] The RICO law was enacted in 1970 to curb organized crime's infiltration of legitimate businesses. The law prohibits a "pattern of racketeering" involving an interstate enterprise, usually fraudulent use of telephones or the mail.

170U-Haul Int'l, Inc. v. Jartran, Inc., 793 F.2d 1034 (9th Cir. 1986).

171Pizza Hut, Inc. v. Papa John's International, Inc., 227 F.3d 489 (5th Cir. 2000), *cert. denied,* 121 S. Ct. 1355 (Mar. 19, 2001).

172George Rosden & Peter Rosden, 3 *Law of Advertising* § 31.05 (1999).

17318 U.S.C. §§ 1961–1968.

In a 2006 fraud and racketeering ruling, a federal court ordered the major cigarette companies to stop the lies, misrepresentations and deceit to the American public "about the devastating health effects of smoking and environmental tobacco smoke."[174] Federal district judge Gladys Kessler enjoined the companies from future acts of fraud and ordered them to issue a series of corrective statements in newspapers, on television, on company websites and on cigarette displays and packages. The judge also ordered the cigarette companies to cease using terms such as "mild," "light," and ultralight," terms the court said falsely implied the cigarettes are less harmful than normal cigarettes. Judge Kessler was barred by earlier court rulings from imposing multibillion dollar penalties that the Justice Department and citizen groups had sought.

Earlier, a federal court in Pennsylvania ruled that consumers could bring a RICO claim against the Ralston Purina Company over advertising that falsely claimed Purina's Puppy Chow would lessen the severity of a disabling bone ailment called canine hip dysplasia.[175] The threat of a RICO suit, with its triple damages, has spurred some companies to settle RICO claims out of court.

◇ Summary ◇

The Federal Trade Commission has several powers and remedies to keep the flow of commercial information clean. The forward-looking powers include staff opinion letters, advisory opinions, industry guides, and trade regulation rules. In addition, the FTC can halt deceptive advertising through consent decrees, cease-and-desist orders, and injunctions. The FTC can also require that advertisements contain statements necessary to leave an accurate impression or to correct misrepresentation. In addition, companies may seek injunctions under the Lanham Act to halt false or misleading advertisements and promotions by competitors. Consumers may not sue advertisers under the Federal Trade Commission Act or the Lanham Act, but they may sue under state law and may eventually prevail in a RICO suit.

Other Federal Regulations

While deception and unfairness are major concerns in the regulation of advertising, consumers claim protection from fraud and misuse of electronic data in the modern media. This section examines regulations on the amount and content of broadcast advertising, the control and security of personal data, and the regulation of contests and the depiction of money in advertising.

Children's Television

Parents and citizen groups often contend that children's television programs contain too much advertising. In response, the 1990 Children's Television Act limits the quantity of advertising aired during children's programs. The 1990 legislation limits commercial time during children's programming to ten and a half minutes an hour on weekends and twelve minutes on weekdays. The FCC said half as much advertising would be allowed during

[174]United States v. Philip Morris USA, Inc., 449 F. Supp. 2d 1 (D.C.D.C. 2006).
[175]Bauder v. Ralston Purina Co., 1989 U.S. Dist. LEXIS 14091 (E.D. Pa. 1989).

half-hour programs. The commission said the commercial limits pertain only to programming for children ages 12 and younger, "children who can neither distinguish commercial from program material nor understand the persuasive intent of commercials."

Television broadcast stations and cable operators must abide by the commercial limits, and they must keep records to verify compliance with the statute. Cable operators are responsible for limiting children's advertising in locally originated programming and cable network programming, but they are prohibited by other laws from editing programming, including advertising, transmitted by over-the-air broadcast licensees. The commercial limits apply to advertising just before and after programming but not to public service announcements and noncommercial miniprograms fewer than five minutes in length.[176]

In 2006 the FCC adopted rules prohibiting the display of website addresses during children's programming if the website is selling a product. A website address may be displayed during programs directed to children ages 12 and under only if it meets four criteria establishing that the site supplements the program and is not a sales promotion:

1. The website offers a substantial amount of program-related content or other non-commercial material;
2. The website is not primarily intended for commercial purposes, including either e-commerce or advertising;
3. The website's home page and other menu pages are clearly labeled to distinguish non-commercial from commercial sections; and
4. The website page to which viewers are directed by the website address is not used for e-commerce, advertising, or other commercial purposes.[177]

The FCC regards the display of the address of a website that sells a product as the "equivalent of a commercial encouraging children to go to the store and buy the product." Thus, including the web address during a program converts the program into a commercial "just as a host telling children to race to their local toy store would," the agency wrote.[178]

Broadcasters are allowed to display the addresses of commercial websites during allowable commercial time. However, during both programs and commercials, broadcasters are not allowed to display the address of a website that uses characters from the program to sell products or services.

The FCC imposes serious fines on broadcasters for violating the commercial time limitations. The FCC fined KTTU (TV) of Tucson $125,000 because the commission found KTTU exceeded commercial limits 581 times in a sixteen-month period.[179] The commission also granted the station only a short-term license renewal of two years. In 1998, the FCC reported that 26 percent of stations seeking license renewal did not comply with the children's television ad limits.[180] As a remedy, the FCC said it would

[176]Children's Television Programming, 6 F.C.C.R. 2111, 68 P & F Rad. Reg. 2d 1615 (1991).
[177]47 C.F.R. § 73.670 (broadcasting); 47 C.F.R. § 76.225 (cable).
[178]Children's Television Obligations of Digital Television Broadcasters, Second Order on Reconsideration and Second Report and Order (FCC 06-143) (Sept. 29, 2006).
[179]Clear Channel Television, Inc., 10 F.C.C.R. 3773 (1995).
[180]Mass Media Bureau Advises Commercial Television Licensees Regarding Children's Television Commercial Limits, 13 F.C.C.R. 10265 (1998).

begin unannounced audits of television stations to discover violations of the commercial time limits. Stations found violating the rule can be reprimanded, fined, or have their license renewal endangered.

PRODUCT-BASED PROGRAMMING AND PROGRAM-LENGTH COMMERCIALS Parents not only protest the quantity of advertising in children's programming but also complain about what they call "program-length commercials," programs based on toys and other commercial products. Citizen groups complain that children's shows featuring commercial products, including *The Adventures of the Gummi Bears* and *Captain N: The Game Master,* are nothing more than program-length commercials for candy, video games, and other products. The groups want the FCC to require that the shows be labeled as commercials, which would mean that the half-hour shows would violate the limits of ten and a half or twelve commercial minutes an hour for children's programming.

The FCC has ruled, however, that a program based on a commercial product is not, by definition, a "program-length commercial." The FCC said that a product-based program is a commercial only if both the show and the ads feature the same character or product. In 1993, the commission fined WFTS-TV of Tampa $10,000 for running a program-length commercial. The station ran two advertisements for G.I. Joe toys during a thirty-minute *G.I. Joe* program featuring cartoons based on the toy. The commission said the entire program counted as commercial time because both the program and the ads sold during commercial breaks in the program featured the same product line.[181]

The FCC said its definition of program-length commercials means that products or services cannot be promoted within the body of a program. Children's programming and commercials during children's programming must be separated.[182] The commission said the definition of program-length commercials reinforced its traditional prohibition against a program host, including a cartoon character, selling a product during the show. The FCC has said previously that children's commercials must be separated from program content with a buffer such as "it's now time for a commercial break," to help children distinguish between advertising and programs.

SPONSOR IDENTIFICATION The FCC also has said companies that give programs to broadcast stations in return for advertising time do not have to be identified as sponsors of the programs under Section 317 of the Communications Act. Section 317, the sponsorship identification requirement, mandates that broadcasters identify anyone who pays to have a commercial or a program broadcast. A station must identify on the air anyone who pays for a program to air or provides a program free if the program promotes a product, service, or trademark. Sponsorship identification is intended to prevent deception by telling viewers who is paying for a program or commercial.

In a case involving one of the most popular children's programs of the late 1980s, the FCC held that broadcast stations did not have to identify the companies providing *He-Man and the Masters of the Universe* to stations if the companies received advertising

[181]Tampa Bay Television, Inc., 8 F.C.C.R. 411 (1993).

[182]Children's Television Programming, 6 F.C.C.R. 2111, 68 P & F Rad. Reg. 2d 1615, *modified on reconsideration on other grounds,* 6 F.C.C.R. 5093, 69 P & F Rad. Reg. 2d 1020 (1991).

time in return. The commission rejected the contention of a citizen group, the National Association for Better Broadcasting (NABB), that KCOP-TV of Los Angeles should have told viewers the program *He-Man* had been given to the station by makers of the toy of the same name. *He-Man,* based on an invincible animated hero, had been given to the station by Mattel and Group W in exchange for two minutes of advertising time during children's programming. The NABB said the *He-Man* cartoon amounted to a gift to the station because the advertising time provided by KCOP-TV was worth only a small proportion of the program's value. Mattel and Group W spent $14 million on the first sixty-five episodes of *He-Man* and received commercials from KCOP-TV worth about $300,000.

In 1989, the FCC said that stations need not identify the source of a program as long as the stations gave something of value, including advertising time, in return. In a decision upheld by a federal appeals court, the commission said a station would have to identify the source of a toy-based program only if it had been given to a station free or for only "trifling" consideration.[183] The more than $300,000 worth of advertising exchanged by KCOP-TV for *He-Man,* the commission said, was of substantial value and not an insignificant, or "trifling," amount. The commission said no single station would be expected to pay the entire cost of a nationally ranked children's program.

Broadcast Advertising

Although advertising can be limited during children's programs, the amount of commercial time in other programming is not restricted. The FCC has said that marketplace forces can better determine the number and length of commercials than FCC rules can. The commission said that if stations air more commercials than the public will tolerate, "the market will regulate itself"—viewers will not watch and advertisers will not buy time.[184]

However, a few federal statutes still regulate commercials. Section 317 of the 1934 Communications Act, for example, requires that broadcasters identify anyone who has purchased broadcast time, a provision that was just mentioned in this chapter.[185] In commercials, use of an advertiser's name or product constitutes sufficient identification of the sponsor. The FCC can waive the sponsorship identification requirement, which it has done for "classified ad" programs and movies produced initially for theaters. Absent the waiver, stations could not broadcast without editing many feature films containing paid-for displays of commercial products.[186]

Two federal statutes ban the advertising of cigarettes, little cigars, and chewing tobacco on all electronic media.[187]

Wine and beer have been advertised on broadcast stations for years, but liquor usually has not been. Liquor advertisements are not prohibited by statute or the FCC; liquor ads have been kept off the air voluntarily by trade associations representing broadcasters and

[183] *In re* Complaint of Nat'l Ass'n for Better Broadcasting against Television Station KCOP(TV), 4 F.C.C.R. 4988, 66 P & F Rad. Reg. 2d 889 (1989), *aff'd,* 902 F.2d 1009 (D.C. Cir. 1990).

[184] Television Deregulation, 98 F.C.C.2d at 1105, 56 P & F Rad. Reg. 2d at 1028.

[185] 47 U.S.C. § 317(a)(1).

[186] 47 C.F.R. § 73.1212(f), (g), (h).

[187] 15 U.S.C. § 1335, 4402(f). The ban on cigarette advertising was upheld in Capital Broadcasting Co. v. Mitchell, 333 F. Supp. 582 (D.C. Cir. 1971), *aff'd without opinion,* 405 U.S. 1000 (1972).

the alcoholic beverage industry. States often place limits on advertising in all media for happy hours, two-for-one specials and other ad content that might encourage irresponsible drinking.

Broadcast beer advertisements are generally aimed at audiences where at least 70 percent of the listeners or viewers are above the legal drinking age. The FTC has ruled that advertisements may be unfair or deceptive if aimed at audiences too young to use the products lawfully. Ads show safe, moderate drinking, in compliance with FTC decisions and trade association rules.[188]

The Food and Drug Administration oversees advertising for prescription drugs, including the pharmaceutical companies' $3 billion yearly advertising campaigns aimed directly to consumers (DTC). Some televised ads raise serious health concerns. Merck and Company's heavily advertised Vioxx enjoyed annual sales of $2.5 billion despite evidence that it caused heart problems.

In 2007, there were 12,600 drug ads for the FDA to review; there were 13 FDA employees to examine DTC drug ads. In 2008, the FDA received $6.1 million to review the mushrooming DTC ads—up from $2.2 million in 2007—but Congress refused to grant the FDA authority to ban DTC advertisements that promote drugs raising serious safety concerns.The FDA can fine pharmaceutical companies for false or misleading advertisements.

Under FDA regulations, direct-to-consumer ads

1. cannot be false or misleading;
2. must present a fair balance between the risks and benefits of the drug;
3. must reveal facts that are material to the representations made in the ad or the consequences of using the product; and
4. must—if printed—disclose the risks listed in the product's labeling or—if broadcast—make "adequate provision" through toll-free telephone numbers, Web sites, brochures, and other means to disclose risks.[189]

Personal Data

With the growth of computerization and the Internet, control of personal data is an increasingly troublesome problem. In one poll, 69 percent of respondents said they were more worried about their identities being stolen than they were of contracting cancer or being hurt in a terrorist attack.[190] In one of the most publicized cases of stolen personal data, it was revealed that sham businesses purchased the personal records—names, addresses, social security numbers—of 150,000 consumers from ChoicePoint, an information services company that sells personal data to credit card companies, mortgage companies, and banks that offer loans and mortgages to consumers.[191] By one estimate, data companies, media

[188]Davis, Wright Tremain, Broadcast Law Blog, www.broadcastinglawblog.com, Nov. 30, 2007.

[189]"Congress Passes FDA Bill Without DTC Ad Limits," Manatt, Advertising Law, Oct. 19, 2007, manatt.com/newsletters; "Prescription Drugs: FDA Oversight of Direct-to-Consumer Advertising Has Limitations," U.S. General Accounting Office, GAO-03-177, October 2002.

[190]Reece Rushing, Ari Schwartz, & Paula Bruenig, "Protecting Consumers Online: Key Issues in Preventing Internet Privacy Intrusions, Fraud and Abuse," Center for Democracy & Technology (2006) at 1, available at http://www.cdt.org.

[191]Steve Lohr, "Surging Losses, but Few Victims in Data Breeches," *N.Y. Times,* Sep. 27, 2006.

companies, universities, and other data handlers collectively fumbled 93,754,333 private records in a recent two years.[192] In addition, major search engines like Google, Yahoo, and MSN collect and store billions of bits of information recording the terms surfers search, what sites they query, and what computer and browser are used.[193] With such vast information, advertisers can profile the preferences of consumers and target ads instantaneously as consumers click on related websites.[194]

Personal data held by financial institutions and data brokers are not "private" in the sense that disclosure reveals intimate family details or medial information. In fact, consumers voluntarily provide much personal information to banks and institutions to acquire a speedy loan, open a bank account, or buy insurance. Web sites collect "behavioral data" on the sites Internet users visit, the icons they click, and the items they purchase online. The privacy issues of personal data include how consumers control what and how information is collected about them and who gets to use it for what commercial purposes.[195]

At the beginning of the computer revolution, the federal government developed a set of Principles of Fair Information Practices intended to increase individuals' control over personal information, limit data collection, and curb abuses of data collectors. The Principles of Fair Information Practices, which have been agreed upon by governments, privacy experts, and industry groups, form the basis for data protection and online privacy laws and policies. The Principles of Fair Information Practices provide:[196]

Notice Data collectors must disclose their information practices before collecting personal information. Failure to have a policy or to abide by its terms may bring action from the FTC for unfair or misleading practices. It may be difficult, however, for companies to make complex legal subject matter understandable to the "average" consumer who is often disinclined to read privacy notices. It is also difficult to format privacy notices for the handheld devices where business is increasingly conducted.

Choice Consumers must be given options on whether and how personal information will be used.

Access Consumers can view and contest the accuracy and completeness of data collected about them.

Security Data collectors must take reasonable steps to assure that information collected is accurate and secure.

American and European governments have adopted data privacy statutes serving the Principles of Fair Information Practices.[197] The federal government has not adopted comprehensive data privacy legislation, but the government has passed a patchwork of legislation

[192]Tom Zeller, Jr., "Link by Link: 93,754,333 Examples of Data Nonchalance," *N.Y. Times,* Sep. 25, 2006.

[193]*See,* Tom Zeller, Jr., "Your Life as an Open Book," *N.Y. Times,* Aug. 12, 2006, at B1.

[194]FTC, "Online Profiling: A Report to Congress, Part 2" (July 2000), at 3.

[195]*See,* Daniel Solove, "Conceptualizing Privacy," 90 *Calif. L. Rev.* 1087 (2002).

[196]FTC, "Online Profiling: A Report to Congress, Part 2" (July 2000), at 3.

[197]For the European directive, see Directive 97/46/EC of the European Parliament and of the Council, 24 Oct. 1995, on the protection of individuals with regard to the processing of personal data and on the free movement of such data, Official Journal of the European Communities, 23 Nov. 1995, No L. 281, p. 31.

that provides consumers some measure of control over how personal data is collected and disseminated:

The Fair Credit Reporting Act (1970)[198] protects consumers from the disclosure of inaccurate personal information held by consumer reporting agencies but does not restrict the amount and type of information collected. Amending the act in 2003, Congress made it easier for consumers to correct credit information and to block fraud. But, one must first be a victim to block fraud. Under the act, victims of fraud can prevent new lines of credit from being established for seven years by placing a fraud alert on their files held by credit reporting agencies, such as Equifax and TransUnion. Fraud victims whose identity has not been stolen can place a fraud alert for 90 days.[199]

The Right to Financial Privacy Act (1978)[200] creates a statutory financial protection for bank records. The act requires that the customers authorize access to their bank records or that the government has a proper subpoena or search warrant.

The Children's Online Privacy Protection Act (COPPA) of 1998 prohibits commercial websites from misusing information acquired from children.[201] The law requires parents' permission before the websites collect information such as names, addresses, and phone numbers from children under thirteen. The FTC's rule implementing the Child Online Privacy Protection Act took effect in 2000, and was renewed without change in 2006.[202] COPPA requires more verifiable measures of ensuring parental consent if the Internet operator wants to provide collected information to third parties or the public. The operator also must post notice online of the company's information practices.

The Gramm-Leach-Bliley Act (1999) regulates the disclosure of personal data by financial institutions.[203] The act requires financial institutions to provide written or electronic notice of the categories of personal information collected, categories of people the information will be disclosed to, and the company's confidentiality policy. The act also codifies protections against pretexting, the practice of obtaining personal financial information through false pretenses. As noted earlier, employees and subcontractors of Hewlett Packard employed pretexting to gain the phone records of dissident HP board members and journalists covering boardroom fights.

Gramm-Leach-Bliley also requires that consumers be told of their rights to opt-out of data distribution programs and requires that safeguards on consumer data be secure. Congress determined controls on the use of personal data should be imposed because the potential for misuse and abuse increased dramatically when financial institutions controlling vast databases of personal data were permitted to merge.

[198] 15 U.S.C. § 1681

[199] To learn more about this and the other statutes cited here, visit the Center for Democracy and Technology, www.cdt.org/privacy/guide.

[200] 35 U.S.C. § 3401.

[201] 15 U.S.C. §§ 6501–6506.

[202] FTC, Children's Online Privacy Protection Rule, 16 CFR § 312, Mar. 15, 2006.

[203] 15 U.S.C. §§ 6801–6810

In important proposed guidelines issued in 2007, the Federal Trade Commission asked Web sites to disclose the behavioral data they collect and to allow consumers to refuse to allow Web sites to collect data for advertisers. Under the guidelines, Web sites would also have to get permission from consumers before collecting "sensitive" medical or children's data and would have to provide reasonable security for the data collected. Some legal experts advised Web site operators to heed the FTC guidelines on collecting behavioral data or risk Congressional intervention.[204]

Lotteries and Contests

For many years, Americans feared that laws prohibiting gambling were needed to "protect the citizen from the demoralizing or corrupting influence" of solicitations to gamble.[205] Therefore, federal law long prohibited all advertising of lotteries.[206] However, as more states conduct lotteries to raise revenue, the federal law has been modified to permit the media to advertise lotteries in states that conduct them. Congress also has adopted other exemptions to the lottery advertising ban.

LOTTERIES A **lottery** has three elements: (1) prize, (2) chance, and (3) consideration. The prize is the reward, money, trip, merchandise, or other remuneration given to the winner. Chance means that luck, not skill, will determine the winner. Consideration, which is often more difficult to recognize than chance or prize, is the effort or expense required of the participant. Consideration is the time one spends to play a game or the money paid to enter a contest. All three elements must be present for a promotion to be considered a lottery.

The ban on lottery advertising was relaxed by two 1988 laws. First, Congress permitted broadcasters to carry ads for legal gambling, including casino gambling, conducted by Native American tribes.[207] Second, Congress permitted publishers and broadcasters operating in states where lotteries are legal to advertise and disseminate information about lotteries in those states and in adjoining states if lotteries are also lawful there.[208]

The media may also print or broadcast advertising and prize lists of lotteries conducted by nonprofit organizations and by commercial companies, if these lotteries are legal under state law. The commercial lotteries, however, must be conducted only occasionally and not be related to the company's usual business.

In 1993, the Supreme Court upheld the constitutionality of the federal prohibition against advertising of lotteries by broadcast stations licensed in states where lotteries are illegal. In *United States v. Edge Broadcasting Co.,* the Court ruled 7-2 that the federal prohibition was constitutional in a case involving WMYK-FM, a station licensed in Moyock, North Carolina, where lotteries are illegal.[209] The station was located only three miles from the state of Virginia, where lotteries are legal. Edge Broadcasting argued that the federal prohibition on lottery advertisements in North Carolina unconstitutionally barred WMYK

[204] "Sites Ignore New FTC Privacy Guidelines at Their Peril," Manatt Advertising Law, Jan. 17, 2008, manatt.com/newsletters.
[205] United States v. Horner, 44 F. 677 (S.D.N.Y. 1891), *aff'd,* 143 U.S. 207 (1892).
[206] 18 U.S.C. §§ 1301–1306.
[207] Indian Gaming Regulatory Act, 25 U.S.C. § 2720.
[208] 18 U.S.C. § 1307.
[209] 509 U.S. 418 (1993).

from broadcasting lawful commercial information, particularly to Virginians who constitute 98 percent of the North Carolina station's audience.

Applying the *Central Hudson* test for commercial speech, the Supreme Court concluded that the federal prohibition on lottery broadcasts advances the significant state interest of discouraging gambling in North Carolina. In dissent, Justice Stevens argued that the government lacks a substantial interest in discouraging gambling in a nation in which more than thirty-five states have legalized lotteries. Whatever the state interest, Stevens said, it does not justify a ban on constitutionally protected commercial speech.

The Supreme Court in 1999 said a ban on radio and television stations carrying ads for legal casino gambling violated broadcasters' First Amendment rights.[210] Louisiana broadcasters argued they should be permitted to carry ads for Louisiana and Mississippi casinos. Writing for the Court, Justice Stevens agreed, saying the ban could not pass the third and fourth parts of the *Central Hudson* test.

The Court said the government's interests were substantial, thus passing the second part of the *Central Hudson* test. The government said its interests were to reduce social costs associated with gambling and protect states in which gambling is illegal. However, the Court said the exemptions Congress adopted—permitting advertising for state-conducted lotteries, casinos operated by Native American tribes, and certain occasional casino gambling—meant the law could not directly advance the government's interests. The Court said it is not clear that permitting advertising for some casino gambling but not others would reduce the number of people who gamble or the amount of gambling. Rather, the Court said, the congressional exemptions only would persuade gamblers to go to one casino rather than another. The law, then, failed to satisfy the third part of the *Central Hudson* test.

The Court also said the law was broader than necessary to serve the government's interest, failing *Central Hudson*'s fourth part. Gambling's social ills will not be reduced by forbidding ads for some casinos while permitting ads for others, the Court said. Thus, banning broadcast casino gambling ads restricted more truthful speech about lawful activities than the law's results could justify, the Court said.

CONTESTS Although publishers and broadcasters may conduct only occasional lotteries unrelated to their businesses, they can conduct promotional contests and advertise the contests of others as long as the promotions are not false or deceptive. To be legal, contests may not consist of all three elements of a lottery: prize, chance, and consideration. Contests may include two elements of a lottery, such as a prize and chance, as long as they do not require the third element, consideration. Many contests avoid the prohibitions on lotteries by basing winning on knowledge or skill rather than chance. Common contests conducted by publishers, broadcasters, and retailers include treasure hunts, drawings, word games, picture coloring, name-that-tune competitions, and cash call-in jackpots.

The FTC generally does not regulate lotteries, but it does issue rules regulating contests, particularly in food retailing and the gasoline industry. The Federal Communications Act of 1934 also regulates contests. The communications act prohibits broadcasters from deceiving the public by providing any "special and secret assistance" to a contestant in a

[210]Greater New Orleans Broadcasting Association v. United States, 527 U.S. 173 (1999).

contest or from fixing or rigging a contest through "any artifice or scheme."[211] In addition, Federal Communications Commission (FCC) rules require broadcasters who conduct or advertise contests to

> fully and accurately disclose the material terms of the contest, and . . . conduct the contest substantially as announced or advertised. No contest description shall be false, misleading or deceptive with respect to any material term.[212]

FCC rules require that stations reveal who is eligible to win, the nature and value of prizes, how to enter, how winners will be determined, and dates of the contest. A disc jockey, television host, or broadcast promotion director could be subject to a fine of $10,000 and a year in jail for participating in a false or misleading contest. Furthermore, a station could lose its license for willful or repeated violation. Contests may also be prohibited under state law.

The FCC revoked the license of WMJX-FM in Miami, Florida, because of deception in two contests. In one, the station announced that contestants could win a $1,000 prize in an Easter egg hunt. The station's program director allowed the promotional announcements to be broadcast even though the station had no prize money to award. In the other contest, the station announced a $500 reward for the listener who found disc jockey Greg Austin, reported to be wandering around the Miami area in a daze, "his mind boggled," after a trip to the Bermuda Triangle. However, station announcers knew that Austin was in the studio, safely returned from a brief charter boat excursion.[213]

Money

The U.S. Supreme Court has ruled that the government can constitutionally regulate the manner in which money is pictured in advertisements and news stories. In *Regan v. Time, Inc.,* the Court upheld a federal statute requiring that money be pictured only in black and white and only either larger or smaller than actual size.[214] The Treasury Department fears that color photos of money in actual size would aid counterfeiters. Therefore, the law prohibits picturing money unless the reproduction is not only black and white but also either less than three-fourths or more than one-and-a-half times the actual size of money.

The *Regan* case arose over a cover picture in *Sports Illustrated* showing a basketball hoop stuffed with $100 bills. The color picture illustrated a story about a basketball point-shaving scandal at Boston University. The Treasury Department tried to seize the plates and other materials used to produce the *Sports Illustrated* cover.

Justice White, in a plurality opinion for the Court, said the government's color and size requirements are not an impermissible content regulation. The Court likened the size and color limitations to limits on the decibel levels imposed on sound trucks or size and height limits on outdoor signs. All of these regulations constitutionally restrict the manner in which a message is presented, not the content of the message.

[211] 47 U.S.C. § 509.
[212] 47 C.F.R. § 73.1216.
[213] WMJX, Inc., 85 F.C.C.2d 251 (1981).
[214] 468 U.S. 641 (1984).

The Court also recognized in *Regan* the government's substantial interest in preventing counterfeiting. Barring color pictures of money makes it harder for counterfeiters to gain access to color negatives that can be altered and used for illegal purposes. Size limitations ensure that the illustrations of money themselves are not used as counterfeit money.

◇ Summary ◇

The Children's Television Act of 1990 limits the amount of time devoted to commercials during children's programming. The FCC also regulates program-length commercials and requires sponsor identification.

The collection, control and dissemination of personal data is regulated by a number of laws that attempt to prohibit fraud and misuse of data.

The media may advertise all official state lotteries in any state that operates one. The media may also print or broadcast advertising and prize lists of lotteries conducted by nonprofit organizations and occasionally by commercial companies if the lotteries are legal under state law and if the commercial lotteries are not related to the company's usual business. A lottery has three elements: chance, prize, and consideration. A contest usually requires the participant to demonstrate a measure of skill or effort. The media may reproduce U.S. money in an advertisement or illustration if the money is pictured in black and white and is either larger or smaller than real money.

Media's Right to Refuse Advertising

It is well established that the media choose what to broadcast or publish. As Chief Justice Warren Burger said in *CBS, Inc. v. Democratic National Committee,* "For better or worse, editing is what editors are for; and editing is selection and choice of material."[215] In *Democratic National Committee,* the Court ruled that a Washington, D.C., television station had a First Amendment right to refuse to sell airtime for a business group's editorial advertisements.

Earlier, the Court had ruled unconstitutional a Florida law requiring newspapers to print replies from political candidates attacked editorially. In *Miami Herald Publishing Co. v. Tornillo,*[216] a political candidate argued that newspapers, which are often monopolies in their cities, should be required to publish responses from candidates the papers criticize. But Chief Justice Burger, writing for the Court, said, "A newspaper is more than a passive receptacle or conduit for news, comment, and advertising." What a newspaper publishes is a matter of editorial judgment that the First Amendment places beyond government control, Burger said.

Before the Supreme Court established the media's First Amendment right to refuse advertising, lower courts had ruled in common law that the media are private businesses free to accept or reject advertising, provided publishers do not violate contracts with their

[215] 412 U.S. 94, 124 (1973).
[216] 418 U.S. 241 (1974).

advertisers, monopolize or restrain trade in violation of the antitrust statutes, or discriminate on the basis of race or sex. In *Chicago Joint Board, Amalgamated Clothing Workers of America, AFL-CIO v. Chicago Tribune Co.,* the U.S. Court of Appeals for the Seventh Circuit ruled that newspapers are private enterprises that can refuse even editorial advertisements.[217]

The First Amendment and the common law do not free the media entirely from required publishing and broadcasting. The Federal Communications Act imposes obligations on broadcasters to provide airtime for candidates during elections. The media are also required to provide access to advertisers with whom contracts have been signed. In addition, media that collude to refuse advertisements may violate the antitrust laws.

◇ Summary ◇

The media may refuse to publish or broadcast advertisements because of First Amendment and common-law precedents. The media's refusal to disseminate an advertisement is not deemed a government refusal in violation of the First Amendment just because the media receive government benefits. However, the media, like other businesses, must honor their advertising contracts, the antitrust laws, and other legal obligations.

Self-Regulation

Despite the elaborate legal apparatus for regulating advertising, self-regulation by the advertising industry has been called the most efficient tool for curbing excesses and illegalities.[218] In the recent era of government deregulation, the FTC also emphasized the importance of regulation from within the advertising industry. With FTC budget cuts and the closure of a number of regional FTC offices, consumers depend on advertisers themselves, more than before, to ensure that advertising is fair and accurate.

Although the zeal for deregulation has abated, regulation of advertising by a number of bureaus and agencies outside of government is still important. These regulatory bodies include associations, such as the American Association of Advertising Agencies; the broadcast networks, all of which have advertising acceptance guidelines; and individual radio and TV stations, newspapers, and magazines.

Some advertisers promote self-regulation to stave off government regulation. The Direct Mail Board of Review, Inc., a trade association formed to help regulate direct mail advertising, has issued a Code of Business Ethics. Similarly, the American Telemarketing Association has adopted "Telemarketing Standards and Ethics Guidelines." The National Infomercial Marketing Association asks members to air only truthful advertisements as required by the association's Marketing Guidelines. A leading regulator of the advertising industry is the National Advertising Division of the National Advertising Review Board (NARB). The NARB was set up by a number of trade associations during the most vigorous period of the consumer movement in the early 1970s.

[217]435 F.2d 470 (7th Cir. 1970), *cert. denied,* 402 U.S. 973 (1971).
[218]George Rosden & Peter Rosden, 3 *Law of Advertising* § 31.02 (1999).

Tobacco Industry Self-Regulation

In 1998, the tobacco industry agreed to limit its advertising and marketing. The agreement was part of a settlement the tobacco industry reached with forty-six states and five United States territories. Four other states previously had arrived at similar agreements with the country's five largest cigarette producers.

The pact bans billboard and transit tobacco advertisements, sales of clothing and other merchandise containing tobacco brand logos, use of cartoon characters such as Joe Camel, and sponsoring sports events and concerts aimed at young people. The agreement permits tobacco companies to use a cigarette brand name to sponsor only one sports event. Human characters such as the Marlboro Man may be used in tobacco advertising under the agreement.

Cigarette manufacturers have committed to financing a $300-million-per-year anti-smoking campaign, aimed primarily at youth.

The tobacco industry and forty states reached an agreement in 1997 limiting lawsuits against cigarette companies, providing for antismoking campaigns, and restricting tobacco advertising and marketing campaigns. The U.S. Food and Drug Administration cannot prevent tobacco companies from advertising cigarettes to young people, the Supreme Court ruled, because Congress has not authorized the FDA to regulate tobacco products—and their advertising—as a drug.[219] Congress rejected the proposal. The 1998 agreement did not need congressional consent.

National Advertising Division

The National Advertising Division and the National Advertising Review Board were established in 1971 to promote truth and accuracy in national advertising. These regulatory bodies were created through the cooperation of the American Advertising Federation, the American Association of Advertising Agencies, the Association of National Advertisers, and the Council of Better Business Bureaus. The National Advertising Division, or the NAD as it is called, is "responsible for receiving or initiating, evaluating, investigating, analyzing, and holding initial negotiations with an advertiser on complaints or questions from any source involving the truth or accuracy of national advertising."[220]

Like the FTC, the NAD investigates advertising claims to determine whether they are substantiated. The NAD says that it "maintains the principle unreservedly" that prior substantiation "is essential for truthful and accurate advertising."[221] Most of the cases NAD reviews involve substantiation of advertising claims.

The NAD deals only with misleading or deceptive national advertisements. It does not get involved in private disputes between competitors and does not take complaints dealing with local advertising or business practices. Furthermore, the NAD does not entertain questions about the basic performance of products, questions of taste, political and issue advertising, or advertising addressed to lawyers, engineers, or other audiences

[219] Food and Drug Administration v. Brown & Williamson Tobacco Corp., 529 U.S. 120 (2000).

[220] NAD/NARB Procedures § 2.1 (Apr. 1, 1990), *quoted in* Keven Plevan & Miriam Siroky, *Advertising Compliance Handbook* 334 (2d ed. 1991).

[221] National Advertising Division, Council of Better Business Bureaus, Inc., "Self-Regulation of National Advertising: Twelfth Year-End Report," in NAD Case Rep., July 15, 1983.

with special expertise. A related organization, the Children's Advertising Review Unit, tries to prevent exploitation of children through misleading ads, messages that children cannot understand, and ads that disregard the risk that children may imitate dangerous product demonstrations.

The NAD's cases come from the organization's own systematic monitoring of national television, radio, and print advertising; complaints from competing advertisers; and complaints from consumer groups, individuals, and the independent Better Business Bureaus. The NAD also reviews claims of deceptive advertising on the Internet, where, an advertising official says, the advertising business can regulate itself more quickly and cheaply than the government can.[222] Consumers and advertisers may report fraud on the Internet via regular mail, e-mail, or the Better Business Bureau's website, http://www.cbbb.org/cbbb. If the NAD is not satisfied that an advertising claim is substantiated, it will negotiate with the advertiser to modify or discontinue the ad. If an agreement cannot be reached, an advertiser can appeal the NAD decision that an ad is deceptive to an impartial five-member panel appointed by the chair of the NARB. The review board has fifty members representing national advertisers, advertising agencies, and the public. Members of the board serve a two-year term. The NAD handled 2,800 cases between 1971 and 1990.[223]

The NAD has no definitive standards defining untrue or inaccurate ads. It decides each case individually. But the NAD brings into the regulatory process the standards of many other agencies and associations, including FTC rules and consent orders, postal regulations, state consumer protection programs, and court decisions, particularly the increasing number of comparative advertising cases. The NAD also relies on the guidelines of the Advertising Research Foundation, network broadcast guides, and professional and trade association guides.

In a typical case, the NAD found there was inadequate substantiation for newspaper ads proclaiming the superiority of Bama Peanut Butter over three other brands that had been compared in taste tests with children in the South. The ad said:

> Peanut Butter lovers say "You Can't Beat Bama!" Jif Can't! Peter Pan Can't! Skippy Can't! In recent taste tests in the South, boys and girls who love peanut butter found Bama Peanut Butter unbeatable! None of the leading brands beat the delicious taste of Bama.

The company's taste tests did show children thought Bama was as good as or better than the other three brands overall, but the kids liked the consistency and the strength of the peanut butter flavor better in one of the competing brands. Because Bama's taste was not preferred in all respects, the NAD found insufficient substantiation for Bama's claim to be preferred by children. The company agreed that claims of Bama's superiority to all three other brands would not be used in future campaigns without more test data to support the claims, but as typically happens, the advertising had already been discontinued.[224]

The NAD has no coercive powers or punitive role, but advertisers nevertheless cooperate with the NAD. Not until 1993 did an advertiser—Eggland's Best, Inc.—refuse to halt

[222]Andrea Sachs, "NAD Turns Ad Monitor to Cyberspace," *Advertising Age,* May 8, 1995, at 20.
[223]George Rosden & Peter Rosden, 3 *Law of Advertising* § 42.02, at 42–43 (1999).
[224]Borden, Inc., NAD Case Report (No. 1931).

an advertisement after participating in the complete process of an NAD investigation, decision, and appeal to the NARB.[225] In those rare cases in which an advertiser refuses to participate in an NAD review or an advertiser refuses to halt a misleading advertisement, the case may be referred to the FTC or another government agency. In 1995, Eggland's Best agreed with the FTC not to disseminate egg advertisements containing misleading and unsubstantiated health claims.[226] Publicity about NAD cases is circulated to the media, businesses, colleges, and government agencies in monthly *Case Reports.*

Media Regulation

In addition to the NARB, advertising is regulated by the networks, newspapers, and other media that sell advertising time and space. The media, like the FTC and the NAD, screen advertisements submitted to them for accuracy and fairness and demand that objective claims be substantiated. So valued are network guidelines that advertising associations regretted network cutbacks in their advertising acceptance departments. There is always a concern that failure of the advertising industry to regulate itself will encourage more government regulation.[227]

For many years, the National Association of Broadcasters' Television Code imposed several limits on members' advertising. These guidelines were more sensitive to the taste and morals of the audience than the law was. To meet the standards of the Television Code, ads not only had to be accurate but also had to be presented "with courtesy and good taste." According to the broadcast code, ads were not supposed to be objectionable "to a substantial and responsible segment of the community."[228] The guides were especially sensitive to the sensibilities of children. The code prohibited advertising hard liquor, firearms except for sport, and fortune-telling. Personal hygiene products were to be advertised "in a restrained and obviously inoffensive manner."

The NAB Code was abandoned after the Justice Department won an antitrust suit challenging the code's provisions barring advertising "clutter." The clutter provisions prohibited the advertising on member stations of two or more products in a single advertisement lasting less than sixty seconds. In other words, thirty-second spots could contain ads for only a single product or two closely related products, such as different models of the same vacuum cleaner. The NAB claimed the clutter provisions saved viewers from the confusion of having to watch several short advertisements at one time. The NAB also contended that the clutter provisions did not violate the antitrust law because the NAB code in which the provisions were contained was a voluntary code adhered to only by members of the National Association of Broadcasters.

The federal District Court for the District of Columbia agreed with the Justice Department that the NAB clutter provisions violated the Sherman Antitrust Act.[229] Although the code was not legally binding on its members, the court said the NAB, in effect, had a

[225]Steven W. Colford, "Paper Tiger Litmus Test: FTC Gets Eggland's, Its First NARB Case," *Advertising Age,* Dec. 20, 1993, at 2.

[226]Eggland's Best, Inc., 59 Fed. Reg. 8638 (1994).

[227]"Networks Hit for Ad Clearance Cuts," *Advertising Age,* Sept. 12, 1988, at 6.

[228]National Association of Broadcasters, "The Television Code," 21st ed., 1980, § IX, in Practicing Law Institute, *Legal and Business Aspects of the Advertising Industry* 1982, at 88.

[229]United States v. National Ass'n of Broadcasters, 536 F. Supp. 149 (D.D.C. 1982).

monopoly on the industry because the most important broadcasting outlets in the country belonged. The court said adherence to the code was not really voluntary because stations that did not abide by the code could be dropped from membership in the association. The court also said that prohibiting an advertiser from advertising more than one product in a thirty-second spot was a restraint of trade that particularly hurt smaller companies that could not afford longer television ads.

After the Justice Department won an antitrust suit against some of the NAB code provisions, the NAB abandoned the broadcast code. However, networks adopted advertising standards that essentially conformed to the abandoned NAB code. All networks have advertising acceptance guidelines requiring truth, good taste, and substantiation of broadcast claims.[230]

◇ Summary ◇

Government regulation is not the only check on the accuracy of advertising. Advertisers themselves and the media monitor advertisements to ensure that the government and public will not find them deceptive. The leading self-regulatory body is the National Advertising Division of the National Advertising Review Board. Many other agencies, as well as the networks and newspapers, monitor advertising. Like the FTC, the National Advertising Division and the media expect advertising claims to be substantiated.

Securities Transactions

Corporations not only have a right to speak but may also be required to speak or publish. A number of laws require banks, insurance companies, and other businesses to disclose to the public the details of their financial offerings and the financial strength of their institutions.

Probably the most far-reaching corporate disclosure laws are the securities acts passed during the Roosevelt administration to eliminate abuses that contributed to the stock market crash of 1929. Under the laws, corporations whose stock is publicly traded must disclose financial information to the government, shareholders, and the public when the corporations register and trade securities.

For public relations practitioners, federal and state disclosure requirements mean jobs writing periodic reports and press releases, preparing for annual stockholders' meetings, and advising corporate executives about their disclosure responsibilities. For business journalists, corporate filings with the Securities and Exchange Commission have been said to compose "the single most intensive research tool" for learning about the operations of American companies.[231]

The fundamental purpose of the federal statutes, the Supreme Court said, "was to substitute a philosophy of full disclosure for the philosophy of *caveat emptor* and thus to achieve a high standard of business ethics in the securities industry."[232] One of the most important securities reforms passed during the New Deal was the Securities Act of 1933,

[230]George Rosden & Peter Rosden, 2 *Law of Advertising* § 17.01[4] (1999).
[231]Donald Kirsch, *Financial and Economic Journalism* 241 (1978).
[232]SEC v. Capital Gains Research Bureau, Inc., 375 U.S. 180, 186 (1963).

which regulates the initial offering and sale of securities.[233] A year later Congress enacted the Securities Exchange Act of 1934, which regulates the trading of securities on stock exchanges after they have been offered.[234] Another relevant measure that was enacted during the Roosevelt administration is the Investment Advisers Act of 1940, which regulates some financial publications.[235]

The securities acts are administered by the Securities and Exchange Commission (SEC), created in 1934. The SEC is an independent, bipartisan, quasi-judicial agency. The SEC has five members, not more than three of whom can belong to the same political party. They are appointed by the president for five-year staggered terms. The SEC oversees the financial disclosure that is required of companies traded on the stock exchanges. Recently, the SEC has also begun to regulate disclosure by cities and public agencies that issue municipal bonds.[236]

Mandated Disclosure

The securities statutes mandate disclosure of financial information about securities that are bought and sold on the stock exchanges. The Securities Act of 1933 requires disclosure in connection with registering securities for sale. The Securities Exchange Act of 1934 mandates corporate disclosure in connection with the trading of those securities. *Security* has been defined broadly under federal law to include stocks, bonds, and a variety of other investment vehicles where the purchaser does not take an active role in managing the investment.[237]

REGISTERING SECURITIES The 1933 Securities Act was passed to provide investors with the information they need to make intelligent decisions when purchasing new stock offerings. To achieve this goal, Section 5(c) of the Securities Act prohibits a company from "going public" by offering its stock for sale before it has filed a registration statement with the SEC containing extensive financial information about the company.[238] A company whose shares are already traded on an exchange must file registration statements if a new stock offering is made. After a company files a registration statement with the SEC, there is a brief waiting period during which a company cannot advertise or offer to sell the securities the company hopes investors eventually will buy. The waiting period allows investors "to become acquainted with the information contained in the registration statement and to arrive at an unhurried decision concerning the merits of the securities." After the waiting period, a company may advertise the shares for sale.

While a company is waiting to offer shares of stock to the public, it may issue press releases, advertise its products, and continue its other usual communications. However, the company may not seek purchasers of its new shares of stock until the SEC declares its registration "effective."

In a famous case, the Arvida Corporation violated Section 5(c) of the Securities Act by inviting investors to purchase Arvida stock before a registration statement had

[233]Ch. 2A, 48 Stat. 74 (codified as amended at 15 U.S.C. § 77a).
[234]Ch. 2A, 48 Stat. 881 (codified as amended at 15 U.S.C. § 78a).
[235]Ch. 2A, 54 Stat. 847 (codified as amended at 15 U.S.C. § 80b-1).
[236]Municipal Securities Disclosure, 59 Fed. Reg. 59,590 (1994).
[237]*See* Donald Langevoort, "What Is a Security?: Some Things You Won't Believe," in *Nuts and Bolts of Securities Law* at 33 (1995).
[238]SEC v. Arvida Corp., 169 F. Supp. 211 (S.D.N.Y. 1958).

been completed.[239] Arvida was formed by the industrialist Arthur Vining Davis when he transferred much of his extensive Florida real estate holdings to the corporation. Davis planned to raise additional capital through an offering of stock to the public. When the financing proposal reached final form but before registration was filed with the SEC, a press release was issued on the letterhead of Loeb, Rhoades & Co., a New York brokerage.

The Loeb, Rhoades press release said Arvida would have assets of more than $100 million. The release also said that Davis would transfer to Arvida more than 100,000 acres near the Florida "Gold Coast" for development. To help ensure wide dissemination of the press release in the most prestigious papers, the public relations counsel for Loeb, Rhoades invited reporters from the *New York Times,* the *New York Herald-Tribune,* and the *Wall Street Journal* to its offices in time to meet the papers' deadlines. A company official told the reporters that the stock would sell for about $10 a share but declined to answer questions about debt on the property, capitalization of Arvida, the company's balance sheet, or control of the corporation. The substance of the press release appeared in the three New York newspapers and numerous other news media throughout the country.

The SEC charged that the release violated Section 5 because it, along with earlier publicity, was calculated "to set in motion the processes of distribution" of stock before registration "by arousing and stimulating investor and dealer interest in Arvida securities."[240] To the SEC, the "arresting references" in the press release to assets in excess of $100 million and to over 100,000 acres on the Florida Gold Coast were part of an illegal selling effort. Indeed, an SEC survey found that within two business days, the publicity had resulted in investor interest worth at least $500,000.

The SEC rejected Loeb, Rhoades's contention that the release and publicity about Arvida were legal because they were legitimate news. Section 5(c), the SEC said, "is equally applicable" whether or not "astute public relations activities" make an illegal stock offering appear to have news value. Indeed, the SEC reasoned, "the danger to investors from publicity amounting to a selling effort may be greater in cases where an issue has 'news value' since it may be easier to whip up a 'speculative frenzy' . . . by incomplete or misleading publicity" and thus aid distribution of an unsound security at inflated prices. This, the SEC concluded, "is precisely the evil which the Securities Act seeks to prevent." The SEC did not want to dam up the normal flow of information, but, the SEC said, the company and its underwriters cannot be part of a publicity campaign that constitutes an offer to sell or solicitation of an offer to buy before registration of a security.

When Arvida's final prospectus was made public, the SEC found support for its decision to enforce Section 5(c). Whereas the press release had stressed the great acreage owned by Arvida, the final prospectus describing the stock revealed that the bulk of the land was not usable in its present condition and was located in areas remote from existing development. The final prospectus also revealed significant debt, indicating that the bulk of the money raised through the stock offering might be used to retire the debt rather than to develop the land. The fuller truth disclosed in the final prospectus proved to the SEC's satisfaction the superiority of the mandated disclosure system over investment decisions "brought about by press releases."

[239] *Id.* at 213–14.

[240] *In re* Carl M. Loeb, Rhoades & Co., 38 S.E.C. 843, 851 (1959).

The *Arvida* case raised no First Amendment issues, but the SEC noted that Section 5(c) of the 1933 act "in no way restricts the freedom of news media to seek out and publish financial news." The Section 5(c) prohibition does not violate the First Amendment rights of underwriters because they are in the business of distributing securities, not news, the SEC said. The restrictions of Section 5(c) do not apply to reporters, who presumably "have no securities to sell."

TRADING SECURITIES Whereas the Securities Act of 1933 is concerned primarily with financial disclosure before a security is traded on an exchange, the Securities Exchange Act of 1934 is principally concerned with the trading of securities from one purchaser to another after distribution on the nation's stock exchanges. Under the 1934 act, large publicly traded corporations are required to file annual, quarterly, and other reports with the SEC about the company's operations.[241] Other sections of the act regulate the solicitation of proxies and tender offers.[242] *Proxy statements* announce annual and special shareholder meetings. *Tender offers* are offers by one company to buy controlling shares of another company.

Annual and Quarterly Reports Annual reports, which must be sent to shareholders and filed for public inspection with the SEC, are one of the most effective media through which information is disseminated to the investment community. Corporate reports contain information about management, net sales, earnings, dividends, and other information about the financial condition of the company. The annual report also contains the "management discussion and analysis" that describes in detail the capital resources, results of company operations, and projected performance. If a projection turns out to be wrong, a businessperson may be protected from a fraud suit if the projection (1) was prepared with a reasonable basis and (2) was disclosed in good faith.[243]

Much of the information in an annual report is updated in required quarterly reports. Between quarterly reports, publicly traded corporations are also mandated to report a few significant developments within fifteen days of their occurrence. Between quarterly reports, companies are required to report to the SEC on form 8-K changes in control of the company, the buying or selling of significant assets, filing for bankruptcy or receivership, changes in the company's certified public accountants, and the resignation of directors.[244] The SEC says that a corporation may, "at its option," report other important occurrences, but the law does not require the company to do so unless disclosure is necessary to avoid fraud.

Although these interim disclosures provide the markets with valuable information, they do not require disclosure of several important corporate and market changes that would be of interest to investors. For example, the SEC does not explicitly require 8-K reports in the event of major litigation against the company. The interim disclosure policies are also weakened by the fifteen-day period in which companies may file their 8-K reports; fifteen days is a long time in fast-moving markets. Furthermore, the effectiveness of the interim reports is undermined by the fact that individual investors are not allowed to sue over violations.[245]

[241] 15 U.S.C. § 78m; 17 C.F.R. § 240.13a-1 et seq.
[242] 15 U.S.C. § 78n; 17 C.F.R. § 240.14a-1.
[243] 17 C.F.R. § 230.175.
[244] 17 C.F.R. § 240.13a-11.
[245] *See* J. Robert Brown, *The Regulation of Corporate Disclosure* 8-16 (1989).

The stock exchanges require much faster disclosure of a much broader range of information than must be disclosed under securities law. The New York Stock Exchange and the American Stock Exchange have adopted rules that generally require rapid disclosure of all material corporate developments.[246] Although listed companies often follow the exchange rules, violations of exchange requirements, like failure to follow SEC regulations, often go unpunished. The enforcement powers of the exchanges are too drastic to be employed frequently or effectively. The New York and American exchanges may halt trading or "delist" companies that disclose too little information. But exchanges competing for corporate listings are reluctant to employ such severe penalties.

Proxies and Annual Meetings Besides reporting regularly in quarterly and annual reports, publicly traded companies must tell shareholders in proxy statements when and where the shareholder meetings will be held and what business will be conducted.[247] Proxy statements must also include extensive information about the compensation of chief executive officers and other highly paid executives. Shareholders who will not attend the annual meeting can vote by proxy on various proposals, including management changes and proposals submitted by shareholders. When shareholders vote by proxy, they give their proxy holder, often a committee designated by management, the authority to vote their shares as they instruct on their proxy statement. Through "proxy fights," dissident directors or minority stockholders may "solicit" shareholders to vote their proxies against management. Through proxy fights, dissident shareholders can sometimes vote management out of office, thus gaining control of a company without buying a majority of shares. Under securities law, neither corporations nor dissident stockholders may issue false or misleading statements to shareholders in an effort to sway their votes.

False or misleading proxy solicitations may be halted whether they are targeted directly at shareholders or are communicated more indirectly through speeches, press releases, and television scripts for the public. The U.S. Court of Appeals for the Second Circuit ruled that even a newspaper advertisement placed by a citizens group might be halted if it contained false statements published in an attempt to influence shareholders in a proxy fight.[248] The case involved a newspaper advertisement purchased by a citizens group opposed to the Long Island Lighting Company, known as LILCO. The citizens group was associated with dissident stockholders who hoped to oust LILCO management in a proxy fight. The ad accused LILCO of mismanagement and of attempting to saddle ratepayers with the needless costs of constructing the controversial Shoreham Nuclear Power Plant. The ad urged that LILCO, a company owned by shareholders, be managed by a public authority.

LILCO tried to halt the advertisement, claiming that it contained false statements attempting to sway LILCO shareholders to vote against management. But a federal district court ruled that the newspaper ad purchased by a citizens group was constitutionally protected political expression.[249] However, the U.S. Court of Appeals for the Second Circuit reversed the lower court. Avoiding the First Amendment issue, the appellate court treated

[246]*Id.* at 76–77.
[247]15 U.S.C. § 78n; 17 C.F.R. § 240.14a-1.
[248]Long Island Lighting Co. v. Barbash, 779 F.2d 793 (2d Cir. 1985).
[249]Long Island Lighting Co. v. Barbash, 625 F. Supp. 221 (E.D.N.Y. 1985).

the case as a narrow issue of securities regulation, noting, "The SEC's authority to regulate proxy solicitations has traditionally extended into matters of public interest." The appeals court remanded the case, asking the lower court to determine whether the ad in a general-circulation newspaper actually solicited shareholders' votes.

Tender Offers Corporate takeovers may be attempted through proxy fights at a company's annual meeting. More often, however, one company buys another by making an offer to stockholders of the other company to tender—or surrender—their shares for a certain price, usually well above the current market price of a stock. Securities law requires that takeover bidders disclose information about themselves to shareholders of the target company. The securities law requires that anyone who rapidly acquires more than 5 percent of another company—and who may be anticipating buying much more—file with the SEC, the target company, and the exchange where the target's stock is traded a statement describing the buyer's "background and identity." Any company that buys a large position in another company must also disclose the source and amount of funds to be used in buying shares, the extent of the buyer's holdings in the target corporation, and the buyer's plans for the target corporation's business or corporate structure.[250]

Summary

The securities laws require stock companies to disclose financial information before shares are offered and while they are being traded. Mandated disclosure includes prospectuses before a stock is offered for sale and periodic reports after trading begins. Although companies must disclose a few significant events if they occur between annual reports, corporations may withhold much information if there is no intent to conceal fraud. Rules regulating communications to shareholders have been held to extend to political advertisements that might affect shareholders' votes.

Fraud

Corporations that knowingly make false or misleading statements in their annual reports, proxy statements, and other communications mandated by the securities acts commit fraud. It is also fraudulent for corporate executives to knowingly make false statements in speeches and press releases if the statements would affect the price of the company's stock. Both federal law and individual states' laws—so-called *blue-sky laws*—outlaw fraud in connection with securities transactions.

Most fraud litigation is brought under Section 10(b) of the 1934 Securities Exchange Act and Rule 10b-5 of the *Code of Federal Regulations.* Section 10(b) makes it unlawful for a corporation or its agent to be manipulative or deceptive in connection with the purchase or sale of securities. Under Rule 10b-5, it is manipulative or deceptive for a company to make a deliberately misleading material statement. It is also fraudulent for a company to fail to clarify a statement to avoid misleading investors. Investors may sue to enjoin deception and to recover money lost because of reliance on deceptive statements.

[250] 17 U.S.C. § 78m(d). *See also* Piper v. Chris-Craft Indus., Inc., 430 U.S. 1, 26–37 (1977).

MATERIALLY DECEPTIVE FACTS For a statement to be fraudulent, it must involve a material fact. Material facts are facts important to the decision of a reasonable investor to buy, sell, or hold a security. A fact is material in a proxy statement, the Supreme Court said, "if there is a substantial likelihood that a reasonable shareholder would consider it important in deciding how to vote." To be material, a fact must not necessarily change an investor's decision to buy or sell. A fact is material if it would be significant to reasonable shareholders in the "total mix" of their information.[251]

Material facts include a sharp change in company earnings, the imminence of a very profitable transaction, and information about a possible merger or bankruptcy.[252]

Material facts also may include the illness or disability of a key executive.[253] A nonmaterial fact would be the color of the chief executive's office. Thus, a company might falsely state the color of the boss's office without committing fraud because the color is not important to investors' decisions to buy or sell.

The merger of two companies is usually important to investors, thus raising the question at what point merger negotiations become material and therefore can no longer be lawfully denied. Are casual lunches at which executives gently probe the possibility of a merger material? Or does a merger become material only when the documents joining two companies are signed?

The Supreme Court has ruled that merger negotiations become material either when they are so advanced as to make a merger very probable or at an earlier point in the discussions if the magnitude of the merger would dramatically alter the company.[254] Thus, discussions of big mergers become material before discussions of insignificant mergers, and discussions that seem likely to result in mergers are material before discussions in which mergers seem improbable. Until mergers and other developments become material, companies can lawfully deny them.

Following major corporate financial scandals, Congress in 2002 passed important legislation to increase corporate accountability and restore confidence in the markets.[255] Just before the fall elections, Congress passed the Sarbanes-Oxley Act to increase trust in corporate accounting, which was undermined repeatedly by unreported sweetheart loans, off-the-books entities, and insider dealing at infamous companies called Enron, Arthur Andersen, ImClone, Global Crossing, WorldCom, and Adelphia.

The major focus of Sarbanes-Oxley is to strengthen independent accounting at publicly traded companies. Sarbanes-Oxley also requires faster and more complete disclosure of important changes at publicly traded companies. From now on, companies must disclose in their annual reports material transactions and special-purpose entities that are not reported on the corporate balance sheet.[256] Other material changes to a company's financial condition must be reported on a "rapid and current basis."

Sarbanes-Oxley also increased criminal penalties greatly. Penalties for corporate mail and wire fraud were quadrupled from five years in prison to twenty years.

[251] TSC Indus., Inc. v. Northway, Inc., 426 U.S. 438, 449 (1976).

[252] Dirks v. SEC, 463 U.S. 646 (1983); Northern Trust Co. v. Essaness Theatres Corp., 103 F. Supp. 954 (N.D. Ill. 1952); *In re* Ward La France Truck Corp., 13 S.E.C. 373 (1943).

[253] Wesley Walton & Charles Brissman, *Corporate Communications Handbook* 4-37 (1990).

[254] Basic, Inc. v. Levinson, 485 U.S. 224 (1988).

[255] Sarbanes-Oxley Act of 2002 (Pub. L. No. 107-204, 116 Stat. 745, also known as the Public Company Accounting Reform and Investor Protection Act of 2002 and commonly called SOX or SarbOx.

[256] 17 C.F.R. §§ 228, 229, 232, 240, 249, 270 and 274.

Misstatements Materially deceptive facts can be positive misstatements or omissions. It was a material misstatement for the director of the Livingston Oil Company to overstate the corporation's income during a speech to securities analysts. The speech was later distributed to shareholders to encourage more sales of stock.[257]

The Supreme Court has ruled it is materially misleading for management to give advice to shareholders that is not based on generally accepted fact. In *Virginia Bankshares, Inc. v. Sandberg*, [258] the Court agreed, 8-1, that a Virginia bank misled minority shareholders when it urged them to approve a buyout of their stock at $42 per share as part of a merger. Management told the shareholders in proxy statements that $42 per share was a "high" value and that terms of the merger were "fair."

Management's "conclusory terms in a commercial context" were misleading, the Court said, because they were not based in fact. The Court agreed with lower-court conclusions that management's statements were misleading because the $42 share price was neither high nor fair "when assessed in accordance with recognized methods of valuation." Management's evaluation, the Court said, "was open to attack by garden-variety evidence."

However, the Court ruled against the shareholders seeking payment above $42 per share from the bank. A five-member majority of the Court ruled that the minority shareholders were not entitled to additional compensation because they could not prove that they lost money as a result of the misleading statements soliciting their proxies. The Court said that the misleading proxy statements did not cost the shareholders money because the shareholders' proxies were not legally necessary for the bank merger to occur.

Public relations firms cannot avoid liability for fraud if they blindly pass along misleading investment information for their corporate clients. A federal judge in Illinois told a corporate financial relations firm it could rely on corporate clients' representations only if the PR firm also made a "reasonable investigation" to satisfy itself that the statements were true.[259] The SEC has reiterated the financial public relations firm's responsibility to withhold corporate information it knows or has reason to know is false.[260]

A 1995 amendment to the federal securities laws provides a "safe harbor" for predictions by corporations as long as they are accompanied by adequate cautionary statements.[261] The safe harbor provision—called a "pirate's cove" by detractors—allows companies to make predictions about earnings or new products without liability for fraud if the predictions are subsequently proven wrong. However, to benefit from the safe harbor, the prediction must caution investors about important factors that could create results different from those envisioned by management.

Omissions More common than misstatements of material facts are deceptive half-truths or omissions. The Electric Autolite Company misled shareholders when it disclosed a proposed merger but failed to tell them in proxy statements that the Autolite board of directors, which recommended a merger with the Mergenthaler Linotype Company, was already under the control of Mergenthaler.[262]

---

[257]Sprayregen v. Livingston Oil Co., 295 F. Supp. 1376 (S.D.N.Y. 1968).
[258]501 U.S. 1083 (1991).
[259]SEC v. Pig 'N' Whistle Corp. [1971–1972 Transfer Binder] Fed. Sec. L. Rep. (CCH) ¶ 93,384 (N.D. Ill. 1972).
[260]*In re* Howard Bronson & Co., SEC Release No. 21138 (July 12, 1984).
[261]104 Pub. L. No. 67, 109 Stat. 737 (1995).
[262]Mills v. Electric Autolite Co., 403 F.2d 429, 434 (7th Cir. 1968), *vacated and remanded,* 396 U.S. 375 (1970).

In one of the most famous public relations fraud cases, the Texas Gulf Sulphur Company (TGS) issued a materially deceptive press release to dampen rumors of a major copper discovery. In its press release, TGS said that press reports of the company's substantial copper discovery in Timmins, Ontario, were exaggerated. The release said public estimates about the size and grade of ore were "without factual basis and have evidently originated by speculation of people not connected with TGS."[263] Relying on this negative release, several investors sold shares in the company, only to learn from a Texas Gulf Sulphur press release twelve days later that the company had made a ten-million-ton ore strike, one of the largest in history.

In court, Texas Gulf Sulphur said it would have been premature and possibly misleading for the company in its first release to speculate on the size and grade of ore at the mining site. The company had not yet had the ore samples analyzed chemically. But a federal appeals court ruled that the known richness of the ore samples even before chemical analysis was material and did not justify a press release as negative as the company first issued. As evidence that the ore samples were material to investors' decisions even before the samples were chemically analyzed, the court noted that several Texas Gulf Sulphur executives bought additional shares of the company before the ore strike was announced.

The U.S. Court of Appeals for the Second Circuit said the TGS press release misleadingly suggested there was no basis for investor optimism. The court did not require a company to issue a press release to quell rumors but said that material facts should be complete and accurate once a company issues a public statement. Instead of saying speculation about a major ore find was without factual basis, Texas Gulf Sulphur should have said nothing, told how promising the ore samples were by visual inspection, or said the situation was in flux.

How much to reveal, if anything, during searches for raw materials, merger negotiations, land acquisitions, and other delicate periods may be a difficult corporate decision. Nevertheless, silence may sometimes be the best policy to keep negotiations on track and to avoid charges of fraud for partial revelations. Silence may be difficult to maintain when a company would like to be forthcoming and when securities analysts and the media are clamoring for information.

Even when a company communicates material facts, statements may be misleading because of the format of presentation. The American-Hawaiian Steamship Company was held to have issued a deceptive proxy statement because the company obscured the truth by scattering material facts through a lengthy document.[264] Use of unnecessarily technical terminology can also be misleading. However, the SEC encourages some businesses, including oil companies, to use technical terms familiar to experienced investors when precision is necessary to avoid deception.

A company's use of a technical term is not deceptive simply because investors might not be familiar with it. The Sable Company was ruled not to be deceptive when it issued a press release announcing the company was filing a new "investigational" application with the Food and Drug Administration (FDA) to develop soft contact lenses. Investigational applications are filed when significant product development is necessary before marketing. The company did not say in its release that it usually takes several years before the government approves an investigational product for the market.

[263]SEC v. Texas Gulf Sulphur Co., 401 F.2d 833, 845 (1968), *cert. denied,* 394 U.S. 976 (1969).
[264]Gould v. American-Hawaiian Steamship Co., 535 F.2d 761, 774 (3d Cir. 1976).

Investors unfamiliar with the lengthy approval process for investigational applications were disappointed that the company's technology would not lead to higher earnings and stock prices for several years. One investor sued Sable for issuing misleading information. However, a federal district court said that a claim that Sable misled investors could not be based on the plaintiff's ignorance. "Where the public can make the evaluation as to how beneficial a certain corporate action will be to the earning picture of that corporation, the omission of information about the decision-making process of a government agency is not a violation of Rule 10b-5," the court said. Indeed, the court said the company probably would have misled investors if it had tried to announce a time at which the FDA would approve the lenses for marketing.[265]

Failure to Disclose Payment for Publicity Another fraud securities law prohibits is failure of publishers and public relations practitioners to disclose payments they receive for corporate publicity affecting a security. Such failure can violate Rule 10b-5 or Section 17(b) of the Securities Act. Section 17(b) makes it illegal to "publish, give publicity to, or circulate any notice, circular, advertisement, newspaper, article, letter, investment service, or communication about a security without revealing payments received."[266] The purpose of the section is to halt articles in newspapers or periodicals that appear to be unbiased opinion about a company but that in fact are purchased.[267]

Stock Market Magazine was charged with fraud for failing to reveal that it published corporate features for companies that bought advertising and story reprints.[268] The U.S. Court of Appeals for the District of Columbia sent the case to a federal district court for a determination as to whether the magazine, which offered financial news to some 12,000 subscribers, was publishing the articles in exchange for corporate purchases of advertising and reprints. If so, the magazine could be required to disclose these payments. The magazine contended there was no quid pro quo that needed to be revealed under the securities laws.

The Court of Appeals told the district court that although the lower court was investigating whether articles were published in return for advertising and reprint sales, the court could not demand to know who wrote the articles in question. The Securities and Exchange Commission had argued that the magazine should be required to reveal not only that it sold advertising and reprints but also that featured companies sometimes wrote the articles, paid public relations firms to write them, or paid editors of *Stock Market Magazine* to write them. The appeals court said the First Amendment prohibits inquiry into who pays a writer or how much of a published article is written by someone outside a magazine. Such inquiry, the court said, would impermissibly interfere with editorial judgments about constitutionally protected content.

The First Amendment protects the publisher's right to determine who writes and edits published material, the court said. Content is protected whether the writer is paid by a publisher, a public relations firm, or a featured company. A magazine might be required to disclose that it received payments or sold advertising and reprints as a condition for

[265]Zucker v. Sable, 425 F. Supp. 658 (S.D.N.Y. 1976).

[266]15 U.S.C. § 77q(b).

[267]H.R. Rep. No. 85, 73d Cong., 1st Sess. 24 (1933), *cited in* United States v. Amick, 439 F.2d 351, 365 n.18 (7th Cir. 1971), *cert. denied*, 404 U.S. 823 (1971).

[268]SEC v. Wall St. Publishing Inst., 851 F.2d 365 (D.C. Cir. 1988), *cert. denied*, 489 U.S. 1066 (1989).

publishing an article, the court said, but the First Amendment bars requiring a magazine to disclose who wrote which parts of a business article.

Public relations practitioners are also supposed to disclose payment from companies they promote. The SEC has warned public relations firms that they violate the Securities Act if they do not reveal payment for preparation and dissemination of material designed to make a new stock offering look like an attractive investment.[269]

IN CONNECTION WITH A PURCHASE OR SALE Under Rule 10b-5, not only must fraudulent statements be material, they must also be "in connection with the purchase or sale of any security." The *in-connection-with* test is met if a corporation issues a materially false or misleading statement on which other investors rely for their purchases or sales. But reliance by investors may be presumed when a company makes materially false or misleading statements. In the *Texas Gulf Sulphur* case, the Second Circuit Court of Appeals said the in-connection-with test was met when Texas Gulf Sulphur issued a misleading statement "reasonably calculated to influence the investing public."[270]

Courts have ruled the in-connection-with requirement is also met when materially false statements are made in corporate annual reports,[271] product promotions,[272] speeches by corporate directors to securities analysts,[273] and advertisements.[274] In each case, investors might rely on the statements when buying or selling securities. The SEC has also warned companies that statements made during rate-filing hearings, during labor negotiations, and in other public circumstances must be factual because they too can be heard and relied on by investors.[275]

DUTY TO CORRECT STATEMENTS ATTRIBUTED TO THE COMPANY A publicly traded corporation has an affirmative duty to correct a published material misstatement if the error originates with the corporation or its agent. In *Green v. Jonhop,* [276] a federal court said that a corporation had an obligation to correct falsely optimistic earnings projections made by an underwriter who marketed the company's securities. Corporate silence in the face of falsely optimistic earnings projections, the court said, could fraudulently encourage investors to rely on the underwriter's statements.

A corporation also has a responsibility to correct misstatements if the company approves or helps to draft reports by stock analysts or public relations firms containing material misinformation. The U.S. Court of Appeals for the Second Circuit noted that corporate officials who review outside analysts' reports engage in "a risky activity, fraught with danger" because officials, by their participation, make "an implied representation that the information they have reviewed is true or at least in accordance with the company's

[269]Howard Bronson & Co., SEC Release No. 21138 (July 12, 1984). *See also* SEC v. Pig 'N' Whistle Corp. [1971–1972 Transfer Binder] Fed. Sec. L. Rep. (CCH) ¶ 93,384 (N.D. Ill. 1972).

[270]SEC v. Texas Gulf Sulphur Co., 401 F.2d 833, 862 (1968).

[271]Heit v. Weitzen, 402 F.2d 909 (2d Cir. 1968), *cert. denied,* 395 U.S. 903 (1969).

[272]SEC v. Electrogen Indus., Inc. [1967–1969 Decisions] Fed. Sec. L. Rep. (CCH) ¶ 92,156 (E.D.N.Y. 1968).

[273]Sprayregen v. Livingston Oil Co., 295 F. Supp. 1376 (S.D.N.Y. 1968).

[274]*See* Donald Feuerstein, "The Corporation's Obligations of Disclosure under the Federal Securities Laws When It Is Not Trading Its Stock," 15 *N.Y. L. Forum* 385, 393 (1969).

[275]SEC Release No. 34-20560 (Jan. 20, 1984).

[276]358 F. Supp. 413 (D. Or. 1973).

views."[277] In addition, corporate officials must treat with caution any activity that suggests that the company has "ratified" a particular analysts' projections. One corporate communication manual suggests that "the company should avoid disseminating analysts' reports."[278]

A corporation may also have a duty to correct its own statements if changing conditions transform accurate statements into misleading statements. A U.S. district court said the A. H. Robins Company had a duty to update statements in its stockholder annual reports indicating that the company's Dalkon Shield contraceptive was safer and more effective than other similar devices on the market. A study that was published after Robins's first reports indicated that the contraceptive was not as safe or effective as Robins first indicated.[279] Another court ruled that the Shattuck Denn Mining Corporation had an obligation to tell investors that a previously announced merger deal had fallen through. Without the update, investors could buy Shattuck's stock with the mistaken belief that the merger would increase profits.[280] Courts have generally been vague about how long an initial corporate communication remains "alive" and thus subject to correction, although it is clear that eventually a statement will become stale and thus not require correcting.[281] One way to limit the "life" of a press release might be to use phrases such as "at present" or "right now."[282]

A corporation generally has no duty to respond to market gossip and rumors not attributable to the company.[283] In the *Texas Gulf Sulphur* case, the court said that the company did not have to respond to speculation about the company's ore discovery because the speculation did not originate with the company. Texas Gulf Sulphur statements were fraudulent because the company responded on its own initiative to rumors in a less than complete statement.

Similarly, a corporation has no duty to respond to an inaccurate interpretive article that is not attributable to the company. The U.S. Court of Appeals for the Second Circuit ruled that the International Controls Corporation (ICC) had no duty to respond to Dan Dorfman's report in the *Wall Street Journal* about ICC's plan to buy the Electronic Specialty Company. The speculation about the plan turned out to be true, but the price per share that Dorfman quoted was considerably higher than ICC was offering. ICC had no duty to respond because the company was not the source of the speculation.[284]

Even if an inaccurate news article is attributed to a company, a corporation probably has no duty to correct the article if information the company provided was accurate. In *Zucker v. Sable,* a federal district court said it would be unreasonable to require a company "to examine every financial publication to ascertain whether the reports of its admittedly accurate press release have been misinterpreted so as to mislead members

[277]Elkind v. Liggett & Myers, Inc., 635 F.2d 156, 163 (2d Cir. 1980).

[278]Wesley Walton & Charles Brissman, *Corporate Communications Handbook* 4-9 (1990).

[279]Ross v. A. H. Robins Co., 465 F. Supp. 904 (S.D.N.Y. 1979), *rev'd,* 607 F.2d 545 (2d Cir. 1979), *cert. denied,* 446 U.S. 946, *reh'g denied,* 448 U.S. 911, *on remand,* 100 F.R.D. 5 (1982).

[280]SEC v. Shattuck Denn Mining Corp., 297 F. Supp. 470 (S.D.N.Y. 1968). *See also* Financial Indus. Fund, Inc. v. McDonnell Douglas Corp., 474 F.2d 514 (10th Cir.) (per curiam) (en banc), *cert. denied,* 414 U.S. 874 (1973).

[281]Wesley Walton & Charles Brissman, *Corporate Communications Handbook* 2-11 (1990).

[282]Donald Langevoort, "Corporate Disclosure and Insider Trading: Keeping Your Client Out of Trouble," in *Nuts and Bolts of Securities Law* at 304 (1995).

[283]*See* John Sheffey, Securities Law Responsibilities of Issuers to Respond to Rumors and Other Publicity: Reexamination of a Continuing Problem, 57 *Notre Dame Law* 755 (1982).

[284]Electronic Specialty Co. v. International Controls Corp., 409 F.2d 937, 949 (2d Cir. 1969). *See also* Greenfield v. Heublein, Inc., 742 F.2d 751 (3d Cir. 1984).

of the public."[285] In *Zucker,* the newspapers had published misleading stories about the Sable company by omitting the word *investigational,* which had been included in Sable's press release. Sable had filed an investigational application with the Food and Drug Administration for development of plastic lenses. The word *investigational* was a critical omission in the news reports because investigational applications, which indicate time-consuming product research is not complete, can take many years for FDA approval.

DUTY TO DISCLOSE INSIDER TRADING Besides a duty to correct its own false or misleading statements, a corporation and its "insiders" also have a duty to disclose material information when they plan to base purchases or sales of company stock on nonpublic information. This duty to disclose to avoid fraud arises from executives' financial responsibility to shareholders and the markets. Publishers of personal investment advisories and some financial journalists may also have a duty to disclose nonpublic information they intend to profit from.

Insiders An assumption underlying the securities laws—although not all legal scholars agree—is that it is unfair for insiders to buy and sell a company's stock for their own benefit if they base their decision on nonpublic material facts. The theory is that every investor should have equal access to material information about a stock. Insiders have a duty to disclose material information before trading because of the fiduciary nature of their positions. Fiduciaries are people who have a position of trust that prohibits them from acting only in their own self-interest. In the corporate context, an executive is entrusted by shareholders with responsibility to manage the shareholders' assets and is therefore supposed to act in the shareholders' interest. To avoid a conflict of interest, Rule 10b-5 imposes a duty on insiders who possess valuable nonpublic information either to disclose the information or to refrain from trading.[286]

Securities statutes do not define *insider,* and congressional attempts to define it have failed. But the Supreme Court, agreeing with the SEC, has defined an insider as one who, by virtue of his or her position with the issuer of stock, has access to nonpublic corporate information that is supposed to be used only for corporate purposes, not for personal benefit.[287] This definition covers corporate officers, directors, controlling stockholders, and corporate public relations executives.

Certain outsiders may acquire the duties of insiders if they "have entered into a special confidential relationship in the conduct of the business of the enterprise and are given access to information solely for corporate purposes."[288] These temporary insiders or quasi-insiders include accountants, lawyers, and public relations counsel who have access to nonpublic material information that is intended only for corporate use. These quasi-insiders, like permanent insiders, are supposed to make true and accurate statements about material aspects of a company and are supposed to abstain from trading if they have not disclosed the material information on which trades might be based.

---

[285] 426 F. Supp. 658, 663 (1976). *See also* Mills v. Sarjem Corp., 133 F. Supp. 753 (D.N.J. 1955).

[286] *See* SEC v. Texas Gulf Sulphur Co., 401 F.2d 833 (2d Cir. 1968), *cert. denied*, 394 U.S. 976 (1969). *But see* Henry G. Manne, *Insider Trading and the Stock Market* (1966).

[287] Dirks v. SEC, 463 U.S. 646, 653 (1983), *citing* Chiarella v. United States, 445 U.S. 222, 227 (1980), and *in re* Cady, Roberts & Co., 40 S.E.C. 907 (1961).

[288] Dirks v. SEC, 463 U.S. at 655, n.14. *See also* Elkind v. Liggett & Myers, Inc., 635 F.2d 156 (2d Cir. 1980); SEC v. Texas Gulf Sulphur Co., 401 F.2d 833 (2d Cir. 1968).

Anthony M. Franco, head of Michigan's largest public relations firm, resigned the presidency of the Public Relations Society of America after the SEC accused him of insider trading. Without admitting guilt, Franco agreed not to trade on inside information. The SEC accused Franco of buying stock in Crowley, Milner and Company just before Franco, as public relations adviser to the company, announced that another company would purchase Crowley.[289]

A variation of illegal insider trading is *tipping*. Tipping is the practice of passing nonpublic material information to friends or brokers so that they can trade. The "tipper" may be liable for fraud along with the "tippee." The *Texas Gulf Sulphur* case is a well-known example of both insider trading and tipping. In *Texas Gulf Sulphur,* the federal appeals court found that executives of the mining company violated insider trading prohibitions by buying stock in the company and also by tipping friends when the insiders learned ahead of the public of the very promising copper ore samples taken at a site in Timmins, Ontario. In ruling that the insiders' stock purchases were illegal, the court said the investing public should have the same access to material corporate information as a corporate insider. Under legislation passed since *Texas Gulf Sulphur* was decided, inside traders may have to repay three times their illegal profits.

In an effort to curb insider trading, Congress passed legislation that increased penalties, extended liability, and encouraged revelation of insider trading. Under the Insider Trading and Securities Fraud Enforcement Act of 1988, not only are illegal traders and tippers liable, but so also are those brokers, investment advisers, and other supervisors who fail to take appropriate steps to prevent illegal trading.[290] The act also increases criminal penalties and allows the Securities and Exchange Commission to pay persons who provide information about insider trading.

Quasi-Insiders People using confidential information to buy or sell securities violate the insider trading laws, even if the traders have no direct association with the company whose shares they trade. The U.S. Supreme Court said that a company owns its nonpublic information just as it does the rest of its property, and the information is for the company's exclusive use.[291] A person violates the securities laws by misappropriating insider information, such as the unpublished fact that a company is targeted for a takeover. The Court's decision came in a case that arose when James O'Hagan bought shares of the Pillsbury Company before the flour miller was purchased by a British company. The Court ruled O'Hagan had misappropriated information belonging to his Minneapolis law firm when he bought the shares. O'Hagan's firm represented Grand Metropolitan PLC (Grand Met), a British company, which hired a Minneapolis law firm to represent it while it was considering its takeover bid for Pillsbury. Pillsbury's share value increased dramatically when Grand Met announced that it would bid for the company. O'Hagan sold his shares for a profit of more than $4.3 million.

Although O'Hagan was not involved directly in representing Grand Met, he was convicted of violating securities, federal mail fraud, and money-laundering laws. The Supreme Court upheld the convictions. The Court said that in addition to the "traditional" theory of insider trading, which is applicable when, for example, a company director or officer uses nonpublic information to trade in the company's stock, there is a second approach—the

[289]SEC v. Franco, Lit. Release No. 11206, 1986 LEXIS 909 (D.D.C. Aug. 26, 1986).
[290]15 U.S.C. § 78u-1. *See also* H.R. Rep. No. 910, 100th Cong., 2d Sess., reprinted in 1988 U.S.C.C.A.N. 6043.
[291]United States v. O'Hagan, 521 U.S. 642 (1997).

"misappropriation" theory. As in the Winans case, a person violates securities laws when she or he "misappropriates confidential information for securities trading purposes in breach of a duty owed to the source of the information."

In the *Grand Met* case, O'Hagan did not represent Grand Met, but his law firm did. The firm's connection allowed O'Hagan to learn nonpublic information: that Grand Met intended to make a bid for Pillsbury. It also created a fiduciary responsibility for him to let Grand Met know he would use that information to purchase Pillsbury stock or to refrain from buying the stock. Because he did neither, he misappropriated Grand Met's information to trade in Pillsbury's stock, and in doing so, he violated insider trading laws. The Court noted, however, if O'Hagan had found in a park trash can information about Grand Met's takeover plans, he would have no fiduciary duty. He could trade freely in Pillsbury stock.

Investment Advisers Stockbrokers and financial advisers have a fiduciary relationship with their clients much like that of a corporate insider with shareholders. Stockbrokers and financial advisers have a personal responsibility to their clients, imposing on the advisers a duty to register with the Securities and Exchange Commission and to avoid misleading customers for personal gain.

Although many publications offer advice about stocks and finances, most financial publications lack the personal relationship to investors and the direct involvement in investors' portfolios that create fiduciary responsibilities. In *Lowe v. SEC,* [292] the Supreme Court ruled that Christopher L. Lowe's *Lowe Stock Advisory* was not an investment advisory that must be registered with the Securities and Exchange Commission. Lowe's newsletter contained general commentary about the securities markets, reviews of investment strategies, and specific recommendations for buying, selling, or holding stocks. Lowe, however, did not manage individual investment portfolios through the newsletter.

A financial publication must register with the SEC as a personal investment advisory, the Court said, only if it offers "individualized advice attuned to any specific portfolio or any client's particular needs." Lowe's newsletter was not a personal investment advisory, the Court said, because it offered completely disinterested advice to the general public on a regular publication schedule. A financial newsletter, the Court said, is not so much like an investment adviser as it is like a newspaper; newspapers, newsmagazines, and general-circulation business publications are exempt from registration requirements of the SEC. The Court in *Lowe* suggested, but did not hold, that a telephone hotline Lowe offered to readers might be subject to the Investment Advisers Act even though his newsletter was not, because the hotline might be considered "personalized advice" about buying and selling securities.

Financial Journalists and Market Insiders There is another level of information processors who have access to corporate information but who do not have the fiduciary duties of a corporate insider, a quasi-insider, or an investment adviser. People in this group include financial journalists, publishers of impersonal financial newsletters, printers, bank employees, public relations practitioners, and employees of financial brokerage houses. These information handlers are sometimes called *market insiders* because they have access to information about mergers, tender offers, and other sensitive financial intelligence, but

[292] 472 U.S. 181 (1985).

they do not have the fiduciary relationship of insiders and quasi-insiders to companies issuing stock or of investment advisers to their clients.[293]

Although market insiders have no fiduciary duty to market traders, courts have ruled that employees of investment banking firms, financial printers, newspaper publishers, and other processors of market information violate Section 10(b) and Rule 10b-5 if they misappropriate information about mergers, acquisitions, and other confidential information for their own gain. Under a theory of misappropriation, market insiders have been ruled to engage in fraud in violation of Section 10(b) by taking market information belonging to their employers and using it to tip and trade for their own enrichment.[294]

By a 4-4 vote, the Supreme Court upheld the securities fraud conviction of R. Foster Winans, a *Wall Street Journal* reporter, who engaged in a form of "scalping."[295] (The 4-4 split means that the appeals court decision is precedent only in the Second Circuit.) A scalper manipulates the market, usually by buying stock, touting it in a publication, and then selling it when the price of the stock rises.[296] Winans passed financial information to a stockbroker, Peter Brant, who acted on the information before it appeared in the *Journal*'s "Heard on the Street" column, a column containing public information about companies' financial prospects. The influence of the *Wall Street Journal* is such that the price of a company's stock might fluctuate because of a favorable or unfavorable mention in the "Heard on the Street" column. Winans's tips resulted in a net profit of $690,000 for Brant and his clients. Winans and his roommate, who was also involved in the scheme, made about $31,000.

The Supreme Court upheld a ruling by the Second Circuit Court of Appeals that Winans violated Section 10(b) by misappropriating information belonging to his employer in violation of the *Journal*'s conflict-of-interest policy. The conflict-of-interest policy forbade staff members to trade on information before it is published. Like most newspapers, the *Wall Street Journal* claims ownership in all information gathered by its staff.[297]

Although Winans was not a corporate insider and was not trading on insider information, he was not exempt from the fraud provisions of the securities law. The Second Circuit said the securities laws are not aimed "solely at the eradication of fraudulent trading by corporate insiders." The fraud provisions also reach trading activity, such as trading on the basis of improperly obtained information, a practice that the court said is "fundamentally unfair."

The court said Winans's duty to abide by the *Journal*'s conflict-of-interest policy created another duty under Section 10(b) to avoid trading or tipping on the basis of misappropriated information. Winans's misuse of the *Journal*'s information before publication defrauded the newspaper, the court said, by sullying its reputation for ethical journalism.

The Second Circuit said that holding a journalist liable under a securities fraud statute did not violate the First Amendment because no government restrictions were placed on publication of the "Heard on the Street" column. The securities law required only that journalists, like other citizens, not engage in fraudulent transactions.

[293]*See* Maria Galeno, "Drawing the Line on Insiders and Outsiders for Rule 10b-5: Chiarella v. United States," 4 *Harv. J. L. & Pub. Pol.* 203, 207 (1981).

[294]SEC v. Materia, 745 F.2d 197 (2d Cir. 1984), *cert. denied,* 471 U.S. 1053 (1985). *See also* United States v. Newman, 664 F.2d 12 (2d Cir. 1981), *aff'd after remand,* 722 F.2d 729 (2d Cir.), *cert. denied,* 464 U.S. 863 (1983).

[295]Carpenter v. United States, 484 U.S. 19 (1987).

[296]SEC v. Capital Gains Research Bureau, Inc., 375 U.S. 180 (1963).

[297]United States v. Carpenter, 791 F.2d 1024 (2d Cir. 1986).

Winans was also convicted of violating federal statutes prohibiting use of interstate mail or wire communication for fraud, a conviction that the Supreme Court unanimously affirmed. The wire and mail fraud statutes prohibit use of either form of interstate communication to obtain money or property by false pretenses. The Court said Winans defrauded the *Wall Street Journal* by taking the publisher's confidential information in violation of an employee pledge and using the mails and telephones to profit from the information. The Court said the *Journal* had an exclusive right to use its property, including confidential business information.

Summary

Publicly traded corporations are subject to fraud suits under Section 10(b) of the Securities Exchange Act of 1934 if they deliberately make a misleading statement of a material fact or fail to disclose material information when they have a duty to do so. Materially deceptive statements include misstatements and omissions that would affect an investor's decision to buy, sell, or hold a security. In addition, a corporation may have a duty to disclose material information if misleading information circulating in the media originated with the corporation. Corporate insiders and publishers of personal investment advisories also have a duty to disclose material information before using it as a basis for buying or selling securities. Financial journalists and market insiders have also been ruled to have a duty not to trade on market information acquired from their employers.

ADEQUATE DISCLOSURE The duty to disclose corporate information includes a requirement that disclosure be timely and broad. When a corporation makes a disclosure, whether it is mandated by statute or is made to avoid fraud, the disclosure must be prompt and adequately distributed so that shareholders and other investors will have time to digest the information before insiders buy and sell.

Breadth of Disclosure Information must be disseminated, the SEC has said, "in a manner calculated to reach the securities marketplace in general through recognized channels of distribution, and public investors must be afforded a reasonable waiting period to react to the information."[298] The procedures to be followed for sufficient dissemination of material information will depend on the market for the corporation's securities. If the corporation has a national market, information should be directed to the national financial press, the major financial communities, and to other areas where the corporation knows there will be interest in its securities.

The New York Stock Exchange says that information must be released "by the fastest available means," including the Dow Jones, Reuters, and Associated Press news services.[299] In addition, the NYSE suggests dissemination to newspapers in New York City and in cities where the corporation has headquarters or plants. As a general rule, one commentator says, "the more media used the better."[300]

[298]*In re* Faberge, Inc., 45 S.E.C. 249, 255 (1973).
[299]NYSE Manual ¶ 202.6(C).
[300]Ian B. Bromberg, "Disclosure Programs for Publicly Held Companies—A Practical Guide," 1970 *Duke L. J.* 1139.

The SEC has said that release of material information over a private wire service to a limited number of institutional subscribers is not adequate dissemination.[301] In *SEC v. Texas Gulf Sulphur Co.*, the U.S. Court of Appeals for the Second Circuit said it was not sufficient for a New York Stock Exchange corporation to publish news of a large mineral discovery only in a Canadian newspaper of limited circulation.[302] In the same case, the Second Circuit said that issuing a news release "is merely the first step in the process of dissemination required for compliance with the regulatory objective of providing all investors with an equal opportunity to make informed investment judgments."

Timeliness While disclosure is supposed to be broad, it is also supposed to be prompt. But the SEC, the courts, and the exchanges permit a company to withhold material information temporarily if the decision to withhold is a good-faith business judgment. Disclosure may be delayed where it would prejudice the ability of a company to pursue corporate objectives or where facts are in a state of flux. The objectives of a corporation might be jeopardized, for example, if negotiations for land were disclosed before acquisition was complete. In the *Texas Gulf Sulphur* case, officers of the company fraudulently misled investors while insiders bought stock, but the appeals court said it was not wrong for the company to withhold disclosure of the promising drilling results until adjoining land could be acquired.[303] Disclosure of information might also be delayed to allow acquisition of another company[304] or liquidation of a portion of a company's business.[305]

When circumstances are in a state of flux, corporations may exercise their business judgment to withhold information until the situation has stabilized. In a rapidly changing situation, a series of press releases could cause undesirable fluctuations in the price of a corporation's stock. In such circumstances, it is better to wait until the situation has calmed.

The U.S. Court of Appeals for the Tenth Circuit ruled that a corporation can wait to release information until it is "available and ripe for publication."[306] The court said that the McDonnell Douglas Corporation did not mislead shareholders when it waited several days for results of an internal evaluation of reduced earnings in the company's aircraft division before issuing a special report. "To be ripe," the court said, information "must be verified sufficiently to permit the officers and directors to have full confidence" in its accuracy. The hazards from an erroneous statement are "obvious," the court said, but it is "equally obvious that an undue delay not in good faith, in revealing facts, can be deceptive, misleading, or a device to defraud." McDonnell Douglas, the court concluded, investigated the expected shortfall as soon as it became known and wasted no time evaluating the information and preparing a release.

◇ Summary ◇

When publicly traded corporations disclose information, it should be disseminated broadly in a timely fashion. But disclosure may be delayed until information is complete and accurate.

[301] *In re* Faberge, Inc., 45 S.E.C. at 255.
[302] 401 F.2d 833, 856 (2d Cir. 1968) (en banc), *cert. denied,* 394 U.S. 976 (1969).
[303] 401 F.2d at 850, n.12.
[304] Matarese v. Aero Chatillon Corp. [1971–1972 Transfer Binder] Fed. Sec. L. Rep. (CCH) ¶ 93,322 (S.D.N.Y. 1971).
[305] Segal v. Coburn Corp. [1973 Transfer Binder] Fed. Sec. L. Rep. (CCH) ¶ 94,002 (E.D.N.Y. 1973).
[306] Financial Indus. Fund, Inc. v. McDonnell Douglas Corp., 474 F.2d 514, 519 (10th Cir. 1973), *cert. denied,* 414 U.S. 874 (1973).

CHAPTER 9

Obscenity and Indecency

"Sex," Justice William Brennan once observed, "has indisputably been a subject of absorbing interest to mankind through the ages." This "great and mysterious motive force in human life," he said, is "one of the vital problems of human interest and public concern."[1] Sex has been a subject of art since humankind originated artistic expression. Even before the Roman Empire, every sexual practice that is today considered acceptable and unacceptable had been sketched, painted, carved, or sculpted.[2]

The commercialization of sex is big business and a significant part of contemporary American mass media. In 2005, the adult entertainment industry generated $12.6 billion in revenue from DVDs, magazines, fantasy phone sex services, Internet sites, satellite and cable services, and hotel pay-per-view services.[3] To put this figure in perspective, revenues of the adult entertainment industry are bigger than the revenue of professional football, basketball, and baseball together, more than Hollywood's domestic box office receipts, and larger than all of the revenues generated by rock and country music recordings.[4] The largest market segment is the sale and rental of adult videos, generating revenues of $4.2 billion in 2005. Adult-oriented Internet sites received 44 million unique visitors a month in 2005 and generated $2.5 billion in revenue. Sexual content is being developed for mobile media, such as cellular telephones and video iPods. Despite the widespread availability of material depicting sexuality, there are sharp cultural and political disputes about the harmfulness of this material and whether government should restrict its availability.

The terms **pornography, obscenity,** and **indecency** are often mistakenly used interchangeably; each term has a distinct meaning. Pornography is a generic reference to sexually explicit material intended to cause sexual excitement. Pornography has no legal definition. Obscenity is legally defined as a narrow class of "hard-core" pornography that is so "offensive" and so lacking in "social value" that it is denied First Amendment protection. Obscene expression is unprotected in all media. Indecent materials are less graphic or erotic than obscenity. Indecency is fully protected in the print media and on the Internet but may be restricted in the more intrusive broadcast media and may be limited in some ways on cable television and in telephone communications. This chapter is largely concerned with two matters: first, discussing the difficult task of defining obscenity, and second, considering the restrictions that may be placed on indecency.

Former Supreme Court Justice William Douglas argued that obscenity should be protected by the First Amendment because obscenity is a matter of taste, which, like matters of belief, is "too personal to define and too emotional and vague" to regulate.[5] But Justice Douglas's liberalism did not prevail in the law of obscenity. Today obscenity, like false advertising and fighting words, is outside of legal protection by the First Amendment and federal or state law.[6]

[1]Roth v. United States, 354 U.S. 476, 487 (1957).
[2]Byrne & Kelley, "Introduction: Pornography and Sex Research," in *Pornography and Sexual Aggression* 2 (Neil Malamuth & Edward Donnerstein eds., 1984).
[3]Free Speech Coalition, *State of the Industry Report* 1 (Jan. 2006).
[4]Gary Allison, "Sanctioning Sodomy," 39 *Tulsa L. Rev.* 95, 148 (2003).
[5]Paris Adult Theatre I v. Slaton, 413 U.S. 49, 70 (1973) (dissenting opinion).
[6]Roth v. United States, 354 U.S. 476 (1957).

Obscenity

Obscenity is the most graphic form of sexual expression and is banned in all media distributed in the United States. Obscenity has not always been of pressing importance in American society. The law in eighteenth-century America as in England was more concerned with preventing blasphemy and heresy than with barring sexual titillation.[7] The first major obscenity law in the United States, and the foundation for today's federal obscenity law, was the Comstock Act of 1873, "An Act for the Suppression of Trade in, and Circulation of, Obscene Literature and Articles of Immoral Use."[8] The movement for an obscenity law was led by Anthony Comstock, a strict New England Congregationalist, who had created a committee at the YMCA in New York for the suppression of vice.

After the Comstock Act was passed, Anthony Comstock was appointed a special agent of the Post Office to enforce the law. He and the New York Society for the Suppression of Vice received a portion of the fines he collected. Comstock claimed he destroyed 160 tons of obscene literature and convicted enough people to fill more than sixty railway passenger coaches holding sixty persons each.[9]

Not until 1957, however, did the Supreme Court rule that punishing obscenity does not violate the First Amendment. Three-quarters of a century after passage of the Comstock Act, the Supreme Court ruled in *Roth v. United States* that obscenity deserves no constitutional protection because it is "utterly without redeeming social importance."[10] Roth was convicted under a federal obscenity statute for mailing an obscene book, circular, and advertising. None of the materials deserved constitutional protection, the Court said, because they made no contribution to the exposition of ideas or truth.

Defining Obscenity

To punish obscene expression—and protect nonobscene material—courts must be able to define *obscenity*. Arriving at a definition has been a difficult task for the courts. Supreme Court Justice Potter Stewart, frustrated by trying to define obscenity, said simply, "I know it when I see it."[11] In *Roth* and later cases, the Supreme Court under Chief Justice Earl Warren established a three-part test for determining whether sexual materials are obscene. The more conservative Court under Chief Justice Warren Burger broadened the three-part test slightly to encompass more sexual materials and make obscenity prosecutions easier. The Burger Court's test for obscenity was set forth in 1973 in *Miller v. California,* the foundation case for discussing obscenity.[12]

California convicted Miller under state law for conducting a mass-mailing campaign to advertise four books—*Intercourse, Man-Woman, Sex Orgies Illustrated,* and *An Illustrated History of Pornography*—and a film entitled *Marital Intercourse.* The advertising brochures contained depictions of men and women, their genitals prominently displayed, engaged in

[7]Frederick Schauer, *The Law of Obscenity* 6–8 (1976).
[8]17 Stat. § 598 (1873).
[9]James Kilpatrick, *The Smut Peddlers* 35 (1960), *quoted in* Frederick Schauer, *The Law of Obscenity* at 13.
[10]354 U.S. 476 (1957).
[11]Jacobellis v. Ohio, 378 U.S. 184, 197 (1964) (Stewart, J., concurring).
[12]413 U.S. 15 (1973).

a variety of sexual activities. The Supreme Court, applying its three-part test, found the materials to be obscene.

To determine whether a work is obscene, the Court said, it is first necessary to establish that "the average person, applying contemporary community standards" would find that the work, taken as a whole, appeals to the prurient interest. Second, the materials must depict or describe sexual conduct in a "patently offensive" way that is specifically defined by state law. Third, the work, taken as a whole, must lack serious literary, artistic, political, or scientific value. The test is "conjunctive"; all three parts must be met if a work is to be ruled obscene and therefore outside of constitutional protection.

PRURIENT INTEREST To be obscene, materials taken as a whole must appeal to the prurient interest as determined by "the average person, applying contemporary community standards." It is not enough that the materials elicit normal, healthy, or lustful thoughts. To be obscene, materials must appeal to a lascivious, shameful, or morbid interest in sex. Materials are not obscene simply because people may find them to be filthy, disgusting, or revolting; they also must have a sexual appeal. The prurient appeal may be presented in advertising, books, magazines, and other works.

The Average Person The Supreme Court required in *Roth v. United States* that obscenity be determined by the average person.[13] This ruling liberalized obscenity law. Although many courts before *Roth* used an average-person standard, the Supreme Court had never before formally rejected the influential *Hicklin* test, which barred sexual materials to everyone if the materials were offensive to children. The *Hicklin* test was the result of a nineteenth-century English case, *Regina v. Hicklin,* in which Lord Cockburn ruled that offensive materials should be judged by the likely effect of the most offensive passages on the most vulnerable members of society, not by the effect of the whole work on the average person.[14]

Lord Cockburn said the intent of the writer of sexual materials, whether to educate or enlighten, was irrelevant if the tendency of the words was to corrupt impressionable minds. Under the *Hicklin* test, a book could be declared obscene if only part of it was found to be obscene to children, the mentally weak, the immature, or other susceptible members of society. Under the *Hicklin* rule, adults who might suffer no ill effects from exposure to pornography could be denied access to sexual materials deemed harmful to children.

In *Miller v. California,* the Supreme Court reiterated its holding in *Roth* that patent offensiveness and prurient interest should be determined by what would be obscene to the average person, not to the youngest and most vulnerable. The average person is the normal adult, not a highly sensitive person.[15] Nor is the average person a prude or a person of strange or perverted tastes.

Community Standard The Supreme Court under Chief Justice Burger and Chief Justice William Rehnquist has reflected the decentralization of power favored by Republican administrations, tending to leave substantial decision-making powers to the states. Each

[13]354 U.S. 476 (1957).
[14]3 Q.B. 360 (1868).
[15]*See, e.g.,* Keaton v. Stanforth, 1997 U.S. App. LEXIS 16407 (6th Cir. 1997).

state, for example, can determine the degree of fault a private person must prove in a libel suit against the media. In the law of obscenity, too, the Burger Court augmented the power of localities by ruling in *Miller v. California* that the average person determining whether sexual materials are obscene is supposed to apply a "contemporary community standard." Jurors can draw on their own understanding of the views of the average person in the community to decide what is patently offensive and prurient.[16] The "community" reflecting the average person's values may be the juror's city, county, or state. The community standard may be interpreted by a public opinion poll. Not surprisingly, urban populations are more tolerant of pornography than are people in smaller communities.[17]

The Warren Court, like the Burger Court, had employed a community standard. But the Warren Court's standard was the same for the whole nation. Chief Justice Burger opposed the national community standard of the Warren years because he thought a single standard for the whole nation was too abstract. It is neither "realistic nor constitutionally sound," Burger said in his *Miller v. California* opinion, "to read the First Amendment as requiring that the people of Maine or Mississippi accept public depiction of conduct found tolerable in Las Vegas, or New York City."[18] The Burger Court admitted that using different state and local standards might cause some distributors to censor their sexual materials to conform to the tastes of the most conservative markets rather than risk prosecution in different communities under different standards.

Although laws proscribing the sale, distribution, or exhibition of obscene materials are substantially alike in all states, the enforcement of those laws varies markedly, reflecting different community values and political realities. In many communities, voters perceive the prosecution of obscenity crimes as being of lesser importance than the prosecution of other types of crimes. In addition, sentences in obscenity cases are often minimal, leading prosecutors to conclude that obscenity prosecutions as "high risk and low reward ventures."[19] At the federal level, enforcement of obscenity laws, such as the ban on the mailing or interstate shipment of obscene materials, varies from administration to administration. In 2005, Attorney General Alberto Gonzales established an Obscenity Prosecution Task Force; prosecutors within the Department of Justice work with the FBI, U.S. Postal Service inspectors, and other agencies to investigate and prosecute the distribution of obscene material.

Because some communities are more conservative than others, federal officials prosecuting pornographers sometimes practice *venue shopping,* picking a jurisdiction—or venue—in which prosecutors think they have the best chance of finding a jury that will convict for obscenity. People connected to the film *Deep Throat,* for example, were prosecuted and convicted under federal obscenity laws in Memphis.[20] Memphis was also the venue of the first conviction for interstate transmission of obscenity over the Internet. A California couple was sentenced to more than two years in prison for distributing digital images of bestiality, incest, rape, and sex scenes involving defecation, urination, and sadomasochistic abuse from their electronic bulletin board on the West Coast to people in Memphis. A federal

[16]Hamling v. United States, 418 U.S. 87 (1974).
[17]Marc Glassman, "Community Standards of Patent Offensiveness: Public Opinion Data and Obscenity Law," 42 *Pub. Opinion Q.* 161 (1978).
[18]413 U.S. 32.
[19]Attorney General's Commission on Pornography: Final Report 55 (1986).
[20]United States v. Battista, 646 F.2d 237 (6th Cir.), *cert. denied,* 454 U.S. 1046 (1981).

court in Memphis sentenced Robert Thomas to thirty-seven months in prison and his wife Carleen to thirty months for transmitting obscenity via a computer network and for selling obscene videotapes through the mail.[21]

Even if materials are never ruled to be obscene, an obscenity prosecution in a conservative jurisdiction may curb national or even world distribution of sexual materials. An Alabama county's obscenity indictment forced a New York City distributor of sex films into bankruptcy when satellite companies stopped beaming the New York firm's movies. Home Dish Satellite Corporation of New York was forced out of business when it was indicted under an Alabama obscenity statute modeled after *Miller v. California.* Home Dish Satellite provided X-rated films that were possibly obscene to 30,000 subscribers nationwide. The company also distributed nonobscene R-rated films to another 1.2 million customers. The indictments were brought in Montgomery County, Alabama, where only about fifty households subscribed to Home Dish Satellite's sexual films.[22]

Also indicted were GTE Corporation, GTE Spacenet Corporation, and United States Satellite, all of which provided the satellite transmission for Home Dish. After the charges were filed, all three satellite transmission firms discontinued their contracts with Home Dish. With no distribution network, Home Dish was forced out of business before any determination of obscenity was made.

With development of the Internet, providers of sexual materials are vulnerable to prosecution under different legal standards around the world. CompuServe, a commercial Internet provider, temporarily shut down more than 200 discussion groups, many dealing with sexually explicit materials, because prosecutors in Bavaria said they violated German pornography laws.[23] To avoid different community standards in every country and community, some online companies would prefer that community standards be determined not by a myriad of local rules but by bulletin board users themselves. Some Internet providers offer filters or screens so that parents can block access to computer discussions containing offensive language.

Minors Although the average adult applying contemporary community standards determines what appeals to prurient interests and otherwise meets the obscenity definition, there is a different or *variable* standard for minors. Protecting the health and welfare of children always has been of special concern to courts and legislatures. The states, the Supreme Court has said, have a compelling interest in "safeguarding the physical and psychological well-being of a minor."[24] Some states prohibit the display of lewd materials where children might see them.[25] In 1996, Congress prohibited a broad range of sexual materials on the Internet in legislation immediately challenged for denying adults access to constitutionally protected expression.

The Supreme Court has approved efforts to protect children under a theory of *variable obscenity,* allowing prohibition of materials that are obscene to children but not to adults. The principle of variable obscenity for adults and children was established in 1968 in *Ginsberg v. New York.*[26]

[21] United States v. Thomas, 74 F.3d 701 (6th Cir.), *cert. denied,* 519 U.S. 820 (1996).
[22] "Obscenity Law Used in Alabama Breaks New York Company," *N.Y. Times,* May 2, 1990, at 1, 11.
[23] Nathaniel Nash, "Holding Compuserve Responsible," *N.Y. Times,* Jan. 15, 1996, at C-4.
[24] New York v. Ferber, 458 U.S. 747 (1982).
[25] *See, e.g.,* Ga. Code Ann. § 16-12-103.
[26] 390 U.S. 629 (1968).

Variable Obscenity In *Ginsberg v. New York,* the Supreme Court upheld the conviction of Sam Ginsberg for selling minors "girlie" magazines that had been found not to be obscene for adults. The magazines showed female buttocks and breasts without full opaque covering as required by a New York statute prohibiting distribution of materials harmful to minors under age seventeen.

Instead of applying the average-person standard in *Ginsberg,* the Court, in an opinion written by Justice Brennan, held that a state might bar materials as obscene if they appeal to the prurient interests of minors, provided the materials also meet the other criteria of obscenity—patent offensiveness to minors and lack of serious social value to minors. Serious literature and objects of art that contain only nudity or sexual information are not obscene to children any more than they are to adults.

The Court in *Ginsberg* did not demand scientific proof that pornography leads to anti-social conduct among children. Instead, the Court deferred to the determination of the New York legislature that materials could be obscene to minors even if they were not to adults. The Court required only that the law defining what is obscene to minors have a "rational relation to the objective of safeguarding . . . minors from harm."

Exploitation of Children To protect young minds and bodies, the Supreme Court also has ruled a state may prohibit the distribution and possession of pictures and films in which children perform sexual acts. It is not necessary to determine whether such sexual materials are obscene, only that the children are exploited sexually, the Court said in *New York v. Ferber.*[27] Ferber was convicted for selling to an undercover police officer two films of young boys masturbating. The Court said that "the exploitative use of children in the production of pornography has become a serious national problem."

In *Ferber*, as in *Ginsberg*, the Court required no scientific proof of harm to children. But, the Court noted, "the legislative judgment, as well as the judgment found in the relevant literature, is that the use of children as subjects of pornographic materials is harmful to the physiological, emotional, and mental health of the child."

Because the distribution of child pornography "is intrinsically related to the sexual abuse of children," the Court said the distributors of children's pornography could be punished even though they did not produce the materials portraying children. Closing the distribution network would cut off the financial incentives essential to pornographic filmmakers, the Court said.

The social interest in protecting children is so compelling the Supreme Court has ruled it is illegal to even possess child pornography.[28] Similarly, a federal court ruled it illegal for a person to receive films depicting teenage girls in provocative poses, even though the girls were wearing bikini bathing suits and underwear.[29] Reporters also are unprotected by the First Amendment if they send and receive child pornography over the Internet while preparing news stories about the child pornography industry.[30]

In 2002 the Supreme Court ruled that the harm-to-children rationale does not support prohibitions of computer-created virtual child pornography or performances involving

[27]458 U.S. 747 (1982).
[28]Osborne v. Ohio, 495 U.S. 103 (1990).
[29]United States v. Knox, 32 F.3d 733 (3d Cir. 1994), *cert. denied* 513 U.S. 1109 (1995).
[30]United States v. Matthews, 209 F.3d 338 (4th Cir.), *cert. denied,* 531 U.S. 910 (2000).

young adults who look like minors. The law can punish the creation, sale and distribution of child pornography, the Court said in *Ashcroft v. Free Speech Coalition,*[31] only if the materials involve real children, not simulations. In *Free Speech Coalition* the Court struck down a section of the Child Pornography Prevention Act of 1996 (CPPA), a law making it illegal to produce, distribute, or receive any visual depiction that "appears to be" of a minor engaging in sexual conduct.[32] The statute, which the Supreme Court ruled was overbroad, was an attempt by Congress to prohibit virtual child pornography that was already proliferating on the Internet.

In *Free Speech Coalition,* the Court distinguished virtual child pornography from explicit depictions of actual children. As the Court had noted in *Ferber*, children are harmed when they are used in the illegal production of pornography. But virtual child pornography, the Court said in *Free Speech Coalition*, "records no crime and creates no victims by its production." The Court also rejected the claim that virtual pornography whets the appetites of pedophiles, finding that the government had not shown a sufficiently strong connection between exposure to virtual imagery and abuse of children. In *Free Speech Coalition,* the Court also struck down a section of the CPPA prohibiting possession of material that had been advertised—or pandered—in a way that conveys the impression that children are engaged in sexual conduct.

Pandering In determining whether sexual materials are obscene, the Supreme Court will consider the methods by which they are marketed. If the materials are aggressively marketed for their prurient appeal, they are more likely to be termed obscene.[33] The assertive marketing of sexual materials for their prurient interest is called pandering. So offensive is pandering to the Supreme Court that the justices have upheld obscenity convictions for the commercial promotion of sexual materials when neither the promotion nor the materials advertised were clearly obscene.

The Supreme Court upheld the obscenity conviction of publisher Ralph Ginzburg in part because of his aggressive marketing of sexual materials. In *Ginzburg v. United States,* one of the most controversial cases in obscenity law, the Supreme Court held that in "close cases" evidence of "commercial exploitation of erotica solely for the sake of their prurient appeal" may be decisive in the determination of obscenity.[34] One of Ginzburg's publications, EROS, a hardbound magazine dealing with sex, featured some explicit material but also photographs described by Professor H. W. Janson, a New York University art historian, as "outstandingly beautiful and artistic."[35] Nonetheless, the Court found an emphasis on prurient appeal in Ginzberg's promotional efforts, such as an advertisement describing EROS as "*the* magazine of sexual candor."

The ads announcing Ginzburg's publications contained no erotic or explicit pictures or foul language, but Justice Brennan, writing for the Court, found pandering because Ginzburg's enterprise was permeated with the "leer of the sensualist." Brennan said that Ginzburg's advertising emphasized the eroticism of his publications, not their literary value. Even the postmark from Middlesex, New Jersey, was suggestive. Furthermore, the Court

[31]535 U.S. 234 (2002).
[32]18 U.S.C. § 1256 (8)(B).
[33]Pinkus v. United States, 436 U.S. 293 (1978); Frederick Schauer, *Law of Obscenity* at 83–84.
[34]383 U.S. 463 (1966).
[35]Peter Magrath, "The Obscenity Cases: Grapes of Roth," 1966 *S. Ct. Rev.* 7, 27.

noted that Ginzburg had first tried to get mailing privileges at Blue Ball and Intercourse, Pennsylvania. Justice Douglas, who dissented, later remarked that Ralph Ginzburg went to jail "not for what he printed, but for the sexy manner in which he advertised his creations."[36]

After the *Ginzburg* ruling, some states amended their obscenity statutes to outlaw the commercial exploitation of erotica solely for the sake of its prurient appeal.[37] The Supreme Court in the 1970s affirmed two obscenity convictions that relied on the pandering concept.[38] In 2002 and 2008, the Court addressed the pandering of child pornography.

In 2002, the Court in *Free Speech Coalition* struck down a provision of the Child Pornography Prevention Act of 1996 (CPPA) that prohibited the possession of a sexually explicit image that is "advertised, promoted, presented, described, or distributed in such a manner that conveys the impression" it depicts a child engaging in sex. The Court said this provision was overbroad because the law not only punished possession of illegal images of child sex that had been advertised as child sex, but the law also punished possession of lawful sexual images *if* the images had been advertised and promoted to "convey the impression" that the materials contained child sex. Thus, possession of a film containing no child sex might be prosecuted criminally if the film trailers conveyed the impression that a viewer would see child sex in the film.

Congress responded to *Free Speech Coalition* by enacting the Protect Act of 2003, outlawing the promotion or advertising of child pornography.[39] In 2008, the Supreme Court upheld the constitutionality of the Protect Act's prohibitions on illegal advertising. Unlike the CPPA, the Protect Act does not criminalize the possession of sexual images because of the way they are advertised. Instead, the Protect Act punishes the advertising of child pornography, regardless of whether a defendant actually possesses child pornography. The Protect Act does not prohibit the advertising of lawful sexual materials, including virtual pornography that does not involve real children and is not obscene.

In *United States v. Williams* the Court ruled that offers to provide or receive child pornography are "categorically excluded from the First Amendment."[40] Advertisers or solicitors of sexual materials can be punished as long as they believe they are offering illegal sexual materials or if they fraudulently offer legal materials they advertise as child pornography. Writing for a seven-person majority, Justice Scalia noted that the constitutional defect the Court found in the pandering provision in *Free Speech Coalition* "was that it went *beyond* pandering" to prohibit possession of protected virtual pornography. In contrast, the Protect Act narrowly focuses on speech that proposes an illegal transaction, where that speech seeks to introduce "material into the child-pornography distribution network."

It is constitutional, the court said, to prohibit the pandering or receipt of pornography involving real children. It is also constitutional to prohibit fraudulent offers of child pornography. Justice Scalia wrote, "an Internet user who solicits child pornography from an undercover agent violates the statute, even if the officer posseses no child pornography. Likewise, a person who [falsely] advertises virtual child pornography as depicting actual

[36]Paris Adult Theatre I v. Slaton, 413 U.S. at 70 (1973) (Douglas, J., dissenting).
[37]*See, e.g.*, Ga. Code § 16–12–80.
[38]Splawn v. California, 431 U.S. 595 (1977); Hamling v. United States, 418 U.S. 87 (1974).
[39]18 U.S.C. § 2252A(a)(3)(B).
[40]2008 U.S. LEXIS 4301 (May 19, 2008).

children also falls within the reach of the statute." Fraudulent offers to provide illegal products are "doubly excluded" from the First Amendment, Justice Scalia noted.

As will be discussed later in this chapter, the FCC considers whether broadcast sexual content is presented in a titillating manner—which the FCC considers pandering—when defining broadcast indecency.

Atypical Tastes Sexual material may be obscene not only if it appeals to average adults and minors but also if it appeals to people with atypical sexual tastes. In Mishkin v. New York, the Supreme Court ruled that pornography that may have little appeal to an "average" person may nevertheless be obscene if it is patently offensive and appeals to the prurient interests of the atypical group to which it is addressed.[41] In Mishkin, the Court upheld the conviction of a man who had helped to produce and sell fifty books, several of which dealt with sadomasochism, fetishism, and homosexuality.

People stimulated by atypical sexual practices argue that there should be no restrictions on the pornography they prefer because it does not appeal to the "average" person. Indeed, the average person might find pornography containing deviant sexual practices to be sickening or disgusting. But, the Court said in *Mishkin*:

> Where the material is designed primarily for and primarily disseminated to a clearly defined deviant sexual group, rather than the public at large, the prurient appeal requirement of the *Roth* test is satisfied if the dominant theme of the material taken as a whole appeals to the prurient interest of the members of that group.

PATENT OFFENSIVENESS Although the Supreme Court lists prurient interest as the first test of obscenity, patent offensiveness is the most distinguishing feature of materials that are obscene. To be obscene, sexually stimulating materials must be more than merely pornographic; they must be more than sexually stimulating or titillating. Many popular sexual materials, including *Playboy* magazine, may be pornographic—and therefore constitutionally protected—without containing the patent offensiveness to be obscene. In *Miller v. California,* the Supreme Court said obscene materials might include (a) patently offensive representations or descriptions of ultimate sex acts, normal or perverted, actual or simulated, or (b) patently offensive representations or descriptions of masturbation, excretory functions, and lewd exhibition of the genitals.

What makes materials patently offensive is their excess of sexual detail, the repetitive nature of the activity, often in a very commercial context. The Supreme Court said it wants to curb "hard-core" pornography. Patently offensive materials usually will include scenes of erection, penetration, or ejaculation. Hard-core pornography also might emphasize homosexuality, bestiality, flagellation, sadomasochism, fellatio, or cunnilingus. Photographs and motion pictures may be the most graphic, but textual material and cartoons also may be "patently offensive."[42] In *Hamling v. United States,* the Supreme Court held that advertising brochures including explicit photographs of heterosexual and homosexual intercourse, fellatio, cunnilingus, masturbation, and group sex were patently offensive.[43]

[41]383 U.S. 502 (1966).
[42]Frederick Schauer, *Law of Obscenity* at 112–13.
[43]418 U.S. 87 (1974).

Mere nudity is not patently offensive. When the Georgia Supreme Court ruled that the nudity in the film *Carnal Knowledge* was obscene, the U.S. Supreme Court reversed. In an opinion written by then Justice William Rehnquist, the Court said the film did not show details of sexually intimate encounters that might be obscene. There was no exhibition "of the actors' genitals, lewd or otherwise."[44] Therefore, the film was not patently offensive.

Similarly, "four-letter words" are not obscene. Four-letter words may be offensive or indecent, but generally they are neither sexually arousing nor patently offensive and therefore are not obscene. For example, the Supreme Court ruled that opposition to the military draft, expressed by the phrase "Fuck the Draft," lacked erotic content.[45] Four-letter words may be part of graphic and lewd sexual portrayals that are patently offensive, but four-letter words by themselves are not obscene.

Because obscenity law focuses on hard-core pornography, it poses few restraints on most journalists, advertisers, and public relations practitioners. One danger for people in the media, however, is using the term *obscenity* too loosely. It is libelous to say a person owns *obscene* materials if the materials in question do not meet the narrow definition of obscenity. If no one has been convicted of selling obscenity, it is safer for the media to refer to *sexual materials* or *erotic magazines,* terms that a jury could say are matters of opinion, not defamatory fact.

SOCIAL VALUE Finally, for a work to be obscene, it must not only be patently offensive and appeal to prurient interests but also lack social value when viewed as a whole.

The Whole Work By requiring that the work be looked at as a whole, the Court in *Miller v. California* reaffirmed its 1957 decision in *Roth* that a determination of obscenity should not be made on the basis of only a few isolated passages or pictures. The *Roth* decision rejected the holding in the nineteenth-century English case, *Regina v. Hicklin,* discussed earlier in this chapter, in which an English court ruled that works could be declared obscene if only a few passages endangered children and other sensitive people. Under the *Hicklin* rule, many literary classics were ruled to be obscene because they contained a few offensive passages. Among the books banned in this country on that basis were James Joyce's *Ulysses,* D. H. Lawrence's *Lady Chatterley's Lover,* and Theodore Dreiser's *An American Tragedy.*

The *Hicklin* rule was challenged in an American court in a case involving the importation of Joyce's *Ulysses.* In a decision upheld on appeal, Judge John Woolsey, a federal judge in New York, ruled that *Ulysses* could be imported because, taken as a whole, the book was not obscene. Judge Woolsey found the book to be a sincere, serious literary effort of which explicit descriptions of sexual acts were a necessary part.[46] The Supreme Court reiterated Judge Woolsey's view when it ruled in *Roth* and in *Miller* that a work should be judged as a whole.

Defining Social Value In First Amendment analysis, courts generally avoid judging the value of expression. In the political arena, for example, the courts make no effort to determine

[44]Jenkins v. Georgia, 418 U.S. 153 (1974).
[45]Cohen v. California, 403 U.S. 15 (1971).
[46]United States v. One Book Called "Ulysses," 5 F. Supp. 182 (S.D.N.Y 1933), *aff'd,* 72 F.2d 705 (2d Cir. 1934).

whether a politician's promises are false, impractical, far-fetched, or naive. Listeners decide the value of what they hear. But in obscenity cases, the Supreme Court always has used a social value test to determine whether materials are constitutionally protected. In the *Miller* decision, the Supreme Court said that to be obscene, sexual content taken as a whole must lack "serious literary, artistic, political, or scientific value."

The Burger Court's standard of social value broadened the definition of obscenity slightly from what it had been during the years of the Warren Court. The Warren Court had required a plaintiff to prove that sexual materials taken as a whole were "utterly without redeeming social value."[47] Liberals on the Warren Court argued that no work should be denied constitutional protection unless it is utterly without value. But Chief Justice Burger in *Miller* said the "utterly without" standard made it too hard for prosecutors to prove that a work was obscene.

The value of sexual expression—unlike its offensiveness and its appeal to prurient interests—is not determined by the average person applying contemporary community standards. In *Pope v. Illinois,* the Supreme Court ruled that the value question of the three-part *Miller* test should be decided by a "reasonable person" rather than by the "average person."[48] Presumably, the Court's decision in *Pope* increases First Amendment protection for sexual materials; the reasonable person might find literary, artistic, political, or scientific value in a work where the average person, representing the majority, might not. In practice, critics, scholars, and other experts frequently help to determine the value of a disputed work.

A federal appeals court reversed a ruling that a rap song was obscene because the lower court judge had not relied on expert opinion to determine the social value of the work. The U.S. Court of Appeals for the Eleventh Circuit overturned a federal district court judge in Florida who used his own judgment to determine that the rap album "As Nasty As They Wanna Be" was obscene.[49] Whereas several music experts testified about the musical and cultural value of the "sampling," "doing the dozens," "boasting," and other techniques used in 2 Live Crew's songs, Broward County (Florida) Sheriff Nick Navarro presented no evidence of obscenity besides a tape recording of the songs. The appellate court said the sheriff had failed to establish that the songs were obscene, a determination the Eleventh Circuit said a judge could not make simply by listening to the tape.

Under the *Miller* standard, courts rule that works dealing with political and historical subjects have social value even if the works are crude and offensive. The movie *Caligula,* for example, was ruled to have artistic value even though it contained endless scenes of tasteless sex and violence. Although a federal court found the film to be patently offensive, the film was not obscene because the violence and sex did not appeal to the prurient interest and because, taken as a whole, the film contained artistic effort and creativity. "*Caligula,*" the court said, "clearly contains political, historical, and social themes and subthemes, including the use and abuse of power, dynastic and institutional struggle, the violence and corruption that attends a society bankrupt in moral values, and the fragility of civilization."[50]

[47]Memoirs v. Massachusetts, 383 U.S. 413 (1966).
[48]481 U.S. 497 (1987).
[49]Luke Records, Inc. v. Navarro, 960 F.2d 134 (11th Cir. 1992).
[50]Penthouse Int'l, Ltd. v. McAuliffe, 7 Media L. Rep. 1798, 1804 (N.D. Ga. 1981), *aff'd by an evenly divided court,* 717 F.2d 517 (11th Cir. 1983), *cert. denied,* 465 U.S. 1108 (1984).

◇ Summary ◇

For a work to be obscene, it must, taken as a whole, appeal to the prurient interest of the average person and be patently offensive applying contemporary community standards. A work appeals to the prurient interest if it is sexually arousing to the average person. Materials that appeal to the prurient interest of minors or deviants may also be obscene to those audiences even though the materials might not be obscene to the average adult. Materials that are not obscene but "pander" in an intense commercial promotion of their sexual appeal also may be prohibited as obscene. Works are patently offensive if they are "hard-core" pornography containing graphic, lewd displays of the genitals or sexual acts. To be obscene, materials also must lack serious literary, artistic, political, or scientific value, as determined by a reasonable person.

Privacy and Possession of Obscenity

Prohibitions on obscenity include bans on the sale, importation, and interstate transport of obscene materials,[51] including child pornography.[52] The U.S. Court of Appeals for the Eighth Circuit has ruled that ordering obscenity through the mail also is illegal.[53] There is, however, a limited right to possess obscene materials in the privacy of the home.

Although the law is quite clear that obscene material cannot be bought or transported lawfully, in 1969 the Supreme Court unanimously ruled in *Stanley v. Georgia* that a First Amendment-based right of privacy protected a citizen who merely possessed sexual materials in the home.[54] Stanley was convicted for possession of obscene films found while police were searching his residence for evidence of illegal bookmaking. In ringing language, Justice Thurgood Marshall wrote, "If the First Amendment means anything, it means that a State has no business telling a man, sitting alone in his own house, what books he may read and what films he may watch. Our whole constitutional heritage rebels at the thought of giving government the power to control men's minds."

In several obscenity cases decided after *Stanley,* such as *United States v. Reidel,* the Court emphasized that the right to possess obscenity in the home did not also mean that someone had a right to distribute or receive obscenity.[55] The limitations placed on the reach of *Stanley* in cases such as *Reidel* prompted Justice Black's comment that *Stanley* would be "good law only when a man writes salacious books in his attic, prints them in his basement, and reads them in his living room."[56]

The right recognized in *Stanley* to possess obscenity is further limited by the Court's ruling in *Osborne v. Ohio* upholding the constitutionality of prohibitions on the possession of child pornography. In *Osborne,* the Court upheld an Ohio statute that prohibited the possession

[51] *See* United States v. Reidel, 402 U.S. 351 (1971); United States v. Thirty-Seven Photographs, 402 U.S. 363 (1971); 18 U.S.C. §§ 1461–65.

[52] Osborne v. Ohio, 495 U.S. 103 (1990).

[53] United States v. Kuennen, 901 F.2d 103 (8th Cir.), *cert. denied,* 498 U.S. 958 (1990). It is illegal for the government to entice citizens to order obscene material through the mails. *See* Jacobson v. United States, 503 U.S. 540 (1992).

[54] 394 U.S. 557 (1969).

[55] United States v. Reidel, 402 U.S. 351 (1971); United States v. Thirty-Seven Photographs, 402 U.S. 363 (1971).

[56] Thirty-Seven Photographs, 402 U.S. at 382 (Black, J. dissenting).

or viewing of materials showing nude minors.[57] The U.S. Supreme Court said the statute was constitutional because the Ohio Supreme Court said it did not prohibit possession of all nude depictions of children. The state law prohibited only those pictures in which the nudity constituted "a lewd exhibition" or a "graphic focus on the genitals." The goal of the Ohio legislature in adopting the statute was to diminish the economic incentives to exploit children in sexually explicit films and pictures by punishing those who possess them.

Whatever tenuous right Stanley had to possess obscenity in his home, the Supreme Court has ruled the right does not extend to areas outside the home, such as public theaters. In *Paris Adult Theatre I v. Slaton,* the Court ruled that a downtown Atlanta theater could be barred from showing two obscene films, *Magic Mirror* and *It All Comes Out in the End,* to willing adults.[58] Signs outside the theater announced that the movies were "mature feature films" for adults 21 and older. "If viewing the nude body offends you," one sign said, "Please Do Not Enter." There was no evidence that minors had entered the theater.

The Supreme Court rejected the theater management's argument that adults should have as much right to attend an explicit movie in a theater as Stanley had to possess obscene materials in his home. A public theater, unlike a home, is not a private place, the Court said. The state can regulate a theater as it can regulate any other business. It was immaterial, the Court said, that the management of the public theater limited the audience to consenting adults. There are many activities, including prostitution, self-mutilation, and bare-fist prizefighting, that the state prohibits even though adults are willing to participate. The state has an interest, the Court said, in protecting "the quality of life and the total community environment, the tone of commerce in the great city centers, and, possibly, the public safety itself."

In a long, detailed dissent to *Paris Adult Theatre,* Justice Brennan argued obscenity laws should do no more than protect unconsenting adults and children, a conclusion arrived at a few years earlier by the first Commission on Obscenity and Pornography, appointed by President Lyndon Johnson. After wrestling with the question of obscenity for more than fifteen years, Justice Brennan decided all definitions of obscenity are too vague to pass constitutional muster.

Brennan also opposed the Court's willingness to permit the government to regulate the moral tone of the community. If the state can create a particular moral tone by proscribing what citizens can read or see, Brennan said, then why cannot the state decree what citizens must read?

In 2003, in *Lawrence v. Texas,* the Supreme Court struck down a Texas homosexual sodomy law, holding that a person's decisions about the intimate relationships he will have in the home are not to be criminalized because society finds such relationships to be immoral.[59] The Court believed decisions about intimate relationships lie within a zone of personal liberty, which the government may not enter. Justice Scalia, in a dissenting opinion, claimed the Court's ruling called into question the nation's obscenity laws, along with other laws based on a state's desire to establish a moral code of conduct.

Lawyers were quick to use *Lawrence* as a defense against prosecutions for distributing obscene materials, but these efforts have not been successful. In 2005, in *United States v.*

[57] 495 U.S. 103 (1990).
[58] 413 U.S. 49 (1973).
[59] 539 U.S. 2003 (2003).

Extreme Associates, the Court of Appeals for the Third Circuit held that federal laws proscribing the distribution of obscene materials do not violate the privacy rights of willing adults.[60] Closely examining the Supreme Court's post-*Stanley* rulings about the distribution of obscenity, the court of appeals found the Court had consistently recognized that the right to possess obscene material in the privacy of the home did not mean there was a correlative right to distribute that material.

The defendants in *Extreme Associates* used various techniques to screen out unwilling adults and children from their Internet site, but the court of appeals found the Internet, like the theater in *Paris Adult Theatre,* was subject to obscenity law. The state has a legitimate interest in stemming the tide of commercialized obscenity, even to consenting adults, the court of appeals said. Moreover, the court of appeals noted the Supreme Court has never suggested that obscenity law does not apply to the Internet. The Supreme Court denied certiorari in 2006.[61]

Due Process and Prior Restraints

Because obscenity is outside First Amendment protection, it can be enjoined before distribution as well as punished afterward.[62] To identify potentially obscene films, local governments have the legal authority to review films before exhibition. However, as was discussed in Chapter 3, local governments no longer do so, largely because the Supreme Court established strict procedural safeguards to protect expression. Injunctions on obscene materials are also rare because of these procedural safeguards.

The Supreme Court has said a prior restraint may be imposed before judicial review only if the restraint is imposed for a specified brief period, a court can review the restraint "expeditiously," and the censor bears the burden of going to court to suppress the speech and prove that the expression is not constitutionally protected.[63] In *Freedman v. Maryland,* the Supreme Court said theater owners and film distributors may not be compelled to prove their productions are not obscene. Rather, the government agency that would stop the expression must prove the materials are obscene.

The due process of prior restraint law requires that administrative decisions be made rapidly and that the administrator not have the final word on what is obscene. Only the courts, the Supreme Court said in *Freedman,* have the necessary sensitivity to freedom of expression to determine when prior restraints might be imposed.[64] Administrators cannot be trusted with the final determination of what is obscene because they, unlike federal judges, are often appointed for short terms to serve immediate political ends. One commentator points out that political appointees do not have the independence and long-term view necessary for determining sensitive First Amendment cases.[65]

Government agents violate a citizen's due process rights if the agents move too slowly to review a prior restraint, which includes the period while a businessperson waits for the

[60]431 F.3d 150 (3rd Cir. 2005).

[61]126 S. Ct. 2048 (2006).

[62]Steven Catlett, "Enjoining Obscenity as a Public Nuisance and the Prior Restraint Doctrine," 84 *Colum. L. Rev.* 1616 (1984).

[63]Freedman v. Maryland, 380 U.S. 51 (1965). *See also* Vance v. Universal Amusement Co., 445 U.S. 308 (1980); Southeastern Promotions, Ltd. v. Conrad, 420 U.S. 546 (1975).

[64]380 U.S. at 58.

[65]Henry Monaghan, "First Amendment 'Due Process,'" 83 *Harv. L. Rev.* 518, 522–23 (1970).

government to issue a business license. Context determines how quickly the government must make a ruling. A theater owner who already has rented films of brief popularity is entitled to a quicker administrative decision than a businessperson who is asking whether the site of a proposed adult bookstore conforms to zoning laws. The Supreme Court said it is constitutional to require that a film distributor wait fourteen days for an appeal of a ruling that his films are obscene but that a delay of forty days may be unconstitutionally long.[66] A federal appellate court ruled that 150 days is too long for the owner of an adult bookstore to wait for administrators to decide whether his store conforms to zoning laws and protects children from obscenity.[67]

If the government is to seize sexual materials, a judge first must rule them to be obscene. In *Fort Wayne Books, Inc. v. Indiana,* the Supreme Court overturned a decision of the Supreme Court of Indiana holding that all sexual materials might be removed from an adult bookstore before a trial for racketeering if officials had reason to believe that the owners were circulating obscenity.[68] The Supreme Court said the risk of prior restraint on constitutionally protected expression is too high if sexual materials may be seized before they are found to be obscene. The Court said officials may seize a single copy of a book or film as evidence, but they may not take all materials from an adult bookstore before an obscenity determination is made.

However, the Supreme Court has ruled that the First Amendment allows the government to seize a defendant's entire entertainment business, including constitutionally protected books and films, after a racketeering conviction. In *Alexander v. United States,* the Court said the government did not violate the First Amendment when it seized thirteen bookstores and video stores and nearly $9 million from Ferris Jacob Alexander after he was convicted of racketeering by transporting and selling obscenity.[69] A five-justice majority rejected Alexander's argument that seizing his entertainment business constituted an unconstitutional prior restraint. First, the racketeering law did not prevent Alexander from selling any particular book, movie, or magazine, nor was he required to obtain government approval before doing so. After forfeiting the assets that were related to his prior racketeering convictions, Alexander was free to open new stores, restock his inventory, and sell sexually explicit materials. Second, the racketeering statute did not target expressive materials; books, like nonexpressive assets such as sports cars and cash, could be forfeited because of their role in the operation of a racketeering enterprise. The Court said the seizure of Alexander's assets, unlike the unconstitutional pretrial seizure in *Fort Wayne Books,* was not premature because a trial court already had determined that Alexander's entertainment business was linked to racketeering in obscenity. However, although the seizure of Alexander's assets did not violate the First Amendment, the Court returned the case to a lower court to determine whether the seizure violated the Eighth Amendment prohibition against "excessive fines."[70]

[66]United States v. Thirty-Seven Photographs, 402 U.S. 363 (1971).

[67]11126 Baltimore Boulevard, Inc. v. Prince George's County, 58 F.3d 988 (4th Cir.), *cert. denied,* 516 U.S. 1010 (1995).

[68]489 U.S. 46 (1989).

[69]509 U.S. 544 (1993).

[70]The trial court's subsequent ruling that the fines were not excessive was affirmed by the Court of Appeals for the Eighth Circuit. Alexander v. United States, 108 F.3d 853 (8th Cir.), *cert. denied,* 522 U.S. 869 (1997).

In a dissent, Justice Anthony Kennedy argued the forfeiture was an unconstitutional prior restraint because it destroyed an entire communication business, denying the public access to lawful expression. The majority's ruling, Kennedy warned, put any bookstore or press at risk of being forfeited to the government.

Summary

The Supreme Court has ruled that adults may receive obscene materials in the privacy of their homes. However, the right to receive and possess obscenity is severely curtailed by constitutional prohibitions on the import, distribution, and sale of obscenity. The right to possess obscenity is further limited by the Court's ruling that possession of child pornography may be barred. The Supreme Court also has held that obscene films may be prohibited in theaters even if admission is limited to adults.

When the government attempts to show a work is obscene, the First Amendment requires due process be followed. This includes placing the burden of proof on the government and providing for rapid judicial review.

Indecency

As was discussed earlier in this chapter, obscene content has no First Amendment protection. If material appeals to the prurient interest, is patently offensive, and has no serious social value, the government may ban the material, criminally punish its creators and distributors, or take a variety of other actions.

Indecent material is sexually oriented but does not meet the *Miller* definition of obscenity. Indecency, much like obscenity, depicts or describes sexual or excretory activities or organs in a patently offensive manner. Indecency, in contrast to obscenity, need not arouse a prurient interest in sex. In addition, an indecent broadcast program, unlike one that is obscene, can have serious value and still violate the law. The FCC has said that the "serious merit" of a program will be considered as a factor, but not necessarily the deciding factor, in determining whether a broadcast is indecent.

Unlike obscenity, indecency receives some First Amendment protection, which varies from medium to medium. Courts analyze indecency regulations according to the technological attributes of a medium and the level of effort required of the reader or viewer to receive messages. For example, the Supreme Court regards the Internet as similar to the highly protected print media because both require affirmative effort by the recipient to receive a message. In contrast, broadcast indecency is restricted because broadcasting is "uniquely accessible to children," even those who are too young to read.

Broadcasting

As was noted in Chapter 3, in 1969, the Supreme Court held in *Red Lion Broadcasting Co. v. FCC* that spectrum scarcity justified regulations designed to promote the presentation of a range of views.[71] If only select licensees may use the public airwaves, those station owners must accept certain public interest obligations not demanded of print media owners.

[71] 395 U.S. 367 (1969).

The regulation of broadcast indecency, however, is not justified on spectrum scarcity grounds. Instead, the Supreme Court's decision in *FCC v. Pacifica Foundation,* upholding the FCC's power to punish a broadcaster for airing indecent content, justifies broadcasting's reduced First Amendment protection in this context because broadcasting is intrusive and accessible to children.[72] Writing for the Court, Justice Stevens said that broadcasting "is a uniquely pervasive presence in the lives of all Americans." Broadcasting "confronts" citizens in public but also "in the privacy of the home, where the individual's right to be left alone plainly outweighs the First Amendment rights of an intruder." Even though listeners could change channels or turn off the receiver after encountering offensive depictions of sexuality, this was "like saying that the remedy for an assault is to run away after the first blow." Justice Stevens also said that society's interest in protecting children, coupled with the ease with which even young children could gain access to broadcasting, justified broadcasting's special treatment. In a dissenting opinion, Justice Brennan questioned whether listening to broadcasts, even in the home, implicated "fundamental" privacy interests.

Although a federal statute outlaws the broadcasting of obscene, indecent, or profane material,[73] the FCC's enforcement has focused on indecency. Broadcasters almost never air hard-core sexual depictions that meet the *Miller* test for obscenity. Also, the statutory reference to profane material has rarely been enforced. In the 1930s, blasphemous statements such as *By God* were regarded as profane.[74] Since the 1960s, however, statements such as *God damn it* have been treated as protected expression.[75] In a 2004 decision treating the word *fuck* as both indecent and profane, the FCC announced a new approach that classifies "vulgar and coarse" language as profane.[76] The FCC left the status of words other than *fuck* unsettled; broadcasters were warned that the agency would analyze other potentially profane words or phrases on a case-by-case basis. Subsequently, in two 2005 decisions discussed below, the FCC ruled that words such as *dick* are not sufficiently graphic to be profane and that blasphemous statements, such as *God damn it,* are not actionable as profanity. In 2006, though, the FCC ruled that *shit* was sufficiently vulgar to be both indecent and profane.

The FCC's new interest in profanity, like its attention to indecency, reflects the ebb and flow of political pressure. In 2001, for example, the FCC received just 346 indecency complaints and the agency levied $91,000 in fines. As shown in Table 9.1, since 2003, indecency and profanity in broadcast programming have been issues of intense political interest. The FCC's enforcement bureau ruled in October 2003 that an isolated utterance of *fuck* in a live entertainment broadcast was not indecent; this ruling prompted 237,215 letters of protest. Amid intense political pressure, the FCC in March 2004 overturned its enforcement bureau and held that even a single utterance of *fuck* in live entertainment programming is indecent and profane. The FCC also received more than 542,000 complaints about Janet Jackson's "wardrobe malfunction" exposing her breast at the 2004 Super Bowl halftime show; in September 2004, the FCC fined CBS-owned television stations $550,000

[72]438 U.S. 726, 748–49 (1978).
[73]18 U.S.C. § 1464.
[74]*See, e.g.,* Duncan v. United States, 48 F.2d 128 (9th Cir. 1931).
[75]Gagliardo v. United States, 366 F.2d 720 (9th Cir. 1966); Raycom, Inc., 18 F.C.C.R. 4186 (2003).
[76]Complaints Against Various Broadcast Licensees Regarding Their Airing of the "Golden Globe Awards," Memorandum Opinion and Order, 18 F.C.C.R. 4975 (2004).

TABLE 9.1

Indecency Complaints and Fines 2000–June 2006

	Number of Complaints	FCC Proposed Fines*
2006 (Jan.–June)	327,198	$3,962,500
2005	233,531	0
2004	1,405,419	2,428,080
2003	166,683	440,000
2002	13,922	99,400
2001	346	91,000
2000	111	48,000

*In some instances, the fine may be reduced or rescinded. Also, the fine may relate to a complaint from a prior year.

Source: FCC Enforcement Bureau

for the Super Bowl broadcast.[77] The agency also negotiated consent decrees with the Viacom, Emmis, and Clear Channel broadcast groups in 2004.[78] In exchange for dismissal of pending indecency cases, these broadcasters agreed to collectively pay $5.5 million in "voluntary contributions" to the U.S. Treasury. Each broadcaster also agreed to implement indecency compliance plans including training of on-air talent and producers, use of time delay equipment on live programming, and suspension or termination of employees involved in future indecency violations. Howard Stern decried the FCC's actions as a "witch hunt" and moved his program in 2006 to Sirius, an unregulated subscription satellite service.

Until recently, FCC fines for indecent broadcasts have been rare and only a small amount.[79] As discussed below, a new law enacted in 2006 increases the amount of fines tenfold. Faced with a difficult regulatory environment and the loss of audience to cable and satellite services that can legally carry graphic programs, like *The Sopranos,* the major television networks in 2006 filed suit against the FCC, claiming it is time to revisit the indecency rules. As discussed below, an appellate court in 2007 held the FCC's new policy toward "isolated expletives" was arbitrary. The Supreme Court accepted this case for its October 2008 Term, its first review of broadcast indecency since 1978.

LIMITING INDECENT BROADCASTS The First Amendment protects indecency because the Supreme Court has said only those sexually oriented materials meeting the *Miller v. California* test for obscenity fall outside constitutional protection. However, in 1978, in

[77]Complaints Against Various Television Licensees Concerning Their February 1, 2004 Broadcast of the Super Bowl XXXVII Halftime Show, Notice of Apparent Liability for Forfeiture, 19 F.C.C.R. 19230 (2004). This case was excluded from the scope of the Viacom consent decree.

[78]Viacom, Inc., Order (FCC 04-268) (Nov. 23, 2004); Emmis Communications Corp., Order (FCC 04-199) (Aug. 12, 2004); Clear Channel Communications, Inc., Order (FCC 04-128) (June 9, 2004).

[79]*See, e.g.,* Frank Aherns, "Delays, Low Fines Weaken FCC Attack on Indecency," *Wash. Post,* Nov. 10, 2005, at A1.

FCC v. Pacifica Foundation, the Supreme Court ruled that the FCC could regulate the times of indecent broadcasts without violating the First Amendment.[80]

The dispute in *Pacifica* began with an afternoon broadcast of a George Carlin monologue, "Filthy Words," on New York City radio station WBAI (FM). A New York father complained to the FCC after hearing the Carlin satire on the use of language while driving with his son.[81] Carlin begins his twelve-minute monologue by saying he will talk about "the words you couldn't say on the public, ah, airwaves, um, the ones you definitely wouldn't say, ever." Then he frequently repeats in a variety of contexts seven "dirty" words: *shit, piss, fuck, cunt, cocksucker, motherfucker,* and *tits.*

The FCC said Carlin's "dirty" words were indecent because they depicted sexual and excretory activities and organs in a patently offensive manner. The commission said the words were "obnoxious, gutter language" that were indecent because they "debased" and "brutalized" human beings "by reducing them to their bodily functions." The commission said Carlin repeated the offensive words "over and over" during the early afternoon when children were "undoubtedly" in the audience.

Although the FCC did not penalize the Pacifica Foundation, the WBAI licensee, for the Carlin broadcast, the commission said additional complaints about indecent programming from listeners could lead to sanctions. Broadcasters airing indecency not only risk fines and the loss of their licenses under the 1934 Communications Act,[82] but they also can be fined and jailed for up to two years under the federal criminal code.[83]

The FCC's decision to warn Pacifica for the broadcast of the Carlin monologue was reversed by the U.S. Court of Appeals for the District of Columbia but reinstated by a divided U.S. Supreme Court. Justice John Paul Stevens, in an opinion supported in part by four other justices, said the FCC's warning to WBAI did not violate the 1934 Communications Act or the First Amendment.

Stevens said the FCC did not censor WBAI's broadcast of the Carlin monologue, as Pacifica contended. As was discussed in Chapter 3, the prohibition on censorship in the 1934 Communications Act has never forbidden the FCC to evaluate broadcasts after they were aired. The commission had not edited the "Filthy Words" monologue in advance. Rather, the FCC had reviewed the program after the broadcast as part of the commission's responsibility to regulate licensees in the public interest. Stevens said review of program content after a broadcast is not censorship.

Stevens also rejected Pacifica's argument that Carlin's monologue could not be regulated because it was not obscene. Pacifica had argued that *obscenity* and *indecency* mean the same thing under federal law. Pacifica contended that indecent language, like obscene language, must appeal to the prurient interest before it can be punished. However, Stevens said the words *obscene* and *indecent* have different meanings when applied to broadcasting. The term *indecent* refers "to nonconformance with accepted standards of morality," the justice said. Hence, the Court accepted the FCC's conclusion that Carlin's monologue was indecent but not obscene.

[80] 438 U.S. 726 (1978).
[81] Pacifica Foundation Station WBAI (FM), 56 F.C.C.2d 94 (1975).
[82] 47 U.S.C. § 312(a)(6).
[83] 18 U.S.C. § 1464.

Justice Stevens said, in a part of the opinion supported by only three other justices, that the First Amendment might have protected the Carlin monologue if it had been offensive political or social commentary. However, Carlin's use of the "seven dirty words" did not deserve absolute First Amendment protection because they were not essential to the "exposition of ideas" and were of such little use in the search for truth that any benefit "is clearly outweighed by the social interest in order and morality." Because the words Carlin used were patently offensive and ordinarily lacked literary, political, or scientific value, they could be regulated in some contexts, Stevens said.

In a part of the opinion in which he again spoke for the Court's majority, Stevens said important considerations in indecency cases include the time of day of the broadcast; the nature of the program containing the offensive language; the composition of the audience; and perhaps the differences among radio, television, and closed-circuit transmissions. The Court said the Carlin monologue could be regulated because of the repetitive use of the offensive words at a time when children could reasonably be expected to be a part of the audience.

Justice Lewis Powell, Jr., joined by Justice Harry Blackmun, concurred with most of the Stevens opinion, including the need to protect children from offensive speech on the broadcast media. However, Powell disagreed with Stevens's attempt to regulate speech on the basis of social value. He said the justices should not be deciding which speech is protected by the First Amendment by assessing the social and political value of its content. The social value of speech "is a judgment for each person to make," said Powell, "not one for the judges to impose on him."

Justice William Brennan, Jr., in a dissenting opinion, said the FCC's regulation of the Carlin speech was unconstitutional. In an opinion joined by Justice Thurgood Marshall, Brennan said the Court's majority was for the first time prohibiting minors from hearing speech that was not obscene and therefore is protected by the First Amendment. Brennan said that "surely" preserving speech entitled to First Amendment protection is important enough that listeners could be required to suffer the "minimal discomfort" of briefly hearing offensive speech before they turned off the radio. Brennan chastised Justice Powell and the majority for "censoring" speech like the Carlin monologue solely because the justices found the words offensive. Brennan accused the Court of attempting "to impose its notions of propriety on the whole of the American people."

All four dissenting justices, in an opinion written by Justice Potter Stewart, said the FCC could not constitutionally regulate the "seven dirty words" because, as the Court determined, the Carlin monologue was not obscene. Stewart said that when Congress passed the law banning "any obscene, indecent, or profane language" from the airwaves, no legislator said that the word *indecent* meant anything different from the word *obscene.*

DEFINING BROADCAST INDECENCY After the *Pacifica* decision, the FCC at first emphasized the limits of its supervision of indecent programming. For more than a decade, the FCC limited its definition of indecency to the frequent repetition of sexual or excretory expletives such as *fuck* and *shit* and did not punish a broadcaster for airing indecent programming.

However, in April 1987, the FCC warned broadcasters that the term *indecent* meant much more than the repetition of George Carlin's "seven dirty words." The commission said, unlike the recent past, any broadcast would be indecent if it included a description or depiction of sexual or excretory activities or organs in a manner patently offensive by contemporary community standards for the broadcast medium. The commission said the context of a broadcast would be an important factor in determining whether the words or depictions are "vulgar" or "shocking" and therefore indecent. Context, the commission said, includes the manner in which the words or depictions are portrayed, whether the portrayal is isolated or fleeting, "the merit" of a program, and whether children might be listening or viewing.[84] The FCC said it would take action against indecent programming when "there is a reasonable risk that children are in the audience." The FCC emphasized broadcasters must precede indecent material with a warning even if children could not reasonably be expected to be in the audience.[85]

The Court of Appeals for the District of Columbia Circuit upheld the FCC's new enforcement policy for indecency. In *Action for Children's Television v. FCC,* the court agreed the FCC's previous policy of limiting indecency actions to programs containing the seven dirty words was an "unduly narrow" interpretation.[86] The court affirmed the FCC's assessment that it made "no legal or policy sense" to regulate Carlin's monologue but not other offensive descriptions or depictions of sexual or excretory activity that avoided the specific words that led to the Supreme Court's *Pacifica* decision. The D.C. Circuit said the commission had rationally decided that a broader definition of indecency was needed.

Under the new indecency policy, the FCC fined dozens of radio broadcasters in the early 1990s for programs featuring bawdy humor and double entendres concerning sexual organs or activities. Infinity Broadcasting paid $1.7 million after the FCC found several broadcasts by Howard Stern were indecent.[87] Stern, the self-proclaimed "King of all Media," frequently talks crudely about sexual activity, discusses his own sexual fantasies, and describes women disrobing in his studio.[88]

The FCC and Evergreen Media Corporation agreed to settle lawsuits filed against each other over the commission's punishment of indecent programming.[89] The FCC agreed to drop several indecency actions against Evergreen and publish a document interpreting its indecency enforcement policies. In return, Evergreen agreed to drop its countersuit and to pay the FCC $10,000. Evergreen also agreed to issue an internal policy memorandum advising employees the company may discipline them if they violate indecency rules.

Eight years later, in 2001, the FCC issued the guidelines Evergreen sought in its agreement with the commission.[90] The guidelines say a radio or television broadcast will be found indecent if, first, it describes sexual or excretory organs or activities and, second, it is patently offensive to an average viewer or listener. The commission said it uses a national standard for determining whether a program is patently offensive, not a local community or statewide test. The FCC also said it considers the "full context" of the program. For example, a newscast employing explicit language might not be indecent, but a disk jockey repeatedly using language implying sexual activity might be indecent programming.

The guidelines reveal that the FCC has no bright-line test to define indecency. Instead, the agency makes case-by-case determinations, balancing several factors to decide whether

[84]*In re* Infinity Broadcasting Corp. 2 F.C.C.R. 2705 (1987).
[85]*In re* Pacifica Foundation, Inc., 2 F.C.C.R. 2698 (1987).
[86]852 F.2d 1332 (D.C. Cir. 1988).
[87]Sagittarius Broadcasting Group. 10 F.C.C.R. 12 (1995).
[88]Mel Karmazin, 8 F.C.C.R. 2688 (1992).
[89]United States v. Evergreen Media Corp., Civ. No. 92-C 5600 (N.D. Ill. Feb. 22, 1994) (agreement for settlement and dismissal with prejudice).
[90]Industry Guidance on Broadcast Indecency, 16 F.C.C.R. 7999 (2001).

Consistent or Inconsistent?

Indecent		***Not Indecent***
Fuck Uttered by U-2's Bono on an awards show. The FCC regarded the remark as "gratuitous."	**Vs.**	**Fuck** Uttered repeatedly by actors during *Saving Private Ryan.* The FCC concluded the language was "integral" to the film.
Shit Uttered by Nicole Richie on an awards show. The FCC regarded the remark as "gratuitous."	**Vs.**	**Bullshitter** Uttered by a *Survivor* contestant during a news interview. The FCC said the news context weighs against indecency findings.
Janet Jackson's Breast Briefly exposed during the *Super Bowl Halftime Show.* The FCC regarded the segment as overtly sexual.	**Vs.**	**Nicollette Sheridan's Naked Back** Shown during an introduction to *Monday Night Football.* Despite the sexually suggestive nature of the segment, there was no graphic depiction of sexual organs.
Howard Stern's discussions of sex Stern discusses various sexual activities such as oral sex. The FCC concluded Stern was pandering to the audience interest in sexuality.	**Vs.**	**Oprah Winfrey's discussions of sex** Winfrey discusses various sexual activities such as oral sex and terms used by teenagers. The FCC claimed the segment was designed to help parents.
A teen-age girl wearing a bra and panites Briefly shown straddling a teen-age boy during an episode of *Without A Trace.* The FCC found the scene to be "highly sexually charged."	**Vs.**	**A couple in bed passionately kissing, caressing, and rubbing** Briefly shown during an episode of *Alias.* The FCC said there was no display of sexual organs.

FIGURE 9.1 Recent FCC Rulings on Indecency

a program is indecent. Critics, who believe the FCC's indecency decisions are arbitrary and inconsistent, claim that indecency determinations reflect "little more than the personal tastes" of the commissioners.[91] Figure 9.1 contrasts recent FCC indecency rulings.

One factor examined by the FCC is the program's explicit or graphic nature. The more explicit the language or pictures, the more likely the program will be found indecent. Thus, the FCC cited Howard Stern's references to testicles, penis size, masturbation, and sodomy and Bubba the Love Sponge's description of oral sex techniques as examples of explicit content. However, the commission also said sexual innuendo, although not explicit or graphic, may be indecent. For example, the FCC sanctioned a radio station for playing a song containing the following lyrics using candy bar names to symbolize sexual activities and organs:

> I whipped out my Whopper and whispered, Hey, Sweettart, how'd you like to Crunch my Big Hunk for a Million Dollar Bar? Well, she immediately went down on my Tootsie Roll and you know, it was pure Almond Joy. I couldn't help but grab her delicious Mounds, this little Twix had the Red Hots.

[91]Stephen Weiswasser and Robert Sherman, "*Oprah* and Spielberg vs. *Without a Trace* and Scorcese: Indecent Inconsistency at the FCC," 24 *Comm. Lawyer* (2006).

To the FCC, the pandering nature of the song made the thought of candy bars "peripheral at best."[92]

In decisions issued in 2004 and 2006, the FCC found that nudity need not be depicted for a television program to be found indecent. A *Married by America* episode featuring topless strippers was found to be indecent even though breasts were digitally obscured. Although the nudity was obscured, "even a child would have known the strippers were topless," the FCC stated.[93] Similarly, an episode of *Without A Trace* briefly depicting partially clothed teenagers at a party was found to be indecent. A teenage girl was shown wearing bra and panties, straddled on top of one male character in a "highly sexually charged" scene.[94]

In contrast, in a 2005 decision, the FCC found that the introduction to a *Monday Night Football* game was not indecent because the nudity shown was not graphic. During the introduction, Nicollete Sheridan, appearing as her *Desperate Housewives* character and wearing only a towel, attempts to seduce Terrell Owens in the Eagle's locker room. After he rebuffs her advances, she drops her towel, prompting Owens to say, "Aw, hell, the team's going to have to win without me," and she leaps into his arms. Sheridan is briefly shown from the back, nude from the waist up. The FCC concluded that although the scene was sexually suggestive, there was no graphic depiction of sexual organs or activities.[95] Also in 2006, the FCC found an episode of *Alias* featuring a couple in bed, "kissing, caressing and rubbing against each other" not to be indecent because there was no display of sexual organs.[96]

A second factor is the persistent repetition of sexual or excretory words such as in George Carlin's recording in the *Pacifica* case. In his "Filthy Words" monologue, Carlin repeats various words such as shit:

> At work you can say it like crazy. Mostly figuratively, Get that shit out of here, will ya? I don't want to see that shit anymore. I can't *cut* that shit, buddy. I've had that shit up to here. I think you're full of shit myself. He don't know shit from Shinola.

The FCC regards repeated sexual or excretory references, such as those in Carlin's monologue, to be indecent. Until 2004, the FCC generally treated isolated expletives, such as a news announcer's on-air blunder, "Oops, fucked that one up," as not indecent. In 2004, however, the FCC announced a new policy, discussed below, that regards even a single utterance of *fuck* to be both indecent and profane. In 2006, the FCC found a single utterance of *shit* was found to be both indecent and profane. For less offensive sexual or excretory language, the FCC requires repetition if the expression is to be deemed indecent.[97]

Brief visual images of nudity can also be indecent, depending on the context. For example, the FCC found the 2004 Super Bowl halftime show to be indecent, even though

[92]WIOD, Inc., 6 F.C.C.R. 3704 (1989).

[93]Complaints Against Various Licensees Regarding Their Broadcast of the Fox Television Network Program "Married By America" on April 7, 2003, Notice of Apparent Liability for Forfeiture, 19 F.C.C.R. 20191 (2004).

[94]Complaints Against Various Television Licensees Concerning Their December 31, 2004, Broadcast of the Program "Without A Trace," Notice of Apparent Liability for Forfeiture, (FCC 06-18) (Mar. 15, 2006).

[95]Complaints Against Various Television Station Licensees Regarding the ABC Television Network's November 15, 2004, Broadcast of "Monday Night Football," Memorandum Opinion and Order (FCC 05-53) (Mar. 14, 2005).

[96]Notices of Apparent Liability and Memorandum Opinion and Order (FCC 06-17) (Mar. 15, 2006).

[97]*See, e.g.*, Infinity Broadcast Operations, Inc., Notice of Apparent Liability for Forfeiture (FCC 04-49) (Mar. 18, 2004).

Janet Jackson's breast was shown for only 19/32 of a second. The segment featured song lyrics and choreography that discussed or simulated sexual activities. After singing "gonna have you naked by the end of this song," Justin Timberlake pulled off part of Ms. Jackson's costume to briefly reveal her breast to the television audience, which included millions of children. Although Jackson and Timberlake claimed the breast exposure was accidental, the FCC concluded that CBS was aware of the "overall sexual nature" of the segment and promoted it as "shocking" to attract viewers.[98]

A third factor is a program's intentional pandering to the audience or intending to shock listeners. The context, or the way in which material is presented, is important in defining indecency. The FCC guidelines contrast Bubba the Love Sponge's monologues with discussions of sex on the *Oprah Winfrey Show*. For example, an *Oprah* program was ruled not to be indecent when a psychologist advised a woman about masturbation:

> You need to at least know how to make your body get satisfied by yourself. Because if you don't know how to do it, how is he going to figure it out? He doesn't have your body parts, he doesn't know.

The FCC concluded that the *Oprah* discussion was not presented in a pandering or titillating manner, unlike the technique of radio "shock jocks." In a 2006 case again involving *Oprah*, the FCC also found a graphic discussion of sexual slang terms used by teenagers not to be indecent. To the FCC, the program was designed to help parents, rather than to titillate. "To the extent that the material is shocking, it is due to the existence of such practices among teenagers rather than the vulgarity or explicitness of the sexual depictions or descriptions."[99]

The FCC also said a news report airing a recording of organized crime figure John Gotti was not indecent, even though Gotti used *fuck* or *fucking* ten times in seven sentences. The FCC believed the explicit language was an integral part of a bona fide news story about organized crime.[100] The commission said it was reluctant to second-guess the editorial judgments of broadcasters "on how best to present serious public affairs programming to their listeners." As will be shown below, in 2006 the FCC again expressed its reluctance to find news programs to be indecent.

Although the FCC is unlikely to challenge expletives in news programs, the commission announced in 2004 that it considers even a single utterance of what it called "the F-word" both indecent and profane in live entertainment programs.[101] In its 2004 ruling, the FCC overturned its own enforcement bureau, which had ruled that U-2's Bono had not expressed indecency when he exclaimed, "This is really, really, fucking brilliant," upon winning the 2003 Golden Globe Award for best original song. The enforcement bureau found that in this context, as in the Gotti broadcast, the word *fucking* did not describe sexual

---

[98]Complaints Against Various Television Licensees Concerning Their February 1, 2004, Broadcast of the Super Bowl XXXVII Halftime Show, Notice of Apparent Liability for Forfeiture, 19 F.C.C.R. 19230 (2004). *See also* Young Broadcasting of San Francisco, Inc., Notice of Apparent Liability for Forfeiture, 19 F.C.C.R. 1751 (2004) (brief exposure of penis found to be indecent).

[99]Complaints Regarding Various Television Broadcasts Between February 2, 2002 and March 8, 2005, Notices of Apparent Liability and Memorandum Opinion and Order, (FCC-06-17) (Mar. 15, 2006).

[100]Peter Branton, 6 F.C.C.R. 610 (1991).

[101]Complaints Against Various Broadcast Licensees Regarding Their Airing of the "Golden Globe Awards," Memorandum Opinion and Order, 19 F.C.C.R. 4975 (2004).

activities. Moreover, drawing upon the 2001 guidelines, the bureau concluded that fleeting and isolated remarks did not warrant FCC sanctions.[102]

In overturning the enforcement bureau's decision, the FCC announced that its precedents allowing isolated or fleeting use of the "F-word" in similar contexts were no longer good law. Any use of the "F-word" inherently has a sexual connotation, the commission said. Furthermore, use of the "F-word" was patently offensive because it "is one of the most vulgar, graphic and explicit depictions of sexual activity in the English language." The FCC described Bono's use of the "F-word" as gratuitous, and indicated that political, scientific, or other uses of the "F-word" might mitigate its offensiveness. The FCC noted that a factor in its decision to target isolated use of the "F-word" was the ease with which broadcasters can delay live broadcasts and bleep offending material. In response to this ruling, many broadcasters began using delays on live broadcasts.

Due to uncertainty about the FCC's standards in the wake of the Bono ruling, sixty-six ABC television network affiliates preempted the November 2004 Veteran's Day broadcast of the film *Saving Private Ryan,* which has numerous uses of the F-word. In early 2005, the FCC dismissed complaints filed against some of the ABC affiliates airing the film, holding the film's coarse battlefield language, unlike that of Bono, was neither gratuitous nor intended to shock. "Indeed, it is integral to the film's objective of conveying the horrors of war through the eyes of these soldiers, ordinary Americans placed in extraordinary situations," the agency stated. ABC provided parents with ample warnings about the film's content; thus, the FCC concluded the presentation was not intended as family entertainment. Also, the FCC ruled that uses of the words *God damn* and similar blasphemous phrases were not profane.[103]

In another decision issued in 2005, the FCC held that the words *dick, penis, testicles, bastard, bitch, hell, damn, orgasm, breast, nipples, pissed,* and *crap* were not profane when used in a fleeting manner in entertainment programs such as *Friends, Will and Grace,* and *Scrubs.* The FCC claimed these words, in context, were not sufficiently graphic to be patently offensive.[104]

In 2006, the FCC ruled that *shit,* "one of the most offensive words in the English language," was both indecent and profane.[105] Nicole Richie, a presenter at the *2003 Billboard Music Awards* program, asked, "Have you ever tried to get cow shit out of a Prada purse?" Even when used in an isolated manner in entertainment programming, the FCC found the S-word was likely to "disturb the peace and quiet of the home." The FCC cautioned broadcasters that only in rare circumstances would the S-word, like the F-word, be regarded as essential to an artistic, educational, or political message. To emphasize its view that the S-word was almost always indecent, the FCC found a documentary about blues musicians airing on a public television station to be indecent. The licensee failed to demonstrate to

[102]Complaints Against Various Broadcast Licensees Regarding Their Airing of the "Golden Globe" Awards, Memorandum Opinion and Order, 18 F.C.C.R. 19859 (Enf. Bur. 2003). *See generally* Anne Marie Squeo, "A Job for Solomon: Was Bono's Blurt a Verb or Modifier?" *Wall Street Journal,* Mar. 11, 2004, at A1.

[103]Complaints Against Various Television Licensees Regarding Their Broadcast on November 11, 2004, of the ABC Television Network's Presentation of the Film "Saving Private Ryan," Memorandum Opinion and Order, 20 F.C.C.R. 4507 (2005).

[104]Complaints by Parents Television Council Against Various Broadcast Licensees Regarding Their Airing of Allegedly Indecent Material, Memorandum Opinion and Order, 20 F.C.C.R. 1931 (2005).

[105]Complaints Regarding Various Television Broadcasts Between February 2, 2002 and March 8, 2005, Notices of Apparent Liability and Memorandum Opinion and Order (FCC 06-17) (Mar. 15, 2006).

the FCC's satisfaction that phrases such as "that shit is crazy" were essential to informing the public about a matter of public importance. In setting aside the artistic judgment of acclaimed filmmaker Martin Scorcese, the FCC said the documentary's educational purpose could have been fulfilled "without the repeated broadcast of expletives."

In an important clarification of its policy on isolated expletives, the commission announced in November 2006 that live news programs provide a context that weighs against an indecency finding. At issue was a live interview on *The Early Show*, a two-hour morning program airing on the CBS television network. During the interview, a contestant in the CBS program *Survivor: Vanuatu,* described another contestant as a "bullshitter." The FCC initially found the broadcast to be indecent, but subsequently concluded its earlier decision did not give "appropriate weight" to the news context of the program. Citing the Gotti case discussed earlier, the FCC explained that news programs were at the core of the First Amendment's protection. The FCC cautioned broadcasters that "there is no outright news exemption from our indecency rules. Nevertheless, in light of the important First Amendment interests at stake as well as the crucial role context plays in our indecency determinations, it is imperative that we proceed with the utmost restraint when it comes to news programming."[106] Commissioner Jonathan Adelstein, in a dissenting opinion, claimed the FCC's reversal of its earlier decision illustrated the "arbitrary, subjective and inconsistent nature" of the FCC's indecency decision making. Further, he questioned the treatment of "infotainment" as news; the segment was merely a promotion of the network's primetime entertainment programming. "The only news here is how far this Commission is willing to stretch the definition of 'news,'" Adelstein stated.

The FCC's campaign against indecency was dealt a severe blow in June 2007 when the Court of Appeals for the Second Circuit ruled the agency's policy punishing isolated expletives violated the Administrative Procedure Act because it was arbitrary.[107] According to the appellate court, the FCC failed to adequately explain why it was departing from precedent when it issued the Bono ruling and the subsequent S-word ruling. The court stated,

> For decades broadcasters relied on the FCC's restrained approach to indecency regulation and its consistent rejection of arguments that isolated expletives were indecent. . . . While the FCC is free to change its previously settled views on this issue, it must provide a reasoned basis for that change. . . . The FCC's decision, however, is devoid of any evidence that suggests a fleeting expletive is harmful, let alone establishes that this harm is serious enough to warrant government regulation. Such evidence would seem to be particularly relevant today when children likely hear this language far more often from other sources than they did in the 1970s when the Commission first began sanctioning indecent speech.

The appellate court also found the FCC's new approach to profanity to be unsupported by a reasoned analysis. The FCC was ordered to provide a fuller explanation of the reasons for its policy shift, but the agency appealed to the Supreme Court instead.

Although the appellate court did not address constitutional issues, in dicta it expressed its doubt that the FCC's "fleeting expletive" policy would pass constitutional

[106]Complaints Regarding Various Television Broadcasts Between February 2, 2002 and March 8, 2005, Order, (FCC 06-166) (Nov. 6, 2006).

[107]Fox Television Stations, Inc. v. FCC, 489 F. 3d 444 (Cir. 2007), *cert. granted* 2008 U.S. LEXIS 2361 (Mar. 17, 2008).

muster. The court said it was sympathetic to the broadcasters' contention that the FCC's indecency test is "undefined, indiscernible, inconsistent, and consequently, unconstitutionally vague." Broadcasters intend to press this issue at the Supreme Court, along with claims that it is no longer possible to describe broadcasting as "uniquely accessible to children." The appellate court suggested that technology controlled by parents may eliminate the need for FCC regulation, an argument broadcasters also intend to emphasize before the Supreme Court.

FINING INDECENCY On June 15, 2006, President Bush signed the Broadcast Decency Enforcement Act, which increased the maximum penalty the FCC can impose per indecency violation from $32,500 to $325,000.[108] This tenfold increase was necessary, President Bush stated, because the prior amount was not a deterrent to many broadcasters, and in recent years "broadcast programming has too often pushed the bounds of decency."

Although Congress sets the maximum amount that can be assessed for an indecency violation, the FCC can impose a lesser amount if it concludes the violation is not egregious. The agency also has substantial discretion in determining whether any fine is assessed. For example, in 2006 the FCC resolved complaints about programs, such as the *2003 Billboard Music Awards* show, involving isolated use of expletives such as *fuck* and *shit*. These programs aired prior to the FCC's decision in the Bono case; the agency found the broadcasts to be indecent but imposed no fines because FCC policy at the time of the broadcasts tolerated isolated use of expletives.[109]

The FCC's discretion also affects its assessment of who is liable for fines. As part of its recent crackdown on indecency, the agency began multiplying the fine by the number of stations carrying a program, but currently the FCC fines only licensees who are the subject of viewer complaints to the FCC. In 2004 the FCC proposed fining all Fox Network affiliates that broadcast an episode of *Married by America* featuring whipped cream, spanking, and strippers, but in 2008 the agency held liable only those 13 Fox affiliates subject to viewer complaints.[110] In another 2008 action, the FCC imposed a $1.2 million fine against 45 ABC Television Network affiliates subject to viewer complaints about a February 25, 2003 episode of NYPD Blue airing at 9 p.m. in the Central and Mountain time zones. In the program, a woman's naked buttocks were shown in several close-range shots, including one the FCC described as "lingering." The maximum fine applicable at the time of the broadcast, $27,500 per station, was levied due to the titillating nature of the scene and because the stations could have declined to air the prerecorded program, the FCC said.[111]

CHANNELING INDECENCY Although the FCC has said broadcasters can air indecency only during the hours when children are not expected to be listening and watching, it has

---

[108] Pub. L. No. 109-235, 120 Stat. 491 (2006).

[109] Complaints Regarding Various Television Broadcasts Between February 2, 2002 and March 8, 2005, Notices of Apparent Liability and Memorandum Opinion and Order at ¶¶ 101–45 (FCC 06-17) (Mar. 15, 2006).

[110] Complaints Against Various Licensees Regarding Their Broadcast of the Fox Television Network Program "Married by America" on April 7, 2003, Forfeiture Order, (FCC 08-63) (Feb. 22, 2008).

[111] Complaints Against Various Licensees Concerning Their February 25, 2003 Broadcast of the Program "NYPD Blue," Forfeiture Order (FCC 08–55) (Feb. 19, 2008).

had difficulty finding a **safe harbor** for indecency that is acceptable to both Congress and the courts. All three branches of government have struggled to find a time for broadcast indecency that shields children from offensive programming but allows adults access to constitutionally protected speech.

In 1995, the U.S. Court of Appeals for the D.C. Circuit held constitutional a restriction of broadcast indecency to the hours of 10 P.M. to 6 A.M. At the same time, the court ruled unconstitutional an attempt by Congress to limit the hours of indecency for most but not all broadcast stations from midnight to 6 A.M.[112] In the Public Telecommunications Act of 1992, Congress had prohibited indecent programming between 6 A.M. and midnight for all broadcast stations except public radio or television stations that left the air at or before midnight. Only the public television stations with shortened hours could begin broadcasting indecency at 10 P.M.

The D.C. Circuit, sitting en banc, voted 7-4 that although a ban of indecency from 6 A.M. to midnight met most constitutional requirements, Congress had not properly justified treating commercial and public broadcasting stations differently. The court said Congress had not explained how the disparate treatment of broadcasters met the compelling governmental interest of protecting children from indecent broadcast programming.

However, the D.C. Circuit's majority said it had to set aside the midnight standard in favor of the 10 P.M. standard—the hour that some public broadcasters could begin airing indecent programming—so all broadcasters would be treated the same. Congress, the court said, did not provide evidence that minors are less likely to be corrupted by sexually explicit material broadcast by a public station than by a commercial station. The court said allowing public broadcasters to air indecency before midnight undermined the argument for prohibiting indecent speech before midnight on other stations.

In separate dissents, Chief Judge Harry Edwards and Judge Patricia Wald argued the statute channeling indecency was unconstitutional; Congress and the FCC had assumed, rather than provided evidence, that indecency harmed children, Edwards and Wald said. Both Edwards and Wald suggested that instead of prohibiting indecency during much of the broadcast day, the government consider equipping television sets with computer technology that would allow parents to block indecent programs from their homes. As discussed later in this chapter, Congress enacted such a requirement, known as the V-Chip, in 1996.

Telephone

For years, there was little concern about content communicated over the telephone. However, when dial-a-porn services proliferated in the 1980s, parents complained the services were readily available to children, who may try to imitate the sexual activities described and who sometimes incurred charges of thousands of dollars listening to dial-a-porn. In 1988, Congress banned obscene and indecent messages delivered via commercial telephone services.

The U.S. Supreme Court held that Congress could constitutionally ban obscene sexual messages provided by commercial telephone services. At the same time, however, the Court said a ban on indecent dial-a-porn services violated the First Amendment.

[112]Action for Children's Television v. FCC (Act III), 58 F.3d 654 (D.C. Cir. 1995), *cert. denied*, 516 U.S. 1043 (1996).

In *Sable Communications v. FCC,* the Supreme Court ruled that sexually explicit phone messages that are indecent but not obscene cannot be banned but can be regulated. The Court said that since indecency, unlike obscenity, is constitutionally protected, Congress invalidly banned indecent dial-a-porn instead of only restricting access by children. Justice White said the 1988 statute was "another case of burning the house to roast the pig."[113]

The Court acknowledged Congress has a legitimate interest in preventing children from being exposed to dial-a-porn. However, the Court said that since indecent speech is constitutionally protected, as the Court first held in *FCC v. Pacifica Foundation,* the regulation of indecent dial-a-porn must be limited so that access by children is restricted without barring access by adults. In *Sable,* the Court distinguished telephone services from broadcasting:

> The context of dial-in services, where a caller seeks and is willing to pay for communication, is manifestly different from a situation in which a listener does not want the received message. Placing a telephone call is not the same as turning on a radio and being taken by surprise by an indecent message. Unlike an unexpected outburst on a radio broadcast, the message received by one who places a call to a dial-a-porn service is not so invasive or surprising that it prevents an unwilling listener from avoiding exposure to it.

Also, telephone service providers were able to use methods such as access codes to make their messages available to adults but not to children.

Shortly after the Supreme Court ruled in *Sable* that a blanket ban on indecent dial-a-porn is unconstitutional, Congress enacted more limited legislation. Congress adopted a statute prohibiting dial-a-porn services from providing indecent messages to persons younger than eighteen years old and to nonconsenting adults.[114] The law also requires telephone companies that bill for adult messages to block indecent dial-a-porn from the phones of customers who have not subscribed to the service in writing. The statute also allows dial-a-porn services to insulate themselves from prosecution by adhering to FCC procedures limiting children's access to explicit sexual messages.

The FCC, under the authority of the law, adopted rules requiring dial-a-porn providers to restrict access to their services by requiring callers to use credit cards or access codes or by scrambling their calls so that they can be heard only through a descrambling device.[115] Two circuits of the U.S. Courts of Appeals, the Second and the Ninth, have upheld the law and the FCC's interpretation of it. Both courts said the rules were narrowly tailored to meet the compelling government interest in protecting the "physical and psychological well-being of minors."[116]

Cable Television

When determining the constitutionality of cable regulations, as when regulating other media, the Supreme Court grapples to protect the First Amendment rights of system operators to control their content, to protect the rights of adults to access constitutionally protected

[113]492 U.S. 115 (1989).
[114]47 U.S.C. § 223.
[115]Regulations Concerning Indecent Communications by Telephone, 5 F.C.C.R. 4926 (1990).
[116]Dial Information Servs. Corp. v. Thornburgh, 938 F.2d 1535 (2d Cir. 1991), *cert. denied,* 502 U.S. 1072 (1992); Information Providers' Coalition for Defense of the First Amendment v. FCC, 928 F.2d 866 (9th Cir. 1991).

content, and to protect children from indecency. At the same time, Congress and the courts want to encourage the development of new technologies.

In some ways, cable is like print, suggesting that cable operators can be accorded maximum First Amendment freedoms without exposing children to great amounts of indecency. Cable systems, like print, offer diverse voices through scores of channels, enough channels to distinguish cable from broadcasting, which is licensed and regulated because of the narrow broadcast band. Cable is also like print because householders control entry of the medium into the home. Cable subscribers, like newspaper and magazine readers, order cable and pay for it regularly. Unlike broadcasting, cable is not as pervasive a "free" medium that enters the home, sometimes intrusively. Cable is also unique because system operators can block channels at the command of individual subscribers, permitting subscribers to protect children from unwanted content.

Although cable can be analogized to print, the medium also embodies qualities of the more ubiquitous and intrusive broadcasting medium, suggesting that cable might be more regulated than print to protect children. The scores of channels offered by the typical cable system can appear every bit as pervasive and intrusive as over-the-air broadcast channels, even though the cable service is invited into the home.

Recently the graphic content on cable program services has drawn fire from politicians. Kevin Martin, chair of the FCC, has argued for extending the indecency rules to the programming included in the expanded basic packages offered by cable and DBS providers. Alternatively, Martin has advocated a change in the way cable systems package their programming so parents can "get Nickelodeon and Discovery without having to buy other adult-oriented fare."[117] In response to Martin's suggestion, Comcast and Time Warner began offering family-friendly packages. The National Cable and Telecommunications Association (NCTA), cable's primary trade association, is opposed to government-mandated programming packages; the NCTA says that parental use of measures such as channel blocking or the V-chip are more appropriate ways to control children's access to indecent programming.

Generally, the courts have ruled that cable operators enjoy nearly the same First Amendment rights as publishers or Internet operators. The Court has noted that cable companies originate programming and exercise editorial discretion.[118] In another case, the Court referred to cable as "part of the press" because cable operators deliver news, information, and entertainment to their subscribers.[119] In yet another case, the court said cable operators are entitled to largely the same First Amendment protection as publishers.[120]

Of course, cable operators, like operators of other media, have no right to disseminate obscenity. But cable operators may transmit indecency. In a case emphasizing the similarity between cable operators and publishers, the Supreme Court upheld lower court rulings that indecency cannot be banned on cable. In *Wilkinson v. Jones,* the Court upheld lower court rulings striking down a Utah statute barring indecency on cable.[121] The federal district court said that cable could not be regulated like broadcasting because cable offered so

[117]Testimony of Kevin Martin before the U.S. Senate Committee on Commerce, Science and Transportation (Nov. 29, 2005).
[118]Los Angeles v. Preferred Communications, Inc. 476 U.S. 488 (1986).
[119]Leathers v. Medlock, 499 U.S. 439 (1991).
[120]Turner Broadcasting Sys., Inc. v. FCC, 512 U.S. 622 (1994).
[121]800 F.2d 989 (10th Cir. 1986), *aff'd without opinion,* 480 U.S. 926 (1987).

many more channels. The court also said that cable, unlike broadcasting, is invited into the home. Indeed, cable viewers pay extra for HBO, Showtime, and other premium channels that sometimes carry sexually oriented programming, the court noted. Furthermore, cable subscribers can control children's access to indecency by installing "lockboxes" provided by cable companies, the court said.

In *United States v. Playboy Entertainment Group, Inc.,* the Court reaffirmed the rights of cable operators by striking down part of a statute designed to protect children from inadvertently being exposed to sexual video and audio.[122] The Court struck down a section of the Telecommunications Act of 1996 that attempted to halt the "bleed" of sexual pictures and dialogue from adult cable channels to channels children might be watching in the basic cable service. The statute required cable operators carrying Playboy channels, AdulTVision, Spice, and other channels "primarily dedicated to sexually oriented programming" either to completely scramble the signals, to block them entirely, or to cablecast them between the hours of 10 P.M. and 6 A.M., to lessen the possibility that children might glimpse a breast or hear suggestive dialogue bleeding from an imperfectly scrambled transmission. Another alternative allowed cable operators to block delivery of the sexually oriented channels only to cable subscribers who requested the block. However, only a tiny fraction of cable subscribers requested the house-by-house block. Most cable systems therefore chose the time-shifting alternative—telecasting indecency after 10 P.M.—because establishing a bleed-proof scrambling technique was too expensive, a complete block ended the transmission of constitutionally protected sexual expression, and few households requested individual blocks.

Playboy and other adult programmers challenged the statute, arguing that even the required time-shifting was unconstitutional because it restricted cable operators, programmers, and adult viewers who desired nonobscene sexual programming before 10 P.M., when 30–50 percent of adult programming is normally viewed. In a 5-4 ruling in which the Supreme Court applied strict scrutiny to the regulations, the Court held that the required scrambling, total blocks, and time-shifting were unconstitutional content restraints because a less restrictive method was available to protect children from a signal bleed, a problem that the Court was not convinced was very serious in the first place. The Court ruled that cable operators' and programmers' First Amendment rights could be served and children protected if cable operators followed the less restrictive alternative of notifying subscribers that the cable companies would block indecent programming to individual homes if subscribers asked. Requiring notification allows subscribers to take advantage of cable's unique technology, the Court said, the ability of cable operators to block individual channels to individual homes. Through notification and blocking, programmers could provide sexual content via cable twenty-four hours a day to adult viewers with a right to view it. At the same time, children would be protected, the Court concluded.

Although cable operators have broad First Amendment rights to control the types of programs they will carry, cable systems are monopolies in most localities and are required to provide channels for voices that the cable operator does not choose. To diversify voices in often-monopolistic cable systems, the federal government requires larger cable systems to lease up to 15 percent of their channels to anyone who will pay to rent a channel.[123]

[122] 529 U.S. 803 (2000).
[123] 47 U.S.C. § 532.

Through local franchises, cities and counties require cable systems to set aside "PEG" channels for public, educational, and government programming.[124] The Supreme Court has ruled that cable operators can ban indecency on leased access channels but not on public, educational, and government channels.

LEASED ACCESS Under a 1984 cable act, Congress requires larger cable systems to designate 10–15 percent of their channels for use by others on a commercial or "leased" basis. Smaller cable systems are not required to lease channels.

A section of a 1992 law permits cable operators to ban indecency on leased channels if the cable system provides written policies that explain the law and the cable company's procedures.[125] The law also allowed cable operators to permit sexually oriented programming over leased channels, but only if the cable operators "segregated" indecent programming on a single channel that would be available within thirty days if subscribers requested it in writing. In a decision affirming the First Amendment rights of cable operators, the Supreme Court ruled that cable operators can permit or forbid indecency on leased access channels but cannot be required to segregate the sexually oriented programming onto a single channel that would be blocked to all subscribers or opened only to those who requested it. In *Denver Area Educational Telecommunications Consortium, Inc. v. FCC* the Court struck down the segregation requirement because it unconstitutionally restricted sexual content of the cable system operators, programmers, and adult viewers.[126]

In a plurality opinion that most justices concurred in, the Court ruled that the law allowing cable operators to ban or allow indecency on cable channels was constitutional. But the portion of the statute requiring the segregation and written request was unconstitutional, the Court said, because it restricted protected programming entirely during the thirty-day period while subscribers were waiting for cable installation. The Court also said the written-request requirement was unconstitutional because it inhibited subscribers whose reputations might be damaged if a cable operator revealed they requested a restricted channel. Furthermore, the Court feared cable operators might forgo disseminating protected sexual expression to avoid the costly and time-consuming government regulations. As for the children, they would be adequately protected, the Court said, through the content decisions of cable operators on leased channels and by technological remedies, including lockboxes.

PEG CHANNELS Local governments may require cable systems to provide public, educational, and government (PEG) channels as a repayment to the community for being allowed to lay cables under city streets and to use city rights-of-way. PEG channels are used for the telecast of city council and school board meetings, educational panels, and public announcements. In *Denver Consortium,* the Supreme Court ruled the First Amendment permits the government to bar cable operators from restricting indecency in PEG channels. The Court concluded that a cable operator's "veto" over indecency was much less necessary to protect children on public access channels than on leased access channels. Unlike leased access channels, which are controlled by a third party who rents a channel, public access channels

[124] 47 U.S.C. § 531.
[125] 47 U.S.C. § 532(b).
[126] 518 U.S. 727 (1996).

typically are operated cooperatively by local community and governmental organizations, often including an access channel manager appointed by the municipality. Elaborate screening and certification processes protect children from indecency on public access channels, the Court concluded, precluding the need for content controls by cable operators.

Internet

In 1996, Congress attempted to prohibit indecency on the Internet, but the U.S. Supreme Court found the law unconstitutional. The Court said the Internet should have the same level of First Amendment protection as the print media have. Because indecency is not prohibited in the print media, it may not be proscribed on the Internet.

The Communications Decency Act (CDA), which was part of the Telecommunications Act of 1996, prohibited deliberately using the Internet to send indecent, patently offensive, or obscene material to people under eighteen years old. The CDA also made it illegal for any person or company—such as America Online—to allow dissemination of obscene or indecent material to minors over Internet facilities it controlled. Violators could be fined or imprisoned for up to two years. Internet providers could defend themselves if they acted "in good faith" to take "reasonable, effective, and appropriate actions" to prevent minors from receiving indecent material through the Internet.[127]

In *Reno v. ACLU,* the Supreme Court found the CDA unconstitutional, saying that the Internet should receive expansive First Amendment protection.[128] The government argued that the Internet should be subject to extensive regulatory control, as is broadcasting. The Court disagreed, stating that the Internet is not as "invasive" as broadcasting. Gaining access to content on the Internet requires a user to take deliberate actions, from turning on a computer to connecting to an Internet Service Provider such as AOL to accessing a specific website. The Court said because certain steps must be taken, it is unlikely that an Internet user would accidentally encounter indecent material.

The Court also distinguished the Internet from broadcasting because there was no spectrum scarcity justifying government regulation. The Internet did not have physical limitations similar to those of broadcasting. At any given time, tens of thousands of people are discussing a range of subjects on the Internet, where content is "as diverse as human thought." And the Internet provides a low-cost means for "publishers" to reach a global audience. The Court recognized that the Internet is used as a worldwide soapbox.

Applying strict scrutiny in the *Reno* decision, the Court agreed the government had a compelling interest in protecting children from obscene and indecent material. But the Court said the CDA was unconstitutional because it was not narrowly drawn to restrict speech as little as possible.

Justice Stevens, writing for the 7-2 Court majority, said important words in the CDA were unconstitutionally vague. The Court said that criminal laws and laws limiting speech—and the CDA was both—must define terms carefully. The CDA was imprecise, the Court said, not allowing Internet users to know what speech was illegal. Communities were left to define *patently offensive* and *indecent* because Congress did not clearly define

[127]Pub. L. No. 104-104, § 502, 110 Stat. 56 (1996).
[128]521 U.S. 844 (1997).

them, the Court said. The word *indecent* is not defined in the law at all. The term *patently offensive* is defined as material involving "sexual or excretory activities or organs" as taken "in context" and "measured by contemporary community standards." The Court said these phrases, meant to give context to "patently offensive," are themselves not defined.

Without clear definitions, the Court said, the words "will provoke uncertainty among speakers about . . . just what they mean." Users might have censored themselves, the Court said, suppressing their speech rather than communicating protected material that they incorrectly feared the CDA might have prohibited. The Court said the statute's undefined terms would cause self-censorship. Some speakers would silence themselves, fearing they would violate the law, even though their "messages would be entitled to constitutional protection," the Court said. Therefore, the Court said, the community using the narrowest, most confining definitions would set the standard for the entire country. Justice Stevens said an e-mail message about birth control a parent sent to a child at college might violate the law if people in the college town considered birth control to be indecent or patently offensive.

The Court also found the CDA was overbroad, prohibiting communications that are constitutionally protected, as well as content that lawfully can be prohibited. The Court noted the CDA constitutionally prohibited obscenity on the Internet but unconstitutionally banned indecent and patently offensive material. The First Amendment does not protect obscene material in any mass medium, including the Internet. But the CDA also banned offensive or indecent material that has literary, artistic, political, or scientific value, the Court said, although that material would be protected for adults if published in other media. Although the Court's obscenity test shelters sexual speech with social value, the CDA did not. Justice Stevens said the CDA might have penalized otherwise protected messages about homosexuality, prison rape, or the First Amendment.

The Court also said the CDA was broader than a New York law protecting children from print indecency that the Court found acceptable. In *Ginsberg v. New York,* discussed earlier in this chapter, the Court upheld a statute making it illegal to sell minors sexually oriented material that would not be obscene if sold to adults.[129] The Court said the New York law was not overbroad but the CDA was too broad because it prohibited not only the sale of indecent material to minors but also the gift of constitutionally protected indecency, even by a parent. Further, the constitutional New York statute barred indecency to anyone under seventeen years old, but the broader CDA barred indecency to anyone under eighteen.

The Court also said the CDA was broader than a statute using zoning laws to restrict where adult movie theaters may be located. In *City of Renton v. Playtime Theatres,* discussed later in this chapter, the Court said it was constitutional for Renton, Washington, to limit adult theaters to certain areas of the city.[130] But the Court said it was not constitutional for the CDA to bar indecency entirely. The zoning law was not an attempt to prohibit content but to channel it to certain places. The CDA was a ban on content, the Court said.

The Court did follow its reasoning in *Sable Communications v. FCC,* discussed earlier in this chapter, in which it upheld a congressional ban on obscene messages transmitted by telephone.[131] But in *Sable* and in the CDA decision, the Court said the First Amendment

[129] 390 U.S. 629 (1968).
[130] 475 U.S. 41 (1986).
[131] 492 U.S. 115 (1989).

protects indecent messages transmitted from adults to adults when users must take affirmative steps to receive indecent material, as both "dial-a-porn" customers and Internet users do.

The Court suggested parental control or blocking software would be constitutionally acceptable ways to prevent children's access to indecent material. The Court majority said a more precisely and narrowly drawn statute preventing children's access to indecent material on the Internet might be constitutional.

After the Court ruled the CDA unconstitutional, Congress attempted to protect children on the Internet with a narrower law. In 1998, Congress enacted the Child Online Protection Act (COPA) prohibiting commercial material "harmful to minors" on the World Wide Web. The overbroad CDA had prohibited noncommercial as well as commercial materials on the whole Internet.

To overcome vagueness and overbreadth, Congress drew on the Supreme Court's ruling in *Miller v. California* to define "harmful to minors" in the Child Online Protection Act. A commercial work is harmful to minors under COPA if jurors applying "contemporary community standards" would find the work as a whole appeals to the prurient interest of minors, is patently offensive and lacks serious value. COPA provides a defense to website operators who use age verification techniques to prevent minors from gaining access to prohibited materials.

An appeals court found COPA to be unconstitutionally overbroad because material disseminated nationally on the World Wide Web might be ruled harmful to minors according to the community standards of a jury in one of the "most puritan of communities." But the U.S. Supreme Court ruled that COPA could not be declared unconstitutional only because different juries would interpret "contemporary community standards" differently. In *Ashcroft v. American Civil Liberties Union,* the Supreme Court ruled that "community standards need not be defined by reference to a precise geographic area."[132]

The Supreme Court sent COPA back to the appeals court to determine whether the statute was sufficiently narrow when all three prongs of the *Miller* test—patent offensiveness, appeal to the prurient interest, and lack of social value—were applied. The Court noted that the overbroad CDA, unlike COPA, allowed punishment of expression that was patently offensive but did not necessarily appeal to the prurient interest or lack social value. "When the scope of an obscenity statute's coverage is sufficiently narrowed by a 'serious value' prong and a 'prurient interest' prong, we have held that requiring a speaker disseminating material to a national audience to observe varying community standards does not violate the First Amendment," the Court said in an opinion written by Justice Thomas.

Eight justices concurred for various reasons that COPA should be remanded to the lower court. Justice Stevens, dissenting, argued that COPA, like CDA, is overbroad. Stevens said that much expression that is lawful for adults will be prohibited if the "contemporary community standards" of conservative communities determines what is patently offensive to minors and appeals to minors' prurient interests. Stevens also argued that juries might bar constitutionally protected expression for adults by easily determining that the work lacks serious value for children.

On remand, the appellate court found COPA to be unconstitutional because the law was not narrowly tailored, nor did it employ the least restrictive means available, such as blocking

[132]535 U.S. 564 (2002).

or filtering technology.[133] The Supreme Court affirmed by a 5-4 vote, holding that the government failed to prove that age verification techniques were more effective than software filters installed by parents. Justice Kennedy, writing for the majority in *Ashcroft v. American Civil Liberties Union II,* noted that COPA was suspect because a blue-ribbon commission created by Congress concluded that filters were more effective than age verification techniques.[134] Kennedy concluded that if Congress promoted the use of filters, parents could control what their children see "without subjecting protected speech to severe penalties."

Justice Breyer argued in a dissenting opinion that COPA's burden on protected speech is modest; it only requires providers of sexual material to restrict minors' access. Moreover, he regarded filters to be faulty, costly, and dependent upon parental willingness to supervise children's use of the web. He claimed that children are often unsupervised or may use computers at friends' homes where parents are more lenient.

The Court remanded the case so the trial court could consider the effectiveness of various technical methods of controlling children's access to harmful material. After a trial, a federal district court in March 2007 held COPA violated the First Amendment because software filters were a more effective, but less restrictive means of blocking access to sexual materials than the age verification schemes authorized by COPA.[135] Additionally, the court ruled that COPA was unconstitutionally vague because it did not define how terms like "as a whole" would apply to the World Wide Web. "There is no question that a printed book or magazine is finite, and, as a result, it is very easy to discern what needs to be examined in order to make an 'as a whole' evaluation," the district court wrote. The same is not true for a webpage or websites since pages and sites are hyperlinked to other pages and sites. A publisher of a website could only guess at what undefined portion of the "vast expanse" of the web would be considered to be the whole work by a court, and this imprecision was unconstitutional, the district court wrote.

Public libraries that accept federal funds may be required to limit access to sexually explicit Internet material, the Supreme Court ruled in 2003. By a 6-3 vote, the Court upheld a federal statute requiring that public libraries use filtering software or risk losing federal subsidies for Internet access.

By 2000, 95 percent of public libraries in the United States provided public Internet access. Patrons of all ages regularly searched for online pornography, often exposing other patrons unwillingly to pornographic images. In 2001, Congress required libraries receiving federal funds to install software filters to block adults from accessing obscenity or child pornography and children from accessing material harmful to minors. But software filters are imprecise, often "overblocking" materials adults and children have a First Amendment right to see. Thus, Congress, in the Children's Internet Protection Act (CIPA), also permitted libraries to disable filters for patrons engaged in "bona fide research or other lawful purposes."[136]

In *United States v. American Library Association*, the Supreme Court upheld CIPA, ruling that libraries may restrict patrons' access to Internet material of "requisite and

[133]ACLU v. Ashcroft, 322 F.3d 240 (3rd Cir. 2003).
[134]542 U.S. 566 (2004).
[135]ACLU v. Gonzales, 2007 U.S. Dist. LEXIS 20008 (E.D. Pa. Mar. 22, 2007).
[136]20 U.S.C. § 9134(f)(3).

appropriate quality," just as librarians have traditionally decided which books to purchase.[137] Writing for the Court, Chief Justice Rehnquist noted that most libraries already exclude pornography from their print collections because they deem it inappropriate. "It would make little sense to treat libraries' judgments to block online pornography differently, when these judgments are made for just the same reason," Rehnquist said.

The majority of the Court concluded that CIPA does not seriously burden library patrons' access to constitutionally protected Internet content. The Court was unsympathetic to the claim that some patrons would be too embarrassed to ask librarians to unblock sites or disable filters. "The Constitution does not guarantee the right to acquire information at a public library without any risk of embarrassment," the Court said.

Justice Souter, in a dissenting opinion joined by Justice Ginsburg, viewed CIPA as unconstitutional censorship. Souter feared that library patrons would be denied access to protected expression by librarians who can refuse under CIPA to unblock sites or disable filters. Justice Souter also disputed Chief Justice Rehnquist's argument that blocking access to Internet sites is analogous to choosing books for library shelves. Souter argued that blocking sites is analogous to cutting pages from an encyclopedia or removing books already purchased. Justice Stevens also dissented, claiming that libraries can allow adults unfettered access to lawful Internet content while protecting other patrons from unwanted exposure to sexual materials by installing privacy screens on terminals or buying recessed monitors.

◇ Summary ◇

Obscenity is prohibited in any medium of expression. The regulation of nonobscene sexual depictions varies from medium to medium. Broadcasters may be punished for airing depictions or descriptions of sexual or excretory activities or organs in a manner that is patently offensive to community standards for the broadcast medium. In *FCC v. Pacifica Foundation,* the Supreme Court ruled that broadcasters can be constitutionally restricted to airing indecency only at those times of day when children are not likely to be in the audience. The current "safe harbor" for broadcasting indecent material is between the hours of 10 P.M. and 6 A.M.

Dial-a-porn services can transmit indecent material at any time of day. However, these services must employ techniques, such as access codes, to limit their audiences to adults. Cable systems may transmit indecent material at any time of day on channels controlled by the cable operator. Cable companies may prohibit indecent material on leased access channels; municipal officials overseeing PEG channels may also prevent these channels from being used for indecent programs. Finally, the Supreme Court has ruled that communicators using the Internet, like print publishers, have a First Amendment right to disseminate indecency.

Violent Pornography

Violence in the media is a recurrent concern among the public and politicians. Congress periodically holds hearings to determine if violence in the media contributes to violence in society. As will be shown later in this chapter, industry organizations have adopted various

[137] 539 U.S. 194 (2003).

systems of labeling comic books, movies, recordings, video games, and Internet sites in response to political pressure. In 1996, Congress passed legislation requiring violent television programming to be labeled and parents to be afforded the technology to block it from home TV screens. In 2005, Congress authorized the use of software to render "imperceptible" portions of films displayed in homes.

American courts have never found that violence alone lacks First Amendment protection. Violence is not included in the definition of obscenity. If violence is combined with sexual content and the material is found to be obscene, it is the sexual matter, not the violence, that is the basis for the finding.

Effects of Violent Pornography

Social science research is not conclusive about the effects of violent pornography. Nonetheless, in 1986 the Attorney General's Commission on Pornography (the Meese Commission) asserted that exposure to violent pornography depicting the degradation, domination, or coercion of women increases aggressive behavior toward women, including sexual violence. The Meese Commission lacked solid scientific proof for this claim and acknowledged that its conclusions were based in part on its members "own insights and experience" with violent pornography.[138] Two commissioners objected to the commission's efforts to "tease the current data into proof of a causal link."[139]

Social scientists questioned the Meese Commission's conclusions, arguing that a causal relationship between exposure to sexually violent images and aggression toward women is found in laboratory studies measuring short-term effects, but that these studies do not support conclusions about long-term effects. Further, it is unclear whether the adverse effects of violent pornography are caused by the combination of violence and sexual imagery, or are due to depictions of violence against women. Social scientific evidence suggests that exposure to violent pornography may increase one's tolerance for sexual crimes, but evidence linking violent crime to pornography is not clear. According to its critics, the Meese Commission used social science studies "selectively to confirm certain moral/political beliefs."[140]

Women and Violence

The Meese Commission advocated stricter enforcement of obscenity law, but feminists claimed that violent and degrading portrayals of women should be illegal even when not obscene. In the 1980s, a number of feminists argued that violent pornography violated women's civil rights; objectionable portrayals of women contributed to discrimination against women in settings such as employment and education.[141] In response, Indianapolis declared the "graphic sexually explicit subordination of women" to be illegal. The ordinance outlawed the verbal or pictorial representation of women in "subordinate" ways, including as sexual objects enjoying pain, humiliation, or rape or in "scenarios of degradation."

[138] Attorney General's Commission on Pornography, Final Report (1986).

[139] *Id.* (separate statement of Commissioners Judith Becker & Ellen Levine).

[140] Daniel Linz, Neil Malamuth, & Katherine Beckett, "Civil Liberties and Research on the Effects of Pornography," in *Psychology and Social Policy* 149 (P. Suedfeld and P. E. Tetlock, eds., 1992).

[141] *See, e.g.,* Catherine MacKinnon, *Only Words* (1993).

The U.S. Court of Appeals for the Seventh Circuit declared the ordinance unconstitutional because it did not assess a work as a whole, nor did it include the elements of patent offensiveness, prurient appeal, and lack of social value as required by *Miller.*[142] Speech treating women in an approved way—premised on equality—was lawful under the ordinance no matter how sexually explicit. "Speech treating women in the disapproved way—as submissive in matters sexual or as enjoying humiliation—is unlawful no matter how significant the literary, artistic, or political qualities of the work taken as a whole," the appellate court wrote. The First Amendment "forbids the state to declare one perspective right and silence opponents."

The Seventh Circuit observed that violent pornography, like racist or anti-Semitic speech, is protected expression even though political majorities find it to be insidious. Otherwise, the government would become "the great censor and director of the thoughts which are good for us."

Video Games

In recent years, the depiction of violence and sexuality in top-selling video games such as *Grand Theft Auto* has become a matter of great concern to social scientists and legislatures.[143] In response to the belief that these games harm children, a number of cities and states have enacted laws limiting or prohibiting children's access to violent and sexually explicit games; each law has been found to be unconstitutional.

In *American Amusement Machine Association v. Kendrick,* the Court of Appeals for the Seventh Circuit found unconstitutional an Indianapolis ordinance limiting the access of minors to video arcade games containing "graphic violence."[144] Although the law also restricted access to games with "strong sexual content," the plaintiffs only challenged the aspects of the law relating to violence.

Because Indianapolis was fearful that violent video games engender aggressive attitudes and behavior, the court of appeals required that the city prove violent video games caused players to commit violent acts. Without strong empirical support, governmental claims about the effects of violent depictions would be a pretext for censorship.

Writing for the court of appeals, Judge Richard Posner found that the social science studies relied on by Indianapolis showed only that violent video games increase aggressive feelings but do not cause anyone to commit a violent act. The city's claim of harm to its children from these games was "wildly speculative."

Posner described video games as a form of constitutionally protected storytelling; the themes presented in games such as *The House of the Dead* are also described in ancient and modern literature. The law was unlikely to reduce children's exposure to media violence, Posner said, because the city was not restricting children's access to violence in other media, such as books and movies.

Children have First Amendment rights, Posner noted, and it was important that children receive "uncensored speech" before they turn eighteen so that their minds are not blank

[142]American Booksellers Ass'n, Inc. v. Hudnut, 771 F.2d 323 (7th Cir. 1985), *aff'd without opinion,* 475 U.S. 1001 (1986).
[143]*See, e.g.,* Craig Anderson et al., "Violent Video Games: Specific Effects of Violent Content on Aggressive Thoughts and Behavior," 36 *Advances Experimental Soc. Psychol.* 199 (2004).
[144]244 F. 3d 572 (7th Cir. 2001).

when they first vote. "People are unlikely to become well-functioning, independent-minded adults and responsible citizens if they are raised in an intellectual bubble," he wrote.

Following *Kendrick,* courts in several states have invalidated laws restricting children's access to video games.[145] For example, in late 2005, an Illinois law prohibiting the sale or rental of violent or sexually explicit video games to minors was ruled unconstitutional.[146] The federal district court carefully reviewed a series of social science studies and concluded that a solid causal link between violent video game exposure and violence had not been established. Applying the *Brandenburg* incitement test discussed in Chapter 2, the court held there was no evidence that violent video game content was "directed to inciting or producing imminent lawless action."

The Illinois law was also flawed because it did not restrict children's access to other media, such as DVDs and CDs, which may portray violence. And because the law banned any sexual imagery in games—even a brief scene—it departed from the traditional requirement that sexual depictions be considered as part of a whole work. "Such a sweeping regulation on speech—even sexually explicit speech—is unconstitutional even if aimed at protecting minors," the district court wrote.

The V-Chip

The FCC has been reluctant to restrict violence in broadcast programming.[147] However, in 1996, Congress adopted legislation requiring ratings of "violent" and "sexual" programming and the installation of computer chips in television sets that would allow parents to block the rated programming.

The so-called V-chip law was enacted as part of the Telecommunications Act of 1996. The law mandates that television receivers with thirteen-inch or larger screens sold in the United States contain a computer chip allowing television set owners to block programs containing violence, sexual content, "or other indecent material about which parents should be informed before it is displayed to children."[148] The law does not define *violence, sexual content,* or *indecency,* although indecency has been defined by the FCC. The V-chip could be coded by parents to automatically block programming that they find objectionable. In 1998, the FCC said V-chips must be installed in half the television receivers made for sale in the United States by July 1, 1999, and in all sets by January 1, 2000.[149]

For the V-chip to block programs, violent or sexually oriented programming must be accompanied by program ratings sent through the television signal. Congress told video program distributors that they had one year to "voluntarily" implement a program rating system that was acceptable to the FCC. Otherwise, the FCC was empowered to create its own advisory committee to develop a ratings system. In March 1998, the FCC gave final approval to the television program rating system developed by the National Association of Broadcasters, the National Cable Television Association, and the Motion Picture

[145]*See, e.g.,* Interactive Digital Software Ass'n v. St. Louis County, 329 F.3d 954 (8th Cir. 2003); Video Software Dealers Ass'n v. Schwarzenegger, 401 F. Supp. 2d 1034 (N.D. Cal. 2005); Entertainment Software Ass'n v. Granholm, 404 F. Supp. 2d 978 (E.D. Mich. 2005); Video Software Dealers Ass'n v. Maleng, 325 F. Supp. 2d 1180 (W.D. Wash, 2004).

[146]Entertainment Software Ass'n v. Blagojevich, 404 F. Supp. 2d 1051 (N.D. Ill. 2005).

[147]Report on the Broadcast of Violent, Indecent, and Obscene Material, 51 F.C.C.2d 418 (1975).

[148]Pub. L. No. 104-104, § 551, 110 Stat. 56 (1996). *See also* 47 U.S.C. § 303 (x).

[149]Blocking of Video Programming Based on Program Ratings, 13 F.C.C.R. 11248 (1998).

Association of America.[150] The ratings, assigned to all television programs except news, sports, and unedited MPAA-rated movies on premium cable channels, alert parents to program material they might not want their children to watch.

The ratings are as follows:

Programs designed for children:

TV-Y	Appropriate for all children
TV-Y7	Programs directed to children seven years old and above
TV-Y7-FV	Fantasy violence may not be appropriate for children under seven years old

Programs designed for general audiences:

TV-G	For general audiences
TV-PG	Parental guidance suggested; the program may contain material unsuitable for younger children. The program also may contain: (V) moderate violence; (S) some sexual scenes; (L) occasional coarse language; or (D) some suggestive dialogue.
TV-14	Parents strongly cautioned; the program may contain material unsuitable for children under fourteen years of age. The program also may contain: (V) intense violence; (S) intense sexual scenes; (L) strong coarse language; or (D) intensely suggestive dialogue.
TV-MA	Mature audiences only; the program may contain material unsuitable for children under seventeen years of age. The program also may contain: (V) graphic violence; (S) explicit sexual scenes; (L) strong coarse language.

Ratings are applied to programs by broadcast and cable networks. Syndicated programs, such as talk shows, are rated by the program distributor. To ensure that program ratings are applied accurately and consistently, the television industry established the Oversight Monitoring Board. The board includes members from broadcast television, cable television, program production, and the public. The board has no enforcement power except public pressure.

Despite being available for nearly a decade, use of the V-Chip is very low. A 2005 study by the Kaiser Family Foundation found that among seventh through twelfth graders, only 6 percent reported parental use of the V-Chip.[151] Low parental use of the V-Chip was recently cited by FCC as a reason for continuing regulation of broadcast indecency.[152]

In an attempt to fend off increased indecency fines on broadcasters and an extension of indecency rules to cable and satellite services, in 2006 a cross-section of media companies and trade associations announced a $300 million national public service advertising campaign to increase parental awareness of the V-Chip. The advertisements encourage parents to visit a website, TheTVBoss.org, which provides information on managing children's television usage.

---

150 Video Program Ratings, 13 F.C.C.R. 8232 (1998).

151 Kaiser Family Foundation, *Generation M: Media in the Lives of 8-18 Year-olds* 20 (2005).

152 Complaints Regarding Various Television Broadcasts Between February 2, 2002 and March 8, 2005, Order at ¶ 51, (FCC 06-166) (Nov. 6, 2006).

The limited effectiveness of the V-Chip and the ratings system, however, was cited by the FCC in an April 2007 report on television violence.[153] The FCC found that of the 280 million television sets in U.S. households, only 119 million sets are equipped with the V-chip. Additionally, the FCC found few parents used the V-Chip and many parents lack understanding of the ratings system. Further, the FCC reported programs are often inaccurately rated.

Although the FCC did not initiate any new rules relating to television violence, it outlined several policy options for Congress to consider. One policy recommended by the FCC was a time-of-day channeling of violent programming, similar to the time channeling of indecency. Such a scheme would require that Congress define violence, an especially nettlesome problem that must include factors such as context, presence of weapons, and realism. Congress had asked the FCC for a definition of violence, a task the agency avoided. This prompted Commissioner Jonathan Adelstein to note that the FCC "has not been able to formulate and recommend a definition of violence that would cover the majority of violent content that is inappropriate for children, provide fair guidance to programmers, and stand a decent chance of withstanding constitutional scrutiny, in light of judicial precedent."

The Family Movie Act of 2005

Congress gave video consumers greater control over the content of movies displayed in private households by enacting the Family Movie Act of 2005 (FMA).[154] The Act allows parents or others to employ software to render objectionable portions of a film "imperceptible" so long as the filtering is controlled by a member of the household and no fixed copy of the altered version of the movie is created.

The Family Movie Act resulted from litigation brought by film directors, such as Steven Spielberg, and Hollywood film studios, against companies that sold unauthorized copies of movies that had been altered to delete "sex, nudity, profanity, and gory violence." The editing techniques included fogging or the use of a black bar to obscure visual content; audio content was redacted or replaced with ambient noise. The directors and studios claimed the edited versions infringed their copyrights. As discussed in Chapter 6, in 2006 a federal district court ruled in favor of the directors and studios and enjoined companies such as Clean Flicks from selling unauthorized edited versions of copyrighted films.[155]

The directors and studios also sued companies that sold filtering software enabling consumers to skip or mute objectionable film content. While the suit was pending, Congress passed the FMA and the defendants selling filtering technology were dismissed from the suit. Companies such as ClearPlay are able to continue selling specially equipped DVD players and filtering software.

ClearPlay produces software that is used in conjunction with an authorized copy of a movie and a specially equipped DVD player. Parents download software for a particular film and are able to customize their preferences by adjusting fourteen different filter

[153]Violent Television Programming and its Impact On Children, Report, (FCC-07-50) (Apr. 25, 2007).
[154]Pub. L. No. 109-9, 119 Stat. 223 (2005) (amending 17 U.S.C. § 110).
[155]Clean Flicks v. Soderbergh, 433 F. Supp. 2d 1236 (D. Colo. 2006).

settings relating to violence, sex and nudity, and language. For example, a parent could mute "Vain references to Deity" "Ethnic and Social Slurs," and "Strong Profanity" in the audio track of a DVD.[156]

◇ Summary ◇

Violent pornography in American media may not be prohibited unless it is obscene. The Meese Commission on pornography said it found a causal link between violent pornography and violence in society, but social scientists generally do not go so far. It also has been ruled unconstitutional to bar violent pornography as an infringement on women's civil rights.

Congress enacted the V-chip requirement in 1996; today, all television sets with a screen thirteen inches or larger sold in the United States are equipped with a computer chip that allows set owners to block programming based on its rating. In 1998, the FCC approved a rating system developed by the broadcast, cable, and motion picture industries. In 2005, Congress authorized the use of software to render "imperceptible" portions of films displayed in homes.

Controlling Nonobscene Sexual Expression

Nonobscene sexual expression may be restricted to certain places or times to protect those who wish to avoid pornography and to preserve the tone of the community. The constitutionality of time, place, and manner restrictions on nonobscene sexual expression depends on the circumstances in each case. Government restrictions on nonobscene sexual expression should be as narrow as possible and should allow alternative avenues by which the nonobscene materials may find their audience.

Generally, the government's power to regulate or prohibit sexual expression increases as the expression merges with conduct. Some conduct, such as nude sunbathing, topless waitressing, and massaging, contains no expression and therefore can be regulated without First Amendment consideration.[157] Other nonobscene conduct, such as nude dancing and nude musicals, contains significant expressive content and therefore may be channeled to certain times and places if not banned.[158] Three acceptable governmental regulations on the distribution of nonobscene sexual materials are zoning, postal, and display laws. The media themselves also self-regulate the sexual content of their offerings.

Zoning Laws

Communities attempt through zoning laws to control the impact of adult theaters and bookstores. Sometimes cities attempt to diffuse the impact of sex establishments by spreading them through different parts of the community or controlling the signs through which they present themselves to the public. Sometimes city zoning concentrates adult bookstores and theaters in one place for easier monitoring and law enforcement.

In 1986, the Supreme Court upheld a Renton, Washington, zoning regulation that prohibited adult movie theaters within 1,000 feet of any residential zone, family dwelling, church, park, or school. In *City of Renton v. Playtime Theatres, Inc.,* the Court ruled the

[156]More information about ClearPlay is available at www.clearplay.com.
[157]*See, e.g.,* South Florida Free Beaches v. City of Miami, 734 F.2d 608 (11th Cir. 1984).
[158]Schad v. Borough of Mount Ephraim, 452 U.S. 61 (1981); Southeastern Promotions, Ltd. v. Conrad, 420 U.S. 546 (1975).

law was a constitutional time, place, and manner regulation even though it singled out adult movie theaters and bookstores for regulation.[159] The regulation was content-neutral, the Court said, because it was aimed at protecting the community from crime and declining trade and property values, not at the content of the films.

The restrictions were needed, the Court said, even though adult theaters in Renton had not presented problems up to that time. Furthermore, the Court was satisfied enough sites remained in Renton where adult businesses could be opened.

Courts used the *Renton* standard in rejecting challenges to changes in New York City zoning laws. The zoning changes largely were limits on where adult businesses may locate and prohibitions on adult businesses clustering together. The new zoning standards effectively shut down all adult business in Times Square, including adult theaters and bookstores. Several courts found the city's intent was to eliminate neighborhood deterioration, crime, and decreased property values that accompany adult businesses. The city's purpose was not to infringe on the adult businesses' speech rights. The courts also said the zoning laws were not broader than necessary to rectify these effects. Finally, courts said the adult businesses had sufficient alternative areas within New York City to conduct their activities.[160]

Although the Supreme Court has approved zoning laws to restrict the location of pornographic theaters and bookstores, the Court generally does not permit zoning laws to ban nonobscene sexual expression. The Court struck down a New Jersey zoning law that barred all commercial live entertainment, including nude dancing, in the Borough of Mount Ephraim. The zoning ordinance was declared unconstitutional because it provided no place where constitutionally protected nonobscene dancing might be performed. The Court said the borough had not demonstrated that permitting nude dancing would create the difficulties with parking, trash collection, and police protection that prompted the ban on commercial live entertainment.[161]

After the *Mount Ephraim* ruling regulating the place, not the content, of nude dancing, the Court twice upheld laws banning public nudity, including dancing. In a 5-4 ruling in *Barnes v. Glen Theatre,* the Court said Indiana could constitutionally adopt a statute requiring otherwise nude dancers to wear pasties and G-strings.[162] The Court upheld a similar Pennsylvania law in *City of Erie v. Pap's A.M.*[163] In both cases, the Court applied the *O'Brien test,* discussed in Chapter 3, concluding that the bans on public nudity were designed to protect public morality and safety, not to suppress freedom of expression, and at most had minimal impact on expressive activity.

Writing for the Court plurality in *Pap's A.M.,* Justice O'Connor said the Erie ordinance protects public morality and prevents the secondary effects of crime and neighborhood decay that adult entertainment establishments engender. The Court acknowledged that requiring pasties and G-strings might minimally diminish the erotic impact of otherwise nude dancing, but, the Court said, the First Amendment does not require a city to permit dancers to convey the erotic message "when the last stitch is dropped." In a concurring opinion, Justices Scalia and Thomas saw no need to apply the *O'Brien test* to an ordinance that was aimed at nudity that the city could ban to further public morality.

[159] 475 U.S. 41 (1986).
[160] *See, e.g.,* Hickerson v. City of New York, 146 F.3d 99 (2d Cir.), *cert. denied,* 525 U.S. 1067 (1998).
[161] Schad v. Borough of Mount Ephraim, 452 U.S. 61(1981).
[162] 501 U.S. 560 (1991).
[163] 529 U.S. 277 (2000).

Zoning laws restricting the showing of nonobscene materials must not be too broad. In a Florida case, the U.S. Supreme Court struck down an ordinance prohibiting drive-in movie theaters from exhibiting films showing bare breasts, buttocks, or pubic areas if the screen were visible from streets and sidewalks. The Supreme Court ruled the ordinance was too broad as applied to adults because it barred adults from seeing nonobscene anatomy on the screen. The Court also said the ordinance was too broad as it applied to children. By preventing the showing of all nudity, the ordinance would have protected children not only from lewd pornography but also from pictures of a baby's buttocks, the nude body of a war victim, scenes from a culture where nudity was common, art exhibitions, and pictures of nude bathers.[164] Such a broad prohibition on content is unconstitutional.

Postal Regulations

Whereas zoning may channel nonobscene communications to certain places, postal regulations protect one's privacy from the assault of unwanted sexual materials. Reflecting the special concern of legislators and courts for protecting children and privacy, the Supreme Court permits homeowners to stop sexually oriented advertisements from being delivered to their mailboxes. Under postal law, people who receive a pandering advertisement can contact the post office and have their names removed from the mailer's list. The law also says that the sender can be required to mark on the outside that the advertisements are sexually oriented. Ads do not have to be obscene to be halted. The Supreme Court upheld the constitutionality of the statute in *Rowan v. United States Post Office Department.*[165] The Supreme Court unanimously agreed no one has a right to press even good ideas on an unwilling recipient. Thus, the mailer's right to communicate stops at the mailbox of the unreceptive addressee.

Display Laws

Statutes and ordinances also may restrict the display to minors of sexually explicit materials that are not obscene for adults. The U.S. Court of Appeals for the Tenth Circuit upheld the constitutionality of a Wichita, Kansas, ordinance barring display of sexual materials to minors but permitting the use of so-called blinder racks that hide the lower two-thirds of the cover of sexual publications. Blinder racks effectively shield minors from sexual materials without unconstitutionally depriving adults of access to legal sexual publications.[166] Similarly, another federal appellate court ruled constitutional a Minneapolis ordinance requiring bookstores to keep materials that are harmful to minors in a sealed wrapper or behind an opaque cover.[167] Adults still have access to the materials by asking a clerk to remove the wrapper, by viewing an inspection copy kept behind the store counter, or by viewing the material in an adults-only bookstore that excludes minors.

Informal Restraints

Injunctions are not the only potentially unconstitutional restraints on sexual materials. Informal government pressures also may unconstitutionally suppress sexual materials.

[164]Erznoznik v. City of Jacksonville, 422 U.S. 205, 213 (1975).
[165]397 U.S. 728 (1970).
[166]M.S. News Co. v. Casado, 721 F.2d 1281 (10th Cir. 1983).
[167]Upper Midwest Booksellers Ass'n v. City of Minneapolis, 780 F.2d 1389 (8th Cir. 1985).

In 1963, the U.S. Supreme Court ruled it was unconstitutional for a state commission to threaten magazine and book distributors with prosecution for materials that had not been determined to be obscene. In *Bantam Books, Inc. v. Sullivan,* the Court ruled that the Rhode Island Commission to Encourage Morality in Youth imposed an unconstitutional prior restraint on magazine and book distributors when the commission sent them notices that some of their publications, including *Playboy* and *Peyton Place,* were "objectionable" for sale or display to youths under age 18.[168] The notices thanked distributors on the list in advance for their cooperation and reminded them that the Rhode Island commission had the duty to recommend prosecution for purveyors of obscenity. Officials were then sent to see what action distributors planned to take.

The Rhode Island commission said it wrote letters and visited distributors simply to advise them of their legal rights. But the Supreme Court said the commission engaged in an informal censorship in violation of the First Amendment. The Court said the Rhode Island commission's threats and coercion unconstitutionally suppressed publications. The Court also said the term *objectionable* in the commission's warning notice was vague, leaving distributors to speculate whether the commission considered a particular publication to be obscene.

In a more recent case, a federal appeals court held that Attorney General Edwin Meese and members of his Commission on Pornography did not violate the First Amendment when they sent letters to distributors of *Playboy* and *Penthouse,* threatening to print allegations that the distributors were selling pornography.[169]

The D.C. Circuit said the Commission on Pornography's letters to convenience stores, asking them to respond to accusations they were selling pornography, were not like the unconstitutional letters sent by the Rhode Island Commission to Encourage Morality in Youth. Unlike the Rhode Island letters, the pornography commission's letters never threatened legal action, the court said. Whereas the Rhode Island letters warned of possible prosecution and were followed by a police visit, the pornography commission's letters only announced the accusations of pornography and asked the companies to respond. Even though the pornography commission was headed by the U.S. attorney general, the court found no threat of prosecution in the letters. The First Amendment is not abridged, the court said, "in the absence of some actual or threatened imposition of governmental power or sanction."

Cutting Funds

Another way for the government to curb nonobscene sexual expression is to bar funding. The government, of course, does not have to support painters, writers, musicians, and other artistic creators. Conservative budget cutters may constitutionally limit or eliminate funding for the National Endowment for the Arts, the National Endowment for the Humanities, and other agencies that support artistic expression. If the government does fund expression, it is not obligated to support art, dance, and writing that is sexually explicit.

In 1998, the U.S. Supreme Court said the government may reject grant proposals for artistic projects that are indecent or do not comply with "values of the American public."[170] The Court said a law requiring the National Endowment for the Arts (NEA) to consider

[168]372 U.S. 58 (1963).
[169]Penthouse Int'l, Ltd. v. Meese, 939 F.2d 1011 (D.C. Cir. 1991), *cert. denied,* 503 U.S. 950 (1992).
[170]National Endowment for the Arts v. Finley, 524 U.S. 569 (1998).

whether artistic projects seeking federal funds show a "respect for diverse beliefs" and are "decent" does not unconstitutionally force the NEA to suppress certain viewpoints.

In 1990, Congress told the NEA to include among criteria for judging grant applications "general standards of decency and respect for the diverse beliefs and values of the American public."[171] Several artists challenged the law, arguing the statute required the NEA to engage in viewpoint discrimination by rejecting artistic projects defying mainstream values or offending generally accepted standards of decency. The 8-1 Court disagreed, saying the law did not prevent the NEA from funding indecent artistic expression if it chooses. The Court said the law does no more than require the NEA "to take 'decency and respect' into consideration." Because words like *decency* and *value* are open to many interpretations, the Court said, Congress did not forbid funding specific viewpoints.

Justice Sandra Day O'Connor, writing for the majority, said there was no substantial risk the law would limit expression because the NEA does not directly apply the required decency criteria to each grant proposal. Rather, the NEA interprets the statute as being satisfied if panel members reviewing grant applications have diverse backgrounds and points of view. Also, the Court said, many factors, including decency, go into judging the quality of artistic projects. When considering funding requests in which decency is not a question, the Court said, the NEA turns down many more applications than it accepts. The law only provides additional criteria—decency and respect for American beliefs and values—the NEA may use to make these decisions, according to the Court.

The Court said it was not deciding whether the NEA's method of applying the law is what Congress intended. But, the Court said, it is "clear" the law "imposes no categorical requirement" that would force the NEA to reject grant proposals because of their viewpoints.

Industry and Citizen Regulation

Politicians frequently blame the media for social ills. These accusations are often accompanied by calls for government regulation of media content, especially portrayals of sex and violence. For example, revelations that the teen-aged killers at Columbine High School had been preoccupied with violent movies and video games led to proposed legislation outlawing the sale of violent material to children.[172] Media organizations, whose PACs are heavy donors to political campaigns, have largely been able to blunt these calls for regulation by claiming that self-regulation is preferable to government regulation. As stated by the Internet Content Rating Association, a private organization that has developed a rating system for Internet sites, labeling sends a clear signal "that the World Wide Web is willing and able to self-regulate, rather than have the heavy hand of government legislation decide what is or is not acceptable."[173] Thus far, the only government regulation of violence is the television program rating scheme discussed earlier in this chapter.

COMICS In April and June 1954, a United States Senate subcommittee investigating juvenile delinquency held televised hearings on the effects of comic books. A prominent witness

[171] 20 U.S.C. § 954(d)(1).

[172] Jeffrey Taylor, "House GOP Tries to Curb Violent Fare," *Wall Street Journal,* June 8, 1999, at A20; Jeffrey Taylor, "How Do You Define Obscene Violence? Congress Might Try," *Wall Street Journal,* June 9, 1999, at A1.

[173] More information about the Internet Content Rating Association is available at its website, www.icra.org.

was Dr. Fredric Wertham, a psychiatrist whose book *Seduction of the Innocent* claimed the lurid portrayal of violent crime in comic books was linked to a rise in juvenile delinquency. In response, comic book publishers formed the Comics Code Authority (CCA) in October 1954; the CCA created content guidelines, a reviewing process, and a seal to be displayed on the cover of approved comics. The industry's self-regulation appeased the Senate subcommittee; its 1955 report was critical of the content of comics, but regarded self-regulation as an adequate solution.

The original code, designed to promote "good taste or decency" covered areas such as crime, violence, sex, nudity, and profanity. For example, the code provided that "passion or romantic interest shall never be treated in such a way as to stimulate the lower and baser emotions." The code also prohibited advertisements for liquor, tobacco, weapons, and gambling. Because most magazine distributors would not carry comics lacking the CCA seal, it became difficult to sell unapproved comics on newsstands.

During the 1980s, the comics market changed as specialty retailers, such as comic book stores, replaced newsstands as primary outlets. Today, more than 80 percent of comics are sold through specialty retailers. In response to this change, the CCA amended its code in 1989. The new code allows adult-themed material to be distributed without a seal if restricted to specialty outlets. Publishers who wish to display the CCA seal must submit comics to the code administrator for review prior to publication. The current code provides that violent behavior is not to be shown as acceptable, drug use is not be depicted in a glamorous way, and graphic sexual activity is not allowed. The CCA claims that its code assures parents that approved comics "uphold basic American moral and cultural values."[174]

Only a small number of publishers currently submit material for CCA approval. These publishers, who still rely on newsstands, include DC, publisher of *Superman;* Archie, publisher of the *Archie, Jughead,* and *Veronica* series; and Bongo, publisher of the *Simpsons* and related titles. Comics published by other companies are either unrated or self-rated by the publisher. For example, Marvel, publisher of the *X-Men* and *Spider-Man* comics, has developed its own rating system; its comics are labeled All Ages, T+, and Parental Advisory. Marvel has also developed a separate line of adult-themed comics published under the Max Comics banner. Max titles are labeled Explicit Content and are not sold on newsstands.

MOTION PICTURES The movie rating system was created in 1968 by the Motion Picture Association of America and the National Association of Theatre Owners. This is a voluntary system; filmmakers are under no legal obligation to have their films rated, nor must theater owners restrict their audiences. However, filmmakers have a powerful economic incentive to have a film rated because most theaters will not exhibit unrated films. Because the ratings symbols G, PG, PG-13, R, and NC-17 are registered trademarks, filmmakers may not self-apply these symbols to films. (The X rating, which has been replaced by NC-17, is not a trademark and is self-applied in various forms, such as XXX to hard-core sexual films.) Theater owners have political incentives to enforce age restrictions. For example, after the Columbine tragedy, theater owners pledged to increase their efforts to restrict audiences for R-rated films, acknowledging that they were doing this to reduce the prospect of onerous legislation.[175] As most

[174]Comics Magazine Association of America, Principles of the Comics Code Authority (1989).

[175]David Rosenbaum, "Theaters in U.S. Will Require ID's at R-Rated Films," *N.Y. Times,* June 9, 1999, at A1.

American teenagers know, enforcement of age restrictions for R-rated films varies from theater to theater. Enforcement has been less strict in large cities and on the East and West Coasts and more strict in small towns and suburbs in the South and Midwest.

Ratings decisions are made by a ratings board whose members are parents who are not affiliated with the film industry. The board reviews each submitted film, estimating what most parents would consider to be an appropriate rating. By majority vote, the board decides on a film's rating. A producer who is seeking a less severe rating may edit the film and resubmit it. Also, producers may appeal a rating decision to a ratings appeal board, consisting of representatives of the motion picture industry. Only by a two-thirds vote may the appeal board overturn a ratings board decision. Since 1968, more than 17,000 films have been rated: 58 percent received R ratings, 21 percent received PG ratings, 12 percent received PG-13 ratings, 7 percent received G ratings, and only 2 percent received NC-seventeen ratings.[176]

In making ratings decisions, the ratings board considers theme, language, violence, nudity, sex, and drug use. Films that are classified as G, or general audience, are for all ages and contain minimal violence and no nudity, sex scenes, or drug use. A PG, or parental guidance rating, means that some material in the film might be inappropriate for young children. Drug use and explicit sex scenes are absent; any nudity is brief, and violence does not exceed moderate levels. A rating of PG-13, or parents strongly cautioned, means that some material in the film is inappropriate for preteens. Some scenes of nudity and drug use may be present, along with isolated use of sexually derived words. Rough violence is absent in a PG-13 rated film. An R-rated film is restricted to those who are at least seventeen years old or accompanied by a parent or guardian. Films rated R may include nudity and sexual scenes, rough and persistent violence, drug use, and coarse language. If a film receives an NC-17 rating, no one age seventeen or under may be admitted to view it. Films that receive this rating have explicit sex scenes, excessive violence, or an accumulation of sexually oriented language. It is important to note that the NC-17 rating is not synonymous with the legal category of obscenity; a film may receive an NC-17 rating because of its violence.

All advertising for films submitted for a rating must be approved by the MPAA. In recent years, the MPAA has restricted the display of guns and other violent imagery in advertising.[177] If a studio were to broadcast or publish an advertisement that had been rejected by the MPAA, the rating of the film would be revoked. Trailers shown in theaters or on home videos must show the rating for the trailer and the rating of the picture being advertised. A trailer that is rated for "all audiences" contains no scenes that caused a film to be rated PG, PG-13, R, or NC-17. Trailers that are rated for "restricted audiences" should precede only films that are rated R or NC-17.

RECORDED MUSIC The recording industry also has a voluntary system of labeling recorded music. In 1985, in response to pressure from the National Parent Teacher Association and the Parents Music Resource Center, the recording industry agreed to place parental advisory labels on recordings that include explicit depictions of violence, sex, or drug use. The Recording Industry Association of America (RIAA) owns the mark "Parental Advisory—Explicit Content" and allows record companies to place this label on the packaging for

[176]Motion Picture Association of America, "US Entertainment Industry: 2005," *MPA Market Statistics* 15 (2006).
[177]Bruce Orwall & John Lippman, "Movie Rating Group Is Frisking Ads for Guns," *Wall Street Journal,* June 14, 1999, at B1.

FIGURE 9.2 Copyright, Motion Picture Association of America. Used by permission.

recordings. No record company is required to label its explicit recordings. If a record company chooses to participate in the labeling program, the decision as to which recordings are labeled is made by the record company in conjunction with the artist. The RIAA states,

> In some instances, record companies ask an artist to re-record certain songs or to revise lyrics because a creative and responsible view of the music demands such a revision. Sometimes songs are simply taken off an album. In other instances, the artist and the record company agree that there is musical and artistic credibility in the whole of the work even when the lyrics may be too explicit for mainstream distribution. In those instances, the RIAA's Parental Advisory label is applied prominently to the outside of the permanent packaging.[178]

The RIAA provides record companies with guidelines to determine when a label should be attached to a recording. The guidelines note that labeling "is not a science" and requires consideration of the "context, frequency, and emphasis" of the lyrics. The guidelines ask record companies to consider whether, "in light of contemporary cultural morals and standards and the choices and views of individual parents, the recording might be one that parents may not want their children to listen to."[179]

The RIAA also recommends that the Parental Advisory label appear in advertisements for labeled recordings. Record retailers are also encouraged to post notices explaining that recordings displaying the Parental Advisory logo "contain strong language or depictions of violence, sex or substance abuse. Parental discretion is advised." The RIAA estimates that an average record store carries 110,000 album titles, and approximately 500 are labeled. Record stores vary in their approach to labeled music. Some retailers will not carry labeled recordings, others will not sell labeled recordings to children, and some sell these recordings without regard to age.

VIDEO GAMES Since 1994, the Entertainment Software Rating Board, created by the interactive software industry, has rated video and computer games.[180] The ESRB rates more than 1,000 games per year. Each game is judged by three raters, such as retired school principals, who have no ties to the interactive software industry. Once a game is rated, a rating icon is displayed on the front of packaging; more detailed content descriptors appear on the back of packaging. Because the ESRB owns its rating icons, game producers may not self-apply the icons to any game that has not been rated by the ESRB.

The ESRB classifies games as follows:

Early Childhood (EC)	Content is suitable for children age three and older. There is no content that parents would find inappropriate.
Everyone (E)	Content is suitable for ages six and older. These games may contain minimal violence. In 1998, this replaced the previously used Kids to Adults (K–A) category.

[178]Recording Industry Association of America, "Parental Advisory "available at http://www.riaa.com/issues/parents/advisory.asp.

[179]*Id.*

[180]Entertainment Software Rating Board, "About ESRB," available at http://www.esrb.org/about/index.jsp.

Everyone 10+ (E10+)	Content suitable for ages ten and over. Games may contain mild violence and/or minimally suggestive themes.
Teen (T)	Content is suitable for ages thirteen and older. Games in this category may contain violent content and strong language.
Mature (M)	Content is suitable for ages seventeen and older. These games include more intense violence or language than games in the Teen category.
Adults Only (AO)	These games include graphic sex and/or violence and are not suitable for those under the age of eighteen.
Rating Pending (RP)	Games have been submitted to the ESRB and are awaiting final rating. This symbol appears only in advertising prior to the release of a game.

The content descriptors include "Blood and Gore," "Use of Drugs," "Strong Language," "Nudity," and "Suggestive Themes."

In July 2005, the ESRB changed the rating of *Grand Theft Auto: San Andreas* from M to AO after it was disclosed that software unauthorized by the game maker enabled players to unlock explicit sexual content hidden in the game. (Apparently the scenes were placed in the game while it was under development; prior to the game's release, the game maker decided against making the scenes easily accessible as a way of avoiding an AO rating.) The ESRB's rating change prompted Wal-Mart and Target, the nation's largest sellers of video games, to pull the game from their shelves; most major chain stores do not carry AO-rated games. The maker of the game claimed the software "patch," produced by an independent programmer, was an unauthorized modification of its game and released a new version that prevents such modification. The ESRB rated the new version of *Grand Theft Auto: San Andreas* as M, and the game returned to the shelves of major retailers.

INTERNET The ESRB also rates online gaming and other websites. Sites that have been rated may display the ESRB icon; content descriptors pop up when the mouse cursor is placed over the icon. In addition, parents may set the security feature on a browser to block access to websites whose ESRB rating indicates the content is inappropriate for their children.

Another prominent system of rating websites has been developed by the Internet Content Rating Association, a private group supported by Internet companies. The ICRA system asks website operators to fill out a questionnaire assessing their site's depiction of nudity, sexual activities, violence, drug use, and gambling. ICRA then generates a label that is added to the site's meta tag, a software code that is not visible to users but is read by the user's browser. Website operators may also display an ICRA logo or "labeled with ICRA" link on the site. ICRA can revoke the use of the trademarked label and logo if a website operator misrepresents the nature of the site's content.[181]

With the ICRA rating system, parents may set the security feature on their browser to block access to unlabeled sites, or they may selectively block certain types of sites. Three

[181] Internet Content Rating Association, "Terms and Conditions," available at http://www.icra.org/legal/#content.

of the most popular web portals, Yahoo!, MSN, and America Online, require that websites featured on these portals carry ICRA ratings.[182]

MOBILE PHONES Users of advanced mobile phones are able to access a wide variety of content including video clips made for mobile devices, music, ring tones, games, images such as background "wallpaper" for the screen, text, photo and video messages, and Internet sites. In November 2005, the nation's leading carriers, in partnership with the Cellular Telecommunications & Internet Association, adopted content guidelines.[183]

The guidelines distinguish between content accessed from the carrier's managed content portal and content accessed from the Internet. Carrier-offered content is divided into two categories: Generally Accessible Carrier Content and Restricted Carrier Content. Content is restricted if it contains intense profanity, intense violence, graphic depictions of sexual activity, nudity, hate speech, graphic depictions of illegal drug use, and activities such as gambling that are restricted by law to those eighteen years of age and older. The carriers have pledged not to provide restricted content until controls are in place allowing parents to restrict access to this type of content.

Another aspect of the guidelines calls for the carriers to develop blocking and filtering technologies allowing parents to block access to the Internet entirely or to block access to specific Internet sites. Although carriers have no control over content not featured on their portals, filtering is intended to give parents the ability to control what children can access via wireless devices.

Content generated by a user, such as text messages, instant messages, and picture mail, is not subject to the content classification system.

MARKETING PRACTICES After the Columbine tragedy, President Clinton asked the Federal Trade Commission to assess whether the motion picture, recorded music, and electronic games industries were marketing to children products that had parental warnings or age restrictions. In 2000, the FTC issued a report concluding that these three industries routinely targeted children under age seventeen in advertising campaigns for restricted material.[184] In 2002, the FTC found that the movie and electronic games industries had reduced the advertising of R-rated movies and M-rated games in media popular with teenagers. The record industry continued to advertise music with explicit lyrics in television shows and magazines popular with teenagers, although advertisements in these outlets increasingly displayed the Parental Advisory warning.[185] In its 2004 report, the FTC found that the music industry had substantially curtailed advertising of explicit music in print media popular with teenagers but continued to place ads on cable music channels popular with teenagers. The motion picture industry returned to advertising R-rated films and DVDs on television programs with large teen viewership, a practice that had previously

[182]Dina El Boghaddy, "AOL, MSN, Yahoo to Label Sites for Questionable Content," *Wash. Post,* Oct. 23, 2001, at E5.
[183]Cellular Telecommunications & Internet Association, Wireless Content Guidelines (Nov. 8, 2005).
[184]FTC, "Marketing Violent Entertainment to Children: A Review of Self-Regulation and Industry Practices in the Motion Picture, Music Recording & Electronic Game Industries" (Sept. 2000).
[185]FTC, "Marketing Violent Entertainment to Children: A Twenty-One Month Follow-up Review of Industry Practices in the Motion Picture, Music Recording & Electronic Game Industries" (June 2002).

declined.[186] The FTC in 2007 expressed concern about advertising on websites popular with children.[187] The agency found advertisements for R-rated films, parental advisory-labeled music, and M-rated video games were frequently placed on websites with substantial audiences of children under seventeen. The FTC refuses to bring any legal action based on these marketing practices, fearing that this would cause these industries to cease self-regulation. The FTC also recognizes that the First Amendment limits its authority to regulate the marketing and sale of violent material. The agency recommends that Congress continue its support for industry self-regulation programs.

CITIZEN ACTION A number of citizens' groups pressure the media, with varying success, to reduce sex and violence. For example, pressure from the Parents Music Resource Center and the National Parent Teacher Association led to the establishment of the record industry's Parental Advisory program. In November 2003, pro-family groups such as Focus on the Family and the American Decency Association called for a boycott of Abercrombie & Fitch clothing stores because the company's Christmas issue of its quarterly magazine featured photographs of naked young men and women in a variety of sexual poses. The company's corporate offices were also flooded with 300 telephone calls per hour from protestors. In response, the company pulled the magazine from its stores.[188] A group known as Enough is Enough seeks to educate the public and policymakers on the dangers of pornography. It also tries to influence companies, stressing the importance of protecting children from pornography. The Parents Television Council claims to have one million members; the PTC works to "ensure that children are not constantly assaulted by sex, violence and profanity" on television and other media. The PTC rates programs as family friendly or unsuitable for children and facilitates complaints to the FCC.[189] Courts have ruled that citizens have a First Amendment right to picket pornographic establishments and to try to intimidate patrons and employees of the stores by threatening to publish their pictures. Such conduct is constitutional as long as the pickets do not trespass or block entrances.[190]

Summary

Sexual communications that are not obscene may be regulated by time, place, and manner restrictions such as zoning ordinances, postal regulations, and restrictions on the display of materials that would be harmful to minors. In addition, citizens may pressure media to curb sex and violence. Letters threatening government legal action against sexual materials may constitute an unconstitutional prior restraint, but critical, nonthreatening letters are constitutional. The government may choose the art it funds, including denying grants based in part on whether the government considers the artistic project to be indecent.

[186]FTC, "Marketing Violent Entertainment to Children: A Fourth Follow-Up Review of Industry Practices in the Motion Picture, Music Recording, and Electronic Game Industries" (July 2004).

[187]FTC, "Marketing Violent Entertainment to Children: A Fifth Follow-up Review of Industry Practices in the Motion Picture, Music Recording, and Electronic Game Industries" (Apr. 2007).

[188]Anne Morse, "'Field Guide' Bye-Bye: Abercrombie and Fitch Stops Selling Porn," available at http://www.nationalreview.com/comment/morse200312010917.asp.

[189]The PTC has an online form for filing an indecency complaint with the FCC. *See* www.parentstv.org/PTC/fcc/fcccomplaint.asp.

[190]Eagle Books, Inc. v. Jones, 474 N.E.2d 444 (Ill. App.), *cert. denied,* 474 U.S. 920 (1985).

CHAPTER 10

The Media and the Judiciary

Thus far, this book has concentrated on law that punishes injurious publication: broadcasts that hurt individual reputations, ads that mislead consumers, and magazine articles that infringe on copyright. This chapter on the media and the courts is the first of three chapters to focus on newsgathering.

News coverage of the courts creates tensions between the advocates of two constitutional rights. The Bill of Rights, in addition to guaranteeing free speech and a free press, also guarantees the right to a fair trial for criminal defendants. The Sixth Amendment provides that anyone who is accused of a crime shall have the right to a trial "by an impartial jury," a jury composed of persons who can decide guilt or innocence on the basis only of the evidence presented in a courtroom. Judges, attempting to ensure fair trials, sometimes curb the speech of lawyers and witnesses and the ability of journalists to obtain information.

In court, judges may control what jurors see and hear. However, outside the courtroom, jurors often see and hear news stories and tidbits of gossip that are protected by the First Amendment but are not allowed into evidence in court. Extensive news coverage may jeopardize the rights of criminal defendants to receive a fair trial, some legal experts contend. Perhaps the most highly publicized criminal case in the 1990s was O. J. Simpson's murder trial. The Simpson criminal case graphically demonstrated many of the problems courts face in attempting to ensure a defendant a fair trial in a highly publicized case. For example, the Simpson trial highlighted the difficult and expensive procedures courts must adopt to seat an impartial jury and then keep the jury uncontaminated by publicity about the case. In addition, despite Simpson's acquittal, many legal experts expressed concern about the media circus that surrounded the trial, as well as both the prosecution and the defense engaging in constant "spin control" in the media as the trial progressed.

In 1966, the U.S. Supreme Court ruled that massive sensational media coverage prevented Dr. Sam Sheppard, an osteopath who lived near Cleveland, Ohio, from receiving a fair trial. Some of the events in the Sheppard case were later fictionalized in a television series and the movie *The Fugitive.* Sheppard's ordeal began on July 4, 1954, when neighbors he had called discovered Marilyn Sheppard's body in the upstairs bedroom of the family home. Sheppard said he woke up in the middle of the night to find a "form" standing by his dead wife. He claimed he struggled with the intruder but was knocked unconscious. Sheppard immediately became the object of sensational pretrial publicity. The media also helped turn his trial into what has been called a "Roman holiday."[1]

Sheppard became a suspect soon after his wife's death, but he was not arrested for about a month. Meanwhile, local newspapers published a barrage of information and opinions that were never admitted into evidence during his trial. Cleveland newspapers accused Sheppard of impeding the police investigation, emphasized his refusal to take a lie detector test, and quoted a police detective who said Sheppard's explanation of the death was suspect. The newspapers said Sheppard was "getting away with murder," and one ran a front-page editorial asking "Why Isn't Sam Sheppard in Jail?" Within twenty-four hours of the editorial, the authorities arrested Sheppard.

During Sheppard's trial in 1954, the judge seated newspaper reporters so close to Sheppard and his attorney that the pair had to leave the courtroom to talk without being

[1]Sheppard v. Maxwell, 384 U.S. 333 (1966).

overheard. Often the movement of reporters into and out of the courtroom made it difficult for the lawyers and witnesses to be heard. Photographers jammed the corridors, taking pictures of jurors, witnesses, lawyers, and Sheppard.

The jury convicted Sheppard of murder. His unsuccessful appeals to three appellate courts were discussed in Chapter 1. Sheppard spent twelve years in jail before the U.S. Supreme Court, in *Sheppard v. Maxwell,* reversed the original verdict on the ground that he did not receive a fair trial. Sheppard was acquitted in a new trial but died a few years later. In 2000, Sheppard's son lost a lawsuit asking a jury to find that Ohio had wrongfully imprisoned his father.[2]

The Supreme Court said that Sam Sheppard did not receive a fair trial because of prejudicial publicity and a carnival-like atmosphere in the courtroom. However, the Court also stressed the media's role in protecting public oversight of the judicial system. In *Sheppard,* the Court emphasized that judges must ensure that defendants receive trials by impartial juries at the same time that they restrict the press as little as possible. The Court's *Sheppard* opinion establishes the framework for much of the rest of the chapter. Although the chapter will focus on the rights of criminal defendants, parties to civil litigation face many of the same issues.

Defining Jury Bias

The U.S. Supreme Court has said that jurors are biased as a matter of law if they are so affected by prejudicial publicity that they cannot set aside preconceived ideas and decide a case solely on evidence presented during a trial. Judges and lawyers often argue that an impartial jury may be impossible to find if a community has been saturated by news reports of a sensational crime and the arrest of a suspect. However, social scientists have been unable to prove that prejudicial publicity causes biased jurors.

The Supreme Court and Jury Prejudice

Criminal law requires that impartial jurors arrive at a verdict of "guilty" or "not guilty" based only on the evidence permitted under the rules of the court. Justice Oliver Wendell Holmes said in 1907 that "the theory of our system is that the conclusions to be reached in a case will be induced only by evidence and argument in open court, and not by any outside influence, whether of private talk or public print."[3] The courts do not require jurors to be completely unaware of the facts and issues of a case. In the treason trial of Aaron Burr, Chief Justice John Marshall first said that impartial jurors might form impressions about a case before trial as long as those impressions could be changed in light of evidence presented in court.[4]

The Supreme Court has said a defendant can receive a fair trial even if every member of the jury knows the defendant's prior criminal record before the trial begins. The criminal defendant in *Murphy v. Florida,* Jack Roland Murphy, had become notorious after he helped steal the Star of India sapphire in 1964. Known as "Murph the Surf," Murphy also attracted attention because of a flamboyant lifestyle. In 1968, he was arrested for robbery and assault. However, before he could be tried on those charges, he was convicted of murder

[2]James Ewin, "Sheppard Verdict Is Challenged," *Cleveland Plain Dealer,* May 2, 2000, at 2B.
[3]Patterson v. Colorado, 205 U.S. 454, 462 (1907).
[4]United States v. Burr, 24 F. Cas. 49 (1807).

and pleaded guilty to the interstate transportation of stolen securities. The events attracted extensive press coverage. When Murphy was later convicted of the 1968 charges of robbery and assault, he appealed on the ground that the jury had been prejudiced by knowledge of his previous criminal record.

Justice Thurgood Marshall, writing for the Court, said jurors need not be "totally ignorant of the facts and issues" of a case.[5] He distinguished between "mere familiarity" with a defendant and a "predisposition against him." Marshall said most of the publicity about Murphy was factual and published at least seven months before the jury was selected, too far in advance to inflame prejudice at the time of the trial. Marshall said that none of the jurors, when questioned before the trial, indicated that Murphy's past was relevant to the case. The trial court did not have difficulty finding jurors who claimed to be impartial. Only twenty of seventy-eight persons questioned were excused because they had prejudged Murphy's guilt, suggesting little overt prejudice against Murphy. Neither the atmosphere in the courtroom nor that in the community was inflamed, the Court said.

The Supreme Court has said a conviction will be overturned because of prejudicial publicity only if the Court finds identifiable bias in individual jurors[6] or such an extraordinary amount of prejudicial publicity in the media that the "presumption of prejudice" is raised.[7] Jon Yount could not convince the Court that publicity had created a "presumption of prejudice" in his second murder trial. In *Patton v. Yount,* the Court upheld Yount's second conviction even though five of the twelve jurors had thought, at least at one time, Yount was guilty.[8] Yount had pleaded not guilty by reason of temporary insanity at his first trial after confessing to the brutal killing of a female high school student. The Pennsylvania Supreme Court overturned Yount's first conviction because the police had not provided him adequate notice of his right to an attorney prior to his confession. Later, Yount was convicted a second time and again appealed, this time contending he did not receive a fair trial because of prejudicial pretrial publicity. A federal appeals court said that 77 percent of 163 people questioned during the jury selection process at the second trial admitted they thought that Yount was guilty.

Yet the U.S. Supreme Court said the trial judge had not erred in finding that the jury was impartial. The Court, in an opinion written by Justice Lewis Powell, Jr., noted that "the extensive adverse publicity and the community's sense of outrage" were at their height before the 1966 trial. The second trial occurred when "prejudicial publicity was greatly diminished and community sentiment had softened." The Court said the two daily newspapers in the county averaged fewer than one article a month, primarily in the form of announcements, about the Yount proceedings before the second trial. Articles during the jury selection process were "purely factual." Furthermore, Powell said, the time between the two trials "had a profound effect on the community and, more important, on the jury, in softening or effacing opinion." The Court decided the lapse of time between the first and second trials rebutted "any presumption of partiality or prejudice that existed at the time of the initial trial."

In contrast, in *Irvin v. Dowd,* the Court overturned a murder conviction because publicity created a "wave of passion" and "pattern of prejudice."[9] The Court found a "build-up

[5]421 U.S. 794 (1975).
[6]*See, e.g.,* Irvin v. Dowd, 366 U.S. 717 (1961).
[7]*See, e.g.,* Estes v. Texas, 381 U.S. 532 (1965).
[8]467 U.S. 1025 (1984).
[9]366 U.S. 717 (1961).

of prejudice" in the case of Leslie Irvin, who was convicted for a December 1954 murder near Evansville, Indiana. Shortly after his arrest in April 1955, the press announced that "Mad Dog Irvin" had confessed to six murders in four months. Headlines announced he had been placed at the scene of at least one of the murders and identified in a police lineup. In many stories, Irvin was referred to as the "confessed slayer of six." Radio, television, and newspaper stories revealed Irvin's criminal history. The local radio station broadcast curbside opinions of Irvin's guilt by members of the public.

U.S. Supreme Court Justice Tom Clark, who wrote for a unanimous Court, said the continued adverse publicity fostered a strong prejudice among the people of the county. Of 430 prospective jurors who were questioned, 90 percent at least suspected Irvin was guilty. A number admitted that if they were in Irvin's place, they would not want themselves on the jury. Of the jurors finally seated, eight of twelve were familiar with the case, including the fact that Irvin was accused of other murders. All eight said they thought he was guilty. Some jurors said they were going to have to be convinced that Irvin was not guilty, contrary to the principle that a defendant is presumed innocent until proven guilty. One juror said he "could not . . . give the defendant the benefit of the doubt that he is innocent." Another said he had a "'somewhat' certain fixed opinion" of guilt. Yet all twelve jurors told the judge they could be impartial.

Justice Clark said the statements of impartiality could be given little weight when "so many" jurors "so many times, admitted of prejudice." The jurors' statements reflected a "'pattern of deep and bitter prejudice' shown to be present throughout the community." The Court overturned Irvin's conviction and death sentence. He was convicted again in a second trial and sentenced to life imprisonment.

Although the evidence of prejudice was discussed in *Irvin v. Dowd,* none was presented in *Sheppard v. Maxwell,* discussed at the beginning of the chapter. In *Sheppard v. Maxwell,* the Court did not require evidence that jurors were unable to base their verdict on what they saw and heard in the courtroom. The Court said only there could be no doubt that the deluge of extremely inflammatory publicity reached at least some of the jurors. Relying on its own impression of the potential impact of publicity, the Court criticized the prejudicial publicity, community pressure, and lack of judicial control over activity in the courtroom that led to Sheppard's conviction.

Prejudicial Publicity, Community Pressure, and Decorum in Court

A Supreme Court justice who was particularly concerned about prejudicial publicity, the late Felix Frankfurter once asked how "fallible men and women" can reach a verdict based only on what they hear in court when their minds are "saturated" by media coverage for months "by matter designed to establish the guilt of the accused."[10] Frankfurter particularly feared pretrial news about criminal proceedings before jurors are selected. In the *Sheppard* case, all but one of the jury members who decided that Sam Sheppard was guilty said during the jury selection process that they had read about the case in the newspapers or heard about it on radio or television.

[10] Irvin v. Dowd, 366 U.S. 729–30, (Frankfurter, J., concurring).

Although legal experts and scholars do not agree on the impact of pretrial publicity, most assume that certain kinds of information may be prejudicial.[11] The U.S. Justice Department, the American Bar Association, and several state bench-bar-press committees have issued similar guidelines designed to limit reporting of crime and court news. Most mention the reporting of the following:

- *Confessions*. The Fifth Amendment protects against persons being required to testify against themselves. A confession may be ruled inadmissible evidence at trial if it was made under duress or if a defendant was not properly advised of his or her right to an attorney. However, jurors may have a hard time ignoring a confession that is printed or broadcast. In *Rideau v. Louisiana,* the Supreme Court overturned the murder conviction of Wilbert Rideau after he confessed to a sheriff in the absence of a lawyer to advise him of his rights. Rideau's filmed confession was seen by an estimated 100,000 television viewers living near Lake Charles, Louisiana. The Supreme Court said the televised confession in a very real sense *was* Rideau's trial—at which he pleaded guilty to murder. The Court added that any subsequent court proceedings would be pointless.[12]
- *Prior criminal records*. A prior criminal record is ordinarily inadmissible because a defendant cannot be convicted on the basis of past criminal history. Prosecutors must prove that defendants committed the crimes for which they are being tried and not past misdeeds. Yet jurors might have a difficult time deciding that a person on trial for burglary or murder is innocent if he or she has been convicted of a similar crime before. In *Irvin v. Dowd,* the media revealed Leslie Irvin's earlier convictions for arson and burglary after he was arrested for murder near Evansville, Indiana. News stories also disclosed Irvin's juvenile record and a court-martial on AWOL charges. The Supreme Court said the stories were part of "a build-up of prejudice" in the community that led the Court to overturn Irvin's 1955 conviction.
- *The results of lie detector tests, blood tests, ballistics tests, and other investigatory procedures*. The results of some tests administered by police investigators might not be admitted into evidence in court because the tests were improperly administered. Some tests used to evaluate evidence produce unreliable results. In addition, the fact that a defendant chooses not to take a test might have no bearing on his or her guilt or innocence. Yet in *Sheppard v. Maxwell,* the Cleveland newspapers headlined Sam Sheppard's refusal to take a lie detector test as if it were evidence he must be hiding his role in his wife's murder. The newspapers also reported the results of blood tests that were never admitted into evidence at the trial.
- *Character flaws or lifestyle*. Comments from neighbors or other acquaintances, often seen in newspapers and newscasts, about a suspect's lifestyle will seldom be admitted into evidence in court. Frequently, the comments reflect rumors or hearsay rather than behavior witnessed firsthand. In the *Sheppard* case, the Cleveland newspapers emphasized that Sheppard had extramarital affairs that were not documented in court. During the trial, the jurors had access to a newspaper story claiming that

[11]*See, e.g.,* John Walton, "From O.J. to Tim McVeigh and Beyond," 75 *Denver U.L. Rev.* 549 (1998).
[12]373 U.S. 723 (1963).

Marilyn Sheppard had said her husband had a "Dr. Jekyll and Mr. Hyde" personality. No evidence of the accusation was presented during the trial.

- *Potential witnesses, testimony, or evidence.* Pretrial statements of potential witnesses may or may not be accurate and may or may not be heard by jurors in court. In the *Sheppard* case, the newspapers quoted a detective who said blood had been washed from the floor of the Sheppard home before investigators arrived but who never testified about the blood in court. Opinions about the credibility of prospective witnesses or the reliability of possible evidence also can mislead potential jurors.
- *Speculation by officials.* Sometimes law enforcement officers and judges are purveyors of prejudicial publicity. They might make statements about the character, innocence, or guilt of defendants that probably will not be admitted into evidence. In the *Sheppard* case, a newspaper headline reported that a police captain had called Sheppard a "bare-faced liar." The police officer was never called to the witness stand to explain the comment. In the *Irvin* case, the media reported that at least two officials were determined to make certain that Leslie Irvin was executed.
- *Other sensational and inflammatory statements.* Judges fear press coverage so inflammatory and pervasive that it contributes to a "deep and bitter pattern" of community prejudice. Although an accumulation of publicity can contribute to a public perception that the suspect is guilty, particular kinds of media coverage can foster community fears and prejudices. The reporting of public opinion polls, like the one conducted by a radio station in the *Irvin* case, can be highly inflammatory and may have little relation to the facts of the case. Media use of nicknames such as "Mad Dog Irvin" can suggest guilt. Headlines that demand the arrest of a suspect, as occurred in the *Sheppard* case, can inflame a community. Strong community bias not only makes selecting impartial jurors difficult but also can pressure jurors into convicting the defendant. When the Cleveland papers published the names of potential jurors, all received calls and letters from "cranks and friends" with opinions about the upcoming trial.

Finally, legal experts contend a defendant not only needs to be tried by jurors who are unaffected by prejudicial publicity but also needs to be tried in solemn and ordered proceedings free of a carnival-like atmosphere. The Supreme Court once said the preservation of an atmosphere in court necessary for a fair trial "must be maintained at all costs."[13] In the *Sheppard* case, the judge did not adequately preserve the decorum of the courtroom when he seated reporters inside the rail that separates the public from the trial participants. Reporters could overhear conversations between Sheppard and his lawyers and between the lawyers and the judge. Reporters also handled exhibits lying on the attorneys' tables. The Court said the arrangements made for the press inside the courtroom caused Sheppard "to be deprived of that 'judicial serenity and calm to which [he] was entitled.'"[14]

Measuring Prejudice

Although courts and others routinely assume some information will be prejudicial, no one knows for certain whether extensive exposure to media coverage of the criminal justice

[13]Estes v. Texas, 381 U.S. 540.
[14]384 U.S. at 355 (quoting Estes v. Texas, 381 U.S. 536).

process has an impact on jury decisions. In contrast to the result of the Sheppard trial, for example, Watergate defendants John Mitchell and Maurice Stans, Cabinet officers in the Nixon administration, were found not guilty in spite of massive nationwide pretrial publicity. William Kennedy Smith was found not guilty after the barrage of pretrial publicity following his arrest on a charge of rape in Palm Beach, Florida. Despite the deluge of pretrial publicity surrounding the O. J. Simpson case, a jury acquitted Simpson after only a few hours of deliberation. Similarly, Michael Jackson was found not guilty of child molestation charges in 2005 following several years of adverse publicity about his relations with children.

Many observers argue that the values of a fair trial and a free press often are compatible. The Supreme Court acknowledges that the press helps ensure fair trials by allowing public scrutiny of the judicial system.[15] Extensive pretrial publicity is relatively rare; the majority of crimes receive little or no press coverage. Also, there is little evidence linking pretrial publicity to jury bias. The impact of the press on potential jurors is exaggerated, and procedural safeguards are effective in limiting the effect of pretrial publicity.

There is little real-life evidence bearing on this issue. The only time researchers listened to actual jury deliberations, they said they found that jurors did not make capricious decisions because of bias.[16] The secretly taped jury discussions were but one aspect of a massive study of jury performance completed in 1954. The director of the study, Harry Kalven, said the jury was "a pretty stubborn, healthy institution not likely to be overwhelmed by a remark . . . in the press."[17]

Soon after the 1954 study, the courts prohibited studies of real juries, fearing the research would influence deliberations. Hence, most research on the impact of crime reporting on jurors comes from studies of public reaction to news stories and research involving mock juries. Human attitudes are difficult to study even when they can be tested directly by procedures well designed for the research questions being asked. Research on juror behavior is particularly imprecise because it is conducted on nonjurors in circumstances that do not effectively duplicate the experiences of jurors. In the studies, subjects usually are asked to react to prejudicial stories immediately. However, in real trials, people sit on juries months after seeing much of the publicity about a case. In addition, researchers often do not take into consideration that judges frequently admonish real juries to ignore what they have previously read or heard about a case. Further, no one knows whether research results would be different if the persons studied in hypothetical situations were making life-and-death decisions about real human beings.

The most one can conclude from such research is that publication of a defendant's confession or criminal record could convince some jurors that a defendant is guilty. However, some studies suggest that careful questioning of the jury pool during the jury selection process can help weed out potential jurors strongly influenced by pretrial publicity.[18]

---

[15] *See, e.g.,* Sheppard v. Maxwell, 384 U.S. 349–50; Cox Broadcasting Corp. v. Cohn, 420 U.S. 469, 491–92 (1975).

[16] Harry Kalven Jr. & Hans Zeisel, *The American Jury* 492–99 (1966). *See also* Rita Simon, "Does the Court's Decision in *Nebraska Press Association* Fit the Research Evidence on the Impact on Jurors of News Coverage?" 29 *Stan. L. Rev.* 515, 518–20 (1977).

[17] Donald Gillmor, "Free Press v. Fair Trial: A Continuing Dialogue—'Trial by Newspaper' and the Social Sciences," 41 *N.D. L. Rev.* 156, 167 (1965).

[18] *See, e.g.,* Geoffrey Kramer et al., "Pretrial Publicity, Judicial Remedies, and Jury Bias," 14 *Law & Hum. Behav.* 409 (1990); Rita Simon, "Does the Court's Decision in *Nebraska Press Association* Fit the Research Evidence on the Impact on Jurors of News Coverage?" 29 *Stan. L. Rev.* 515, 520–26 (1977).

In addition, a factor often forgotten by commentators concerned about the impact of prejudicial publicity is people's inability to absorb everything that is published or broadcast. Some people pay little attention to news. Even regular news consumers watch and read selectively and forget much of what they have heard or read as time passes. One federal appeals court judge said he conducted a study in which 94 percent of jurors could not remember stories published about highly publicized cases. The other 6 percent remembered only that they had read "something." Fewer than 1 percent of the jurors could remember what they had read. Fewer than half of the 1 percent had determined guilt or innocence on the basis of what they had read.[19]

Regardless of the lack of research evidence establishing that media coverage of criminal cases influences jurors, courts try to protect defendants against prejudicial publicity.

Summary

The Sixth Amendment guarantees criminal defendants the right to a trial by an impartial jury. The Supreme Court has said that an impartial juror is one free from strong impressions that close the mind to evidence presented in court. Jurors can know something about a defendant as long as they can decide a case on evidence they hear in court. However, the Court has overturned criminal convictions on evidence of massive publicity that has created a "presumption of prejudice" among jurors. Many judges and lawyers contend that information published before a trial but not introduced into evidence can lead to a biased jury. Prejudicial publicity can include news about confessions, criminal records, results of police tests, and reports of character flaws. It also can include derogatory nicknames, curbside opinion polls, and comments by neighbors and investigating officers. Judges and lawyers also are concerned about the impact of community pressure on jurors. In addition, maintaining order in the courtroom itself is considered essential to guarantee the rights of a defendant. However, there is no reliable evidence indicating that extensive pretrial news coverage of arrests and pretrial proceedings will endanger the rights of a defendant to an impartial jury.

Remedies for Prejudicial Publicity

The Supreme Court's decision in *Sheppard v. Maxwell* in 1966 marked the fifth time in seven years that the Court had reversed a criminal conviction because of prejudicial publicity or press behavior in the courtroom.[20] In *Sheppard,* the Court responded to the issues raised by prejudicial publicity not by lecturing the press but by delivering a stinging rebuke to the trial judge for failing to protect Sheppard's right to a fair trial.

Justice Clark, backed by seven of eight other justices, said the trial court judge had not adequately protected Sheppard's right to a trial by an impartial jury. Clark said that given "the pervasiveness of modern communications and the difficulty of effacing prejudicial

[19] Remarks by Judge William Bauer in "Newspapers under Fire," in American Society of Newspaper Editors, *Problems in Journalism* 226–27 (1976).

[20] *See also* Marshall v. United States, 360 U.S. 310 (1959); Irvin v. Dowd, 366 U.S. 717 (1961); Rideau v. Louisiana, 373 U.S. 723 (1963); Estes v. Texas, 381 U.S. 532 (1965).

publicity from the minds of jurors," trial courts must ensure that the accused can still receive a trial by an impartial jury, free from outside influences.

Clark said the Supreme Court did not want to impose direct limitations on the reporting of public trials because of both the First Amendment and the role of the press in guarding against abuses in the criminal justice system. Clark said justice cannot survive secret trials. He also said that the press guards against the miscarriage of justice by subjecting the police, prosecutors, and the entire judicial process to public scrutiny. But, he continued, no one ought to be punished for a crime without being "fairly tried in a public tribunal free of prejudice, passion, excitement, and tyrannical powers."

The Supreme Court said the trial court judge in the *Sheppard* case had failed to protect the defendant in three ways, including two involving the judge's lack of control over the trial itself. The Court said the trial judge (1) did not control the atmosphere of the courtroom and (2) did not control information released to the press during the trial. Both concerns will be discussed later in the chapter.

The third judicial error, said the *Sheppard* Court, was the judge's failure to protect jurors from the impact of prejudicial pretrial publicity. The Court recommended remedies for prejudicial publicity that generally do not directly interfere with reporting court news. The remedies include changing the location of the trial, importing a jury, delaying the trial, and conducting different trials for defendants charged with the same crime. Other judicial tools for preventing prejudicial publicity from influencing jurors are excusing potential jurors who demonstrate bias, admonishing jurors, sequestering the jury, and scheduling a new trial. These remedies do not prevent extensive coverage of criminal proceedings but may limit the impact of pretrial news on jurors.

Change of Venue

One of Justice Clark's suggestions for protecting a trial against the impact of news stories is a **change of venue,** which means a shift in the location of the trial. Judges have the authority, within limits specified by state law, to move a trial from the jurisdiction of the crime to one nearby. Moving a trial can be expensive for the county responsible. However, changing the location of a trial is supposed to move the trial away from the scene of the most damaging publicity.

In *Rideau v. Louisiana,* the Supreme Court held that the trial court's denial of a change of venue for Wilbert Rideau violated his constitutional right to a "fair and impartial trial." Rideau had asked that the trial be removed from the Calcasieu Parish trial court after his confession was televised three times in the county. Justice Potter Stewart, writing for the Supreme Court, said the televised confession became Rideau's trial to "tens of thousands of people." Stewart said further court proceedings "in a community so pervasively exposed to such a spectacle could be but a hollow formality."

The success of changing venue depends on the extent and nature of the news coverage about a case. Frequently, if a crime is notorious enough to trigger extensive publicity, it may be difficult to move the trial far enough away to find unaffected jurors. Nonetheless, national coverage of an event may differ from local coverage where the event takes place, suggesting that a change of venue may result in greater impartiality among potential jurors. For example, in early 1996, a federal judge moved the trial of Timothy McVeigh and Terry Nichols, charged in the 1995 bombing of the federal office building in Oklahoma City, from Oklahoma City to Denver.[21] The judge noted that the bombing had generated enormous national publicity but reasoned that the national news coverage of the tragedy was significantly different from the local coverage. The national coverage, the judge said, was more "factual," pertaining to the "who, what, where, why, and when" of the bombing. The local coverage in Oklahoma, by contrast, was more "personal, providing individual stories of grief and recovery," as well as being more intense than the national coverage. The judge concluded that these differences suggested that a more impartial jury could be found outside the Oklahoma City area, even though no part of the country was unfamiliar with the bombing. On the other hand, a change of venue to a nearby community might be less effective. In the *Irvin* case mentioned earlier, the trial was moved to a county adjacent to the one where the murder had been committed, but the move did not substantially improve the defendant's chances of receiving a fair trial. Although a transfer might move the trial from the community with the most at stake, the publicity sometimes follows.

Change of Venire

A change of **venire** changes the jury pool rather than the location of a trial. Occasionally, a judge will request that potential jurors be brought in from a nearby community. In the sensational murder trial of John Wayne Gacy, accused of the sex-related murders of thirty-three boys and young men in 1979, jurors were bused from Rockford, Illinois, to Chicago.

In 1995, a state appellate court affirmed a Trenton, New Jersey, judge's order that a jury from a nearby county should be bused in to consider a highly publicized murder trial, although the appellate court also ruled that the racial demographics of the potential jury pool must be carefully examined to ensure fairness. A Trenton newspaper had engaged in a "stream of invectives" against the defendant, an African American man accused of raping and murdering a white female artist. The *Trentonian* had referred to the defendant as "monster," "maggot," and "artist slayer" and stated that the defendant would eventually be put to death and that "the world will be a better place for his passing."[22] On appeal, a New Jersey appellate court agreed that the trial judge had properly decided, on the basis of the prejudicial publicity, that the case should be tried before a jury from another county. However, the appellate court held that the judge should have considered the racial composition of the county from which the jury would be drawn.[23]

Theoretically, jurors who have been imported have had less exposure to potentially damaging publicity. However, regional newspapers and national television news ensure that information about major crimes achieves widespread circulation. Importing a jury also can be expensive for the county responsible for the trial.

Continuance

A judge who believes that publicity might damage the chances for a fair trial can postpone the trial until publicity subsides. **Continuance,** the legal term for postponement, was mentioned

---

[21]United States v. McVeigh, 910 F. Supp.1467 (W.D. Okla. 1996).

[22]"Judge Lambasts Paper's 'Invective' in N.J. Murder," *Editor & Publisher,* May 13, 1995, at 23; Michael Booth, "Race Demographics Must Be Considered in Venue Challenges," *N.J.L.J.,* June 19, 1995, at 1.

[23]State v. Harris, 660 A.2d 539 (N.J. App. Div. 1995).

by Justice Clark in *Sheppard v. Maxwell* as an alternative when a trial judge is faced with "a reasonable likelihood that prejudicial news prior to trial will prevent a fair trial." The Court noted in *Irvin v. Dowd* when reversing the conviction of Leslie Irvin for six murders that the trial court had denied eight motions for a continuance.

Postponement can effectively remove the trial from the publicity surrounding the arrest. Of course, there is likely to be renewed publicity when the trial finally takes place. There are other practical problems. Defendants asking for a postponement might have to waive their constitutional right to a speedy trial. In addition, defendants unable to raise bail wait in jail during the continuance. Furthermore, the longer a trial is postponed, the more likely witnesses or evidence will disappear.

Lawyers for Timothy McVeigh, charged with the Oklahoma City federal building bombing, argued news stories—in particular, reports in the *Dallas Morning News* and several other publications that McVeigh had confessed to his lawyers—had made a fair trial impossible. McVeigh's lawyers asked Judge Richard Matsch, who presided over McVeigh's trial, to grant a year's continuance, among other suggested procedural remedies. Matsch denied the requests.[24] The judge conceded the media had covered "every angle of the story," but he said the process of criminal prosecution goes far to ensure fairness. He said he had "full confidence that a fair minded jury" would "return a just verdict based on the law and evidence presented to them." The jury found McVeigh guilty of eleven counts of murder and conspiracy.

Severance

Severance is a remedy available only when more than one person has been charged with the same crime or related crimes. Two or more defendants are tried separately in an attempt to prevent the publicity related to one trial from affecting the other.

Voir Dire

Voir dire is the term used for the process of questioning potential jurors before selecting a jury for a trial. Potential jurors are asked questions designed to detect bias. The prospective jurors might be asked whether they know the defendant or any of the witnesses. They also might be asked about their occupation, reading habits, or religious beliefs. They might be asked whether they have racial prejudices or believe in the death penalty. In theory, the purpose of voir dire is to find persons able to judge a defendant only on the basis of information presented in the courtroom. In practice, each lawyer looks for jurors who might lean toward his or her client or who might be suspicious of the opposing lawyer. In many federal courts, the judge asks the questions. In state courts, the opposing attorneys usually ask the questions during voir dire.

The lawyers on each side of a case can challenge any number of jurors "for cause." Prospective jurors will be excused if the judge is convinced they are unfit to serve. For example, a juror might be dismissed for an obvious prejudice or because he or she is a relative of the crime victim. The Supreme Court noted in *Rideau v. Louisiana* that the trial judge had wrongly refused to excuse two deputy sheriffs from the jury in spite of the fact that Rideau had confessed to the sheriff.

[24] United States v. McVeigh, 955 F. Supp. 1281 (D. Colo. 1997).

In addition to the challenges for cause, each side in a case also can dismiss a limited number of jurors through **peremptory challenges** without giving a reason. The number of peremptory challenges varies with the state and with the nature of the case. Lawyers use peremptory challenges to excuse prospective jurors when the lawyers cannot persuade a judge to excuse them for cause. Attorneys might excuse a juror because they have a "gut feeling" that a potential juror has hidden biases. The gut feeling could be based on answers to questions, facial expressions, clothes, or rumor. Peremptory challenges are also used to excuse jurors who have socioeconomic characteristics that suggest a probable bias, though one that might be hard to detect. For example, the attorney of a man accused of sexually abusing children will often want to excuse mothers from the jury. The Supreme Court has held, however, that discriminatory use of peremptory challenges based on race or gender violates the Fourteenth Amendment's equal protection clause.[25]

In *Irvin v. Dowd,* 430 prospective jurors were examined in a lengthy voir dire that is unusual except in sensational cases receiving widespread publicity. In a voir dire lasting four weeks, 268 prospective jurors were excused for cause because of their belief that Irvin was guilty of murder. More than one hundred potential jurors were excused because they opposed the death penalty. Dowd's counsel excused twenty through peremptory challenges, the prosecution ten. Both used all of the peremptory challenges allowed by Indiana law. Other prospective jurors were excused on personal grounds such as health.

The Supreme Court has ruled that the Sixth Amendment does not require that potential jurors be asked to disclose their exposure to prejudicial publicity. In *Mu'Min v. Virginia,* the Court rejected a convicted murderer's contention that the right to an impartial jury requires that judges ask potential jurors specific questions about their exposure to pretrial publicity. The Court said it was constitutionally sufficient for a judge to ask prospective jurors generally whether they could decide guilt on the basis of courtroom testimony, without asking them specifically what they knew about the case. The Court said judges do not necessarily have to ask such questions as "What have you seen, read, or heard about this case?" It is sufficient for a judge to ask, "Given what you have seen, read, or heard about this case, can you enter the jury box with an open mind and be impartial in this case?" Judges can ask more precise questions if they choose, the Court said, but the Sixth Amendment does not require them to do so.[26]

Voir dire gives attorneys some control over the nature of the jury that will hear a case. However, some critics assert that voir dire is not very effective. Many judges and lawyers contend that potential jurors say what they believe the attorneys want to hear. The critics say potential jurors can hide bias.

As part of a recent trend to abbreviate the jury selection process, courts in high-profile cases have engaged in a two-step voir dire process. Questionnaires are sent to potential jurors; the answers are then used to reduce the number of potential jurors questioned in person. For example, 400 potential jurors in the 2006 criminal trial of former Enron executives Kenneth Lay and Jeffrey Skilling received questionnaires asking detailed questions about their opinions of Enron, Lay, and Skilling. Based on the answers, 300 people were eliminated from the jury pool. The remaining one hundred were summoned to court where they received

[25]Batson v. Kentucky, 476 U.S. 79 (1986) (race); J.E.B. v. Alabama, 511 U.S. 127 (1994) (gender).
[26]500 U.S. 415 (1991).

additional questioning.[27] Questionnaires were also used as part of the voir dire process in the Martha Stewart case. In post-trial motions, Stewart's lawyers claimed a juror gave misleading answers to a selection questionnaire. The trial judge found there was no proof the juror was biased against Stewart; this ruling was sustained by the Second Circuit Court of Appeals.[28]

In some trials, behavioral scientists have been used as "jury consultants" to help lawyers choose jurors. These jury consultants conduct extensive research in an attempt to determine what kind of jurors might be sympathetic to the lawyer's case. Then the lawyer tries to seat jurors who fit the profile. In the O. J. Simpson murder trial, for example, defense lawyers and prosecutors used jury consultants in an attempt to choose a sympathetic jury.

Sequestration

Sequestration is the "locking up" of the jury during a trial. A judge can order that the jurors be isolated under guard. They usually are housed together at a hotel at government expense. They are generally not allowed to see friends or family or to see news stories about the case. Guards screen and monitor phone calls.

Sequestration prevents jurors from hearing others evaluate the evidence or predict the outcome of the trial. Although sequestration cannot be used until a jury is chosen, it effectively keeps jurors from obtaining information from outside the courtroom during the trial. The Supreme Court implied that the judge in the Sheppard trial should have sequestered the jury. Because the judge did not sequester jurors, they were exposed to rumors and opinions during the trial as well as before. Two jurors heard a woman tell Walter Winchell on the radio that Sheppard had fathered her illegitimate child.

However, sequestration is very expensive, and it seriously disrupts the lives of jurors, particularly during long trials. The jurors in the O. J. Simpson prosecution, for example, suffered significant hardship during their nine-month sequestration. One Simpson juror, who had to be treated for high blood pressure during the trial, told the *Los Angeles Times* that the sequestration made him "stir-crazy."[29] Defense attorneys often worry that a sequestered jury will resent the defendant for keeping them from family and friends. Moreover, questions have been raised about sequestration's effectiveness. Some experts contend that even sequestered jurors are rarely completely isolated from prejudicial information, which can seep in to affect jurors despite the best safeguards.[30]

Judicial Admonition

Once a jury has been chosen, a judge can instruct jurors to render their verdict on the basis of evidence presented in the courtroom. A judge may tell jurors to avoid reading, watching, or listening to anything about the trial.

The Supreme Court criticized as inadequate the **admonitions** to the jury issued by the Sheppard trial court judge. He "suggested" and "requested" that jurors avoid reading newspapers, listening to the radio, or watching television. He said that "we shall all feel very

[27]Paul Davies and John Emshwiller, "Split Verdict on Selecting Juries Quickly," *Wall Street Journal*, Feb. 1, 2006, at B1.
[28]United States v. Stewart, 433 F.2d 273 (2d Cir. 2006).
[29]"The Simpson Legacy," *Los Angeles Times*, Oct. 8, 1995, at S4.
[30]"Sequestering Juries," *N.J.L.J.*, Oct. 9, 1995, at 26.

much better" if the jurors paid no attention to the media. But, the Court said, the judge failed to "instruct" or "admonish" jurors to avoid the media.

Judges who admonish jurors want to keep them from seeing or hearing information and commentary that may affect their decisions while at the same time avoiding the cost and inconvenience of sequestration. The judicial admonition may be the most frequently used but least binding of the remedies discussed. However, many judges believe, and one important study found, jurors take such admonitions very seriously.[31]

New Trial

As a last resort, a criminal conviction can be overturned, as occurred in *Irvin, Sheppard,* and *Rideau.* A retrial involves all the expense and personal trauma of the first trial. Defendants may have to remain in jail if they cannot post bond. In his *Sheppard* opinion, Justice Clark noted that

> reversals are but palliatives; the cure lies in those remedial measures that will prevent the prejudice at its inception. The courts must take such steps by rule and regulation that will protect their processes from prejudicial outside interferences.

Summary

The majority opinion in *Sheppard v. Maxwell* criticized the trial court judge for failing to protect against prejudicial pretrial publicity, failing to control the courtroom, and failing to restrict the release of prejudicial information during the trial. The Supreme Court's opinion suggested that the judge in the Sheppard trial should have used tools available to judges to protect against prejudicial pretrial publicity. The devices available include change of venue, change of venire, continuance (postponement), severance of related trials, voir dire, sequestration, admonitions to the jury, and a judicial order for a new trial.

Controlling Conduct in Court

The Supreme Court stressed in *Sheppard v. Maxwell* that judges must ensure a dignified atmosphere in the court, including control over the behavior of journalists. Justice Tom Clark's majority opinion said the judge in the Sheppard trial should have better controlled the conduct of reporters in the courtroom. He also should have kept reporters from areas of the courtroom where they could disrupt the defendant, lawyers, and jurors. The Supreme Court said reporters should not have been allowed to sit near the defendant or jurors and should not have been allowed to handle court exhibits. The number of reporters in the courtroom should have been reduced when it became evident they were disrupting the trial, the Court said.

Judges also can control the use of cameras in court. However, restrictions on cameras in state courts have been significantly relaxed in the last twenty-five years.

Both television and still cameras have long been perceived by some judges and lawyers as a threat to the dignity of courtrooms. In fact, photographers were not allowed in court during trials for most of the twentieth century, a restriction that the U.S. Supreme

[31] Harry Kalven, Jr., & Hans Zeisel, *The American Jury* (1966).

Court held to be constitutional. But in the last twenty-five years, most states have adopted rules allowing camera coverage of trials. The Supreme Court has said that states can develop their own rules as long as the presence of cameras does not violate a defendant's right to a fair trial. Cameras still were prohibited in federal trial courts in 2008, even though an experimental program in a few federal courts in the early 1990s had resulted in generally favorable evaluations by lawyers and judges.

The Early Ban on Cameras

The hostility to cameras in court is often traced to the sensational trial of Bruno Hauptmann in 1935. Hauptmann was accused of kidnapping and killing the eighteen-month-old son of Charles Lindbergh, who had become famous when he was the first person to fly non-stop across the Atlantic. More than 800 journalists from around the world attended the trial. The journalism trade publication *Editor & Publisher* reported newspaper circulation figures during the trial. The press hired messengers who disrupted the trial by running into and out of the courtroom with copy. Reporters and photographers who could not get into the courtroom jammed the halls. However, only a few cameras were allowed inside the courtroom, and photographers largely obeyed a judicial order barring pictures while court was in session.[32]

Yet in 1937, two years after Hauptmann's conviction, the American Bar Association (ABA) recommended banning cameras in courtrooms as one of several efforts to curb trial publicity. Canon 35 of the ABA's Canons of Professional and Judicial Ethics said cameras and broadcasts of trials should be banned because they "detract from the essential dignity of the proceedings, degrade the court and create misconceptions . . . in the mind of the public." Although ABA recommendations are not law, they are significant because states often adopt them as rules governing court proceedings. State bar associations also adopt ABA rules when writing enforceable codes of ethics. In addition, the ABA's rules are considered by judges writing court opinions.[33]

The ABA's opposition to cameras continued for more than forty years. For most of that time, photographers were generally kept out of courtrooms. In the mid-1950s, only one state—Colorado—allowed cameras in court. In the early 1960s, Texas also permitted courtroom television and still photography. In 1962, televising live events was still relatively new and spectacular, and television coverage of the trial of Billie Sol Estes created a major controversy.

Estes, a Texas grain dealer, became the focus of national media attention when he was charged with fraudulently inducing farmers to buy nonexistent fertilizer tanks. A two-day pretrial hearing in Tyler, Texas, was broadcast live by radio and television. The scene was vividly described by the *New York Times*:

> A television motor van, big as an intercontinental bus, was parked outside the courthouse and the second-floor courtroom was a forest of equipment. Two television cameras had

[32]*See generally* State v. Hauptmann, 180 A. 809, 827, *cert. denied,* 296 U.S. 649 (1935); Marjorie Cohn & David Dow, *Cameras in the Courtroom* (1998); Ronald Goldfarb, *TV or Not TV: Television, Justice and the Courts* (1998).

[33]*See* Criminal Justice Standards Committee of the American Bar Association, *ABA Standards for Criminal Justice; Fair Trial and Free Press* 10–12 (3d ed. 1992).

> been set up inside the bar and four more marked cameras were aligned just outside the gates.
>
> A microphone stuck its 12-inch snout inside the jury box, now occupied by an overflow of reporters from the press table, and three microphones confronted Judge Dunagan on his bench. Cables and wires snaked over the floor.[34]

By the time the trial itself began, the judge had moved television cameras to a booth constructed in the back of the courtroom. This prompted Estes's counsel to remark, "This doesn't look like a courtroom to me, it looks like a movie theater."[35] Live coverage was permitted only occasionally during the trial, and reports of the trial were confined primarily to news programs. However, in spite of the more limited camera coverage, Estes appealed his conviction on the ground that broadcast coverage denied him a fair trial. The Supreme Court agreed, 5-4, and ordered a retrial. Estes later was convicted again.

The Supreme Court's majority in *Estes v. Texas* said the press must be allowed as much freedom to report court proceedings as possible, but the preservation of the atmosphere necessary to guarantee a fair trial "must be maintained at all costs."[36] Four of the five justices in the majority believed that the mere presence of television cameras in court violated the defendant's Sixth Amendment guarantee of a fair trial. The fifth justice, John Harlan, said television coverage must be banned at that time in criminal trials of "widespread public interest" and "great notoriety."

Justice Clark, who wrote the Court's majority opinion, listed the concerns still voiced by those opposing cameras in court. Cameras and their "telltale red lights" would distract jurors and inevitably lead to the pressure "of knowing their friends and neighbors have their eyes upon them." Cameras were also a form of mental harassment resembling a police line-up, Clark said. A defendant "is entitled to his day in court, not in a stadium or a city or nationwide arena," he added. Clark also said the presence of cameras impaired the quality of testimony because it could frighten some witnesses and encourage others to exaggerate.

In addition, Clark said, cameras added to the concerns of judges in ensuring that defendants received a fair trial. Judges had to supervise the use of cameras in court and were subject to the "ever-present distraction" of the presence of cameras. Clark also said that elected judges would want to use televised trials as a political weapon. He said the "heightened public clamor resulting from radio and television coverage will inevitably result in prejudice."

Whereas four of the justices in the majority suggested television cameras inherently endangered the constitutional rights of any criminal defendant, Justice Harlan said in a concurring opinion that he was limiting his judgment to only "heavily publicized and highly sensational" trials. Harlan, whose vote was necessary to overturn the first Estes conviction, suggested he might permit cameras in "run-of-the-mill" criminal trials and for educational purposes. Harlan did not want to prohibit the states from experimenting with cameras in the courtroom. He said that television may eventually become "so commonplace an affair in the daily life of the average person" that it would not likely damage the judicial process.

Harlan agreed with the rest of the majority that the First Amendment did not guarantee the right of broadcasters to take television cameras into courtrooms. The majority rejected

[34]Homar Bigart, "Estes Goes on Trial in Texas with TV in Courtroom," *N.Y. Times,* Sept. 25, 1962, at 46.
[35]*Newsweek,* Nov. 5, 1962, at 5.
[36]381 U.S. 532 (1965).

the argument that courts treated the print media more favorably than the broadcast media. Both print and broadcast reporters were permitted in courtrooms, Clark said.

Cameras Move into Courtrooms

After the *Estes* decision, every state but Colorado barred cameras from court for nearly a decade. Meanwhile, cameras became smaller and quieter and therefore less intrusive. They became less dependent on special lighting. The media kept pushing for the acceptance of cameras in court. By the mid-1970s a number of states had experimented with cameras in courtrooms. Among the first were Alabama, Georgia, New Hampshire, Texas, and Washington. By the end of 1980, twenty-two states had experimented with cameras and another dozen were studying the issue.[37]

A pilot program in Florida led to the Supreme Court test of whether states could allow cameras in court. Florida had first tried to experiment with cameras in 1976. However, the 1976 rules required the consent of all participants, and defendants consistently refused to permit cameras in court. Then in July 1977, the Florida Supreme Court initiated a one-year test that did not require the consent of everyone photographed during a court proceeding but only the consent of the judge. The other rules of the pilot program were similar to procedures adopted in many other states both before and since. For example, Florida allowed only one television camera and two still cameras, all in fixed positions in court. If several publications and broadcast stations wanted trial coverage, a pooling agreement had to be arranged. Film and lenses could not be changed while court was in session. No artificial lighting was allowed. The media had to use existing courtroom audio recording equipment and could not record bench conferences between judges and attorneys.

After the year-long Florida experiment, a study found cameras did not affect the behavior of those in court. Many of the trial participants surveyed believed that jurors and witnesses were slightly self-conscious in front of cameras but also slightly more attentive. Although a few witnesses refused to testify in front of cameras, the Florida Supreme Court said that physical disturbance by the cameras "was so minimal as not to be an arguable factor" during trials.[38]

Florida's rules were challenged by two defendants who had objected to the presence of cameras at their trial. During the first month of Florida's experiment, two Miami Beach police officers were charged with burglarizing a well-known restaurant. An amateur radio operator overheard the two officers talking on their walkie-talkies during the burglary and taped the conversation. At the officers' trial, the judge allowed cameras in the courtroom over the objection of the defense. The jury was not sequestered, but jury members were told not to read about the case or watch the local television news. Actually, only two minutes and fifty-five seconds of the trial were broadcast, depicting only the prosecution's side of the case. The policemen were convicted and appealed on the ground that they had not received a fair trial because cameras were in the courtroom. The Florida District Court affirmed the convictions, and the Florida Supreme Court declined to review the case.[39]

On appeal, the U.S. Supreme Court held 8-0 that the Constitution does not prohibit states from experimenting with cameras in state courts. In *Chandler v. Florida,* the Court said it

[37]Chandler v. Florida, 449 U.S. 560, 565 nn.5-6 (1981).
[38]*In re* Post-Newsweek Stations, Inc., 370 So. 2d 764 (Fla. 1979).
[39]Chandler v. Florida, 449 U.S. at 568-69.

had no reason to "endorse or to invalidate" Florida's rules permitting cameras in court unless criminal defendants can prove their Sixth Amendment rights to a fair trial were violated. Chief Justice Burger, a strong critic of cameras in court, wrote the opinion.[40]

Burger noted in *Chandler* that only four justices in *Estes* had declared that cameras in the courtroom automatically denied a defendant a fair trial. The Court in *Estes* therefore fell one vote short of ruling that the presence of cameras in court violated the Sixth Amendment. Burger, in asking again whether cameras in court violated the rights of criminal defendants, noted technological changes since *Estes* and the procedural protections in Florida designed to protect the rights of defendants. He acknowledged there was still a heated controversy over whether the mere presence of cameras in court "invariably and uniformly affected the conduct of participants so as to impair fundamental fairness." Yet, said the chief justice, whatever potential cameras had for interfering with the judicial process, no one had presented data establishing that the "mere presence" of broadcast media "inherently has an adverse effect on that process."

The Supreme Court said a complete constitutional ban of cameras could not be justified simply because a fair trial might be jeopardized in some cases. To overturn a conviction in a trial with cameras present, a defendant must demonstrate the cameras impaired a jury's ability to decide his or her case fairly, the Court said, or a defendant must establish that the presence of cameras or the possibility of televised coverage adversely affected any participants, including witnesses. In the *Chandler* case, the majority opinion noted, the police officers had not provided any evidence that their trial was tainted by broadcast coverage.

Chief Justice Burger, in the majority opinion, said the U.S. Supreme Court is empowered to intervene in state procedures only when fundamental constitutional guarantees are being violated. Therefore, Florida and the other states were free to allow cameras in state courts even though "dangers lurk in this, as in most, experiments."

Shortly after the *Chandler* decision, the ABA modified its ban on cameras in Canon 35, which had become Rule 3A(7) of the ABA Code of Judicial Conduct. The new rule still prohibits broadcasting, televising, recording, and photography in, or adjacent to, a courtroom unless an appellate court "or appropriate authority" approves. Then a judge can allow camera coverage only under supervision that ensures it is "unobtrusive, will not distract trial participants, and will not otherwise interfere with the administration of justice."[41]

By 2008, forty-three states allowed television coverage of trials and appellate proceedings. Seven states—Delaware, Illinois, Indiana, Louisiana, New York, South Dakota, and Utah—limited camera coverage to appellate arguments, which are heard solely by judges. Only the District of Columbia banned cameras from trial and appellate proceedings. Recently, the New York statute banning cameras in trial courts was found constitutional by New York's highest court, which stated the law was merely a restriction on the means of gathering news, not a restriction on the openness of court proceedings.[42]

As part of the general trend toward more camera coverage of judicial proceedings, a number of state supreme courts have recently begun live webcasting of their oral arguments.

[40] 449 U.S. 560 (1981).
[41] American Bar Association, *Code of Judicial Conduct* Canon 3A(7) (1982).
[42] Courtroom Television Network v. New York, 833 N.E. 2d 1197 (N.Y. 2005).

These include the supreme courts of Alaska, Florida, Indiana, Michigan, Mississippi, Missouri, North Dakota, Washington, and West Virginia.[43] In some instances, the oral arguments are also carried on cable television systems. For example, oral arguments of the Michigan Supreme Court are transmitted to cable systems throughout Michigan by MGTV, a C-SPAN-type service created by Michigan cable operators. Some courts, such as Florida's, have placed archives of recordings on the Internet, allowing citizens to view arguments in noteworthy cases such as Al Gore's challenge to Florida's 2000 presidential election procedures.

States vary in the nature of trial coverage allowed, as is illustrated in Table 10.1. Ostensibly to preserve a fair trial, some states prohibit or limit camera coverage of criminal trials. For example, Pennsylvania prohibits any broadcast coverage of criminal trials, and Maine allows broadcast coverage only of nontestimonial aspects of criminal proceedings, such as arraignments and sentencing. Other states generally allow coverage of criminal and civil proceedings but protect privacy by prohibiting coverage of sensitive cases or vulnerable witnesses. Virginia, for example, prohibits broadcast coverage of sex offense cases, and Missouri prohibits coverage of domestic relations and child custody cases. Kansas and Ohio prohibit coverage of witnesses who object. Many states leave broad discretion with the trial judge to determine what cases or witnesses will be subject to broadcast coverage. In Florida, a judge can exclude electronic media coverage only if it will have a "substantial effect" that would be "qualitatively different" from that of other media coverage.

Judges in recent high-profile cases, wary of the circus-like atmosphere of the O. J. Simpson case, have prohibited or sharply restricted electronic coverage of courtroom proceedings. For example, electronic coverage was not allowed in Michael Jackson's 2005 child molestation trial. In the 2004 Scott Peterson murder trial, the electronic media were limited to audio coverage of the reading of the verdict. The judge handling the criminal case against Kobe Bryant ruled that video and audio coverage of the trial would be allowed only during the attorneys' closing arguments; the trial was averted when the sexual assault charges were dismissed.

To ensure the dignity of court proceedings, state court rules typically limit the number of photographers and electronic media personnel and their location in the courtroom and specify the types of equipment that may be utilized. For example, Florida allows one television camera at trials and appellate proceedings; only one still photographer is allowed at trials and appellate proceedings. The cameras must not produce distracting sound or produce artificial light. Media personnel are not allowed to move around the courtroom while court is in session. To protect attorney-client privilege, no audio pickup is allowed of conferences between attorneys and their clients, between cocounsel, or between the judge and the attorneys held at the bench.[44]

As of 2008, cameras were not allowed in federal trial courts. The Judicial Conference of the United States, the policymaking body for the federal courts, authorized in 1991 a three-year experiment allowing still photography and radio and television coverage of civil trials and appeals in about a half-dozen courts. Although the program ended with a largely

---

[43]Web addresses for state supreme court oral arguments include the following: Florida, http://wfsu.org/gavel2gavel; Michigan, http://www.mgtv.org; and Mississippi, http://www.mssc.state.ms.us.

[44]"Technological Coverage of Judicial Proceedings," Fla. R. Jud. Admin. 2.280 (2007).

TABLE 10.1

Cameras in Courts

TIER 1: STATES THAT ALLOW THE MOST COVERAGE		
California	Montana	Vermont
Colorado	Nevada	Washington
Florida	New Hampshire	West Virginia
Georgia	New Mexico	Wisconsin
Idaho	North Dakota	Wyoming
Kentucky	South Carolina	
Michigan	Tennessee	
TIER II: STATES WITH RESTRICTIONS PROHIBITING COVERAGE OF IMPORTANT TYPES OF CASES, SUCH AS SEXUAL OFFENSE, OR PROHIBITING COVERAGE OF ALL OR LARGE CATEGORIES OF WITNESSES WHO OBJECT TO COVERAGE OF THEIR TESTIMONY		
Alaska	Massachusetts	Oregon
Arizona	Mississippi	Rhode Island
Connecticut	Missouri	Texas
Hawaii	New Jersey	Virginia
Iowa	North Carolina	
Kansas	Ohio	
TIER III: STATES THAT ALLOW APPELLATE COVERAGE ONLY OR THAT HAVE SUCH RESTRICTIVE TRIAL RULES THAT COVERAGE IS LARGELY PREVENTED		
Alabama	Louisiana	New York
Arkansas	Maine	Oklahoma
Delaware	Maryland	Pennsylvania
Illinois	Minnesota	South Dakota
Indiana	Nebraska	Utah

The District of Columbia is the only jurisdiction that prohibits trial and appellate coverage entirely.

For detailed information about each state's rules, see http://www.rtnda.org/fol/scc.html.

favorable evaluation by lawyers and judges,[45] the Judicial Conference voted in 1994 to continue the ban on cameras in federal trial courts.[46] The rules banning cameras in federal trial courts[47] have withstood First Amendment challenges.[48]

The Judicial Conference in 1996 passed a resolution allowing federal courts of appeal to decide for themselves whether to allow still photographs or radio and television coverage of appellate arguments.[49] Two U.S. Courts of Appeals—the Second and Ninth Circuits—have permitted cameras in appellate arguments on a case-by-case basis.

The Judicial Conference's resolution does not apply to the U.S. Supreme Court, whose members are vehemently opposed to television coverage of the Court's proceedings. Justice David Souter, for example, stated in 1996, "The day you see a camera in our courtroom, it's going to roll over my dead body."[50] Legislation requiring the Court to televise its proceedings passed the Senate Judiciary Committee in 2006 and 2007, prompting five members of the Court to publicly express their opposition. For example, Justice Kennedy stated the proposed legislation raised sensitive separation of powers issues. "We feel very strongly that we have intimate knowledge of the dynamics and mood of the court, and we think that proposals mandating and directing television in our court are inconsistent with the deference and etiquette that should apply between the branches," Kennedy stated.[51] Justice Scalia was more blunt. "We don't want to become entertainment," he said.[52] Chief Justice Roberts acknowledged the argument that the public would benefit greatly from televised proceedings, but added, "We don't have oral arguments to show people how we function. We have them to learn about a particular case, in a particular way that we think is important."[53]

Journalists made some progress in December 2000, when the Supreme Court released audiotapes of the oral argument in the challenge to Florida's handling of presidential ballots.[54] The Court released the tapes immediately after the argument was finished—the first time the Court made audiotapes public before announcing its decision in a case. Since 2003, the Court has released audiotapes immediately after hearing arguments in important cases challenging affirmative action, federal election laws, the war on terrorism, and restrictions on abortion. "Routine, quick release of all oral-argument audiotapes still seems some distance away," wrote veteran Supreme Court reporter Tony Mauro.[55]

---

[45]"Electronic Media Coverage of Federal Civil Proceedings: An Evaluation of the Pilot Program in Six District Courts and Two Courts of Appeals," Report of the Federal Judicial Center to the Committee on Court Administration and Case Management of the Judicial Conference of the United States (1993).

[46]"Judicial Conference Votes Down Cameras," *News Media & L.*, Fall 1994, at 3.

[47]Fed. R. Crim. P. 53.

[48]*See, e.g.*, United States v. Hastings, 695 F.2d 1278 (11th Cir.), *cert. denied*, 461 U.S. 931 (1983).

[49]Linda Greenhouse, "Reversing Course, Judicial Panel Allows Televising Appeals Courts," *N.Y. Times*, March 13, 1996, at A1.

[50]Robert Greenberger, "High-Court Shift: Speedy Sound Bits, for Now, but No TV," *Wall Street Journal*, April 30, 2004, at B4.

[51]Linda Greenhouse, "2 Justices Indicate Supreme Court Is Unlikely to Televise Sessions," *N.Y. Times*, Apr. 5, 2006, at A16.

[52]"Scalia Bars Reporters from Speech to Insurance Execs," Associated Press, Oct. 13, 2005.

[53]Tony Mauro, "Glimmers of Greater Openness at Secretive Court," (Oct. 9, 2006) *available at* http://www.fac.org/analysis.aspx?id=17509.

[54]"The Supreme Court Arguments," *N.Y. Times*, Dec. 2. 2000, at A18. Audio recordings of oral arguments in historic Supreme Court cases are available at http://www.oyez.org.

[55]Tony Mauro, "Glimmers of Greater Openness at Secretive Court, (Oct. 9, 2006) *available at* http://www.fac.org/analysis.aspx?id=17509.

In 2006, the Court announced it would release publicly the transcripts of oral arguments within hours after they conclude. Previously, free transcripts were posted on the Court's website two weeks after oral argument.[56]

Summary

Judges have the authority to control the behavior of the press within the courtroom. Whether cameras are allowed in state courtrooms depends on the rules of individual states. Many states allow restricted use of cameras in court, a practice permitted by the U.S. Supreme Court as long as the right of a defendant to a fair trial is not violated. Cameras were experimented with in federal courtrooms in the early 1990s, but they are still banned in most federal courts.

Controlling Prejudicial Publicity

In *Sheppard v. Maxwell,* Justice Clark's majority opinion stressed that judges, in addition to protecting the jury from prejudicial publicity and controlling courtroom conduct, must control publicity about the trial. Clark emphasized the need to control the disclosure of information by trial participants. At the same time, however, he asserted that the press cannot be prevented from reporting the trial itself. The tolerance for "gagging" trial participants and intolerance for restricting press reports of trials continues to be the Court's policy after nearly forty years of litigation. In addition, the Supreme Court has held since *Sheppard v. Maxwell* that the press cannot ordinarily be punished for reporting lawfully obtained information about the judicial process.

Restraints Imposed on News Sources

In the *Sheppard* opinion, Justice Clark said the trial judge in the case should have tried to control the release of information to the press by lawyers, police, and witnesses. Clark said no one who was a part of the trial process, and therefore under the direct jurisdiction of the court, "should be permitted to frustrate" a court's responsibility to ensure a trial "by an impartial jury free from outside influences." Collaboration between attorneys and the press involving information affecting the fairness of a criminal trial is not only subject to regulation but also highly censurable and worthy of disciplinary measures.

Clark applauded the *Sheppard* trial judge's threat to bar from the courtroom one defense witness, Sheppard's brother, who was accused of trying the case in the newspapers. Clark said the judge would have been within his authority to forbid any lawyer, party, or witness to discuss the case with the press. He said the judge could have barred any participant in the case from revealing Sheppard's refusal to take a lie detector test, the identity of prospective witnesses, the contents of probable testimony, comments about Sheppard's guilt or innocence, or any other statements related to the merits of the case. The court also could have requested local government officials to instruct their employees not to disseminate information about the case, Clark said in *Sheppard.*

Even before *Sheppard,* the U.S. Department of Justice had issued a 1965 policy statement governing the release of information by its personnel. Commonly known as the Katzenbach Rules, after then-Attorney General Nicholas Katzenbach, the statement condemned the release

[56]Charles Lane, "High Court to Post Same-Day Transcripts," *Wash. Post,* Sept. 15, 2006, at A8.

of information designed to influence the outcome of a trial. The rules, still federal policy in 2007, instruct Justice Department personnel not to make statements about investigative procedures, evidence, prospective witnesses, confessions, a defendant's character, or arguments to be used in the case. Nor were members of the Justice Department to volunteer information about a defendant's prior criminal record or encourage the news media to obtain photographs of defendants in custody. Authorized personnel could release a defendant's identity, age, and residence; the criminal charge; the identity of the investigating and arresting agencies; the length of the investigation; and the circumstances surrounding the arrest.[57]

Shortly after the *Sheppard* decision, judges and lawyers released their own recommendations designed to prevent the publication of information similar to that discouraged by the Katzenbach Rules. In 1968, the American Bar Association recommended contempt citations for lawyers, defendants, witnesses, court personnel, and law enforcement officers who made out-of-court statements designed to affect the outcome of a trial or who violated a court order not to reveal information disclosed in a closed courtroom.[58] Also in 1968, the Judicial Conference of the United States, the agency responsible for developing policy for the federal courts, adopted similar guidelines for the release of information.[59]

When the guidelines of the ABA and judicial conference were published, judges began to issue more orders restricting trial participants, lawyers, and court personnel from releasing information to the press. Since the 1960s, the ABA and the judicial conference have revised their recommendations to allow for the release of more information than the 1968 documents allowed, but both still encourage restrictive orders, particularly for lawyers.[60] The U.S. Supreme Court has refused several opportunities to declare unconstitutional what judges call restrictive orders and what journalists call "gag" orders. In fact, in 1991, the U.S. Supreme Court said lawyers' comments about criminal proceedings can be restricted because lawyers, as officers of the court, are bound to protect the integrity of the legal system. In *Gentile v. State Bar of Nevada,* the Court said restrictions of attorneys' comments during trials, in particular, are subject to less First Amendment scrutiny than constraints on the expression of the press or public in general.[61] The Court said that the speech of lawyers such as Dominic Gentile, representing a client indicted for the theft of cocaine and $300,000 out of a safety deposit box, can be restricted if there is a "substantial likelihood" their statements would prejudice a criminal proceeding. Chief Justice Rehnquist, writing for a majority, said lawyers' speech may be restricted more than that of the public and press because attorneys have special access to information about judicial proceedings and the discovery process. Rehnquist said lawyers' out-of-court statements could threaten the fairness of proceedings because the public is likely to consider lawyers' statements "especially authoritative."

In spite of the Court's decision that the speech of lawyers could be limited, a majority of the Court said the speech of Dominic Gentile had been unconstitutionally punished. Gentile had been reprimanded by the Nevada State Bar after telling reporters after a press

[57]*See* 28 C.F.R. § 50.2.

[58]American Bar Association Legal Advisory Committee on Fair Trial and Free Press, *The Rights of Fair Trial and Free Press* (1969).

[59]*See* Report of the Committee on the Operation of the Jury System on the "Free Press-Fair Trial" Issue, 45 F.R.D. 391 (1968).

[60]*See* Criminal Justice Standards Committee of the American Bar Association, *ABA Standards for Criminal Justice; Fair Trial and Free Press* (3d ed. 1992); Revised Report of the Judicial Conference Committee on the Operation of the Jury System on the "Free Press-Fair Trial" Issue, 87 F.R.D. 519 (1980).

[61]501 U.S. 1030 (1991).

conference that the people who were accusing his client of theft were convicted money launderers and drug dealers, most of whom were trying to work out a deal with the police in exchange for their testimony. A majority of the Court declared unconstitutionally vague a provision of Nevada's bar rules allowing lawyers to explain publicly the "general nature" of their client's case "without elaboration." The Court held that lawyers cannot know for certain when comments about a case no longer are of a "general nature" but instead have become an "elaboration" that is prohibited.

Restrictive orders prohibiting trial participants, and particularly lawyers, from providing information to the press take a variety of forms. They can ban all, or only some, of the persons involved in a trial from discussing a case with journalists. They can prohibit giving the media specific kinds of information or any information at all. In one notorious double murder trial in Arizona, one with "overtones of organized crime and contract killing," the trial court judge ordered all participants in the case to keep away from news personnel during the proceeding. He said massive publicity since the two murders, including allegations of professional killings and brutality, made it necessary to control discussion of the case outside the courtroom. The judge said that the **gag order** was the least restrictive means to protect the defendants' Sixth Amendment rights to a fair trial.[62]

One of the most intense cases of prejudicial publicity began on February 15, 2002, when law enforcement officers, acting on an anonymous tip, discovered fifty decomposing bodies at the Tri-State Crematorium in Noble, Georgia. There was no state law specifically dealing with this circumstance. Instead, the proprietor of the facility, Tommy Ray Brent Marsh, was arrested and charged with theft by deception because he had received payment but had not performed the cremations. State law enforcement officials and news reporters converged on the gruesome scene; as several hundred more bodies were discovered, state officials, including the governor, gave news conferences in which they expressed their shock and outrage and promised to enact strict laws affecting cremation. After touring the scene, one legislator described the sight of piles of bodies as something out of a Stephen King novel. News coverage included reports of death threats against Marsh by individuals who thought their deceased relatives had been cremated. Before a bond hearing, Marsh was photographed and televised being led into court in handcuffs and a bulletproof vest surrounded by deputies.

On February 21, 2002, William Ralph Hill, Jr., a superior court judge, issued a broad restraining order that precluded officials even from notifying family members about the recovery and identification of the remains of deceased family members. On March 7, the court modified the order to facilitate communication between public officials and family members. The order was also modified to allow state officials to discuss publicly the results of environmental tests and the progress of the cleanup of the crematorium. The modified order, like the original order, restrained law enforcement officials from making public statements concerning matters such as their opinion of Marsh's guilt; attorneys were prohibited from making prejudicial statements.

Judge Hill's modified order, printed in part as Figure 10.1, was necessary, he said, because the intense pretrial publicity so inflamed potential jurors that it created a clear and

[62]KPNX Broadcasting Co. v. Maricopa County Super. Ct., 678 P.2d 431, 434 (Ariz. 1984).

SUPERIOR COURT OF WALKER COUNTY
STATE OF GEORGIA

ORDER RESTRICTING EXTRA JUDICIAL STATEMENTS

IT IS **ORDERED AND DIRECTED** that during the pendency of the above cases and until their final determination in this Court the District Attorney and his assistant prosecutors, counsel for the Defendant and all persons affiliated with them, the Court staff, the Walker County Sheriff and his lawful deputies, agents and employees of the Georgia Bureau of Investigation and the Walker County Coroner involved in this investigation shall not release, make or authorize the release any extra judicial statement by any means of public communication and news media relating to: (a) the prior criminal record (including arrests, indictments or other charges of crime) if any exists, or the character or reputation of the accused; (b) the existence or content of any confession, admission or statement given by the accused or any co-defendant, if any exists or the refusal or failure of the accused or any co-defendants to make any statements; (c) the accused's refusal or failure to submit to any examination or tests; (d) the possibility of a plea of guilty to the offense charged or a lesser offense; (e) any opinion as to the guilt or innocence of the accused and his conduct in the matters under investigation or as to the merits of the case or any evidence in the case; (f) any opinion as to the fairness of the proceedings, the probability of a fair trail of this case in this venue, the presence or absence of prejudice in this venue regarding this case or the Defendant, (g) any personal remarks concerning counsel, the trial judge, the accused or officers of the Court, (h) the identity, testimony or credibility of prospective witnesses.

(2) This Order of the Court shall not preclude in any way the aforesaid persons from the dissemination of facts and information to family members regarding the recovery and identification of the remains of deceased family members by any of the above persons nor shall it interfere with or prohibit communication in any way between the above agents and family members in answering specific questions family members may have concerning the investigation. The Court intends for all family members or potential family members with possible remains recovered from the crematorium or elsewhere to receive any and all information developed by the investigation consistent with the District Attorney's discretion to reveal information in accordance with Georgia Code of Professional Conduct 3.6. The Court's Order has never been intended to in any way interfere with the flow of information they seek.

(3) This Order of the Court shall not preclude the dissemination by public communication and the news media of information concerning the results of any scientific tests or examination addressing any public health, safety or environmental risks or any other information concerning health or environmental risks or the progress of the clean up of the crematorium site and cost estimates of the public works project.

(4) Counsel for the State and the Defense hereby are reminded of their obligations under Georgia Rule of Professional Conduct 3.6 ("Rule 3.6") and are ordered to follow strictly Rule 3.6. Rule 3.6 states:

> A lawyer who is participating or has participated in the investigation or litigation of the matter shall not make any extra judicial statement that a person would reasonably believe to be disseminated by means of public communication if the lawyer knows or reasonably should know that it will have a substantial likelihood of materially prejudicing an adjudicative proceeding in the matter.

(Continued)

(5) This Order shall not preclude the press or media from reporting events as they transpire in open Court or any matters of public record in this Court and shall not be construed to preclude any attorney or court office from quoting or referring without comment to public records of the Court in the case, from announcing the scheduling or result of any stage in the judicial process; or from announcing without further comment that the accused denies the charges made against him.

(6) The Court reserves the right to impose additional restrictions or modifications, upon notice to affected parties and a hearing on the matter, should the Constitutional rights of the Defendant or the needs or interests of the State of Georgia or the Movants warrant rehearing on the matter.

This Order is effective from the date of this Order until the conclusion or termination in the trial court or until further Order of the Court.

The Order may be enforced by the contempt powers of the Court.

SO ORDERED, in LaFayette, Walker County, Georgia, this 7th day of March, 2002.

Wm. Ralph Hill, Jr.
Judge, Superior Courts
Lookout Mountain Judicial Circuit

FIGURE 10.1 Restrictive order.

present danger to Marsh's right to a fair and impartial jury, not only locally but also throughout Georgia. Judge Hill concluded that in addition to the gag order, alternatives such as change of venue and a searching voir dire examination of potential jurors might have to be used at a later time to protect the fairness of the trial in this highly unusual case.[63]

A trial was averted when a plea agreement was reached between Marsh and the state of Georgia; on January 31, 2005, Marsh was sentenced to twelve years in prison.

A restrictive order is likely to be overturned if an appellate court decides that the trial judge did not consider alternatives to the order and the order was broader than necessary to protect the rights of a defendant. For example, a federal district court in Connecticut overturned a state court's order prohibiting attorneys from making "any public statement" to the press during a sensational chain-saw murder trial. Richard Crafts was accused of cutting his wife up with a chain saw, then putting her body through a woodchipping machine. The federal court acknowledged that because of the extensive media coverage the case had already received, trial judge Howard Moraghan "could reasonably conclude" that further publicity might endanger the defendant's right to a fair trial. However, the federal court declared the restrictive order unconstitutionally overbroad because it prohibited "any" statements by lawyers about the case rather than only those statements that might "reasonably" be prejudicial. In addition, the federal court said, gag orders must be accompanied by evidence that a judge had considered alternatives to restricting the speech of the attorneys. The federal court said Moraghan provided no evidence that he had considered alternatives to the restrictive order, such as admonishing or sequestering the jury.[64]

[63]State v. Marsh, 30 Media L. Rep. 1507 (2002).
[64]Connecticut Magazine v. Moraghan, 676 F. Supp. 38 (D.C. Conn. 1987).

Appellate courts are more likely to overturn restrictions on participants' speech in civil trials and after legal proceedings are concluded. In 1990, the U.S. Supreme Court found unconstitutional a Florida law that punished **grand jury** witnesses who disclosed their own grand jury testimony. In *Butterworth v. Smith,* Michael Smith, a reporter for the *Charlotte Herald-News,* wanted to include in a news story or book his own testimony before a special grand jury investigating the Charlotte County State Attorney's Office and Sheriff's Department.[65] Smith was called to testify after writing news stories about alleged misconduct relevant to the grand jury's investigation. The prosecutor conducting the grand jury investigation warned Smith that he could be prosecuted under Florida law if he revealed any of his testimony. When the grand jury concluded its investigation, Smith claimed a First Amendment right to publish his own testimony. The state of Florida argued in part that grand jury testimony should remain secret so that persons exonerated by grand juries would not be held up to ridicule, witnesses would not fear retribution, and persons about to be indicted would not flee.

The U.S. Supreme Court held unanimously that the First Amendment protects the right of grand jury witnesses to publish their own testimony once the term of a grand jury ends. The majority opinion, written by Chief Justice Rehnquist, said the Florida statute was unconstitutional because it provided for the punishment of speech central to First Amendment values. Rehnquist noted that under the Florida ban on discussion of grand jury testimony, critics of government could be silenced by calling them before grand juries. In contrast, Rehnquist said, some of Florida's reasons for grand jury secrecy did not apply to the release of a witness's own testimony after a grand jury had been discharged. Any remaining reasons, Rehnquist said, were insufficient to justify the permanent ban on testimony. The Court did not decide whether grand jury witnesses could publish their own testimony while a grand jury is still sitting or discuss what they had learned about the grand jury proceedings from being a witness, such as the scope and details of the investigation.

◇ Summary ◇

Judicial orders restricting officers of the court and others involved in a case from talking to the press were widely encouraged in the late 1960s. Court orders restricting witnesses, law enforcement officers, lawyers, and litigants are usually upheld by appellate courts if the trial judge decides there is a reasonable likelihood that the jury may otherwise be biased and the judge has considered alternatives.

Restraints Imposed on the Media

Although Justice Tom Clark, in *Sheppard v. Maxwell,* authorized restraints on trial participants' contacts with the news media, he did not say reporters could be restricted from publishing information they obtained about the criminal proceedings. In fact, consistent with the Supreme Court's general intolerance of prior restraints on publication, Clark said the Supreme Court had not authorized restrictive press reports of proceedings in open court.

[65] 494 U.S. 624 (1990).

The Supreme Court's prohibition of prior restraints directed at the news media in criminal proceedings might seem curious considering the Court's tolerance of restrictive orders on news sources such as lawyers, witnesses, and law enforcement officers. A gag on either a reporter or a reporter's source has essentially the same impact: Less information reaches the public. But the Court frequently draws a line between restricting press access to information and prior restraint, saying that although the First Amendment does not give reporters an absolute right to gather news, it does create an almost insurmountable bar to prior restraints once material is in the hands of the press.[66]

Protection of the media's right to publish information about criminal proceedings was reinforced in 1976 when five Supreme Court justices said they were not likely to tolerate prior restraints on the news media to stop prejudicial pretrial publicity. In *Nebraska Press Association v. Stuart,* the Court held that a Nebraska court's restrictions on the reporting of a murder investigation and subsequent legal proceedings violated the First Amendment.[67]

The case began with a mass murder in the tiny prairie town of Sutherland, Nebraska, on the night of October 18, 1975. The 850 town residents were told to stay off the streets and to be careful whom they admitted to their homes after six members of the Henry Kellie family had been killed. The next day, a neighbor of the murdered family, thirty-year-old Erwin Charles Simants, confessed to law enforcement officers. Simants, charged with six counts of premeditated murder, immediately became the focus of nationwide news coverage.

After four days of publicity, County Judge Ronald Ruff issued an order prohibiting the publication of news obtained during public pretrial proceedings. Members of the press also were ordered to observe supposedly voluntary Nebraska Bar-Press Guidelines. The guidelines, agreed to by representatives of the state bar and news media, discouraged the reporting of confessions, opinions about guilt or innocence, statements that would influence the outcome of a trial, the results of laboratory tests, comments on the credibility of witnesses, and evidence presented during the trial outside the presence of a jury. Ruff's order, upheld by District Judge Hugh Stuart, was intended to suppress publication of Simants's confession, statements he had made to relatives, and the results of medical tests related to a sexual assault. When the Nebraska Press Association appealed, the Nebraska Supreme Court upheld the key elements of the Stuart order. Simants was convicted of first-degree murder in January 1976.

Five months later, a unanimous U.S. Supreme Court said the Nebraska court order barring publication of Simants's confession and other information about the case was unconstitutional. Chief Justice Warren Burger, who wrote for five of the nine justices, did not say that prior restraints could never be imposed to protect the rights of a defendant. However, he said, anyone wishing to restrain the media would have the "heavy burden" of demonstrating that a fair trial would not be possible without prior restraint. Burger refused to consider the First Amendment to be more important than the Sixth or vice versa. Yet he said a prior restraint on publication was "one of the most extraordinary remedies known to our jurisprudence" and should be difficult to obtain. He said that a prior restraint did more than "chill" speech—it "froze" it, at least for a time.

To determine whether a prior restraint was warranted in the Simants case, Burger applied a form of the clear-and-present-danger test once used in sedition cases. He said the

[66]*See, e.g.,* Pell v. Procunier, 417 U.S. 817 (1974).
[67]427 U.S. 539 (1976).

question was whether the "gravity of the evil" of pretrial publicity, "discounted by the improbability" of its occurrence, merited a prior restraint. Burger looked at three factors:

1. the nature and extent of pretrial news coverage
2. whether other measures would likely mitigate the effects of unrestrained pretrial publicity
3. the effectiveness of a restrictive order in diminishing the effect of prejudicial publicity

Considering the first factor, Burger affirmed trial judge Ronald Ruff's judgment that there would be "intense and pervasive" pretrial publicity that might impair the defendant's right to a fair trial. However, Burger did not believe there was enough evidence that unchecked publicity would have impaired jurors' abilities to judge Simants fairly. Burger noted that Ruff found only that the publicity could *possibly* have constituted a clear and present danger to a fair trial. Burger said Ruff's conclusion was necessarily speculative because the judge was dealing with factors "unknown and unknowable." Burger seemed to suggest that it might be impossible to prove that pretrial publicity would lead to a prejudiced jury and thus impossible to meet the burden of proof necessary to justify a prior restraint.

Second, Burger said Ruff had not indicated whether alternatives to prior restraint would have protected Simants. Ruff had not said that remedies such as a change of venue or the questioning of jurors during voir dire would have failed to protect a fair trial. Nor had Ruff closed the courtroom, an alternative that Burger implicitly approved in his opinion.

Finally, Burger said, it was not clear that a prior restraint on publication would have halted pretrial publicity in Sutherland. In a town of 850, word of mouth could be more damaging than news media accounts, Burger said. In addition, by law, Judge Ruff could legally try to limit the publicity only within the county. As a county judge, he did not have jurisdiction over network television news and the national wire services.

Although Burger imposed a form of the clear-and-present-danger test on defendants who want to restrain the press, at least three of the Court's justices would have provided even greater protection for the press. Justice William J. Brennan, Jr., who had concurred only in the judgment in the case, said in a separate opinion that prior restraint could never be permitted to ensure a fair trial. Justices Potter Stewart and Thurgood Marshall joined in Brennan's concurring opinion. In addition, Justices Byron White and John Paul Stevens indicated in separate concurring opinions that they might eventually agree to Brennan's absolutist approach.

Meanwhile, Simants's first murder conviction was overturned on the ground that a sheriff supervising the sequestered jury members had tried to influence them. When Simants was retried, he was found not guilty by reason of insanity.

A year after the Supreme Court's decision in *Nebraska Press Association,* the Court affirmed its reluctance to allow prior restraints on court coverage. In *Oklahoma Publishing Co. v. District Court,* a trial judge had allowed the press to attend the detention hearing of an eleven-year-old boy who had been arrested for the murder of a railroad switchman.[68] A few days later, the judge prohibited the media from publishing the boy's name, obtained during the open hearing, and a picture, taken immediately afterward without any objections.

[68] 430 U.S. 308 (1977).

The Supreme Court noted that, by statute, juvenile proceedings in Oklahoma were private unless explicitly ordered open. However, the Court said in a per curiam opinion that because the press was permitted to attend the hearing, an order to prohibit the publication of information and pictures obtained there was unconstitutional.

The *Nebraska Press Association* decision has largely meant that prior restraints on court coverage have not been allowed by lower courts. In 1994, for example, a federal court refused to grant a prior restraint on a television docudrama based on Lyle and Erik Menendez's involvement in the death of their parents. Although the brothers' lawyers argued that the Fox Broadcasting docudrama would inevitably taint the jury pool, the court declined to enjoin the program. The court based its decision on the *Nebraska Press Association* test, reasoning that alternatives such as careful voir dire of jurors could protect the brothers' fair trial rights.[69]

Similarly, in 2005 the Court of Appeals for the Second Circuit ruled unconstitutional a judge's order barring publication of the names of potential jurors in the trial of Wall Street figure Frank Quattrone.[70] Shortly before Quattrone's trial in April 2004, a state court judge declared a mistrial in the separate prosecution of Dennis Kozlowski, a former high-profile executive of Tyco Corporation. Near the close of Kozlowski's fraud trial, the *Wall Street Journal* and other publications published the name of a juror who in court flashed an apparent O.K. sign to Kozlowski. Soon after, the juror received a frightening letter and the state court judge declared a mistrial.[71] Jury selection began in the Quattrone case less than two weeks later.

To avoid a mistrial, federal district judge Richard Owen ordered the press not to disclose the names of prospective jurors in the Quattrone case, even though the names were stated in open court. The court of appeals held the order unconstitutional because it failed to meet the standards of *Nebraska Press Association*. First, Owen did not make factual findings that publicity would harm Quattrone's right to a fair trial. Owen based his order solely on the incidents in the Kozlowski trial, and the appellate court held that a prior restraint may not be based on incidents that occurred in a completely separate and unrelated trial. Second, the record did not demonstrate that Owen had sufficiently considered measures other than a prior restraint. Finally, the appellate court held the ban to be ineffective because it did not prevent members of the public from disseminating the jurors' names.

Despite the generally broad protection against prior restraints granted in *Nebraska Press Association*, the Supreme Court has in rare instances allowed prior restraints involving court coverage to stand. In 1990, the U.S. Supreme Court denied certiorari when a trial court imposed a **temporary restraining order** on the Cable News Network (CNN) in *United States v. Noriega*.[72] The Supreme Court, typically, did not explain why it refused to review the case, and a denial of certiorari does not establish precedent. Two justices dissented from the denial of certiorari, arguing that the restraining order in the Noriega case conflicted with the Court's decision in *Nebraska Press Association*.

[69]Menendez v. Fox Broadcasting Co., 22 Media L. Rep. 1702 (C.D. Cal. 1994).

[70]United States v. Quattrone, 402 F.3d 304 (2d Cir. 2005).

[71]*See* Jess Bravin & Kara Scannell, "Behind the Tyco Mistrial," *Wall Street Journal*, Apr. 5, 2004, at B1; Andrew Ross Sorkin, "No O.K. Sign and No Guilty Vote by Juror No. 4," *N.Y. Times*, Apr. 7, 2004, at A1.

[72]United States v. Noriega, 752 F. Supp. 1032 (S.D. Fla.), *aff'd sub nom. In re* Cable News Network Inc., 917 F.2d 1543 (11th Cir.), *cert. denied*, 498 U.S. 976 (1990).

In *Noriega,* the Supreme Court let stand a federal district court order that CNN not broadcast tape-recorded conversations between deposed Panamanian dictator Manuel Noriega and his defense team until the district court could review them. Attorneys for Noriega, who was brought to the United States to face drug-trafficking charges, sought the restrictive order after being asked by CNN to comment on the tapes that prison officials had recorded. Judge William Hoeveler wanted the tapes reviewed to determine whether broadcasting their contents would damage Noriega's Sixth Amendment right to a fair trial. His temporary restraining order was not a ruling on the merits of Noriega's claim. Rather, it was intended to protect the status quo until the court could determine if a prior restraint was justified.

CNN subsequently turned the Noriega tapes over to Hoeveler after losing its appeals. After reviewing the tapes, Hoeveler vacated the restraining order, finding that Noriega could not prove, using the three-point *Nebraska Press Association* test, that broadcast of the conversations would undermine Noriega's right to an impartial jury.[73] As will be discussed later in the chapter, CNN was later held in contempt for cablecasting some of the tapes while the restraining order was in effect.

In 1984, the Supreme Court specifically approved an exception to its virtual ban of prior restraints on journalists, an exception triggered when media personnel obtain information because they are participants in a trial. In *Seattle Times Co. v. Rhinehart,* the Court said that two Washington state newspapers could be restrained from publishing information they acquired only because they were defendants in a libel suit.[74] The two papers, the *Seattle Times* and the *Walla Walla Union-Bulletin,* had been sued for $14 million by Keith Rhinehart, the leader of a religious group called the Aquarian Foundation. During the pretrial discovery process, the newspapers questioned whether the foundation had been damaged by stories reporting that Rhinehart treated inmates in a state prison to entertainment that included women who "shed their gowns and bikinis." They asked the judge to order the foundation to reveal the names of its members and donors for the previous ten years in order to determine whether donations declined after the stories. The foundation countered that such an order would violate the First Amendment rights of members and donors to privacy, freedom of association, and freedom of religion. The foundation argued that its members would be harassed and donations would drop.

The trial court judge ordered the Aquarian Foundation to provide the names of members and donors but prohibited the newspapers from publishing the information. The newspapers appealed the restriction on publication, but the order was upheld by a unanimous U.S. Supreme Court. Justice Lewis Powell, Jr., writing the Court's opinion, said the restraint on publication inherent in the trial court's order was not the "classic prior restraint that requires exacting First Amendment scrutiny." Although the order prohibited publication of information obtained through discovery, the same information could be published if acquired in another way, Powell said.

However, Powell continued, even if *Rhinehart* was not a classic prior restraint case, the newspaper's First Amendment rights could be restricted only if an important government interest was at stake. The Court decided that the state of Washington had demonstrated a "substantial" government interest: to prevent information acquired during discovery from

[73]United States v. Noriega, 752 F. Supp. 1045 (S.D. Fla. 1990).
[74]467 U.S. 20 (1984).

being used for other purposes. Court rules requiring litigants to reveal any information relevant to a suit, the Court said, force trial participants to provide material that may damage an individual's privacy or reputation if published. The Supreme Court accepted the findings of the Washington courts that the publication of the names of Aquarian Foundation members and donors could lead to their being annoyed, embarrassed, or even discriminated against. The Supreme Court said the Washington courts did not abuse their discretion by deciding that an order requiring the foundation to reveal private financial records could also prohibit publication of that information. The courts could limit the use of the information because it was made available by court order only so that the newspapers could defend themselves in a libel suit.

Recently, in *People v. Bryant,*[75] the Colorado Supreme Court modified and upheld an order prohibiting media publication of intimate information about Kobe Bryant's accuser. After the trial court held an **in camera** pretrial hearing to determine the relevance of evidence of the accuser's sexual conduct, the court reporter mistakenly sent a transcript of this hearing via e-mail to seven media entities such as the Associated Press. When this mistake was discovered, the judge issued an order prohibiting the recipients from publishing any information contained in the transcript. The state supreme court agreed with the trial court's determination that preserving the privacy of the accuser's sexual conduct was an interest of the highest order. The state supreme court believed this case was analogous to *Rhinehart;* the hearing transcript was not a public component of a trial, nor was the information acquired through the media's investigative efforts.

The Colorado Supreme Court narrowed the trial court's order, ruling that those portions of the transcript that were admissible at trial could be published. Further, the state high court emphasized the gag order did not apply to information the press acquired through investigative techniques.

Three justices dissented because detailed information about the accuser's sexual conduct was available through public documents and had been widely reported by the media.[76] Thus, the prior restraint would not protect the privacy of the accuser. Further, the media did nothing wrong in obtaining the transcript and should be permitted to publish this lawfully acquired information, the dissenters said.

Summary

The Supreme Court, in *Nebraska Press Association v. Stuart,* said that prior restraints on publication to protect the right to a fair trial are ordinarily unconstitutional. The Court said that before trial judges issue prior restraint orders, they must consider the nature and extent of pretrial news coverage, alternative measures to protect Sixth Amendment rights, and whether a prior restraint order would be effective. However, the Court has approved a prior restraint order in a case in which newspapers obtained information only because they were parties in a lawsuit.

[75]94 P.3d 624 (Colo.), *stay denied,* 125 S. Ct. 1 (2004).

[76]*Id.* at 639 (Bender, J., dissenting). *See generally* Kirk Johnson, "The Bryant Trial: Anatomy of a Case That Fell Apart," *N.Y. Times,* Sept. 3, 2004, at A14.

Punishment after Publication

The Supreme Court, in addition to holding that it is ordinarily unconstitutional to prevent the publication of news about court proceedings, has also ruled it unconstitutional to punish the media after publication for news about the judicial system. In two cases, the U.S. Supreme Court ruled unanimously that government could not punish the media for truthful news stories about the judiciary or the criminal justice system absent a compelling government need. The Court held that states could not punish the media even for printing information declared confidential by state law.

In *Landmark Communications v. Virginia,* the Court said the state could not justify the punishment of a newspaper for printing information about a confidential judicial inquiry.[77] The case arose in 1975 when the *Virginian Pilot,* owned by Landmark Communications, identified a judge who was being investigated by the Virginia Judicial Inquiry and Review Commission, which reviews complaints about the disability or misconduct of judges. An article in the *Pilot* accurately reported that the commission had not filed a formal complaint against the judge. A month after the article, a grand jury indicted Landmark for divulging the judge's name in violation of state law. A Virginia statute provided that dissemination of the confidential information was a misdemeanor. Landmark was found guilty and fined $500.

The Supreme Court of Virginia affirmed the conviction, but the decision was reversed by the U.S. Supreme Court. Chief Justice Burger, writing the Court's opinion, did not discount the need for confidentiality by the judicial review commission. He noted that forty-eight states, including Virginia, provided for confidential investigations of judicial conduct. Burger said confidentiality encouraged citizens to participate in investigations. It also protected the credibility of individual judges and the reputation of the judicial system from public disclosure of unsubstantiated complaints.

Although the Court recognized the legitimacy of confidential judicial inquiries, Burger said the Constitution severely limited fining the press for truthful publications. Burger said accurate reporting of the conduct of public officials "lies near the core of the First Amendment." He said the article published by the *Virginian Pilot* "clearly served those interests in public scrutiny and discussion of governmental affairs which the First Amendment was adopted to protect." Before discussion of the court system can be punished, Burger said, the danger to the administration of justice "must be extremely serious and the degree of imminence extremely high before utterances can be punished."

In contrast, Burger said, Virginia's interest in encouraging participation in the investigation of judges and protecting both the reputation of individual judges and respect for the judicial system did not justify the encroachment on the freedom of the press. Virginia argued that the state's effort to protect confidentiality encourages complainants, witnesses, and judges to take part in the investigations. But Burger noted that more than forty of the forty-seven states with review boards did not punish breaches of confidentiality by criminal sanction. In addition, Burger said, the Court had established in libel cases that it would not repress speech that damaged public officials' reputations.

A year later, the Supreme Court told the state of West Virginia it could not punish the *Charleston Daily Mail* and the *Charleston Daily Gazette* for printing the name of a

[77] 435 U.S. 829 (1978).

juvenile defendant. The two papers identified a fourteen-year-old who shot and killed a classmate at a junior high school in St. Albans, a small community outside Charleston. Reporters obtained the name by asking witnesses, the police, and an assistant prosecuting attorney at the scene of the incident. A grand jury indicted the two newspapers for violating a West Virginia law prohibiting newspapers from publishing the names of youths charged as juvenile offenders. Under the law, newspapers, but not broadcast stations, could be fined $100 and editors and reporters jailed for up to six months. The West Virginia Supreme Court prohibited county officials from acting on the indictment, and the U.S. Supreme Court, in *Smith v. Daily Mail Publishing Co.,* upheld that judgment.[78]

The U.S. Supreme Court said a state could punish "truthful information about a matter of public significance" only "to further a need of the highest order." The Court's majority opinion acknowledged the validity of West Virginia's interest in facilitating the rehabilitation of youthful offenders by protecting their anonymity. The publicity from one crime could create a stigma that would block employment opportunities, the state argued.

However, the Court said, the state's interest in anonymity was not sufficient to overcome First Amendment rights threatened by imposing criminal penalties for the publication of the names of juveniles. The Court noted that every state protected the anonymity of juveniles but forty-five of the fifty accomplished that objective without criminal penalties. Moreover, the Court said, the statute was unconstitutional because it restricted only newspapers and not the electronic media, thus not accomplishing its purpose of protecting the identity of juveniles. Three radio stations had also revealed the name of the fourteen-year-old St. Albans youth who killed his classmate, but none of the stations could be prosecuted under the West Virginia law.

Summary

The Supreme Court has indicated that the First Amendment ordinarily prohibits punishment of the press for the publication of news stories about judicial proceedings. The Court has declared that absent a compelling governmental interest or an extremely serious and imminent threat to the administration of justice, states cannot punish the media for publishing stories based on information that is otherwise protected by law.

Access to Courtrooms

After the Supreme Court demonstrated in 1976 and 1977 its intolerance for prior restraints on publication, at least some trial court judges noted Justice Burger's suggestion in *Nebraska Press Association* that judges might close courtrooms to ensure a fair trial. In the late 1970s, several trial court judges tried to close courtrooms to prevent reporters from acquiring information that could prejudice the outcome of a trial. Indeed, the Supreme Court seemed to sanction court closures in 1979 when it ruled that the press and the public did not have a constitutional right to attend **pretrial hearings.** However, in the 1980s, the Supreme Court reversed direction and held that the public and the press do have a qualified First Amendment right of access to trials and the jury selection process as well as to pretrial hearings.

[78] 443 U.S. 97 (1979).

TRIALS The Supreme Court first ruled in 1980 that the press and the public have a constitutional right of access to courtrooms. In *Richmond Newspapers v. Virginia,* seven justices agreed the public has a limited First Amendment right to attend criminal trials.[79] *Richmond Newspapers* marked the first time the Supreme Court has held that the public has a First Amendment right to observe government proceedings and records.

Richmond Newspapers arose from a series of circumstances that understandably could frustrate a judge. In July 1976, John Stevenson was convicted of the murder of a hotel manager. A few months later, the Virginia Supreme Court overturned the conviction, holding that a bloodstained shirt had been improperly admitted into evidence. A second trial ended in a mistrial in May 1978 when a juror asked to be excused and no alternate juror was available. Stevenson's third trial, in June 1978, also ended in a mistrial when one prospective juror told others about the history of the case.

Before the beginning of the fourth trial, still in 1978, Judge Richard H. C. Taylor closed the trial at the request of the defense. He had previously said he would agree with defense requests if he believed the rights of the defendant were infringed "in any way" and the rights of "everyone else" were not "completely" overridden. Richmond Newspapers, the corporate parent of the *Richmond Times-Dispatch* and the *Richmond News-Leader,* unsuccessfully protested the closure. Stevenson was found not guilty after a closed trial. Richmond Newspapers' posttrial appeal of the closure was denied by the Virginia Supreme Court, but the U.S. Supreme Court granted certiorari.

Although a majority of the Court agreed that the Virginia closure order violated the public's right to an open trial, the Court was otherwise divided. No more than three justices agreed to join any one opinion. Chief Justice Burger, writing the opinion for the Court, said that although the First Amendment does not explicitly mention a public right to attend criminal trials, such a right is implied. The rights specifically guaranteed in the First Amendment, Burger said, such as freedom of speech and press, the right to assemble peaceably, and the right to petition the government for a redress of grievances, ensure free communication about government. "Plainly it would be difficult to single out any aspect of government of higher concern and importance to the people than the manner in which criminal trials are conducted," he added.

Burger said the Bill of Rights was enacted after a long tradition of openness in the Anglo-American judicial system, a tradition based on the indispensable role public trials play in the criminal justice system. Burger, supported only by Justices White and Stevens, said criminal trials have been open "to all who cared to observe" since before the Norman conquest of England. Trials have long been presumptively open, Burger said, because public trials discourage perjury and official misconduct during the proceedings. Open trials also inspire public confidence in the criminal justice process. Burger said that when trials are open, citizens know they can observe the system at work to see whether it is fair. In addition, public trials allow the public to see "justice done," helping to defuse community outrage after major crimes.

For Burger, the First Amendment right of the press to report court news would lose its meaning if access to courtrooms could be denied. He said that freedom of the press "could be eviscerated" without some protection for gathering news. Although Burger emphasized

[79] 448 U.S. 555 (1980).

the First Amendment right to attend trials belongs to the public as a whole and not specifically to the press, he also said that the press often acts as a surrogate for the public, informing people about court activity. He noted that while public attendance in court had once been common, people now rely on the media for their information about trials. Therefore, even though journalists have no greater right of access to courts under the First Amendment, "they often are provided special seating and priority of entry so that they may report what people in attendance have seen and heard."

Burger based the right of access to courts not only on the First Amendment right of the public to have information about the courts but also on an expansive interpretation of the First Amendment right to assemble. Burger said that trial courtrooms—like public streets, sidewalks, and parks—are public places where the public and representatives of the media have a right to exercise their First Amendment rights. People assemble in public places, Burger said, "not only to speak or to take action, but also to listen, observe, and learn." He added that people exercising their First Amendment right to be present in a courtroom historically have been thought to enhance "the integrity and quality of what takes place."

Because the press and the public have a constitutional right to attend court, Burger said, the trial in a criminal case can be closed only if the state interest in a fair trial overrides the rights of the press and public to attend. Burger criticized Judge Taylor in the *Stevenson* case for failing to explain the need for closure. Burger said, "No inquiry was made as to whether alternative solutions would have met the need to ensure fairness; there was no recognition of any right under the Constitution for the public or press to attend the trial."

Burger did not explain what circumstances and evidence would demonstrate the "overriding interest" that would justify closing the court. However, in a separate opinion, Justice Stewart suggested that courts might be closed to protect trade secrets or youthful rape victims. Justice Brennan, in a separate opinion joined by Justice Marshall, said that national security might warrant closure.

Just two years after the Court decided *Richmond Newspapers,* a 6-3 majority affirmed the Court's commitment to public trials. In 1982, in *Globe Newspaper Co. v. Superior Court,* five justices said states could not require that courts be closed routinely during the testimony of minors in sex offense cases.[80] The Court's opinion said closure could be based only on a "compelling" need in individual cases and could last no longer than necessary.

In *Globe Newspaper Co.,* a Massachusetts statute provided that a judge "shall exclude the general public from the courtroom" during a criminal trial "for rape, incest, carnal abuse," or other sex-related crimes when the victim was less than eighteen years old. Relying on the statute, a trial court judge in Norfolk County ordered a rape trial closed in 1979. The defendant had been charged with the rape of two sixteen-year-olds and a seventeen-year-old. When the Supreme Judicial Court of Massachusetts dismissed an appeal by the *Boston Globe,* the U.S. Supreme Court granted certiorari.

Justice Brennan, who wrote the Court's majority opinion, agreed the first of two reasons the state offered for the statute was compelling. The state said it wanted to close courtrooms to protect young victims of sex crimes from further trauma and embarrassment. However, Brennan said, as compelling as that interest was, it did not justify the

[80] 457 U.S. 596 (1982).

mandatory closure required by the state statute. Rather, he said, the need for closure must be made on a case-by-case basis. Brennan said the need for closure would depend on the minor's age and psychological maturity, the nature of the crime, the need for the testimony, and the interests of close relatives. He said the court should not be closed if the names of the minors were already in the public record or if the minors indicated they were willing to testify in the presence of the press.

Brennan also said the state had not sufficiently proven its second justification for the statute: that automatic closure encourages minor sex-crime victims to cooperate with law enforcement officials. Brennan said officials may be able to prove in individual cases that sex-offense victims would testify only if they could do so in closed court. However, the Massachusetts law requiring closed courts did not guarantee that the testimony would be kept secret. Massachusetts still provided the press with access to court transcripts containing testimony.

Chief Justice Burger dissented vigorously from Brennan's opinion. Burger said the decision undercut the state's authority and duty to protect minor victims of crimes.

The decision in *Globe Newspaper Co.* has generally not affected state efforts to keep juvenile proceedings closed. In *Globe,* the Court said the state may not automatically close the trial of an adult when juvenile witnesses may be called. But the Court did not say that all juvenile proceedings are presumptively open. In fact, juvenile proceedings are presumptively closed to the public in a majority of the states. Juvenile proceedings are presumptively open in relatively few states, although in recent years, a number of state legislatures have considered proposals expanding access to the juvenile justice system. Several states base access on the seriousness of the offense, the youth's age, or both. States often avoid prosecuting youths in open court as part of an effort to avoid stigmatizing them for life as criminals. States try to avoid treating juveniles as adult criminals so that efforts to rehabilitate them might be more effective. The Supreme Court has not ruled that closing courts during juvenile proceedings violates the First Amendment rights of the public and press.[81]

Opponents of closed juvenile justice proceedings say public access to ensure against abuse is as important in the juvenile justice system as it is in adult courts. Indeed, many observers question whether youths who are arrested for violent crimes and repeat offenders should not be treated as adults.

Several state appellate courts have affirmed trial court decisions to open juvenile proceedings to the public. In Ohio, the supreme court said state law allows trial judges to admit the public. The Ohio Supreme Court said a juvenile court judge did not abuse his discretion when he opened a hearing held to consider whether two juveniles should be tried as adults. The juveniles, arrested on charges of murder, argued that their Sixth Amendment rights to a fair trial would be jeopardized if evidence presented in an open hearing was ruled inadmissible during their trial. However, the juvenile court judge said the public's First Amendment right to attend trials includes juvenile proceedings. He said the juveniles had not demonstrated that closing the hearing was necessary to protect their Sixth Amendment rights.[82]

[81]For an argument favoring opening juvenile proceedings, see Joshua Dalton, "At the Crossroads of *Richmond* and *Gault*: Addressing Media Access to Juvenile Delinquency Proceedings through a Functional Analysis," 28 *Seton Hall L. Rev.* 1155 (1998).

[82]Ohio *ex rel.* Fyffe v. Pierce, 531 N.E.2d 673 (1988).

Some federal courts have also noted the value of openness in juvenile proceedings. In 1994, a federal appellate court ruled that the Juvenile Delinquency Act does not require that federal juvenile hearings be closed to the press and public.[83] The U.S. Court of Appeals for the Third Circuit held that judges may decide on a case-by-case basis whether to grant access to juvenile proceedings. The case arose when the *Pittsburgh Post-Gazette* sought access to the detention hearing of two juveniles arrested in connection with gang-related armed robberies. After being denied access, the newspaper appealed to the Third Circuit.

The parties to the case disputed the meaning of key sections of the Juvenile Delinquency Act, one section of which suggested that judges had discretion to hold juvenile hearings in open court or in chambers. The appeals court, noting the many civic advantages of open trials pointed out in the *Richmond Newspapers* case, reasoned that mandatory closure of juvenile hearings was unconstitutional. Instead, the Third Circuit ruled that the judge in each case should balance the public interest in openness against the interests of the juvenile, including the harm to rehabilitation that publicity might cause. The appeals court stated that judges who close juvenile proceedings must provide "factual findings related to the circumstances of this particular case" that warrant closure.

If the Supreme Court has not declared that juvenile proceedings must be open to the public, neither has it said that civil trials must be open to the public. However, Chief Justice Burger noted in *Richmond Newspapers* that both civil and criminal trials have historically been presumed to be open.

Civil court cases can often be more important to the public than the prosecution of individual criminals. Civil trials often involve such issues as discrimination, voting rights, antitrust, government regulation, and bankruptcy. They also often involve the dangers of cigarettes, drugs, automobiles, and chemical-processing plants. News reports of civil litigation may provide the public with information about corporate products and industrial processes normally kept secret. Also, in civil cases, judges, although not unconcerned with fairness, do not have to safeguard a criminal defendant's Sixth Amendment right to a fair trial.

Several appeals court opinions have recognized the public's First Amendment right of access in civil as well as criminal cases. Appeals courts often require judges to demonstrate a compelling need before closing civil hearings or trials. Judges must also show a potential for harm to litigants or persons not party to a case and severely limit the closure. In 1988, a Maryland appellate court said a trial court unconstitutionally closed court proceedings arising out of a state investigation into fraudulent automobile repairs. The Maryland attorney general sued Cottman Transmission Systems, which franchised 150 auto transmission repair centers, for defrauding consumers. Cottman employees allegedly induced customers to authorize and pay for unnecessary repairs. When the state issued a press release announcing its accusations, Cottman sales dropped 35 percent, and a circuit court judge ordered that all proceedings be closed.

On appeal, the Maryland Court of Special Appeals noted the same policy considerations for keeping criminal courts open, such as allowing the public to check for government abuse and fostering public respect for the judicial process, apply to civil courts. The Maryland appeals court said Cottman Transmission had not demonstrated an interest sufficiently

[83]United States v. A.D., 28 F.3d 1353 (3d Cir. 1994). *See also* United States v. Doe, 22 Media L. Rep. 1693 (E.D. Wis. 1994).

Protesting Court Closures

If a motion is made to close a court proceeding, you should raise your hand, stand and say:

"Your honor, I am (your name), a reporter for the (your newspaper). I respectfully request the opportunity to register on the record an objection to the motion to close this proceeding to the public, including the press. Our legal counsel has advised us that standards set forth in recent state and federal court decisions give us the opportunity for a hearing before the courtroom is closed. Accordingly, I respectfully request such a hearing and a brief continuance so our counsel can be present to make the appropriate arguments. Thank you.'

FIGURE 10.2 This is a sample statement journalists often read to judges if a motion is made to close a court proceeding. A legal confrontation with judges over courtroom closure can often be avoided if journalists ask judges before court proceedings that their media organizations be allowed to challenge motions for closure. Many media lawyers recommend that reporters call their editors as soon as possible after the issue of closure is raised so that editors have the option of calling an attorney. This sample statement is provided by the First Amendment Foundation, Tallahassee, Florida.

compelling to close the court proceedings. Cottman, said the court, only wanted to minimize the damage to its reputation and business, a desire of every business and professional sued. The court said that "possible harm to a corporate reputation does not serve to surmount the strong presumption in favor of public access to court proceedings and records." Every business is "entitled to a fair trial, not a private one," the Maryland court said.[84]

JURY SELECTION A unanimous Supreme Court declared that the selection of the jury, as well as the trial itself, must ordinarily be open to the public. In fact, in the first of two closed-courtroom cases named *Press-Enterprise Co. v. Riverside County Superior Court,* the Court treated jury selection as part of the trial.[85] The Court said, in effect, that public confidence in the criminal justice system derives in part from public access to the questioning of potential jurors. Public confidence in the courts generally should be given priority over undocumented concerns about the right to a fair trial for the defendant or violations of the privacy of citizens asked to be jurors, the Court said.

In what is known as *Press-Enterprise I,* the Press-Enterprise Company of Riverside, California, successfully appealed the closing of jury selection before the trial of Albert Greenwood Brown, Jr. Brown, an African American, had been charged with the rape and murder of a white teenage girl in California. He had been convicted previously of raping a white adolescent girl. The judge refused to allow the voir dire examination of jurors to be open to the public and the press for two reasons. He wanted to protect Brown's right to a fair

[84]State v. Cottman Transmission Sys. Inc., 542 A.2d 859 (Md. Ct. Spec. App. 1988). *See also* Publicker Indus. v. Cohen, 733 F.2d 1059 (3d Cir. 1984); Newman v. Graddick, 696 F.2d 796 (11th Cir. 1983).

[85]464 U.S. 501, 508 (1984). *See also* ABC, Inc. v. Stewart, 360 F.3d 90 (2d Cir. 2004) (closure of voir dire was invalid).

trial and the privacy rights of jurors who "had some special experiences in sensitive areas that do not appear to be appropriate for public discussion." After a voir dire lasting six weeks, all but three days of which were closed to the press, the judge also refused to release the transcripts of the questioning. California appellate courts refused to review the case, but the U.S. Supreme Court vacated the judge's order and remanded the case for further consideration.

Chief Justice Burger, writing for eight of the nine justices, said the process of jury selection has been presumptively open to the public since the development of trial by jury. Burger contended the selection of jurors has always been an integral part of the public trial. At times, the courts even selected jurors from members of the public attending the trial. Although Burger said, "no right ranks higher than the right of the accused to a fair trial," he contended the right of the accused and the right of the public to attend the voir dire were closely connected. Burger said:

> The value of openness lies in the fact that people not actually attending trials can have confidence that standards of fairness are being observed; the sure knowledge that *anyone* is free to attend gives assurance that established procedures are being followed and that deviations will become known.

To overcome the presumption that jury selection must be open, Burger said, a judge first must specify an overriding interest, such as the defendant's right to a fair trial or jurors' rights to privacy. Second, the judge must establish that the overriding interest cannot effectively be protected except through closure. For example, Burger said, a judge may decide that closure is the only way to protect the privacy of a prospective juror who, during the voir dire, is asked whether he or she has ever been sexually assaulted. Third, the judge must document in writing why closure is essential to protect a "higher value." That is, the judge will need to explain why the answer of the prospective juror is entitled to privacy. Fourth, the closure can last only as long as necessary to meet the needs of the single juror. Burger said the California trial judge in *Press-Enterprise I* had not supported his closure order by findings that either Brown's right to a fair trial or the privacy of the jurors was threatened by questioning the jurors in public.

PRETRIAL HEARINGS Since 1984, the Supreme Court has extended a First Amendment right of access to hearings held before the trial begins. Although pretrial hearings are not technically part of trials, they often take on the significance of trials. Legal authorities contend that 90 percent of criminal cases never reach the trial stage, often because they are resolved as a result of pretrial hearings. Consequently, a pretrial hearing often presents the only opportunity for a public proceeding in a criminal case.

Pretrial hearings are often held to determine whether there is enough evidence for a judge to find "probable cause" that a defendant committed a crime. Judges may also hold pretrial hearings to consider whether potential evidence, such as a confession or a weapon, may be presented to a jury during a trial. Judges also hold hearings to consider whether bail should be denied or the courtroom closed.

If a pretrial hearing is reported in the media, potential jurors can read about, and perhaps be influenced by, information such as a confession that might not be admissible as evidence during a trial. Because jurors are not selected until a case comes to trial, judges cannot sequester them or order them not to read or listen to news reports about pretrial hearings.

In the early 1980s, trial courts were reluctant to open pretrial hearings to the public, in part because of a 1979 U.S. Supreme Court decision. In 1979, before recognizing a First Amendment access to courtrooms, the Court said in *Gannett Co. v. DePasquale* that the press and public do not have a right to attend pretrial hearings.[86] Only one year after *Gannett,* the Supreme Court ruled in *Richmond Newspapers* that trials are presumptively open under the First Amendment. However, the Court did not overrule *Gannett* in *Richmond Newspapers, Globe Newspaper Co.,* or *Press-Enterprise I.* In 1986, the Court ruled in *Press-Enterprise II* that the public and the press have a First Amendment right to attend pretrial hearings held to determine whether there is probable cause to believe a suspect has committed a crime. Although the Supreme Court did not directly overrule *Gannett* in *Press-Enterprise II,* the Court's reliance on the First Amendment right of access cast considerable doubt on *Gannett*'s continued validity.[87]

In *Press-Enterprise II,* a magistrate in Riverside, California, excluded the press from a preliminary hearing scheduled to determine whether there was probable cause that a nurse had murdered a dozen hospital patients. Nurse Robert Diaz was charged with killing the patients with massive doses of the heart drug lidocaine. The magistrate said closure was necessary because Diaz's case had attracted national publicity and "only one side may get reported in the media." After a forty-one-day hearing, the magistrate ordered a trial because he determined there was probable cause to believe that Diaz committed the murders. The magistrate refused to release transcripts of the hearing.

The California Supreme Court, upholding the magistrate's order to close the courtroom, said that defendants must demonstrate only a "reasonable likelihood" that a public hearing would prejudice their right to a fair trial. However, the U.S. Supreme Court, by a 7-2 margin, said the First Amendment requires that defendants seeking to close pretrial hearings must demonstrate a greater danger to their rights than a "reasonable likelihood."[88] Instead, the Court said, defendants must provide specific evidence that an open courtroom would present a "substantial probability" of endangering their rights to a fair trial. In addition, echoing *Press-Enterprise I,* the Supreme Court said judges must consider whether alternatives to closure could protect the rights of the defendant. Further, closure must be for only as short a time as necessary to ensure a fair trial.

Chief Justice Burger, again writing for the Court, said the public ought to have access to pretrial hearings for the same reasons that access is important for criminal trials and jury selection. Most preliminary hearings, including those in California, are traditionally open, Burger said. In addition, preliminary hearings are enough like trials that the Court could conclude that public access is as essential to success of the hearings as it is to the success of trials. As in trials, Burger said, preliminary hearings in California afford the accused the right to appear before a magistrate, to be represented by an attorney, to cross-examine hostile witnesses, to present evidence on behalf of the defense, and to challenge illegally obtained evidence.

Burger said the preliminary hearing in California "is often the final and most important in the criminal proceeding" and sometimes the only chance for the public to observe the

[86]443 U.S. 368 (1979).
[87]*See also* El Vocero de Puerto Rico v. Puerto Rico, 508 U.S. 147 (1993) (per curiam).
[88]478 U.S. 1 (1986).

criminal justice system at work in a given case. The attendance of the public and the press at open hearings is also important because, unlike a trial, there is no jury to guard against the "corrupt or overzealous prosecutor" and "the compliant, biased, or eccentric judge."

However, as forcefully as the Supreme Court emphasized the importance of access in *Press-Enterprise II* and the other decisions, the Court will not stop all court closures. First, the Supreme Court has said the right of access is not absolute. Trial judges can constitutionally close courts if they can document an overriding interest that cannot be protected by alternative means and if they can narrowly restrict the closure as required in the *Press-Enterprise* cases. In addition, state courts are still apt to be influenced by state constitutions, statutes, and common-law traditions that may have more relaxed standards for closure than the relatively new First Amendment guarantees. Although state law cannot contradict the First Amendment, substantial leeway for interpretation in individual cases remains after the recent Supreme Court opinions.

In addition, the Supreme Court's recent emphasis on the presumption of openness for trials and pretrial hearings should not affect the historic secrecy of grand juries. Because grand juries prepare indictments, rather than determine guilt, they play a different role in the legal system than pretrial hearings and trials. Reports about grand jury proceedings could disseminate unsubstantiated charges and hearsay that might not lead to an indictment. No judge is present in a grand jury hearing to ensure that the evidence sought is relevant to the investigation. Further, those who testify generally do not have the right to counsel or the right to cross-examine others who testify, as they would during pretrial proceedings and trials. In *Press-Enterprise II,* all nine justices supported opinions emphasizing the importance of secrecy for grand jury proceedings.

The press has no First Amendment or common-law right of access to judicial hearings or documents connected to grand jury proceedings, the U.S. Court of Appeals for the District of Columbia said.[89] The court denied media access to grand jury hearings and documents that would reveal grand jury issues or processes in the investigation of President Clinton's relationship to former White House aide Monica Lewinsky. Neither the First Amendment nor the common law permits violating grand jury secrecy, the court said.

◇ Summary ◇

In four rulings over six years in the early 1980s, the U.S. Supreme Court emphasized the First Amendment right of the public and press to attend judicial proceedings. In 1980, in *Richmond Newspapers v. Virginia,* the Court said that the public and the press have a First Amendment right to attend trials, which are presumptively open unless the state can document an overriding interest in closure. In *Globe Newspaper Co.,* the Court said that statutes providing for automatic closures are unconstitutional. In *Press-Enterprise I,* the Court said that the First Amendment protects against the closure of the jury selection process. In *Press-Enterprise II,* the Court extended the presumption of openness to pretrial hearings. In the series of courtroom-closure cases, the Court has established that judicial proceedings can ordinarily be closed only for compelling reasons that are carefully substantiated. A judge must consider alternatives to closure and must limit closure to only as

[89] *In re* Motions of Dow Jones & Co., Inc., 142 F.3d 496 (D.C. Cir.), *cert. denied,* 525 U.S. 820 (1998).

long as necessary. Thus far, most courts considering closure have not distinguished between criminal and civil cases. Grand jury proceedings remain closed, however. Juvenile court proceedings, traditionally closed, are sometimes open to the public.

Access to Court Records

Official court records long have been open for inspection and copying by the public and the press under common law. Recently, many appellate courts have said access to records also is guaranteed by the First Amendment. The Supreme Court has not directly established a First Amendment right of access to judicial records, but the *Press-Enterprise* cases establishing a right of access to jury selection and pretrial hearings also included access to sealed transcripts. Chief Justice Burger's majority opinions in both cases seemed to assume that the public has the same right of access to the transcripts of the pretrial hearings as it has to the hearings themselves.

Both state and federal appellate courts usually support a right of access to official court documents, particularly to those used as evidence in court, unless a compelling need for nondisclosure is demonstrated. In a government attempt to prosecute automobile maker John DeLorean on charges of conspiring to import cocaine, the U.S. Court of Appeals for the Ninth Circuit said that court records could be sealed only if "strictly and inescapably necessary" to ensure a fair trial for the defendant.[90] The Ninth Circuit said a district court judge had improperly closed records pertaining to whether DeLorean should be confined before his trial and documents containing allegations of government misconduct during the DeLorean investigation.

The Ninth Circuit said such pretrial documents often are important to a public understanding of the judicial process. The appeals court said the district court failed to satisfy all three of the tests that must be applied before documents could be sealed. First, the judge had not demonstrated there was a substantial probability DeLorean would not receive a fair trial if the documents were released. Second, the judge had not established that alternatives to closure would inadequately protect DeLorean's rights. Finally, the judge did not demonstrate a substantial probability that closure would be effective in protecting DeLorean's rights.

Several federal courts have found that the presumption of openness extends to the right of broadcasters to copy tapes used as evidence in court. For example, the U.S. Court of Appeals for the Third Circuit said broadcasters could not be prohibited from copying tapes made during a controversial FBI "sting" operation known as Abscam.[91] The three major broadcast networks and Westinghouse Broadcasting, Inc., sought video and audio tapes played in open court during the bribery trial of two Philadelphia city council members. The Third Circuit said the broader dissemination of information already made public increased the chance that the Abscam trial could provide a catharsis for community hostility and ensure that the defendants were treated fairly by judges and lawyers, goals emphasized in the Supreme Court's decision in *Richmond Newspapers.* The Third Circuit said broadcasts of the tapes would give persons other than those who attended the trial a chance to observe a significant public event. The court said defense arguments that

[90]Associated Press v. U.S. Dist. Court, 705 F.2d 1143 (9th Cir. 1983).

[91]*In re* NBC, 648 F.2d 814 (3d Cir. 1981). *See also In re* Application of NBC [United States v. Myers], 635 F.2d 945 (2d Cir. 1980); United States v. Jenrette, 653 F.2d 609 (D.C. Cir. 1981).

additional publicity could prejudice a new trial were only speculative. Even if a new trial were necessary, the court said, the voir dire examination of potential jurors could be employed to avoid seating biased jurors. The Third Circuit also said that tapes could be edited to protect nondefendants whose reputations might otherwise be damaged.

In contrast, both the Fifth and Sixth Circuits of the U.S. Courts of Appeals turned down requests to copy tapes because of perceived risks to the defendants' Sixth Amendment rights.[92] Both courts said that a right of access was only one of many issues to be considered. Both courts relied on *Nixon v. Warner Communications, Inc.*, a 1978 Supreme Court decision that prevented the copying of White House tapes of former president Richard Nixon. In *Nixon,* the Supreme Court held that broadcasters and record companies did not have the right to copy the Nixon tapes for broadcasting and sale to the public. The tapes had been used as evidence at the trials of presidential aides charged with obstructing justice during the Watergate investigation. The Supreme Court acknowledged "a general right to inspect and copy public records and documents" at the discretion of the judge.[93] However, the Court held that the public's common-law right of access had been superseded by congressional action creating a procedure for processing and releasing the tapes to the public.[94] The First Amendment had not been violated because the press had been allowed to listen to the tapes and had been given transcripts during the trial.

Federal appeals courts have been divided not only on the right of broadcasters to copy tapes but also on the media's right of access to records that have not been introduced into evidence in court. Many of the conflicts over access to records involve materials used by lawyers during the discovery process in cases that never come to trial. Chapter 1 of this book discussed the discovery process, which allows both parties in a legal dispute to investigate documents and question witnesses that might be material to a case. A court can compel one party to disclose discovery information to the other, sometimes accompanying the order with a confidentiality order guaranteeing that the information will not be made public.

A Supreme Court case involving both compelled discovery and a protective order, *Seattle Times v. Rhinehart,* has strongly influenced lower courts since it was decided in 1984. In *Rhinehart,* discussed earlier in this chapter, the Supreme Court said a trial court did not violate the First Amendment when it prohibited newspapers from publishing information obtained during discovery in a libel suit. The Court said that prohibiting the publication of information obtained only because of a court order was not a classic prior restraint that almost always violates the First Amendment. Even so, the Court said, the First Amendment right to publish could be restricted only if a substantial governmental interest was at stake. In *Rhinehart,* the Court said the need to prevent the abuse of the rules requiring compelled discovery overrode First Amendment values. The Seattle and Walla Walla newspapers could not claim a First Amendment right to publish information that might invade privacy and damage reputations if those materials were obtained only because the newspapers were litigants in a civil suit.

[92]United States v. Beckham, 789 F.2d 401 (6th Cir. 1986); Belo Broadcasting Corp. v. Clark, 654 F.2d 423 (5th Cir. 1981). *See also* Oregon *ex rel.* KOIN-TV, Inc. v. Olsen, 711 P.2d 966 (Or. 1985); United States v. Edwards, 672 F.2d 1289 (7th Cir. 1982).

[93]435 U.S. 589 (1978).

[94]Presidential Recordings and Materials Preservation Act, Pub. L. No. 93-526, 88 Stat. 1695 (1974).

Before and after *Rhinehart,* some courts have ruled that the need to protect such social and economic values as privacy and trade secrets might overcome the right of access to certain court documents. In 1983, the year before *Rhinehart* was decided, the U.S. Court of Appeals for the Sixth Circuit upheld an order protecting information about 423 questionable loans made by the United American Bank. The documents included the names of borrowers, the amounts of each loan, and "extensive discussion of each borrower's financial condition, prospects and personal life." The documents had been sealed under a protective order by a district court judge when they were filed in a suit trying to stop the Federal Deposit Insurance Corporation from closing the bank. When the *Knoxville News-Sentinel* and the *Knoxville Journal* appealed, the Sixth Circuit ruled "the long established" presumption of public access had to yield to statutory restrictions on the disclosure of bank records. The court cited several federal statutes to support the argument that Congress intended that "the banking records of individuals be kept in strict confidence." The court said the borrowers were not responsible for the litigation and their interest in privacy was "sufficiently compelling to justify nondisclosure." The borrowers had a "justifiable expectation" that their names and financial records would not be revealed to the public.[95]

However, many courts hold that documents in both criminal and civil courts cannot automatically be sealed, even when the information contained in them might not be offered in evidence at trial. For example, the U.S. Court of Appeals for the First Circuit has said the federal rules governing civil suits create a presumption that pretrial discovery should take place in public. Therefore, in *Public Citizen v. Liggett Group,* the First Circuit said that documents surrendered in pretrial discovery to the relatives of a lung cancer victim could be made public.[96] The court upheld a lower court decision to release to health associations eighteen boxes of research documents prepared by a consultant for Liggett & Meyers Tobacco Company even though a trial was never held.

Liggett & Meyers claimed a general right of privacy in the documents and argued that allowing public access to pretrial discovery materials would excessively disrupt future litigation. The Public Citizen Litigation Group, representing the health organizations, said the public should know as much as possible about the hazards of smoking.

The First Circuit said federal rules permit the courts to seal pretrial documents in civil suits for "good cause" to protect persons "from annoyance, embarrassment, oppression or undue burden or expense." However, the court said the rules also require that pretrial discovery be public unless compelling reasons justify denying public access. The court noted Liggett & Meyers had not argued that documents sought by the health organizations contained trade secrets or other "specifically confidential material" that would have prevented them from being made public.

The Liggett & Meyers case represents a significant development in access litigation. Although judicial decisions affecting access to pretrial and trial documents have not yet changed substantially in light of *Richmond Newspapers* and its progeny, the fight for the disclosure of sensitive court documents has intensified. A few states have adopted laws or court rules that limit the power of courts to seal records connected to litigation.[97] Public interest groups

[95] *In re* Knoxville News-Sentinel, 723 F.2d 470, 477 (6th Cir. 1983).
[96] 858 F.2d 775 (1988), *cert. denied,* 488 U.S. 1030 (1989).
[97] *See, e.g.,* Fla. Stat. § 69.081; Tex. R. Civ. P. 769.

and the media have become increasingly aware that enormous amounts of information about public issues, such as the health hazards of smoking, are collected by attorneys in civil suits.

In addition, the press in particular has been aggressive in seeking documents during the criminal trials of such well-known persons as Terry Nichols, who, along with Timothy McVeigh, was tried for the Oklahoma City bombings.[98] The trial judge sealed inadmissible evidence, such as a report of Nichols's nine-hour statement to the FBI, which the court found to be hearsay.

The U.S. Court of Appeals for the Tenth Circuit sustained the trial court's action, using a form of the *Press-Enterprise II* test. The court said the press and public historically have not had access to evidence ruled inadmissible for presentation at trial. Nor is there any reason the press and public should know what evidence is inadmissible, the court said. Knowing about the inadmissible evidence will not help the public to better understand the criminal justice process, the court said.

Whether juror names have been traditionally publicly available was prominent during the high-profile 2007 trial of media tycoon Conrad Black at which Black was convicted of obstruction of justice and mail fraud stemming from complicated maneuvers diverting money to him from Hollinger International shareholders. To accommodate the more than 400 journalists covering the trial, the judge reserved half of the courtroom seats for journalists and arranged a live audio and video feed in two overflow courtrooms.

During the trial, the judge refused to publicly release the names and addresses of the jurors, claiming disclosure of this information in such a highly publicized case would create the risk that jurors would be subjected to prejudicial contact.[99] Voir dire had been open to the public, as required by *Press-Enterprise I.* But unlike public access to voir dire, which promoted the fairness of the proceedings, the court said disclosure of juror names raised the prospect of jury tampering and other contact harmful to a fair trial. Moreover, the court found protecting juror privacy during a trial was a well-established practice. Even assuming there was a First Amendment right to the information, it was outweighed by the defendant's right to a fair trial.

After the verdict, the jurors' names and addresses were released. When reporters gathered for an expected press conference with the jury members, a bailiff announced, "The jury has elected not to speak to the press."

◇ Summary ◇

Most court records are presumed by appellate courts to be open. However, lower court judges may seal records, particularly if the records have not been introduced into evidence in court. Courts have disagreed when asked to decide whether broadcasters may copy videotapes introduced into evidence in court.

Interviewing Jurors

In extraordinary cases such as those involving organized crime figures, juror anonymity is protected, and journalists are prohibited from initiating interviews with jurors who wish to remain anonymous after the verdict. In other high-profile cases in which juror identity is

[98]United States v. McVeigh, 119 F.3d 806 (10th Cir. 1997), *cert. denied,* 522 U.S. 1142 (1998).
[99]United States v. Black, 483 F. Supp.2d 618 (N.D. Ill. 2007).

known, judges may still seek to restrict press interviews with jurors. Appellate courts have upheld reasonable restrictions on postverdict press interviews with jurors.

A federal appellate court upheld a restriction on juror interviews in a highly publicized Louisiana racketeering case. The trial judge prohibited interviews with jurors concerning their deliberations but allowed interviews concerning their general reactions or the verdict. The U.S. Court of Appeals for the Fifth Circuit said journalists do not have a special First Amendment right of access to matters unavailable to the public. Because the public is not entitled to information about jury deliberations, the court said, neither is the press. To hold otherwise, the court said, would be to compromise jury secrecy, necessary for candid discussions.[100]

In another highly publicized Louisiana case, an anonymous jury was empaneled because two of the defendants had previously pled guilty to witness tampering. At the conclusion of the trial, the judge told the jurors that their anonymity would be protected unless they chose to be publicly identified. The judge also prohibited jurors from publicly discussing their deliberations but said they could discuss their general reactions to the trial. None of the jurors wished to be identified publicly. The Fifth Circuit upheld the trial court's action, concluding that the interest in protecting jurors from postverdict harassment and invasions of privacy justified the restriction on newsgathering. The appellate court added, "If jurors voluntarily waive their anonymity and consent to interviews on matters other than jury deliberations, so be it. They need not become unwilling pawns in the frenzied media battle over these cases."[101]

Recently, the New Jersey Supreme Court upheld a trial court's order prohibiting media representatives from interviewing jurors after a highly publicized murder trial ended in a mistrial.[102] The trial court feared that interviews with jurors in the mistrial case would chill the free exchange of ideas among jurors in a retrial. The state supreme court found this fear to be too speculative a basis to justify the restriction. However, the supreme court believed that juror interviews "might reveal some insight into the jury's deliberative process" that would give the prosecution a significant advantage at the retrial and violate the defendant's Sixth Amendment rights. The risk that juror interviews would benefit the prosecution was sufficiently important to justify the interview ban. Moreover, the supreme court noted that the ban expired on the return of a verdict in the retrial.

A ban on juror interviews that is not narrowly tailored to serve a sufficiently important interest will be found unconstitutional. For example, the U.S. Court of Appeals for the Tenth Circuit found impermissibly overbroad a judge's order that prevented jurors from discussing the case with anyone.[103] The judge offered no reason for the restriction, nor was the order tailored to protect the confidentiality of jury deliberations. The Tenth Circuit stated:

> It would have been constitutionally permissible for the court routinely to instruct jurors that they may refuse interviews and seek the aid of the court if interviewers persist after they express a reluctance to speak. It could have told the jurors not to discuss the specific votes and opinions of noninterviewed jurors in order to encourage free deliberation in the jury room. But the court could not issue a sweeping restraint forbidding all contact between the press and former jurors without a compelling reason.

[100] United States v. Cleveland, 128 F.3d 267 (5th Cir. 1997), *cert. denied,* 523 U.S. 1075 (1998).
[101] United States v. Brown, 250 F.3d 907 (5th Cir. 2001).
[102] State v. Neulander, 173 N.J. 193, 801 A.2d 255 (N.J. 2002), *cert. denied,* 537 U.S. 1192 (2003).
[103] Journal Publishing Co. v. Mechem, 801 F.2d 1233 (10th Cir. 1986).

While acknowledging the trial court's power to impose limited restrictions on juror interviews, the Tenth Circuit concluded that the order impermissibly interfered with the news media's First Amendment right to gather information.

Summary

Judges have the authority to reasonably restrict interviews with jurors. However, these restrictions must be narrowly tailored to serve an important interest, such as preserving the confidentiality of jury deliberations. In cases where an anonymous jury is empaneled, judges may prevent the press from contacting jurors who wish to remain anonymous.

Voluntary Cooperation

An informal remedy for prejudicial publicity is voluntary cooperation among the courts, law enforcement agencies, and the press. In several states, lawyers, judges, law enforcement officers, and journalists have agreed to voluntary guidelines for the handling of criminal pretrial publicity. In the early 1970s, at least two dozen states adopted guidelines that encouraged the release of basic information about arrests and discouraged the publication of information prejudicial to the rights of criminal defendants. The guidelines varied widely, but most substantially paralleled the Katzenbach Rules mentioned earlier in the chapter. The guidelines recognized the right of the public to be informed about activities in the criminal justice system and the right of editors to decide what to print. But they also recognized that an accused person is presumed innocent until proven guilty and has the right to a trial by an impartial jury under the Sixth Amendment.

Most of the guidelines, such as those still used in New York, said that law enforcement officers should release to the press a suspect's name and address, the identity of the investigating agency, the text of the charge, and circumstances directly related to the arrest. The New York guidelines, like most others, warn against the publication of confessions, the possibility of a guilty plea, opinions about the character or reputation of a defendant, opinions about evidence and potential witnesses, and the results of such investigative techniques as ballistics tests and lie detector tests. The New York guidelines warn that the latter information "may tend to create dangers of prejudice without serving a significant law enforcement function."[104] However, most guidelines, like those in New York, include statements emphasizing that only the media have the right to decide what to publish. The guidelines do not provide for sanctions for violations of the guidelines other than adverse publicity and peer disapproval.

Most of the guidelines were adopted in the wake of the 1966 Supreme Court opinion *Sheppard v. Maxwell.* Press-court relations deteriorated rapidly after the Supreme Court ordered a retrial for Cleveland osteopath Dr. Sam Sheppard and admonished the judge in Sheppard's first trial for not adequately protecting the defendant against sensational news coverage. Soon after *Sheppard,* the American Bar Association, the U.S. Department of Justice, and the Judicial Conference of the United States adopted recommendations leading to restrictions on press coverage.

The Supreme Court's *Sheppard* decision also reinforced the findings of a 1964 presidential commission headed by Supreme Court Chief Justice Earl Warren. The Warren

[104]New York Fair Trial Free Press Conference, *New York Fair Trial Free Press Conference Principles and Guidelines 1993,* at 1–2.

Commission had strongly criticized the media for their lack of self-discipline in the news coverage of the assassination of President John F. Kennedy and the subsequent shooting of Lee Harvey Oswald by Jack Ruby. The commission had called for a professional code of conduct that demonstrated the press was sensitive to the rights of defendants to receive fair trials.[105]

Both the Warren Commission and the ABA recommended that representatives of the bar and the media develop standards for reporting criminal investigations and court proceedings.[106] Much of the press feared that formal standards of acceptable and unacceptable criminal reporting might lead to reduced press freedom. However, some media representatives preferred cooperation with law enforcement officers and court officials to officially imposed restrictions on information about trials. As a result, unofficial groups of lawyers, judges, law enforcement officers, and news media personnel in some states developed informal guidelines, such as those in New York. The guidelines generally recognized the problems that some reporting practices created for the criminal justice system without mandating what the media should print or broadcast. In some states, what became known as bench-bar-press discussions not only produced guidelines but also helped to reduce animosity and develop a spirit of cooperation. Some of the bench-bar-press groups established in the 1960s still operate.

However, in 2008, journalists, judges, and lawyers no longer sense the urgent need for the cooperation of the earlier era. In some cases, the bench-bar-press guidelines have been forgotten by the press. More often, guidelines are ignored in sensational cases. Press interest in guidelines waned when judges turned voluntary guidelines into court-imposed orders. *Nebraska Press Association v. Stuart,* discussed earlier in this chapter, arose out of Judge Stuart's order that the press observe the Nebraska Bar-Press Guidelines. In Washington State, a judge turned guidelines into requirements for access to his courtroom.

The Washington case was especially significant because the state had long been a leader in press-bar cooperation. Washington's Bench-Bar-Press Committee adopted guidelines in 1966. However, in 1981, Superior Court Judge Byron Swedburg told reporters they would not be admitted to a pretrial hearing unless they signed an agreement to abide by Washington's bench-bar-press guidelines. Swedburg wanted to limit pretrial news coverage after the arrest for attempted murder of the girlfriend of the "Hillside Strangler," a man notorious for multiple murders in Washington and California. The judge did allow that members of the public who were not journalists could attend the hearing without signing an agreement.

Many reporters refused to agree to Swedburg's conditions, believing that his order was a prior restraint. However, in *Federated Publications, Inc. v. Swedburg,* the state supreme court said Swedburg's order was not a prior restraint, particularly since the judge had set no penalty for violating the agreement.[107] The court said the order was a reasonable means of avoiding a closed hearing. The U.S. Supreme Court refused to review the case.

The implications of *Swedburg* became a major concern for the press. The state's media associations withdrew their support for the guidelines. In addition, the Washington case troubled the news media in other parts of the country. For example, the Arizona Newspaper Association withdrew its approval of the Arizona guidelines following *Swedburg.* In North

[105]*Report of the President's Commission on the Assassination of President John F. Kennedy* 241 (1964).

[106]American Bar Association Legal Advisory Committee on Fair Trial and Free Press, The Rights of Fair Trial and Free Press (1969).

[107]633 P.2d 74 (1981), *cert. denied,* 456 U.S. 984 (1982).

Carolina, guidelines were revised to stress the voluntary nature of the bench-bar-press agreements. Even more important, many media representatives to bench-bar-press groups across the country believed the spirit of cooperation had been undermined.

The media reaction to *Swedburg,* however, overlooks the fact that journalists frequently obtain access to information or to court proceedings by agreeing to conditions. In North Carolina, for example, judges sometimes permit reporters to attend juvenile proceedings only on the condition that names not be revealed. Judges by statute can exclude the public from a juvenile hearing unless the juvenile requests that the proceeding be open.[108]

Summary

In the late 1960s, lawyers, judges, and news media representatives met in many states to try to reduce tensions that had arisen over prejudicial pretrial publicity. More than twenty of these groups developed guidelines for the release, and reporting, of information related to criminal justice activity. Once the tension of the 1960s subsided, many of the guidelines fell into disuse. Media cooperation was, in part, threatened when judges required adherence to the guidelines in exchange for access to courtrooms.

Contempt Power

Judicial Authority

Members of the news media agreed to guidelines for the reporting of criminal proceedings in part because of the power of judges to control the courts. Judges can exercise the kind of control over a trial that was recommended in the 1966 Supreme Court decision *Sheppard v. Maxwell* because judges have the power to punish anyone who disobeys a judicial order.

American judges inherited from the English courts the power to cite for **contempt of court** any acts of disobedience or disrespect and any acts that interfere with the judicial process.[109] A single judge—often the same judge who was the object of the contempt—can decide what kind of conduct constitutes contempt of court, accuse a person of being in contempt, determine that person's guilt, and assess the punishment. In a matter of minutes, a person can be fined or sentenced to jail.

The judicial power to *summarily* cite for contempt of court is an unusual concentration of authority in our system of government. A holdover from authoritarian rule in England, the contempt power ensures judicial authority and order in the court. It gives judges the enforcement power necessary to protect the constitutional rights of persons under the jurisdiction of the courts. Anyone who disobeys a judge, including a journalist, may be faced with a contempt citation. Even if an appeals court later decides that a contempt order was unconstitutional, it may well uphold the fine or jail term imposed by the trial judge. The appellate courts do not want to encourage doubts about judicial authority in the courtroom.

However, there are limits on the contempt power that curb its abuse. Most of those limits apply to both civil and criminal contempt.

[108]N.C. Gen. Stat. § 7A-629. *See also* Sacramento Bee v. U.S. Dist. Court, 656 F.2d 477 (9th Cir. 1981), *cert. denied*, 456 U.S. 983 (1982).

[109]*See* Ronald Goldfarb, *The Contempt Power* 1 (1971).

Civil Contempt versus Criminal Contempt

The differences in the two kinds of contempt, civil and criminal, do not parallel the distinctions between civil and criminal law. Rather, civil and criminal contempt can be distinguished by the purpose of a contempt order and a difference in the assessment of penalties.[110]

A civil contempt citation is coercive; it is applied to get someone to do something. The penalty stays in force until the court's directives are obeyed or become moot. Civil contempt is usually imposed on a person who refuses to obey an order intended to protect one of the parties in a court case. In mass media law, judges most often use civil contempt when a reporter refuses to reveal confidential news sources. Journalists are cited for contempt because they refuse to give possible evidence to one of the parties in a legal dispute. Myron Farber of the *New York Times* was sentenced to jail and fined $1,000 a day for civil contempt after he refused to divulge his notes in a murder trial. Farber spent forty days in jail after refusing to let the judge review the notes.

In civil contempt, a judge can order the person charged with contempt to be locked up until he or she agrees to obey the court. In a sense, people charged with civil contempt hold the keys to their own cells. They can free themselves by complying with the court order. Many states have limited the amount of time a person can serve in jail.

In contrast, a criminal contempt citation punishes disrespect for the court, such as obstruction of court proceedings or verbal abuse of the judge. The penalty could be a fine, a jail sentence, or both. In Colorado, a court held two reporters and their newspaper, the *Boulder Daily Camera,* in contempt after the reporters questioned jurors in a murder trial. As a result of the reporters' actions, the jurors were dismissed and jury selection had to be repeated. In lieu of a fine, the reporters and the newspaper were ordered to reimburse the parties in the case and the state judicial department for the costs of four additional days of trial. The reporters and the newspaper also had to pay the costs incurred by the state for prosecuting them for contempt.[111]

A journalist who refuses to reveal confidential sources could be cited for both civil and criminal contempt. A judge can cite a reporter for civil contempt in an effort to coerce a reporter to reveal sources and for criminal contempt for disobeying an order of the court. This happened in the case of Myron Farber, the *New York Times* reporter mentioned earlier. In addition to his fine and jail sentence for civil contempt, Farber was fined $1,000 and ordered to spend six months in jail—a sentence later suspended—for disobeying the court.

The Supreme Court has ruled that those sentenced to jail for criminal contempt for more than six months have a right to a jury trial.[112] Additionally, in cases involving "serious" fines, such as the $64 million fine imposed on a union for out-of-court violations of an injunction, the Court has ruled criminal procedural protections, such as trial by jury, the right to counsel, and proof beyond a reasonable doubt, are necessary to prevent the arbitrary exercise of judicial power.[113] The Court has not yet granted the same procedural right to persons cited for civil contempt.

[110]*See* Luis Kutner, "Contempt Power: The Black Robe; A Proposal for Due Process," 39 *Tenn. L. Rev.* 1, 8 (1971).
[111]*In re* Stone, 703 P.2d 1319 (Colo. Ct. App. 1985).
[112]Bloom v. Illinois, 391 U.S. 194 (1968).
[113]United Mine Workers of America v. Bagwell, 512 U.S. 821 (1994).

Limits on Judicial Power

The U.S. Constitution and federal law limit the power of judges to cite for contempt of court, particularly for behavior outside of the judge's presence. The limits are important to journalists because they protect the publication of information and comment about the courts.

FIRST AMENDMENT Supreme Court decisions in the 1940s virtually eliminated the use of contempt citations to punish publications or broadcasts about court proceedings, especially for the criticism of judicial behavior. In *Bridges v. California,* the Supreme Court ruled that contempt citations issued in response to published criticism of judges violated the First Amendment.[114] By a 5-4 margin, the Court said that judges could not hold journalists or speakers in contempt absent a clear and present danger of a miscarriage of justice.

In *Bridges,* an official of the International Longshoremen-Warehousemen's Union was held in contempt after newspapers reported that he said that a judge's decision in a union dispute was "outrageous." At about the same time, the *Los Angeles Times* published three editorials commenting about cases pending before judges; the newspaper was found guilty of contempt of court and fined. The convictions of the union official and the newspaper were upheld by the California Supreme Court but overturned by the U.S. Supreme Court. Justice Hugo Black, writing the Court's majority opinion, said "the only conclusion supported by history" is that those who adopted the Constitution "intended to give to liberty of the press . . . the broadest scope that could be countenanced in an orderly society." Black said the contempt citations punished speech about important controversial topics "at the precise time" when the public interest in those issues would be at its peak. Drawing on language used by the Supreme Court in sedition cases, Black said the criticism of pending court cases could be punished only if there was an "extremely high" degree of imminence of an "extremely serious" evil. Black said neither the union official's remarks nor the newspaper editorials met this standard.

Five years later, in *Pennekamp v. Florida,* the Supreme Court said inaccurate editorials about a rape case before a Florida court did not present a clear and present danger to the administration of justice.[115] In the editorials, the *Miami Herald* accused judges of protecting criminals more than the law-abiding public. Justice Stanley Reed, writing for a unanimous Court, said, "Free discussion of the problems of society is a cardinal principle of Americanism—a principle which all are zealous to preserve." Reed said that discussing a case only after its conclusion might not adequately alert the public to the danger of "supposedly wrongful judicial conduct."

One year after *Pennekamp,* the Court again overturned journalists' contempt convictions in *Craig v. Harney*.[116] A trial judge concluded newspaper coverage and editorials about a pending case were intended to falsely present to the public the nature of the proceedings and influence the court. The Supreme Court reversed, stating there "is no special perquisite of the judiciary which enables it, as distinguished from other institutions of democratic government, to suppress, edit, or censor events which transpire in proceedings before it."

Bridges, Pennekamp, and *Harney* made it clear that the Supreme Court expects judges to have thick skins and that the criticism of judges should not lead to contempt of court

[114] 314 U.S. 252 (1941).
[115] 328 U.S. 331 (1946).
[116] 331 U.S. 367 (1947).

charges. As the Court stated in *Harney,* "the law of contempt is not made for the protection of judges who may be sensitive to the winds of public opinion. Judges are supposed to be men of fortitude, able to thrive in a hardy climate." However, courts might uphold contempt citations for other kinds of publications. For example, courts might be less tolerant of publications that seek to influence jury decisions. Courts might decide that jurors could be more easily intimidated than judges. In addition, *Bridges, Pennekamp,* and *Harney* did not involve prejudicial pretrial publicity or the violation of a judicial order.

JUDICIAL REACH AND DUE PROCESS The Supreme Court has not been alone in limiting the use of the judicial contempt power. Congress and many state legislatures have passed laws limiting the ability of judges to hold journalists in contempt for the publication of unfavorable stories or commentary. As early as 1831, Congress enacted a statute restricting federal judges to holding persons in contempt only if they refused to obey a judicial order or if their behavior in or near the courtroom could "obstruct the administration of justice."[117] The word *near* probably refers to the hallway outside the courtroom and maybe the sidewalks or grounds just outside the courthouse.[118]

In addition, persons cited by federal judges for contempt for activity taking place outside a courtroom ordinarily have a right to a notice of the nature of the charge and a hearing. In federal courts, persons who are cited for contempt have the right to an attorney, the right to cross-examine witnesses, the right to offer testimony, and frequently the right to a jury trial. If the contempt involves criticism or disrespect of a judge, that judge is disqualified from the proceeding.[119]

Limits on Appeals

The power of judges to cite for contempt of court with only limited opportunities for appeal presents particular problems for journalists when a judge has issued a prior restraint order—that is, a judge has ordered reporters not to print or publish a news story. After the Supreme Court's decision in *Nebraska Press Association,* most prior restraint orders would be considered unconstitutional by appellate courts. However, if reporters do not print the news until they can appeal a judge's order, a story may lose its news value. If journalists do print the story in violation of a judge's order, they may be cited for contempt of court. The rule in most parts of the United States is that a citation for contempt of court stands even if an appellate court declares the original prior restraint order unconstitutional. In other words, a journalist can be jailed or fined for violating an order that infringes on the First Amendment. The reason is that appellate courts want to protect the authority of the trial courts even when the trial courts are wrong. As the U.S. Supreme Court stated in 1967, "respect for judicial process is a small price to pay for the civilizing hand of the law. . . ."[120]

The traditional rule upholding contempt citations—known as the Dickinson Rule—resulted from a decision of the U.S. Court of Appeals for the Fifth Circuit in 1972. The incident leading to *Dickinson v. United States* began when two reporters in Baton Rouge,

[117]18 U.S.C. § 401.
[118]Nye v. United States, 313 U.S. 33 (1940).
[119]Fed. R. Crim. P. 42(a) (3). *See* Ronald Goldfarb, *The Contempt Power* 68 (1971).
[120]Walker v. City of Birmingham, 388 U.S. 307 (1967).

Louisiana, tried to cover the hearing of a government-sponsored civil rights volunteer accused of conspiring to murder the mayor. A federal district judge ordered the news media not to report testimony given in the public proceedings, an order the two reporters disobeyed. The judge found the reporters in contempt of court and fined them $300 each. The reporters appealed.

The U.S. Court of Appeals for the Fifth Circuit agreed with the reporters that the judge's order was a prior restraint that violated the First Amendment. The Fifth Circuit said that a blanket ban on publication "cannot withstand the mildest breeze emanating from the Constitution."[121] However, the appeals court refused to overturn the contempt order.

Chief Judge John Brown said the principle that an injunction must be obeyed, regardless of the ultimate validity of the court order, was "well-established." Brown suggested that the reporters should have appealed the order rather than violating it. He acknowledged that an appeal created "thorny problems" given the timely nature of news. Brown concluded, however, that a judicial order must be obeyed absent a showing that it was "transparently invalid" or "patently frivolous." He said that the First Amendment does not give reporters the right to violate a judicial order with impunity without "strong indications that the appellate process was being deliberately stalled."

The case against the two reporters was returned to the district court judge to determine whether the punishment for contempt was "appropriate" given that the order disobeyed had been unconstitutional. The trial judge upheld his previous contempt order and the fines. The Fifth Circuit affirmed the lower court for the second time.[122]

In 1986, however, the U.S. Court of Appeals for the First Circuit overturned a contempt conviction of a newspaper that disregarded a judge's prior restraint order. In 1986 and in a related opinion in 1987, the court ruled that it was permissible to violate a "transparently unconstitutional" court order if a quick appeal to the order was not available.[123] The First Circuit reversed a contempt citation issued by the U.S. District Court for Rhode Island against the *Providence Journal* for printing, contrary to a judicial order, information about Raymond Patriarca, a reputed crime boss in New England. After Patriarca died in 1985, the paper obtained from the FBI the results of an illegal wiretap on Patriarca's phone in the 1960s. However, Patriarca's son obtained a court order barring publication in the *Journal* on the grounds that his own right of privacy would be violated. The *Journal* was cited for contempt of court in November 1986 when it printed a story based on the FBI file in violation of the court order.

A three-judge panel of the First Circuit reversed the contempt order in December 1986. The panel said the order was a "transparently invalid" infringement of the First Amendment because the federal district judge had failed to meet the heavy burden of proof required by the U.S. Supreme Court before imposing a prior restraint. The court acknowledged the "bedrock principle" that court orders—even those later found to be unconstitutional—must be obeyed. However, the panel of judges said that when a court order "transparently" violates the First Amendment, the court "is acting so far in excess of its authority that it has no right to expect compliance," and the interest in preserving the integrity of the judicial system is not served by requiring it.

[121]465 F.2d 496 (5th Cir. 1972).

[122]Dickinson v. United States, 476 F.2d 373, *cert. denied,* 414 U.S. 979 (1973).

[123]*In re* Providence Journal, 820 F.2d 1342 (1st Cir. 1986), *modified,* 820 F.2d 1354 (1st Cir. 1987), *cert. dismissed,* 485 U.S. 693 (1988).

In May 1987, the First Circuit, after rehearing the case en banc, affirmed the panel's opinion but attached a modification. The full court said that editors in the future who are ordered not to print a story must make a "good faith effort" to appeal a prior restraint before they publish in violation of the order. When editors are ordered not to print a story, the court said, they may publish and still challenge the constitutionality of an order only "if timely access to the appellate court is not available or if [a] timely decision is not forthcoming."[124]

The U.S. Supreme Court dismissed *United States v. Providence Journal* on procedural grounds, leaving intact the First Circuit's ruling in favor of the newspaper.[125] However, the rule in *Providence Journal* holds only for the First Circuit and does not overturn *Dickinson* in the Fifth Circuit. Nor does the First Circuit's decision change the general judicial bias toward upholding a contempt of court order even if it is unconstitutional. Only a few state appellate courts—including those in Illinois,[126] Kansas,[127] and Washington[128]—have joined the First Circuit in allowing publishers who defied injunctions to challenge the validity of their contempt citations.

The limited application of the *Providence Journal* ruling is illustrated by contempt proceedings against CNN. As discussed earlier in this chapter, CNN was temporarily ordered not to broadcast audiotapes of deposed Panamanian president Manuel Noriega's prison telephone calls. While CNN's appeal of the order was pending before the Eleventh Circuit, the network repeatedly cablecast the tapes. Even though the restraining order was eventually vacated, Judge William Hoeveler found CNN to be in criminal contempt of court.[129] In late 1994, Judge Hoeveler gave CNN the option of paying a "substantial" fine or airing an apology and paying a smaller fine. The network chose to pay an $85,000 fine and air the apology, which was drafted by the judge. The apology stated that CNN "realizes that it was in error in defying the order of the court" and that the network should have awaited the results of its appeal rather than violating the court's order. The apology concluded, "Our justice system cannot long survive if litigants take it upon themselves to determine which judgments or orders of court they will or will not follow. . . . In the event unfavorable judgments are rendered, the right of appeal is provided. This is the course on which we should have relied. We regret that we did not."[130]

◇ Summary ◇

Judges have substantial authority to cite individuals for contempt of court. Criminal contempt citations are used to punish disruptive behavior. Judges issue civil contempt citations to coerce people into following a court order, such as revealing confidential news sources. Congress, state legislatures, and the courts have provided substantial protection against contempt citations for persons writing about the courts. However, persons ordered not to publish information about court activity may be punished for contempt even if the order itself is ultimately declared invalid.

[124]820 F.2d 1354 (1st Cir. 1987).
[125]485 U.S. 693 (1988).
[126]Cooper v. Rockford Newspapers, Inc., 365 N.E.2d 746 (Ill. App. Ct. 1977).
[127]State v. Alston, 887 P.2d 681 (Kan. 1994).
[128]State *ex rel.* Superior Court of Snohomish County v. Sperry, 483 P.2d 608 (Wash.), *cert. denied,* 404 U.S. 939 (1971).
[129]United States v. Cable News Network, Inc., 865 F. Supp. 1549 (S.D. Fla. 1994).
[130]"CNN Is Sentenced for Tapes and Makes Public Apology," *N.Y. Times,* Dec. 20, 1994, at B7.

CHAPTER 11

Protection of News Sources, Notes, and Tape

In addition to the conflicts between the courts and the press in the free press–fair trial debate discussed in the previous chapter, the dispute festers over court orders demanding the release of journalists' notes, tapes, and confidential news sources. On one side, many judges and lawyers believe that reporters should be required to testify in court like everyone else.

On the other side, journalists argue that their ability to report the news often depends on protecting the confidentiality of news sources.

In fact, reporters are frequently willing to go to jail, pay fines, or perform court-ordered community service rather than obey court orders requiring them to reveal the names of confidential sources. In one of the most famous cases, *New York Times* reporter Myron Farber spent forty days in jail and the *Times* paid $286,000 in fines when Farber refused to produce notes of his investigation into suspicious deaths in a New Jersey hospital. Farber's stories led to the murder indictment of Dr. Mario E. Jascalevich, who wanted to see Farber's notes for the preparation of his defense.

Farber said he refused to give up his notes because they would have revealed confidential sources he used to prepare his stories. Farber and other journalists argue that news sources will not talk to the media if they suspect their identities will be revealed. Unless reporters can promise confidentiality, they say, people who know about official corruption and criminal activity will keep quiet because they fear for their jobs or their safety if they "blow the whistle." If reporters cannot promise confidentiality to sources, Farber said, there would be less information for the public "on a variety of important and sensitive issues, all to the detriment of the public interest."[1]

However, judges order journalists to turn over notes and the names of sources to protect significant social interests such as the Sixth Amendment right of criminal defendants to obtain evidence in their favor and to confront witnesses against them. In the case of the *New York Times's* Myron Farber, Jascalevich wanted to know what the reporter was told by potential witnesses in his murder trial. Accused of poisoning hospital patients, Jascalevich wanted to know, for example, what Farber was told by Dr. Stanley Harris, the physician for several of the patients who died and who Jascalevich believed to be his "principal accuser."

In addition, law enforcement officials contend that journalists have a civic duty to testify against criminal suspects. Officials are frustrated when journalists write stories about drug possession and trafficking but will not contribute information to criminal investigations or testify in court. Reporter Robin Traywick was fined $1,400 because she refused to tell a grand jury the sources for stories about cocaine use she published in the *Richmond Times-Dispatch.* The grand jury was convened to investigate allegations in Traywick's stories that lawyers, judges, and other public officials were using cocaine and that some defendants arrested on drug-related charges were inexplicably receiving lenient treatment. Traywick's articles quoted sources who had been promised confidentiality.[2]

Finally, plaintiffs and defendants in civil suits sometimes contend that journalists possess information that could determine who wins and who loses their litigation. Plaintiffs suing the media for libel want access to story sources in order to prepare their cases. Richard Hargraves, an editorial writer for the *Belleville (Illinois) News-Democrat,* spent fifty-four hours in jail for refusing to reveal the names of sources for an editorial accusing a county official of lying to the public. The official, Jerry Costello, sued for libel and tried to learn the names of Hargraves's sources in order to prove that the editorial was false. Hargraves was released only when his sources revealed themselves.[3]

[1] *In re* Farber, 394 A.2d 330 (N.J. 1978).

[2] "Journalist Fined $1,400 for Refusing to Testify," *News Media & L.,* Mar.–Apr. 1983, at 46.

[3] "Column Leads to Jail," *News Media & L.,* Nov.–Dec. 1984, at 36.

Similarly, the testimony of five reporters was deemed to be critical to Wen Ho Lee's suit against the Departments of Justice and Energy for violating Lee's rights under the federal Privacy Act. Anonymous sources revealed to the press that Lee was the target of an investigation into security breaches at the Los Alamos nuclear research facility. Lee claimed these leaks, which included information about his employment history, finances, and results of polygraph examinations, violated the Privacy Act. When government officials proved to be evasive and uncooperative in helping Lee identify the leakers, a court ruled the testimony of reporters was necessary. The reporters balked and were held in contempt of court, a ruling sustained by the Court of Appeals for the District of Columbia Circuit.[4] The reporters avoided jail and fines when their news organizations paid Lee $750,000 to settle the case.

For many years, judges and legislatures have tried to reconcile the need for evidence in court with the desire of communicators to preserve the anonymity of their sources. The result so far is an uneasy compromise. In most states, reporters may withhold sources or notes unless a criminal defendant, a prosecutor, or a party in a civil suit proves a compelling reason for demanding them. Hence, much of the protection for reporters is provided on a case-by-case basis only after a court battle.

This chapter will discuss the statutes and judicial opinions that shield journalists from contempt citations if they refuse to testify. The chapter also will discuss congressional subpoenas, government access to journalists' telephone records, and police searches of newsrooms.

Protection under the Common Law

Before the 1970s, courts usually held that journalists deserved no special protection when ordered to reveal the names of confidential sources. The courts have generally not extended to journalists the common-law privilege that protects the confidential relationships between lawyers and clients, doctors and patients, and priests and penitents.

Lawyers and doctors, for example, are usually not required to testify in court about their clients or patients because society recognizes they render essential services that depend on confidentiality. Lawyers and doctors cannot effectively provide legal advice or practice medicine if clients and patients cannot be candid, assured that their confidences will not be revealed. Lawyers need to know all information pertinent to a criminal charge in order to provide the best defense. Doctors sometimes need to know intimate details about a patient's behavior to provide a correct diagnosis. Clients and patients will not be open and forthright, or might not seek help in the first place, if they believe that embarrassing or incriminating information might be made public.[5]

However, judges and legal scholars argue that few should be exempted from the responsibility of testifying in court. As more people are excused from telling what they know, fewer remain to contribute evidence in the search for truth in court. Courts traditionally have refused to excuse reporters from testifying because news sources do not depend on journalists for their personal welfare in the same way that patients depend on doctors or clients depend on lawyers. The privilege for journalists, when recognized, is not based as

[4]Lee v. DOJ, 413 F.3d 53 (D.C. Cir. 2005), *cert. denied,* 126 S.Ct. 2351 (2006).
[5]*See, e.g.,* John Henry Wigmore, 8 *Evidence in Trials at Common Law* §§ 2291, 2380a (McNaughton rev. ed. 1961).

much on a source's need to talk to a reporter as on the need for the public to receive information about crime and corruption that might otherwise remain unpublished.

In addition, critics of a journalistic privilege contend that reporters do not have the same professional preparation and oversight as lawyers and doctors do. Doctors and lawyers, unlike journalists, have at least three years of professional education in addition to a bachelor's degree. Doctors and lawyers have to meet educational requirements or pass tests before they can serve patients and clients. Doctors and lawyers are certified by state governments and subject to review by their peers.

Despite the courts' reluctance to protect the confidentiality of the journalist–news source relationship, a limited common-law privilege has emerged in a few state courts.[6] While some federal courts have recognized a federal common-law privilege,[7] recent cases, discussed later in this chapter, offer little hope for widespread federal judicial recognition of a common law-based privilege. Journalists have had more success relying on the U.S. Constitution and state statutes to rebuff subpoenas, judicial orders to testify in court (*subpoena ad testificandum*) or to produce notes, tapes, or documents in court (*subpoena duces tecum*).

Protection under the First Amendment

Although most courts do not recognize a common-law privilege for reporters who refuse to reveal confidential sources, many provide a limited First Amendment privilege. Strangely enough, the source of these rulings is *Branzburg v. Hayes,* a Supreme Court decision that appeared to say that journalists do not have constitutional protection when they refuse to reveal their news sources. However, lower courts have relied on the peculiar configuration of concurring and dissenting opinions in *Branzburg* to create a limited First Amendment privilege for journalists.

The Supreme Court

In *Branzburg v. Hayes,* a 5-4 majority of the U.S. Supreme Court rejected a privilege under the First Amendment for three reporters who had refused to testify before three different grand juries.[8] The Supreme Court decided the cases from Kentucky, California, and Massachusetts with one opinion.

One of the reporters, Paul Branzburg of the *Louisville Courier-Journal,* was appealing two court orders to testify before different grand juries investigating drug use and sales. In 1969, Branzburg had written about two young men he watched making hashish near Louisville. Branzburg promised not to reveal the men's identities and refused to identify them when called to appear before a grand jury. In a second article, in 1971, Branzburg described the two weeks he spent watching and interviewing several dozen unnamed drug users in Frankfort, Kentucky. He again refused to testify after being subpoenaed by a grand jury to discuss criminal activity he had witnessed. Although a Kentucky law protects reporters from being forced to reveal sources, a state appellate court said the statute did not protect journalists who personally observe criminal acts.

[6]*See, e.g.,* Senear v. Daily Journal-American, 641 P.2d 1180 (Wash. 1982).
[7]*See, e.g.,* Riley v. City of Chester, 612 F.2d 708 (3rd Cir. 1979).
[8]408 U.S. 665 (1972).

In a case decided at the same time as *Branzburg*, Earl Caldwell of the *New York Times* was subpoenaed to appear before a federal grand jury in Oakland, California. The grand jury ordered Caldwell, who covered the militant black organization known as the Black Panther party, to bring notes and audiotapes of interviews with Panther officers and other representatives. The grand jury was investigating allegations of Panther threats against President Nixon, Panther involvement in assassination plots, and Panther participation in riots. Caldwell refused to appear and was found in contempt of the grand jury. The U.S. Court of Appeals for the Ninth Circuit reversed the contempt order, and the U.S. government petitioned for certiorari.

The third case before the Supreme Court at the time of *Branzburg* also involved a journalist who had refused to answer grand jury questions about the Black Panthers. Paul Pappas, a television news reporter-photographer, covered civil disorders in New Bedford, Massachusetts, in 1970. He had been allowed into a barricaded store serving as the headquarters for the Black Panthers while they waited for a police raid. Two months later, Pappas told a grand jury what he had witnessed outside the Black Panthers' headquarters, but he refused to answer questions about what took place inside.

The three reporters told the grand juries that the First Amendment protected them from being forced to disclose confidential information. The reporters argued that if journalists were forced to reveal their confidential sources, people would be reluctant to speak to reporters. The First Amendment interest in a "free flow of information" would suffer. Caldwell refused even to enter the grand jury room, arguing that his appearance, even if he said nothing, would destroy his working relationship with the Black Panthers. Because grand jury proceedings are secret, Caldwell said, the Black Panthers could never be sure what he had said or refused to say behind closed doors. Caldwell said that his source's uncertainty about his grand jury appearance would drive "a wedge of distrust and silence between the news media and the militants," resulting in less public knowledge about Panther activities.

Denying a First Amendment privilege for journalists, a divided Court in *Branzburg* contrasted the rights of the press with the obligation of every citizen to answer questions relevant to a criminal investigation. Justice Byron White, writing a majority opinion for the Court, said he could not see why the public interest in law enforcement should be overridden by "the consequential, but uncertain, burden on news gathering" that might result from insisting that reporters testify before grand juries.

White, supported by four other justices, emphasized the importance of the long-standing principle that the public "has a right to every man's evidence," particularly during grand jury proceedings. He said that stopping drug trafficking, assassination plots, and violent disorders was a "fundamental function" of government. Grand juries, which determine whether there is reason to believe a crime has been committed and whether there is sufficient evidence to bring charges, play "an important role in fair and efficient law enforcement." White did not think that reporters should be protected from testifying about someone who had committed a crime or someone who had evidence of criminal conduct. He said the Court could not adopt the theory "that it is better to write about crime than to do something about it."

White said the journalists had not demonstrated that substantial numbers of sources would remain silent if journalists were forced to testify before grand juries. White claimed sources such as representatives of minority political groups would continue to speak to reporters because they needed the media to disseminate their views. He asserted that sources who were afraid of losing their jobs or who feared for their safety could trust their stories to officials as much as they could to the press.

White rejected the arguments of reporters Branzburg, Caldwell, and Pappas even though the three argued only for a qualified, rather than an absolute, privilege for reporters to withhold the names of sources. The reporters said they should not have to testify unless the government could establish that (1) a reporter had information relevant to a crime being investigated, (2) the information was not available from other sources, and (3) the need for the information was sufficiently compelling to override First Amendment concerns. But White said that although the privilege recommended by Branzburg, Caldwell, and Pappas would presumably reduce the number of times that reporters would have to testify, the conditional privilege would not provide the press with the certainty of confidentiality necessary to satisfy sources. Because the proposed privilege was conditional, White said, the press could never guarantee a source that confidentiality would be protected by a court.

In addition, White said, establishing the qualified privilege recommended by the three reporters would mean a substantial burden for judges. White said the privilege would force judges to resolve several legal issues each time a reporter was subpoenaed to testify. The courts would have to answer such questions as whether the reporter possessed useful confidential information or whether the law enforcement interest in the information outweighed First Amendment values.

White also did not want to force judges to decide who would qualify for a constitutional press privilege. Defining who was a journalist, he said, was "a questionable procedure in light of the traditional doctrine that liberty of the press is the right of the lonely pamphleteer who uses carbon paper or a mimeograph." He said that lecturers, political pollsters, scholars, and novelists, as well as newspaper publishers, disseminate information gathered from confidential sources. He added,

> Almost any author may quite accurately assert that he is contributing to the flow of information to the public, that he relies on confidential sources of information, and that these sources will be silenced if he is forced to make disclosures before a grand jury.

White said newsgathering, including the protection of confidential sources, is "not without its First Amendment protections." He said there is "no justification" for officials to harass the press in efforts to disrupt a journalist's relations with news sources. However, White said that legislators, rather than the courts, should weigh the need to protect confidential sources against the need for testimony. Congress and the state legislatures have the power to develop a statutory privilege. The task of judges is to uphold the law rather than to make it, White said.

Justice Lewis Powell, Jr., although the fifth vote in the *Branzburg* 5-4 decision, wrote a separate concurring opinion to emphasize "the limited nature" of the Court's ruling. Although Powell voted against Branzburg, Caldwell, and Pappas, he implied that journalists have more First Amendment protection than White had conceded. Unlike White, Powell said the needs of law enforcement and of journalists should be balanced on a case-by-case basis. He said news personnel might contest subpoenas if the information sought bears "only a remote and tenuous relationship to the subject of the investigation" or does not serve "a legitimate need of law enforcement."

Justice Potter Stewart, writing a dissenting opinion, would have granted the three reporters in *Branzburg* the qualified privilege they sought. Stewart, in an opinion supported by Justices William Brennan and Thurgood Marshall, rebuked the "Court's crabbed view of the First Amendment." He said that the "delicate and vulnerable" nature of First Amendment freedoms requires special safeguards. Stewart said reporters have a limited First Amendment right to refuse to reveal sources, a right that stems from society's interest "in a full and free flow of information to the public." Stewart, in contrast to White, said the right to publish information would be severely curtailed without protection to obtain it in the first place.

Stewart said confidential sources are particularly important for "sensitive" stories involving government officials, political figures, dissidents, and minority groups. Stewart said the Court's *Branzburg* decision would mean that "a public-spirited citizen, who is not implicated in any crime, will now be fearful of revealing corruption or other governmental wrongdoing." Because journalists could be forced to identify sources under court order, whistle-blowers might have to choose "between risking exposure by giving information or avoiding the risk by remaining silent."

Stewart said the Court's decision in *Branzburg* forces journalists into a choice between two bad alternatives. Journalists can risk a contempt of court citation for failing to reveal news sources, or they can violate professional ethics by disclosing the name of a confidential source. Journalists who disclose confidential sources would have difficulty establishing future confidential relationships, Stewart suggested.

Stewart acknowledged that grand juries must be able to compel "every man's relevant evidence" if the criminal justice system is to function fairly. But Stewart thought it would serve a greater public good if journalists had a partial exception to the rule that everyone must testify. Stewart said a qualified privilege for journalists would serve a public interest that parallels the interest served by the privilege accorded doctors and lawyers to withhold confidential information about their patients and clients. A reporter's privilege would "insure nothing less than democratic decision-making through the free flow of information to the public," Stewart said.

Stewart argued journalists should have a First Amendment privilege to withhold names and information unless officials satisfy "a heavy burden of justification" overcoming the privilege. Stewart said he would require the government to demonstrate there is:

1. a probable cause to believe that a reporter has information "clearly relevant" to a specific violation of law
2. evidence that the information sought cannot be obtained by alternative means less destructive of First Amendment values
3. "a compelling and overriding interest in the information"

Two of Stewart's points parallel those in Powell's concurring opinion. Both Stewart and Powell would require that a request for confidential sources be relevant to a specific investigation. Stewart said the relevance requirement prevents the government from conducting a fishing expedition for information at the expense of the media. Stewart said that in the case of *New York Times* reporter Earl Caldwell, the government had not shown that the grand jury was investigating any specific crime. The relevance requirement also could prevent harassment of reporters and sources.

Stewart also agreed with Powell that the government must demonstrate a need for a journalist's confidential information. However, Stewart would have imposed a heavier burden of proof on the government than Powell. Powell required only that a request for information serve a "legitimate need" of law enforcement rather than the "compelling and overriding" interest specified by Stewart.

Stewart agreed with the Ninth Circuit that the government had not established a compelling interest in Caldwell's testimony. Stewart said there was no evidence that Caldwell had information about illegal activities of the Black Panthers that he could give to the grand jury. On the other hand, Stewart believed that Caldwell had demonstrated that his ability to report on the Black Panthers would be impaired if he were required to appear before a grand jury.

Finally, Stewart said officials should have to prove they could not obtain the necessary information without forcing a journalist to testify, a point that Powell had not mentioned. Stewart said that if journalists were required to provide information that was available elsewhere, the flow of information to the public would be disrupted without a resulting benefit to the courts. In the *Caldwell* case, Stewart said, the government had not shown that it had tried alternative means to acquire the information it was seeking. Stewart wanted the government to show that the information it was seeking could not be obtained through police informants, other law enforcement agencies, or other witnesses.

Justice William Douglas, the fourth dissenter in *Branzburg,* argued that the First Amendment prohibited the government from requiring journalists to testify. His views, coupled with those of Stewart, Marshall, and Brennan, added up to four justices who believed in at least limited First Amendment protection for journalists who refused to reveal their sources. Justice Powell's concurring opinion, which arguably implied that some form of reporter's privilege should be recognized, muddied the waters. Justice Stewart later described the vote in *Branzburg* as perhaps "a vote of four and a half to four and a half."[9]

Due to *Branzburg*'s ambiguities, many lower courts began to create a qualified First Amendment privilege for journalists who refuse to disclose confidential information. Other courts, however, have followed the view of the majority in *Branzburg,* which denied a constitutional privilege, particularly when the facts of cases mirror the circumstances of Branzburg, Caldwell, and Pappas.

Lower Court Denial of Privilege

Courts are most likely to follow the precedent of Justice White's majority opinion in *Branzburg* when journalists are subpoenaed by grand juries, when they are asked to testify about something they witnessed, and when they are being asked to produce nonconfidential information rather than sources or information obtained because they promised confidentiality.

Courts ordinarily follow *Branzburg*'s majority when asked to decide whether a reporter should testify in front of a grand jury. When the Supreme Court held that reporters do not have a First Amendment right to refuse to testify before grand juries, the Court emphasized the importance of grand juries to effective law enforcement and the need for "every man's evidence." Lower courts have since contended that journalists deserve First Amendment protection against testifying only if they can establish that grand jury requests

[9]Potter Stewart, "Or of the Press," 26 *Hastings L.J.* 631, 635 (1975).

for testimony are conducted in bad faith or constitute harassment.[10] Reporters who are unable to meet this burden of proof are uniformly required to testify about the selling of drugs, the possession of weapons, or assaults.

Courts also frequently require reporters to testify when they are asked about events they witnessed rather than about the names of sources or information given to them by sources. In these cases, the reporters themselves are, in a sense, their own sources. Reporters Branzburg, Pappas, and Caldwell had been asked to reveal what they witnessed. In *Miami Herald Publishing Co. v. Morejon,*[11] the Florida Supreme Court held that the First Amendment did not protect a *Herald* reporter who refused to testify about events he had witnessed. Accompanying airport police officers, reporter Joe Achenbach watched the arrest of Aristides Morejon for smuggling four kilograms of cocaine into the country. The Florida court, relying on the majority in *Branzburg,* said that there is no privilege for reporters who are subpoenaed for their eyewitness observations of an event relevant to a court proceeding. The court refused to apply the Stewart three-part test because it said Achenbach was not relying on a confidential source that might "dry up" if revealed.

For many years, prosecutors, defendants, and judges frequently requested reporters' notes, tapes, and other information, but usually not journalists' sources. But subpoenas for sources and contempt citations for uncooperative journalists have increased dramatically, especially since September 11, 2001. Prosecutors investigating leaks of classified or restricted information have been especially aggressive in seeking the identity of journalists' sources. As the subpoenas and contempt citations mounted, both houses of Congress in 2005, 2006, and 2007 considered enacting federal shield statutes for the first time in decades.

In Providence, Rhode Island, Channel 10 reporter James Taricani was sentenced to six months home confinement for refusing to reveal the source of a leaked video showing a city hall official taking a bribe; the prosecutor had already deduced the identity of the source.[12] A heart transplant recipient with a pacemaker, Taricani was allowed to leave his home only for medical appointments. He was required to wear an electronic monitoring device around this ankle. Taricani was also prohibited from engaging in any business or profession, giving interviews, appearing on radio or television, and using the Internet. His six-month sentence was reduced after four months because he had fully complied with the conditions of confinement.

Two reporters for the San Francisco Chronicle, Mark Fainaru-Wada and Lance Williams, were sentenced to jail for a period of up to eighteen months in September 2006 for their refusal to comply with grand jury subpoenas. The reporters, who obtained secret grand jury transcripts about a government investigation of the distribution of steroids to prominent athletes, were asked to identify their sources in a subsequent investigation into the leak.[13] The judge stayed their imprisonment until the Court of Appeals for the Ninth Circuit could consider an appeal. While the case was on appeal, Troy Ellerman, a lawyer for an executive with the laboratory under investigation, identified himself as the reporters' source. Ellerman agreed to plead guilty to obstruction of justice and disobeying court orders. As part of the plea deal, prosecutors ceased their attempt to imprison the reporters.

[10]*See, e.g., In re* Lewis, 377 F. Supp. 297 (C.D. Cal.), *aff'd,* 501 F.2d 418 (9th Cir. 1974), *cert. denied,* 420 U.S. 913 (1975).
[11]561 So.2d 577 (1990).
[12]*In re* Special Proceedings, 373 F.3d 37 (1st Cir. 2004).
[13]*In re* Grand Jury Subpoenas to Fainaru-Wada and Williams, 438 F. Supp. 2d 1111 (N.D. Cal. 2006).

Journalists in Jail
2001–2008

Journalist	*Year*	*Time in Jail*	*Reason for Release*
Josh Wolf	2006–07	226 days	Provided video
Judith Miller	2005	85 days	Agreed to testify
Jim Taricani	2004–05	122 days	Complied with conditions of confinement
Vanessa Leggett	2001–02	168 days	Grand Jury term expired

FIGURE 11.1 Journalists jailed since 2001.

In Washington, a three-judge panel of the U.S. Court of Appeals unanimously ruled that two journalists must testify before a federal grand jury investigating unauthorized disclosure of undercover CIA operative Valerie Plame, whose name was leaked to Washington columnist Robert Novak, possibly in violation of federal law.[14] In each case, courts ruled that *Branzburg* precluded recognition of a journalist's privilege.

For more than thirty years, media lawyers have claimed that *Branzburg* does not preclude a qualified First Amendment privilege for journalist-source relationships, especially in cases not involving grand juries. In particular, media lawyers have claimed that Justice White's opinion for the *Branzburg* Court was a plurality opinion, and the crucial opinion was Justice Powell's concurring opinion, which arguably implied that some form of reporter's privilege should be recognized.[15] The court of appeals in the Plame case, however, characterized Justice White's *majority* opinion as "authoritative precedent," which "in no uncertain terms" rejected a reporter's privilege. Moreover, the court of appeals read Justice Powell as emphasizing that a First Amendment privilege to withhold source identity was available only in rare cases of bad faith investigations—a protection available to the public as well as the press. "The Constitution protects all citizens, and there is no reason to believe that Justice Powell intended to elevate the journalistic class above the rest," the appeals court wrote.

The appeals court concluded that the Supreme Court's *Branzburg* ruling precluded a First Amendment privilege in the grand jury setting. The appeals court wrote:

> We have pressed appellants for some distinction between the facts before the Supreme Court in *Branzburg* and those before us today. They have offered none, nor have we independently found any. Unquestionably, the Supreme Court decided in *Branzburg* there is no First Amendment privilege protecting journalists from appearing before a grand jury or otherwise providing evidence to a grand jury regardless of any confidence promised by the reporter to any source. The Highest Court has spoken and never revisited the question. Without doubt, that is the end of the matter.

[14] *In re* Grand Jury Subpoena, Miller, 397 F.3d 964 (D.C. Cir.), *cert. denied,* 125 S. Ct. 2977 (2005). *See generally* Douglas McCollam, "Attack at the Source," *Columbia Journalism Rev.,* March–April 2005, at 29.

[15] *But see* McKevitt v. Pallasch, 339 F.3d 530, 532 (7th Cir. 2003) (questioning lower court decisions recognizing a First Amendment-based journalist's privilege).

As will be discussed later in this chapter, the appeals court did not decide whether a federal common-law privilege exists for journalists. But the court concluded that the government's need for the journalists' testimony outweighed any common-law privilege that might exist.

The prosecutor complicated the Plame case by acquiring "waivers" of confidentiality from key officials. In what promises to be an increasingly popular tactic, officials waive confidentiality, thus allowing journalists to discuss with prosecutors conversations the journalists might have had with officials. Some journalists assert the waivers are coerced by the administration and thus should be ignored by the courts. However, Matthew Cooper of *Time* testified before the grand jury investigating the Plame leak in July 2005 after his source urged him to do so. Judith Miller of the *New York Times* initially refused to testify and was jailed for contempt. While in jail, Miller sought assurances from her source, "Scooter" Libby, Vice President Cheney's chief of staff, that the waiver Libby signed was voluntary. Libby urged her to testify and on release after spending 85 days in jail, Miller testified about her conversations with Libby.[16]

Based in part on the testimony of Miller and Cooper, Libby was indicted in October 2005 on obstruction of justice, false statement, and perjury charges for allegedly lying to FBI agents and the grand jury investigating the Plame leak. During the pretrial discovery process, Judge Reggie Walton ruled that *Time* magazine must produce drafts of an article by Cooper, along with internal correspondence, to Libby's attorneys. Drawing upon *Branzburg,* Walton rejected the claim that a journalist has a First Amendment privilege to withhold documents from a criminal defendant. Because the indictment of Libby claimed discrepancies exist between Libby's grand jury testimony and that of reporters such as Cooper, the court ruled the "First Amendment does not protect news reporters or news organizations from producing documents when the news reporters are themselves critical to both the indictment and prosecution of criminal activity."[17] After a trial at which Miller, Cooper, and other journalists testified, a jury in March 2007 concluded Libby had falsely testified that he learned of Plame's CIA affiliation from reporters and did not leak information about Plame. He was convicted on four counts of obstruction of justice, perjury, and making false statements.

Lower Court Reliance on a Three-Part Test

In situations not involving grand juries, appellate courts have recognized a limited First Amendment privilege based on the three-part test advocated by Justice Stewart in his *Branzburg* dissent. Persons who seek confidential information from reporters are usually asked to demonstrate that the information is relevant to their case, they cannot obtain the information from alternative sources, and their need for the information is "compelling" and should override the First Amendment interest in protecting news sources. The Supreme Court has passed up several opportunities to overturn the lower courts' grant of a constitutional privilege to journalists.

The practical application of a qualified privilege for reporters varies greatly by jurisdiction. Courts disagree over whether the privilege should apply when a criminal defendant

[16] *See generally* William Lee, "The Priestly Class: Reflections on a Journalist's Privilege," 23 *Cardozo Arts & Enter. L.J.* 635 (2006).

[17] United States v. Libby, 432 F. Supp.2d 26 (D.D.C. 2006).

is seeking information, when the information is being sought in a libel suit, or when documents and videotape are obtained without a promise of confidentiality.

Not all states base the qualified privilege on the U.S. Constitution. A few state courts have recognized a privilege in their state constitutions[18] or state common law.[19]

CRIMINAL PROCEEDINGS The Reporters Committee for Freedom of the Press found that more than half of the subpoenas issued to reporters in 2001 were from criminal defendants in state court proceedings.[20] In most criminal trials, courts use a three-part constitutional test to determine whether reporters are required to reveal confidential sources or information in their possession. Usually, the deciding factor is whether the person seeking the information can demonstrate a compelling need.

During criminal trials, prosecutors are frequently able to convince judges that journalists have information needed to convict a criminal defendant. However, criminal defendants trying to subpoena reporters often do not obtain the information they seek, in spite of the Sixth Amendment right to compel testimony in their favor. Criminal defendants seldom succeed because they can rarely meet all three parts of Stewart's test in *Branzburg*. For example, a federal appeals court affirmed the quashing of a subpoena served on *Sports Illustrated* because a defendant in a college basketball point-shaving scandal could not demonstrate that the information he sought was necessary to his defense. The U.S. Court of Appeals for the Second Circuit said that James Burke, who had been convicted, also had not shown that he had tried to obtain the information from sources other than *Sports Illustrated*.[21]

The Second Circuit blocked Burke's attempt to obtain nearly all of the documents and tapes related to a 1981 *Sports Illustrated* article, "How I Put the Fix In," coauthored by Douglas Looney, a staff writer, and Henry Hill, a career criminal. In the article, Hill told his version of a scheme to fix Boston College basketball games during the 1978–79 season. According to Hill, brothers Rocco and Tony Perla had purchased the cooperation of two key Boston College basketball players, Richard Kuhn and Ernie Cobb. The two players were paid if Boston College fell short of the point spread set by the bookmakers. Henry Hill and James Burke, a reputed mob boss, were to provide protection if the bookmakers discovered they were being swindled.

The scheme to fix Boston College games collapsed when the team came closer than planned to beating Holy Cross and the conspirators lost substantial sums of money. Soon afterward, Hill testified against his partners in exchange for immunity from prosecution. Burke was sentenced to twenty years in prison. Burke appealed, contending that the trial judge made several errors. One error, Burke argued, was the judge's failure to require that *Sports Illustrated* turn over the documents and tapes related to the Hill-Looney article.

When the Second Circuit applied a version of Stewart's three-part test in *United States v. Burke,* the court said Burke satisfied only one prong: that the information sought was relevant to his defense. The court agreed that the documents and tapes being sought could have been relevant because they might have contradicted the trial testimony of Henry Hill.

[18]*See, e.g.,* Zelenka v. State, 266 N.W.2d 279 (Wis. 1978).

[19]*See, e.g.,* Senear v. Daily Journal-American, 641 P.2d 1180 (Wash. 1982).

[20]Reporters Committee for Freedom of the Press, *Agents of Discovery: A Report on the Incidence of Subpoenas Served on the New Media in 2001* at 7 (2003).

[21]United States v. Burke, 700 F.2d 70 (2d Cir.), *cert. denied,* 464 U.S. 816 (1983).

But Burke failed to satisfy the second requirement of the three-part test, the court said, because Burke could not prove that the materials were "necessary or critical" to his defense, an adaptation of the Stewart requirement that there be a "compelling and overriding interest" in the information. The *Sports Illustrated* documents and tapes were not critical to Burke's case because he wanted to use them only to attack Hill's credibility. The court said that there was already ample evidence to destroy Hill's credibility as a witness. The court said Hill had been convicted of loan-sharking, extortion, and drug trafficking. He also had admitted to armed robbery, arson, and hijacking.

The Second Circuit said that Burke could not fulfill the third requirement of the Stewart test either. Burke had not sought the information from other available sources. For example, he had not subpoenaed a witness to the interviews of Hill by the *Sports Illustrated* writer Looney.

Sometimes the application of the three-point test results in a journalist being required to testify, as occurred in *United States v. Criden*.[22] In 1980, a federal appeals court upheld an order holding reporter Jan Schaffer of the *Philadelphia Inquirer* in contempt of court after she refused to testify during a trial arising from the FBI's Abscam operation. The defendants in the trial, a lawyer and three Philadelphia city council members, were charged with receiving bribes from FBI agents posing as Arab sheiks. The defendants argued that the bribery charges should be dismissed because the prosecutors purposely released "sensational and prejudicial information," making a fair trial impossible.

After one of the prosecutors, U.S. Attorney Peter F. Vaira, admitted giving Schaffer information, the defendants wanted to ask the reporter what she thought about Vaira's motivation and credibility. Schaffer refused to say whether she had talked with Vaira, arguing that any answers might lead to a disclosure of sources. However, the U.S. Court of Appeals for the Third Circuit said that Schaffer's claim to a First Amendment privilege had to be balanced against the defendants' Sixth Amendment right to compel testimony in their favor.

The Third Circuit, employing a version of the three-part test, said the information sought from Schaffer was both relevant and important. Information about Vaira's motivations and credibility was central to the question of misconduct by the prosecution. In addition, the defendants had demonstrated that they had tried to get the pertinent information from other sources. They had called Vaira to testify, and they had unsuccessfully tried to obtain a report of an investigation of Abscam leaks undertaken by the U.S. Justice Department. They had convinced the court that "only Schaffer" could testify to Vaira's credibility during telephone conversations between the two of them.

Courts have applied the reporters' constitutional privilege not only to the mass media but also to specialized publications and book authors. For example, the same court that decided the *Burke* case allowed a privilege claim when several states subpoenaed documents from an oil industry news service. The U.S. Court of Appeals for the Second Circuit said that a trial court improperly cited *Platt's Oilgram Price Report* for contempt when the publication refused to provide the states with information about prices for petroleum products to use in antitrust litigation. The states argued that oil companies conspiring to fix gasoline prices might have communicated price information through *Platt's* reporters. *Platt's* refused to provide documents containing confidential news sources. The Second

[22] 633 F.2d 346 (3d Cir. 1980), *cert. denied,* 449 U.S. 1113 (1981).

Circuit said the states provided no evidence that the names of confidential sources were relevant to the antitrust claims. Further, the states failed to establish that the information could not be obtained elsewhere.[23] Courts have also applied the privilege in cases involving an investigative book author,[24] a medical newsletter,[25] documentary filmmakers,[26] and Wall Street investment analysts.[27]

CIVIL TRIALS The Reporters Committee for Freedom of the Press reported that subpoenas in civil suits accounted for 36 percent of the subpoenas issued in 2001 to news media responding to a survey. Nearly 97 percent of those subpoenas were sought by litigants in lawsuits in which the media entity was not a party to the suits.[28] If the newspaper or broadcast station fighting a subpoena is not the defendant in a civil suit, the courts frequently recognize the constitutional privilege and decide in favor of the news medium. In the recent Wen Ho Lee case, however, the Court of Appeals for the District of Columbia Circuit upheld a lower court ruling that journalists had to reveal the identity of their confidential sources.

Journalist as Third Party Writers or editors are least apt to be required to disclose information when it is being sought by parties in civil suits that do not directly involve the journalists being subpoenaed. The courts regularly decide that the civil litigants seeking notes or the names of sources in such cases cannot meet the requirements of the three-part test.

Litigants in civil suits often cannot establish that the information they seek is available only from journalists, one of the prongs of the Stewart test. Because the journalists were able to discover the information, judges often reason, attorneys for civil litigants ought to be able to do the same. Civil litigants also have a more difficult time than criminal defendants in proving a compelling need for the information. The Constitution does not provide civil litigants with the same power to require testimony on their own behalf as it does for criminal defendants. In addition, because defendants in civil suits do not face the possibility of jail or death, they might have less at stake if journalists withhold information. That is, judges often view the interests of parties in civil suits, which are primarily monetary, as less compelling than those in criminal cases. Furthermore, many civil suits involve private disputes such as compensation in accidental injury cases that do not have a direct and substantial impact on public health and safety.

A federal appeals court decided one of the most significant civil cases involving confidential news sources in 1972, less than six months after the Supreme Court decided *Branzburg*. In *Baker v. F & F Investment,* the U.S. Court of Appeals for the Second Circuit used a variation of the three-part test to uphold the right of a prominent magazine journalist to refuse to reveal his source.[29] The court said litigants seeking the source of an article by journalist Alfred Balk had not established the need for the information or that they

[23]McGraw-Hill, Inc. v. Arizona, 680 F.2d 5 (2d Cir. 1982).
[24]Shoen v. Shoen, 5 F.3d 1289 (9th Cir. 1993).
[25]Apicella v. McNeil Laboratories, Inc., 66 F.R.D. 78 (1975).
[26]Silkwood v. Kerr-McGee Corp., 563 F.2d 433 (10th Cir. 1977).
[27]Summit Tech. Inc. v. Healthcare Capital Group, Inc., 141 F.R.D. 381 (D. Mass 1992).
[28]Reporters Committee for Freedom of the Press, *Agents of Discovery: A Report on the Incidence of Subpoenas Served on the New Media in 2001* at 7 (2003).
[29]470 F.2d 778 (2d Cir. 1972), *cert. denied,* 411 U.S. 966 (1973).

could not find the information in other ways. Balk wrote "Confessions of a Block-buster" for the *Saturday Evening Post* in 1962. He based the story, which documented discriminatory real estate practices in Chicago, on information supplied by an anonymous source given the pseudonym "Norris Vitcheck." The source told Balk how he scared whites living near African American neighborhoods into selling their houses to him at low prices. "Vitcheck" then sold those houses to African Americans for substantial profits. Several years after the article appeared, a group of African Americans sued about sixty landlords, real estate companies, and real estate investors, contending that they sold homes to blacks for excessive prices. The plaintiffs wanted Balk to identify "Vitcheck."

The Second Circuit said the plaintiffs had not demonstrated a sufficiently compelling need for the information to override the First Amendment values at stake. In civil cases, the court said, the public interest in protecting a journalist's confidential news sources "will often be weightier than the private interest in compelled disclosure." In the case at hand, the Second Circuit did not mention the Stewart three-part test but relied on similar criteria. The court said the identity of the source "did not go to the heart" of the case, a phrase often used when confidential sources are either not relevant or not necessary to a case. The Second Circuit also noted that according to the trial court judge no alternatives to identifying Balk's source had been tried.

In contrast, the courts addressing Wen Ho Lee's efforts to force journalists to reveal their confidential sources all found that a qualified First Amendment privilege in civil cases had been overcome. The prevailing precedent in the District of Columbia Circuit, *Zerilli v. Smith* requires that civil litigants seeking information from a non-party journalist must meet two requirements; they must show that the information sought goes to the "heart of the matter" and that they have exhausted all reasonable alternative sources of the information.[30] In the *Lee* case, the court of appeals held that the lower court properly applied *Zerilli*. The information Lee sought was critical to proving that federal officials violated his rights under the Privacy Act. If Lee were unable to identify the leakers, he would have also been unable to prove the other elements of a Privacy Act claim, such as willfulness and intent. Before seeking information from journalists, Lee used every tactical device in the Federal Rules of Civil Procedure to extract evidence from the government. For example, Lee deposed twenty government officials, including the Secretary of Energy and the Director of the FBI. These depositions revealed "a pattern of denials, vague or evasive answers, and stonewalling." Lee's extensive efforts, combined with the unwillingness of government officials to admit to the leaks, meant the testimony of the journalists was necessary, the court said.

In a case similar to *Lee*, a federal judge in March 2008 held reporter Toni Locy to be in contempt for failing to identify her sources for stories about Steven Hatfill, a former Army scientist who claims federal officials illegally leaked information about him. Graduated fines, up to $5,000 each day, were stayed when an appellate court agreed to hear Locy's appeal.[31]

Libel Suits Courts are more reluctant to protect journalists' confidential news sources in civil suits involving media defendants than in suits in which the media are not parties.

[30] 656 F.2d 705 (D.C. Cir. 1981).

[31] United States v. Lee, 413 F.3d (D.C. Cir. 2005), *cert. denied*, 547 U.S. 1187 (2006); Hatfill v. Mukasey, 2008 U.S. Dist. LEXIS 17756 (D.D.C. Mar. 7, 2008), *stay granted*, 2008 U.S. App. LEXIS 5755 (D.C. Cir. Mar. 11, 2008).

Courts frequently order journalists to reveal sources and notes when they are subpoenaed by libel plaintiffs. Judges generally insist that libel plaintiffs must have the opportunity to prove that newspapers or broadcast stations acted negligently or with actual malice when preparing defamatory stories.

Judges often conclude that it is unfair for journalists to claim that they acted properly in preparing a story and at the same time refuse to divulge sources that would allow a libel plaintiff to prove otherwise. For example, in *Star Editorial, Inc. v. United States District Court,* a federal appeals court said the only way a libel plaintiff could meet his burden of proof in a libel case was to know who had accused him of lewd and drunken conduct. The U.S. Court of Appeals for the Ninth Circuit ordered the *Star,* a weekly supermarket tabloid, to disclose confidential informants used in preparing a story.[32] The *Star* had published a story claiming that the plaintiff, comedian Rodney Dangerfield, had been drunk in a Las Vegas hotel room with two naked women, had "trashed" the hotel room, and had chased a female hotel employee around his room with ice tongs stating that he hoped to rip her clothing off.

Applying a constitutional privilege drawn from *Branzburg* and the California constitution, the court decided that the *Star* must disclose its confidential sources. The Ninth Circuit said the sources for the Dangerfield allegations, sources the *Star* said were employees of Caesar's Palace hotel, were relevant to Dangerfield's libel suit. The court also said that Dangerfield had an important interest in discovering the *Star*'s confidential sources because the comedian, as a public figure, had to prove the tabloid acted with *New York Times* actual malice. The court said Dangerfield had to know the source of the story to demonstrate that the story was false or that the *Star* had recklessly relied on the sources. This could be demonstrated, the court noted, by showing that the sources were unreliable or that there were in fact no sources. Without knowing the identity of the sources, however, Dangerfield would have an extremely difficult time proving his case.

Courts considering the constitutional privilege in libel cases frequently point out that the U.S. Supreme Court ruled in 1979 that journalists have no First Amendment right to refuse to testify when a libel plaintiff is seeking evidence of *New York Times* actual malice. In *Herbert v. Lando,* discussed in Chapter 4, the Supreme Court ruled that journalists do not have a First Amendment privilege to refuse to provide information about how a story is investigated and written. In *Herbert,* which did not involve confidential sources, *60 Minutes* producer Barry Lando was required to tell Lieutenant Colonel Anthony Herbert how he decided what to include in a broadcast critical of the army officer. The Supreme Court said such an exploration into the journalistic process was justified because public-figure libel plaintiffs could not show knowing falsehood or recklessness if they did not know what writers and editors were thinking when they put a story together.[33] Lower courts have relied on *Herbert* to require journalists to reveal not only nonconfidential notes and newsroom memos but also confidential sources.[34]

In addition, courts have relied on *Herbert* to justify punitive measures against the media if they refuse to reveal confidential sources and other materials. Several courts after

[32] 7 F.3d 856 (9th Cir. 1993).
[33] 441 U.S. 153 (1979).
[34] *See, e.g.,* Cape Publications, Inc. v. Bridges, 387 So.2d 436 (Fla. Dist. Ct. App. 1980).

Herbert ruled that news organizations refusing to reveal confidential news sources have to defend themselves in libel suits as if the sources did not exist.

In New Hampshire, for example, the state supreme court not only affirmed a lower court ruling to compel disclosure of a newspaper's sources but also said the lower court could punish the paper's refusal to reveal the source by assuming that the source did not exist. In *Downing v. Monitor Publishing Co.,* former police chief Clayton Downing of Boscawen sought the names of sources who had told the *Concord Monitor* that he had failed a lie detector test. The New Hampshire Supreme Court relied heavily on *Herbert* when it said that there is "no absolute privilege" that allows the press to refuse to reveal sources of information "essential" to a libel plaintiff's case.[35]

The New Hampshire Supreme Court noted that reporters held in contempt for refusing to reveal sources often choose to go to jail rather than to obey court orders to provide information. Putting journalists in jail "in no way" helps libel plaintiffs obtain sufficient information to prove their cases, the court said. Therefore, the court decided, if a journalist refuses to reveal a source, the court would assume no source was used. Thus, a newspaper or broadcast station might have to prove the lack of recklessness or negligence without using the information gained from the confidential source and even without saying in court that a source existed.

The more uncompromising approaches, like that of *Downing,* have been limited to a minority of cases that became less frequent during the 1990s. However, many courts do not rely on the three-part constitutional test in libel suits, and journalists are usually ordered to disclose their confidential sources in cases before those courts.

Therefore, in libel suits, journalists not only have to weigh the possibility of fines or jail sentences when deciding whether to make promises protecting the confidentiality of sources but also have to consider the possibility of harm to their libel defenses. Before publishing a defamatory story, journalists should be confident they can prove to a jury that they are accurate and have exercised sufficient care in the preparation of the article without reliance on confidential sources. On occasion, newspapers and broadcast stations may face the dilemma of having to decide whether to break a promise of confidentiality or risk losing a libel case.

The First Amendment is not, of course, the only source of protection for journalists who want to refuse to reveal confidential news sources. There are also state statutes and federal court rules and guidelines.

Summary

The Supreme Court decided 5-4, in *Branzburg v. Hayes,* that reporters do not have First Amendment protection to refuse to testify before grand juries. Justice White, writing the majority opinion, said that journalists had not demonstrated that they should be accorded a privilege under the First Amendment that would allow them to refuse to reveal confidential sources. However, Justice Powell, casting the deciding vote, implied that journalists might be entitled to protection in limited instances. Justice Stewart, in dissent, said that to compel testimony from journalists the First Amendment should be interpreted to require

[35]415 A.2d 683 (N.H. 1980).

government officials to prove that there is probable cause to believe the information is relevant to a specific investigation, that the need for the information is compelling, and that no alternative way of acquiring the information is available.

Since *Branzburg,* a First Amendment privilege is seldom granted when journalists are subpoenaed to testify before grand juries, discuss an event they witnessed, or provide nonconfidential information or sources. However, some appellate courts have added Justice Powell's vote to that of the four dissenters in *Branzburg* and have recognized a qualified First Amendment privilege for reporters who refuse to disclose confidential sources. Most appellate courts require persons who want to subpoena a journalist to meet a three-part test based on Stewart's *Branzburg* dissent. Through the protection afforded in the three-part test, appellate courts often decide that journalists do not have to testify in criminal trials. Reporters are required to testify even less often when information is being sought by parties to civil suits that do not directly involve the media. The courts are more reluctant to grant the privilege and to rule in favor of journalists when a newspaper or broadcast station is being sued for libel.

A Federal Common-Law Privilege?

Three years after the *Branzburg* decision, Congress enacted the Federal Rules of Evidence, including Rule 501, which provides the privilege of a witness "shall be governed by the principles of the common law as they may be interpreted by the courts of the United States in the light of reason and experience."[36] In *Jaffee v. Redmond,* the Supreme Court held that confidential communications made to licensed psychotherapists were protected by a federal common-law privilege. In doing so, the Court adopted a multipart test to guide lower courts in other cases in which a common-law privilege is asserted. The test asks whether the asserted privilege would serve significant private and public interests, whether these interests outweigh any evidentiary benefit resulting from rejection of the privilege, and whether the privilege has been widely recognized by the states.[37]

As shown in contemporary cases, such as those involving Wen Ho Lee and Valerie Plame, judicial skepticism toward a First Amendment-based journalist's privilege has markedly increased since 2001. To provide judges with an alternative basis for protecting journalists, media lawyers have argued for a qualified reporter's privilege based on federal common law. These recent efforts have uniformly failed. Appellate courts for the second circuit[38] and the District of Columbia circuit[39] recently ruled that even if a common-law privilege existed, it was overcome by the government's need for the journalists' information. The district courts handling the cases of former White House official "Scooter" Libby[40] and the reporters covering the baseball steroids scandal[41] similarly rejected the common-law privilege arguments.

In 2006, the Court of Appeals for the Second Circuit reversed a lower court ruling that a common-law privilege protected the telephone records of two *New York Times* reporters.

[36]Fed. R. Evid. 501.
[37]518 U.S. 1 (1996).
[38]N.Y. Times Co. v. Gonzales, 459 F.3d 160 (2nd Cir. 2006), *stay denied,* 2006 U.S. LEXIS 9194 (Nov. 27, 2006).
[39]*In re* Grand Jury Subpoena, Miller, 397 F. 3d 964 (D.C. Cir. 2005).
[40]United States v. Libby, 432 F. Supp.2d 26 (D.D.C. 2006).
[41]*In re* Grand Jury Subpoenas to Fainaru-Wada and Williams, 438 F. Supp. 2d 1111 (N.D. Cal. 2006).

The appellate court agreed with the district court that any common-law privilege would be qualified, but concluded the privilege would be overcome on the facts of this case. Consequently, it was unnecessary for the appellate court to rule on whether such a privilege exists under Rule 501. The appellate court said that even applying Justice Stewart's test, the government had a compelling interest in acquiring the telephone records of the *Times* reporters to learn the identity of government officials who leaked information about upcoming FBI searches of Islamic charities.[42]

In the 2005 case involving Judith Miller and Matthew Cooper, the Court of Appeals for the District of Columbia Circuit held that *if* there were a common-law privilege, it was not absolute and was overcome by the special prosecutor investigating the leaking of Valerie Plame's CIA affiliation.[43] Judge Tatel's separate opinion offered the strongest support for a journalist's federal common-law privilege. Tatel argued that "reason and experience," as evidenced by state shield laws, supported judicial acknowledgement of a qualified common-law privilege. Judge Tatel proposed a balancing test for leak cases that examined the government's need for the information, exhaustion of alternative sources, and weighed the harm caused by the leak against the leaked information's value. In this case he believed the news value of Plame's CIA affiliation was marginal. Tatel's test has been incorporated into legislative proposals for a federal shield law.

Judge Tatel's balancing test was sharply criticized by Judge Rosemary Collyer in a contempt proceeding against Walter Pincus of the *Washington Post*.[44] Pincus relied on anonymous government sources in articles about Wen Ho Lee, a nuclear weapons researcher who was investigated for espionage. (First Amendment aspects of the Lee case were discussed earlier in this chapter.) Pincus claimed that Judge Tatel's common-law balancing test should be followed. Judge Collyer found this test to be inherently unworkable and declined to create a federal common-law privilege. She wrote, "Submission of a reporter's privilege to a judge's determination of the newsworthiness of his or her story . . . would create a subjective and elastic standard whose outcome could not be predicted. . . . Courts are ill-suited to decide the degree to which information is beneficial or unimportant to the common weal." As noted earlier in this chapter, the *Washington Post,* along with other media organizations, paid Lee $750,000 in 2006 as part of a settlement that ended contempt citations against Pincus and four other journalists.

Protection under State Statutes

Although the Supreme Court in *Branzburg* said the First Amendment does not protect reporters from being compelled to testify before grand juries, the Court did not say the Constitution prohibits legislative protection for confidential sources. As a general matter, legislative protection of newsgathering and dissemination can nearly always exceed the minimum protection guaranteed by the Constitution. In *Branzburg,* Justice White invited legislatures to "fashion standards and rules as narrow or as broad as deemed necessary. . . ." At the time of *Branzburg,* seventeen states had shield laws. By 2008, thirty-five states had

[42]N.Y. Times Co. v. Gonzales, 459 F.3d 160 (2nd Cir. 2006), *stay denied,* 2006 U.S. LEXIS 9194 (Nov. 27, 2006).
[43]*In re* Grand Jury Subpoena, Miller, 397 F. 3d 964 (D.C. Cir. 2005).
[44]Lee v. DOJ, 401 F. Supp. 2d 123 (D.D.C. 2005).

shield laws. Congress has considered a federal shield law, most recently in 2007, but has not yet enacted such a measure.

States that have adopted "shield laws" protecting journalists are Alabama, Alaska, Arizona, Arkansas, California, Colorado, Connecticut, Delaware, Florida, Georgia, Hawaii, Illinois, Indiana, Kentucky, Louisiana, Maine, Maryland, Michigan, Minnesota, Montana, Nebraska, Nevada, New Jersey, New Mexico, New York, North Carolina, North Dakota, Ohio, Oklahoma, Oregon, Pennsylvania, Rhode Island, South Carolina, Tennessee and Washington. California is the only state to provide for a privilege in its state constitution. A shield law has also been adopted by the Council of the District of Columbia. A survey of news organizations by the Reporters Committee for Freedom of the Press found that shield laws provided the basis for more than half of the successful media challenges to subpoenas in 2001.[45]

State shield laws vary widely; about a dozen state statutes are similar to Alabama's, which is considered to be "absolute" because it does not qualify the reporters' privilege:

> No person engaged in, connected with or employed on any newspaper, radio broadcasting station or television station, while engaged in a news-gathering capacity, shall be compelled to disclose in any legal proceeding or trial, before any court or before a grand jury of any court, before the presiding officer of any tribunal or his agent or agents or before any committee of the legislature or elsewhere the sources of any information procured or obtained by him and published in the newspaper, broadcast by any broadcasting station, or televised by any television station on which he is engaged, connected with or employed.[46]

Although the Alabama statute is absolute in the sense that it does not list exceptions to the privilege, the law does not shield all journalists. For example, it does not protect the authors of articles written for magazines. This limitation was an important aspect of a recent libel lawsuit brought by former University of Alabama football coach Mike Price against *Sports Illustrated.* The centerpiece of a May 2003 *Sports Illustrated* article about Price was a description of a hotel room incident between Price and two women he had earlier met at a Pensacola, Florida, strip club. The article included the following:

> He eventually met up with two women, both of whom he had earlier propositioned for sex, according to one of the women, who agreed to speak to SI about the hotel-room liaison on the condition that her name not be used. The woman, who declined comment when asked if she was paid for the evening, said that the threesome engaged "in some pretty aggressive sex." She said that at one point she and her female companion decided to add a little levity to the activity: "We started screaming 'Roll Tide!' and he was yelling back, 'It's rolling baby, it's rolling.'"

Price admitted visiting the strip club, but denied having sex with anyone mentioned in the article. In a subsequent libel suit, he sought the identity of the confidential source to establish that *Sports Illustrated* acted with actual malice. The Court of Appeals for the Eleventh Circuit concluded that *Sports Illustrated,* as a magazine, was not covered by the Alabama

[45]Reporters Committee for Freedom of the Press, *Agents of Discovery: A Report on the Incidence of Subpoenas Served on the New Media in 2001* at 10 (2003).

[46]Ala. Code § 12-21-142.

shield law.[47] However, because a qualified First Amendment privilege applied to the magazine, Price was required to depose four women who had knowledge of the confidential source's identity before the article's author would be compelled to reveal his source. Shortly after this ruling, Price and the magazine settled the suit.

The Alabama statute also appears to require publication before any protection is provided. Unpublished notes and tapes may be subpoenaed. Further, the statute on its face would appear to protect only a journalist who refuses to reveal the name of a source and not a journalist who refuses to reveal information from notes.[48] The limitations the Alabama legislature has imposed on the statutory privilege are typical of the laws of many states.

Seven of the more important points to consider in evaluating a shield law are who is protected, whether confidentiality is required for protection, what kind of information is protected, whether publication is required, in what legal forums can the privilege be asserted, whether the privilege can be waived, and whether exceptions to the privilege are specified.

People Protected

Justice White's majority opinion in *Branzburg* questioned how judges could define a journalist entitled to a constitutional privilege. White implied that determining who should be protected by a privilege and who should not would be difficult because a variety of communicators, such as "lecturers, political pollsters, novelists, academic researchers, and dramatists" contribute to public knowledge. Legislators adopting shield laws have the difficult task of specifying who ought to be shielded from disclosing sources or information in court. The list must be limited, or it could prove to be a haven for anyone who does not want to testify in court, frustrating legitimate attempts to compel needed testimony.

Most of the thirty-three states with shield laws allow protection for those connected to "newspapers, radio, and television" or the "news media." About a dozen states appear to protect *anyone* employed by the news media. Another dozen protect only persons involved in the news process, including editors and photographers. One state statute, Alaska's, applies only to "reporters."[49]

Most shield laws exclude book authors, freelance writers, academic researchers, and others not working directly in news organizations. Many states, such as Alabama, exclude magazine writers. Michigan amended its shield law in 1986 to protect broadcast journalists for the first time.[50] A few states, including Alaska, Illinois, and Louisiana—but not California—shield persons engaged in reporting or editorial activities for "motion picture news."[51]

Minnesota and Nebraska have adopted among the broadest descriptions of persons covered by shield laws. The statement of principle in the Minnesota shield law asserts that the statute was written to provide a privilege against the disclosure of news sources and other information for the "news media." The law protects any person "directly engaged in

[47]Price v. Time, Inc., 416 F.3d 1327 (11th Cir. 2005). *See generally* Stefan Fatsis, "Playing Defense: A Coach's Lawsuit Poses Challenges for Time, Inc.," *Wall Street Journal,* July 13, 2005, at A1.

[48]*But see* Brothers v. Brothers, 16 Media L. Rep. 1031 (Ala. Cir. Ct. Marshall Co. 1989).

[49]Alaska Stat. § 09.25.300.

[50]Mich. Comp. Laws § 767.5a (2005). This modification was prompted by judicial rulings that broadcast journalists were not covered by the state's shield law. *In re* Contempt of Stone, 397 N.W.2d 244 (Mich. Ct. App. 1986).

[51]Alaska Stat. § 09.25.390 (1) (A) (ii); 735 Ill. Compiled Stat. Ann. 5/8-902; La. Rev. Stat. § 45:1451(f); Cal. Evid. Code § 1070.

the gathering, procuring, compiling, editing or publishing of information for the purpose of transmission, dissemination or publication to the public."[52] Nebraska's law may be even broader than Minnesota's. It protects persons engaged in "procuring, gathering, writing, editing, or disseminating" not only news but also "other information." In addition, the Nebraska statute applies to "any medium of communication," which includes, but is not limited to, "any newspaper, magazine, other periodical, book, pamphlet, news service, wire service, news or feature syndicate, broadcast station or network, or cable television system." The Nebraska statute appears broad enough to apply to work of communicators such as public relations professionals.[53]

The growth of Internet-based journalism poses interesting statutory interpretation problems for courts. Laws that narrowly specify protected media, such as Alabama's reference to newspapers, radio, and television stations do not cover journalists producing material solely for websites. Laws that use expansive terms, such as Nebraska's reference to "any medium of communication" cover web journalists. In between these two extremes are state laws that use ambiguous terms, such as "periodical publication" that may be sufficiently expansive to protect web journalists.

The California Court of Appeals for the Sixth Appellate District ruled in 2006 that the state's shield law covered Jason O'Grady, owner and editor of PowerPage, a website devoted to news about Apple computer products.[54] Over a period of several days in November 2004, O'Grady published articles on his website providing details about an Apple product that was under development. Apple claimed O'Grady published its trade secrets, obtained through an Apple employee's breach of confidentiality, and sought to discover the identity of O'Grady's source.

The appellate court easily concluded that O'Grady was an editor/reporter engaged in the dissemination of news. The more difficult question was whether the shield law's protection for journalists working for a "newspaper, magazine, or other periodical publication" applied to PowerPage. The court concluded that PowerPage was not a newspaper because that term means a regularly appearing publication printed on inexpensive paper. Because the term *magazine* or *e-zine* is now widely used to describe websites that offer regularly updated news, the appellate court concluded that PowerPage could be classified as a magazine. The court stated that webpages like PowerPage "are highly analogous to printed publications: they consist predominately of text on 'pages' which the reader 'opens,' reads at his own pace, and 'closes.'" Even if PowerPage could not properly be classified as a magazine for the purposes of the shield law, the appellate court concluded the legislature "intended the phrase 'periodical publication' to include all ongoing, recurring news publications while excluding nonrecurring publications such as books, pamphlets, flyers, and monographs. . . . [The legislature] must have intended that the statute protect publications like petitioners', which differ from traditional periodicals only in their tendency, which flows directly from the technology they employ, to continuously update their content."

[52]Minn. Stat. Ann. § 595.023.
[53]Neb. Rev. Stat. § 20-144.
[54]O'Grady v. Superior Court of Santa Clara County, 130 Cal. App. 4th 1423 (Cal. Ct. App. 2006).

Video blogger Josh Wolf is also arguably covered by the California shield law in state cases. However, in April 2006, a federal judge ruled that California privilege law was irrelevant in federal proceedings. A federal grand jury subpoenaed Wolf, seeking video he shot in 2005 of a San Francisco protest march in which a policeman was injured. Wolf filed a motion to quash, arguing that the California shield law provided an absolute barrier to the subpoena. The district court ruled that *Branzburg,* not the state shield law, governed this case and Wolf was ordered to testify.[55] Wolf refused to do so and was imprisoned on August 1, 2006 and briefly released on September 1 while his case was appealed to the Court of Appeals for the Ninth Circuit. After the appellate court affirmed the contempt order,[56] Wolf returned to jail on September 22. Wolf was released in April 2007 in a deal with prosecutors. Wolf provided the video to the court and in a statement swore he had no information relating to the injury of the police officer. Wolf's incarceration for 226 days is a record for an American journalist held in contempt of court.

Confidentiality Requirement

A few state shield laws specify that a reporter must have promised confidentiality to a source to be protected by the statute. However, most of the state statutes, like that of Alabama, do not explicitly say whether a promise of confidentiality is required for a journalist to be protected under the law.

The Tennessee Supreme Court, among others, has ruled that the state's statute protecting "any information or the source of any information" from disclosure protects journalists whether or not they promise confidentiality. The Tennessee court's opinion said the statutory protection for "any" information means that "all" information is protected.[57] The court noted that the legislature had not qualified its protection of "any information" in the statute by requiring that a promise of confidentiality be made. The Tennessee Supreme Court reversed a lower court decision that would have required Memphis newspapers to disclose "any and all correspondence, studies, reports, memoranda, or any other source material" for stories about a bridge collapse.

On the other hand, the Rhode Island Supreme Court strictly construed a state shield law that protects reporters only from testifying about a "confidential association," "confidential information," or the "source of any confidential information."[58] In *Outlet Communications Inc. v. Rhode Island,*[59] the court said the statute did not shield a Providence television station from a grand jury subpoena seeking portions of an on-camera interview that had not been broadcast. The televised interview had taken place on a public sidewalk with a man who had asked the station for a chance to "tell his side of the story" before turning himself in to police. His sidewalk arrest immediately after the interview was also broadcast. The Rhode Island court said the television station could not rely on the statute because the interview "was anything but secret or confidential."

[55]*In re* Grand Jury Investigation, Wolf, No. CR 06-90064 MISC MMC (N.D. Cal. Apr. 5, 2006).

[56]2006 U.S. App. LEXIS 23315 (9th Cir. Sep. 8, 2006).

[57]Austin v. Memphis Publishing Co., 655 S.W.2d 146 (Tenn. 1983). *See also, e.g.,* Aerial Burials Inc. v. Minneapolis Star & Tribune Co., 8 Media L. Rep. 1653 (Minn. Dist. Ct. Hennepin Co. 1982); Brothers v. Brothers, 16 Media L. Rep. 1031 (Ala. Cir. Ct. Marshall Co. 1989).

[58]R.I. Gen. Laws § 9-19.1-2.

[59]588 A.2d 1050 (R.I. 1991).

Information Protected

States are divided over whether to shield reporters from revealing notes and other information as well as sources. Some states protect reporters from testifying only when the journalists want to withhold the name of a source. Other states offer protection against disclosure of any information in the possession of a reporter or other media employee. Only a few state statutes specifically say that outtakes, film, and photographs are protected from forced disclosure.

The Alabama shield law quoted earlier, if strictly interpreted, would protect only "the sources" of information obtained by news personnel, that is, the identity of confidential sources.[60] The Tennessee statute applies to "any information" as well as "the source of any information" obtained for publication or broadcast.[61] Nebraska protects sources; information; and "all notes, outtakes, photographs, film, tapes, or other data."[62]

Although the text of the Pennsylvania shield law provides protection only against the disclosure of "the source of information," the state's supreme court has interpreted the language broadly. The Pennsylvania Supreme Court said the "source of information" includes all sources of information, including tape recordings, memoranda, notes, and reports.[63]

Most statutes do not protect reporters who have been called to testify about events they have seen rather than to reveal a source or information given to them by a source. More than one court has held that a statute shielding confidential news sources from disclosure does not protect a reporter who witnessed a crime from testifying. Paul Branzburg, the *Louisville Courier-Journal* reporter of *Branzburg v. Hayes,* tried to avoid appearing before two grand juries by arguing he was protected by the Kentucky shield law. Although the Kentucky statute provides without qualification that reporters do not have to reveal their sources, the Kentucky Court of Appeals said the law did not apply to Branzburg's case because Branzburg's own observation was the source of the story. Branzburg was subpoenaed to testify about criminal acts, the making and using of drugs, that he had witnessed.[64] The court said he could not protect the identity of the young men who had made the drugs even though he would have had no story without his promise to maintain their anonymity. Branzburg could have been jailed or fined had he remained in Kentucky. However, he had moved to Michigan by the time his case was considered by the U.S. Supreme Court, and Michigan refused to extradite him.

Publication Requirement

Slightly more than half of the thirty-three state shield laws appear to provide protection whether or not the subpoenaed information is published. About a half-dozen statutes, including Alabama's, require publication in order for the statutory protection to be triggered. State statutes that require publication will not ordinarily protect information or pictures that reporters and editors leave out of newspapers and news broadcasts.

[60]Ala. Code § 12-21-142. *But see* Brothers v. Brothers, 16 Media L. Rep. 1031 (Ala. Cir. Ct. Marshall Co. 1989).
[61]Tenn. Code Ann. § 24-1-208(a).
[62]Neb. Rev. Stat. § 20-145(5).
[63]*In re* Taylor, 193 A.2d 181 (Pa. 1963).
[64]Branzburg v. Pound, 461 S.W.2d 345 (Ky. 1970), *aff'd sub nom.* Branzburg v. Hayes, 408 U.S. 665 (1972).

In contrast, Minnesota's shield law protects against the disclosure of "any unpublished information," and therefore a state court quashed a subpoena for half a page of notes a reporter said she did not use or rely on for a story. Minneapolis freelance journalist Joanna Conners turned over to a plaintiff in a libel case her handwritten notes and a transcription of a tape-recorded interview that contained published information. She deleted from the notes and transcripts information she said she did not use.[65]

Forums Where Privilege Can Be Asserted

Most shield laws appear to protect journalists from a subpoena initiated by any legal authority. Others prevent subpoenas only in a narrow range of circumstances.

Most shield laws protect newspersons asked to testify before any administrative, judicial, or legislative body. Some, like the one in Alabama, are more detailed. Alabama protects reporters before "any legal proceeding or trial, before any court or before a grand jury of any court, before the presiding officer of any tribunal or his agent or agents or before any committee of the legislature or elsewhere," which includes administrative hearings. A few state statutes cover only civil proceedings or only criminal proceedings. Some indicate that they do not allow a newsperson to refuse to testify in a libel suit. Therefore, *Belleville News-Democrat* editorial writer Richard Hargraves, mentioned in the chapter introduction, argued unsuccessfully that the Illinois shield law protected him from being forced to reveal his sources. County official Jerry Costello had sued Hargraves and his paper for libel and wanted to know the sources of an editorial that had accused him of lying. Although the Illinois shield law provides a qualified privilege protecting reporters from revealing sources' names, it specifically exempts libel suits.[66]

Waiver

Most state shield laws do not address whether a journalist's privilege is lost, or *waived,* if the source becomes known or if the journalist discloses part of a confidential conversation. A few statutes indicate that limited disclosure, publication, or testimony by a journalist does not waive the privilege protecting against the forced disclosure of additional information. However, a few shield laws provide that informants can destroy the privilege of a newsperson by revealing their own identity.

Although the New Jersey shield statute does not contain a waiver provision, the state's rules of evidence do. The New Jersey shield law provides for a privilege for information "whether or not it is disseminated." However, the state's evidence rules declare that a person claiming a privilege cannot refuse to testify if any part of the confidential information is disclosed. In the case *In re Schuman,* the New Jersey Supreme Court ruled that the shield law controlled. The court said *New Jersey Herald* reporter Evan Schuman did not have to appear in court simply to affirm the truth of a story he wrote about a murder confession. The court said that Schuman was protected from compelled testimony because the state shield law explicitly covered information already disseminated. The court also recognized

[65] Aerial Burials Inc. v. Minneapolis Star & Tribune Co., 8 Media L. Rep. 1653 (Minn. Dist. Ct. Hennepin Co. 1982).
[66] 735 Ill. Compiled Stat. Ann. § 5/8-903; "Column Leads to Jail," *News Media & L.,* Nov.–Dec. 1984, at 36.

that the "legislature has continuously acted to establish the strongest possible protection from compulsory testimony for the press."[67]

Sometimes reporters, such as Jan Schaffer of the *Philadelphia Inquirer,* mentioned earlier, refuse to acknowledge a source even though the source is otherwise revealed. In *United States v. Criden,* Schaffer contended that if she confirmed or denied that she had talked to one source, investigators could determine whether she had talked to other confidential sources. However, the U.S. Court of Appeals for the Third Circuit ruled that Schaffer had to testify after criminal defendants satisfied a three-part test.[68]

Exceptions

Some shield laws, like that of Alabama, are absolute in the sense that they do not qualify or limit a journalist's privilege or list exceptions to the statutory protection against the disclosure. In states that list exceptions to their shield laws, the most frequent limitation is a three-part test similar to the one advocated by Justice Stewart in *Branzburg v. Hayes.* In Tennessee, for example, the state shield law protects a journalist from compelled testimony unless the person seeking the information can demonstrate that (1) the information sought relates to a specific, probable violation of law, (2) the information cannot be obtained through alternative means, and (3) there is a compelling and overriding public interest requiring disclosure.[69] Journalists are shielded from testifying if persons seeking the information cannot meet all three criteria.

A few states require disclosure when necessary to prevent "a miscarriage of justice,"[70] a provision that could be used if a judge believed a reporter's testimony was critical to the defense of a criminal defendant. Some states simply indicate that the privilege can be revoked if disclosure is essential to the public interest.[71]

Pros and Cons of Shield Laws

The benefits of shield laws tend to be too easily dismissed and too often overestimated. Journalists sometimes overlook the protection of shield laws because they would prefer protection under the First Amendment. Reporters and editors note that shield laws adopted by legislatures can also be rescinded by legislatures. A constitutional privilege, journalists contend, is taken more seriously by the courts than legislated protection.

Reporters and editors also argue that the protection against testifying afforded by statutes is necessarily limited because statutes must define who should be protected and under what conditions. Many news personnel would prefer a broadly stated privilege under the First Amendment that can be interpreted on a case-by-case basis in the courts. The courts could determine when a privilege under the First Amendment should apply without predetermined exceptions.

However, First Amendment protection has its limits as well. Because of the *Branzburg* precedent, a constitutional privilege is unlikely to protect journalists subpoenaed to testify

[67]552 A.2d 602 (N.J. 1989).
[68]633 F.2d 346 (3d Cir. 1980).
[69]Tenn. Code Ann. § 24-1-208. *See also* Fla. Stat. § 90.5015 (2) (using a similar three-part test).
[70]*See, e.g.,* N.D. Cent. Code Ann. § 31-01-06.2.
[71]*See, e.g., La. Rev. Stat.* § 45:1453.

before grand juries or journalists who witness criminal activity. The constitutional privilege might not be available in libel litigation because courts are reluctant to allow journalists "to hide" information that could be used against them. In addition, journalists cannot predict when a court will use the three-part test and how it will be applied in an individual case.

In the absence of a clearly defined constitutional protection for journalists, reporters in states with shield laws know that they will not be compelled to testify at least in some circumstances. Although shield laws are not usually absolute, journalists can often determine before they promise confidentiality whether a shield law will protect them. The mere existence of shield laws might help to thwart subpoenas. For example, lawyers might be less likely to seek a subpoena for the purpose of "fishing" for information when a state statute clearly grants a reporter a shield against testifying.

Journalists working in states with shield laws should be cautious before relying on the states' statutes, however. Shield laws are limited not only by a myriad of exclusions and exceptions but also by judges who tend to interpret them strictly. Many journalists and sources who have counted on a shield law found out too late that the statute did not apply to them. Many reporters therefore have faced penalties, including jail, that they had not anticipated and might not have risked had they known no protection existed. A reporter must know not only what a state shield law says but also how the courts could interpret that law. Moreover, as Josh Wolf recently discovered, a strong state shield law is inapplicable in federal proceedings.

Adding to the inherent judicial concern about shield laws limiting the availability of important testimony is a concern for the separation of powers among the branches of government. A few courts have declared that shield laws represent illegal interference by a legislature in the affairs of the judiciary. For example, New Mexico's Supreme Court ruled that the state's shield law violated the state constitution because the legislature could not establish rules for the courts.[72] In addition, courts sometimes rule that shield laws unconstitutionally interfere with the Sixth Amendment rights of criminal defendants. The New Jersey Supreme Court ruled that *New York Times* reporter Myron Farber had to produce subpoenaed materials in the murder trial of Dr. Mario E. Jascalevich despite the state's shield law. The New Jersey court agreed that it was "abundantly clear" that Farber fell under the New Jersey law providing news media employees the privilege of refusing to reveal information collected during their professional activities. However, the court said the state's shield law had to yield to both federal and state constitutional provisions that gave defendants the right "to have compulsory process for obtaining witnesses" in their favor.[73]

The lack of complete protection for confidential sources means that a journalist should consider carefully any promise not to reveal the identity of sources. A reporter may want to promise only conditional confidentiality. That is, a reporter will promise to protect the identity of a source unless ordered to reveal it by a court. Moreover, some lawyers suggest that reporters require sources to sign affidavits as evidence the source exists. Many news organizations require that editors be consulted when reporters wish to promise confidentiality to news sources. Editors might disagree with the promise of confidentiality after the

[72]Ammerman v. Hubbard Broadcasting, Inc., 551 P.2d 1354 (N.M. 1976). The same New Mexico Supreme Court later promulgated a rule providing journalists a limited privilege. N.M. R. Evid. § 11-514.
[73]*In re Farber,* 394 A.2d 330 (N.J. 1978).

reporter has legally obligated the newspaper, a problem discussed later in the chapter. In addition, news organizations might refuse to help reporters fight subpoenas if the reporters do not adhere to company policy on confidentiality.

◇ Summary ◇

Thirty-three states and the District of Columbia have adopted statutes protecting journalists from revealing news sources. These statutes vary greatly, but none protects every writer in all circumstances. Most apply only to news media employees. A few specify that they apply only when confidentiality has been promised. About half of the statutes apply only to the disclosure of sources and not to notes and other information. The rest protect other information that reporters possess as well. Journalists need to be aware of the limitations of their state's shield laws before relying on them for protection against a court order to testify.

Protection under Federal Statutes and Regulations

No federal statute explicitly protects reporters from being ordered to testify in court. Shortly after *Branzburg* was decided, both the House and Senate held extensive hearings on proposed shield legislation. The move to enact a federal shield law collapsed because press organizations could not agree on whether the privilege should be qualified or absolute and the Department of Justice opposed the proposed legislation.[74] By 1975, the sense of urgency had passed as lower courts began recognizing a qualified First Amendment privilege.

As a result of recent high-profile cases, such as the Plame and Lee cases discussed earlier in this chapter, the House of Representatives approved a bill protecting journalist-source relationships on October 16, 2007;[75] a similar bill was approved by the Senate Judiciary Committee on October 4.[76] The most controversial aspect of these proposals is the qualified protection of the identity of confidential sources leaking to journalists classified national security information. Relying on Judge Tatel's balancing test discussed earlier in this chapter, the bills would require the government to prove a leak caused "significant" harm to national security and the interest in disclosure of the source's identity outweighs the interest in the free flow of information. The Bush administration has threatened a veto because these proposals place a burden on tracing sources of national security leaks. Supporters, though, claim a shield law is necessary to protect the disclosure of government wrongdoing, such as warrantless wiretapping. Senate action is unlikely in 2008 due to the pending elections.

Despite the absence of a federal shield law, rules governing the federal courts and regulations issued by the Department of Justice and the Securities and Exchange Commission restrict the use of subpoenas served on reporters.

[74]*See generally Newsmen's Privilege: Hearings before the Subcomm. on Constitutional Rights of the Senate Comm. on the Judiciary,* 93d Cong. (1973); *Newsmen's Privilege: Hearings before Subcomm. No. 3 of the House Comm. on the Judiciary,* 93d Cong. (1973).

[75]Free Flow of Information Act of 2007, H.R. 2102, 110th Cong. (2007).

[76]Free Flow of Information Act of 2007, S. 2035, 110th Cong. (2007).

Several courts have protected reporters from subpoenas under rules of evidence Congress adopted for use in the federal courts. Section 403 of the Federal Rules of Evidence, for example, allows judges to quash subpoenas if information sought from reporters would duplicate information already available. Therefore, a federal judge must consider whether alternative sources of information exist even if the judge does not recognize the qualified privilege developed in the Stewart dissent in *Branzburg*.

In addition to the rules governing the federal courts, the U.S. attorney general issued guidelines in 1973 to limit requests for journalists' confidential sources by members of the Department of Justice. The guidelines were written "to strike the proper balance" between the public interest in an unrestricted flow of information and the public interest in fair and effective law enforcement. The guidelines apply to civil litigation as well as criminal investigations.[77]

The guidelines reflect the protections for journalists recognized in Stewart's three-part test in *Branzburg v. Hayes*. The guidelines state that before subpoenaing journalists, Justice Department employees must seek alternative sources and negotiate with the media when possible. The guidelines specify that the government should seek subpoenas only when there are "reasonable grounds" to believe that the information is relevant and essential to an investigation or case. The scope of the subpoena should be as narrow as possible, limiting the amount of material requested. No subpoena is to be issued without the authorization of the U.S. attorney general.

The guidelines do not define the terms *reporter* or *news media*. Nonetheless, Department of Justice officials make distinctions about the people subject to the guidelines. For example, aspiring book author Vanessa Leggett was not considered to be a journalist by the DOJ; as an unpublished freelancer working on a book about a high society murder, Leggett lacked an employer or a contract for publication. Consequently, *all* of her notes and tape recordings relating to the murder were subpoenaed by a grand jury without any negotiation between Leggett and the DOJ. A federal appeals court ruled that even if Leggett were a "journalist," she was required to comply with the subpoena absent evidence of harassment or oppression. While the subpoena was not as "narrowly tailored as would be ideal," the appellate court held it was not overly broad. Leggett spent 168 days in federal prison—for refusing to turn over her notes and tape recordings.[78]

The Justice Department guidelines also limit subpoenas for journalists' long-distance telephone records. The restrictions were added after a federal appeals court ruled that the news media had no constitutional right to be notified before telephone companies surrendered the records of journalists' long-distance phone calls to law enforcement officers. In *Reporters Committee for Freedom of the Press v. AT&T,* several reporters, two newspaper companies, and the Reporters Committee for Freedom of the Press tried to block government access to reporters' long-distance billing information if the journalists were not told beforehand.[79] The journalists sued AT&T after the company released toll-call records to government officials five times without informing the media. In one case, the FBI used phone records to try to link Daniel Ellsberg to the publication of the Pentagon Papers, discussed in Chapter 3. In another, the Internal Revenue Service sought evidence to confirm

[77]28 C.F.R. § 50.10.
[78]*In re* Grand Jury Subpoenas, 29 Media L. Rep. 2301 (5th Cir. 2001), *cert. denied* 535 U.S. 1011 (2002).
[79]593 F.2d 1030 (D.C. Cir. 1978), *cert. denied,* 440 U.S. 949 (1979).

that an IRS employee had illegally divulged information to *New York Times* reporter David Rosenbaum.

The U.S. Court of Appeals for the D.C. Circuit, citing the Supreme Court's decision in *Branzburg,* said that the media have no First Amendment right to prevent the government from seeing telephone records that allow the identification of a news source. In *Reporters Committee,* the court said the First Amendment does not guarantee anyone, including journalists, the right to collect information immune from good-faith investigations by the government. No one, said the court, is insulated from the inhibitions that result from knowing the government has the authority to investigate criminal activity. The court added:

> All citizens when they choose to act surreptitiously are put to some inconvenience; they must lower their voices, put little or nothing in writing, speak and meet outside the presence of third parties; these simple precautions are commonly used, whether the ends be lofty or evil. Plaintiffs are no exception simply because they are "journalists."

In addition, the court said that telephone records are not protected by Fourth Amendment restrictions on government searches. The Fourth Amendment, as discussed in Chapter 5, protects citizens "against unreasonable searches and seizures" of their person, house, papers, and effects and declares that no warrants should be issued "but upon probable cause" specifically "describing the place to be searched, and the persons or things to be seized." The D.C. Circuit said that persons using the phone system knowingly expose their actions to third parties, thus surrendering Fourth Amendment rights protecting private affairs from unreasonable government encroachment. The court said the government was free to investigate criminal activity by examining the telephone records of persons who might have been in contact with a suspect.

The Justice Department guidelines, amended after *Reporters Committee,* limit any federal subpoena for telephone records to specific and relevant information essential to an investigation. The guidelines also say the government should pursue alternative approaches to obtaining the information being sought before officials seek a subpoena. The government need not notify the media before subpoenaing telephone records if prior notice poses "a substantial threat to the integrity" of an investigation. However, if a news organization is not warned before a subpoena for telephone records, it must be notified within ninety days of the time the subpoena is issued. The U.S. attorney general must ordinarily approve a subpoena for telephone records.

Department of Justice attorneys who do not follow the guidelines are subject to internal disciplinary action, but the guidelines specifically state they are "not intended to create or recognize any legally enforceable right in any person." Recently, the *New York Times* argued the government failed to comply with the guidelines when seeking the telephone records of two *Times* reporters and, as a result, should be barred from receiving the records. A federal district court rejected this argument, holding the guidelines "are just that— touchstones to assist the DOJ in its exercise of prosecutorial discretion— and confer no substantive rights or protections" that may be privately enforced.[80] Similarly, in the case of journalists Matthew Cooper and Judith Miller, discussed earlier in this chapter, the Court of Appeals for the District of Columbia Circuit held the guidelines, not required by any constitutional or statutory provision, merely "exist to guide the Department's exercise of

[80]N.Y. Times Co. v. Gonzales, 382 F. Supp.2d 457 (S.D.N.Y. 2005), *rev'd on other grounds,* 459 F.3d 160 (2d Cir. 2006), *stay denied,* 2006 U.S. LEXIS 9194 (Nov. 27, 2006). The *Times* did not appeal this aspect of the lower court's ruling.

its discretion in determining when to seek the issuance of subpoenas to reporters, not to confer substantive or procedural benefits upon individual media personnel."[81]

In 2006, the Securities and Exchange Commission issued guidelines concerning subpoenas to members of the news media. The guidelines were prompted by an SEC investigation into stock manipulation by Gradient Analytics in which SEC investigators subpoenaed two Dow Jones reporters who had covered the firm. Since the insider trading scandals of the 1980s, discussed in Chapter 8, when reporters were the subject of investigations, the SEC had not subpoenaed any journalists. News of the 2006 subpoenas caused SEC Chair Christopher Cross to publicly scold his staff for failing to give the commissioners prior notice of the subpoenas. Although the SEC had no formal policy in place, Cox stated that "the issuance of a subpoena to a journalist which seeks to compel production of his or her notes and records of conversations with sources is highly unusual." Following Cox's remarks, the SEC decided not to enforce the subpoenas.[82]

In response to the Dow Jones incident, the SEC in April 2006 adopted guidelines for issuing subpoenas to journalists. Like the Department of Justice guidelines, the SEC guidelines require staff members to seek the information from non-media sources and to negotiate with news media to obtain information through informal methods, such as voluntary production, informal interviews, or written summaries. A subpoena will be issued only in cases where the requested information is essential to an investigation and all alternative means of obtaining the information have been exhausted. Only the director of the Division of Enforcement, in consultation with the General Counsel, may authorize a subpoena and the chair of the SEC must be promptly notified. As with the Department of Justice guidelines, the SEC guidelines are not intended to create any legally enforceable rights in any person.[83]

Although no federal agencies other than the Department of Justice and the Securities and Exchange Commission have formal policies concerning news media subpoenas, it is rare for administrative agencies to seek information from the press. In 2005 and 2007, however, two federal judges ruled that *Platts*, a publisher of energy prices and transaction data, was required to comply with administrative subpoenas issued by the Commodity Futures Trading Commission (CFTC); the CFTC was investigating whether an energy marketing company had submitted false data to *Platts* in an effort to manipulate natural gas prices. *Platts* was covered by a qualified reporter's privilege because it engaged in journalistic analysis and judgment, in addition to simply reporting data, the courts ruled. However, the privilege was more limited than in a civil case because the CFTC's investigatory authority was similar to that of a grand jury. Both courts concluded the CFTC proved that most of the information sought was critical to the investigation and could not be obtained through alternative sources. In the 2005 case, however, the court modified the subpoena so that *Platts* did not have to divulge information obtained from firms other than the target of the investigation.[84] In the 2007 case, the court refused to enforce that portion of the subpoena seeking all complaints received by *Platts* about the alleged price manipulation, noting this was a "fishing expedition."[85]

[81]*In re* Grand Jury Subpoena, Miller, 397 F. 3d 964 (D.C. Cir. 2005).

[82]Kara Scannell, "Cox Knocks Journalist Subpoenas," *Wall Street Journal,* Feb. 28, 2006, at C5.

[83]17 C.F.R. § 202.10.

[84]United States Commodity Futures Trading Comm'n v. McGraw-Hill, 390 F. Supp. 2d 27; 403 F. Supp. 2d 34 (D.D.C. 2005).

[85]507 F. Supp. 2d 45 (D.D.C. 2007).

◇ Summary ◇

There is no federal shield law. However, several courts have recognized a privilege for reporters under federal rules of procedure adopted by Congress for the federal courts. In addition, the Department of Justice and the Securities and Exchange Commission have adopted guidelines designed to limit the use of subpoenas served on journalists.

Congressional Authority

The judicial branch is not the only arm of the federal government with the power to subpoena reporters and cite journalists for contempt for refusing to disclose sources or information. Although no reporter has been found in contempt of Congress in the last thirty years, a few have been threatened with contempt citations for refusing to testify during congressional investigations.[86] In 1992, for example, a special counsel appointed by the Senate tried to obtain congressional authority to compel the testimony of Nina Totenberg of National Public Radio and Timothy Phelps of *Newsday*. The two refused to disclose the sources of their stories reporting that law professor Anita Hill had told Senate investigators that she had been sexually harassed by Judge Clarence Thomas, a nominee to the U.S. Supreme Court. Although Thomas was eventually confirmed, the disclosure of Hill's charges led to nationally televised committee hearings that included testimony from Hill and Thomas. However, the leadership of the Senate Rules Committee decided not to require Totenberg and Phelps to testify or face contempt charges. Rules Committee chairman Senator Wendell H. Ford said that requiring the reporters to testify "could have a chilling effect on the media and could close a door where more doors need opening."[87]

Search Warrants

In the 1970s, a few media personnel faced a new legal weapon, the **search warrant,** more threatening to confidentiality than a subpoena. Although subpoenas require reporters to testify in court or produce documents for the court, the recipient of a subpoena can challenge it during a hearing before complying. In contrast, a search warrant allows no opportunity for a journalist to prepare a response and no opportunity for a court challenge. A search warrant authorizes law enforcement officers to make unannounced searches for journalists' notes and photographs.

Many law enforcement officers prefer search warrants to subpoenas because the officers believe journalists will seek to quash subpoenas. In addition, the officials fear that journalists will destroy or hide evidence while fighting a subpoena. News personnel fear search warrants because they believe a proliferation of newsroom searches will intimidate potential confidential sources. If law enforcement officers could easily acquire warrants authorizing searches, sources could reasonably conclude that journalists could not honor promises to keep information confidential.

86For a discussion of legislative use of the contempt power, see Ronald Goldfarb, *The Contempt Power* 22–41 (1971).
87Clifford Kraus, "Senate Panel Rebuffs Prosecutor in Leak Inquiry," *N.Y. Times*, Mar. 26, 1992, at B12.

Thus far, however, newsroom searches by law enforcement officers have been relatively rare. In addition, state and federal statutes have largely neutralized a 1978 Supreme Court opinion that permitted police to conduct unannounced searches of newsrooms.

In *Zurcher v. Stanford Daily,* the Supreme Court said the U.S. Constitution permits the police to search without warning the homes and offices of people who are not criminal suspects.[88] The Court said that neither the First nor the Fourth Amendment prohibits law enforcement officers with a search warrant from searching for criminal evidence on property used or owned by law-abiding citizens. The 5-3 decision permitted searches of newsrooms, corporate offices, and private homes and cars.

In *Zurcher,* the Stanford University student newspaper challenged a 1971 search of its office. The search occurred after *Stanford Daily* photographers took pictures of a student takeover of Stanford University Hospital's administrative offices. When police officers tried to remove the demonstrators, violence erupted, and several officers were hurt. The injured officers could not identify most of the people involved. Police photographers did not see the violence.

When the Santa Clara County district attorney saw pictures of the incident in the *Stanford Daily,* he obtained a warrant from the municipal court for a search of the paper's offices for film, negatives, and prints showing the events at the hospital. The warrant said officials had probable cause to believe that the *Stanford Daily* offices contained "material and relevant" evidence helpful to identifying the persons involved in the violence. Police did not contend that anyone connected with the paper had violated the law. Indeed, the search of the student newsroom did not produce anything that had not been published. The *Stanford Daily* and members of the staff complained that the search violated their rights under the First, Fourth, and Fourteenth Amendments. The students argued that warrants authorizing searches of places occupied by "third parties," persons not directly suspected of crimes, should not ordinarily be allowed.

The Supreme Court said in *Zurcher* that the Fourth Amendment provides no special exemption for searches involving third parties when authorities have probable cause to believe that they can find criminal evidence. In addition, said Justice Byron White, writing for the Court, the First Amendment does not protect the news media from searches. White said the First Amendment requires only that the courts adhere to Fourth Amendment requirements with "particular exactitude." He said the preconditions for a warrant—probable cause, specificity with respect to the place to be searched and the things to be seized, and overall reasonableness—should provide adequate protection for journalists. Justice White also said that the legislative and executive branches could adopt laws and regulations protecting against the abuse of search warrants.

Journalists feared that the Supreme Court's *Zurcher* opinion would encourage law enforcement officers to use search warrants rather than subpoenas, fears fueled by a few searches conducted shortly after *Zurcher* was announced. In Boise, Idaho, for example, a prosecutor armed with a search warrant rummaged through the desks and files of television station KBCI-TV until he found film of a prison riot.[89] The news media launched a major lobbying campaign to encourage state legislatures and the U.S. Congress to adopt statutes to curb searches triggered by the Supreme Court's opinion in *Zurcher.*

---

[88] 436 U.S. 547 (1978).
[89] Wayne King, "TV Tapes Are Seized in an Idaho Inquiry on Prison Uprising," *N.Y. Times,* July 27, 1980, at A1.

In response to the concerns of the news media, several state legislatures and the Congress adopted legislation to protect newsrooms from searches. The federal law, the Privacy Protection Act of 1980, severely restricts the use of search warrants to look for or seize information in the possession of public communicators. Under the Privacy Protection Act, federal, state, and local law enforcement officers can search only in exceptional circumstances for criminal evidence in the offices of the news media, book authors, and others who intend to disseminate information to the public.

The Privacy Protection Act puts more severe restrictions on searches for "work product materials" obtained and prepared for public dissemination. Work product materials are notes, story drafts, mental impressions, and opinions. The statute prohibits searches for work product materials unless federal and state law enforcement officers can establish beforehand that (1) there is probable cause to believe a reporter has committed a crime, (2) there is reason to believe that seizure of the materials is necessary to prevent an injury or death, or (3) the materials contain information "relating to the national defense, classified information, or restricted data" as defined under federal espionage laws. The government needs to prove only one of the three to meet its obligation under the statute.[90]

In 1993, a federal district court ruled that Secret Service agents violated the Privacy Protection Act when they searched the offices of Steve Jackson Games, Inc., and seized work product materials. The U.S. District Court for the Western District of Texas awarded Steve Jackson Games $51,000 in expenses and damages to the business after the Secret Service obtained a search warrant to look for a proprietary computer document stolen from Bell South. The court noted that federal agents seized 300 computer disks, including a draft of the book *Gurps Cyberpunk,* the drafts of several magazine articles about games, and an electronic bulletin board. The Secret Service had no evidence that the company had committed a crime, the court said.[91]

The Privacy Protection Act allows officials to search for "documentary materials" under more circumstances than they may search for "work product materials." Documentary materials are pieces of information recorded in tangible form that are obtained during the preparation of a story. This category includes videotapes, audiotapes, photos, and other raw materials of the newsgathering process. Documentary materials do not qualify as work product materials because they do not contain journalists' ideas. Law enforcement officials may search for and seize "documentary materials" not only when there is reason to believe a journalist has committed a crime, when there is reason to believe a life can be saved, or when there is national security information to protect, but also when a journalist does not produce the materials in response to a subpoena. In addition, law enforcement officers can search for documentary materials if they can demonstrate they have a reason to believe the materials would be altered, destroyed, or hidden if a reporter were served with a subpoena.

In a 1995 case involving documentary materials, a Missouri federal district court held that a police seizure of a videotape from a television newsroom violated the Privacy Protection Act.[92] The judge ordered the prosecutor to pay the television station $1,000, the minimum penalty under the act. The controversy began when WDAF-TV of Kansas City, Missouri,

[90]42 U.S.C. § 2000aa.

[91]Steve Jackson Games, Inc. v. United States Secret Service, 816 F. Supp. 432 (W.D. Texas 1993), *aff'd,* 36 F.3d 457 (5th Cir. 1994).

[92]Tom Jackman, "Seizure of Videotape Ruled Improper," *Kansas City Star,* Feb. 2, 1995, at A1.

obtained a videotape from a tourist that showed a man dragging a woman by the hair across a Kansas City street. The woman was later found murdered. After WDAF aired the tape, police sought a search warrant because they said the evidence contained in the tape was crucial in order to charge the man with the murder before Missouri law required that he be released.

The court ruled that the search warrant violated the Privacy Protection Act because the request for the search warrant failed to state that a search would prevent a death or injury or fulfill other provisions of the act permitting a search for documentary materials. The court rejected officials' attempts to justify the search warrant after the fact.

The Privacy Protection Act and similar state laws provide public communicators substantial protection against unannounced searches. Although the Privacy Protection Act limits searches by state and local officials as well as by federal officials, several states have enacted provisions that are more stringent than the federal statute.[93] Law enforcement officers ordinarily will have to rely on a subpoena rather than a search warrant to obtain confidential information from the media. However, some exceptions remain. For example, the provision in the federal law allowing searches for national security information would have allowed an unannounced search of the *New York Times* offices for the Pentagon Papers.

The FBI's power to engage in electronic surveillance or to examine records, papers, and documents was expanded by the USA Patriot Act, enacted in response to the terrorist attacks of September 11, 2001. Under this act, the FBI may obtain information relating to investigations of "international terrorism or clandestine intelligence activities."[94] The FBI, however, is prohibited from investigating someone "solely upon the basis of activities" protected by the First Amendment, such as speaking against government policy. Under the law, FBI agents could subpoena customer records from telephone companies and Internet service providers (ISPs), as well as customer records held by other businesses.

One type of FBI subpoena is known as a National Security Letter (NSL). Requests for NSLs are approved by Special Agents in charge of the FBI's fifty-six field offices. Prior to the Patriot Act, NSL requests were approved by senior FBI officials at FBI headquarters. A March 2008 report issued by the Inspector General of the Department of Justice found the FBI's use of NSLs has grown dramatically since enactment of the Patriot Act.[95] The FBI issued approximately 8,500 NSL requests in 2000. After the passage of the Patriot Act in 2001, the number of NSL requests has averaged approximately 48,000 a year during the 2003–2006 period. The majority of NSLs sought telephone billing records and other records relating to electronic communication. Another type of subpoena, known as a Section 215 order, has rarely been used by the FBI. Section 215 of the Patriot Act allows the FBI to seek orders from the Foreign Intelligence Surveillance Court for "any tangible things" including books, records, and other items from any business or organization provided the items are for an authorized investigation to protect against terrorism or clandestine intelligence activities. In 2005, the FBI obtained 162 Section 215 orders for a variety of records such as apartment leasing records and credit card records. Despite widespread fear that the FBI would use its authority to obtain

[93]*See, e.g.*, Tex. Code Crim. Proc. Art. 18.01 (e).
[94]50 U.S.C. § 1861; 18 U.S.C. § 2709.
[95]U.S. Dept. of Justice, Office of the Inspector General, *A Review of the Federal Bureau of Investigation's Use of National Security Letters* (Mar. 2008).

library records, a March 2007 report showed the FBI did not obtain any Section 215 orders for library records between 2003 and 2005.[96]

In enacting the Patriot Act, Congress forbade all persons or organizations faced with FBI requests for information from telling others about the investigation. In 2005, Congress renewed key provisions of the Patriot Act and altered the provisions relating to FBI subpoenas. Instead of a blanket prohibition on disclosure, under the new law FBI officials could determine which recipients of subpoenas were gagged, based on FBI assessment of factors such as danger to national security.[97] Nonetheless, in 2007 a federal district court found the amended law was an unconstitutional content-based restriction on speech.[98] The law excluded the first-hand experiences of NSL recipients from public debate about government intrusion into private lives. Also, the FBI's power to choose which NSL recipients were gagged raised the danger of the FBI silencing only those recipients likely to speak out against the use of NSLs.

Summary

The U.S. Supreme Court decided in *Zurcher v. Stanford Daily* that the First Amendment does not protect communicators from authorized searches for criminal evidence, even when they are not suspected of criminal activity. The impact of the decision has been blunted by state and federal statutes encouraging the use of subpoenas rather than search warrants in most circumstances. The Privacy Protection Act limits searches for work products and documentary materials.

Breaching Confidentiality

This chapter has focused on the efforts of journalists to honor their promises of confidentiality to news sources. Occasionally, however, reporters or editors reveal the names of sources to whom they have promised anonymity. In 1991, the U.S. Supreme Court said journalists are not protected by the First Amendment when sued by victims of broken promises. In *Cohen v. Cowles Media Co.*, the Supreme Court upheld the constitutionality of a Minnesota state law permitting persons who are injured because of a broken promise to recover damages.[99] Subsequently, when the same case was remanded to the Minnesota Supreme Court, the court awarded $200,000 to Dan Cohen, who lost his public relations job after newspapers revealed his name in violation of a promise of confidentiality.

Cohen, a public relations consultant and spokesperson for the 1982 Independent-Republican gubernatorial candidate in Minnesota, sued the *Minneapolis Star & Tribune* and the *St. Paul Pioneer Press Dispatch*. Even though reporters for the two papers had promised him confidentiality, Cohen was identified as the source of a story reporting that the candidate for the Democratic-Farm-Labor party had been convicted twelve years before of shoplifting $6 worth of merchandise.

Editors of the *Star & Tribune* and the *Pioneer Press Dispatch* named Cohen as the source of the story because, they said, readers needed to know that the shoplifting story came

[96]U.S. Dept. of Justice, Office of the Inspector General, *A Review of the Federal Bureau of Investigation's Use of Section 215 Orders for Business Records* (Mar. 2007).
[97]18 U.S.C. § 2709 (c); *see also* 18 U.S.C. § 3511.
[98]Doe v. Gonzales, 500 F. Supp. 2d 379 (D.D.C. 2007).
[99]501 U.S. 663 (1991).

from the opposing candidate's campaign staff. The editors argued that a story revealing that one candidate's campaign released "eleventh hour information" about an opponent was more important than a story about a twelve-year-old shoplifting charge that had been vacated.

When the newspapers printed Cohen's name, he lost his job as a public relations executive with an advertising firm and sued the newspapers. Cohen charged that the newspapers breached an oral contract and claimed the reporters and editors misrepresented the commitment of the newspapers to protect confidential sources. A jury awarded Cohen $200,000 in compensatory damages for both claims and $500,000 in punitive damages for misrepresentation. In 1989, the Minnesota Court of Appeals upheld Cohen's contract claim and the $200,000 award for compensatory damages. However, the appeals court overturned the award for punitive damages, saying that the reporters had not misrepresented their intentions at the time the promise of confidentiality had been made.[100]

In 1990, the Minnesota Supreme Court reversed the verdict, saying that the reporters' promises to Cohen constituted neither misrepresentation nor a breach of contract.[101] The court said the publication of Cohen's name was not a breach of contract because both reporters and their sources "understand that a reporter's promise is given as a moral commitment" rather than as a binding offer and acceptance of an offer. Because no genuine contract existed, the newspapers could not have breached a contract.

The Minnesota Supreme Court also refused to enforce the promises of confidentiality to Cohen through a common-law doctrine protecting people who rely on promises. The doctrine, called *promissory estoppel,* requires that courts enforce a promise if breaking the promise creates an injustice that should be remedied by law. The Minnesota court said that enforcing promissory estoppel against the newspaper would violate the First Amendment because Cohen was a political source in a political campaign, a "classic First Amendment context." The specter of civil damages arising from promises made during election coverage would chill the public debate, the court said.

The U.S. Supreme Court, in a 5-4 decision, overruled the Minnesota court. The U.S. Supreme Court's majority said the First Amendment does not prohibit the use of Minnesota's common law of promissory estoppel when journalists break promises made to sources.[102] Justice White, writing for the Court's majority, said that a long line of cases had established that the First Amendment does not immunize the press from laws that apply to everyone. White noted that reporters, like all citizens, cannot break and enter an office or residence to gather news. Nor can reporters refuse to reveal a confidential news source before a grand jury. Similarly, White said, reporters, like other citizens, may be held responsible for commitments they break.

The Court's majority discounted as "constitutionally insignificant" any impact of Minnesota's doctrine of promissory estoppel on reporting, including possible self-censorship by the press. Any effect of promissory estoppel to limit news coverage, the Court said, was an "incidental" consequence of equally applying laws that ensure promises are kept.

In separate dissenting opinions in *Cohen,* Justices Souter and Blackmun said that Minnesota's doctrine of promissory estoppel violated First Amendment rights even though it applied to media and non-media alike. The dissenters argued that the importance of

[100] 445 N.W.2d 248 (Minn. Ct. App. 1989).
[101] 457 N.W.2d 199 (Minn. 1990).
[102] 501 U.S. 663 (1991).

political speech—essential to citizens in a democracy—should override Minnesota's practice of enforcing informal promises, at least in this case.

The Supreme Court remanded *Cohen* to the Minnesota Supreme Court to determine whether Cohen could establish that he met Minnesota's promissory estoppel requirements. The Minnesota court, in its second review of the *Cohen* case, upheld the jury's award to Cohen of $200,000 in compensatory damages, ruling that Cohen met all three requirements for promissory estoppel.[103]

First, Cohen had documented that the reporters clearly promised confidentiality. Second, the Minnesota high court said, Cohen relied on the reporters' promise to his detriment when he handed them the papers documenting the conviction of the Democratic-Farm-Labor candidate. The resulting stories, using Cohen's name as the source, cost him his job. Finally, the Minnesota Supreme Court said, the broken promises by the newspapers led to an injustice that should be remedied through the common law of promissory estoppel. The court said that denying Cohen any recourse for the loss of his job would be unjust, given the long journalistic tradition of protecting confidential sources and the absence of a compelling need "in this case" to break the promise.

In the initial wake of the *Cohen* case, a number of other sources filed lawsuits against the press, claiming that confidentialty promises were broken. In 1993, a federal appellate court remanded for trial a second Minnesota suit brought by a plaintiff who said her identity could be recognized in a story although she had been promised anonymity. The U.S. Court of Appeals for the Eighth Circuit, reversing a summary judgment issued by a federal district court, said a jury ought to decide whether Jill Ruzicka was unjustly harmed under the common-law doctrine of promissory estoppel. The Eighth Circuit said that a confidentiality promise made to Ruzicka by a *Glamour* magazine writer was "sufficiently specific" to qualify as a "clear and definite" promise, one of the requirements of promissory estoppel.[104]

The Eighth Circuit said "there is nothing vague or ambiguous" about a promise to keep a source from being identified in a story. The court relied on a dictionary meaning of *identifiable* as "subject to identification; capable of being identified." The court said the "plain meaning" of a promise that a source would not be identifiable was that the source's identity would be masked so that "a reasonable reader" could not recognize her. The Eighth Circuit said it was up to a jury to determine at trial whether Ruzicka could be reasonably identified in the story, which did not name her but described her career and discussed her allegations of sexual abuse, using her first name and a pseudonym for her last name. The Eighth Circuit also said a jury should determine whether the promise of anonymity must be enforced to prevent an injustice.

On remand, the case was settled for $250,000.[105]

◇ Summary ◇

The U.S. Supreme Court has said the First Amendment does not protect journalists who reveal the names of sources promised confidentiality. The Court said that the state of Minnesota could enforce its doctrine of promissory estoppel, a common-law doctrine protecting people who rely on promises to their detriment.

[103] 479 N.W.2d 387 (Minn. 1992).
[104] Ruzicka v. Conde Nast Publications, Inc., 999 F.2d 1319 (8th Cir. 1993).
[105] Ruzicka v. Rothenberg, 83 F.3d 1033 (8th Cir. 1996).

CHAPTER 12

Access to Information

Although the First Amendment protects the right to publish information about public issues, it does not guarantee the right to collect information about the government. The U.S. Supreme Court has refused to provide First Amendment protection for newsgathering beyond the access to criminal trials discussed in Chapter 10. The First Amendment does not ensure that a reporter can gain entry to a city council meeting, obtain a consultant's report about the quality of drinking water, or visit the site of a nuclear power plant accident.

If the U.S. Constitution does not guarantee a communicator's access to information, neither does the common law. Judges traditionally have not required that governmental bodies meet publicly or allow everyone to inspect government records. Nevertheless, many government records and meetings have historically been open to the public. This openness has been codified over the last fifty years in federal and state open records and meetings statutes.

Access law, like the right to publish, is grounded in American political theory. Because government in the United States is based on the will of the public, citizens need to know what government is doing. Thomas Jefferson said that only an informed electorate could govern effectively.[1] Professor Alexander Meiklejohn wrote that citizens who are denied information will make decisions that are "ill-considered" and "ill-balanced."[2] Professor Thomas Emerson said a democracy without an informed public is a contradiction.[3] An informed public must have access to information not only about government, but also about health, safety, consumer information, ecology, and global warming.

Just as access to information is important to our system of government, so is the security of government records, the effectiveness of law enforcement departments, and the privacy of citizens. Therefore, not all government records and meetings are open. National defense sometimes hinges on secret military tactics and capabilities. Law enforcement officers would have difficulty catching criminals if suspects could demand to see police evidence and learn investigatory strategies. Likewise, government would infringe citizens' privacy if it disclosed information about the health or taxes of individuals.

Since September 11, 2001, the government has closed records, websites, and proceedings in order to deny information to terrorists who might try to harm the United States. Many journalists and civil libertarians think too many records have been stamped classified, so many that American citizens are denied needed information about how the government conducts the war on terror.

However numerous the government's reasons for withholding information, Americans probably have more access to government information than citizens in any other country. In the United States, citizens may see criminal arrest records, property records, and census reports. The public also can acquire scientific data on the side effects of prescription drugs and learn how the CIA and the FBI have monitored citizens illegally.

British journalist William Shawcross was impressed with the information he could acquire through freedom-of-information requests for a critical book he wrote about American military actions. Shawcross noted he could not acquire similar information in Great Britain.[4]

This chapter discusses the law of access to the legislative and administrative branches of government and to news events. The chapter begins with a discussion of the Supreme Court's First Amendment rulings on access to government-controlled installations. Then the chapter discusses the law of access to public property, quasi-public property, and war zones. Next, the chapter treats federal and state laws controlling access to government records and meetings.

[1]*E.g.*, Letter to Edward Carrington, Jan. 16, 1787, in 11 *The Papers of Thomas Jefferson* 48–49 (Julian P. Boyd ed., 1955).
[2]*Free Speech* 26 (1948).
[3]"The Danger of State Secrecy," *The Nation,* Mar. 30, 1974, at 395.
[4]*All Things Considered,* National Public Radio, July 7, 1989.

Access and the Constitution

For many scholars and journalists, the freedom to publish news means little without the ability to gather information. However, the U.S. Supreme Court has ruled that the First Amendment does not guarantee public access to news to the same degree it guarantees the media the right to publish and broadcast. The Court did rule, however, in *Richmond Newspapers v. Virginia,* that the public and the press have a constitutional right to attend trials. The Court might have extended the rationale of its decision in *Richmond Newspapers* to other governmental settings. If citizens have a constitutional right of access to courts because courts have historically been open, it could be argued that citizens should also have a constitutional right of access to legislatures and city council meetings. If citizens have a constitutional right of access to the courts because of the important governing decisions made there, it could be argued that citizens should have a similar right of access to legislatures and other governing institutions. Although a few federal courts have recognized citizens' First Amendment rights to government functions and records, the Supreme Court has not extended a citizen's constitutional right of access beyond proceedings in the courts. Journalists therefore depend on statutes to gain access to government records and meetings. In a series of cases involving access to prisons, the Supreme Court explained why citizens cannot demand access to governmental buildings and activities in the name of the First Amendment.

The Supreme Court

In the handful of newsgathering cases the Supreme Court has decided, it has set forth three principles: First, the First Amendment does not guarantee the public or the press a right to obtain information. Second, journalists have no greater rights of access to information than anyone else. Third, the public's need for access to information will be balanced against sometimes conflicting social needs, such as effective law enforcement and individual privacy.

The Supreme Court said as early as 1972 that

> it has generally been held that the First Amendment does not guarantee the press a constitutional right of special access to information not available to the public generally. . . . Despite the fact that news gathering may be hampered, the press is regularly excluded from grand jury proceedings, our own conferences, the meetings of other official bodies gathered in executive session, and the meetings of private organizations. Newsmen have no constitutional right of access to the scenes of crime or disaster when the general public is excluded.[5]

The Supreme Court has denied journalists a First Amendment right of access to newsworthy information in three prison cases. In the first two, which were decided on the same day, the Court upheld the constitutionality of prison rules restricting reporters' interviews

[5]Branzburg v. Hayes, 408 U.S. 665 (1972).

with inmates. The Court said that the First Amendment does not guarantee the press more access to prisons and inmates than is available to the general public.

In one of the cases, *Pell v. Procunier,* reporters claimed a First Amendment right to interview specific California prisoners.[6] Before 1971 in California, journalists could conduct face-to-face interviews with prisoners on request. However, state prison officials said that the policy of unrestricted interviews was partly responsible for a breakdown in prison discipline. Particularly damaging to prison discipline, officials said, was media attention showered on the Soledad Brothers, three black inmates accused of killing a white prison guard. The Soledad Brothers' influence over fellow prisoners grew with their celebrity, officials claimed, reducing the ability of guards to control the prisons. An escape attempt in 1971 resulted in five deaths.

To tighten control by reducing the celebrity of inmates, California officials revised the corrections manual to prohibit "media interviews with specific individual inmates." In *Pell v. Procunier,* the Supreme Court ruled 5-4 that the new restrictions on reporters' access to prisoners did not abridge the First Amendment rights of the press. The Court came to the same conclusion in *Saxbe v. Washington Post,* a case decided at the same time as *Pell* involving similar regulations at federal prisons.[7]

In *Pell,* the Court said that although the First and the Fourteenth Amendments prevent the government from interfering with a free press, the Constitution does not require the government to provide the press access to information not available to the average citizen. Writing for the Court, Justice Potter Stewart said:

> It is one thing to say that a journalist is free to seek out sources of information not available to members of the general public. . . . It is quite another thing to suggest that the Constitution imposes upon government the affirmative duty to make available to journalists sources of information not available to members of the public generally.[8]

Stewart said the Court would defer to the judgment of corrections officials as long as there was no evidence that prison rules were adopted to control specific kinds of expression. Prison officials have the responsibility to control conduct in the prisons, and they have the expertise to determine which forms of prisoner communications do not interfere with prison security, Stewart said.

Justice William O. Douglas, writing a dissent backed by Justices William J. Brennan Jr. and Thurgood Marshall, argued that barring the press from selecting prisoners to interview violates the First Amendment. Douglas said a ban on press interviews with specifically designated prisoners was unconstitutional because it was "far broader" than necessary to protect prison discipline. Douglas said a prohibition on selected interviews was unnecessary because prison discipline and order could be maintained with "reasonable" regulations on the time, place, and manner of prisoner interviews.

Douglas, quoting his own dissent in a previous case, said the press has a preferred position under the Constitution "to bring fulfillment to the public's right to know," which

---

[6]417 U.S. 817 (1984).
[7]417 U.S. 843 (1974).
[8]417 U.S. 834 (1974).

is "crucial to the governing powers of the people." Douglas said the public is responsible for prisons and needs to be informed about their condition:

> It is . . . not enough to note that the press . . . is denied no more access to the prisons than is denied the public generally. . . . The average citizen is most unlikely to inform himself about the operation of the prison system by requesting an interview with a particular inmate. . . . He is likely instead, in a society which values a free press, to rely upon the media for information.

A few years later, the Court again upheld restrictions imposed on jail visits, this time regulations adopted by Alameda County, California, Sheriff Thomas Houchins. In *Houchins v. KQED*, the Court denied access to a television station that wanted to see the portion of the Santa Rita jail where an inmate was reported to have committed suicide. A psychiatrist claimed that some of his patient-prisoners were ill because of the conditions there.

Chief Justice Warren E. Burger, writing the opinion of the 4-3 majority, said the Court had "never intimated" a First Amendment right of access to all sources of information under government control. He said that a constitutional right to enter the jail could not be based on the public's concern for the condition of jails and the media's role in providing information. The issue in the case was not the right of citizens to receive ideas, Burger continued, but a claim by the press of a special privilege of access that the Court had rejected in *Pell* and *Saxbe*. The media have no right of access "different from or greater than" that afforded the public in general, Burger said.

Burger said reporters can learn of prison conditions by interviewing prison visitors, public officials, prison personnel, and prisoners' lawyers. He suggested that the public interest in prisons is protected when the Board of Corrections and health and fire officials inspect and report on prisons. Burger said the Constitution left the issue of public access to the "political process." It is a legislative matter, he said, quoting a speech by Justice Stewart. Burger asserted:

> The Constitution itself is neither a Freedom of Information Act nor an Official Secrets Act.
>
> The Constitution . . . establishes the contest [for information], not its resolution. Congress may provide a resolution, at least in some instances. . . . For the rest, we must rely, as so often in our system we must, on the tug and pull of the political forces in American society.[9]

In addition, Burger said, the Constitution provides no standards for determining when access is appropriate. Burger said that he did not want the courts deciding who should have access to what governmental information and under what conditions.

Lower Federal Courts

Although the Supreme Court has not recognized a First Amendment right of access to prisons or other news venues—except the courts—a few lower courts have noted a First Amendment newsgathering right in public places. Several courts have ruled that restrictions on press access cannot be over broad or capricious. One court said the National Transportation Safety Board violated the First Amendment when it severely restricted access to Logan International Airport after a DC-10 slid off an icy runway, killing two people.

[9]438 U.S. 1 (1978) (quoting a speech found in Potter Stewart, "Or of the Press," 26 *Hast. L.J.* 631, 636 (1975)).

The court said the board violated the First Amendment because it offered no "reasonable basis" for limiting press access to one hour per day.[10] However, it would be inaccurate to say that journalists have a First Amendment right of access to news scenes.

Courts have ruled that restrictions on access cannot be too broad. Courts in at least seven states struck down broad restrictions on the access of journalists and pollsters to voting locations. The restrictions were adopted to limit "exit interviews" of voters as they left the polls. The statutes were designed to impede the television networks' projections of winners in presidential elections before the polls close in all states. Officials in Western states argued that voters often failed to vote in local elections when East Coast media projected national winners long before the voting booths closed in California, Oregon, and Washington. Officials contended that citizens did not vote if they already knew the winner of the presidential race.

A federal appeals court ruled unconstitutional a Washington State statute prohibiting interviews of voters within 300 feet of a polling place. In *Daily Herald v. Munro,* the U.S. Court of Appeals for the Ninth Circuit said the First Amendment protects the discussion of governmental affairs and the gathering of news that takes place in exit interviews.[11] Therefore, the court said any law regulating exit polling must be narrowly tailored to accomplish a compelling governmental interest. The Ninth Circuit said the state's statute prohibiting exit interviews within 300 feet of a polling place—the length of a football field—was too broad for the state's purpose of maintaining peace and order at polling places. Although an appropriately narrow regulation might prohibit disruptive exit polling, the court said, the unconstitutionally broad statute in Washington prohibited all exit polling. Several laws similar to Washington's have been overturned by federal and state courts.[12]

Broadcast networks promised to be more careful after falsely projecting Al Gore the winner in the key state of Florida in the 2000 presidential election. Several networks made the error because they relied on a single source of information for exit polls. Following the Florida embarrassment, networks promised to acquire exit poll data independently. They also promised to curb their competitiveness to call winners first, agreeing to call winners in a state only after the polls close in that state.[13]

Governments may not bar journalists' access arbitrarily or capriciously. In Iowa, a federal court said that a police department acted without justification when it refused to show public records to one newspaper after showing them to another.[14] Similarly, a court ruled that a female reporter could not be denied access to a locker room in a city-owned baseball stadium where male reporters were allowed. The exclusion from the New York Yankees' locker room violated the right of *Sports Illustrated* reporter Melissa Ludtke to pursue her profession, the court said. The court said the privacy of male baseball players could be protected while Ludtke was allowed to pursue her profession.[15]

[10] Westinghouse Broadcasting Co. v. National Transp. Safety Bd., 670 F.2d 4 (D. Mass. 1982).
[11] 838 F.2d 380 (9th Cir. 1988).
[12] *E.g.*, NBC v. Cleland, 697 F. Supp. 1204 (N.D. Ga. 1988); CBS v. Growe, 15 Media L. Rep. 2275 (D. Minn. 1988).
[13] Jim Rutenberg, "TV Networks Act to Avoid More Blunders in Vote Tallies," *N.Y. Times,* Oct. 22, 2002, at 28.
[14] Quad-City Community News Serv., Inc. v. Jebens, 334 F. Supp. 8 (S.D. Iowa 1971).
[15] Ludtke v. Kuhn, 461 F. Supp. 86 (S.D.N.Y. 1978).

Courts also have ruled that the First Amendment prohibits officials from retaliating or punishing reporters by denying them access to press conferences or sessions of state legislatures. A federal district court in Hawaii said Honolulu Mayor Frank Fasi could not deny access to his press conferences to Richard Borreca because the mayor disliked Borreca's coverage of his administration. Fasi said Borreca's stories in the *Honolulu Star-Bulletin* were "irresponsible, inaccurate, biased, and malicious." The court said that officials could criticize the work of reporters, but officials violate the First Amendment, the court said, if they intimidate or discipline reporters without a compelling reason.[16]

While the government may not discriminate or retaliate against reporters by excluding disfavored journalists from public meetings and press conferences, government officials may favor some reporters over others when discussing policy, suggesting stories, and disclosing information. Every president and governor has favored some reporters over others with news tips and exclusive interviews. The U.S. Court of Appeals for the Fourth Circuit ruled that Maryland Governor Robert Ehrlich continued this constitutional tradition of discretionary disclosure when the governor issued a directive barring members of his administration from talking with two *Baltimore Sun* journalists who the governor concluded were not "objective." The governor told his administration not to return calls or comply with requests of the two *Sun* journalists, but the administration did allow the journalists to be notified of, and to attend, public press conferences.[17]

The appeals court said the governor's directive reflected the practice that government administrators have discretion over how and to whom they release information. The directive, the court said, did not unconstitutionally inhibit the journalists' ability to gather information through their enterprise and to write critically about the governor and his administration. Nor did the directive ban officials from returning the phone calls of other journalists, including those from the *Sun*. "Government officials frequently and without liability evaluate reporters and reward them with advantages of access," the court said. After the Ehrlich directive, officials in several communities issued similar notices.[18]

◇ Summary ◇

Although the Supreme Court has recognized a First Amendment right of access to criminal trials, it has ruled in cases involving access to prisons that the First Amendment does not guarantee a right to gather news. The Court has also said that journalists have no constitutional right of access to government facilities beyond that of the public. Other federal courts have said that the First Amendment prohibits officials from arbitrarily denying access or retaliating against journalists by denying access to news conferences. A federal appeals court, however, has ruled the executive branch can favor some journalists over others with interviews and conversations.

[16] Borreca v. Fasi, 369 F. Supp. 906 (D. Haw. 1974).
[17] Baltimore Sun v. Ehrlich, 437 F.3d 410 (4th Cir. 2006).
[18] Kirsten Mitchell, "Ehrlich's Edict," 29 *News Media & the Law* (Spring 2005) at 17.

Access to Events

The limited constitutional protection for newsgathering means that officials are generally not required to grant reporters access to news events on public property, on quasi-public property, or in war zones.

Public Property

Everyone, including members of the press, generally has access to public streets, sidewalks, parks, and public buildings. Several courts have recognized a common-law right for everyone to observe, photograph, and record what can easily be seen or overheard in a public place.[19] However, public officials have the authority to deny access to public property when it becomes the scene of a public disorder or disaster such as an automobile accident or fire. Public safety officers often exclude journalists from the scene, sometimes unnecessarily. However, courts often avoid second-guessing police and fire officials who have to make snap judgments while trying to save lives and property.

Anyone who disobeys an official order to move away from the scene of a calamity may be charged with criminal trespass, obstruction, or resisting arrest.[20] The First Amendment seldom provides protection in such a situation.[21] Although police and fire officials are not supposed to act arbitrarily or capriciously, the courts tend to provide them with wide discretion during emergencies. California and Ohio are two states that have adopted legislation permitting journalists access to the scenes of disasters.[22]

Journalists have few options if they confront authorities at accident and disaster scenes on public property. If journalists refuse to move when ordered to, they may be arrested for interference, disorderly conduct, assault, failure to move on, or other violations, even if their presence poses no hindrance to officials. Sometimes police and fire officials do not fully appreciate the value of news coverage or do not know the laws protecting news reporting.

The New Jersey Supreme Court upheld the conviction for disorderly conduct of a newspaper photographer who refused to obey a state trooper at the scene of an automobile accident. Harvey Lashinsky, a photographer for the *Newark Star-Ledger,* had stopped at the scene of an accident in the median of the Garden State Parkway. Inside a car, a girl was pinned against the corpse of her decapitated mother. Lashinsky took pictures until he was told to back away by a New Jersey state trooper who feared that spilled fuel might ignite or that the gathering crowd might steal property or destroy evidence. When Lashinsky was told to move, he argued with the trooper and was arrested. Although Lashinsky said he did not intend to interfere with the officer, he was convicted under a New Jersey statute for refusing to move, for arguing with the officer, and for attracting a crowd to the scene.[23]

---

[19] *E.g.,* Harrison v. Washington Post Co., 391 A.2d 781 (D.C. Ct. App. 1978); Jacova v. Southern Radio & Television Co., 83 So. 2d 34 (Fla. 1955).

[20] *See generally* Kent R. Middleton, "Journalists' Interference with Police: The First Amendment, Access to News and Official Discretion," 5 *COMM/ENT* 443 (Spring 1983).

[21] *But see, e.g.,* Connell v. Hudson, 733 F. Supp. 465 (D. N.H. 1990).

[22] Cal. Penal Code § 409.5(d); Ohio Rev. Code Ann. 2917.13.

[23] State v. Lashinsky, 404 A.2d 1121 (N.J. 1979).

President Clinton signed a law making it more difficult for the media to report on airplane crashes. The Aviation Disaster Family Assistance Act requires the National Transportation Safety Board to obtain from the airlines lists of passengers on downed craft and release information only to passengers' families. The act also provides for areas where passengers can grieve in private without questions from the media. A task force will recommend ways to ensure that journalists and attorneys do not "intrude on the privacy of families of passengers involved in an aircraft accident."[24]

Quasi-Public Property

The media's right of access to quasi-public property is even less secure than its right of access to public property. Quasi-public property is land that serves a public purpose but is not available for use by the general public. Army bases are quasi-public property. They belong to the public, but unlike public parks, they are not open for regular public use. The site of a nuclear power plant also might be considered quasi-public. The land and buildings may be owned by either the state or a private company, but the facility is dedicated to a public use and is usually regulated and financed by a public agency. The site of a nuclear power plant is not public land in the sense that it is dedicated to public use for recreation, communication, or another public purpose.

The administrator of quasi-public property, such as a utility, can restrict use to the purposes for which the property is dedicated. In 1984, the U.S. Supreme Court refused to review the criminal trespass convictions of nine reporters covering a demonstration at the Black Fox nuclear power plant in Oklahoma. The journalists had accompanied antinuclear demonstrators through a hole in a fence at the plant instead of staying at a company-approved viewing site on the property. The journalists complained that they would have missed much of the story if they were restricted to the observation site provided by the Public Service Company of Oklahoma (PSO), which ran the nuclear power plant. Indeed, the PSO, which had been stung by bad publicity from an earlier antinuclear protest, said it wanted to minimize coverage of the demonstration by restricting press access.

The Oklahoma Court of Criminal Appeals said that the press had no special right of access. The Public Service Company, the court said, had the power to regulate the quasi-public property to conform to designated uses. Because the Black Fox facility was not dedicated to use by demonstrators, nine reporters were fined $25 each for trespassing with the demonstrators.

The majority of the Oklahoma court rejected Judge Tom Brett's dissenting argument that journalists who are peacefully gathering news on quasi-public property should not be held to strict liability for trespass. Judge Brett argued that journalists' interests in newsgathering should be balanced against the threat to property and order. Brett did not see that the press posed a threat to public order or property at the Black Fox plant.[25]

Because journalists have limited rights of access to public and quasi-public property, they need to work with public officials to develop access guidelines before emergencies occur. Reporters will more likely be allowed to do their jobs at the scenes of accidents and

[24] "Media Access to Information During Air Disasters Restricted," *News Media & Law,* Fall 1996, at 38.
[25] Stahl v. State, 665 P.2d 839, 9 Media L. Rep. 1945 (Okla. Crim. App. 1983), *cert. denied,* 464 U.S. 1069 (1984).

protests if journalists and officials meet beforehand to discuss each other's responsibilities and agree to conditions and limits on access. Many news organizations have developed access guidelines with state and local law enforcement officers. The media are trying to use a similar tactic to obtain access to war zones.

War Zones

Journalists covering news in foreign countries usually need permission of the host government. However, when journalists cover wars involving U.S. troops, they are also subject to the constitutional authority of the U.S. president as commander-in-chief of the military. Over the course of American military history, press access to combat operations has varied considerably, depending on the attitudes of the president, secretary of defense, and military commanders in the field.

Extensive press coverage of war began during the Civil War, when reporters lived and traveled with troops. During World War I, newspapers sent reporters to the trenches of all major battles.[26] The tradition of reporters accompanying troops into combat continued with World War II and Vietnam.

However, when Marines landed on Grenada in 1983 to "liberate" the island, they were not accompanied by journalists.[27] Media protests led to the establishment of the Sidle Commission, which was created to draft rules governing combat reporting. The rules included a recommendation that reporters be organized into pools to be escorted by military information officers while covering military operations.[28]

The media loudly criticized American restrictions on news coverage of the Panama invasion of 1989 and the Persian Gulf War in 1991.[29] Most journalists accept standard wartime restrictions on reports of troop locations and the dates of troop movements, reports that might jeopardize operations and endanger lives. However, the media sharply criticized being confined to press pools during the Persian Gulf War. Only three pools of seven reporters each were allowed into the combat zone during some of the Persian Gulf fighting. The military escorts accompanying pool reporters helped to choose people to be interviewed and monitored interviews, sometimes interrupting them. Reporters also objected to the military's "security review" of all press pool reports. Although guidelines stated that material would not be censored because it might "express criticism or cause embarrassment," reporters complained that military reviewers suggested changes designed to support the war effort. In one widely reported incident, a military reviewer barred Frank Bruni, Jr., of the *Detroit Free Press* from reporting that some of the young Stealth-bomber pilots were returning from their first combat missions in a "giddy" mood. The military reviewer replaced "giddy" with "proud." Bruni convinced the reviewer to settle for "pumped up." Additionally, appeals of censors' decisions delayed press reports of the war, reducing their news value. Bruni's story describing the pilots was delayed for two days while he appealed the reviewer's changes.[30]

[26]Drew Middleton, "Barring Reporters from the Battlefield," *N.Y. Times Magazine,* Feb. 5, 1984, at 37.
[27]Phil Gailey, "U.S. Bars Coverage of Grenada Action, News Groups Protest," *N.Y. Times,* Oct. 27, 1983, at A1.
[28]Department of Defense, Joint Chiefs of Staff Media-Military Relations Panel, *Final Report* (1984) (Sidle Report).
[29]Department of Defense, "Operation Desert Shield Ground Rules" and "Guidelines for News Media," Jan. 14, 1991. Also see "Pentagon Manipulates War Coverage," *News Media & L.,* Winter 1991, at 2–3.
[30]Sydney H. Schanberg, "Censoring for Political Security," *Wash. Journalism Rev.,* Mar. 1991, at 23–25.

News executives said the Defense Department's restrictions made it impossible for reporters and photographers to tell the public the full story.[31] Critics of the restrictions said the military wanted to manipulate public opinion by presenting a sanitized view of the war. However, General Colin L. Powell, then chairman of the Joint Chiefs of Staff, said the press policies were necessary in an era of rapid worldwide communications. If an officer "sat around in his tent and mused" with a few reporters, Powell said, reports of the conversation would be in the capitals of 105 countries "one minute later."[32] Shortly after the Gulf War, a federal district court dismissed as no longer relevant two media challenges to the constitutionality of the Defense Department's Persian Gulf rules.[33]

In 1992, military officials and executives of major news organizations agreed to a set of nine principles for media coverage of military operations. The principles begin with the statement that "open and independent reporting will be the principal means of coverage of U.S. military operations." Restricting reporters to well-supervised pools of reporters is not supposed to be the "standard means" of covering military operations, the principles say. Pools "may sometimes provide the only feasible means of early access to a military operation" but should disband within thirty-six hours "when possible."

During the opening stages of Operation Enduring Freedom, journalists were granted access to Navy ships in the Arabian Sea but were not allowed to accompany American forces operating in Afghanistan. Larry Flynt, publisher of *Hustler,* claimed that the Pentagon's policy interfered with the right to gather information. A federal district court refused to issue an injunction requiring access and later dismissed the case.[34] The Court of Appeals for the District of Columbia Circuit affirmed, holding that there was no First Amendment right of media access to combat operations.[35]

In a case challenging U.S. military restrictions on press access to prisoners held as "unlawful combatants," a federal district judge ruled that the Pentagon was not required to establish press pools. The court deferred to the judgment of military authorities, concluding that "in light of the unique military context," press access to the prisoners was not guaranteed by the First Amendment.[36]

As part of the preparations for Operation Iraqi Freedom, Pentagon officials developed a plan to embed at least 500 journalists with military units. This extensive access was designed to allow coverage, shape public opinion about the conduct of the war, and counter anticipated Iraqi claims of American atrocities. The Pentagon's policy required embedded journalists to agree to a lengthy set of ground rules to protect operational security; violation of the ground rules could result in removal from the war zone. (A summary of the ground rules appears in Figure 12.1) For example, embedded reporters had to agree not to report information about future operations, tactics, or specific numbers of troops or equipment. Information about ongoing battles was not to be released until authorized by the on-scene commander.

---

[31]"15 Top Journalists Object to Gulf War Curbs," *N.Y. Times,* May 2, 1991, at A17.

[32]Jason DeParle, "Long Series of Military Decisions Led to Gulf War News Censorship," *N.Y. Times,* May 5, 1991, at A1.

[33]The Nation v. Department of Defense, 762 F. Supp. 1558 (1991); Agence France-Presse v. Department of Defense, 762 F. Supp. 1558 (1991).

[34]Flynt v. Rumsfeld, 180 F. Supp. 2d 174 (D.C. 2002) (refusing request for injunction); 245 F. Supp.2d 94 (D.C. 2003) (granting motion to dismiss).

[35]355 F.3d 697 (D.C. Cir. 2004).

[36]Getty Images News Services v. Department of Defense, 193 F. Supp.2d 112 (D.C. 2002).

To be embedded with U.S. military units during Operation Iraqi Freedom, journalists agreed to follow an extensive set of ground rules. The Pentagon required journalists to sign an agreement acknowledging that failure to follow the rules "may result in the immediate termination of the embed and removal" from the war zone. The following is a sampling of the ground rules.

What's Allowed

- Approximate friendly-force strength figures
- Confirmed numbers of captured enemy personnel
- Types of ordinance expended in general terms
- Generic description of origin of air operations, such as "land-based"
- Date, time, location, and results of previous conventional military missions and actions, only if described in general terms
- Number of aerial missions
- Service members' names and hometown with the individuals' consent

What's Not Allowed

- Specific numbers of troops, aircraft, ships, equipment, or supplies
- Information on special operations units, unique tactics
- Information regarding future operations
- Information regarding force protection measures at military installations
- Live broadcasts from airfields or aircraft carriers until safe return of aircraft or until authorized by unit commander
- Photographs or television coverage showing the recognizable face or nametag of a prisoner of war
- Specific information on friendly-force troop movements during an operation that would jeopardize operational security
- Rules of engagement
- Information on intelligence collection activities
- Information on missing or downed aircraft while rescue operations are underway

FIGURE 12.1 Ground Rules for Embedded Media in Operation Iraqi Freedom.

Military officials were to practice "security at the source," meaning that classified information was not to be disclosed to the press. However, the Pentagon's policy provided that classified information could be disclosed to reporters who agreed to security review of their coverage. The Pentagon's policy stated that security review "will not involve any editorial changes; it will be conducted solely to ensure that no sensitive or classified information" is included in news reports.[37]

[37]Office of Assistant Secretary of Defense for Public Affairs, "Public Affairs Guidance on Embedding Media During Possible Future Operations/Deployments in the U.S. Central Commands Area of Responsibility," Feb. 10, 2003. www.defenselink.mil/news/Feb2003/d20030228pag.pdf.

As the protracted Iraq war became increasingly dangerous, the number of embedded journalists declined—to 92 in May 2007—and their ability to travel constrained. In 2006, the military required journalists to get written permission from wounded American soldiers before publishing their pictures, a requirement, in effect, prohibiting publication.[38]

◇ Summary ◇

Courts are often inclined to accept the discretion of officials when they deny journalists access to public and quasi-public property. State statutes specify punishment for those who obstruct authority. The Defense Department, acting under the auspices of the president, controls access to war zones. The Defense Department embedded reporters in military units during Operation Iraqi Freedom.

Access to Records

Although the law seldom guarantees press access to public places, all states and the federal government have adopted statutes mandating public access to many government records and meetings. Most records laws begin with a statement declaring a government policy to maximize the availability of records for the public. When deciding close cases, courts often rule for openness when they can site statutes in which legislatures have committed the state to open records and meetings. Most laws define *public record* and describe the government agencies covered by the law, the criteria for individual access to records, the procedures for obtaining public records, the charges for obtaining records, the records that are exempt from disclosure, and the penalties for officials who improperly withhold public records.

The discussion of records laws begins with an analysis of the federal Freedom of Information Act, the law controlling documents held by federal agencies. Most issues raised by the federal law are also pertinent to state laws.

Federal Freedom of Information Act

The Freedom of Information Act (FOIA), as amended in 1996, requires that federal agencies provide any person access to records, both paper and electronic, that do not fit one of nine exempt categories (described in a later section).

HISTORY AND PURPOSE Congress adopted the Freedom of Information Act in 1966 as a bipartisan effort to increase public access to federal documents. The Electronic Freedom of Information Act Amendments, adopted in 1996, extend the open records law to digital information held by federal agencies.[39] The original FOIA replaced a 1946 act that recognized the public nature of government records but was treated by federal agencies as authorization to withhold records. Beginning in 1955, First Amendment scholar Harold

[38]David Carr, "Not to See the Fallen Is No Favor," *N.Y. Times*, May 28, 2007 at C1.
[39]Pub. L. No. 104-231, 110 Stat. 3048, *amending* 5 U.S.C. § 552.

Cross and California Congressman John Moss organized advocates for reform. Cross and Moss were joined by the media and various reform organizations seeking greater government accountability.

Recognizing the rapid growth of digital information, Congress passed the Electronic Freedom of Information Act in 1996 to "maximize the usefulness of agency records and information collected, maintained, used, retained, and disseminated by the Federal Government."[40] By improving public access to agency information, the Electronic Freedom of Information Act was supposed to "foster democracy." But federal records are public whether or not their disclosure promotes some obvious democratic purpose. Federal records are open to any person "for any public or private use," Congress said.

The FOIA establishes that the government should disclose whenever possible and withhold only when necessary. Congress included nine exemptions in the law to balance the government's need to maintain privacy and confidentiality with the public's right to be informed. The Supreme Court has said that the exemptions do not obscure that "disclosure, not secrecy" is the "dominant objective" of the act.[41]

Since its passage, the FOIA has allowed journalists and writers to uncover a wide range of information important to the public welfare. Journalists used the FOIA to document how the Department of Housing and Urban Development during the Reagan administration used government funds to finance projects for prominent Republicans, former colleagues, and friends. Documents obtained through the FOIA also revealed how the FBI harassed Dr. Martin Luther King, Jr., and how the CIA illegally monitored domestic political groups and experimented on prisoners with mind-control drugs. The Freedom of Information Act has also been used to disclose unsanitary conditions in food-processing plants, the fat content of hot dogs, safety hazards at nuclear power plants, the increased incidence of cancer among plutonium workers, the presence of poisonous wastes in drinking water, and the compliance of school districts with antidiscrimination laws.

Still, the act has been heavily criticized. Journalists charge that agencies withhold information by interpreting exemptions too broadly and that agencies unnecessarily delay disclosure. Journalists also complain that agencies "lose" documents and hire insufficient staff to process FOI requests. Law enforcement officers, businesses, and others contend the act allows too much disclosure, is unfair to businesses submitting information to the government, and is an undue burden on government.[42]

President George W. Bush and Attorney General John Ashcroft reduced the presumption of openness that former President Clinton and his Attorney General Janet Reno set forth. Reno encouraged agencies to release information even if records might fall under an FOIA exemption, unless disclosure created a "foreseeable harm."[43] Reno directed the

[40]Section 2. Findings and Purposes, 110 Stat. 3048.

[41]Department of Air Force v. Rose, 425 U.S. 352 (1976).

[42]*See* Harold Relyea, "The Administration and Operation of the Freedom of Information Act: A Retrospective," 11 *Gov't Info. Q.* 285 (1994); "Non-Denial Denial: How Attitudes and Inertia Combine to Subvert the Freedom of Information Act," *Kiplinger Program Report,* Summer 1994 (available from School of Journalism, Ohio State University, Columbus, Ohio).

[43]Dept. of Justice, "Applying the 'Foreseeable Harm' Standard under Exemption Five," *FOIA Update,* Spring 1994, at 3.

Department of Justice to presume that documents should be disclosed when the department reviewed the correctness of a federal agency's decision to withhold information.

The Bush administration took a less expansive view of openness, particularly after the attack on the World Trade Center and the Pentagon on September 11, 2001. In a memo from Attorney General Ashcroft, the Bush administration said that it would defend agencies that withheld records for any "sound legal basis." The Ashcroft memo emphasized the importance of protecting national security, personal privacy, and the confidentiality of sensitive business information contained in government records.[44] Ashcroft also announced an interagency task force to reduce the leaks of classified information from government agencies.

Access advocates and politicians criticize the Bush administration for vastly increasing the number of secret government documents. In 2004, the government classified 15.6 million documents—about 125 per minute—nearly double the number in 2001. Thousands are classified under vague categories such as "sensitive security information." At the same time, the Bush administration has greatly slowed the declassification of documents.[45]

DEFINING "AGENCY" The FOIA requires that "agency" records be open. The term *agency* includes

> any executive department, military department, Government corporation, Government controlled corporation, or other establishment in the executive branch of the government, . . . or any independent regulatory agency.[46]

The act applies to cabinet offices such as Defense, Treasury, and Justice and agencies such as the FBI and Internal Revenue Service that report to them. Federal records are public whether housed in Washington, D.C., or in regional offices in Atlanta or San Francisco. Independent regulatory agencies subject to the law include the Federal Communications Commission, Federal Trade Commission, Securities and Exchange Commission, and Consumer Product Safety Commission. The act pertains to presidential commissions, the U.S. Postal Service, and Amtrak. It applies to the Executive Office of the President, including the Office of Management and Budget, but not to the president himself or to the president's advisers. Therefore, the act does not apply to the Council of Economic Advisers or other agencies established only to advise and assist the president.[47] In addition, the act does not apply to records of Congress or the federal courts.

DEFINING "RECORD" The original FOIA did not define records, but the Electronic Freedom of Information Act of 1996 includes in the definition of a record any nonexempt information maintained by an agency "in any format, including an electronic format." Federal records include most information that functions as a record of government activity

[44]Dept. of Justice, "New Attorney General FOIA Memorandum Issued," Oct. 15, 2001, www.usdoj.gov/oip/foiapost/2001foiapost19.htm.

[45]Scott Shane, "Since 2001, Sharp Increase in the Number of Documents Classified by the Government," *N.Y. Times*, July 3, 2005, at 14.

[46]5 U.S.C. § 552(f).

[47]*See* Rushforth v. Council of Economic Advisers, 762 F.2d 1038 (D.C. Cir. 1985).

and can be reproduced. Paper documents, tape recordings, photographs, and computerized printouts are records because they chronicle government activity and can be reproduced. Physical objects, such as weapons, are not records.

Under the Electronic Freedom of Information Act, or EFOIA, as it is called, requesters are supposed to receive records in the format they choose if that format is readily available. Thus, requesters should be able to receive electronic copies of databases and database queries. An agency is also supposed to make new records available online if the agency has online capabilities. If an agency lacks online capacities, the agency must make the new information available on CD-ROM, diskette, or other electronic format. Congress's decision in EFOIA to allow requesters to choose the format of records they receive overturns a federal precedent allowing administrators, not the requesters, to determine the format in which records would be released.[48]

EFOIA also requires federal agencies to make reasonable efforts to search for requested records in electronic form unless a search would "significantly interfere" with agency operations. To search electronic databases, agencies may have to engage in at least limited programming. But the law does not require agencies to create "new" records. Administrators may redact electronic records, as they can paper records, to remove private, proprietary, or security information before releasing records. However, the EFOIA requires an agency to tell how much of a document, if any, has been deleted.

A study of the effectiveness of the EFOIA concluded that many federal agencies have failed to make electronic records available to the public.[49] The study by OMB Watch, a nonprofit organization involved in information policy, reported that thirteen of fifty-seven agencies had met no EFOIA requirements to allow easy public access to electronic records. Three-quarters of the other agencies studied had complied with some requirements of the EFOIA, but none of them had complied completely.

Regardless of the physical form or format of a record, an agency must both possess and control a record for it to be subject to disclosure under the FOIA. In a ruling that especially limits public access to studies prepared by private consultants for the government, the Supreme Court said a report about diabetes treatments was not an agency record because a federal agency did not possess it. However, government records maintained by private firms under government contract are open.[50]

The Supreme Court has also ruled that an agency cannot be forced to obtain documents that would fall under the FOIA if the agency possessed them. Thus, the State Department was not required to retrieve transcripts of Henry Kissinger's telephone conversations while he was Secretary of State and National Security Adviser. Earlier, Kissinger donated the transcripts to the Library of Congress—which is not subject to the FOIA—with an agreement that substantially limited public access.[51] A Court has also ruled an agency may have to make records available to requesters even if the same records can be found elsewhere.[52]

[48]Dismukes v. Dept. of Interior, 603 F. Supp. 760 (D.D.C. 1984).
[49]OMB Watch, *Government Information Insider* 2 (Winter–Spring 1998).
[50]Forsham v. Harris, 445 U.S. 169 (1980).
[51]Kissinger v. Reporters Committee for Freedom of the Press, 445 U.S. 136 (1980).
[52]Department of Justice v. Tax Analysts, 492 U.S. 136 (1989).

ACCESS FOR WHOM? Under the FOIA, "any person" may submit a request for a federal record.[53] "Any person" includes citizens of foreign countries and persons acting on behalf of organizations such as defense contractors, media companies, and public interest groups.[54]

A federal agency generally cannot consider the purpose of an FOIA request when deciding whether to disclose records.[55] A requester does not have to explain or justify a request. If an agency possesses a public record, it should disclose it if asked to. If release of records depended on an official's definition of the "public interest," agency personnel could withhold documents because they disapproved how the information might be used. As one judge put it, the FOIA grants "the scholar and the scoundrel equal rights of access to agency records."[56]

FOI REQUESTS The FOIA mandates that agencies respond to requests promptly and requires only commercial users of the act to pay full search and copying costs. Denials of FOIA requests can be appealed.

Filing Requests Anyone seeking information from a U.S. government agency may be able to obtain it informally. Persons can ask an agencies public information officer, even at a local or regional office, without making a formal FOIA request. This informal approach, when it works, is quick and inexpensive.

If informal requests do not succeed, a person can file a formal, written request for the information under the FOIA. Each agency must publish a description of its organization and a list of the people a citizen should contact when making an inquiry under FOIA. The agency must explain its FOIA procedures and provide electronic indexes of popular records.[57] A sample request letter is printed as Figure 12.2. Additional information for preparing a request is available in an online booklet, "How to Use the Federal FOIA Act," published by the Reporters Committee for Freedom of the Press.[58]

Once a formal FOIA request has been made, an agency must release the documents or demonstrate that they fall into one of the exempt categories. Although the law requires the requester only to "reasonably" describe the documents sought, requests are more likely to be fulfilled quickly, cheaply, and completely if the requester describes with some precision the records he or she seeks. When possible, a requester should describe a document by number, date, title, and author.

If an agency decides that some of the information requested falls under one of the nine exemptions, only that information can be deleted. The rest of the document should be disclosed.

Response Deadlines Under the FOIA, agencies have twenty days to determine whether to grant or deny a request for records. If an agency cannot fulfill a request within the

[53]5 U.S.C. § 552(a)(3).

[54]James O'Reilly, 1 *Federal Information Disclosure* ¶ 4.06, at 4-24, 4-25 (2d ed. Nov. 1990).

[55]*See* Department of Justice v. Reporters Comm. for Freedom of the Press, 489 U.S. 749 (1989) and *see, e.g.,* Justin Franklin & Robert Bouchard, *Guidebook to the Freedom of Information and Privacy Acts* ¶ 1.03, at 1-26, 1-27 (2d ed. Aug. 1995).

[56]Durns v. Bureau of Prisons, 804 F.2d 701, 706 (D.C. Cir. 1986).

[57]5 U.S.C. § 552(a)(2)(C)(D)(E).

[58]http://www.rcfp.org.

Your address
Daytime phone number
Date

Freedom of Information Office
Agency
Address

FOIA Request

Dear FOI Officer:

Pursuant to the federal Freedom of Information Act, 5 U.S.C. § 552, I request access to and copies of ***(here, clearly describe what you want. Include identifying material, such as names, places, and the period of time about which you are inquiring. If you think they will help to explain what you are looking for, attach news clips, reports, and other documents describing the subject of your research.)***

(Optional:) I would like to receive the information in electronic ***(or microfiche)*** format.

I agree to pay reasonable duplication fees for the processing of this request in an amount not to exceed $***(state amount)***. However, please notify me prior to your incurring any expenses in excess of that amount.

(Suggested request for fee benefit as a representative of the news media:) As a representative of the news media I am only required to pay for the direct cost of duplication after the first 100 pages. Through this request, I am gathering information on ***(subject)*** that is of current interest to the public because ***(give reason)***. This information is being sought on behalf of ***(give the name of your news organization)*** for dissemination to the general public. ***(If a freelancer, provide information such as experience, publication contract, etc., that demonstrates that you expect publication.)***

(Optional fee waiver request:) Please waive any applicable fees. Release of the information is in the public interest because it will contribute significantly to public understanding of government operations and activities.

If my request is denied in whole or part, I ask that you justify all deletions by reference to specific exemptions of the act. I will also expect you to release all segregable portions of otherwise exempt material. I, of course, reserve the right to appeal your decision to withhold any information or to deny a waiver of fees.

As I am making this request as a journalist ***(or author, or scholar)*** and this information is of timely value, I would appreciate your communicating with me by telephone, rather than by mail, if you have questions regarding this request.

(If you are a reporter or a person who is "primarily engaged in disseminating information," and your request concerns a matter of "compelling need," a request for expedited review may be honored. If so, include the next three paragraphs:)

Please provide expedited review of this request which concerns a matter of urgency. As a journalist, I am primarily engaged in disseminating information.

The public has an urgent need for information about ***(describe the government activity involved)*** because ***(establish the need for bringing information on this subject to the public's attention now.)***

I certify that my statements concerning the need for expedited review are true and correct to the best of my knowledge and belief.

I look forward to your reply within 20 business days, as the statute requires.

Thank you for your assistance.

Very truly yours,

FIGURE 12.2 Sample FOI Act Request Letter, Reporters Committee for Freedom of the Press.

twenty days because of "unusual circumstances," the requester may narrow the request so that an agency can fulfill it within twenty days, or the requester and the agency may negotiate a time at which the request will be fulfilled. "Unusual circumstances" are not supposed to include the lengthy backlogs that delay disclosures at several federal agencies.

To speed delivery of information, agencies can abandon the usual procedure of always serving the first customer in line. Under EFOIA, agencies can develop multitrack policies, fulfilling simple requests quickly on one track and more complex requests more slowly on another track. Under this plan, citizens with simple requests should not have to wait while more complex requests are being filled.[59]

Further expediting release of information, EFOIA reduces the number of formal requests that citizens must file by requiring agencies to make popular records readily available. Under EFOIA, agencies are required to make publicly available records already requested by other parties if the agency thinks the records are likely to be requested often. Agencies are also required to create a Government Information Locator Service, or indexes of all major information systems.

Agencies are also required to expedite a request when the requester demonstrates a compelling need for the records. Agencies will expedite requests when delay poses an imminent threat to an individual's life or safety or when "a person primarily engaged in disseminating information" can show an "urgency to inform the public concerning actual or alleged federal government activity."[60]

The Center for National Security Studies has reported that some agencies meet FOIA time limits, but some do not respond to requests for years. This is particularly true of the CIA, the FBI, and the State Department.[61] A survey of 22 agencies by Journalists for Open Government revealed 148,000 unprocessed requests at the end of 2005, or 31 percent of the total number handled.[62] To reduce delays, Congress adopted legislation in 2007 requiring agencies who fail to meet the twenty-day deadline for producing records to refund from their operating budgets the search costs incurred fulfilling a request. The law also allows requesters to track requests by phone or Internet if fulfilling a request will require more than ten days.[63]

The 2007 law also created an ombudsman to mediate disputes between record requesters and agencies, but President Bush, who signed the new law, failed to fund the new ombudsman's office in the neutral National Archives and Records Administration.

Fees Generally, federal agencies are supposed to charge requesters only the actual costs of finding and copying information, including computerized information.[64] The FOIA requires that only persons seeking information for commercial uses pay full search and copying costs as well as the costs for officials to review information for possible deletions. All other

[59]5 U.S.C. § (a)(6)(D).
[60]5 U.S.C. § 552(a)(6)(E).
[61]*E.g., Litigation under the Federal Open Government Laws 2002* at 25 (Harry A. Hammitt et al., eds.).
[62]Journalists for Open Government, "Federal Government Continues to Fall Behind in Responding to FOIA Requests, CJOG Finds," June 30, 2006.
[63]Openness Promotes Effectiveness in our National Government Act, codified at 5 U.S.C. §§552(a)(4) and (6).
[64]Paperwork Reduction Act of 1995, *codified at* 44 U.S.C.S. § 3501 *et seq.*

requesters pay nothing for the first two hours of search time and the first one hundred pages copied. Furthermore, requesters using the information for noncommercial purposes cannot be charged for the review for deletions.

The 1986 FOI Reform Act also specifies that all fees will be reduced or waived if the disclosure of the information is in the public interest because dissemination is likely to contribute significantly to public understanding of the operations or activities of the government and is not primarily in the commercial interest of the requester.[65] A federal court ruled that news media entitled to an exemption from search fees include any FOIA user who "gathers information of potential interest" to the public, uses editorial skills to create a distinct work, and publishes or otherwise distributes the work. The court upheld a fee waiver for the National Security Archive, a nonprofit research institute that disseminates information about defense and international economic policy.[66] The court said the Archive is a news medium because it obtains information from several sources, exercises editorial judgment, creates indexes and other research tools, and makes its work available to the public. In 2007, Congress amended the law to permit free searching and copying for freelancers and potentially for bloggers. The law permits waivers for "any person or entity that gathers information of potential interest to a segment of the public, uses its editorial skills to turn the raw materials into a distinct work, and distributes the work to an audience."

Persons seeking information through the FOIA should request a fee waiver in the initial request if they believe they are eligible. Before agencies begin their searches, requesters should establish a limit on the money they are willing to spend for searching and copying.

APPEALS AND PENALTIES If an agency head denies an appeal for access to a record, or if the agency does not respond within twenty days, a person requesting information can file a complaint in federal district court. The FOIA provides that a suit under the act should be given precedence over most other litigation. A court has the authority to examine the documents at issue to decide whether an agency has improperly withheld records.[67] The court's decision can be appealed to one of the circuits of the U.S. Courts of Appeals. The judicial examination of documents, known as **in camera review,** was expanded by Congress in 1974 to include even classified information related to national security. President Ford vetoed the 1974 legislation, contending that the courts should not have the authority to overrule the executive branch on what documents should be classified. Congress overrode the president's veto, asserting that a check on executive branch secrecy was necessary.

If a person seeking information wins in court, a judge can assess the government the requester's attorney's fees and other litigation costs.[68] Under a 2007 amendment, a requester might also win attorney's fees from an agency before litigation if a judge orders disclosure or an agency changes its mind.[69]

[65] 5 U.S.C. § 552(a)(4)(A)(iii).
[66] National Sec. Archive v. Department of Defense, 880 F.2d 1381 (D.C. Cir. 1989), *cert. denied,* 494 U.S. 1029 (1990).
[67] 5 U.S.C. § 552(a)(4)(B).
[68] 5 U.S.C. § 552(a)(4)(E).
[69] *Id.*

◇ Summary ◇

The Freedom of Information Act makes federal records available to any person. The statute opens paper and digital records of the executive branch, with the exception of the White House, but not records of Congress or the federal courts. A document is a record of a federal agency only if the agency both possesses and controls it. An agency must respond to a written request for a record within twenty working days. When a citizen appeals inaction or denial, an agency head is supposed to answer within twenty working days. Agencies can charge for searches and copying, but fees are waived if a request is in the public interest.

EXEMPTIONS An agency *must* disclose any record that does not fall within one of the nine categories of information exempted from disclosure under the FOIA. But the Supreme Court has ruled that the exemptions permit, but do not require, a federal agency to withhold documents.[70] An agency *may* disclose a document that fits one of the nine exemptions if another statute does not require the information be withheld.

The most important exemptions for journalists are exemption 1, national security; exemption 6, personnel and medical files; and exemption 7, law enforcement investigation records. The most important exemption for businesses is exemption 4, protecting confidential business information. Businesses are also protected by exemption 8, banking reports; and 9, information about wells. The other FOIA exemptions are 2, internal rules and agency practices; 3, matters required to be withheld by other statutes; and 5, interagency or intra-agency memoranda.

(1) National Security Exemption 1 protects from disclosure information that could damage the national defense and foreign policy. The FOIA grants the executive branch more discretion to withhold national security information than any other category. Exemption 1 is the only exemption that allows the executive branch, rather than Congress, to determine the criteria for the release of documents.

In 1995, President Clinton released a long-awaited reform of the classification process for national security and foreign policy documents, a reform that was welcomed by critics of government secrecy.[71] A president's executive order dictates how federal officials classify information that should be protected from disclosure under exemption 1 of the Freedom of Information Act. Clinton's order has been largely upheld by President George W. Bush.

Like previous presidential classification orders, the Clinton order recognized that "democratic principles require that the American people be informed of the activities of their Government." The Clinton order required officials who classify information to explain not just whether a document fit into a category exempt from disclosure but also why the release of a document could reasonably be expected to damage national security. The Clinton order told officials that if they were uncertain of the appropriate level of classification, they should classify a document at the lower level. If officials harbored "significant

[70]Chrysler Corp. v. Brown, 441 U.S. 281 (1979).
[71]Exec. Order No. 12,958, 60 Fed. Reg. 19,825 (Apr. 20, 1995).

doubt" about the need to classify information, the order said the information should not be classified.

For documents falling into one of the categories of exceptions, agencies were required to establish a program for "systematic declassification review." Newly classified documents were to remain classified for only ten years, and the order required automatic declassification of most documents classified for twenty-five years.

The Clinton classification order provided for three levels of classification: top secret, secret, and confidential. All levels protect the records from public disclosure, and the level of classification controls which government officials have access to the documents. The categories of information that can be classified included military plans, weapons, or operations; intelligence activities; programs for safeguarding nuclear facilities; U.S. foreign relations; and information about foreign governments. Even information in these categories could not be classified unless it met the other specifications of the order.

A new classification category, "Sensitive Security Information," has emerged since 9/11. Under this broad, informal classification, the government withholds a wide range of information, presumably essential to the preservation of national security. Government agencies often withhold Sensitive Security Information under exemption 3, which provides for withholding information declared confidential by statute.

In 2003, President George W. Bush amended, but did not radically change, the Clinton classification order.[72] Bush retained Clinton's classification categories and Clinton's program of declassification review. Like Clinton, the Bush order promised not to classify records to conceal violations of law, to prevent embarrassment, or to cause delay. However, the Bush order removed the "significant doubt" clause, thus allowing officials to classify information even if they doubted classification was necessary. Bush also postponed until December 31, 2006, the time at which documents classified for twenty-five years would be automatically declassified. Bush, unlike Clinton, also allowed public documents to be reclassified if an agency head deemed it necessary.[73]

The Bush administration took other measures to curb the flow of information related to national security. In October 2001, shortly after the terrorist attack at the World Trade Center and the Pentagon, Attorney General John Ashcroft issued a memo telling federal agencies that the Justice Department would support withholding information if an agency had a "sound legal basis." Ashcroft's predecessor, Janet Reno, had ordered agency administrators to disclose records unless disclosure presented a "foreseeable harm."[74] In 2002, White House Chief of Staff Andrew Card Jr. ordered federal agencies to withhold "sensitive" information to protect national security even if it was unclassified. Card's order resulted in agencies removing information from government websites about water resources, the operation of power plants, and other subjects.

The FOIA authorizes judges to review classification decisions, but the courts rarely order the release of information that the executive branch says should be classified. Judges ordinarily defer to the president, who is given the power by the Constitution to conduct foreign

[72]Executive Order No. 13292, 68 Fed. Reg. 15315, Mar. 28, 2003.

[73]Reporters Committee for Freedom of the Press, "Presidential Directive Changes 'Tone' of Classification Rules," http://www.rcfp.org/news/2003/0326amendm.html.

[74]Reporters Committee for Freedom of the Press, *Homefront Confidential*, 3d ed., Mar. 2003, at 50.

policy and to supervise national security. In addition, most courts seem to share the sentiment of the judge who said that "few judges have the skill or experience to weigh the repercussions of disclosure of intelligence information."[75]

In 2006, a federal district court allowed the Department of Defense to withhold under exemption 1 photographs identifying past and present detainees at Guantanamo Bay. The court ruled that disclosure of photographs would provide "conclusive identification" of detainees in ways that release of detainees' names—many of which are the same—would not.[76] The court saw damage to national security if the photos were released because the detainees and their families would be more exposed to retaliation, thus reducing the likelihood the detainees would cooperate with Americans gathering intelligence.

(2) Agency Rules and Practices Exemption 2 allows agencies to withhold documents "related solely" to internal personnel rules and practices. Among the records fitting the exemption are regulations governing filing, parking, cafeteria use, and sick leave.

The courts have said exemption 2 protects the withholding of only those records of little or no concern to the general public.[77] In the most significant exemption 2 case, *Department of the Air Force v. Rose,* the Supreme Court said the exemption does not allow the government to withhold documents involving issues of a "genuine and significant public interest." The Court said that exemption 2 did not permit the U.S. Air Force Academy to withhold summaries of honors and ethics hearings with the identification of the participants deleted. *New York University Law Review* editors wanted the summaries for an article about discipline at the military academies. Justice Brennan, writing for a majority of the Court, said the

> general thrust of the exemption is simply to relieve agencies of the burden of assembling and maintaining for public inspection matter in which the public could not reasonably be expected to have an interest. The case summaries plainly do not fit that description. They are not matter with merely internal significance. They do not concern only routine matters. Their disclosure entails no particular administrative burden.

Brennan said the public interest in discipline at the Air Force Academy was obvious, given the importance of discipline to military effectiveness.

Courts have tended to protect the withholding of law enforcement agency staff manuals, such as instructions telling agents of the Bureau of Alcohol, Tobacco, and Firearms how to conduct searches and raids.[78] Also protected from disclosure have been federal agency computer plans[79] and agency tests and hiring criteria for job applicants.[80]

(3) Statutory Exemptions The third exemption applies to documents that Congress has declared in other statutes to be confidential. The third exemption is often called the

[75] "2 Tell of Radiation Experiments on Them as Boys," *N.Y. Times,* Jan. 14, 1994, at A12.
[76] Associated Press v. U.S. Dept. of Defense, 462 F. Supp.2d 573 (S.D.N.Y. 2006).
[77] *See* Department of the Air Force v. Rose, 425 U.S. 352 (1976).
[78] Caplan v. Bureau of Alcohol, Tobacco & Firearms, 587 F.2d 544 (2d Cir. 1978); Hardy v. Bureau of Alcohol, Tobacco & Firearms, 631 F.2d 653 (9th Cir. 1980).
[79] Schreibman v. Department of Commerce, 785 F. Supp. 164 (D.D.C. 1991).
[80] *See, e.g.,* Patton v. FBI, 626 F. Supp. 445 (M.D. Pa. 1985), *aff'd,* 782 F.2d 1030 (3d Cir. 1986).

"catchall" exemption because it exempts from disclosure any records Congress has decided to exclude from the general policy of openness under the FOIA.

The exemption applies to Census Bureau records, tax returns, and patent applications. Exemption 3 allows for the withholding of records by such agencies as the U.S. Postal Service, Central Intelligence Agency, Department of Agriculture, and the Federal Trade Commission. The Central Intelligence Agency Act of 1949 provides that the names, titles, and salaries of CIA employees and the number of personnel employed by the agency are exempt from disclosure.[81] Statutes permit the government to withhold information if disclosure would compromise homeland security and privacy.

Homeland Security One of the most important restrictions on access to records is found in Section 214 of the Homeland Security Act, the act that creates the cabinet level Department of Homeland Security. Section 214 prohibits the department from disclosing critical infrastructure information provided by agencies and private businesses. Under the Homeland Security Act, private sector companies in chemicals, nuclear energy, water, finance, and communications can avoid public disclosure if they submit vulnerabilities in their critical infrastructure to the Department of Homeland Security. Critical infrastructure includes vital systems and assets whose incapacity would have debilitating impact on security, the economy, and public health or safety. Once the DHS possesses information regarding the security of critical infrastructure, the information is private and not to be disclosed or used against a company for wrongdoing.[82]

While the Homeland Security Act will in some cases keep important information from terrorists, critics fear Section 214 will allow corporations to dump embarrassing—perhaps even criminal—information on the Department of Homeland Security with assurance that it will never be made public. As an example of a potential misuse of the law, Senator Patrick Leahy warned that DHS would have to acquire consent from a medical laboratory to warn the public of anthrax released from the lab if the lab had told DHS about the vulnerability of this critical infrastructure information.

After passage of the Homeland Security Act, agencies greatly expanded the "Sensitive Security Infomation" they withhold, information that is sensitive but not classified. SSI is usually protected by statute or regulation. Often sensitive information is stamped "For Official Use Only." Employing the catchphrase "sensitive information," the Nuclear Regulatory Commission removed its website after 9/11. Citing security, the military refused to release the names of enemy combatant detainees who escaped in Afghanistan, identities disclosed a short time later by Afghan authorities. Acquiescing to a request by the Department of Homeland Security, the Federal Communications Commission blocked public access to disruptions in telecommunications service, information said to supply a "roadmap for terrorists."[83]

Privacy Under the Privacy Act of 1974, individuals have the right to obtain and amend government files containing personal information about them. In addition, the Privacy Act

[81]50 U.S.C. § 403g.
[82]*See,* Reporters Committee for Freedom of the Press, *Homefront Confidential* 3d ed., Mar. 2003, at 55–57.
[83]Reporters Committee for Freedom of the Press, *Homefront Confidential, Freedom of Information,* 6th ed., 2005, at 22–25.

permits government agencies to use a "personally identifiable record" only for the reasons it was collected or for reasons specifically listed in the act itself. Agencies are otherwise prohibited from disclosing personal information without the written consent of the person involved. Agencies must keep track of each disclosure.[84]

In 1984, Congress passed legislation stating that a government agency could not use the Privacy Act to deny access to information that should be available under the FOIA.[85] If there is a conflict between the Privacy Act and the FOIA, the FOIA is supposed to prevail. But even after the congressional action, agencies are cautious about releasing an individual's records under the FOIA. An agency may be sued under the Privacy Act if it improperly releases personal records under FOIA.

Student Educational Records Another federal statute that protects privacy is the Family Educational Rights and Privacy Act, often called FERPA or the **Buckley Amendment.**[86] FERPA permits students over age eighteen—or parents of younger students—to see and correct their "educational records." FERPA also prohibits educational institutions from releasing educational records to the public under threat of losing federal funding.

Universities, colleges, and high schools are permitted by FERPA to release "directory information" unless students object. Directory information includes a student's name, address, telephone number, date and place of birth, attendance record, field of study, degrees, and participation in official activities, including sports. Educational institutions can release the weight and height of members of athletic teams. Grades and health information may not be released.

Student Law Enforcement Records Federal law requires that most campus crime be disclosed, either as individual incidents or in statistical summary, if the crimes are recorded in law enforcement records. The law says law enforcement records at state college and university police stations—records of arrests, charges, and incidents—are public, just as law enforcement records are public at city police stations.[87] Law enforcement records do not become exempt educational records if they are stored in the office of student affairs or other non–law enforcement offices.

Under federal law, all public and private colleges and universities that receive federal funding must maintain public logs of criminal incidents reported to their police or security offices.[88] Within two days of an incident, record custodians must add to the log the nature, date, time, location, and disposition of each criminal complaint. However, campus officials may withhold information that would jeopardize ongoing investigations or reveal the identity of victims of sex crimes. Federal law also requires institutions receiving federal money to annually report statistics for campus crimes, including murder, manslaughter, sex offenses, robbery, aggravated assault, burglary, motor vehicle theft, and arson.

[84] 5 U.S.C. § 552a(b), (c), (d).
[85] 5 U.S.C. § 522a(t).
[86] 20 U.S.C. § 1232g.
[87] 20 U.S.C. § 1232g(a)(4)(B)(ii).
[88] 20 U.S.C. § 1092(f).

Student Disciplinary Records Citing FERPA, college and university officials have frequently closed student disciplinary records. College officials, supported by the Department of Education, argue that records of student disciplinary proceedings, often conducted in student judicial courts, should remain closed so that youthful offenders can be educated and rehabilitated, shielded from the glare of publicity. Universities also argue that students who violate laws and regulations should not be required forever to carry the stigma of "guilty" because of youthful indiscretions.

Campus judiciaries often try cases involving university rules and conduct standards, including those that proscribe cheating, hazing, or destroying dormitory property. But disciplinary records may also include criminal activity not reported to law enforcement officials. Indeed, colleges often channel some criminal complaints into the student disciplinary process to avoid the requirement of disclosing law enforcement records. The media and access advocates argue that student judiciary records and proceedings dealing with campus rules violations and crimes should be open to ensure that justice is served and that the public knows whether a campus is dangerous.

Federal law says student judiciary records are not "educational records" exempt from disclosure if the records document charges of violent crime or unforced sex crimes, such as consensual sex with a minor. Thus, universities will not jeopardize federal funding if they release student judiciary records of violent crimes and unforced sex acts. But colleges and universities are not required to release the records under federal law. Colleges and universities may be required under state open records acts to disclose noneducational records of violent crimes. Of course, records of violent crimes will be open at campus police stations if criminal reports are filed with law enforcement officials.

Student judiciary records involving nonviolent crimes and university rules may be withheld at most campuses as "educational records." The federal Department of Education argues that student judiciary records involving nonviolent crimes are educational records that should be exempt from disclosure. In 1998, the DOE sued Miami University and Ohio State University to prevent them from releasing campus judiciary records containing students' names. A federal court ruled for the Department of Education.[89] Earlier, the Supreme Court of Georgia ruled that student judiciary records and meetings are open under state open records and meetings acts, even if the records reveal the names of students.[90]

If a university unlawfully reveals educational records, it might lose federal funding, but FERPA does not allow the injured student to sue the university under FERPA.[91] The Supreme Court overturned a Washington Supreme Court ruling that Gonzaga University should pay a Gonzaga student $1.5 million for unlawfully revealing his educational records and refusing to attest to his good character. The university told representatives of the state teacher-certificate office that the student had been accused of raping another student. However, no charges were filed against the student. The student claimed the university's revelation of false accusations and failure to attest to his good character defamed him, invaded his privacy, and cost him a job. The student could sue for defamation or invasion of privacy, but could not sue under FERPA, the Court said.

[89]United States v. Miami University, 91 F. Supp. 2d 1132 (S.D. Ohio 2000).
[90]Red & Black Publishing Co. v. Bd. of Regents, 427 S.E.2d 257 (Ga. 1993).
[91]Gonzaga Univ. v. Doe, 536 U.S. 273 (2002).

Driver's Records In addition to the Buckley Amendment and the Privacy Act, Congress passed a law prohibiting states from releasing personal information from motor vehicle records without a driver's consent. The Driver's Privacy Protection Act of 1994 was passed to protect vehicle owners from being stalked and to curb widespread commerce in personal information gleaned from drivers' records.[92] Under the law, state agencies can be fined if they release to the public such information as a driver's name, address, social security number, telephone number, or medical information without the driver's consent. Any individual who violates the act can be sued. The act does not restrict the release of information about accidents, driving violations, or a driver's legal driving status. The act provides several exemptions, authorizing states to provide personal information to both businesses and government agencies or for such purposes as market surveys and other research, product recalls, vehicle performance monitoring, protection against business fraud, and criminal prosecutions.

Sponsors of the Driver's Privacy Protection Act, including Senator Barbara Boxer, a California Democrat, intended the bill to block access to the identities of license tag holders that stalkers might use to trace women, doctors, police officers, and celebrities. Senator Boxer also fought for the act to prevent murders similar to that in 1989 of actress Rebecca Schaeffer, killed by an obsessed fan who obtained her address through a private detective who examined motor vehicle records.[93] Opponents of the law, including journalists, charge that it curbs legitimate uses of information from drivers' records and does not curb stalkers. Journalists have used drivers' information to find fathers avoiding child support payments and to identify witnesses and participants in demonstrations and illegal conduct.[94] Some states argued that Congress, when it adopted the law, exceeded its authority in violation of the Tenth Amendment by restricting state control of drivers' records kept by the states.

In 2000, the U.S. Supreme Court upheld the Driver's Privacy Protection Act from state challenges to the constitutionality of the statute under the Tenth Amendment. The Supreme Court said that Congress constitutionally regulated commercial databases in interstate commerce. The Supreme Court did not discuss privacy and access issues of concern to journalists and the public.

(4) Confidential Business Information Regulated businesses such as broadcast stations and drug-manufacturing companies must submit voluminous amounts of information to regulatory agencies. In addition, businesses seeking government contracts must provide government officials with proprietary information that could be valuable for competitors and journalists. Exemption 4 protects (1) trade secrets and (2) commercial or financial information that businesses submit to government agencies on a confidential basis.

Businesses seeking information about government regulations and their competitors use the FOIA more than any other group of requesters. Businesses have obtained, through the FOIA, information about government agency procedures, inspection plans, and enforcement policies. For example, food-processing plants and drug companies obtain

[92]18 U.S.C. § 2721-25.

[93]*See, e.g.*, "The Boxer Driver's Privacy Protection Act of 1993," News from U.S. Senator Barbara Boxer (Oct. 28, 1993).

[94]"Bill Would Close Access to Drivers' Records," *News Media & L.*, Winter 1994, at 9.

inspection procedures of the Food and Drug Administration in preparation for visits by FDA personnel.

Businesses also use the FOIA to engage in "industrial espionage," obtaining information about their competitors that is not otherwise available. For instance, Suzuki Motor Company acquired copies of records submitted to the U.S. government by Toyota, information that Suzuki could not obtain from the Japanese government.[95]

Businesses complain that they are required to provide the government economically sensitive information without being able to control who will see it. Indeed, the FOIA allows government agencies the discretion to disclose confidential business information, and agencies sometimes knowingly release confidential business records in response to an FOIA request. In addition, agencies sometimes accidentally release sensitive information. For example, the EPA gave the secret formula for Roundup weed killer, a Monsanto herbicide, to a competitor because of an agency processing error. Roundup had provided 40 percent of Monsanto's profits during the previous year.[96]

The less used of the two provisions in exemption 4 allows agencies to withhold documents that contain trade secrets, such as the formula for Coca-Cola. Most of the exemption 4 litigation has focused on protecting confidential "commercial or financial information." Agencies are allowed to withhold commercial information about such things as business sales and operating costs, a company's financial condition, and data about a company's workforce if disclosure is likely to impair the government's ability to obtain necessary information in the future or cause "substantial" harm to the competitive position of the company providing the information.[97]

A court upheld the Defense Department's refusal to reveal information provided by Norris Industries about ammunition the company manufactures. Norris had submitted financial data, including production costs, for the M549 warhead for artillery. An appeals court ruled that disclosure of Norris's financial data would harm Norris's competitive position by allowing competitors to calculate Norris's future bids and pricing structure.[98]

Although federal agencies may choose to withhold confidential business information under the FOIA, companies can rarely force the government to withhold information under a "reverse FOIA" suit. In *Chrysler Corp. v. Brown,* the Supreme Court said the FOIA provided no mechanism that allows a company to stop an agency from releasing information, even if the documents qualified for exemption 4. In *Chrysler,* the auto company tried unsuccessfully to block the government's release of detailed employment records of a Delaware assembly plant, data that Chrysler claimed would allow competitors to raid Chrysler employees and determine technology and equipment being used.[99] Under an

[95]James O'Reilly, Regaining a Confidence: Protection of Business Confidential Data through Reform of the Freedom of Information Act, 34 *Admin. L. Rev.* 263 (1982).

[96]Pete Earley, "EPA Lets Trade Secret Loose in Slip-Up, to Firm's Dismay," *Washington Post,* Sept. 18, 1982, at A1. *But see* Russell B. Stevenson, Jr., Protecting Business Secrets under the Freedom of Information Act: Managing Exemption 4, 34 *Admin. L. Rev.* 207, 220 (1982).

[97]National Parks & Conservation Ass'n v. Morton, 498 F.2d 765 (D.C. Cir. 1974). *But see* Critical Mass v. Nuclear Regulatory Comm'n, 975 F.2d 871 (D.C. Cir. 1992), *cert. denied*, 507 U.S. 984 (1993) (recognizing protection for documents that do not fit the first two prongs).

[98]Gulf & Western Indus., Inc. v. United States, 615 F.2d 527 (1979).

[99]Chrysler Corp. v. Brown, 441 U.S. 281 (1979).

executive order issued by President Ronald Reagan, agencies contemplating release of business information must allow a business time to object to disclosure, and the agency must explain its reasons if it releases the business information anyway.[100]

(5) Agency Memoranda The widely used exemption 5 protects the deliberative policy-making process of executive agencies. Exemption 5 incorporates into the FOIA what is known as "executive privilege." It exempts from disclosure working documents, circulated within an agency or between agencies, that historically have been considered privileged government communications under common law. Exemption 5 protects opinions and recommendations in order to encourage open and frank discussion on policy matters.

Officials contend that sensitive issues can be discussed more thoroughly in preliminary stages outside the glare of publicity. Decision makers are more likely to suggest unconventional ideas, officials argue, if records of their discussions will not be disclosed. Officials also contend that "premature publicity" confuses the public by revealing issues and arguments that have little or nothing to do with final decisions.

However, advocates of government disclosure contend the public needs to be a part of the policymaking process before decisions are made. Important issues may be overlooked or deemphasized, it is argued, if officials make up their minds without public debate.

Exemption 5 shields from disclosure policy drafts, staff proposals, studies, and investigative reports. The courts have held the exemption also protects from disclosure reports from consultants and internal investigations used in policy preparation and self-criticism.[101] A federal appeals court ruled that exemption 5 prevented a non-profit legal organization from acquiring records of a consulting firm that advised the Department of Defense on setting up commissions to try terrorists.[102]

(6) Personnel, Medical, and Similar Files Exemption 6 protects from disclosure a very wide array of information in personnel, medical, and "similar" files that, if released, "would constitute a clearly unwarranted invasion of personal privacy." Agencies have to balance the interest in an individual's privacy against the public interest in monitoring the activities of government. The Supreme Court has interpreted the privacy exemption very broadly.

The threshold issue in an exemption 6 case is whether a record falls within the definition of "personnel," "medical," and "similar" files. "Personnel files" are employment records, including performance evaluations and reports on disciplinary proceedings. "Medical files" encompass any individual's medical records held by federal agencies.

"Similar files" include documents that reveal an individual's social security number, marital status, financial status, or welfare payments.[103] In addition, courts have said that "similar files" encompass the addresses of federal employees, persons taking federal

[100]Exec. Order No. 12,600, 3 C.F.R. 235.

[101]Justin Franklin & Robert Bouchard, *Guide book to the Freedom of Information and Privacy Acts,* ¶ 15.11, at 15-27, 15-28; ¶ 15.16, at 15-38.

[102]Nat'l Inst. of Military Justice v. Dept. of Defense, 512F.3d 677 (D.C. Cir. 2008).

[103]*See, e.g.,* Justin Franklin & Robert Bouchard, *Guidebook to the Freedom of Information and Privacy Acts* ¶ 1.09[4], at 1-231.

exams, and persons holding Veterans Administration loans.[104] The Supreme Court has said that the term *similar files* applies to any information about a specific individual held by the federal government. In *Department of State v. Washington Post Co.,* eight of the nine justices said a file does not have to contain intimate information to be withheld. Justice William H. Rehnquist said exemption 6 was intended "to protect individuals from the injury and embarrassment that can result from the unnecessary disclosure of personal information."[105]

In 1994, the U.S. Supreme Court ruled in *Department of Defense v. Federal Labor Relations Authority* that disclosure of the home addresses of government employees to unions requesting the addresses would constitute a clearly unwarranted invasion of the right of federal employees to privacy in their homes.[106] At the same time, the Court said releasing the addresses of government employees to unions "would not appreciably" advance citizens' rights to be informed about the activities of federal government agencies. Eight of the nine justices on the Court said that "privacy of the home . . . substantially outweighs" a "negligible" public interest in the disclosure of the home addresses, a disclosure that would not help the public understand government operations. The Court said release of the home addresses might facilitate collective bargaining by allowing unions to communicate more effectively with the federal employees they represent but would reveal "little or nothing" about the activities of the government, in this case the Army, Navy, and Air Force.

Although the Supreme Court has said that exemption 6 protects a wide range of information about individuals, it has also held the exemption does not create an absolute right to privacy for personnel, medical, or similar files. Privacy interests must be balanced against the public interest in knowing about the activities of government, an interest that the Supreme Court has said is the "core purpose" served by the Freedom of Information Act. The Court has said the release of private information is unwarranted unless the information sought "sheds light" on government performance.[107]

In 2006, a federal judge rejected Defense Department claims that names of detainees at Guantanamo Bay should be withheld to protect the privacy of the detainees and their families. Judge Jed Rakoff ordered transcripts of detainees' appearances before a military tribunal released after a survey of detainees revealed that only 17 of 317 objected to disclosure of their identities. Neither the detainees nor their families had any reasonable expectation of privacy in their participation in the tribunals, Rakoff said.[108]

Later in the year Judge Rakoff ordered the release to the Associated Press identifying information and documents of allegations and accounts of detainees'mistreatment at Guantanamo—such as assaults, use of pepper spray, and verbal abuse—and the disciplinary actions taken. Rakoff said most detainees would want the records released as evidence of their abuse.[109] The court saw a public interest in disclosing records shedding light on American treatment of detainees. Similarly, Judge Rakoff ordered disclosure of the

[104]*See, e.g.,* James O'Reilly, 2 *Federal Information Disclosure* ¶ 16.06, at 2S-4, 2S-5 (2d ed. June 1995).
[105]456 U.S. 595 (1982).
[106]510 U.S. 487 (1993).
[107]Department of Justice v. Reporters Comm. for Freedom of the Press, 489 U.S. 749 (1989).
[108]Associated Press v. Dept. of Defense, 410 F. Supp.2d 147 (S.D.N.Y. 2006).
[109]Associated Press v. U.S. Dept. of Defense, 2006 U.S. Dist. LEXIS 67913 (S.D.N.Y. Sep. 20, 2006).

heights and weights of detainees involved in hunger strikes, information that would shed light on American treatment of detainees.[110] However, Judge Rakoff refused to order the release of information identifying the wife of a detainee.[111] The judge ruled the woman retained an expectation of privacy in letters she wrote to her husband.

A federal appellate court also authorized the release of federal employee's sick-leave records because they would help explain how the government works—or doesn't. The court said the public interest in the disclosure of sick-leave records of a federal administrator would outweigh the individual privacy interest in the documents. The appellate court said that the release of sick-leave and work-attendance records of an employee at the Federal Communications Commission serves the public interest in obtaining information about potential government misconduct.[112]

(7) Law Enforcement. Exemption 7 of FOIA permits the government to withhold information compiled for law enforcement purposes. Exemption 7 allows information to be withheld if disclosure would interfere with law enforcement investigations, disclose the identity of confidential sources, endanger lives, invade privacy, deprive a defendant of a fair trial, or reveal law enforcement techniques.[113]

Agencies cannot withhold records under exemption 7 if the records are not compiled for law enforcement purposes. A federal appeals court ruled the FBI had to disclose documents collected about the Free Speech Movement at the University of California because they were not compiled—contrary to a government claim—for the legitimate law enforcement purpose of investigating Communist subversives. Rather, the records were compiled to gain information on a leader with a "contemptuous attitude" and to harass liberal faculty members.[114]

The Supreme Court has interpreted the privacy exemption very broadly in exemption 7 cases, undermining federal and state precedent establishing that records are presumptively open to anyone for any purpose. In two exemption 7 cases, the Court has ruled that requesters will gain access to records containing private information only if they can demonstrate the records will clarify government operations or reveal misconduct. The Court has also allowed the family of a dead official to assert privacy claims in government records.

In *Department of Justice v. Reporters Committee for Freedom of the Press,* the Court ruled that computerized FBI "rap sheets" on private individuals are exempt from disclosure even though much of the information contained in rap sheets can be found in public records in police stations around the country.[115] The FBI's rap sheets at issue in *Reporters Committee* are national computer compilations of criminal records that have traditionally been kept confidential. The rap sheets combine information about arrests, indictments, acquittals, and convictions, information that individually is often a matter of public record in local and state law enforcement agencies and courthouses. The rap sheets are accumulated

[110]Associated Press v. U.S. Dept. of Defense, 462 F. Supp.2d 573 (S.D.N.Y. 2006).
[111]Associated Press v. U.S. Dept. of Defense, 2006 U.S. Dist. LEXIS 67913 (S.D.N.Y. Sep. 20, 2006).
[112]Dobronski v. FCC, 17 F.3d 275 (1994).
[113]5 U.S.C. § 552(b)(7).
[114]Rosenfeld v. United States, 57 F.3d 803 (9th Cir. 1995).
[115]489 U.S. 749 (1989).

through a nationwide network of local, state, and federal law enforcement agencies that share criminal history information under strict rules governing its use. The rap sheets sometimes contain information that is incorrect or incomplete because it may not be updated. Although most states release information about convictions, most states restrict the disclosure of criminal complaints and arrests that do not result in a conviction. Many states withhold information about individuals in the prison system.

The Court's decision in *Reporters Committee* ended a decade-long search by the Reporters Committee and CBS correspondent Robert Schakne for the criminal records of Charles Medico and his three brothers. Medico Industries, a family company, had been described by the Pennsylvania Crime Commission as "a legitimate business dominated by organized crime figures." Schakne wanted to know the connection between the company's defense contracts and bribery allegations against former Representative Daniel Flood, a Democrat from Pennsylvania. The FBI refused to release records of the only living brother, Charles Medico. Schakne and the Reporters Committee argued the information in the FBI rap sheets was a matter of public record in local government files and therefore ought to be released by the federal government.

The U.S. Supreme Court, balancing the importance of individual privacy against the public interest in understanding government operations, unanimously ruled that the FBI could withhold Medico's records. The Court's opinion, supported by seven justices, said that the federal government's computerized database of rap sheets was private because, in effect, the facts and incidents from which it was compiled were private. Even though journalists might find much criminal information about citizens in American courthouses and police stations, the Court said the information was effectively private because it was hard to locate.

Writing for the majority, Justice Stevens said bits and pieces of criminal information scattered through counties and states enjoy a "practical obscurity" that would be lost if that information were disseminated from a centralized database. "Plainly there is a vast difference," Stevens said, "between the public records that might be found after a diligent search of courthouse files, county archives and local police stations throughout the country and a computerized summary located in a single clearinghouse of information."

If the information in the rap sheets were "freely available" in other locations, Stevens said, Schakne and the Reporters Committee could have easily acquired it without using the FOIA. Stevens also said that Congress had demonstrated it intended to protect the privacy of rap sheets by authorizing only a limited use of rap sheets by law enforcement agencies, banks, and the nuclear power industry. In addition, Stevens said, the FBI's regulations specify that it can stop sharing rap sheet information with any agency that discloses the data.

The Supreme Court said in exemption 7 cases the public interest in disclosure might outweigh privacy interests if disclosure revealed how the government operates. Indeed, the Court said the basic policy of full agency disclosure focuses on the citizens' right to be informed about "what their government is up to." However, disclosure of rap sheets on private citizens reveals "little or nothing" about the conduct of a government agency, the Court said. The Court argued that disclosure of Medico's personal criminal records would say "nothing directly" about Representative Flood's behavior or the conduct of the Defense Department when it awarded contracts to Medico Industries.

After *Reporters Committee,* a Senate report contested the Supreme Court's assertion that the basic purpose of FOIA is to reveal what the government is up to. Government agencies are not required to release records only when information will shed light on government operations, the report said.[116] The purpose of open records laws is much broader, the Senate report said. Federal agencies must honor records requests "of any person for any public or private use."

The Supreme Court was not impressed with Senate reminders of the broad purposes of the open records law. In a significant decision in 2004, the Supreme Court narrowed the range of records a requester might acquire if those records contain private information. In *National Archives and Records Administration v. Favish,* a unanimous Court extended privacy rights under exemption 7 to living relatives of a dead official and required a plaintiff seeking photos of a suicide scene to assert not just that the records would reveal what the "government is up to," but would provide evidence of government misconduct.[117]

In an opinion written by Justice Kennedy, the Court denied the request of Allan J. Favish, a California lawyer who sought death scene photographs of Vincent Foster, deputy counsel to President Clinton. Foster was found dead in Fort Marcy Park near Washington. One photo showed a gun in Foster's hand. Five investigations concluded Foster committed suicide, but Favish argued the government's investigations were "grossly incomplete and untrustworthy."

The Court did not view the Foster photographs as presumptively open records of a completed investigation into the death of a public official. Rather, the Court ruled the photographs could be withheld under exemption 7 because disclosure could result in an unwarranted invasion of the privacy of Foster's close relatives. Law and tradition recognize the right of family members to control the body and death images of the deceased, the Court said.

The invasion of the family's privacy was "unwarranted" because privacy interests were not outweighed by public interests in disclosure. Indeed, the Supreme Court placed considerable new burdens on a requester trying to acquire federal law enforcement records containing private information. When the privacy of a suicide's close relatives is at stake, it is not enough for a requester to demand information for its own sake, or to show "what the Government is up to," the Court said. The requester must show that the "the public interest sought to be advanced is a significant one," and that the "information is likely to advance that interest." Favish claimed a significant public interest—disclosure of government misconduct—but he lacked evidence, the Court said.

Favish presented a "bare suspicion" of government impropriety, not evidence "that would warrant a belief by a reasonable person that the alleged Government impropriety might have occurred." Disclosure of the Foster photos would be unlikely to reveal government impropriety, the Court reasoned, noting that five investigations into Foster's death had found no impropriety.

Critics of the *Favish* decision object that the Court reverses traditional FOI law when it requires the requester to present evidence of government wrongdoing to override the privacy rights of third parties in photographs of death scenes. The government previously has borne the burden of justifying closure of records.[118]

[116]Sen. Rep. No. 104-172, 104th Cong., 2d Sess. 26–27 (1996).

[117]541 U.S. 157.

[118]*See, e.g.,* Tony Mauro, "Supreme Court's Ruling Marks Blow to Public's Right to Know" (posted 4/6/04) http://www.usatoday.com/news/opinion/editorials/2004-04-06-scotus-edit_x.htm.

In 2005, a federal district judge ruled that disclosure of redacted photographs of abused prisoners at Abu Ghraib prison in Iraq would not invade the privacy of the prisoners. Judge Alvin Hellerstein ordered the Department of Defense to disclose the photographs of prisoner abuse taken by reservist Joseph Darby. With identifying characteristics redacted, any privacy invasion, the court said, would be "minimal" and not "unwarranted" in light of the public interest in disclosure at the heart of the Freedom of Information Act. The court also rejected government claims that disclosure might incite violence against U.S. troops, in violation of exemption 7(F), which permits the withholding of law enforcement records to protect personal safety. Exemption 7(F) was enacted to protect the safety of individuals involved in law enforcement investigations, Hellerstein said, not to block disclosure and discussion of important governmental activities such as the improper conduct of U.S. soldiers. "Our nation does not surrender to blackmail," Hellerstein said.[119]

Exemption 7 of the Freedom of Information Act also allows agencies to withhold records that could reasonably be expected to disclose the identity of a confidential source, including victims, prisoners, businesses, and state or local law enforcement agencies.[120] It also protects information furnished by a confidential source during a criminal investigation or a national security intelligence operation. One court said the identity of confidential sources should be withheld "not only to protect those citizens who voluntarily provide law enforcement agencies with information, but also to ensure that such persons remain willing to provide such information in the future."[121] The Supreme Court has ruled the FBI can claim confidentiality for its sources only if the sources "spoke with an understanding" that their confidentiality would be protected.[122]

(8) Banking Reports Exemption 8 protects from required disclosure a number of financial reports and audits of banks, trust companies, investment banking firms, and other federally regulated financial institutions. The records are held by such agencies as the Federal Reserve System, the Comptroller of the Currency, and the Federal Home Loan Bank Board. The exemption has been construed broadly by the courts to convince bankers that the information they give the government will be kept confidential.

(9) Information about Wells Exemption 9 protects geological and geophysical information, including maps concerning oil, gas, and water wells. Exemption 9 prevents speculators from easily acquiring valuable information that competitors have collected about the location of gas and oil wells. Exemption 9 is the least invoked exemption.

◇ Summary ◇

In an effort to balance the government's need for secrecy with the presumption of openness that pervades the Freedom of Information Act, the FOIA provided nine categories of information that can be exempt from disclosure to the public. An agency must disclose

[119]American Civil Liberties Union v. Dept. of Justice, 389 F. Supp.2d 547 (S.D.N.Y. 2005).
[120]Justin Franklin & Robert Bouchard, *Guidebook to the Freedom of Information and Privacy Acts* ¶ 1.10 [4], at 1-299.
[121]Maroscia v. Levi, 569 F.2d 1000, 1002 (7th Cir. 1977).
[122]United States v. Landano, 508 U.S. 165 (1993).

any record that does not fall under one of the exemptions and may disclose information falling into an exempt category. Exemption 1, the national security exemption, protects from forced disclosure items properly classified according to criteria established by the president. Even though Congress has given the courts the authority to review whether the government has properly classified records, the courts have been reluctant to second-guess the executive branch on matters of national security. Exemption 2 protects agency management records of little concern to the general public, such as parking and sick-leave regulations. Exemption 3 allows the government to withhold documents Congress has authorized to be confidential in other statutes either by enumeration or by use of criteria. The Homeland Security Act protects critical infrastructure information. The Privacy Act of 1974 limits federal agency use of personal information but does not restrict the release of information available through the Freedom of Information Act. FERPA provides that colleges and universities that improperly release "education records" could lose their federal funding. Congress has said that campus police records are not "education records" and that universities must report campus crimes. State colleges and universities can also release disciplinary records of violent crimes and non-forced sex crimes. The Driver's Privacy Protection Act of 1994 punishes state agencies that release personal driver's information to the public.

Exemption 4 protects trade secrets and confidential commercial and financial information. Trade secrets include commercially valuable information and formulas used and kept secret by a business. Commercial and financial information can be withheld only if disclosure would impair an agency's ability to obtain information in the future or cause substantial competitive harm to the business submitting the data. Many businesses are concerned that the FOIA does not adequately protect from competitors information they are required to give the government. Exemption 5 allows government agencies to withhold information used in their decision-making processes as long as documents are not publicly revealed to be the bases for decisions. Exemption 6 protects information in personnel, medical, and similar files that "would constitute a clearly unwarranted invasion of personal privacy." The courts balance the personal interest in nondisclosure against the public interest in the information about government activities. Exemption 7 applies to records compiled for law enforcement purposes that, if disclosed, could reasonably be expected to interfere with law enforcement efforts, constitute an unwarranted invasion of privacy, disclose the identity of a confidential source, or endanger the safety of law enforcement personnel. Exemption 8 protects banking reports submitted to the federal government. Exemption 9 applies to maps of oil and gas wells.

State Records Laws

The FOIA attracts so much attention that it might be easy to forget that it applies only to federal records, albeit federal records that are located all over the country. Many reporters, however, rely daily on state laws that give them access to state, county, and municipal government records. Reporters depend on state laws to provide them access to county budgets, city data about the number of housing starts, and reports on the quality of water leaving the local sewage treatment plant.

In most states, the common law requires that government records be open. Access to records through the common law, however, has two major limitations. First, the only persons who can obtain access are those with a legal interest in them—that is, those who would be directly affected by them, often because of a lawsuit. The general public and press do not have access to records when they are available only to persons with a legal interest in them. A second limitation of the common law is that a "public record" is not subject to disclosure unless it is "required to be kept" or is specifically listed by state law as a public record.[123] Many government documents have not been officially designated as public records.

To augment the access provided by common law, all fifty states have adopted statutes requiring disclosure of public records held by state, county, and municipal governments. The provisions and effectiveness of these laws vary significantly. In addition, state records laws are frequently adjusted through amendment and court interpretation.

Most open records laws begin with a policy statement expressing the need for government officials to be accountable. West Virginia's statute bluntly declares, "The people, in delegating authority, do not give their public servants the right to decide what is good for the people to know and what is not good for them to know."[124]

State records laws routinely apply to executive and administrative agencies of the state, county, and municipal governments. Most states have separate laws or policies regulating access to the records of courts and legislatures. New York's FOI law, for example, covers

> any state or municipal department, board, bureau, division, commission, committee, public authority, public corporation, council, office or other governmental entity performing a governmental or proprietary function for the state or any one or more municipalities thereof, except the judiciary or the state legislature.[125]

Public funding often determines whether an agency must abide by the public records statute. Under Kentucky law, for example, a "body" must conform to the state's open records law if a state or local government created the agency or provides at least 25 percent of its funds.[126]

Most laws adopted recently require the government to disclose records in almost any physical form, including computer tapes and disks. For example, South Carolina's FOI law defines public records to include "all books, papers, maps, photographs, cards, tapes, recordings or other documentary materials regardless of physical form or characteristics."[127] However, some local officials are reluctant to produce computerized records, want to charge more than the cost of reproduction, or refuse to provide electronic copies of the records instead of paper printouts.

Only a few state open records statutes have authorized direct public access to government data banks. Florida, often at the forefront of access law, encourages government agencies to provide electronic access through private computer terminals to public records "in the most cost-effective and efficient manner available."[128] New York has established the

[123] *See* Burt Braverman & Frances Chetwynd, 2 *Information Law* ¶ 24-2.1, at 897 (1985).
[124] W. Va. Code Ann. § 29B-1-1.
[125] N.Y. Pub. Off. Law § 86(3).
[126] Ky. Rev. Stat. Ann. § 61.870(1)(g), (h).
[127] S.C. Code Ann. § 30-4-20(c).
[128] 1995 Fla. Laws ch. 296.

Legislative Retrieval Service, a computerized database providing access to pending legislation and related information.[129]

States define public records not only by their physical form but also in terms of their origin, nature, and purpose. Some states define public records expansively to include anything in the possession of a state agency, or a public record can be any record made or received in connection with a state law or the transaction of public business. In contrast, some states still define records more restrictively, limiting public records to only those identified specifically by law as public records.[130]

All states provide a number of exemptions to records disclosure. Some records laws are more restrictive than they first appear. For example, Florida's highly touted and broadly stated open records law is limited by more than 625 statutory exemptions.[131] Most, if not all, states restrict access to personal records and law enforcement and investigatory information. Several states also exempt trade secrets and other business information, department memoranda, and tax return data. States are divided between those that mandate withholding any record exempted from disclosure and those that give an agency discretion to disclose exempted material, as the FOIA does.[132]

State laws either allow "any person" access to state records or limit access to state citizens.[133] A "person" includes corporations, citizens groups, and associations. Journalists have no greater rights of access than others.[134] In all but a few states, access is not dependent on the reason that a person wants to see a document. For example, a Pennsylvania court said a school district must disclose the names and addresses of incoming pupils to parents opposed to the scheduling of kindergarten classes. The court said the parents had a right to the information even though the parents wanted it to enlist opposition to school policy.[135] However, at least a few states restrict access for "commercial" use.[136]

In 1999, the U.S. Supreme Court upheld a California law denying commerical users access to addresses on police records. In a 7-2 vote, the Supreme Court ruled that the law does not unconstitutionally restrict the speech of lawyers, bail bondsmen, and social workers who would use the addresses from police records to seek clients. The law permits access to the addresses for five noncommercial purposes, including journalism.

In *Los Angeles Police Dept. v. United Reporting Publishing Co.*[137] the Court ruled the California statute is not an unconstitutional content regulation because it does not bar speakers from disseminating information they already possess. Rather, the statute limits who may have access to the information, the Court said. The Court said the state, which has the authority to deny records to all users, has the authority to deny access to citizens who would use them for commercial purposes.

[129]*See* Legi-Tech v. Keiper, 766 F.2d 728 (2d Cir. 1985).

[130]Burt Braverman & Frances Chetwynd, 2 *Information Law* ¶ 24-4.2.2.2, at 915-16 (1985 & Supp. 1990). *See also* Reporters Committee for Freedom of the Press, *Open Government Guide.*

[131]*E.g.*, Associated Press, "Exemptions Chip Away at Sunshine Law," *St. Petersburg Times,* Sept. 11, 1995.

[132]*See generally* Reporters Committee for Freedom of the Press, *Open Government Guide.*

[133]*See* Burt Braverman & Frances Chetwynd, 2 *Information Law* ¶ 24-3.1, at 903-04 (1985 & Supp. 1990).

[134]*See* James O'Reilly, 2 *Federal Information Disclosure* ¶ 27.03, at 27-8 (2d ed., June 1991).

[135]Wiles v. Armstrong Sch. Dist., 66 Pa. D. & C.2d 499 (1974).

[136]*See, e.g.,* Ariz. Rev. Stat. Ann. § 39-121.03; R.I. Gen. Laws § 38-2-6.

[137]528 U.S. 32 (1999).

Few state statutes specifically outline procedures citizens can follow to request a record. Some states require that a government agency provide an explanation for nondisclosure. Most states provide for judicial review of a record custodian's denial of a disclosure request. Many states require, and others permit, a citizen to appeal a denial of a records request within the agency before seeking a judicial appeal.

About ten states provide for reimbursement of attorney's fees and related expenses to successful plaintiffs.

◇ Summary ◇

Every state has an open records law for executive and administrative agencies of state, county, and municipal governments. Most laws begin with statements establishing a state policy of openness. Most state records laws apply to any document in the possession of a state agency, with specifically named exemptions. The most common provisions restricting the disclosure of public documents protect privacy and law enforcement investigations. More recently written laws tend to apply to records in any physical form, including in electronic format. Most states provide for fines or jail terms for officials who do not comply with the state law, although such stern sanctions are seldom imposed.

Access to Meetings

Neither the First Amendment nor the common law provides the press and the public access to the meetings of federal, state, or local governing bodies. Hence, access can be obtained only through statute.

A strong statute will declare that the purpose of the law is to open deliberations to the public as much as possible and that the law should be interpreted by the courts accordingly. The statute should describe the government agencies that are subject to the law. It will tell how many members must be present for a meeting to be official. It will explain how an agency may close a meeting and under what conditions closure is allowed. It should explain how a citizen can contest a closed meeting and what remedies are available if the law has been violated.

Federal

A federal "sunshine law" requires several executive agencies to meet in public. Congress has adopted separate internal rules opening up most of its sessions and most of its committee meetings to the public.

SUNSHINE ACT In 1976, Congress passed legislation requiring about fifty federal agencies, commissions, boards, and councils to meet in public. The Sunshine Act also covers the deliberations of agency subdivisions "authorized to act on behalf of the agency." The Sunshine Act declares that the public "is entitled to the fullest practicable information" about the "decision-making processes" of the federal government.[138] With ten exceptions,

[138]Government in the Sunshine Act, 90 Stat. 1241 (1976) (declaration of policy).

any meeting at which a sufficient number of members are required to take action is presumed to be public.

The Sunshine Act pertains only to agencies subject to the Freedom of Information Act. In addition, the agencies must be headed by boards of two members or more, a majority of whom are appointed by the president.[139] Among the agencies subject to the statute are the Federal Trade Commission, Federal Communications Commission, Securities and Exchange Commission, and National Labor Relations Board.

The Sunshine Act allows public access to discussions prior to official actions. The U.S. Court of Appeals for the D.C. Circuit has said Congress intended that the decision-making process of government be conducted in the open. The court in 1982 rejected arguments of the Nuclear Regulatory Commission that discussions of budget proposals should be closed. The court said that although the FOIA exempted documents prepared as a part of the decision-making process, Congress decided that the discussion of issues prior to decisions must be exposed to public scrutiny.[140]

To close a meeting, a federal agency must determine that remaining open would lead to a disclosure of information protected by one of the Sunshine Act's ten exempt categories. The agency also must determine that the public interest does not require that the meeting be open. Seven of the ten exemptions to the presumption of open meetings parallel exemptions of the FOIA: national security, agency rules, matters exempted by other statutes, business information, matters of personal privacy, investigatory records, and the reports of financial institutions. The Sunshine Act also exempts accusations of criminal activity or formal reprimands to protect the reputations of persons accused but not yet formally charged. In addition, an exemption permits closure for agencies regulating financial matters if a discussion would (1) lead to financial speculation, (2) "significantly endanger" the stability of a bank, or (3) frustrate the implementation of an agency action.

A final exemption to the Sunshine Act allows closed meetings to discuss an agency's issuance of a subpoena or its participation in a court or administrative proceeding.[141] The exemption is intended to ensure that a premature announcement does not allow people to effectively counter agency plans. The Nuclear Regulatory Commission (NRC) used the last exemption to block public access to a discussion about the reopening of the nuclear power plant at Three Mile Island in Pennsylvania. In 1979, a cooling system at the power plant failed, spreading radiation in the atmosphere up to ten miles away. Four years later, the *Philadelphia Inquirer* wanted to attend NRC meetings dealing with procedural steps for deciding whether to reopen a portion of the plant. A federal district court ruled that the meetings could be closed because they involved preparation for a formal administrative hearing.[142]

The Sunshine Act requires agencies to place a public notice of meetings in the *Federal Register* at least one week in advance. If an agency chooses to close a meeting, it must do so by a recorded vote of its members, and it must provide reasons in advance. Anyone who objects to a closure can file a suit in a federal district court. A court can enjoin a closed meeting or require that similar meetings be open in the future. The agency must maintain

[139] 5 U.S.C. § 522b(a)(1).
[140] Common Cause v. Nuclear Regulatory Comm'n, 674 F.2d 921 (D.C. Cir. 1982).
[141] 5 U.S.C. § 552b(c)(10).
[142] Philadelphia Newspapers, Inc. v. Nuclear Regulatory Comm'n, 727 F.2d 1195 (D.C. Cir. 1983).

a transcript or recording of any closed meetings. Anyone can sue to obtain a transcript, which can be examined by a judge in chambers to determine if it should be open.

Even if a suit under the act is successful, no financial penalty can be levied against individual members of an agency, and no agency action can be invalidated. However, the government can be forced to pay court costs and lawyers' fees. A person who sues under the act can be assessed court costs and lawyers' fees if the suit is found to be "dilatory or frivolous."[143]

One federal agency commissioner who has argued that the Sunshine Act must be reformed has acknowledged that members of many federal governing bodies often do not debate issues during public meetings. Securities and Exchange Commissioner Steve Wallman said decisions are made out of public view through staff discussions, written memos, and one-on-one conversations.[144]

Although some government agencies are subject to the Sunshine Act, government advisory boards—composed of citizens rather than government officials and employees—are subject to a different law requiring open meetings. The Federal Advisory Committee Act (FACA) requires that advisory boards meet in public so that advice to government officials by "outsiders" is open to public scrutiny. A federal appellate court ruled that the meetings of President Clinton's Task Force on National Health Care Reform, headed by Hillary Rodham Clinton, need not be open to the public.[145] The court said the task force's meetings were not subject to FACA because Clinton, as the president's spouse, was considered an "officer or employee of the government" rather than a member of the general public.

The U.S. Supreme Court did not rule on whether public interest organizations could seek records of meetings of an energy task force chaired by Vice President Dick Cheney. Public interest organizations, including press groups, sought information under FACA about meetings of a national task force in which executives from the energy industry participated. The groups wanted to learn if private energy companies significantly influenced federal energy policy. Vice President Cheney argued courts would intrude unconstitutionally into the operations of the executive branch even by seeking documents about the membership and structure of the task force. On remand from the Supreme Court, a federal appeals court ordered the complaints be dismissed after ruling that FACA disclosure requirements did not apply to the task force because the energy executives who participated had no vote in, or veto over, task force decisions.[146] Supreme Court Justice Antonin Scalia refused to recuse himself from the case after it was revealed he went duck hunting with the vice president.[147]

CONGRESS The U.S. Constitution provides that each house of Congress should publish "a Journal of its Proceedings . . . excepting such Parts as may in their Judgment require Secrecy."[148] Otherwise, the Constitution specifies that each house may determine its own rules. The rules determine which sessions should be open to the public and whether cameras ought to be allowed.

143 5 U.S.C. § 552b(g), (h), (i).
144 Lucy Dalglish, "Federal Agencies Look for Shade from Sunshine Laws," *Quill,* Sept. 1995, at 18.
145 Association of American Physicians & Surgeons v. Clinton, 997 F.2d 898 (D.C. Cir. 1993).
146 *In re* Cheney 542 U.S. 367, *on remanded,* 406 F.3d 723 (D.C. Cir. 2005).
147 Cheney v. Dist. Court, 541 U.S. 913 (2004).
148 U.S. Const. art. I, § 5.

Most sessions of the Senate and House are open to the public. The House of Representatives in 1995 voted to require that all committee meetings also be open to the public unless the committee votes to the contrary. Under the rule, House committee meetings can be closed to prevent disclosure of information that would "endanger national security," "compromise sensitive law enforcement information," "tend to defame, degrade or incriminate" someone, or violate a law or rule of the House.[149] The Senate operates under rules adopted in the mid-1970s, rules that require committee and subcommittee meetings—including bill-drafting sessions—be open to the public unless a majority votes in public to close. The House and Senate have agreed to open conference committee meetings, where representatives of the House and Senate try to reconcile different versions of a bill. A conference committee meeting can be closed only by a vote in public of a majority of the Senate conferees or by a vote of the entire House of Representatives.[150]

Both the House of Representatives and the Senate allow radio and television coverage of their proceedings. The two chambers control the cameras and allow broadcasters to use the footage. The committee hearings of both houses are generally open to broadcast coverage.

Summary

The Sunshine Act requires about fifty federal agencies to meet in public. The act applies to agencies subject to the FOIA and headed by a board appointed by the president. The act allows access to discussions prior to official actions. The act provides for exceptions to openness when the agencies are dealing with any of ten topics, most of them mirroring the FOIA exemptions. Each house establishes its own rules for access. Most sessions of the bodies and most congressional committee meetings are now open. Both the House of Representatives and the Senate permit broadcast coverage.

States

All fifty states have adopted open meetings laws—many in the last fifteen years. Only Alabama had a modern open meetings law in 1950. By 1962, only twenty-eight states had open meetings laws.[151] The states' open meetings requirements change often through legislative amendment and court interpretation. Reporters and public relations personnel need to keep track of legal developments in the state where they work.

Many scholars assert that one of the most important aspects of a strong open meetings statute, as well as a strong records law, is a legislative declaration that the law is intended to open government deliberations and actions to the people.[152] One of the most explicit declarations is from the state of Washington:

[149]House Information Resources, 104th Cong., 1st Sess., House Rules XI-2 (g)(1) (Sept. 29, 1995).
[150]Congressional Quarterly, *Guide to Congress* 59, 67, 112-13, 458-59, 464 (4th ed. 1991).
[151]William Wright II, "Comment, Open Meetings Law: An Analysis and a Proposal," 45 *Miss. L.J.* 1151 (1974).
[152]*E.g., id.* at 1162; Douglas Wickham, "Let the Sunshine In! Open-Meeting Legislation Can Be Our Key to Closed Doors in State and Local Government," 68 *Nw. U. L. Rev.* 480 (1973).

> The legislature finds and declares that all . . . public agencies of this state and subdivisions thereof exist to aid in the conduct of the people's business. It is the intent of this chapter that their action be taken openly and that their deliberations be conducted openly.
>
> The people of this state do not yield their sovereignty to the agencies which serve them. The people, in delegating authority, do not give their public servants the right to decide what is good for the people to know and what is not good for them to know. The people insist on remaining informed so that they may retain control over the instruments they have created.[153]

Some states indicate that the meetings of all agencies supported by public funds or performing governing functions are open except for explicitly named exceptions. The other states list or enumerate the kinds of agencies that must hold open meetings. The New York open meetings law, like its records law, applies to

> any state or municipal department, board, bureau, division, commission, committee, public authority, public corporation, council, office or other governmental entity performing a governmental or proprietary function for the state or any one or more municipalities thereof, except the judiciary or the state legislature.[154]

Some open meetings statutes, which list the agencies that must comply but which are less inclusive than New York's, leave the status of any unlisted agencies unclear. For example, a law may enumerate "boards and commissions" but not "councils." Many state laws exempt jury proceedings and parole and pardon boards from their meetings laws. Most state legislatures are required to be open.

A comprehensive definition of the word *meeting* in a state law can help the public and officials know what kind of gathering triggers the statute. For example, the Texas statute defines *meeting* as

> a deliberation between a quorum of a governmental body, or between a quorum of a governmental body and another person, during which public business or public policy over which the governmental body has supervision or control is discussed or considered, or during which the governmental body takes formal action.[155]

A *quorum* is the number of members who must be present at a meeting before an agency can conduct official business. In Texas, a majority of the members of a public body constitutes a quorum. In 1990, the Texas Supreme Court said that two of the three members of the Texas Water Commission were in a "meeting" when they discussed a case in the restroom.[156] States usually require either a quorum or a majority to be present for the meeting to qualify under the law. A majority may or may not be a quorum. In some states, any two members talking to each other is sufficient for a meeting under the law, regardless of the size of the government body.

[153]Wash. Rev. Code Ann. § 42.30.010.
[154]N.Y. Pub. Off. Law § 86(3).
[155]Tex. Gov't Code 551.001(4).
[156]Acker v. Texas Water Comm'n, 790 S.W.2d 299 (Tex. 1990).

What if members of a public body discuss public business at lunch, during a round of golf, or at a retreat? Social gatherings can be an excuse to do the public's business without the public watching. On the other hand, even many advocates of open meetings believe that a law should not prevent officials from socializing. The Texas open meetings law specifically excludes from its requirements any "social functions unrelated to the public business" and attendance at conventions and workshops as long as there is no public business conducted and if "discussion of public business is incidental to the social function, convention, or workshop." Some states provide no exclusion for social affairs or retreats or conferences. In most states, if a meeting is open to the public, cameras and audio equipment are usually allowed.

All states allow executive, or closed, sessions. Executive sessions are most commonly allowed for discussions of the hiring, firing, and disciplining of personnel; real estate transactions; official investigations; security or safety discussions; labor negotiations; and legal suits. Some states also allow executive sessions for discussions that would tend to damage individual reputations.

Journalists frequently object when public officials appear to stretch the meaning of the "personnel" exemption when they close a meeting. In 1989, the Mississippi Supreme Court said a majority of the Hinds County Board of Supervisors repeatedly violated the state's open meetings law when they went into executive session to discuss "personnel." The court held that under the Mississippi statute, the exemption for "personnel matters" was restricted to "dealing with employees hired and supervised by the board." The board had illegally entered executive session to discuss hiring an architect, an independent professional who was not an employee of the board, the court said. The court added that another item discussed in executive session, an appointment to fill a vacancy on the board itself, was not a "personnel matter" as defined by the court either.[157]

Advocates of open government argue that a decision to close meetings should be a public vote, with the reasons for closure on the record. Although the Mississippi open meetings law requires that votes for closure be public, the Mississippi Supreme Court said the Hinds County Board of Supervisors did not always comply. In addition, the court said, the board violated the law by discussing in executive session business that had not been included in its stated reasons for closure. The court also said the board inadequately explained its reasons for going into executive session because the board "tells nothing" about the reasons for closing a meeting when it "simply" says "personnel matters" or "litigation." In an expansive reading of the Mississippi law, the supreme court said the requirement that the reason for closure be announced means that a reason must be "of sufficient specificity to inform those present that there is in reality a specific, discrete matter" that needs to be discussed in executive session.

Advocates of open government want not only votes to close meetings to take place in public, but also all final votes on public policy to be in the open. The Mississippi Supreme Court said the Hinds County Board of Supervisors illegally voted to hire an architectural firm in an executive session.

[157]Hinds County Bd. of Supervisors v. Common Cause, 551 So.2d 107 (Miss. 1989).

Open meetings laws, to be effective, must include a requirement that the public be notified of meetings. Requirements that meetings be open are meaningless if no one knows when and where the meetings are held. Many statutes require that the times of regularly scheduled meetings be posted and sent to the media. States often mandate that the media, or persons requesting notification, be advised of special or emergency meetings in enough time to attend.[158]

Virtually every state provides a mechanism to enforce the open meetings law, but the enforcement mechanisms are seldom used in many states. Prosecutors are reluctant to take action against fellow officials, and citizens seldom make the effort or spend the money to challenge closed meetings. Observers believe the number of Florida officials successfully prosecuted for open meetings law violations—eighty-six since 1977—is unusually high.[159]

Several state statutes provide for short jail sentences or fines for officials responsible for closing meetings illegally. In 1989, three Longwood, Florida, officials were fined $500 each for discussing outside of an official meeting a proposal for the city to purchase a utility.[160] Florida's law and laws in other states also provide for civil penalties, eliminating the stigma attached to a criminal conviction.

Some states allow a court to enjoin officials from closing a meeting when the officials' intent to do so is known in advance. Other states provide for the nullification of any law or ordinance passed in an illegally closed meeting. A few innovative states remove from office officials involved in illegally closing meetings. One of the Longwood, Florida, officials mentioned earlier, City Commissioner Rick Bullington, was removed from office by the governor under a provision in Florida's general statutes after Bullington participated in policy discussions outside of an open meeting.[161]

◇ Summary ◇

Every state has an open meetings law. The laws that best protect the public's interest in openness specify that meetings be open during consideration of issues as well as when formal action is taken. Strong state open meetings laws also provide for public notice of meetings. At least a few state laws prohibit public officials from conducting business at social occasions. Many states permit closed sessions for discussing personnel matters, real estate transactions, official investigations, security, and labor negotiations. Enforcement of the open meetings statutes is a problem in many states, although most have statutory mechanisms, such as fines or short jail sentences, for illegal closure.

Obtaining Access: A Final Word

Laws requiring access help journalists. Because of open meetings and open records laws, reporters do not have to rely totally on their own devices to gain access to government meetings and records. However, laws themselves do not guarantee access to records or meetings. Many officials are not aware of the laws. Others may try to ignore or evade them.

---

[158] *E.g.*, Ark. Stat. Ann. § 25-19-106(b)(2).

[159] *See* "Sunshine Prosecutions and Fee Awards Continue Growth," *Brechner Report*, Feb. 1992, at 1.

[160] "Two Convicted of Sunshine Violations; One Ousted," *Brechner Report*, Nov. 1989, at 1.

[161] *Id. See* Fla. Stat. § 112.52.

Successful reporters learn that access depends on effectively cultivating sources. Officials are more likely to help reporters they know and trust. Reporters should discuss with public officials the importance of conducting business in the open and make an effort to understand why sources are sometimes reluctant to disclose information. Journalists should develop guidelines with local officials for coverage of news events.

Many reporters also have learned that persuasion, either friendly or stern, is often more likely to open a meeting or a record than the enforcement provision of the state law. Persuasion is more immediate and also less expensive than filing a lawsuit or seeking criminal charges. Sometimes, a reluctant official needs only to be convinced that access is required by law. But journalists can best use persuasion if they know access laws themselves. In many states, press associations distribute wallet-sized copies of open meetings and records laws for reporters to carry to meetings.

Reporters also should consult with lawyers to find out how best to achieve access in their states. The best route in some states may be speaking up when asked to leave a meeting. But in North Carolina, a reporter can be fined and jailed for intentionally disrupting a meeting and then refusing an order to leave. Journalists usually need to record the official reasons given for closure in order for lawyers to challenge it.

If it appears that access has been denied illegally, a reporter should consult first with an editor and then with a lawyer. Only they can decide whether a publication wants to pursue legal action. Sometimes a paper will write stories about closure and leave blank spaces where a story would have been published had the reporter been able to attend, or a broadcast station will use a picture of a closed door to pressure officials to keep meetings open. Few public officials want the voters to believe that they make decisions in closed, "smoke-filled" rooms.

Appendix A

Finding and Reading the Law

American legal sources, including cases, statutes, regulations, and commentary, are generally easy to find and cite. This appendix describes how to locate printed and online sources for most cases and legislative and administrative materials that comprise communication law. The appendix also explains how to read and write legal citations and how to read a judicial opinion.

Finding Court Documents

Most legal citations contain, in order, the name of the parties to the legal action, the volume of the legal reporting service containing information about the action, the abbreviation for the legal reporting service, the first page of the information cited, the name of the court issuing the opinion, and the year of the action.

Footnote 38 in Chapter 1 refers to *Hutchinson v. Proxmire,* 443 U.S. 111 (1979). The first name in the citation, *Hutchinson,* refers to the party initiating the legal action, whether the party is filing a complaint or an appeal. The second name, *Proxmire,* refers to the object of the action. The rest of the citation tells where the legal document can be found. The abbreviation between the numbers refers to the court reporter where the case is found. The "U.S." in the example stands for *United States Reports,* the official reporter for decisions of the U.S. Supreme Court. The number in front of the "U.S.," 443, refers to the volume in which the case can be found. The number after the "U.S.," 111, refers to the page on which the case begins. Therefore, *Hutchinson v. Proxmire* can be found in volume 443 of *United States Reports,* beginning on page 111. The final number in the citation for *Hutchinson v. Proxmire* is the year the opinion was issued, 1979.

Any government or academic law library should have the *United States Reports*. However, the same legal opinions that are published in *United States Reports* are also reported commercially in reporting systems such as West's *Supreme Court Reporter*. West has published legal reports since the 1800s. West's report of *Hutchinson v. Proxmire* can be found at 99 S. Ct. 2675 (1979), that is, volume 99 of West's *Supreme Court Reporter,* beginning on page 2675. It is the exact same case found in the *U.S. Reports,* but the *Supreme Court Reporter* version is a less official—but faster—commercial printing of the case. A third commercial source for court decisions—and there are others—is the *Media Law Reporter,* a commercial service focusing on communication law decisions. *Hutchinson v. Proxmire* is reprinted in volume 5 of the *Media Law Reporter,* beginning on page 1279, i.e., 5 *Media L. Rep.* 1279. *Media Law Reporter* is available in many law libraries and some journalism libraries. Court opinions are available much sooner in *Media Law Reporter* than they are in the official *United States Reports*.

Recent opinions of the thirteen circuits of the U.S. Courts of Appeal can be found in the *Federal Reporter,* also published by West. Citations use the abbreviation "F." to represent the *Federal Reporter*. The federal appeals court opinion in the *Hutchinson* case can be found at *Hutchinson v. Proxmire,* 579 F.2d 1027 (7th Cir. 1978). The "2d" means that volume 579 is in the second series of volumes of the *Federal Reporter*. If the abbreviation had been "F." and not "F.2d," the case would have been found in the first series.

The first series of the *Federal Reporter* was issued from 1880 to 1924 and stopped with volume 300. The second series ended with volume 999 in 1993, when the third series (F.3d) began. In the *Federal Reporter* citation for *Hutchinson,* there is an abbreviation within the parentheses next to the date. The "7th Cir." stands for the U.S. Court of Appeals for the Seventh Circuit, the court that heard the case. When the court that issues a decision is not mentioned in the text, it is named next to the date in the footnote citation.

The most comprehensive collection of federal district court decisions is found in the *Federal Supplement.* The summary judgment issued by the federal district court judge in *Hutchinson v. Proxmire* can be found at 432 F. Supp. 1311 (W.D. Wis. 1977). The abbreviations within the parentheses indicate which court heard the case, in this instance, the U.S. District Court for the Western District of the state of Wisconsin. Reports of federal court cases below the U.S. Supreme Court from 1789 to 1879 were reported in *Federal Cases,* abbreviated "Fed. Cas." in footnotes.

This book frequently refers to state court cases. Although most state trial court opinions are not published, state appellate opinions are—sometimes in both the official state reports and in a West version. *State v. Sheppard,* 100 Ohio App. 345 (1955) is the citation for the official report of the Ohio Court of Appeals. *State v. Sheppard,* 128 N.E.2d 471 (Ohio Ct. App. 1955) cites the same case published in West's *Northeastern Reporter,* second series. In the opinion, the court denied the first appeal by Sam Sheppard after he was convicted of murdering his wife. The Sheppard case is discussed in Chapters 1 and 10.

West prints state cases in seven "regional" reporters. "N.E." stands for the Northeastern region, "S.E." for the Southeastern region, "P." for the Pacific, and so forth (see Figure A.1). Again, the "2d" refers to the second series, in this case of the Northeastern reporter.

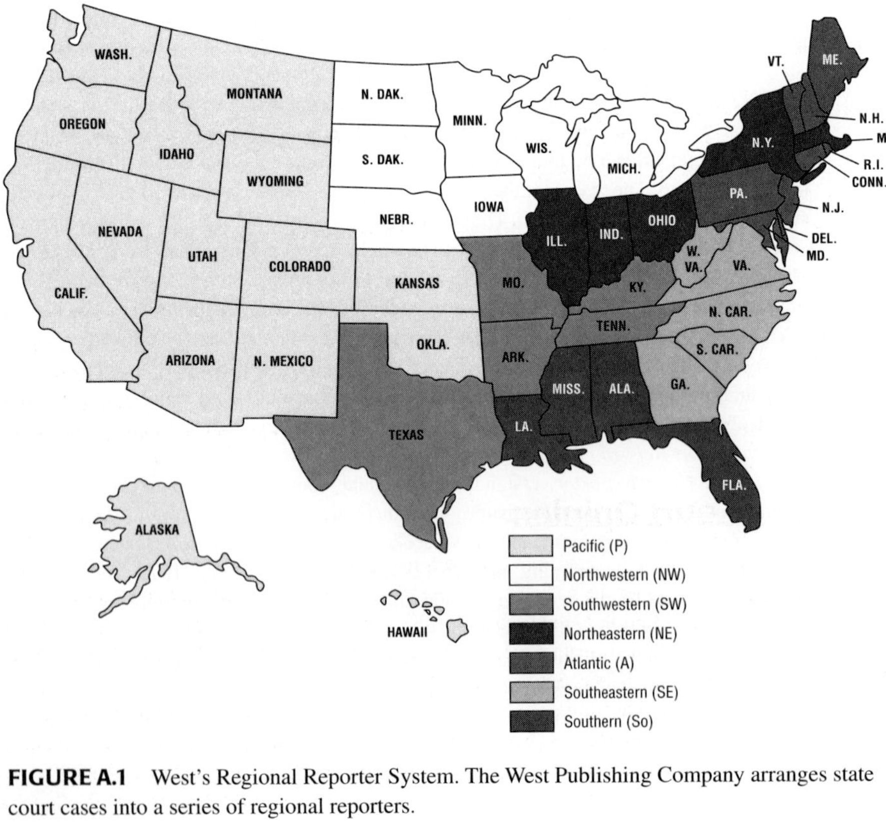

FIGURE A.1 West's Regional Reporter System. The West Publishing Company arranges state court cases into a series of regional reporters.

West also publishes a few individual state reporters in large states with many court decisions. For example, the *California Reporter,* abbreviated "Cal. Rptr.," provides state appellate court decisions for California. The state-published *California Reports,* for the California Supreme Court, and *California Appellate Reports,* for the California Courts of Appeal, are abbreviated "Cal." and "Cal. App.," respectively. The *New York Supplement,* or "N.Y.S.," reports New York appellate court decisions and some lower court opinions. The official *New York Reports,* abbreviated "N.Y." in citations, reports decisions of the New York Court of Appeals, the state's highest court. The *Appellate Division Reports,* "A.D.," provide the opinions of the Appellate Division of the Supreme Court in New York. In New York, the trial courts are named the Supreme Court.

Most of the case opinions cited in the book are also found in computerized databases found in most law libraries and other locations. The two commercial databases that specialize in legal material, LEXIS and Westlaw, provide court opinions more quickly than the print services and provide extensive capabilities for searching for specific subjects. LEXIS and Westlaw are cited in the footnotes in this book when they are the only sources for a court opinion at the time of publication.

Many court decisions and other legal documents can also be found on the Internet. One comprehensive source is the Legal Information Institute at Cornell Law School, http://www.law.cornell.edu. Many university and public libraries subscribe to LexisNexis Academic Universe, a scaled-down web version of the more comprehensive and expensive LexisNexis database. Court opinions can also be found at FindLaw.com and other sites. Many courts operate websites where recent opinions are posted. For example, the U.S. Supreme Court's website, supremecourtus.gov, posts opinions shortly after they are issued.

Some of the footnotes in this book cite court rules rather than court decisions. The abbreviation "Fed. R. Crim. P." stands for *Federal Rules of Criminal Procedure,* rules adopted by the U.S. Supreme Court to guide and regulate the conduct of the federal courts for criminal proceedings. "Fed. R. Civ. P." are the federal rules governing civil proceedings. *The Federal Rules Decisions,* abbreviated "F.R.D.," report federal district court decisions that interpret the federal rules of civil and criminal procedure. In 1974, Congress passed Federal Rules of Evidence (Fed. R. Evid.) to bring uniformity to federal rules governing admissibility of evidence in court. Each state also has its own set of rules.

The legal citations in this book and elsewhere not only reveal where to find a court case but also often provide a case history. Citations therefore will include a short description of the action taken by courts and administrative agencies. For example, the abbreviation "aff'd" indicates that an appellate court affirmed a lower court action. "Rev'd" stands for "reversed." "Cert. denied" means that the U.S. Supreme Court rejected the petition for *certiorari.* "Sub nom." means that a different name is being used for the same case.

In a citation in Chapter 1, footnote 45 tells the reader that a decision in the case *State v. Sheppard* by the Court of Appeals of Ohio was affirmed by the Ohio Supreme Court. The citation: State v. Sheppard, 128 N.E.2d 471 (Ohio Ct. App. 1955), *aff'd* 135 N.E.2d 340 (Ohio 1956), *cert. denied* 352 U.S. 910 (1956). The abbreviation for the state of Ohio in parentheses with the date indicates that the decision was made by the state's supreme court. Footnote 45 also indicates that the U.S. Supreme Court refused to take the case. There was no change in the case name as the dispute traveled through the court system.

Reading a Court Opinion

Once a court opinion is found, the next task is to make sense of it. One aid often available is a collection of small paragraphs just under the name of the case. These "headnotes" summarize major legal points addressed in the opinion. In addition to the headnotes, many reporting systems provide a syllabus for the case. The syllabus summarizes the principal facts of the case and the decision of the court. Neither the headnotes nor the syllabus are "official" because they are not written by the courts.

Following the headnotes, the syllabus, and a list of attorneys involved in the case, the reporting system will usually indicate who wrote the opinion of the court. In many reporting systems, the votes of the other judges or justices are recorded only if they dissented or wrote a concurring opinion. If a judge is not listed as concurring or dissenting and is not listed as absent, it can be assumed that he or she voted for the court opinion. In the Supreme Court case *Hutchinson v. Proxmire,* Chief Justice Burger wrote the majority opinion. (Justice Stewart joined the majority opinion, except that he disagreed with one footnote.) Justice Brennan wrote a dissenting opinion. Because there is no note indicating that a justice did not participate in deciding the case, all nine voted in the case. Therefore, a reader can conclude that the Court decided all the issues in *Hutchinson*—except for the footnote objected to by Justice Stewart—by an 8-1 vote.

A student reading a court opinion should first look for the issue, or issues, that the court is addressing. Sometimes a court opinion will say, "The issue before the court is . . ." At other times, the issue may be obscured in the language of an opinion. Sometimes a court opinion will not clearly address any one issue. In some cases, the justices disagree on the major issue being addressed. Still, understanding the issues helps a reader determine what is important in an opinion.

Knowing the issue, or the question, as it is often called, also helps to locate the resolution, or holding, of the case. When a reader knows the legal question a court is posing, the court's answer is easier to find. One of the questions in *Hutchinson v. Proxmire* was whether Hutchinson, a research scientist receiving federal funds for his work, was a "public figure" as defined by the Court. The holding for that issue was "no," Hutchinson was not a public figure. The holding of a case should lead to the point of law, a brief statement of the meaning of the opinion. The libel chapter discusses the Court's ruling in *Hutchinson v. Proxmire.* The Court ruled that research scientists are not public figures in libel suits just because they receive large government funding.

In addition to identifying the issue and the holding, it is important to find the major reasons, or the rationale, for a court's decision. A court may support its rulings by referring to previous court decisions, its interpretation of a statute, legislative documents leading up to the passage of a statute, a court's understanding of history, or its understanding of good public policy. When the Supreme Court ruled in *Hutchinson v. Proxmire* that Hutchinson was not a public figure, it relied on language in previous Supreme Court opinions discussing the definition of public figure.

As was mentioned earlier in this appendix, some court decisions cannot be fully understood without reading concurring and dissenting opinions. Brennan's lone dissent in *Hutchinson* was not a major factor in the disposition of the case.

The importance of a court opinion varies with the level of the court. An opinion by a federal district court judge does not have the same impact on the law as an opinion by the U.S. Supreme Court. Opinions by trial courts, such as a federal district court, generally have the least influence on other courts. Decisions in a trial court are more apt to be dependent on the facts of an individual case than at other levels of the court system. The decisions are often made by juries rather than judges, who are legal professionals. Trial courts set precedent over the smallest geographical jurisdictions, and trial court opinions are the least likely to be reported or published.

Opinions by intermediate appellate courts carry more precedential value. Judges rather than juries are examining cases in light of the law as a whole. Appellate courts review the decisions of several trial courts. Most appellate court opinions are officially reported. Of course, Supreme Court decisions carry the most weight.

Finding Legislative Documents

Court opinions are not the only place where law is found. There are several important legal documents generated by the legislature.

The most important documents produced by the legislative process, statutes, are compiled by the federal government and each state government. Statutes passed by Congress are published in chronological order for each session of Congress in *United States Statutes at Large*. The citation for the 1934 Communications Act, as originally adopted, is 48 Stat. 1064 (1934). The 1934 Communications Act can be found on page 1064 of volume 48 of *United States Statutes at Large*. The Communications Act and other federal statutes can also be found in the *United States Code,* a compilation of active federal law. The code is arranged by fifty topics, or "titles," and is published about every six years. The 1934 Communications

Act, as amended, can be found in Title 47 of the *United States Code*. The citation for the section requiring that broadcasters provide equal opportunities for political candidates is 47 U.S.C. § 315.

West and the Lawyers Co-operative Publishing Company publish annotated versions of the statutes that provide references to historical changes in the laws, notes about court decisions interpreting the statutes, and a list of pertinent publications discussing the law. West prints the *U.S. Code Annotated,* and the Lawyers Co-op prints the *U.S. Code Service*. Citations to the equal opportunities section of the 1934 Communications Act are 47 U.S.C.A. § 315 and 47 U.S.C.S. § 315, respectively. Both services provide a "popular name index" so that statutes can be found if only the commonly used, rather than legal, name is known. The Trademark Act of 1946, for example, can be found by looking under "Lanham Act," the commonly used name. Statutes and annotations are also found on LEXIS, some state and federal government Internet home pages, and other online sources.

Proposed legislation, committee reports, hearings, and floor debates for the U.S. Congress are readily available on most major university campuses. Libraries that serve as one of nearly 1,400 federal document depositories keep a copy of every bill submitted to each house of Congress. The depositories receive most of the documents printed by the U.S. Government Printing Office, including the transcripts of congressional hearings, committee reports on legislation, and other committee staff studies. The committee reports—which document the history, purpose, and explanations of bills passed by the committees—are available in a West publication, *United States Code Congressional and Administrative News* (U.S.C.C.A.N.). The *Congressional Record* (Cong. Rec.) is the official amended version of what is said on the floor of the U.S. House and Senate. The floor debates, committee hearings, and committee reports constitute what is called the legislative history of a bill. The Library of Congress provides many bills, resolutions, and committee reports, as well as the *Congressional Record* online at http://thomas.loc.gov. In contrast to the extensive legislative history available for congressional action, information about state legislative activity is sometimes scarce.

Commerce Clearing House publishes the *Congressional Index* (CI), an excellent place to find the status of bills introduced in Congress, including information about hearings and committee votes. The *Congressional Quarterly Weekly Report* (Cong. Q. Wkly. Rep.) provides regular updates on the progress of legislation and reports on votes in both houses. Another good index for congressional materials is the *Congressional Information Service Index*. The *Monthly Catalog* of United States Government Publications indexes most documents published by the government. Legislative information, including the status of bills, can be found on the Internet at http://thomas.loc.gov.

Finding Administrative Documents

The rules and regulations of the administrative agencies are printed in the *Federal Register,* published daily by the government. The *Federal Register,* abbreviated FR in textual matter and "Fed. Reg." in citations, also publishes proposed rules, federal legal notices, documents ordered published by Congress, and presidential proclamations and executive orders. The Congressional Information Service provides an effective index to the *Federal Register*. The *Federal Register* can be found at the Government Printing Office website, "GPO Access," http://www.access.gpo.gov/.

A compilation of administrative regulations can be found in the *Code of Federal Regulations,* or "C.F.R." The CFR, a commercial service updated annually, is to administrative law what the United States Code is to statutory law. The regulations of the administrative agencies are organized into fifty "titles" parallel to the titles of the United States Code. Regulations adopted by the Federal Communications Commission to enforce the 1934 Communications Act can be found in Title 47 of the CFR. The *Code of Federal Regulations* is also available on the website of the Government Printing Office, www.gpoaccess.gov.

Each of the federal administrative agencies publishes official reports containing agency decisions. The FCC used to call its official reports the *Federal Communications Commission Reports,* abbreviated "F.C.C." in a citation. Since 1986, the FCC has instead published the *FCC Record* (F.C.C.R.). The FTC publishes *Federal Trade Commission Decisions* (F.T.C.). Other publications important to communication law include *Securities and Exchange Commission Decisions and Reports* (S.E.C.) and *Copyright Decisions* (Copy. Dec.), published by the Copyright Office of the Library of Congress. The FCC, the FTC, the Copyright

Office, and other federal agencies have excellent websites containing statutes, regulations, administrative rulings, proposed regulations, press releases, commissioners' speeches, and many other resources.

In addition, numerous commercial services provide excellent research resources for students studying administrative agencies. For the study of telecommunications, the best service is Pike & Fischer's Radio Regulations (Rad. Reg.), a privately published loose-leaf service updated regularly. Commerce Clearing House publishes a few legal services used in this book, including the Federal Securities Law Reports (Fed. Sec. L. Rep.), the Trade Regulation Reporter (Trade Reg. Rep.), and the United States Patents Quarterly (U.S.P.Q.). The Bureau of National Affairs publishes the Securities Regulation & Law Report (Sec. Reg. & Law Rep.).

Other Resources

There also are general resource materials that can be helpful in finding and understanding the law. The two major legal encyclopedias are *American Jurisprudence* 2d (cited as Am. Jur. 2d) and *Corpus Juris Secundum* (C.J.S.). Although the titles are formidable, both can provide extensive subject indexes that lead to short legal summaries and pertinent legal citations.

A good way to find all the cases related to a particular topic is to use one of the many legal digests. West Publishing Company, in particular, provides digests for the Supreme Court, for all federal courts, for individual states, and for groups of states. The digests contain brief case summaries.

One way to begin a search is through computerized indexes such as LEXIS and Westlaw, mentioned earlier. Another way is to examine extensively footnoted law review articles, which can be accessed on LEXIS and Westlaw. The two major indexes to law reviews are *Current Law Index* and *Index to Legal Periodicals*. In footnotes in this book, law reviews ordinarily can be recognized by the abbreviation "L. Rev." in a citation. For example, the abbreviation of *Harvard Law Review* is "Harv. L. Rev." Other excellent online sources are provided by the Radio Television News Directors Association, the Reporters Commitee for Freedom of the Press, the Electronic Frontier Foundation, the Center for Democracy and Technology, the Berkman Center for Internet and Society, and many others.

Volumes of legal documents and other legal resources are available online. *The Lawyer's Guide to the Internet,* by G. Burgess Allison, provides a good and readable introduction to the Internet and lists of several Internet addresses. An easy-to-understand guide to legal research is *The Legal Research Manual: A Game Plan for Legal Research and Analysis,* by Christopher and Jill Wren. An indispensable tool for legal writing is *The Bluebook: A Uniform System of Citation,* the authority in legal style. Not only is the *Bluebook* a convenient guide for legal citations, it is also a guide to outlets for publication. The *Bluebook,* which has a blue cover, is published by the Harvard Law Review Association.

Anyone doing legal research should also be acquainted with *Black's Law Dictionary,* the most widely used dictionary for legal terminology.

Updating

Law is constantly changing. The bound volumes of statutes, regulations, and court opinions frequently become outdated soon after they reach the shelves. To keep up with new developments, legal researchers rely extensively on "advance sheets," "pocket parts," and *Shepard's Citations.*

Advance sheets are early paperback versions of opinions or other legal research materials that eventually will be available in hardbound books. Pocket parts are paperback supplements to statutes, codes, and regulations, usually found in a back "pocket" of a bound volume. Anyone using legal research materials should be sure to check for advance sheets or pocket parts in order to ensure that the law has not been changed.

Shepard's Citations allows anyone studying the law to be certain that a specific court opinion or administrative agency ruling is still valid law. *Shepard's* tells a legal researcher when an opinion such as *Hutchinson v. Proxmire* has been mentioned in subsequent court decisions. *Shepard's* can be used to determine if a court opinion has been overturned or to see how the law has developed since the opinion being "shepardized" was decided.

Appendix B

The First Fourteen Amendments to the Constitution

Amendment I

Congress shall make no law respecting an establishment of religion, or prohibiting the free exercise thereof; or abridging the freedom of speech, or of the press; or the right of the people peaceably to assemble, and to petition the Government for a redress of grievances.

Amendment II

A well regulated Militia being necessary to the security of a free State, the right of the people to keep and bear Arms, shall not be infringed.

Amendment III

No Soldier shall, in time of peace be quartered in any house, without the consent of the Owner, nor in time of war, but in a manner to be prescribed by law.

Amendment IV

The right of the people to be secure in their persons, houses, papers, and effects, against unreasonable searches and seizures, shall not be violated, and no Warrants shall issue, but upon probable cause, supported by Oath or affirmation, and particularly describing the place to be searched, and the persons or things to be seized.

Amendment V

No person shall be held to answer for a capital, or otherwise infamous crime, unless on a presentment or indictment of a Grand Jury, except in cases arising in the land or naval forces, or in the Militia, when in actual service in time of War or public danger; nor shall any person be subject for the same offence to be twice put in jeopardy of life or limb; nor shall be compelled in any criminal case to be a witness against himself, nor be deprived of life, liberty, or property, without due process of law; nor shall private property be taken for public use, without just compensation.

Amendment VI

In all criminal prosecutions, the accused shall enjoy the right to a speedy and public trial, by an impartial jury of the State and district wherein the crime shall have been committed, which district shall have been previously ascertained by law, and to be informed of the nature and cause of the accusation; to be confronted with the witnesses against him; to have compulsory process for obtaining witnesses in his favor, and to have the Assistance of Counsel for his defence.

Amendment VII

In Suits at common law, where the value in controversy shall exceed twenty dollars, the right of trial by jury shall be preserved, and no fact tried by jury, shall be otherwise reexamined in any Court of the United States, than according to the rules of the common law.

Amendment VIII

Excessive bail shall not be required, nor excessive fines imposed, nor cruel and unusual punishments inflicted.

Amendment IX

The enumeration in the Constitution, of certain rights, shall not be construed to deny or disparage others retained by the people.

Amendment X

The powers not delegated to the United States by the Constitution, nor prohibited by it to the States, are reserved to the States respectively, or to the people.

Amendment XI

The Judicial power of the United States shall not be construed to extend to any suit in law or equity, commenced or prosecuted against one of the United States by Citizens of another State, or by Citizens or Subjects of any Foreign State.

Amendment XII

The Electors shall meet in their respective states and vote by ballot for President and Vice-President, one of whom, at least, shall not be an inhabitant of the same state with themselves; they shall name in their ballots the person voted for as President, and in distinct ballots the person voted for as Vice-President, and they shall make distinct lists of all persons voted for as President, and of all persons voted for as Vice-President, and of the number of votes for each, which lists they shall sign and certify, and transmit sealed to the seat of the government of the United States, directed to the President of the Senate;—The President of the Senate shall, in the presence of the Senate and House of Representatives, open all the certificates and the votes shall then be counted;—The person having the greatest number of votes for President, shall be the President, if such number be a majority of the whole number of Electors appointed; and if no person have such majority, then from the persons having the highest numbers not exceeding three on the list of those voted for as President, the House of Representatives shall choose immediately, by ballot, the President. But in choosing the President, the votes shall be taken by states, the representation from each state having one vote; a quorum for this purpose shall consist of a member or members from two-thirds of the states, and a majority of all states shall be necessary to a choice. And if the House of Representatives shall not choose a President whenever the right of choice shall devolve upon them before the fourth day of March next following, then the Vice-President shall act as President, as in the case of the death or other constitutional disability of the President.—The person having the greatest number of votes as Vice-President, shall be the Vice-President, if such number be a majority of the whole number of Electors appointed, and if no person have a majority, then from the two highest numbers on the list, the Senate shall choose the Vice-President; a quorum for the purpose shall consist of two-thirds of the whole number of Senators, and a majority of the whole number shall be necessary to a choice. But no person constitutionally ineligible to the office of President shall be eligible to that of Vice-President of the United States.

Amendment XIII

Section 1. Neither slavery nor involuntary servitude, except as a punishment for crime where of the party shall have been duly convicted, shall exist within the United States, or any place subject to their jurisdiction.

Section 2. Congress shall have power to enforce this article by appropriate legislation.

Amendment XIV

Section 1. All persons born or naturalized in the United States, and subject to the jurisdiction thereof, are citizens of the United States and of the State wherein they reside. No State shall make or enforce any law which shall abridge the privileges or immunities of citizens of the United States; nor shall any State deprive any person of life, liberty, or property, without due process of law; nor deny to any person within its jurisdiction the equal protection of the laws.

Section 2. Representatives shall be apportioned among the several States according to their respective numbers, counting the whole number of persons in each State, excluding Indians not taxed. But when the right to vote at any election for the choice of electors for President and Vice President of the United States, Representatives in Congress, the Executive and Judicial officers of a State, or the members of the Legislature thereof, is denied to any of the male inhabitants of such State, being twenty-one years of age, and citizens of the United States, or in any way abridged, except for participation in rebellion, or other crime, the basis of representation therein shall be reduced in the proportion which the number of such male citizens shall bear to the whole number of male citizens twenty-one years of age in such State.

Section 3. No person shall be a Senator or Representative in Congress, or elector of President and Vice President, or hold any office, civil or military, under the United States, or under any State, who having previously taken an oath, as a member of Congress, or as an officer of the United States, or as a member of any State legislature, or as an executive or judicial officer of any State, to support the constitution of the United States, shall have engaged in insurrection or rebellion against the same, or given aid or comfort to the enemies thereof. But Congress may by a vote of two-thirds of each House, remove such disability.

Section 4. The validity of the public debt of the United States, authorized by law, including debts incurred for payment of pensions and bounties for services in suppressing insurrection or rebellion, shall not be questioned. But neither the United States nor any State shall assume or pay any debt or obligation incurred in aid of insurrection or rebellion against the United States, or any claim for the loss or emancipation of any slave; but all such debts, obligations, and claims shall be held illegal and void.

Section 5. The Congress shall have power to enforce, by appropriate legislation, the provisions of this article.

Glossary

Absolute privilege A libel defense protecting false and defamatory statements made by certain individuals, such as government officials acting in their official capacities, or in certain documents, such as those filed with courts.

Absolutism A theory of freedom of expression holding that the First Amendment prevents all government interference with speaking or publishing. The absolutist position is associated with Justice Black. See also **ad hoc balancing, bad-tendency test, clear-and-present-danger test,** and **definitional balancing.**

Actual damages Money awarded in a libel suit to a plaintiff who can demonstrate evidence of harm to reputation. Actual damages can include evidence of emotional distress as well as proof of monetary loss.

Actual malice (common law) In libel, publication with improper motive such as hatred, spite, vengeance, or ill will. Proof of common-law actual malice has traditionally defeated common-law defenses such as the reporter's privilege to report official proceedings and fair comment and opinion. Proof of common-law actual malice also is often required by persons suing for trade libel or *libel per quod.*

Actual malice (*New York Times*) In libel, publication with the knowledge of the falsity of a story or with reckless disregard for the truth. The U.S. Supreme Court has said that both public officials and public figures must prove *New York Times* actual malice in order to win libel suits.

Ad hoc balancing A judicial weighing, case by case, of reasons for and against publishing to determine whether expression may be halted or punished. Ad hoc balancing is flexible but unpredictable because it relies little on previous cases or set standards. See also **absolutism, bad-tendency test, clear-and-present-danger test,** and **definitional balancing.**

Adjudicate To settle a matter.

Administrative law Rules and decisions of administrative agencies such as the Federal Communications Commission (FCC) and the Federal Trade Commission (FTC).

Admonition A judge's warning to jurors about their duties or conduct, such as instructing jurors to ignore prejudicial publicity when deciding on their verdict.

Appeal Asking a higher court to review a lower court's decision.

Appellate court A court that reviews the actions of a lower court after an appeal by one of the parties in a case. Appellate courts consider only errors of law or legal procedure and do not reevaluate the facts of a case.

Bad-tendency test A discredited judicial test halting or punishing speech that presents only a remote danger to a substantial individual or social interest. See also **absolutism, ad hoc balancing, clear-and-present-danger test,** and **definitional balancing.**

Buckley Amendment Family Educational Rights and Privacy Act that prohibits federally funded institutions from disclosing student educational records to the public.

Burden of proof The responsibility imposed on one side in a legal conflict to prove its version of the facts.

Certiorari The name of a writ asking the U.S. Supreme Court to review a case. If the writ is granted, the Court will order the lower court to provide the record of the case for review.

Change of venue Moving a trial from one geographical area to another to, for example, lessen the effects of prejudicial publicity.

Clear-and-present-danger test A judicial test that, if applied literally, halts or punishes expression only where there is objective evidence of an imminent, substantial danger to individual or social interests. Sometimes the test has been used to halt speech that presents no clear, imminent danger. See also **absolutism, ad hoc balancing test, bad-tendency test,** and **definitional balancing.**

Coaxial cable Used by cable television companies to transmit signals to customers. Progressively being replaced by **fiber-optic cable.**

Collective work In copyright law, a gathering of preexisting works, which may already be copyrighted, into a new work, such as a magazine or anthology.

Color of law Journalists and others act under color of law when they willingly act in concert with officials, becoming like officials themselves.

Common carrier In communications, a regulated monopoly, guaranteed profits by the government, that is expected to provide message delivery service to anyone for a fee, without interfering in the content of the message.

Common law The body of law developed from custom and tradition as recognized by judicial decisions. Common law is largely based on previous court decisions.

Common-law malice Hatred, ill will, spite.

Compilation A copyrightable work formed by selecting, coordinating, or arranging preexisting works into a new, original work, such as a database.

Concurring opinion An opinion written by an appellate court judge stating why the judge agreed with other judges.

Consent decree An agreement between a defendant and the government that the defendant will cease allegedly illegal activities.

Contempt of court Acting impermissibly to interfere with a legal proceeding. Punishable by fine or imprisonment.

Content regulation The regulation of expression based on what is said as opposed to where or when it is said. First Amendment doctrine predisposes courts to consider content regulations unconstitutional. See also **time, place, and manner test, strict scrutiny.**

Continuance Postponing a trial, such as to ameliorate the effects of prejudicial publicity.

Corporation An artificial entity created under the power of law. Corporations have some, but not all, protections the Bill of Rights gives individuals.

Damages Money awarded to a winning plaintiff in a civil lawsuit. See also **actual damages, special damages,** and **punitive damages.**

Defamation Injury to reputation.

Defendant In civil law, the party against whom a lawsuit is brought. In criminal law, the party accused of a crime by the state.

Definitional balancing Judicial balancing of interests after freedom of expression is broadly defined to give it extra weight. Definitional balancing provides more predictable protection to freedom of expression than ad hoc balancing. See also **absolutism, ad hoc balancing, bad-tendency test,** and **clear-and-present-danger test.**

Derivative work In copyright law, a transformation or adaptation of an existing work, such as the creation of a filmscript from a novel.

Discovery The process before a trial of gathering information that can be used as evidence in a court case. Discovery includes the exchange of information by the two parties to a case.

Dissenting opinion An appellate judge's opinion explaining the judge's disagreement with the court majority's decision.

En banc A French term used when all of the judges of an appellate court decide a case. More typically, a single judge or a small number of judges, called a panel, decide a case.

Equal opportunities Section 315 of the Communications Act requiring broadcast stations and cable systems to offer a legally qualified candidate access to approximately the same size and type of audience for approximately the same amount of time as the station or system provided the candidate's opponent.

Equity A source of law that allows courts to fashion remedies appropriate to the case at hand. The law of equity enables courts to provide legal remedies other than money damages.

Fault Frequently used to mean the media error that the plaintiff must prove to win a libel suit. Plaintiffs who are judged to be public officials or public figures must prove *New York Times* actual malice. Individual states can determine the level of fault that must be proven by other plaintiffs, but most states have chosen negligence.

Fiber-optic cable Hair-sized strands of clear flexible tubing, predominantly made of glass, that allow information to be sent through impulses of light.

Fighting words Unprotected words that by their very utterance inflict injury or tend to incite an immediate breach of the peace.

First Amendment due process First Amendment procedural requirements that the government justify prior restraints and other restrictions and that hearings be held at which restrictions may be contested. See also **prior restraint.**

Fourteenth Amendment Amendment to the Constitution making states, in addition to the federal government, liable for violation of rights protected by the Bill of Rights. A state government that violates the Bill of Rights usually also violates a citizen's right of due process guaranteed by the Fourteenth Amendment. See also **incorporation.**

Franchise Agreement between a city, county, or state and a cable system operator allowing the operator to provide cable television service.

Gag order See **restraining order.**

Grand jury A jury determining whether there is sufficient evidence to charge a criminal suspect, or otherwise inquiring into possible criminal activity.

In camera review A judge's review of documents or testimony in private or in the judge's chambers, without the public present.

Incorporation A series of cases in which the Supreme Court made state governments liable for violating the Bill of Rights. The Court incorporated the Bill of Rights into the Fourteenth Amendment by holding that state infringements of free speech and other rights violate a citizen's right to due process, guaranteed by the Fourteenth Amendment. See also **Fourteenth Amendment.**

Indecency Non-obscene material depicting or describing sexual or excretory activities or organs. The level of protection for indecency varies; broadcast indecency receives the least protection, Internet indecency receives the strongest protection.

Indictment An accusation issued by a grand jury that charges an individual with a crime and requires the person to stand trial.

Injunction Order from a court telling a person or company to perform or refrain from some act, such as publishing. An injunction is an equitable remedy. See also **equity, prior restraint.**

Innocent construction rule A rule stating that material must be defined as innocent rather than defamatory if an innocent construction is possible.

Innuendo Implied defamation.

Jurisdiction The authority of a court. A court has jurisdiction over a person when that person must obey the orders of the court. A court has jurisdiction over subject matter when constitutions or statutes give the court the power to decide cases relating to the subject.

Liability Being legally responsible for an act.

Libel Printed or, in some states, broadcast defamation.

Litigant A party in a lawsuit; a participant in litigation.

Lottery A contest involving a prize, chance, and consideration.

Negligence Not acting as a reasonable person would. In some states, a journalist not acting as a reasonable journalist would.

Neutral reportage A libel defense in a few jurisdictions. Neutral reportage may be found if the defamatory charges are newsworthy and related to a public controversy, made by a responsible person or organization, about a public official or public figure, and accurately and neutrally reported, and if the story includes opposing views.

Obscenity Material that appeals to the prurient interest, is patently offensive, and is without serious social value.

Opinion A court's written statement explaining its decision, or a judge's written statement explaining agreement or disagreement with a court's decision.

Original jurisdiction A court of original jurisdiction is the first court to decide a case, rather than a court hearing a case on appeal.

Overbreadth A First Amendment doctrine by which courts determine that legislation is unconstitutional because it restricts more expression than necessary. See also **strict scrutiny, vagueness.**

Participant monitoring Secret recording or transmitting of a conversation in which one party to the conversation is aware of the recording.

Party A participant in a legal action.

Per curiam An opinion issued by and for the entire court rather than by one judge writing for the court.

Peremptory challenge An attorney's right to challenge seating a juror without offering a reason.

Petitioner A person who petitions a court to take action, including the initiation of a civil suit or the initiation of an appeal.

Plaintiff The party bringing the lawsuit; the person complaining.

Plurality With reference to the U.S. Supreme Court, the opinion that is supported by more justices than any other opinion in a single case but not supported by a majority of the justices.

Political action committee (PAC) An organization established by a corporation, union, or others to solicit and spend money on behalf of political candidates and issues.

Pornography Sexually explicit material that is not obscene.

Precedent An established rule of law set by a previous court opinion. A precedent for an individual case is the authority relied on for the disposition of the case. The precedent usually comes from a case involving similar facts and raising similar issues as the case at hand.

Preemption The doctrine that allows the federal government to preclude local or state governments from regulating a specific activity.

Pretrial motions or hearings Conferences among attorneys and the judge before a trial begins attempting, for example, to narrow issues or determine what exhibits will be permitted at trial.

Prior restraint Restriction on expression before publication or broadcast by injunction, agreement, or discriminatory taxation. First Amendment doctrine favors punishment after publication instead of prior restraint. See also **injunction.**

Private figure A libel plaintiff who is not a public figure or public official. In most states, a private figure libel plaintiff need prove only that the defendant acted negligently.

Probable cause A legal standard used by judges, police officers, and grand juries to determine whether there are reasonable grounds for believing that a person committed a crime.

Product disparagement See **trade libel.**

Public figure The U.S. Supreme Court has said that people become public figures for the purpose of libel suits only if they (1) possess widespread fame or notoriety or (2) have injected themselves into the debate of a controversial public issue for the purpose of affecting the outcome of that controversy.

Public forum Public property dedicated to public discourse, such as a speaker's corner, or public property traditionally open to public debate, such as streets and sidewalks. The law also recognizes a nonpublic forum in public property, such as an army base, dedicated to purposes other than free speech.

Public interest The standard the Federal Communications Commission uses to make decisions, according to the Communications Act of 1934.

Puffery Exaggerated advertising claims that are not misleading, deceptive, or false.

Punitive damages Money damages awarded to punish a defendant rather than to compensate a plaintiff for loss of money or reputation.

Qualified privilege A journalist's libel defense based on another's absolute privilege. A qualified privilege may be lost if the story is not fair and accurate or if the defamatory statements are not accurately attributed.

Referendum A ballot issue allowing voters to accept or reject a state constitutional amendment or a state law.

Remand When an appellate court sends a case back to a lower court, directing the lower court to decide the case consistent with the higher court's opinion.

Reputation What others think of a person or entity.

Respondent An appellee, a party opposing the grant of a petition before a court.

Restatement of Torts A publication of the American Law Institute that attempts to provide a comprehensive statement of the law of torts.

Restraining order An order issued by a judge commanding reporters and editors not to publish stories about a legal proceeding. A restraining order—often called a gag order by the press—also may restrict trial participants from talking with journalists.

Rule making A formal process of making administrative law used by such agencies as the Federal Communications Commission and the Federal Trade Commission. An agency must publish a proposed rule in the *Federal Register* and review comments. The rule as finally adopted must also be published.

Safe harbor In the context of broadcast regulations, the time period from 10 P.M. to 6 A.M. when radio and television stations may air indecent material without incurring Federal Communications Commission sanctions.

Search warrant An order issued by a magistrate directing a law enforcement officer to search a place for unlawful property.

Security review Prepublication review by military officials of wartime press reports to ensure classified information is not disclosed.

Seditious libel Defaming the government.

Sequestration Physically isolating jurors during a trial. Housing jurors under guard so that they will not be exposed to information or opinions about a case outside of the courtroom.

Slander Spoken defamation. However, in most states, defamation spoken on broadcast stations or in motion pictures is considered libel.

SLAPP suits (Strategic Lawsuit Against Public Participation) Libel suits filed against citizen activists to stop political expression.

Special damages Money damages compensating for the loss of reputation that are awarded only on proof of out-of-pocket monetary loss.

Spectrum A physical property allowing radio and television signals to be sent from a transmitter to a receiver.

Stare decisis The foundation of common law, the doctrine that judges should rely on precedent when deciding cases in similar factual situations.

Statute of limitations Time limits established by statute during which lawsuits may be filed or criminal charges brought.

Statutory law The law made by statutes passed by legislative bodies.

Strict scrutiny The judicial requirement that a restriction on protected contents be justified by a compelling government interest and that the regulation not be overbroad or vague. See also **overbreadth, vagueness.**

Subpoena A court document requiring a person to appear in court and testify at a given time and place.

Summary judgment A ruling by a judge that there is no dispute of material fact between the two parties in a case, and that one party should win the case as a matter of law. A summary judgment precludes the need for a trial.

Temporary restraining order A court order temporarily preventing action. It is an emergency remedy that is possible only while the court considers a more permanent solution to a legal problem. A temporary restraining order can be issued only for a brief time in exceptional circumstances.

Third-party monitoring Bugging, wiretapping, or eavesdropping on a conversation without knowledge of the parties to the conversation.

Time, place, and manner test Regulation of where and when expression is made as opposed to what is said. First Amendment doctrine is more tolerant of time, place, and manner restrictions than of content regulations. See also **content regulation.**

Tort A legal wrong, other than a crime or a violation of a contract, that is committed by one person against another. Torts include libel, invasion of privacy, and trespass. Relief for a tort is usually sought through monetary damages.

Trade libel Intentionally defaming product quality causing the product manufacturer to lose money.

Vacate To set aside the opinion of a lower court; to rescind, annul, or render a decision void.

Vagueness The doctrine by which courts determine that laws are unconstitutional because average persons would not know ahead of time whether their expression would violate the law. Vague laws affecting expression violate the First Amendment because the uncertainty they create leads to self-censorship. See also **overbreadth, strict scrutiny.**

Venire The pool of people from which a jury is selected.

Viewpoint discrimination Unconstitutional government regulation of speech expressing a particular view on a subject.

Voir dire The examination of prospective jurors to determine whether they are qualified to sit on a jury.

Work for hire In copyright law, a work prepared by an employee "within the scope of his or her employment," or a commissioned work, perhaps from a freelancer, for which a work-for-hire contract is signed. In either case, the employer owns all rights in the work.

Case Index

Subject Index